Taking Food Public

The field of food studies has been growing rapidly over the last thirty years and has exploded since the turn of the millennium. Scholars from an array of disciplines have trained fresh theoretical and methodological approaches onto new dimensions of the human relationship to food. This anthology capitalizes on this particular cultural moment to bring to the fore recent scholarship that focuses on innovative ways people are recasting food in public spaces to challenge hegemonic practices and meanings. Organized into five interrelated sections on food production, consumption, performance, diasporas, and activism, articles aim to provide new perspectives on the changing meanings and uses of food in the twenty-first century.

Psyche Williams-Forson is Associate Professor of American Studies at the University of Maryland College Park and an affiliate faculty member of the Women's Studies and African American Studies departments and the Consortium on Race, Gender, and Ethnicity. She authored the award-winning book (American Folklore Society), *Building Houses Out of Chicken Legs: Black Women, Food, and Power* (2006). Her new research explores the role of the value market as an immediate site of food acquisition and a project on class, consumption, and citizenship among African Americans by examining domestic interiors from the late nineteenth century to the early twentieth century.

Carole Counihan is Professor of Anthropology at Millersville University and editor-in-chief of *Food and Foodways* journal. She is author of *The Anthropology of Food and Body* (1999), *Around the Tuscan Table: Food, Family and Gender in Twentieth Century Florence* (2004), and *A Tortilla Is Like Life: Food and Culture in the San Luis Valley of Colorado* (2009). She is editor of *Food in the USA* (2002) and, with Penny Van Esterik, of *Food and Culture* (1997, 2008). She has been a visiting professor at Boston University, the University of Cagliari, the University of Gastronomic Sciences (Italy), and the University of Malta. Her new research focuses on food activism in Italy.

Taking Food Public

Redefining Foodways in a Changing World

EDITED BY

Psyche Williams-Forson

Carole Counihan

Routledge
Taylor & Francis Group

NEW YORK AND LONDON

Please visit the book's companion website at
www.routledge.com/textbooks/9780415888554
A comprehensive set of test items for each reading in this book is available to
instructors by e-mailing Routledge at saleshss@taylorandfrancis.com

First published 2012
by Routledge
711 Third Avenue, New York, NY 10017

Simultaneously published in the UK
by Routledge
2 Park Square, Milton Park, Abingdon, Oxon OX14 4RN

Routledge is an imprint of the Taylor & Francis Group, an informa business

© 2012 Taylor & Francis

Library of Congress Cataloging-in-Publication Data
  Taking food public: redefining foodways in a changing world/edited by Psyche
Williams-Forson, Carole Counihan.
    p. cm.
  Includes bibliographical references.
  1. Food—Social aspects. 2. Food supply. 3. Food habits. 4. Nutrition policy.
  5. Food industry and trade.   I. Williams-Forson, Psyche A. II. Counihan, Carole, 1948–
  GT2850.T326 2011
  306.4—dc23
                                                                    2011031165

ISBN: 978-0-415-88854-7 (hbk)
ISBN: 978-0-415-88855-4 (pbk)

Typeset in Sabon
by RefineCatch Limited, Bungay, Suffolk, UK

Printed and bound in the United States of America on acid-free paper by Sheridan Books, Inc.

CONTENTS

SECTION 1. RETHINKING PRODUCTION

SECTION 2. RETHINKING FOOD CONSUMPTION

SECTION 3. PERFORMING FOOD CULTURES

SECTION 4. FOOD DIASPORAS: TAKING FOOD GLOBAL

ACKNOWLEDGMENTS

We launched this project at a small restaurant in State College, PA, in May 2009 during the annual meeting of the Association for the Study of Food and Society. Psyche suggested we do a collection of cutting edge articles in food studies and Carole said yes! We spent several months communicating back and forth about what we wanted to include and why, what the key themes would be, and how we would structure the book. We penned a proposal and an initial table of contents, sent it to Steve Rutter at Routledge, and soon received ten reviews. We are grateful to Steve and the reviewers for their invaluable feedback, article suggestions, and provocative questions. Specifically, we would like to thank:

Deanna Pucciarelli of Ball State University
Marie Hopwood of DePauw University
Erick Castellanos of Ramapo College
Chanasai Tiengtrakul of Rockhurst University
Cherubim Quizon of Seton Hall University
Karl Schmid of Trent University
Jeff Haydu of University of California, San Diego
Julie Velasquez Runk of University of Georgia
Fuji Lozada of Davidson College

Psyche Williams-Forson would like to acknowledge the Department of American Studies at the University of Maryland College Park and especially, department chair Nancy Struna for lending time and assistance to this project as well as the staff and students in the Deparment, especially Manwah "Betsy" Yuen. There are a number of food studies scholars who have contributed to my thinking on this book as well as undergraduate and graduate students. Among these is Jessica Walker who lent research assistance. This book could not be completed without my family—husband Kwame and daughter, AbenaAnn. They are a constant reminder of the things that really matter in life and the importance of prioritizing. Psyche would most especially like to thank her co-editor Carole Counihan for hearing my idea and not only encouraging me to run with it, but also coming aboard and seeing it through. You are an invaluable mentor, friend, and colleague, and I thank you!

Carole Counihan would like to thank Millersville University for support for this project, especially the Faculty Grants Committee; my congenial and supportive colleagues in the Sociology-Anthropology department, especially department chair Mary Glazier and secretary Barbara Dills; and my students, who have contributed to my thinking in many ways. I especially want to thank student Erin Patterson, for her efficient, congenial, and organized work as editorial assistant on this project. I thank my valued comrades-in-arms Tracey Weis, Theresa Russell-Loretz, Barb Stengel, and Kathy Brown for being there; my husband and fellow-anthropologist Jim Taggart for his cheerful and steadfast support; and my children and grandchildren for keeping me grounded. I thank all the many food studies colleagues whose work has motivated and challenged me over the years, especially my co-editor, Psyche Williams-Forson, whose intelligence, good humor, and penetrating insights have made this project both a pleasure and an inspiring intellectual journey.

PREFACE

Food has always been a public object and activity as well as a domestic concern. From the emergence of hucksters, hawkers, and street peddlers to grocery stores, markets, and restaurants, groups of people large and small have always produced and consumed food publically. Recently, however, the *public* discourses around food have become louder, more diverse, and more pronounced. Conversations and debates are taking place in coffee shops, on street corners, and in academic venues. People are discussing questions such as: how do I eat more nutritious foods, where do I find "good" foods and how do I cook them, what do local and organic mean, and what are the consequences on my health and the environment of the foods I eat? The growth of four journals devoted specifically to the social, cultural, aesthetic, and political dimensions of food has also expanded the public reach of these conversations.[1] The *deliberateness* of these verbal exchanges reflects our reasons for including the discussions you will find in *Taking Food Public*.

The most important reason for selecting articles for this volume was their contribution to the theme of taking food public in thoughtful and innovative ways. Most of the articles were previously published in scholarly journals or books; a few were written expressly for this volume. All articles are recent and published since 2002. Articles were chosen for being clear and accessibly written, with descriptive data and thoughtful analysis. Some articles are by established scholars, and others are by new voices in the field. There were many excellent articles we considered but could not include for lack of space. Our goal was to put together a selection of articles that describe and critique a range of issues in the global agro-industrial food system and alternatives to them.

To accompany this book, we have come up with a collection of model test questions in a form that instructors can easily edit to suit their teaching needs. To receive these, please contact saleshss@taylorandfrancis.com. Please also visit the book's companion website at www.routledge.com/textbooks/9780415888554

Psyche Williams-Forson and
Carole Counihan

NOTE

1. The four scholarly journals devoted to food studies are: *Food and Foodways*, *Food, Culture and Society*, *Gastronomica*, and the online journal *The Anthropology of Food*.

Taking Food Public

Psyche Williams-Forson and Carole Counihan

What does it mean for food to go public? For us, it means that well beyond the academy people across the globe are consciously shaping food in the public sphere, contesting the status quo, and promoting creative options. With the choices they make come burdens and responsibilities that bear thinking through. We chose the name *Taking Food Public* over time as we developed the book to focus on the increasingly important topic of how people take food public in myriad ways. To this end, we have organized the discussions in this volume into five sections that focus on production, consumption, performance, diaspora, and activism.

PRODUCTION

We begin with production because it forms the foundation of every society and food is at the core of every economy. Since World War II, as Tim Lang's "Food Industrialisation and Food Power" describes, the industrial agrofood system has emerged, transforming land, labor, agriculture, diet, food culture, and the environment across the globe. Concentration, long-distance trade, high chemical and fossil fuel inputs, nonsustainability, and profit-making characterize the global agrofood system. Today, 80% of the world's poor still rely on agriculture for their survival, yet the majority of the world's population increasingly crowds into cities,

and food production is increasingly more globalized and concentrated.

Many articles in this volume discuss how women, small farmers, ethnic minorities, displaced persons, and the poor are coming up with new ways to advocate for changes in food production from gleaning to food stands to urban gardens and sustainable agriculture.

Because women are still primary food providers all over the world, we included Patricia Allen and Carolyn Sachs's important article on "Women and Food Chains." They take a feminist approach to food and look at how gender affects understandings of the body, nurturance, labor, power, and food activism. Larch Maxey addresses directly the question of whether family farmers can carry on sustainable agriculture in the global North by examining two small farms in Canada and the United Kingdom. Hanna Garth provides another, different case study of alternative production in her descriptive ethnographic study of food availability in Santiago de Cuba after the collapse of the Soviet Union and the concomitant demise of Cuban agriculture. She finds that small-scale sustainable agriculture can provide adequate, healthy, and culturally appropriate food for the Cuban population and a successful alternative to the highly industrialized agriculture that previously dominated the Cuban landscape.

Focusing on rural Western Oregon, Joan Gross examines those returning to pre-capitalist ways of food acquisition as resistance to the global food system. Gross discusses two groups—the back-to-the-landers relying on subsistence agriculture, and freegans—modern day foragers living off the waste of others and on what they can gather in the wild. These extreme practices call into relief how the foodshed can be expanded beyond the reach of corporate agriculture. Laura Lawson looks at another emerging form of public food production—urban gardens—in her article on the Los Angeles South Central Farm established in the heart of the city by mainly Mexican and Central American immigrant gardeners on city land that later was successfully claimed by powerful developers. The article raises important questions about the challenges to producing food in urban spaces. Meredith Abarca uses a method of "culinary chats" to explore Mexican women's "public kitchens"—small-scale food businesses based on women's knowledge of budgeting, preparing, and serving food. They convert their home cooking abilities into an economic resource to support themselves and their families and also create "family wealth," a network of extra-economic support of food gifts, labor exchanges, jobs, and moral support.

CONSUMPTION

An important dimension of taking food public is consumption, which is inevitably tied to production. Food studies are well served by taking an approach that examines both production and consumption as two sides of the same coin, mutually determining each other. Consumption choices are powerful and where they exist they are often based on several considerations including personal values, economic considerations, politics, convenience, and knowledge of health and nutrition. Daily, we are confronted with the reality that more and more people find themselves in food insecure situations while others have abundant resources and overflowing

larders. Reasons for food insecurity addressed in this volume range from the lack of whole and healthy food choices and/or the inability to access these choices due to disabilities, poverty, lack of transportation, and emigration. In addition, there are a number of pervasive and powerful influences from advertising to marketing that shape people's food beliefs and choices. Yet through alternative forms of consumption—such as dumpster diving or veganism—people challenge the status quo and promote alternative meanings and forms of food acquisition and consumption.

But what options remain for healthy eating when choices are limited? Kwate, Yau, Loh, and Williams consider this question in their study of the high prevalence of obesity in African American populations, which they argue is due in no small part to the density of fast food restaurants in many predominantly African American urban areas. Popular opinions often lead to misinformed judgments about the choices people make to participate in sustainable food consumption. Despite the barriers of cost, geography, and lack of knowledge, many still wish to feed their families healthy foods. Webber, Sobal, and Dollahite take on some misperceptions about food choices in their examination of physically impaired and disabled food shoppers from low-income households who desired to eat healthy foods but found themselves hampered by their health conditions and disabilities.

Consumption links individuals and households to the outside world in myriad ways. Psyche Williams-Forson describes the meeting of African American and Ghanaian cultures and cuisines inside her household and the complex gender issues at play as she and her Ghanaian husband negotiate culinary practices. By reflecting on the tensions involved when other women cook for her husband, Williams-Forson uses theory and auto-ethnography to question how the broad sociopolitical forces of gender, race, class, and diaspora play out around meals in her home. A. Breeze Harper also looks at how social and economic statuses affect food choices by examining Black female vegans. Harper details how some women of color have made veganism an explicit political choice to promote greater health and equity for food and the planet. Writing from a similar standpoint of consciousness, Rouse and Hoskins articulate the ways food consumption helps followers of Sunni Islam conform to and express publically Islamic notions of purity and holiness. Edwards and Mercer continue the discussion of alternative consumption through their study of young people in Australia who, primarily for political reasons, choose dumpster diving as one means of obtaining food. They also participate in Food Not Bombs, collecting past-prime produce free from markets, which they cook into soup and serve to the homeless. Julie Guthman also examines how food conveys political ideology by considering how farmers' markets and community supported agriculture project a discourse that often alienates people of color. Ethical issues are at the heart of these articles on food consumption.

PERFORMANCE

Our section on performance focuses on the ways people have taken food "on the road" to disrupt conventions and transform meanings in and through performances—public, structured, and explicit enactments of food ideologies. What does it mean to perform food? In their special issue on food of *Text and Performance Quarterly*, Laura Lindenfeld and Kristin Langellier write that food, cooking, and eating constitute "a complex system of performance practices and epistemologies."[1] The things we do with food—acquire, prepare, create, consume— are, they argue, performative by nature. They go on to cite what Barbara

Kirshenblatt-Gimblett defines as three junctures at which food and performance intersect: doing, behaving, and showing. The question becomes how and what do food performances mean and reflect?[2]

In the category of performance we include literature, art, competitive eating, firehouse cooking, ambulatory food vendors, and other forms of public food displays. Anita Mannur analyzes Asian literature and film to think through how family norms and domestic routines define and constrain men's and women's sexual identity and longing in heteronormative ways, and how public food production in diverse Diasporic locations can offer potential routes to liberation. Julia Ehrhardt also uses literature to think through the performance of identity—specifically how queer studies can inform the ways "food practices and beliefs reinforce and resist heterosexual gender ideologies." C. Wesley Buerkle further complicates hegemonic gender identities by disrupting the dichotomies between masculine and feminine in his discussion of metrosexual masculinity. Metrosexuals are men concerned with self-image, personal grooming, fashion, and aesthetics—attributes stereotypically associated with heterosexual women and gay men. Buerkle argues that meat consumption and advertising counter this suspect sexuality and celebrate a "retrograde masculinity" that reinforces heteronormativity and reinscribes dichotomized gender divisions through food consumption.

Continuing the theme of performing gender identity through food practices, Deutsch examines how urban firemen use sexual humor to assert their masculinity while they negotiate the stereotypically feminine tasks of cooking, shopping, and meal planning in the public/private space of the firehouse. Taking a different tack, Adrienne Johnson considers "gurgitators," men and women who risk mind, body, and soul to perform competitive eating. Johnson asks why they are motivated and provoked into such performances and why we, as spectators, find them fascinating.

Another kind of consumption linking performance, gender, reproduction, and the body is explored in Penny Van Esterik's "Vintage Breast Milk." This article considers the social and symbolic meanings of Toronto performance artist Jess Dobkin's controversial "Lactation Station Breast Milk Bar" where breast milk tastings mimic conventional wine tastings and disrupt taken-for-granted assumptions about private and public, (re)production and consumption.

Public food consumption always communicates meanings, values, and identities. How do meanings surrounding food assistance change when the recipient is living with disabilities? Denise Lance raises these kinds of questions in her article, "Do the Hands That Feed Us Hold Us Back?" She explores the challenges faced by those who need eating assistance and the ways they try to balance dependence, potential embarrassment, and intimacy of assisted eating.

New ways of eating and receiving food are also at the heart of Alison Caldwell's essay "Will Tweet for Food." Caldwell explores the intersections of new media, urban spaces, gourmet-like foods, and food carts to illustrate the ways in which Twitter has increased interactions with mobile food consumption and heightened the levels of performance involved in the acquisition of such foods. Considering another form of new media, Melissa Salazar raises our awareness of the benefits of using visually based research methods to capture and explore food behaviors, interactions, and implications. The work of Caldwell and Salazar, goes a long way toward redefining "public" interaction with food in a rapidly changing technological era. Taken together, the articles in the performance section reveal that there is an increasingly public and politicized moral discourse around food and a growing need to address class issues embedded in hegemonic meanings. Articles in this section provoke discussion and enlarge considerations of "alternative"

food in ways that are democratic and inclusive rather than elitist and exclusive.

DIASPORA

A global perspective enlarges the meaning of taking food public. This section explores how global movement has characterized and shaped peoples and foods in the late twentieth and early twenty-first century, displacing cultures, transforming diets, creating new identities, and altering meanings embedded in food. It examines the movement of foods not only as commodities like coffee, corn, and Coca-Cola, but also as capsules of culture, homeland, and nostalgia for people in the diaspora—like the *envios* food packages common among Mexican emigrants or kosher foods for Jews in the southern United States. As foods and their production and consumption travel around the world, their meanings change; like Spam in the Philippines or matzah in Mississippi, they become both globalized and localized. They may represent corporate power, transnational identities, and cultural imperialism, but also local power, cultural resistance, and the grassroots politicization of food.

Starting off this section is Daniel Reichman's study of the global coffee market and three ways it is regulated: through violence in Honduras against coffee farmers, in fair trade consumer initiatives, and by international regulatory treaties. By looking at these three forms together, he exposes the strengths and limitations of political power, the ways citizens are developing grassroots efforts for economic justice, and coffee can be a symbol of people's stance towards and place in the global economy. Exposing another fascinating dimension of food on the move, Valerie Imbruce gives rich detail on the Chinese vegetable trade in New York City, which imports vast quantities of fruits and vegetables from all over the globe and furnishes them to independent greengrocers and ambulatory vendors in NYC's several Chinatowns. This business provides an alternative form of food globalization characterized by multiple small traders, intense competition, resistance to consolidation, and high-quality produce at reasonable prices. Ty Matejowsky focuses on one of the most successful global industrial foods—the canned chopped pork known as Spam—and its consumption in the Philippines to interrogate food globalization and show how local populations incorporate global foods into local cultures and give them sometimes surprising meanings. James Grieshop examines another fascinating case of transnational migration, food globalism, and small-scale entrepreneurship—*envios*—the small-scale package services sending food and other culturally meaningful goods from Mexico to far-flung citizens in the United States. The *envios* demonstrate the enduring importance of food as a cultural glue linking migrants to their homeland and to each other in the diaspora.

Furthering the discussion of transnationalism, indigeneity, and consumables, June Nash illustrates the evolution of ways in which water, rum and now cola have had a profound effect on the lives of Mesoamerican people. Marcie Cohen Ferris takes up a similar yet different evolution of food and foodways involving religious and secular practices in her discussion of Jews in the Mississippi Delta. Her article begs the question of how landscapes can have an impact on Diasporic peoples and how they in turn change and affect their host communities by bringing in new foods and folkways. Julie Botticello asks the same question in decidedly different ways. In her essay on "The Yoruba Body," Botticello takes note of the steadily increasing population of Nigerians in the UK. Focusing on a variety of foodstuffs including medicinals, Botticello notes how the Yoruba people have used food through the process of

market selling with makeshift stalls and barrows to assist in their resettlement. Gaytán takes up this thread in her recognition of tequila as a powerful symbol of Mexican national identity. More than an inebriant, tequila is a material culture artifact used in most every ritual and activity central to this culture. Elizabeth Fitting rounds out this group of essays by calling into question the discussions of maize production in Mexico. Fitting argues that genetically modified maize production is much more complex than the dichotomous debates that currently surround its discussion.

ACTIVISM

While food has always been a key piece of governmental domestic and foreign politics, it has increasingly become a channel for counter-hegemonic political actions, which we call food activism. Where food is concerned, the personal is indeed political. The ingestion of food forces us to consider the consequences of what we eat for our bodies and the environment. Citizens are striving for food democracy and more just food systems through personal choices like eating vegan and buying at farmers' markets, to collective solutions like participating in food banks and community kitchens, to global movements like joining Slow Food, Via Campesina, and the anti-GMO movement.

Articles in this section examine both individual and collective efforts to change the world by changing the way food is produced, distributed, and consumed. Hassanein defines and discusses the important concept of "food democracy" and asks whether small changes in foodways can lead to transforming the dominant agrofood system to be both more democratic and more sustainable. Rebecca Sims analyzes another very different effort to promote good local food in her article on sustainable tourism in two regions of the United Kingdom. She explores the concept of authentic food and the value of embedding it in geographical place to enhance the tourism experience as well as to promote local and sustainable agriculture. Carole Counihan examines the continuum between women's food roles in the home with those in public and explores how food can be both a symbol of women's oppression and a channel to public power. Kathleen Schroeder looks at community kitchens in Peru and Bolivia and shows how they simultaneously empower and oppress the women who run them. These community kitchens foster initiative and self-sufficiency at the same time as they perpetuate the neo-liberal market economy that denies resources to women of marginal income and social status. Hayes-Conroy and Hayes-Conroy examine links between public activist work and the most private corporeal experience of eating, suggesting that attention to "visceral differences" among people may make the efforts of activist groups like Slow Food more successful.

Farmers' markets, recently burgeoning alternative agrofood institutions, are the topic of Lisa Markowitz's article, which ponders their relative lack of success in reaching economically vulnerable and racially and ethnically diverse populations. Using ethnographic research in Louisville, Kentucky, Markowitz explores the factors that have contributed to and detracted from farmers' markets ability to enhance food access to all citizens. Carol Morris and James Kirwan take an interesting approach to vegetarianism by asking if a movement based on such an individually focused act of consumption can really transform the food system and promote the alternative food economy. Denise Copelton looks at another individually rooted form of food activism around the autoimmune reaction to gluten known as Celiac Disease (CD). Drawing on field research with CD support groups, national CD conferences, and interviews, she explores the search for gluten-free foods and the determinants of everyday activism,

and she compares those who embrace their daily activism with those who resent and reject it.

Chad Lavin offers the provocative suggestion that "the focus on food immerses consumers in the contradictions of capital." He challenges us to ponder if the focus on food consumption and ethics in food activism may detract from its potential for real political transformation. The book's final essay is by Eric Holt-Giménez who uses the important concept of food sovereignty to define the challenge of social movements. His essay is a scathing indictment of the global food system and its production of global hunger. He counters this with a hopeful depiction of the converging efforts of peasants and small farmers to promote food democracy and sustainable agriculture through case studies of Via Campesina, Campesino to Campesino organizations, and the Brazil Landless Workers' Movement. Ending this book with producers' movements brings us full circle from our initial focus on alternative forms of production. The diverse, widespread and growing ways people are trying to change the food system through public participatory politics offers hope for a more democratic future.

WAYS TO USE THE BOOK

Our goal was to compile a compelling array of articles that would interest general readers and serve as a text for advanced undergraduate and graduate level courses. Articles can be read from start to finish following the organizational logic of the book, but they can also be read in a number of different ways for diverse courses such as: Food Activism, The Global Food System, Food and Inequality, Food and Society, Food and Culture, and others. For example, a course on Food Activism could include the ten articles in the food activism section, but also several from sections 1–4.[3] A course on The Global Food System could pick from among the eighteen articles with an international perspective and contrast them with the other twenty-five that focus on the USA.[4] A course on Food and Inequality could include some or all of the twenty-four articles on how the statuses of gender, race, class, disability, and obesity construct people's place in the social hierarchy.[5] Instructors can use the book creatively, assigning some of the articles to all students and using others for individual assignments and as resources for student papers.

At the time this book is going to press, *The Atlantic* has an article by Corby Kummer titled, "The Great Grocery Smackdown: Will Walmart, not Whole Foods, Save the Small Farm and Make America Healthy?" the gist of which challenges our wholesome sensibilities about where "good food" comes from, the role of the small farmer, industrialization, and notions of alternative food. What Kummer reveals is what we have tried to bring to the fore in this book—food matters, yes, and food discussions are very complex. It is important that we constantly talk about what is happening in our homes, communities, and businesses with regard to food because changes are occurring rapidly and furiously—and they are happening in public forums, in chat rooms, on blogs, in Tweets, and on other social networking sites. These conversations are publically happening in classrooms, on television stations, and in the proliferation of reading material being produced in newspapers and magazines, sometimes

so that they bring folks to shouting matches. Take, for instance, one of Kummer's final assertions: "in an ideal world, people would buy their food directly from the people who grew or caught it, or grow and catch it themselves. But most people can't do that. If there were a Walmart closer to where I live, I would probably shop there." The implications of such a statement published for all the world to see has the capacity not only to challenge those who hate the likes of Walmart but also encourage others to take another look at the oft demonized retail giant as a viable alternative. The point is that this is an important cultural moment with regard to food and we want generations of readers to be aware of these changing food times. We have sought to capture some of these debates and conversations in this volume and we hope that you, the reader, will find some usefulness in them both now and in the future!

NOTES

1. Laura Lindenfeld and Kristin Langellier, "Introduction," *Text and Performance Quarterly* 29. 1 (January 2009): 1–4.
2. Ibid, 2–3.
3. Articles that discuss diverse forms of food activism are: 3–7, 12, 14, 15, 21, 25, 33, 34–43.
4. Articles that focus on the USA are: 3, 6, 7, 9, 10, 11, 12, 13, 15, 17, 18, 19, 20, 22, 23, 24, 26, 30, 34, 36, 38, 39, 40, 41, 42. Articles with an international focus are: 2, 4, 5, 8, 14, 16, 21, 25, 26, 27, 28, 29, 31, 32, 33, 35, 37, 43.
5. Articles that focus on how gender constructs social position are: 3, 8, 11, 12, 16, 17, 18, 19, 21, 36, 37. Articles that focus on how by race, class, disability, and obesity construct social position are: 6, 7, 9, 10, 11, 12, 14, 15, 22, 25, 28, 29, 39, 41, 43.

SECTION 1

Rethinking Production

2

Food Industrialisation and Food Power: Implications for Food Governance

Tim Lang

The twentieth century witnessed a revolution in the nature of the food supply chain, the implications of which are only now being worked through at policy and institutional levels. The period was characterised by unprecedented changes in how food is produced, distributed, consumed and controlled – and by high levels of concentration of market share. After a period in which the state in developed countries actively promoted the restructuring of supply chains in the name of efficiency and output maximisation, adverse public reaction to these changes in the West is now forcing governments to respond differently, taming rather than forcing the pace and scale of change. The state is caught on the horns of a policy dilemma: on the one hand, actively promoting the development of efficient modern food supply chains; on the other hand, having to develop processes of food governance which can respond to and retain public trust in food.

The struggle over the direction of the food supply chain now going on in many developed countries has lessons for the developing world, still heavily focused on trade issues such as market access, the subsidies of the European Union's Common Agricultural Policy and economic protectionism. Important though these issues are, the emergence of another discourse is potentially both more threatening and important for the developing world. A policy choice looms.

This article explores the conflict and the choice, drawing mainly on the European experience, and particularly on the British. The UK is interesting not just because it was the first industrial nation and thus the first to sever its people from the land in a systematic and mass manner, but because it has had to grapple with the peculiarities of a post-colonial political transition into a European Member State.

CHANGES IN INDUSTRIAL AND POST-INDUSTRIAL FOOD SUPPLY CHAINS

The last half century ushered in a period of unprecedented and rapid change in the food system, whose impact is on a par with that of the so-called Columbian exchange half a millennium ago, or the impact of British nineteenth-century colonialism which used foreign lands both to feed trade and to home populations on a massive scale; or the impact of the internal combustion engine, in particular the tractor, and its substitution for animal traction power; or that of the chemical revolution on soil management. The new era of food supply management has redrawn the spatial as well as the cultural food map.

Developed world consumers have been able to transcend the seasons, with a cornucopia of year-round fruit and vegetables arriving in tightly planned waves from Europe, the Americas, Africa, and Australasia. Although the new food system has new characteristics, explored below, it could not have been ushered in without previous technical and social transformations. In particular, the twentieth-century agricultural revolution drew on patient and much slower transformations in the understanding of chemistry, plants, animals and engineering. In the late nineteenth century, for example, there had been a shift from milling grains using hands, animals, wind and water to the faster steam or electric roller mills. But in the 1960s, another quantum leap was made with the 'Chorleywood process' which allowed bakers to emulate car manufacturers in the organisation of their throughput. The new process whipped bread to rise in a few minutes, where, for the previous four millennia, bakers had had to wait hours. Yeast was added purely for taste.

Among the core characteristics of the twentieth-century revolution in the food supply chain are its integration, control systems and astonishing leaps in productivity, as measured in labour and capital use. The resultant restructuring has included changes in:

- how food is grown – for example, mass use of agrochemicals, hybrid plant breeding;
- how animals are reared – for example, factory farms, intensive livestock rearing, prophylactic use of pharmaceuticals to increase weightgain;
- the emergence of bio-technology – as applied to plants, animals and processing;
- food sourcing – for example, a shift from local to regional and now global supply points, with a blurring of the notion of seasonality and a tendency to monoculture on the farm belying the biodiversity on the supermarket shelf;
- means of processing – for example, use of extrusion technology, fermentation, wholesale use of cosmetic additives to disguise products and yield consistency;

- use of technology to shape quality – the goal of mass production to deliver consistency and regularity (uniformity) is now focused on the development of niche products with 'difference';
- the workforce – for example, a dramatic shedding of labour on developed-world farms but a retention of pools of cheap labour (immigrants) to do the manual tasks such as grading and picking; also a strong push to 24-hour working;
- marketing – a new emphasis on product development, branding and selling has accompanied a dazzling display of apparent choice, with thousands of products vying for attention;
- retailers' role – they have emerged as the main gateways to consumers, using contracts and specifications to gate-keep between primary producers and consumers;
- distribution logistics – for example, use of airfreight, regional distribution systems, 'trunker' (heavy lorry) networks, satellite tracking;
- methods of supply chain management – for example, centralisation of ordering, application of computer technology, application of batch/niche production to mass lines ('flexible specialisation');
- moulding of consumer tastes and markets – for example, mass marketing of brands, the use of product placement methods, huge investments in advertising and marketing and the targeting of particular consumer types;
- level of control over markets – for example, rapid regionalisation and moves towards globalisation, and the emergence of cross-border concentration.

As the twentieth century unfolded, the industrial approach was applied from farm to retailing to food service/catering. A new human geography of food emerged. In developed countries such as the UK, more people now work in catering than in the entire rest of the food supply – though in catering, too, there is now pressure to shed labour and introduce pre-processed products into the kitchen.

Meat production is one sector with many advanced industrial characteristics. It has witnessed the application of factory methods of management, production and control, not just in the meat packing plants of Buenos Aires or Chicago, but in the rearing of animals themselves. This is illustrated by the emergence of huge feed-lots where land was cheap (the Americas), or caged poultry and pig production and intensive dairy production units where land and/or weather demanded it. Productivity of animals, land and labour has risen to unprecedented levels. Dairy cattle have been bred to achieve a doubling and trebling of milk output, for instance. This industrial meat production regime is now being transferred to the developing world. The Indian broiler industry, for example, has grown from 31 million birds a year in 1981 to 800 million two decades later (Gold, 2003).

The role of Information Technology is another important new feature. Laser bar codes and Electronic Point of Sale (EPOS) systems in retailing are, to the consumer, the visible end of a sophisticated techno-logical web covering the supply chain (Brown 1997). Computers enable the application of 'just-in-time' distribution systems (which minimise build-up of stocks and allow the application of an Efficient Consumer Response ethos to deliver business-to-business efficiencies), robotic warehouses, satellites for moni-toring crops in distant places and the management of shipments and lorry delivery schedules. A retailer with annual sales of £17 billion cannot afford to run out of key food products or it will lose consumer credibility. Computers are central to this industrialised management approach.

By the late twentieth century, such was the tightness of control of the managerial

revolution in the food sector, that it had replaced the motor industry as the bench-mark for efficiency. Retail management was being offered to other service sectors as varied as hospitals and education as the ideal customer-oriented approach.

REDEFINING THE MARKET: THE EMERGENCE OF HIGH LEVELS OF CONCENTRATION

The food sector has been concentrating rapidly. The sectors vary in their dynamics. Land ownership is locked by the fact that land cannot move. Food manufacturers, by contrast, can relocate production outside their parent country, yet still have access to 'home' consumer markets. Thus, and following the creation of the Single European Market in the late 1980s, a company like European giant Unilever was able to rationalise its product mix, recipes and factories, to make maximum use of European scale and transport systems. In the United States, a similar regional market, the market share of the top 20 food manufacturers has doubled since 1967 (Connor, 2003); 100 firms now account for 80% of all value-added in the sector. European levels are not dissimilar to those of the US. Globally, a group of global players with enormous purchasing power has emerged among manufacturers (Table 2.1) and retailers (Table 2.2).

The situation among retailers is changing particularly rapidly. In the period 1993–9, the aggregate concentra-tion of the top 10 grocery retailers in the EU grew by 24.9%, whereas the market share of the bottom 10 companies in the EU Top 50 declined by 72.2%. The larger are getting larger and the small (even though large in relative historical terms) are being squeezed (Dobson, 2003). In Europe, retailers are now concentrating regionally, perhaps due to the fact that home markets were already concentrated.[1] There are some emerging

Table 2.1 World top 10 food manufacturers, 2002

Sector rank	Global rank	Company	Country	Market value $m	Turnover ($m)
1	34	Nestle SA	Switzerland	88,112.0	50,615.8
2	62	Unilever	UK & Netherlands	56,394.0	48,505.0
3	201	Kraft Foods	US	21,450.8	33,875.0
4	240	General Mills	US	17,843.9	7,077.7
5	266	Danone	France	16,706.2	12,687.3
6	272	Sara Lee	US	16,304.7	17,747.0
7	305	Heinz (H J)	US	14,539.7	9,430.4
8	311	Cadbury Schweppes	UK	14,202.0	7,898.8
9	325	Kellogg	US	13,685.9	8,853.3
10	347	Conagra Foods	US	13,026.8	27,194.2

Source: Financial Times FT500 (2002).

European giants such as Carrefour, Aldi, Tesco and Ahold.[2] The UK's Tesco, for instance, is now structured into three divisions: UK and Ireland, Central Europe and the Far East.

These trends are likely to continue. The Institute of Grocery Distribution, a food sector research institute, predicts that, based on historical growth rates in European turnover for the last 5 years, the top ten retailers will increase market share from 37 to 60% by 2010. Their combined European grocery turnover will grow from €337.1bn in 2000 to €461.7bn by 2005 and €669.7bn by 2010 (IGD, 2001).

Much current market concentration has occurred not by slow gains due to superiority of product or consumer appeal, but by buy-outs. Mergers and acquisitions have been rife from the 1980s on both sides of the Atlantic, as already large companies snapped up competitors. The results have changed both the architecture of the food supply chain and its public face. For example, a 'national' brand like Kit-Kat (once owned by former Quaker confectioner Rowntree's of York) could be bought by Swiss based Nestlé and turned into a global brand.

Similar trends occur in other sectors. Concentration is probably at its most advanced in agrochemicals, a key infrastructural sector. In the late 1980s, the top

20 firms worldwide accounted for around 90% of sales (Lang and Clutterbuck, 1991). By the late 1990s, this level was held by 10 firms. Today it is just seven (see Table 2.3).

There are also strong links between sectors. Chemical companies have diversified into seeds and biotech. In the US, the top four beef packers already controlled around a quarter of the market in the mid-1970s. Today, just 20 feedlots feed half of the cattle in the US and these are directly connected to the four processing firms that control 81% of the beef processing either by direct ownership or through formal contracts (Connor, 2003; Hendrickson et al., 2001).

Concentration is strongly linked to power and the concentration of power over the food system is now remarkable, whether one looks nationally, regionally or globally. A web of contractual relationships turns the farmer into a contractor, providing the labour and often some capital, but never owning the product as it moves through the supply chain. Farmers never make the major management decisions. Table 2.4 gives the level of concentration in the US for each sector held by the top three or four firms in some key meat, cereal, processing and retail sectors.

Rapid concentration throughout the supply chain also has implications for

Table 2.2 World top 30 food retailers, 2002

Rank	Company	Country	Turnover ($m)	No. of Countries	Foreign Sales (%)	Ownership
1	Wal-Mart	US	180,787	10	17	Public
2	Carrefour	France	59,690	26	48	Public
3	Kroger	US	49,000	1	0	Public
4	Metro	Germany	42,733	22	42	Public/family
5	Ahold	NL	41,251	23	83	Public
6	Albertson's	US	36,762	1	0	Public
7	Rewe	Germany	34,685	10	19	Co-operative
8	Ito Yokado (incl. Seven Eleven)	Japan	32,713	19	33	Public
9	Safeway Inc.	US	31,977	3	11	Public
10	Tesco	UK	31,812	9	13	Public
11	Costco	US	31,621	7	19	Public
12	ITM (incl. Spar)	France	30,685	9	36	Co-operative
13	Aldi	Germany	28,796	11	37	Private
14	Edeka (incl. AVA)	Germany	28,775	7	2	Co-operative
15	Sainsbury	UK	25,683	2	16	Public/family
16	Tengelmann (incl. A&P)	Germany	25,148	12	49	Private/family
17	Auchan	France	21,642	14	39	Private/family
18	Leclerc	France	21,468	5	3	Co-operative
19	Daiei	Japan	18,373	1	0	Public
20	Casino	France	17,238	11	24	Public
21	Delhaize	Belgium	16,784	11	84	Public
22	Lidl & Schwartz	Germany	16,092	13	25	Private
23	AEON (formerly Jusco)	Japan	15,060	8	11	Public
24	Publix	US	14,575	1	0	Private
25	Coles Myer	Australia	14,061	2	1	Public
26	Winn Dixie	US	13,698	1	0	Public
27	Loblaws	Canada	13,548	1	0	Public
28	Safeway plc	UK	12,357	2	3	Public
29	Lawson	Japan	11,831	2	1	Public
30	Marks & Spencer	UK	11,692	22	18	Public
TOTAL			**930,537**			

Source: IGD (2002).

Table 2.3 World top 7 agrochemical companies, 2001

Rank	Company	AgChem Sales 2001 (US$m)
1	Syngenta	5,385
2	Aventis	3,842
3	Monsanto	3,755
4	BASF	3,105
5	Dow	2,612
6	Bayer	2,418
7	DuPont	1,917

Source: Agrow (2002).

how a 'market' is defined in competition policy. Should a market be defined by consumers' travel-to-shop time, as the UK's Competition Commission suggested when reviewing the UK retail sector in 2000? Is a market national? Or is it a regional entity (for example, European/US)? Or global? Should consumers or regulators decide how to define a market? These questions illustrate policy dilemmas that will shape the governance of food policy in the twenty-first century – and to

Table 2.4 Concentration in the US food processing sectors

Sector	Concentration ratio (%)	Companies involved
Beef Packers	81	Tyson (IBP), ConAgra Beef Cos, Cargill (Excel), Farmland National Beef Pkg. Co
Pork Packers	59	Smithfield, Tyson (IBP), ConAgra (Swift), Cargill (Excel)
Pork Production	46	Smithfield Foods, Premium Standard Farms (ContiGroup), Seaboard Corp., Triumph Pork Group (Farmland Managed)
Broilers	50	Tyson Foods, Gold Kist, Pilgrim's Pride, ConAgra
Turkeys	45	Hormel (Jennie-O Turkeys), Butterball (ConAgra), Cargill's Turkeys, Pilgrim's Pride
Animal Feed Plants	25	Land O'Lakes Farmland Feed LLC\Purina Mills, Cargill Animal Nutrition (Nutrena), ADM (Moorman's), J.D., Heiskell & Co
Terminal Grain Handling Facilities	60	Cargill, Cenex Harvest States, ADM, General Mills
Corn Exports	81	Cargill-Continental Grain, ADM, Zen Noh
Soybean Exports	65	Cargill-Continental Grain, ADM, Zen Noh
Flour Milling	61	ADM Milling, ConAgra, Cargill, General Mills
Soybean Crushing	80	ADM, Cargill, Bunge, AGP
Ethanol Production	49	ADM, Minnesota Corn Producers (ADM has 50% Equity Stake), Williams Energy Services, Cargill
Dairy Processors	n/a	Dean Foods (Suiza Foods Corp.), Kraft Foods (Philip Morris), Dairy Farmers of America, Land O'Lakes
Food Retailing	38	Kroger Co., Albertson's, Safeway, Wal-Mart, Ahold

Source: Hendrickson et al. (2001).

which developing countries will not be immune.

THE ROLE OF THE STATE

Government action has often lagged behind technological, managerial and industrial changes in food supply. Traditionally, food policy was addressed in discrete analytical boxes such as 'farming', 'fisheries', 'development', 'health', 'environment', 'transport', 'consumer affairs',

etc. But a series of public crises have driven change. A new consciousness began first at the social fringes in the 1970s, with regard to concerns about quality (for example, contaminants, residues, pathogens) and among epidemiologists (for example, about the impact of diet on health). By the 1990s it was mainstream, aided by a series of crises and food scandals in Europe. Slack had been so cleverly taken out of the system that if something went wrong, it did so catastrophically, as was seen with the UK's BSE (1986–) and Foot and Mouth

Disease (2001) outbreaks, and with the numerous food safety scandals from the late 1980s.

Governments and food scientists and technologists, as well as the now high-profile market leaders, were increasingly forced onto the defensive, having to justify why, when they had such power and spoke in terms of meeting consumer needs, consumer interests had apparently been somewhat marginalised in pursuit of industrial efficiencies. While companies introduced tougher specifications for suppliers and new traceability controls ('plough to plate'), governments introduced reforms ranging from the creation of food agencies to wholesale shake-ups of ministries. The UK, for instance, set up a Food Standards Agency in 2000, and effectively abolished its Ministry of Agriculture in 2001 (Barling and Lang, 2003). In 2003, the European Union launched a new multi-state European Food Safety Authority.

An important duality has emerged. On the one side, we find a state system of regulations, on the other a system of self-regulation, largely driven by the major forces in supply chain management, the food retailers in particular (Barling and Lang, 2003).

But this state-corporate duality has compounded policy incoherence, because it fails to address a central feature of food policy, its inter-connectedness. The UK has not solved this problem. For example, in the wake of the Foot and Mouth Disease debacle that cost the taxpayer nearly £3 billion, the government set up a Commission into the Future of Farming and Food (Curry, 2002). But in the end, the problem was framed as primarily about cost and efficiency. The problem with UK farming, the report argued, was that it was not efficient enough. Better co-ordination and information flow was essential if the UK food supply chain was to compete with cheap imports. The Commission acknowledged that if consumers wanted improvements in the conservation and environmental aspects of farming (wildlife, biodiversity, land management, reduction of pesticide use, etc.), this had to be paid for. It recommended an increase of £500 million in subsidies to engineer the transition to this new policy package of efficiency with environmentalism.

Inter-connectedness means that trust is a central issue in food policy. This is perhaps most clearly seen in times of war or crisis, when food's multi-sectoral impact emerges from the analytical and practical shadows to take centre stage in political life (see for the UK: Beveridge, 1928; Le Gros Clark and Titmus, 1939; Hammond, 1950). Food can have a direct impact on morale. This has been acknowledged by the military for millennia, but with the severance of a majority of people from the land, this factor is now increasingly important in civil society too. The need for a multi-sectoral approach in food policy is also well appreciated in both the study and management of famine and hunger, and other deficiency situations in the development process.

THE COMPLEXITY OF CONSUMER SOVEREIGNTY

Focus on the issue of trust reminds us that consumers have played an important part in the evolution of food policy (Marsden et al., 2000). The period of public crises (1980–2000) included concerns about unnecessary use of food additives, the impact of pesticides, weak microbiological standards (particularly for food-borne pathogens), limited labelling and the role of diet in degenerative diseases such as heart disease, diabetes and some cancers. Consumer scepticism is rife (Gabriel and Lang, 1995). By the end of the last century, the nature of production, distribution and consumption, even cooking, was being subjected to considerable scrutiny and was sparking debate in most developed economies (Lang, 1996).

The relationship between industry and consumers is complex, however. Rhetoric suggests that the food supply chain is consumer-led, but this phrase disguises more complex impetuses. Consumers, as most observers note, are at the heart of the battles not just for global brands (Grievink, 2003), but for minds. The top 20 food brands in the UK spend over £105 million a year on marketing (Marketing, 2002). While the UK Government spends around £5 million on healthy eating advice, Coca-Cola alone spends £27 million in the UK yearly. It spends $1.4 bn on advertising worldwide, as does McDonalds (Ad-Brands, 2003).

Kinsey (2003) has argued that the old supply-demand chain is now a loop, where intelligence is gathered about consumers but shaped by supply requirements coming back up the supply chain. US and European food sectors have for a decade espoused a management goal known as 'Efficient Consumer Response', the purpose of which is improved co-ordination and waste reduction. The old policy framework which pursued regularity and risk reduction as farmers struggled against the vagaries of nature is now being replaced by a battle over marketing. The product innovation and quality controller for one of Britain's top five retailers informed this author: '. . . sometimes we have to do things before the customer even knows what they want'.

Advertising expenditure is not the only additional cost borne by consumers when purchasing. While the relative price of food might have dropped in many societies, health costs associated with diet have risen dramatically compared with the 1940s. Life expectancy has risen, of course, but so has evidence about the impact of diet-related diseases like cancers, heart disease and diabetes from which consumers die prematurely. Political attention for the last decade has been on food safety but the real crisis comes from food's role in degenerative

diseases. The World Health Organization's Cancer Report (WHO, 2003) expects a steep rise in cancers in part due to poor diets – eating too much fat and not enough fruits and vegetables. There are no incentives for processors to sell only simple foods: for example, value-added fruit juices (lots of water plus a little fruit) make more money.

The health toll of diet-related disease is a very large financial problem for affluent countries. Table 2.5 gives a breakdown of the direct and indirect costs for a number of key diseases related to diet in the United States. These costs are immense, even for a rich society like the United States. Table 2.6 shows how general healthcare costs are rising rapidly in many developed economies. The growth of health expenditure is sometimes higher than the growth of GDP. The UK healthcare system, for instance, costs £68 billion for a population of just under 60 million people, costs that the Treasury expects will rise to between £154 bn ($231 bn) and £184 bn ($276 bn) by 2022–3 in 2002 prices (Wanless, 2002). At constant prices, the healthcare costs are doubling.

The WHO has now stepped up its appeal to both developed and developing country governments to act to prevent the double burden of food-related ill-health problems associated with under- and over-consumption coinciding in the same countries. In effect, the WHO and the FAO are now in agreement that the productionist era in food policy has come to an end. Mere quantity is an inadequate policy goal. Quality, distribution and externalised social costs also have to be central to the policy framework (WHO/FAO 2003).

The enticing possibility is that realisation of the size of health and other external costs could change the politics of food. Concern about rising health costs could explain why many Finance Ministries are so concerned about diet-related ill-health. The insurance industry is also worried, one factor behind President George W.

Table 2.5 Economie costs of diet- and exercise-related health problems, US

Disease	Direct costs US$ bn (medical expenditures)	Indirect costs US$ bn (productivity losses)	Total costs US$ bn
Heart disease	97.9	77.4	175.3
Stroke	28.3	15.0	43.3
Arthritis	20.9	62.9	83.8
Osteoporosis	n/a	14.9	14.9
Breast cancer	8.3	7.8	16.1
Colon cancer	8.1	n/a	8.1
Prostate cancer	5.9	n/a	5.9
Gall bladder disease	6.7	0.6	7.3
Diabetes	45.0	55.0	100.0
Obesity	55.7	51.4	107.1
Total			**561.8**

Note: Costs are expressed in constant 1998 US$, using the Consumer Price Index.
Source: Kenkel and Manning (1999).

Table 2.6 Growth of expenditure on health, 1990–2000

	Real per capita growth rates, 1990–2000 (%)		Health spending as % of GDP		
	Health Spending	GDP	1990	1998	2000
Australia	3.1	2.4	7.8	8.5	8.3
Austria	3.1	1.8	7.1	8.0	8.0
Belgium	3.5	1.8	7.4	8.5	8.7
Canada	1.8	1.7	9.0	9.1	9.1
Czech Republic	3.9	0.1	5.0	7.1	7.2
Denmark	1.7	1.9	8.5	8.4	8.3
Finland	0.1	1.8	7.9	6.9	6.6
France	2.3	1.4	8.6	9.3	9.5
Germany	2.2	0.2	8.7	10.6	10.6
Greece	2.8	1.9	7.5	8.7	8.3
Hungary[a]	2.0	2.7	7.1	6.9	6.8
Iceland	2.9	1.6	7.9	8.3	8.9
Ireland	6.6	6.4	6.6	6.8	6.7
Italy	1.4	1.4	8.0	7.7	8.1
Japan	3.9	1.1	5.9	7.1	7.8
Korea	7.4	5.1	4.8	5.1	5.9
Luxembourg[b]	3.7	4.5	6.1	5.8	6.0
Mexico	3.7	1.6	4.4	5.3	5.4
Netherlands	2.4	2.3	8.0	8.1	8.1
New Zealand	2.9	1.5	6.9	7.9	8.0
Norway	3.5	2.8	7.8	8.5	7.5
Polandb	4.8	3.5	5.3	6.4	6.2
Portugal	5.3	2.4	6.2	8.3	8.2
Slovak Republic	. .	4.0	. .	5.9	5.9
Spain	3.9	2.4	6.6	7.6	7.7
Switzerland	2.5	0.2	8.5	10.6	10.7
United Kingdom	3.8	1.9	6.0	6.8	7.3
United States	3.2	2.3	11.9	12.9	13.0
OECD Average[c,d]	**3.3**	**2.2**	**7.2**	**8.0**	**8.0**
EU Average	**3.1**	**2.3**	**7.4**	**8.0**	**8.0**

Notes: a) 1991–2000; b) 1990–9; c) Excludes the Slovak Republic because of missing 1990 estimates; d) unweighted averages. No recent estimates available for Sweden and Turkey.
Source: OECD Health Data (2002:1). Available at www.oecd.org/pdf/M00031000/M0003113O.pdf.

Bush's launch of a high-profile US initiative against rampant obesity.

POSSIBLE SOURCES OF CHANGE

The costs of diet-related ill health and the fiscal burden of healthcare may seem unlikely triggers for a re-think about the political economy of food and about the attractions of the industrial and intensive approach to the food supply. But fiscal pressure, driven in part by rising numbers of post-retirement elderly, is already proving a strong motivation for states to re-think pension systems and promises of old-age retirement, made in the great era of affluence of the late twentieth century when stock markets were booming and there seemed no end to the consumerist bargain. Framing the food supply chain to help reduce healthcare costs will become increasingly pressing as those costs rise in affluent societies, and as degenerative diet-related ill-health grows in societies without sufficient GDP to afford expensive healthcare and health insurance systems.

Another potential source of change is public pressure, the preparedness of consumers to act, not just think, like citizens with long-term commitments beyond the checkout counter/point of sale. The appeal to consumers to act differently and to see beyond cheapness can come from various sources. It ranges from individual survival ('your or your family's health') to ecological sustainability ('the planet'). To take one example, the rapid rise in meat consumption that accompanies rising disposable income has implications for land use and grain production to feed the demand for meat. Meat production is an industry already under some consumer scrutiny for factory farming, associations with burger culture (cheap products, high fat, poor ecological impact), and for public health problems (for example, prophylactic use of antibiotics weakening their viability for real human health need).

Public pressure can be highly effective. If food power is concentrating, even large corporations are vulnerable and exposed to sudden changes in public sympathy. When European food safety procedures were found wanting in the 1990s, arguments from consumer campaigners for more ecological systems of food production found popular resonance and moved from the fringe to centre-stage in public policy (Lang, 1996). Politicians intervened in the supply chain because consumers realised that they had little control at the point of sale. The consumerist bargain (cornucopia without consequences) looked momentarily shaky. In the EU, this culminated in the crisis over BSE (mad cow disease) which forced the President and Council onto the defensive (Santer, 1997; Lobstein et al., 2001). Other crises, for example, over contaminated feed in Belgium and a wave of food safety scandals in the UK, for instance, highlighted the vulnerability of the industrial food system. The policy question was raised that prices might be cheap, but at what social, health and environmental cost? The implications of this question are still being struggled over within the supply chain, with companies investing hugely in traceability systems while consumer and health analysts argue that the externalised costs are not just microbiological. Indeed, these represent a small fraction of the total burden (Pretty et al., 2003).

Environmental pressures such as climate change and global water shortages could also pose direct and real threats to affluent countries. Water becomes highly sensitive not just for direct human consumption but for use in intensive irrigation and cropping systems (UNEP, 2002; Barlow and Clarke, 2002). The implications of climate change are still unclear but some academic prognoses suggest that cash crops such as tea and coffee – central to the development agenda, let alone the taste buds of affluent consumers – could fall by significant amounts; a one degree rise in temperature can lead to 10% yield reductions in tropical crops (UNEP, 2001). The impact on the economies of countries like Uganda or Kenya, already vulnerable to mono-commodity production downturns, could be serious.

In conclusion, although this article has argued that industrialisation and concentration have developed in a mutual cycle of development, it has also argued that some fragility is discernible in the fabric of efficiency that has been woven throughout the food supply chain. It would be foolish (and historically myopic) to pronounce an end to the industrialised system. Indicators suggest continued rural depopulation, capital investment, application of technology, intensification – all the features of industrialisation summarised earlier in this article. And yet, the crises in rich countries suggest the need to give more attention to the potential impact of currently marginal policy issues such as public health, ecological strains and consumer reaction. It would be unwise for developing countries to dismiss these concerns as the luxuries of the affluent.

NOTES

1. The share held by the top three firms in EU countries ranges from 40% (Germany, UK) to over 80% (Finland and Ireland). But the largest countries are now poised to emulate the smaller ones (Grievink, 2003).
2. The last was hit by a crisis of fraudulent accounting after falsely claiming $880 m. higher earnings than had happened (Bickerton, 2003).

REFERENCES

Ad-Brands (2003). http://www.mind-advertising.com/us/index.html

Agrow (2002). 'Gap narrows between prospective agrochemical market leaders', *AGROW World Crop Protection News*, 397, 29 March, p.l

Barling, D. and Lang, T. (2003a) 'A Reluctant Food Policy?', *Political Quarterly* 74 (1): 8–18.

Barlow and Clarke (2002). *Blue Gold: the battle against corporate theft of the world's water*. Toronto: Stoddart

Beveridge, W. (1928) *British Food Control*. Oxford: Oxford University Press.

Bickerton, I. (2003) 'New Scandal Hits Embattled Ahold', *Financial Times*, 27 May, p.22.

Brown, S. A. (1997) *Revolution at the Checkout Counter: the Explosion of the Bar Code*. Cambridge, MA: Harvard University Press.

Connor, J. (2003) 'The Changing Structure of Global Food Markets: Dimensions, Effects, and Policy Implications'. Paper presented at OECD Conference on Changing Dimensions of the Food Economy, The Hague, 6–7 February.

Curry, D. (2002) *Report of the Commission of Inquiry into the Future of Farming and Food*. London: Cabinet Office.

Dobson, P. (2003) 'Buyer Power in Food Retailing: the European Experience'. Paper presented at OECD Conference on 'Changing Dimensions of the Food Economy', The Hague, 6–7 February.

Gabriel, Y. and Lang, T. (1995). *The Unmanageable Consumer* London: Sage.

Gold, M. (2003) *M-Eatless*. Petersfield, UK: Compassion in World Farming.

Grievink, J.-W. (2003) 'The Changing Face of the Global Food Supply Chain'. Paper presented at OECD Conference on Changing Dimensions of the Food Economy, The Hague, 6–7 February.

Hammond, R. J. (1950) *Food*. London: HMSO and Longmans.

Hendrickson, M., Heffernan, W. D., Howard, P. H. and Heffernan, J. B. (2001) *Consolidation in Food Retailing and Dairy: Implications for Farmers and Consumers in a Global System. Report to National Farmers Union (USA)*. Columbia, MO: Department of Rural Sociology, University of Missouri.

IGD (2001) *European Grocery Retailing: Now and in the Future*. Letchmore Heath: Institute of Grocery Distribution.

Kenkel and Manning (1999) 'Economic Evaluation of Nutrition Policy Or There's No Such Thing As a Free Lunch', *Food Policy*, 24, pg. 148

Kinsey, J. (2003) 'Emerging Trends in the New Food Economy: Consumers, Firms and Science'. Paper presented at OECD Conference on Changing Dimensions of the Food Economy, The Hague, 6–7 February.

Lang, T. (1996) 'Going Public: Food Campaigns during the 1980s and 1990s', in David Smith (ed.) *Nutrition Scientists and Nutrition Policy in the 20th Century*. London: Routledge.

Lang, T. and Clutterbuck, C. (1991) *P is for Pesticides*. London: Ebury.

Le Gros Clark, F. and Titmus, R. M. (1939) *Our Food Problem and its Relation to Our National Defences*. Harmondsworth: Penguin.

Lobstein, T., Millstone, E., Lang, T. and van Zwanenberg, P. (2001) *The Lessons of Phillips: Questions the UK Government Should be Asking in Response to Lord Phillips' Inquiry into BSE*. A Discussion Paper. London: Food Commission/Centre for Food Policy/Science Policy Research Unit, University of Sussex.

Marketing (2002) 'Biggest Brands 2000: Top 50' *Marketing* (available at www.marketing.haynet.com/feature00/bigbrands00/to p50.htm).

Marsden, T., Flynn, A. and Harrison, M. (2000) *Consuming Interests*. London: UCL Press.

Pretty, J., Griffin, M., Sellens, M. and Pretty, C. (2003). *Green Exercise: Complementary Roles of Nature, Exercise and Diet in Physical and Emotional Well-Being and Implications for Public Health Policy*. CES Occasional Paper 2003–1. Wivenhoe: University of Essex Centre for Environment and Society.

Santer, J. (1997) 'Speech by Jacques Santer, President of the European Commission at the Debate in the European Parliament on the report into BSE by the Committee of Enquiry of the European Parliament'. 18 February. Speech 97/39.

UNEP (2001) 'Climate Change: Billions Across The Tropics Face Hunger And Starvation As Big Drop In Crop Yields Forecast Soaring Temperatures Force Coffee and Tea Farmers to Abandon Traditional Plantations'. News Release 01/107, 8 November (available at www.unep.org/documents/default.asp?DocumentID=225 &ArticleID=2952).

UNEP (2002) *Global Environment Outlook*. London: Earthscan and New York: United Nations Environment Programme.

Wanless (2002) *Securing Our Future Health: Taking a Long-Term View. Final Report*. London: H M Treasury. April

WHO (2003) *World Cancer Report*. Geneva: World Health Organisation and International Agency for Research on Cancer

WHO/FAO (2003) *Diet, Nutrition and the Prevention of Chronic Diseases*. Report of a consultation. Technical Series Report 916. Rome: Food and Agriculture Organisation and Geneva: World Health Organization, 23 April.Section 1

3

Women and Food Chains[1]: The Gendered Politics of Food

Patricia Allen and Carolyn Sachs

INTRODUCTION

Throughout history, the social relations of food have been organized along lines of gender. Today, in most societies women continue to carry the responsibility for the mental and manual labor of food provision—the most basic labor of care. Women's involvement with food constructs who they are in the world— as individuals, family members, and workers—in deep, complex, and often contradictory ways. Women perform the majority of food-related work, but they control few resources and hold little decision-making power in the food industry and food policy. And, although women bear responsibility for nourishing others, they often do not adequately nourish themselves. These longstanding contradictions are seemingly immune to the dynamism that characterizes nearly every other aspect of the agrifood system[2] in this era of globalization and innovation.

In this article we reflect on these contradictions, taking up three questions about gender relations in the contemporary agrifood system. First, we ask how the subordination of women and sublimation of feminist consciousness in relation to food has been engaged and explained in agrifood and feminist scholarship. We find a rich literature on body politics and gendered eating patterns, but substantial gaps in the areas of structural issues and social change. Second, we ask what are the configurations of food-connected

gender relations? We discuss this within a framework of what we call food domains—material, socio-cultural, and corporeal—that define women's relationships to food. We find, unsurprisingly, that women are disadvantaged in each of these domains. This leads to our next question, what actions are being taken to change gender relations in the agrifood system? We look at the locations of women's agency in improving social and economic conditions in these three domains. While women are engaging in numerous important efforts to change the food system, these efforts are rarely coordinated. Neither are they generally identified as feminist projects, in the sense of being strategically oriented toward improving gender relations.

How can we work to better understand the complicated and contradictory connections between gender and food? Avakian and Haber (2006) have called for a new field of feminist food studies. For this field of study to emerge, the connections between women's food work in the labor market (material), their responsibility for food-related work in the home (socio-cultural), and their relationship with eating (corporeal) must be studied and adequately theorized. Until recently, these areas have been both understudied and unconnected, with little integration of the material, socio-cultural, and corporeal domains. Currently, feminist studies in the corporeal domain help to explain why gender relations remained so static in the food system despite the progress that women have made in many other arenas, such as medicine, law, and politics. However, other gender issues, including the relative absence of a feminist agenda despite women's increasing involvement in leadership roles in the food system, remain neglected. We suggest that weaving the strands of feminist studies together with political economy and sociology can provide strong theoretical grounding for a feminist food studies that would illuminate causes, conditions, and possibilities for change in gender relations in the agrifood system.

THEORIZING THE CONNECTIONS BETWEEN GENDER AND FOOD

Women are occupied in and preoccupied with food on a daily basis, irrespective of class, culture, or ethnicity. While the edges of these occupations and preoccupations can blur, we find it useful to distinguish women's involvement in the food system in terms of material, socio-cultural, and corporeal. In discussing the material domain, we focus on women's labor in the formal labor force—women's productive labor outside the home and in the public sphere. In the socio-cultural domain, we are concerned with women's reproductive (usually unpaid) labor in the home and with their families, i.e., their work in the private sphere. Finally, the corporeal domain incorporates women's physical and emotional connections to eating and food, including the cultural forces that condition these connections.

Women remain disadvantaged in the material, socio-cultural, and corporeal domains of the agrifood system. Yet, while women engage in significant and far-reaching efforts to change the system, few of these efforts focus specifically on improving gender relations. How have these conditions been engaged and explained? Here we review scholarly contributions to our understanding of gender relations in the agrifood system. The most developed areas in terms of theorizing the connections between food and gender are the corporeal and socio-cultural domains, with fewer contributions in the material domain.

The Corporeal Domain

Feminist scholars have described and explained the ways in which women obsess about and are tormented by food. Women's identities are clearly tied to their often problematic relationship with food. Bordo (1998) suggests that women seek emotional heights, intensity, love and thrills from food. She also points out that the restriction of food and denial of hunger serve as central features of the construction of femininity (Bordo 1998). Bordo argues that most women who can afford to eat well are dieting and hungry almost all of the time.

Dieting, anorexia nervosa, bulimia, and obesity—all on the rise—mark the confused messages that women should have perfect (thin) bodies at the same time that they are encouraged to over consume and indulge in junk food. Advertising and media play an enormous role in perpetuating women's obsession with thinness. The media constructs idealized images of the thin and well-toned body and also promotes consumer products that help people, especially women, achieve this well-maintained body (Ballentine and Ogle 2005). Counihan (1998) points to many women's transformation fantasy— once I am thin everything will be fine. Being thin becomes a panacea; women are socialized to believe that their problems come from being too fat. Counihan describes the quest for becoming thin as a pathetically reductionist channel for dealing with institutionalized powerlessness. Bordo's (2003) analysis of advertisements geared towards women finds that contemporary advertisements reveal continual and astute manipulation of women's dilemmas with conflicting role demands and time pressure. Messages for women emphasize mastery and control of the self compared to ads targeted towards men that emphasize mastery and control over others.

While the push for thinness may be media driven, women's social networks with partners, families, and friends also reinforce the media's message for acceptable bodies (Paquette and Raine 2004). Taken for granted and often well-intentioned social conventions of friendship and caring strongly influence women's body image. Women's body images are disciplined not by force, but through their own and others' critical gaze and surveillance. Thus, Paquette and Raine (2004) suggest that women will not be able to take control over their bodies only by resisting the enormous power of fashion, cosmetic, and diet industries. Everyday social relations and conventions and relationships with health care professionals must also change.

The Socio-Cultural Domain

Obsession with food is connected to another area of feminist food scholarship that centers on women's responsibility for feeding others. Food studies scholars hold contrasting perspectives on whether women's food work gives them power in the family or reinscribes their subordinate gender roles. Women's food provisioning represents their ties to family and also maintains cultural traditions that are at the heart of many women's identities. Anthropological studies of various countries, regions, and ethnic groups reveal how women construct their identities, cultures and class positions through food work (Counihan 2004; Devasahayam 2005). Women's daily work with food connects them in intimate ways with close relatives and friends. For example, newly arrived immigrant women in the USA attempt to maintain their culture by cooking Dominican or Indian meals, while women from upper-middle class families serve fresh fruits and vegetables and fine wines through which they display their class positions.

One of the first scholars to study women's work with food, Lewin (1943), argued that this feeding responsibility gives women power because they act as gatekeepers who control the flow of food into their households. Although Lewin's view of women as gatekeepers held sway for over fifty years, recent scholars of household food provisioning (e.g., McIntosh and Zey 1998) question how much power women gain from their roles as food providers. Food work can reinscribe women's subordination in the home as they put in long, often unrecognized hours working for others. In her 1991 hallmark study, *Feeding the Family*, DeVault documents women's central responsibility for feeding others. She argues that feeding work encompasses both physical and mental labor, although women often deny that feeding the family is work. She also observed that most women try to construct an "ideal family" through their caring/feeding work. Although as Kemmer (2000) points out, even though many women continue their efforts to construct this "ideal family," the structure of many families is not the traditional family, and women's service to their families reinforces women's subservience and other family members' entitlement.

Feminist theory has made multiple strides in examining the intersections between gender, race, ethnicity and class (Narayan 1995; hooks 1998). Rather than viewing women as a unified category, awareness of this intersectionality provides a more complex stance to understand women's work and lives. These intersections of gender, race, ethnicity, and class define who does what work in the food systems and under what conditions. White, upper-middle class women's entrance into the labor force has been facilitated by transferring their care work to other women who are often poor, immigrants, and women of color (Tronto 2002; Duffy 2005). Much of the preparation and serving of food has now been transferred from women's reproductive labor in the home to other women, often poor women of color, who prepare food in processing plants, grocery stores, and restaurants. Race and ethnicity also define the spaces where women work. White women tend to be concentrated at the public face of reproductive labor in the paid labor force, especially in jobs that require interaction; by contrast, women of color are disproportionately represented in dirty, back room jobs (Nakono Glenn 1992). Recent feminist work also explores how images and symbols related to food are intricately tied up with gender and race (Inness 2001).

The Material Domain

In the material domain, a number of studies of women in agricultural production have been conducted in recent years (see, for example, Whatmore 1991; Sachs 1996; Chiappe and Flora 1998). However, very few studies explore the material aspects of gender relations throughout the food system, despite an explosion of studies of commodity chains and globalization (e.g., Friedland 1984; Tanaka and Busch 2003; Gereffi and Korzeniewicz 1994). Since these analyses highlight who controls and who is vulnerable in global commodity chains, commodity chain analysis is ideal for studying gender relations in the food system. In practice, however, other than studies by Barndt (1999) and Dolan (2004), few efforts call attention to women's disadvantaged positions in the agrifood system. Gender analysis remains on the margins of the sociology of agriculture.

As the sociology of agriculture moves more towards a focus on consumption[3], it would seem that gender relations would emerge as an obvious key problematic. Agrifood studies of consumption regard

consumers as active agents in shaping the food system (Goodman 2003), and consumers, especially food purchasers, are typically women. Yet, the gendered construction of production and consumption practices remains a major omission in the debates over the relationship between production and consumption (Lockie and Kitto 2000). Studies of consumption in the sociology of agriculture typically view consumers as ungendered subjects. This focus on consumption is driven by a shift in the politics of resistance in the food system. With the diminished power of unions and the erosion of production-based politics, some view consumers as the new actors in challenging institutions (Gouveia and Juska 2002).[4] This scholarly turn towards consumption presents an excellent opportunity for increasing our understanding of women's connection to food.

RESISTANCE AND FEMINISM

Feminist scholarship also provides complex understandings of resistance strategies. Resistance to neo-liberal globalization in the food system and gender relations with food comes in heterogeneous forms that are not necessarily connected to each other (Della Porta and Diani 2006). As with resistance to neo-liberal globalization in general, these activities include individual acts, workers' movements including organizing union activities, and organizing in the form of new social movements that focus on gender, environment, race, ethnicity, and consumer movements.

Women's efforts to resist and reshape the food system take multiple forms. Molyneux's (1985) distinction between practical and strategic gender needs forms the basis of much gender and development analysis (Moser 1989), but is rarely applied to women's resistance in developed countries. In the case of food, this distinction between practical and strategic efforts proves useful in the U.S. context. Women may act to meet their practical needs, such as access to healthy food, without altering gender power relations. These resistance efforts focus on helping women survive within the current structure. Women also act to meet their strategic needs—acts that involve altering gender power relations—such as equity in the workplace, shared responsibility for cooking, and healthy approaches to women's bodies. These efforts strive to change the core of the structure that subordinates women in the first place.[5] Attempts at resistance to the food system occur in both production and consumption politics. In the USA, many of these efforts are often not explicitly feminist or part of the feminist movement.

How do we explain the perplexing absence of a feminist agenda in women's actions in food-system work? One key factor is agrarian ideology, which tends to support and reinforce the subordination of women. Fink (1992: 196) characterizes the exclusionary nature of agrarian ideology stating that it has been "a white male vision that has failed to consider the full human integrity of other persons." she points out that agrarianism is a gendered ideology that projects different ideals for men and women. Women have been expected to support the farm, men, and children ahead of their own needs or aspirations. Focused on the nuclear family and the male farmer, agrarian ideology embodies traditional gendered roles and can pose a roadblock to raising issues of gender equality for both men and women. And, even though agrarian populism emphasizes the importance of democracy, populist organizing and solidarity were based on a traditional gender division of labor (Naples 1994). Women have long been rendered irrelevant in their roles as farmers. Several studies explore the simultaneous centrality and invisibility of women's labor in agricultural production and also highlight the continual dominance of patriarchal family farms in shaping women's access to land, capital, and credit in the global food system (see Sachs 1996; Whatmore 1991, Friedmann 1986, Brandth 2002). Studies of masculinities and farming also emphasize how gender constructs both men's and women's identities on farms (Brandth 1999). Hassanein (1999) points out that the limitations women face in agricultural environments come not only from overt discrimination or institutional barriers but also from their socialization in rural communities and unequal gender relations experienced in daily life. Women farmers report that they are often not taken seriously or treated respectfully by other farmers, family members, and agricultural professionals (Trauger and Sachs 2006).

DOMAINS OF GENDERED RELATIONS IN FOOD

Here we examine gender relations in the food system in the material, sociocultural, and corporeal domains. Beginning with the material domain, we trace women's labor from field to table within the agrifood system in the USA. Certainly these issues of gender and food are global, cross-borders, and are not confined to any one country. We focus principally on the USA to set boundaries to our study. The USA is a particularly interesting case in terms of the political economy of the food system since it often wields control in terms of globalization of the food system and has high levels of concentration in production, processing, and retailing.

The Material Domain: Women's Paid Labor in the Agrifood System

Increasing concentration and globalization of food production, processing, distribution, and retailing characterize the food industry. These changes have shifted the jobs in the food industry, the largest industrial sector in the USA, from production and manufacturing to service. In this section we document how material relations in the agrifood system are highly gendered from field to table.

The dramatic restructuring and concentration of production agriculture has resulted in fewer farms and farmers in the USA. The size of farms has increased at the same time that smaller family farms continue to go out of business. Despite, or maybe because of, these trends, more women are farming today than in the past. The percentage of women farmers doubled from 5 percent in 1978 to 10 percent in 1997 to 12 percent in 2002 (U.S. Census of Agriculture 2002). In addition, the Census of Agriculture began to count multiple operators on farms in 2002 and reported that 27 percent of farmers were women. Women farmers remain underrepresented relative to their proportion in the population, however. In addition, women farmers typically own smaller, less-capitalized farms and have lower farm incomes and farm sales than men farmers (U.S. Census of Agriculture 2002).

While women farmers face difficulty in terms of gaining access to land, capital, credit, and knowledge, women farm laborers are certainly even more disadvantaged. Women farm laborers earn extremely low wages and are often subject to sexual harassment. Among U.S. farm workers, women are more vulnerable to exploitation than men, and they are paid even lower wages and given fewer benefits than their male family members (Kearney and Nagengast 1989). Women farm workers median yearly earnings were between $2,500 and $5,000 compared to men farm workers whose median yearly earnings were between $5,000 and $7,5000 (U.S. Department of Labor 2005).

Gender divisions of labor also characterize food processing and manufacturing. Global commodity chains, especially in horticulture, rely on women as disadvantaged workers in processing and packinghouses (Dolan 2004; Collins 1995; Barndt 1999; Barrientos 2001). Women are preferred workers in vegetable and fruit production, which is seasonal, part-time, and flexible. Increasingly, fresh fruits and vegetables are tended and harvested by women in Southern countries for export to the USA and Europe. In the USA, women are the preferred workers in the lower echelons of food processing, where they tend to dominate low-level, high-intensity jobs, while men dominate supervisor and driver jobs. According to the U.S. Department of Labor and the U.S. Bureau of Labor Statistics (2005), women comprised 75 percent of graders and sorters of agricultural products, but only 20 percent of meat processing workers; in both cases their earnings were approximately three-fourths of men's earnings. Indeed, the lowest paying occupation for women in the USA in 1998 was farming, fishing, and forestry occupations with median earnings of only $302 per week for full-time work (Bowler 1999).

With shifts in diet, farm-export policies, and retail stores demand for prepackaged meat, processors have deskilled jobs and shifted plants from unionized areas to rural areas with cheaper land and labor. The meat industry has changed with changes in diet—the shift from beef consumption to poultry consumption due to health concerns has resulted in poultry processing becoming the largest sector of the meat industry (Kandel 2006). Women, immigrants, and Hispanics have become preferred workers in these low-paying, difficult, and dangerous jobs.[6] These jobs fit the International Labor Organization's definition of 3D jobs: jobs that are dirty, dangerous, and degrading.

In food retailing, globalization has led to dramatic restructuring, with the 10 largest food companies now controlling 49 percent of food sales. Grocery stores ranked among the largest industries in the USA in 2002, providing 2.5 million jobs. Food retailers rely heavily on women workers. In 2002, women worked 49 percent of the hours in grocery stores (Clarke 2003). In their efforts to be competitive, retailers' cost-cutting strategies often translate into low pay for the women workers on whom they rely. For example, 72 percent of sales workers at Wal-Mart are women, who average $7.50 per hour with no health benefits. At the other end of the spectrum, management in the food retailing industry has been male dominated, so much so that one large grocery chain recently instituted policies to increase the number of women in management.[7]

One of the major shifts in food labor results from increased dining outside the home—in restaurants and other institutions such as schools, hospitals, and prisons. The percent of food expenditures for food eaten outside the home increased from 33 percent in 1970 to 49 percent in 2005 (Economic Research Service 2006). This shift away from domestic food preparation is due in large part to the entry of more women into the labor force and their lack of time to prepare food at home. As more and more people eat out, the number of jobs in food service increases. Women hold most of the jobs in food service. The 2002 U.S. Census reports that women comprise 77 percent of the 6.5 million workers in food preparation and service. Sixty-eight percent of food servers and 78 percent of restaurant greeters are women (U.S. Bureau of Labor Statistics 2005b). The number of jobs in the food service industry is predicted to increase, but these are not necessarily "good" jobs. Many of these food service workers are entry-level employees who often work long shifts in temporary positions and wield very little power in terms of their schedules or other terms of employment. Many of the jobs held by women in food service are part-time, flexible positions in which the workers earn relatively low wages with few benefits. Part-time work is more common among food and beverage serving workers than among workers in almost any other occupation. In 2004, half of all food servers worked part-time schedules (U.S. Bureau of Labor Statistics 2005a). Jobs in the food sector are also often

"contingent," in that they are conditional, transitory, and irregular.

In the commercial kitchen, we might expect women to outnumber men as cooks. After all, cooking is almost universally coded as women's work in the home. Yet women are less likely than men to work as cooks in restaurants—whether McDonald's or five-star restaurants. Women comprise less than 40 percent of paid cooks and less than 20 percent of head cooks and chefs (U.S. Bureau of Labor Statistics 2005a). Wages of chefs and cooks vary significantly by type of eating establishment. In 2002, median hourly earnings of chefs and head cooks, jobs that men dominate, were $13.43 with the highest 10 percent earning more than $25.86 per hour. By contrast, women cooks often work in institutions and cafeterias earning an average of $8.72 per hour. Fast-food cooks earned the least—$6.90 per hour (U.S. Bureau of Labor Statistics 2005a). Not surprisingly, women in the cooking occupations predominate in places with lower earnings.

Women are not well represented in the leadership of agribusinesses. Even though the number of women-owned businesses in agriculture has almost doubled since 1980, only one business sector (the transportation, communication, and utilities sector), reported fewer women-owned businesses than agriculture. In 1997, women owned only 16 percent of agricultural service businesses, 20 percent of food manufacturing businesses, 21 percent of retail food stores, and 23 percent of retail drinking and eating places (U.S. Census Bureau 1997). In addition, of 11 major U.S. industries, agriculture has historically been the least likely to employ women as managers, executives, or administrators (U.S. Department of Labor 1989). Women employed in these positions made up less than one percent of the total managerial force in the agricultural industry. The food industry, national governments, international trade organizations, and multilateral organizations set policies about food. In

1992, 82 percent of managers in the U.S. Department of Agriculture were male (U.S. Office of Personnel Management 1992), and the percentage was even higher in senior executive positions.

Decisions related to agriculture and food often rely on science and scientific data about agricultural production and food that contain little input from women. Feminist critiques of agricultural science suggest that women's knowledge is often devalued (Feldman and Welch 1995; Sachs 1996). Agricultural and food-related sciences are historically extremely gendered, with men predominating in agricultural science and women finding a place in nutrition or home economics. For example, in 1976, nearly all (99.6 percent) of agricultural scientists were male (Busch and Lacy 1983). While women have historically been excluded from scientific professions in general, their exclusion continues to be particularly glaring in the agricultural sciences. In 1995, women comprised 13 percent of employed agricultural scientists compared to 28 percent of biological scientists (Buttel and Goldberger 2002). However, the under-representation of women in the agricultural sciences is shifting, with the percentage of women receiving their Ph.D. degrees in agricultural sciences increasing substantially in the past ten years from 23 percent in 1995 to 36 percent in 2005 (National Science Foundation 2006).

Women are increasingly performing labor in the formal labor force on farms, processing plants, grocery stores, and restaurants. Much of this work has shifted from labor previously performed by women in the domestic sphere. Women are overrepresented among low-wage food workers, but are underrepresented in the areas of management and science. Food work, earlier performed by middle and upper-middle class women in the home, has been transferred to low-wage workers, often women of color, in the labor force. This imbalance of power between men and women is similarly evident in the domestic sphere. After all, it is in the home and the family—the next domain we discuss—where gender differences in treatment of individuals and access to resources begin (Engberg 1996).

The Socio-Cultural Domain: Nourishing Others

Although women rarely work as chefs and head cooks in restaurants, they almost always hold the position of head cook in their homes. Regardless of culture, class, or ethnicity, the majority of women cook and serve food for their families—a cultural universal of care and sustenance. Food work involves physical, mental, and caring labor. Women go to the store, shop, unpack groceries, prepare food, cook meals, serve food, wash dishes, and clean the kitchen. Food work is not merely physical but involves relentless mental and caring labor—planning meals, worrying about nutrition, and arranging and serving meals (DeVault 1991). Women must know the food likes and dislikes of their family members, plan the timing and location of meals, and keep up with complicated and ever-changing news on nutrition and food safety. DeVault likens this work of feeding the family to solving a puzzle. DeVault addresses class differences between women, she suggests that in solving the puzzle of what's for dinner, middle-class women consult recipes and working-class women rely on tradition. However, she neglects to consider how race and ethnicity effect women's cooking efforts (Avakain and Haber 2006). Gullah women, African American women, and Jewish women also attempt to maintain their marginalized cultural traditions through food production (Betts 1995; Harris 1995; Kirshenblatt-Gimblettt 1997).

In solving the food-provision puzzle women typically select food that pleases other family members, especially their husbands (Sutor and Barbour 1975; Burt and Hertzler 1978; Schafer and Bohlen

1977). Furthermore, since men's needs dominate the organization of cooking and eating in terms of the composition and timing of meals, many women face serious repercussions if food is not prepared correctly and on time (Bell and Valentine 1997). Women who fail to please their husband's food preferences often experience negative consequences ranging from small arguments to domestic violence. Indeed, the purchase, preparation, and serving of food often serves as a key instigator of violent incidents in the home (Ellis 1983; Murcott 1983). Thus, although women choose the food from supermarket shelves, their decisions often reflect the preferences of others. And, if they make the "wrong" decision, tension, arguments, or violence may ensue. As with other household work, women experience a fundamental ambivalence between the tedium and marginalizing aspects of their work and the love and caring they feel for their families. Such work can be pleasurable or onerous depending on circumstances such as time or financial pressure.

While women remain responsible for food provision in the home, the nature of this caring work of feeding others has shifted over time. Few families or individuals in households eat all of their meals together. Household members who work, go to school, or spend time outside the home often eat breakfast, lunch, and sometimes dinner away from home in restaurants, cafeterias, or other food establishments. Women who work outside the home have less time to prepare food for their families. Much of food processing and cooking activities for food eaten at home now takes place in the market. Convenience foods, such as pre-cooked meals, save women time preparing meals and bring increased profits to the processing, retailing and restaurant industries. But, convenience foods are expensive, stretching the budgets of low-income women. And as we discussed in the previous section, the labor to produce these convenience foods is often provided by women, often women of color, working for low wages in difficult working conditions (Julier 2006).

Still, despite the increasing entry of women into the labor force, women spend at least twice as much time as men doing domestic chores, an imbalance particularly marked in food labor. Even when men share more domestic labor in the home, they are only marginally involved with food provisioning activities (Engberg 1996). Studies show that mothers, still considered the experts on children, do the majority of work in taking care of children, including feeding them (Zimmerman et al. 2001; Coltrane 1996).

Another aspect of the entry of women into the labor force is that in upper-middle and middle-class U.S households employed women lack the time to do housework and child care. Male household members rarely step in. Women either work almost around the clock or, if they can afford it, hire domestic help. Affluent career women increasingly maintain the illusion of "doing it all" by hiring domestic workers and nannies to clean the house, feed the children, and magically disappear from sight (Ehrenreich and Hothschild 2002). While most women in U.S. households maintain responsibility for cooking and serving food, the dislocation of third-world women to the USA and other industrialized countries enables relatively affluent women to hire immigrant women to perform domestic work while they work outside the home (Mack-Canty 2004). White, upper-middle class women transfer their care work to other women—often poor, immigrants, and women of color (Tronto 2002; Duffy 2005).

The Corporeal Domain: Embodied Politics

While women have primary responsibility for feeding others, they often fail to take care of their own nutritional needs. Many women, regardless of their age or weight are dissatisfied with their bodies (Paquette and Raine 2004). Seventy-five percent of "normal" weight women consider themselves overweight, and 90 percent of women overestimate their body size. The average woman sees 400 to 600 advertisements per day and by the time a girl is 17 years old, she has received over 250,000 commercial messages. Most of these messages directly or indirectly promote physical attractiveness, including being thin. Nearly three-quarters of girls report that magazine models influence their concept of an ideal body shape, yet a woman between the ages of 18 and 34 has only a one percent chance of being as thin as a supermodel. Body discontent leads to dieting by normal weight women, unhealthy weight loss practices, restrained eating, eating disorders, depression, and poor self-esteem (Paquette and Raine 2004).

Within the agrifood system, the diet industry profits enormously from women's obsession with thinness and attempts to maintain unattainable body weights. The numbers of girls and women on diets has skyrocketed. Dieting, now a normal female lifetime preoccupation, begins with girls in pursuit of the perfect body. In a 1986 study of five hundred schoolgirls, 81 percent of ten-year-olds reported they had dieted at least once (Mellin et al. 1992). That the perfect body is, by definition, unattainable, traps many women and girls in a relentless cycle of failure. The proliferation of eating disorders, heavily gendered, is also class specific. Bordo (1998) claims that many women, who can afford to eat well, diet and go hungry most of the time. Girls and women, especially from the upper and upper-middle classes, deny themselves food as they tie their hopes for happiness on being thin.

On the other end of the weight continuum, the number of women who are overweight and obese is increasing. Sixty-two percent of women in the USA are overweight and 28 percent are obese (National Institutes of Health 2006).

Gender, class, ethnicity, and race intersect in defining who is likely to be overweight or obese. A negative correlation exists between income and weight; as incomes go down weight goes up. People with low incomes find that foods high in sugar and fat are cheap and readily available, while "healthy" foods are relatively expensive and not necessarily available in their local stores (Morton et al. 2005). Obesity in women is also correlated with race and ethnicity. Obesity is most prevalent among non-Hispanic black women (49 percent) compared with Mexican-American women (38 percent) and non-Hispanic white women (31 percent) (National Center for Health Statistics 2004). For men, however, there is very little difference in obesity levels based on race/ethnicity (National Center for Health Statistics 2004). Obesity is connected to many health problems and the link between obesity and diabetes is particularly high in women. Obesity among children is also on the rise. Mothers often take the blame for their failure to provide their children with nutritious foods. Women with children are caught in a double bind as they are enjoined to make their children happy by feeding them junk food while they are simultaneously exhorted to be "good mothers" by ensuring the nutritional health of their children.

Eating disorders, whether resulting in being too thin or too fat, have been analyzed and treated principally as individual, psychological, and medical problems. Studies of obesity similarly focus the problem on individual eating behaviors rather than the food industry, limited access to nutritious food, or the increasing loss of public space for physical activity. Medicalization and individualization of public health and social problems obscure the food industry's role in constructing people's food desires and behaviors and blame the individual. Since food is women's responsibility, the corollary of the individuation of food-related health problems is that women are to blame.

Women cannot help but be caught up in some form of schizophrenic positioning with regard to food—eat more, eat less; eat well, eat badly—due to the contradictory and simultaneous marketing of thinness and food indulgence. At the same time that fashion advertising tells women to be thin, food advertising advocates indulgence, including eating junk food. Despite, or maybe due to, their schizophrenic position, women are leading efforts to create change in the agrifood system. We highlight some of these efforts in the next section.

WORKING AGAINST HOMEOSTASIS

Gender relations in the agrifood system have remained surprisingly static despite sea changes taking place in other dimensions of the agrifood system. One thing that has changed, however, is the extent of women-led initiatives. While women have always been involved in the food system, they now are playing expanded roles in changing material, socio-cultural, and corporeal conditions. Their efforts take multiple forms ranging from individual-level actions to collective resistance in the form of union organizing or involvement in agrifood social movements.

Women have taken the lead in resisting the repressive and exploitative conditions women face as hired labor in the food system. For example, women farm workers have organized for the rights of women farm workers, farm worker health, and day care and schools for migrant children. One group, Organización en California de Lideras Campesinas (Farm worker Women's Leadership Network), organized in 1992, trains and organizes farm worker women on health issues, nutrition, pesticide issues, domestic violence, and economic development. Women have also taken the lead in the retail workers movement, beginning in 2000 when Betty Dukes filed a sex discrimination claim against Wal-Mart, her employer.[8] Wal-Mart is the largest food retailer in the United States as well as one of the largest employers in many regions of the country.[9] The suit charged Wal-Mart with discriminating against women in promotions, pay and job assignments, and that the company was in violation of the Civil Rights Act (Featherstone 2004).[10] Dukes vs. Wal-Mart Stores, Inc., eventually expanded to represent 1.6 million women, making it the largest civil rights class-action suit in history. Recognizing the central importance of Wal-Mart policies on American women, National Organization of Women (NOW) actively supports this legal action.

In the public domain, women have worked to reshape the food system through organizing around livelihood issues and claims made on the state. Women were instrumental in establishing and managing federal food assistance programs to combat hunger and poor nutrition, and they continue to lead the fight to hold the line on cutbacks in public programs that provide assistance to impoverished families in the USA. For example, the National Council for Women's Organizations has a food security program that works to protect and expand the Food Stamp Program, the WIC Program (Women, Infants, and Children), and other supplemental food programs.

Women have also played central roles in shaping and furthering alternative agrifood movements and institutions. For example, women have led the National Campaign for Sustainable Agriculture, the California Campaign for Sustainable Agriculture, the California Food and Justice Coalition, the USDA Community Food Projects program, and the USDA SARE program. Peter et al. (2000) found that women are better represented and more prominent in sustainable agriculture organizations than they are in conventional agricultural organizations. Women often take the lead in urban agriculture, developing community gardens in diverse, low-income communities (Hynes 1996). For example, women have created

Grow Pittsburgh, an organization that works to reclaim abandoned urban lots, build kitchen gardens to improve nutrition, and engage youth in food system work (Grow Pittsburgh 2006).

In Vermont, Maine, Iowa, and Pennsylvania women farmers have formed new types of networks for educational, social, and entrepreneurial support to empower women in sustainable agriculture and food-related businesses (Trauger 2005). For example, the Pennsylvania Agricultural Women's Network began in 2003 as a fledgling organization of women farmers and agricultural professionals with the goals of creating an empowering learning environment and network. The network's rapid growth surprised the organizers. As of 2006, more than 600 members participate in the network, the majority who work as farmers on small or medium-sized operations. Women farmers often lead the way for environmental sustainability and innovative entrepreneurship on farms. For example, in DeLind and Ferguson's (1999) study of community supported agriculture, they discovered that women were the primary workers on CSAs. Other women farmers, frustrated with working so hard to raise crops and livestock with very little return, form nonprofits or educational programs on their farms—one woman runs a farm camp for girls and several women involve at-risk children on their farms (Sachs 2006).

Women also lead broad-scale efforts to create, healthy, environmentally sustainable, and socially just food cultures and systems. For example, women are key leaders in pushing for changes in food and agriculture issues in the anti-globalization struggle (Mohanty 2003; Shiva 2002). While some organizing efforts engage the state, most fall into the domain of the consumer politics of food. Women are at the forefront of ethical buying, supporting fair trade, humane, organic, and local food. Some of these efforts are individual acts by consumers and business owners, others are collective actions, and some combine individual and collective actions. For example, Judy Wickes, owner of the White Dog Café in Philadelphia, works with her restaurant and her Fair Food Foundation to strengthen and connect locally owned businesses and farms committed to working in harmony with natural systems, providing meaningful living wage jobs, supporting healthy community life, and contributing to economic justice (White Dog Café 2006). Her efforts are tied more broadly to the fair trade, sustainable agriculture, and local food movements. One of their innovative projects, the Sister Restaurant Project develops "sister" relationships with African-American owned restaurants. They promote visits to their sister restaurants to encourage their customers to visit neighborhoods they otherwise might not go to in order to increase understanding, build citywide community, and support minority businesses and cultural institutions.

In the corporeal realm, women's organizations combat the cultural impositions such as advertising that contribute to the destructive eating behaviors of many women and girls. The concern with eating disorders is the major food-related issue that has been taken up by the feminist movement. For example, the National Organization for Women organizes a "Love Your Body Day" to provide a forum for people to speak out against advertising and images of women that are harmful or offensive. Millman's now classic book, "Such a pretty face: Being fat in America" (1980) explored stereotypes of overweight women and inspired scholarship and activism around issues of body image and feminism.

Despite all of these women-led efforts in the agrifood system, there is a curious absence of feminism per se in women's efforts to create change in the agrifood system, with the exception of corporeal politics. This is true in three ways. First, while the efforts described above are by women, they are not necessarily consciously "feminist" in the sense of resisting the oppressive nature of gender relations. Second, some of the efforts may be counter to a feminist agenda. Third, the feminist movement rarely takes up issues relating to women and food in material and domestic realms.

Women's efforts to change the food system rarely take an explicitly feminist approach. The leader of the farm women's network studied by Hassanein (1999) emphasized that it was not a "feminist" organization. Luminary women such as Dolores Huerta played strong roles in the farm labor movement. While Huerta was herself a feminist,[11] the farm labor movement, infused with a machismo culture, rarely addresses women's issues. In some cases, women may be instigators, but still play support roles. For example, a study of women in the sustainable agriculture movement in California found that while women were active in the movement, particularly at the grassroots level, men tended to hold the more visible leadership and decision-making positions (Sachs 1996). A Minnesota study found that men acted as teachers, leaders, and decision makers in the sustainable agriculture movement while women involved in the movement tended to occupy support roles such as providing food, working registration tables, and sending mailings (Meares 1997). Men are disproportionately represented in leadership roles in sustainable agriculture such as project directors, conference speakers, and authors just about everywhere. Women have been correspondingly overrepresented in social cohesion roles such as organizing conferences, coordinating community endeavors, and fostering networks among different groups. The "traditional" roles played by women in these movements may serve to reinscribe and normalize gendered relations.

Beyond this, agrifood women activists have also historically tended to overlook their needs or subordinate themselves. For example, rural women in the USA have tended to join organizations that support their families or farm organizations rather than participating in organizations dedicated to women's empowerment (Sachs 1996). For example, one supporter of the California Women for Agriculture in the 1980s said that the women were involved basically on behalf of their men, from whom they get their ideas (Friedland 1991).

In other ways, some of women's food-system efforts are contradictory—or at least ironic—in terms of a feminist agenda. For example, some practices advocated by alternative agrifood movements, such as farmers' markets and CSAs, can add both to the workload of farm women and to women's already overburdened workload in food procurement and preparation in the home (Allen 1999). Some of the women in Meares' (1997) study of the sustainable agriculture movement reported that their workloads had increased as a result of their partners' participation in the movement, but that the workloads of their male partners had not increased. And, the Slow Food movement, a shining light of contemporary food movements, promotes the leisurely consumption of elaborate, home-prepared meals without acknowledging that time pressures for the women who are the traditional preparers of food have tightened. On the other hand, a woman resisting domestic servitude in the kitchen might turn to fast foods to feed her children and then feel guilty. And, the body-acceptance movement rightly resists cultural stereotypes of thinness for women, but may lead women to accept obesity, a condition that negatively affects their health.

The feminist movement has taken on issues with regard to women and food in the corporeal domain, but has attended far less to the material and socio-cultural domains. Rather, feminist organizing efforts have focused more on women's involvement in the formal economy, formal politics, and concerns with women's bodies and reproductive rights. In the private sphere of the home, the major feminist issue has focused on domestic violence, although rarely is it linked to the apparently crucial trigger of food and meals. Changing the division of labor in the home or kitchen has largely been a struggle for women at the individual level of negotiating with their partners and other family members, as opposed to an organized feminist struggle.

CONCLUSION

Nearly all women spend a significant portion of their day occupied and preoccupied with food. This responsibility, a key component of women's identity, also serves as a key component of their exploitation, oppression, and, accordingly, their resistance. Women do the majority of food-related work, but have little power. Women feed others and deprive themselves. For Western women and girls, dieting serves as a normal and often lifetime activity. In conditions of food shortage, women and girls go hungry more often than men and boys. Gender discrimination and contingency is enabled by an accepted cultural orientation that undervalues women and their labor. Despite these conditions and their seemingly immutable character, women are taking action to create change. Women's subordination is locked into food, but their resistance in the material, socio-cultural, and corporeal domains of food challenges global capitalism and male privilege. As women work to reshape the food system in the interest of better health, social justice, and environmental soundness, they are also creating possibilities for women to gain control of their bodies and their lives.

We suggest that gender relationships in the food system can be understood through exploring three intersecting and overlapping domains: the material, the socio-cultural, and the corporeal. Feminist scholarship's focus on the connections between gendered divisions of labor in the home and in the labor market and distinctions between the private and public realms prove useful in understanding women's relationship to food. Women's work with food spans the formal economy, informal economy, and household economy. Thus, in studying women's connections to food, we have examined their work in both the formal economy and the household.

Barndt's (1999) Tomasita project is an example of this type of interaction that combines research and action. In the commodity chain tradition, the research traces women's work with tomatoes from the fields and processing plants in Mexico to the supermarkets and fast food restaurants in Canada. This research shows how labor practices of Maquilization and McDonaldization have resulted in the feminization of the workforce as deskilled, part-time, low-wage women workers replaced skilled, permanent, often male, workers. What makes Barndt's project particularly important is the way in which it went beyond research to bring Mexican and Canadian women workers and scholars together to discuss strategies for action and resistance.

Women's experiences in the food system also must be examined through feminist standpoint theory, which holds that feminist social science should be conducted from the standpoint of women in order to examine and understand the systematic oppressions of women in society. Sometimes a source of power, more often one of subordination, the fact remains that we need to understand much more about gender relations in the food system. We need to know much more about who women food activists are, their motivations, and their visions for the food system. We have much to learn about the possibilities for changing gender relations and the emerging field of feminist food studies can lead the way through weaving together feminist studies of food and the body with feminist work in the sociology and political economy of agriculture.

ACKNOWLEDGMENTS

The authors would like to that Hilary Melcarek for her invaluable research support and the anonymous reviewers for their insightful comments and suggestions.

NOTES

1. We use the term "food chains" in a double sense. First, we are drawing on the scholarship of commodity food analysis (Barndt 1999; Dolan 2004). Second, we suggest that women's inescapable responsibility for reproductive work with food for their families and their relationship to food and eating, metaphorically "chains" them to food.

2. The agrifood system is the complex of institutions and organizations that define, regulate, and shape the organization of agriculture and food from field to table.

3. The sociology of agriculture has long neglected the relationship between the production and provision of food. Scholars have typically viewed production as determining consumption, thereby justifying the neglect of consumers (Lockie and Kitto 2000). Despite the historical disregard of consumption by agrifood studies, efforts to locate food production and consumption in a more symmetrical analytic framework are currently underway (Goodman 2003). Recently, agrifood studies attempts to bring the consumer in through research on systems of provision (Fine et al. 1996) and actor-network theory (Murdoch 1994).

4. Gouveia and Juska (2002) point out how production and consumption politics divide along race lines in the food system, particularly in the meat industry, with mobilization around production issues primarily led by Latino groups and consumer resistance largely led by non-Hispanic whites.

5. As Gouveia and Juska (2002) remind us, these resistance efforts are not only gendered, but also defined by race and ethnicity.

6. While in 1980, 74 percent of meat processing workers were white, by 2000, 49 percent of meat processing workers were Hispanic (Kandel and Parrado 2005).

7. Between 2000 and 2005, Safeway increased the number of women store managers by 40 percent, 34 percent for white women and 65 percent for women of color. During the same period of time, the number of women in vice-president positions increased from 12 percent to 25 percent (Catalyst 2006).

8. Specifically, Dukes claimed that despite her hard work and excellent performance, she was denied the training she needed to advance to a higher, salaried position.

9. For example, Wal-Mart is the largest employer in Pennsylvania.

10. In February, 2007, a Federal Appeals Court in San Francisco upheld a lower court ruling granting class action status to the lawsuit against Wal-Mart.

11. Huerta worked diligently with Cesar Chavez to organize farmworkers in the United Farm Workers of America, AFL-CIO (UFW) until his death in 1993. At age 75, Huerta continues her work organizing farmworkers as Secretary-Treasurer Emeritus of the UFW and also organizes on feminist issues in her position as a board member of the Feminist Majority Foundation (Dolores Huerta Foundation, 2003–2006).

REFERENCES

Allen, Patricia. 1999. "Reweaving the Food Security Safety Net: Mediating Entitlement and Entrepreneurship." Agriculture and Human Values 16 (2): 117–129.

Avakian, Alrene Voski, and Barbara Haber. 2006. "Feminist Food Studies: A Brief History." Pp 1–26 in From Betty Crocker to Feminist Food Studies: Critical Perspectives on Women and Food, edited by A. V. Avakian and B. Haber. Amherst, MA: University of Massachusetts Press.

Ballentine, Leslie and Jennifer Ogle. 2005. "The Making and Unmaking of Body Problems in Seventeen Magazine, 1993–2003." Family and Consumer Sciences Research Journal 33 (4): 281–307.

Barndt, Deborah, ed. 1999. Women Working the NAFTA Food Chain: Women, Food and Globalization. Toronto, ON: Sumach Press.

Barrientos, Stephanie. 2001. "Gender, Flexibility and Global Value Chains." Institute of Development Studies Bulletin 32(3): 83–94.

Bell, David and Gill Valentine. 1997. Consuming Geographies. London, UK: Routledge.

Beoku-Betts, Josephine. 1995. "We Got Our Way of Cooking Things: Women Food and Preservation of Cultural Identity among the Gullah." Gender and Society 9(5): 535–555.

Bordo, Susan. 1998. "Hunger as Ideology." Pp 11–35 in Eating Culture, edited by R. Scapp and B. Sietz. Albany, NY: State University of New York Press.

Bordo, Susan. 2003. Feminism, Western Culture, and the Body. Berkeley, CA: University of California Press.

Bowler, Mary. 1999. "Women's Earnings: An Overview." Monthly Labor Review December: 1–21.

Brandth, Berit. 1999. "Modernity, Feminism and Farm Women." Unpublished paper given at

Gender and Transformation in Rural Europe, Wageningen, Netherlands, 14–17 October 1999.

Brandth, Berit. 2002. "Gender Identity in European Family Farming: A Literature Review." Sociologia Ruralis 42 (3): 181–200.

Burt, J. V. and A. V. Hertzler. 1978. "Parental Influence on the Child's Food Preference." Journal of Nutrition Education 10: 123–134.

Busch, Lawrence, and William B. Lacy. 1983. Science, Agriculture, and the Politics of Research. Boulder, CO: Westview Press.

Buttel, Frederick and Jessica Goldberger. 2002. "Gender and Agricultural Science: Evidence from Two Surveys of Land Grant Scientists." Rural Sociology 57 (10): 24–46.

Catalyst. 2006. "Safeway's Championing Change for Women: An Integrated Strategy." http://www.catalystwomen.org.

Chiappe, Maria B. and Cornelia Butler Flora. 1998. "Gendered Elements of the Alternative Agriculture Paradigm." Rural Sociology 49:183–209.

Clarke, Cynthia M. 2003. "Workplace Illnesses and Injuries in Grocery Stores." Washington, DC: Bureau of Labor Statistics, http://www.bls.gov.

Collins, Jane. 1995. "Transnational Labor Process and Gender Relations: Women in Fruit and Vegetable Production in Chili, Brazil, and Mexico." Journal of Latin American Anthropology 1(1): 78–99.

Coltrane, Scott. 1996. The Family Man: Fatherhood, Housework, and Gender Equality. New York, NY: Oxford University Press.

Counihan, Carole M. 1998. "What Does It Mean to Be Fat, Thin, and Female in the United States: a Review Essay." Pp. 145–162 in Food and Gender: Identity and Power, edited by Carol M. Counihan and Steven L. Kaplan. Åmsterdam, Netherlands: Harwood Academic Publishers.

Counihan, Carole M. 2004. Around the Tuscan Table: Food, Family and Gender in Twentieth Century Florence. New York, NY: Routledge.

Della Porta, Donatella and Mario Diani. 2006. Social Movements: An Introduction. London, UK: Blackwell.

DeLind, Laura and Anne Ferguson. 1999. "Is This a Woman's Movement?: The Relationship of Gender to Community-Supported Agriculture in Michigan." Human Organization 58: 190–200.

Devasahayam, Theresa. 2005. "Power and Pleasure Around the Stove: The Construction of Gendered Identity in Middle-class Hindi South Indian Households in Urban Malaysia." Women's Studies International Forum 28(1): 1–20.

DeVault, Marjorie L. 1991. Feeding the Family: The Social Organization of Caring as Gendered Work. Chicago, IL: University of Chicago Press.

Dolan, Catherine. 2004. "On Farm and Packhouse: Employment at the Bottom of a Global Value Chain." Rural Sociology 69 (1): 99–126.

Dolores Huerta Foundation. 2003–2006. Dolores Huerta Biography. http://www.doloreshuerta.org//dolores_huerta_foundation.htm.

Duffy, Mignon. 2005. "Reproducing Labor Inequalities: Challenges for Feminists Conceptualizing Care at the Intersections of Gender, Race, and Class." Gender and Society 19 (1): 66–82.

Economic Research Service. 2006. "Food Consumer Price Index, Prices, and Expenditures: Food Expenditure Tables." Washington, DC: United States Department of Agriculture, https://www.ers.usda.gov

Ehrenreich, Barbara and Arlie R. Hochschild. 2002. Global Woman: Nannies, Maids and Sex Workers in the New Economy. London, UK: Granta Books.

Ellis, Rhian 1983. "The Way to a Man's Heart: Food in the Violent Home." Pp. 164–171 in The Sociology of Food and Eating: Essays on the Sociological Significance of Food, edited by A. Murcott. Aldershot, UK: Gower.

Engberg, L. 1996. "Livelihood and Food Security: Issues for Women and Families." NGO Comments on WFS Policy and Plan of Action. http://www.unac.org.gnfs/ngolila.htm.

Featherstone, Liza. 2004. Selling Women Short: The Landmark Battle for Workers' Rights at Wal-Mart. New York, NY: Basic Books.

Feldman, Shelley and Rick Welsh. 1995. "Feminist Knowledge Claims, Local Knowledge and Gender Divisions of Agricultural Labor." Rural Sociology 60 (1): 23–43.

Fine, Ben, Michael Heasman, and Judith Wright. 1996. Consumption in the Age of Influence: The World of Food. London, UK: Routledge.

Fink, Deborah. 1992. Agrarian Women: Wives and Mothers in Rural Nebraska. Chapel Hill, NC: University of North Carolina Press.

Friedland, William H. 1984: "Commodity Systems Analysis: An Approach to the Sociology of Agriculture." Pp. 221–235 in Research in Rural Sociology and Development, Focus on Agriculture. Vol. 1, edited by H. K. Schwarzweller. Greenwich, CT: JAI Press.

Friedland, William H. 1991. "Women and Agriculture in the United States." In Towards a New Political Economy of Agriculture, edited by W.H. Friedland, L. Busch, F. Buttel, and A. Rudy. Boulder, CO: Westview Press.

Friedmann, Harriet. 1986. "Property and Patriarchy: A Reply to Goodman and Redclift." Sociologia Ruralis 26: 186–193.

Gereffi, Gary and Miguel Korzeniewicz. 1994. Commodity Chains and Global Capitalism. Westport, CT: Greenwood Press.

Goodman, David. 2003. "The Quality 'Turn' and Alternative Food Practices: Reflections and Agenda." Journal of Rural Studies 19 (1): 1–7.

Gouveia, Lourdes and Arunas Juska. 2002. "Taming Nature, Taming Workers: Constructing the Separation Between Meat Consumption and Meat Production in the U.S." Sociologia Ruralis 42(4):370–38.

Grow Pittsburgh. 2006. http://www.growpittsburgh.org.

Harris, Jessica. 1995. The Welcome Table: African American Heritage Cooking. New York: Simon & Schuster.

Hassanein, Neva. 1999. Changing the Way America Farms: Knowledge and Community in the Sustainable Agriculture Movement. Lincoln, NE: University of Nebraska Press.

hooks, bell. 1998. "Eating the Other: Desire and Resistance." In Eating Culture, edited by R. Scapp and B. Seitz. Albany, NY: State University of New York Press.

Hynes, H. Patricia. 1996. A Patch of Eden: America's Inner City Gardeners. Boston, MA: Chelsea Green.

Inness, Sherrie A. 2001. Dinner Roles: American Women and Culinary Culture. Iowa City, IA: University of Iowa Press.

Julier, Alice. 2006. "Hiding Gender and Race in the Discourse of Commercial Food Consumption." Pp 27–46 in From Betty Crocker to Feminist Food Studies: Critical Perspectives on Women and Food, edited by A. V. Avakian and B. Haber. Amherst, MA: University of Massachusetts Press.

Kandel, William. 2006. "Meat Processing Firms Attract Hispanic Workers to Rural America." Amber Waves, June. Washington, DC: United States Department of Agriculture, Economics Research Service.

Kandel, William and Emilio A. Parrado. 2005. "Restructuring of the US Meat Processing Industry and New Hispanic Migrant Destinations." Population and Development Review 31 (3): 447–471.

Kearney, Michael and Carol Nagengast. 1989. "Anthropological Perspectives on Transnational Communities in Rural California." Working Group on Farm Labor and Rural Poverty Working Paper no. 3. Davis, CA: California Institute for Rural Studies.

Kemmer, Debbie. 2000. "Tradition and Change in Domestic Roles and Food Preparation." Sociology 34 (2): 323–333.

Kirshenblatt-Gimblett, Barbara. 1997. "The Temple Emanuel Fair and Its Cookbook, Denver 1888. In Recipes for Reading." Anne Bower (ed). Amherst: University of Massachusetts Press.

Lewin, Kurt. 1943. "Forces Behind Food Habits and Methods of Change." Pp. 35–65 in The Problem of Changing Food Habits. Bulletin 108. Washington, DC: National Academy of Science, National Research Council.

Lockie, Stewart and Simon Kitto. 2000. "Beyond the Farm Gate: Production-Consumption Networks and Agri-Food Research." Sociologia Ruralis 40 (1): 3–19.

Mack-Canty, Colleen. 2004. "Third-Wave Feminism and the Need to Reweave the Nature/Culture Duality." NWSA Journal 16 (3): 154–174.

McIntosh, Wm. Alex and Mary Zey. 1998. "Women as Gatekeepers of Food Consumption: A Sociological Critique." Pp. 125–144 in Food and Gender: Identity and Power, edited by C. M. Counihan and S. L. Kaplan. Amsterdam, Netherlands: Harwood Academic Publishers.

McMichael, Philip. 2000. "The Power of Food." Agriculture and Human Values, 17 (1): 21–33.

Meares, A.C. 1997. "Making the Transition from Conventional to Sustainable Agriculture: Gender, Social Movement Participation, and Quality of Life on the Family Farm." Rural Sociology 62 (1): 21–47.

Mellin, L.M., CE. Irwin, and S. Scully. 1992. "Prevalence of Disordered Eating in Girls: A Survey of Middle Class Children." Journal of the American Dietetic Association, 92 (7): 851–853.

Millman, Marcia. 1980. Such a Pretty Face: Being Fat in America. New York, NY: Norton.

Mohanty, Chandra. 2003. Feminism Without Borders: Decolonizing Theory, Practicing Solidarity. Durham, NC: Duke University Press.

Molyneux, Maxine. 1985. "Mobilization Without Emancipation: Women's Interests, The State, and Revolution Within Nicaragua." Feminist Studies 11 (2): 227–254.

Morton, Lois Wright, Annette Bitto Ella, Mary Jane Oakland, and Mary Sand. 2005. "Solving the Problems of Iowa Food Deserts: Food Insecurity and Civic Structure." Rural Sociology 70(1): 94–112.

Moser, Charlotte. 1989. "Gender Planning in the Third World: Meeting Practical and Strategic Gender Needs." World Development 17 (11): 1799–1825.

Murcort, Ann. 1983. "It's a Pleasure to Cook for Him . . . : Food, Mealtimes and Gender in Some South Wales Households." Pp. 97–107 in The Public and the Private, edited by. E. Garmarnikov. London, UK: Heinemann.

Murdoch, Jonathan. 1994. "Some Comments on 'Nature' and 'Society' in the Political Economy of Food." Review of International Political Economy 1 (3): 571–577.

Nakono Glenn, Evelyn. 1992. "From Servitude to Service Work: Historical Continuities in the Racial Division of Paid Reproductive Labor." Signs: Journal of Women in Culture and Society 18: 1–43.

Naples, Nancy A. 1994. "Contradictions in Agrarian Ideology: Restructuring Gender, Race-Ethnicity, and Class." Rural Sociology 59 (1): 110–135.

Narayan, Uma. 1995. "Eating Cultures: Incorporation, Identity and Indian Food." Social Identities 1 (1): 63–86.

National Center for Health Statistics. 2004. "Obesity Still a Major Problem." Atlanta, GA: Center for Disease Control, http://www.cdc.gov/nchs/pressroom/04facts/obesity

National Institutes of Health. 2006. "Weight Control Information Network." Washington, DC: U.S. Department of Health and Health Services. http://win.niddk.nih.gov/statistics

National Science Foundation. 2006. "Women, Minorities, and Persons with Disabilities in Science and Engineering." http://www.nsf.gov/statistics

Paquette, Marie-Claude and Kim Raine. 2004. "Sociocultural Context of Women's Body Image." Social Science & Medicine 59: 1047–1058.

Peter, Greg, Michael M. Bell, and Susan Jarnagin. 2000. "Coming Back Across the Fence: Masculinity and the Transition to Sustainable Agriculture." Rural Sociology 65 (2): 215–233.

Sachs, Carolyn E. 1996. Gendered Fields: Rural Women, Agriculture, and Environment. Boulder, CO: Westview Press.

Sachs, Carolyn E. 2006. "Going Public: Networking Globally and Locally." Presidential Address at Rural Sociological Society Annual Meeting, Louisville, KY, August, 2006.

Schafer, Robert and Joe M. Bohlen. 1977. "The Exchange of Conjugal Power and Its Effects on Family Food Consumption." Home Economics Research Journal 5: 124–134.

Shiva, Vandana. 2002. Sustainable Agriculture and Food Security: The Impact of Globalization. Thousand Oaks, CA: Sage Publications.

Sutor, Carol. B. and Helen F. Barbour. 1975. "Identifying Food Related Values of Low-Income Mothers." Home Economics Research Journal 3: 198–204. Tanaka, Keiko and Lawrence Busch. 2003. "Standardization as a Means for Globalizing a Commodity: The Case of Rapeseed in China." Rural Sociology, 68 (1): 25–45.

Trauger, Amy K. 2005. Social, Economic, and Environmental Justice: a Network Analysis of Sustainable Agriculture in Pennsylvania. PhD dissertation, Department of Geography, Penn State University.

Trauger, Amy and Carolyn Sachs. 2006. "Understanding Effective Educational Programming for Women Farmers in the Pennsylvania Women's Agricultural Network." Paper presented at Rural Sociological Society Annual Meeting, Louisville, KY, August 2006.

Tronto, Joan C. 2002. "The 'Nanny' Question in Feminism." Hypatia, 17(2): 34–51. U.S. Bureau of Labor Statistics. 2005a. Occupational Outlook Handbook. Washington, DC: U.S. Department of Labor, http://www.bls.gov

Tronto, Joan C. 2005b. Women in the Labor Force: A Data Book., Report 95. Washington, DC: U.S. Department of Labor. http://www.bls.gov/cps/wlf-databook-2005.pdf

U.S. Census of Agriculture. 2002. U.S. Census of Agriculture. Washington, DC: United States Department of Agriculture.

U.S. Census Bureau. 1997. 1997 Economic Census: Minority- and Women-Owned Businesses, United States. Washington, DC: U.S. Census Bureau. http://www.census.gov/epcd/mwb97/ca/CA.html#Total%20minorities

U.S. Department of Labor. 1989. Facts on Working Women. Report 89–4. Washington, DC: U.S. Government Printing Office.

U.S. Department of Labor and U.S. Bureau of Labor Statistics. 2005. Highlights of Women's Earnings in 2004. Washington, DC: US Department of Labor. http://www.bls.gov/cps/cpswom2004.pdf#search=%22%22highlights%20of%20women's%20earnings%22%22

U.S. Department of Labor. 2005. "Income and Poverty, Chapter 3 in National Agricultural Workers Survey. http://www.dol.gov/asp/programs/agworker/report/ch3.htm

U.S. Office of Personnel Management. 1992. Federal Civilian Workforce Statistics: Demographic Profile of the Federal Workforce. PSO-OWI-5. Washington, DC: U.S. Government Printing Office.

Whatmore, Sarah. 1991. Farming Women: Gender, Work, and Family Enterprise. London, UK: Macmillan.

White Dog Café. 2006. http://www.whitedogcafe.com

Zimmerman, Toni Schindler, Shelly A. Haddock, Scott Ziemba, and Aimee Rust. 2001. "Family Organizational Labor: Who's Calling the Plays?" Journal of Feminist Family Therapy 13 (2–3), 65–90.

4

Can We Sustain Sustainable Agriculture? Learning from Small-scale Producer-suppliers in Canada and the UK

Larch Maxey

INTRODUCTION

> . . . geographers need to continue to delve into the micro-politics of delivering new sustainability mechanisms.
>
> O'Riordan 2004, 238

There is a growing willingness to question the sustainability of the systems and assumptions underlying human society, particularly within the western, or Minority World[1], where 20% of the world's population is responsible for 80% of the world's resource consumption and pollution (Chambers *et al.* 2000). This paper suggests that the notion of sustainability is a potent concept when it comes to understanding and addressing a series of overlapping contemporary issues from climate change (Hulme and Turnpenny 2004) to socio-cultural change. Collectively these issues constitute the sustainability crises, a series of inter-related crises which sustainability can help us understand, place in context and begin to address (Maxey 2003). Many of these crises and responses to them can be seen through the locus of food. Drawing on the heterogeneity of food networks the paper introduces the notion of sustainable food as a tool to access and shape wider societal debates.

Interest in food and its wider social, cultural, economic and environmental implications has flourished amongst policymakers and academics over the last 10 years (Smithers and Johnson 2004; Smithers *et al.* 1998; Morris and Evans 2004; Winter 2004). Within academic geography much of this discussion has revolved around notions of 'alternative' food. Responding to calls for more in-depth research on these alternative food networks (Goodman and Dupais 2002; Goodman 2003; Morris and Evans 2004; Winter 2005), this paper presents results from ethnographic research carried out over seven years from 1998 to 2005. The research reported here draws upon grounded theory, participatory research and actor-network theory to explore the experiences of practitioners themselves, those engaged in attempts to sustain networks of putative 'sustainable food' in six particular settings within Canada and the UK. The cross-continental contexts of the research case studies highlight the global nature of food networks and the overlapping experiences of those seeking to create direct producer-supplier networks in Minority World areas.

SUSTAINING SUSTAINABILITY?

Since the notion of 'sustainable development' came to prominence within popular and policy discourses, it has been simultaneously highly controversial, hotly contested and more recently a 'self-evident good' (Engel and Engel 1990). The concept and practice of 'sustainability', however, warrants separation from the equally controversial notion of 'development'. Following post-colonial and

Foucauldian critiques, 'development' can be seen as a heavily laden term through which predominantly middle class, white, western values and norms have been privileged (Hart 2004). Indeed, many of the values, norms and practices embedded within hegemonic notions of 'development' are those driving the sustainability crises (Sachs 1999). Relieved of the burden of 'development', it may become more common to research and implement sustainability within Minority World contexts, rather than within 'developing' world contexts as has been most common to date (Williams and Millington 2004).

The concept of sustainability, however, offers valuable insights into and routes out of our contemporary crises. A deeper understanding of and engagement with sustainability within, for example, research, policy and personal spheres presents great promise if we are to move towards a more just, diverse and harmonious world in which people of every culture can flourish alongside other species and the ecosystems which support them (O'Riordan 2004). At an absolute minimum sustainability involves looking at issues and making decisions in which environmental, economic, and sociocultural factors are considered *together*; this does not imply, however, trading off between these three elements. Given the current hegemony of neoliberalism, that would leave the economy in its current position of dominance (Douthwaite 1996; McDowell 2004). Sustainability requires all three elements to be simultaneously satisfied. This highlights how misleading it can be to describe something as 'economically sustainable', as many commercial actors do, or 'environmentally sustainable' (Agyeman and Evans 2004). To be sustainable something must be simultaneously economically, socially *and* environmentally sustainable (Bowler 2002).

Sustainability's triple bottom line is deceptively simple. In practice, however, it requires a paradigm shift from currently dominant neoliberal thinking (Sachs 1999; O'Riordan 2004). A key

contribution of sustainability, therefore, is its emphasis on connections and the ways in which modernist boundaries between, for example, environment and society, academic disciplines and different spheres of life are breaking down (Bowler 2002; Whatmore 2002). Thus sustainability is proposed as a tool to facilitate questioning, analysis and action. It is understood in this paper as a *process* rather than a definitive end point and key to this process is opening up not only active engagement but also the construction of norms and agendas to all actors (Maxey forthcoming). This view of sustainability as a process mirrors John Law's claim that network ordering 'is better seen as a verb – a somewhat uncertain process of overcoming resistance – rather than as the fait accompli of a noun' (2006, 1).

Approached in this way, sustainability has much affinity with Actor-Network Theory (ANT). ANT is an emergent and contested set of ideas and practices with its roots in the work of Michel Callon (1986), Bruno Latour (1987 2005), John Law and others (1987; Law and Hassard 1999). A key contribution of ANT is that it assumes the radical indeterminacy of the actor. From this starting point ANT has been used to analyse the progressive constitution of heterogeneous *actor-networks* made up of human and non-human actors and the negotiations and interactions they involve. An actor-network, then, is the act linked together with all of its influencing factors, which are also linked, producing an actor-network. This concern to explore and understand the connections and links between actors, actions and effects offers much overlap with, and potential to inform, process-based sustainability.

ANT emphasizes that actor-networks are continually being (re)made and (re)negotiated, stabilized and undermined. In this way ANT emphasizes the immanent fragility of networks and raises the challenge of studying reality as transitional in its becoming, and as trajectories of creation. These ideas of immanent fragility, becoming and change are also central to process-based approaches to sustainability (Maxey forthcoming), as illustrated by O'Riordan and Voisey's (1998) call for a 'sustainability transition'. Equally, ANT's principle of generalized symmetry has much to offer sustainability analysis. ANT's insistence that the differences between, for example, human and non-human actors are generated in the network of relations, and should not be presupposed, opens up multiple possibilities for bringing the non-human world into thought and practice. This could, for example, help address the anthropocentric root of many aspects of the sustainability crises. ANT can also help to identify and analyse the ways in which sustainability is politically constituted. Following ANT, sustainability itself could, for example, be seen as an actor-network and an effect. Equally, sustainability has considerable scope to inform and stimulate the use of ANT. Sustainability analysis, for example, could help to broaden 'the problem of selection'[2] within ANT-informed research.

Beginning to explore some of these potential links between ANT and sustainability, this paper considers the notion of sustainable food, recognizing that food, like everything else, is embedded in a host of heterogeneous processes and contexts. Indeed, one of ANT's seminal texts concerned food procurement as Michel Callon studied the interactions between marine biologists, scallops, fishermen and others in the St Brieuc Bay, France (Callon 1986). This paper seeks to draw on the understandings and insights of sustainability outlined above to look at food networks generally, and locally based producer-supplier networks within the Minority World specifically.

SUSTAINABLE FOOD NETWORKS?

Noting the caveat that food, like everything else, should not be overly compartmentalized, food offers rich opportunities for nourishing sustainability analysis and practice. Eating is something that connects us all. Everything we eat instantly places us into a series of socio-economic, cultural, even spiritual positions and enmeshes us within webs of relationships extending across time and space. Food's vital and varied roles partially account for the growing interest in the topic amongst geographers over the last 10 years (Essex et al. 2006; Smithers and Johnson 2004; Winter 2004 2005; Whatmore 2002; Marsden et al. 1999). Interests ranging from global-local economics (Jones 2003; Potter and Tilzey 2005), issues of identity (Bell and Valentine 1997; Curry-Roper 2000; Morris and Young 2000) and rural change (Marsden 2003; Morris and Buller 2003; Renting et al. 2003) have all been approached through geographies of food.

Geographers have highlighted important shifts within contemporary food geographies, including an increase in imported, 'luxury' and 'novelty' foods (Barrett et al. 1999), rising sales of convenience food and ready meals (Yakovleva and Flynn 2005) and the concentration of these food sales through large multiple supermarket and fast food restaurant chains (Smith and Marsden 2004; Guthman 2004; Michaels 2004). Research has also begun to explore how global trends such as neoliberal economic policies and globalization translate into local, national and international food policies and practices (Cook et al. 2004; Defra 2005; Millstone and Lang 2003; Winter 2004; Potter and Tilzey 2005; Troughton 2005). Helpfully, some of this research begins to highlight ways in which apparently unassailable hegemonic discourses such as neoliberal globalization begin to break down, fray and fragment in practice (Cook and Harrison 2003; Pritchard and Burch 2003; Wilson and Rigg 2003). Work such as this illustrates the importance of more in-depth studies capable of teasing out the subtle and particular ways in which broader trends and ideas are enacted and experienced on the ground.

Closely linked to work highlighting such trends has been a surge of research on 'alternative' food networks. This work has covered a varied range of food networks and employed a plethora of analytical approaches. In North America, for example, Goodman (2003) has looked at 'alternative agro-food networks' and Allen et al. (2003) investigated 'alternative food initiatives' (AFIs). Within the UK, Renting et al. (2003) have advocated short food supply chains (SFSCs) and Buller and Morris (2004, 1067) considered the potential of 'market orientated initiatives for environmentally sustainable food production' (MOIs) to offer alternatives to those wider food trends. Such work fits comfortably with analysis by many commentators including Hassanein (2003), Hinrichs (2003) and Roberts et al. (1999) in North America and Renting et al. (2003), Seyfang (forthcoming) and Douthwaite (1996) in the UK, who argue that 'shorter', more localized food networks offer exciting possibilities. These 'possibilities' (Holloway et al. 2006) include greater food democracy, reduced environmental impact associated with food, healthier food and circulating wealth more efficiently within local economies. These advantages and others are well rehearsed within the literature on sustainable. agricultural systems on both sides of the Atlantic (Pretty et al. 2001; Roberts et al. 1999) and increasingly within food geography research. What is still largely missing from this literature, however, is research into how these principles are translated and experienced in practice.

'Alternative' food networks are often presented as part of the answer to the unsustainable excesses of market-driven globalization, by policymakers, academics and farmers on both sides of the Atlantic (Fearne et al. 2005; Roberts et al. 1999; Michaels 2004). However, there has been insufficient research exploring the ways such networks are constructed, experienced and maintained (Larson and Duram 2001). Michael Winter, for example, in a recent review of geographies of food, notes that the social dimension of sustainable agriculture 'remains largely unexplored' (2005, 614). Carol Morris and Nick Evans go further in their argument for greater attention to cultural concerns within 'agri-culture' studies, suggesting 'there is room for far greater diversity of ethnographies, focus group work, and participation activities to name but a few' (2004, 107). Equally, there have been a growing number of calls for research which does not focus on producers in isolation, but considers their roles within wider contexts (Goodman and DuPais 2002; Goodman 2003; Holloway et al. 2006). ANT is well placed to support such approaches. The body of work on alternative food networks within North America and the UK is growing. However, there have been very few studies directly comparing experiences across continents. There has been even less research investigating the grounded experiences of producer-suppliers through in-depth, longitudinal research.

Cross-country studies in this area are particularly pertinent for at least three key reasons. Firstly global, or at least transnational, food networks are increasingly important and trends in shaping food are increasingly global (Barret et al. 1999; Potter and Tilzey 2005). Secondly, sustainability requires awareness of impacts and opportunities at every scale and cross country comparisons open up more scope for this. Finally, several 'alternative' models of food provisioning, including farmer's markets and Community Supported Agriculture schemes have emerged from North America and are gaining momentum both there and in other countries such as the UK. A study engaging with these phenomena in both the UK and Canada, therefore, offers opportunities to begin exploring the particular ways these approaches are played out, experienced in different contexts and their potential contribution to sustainability.

METHODOLOGY AND CASE STUDIES

The research reported here was carried out over a seven year period from 1998 to 2005, drawing upon grounded theory and participatory research methods. The adoption of an abductive research strategy (Mason 2002) allowed the field data to shape research questions and foci (Pain 2004; Pain and Francis 2003; Glaser 1992 1998; Cope 2003; Maxey 2003). This research strategy was important in addressing some of the gaps identified in the literature and in supporting the theoretical approach to sustainability and ANT outlined above. In-depth research required the selection of relatively few case studies to allow access to richer, more subtle and nuanced data so vital in supplementing more aggregate research and commentary (Cope 2003). The longitudinal approach supported these aims as well as addressing a further gap in the literature, which is generally composed of snap-shot, one-off research (Winter 2005). The six case studies[3] were chosen to reflect the research's wider epistemo-logical concern to engage with putative sustainable food networks which have received little detailed qualitative empirical research attention to date, despite forming part of those commonly hailed 'answers' to contemporary food crises (see above). Furthermore, there was a concern to address the lack of detailed ethnographic studies which directly compare cross-country experiences. This is particularly pertinent given the trans-national nature of contemporary food trends. In order to address specific gaps in the research two key features were identified as selection criteria. Firstly, each case study performed the dual role of producer and supplier, and

secondly, each dealt with small-scale vegetable production and distribution. The case studies were also very small scale with 3–22 acres used for vegetable growing. All the farms studied were also located within an hour's drive of an urban area which provided at least some of their market.

The research methodology adopted was emergent and progressive with more intensive methods employed as research relationships became established (Clifford and Valentine 2003). Trust was built up slowly with each case study and the ethical and epistemological commitment to participation helped this (Kitchin and Tate 2000; Maxey 1999). A range of roles and research methods were employed in each case study, including initial contact through wider related networks, exploratory and largely observational visits, followed by in-depth interviews and participant observation. The latter two methods formed the bulk of the data-gathering techniques, with semi-structured interviews of 1–2½ hours triangulated with observation and participatory practice in each case study. Participation in each case study was extensive and involved a succession of visits which varied in length from one hour to three weeks. Research-related roles performed by the researcher included production side practices, distribution and sales side, including attending farmers' markets and acting as a food box coordinator and customer.

Three of the case studies were, and still are, located in the predominantly rural region of south Wales, UK within a 20 km radius of Swansea (see Figure 4.2). These include the following:

1. Jade Gate, an 8–3[4] acre organic farm established in 1997, which distributes produce through a box scheme. On a weekly basis 80 boxes were either delivered by horse and cart or placed in a straw-bale shed for customers to pick up.

2. Crickton Farm Shop sells fruit and vegetables grown on 22 acres. The family have been farming the land for three generations. The farm shop was established by the father of the present farmer in 1965. In addition to selling through the farm shop, produce is sold at farmers' markets in Swansea, and on Gower and, beginning in 2005, through direct delivery by van to customers' doors.

3. Organics To Go (OTG) was established in 1998. It is based on a 70 acre holding which houses Fox Housing Cooperative and an embryonic 'eco-village'. OTG distributes organic produce grown on 20 acres as well as that supplied by eight other small-scale farmers in west Wales. Produce is distributed to 100–2000[5] households by vans run on biodiesel and LPG, both locally and as far as London (270 miles).

The other three case studies are located in southern Ontario, Canada, within a 100 km radius of Toronto, on the fringes of a metropolitan region of over 5 million people. Each farm sells some of its produce within Toronto as well as to more localized markets, including Hamilton in the case of Plan B and Hillsburgh in the case of Everdale. The Canadian case studies include the following:

1. Plan B Organic Farm, established in 1997, runs a Community Supported Agriculture (CSA) scheme (Plan B 2005) on 12 acres. On average, 100 members buy a seasonal 'share' in the farm's produce and pick up produce weekly throughout the season.

2. Everdale Organic Farm received organic certification in 1997 and grows a range of fruits and vegetables on 15 acres, part of a larger 50 acre site which houses Everdale Environmental Learning Centre (Everdale 2005). Produce is distributed through Everdale Farm Store, local organic distributors and an 80% share CSA.

3. Bowman's Farm is a third generation, Old Order Menonite sheep farm of 100 acres of which 3 acres is certified organic for fruit and vegetable growing. Produce is sold from a roadside stall at the front of the house and, since 1994, through FoodShare's Good Food Box. Established in 1994, FoodShare's Good Food Box delivers 4000 boxes each month through 200 neighbourhood-based volunteer coordinators (FoodShare 2005). The author was a Good Food Box coordinator from 1999 to 2001. Bowman's Farm is one of a growing number of Ontario growers distributing fruit and vegetables through the Good Food Box.

In the text that follows the quotations from farmers have been coded, with the code appearing after each direct quotation. Thus W1 5 refers to Welsh case study 1, interview number 5. This coding ensures anonymity of respondents and was used in the data analysis (Cope 2003).

PATHWAYS TO SUSTAINABLE AGRICULTURE

The case studies can be divided broadly into two groups according to the paths through which their main protagonists came to be engaged in growing and directly distributing food. The first pathway involved inheritance. Two case studies, one in each country, were run by third generation farmers and in both instances there had been an assumption that they would continue the farm:

> I think when you were 15 going back 35, 36 years, most farmers' sons were almost expected to carry on the business.
>
> W3 1

Although elements of obligation and tradition thus informed these farmers' entry into farming, they did not simply continue farming in the same ways their ancestors had done. Rather, these farmers made a series of changes, including reducing the amounts of chemical pesticides and fertilizers used and/or shifting to organic farming methods, as well as introducing new crop varieties, marketing and distribution techniques.

The second pathway involved people coming into farming with little or no prior experience, as 'city kids', to adopt the terminology of several members of this group. Surprisingly, only one member of this group had any experience of growing food as a child. In each case farming was a conscious choice they made as adults. This often involved a significant change in direction. Previous occupations included welding, nursing, academic research and 'middle management in a large corporate business' (C1 3).

Despite these contrasting backgrounds, similarities between case studies were strong and recurrent features of the research. Within both country contexts, for example, each case study underwent a series of sharp learning curves. Although these learning curves were often steeper for the 'city kids', they were certainly present for third generation farmers too, as a FoodShare worker recounted in 2004:

> Tom's first delivery of leeks to us ten years ago arrived in a washing machine box and they were 6 feet tall!
>
> C3 2

As this quotation suggests, the challenges involved in running these sustainable food ventures were not limited to growing, but included marketing, presentation and business skills. In some respects the 'city kids' had an advantage in these areas as they generally had more recent direct experience of living, working, buying and eating in cities and thus found it easier to market and prepare produce for the city-based markets to which most produce went.

ETHICAL AND EMOTIVE MOTIVATIONS

Overlaps and commonalities between case studies were stronger than differences when one considers participants' motivations. Across both country contexts farmers expressed a similar range of drivers. There was, however, a slight difference in emphasis across case studies, with multi-generational and women farmers tending to emphasize the fulfilment and pleasure they received from both growing food and meeting customers. In contrast, the newer male farmers tended to emphasize ethico-political motivations. The founder of Jade Gate, for example, which during the study period switched over to using a horse for most farm work and all deliveries, suggested that for him the foremost concern was to provide 'clean, carbon neutral food', reflecting quite closely concerns expressed by a key male protagonist at Plan B. In terms of an ecological footprint (Chambers et al. 2000), Jade Gate was the most sustainable of the six. A high level of concern for the environmental component of sustainability was found within each case study, however. Without exception participants were motivated by a concern to reduce negative environmental impacts of food and enhance positive impacts by reducing food miles and external inputs and encouraging biodiversity, for example.

Although not all participants were aware of sustainability's 'triple bottom line', on each farm people were motivated by social and economic as well as environmental concerns and often emphasized that all three overlapped. A leading member of OTG, for example, suggested:

> My main focus is to support growers, it's not that I don't like customers, but consumers have too much power. Also, because I'm interested in growing and I want to support other people who're growing, as it's a challenging life choice.
>
> W3 2

This quotation introduces the tensions which became apparent during the research between growers and consumers, although these tensions have received little attention from researchers to date, particularly in the context of Minority World 'alternative' agriculture[6]. This gap is particularly noteworthy given the extent to which researchers in the recent past have referred to 'consumers' and 'consumer demand' rather uncritically as though this were monolithic, universal and detached from the murky world of advertising and peer group pressure[7]. Drawing on Clive Potter and Mark Tilzey's (2005, 581) call for research exploring the way 'deep-set structural tendencies and policy trends . . . are constituted in relation to, and mediated through, the agency of individual land managers and other actors', this paper identifies tensions between 'consumers' and farmer-suppliers as a significant component of the way such macro trends shape attempts to manage land sustainably. Indeed, these tensions were found in both country contexts and increased during the research period. The Canadian case studies showed higher levels of tensions at the outset of the research and those in Wales exhibited the greatest increase in tensions, so that by the end of the study period they were quite evenly matched across continents. Such tensions, then, are amongst the very real, but underanalysed impacts of neoliberal policies, experienced by actors as they attempt to grow, sell, buy and eat sustainable produce.

The above quotation (W3 2) also indicates the extent to which working with the case studies involved conscious lifestyle choices. Even those who initially chose farming as it was their parents' profession had made a series of conscious decisions to stay in farming and develop more sustainable farming and often did so against a backdrop of challenging economic and social constraints.

Participants' motivations also changed over time in both country contexts. Concerns such as 'climate change', food security and reconnecting people with food often provided significant initial motivations for the male 'city kids' group in particular. After several years, however, more mundane, personal and experiential motivations generally came to the fore even within this group. In each case study, for example, people spoke of the personal dietary benefits of growing fresh fruit and vegetables, 'We all eat so well, it's really fresh, organic produce' (C2 3), as a male member of Plan B put it. That is not to suggest that what I have termed ethico-political motivations became irrelevant or even weakened over time. Rather, their relative significance within day-to-day motivations and sense making declined relative to other factors. As noted above, there was a gender as well as temporal component to this, with female workers as well as longer serving male workers tending to emphasize more practical, mundane and sensory motivations. As a female worker at Jade Gate explained:

> I just love working out here, you know, no one gives you any shit and it's so great when you see the plants coming on so well. I'm very proud of my brasicas this year!
> W1 4

This finding supports work that has been done on female farmers within sustainable agriculture (Panelli and Pini 2005; Traugher 2004; Troughton and Mitchell 2000; Chiappe and Flora 1998).

INDEPENDENT INTERDEPENDENCE

Women and longstanding male farmers gained the greatest fulfilment from the very process of growing. However, a love of growing was common to all those involved. Indeed, participants demonstrated a range of largely shared values, understandings, practices and norms, which coalesced around a strong sense of independent interdependence. A determined independence informed attitudes and practices within each case study, combined with their – to some extent – self-acknowledged interdependence within a series of 'heterogeneous networks' or 'rhizomes' (Winter 2005, 610). The independence of case studies took a range of forms, including independence of thought, economic independence and agricultural independence.

Independence of thought can be seen in individuals' and groups' preparedness to both be 'different' and to take risks, innovate and change methods and approaches. Economic and agricultural independence flowed from participants' desire to sever disempowering links of dependency upon macro structures, including the state and commercial agricultural and retail corporations. Whilst these different forms of independence informed, on a daily basis, land managers' construction and negotiation of their roles, they were complicated, coloured and imbued with a series of interdependences. These included socio-cultural, economic and agricultural interdependences as each venture was situated within a wider series of rhizomes, made up of human and non-human actors and the discourses they gave rise to.

The fluid inter-relationships between human actors can be seen in their location within a complex series of wider spatial and socio-cultural contexts, relationships and positions. Each project drew upon voluntary and/or paid labour, for example. Although this was generally supplied locally through more informal contacts, at times labour supply formed part of more formal national and international networks such as WWOOF (2005)[8]. The case studies were, in many respects, all highly independent. For example, they each grew, marketed and distributed their own products, interacted, and built up mutually supportive relationships with, additional producers and/or distributors. Again this was found to be mirrored to a remarkable extent across both country contexts. Crickton Farm Shop and Everdale Organic Farm Shop, for example, both stocked a range of local produce from beyond their farms, including traditional and organic meat and dairy products, as well as fruit and vegetables grown by other farms. Initially motivated by a concern to help similarly positioned (more sustainable) producers market and sell their produce, carrying these items also added to the shops' attraction. Customers who cared enough about local provenance, food quality, etc. to shop there in the first place generally appreciated the availability of a wider range of similarly sourced products. Such synergies and mutual aid within and between small-scale suppliers and distributors has not received significant attention to date and appears an important component of future work in this area, particularly as the other case studies appeared set to move in this direction. OTG introduced such measures in 2006 and Plan B had similar intentions.

Such layers of connection demonstrate the hybridity and complexity of more sustainable agricultural systems within the Minority World. Perhaps the deepest and most complex forms of interdependence, however, concerned non-human actors. An unexpected finding of the research was the frequency with which spirituality emerged as a component of these agricultural systems. Exploring spirituality within putative sustainable food systems was not originally part of the research design, but something which emerged during the research process, with participants in all but one case study describing a spiritual connection with the farm, land and process of growing food. The spiritual component was heterogeneous and in many cases quite subtle, personal, even private. For most farmers spiritual connections built up over time in their daily actions and were embodied and performative, emerging from wider senses of interdependences with actors such as the soil, landscape, weather and seasons, plants and animals as well as various human actors. Each of these actors, it was clear, had their own agency and role within the agricultural system. Although a somewhat surprising feature of the research, this spirituality and the wider interdependence from which it flows has considerable resonance with both sustainability's emphasis of connections and interdisciplinarity (O'Riordan 2004; Agyeman and Evans 2004) and ANT's sensitivity to non-human actors within hybrid and shifting constellations or rhizomes (Drummond and Marsden 1999).

Despite participants' attempts to reconcile tensions between in/inter-dependence, these were, at times, problematic. Strong personalities, so valuable in the pioneering work and approaches found in the case studies, were prone to clash. Perhaps the greatest tensions though were with rhizomes extending out beyond the farm, involving macro-scale actors such as government bodies, corporations and, unexpectedly, organic certification bodies, as we shall explore below.

BARRIERS TO SUSTAINABLE FOOD OPERATIONS AND THEIR SOLUTIONS

Despite high levels of competence, ingenuity, commitment and hard work, with working weeks ranging from 60 to 100 hours in the summer, for example, the case studies were highly fragile in many respects. Farmers suggested this vulnerability stemmed from a range of barriers they encountered. Through participant observation in particular a bleak picture emerged, with the coincidence of two or more problems capable of threatening the entire farm operation. In each case study, at some point during the research period, participants felt obliged to question whether the farm could even keep running. This actually helped reaffirm participants' conscious, shared commitment to run the farms sustainably in many respects. Actively struggling to maintain the operation's very existence often facilitated and

rendered explicit what ANT may refer to as translation, the process by which actors come together to create and maintain a forum or central network (Callon 1986). Within all the case studies this forum was based around notions of sustainability and healthy local food networks. Therefore, the first moment of translation – problematization – was ongoing and linked to the motivations mentioned above. However, during these crisis points additional problems were identified, with an often rapid process of interessement and enrolment, in which actors negotiated and adopted roles in the pursuit of the problems identified. This enhanced process of translation, however, was often afforded at considerable personal cost to all those involved, and particularly the lead protagonists. This illustrates the pressure experienced by those seeking to establish sustainable food systems in the Minority World. Whilst financial strains informed, if not drove, all of these moments of crisis and translation, they were informed more by a loss of heart than a loss of money. To appreciate this it is helpful to consider the financial context in which these projects operated.

All six case studies have survived that 'difficult first five years' (W1 1) of commercial operation and can thus be regarded as within the minority of 'successful' sustainable food ventures which do not fold in this period. These 'successful businesses', however, were dependent on the labour of either volunteers, including family members, or low-paid workers. In every case study those running the operations were the ones who worked hardest, yet calculated as an hourly rate few of the case studies generated economic activity at the minimum wage. Participants were 'working poor' (C1 4) in the words of a Plan B farmer, which in Canada covers those in full-time work, but earning less than Cn$15 000/ year. Although low wages and long hours are common to most forms of farming in the Minority World, this finding highlights the need to look beyond claims that 'alternative' approaches to food procurement offer easy answers. They also indicate some of the differences between such approaches and more 'mainstream' food procurement, as the most common response to this marginal economic position within the case studies was 'simple living' as an Old Order Menonite farmer described it (W3 4). It may be expected that a religious order dubbed 'the Plain People' (Ober 2005) due to their frugal lifestyle is well placed to adopt such a strategy; however, participants throughout the case studies had a remarkably similar 'simple life'. Across both country contexts residents' diets were based on home-grown food and critical attitudes towards conspicuous consumption – buying second-hand clothes and repairing goods were the norm. 'Keeping our expenses low is another way of making money, right?' as an Everdale Farm worker put it (C2 4). The extent to which this strategy was adopted across all case studies illustrates both their tight economic margins and the importance participants placed upon independence from macro politico-economic structures and forces.

As economic geographers have noted, the phenomenon of 'working poor' is becoming increasingly common under the influence of neoliberal globalization (McDowell 2004). It is ironic, therefore, that a feature associated with highly exploitative corporate practice in this situation arises from discourses and practices around sustainability in which individual and small businesses/community enterprises are involved. There is considerable scope for further research exploring the self-regulation and governmentality inculcated within such pioneering sustainable ventures. Far from operating in a vacuum, these businesses are located within increasingly globalized networks in which Minority World producers compete with global corporations capable of importing food and thus exporting labour and other

costs to regions with far lower wages (Barrett *et al.* 1999; Norberg-Hodge *et al.* 2002; Millstone and Lang 2003). An awareness of the way in which increased neoliberal globalization has made it increasingly difficult to operate more sustainable food systems infused each case study and led to comments such as this one:

> One of the worst things in farming is refrigeration because you can refrigerate food from New Zealand to here [Wales] and supermarkets can refrigerate food, or keep it chilled for weeks or months.
>
> W2 5

As Barrett *et al.* (1999) have shown, refrigeration continues to play an important role in the increased globalization of food. However, individual technologies such as refrigeration need not necessarily contribute to this agenda. Indeed, one case study uses refrigeration of certain produce at certain times and felt this helped improve the quality of their food.

Although relationships with different technologies varied considerably, what came out most strongly from the research was participants' identification of supermarkets and industrial, Fordist agriculture as the greatest obstacle to running economically viable, sustainable food businesses. 'It's just being squeezed by the supermarkets', as one farmer put it (W3 1). The asymmetry of power relations between farmers and supermarkets was central to this:

> Dealing with the supermarkets is too hard, you have a contract to supply, so if you have a failed crop you have to import or buy in from a different area to keep the contract! The supermarkets don't want to know if it poured with rain all day when you're trying to cut, or if there's been a drought.
>
> W3 3

Supermarket purchasers were seen as divorced from the complex interdependence negotiated by farmers on a daily basis. There is great potential for future research which draws upon non-representational approaches and ANT to help explore these interdependencies, by focusing attention on their performativity and the roles of non-human actors, for example. Within food geographies research, ANT has been criticized for privileging 'local contexts' and 'immediate concerns' (Potter and Tilzey 2005, 583) as well as its potential to divert attention from investigating why actors come into certain relations and the different power relations they bring to these situations (Potter and Tilzey 2005; Bieler and Morton 2001). Such limitations, however, are not inherent to these approaches. Indeed, ANT is centrally concerned with the ways in which hierarchy and power is enacted and may be disrupted (Law 2006). Equally, as Lemke (2000) has shown, the topology of networks is in general nonlocal and ANT can form part of a wider inquiry into scale-respecting vs. scale-breaking dynamics.

One way to begin filling the gaps between agency, performance and connectivity suggested by participants was to (re) connect people with food/growing. This is more commonly discussed in the literature on sustainable/alternative food in terms of reconnecting consumers with the food they eat (Norberg-Hodge *et al.* 2002). Within the research, though, it was also discussed in terms of reconnecting other actors such as food purchasers and distributors, as this story about FoodShare's new distributor's visit to Bowman's farm illustrates:

> I don't think he's ever done any growing or planting, but grew up in the city and grew up in his father's distribution business, he's always dealt with produce from the farm gate and never gone out into the fields and seen how it's grown, until he was out here on that visit [organized by FoodShare] and X said that was a life changing day for him . . . so we were hoping that might get him to loosen up on us a bit, but we're still waiting to see any changes.
>
> C3 4

Neoliberalisms' deepening, insidious influence on sustainable food systems was highlighted by farmers' growing discomfort with the roles played by third-party organic certification bodies. Several farmers were highly critical of what they described as the high costs of registration, combined with growing surveillance, formalization and paperwork:

> The paperwork is getting worse every year, because they don't trust what you're doing, they want everything down on paper to prove it.
>
> C1 6

Complaints about excess paperwork are common to farmers and small businesses throughout the Minority World. However, the case studies expressed concern over the additional burdens associated with organic certification, which in some cases felt particularly onerous. This provides a further example of the ways in which putative solutions to the sustainability crises, in this case organic production, may be problematic in practice. Another concern expressed by respondents, particularly those in smaller operations, was that the larger third-party organic verification bodies, such as the Soil Association in the UK and the OCPP (Organic Crop Processors and Producers) in Canada, were complicit in promoting supermarkets' neoliberal, industrialized approaches to agriculture. Several respondents felt they were seeking to increase the size of the organic market and productive area by pushing organics within supermarkets:

> The big chains are increasingly handling organics and trying hard to push them from a product to a commodity, as soon as it's a commodity you need to shift volume, whereas with a product you have a greater margin.
>
> C3 8

Responses proposed by participants included developing direct supply networks, building trust with customers, reforming all food labelling and using smaller, more responsive third-party verification bodies such as Demeter (2005) and Organic Centre Wales (2005):

> I shouldn't have to pay the Soil Association £500/year for putting nothing into my food, all food should be labelled, what pesticides it has in it, what GM ingredients it has, everything should be fully labelled.
>
> W1 7

Several organizations are exploring different aspects of labelling reform, including grassroots direct action campaigns in France and the UK which involve placing stickers on produce in supermarkets indicating the farm gate price, calls for the C02 consumption equivalent to be shown alongside ingredients and the development of broader sustainability labels, rather than 'just' organic labelling (Wakeman 2005).

Neoliberal values and the influence of supermarkets presented barriers within many aspects of the case studies' operations. Several farmers suggested, for example, that tensions between consumers and suppliers were rooted in supermarket marketing and purchasing policies which led people to expect to pay less for food and emphasize appearance, convenience and quantity, all of which worked against more sustainable concerns.

> I had a customer this morning and he said: 'oh, I'm going on holiday to Mallorca', and he had a nice new car, and those are the main priorities. They wouldn't give up their holidays to buy food for 52 weeks of the year that's better quality food.
>
> W2 1

Supermarket policies take shape within the context of Fordist agriculture pursued particularly in the Minority World since 1945. Thus government policies which continue to shape this post/neo-Fordist agriculture also contribute to barriers experienced within the case studies. Farmers particularly identified 'subsidies'

as a problem. Despite the commonly held view that organic farmers now receive generous subsidies, none of the farms studied received any subsidies during the research period. Indeed, one respondent refused on principle because the amount was 'derisory' and hid the wider inequalities the subsidies system reinforced, giving most money to those with most land. In the UK, for example, 80% of farm subsidies go to the 20% of farmers with the largest land holdings (Cahill 2001). Indeed, participants were unanimous in calling for an end to all agricultural subsidies, creating a level playing field, rather then the present 'tokenistic support for organic' (C3 3).

The context of state supported Fordist agriculture was also identified as contributing to the problem of finding affordable labour:

> Lots of people don't work fast enough, we've lost the skills base and horticultural traditions since everyone switched from mixed farms to dairy after the War.
>
> W3 4

Solutions to this problem proposed by participants included creating apprenticeships, with Everdale Organic Farm running a successful series of courses and apprenticeships. Another proposal was for a change in planning regulations to allow low-impact accommodation for volunteers/farm labour. Whilst there is a growing recognition of the role low-impact development may have in contributing to sustainability there has been very little discussion of its potential role in supporting sustainable agriculture (Fairlie 1996; Maxey 2005).

CONCLUSIONS

Each case study discussed in this paper is in many ways a highly sustainable business, combining longstanding commercial viability with deep commitments to social and environmental concerns. As such, each begins to explore some of the ways in which food can contribute to a sustainability transition. Indeed, any one of the case studies could be found within literature on the sustainability transition as an example of best practice (Douthwaite 1996; Norberg-Hodge *et al.* 2002; Lovins *et al.* 2004). A closer look at how these projects are experienced and maintained, however, demonstrates their immanent fragility. Although each project has scope for improvement on many levels, this finding of fragility is not an indictment of the case studies, but of the wider social, political and economic contexts within which they operate. By implication, therefore, the research reported in this paper points to how unsustainable food systems have become. The research has also identified a number of recurrent features within the case studies, recommendations for personal and policy changes and directions for future research.

Key amongst the findings this paper identifies is the cumulative impact of barriers and challenges each operation faced. These included the tensions between 'consumers' and farmer-suppliers, the need to negotiate marketing, presentation and business skills, changing weather patterns, availability of supplies and consumer preferences. The extent to which neoliberal policies generally, and supermarket practices specifically, continued to impact on these actor-networks was surprising given that each is based around direct supply systems which avoid supermarkets and are often ascribed an 'alternative economic' position (Wakeman 2005; Norberg-Hodge *et al.* 2002; Roberts *et al.* 1999). Neoliberalism's influences extended throughout these networks, as is illustrated by the uncertainty of several farmers over the role of third-party organic verification bodies. In addition to illustrating the burdens placed upon these ventures due to their attempts to be more sustainable, the case of organic certification demonstrates farmers' valuable contribution to the

search for solutions to such problems. Thus farmers proposed using smaller bodies with lower costs and more sensitivity to individual producers' particular needs and concerns. Furthermore, these farmers drew upon wider sustainability analysis to question the underlying causes of such problems. It was suggested, for example, that third-party verification becomes particularly important within stretched food networks, where trust and intimacy between producers and consumers has broken down. As these operations existed to try and reinvigorate that trust, new approaches to quality assurance and verification may be appropriate.

Exploring the possibility of such approaches is just one area of future research suggested by the current study. Others include exploring the tensions between consumers and producers. There is a lack of geographical research on food which critically engages with the shaping of consumer choices. Sustainability analysis can contribute to this through its concern with consumerism's underlying causes and trends. Equally, ANT-informed approaches could usefully contribute to such work.

Connected with this is the scope for research which explores the broader ways in which neoliberalism impacts upon attempts to develop more sustainable food networks, including its inculcation of self-regulation. Changing national and international regulatory frameworks, as illustrated by the introduction of the single farm payment in EU countries, also demand investigation into their impacts on sustainable food networks.

There is considerable scope for learning across different contexts. There has already been a significant degree of interchange within sustainable food networks, with CSAs and farmer's markets increasingly taking off in European and other countries, having originated in North America. Further work into the ways these approaches are experienced in practice could help to highlight the potential for further exchange. FoodShare's Good

Food Box and other programmes, for example, offer a number of possibilities which could be drawn upon in the UK context.

The gendered and temporal component to sustainable food is an area that warrants further cross-national research, as do the synergies and mutual aid practiced within and between small-scale suppliers and distributors, their spirituality and the wider interdependences from which it flows. Such work has considerable potential to inform existing geographical debates such as those concerning the roles of animals (Buller and Morris 2003).

As attitudes towards fridges and road transport illustrate, there is considerable scope for further analysis of the way technologies shape the negotiation of sustainable food networks; ANT, with its origins in science and technology studies, has considerable potential to contribute to this (Latour 1987 2005; Law 1987).

An overriding requirement if we are to move to more sustainable food systems is economic reform, which ensures all 'external' costs are fully internalized with the food we eat (Pretty *et al.* 2001). Only once this is achieved will more sustainable approaches to food provisioning operate in a fair and efficient market. The process of internalizing externalities in this way will be slow and resisted at various points (Potter and Tilzey 2005). In the meantime, much can be done to begin supporting ventures such as these which, by their nature, are already beginning to reflect their full costs within the prices customers pay. Listening to those involved in such projects and engaging in detailed qualitative and quantitative longitudinal work with them can inform this process.

ACKNOWLEDGEMENTS

This paper has benefited considerably from feedback provided at the third seminar 'International Dimensions on Sustainable Farmland Management' in the ESRC seminar series 'Approaches to Sustainable Farmland Management' (16 September 2004), at which an earlier draft of this paper was presented, as well as from the comments of three anonymous reviewers. The research on which this paper is based was made possible by the patience, commitment and cooperation of participants in the six case study farms, to whom a great debt of thanks is owed.

NOTES

1. In this paper the term 'Minority World' is used to denote what are often described as 'western', 'First World' or 'developed' countries and 'Majority World' is used instead of 'developing', 'less developed' or 'Third World' countries. This encourages actors to question and at times reverse the normative assumptions and hierarchical relations implied by such terms.
2. 'The problem of selection' here refers to the choice researchers make when trying to identify all of the heterogeneous elements in an actor-network. As this is often an almost limitless task, the researcher necessarily makes choices as to which components are considered. Sustainability can help inform these choices.
3. In order to protect individuals' privacy all quotations are given anonymously and individuals' names have been changed.
4. When a range is given for figures this indicates the change over the study period.
5. When a range is given for figures this indicates the change over the study period.
6. For some discussion of this in the context of imported produce, see Barrett *et al.* (1999) and Cook *et al.* (2004).
7. This provides another example of how critical sustainability-based perspectives can support food analysis, as these have often shown greater sensitivity to the ways in which demand is created and shaped within the context of sustainable food; see, for example, Norberg-Hodge *et al.* (2002) and Michaels (2004).
8. WWOOF (Willing Workers On Organic Farms) was one of a range of organizations through which the case studies secured volunteer labour.

REFERENCES

Agyeman J and Evans B 2004 'Just sustainability': the emerging discourse of environmental justice in Britain? *The Geographical Journal* 170 155–64

Allen P, Fitzsimmons M, Goodman M and Warner K 2003 Shifting plates in the agrifood landscape: the tectonics of alternative agrifood initiatives in California *Journal of Rural Studies* 19 61–75

Barrett H, Ilbery B, Browne A and Binns T 1999 Globalization and the changing networks of food supply: the importation of fresh horticultural produce from Kenya into the UK *Transactions of the Institute of British Geographers* 24 159–74

Bell D and Valentine G 1997 *Consuming geographies: we are where we eat* Routledge, London

Bieler A and Morton A 2001 The Gordian knot of agency and structure in international relations: a neo-Gramscian perspective *European Journal of International Relations* 7 5–35

Bowler I 2002 Developing sustainable agriculture *Geography* 87 205–12

Buller H and Morris C 2003 Farm animal welfare: a new repertoire of nature-society relations or modernism embedded? *Socioligia Ruralis* 34 216–37

Buller H and Morris C 2004 Growing the goods: the market, the state, and sustainable food production *Environment and Planning A* 36 1065–84

Cahill K 2001 *Who owns Britain?* Canongate, London

Callon M 1986 Some elements of a sociology of translation: domestication of the scallops and the fishermen of St Brieuc Bay in Law J ed *Power, action and belief: a new sociology of knowledge* Routledge & Kegan Paul, London 196–233

Chambers N, Simmons C and Wackernagel M 2000 *Sharing nature's interest: ecological footprints as an indicator of sustainability* Earthscan, London

Chiappe M and Flora C 1998 Gendered elements of the sustainable agriculture paradigm *Rural Sociology* 63 372–93

Clifford N and Valentine G 2003 eds *Methods in human geography* Sage, London

Cook I and Harrison M 2003 Cross over food: re-materializing postcolonial geographies *Transactions of the Institute of British Geographers* 28 296–17

Cook I *et al.* 2004 Follow the thing: papaya *Antipode* 36 642–64

Cope M 2003 Coding transcripts and diaries in Clifford N and Valentine G eds *Methods in human geography* Sage, London

Curry-Roper J 2000 Embeddedness in place: its role in the sustainability of a rural farm community in Iowa *Space and Culture* 4 204–22

Defra 2005 The validity of food miles as an indicator of sustainable development (http://statistics.defra.gov.uk/esg/reports/foodmiles/default.asp) Accessed 28 November 2005

Demeter 2005 Demeter-International e.v. – a worldwide network (http://www.Demeter.net/) Accessed 15 December 2005

Douthwaite R 1996 *Short circuit: strengthening local economics for security in an unstable world* Lilliput Press, Dublin

Drummond I and Marsden T 1999 *The condition of sustainability* Routledge, London

Engel J R and Engel J G eds 1990 *Ethics of environment and development: global challenge, international response* The University of Arizona Press, Tucson

Essex S, Gilg A, Yarwood R, Smithers J and Wilson R eds 2006 *Rural change and sustainability: agriculture, the environment and communities* Oxford University Press, Oxford

Everdale 2005 Everdale Organic Farm and Environmental Learning Centre (http://www.everdale.org/) Accessed 11 December 2005

Fairlie S 1996 *Low impact development: planning and people in a sustainable countryside* Jon Carpenter, Charlbury, UK

Fearne A, Duffy R and Hornibrook S 2005 Justice in the UK supermarket buyer-supplier relationships: an empirical analysis *International Journal of Retail and Distribution Management* 33 570–82

FoodShare 2005 What is the good food box? (http://www.foodshare.net/goodfoodbox01.htm) Accessed 31 December 2005

Glaser B 1992 *Basics of grounded theory analysis: emergence vs forcing* Sociology Press Mill, Valley, CA

Glaser B 1998 *Doing grounded theory: issues and discussions* Sociology Press, Mill Valley, CA

Goodman D 2003 Editorial: the quality 'turn' and alternative food practices: reflections and agenda. *Journal of Rural Studies* 19 1–7

Goodman D and DuPais E 2002 Knowing food and growing food: beyond the consumption-production debate in the sociology of agriculture *Sociologia Ruralis* 4 5–22

Guthman J 2004 *Agrarian dreams: the paradox of organic farming in California* California Studies in Critical Human Geography 11, University of California Press, California

Hart G 2004 Geography and development: critical ethnographies *Progress in Human Geography* 28 91–100

Hassanein N 2003 Practicing food democracy: a pragmatic politics of transformation *Journal of Rural Studies* 19 77–86

Hinrichs C 2003 The practice and politics of food system localization *Journal of Rural Studies* 20 33–45

Holloway L, Kneafsey M, Venn L, Cox R, Dowler E and Tuomainen H 2006 Possible food economies: food production-consumption arrangements and the meaning of 'alternative' cultures of consumptions Working Papers Series No. 25 (http://www.consume.bbk.ac.uk/publications.html) Accessed 15 February 2006

Hulme M and Turnpenny J 2004 Understanding and managing climate change: the UK experience *The Geographical Journal* 170 105–15

Jones A 2003 'Power in place': viticultural spatialities of globalization and community empowerment in the Languedoc *Transactions of the Institute of British Geographers* 28 367–82

Kitchin R and Tate N J 2000 *Conducting research into human geography* Prentice Hall, New York

Larson K and Duram L A 2001 Information dissemination in alternative agricultural research: an analysis of researchers *American Journal of Alternative Agriculture* 15 171–80

Latour B 1987 *Science in action* Harvard University Press, Cambridge, MA

Latour B 2005 *Reassembling the social: an introduction to actor-network theory* Oxford University Press, Oxford

Law J 1987 Technology and heterogeneous engineering: the case of Portuguese expansion in Bijker W E, Hughes T P and Pinch T J) eds *The social construction of technological systems: new directions in the sociology and history of technology* MIT Press, Cambridge, MA

Law J 2006 Notes on the theory of the actor network: ordering, strategy and heterogeneity (http://web.archive.org/web/20040214135427/http%3A//www.comp.lancs.ac.uk/sociology/soc054jl.html) Accessed 5 June 2006

Law J and Hassard J eds 1999 *Actor network theory and after* Blackwell and the Sociological Review, Oxford and Keele

Lemke J 2000 Material sign processes and ecosocial organization in Andersen P B, Emmeche C and Finnemann-Nielsen N O eds *Downward causation: self-organization in biology, psychology, and society* Aarhus University Press, Aarhus, Denmark 181–213

Lovins A, Datta E K, Odd-Even Bustnes, Koomey J G and Glasgow N J 2004 *Winning the oil endgame: innovation for profits, jobs and security* Rocky Mountain Institute, Colorado (http://www.oilendgame.com/) Accessed 5 June 2006

Marsden T 2003 *The condition of rural sustainability* Royal Van Gorcum, Assen, The Netherlands

Marsden T, Murdoch J and Morgan K 1999 Sustainable agriculture, food supply chains and regional development *International Planning Studies* 4 295–301

Mason J 2002 *Qualitative researching* Sage, London

Maxey I 1999 Beyond boundaries? Activism, academia, reflexivity and research *Area* 31 199–208

Maxey L 2003 One path forward? Three sustainable communities in England and Wales Unpublished PhD thesis, Department of Geography, Swansea University

Maxey L 2005 'Low impact development: creating a truly sustainable countryside?' Presented at the RGS-IBG International Conference 1 September (copies available from the author)

Maxey L Forthcoming From organic to sustainable agriculture? The social, cultural and ecological construction of 'sustainable' food chains in Holloway L, Kneafsey M and Maye D eds *Constructing 'alternative' food geographies: representation and practice* Elsevier, Camberley, UK

McDowell L 2004 Work, workfare, work/life balance and an ethic of care *Progress in Human Geography* 28 145–63

Michaels L 2004 *What's wrong with supermarkets?* Corporate Watch, Oxford (http://www.corporatewatch.org/?lid=705) Accessed 5 June 2006

Millstone E and Lang T 2003 *The atlas of food: who eats what where and why* Earthscan, London

Morris C and Buller H 2003 The local food sector: a preliminary assessment of its form and impact in Gloucestershire *British Food Journal* 105 559–66

Morris C and Evans N 2004 Agricultural turns, geographical turns: retrospect and prospect *Journal of Rural Studies* 20 95–111

Morris C and Young C 2000 'Seed to shelf, 'barley to beer', 'womb to tomb', 'teat to table': an analysis of discourses of quality in the UK farming media *Journal of Rural Studies* 16 103–15

Norberg-Hodge H, Merrifield T and Gorelick S 2002 *Bringing the food economy home: local alternatives to global agribusiness* Zed Books, London

Ober H K 2005 The plain people of Lancaster county, Pennsylvania (http://www.horseshoe.cc/pennadutch/religion/plainpeople/plainp.htm) Accessed 10 December 2005

Organic Centre Wales 2005 Organic standards (http://www.organic.aber.ac.uk/farmers/standards.shtml) Accessed 21 December

Organics To Go 2006 Welcome to Organics To Go (http://www.organicstogo.info/) Accessed 5 June 2006

O'Riordan T 2004 Environmental science, sustainability and politics *Transactions of the Institute of British Geographers* 29 234–47

O'Riordan T and Voisey H 1998 *The transition to sustainability: the politics of Agenda 21 in Europe* Earthscan, London

Pain R 2004 Social geography: participatory research *Progress in Human Geography* 28 652–63

Pain R and Francis P 2003 Reflections on participatory research *Area* 35 46–54

Panelli R and Pini B 2005 'This beats a cake stall!': farm women's shifting encounters with the Australian state *Policy and Politics* 33 489–503

Plan B 2005 What is a CSA? (http://www.angelfire.com/ca/planBcsa/page2.html) Accessed 21 December 2005

Potter C and Tilzey M 2005 Agricultural policy discourses in the European post-Fordist transition: neoliberalism, neomercantilism and multifunctionality *Progress in Human Geography* 29 581–600

Pretty J 1995 Participatory learning for sustainable agriculture *World Development* 23 1247–63

Pretty J, Brett C, Gee D, Hine R C, Mason C, Morsion J, Raymen M, van der Bijl G and

Dobbs T L 2001 Policy challenges and priorities for internalizing the externalities of modern agriculture *Journal of Environmental Planning and Management* 44 263–83

Pritchard B and Burch D 2003 *Agri-food globalization in perspective: international restructuring in the processing tomato industry* Ashgate, Aldershot

Renting H, Marsden T and Banks G 2003 Understanding alternative food networks: exploring the role of short food supply chains in rural development *Environment and Planning A* 35 393–411

Roberts W, MacRae R and Stahlbrand L 1999 *Real food for a change: how the simple act of eating can boost your health and energy, knock out stress, revive your community, clean up your planet* Random House, Canada

Sachs W 1999 *Planet dialectics: explorations in environment and development* Zed Books, London

Seyfang G forthcoming Ecological citizenship and sustainable consumption: examining local organic food networks *Journal of Rural Studies*

Smith E and Marsden T 2004 Exploring the 'limits to growth' in UK organics: beyond the statistical image *Journal of Rural Studies* 20 345–57

Smithers J and Johnson P 2004 The dynamics of family farming in North Huron County, Ontario. Part I. Development trajectories *The Canadian Geographer* 48 191–208

Smithers J, Wall E and Swanton C J 1998 A framework for assessing the sustainability of North American farming systems in Epps R ed *Sustaining rural systems in the context of global change* Proceedings of the Joint Conference of the IGU commission on the Sustainability of Rural Systems and the Land Use/Land Cover Change Group University of New England, Armidale 265–75

Traugher A 2004 'Because they can do the work': women workers in sustainable agriculture in Pennsylvania *Gender, Place and Culture* 11 289–307

Troughton M 2005 Fordism rampant: the model and reality, as applied to production, processing and distribution in the North American agro-food system in Essex S, Gilg A and Yarwood R eds *Rural change and sustainability: agriculture, the environment and communities* CAB International, Wallingford UK 13–27

Troughton M and Mitchell N 2000 Problems, issues and experiences of rural women in Southern Ontario in Ogilvie J, Smithers J and Wall H eds *Sustaining agriculture in the 21st century* University of Guelph, Guelph ON 291–300

Wakeman T 2005 East Anglia Food Link: an NGO working on sustainable food presented at Grassroots Initiatives for Sustainable Development Conference 10 January, UCL (copies available from the author)

Whatmore S 2002 *Hybrid geographies: natures cultures space* Sage, London

Williams C and Millington A 2004 The diverse and contested meanings of sustainable development *The Geographical Journal* 170 99–104

Wilson G A and Rigg J 2003 'Post-productivist' agricultural regimes and the South: discordant concepts? *Progress in Human Geography* 27 681–707

Winter M 2004 Geographies of food: agro-food geographies – farming, food and politics *Progress in Human Geography* 28 646–70

Winter M 2005 Geographies of food: agro-food geographies – farming, nature, farmers and agency *Progress in Human Geography* 29 609–17

WWOOF 2005 World-wide opportunities on organic farms (http://www.wwoof.org/) Accessed 1 December 2005

Yakovleva N and Flynn A 2004 Innovation and sustainability in the food system: a case of chicken production and consumption in the UK *Journal of Environmental Policy & Planning* 6 227–50

5

Things Became Scarce: Food Availability and Accessibility in Santiago de Cuba Then and Now

Hanna Garth

Global food security has become an increasing concern across the world. The World Food Program (WFP) states that rates of hunger in Cuba are "extremely low" (WFP 2009). Cuba has had a nationalized food rationing system since 1962, and has been lauded for exemplary food security innovations in the face of national financial hardship (Food and Agriculture Organization of the United Nations 2009). This project examines the present day Cuban food system and how Cubans living in Santiago de Cuba experience the process of food acquisition. This article highlights individual struggles to acquire food products in the face of low availability and decreased accessibility compared to previous time periods in Cuba. In many ways this work revisits Benjamin and colleagues' mission to "get beyond polemics and investigate firsthand the food realities in Cuba today," over 20 years later and on a much smaller scale (Benjamin et al. 1984:302).

There are many ways to measure food security, access to food, and hunger. This project focuses on individual accounts of food access and acquisition. The United States Department of Agriculture (USDA) has noted the difficulty in measuring and characterizing food access (Ver Ploeg et al. 2009) given many levels of decision making such as how much time to allocate to food acquisition and other food related activity, choosing where and how food is acquired, and choosing what to eat. This research project suggests that the process of food acquisition is a complicated and time-consuming task for Santiago households. To understand food acquisition as a complex, multilayered process this project explores subjects' perceptions of food accessibility and availability as well as the difficulties of navigating the food system in Santiago de Cuba.

This work focuses on Cuba's second largest city, Santiago, which is located in the southeastern part of the island. Santiago's tropical climate provides ideal growing conditions for many crops, including sugar, tobacco, coffee, and fruit. In spite of the fact that Santiago has a population of about 500,000 people, Santiagueros often self-identify as *guajiros* or peasants. Santiago is known for its vibrant Afro-Cuban culture; many Santiagueros are proud to maintain what they perceive to be African traditions not only through music, dance, and ritual forms but also through culinary practices. Santiago provides an urban setting through which to view urban food cultivation and food acquisition in a very distinct cultural and social context compared to Havana. Havana is often used as a point of comparison not only because it is where the majority of ethnographic work has taken place but also because Santiagueros usually draw on Havana as a comparison to their own situations.

Cuba's current food system was borne of a complex history of strained economic periods and the need to innovate solutions in the face of deficient international trade relationships (Premat 1998; Stricker 2007). At the inception of Cuba's food rationing system, Fidel Castro noted that a supply and demand price policy "would have been nothing short of ruthless sacrifice on the part of the poor population with the lowest income," and according to Benjamin et al., "such a policy was accepted for luxury and nonessential goods but never for the necessities" (1984:15). Because of the collapse of the Soviet Union, beginning in the late 1980s Cuba suffered a period of economic hardship known as the "Special Period in Time of Peace" (Alvarez 2004; Powell 2008). During this period Cubans barely maintained access to basic foods and luxury and nonessential goods were nearly impossible to find. The collapse of the Soviet Union was extremely devastating for Cuba not only because of their heavy reliance on the Soviet Union as a trade partner but also because the Soviets subsidized the price that Cuba paid for petroleum and supplied free weapons to Cuba. The Soviets also provided low interest loans to cover several Cuban development projects (Dominguez 2005:12). During the period of Soviet financial and material aid, there was an abundance of cheap imported food products and other goods that were accessible even to poor Cubans. The Special Period brought an end to these cheap imports and subsequent food scarcity. Although the end of the Special Period is widely debated, many Santiagueros argue that Cuba is still immersed in the Special Period. Mesa-Lago argues that among decreasing wages and purchasing power, and exceedingly high prices for essential goods and in agricultural free markets, the reduction in food rations from one month's supply to only about 10 days' supply, contributed to today's decline in the Cuban standard of living (2005).

Despite the fact that Cuba's health and social indicators remained noteworthy in the 1990s, "caloric intake fell by 27% between 1990 and 1996" (Dominguez 2005:14). During these years food products became scarce and those that did exist were difficult for average Cubans to access because of their increased prices. Additionally school cafeterias, day care centers, and government job sites provided fewer and lower-quality foods than they had before (Messina 2004). These scarcities of the early 1990s coupled with the creation of the Convertible Unit of Currency (CUC), which I discuss below, led to an increasing lower class in Cuba in the 1990s where "12 percent of urban Cubans earned less than 100 pesos per month (less than $5 per month at the prevailing exchange rate), had no access to dollars, grew no food and received no food subsidies" (Dominguez 2005:15).

In 1993, the government began to allow Cubans to legally use foreign currency; previously the possession of hard currency was a punishable crime. Cuba operated on a dual U.S. dollar–Cuban peso economy until 2004 when dollars ceased to be accepted and the Convertible Cuban Peso (CUC or *Chavitos*) came into circulation. At the time of my research the CUC was equivalent to one dollar and eight cents. However, Cubans do not get paid in CUC; Cuba's second currency, the Cuban national peso is the currency that most Cubans are paid in. There are 25 national pesos per CUC. Whereas there used to be many stores that accepted the national peso, these stores are increasingly converting to CUC, thus forcing Cubans to convert their Cuban national pesos into CUC to make their purchases (Centero et al. 1997; De La Fuente and Glasco 1997; Phillips 2009). Many find the dual currency system to be exhausting and discriminatory in that some see it as creating a two-tiered society—one with access to CUC and one with the national peso.

This project was initially conceived of as follow up research on the literature on the wide spread usage of community gardens in Cuba published in the 1990s; however, I quickly found that compared to other forms of food procurement these gardens are not as central in the everyday lives of people in Santiago de Cuba today as they were reported in the literature. I shifted my research to focus more broadly on the daily processes of food acquisition in addition to the uses of community gardens in Santiago. I found that households generally acquire foods in five basic ways: the government food rations, gifts and trades, black market purchases, peso purchases, and convertible currency (CUC) purchases.

In this article I juxtapose two different memories of food abundance to show the varying ways in which individuals conceptualize food accessibility. The memories articulated in this work are part of the way that Santigueros relate past practices to the current shifts in food accessibility (Garro 2000b). For Santiagueros, the making of a meal is deeply tied with remembered histories of their Spanish, African, Indian, and Haitian ancestors (Sahlins 1990:95). The memories recounted here may facilitate an understanding of the past that helps Santiagueros comprehend their lives in the present and help them to cope with the difficult circumstances that they face today (Bruner 1990:340).

Many Santiagueros express that the transition to state control over food production caused a great shift in the everyday eating of a typical Cuban household, yet when asked what typical Cuban meals consisted of before the 1959 revolution most respond that the standard foods—rice, black beans, pork, and tubers—has in fact not changed. It is true, however, that for many Santiagueros the acquisition of these essential ingredients has become increasingly difficult. Food acquisition is a daily, interdependent activity that forces cooperation among individual community members. My research resonates with P. Sean Brotherton's work on Cuba's health care

system. Brotherton's work theorizes about a relatively recent shift in individual Cubans' orientation to the state public health and medical system; as macroeconomic shifts place strain on the system individual Cubans must work harder to make the system work for themselves (Brotherton 2005:178). The frustration that participants express with the Cuban food system shows, as Brotherton has demonstrated with respect to Cuba's health care system, how hard Cubans must struggle on a daily basis to make the system work (Brotherton 2005).

In the following sections, after explaining the general ways in which Santiagueros acquire food, ethnographic data is provided to show Santiagueros' perceptions of the difficulties of the daily chore of acquiring food in present day Santiago de Cuba. I then present two interlocutors' very different memories of periods in Santiago's history where food products were more widely available and more easily accessed by the local population. These memories of what are perceived to have been better days are one way that Santiagueros use the past to make sense of the present (Bruner 1990:340; Garro 2000a:339; Pilcher 1998:64; Prager 1998:312). Through the juxtaposition of present day struggles with food acquisition and remembered times of a perceived lack of struggle in food acquisition this article illuminates the struggle of individual Santiagueros to make the Cuban food system work.

METHODOLOGY

This research is based on 10 weeks of fieldwork in Santiago de Cuba during the summer of 2008. Using participant-observation, I studied the work carried out for and discourse around the daily acquisition of food for households in various parts of the city. In addition to direct observation, informal, semistructured interviews were conducted across a diverse section of Santiago residents. Through these informal conversations I gained a deeper understanding of local food folklore and symbolic interpretations, in addition to ascertaining the level of local concern over food matters. I interviewed 25 people, some of whom I interviewed multiple times. Most of the interviews were audio recorded when participants consented, and written notes were taken during the conversations. I conducted all of the research in Spanish and transcribed selected interviews myself. Transcripts were analyzed for themes and related quotations; themes were determined based on issues that subjects consistently raised in the interviews.

A community mapping exercise was used to identify how participants spatially locate food sources (markets, ration stations, gardens, farms, etc.) in relation to subjects' homes and other important establishments (markets, schools, clinics, transportation routes). This exercise also illuminated the difficulties faced, the time spent, and the amount of work my interlocutors viewed as necessary to access food. I also acted as a participant-observer in homes and kitchens. Through this context, I observed what foods were served, how they were prepared, as well as discourses surrounding these foods and their access as the meals were being consumed. This was also a way to measure which foods are most commonly consumed in the home.

RESULTS

In the sections that follow I first describe the primary ways in which Santiagueros

acquire food: government food rations, peso purchases, CUC purchases, black market purchases, and gifts and trades. I then expand on the results of the community mapping exercise to highlight the difficulties for many Santiagueros in planning and carrying out food acquisition. This example illustrates the amount of effort involved in these processes of food acquisition. Following this outlining of the process of food acquisition I juxtapose two contrasting views of food scarcity to show different local interpretations of what it means to have adequate access to food.

URBAN FOOD ACQUISITION

In this section, I lay out the basic forms of food acquisition for most of my interlocutors and their evaluation of the affordability, availability, and quality of each form of procurement to show their advantages and disadvantages (see Table 5.1).

Government Rations

The most common way in which food is acquired is through Cuba's national food rationing system. Since 1962, the Cuban government has centrally collected and distributed food throughout the country; complaints about Cuba's food rationing system have persisted since its inception. Every Cuban is eligible for a ration card, with which they can purchase basic food items. The ration prices are very heavily subsidized. The monthly ration includes five eggs, five pounds refined sugar, five

Table 5.1 Advantages and Disadvantages of Basic Forms of Food Procurement in Santiago

	Rations	CUC Stores	Peso Markets	Black Market	Gifts and Trades
Affordable	+	−	+	+/−	+
High Quality	−	+	−	+/−	+/−
Available	−	−	−	−	−

pounds raw sugar, five pounds white rice, five pounds of beans, 0.4 pints cooking oil, a loaf of bread per day, and 200g–500g pork or ground beef mixed with soy.[1] All of these items cost about 25 national pesos a month, or about one dollar—the ration is essential for making ends meet in most Santiago households. Still, complaints about insufficient food products in the monthly ration are widespread in Cuba (Gjelten 2008:180).

During summer of 2008, I quickly found that one of the foremost concerns of many Santiagueros is supplementing their monthly food ration with food items that they view as essential to maintain their ideal Cuban cuisine, in particular: pork, beef, additional rice, black beans, red beans and chick peas, particular spices, eggs, milk, and probably most importantly, cooking oil. Although fresh produce is something that many desire, these other items usually take precedence over the fresh fruits and vegetables.

The government rations are extremely inexpensive, extremely convenient to access given that there is a ration station on nearly every other block, but the supply is often inconsistent in terms of what is available and the quality of the foods. Additionally, the food in the ration is not sufficient for caloric and micronutrient needs.

National Peso Markets

There are many ways to make food purchases with the Cuban national peso. In Santiago there are five large markets that sell goods only in the national peso. Many of the people that I interviewed noted that these markets are very expensive for them, so much so that they try to only shop at these markets when absolutely necessary, that is once they have consumed everything provided by the ration and any foods they can acquire in cheaper ways. Although these markets often have irregular and inconsistent goods, these are often the only

places where certain types of food items are available such as lettuce, tomatoes, and other fruits and vegetables that easily perish or are not conducive to street vendors. Those with more resources use these markets more, but complain of their limited and irregular supply.[2] The prices at these markets vary greatly. During the summer of 2008 I calculated the average prices of some foods: okra, five pesos per piece ($0.23); small cucumbers, three pesos ($0.14); small slices of squash, one peso ($0.05); malanga, nine pesos per pound ($0.41); yucca, 2.50 per pound ($0.11); small plantains, 7.50 per pound ($0.34); and tomatoes, four pesos per pound ($0.18). Some of these items are also available through street vendors, however because of the small quantity they are able to carry they often run out of popular items.

In addition to peso markets, street vendors, whether or not they have a permit to legally sell food, accept pesos for their goods. Many black market purchases are made in pesos, although illicit vendors increasingly demand CUC for their products. Food sales between friends and family normally use the national peso.

CUC Purchases

Currently, CUC purchases are the only way to acquire many of the products Cubans consider necessary, including additional cooking oil, imported spices, and bouillon cubes, and personal hygiene products such as deodorant. Items in the CUC market are priced similarly to U.S. prices: a can of soda is 75 cents, a bar of soap one CUC, a liter of cooking oil one CUC and ten cents, or 16oz of pasta for two CUC.[3] Most of the Santiagueros that I interviewed were able to make very few CUC purchases each month. Many essential items that used to be sold in pesos are increasingly only available in CUC; however, individual access to CUC has not increased. Many cited soap and deodorant as their most important monthly CUC purchases and very few people mentioned purchasing the food items available in the CUC stores.

Black Market Purchases

Figures on black market activity are nearly impossible to come by (Benjamin et al. 1984; Brotherton 2005; Centero et al. 1997; Phillips 2009); I was lucky to acquire some ethnographic data on the black market. Although I cannot draw generalizable conclusions about this data, information of this kind is essential for understanding food security. The category of black market purchases includes not only situations where the possession, consumption, or sale of the product is illegal but also where the manner in which the product is acquired is illegal. Frozen, imported lobster, shrimp and other seafood, often originally destined for hotels and resorts, are also traded on the black market. These foods along with myriad other items, from industrial sized cans of vegetables or capers, to U.S. cigarettes and foreign beer, are all goods stolen from the hospitality industry and constitute a great proportion of the black market goods in Cuba. Additionally, tourists and relatives who are living abroad provide a category of goods bought and sold on the black market, some of which are legal to possess, canned or freeze dried foods, while others are not, such as certain appliances (see Table 5.1).

Black market goods sold directly from farmland are also quite common in Santiago. Legally a certain proportion of crops harvested are to be sold to the government, but many farmers hoard parts of their harvests to sell directly to the public. Farm fresh eggs and freshly ground coffee are among the many direct from the farm specialties commonly sold in Santiago's streets. These goods are usually sold clandestinely through social

networks. However, those households that post a sign on the door or window advertising their goods must have a permit to do so and thus are selling goods legally.

Black market beef was probably the most sought after and most important black market food product at the time of this research. Although beef is unavailable to the general public, except on rare occasions, Cubans with certain diseases, including HIV/AIDS, diabetes, and kidney disorders receive beef in their rations. Based on my informal conversations with a local black market beef trader in Santiago, I suspect that some Cubans are able to get beef by purchasing from or trading with those who have the special diet ration.

Informal Trades, Self-Production, and Gifts

Informal trading and gifts are another essential way in which Santiagueros acquire food. The general scarcity of goods and the extreme irregularity of product availability in Santiago means the hoarding and trading within social networks are essential to overcoming household hardships during times of scarcity. Those with more resources buy products in bulk when they are available in the stores and markets; later they sell or trade these items to friends, family, and extended social networks. Reliance on a network of *socios*, that is, friends, family, neighbors, coworkers, and godparents, is absolutely necessary to keep from going hungry in Santiago.

Food can also be acquired through *pregoneros*, who, known for their *pregones*, or jingles, navigate Santiago streets from sunup to sundown singing songs of the quality of their goods. Some street vendors sell and acquire their goods legally; others do not. Although *pregoneros* are quite convenient given that they come to your home, their prices are marked up and their goods irregular and inconsistent.

This description of the various ways in which Santiagueros acquire food for household consumption illuminates the complexities entailed and the difficulty of navigating the task of food acquisition. This description is necessary to show that, although basic foods are widely available, there are varying degrees of individual accessibility. In the following section, I present some ethnographic data regarding local notions of scarcity in Santiago. The following articulations of food scarcity and abundance show how the concepts of access and availability discussed above relate to individuals' differing ideas about what food security means.

THE WORK OF FOOD ACQUISITION: RESULTS OF COMMUNITY MAPPING EXERCISE

My research indicates that although basic foods are widely available to Santiagueros, individual community members must put forth a great deal of effort and spend a lot of time on food acquisition. The time and energy of individual efforts to make the system work for themselves is often not taken into account when conceptualizing food security. One afternoon during my fieldwork, Mickey hurriedly came by to get me: "Let's go, Hanna." When I asked where we were going, Mickey explained: "we are going to the train station. The train from Guantanamo just arrived; I got a big box of food from my friends in Guantanamo on the train." My puzzled look led Mickey to further explain:

Certain kinds of foods are always cheaper in Guantanamo, like malanga, sweet potatoes, potatoes, some fruits, so we send money to our friends there and they can put a box of food on the train for us for free. It's like, for example, when you go to the state market here and they only have the things that are in the ration, nothing else, no malanga, no cabbage, no garlic, so you have to run all over town looking for it and you are always looking for the cheap price but you don't want to risk not buying

something and then not finding it somewhere else. It's not easy. There is no solution. But here [with shipping food from Guantanamo] we have a solution.

Here Mickey describes his solution to the common situation of "having to run all over town looking" for food. Although Mickey's solution of having food sent to him via train from another province is atypical, if not extreme, the frustration of food acquisition and the feeling that "there is no solution" is very common among Santiagueros. The following ethnographic example illuminates a typical amount of effort individuals must put forth to acquire food in Santiago. Here, I used participatory mapping exercise to attempt to understand individual efforts to acquire foods, including travel time and distance as well as the number of locations from which people acquired food. Community mapping exercises have been widely used in food security research (Coveney and O'Dwyer 2009; Hyman et al. 2005; Sharkey 2009).

About half of the people whom I asked to participate in my mapping exercise agreed to participate and some would only orient to the space verbally and through gesture.[4] They explained to me that the market they used was right up the road, or at the edge of town, often pointing in the direction of the location of reference. My questions regarding how long travel takes were met with some difficulty; travel time varies greatly depending on the mode of transportation. Those who drew or used the map that I purchased to point out their route often had to think for quite a while about where certain points were located.

One interlocutor, Alex, explained to me that he felt it was not very effective to use this mapping exercise as away of gauging the distance that people must travel to acquire food. He felt that a better method would be to ask people what forms of transportation they use, where they go to wait for them, how much they cost and how long they take. I agreed that this would be a wonderful way to garner a deeper understanding of the amount of effort that went in to food shopping and asked him to explain this process for his own process of food acquisition. He explained that in his case to get to the cheapest market located out the outskirts of town he first walked from his house to the other side of the city center. This walk took him about 30 minutes. He then waited for a horse drawn carriage to take him to the edge of town. This was his transportation of choice because it is very cheap, only 0.20 pesos, or just under $0.01. Unfortunately, he often had to wait for 45 minutes to one hour before catching a carriage. The length of time on the carriage varies depending on the number of passengers that get on and off. He explained to me that he could probably walk out to the market but the energy he would "lose" from the walking and sweating in the heat would cost him more in the food he would have to eat and the water he would drink.

This ethnographic articulation of food accessibility illuminates the intricacies of food access, and is essential to understanding local concepts of scarcity and abundance. This data demonstrates that considerable time, energy, and financial resources have to be invested in the procurement of food for a typical Santiago household. Additionally, this data shows that we cannot necessarily assume that the proximity of households to food vendors is the distance that individuals will travel to acquire food; other factors about individual choices informing food purchases must be taken into account.

FOOD SCARCITY: ABUNDANCE FOR SOME VERSUS JUST ENOUGH FOR EVERYONE

When I asked Juan, a Santiguero in his late 50s who grew up in an upper class Cuban home prior to the 1959 revolution, to describe a typical meal from his childhood, he replied:

> People almost always eat rice and beans, in other words typical Cuban food: fried plantains, *tostones*, meat, salad, etc. Children always had a glass of milk. Now they say [milk] is not good for digestion. [Milk] has another way; the lactose takes a different amount of time to digest than other food. Before we always had a glass of milk . . . it was easy to get. The [milkman] brought it to your house, left it in front of your door and there was never a problem with people taking it. The milkman came every day. Kids drank milk four times a day: breakfast, lunch, dinner and before bed.

I commented that even by today's standards that is a lot of milk. Juan continued:

> Before kids were fat, if you see photos of kids in school before [the revolution] you will see fat kids—uh in private school. I'm referring to *private school*, because other kids didn't have these possibilities. Still, in general kids were well nourished. Before [the revolution] you could either go home to eat lunch or your parents gave you money to buy whatever was there—a sandwich, a soda—whatever there was that day.

I asked Juan to tell me about the changes that happened after the revolution and he lamented, "Things became scarce." When he elaborated on the scarcity he recounted that starting in 1959 or 1960, for example, "Corn flakes, a cereal just for kids was not too expensive before but suddenly it was off the shelves and has not come back since."

In addition to U.S.-made cereals such as Corn Flakes, when asked about what changes occurred with respect to food after the revolution my interlocutors listed the following foods as essential to prerevolutionary Cuban cuisine and now scarce: Beef of any sort, "real" (not powdered or canned) dairy products, lettuce, capers, olives, chicken, turkey, duck, lobster, crab, calamari, and shrimp among others.

However, those who longed for these food items tended to come from higher socioeconomic backgrounds prior to the 1959 revolution. I found that Santiagueros from poorer backgrounds reminisced about a period in the early 1980s when luxury items were scarce, but in their memories basic needs were taken care of for all.

One night after sharing a pork leg dinner at his house Rafael began to recall a time when

> things were simpler . . . young people were happy with simple shoes for 20 pesos and didn't care about the American style 20 CUC shoes like the youth today. Because people didn't chase after fancy things everyone was able to have something. Everyone had what they needed; things were equal. Everyone had the same food and it was cheap.

When I asked him how all of this was possible, Rafael replied: "Because of the Soviet Union. Those were the best years of the revolution, the 1980s. In the 1980s here no one lacked anything."

DISCUSSION

In the ethnographic examples presented above, Juan reminisces about a period during his childhood before scarcity was an issue that his family faced. Juan is remembering a time before the 1959 Cuban revolution, a time before food and agriculture was completely controlled by the state. Prompted only by my question about the typical meals of his childhood Juan fixates on the abundance of milk that was available during his childhood and he later adds that Corn Flakes were once available and accessible for his family. Fresh cow's milk is still to this day intensely sought after; the Cuban government regulation of all beef products continues to limit people's access to milk products. I suspect that because of the milk scarcity at the time of our interview,

Juan's memories of his milk-filled childhood were more salient than had there not been a milk scarcity at the time. That is to say, individual concepts of which food items are necessary and desired may vary with food scarcity and abundance.

Juan is aware that "others did not have [the] possibilities" to access the same luxury goods as his family did. He notes that he is referring to "private school," which is along with Corn Flakes another luxury that no longer exists in postrevolutionary Cuba. Juan reflected that after the revolution "things became scarce." Although he does not explicitly state it, in his mentioning of private school he implies an awareness of the fact that, at the same time certain things became scarce for his family, other things became available and accessible to other poorer families in Santiago and throughout Cuba.

Rafael also reflects on a period of his life during which food products and consumer goods in general were much more abundant than what he experiences today. Rafael however reflects on a period after the 1959 revolution during which there was an abundance of goods available at low enough prices that they were accessible to almost all Cubans. Other interlocutors also reminisced about the availability of imported goods from the Soviet Union, China, and other parts of the world during the 1980s. Rafael's family comes from a poor socioeconomic background, which may contribute to his reflection on the period during the 1980s as the best years of the revolution. For his family, this was a period when things were most widely accessible to them. Rafael also stresses the equality of accessibility of goods during this time: "Everyone had the same food and it was cheap."

The distinct viewpoints of Juan and Rafael raise questions about the role of the distribution of resources and the type and quality of those resources. These two points of view raise questions about the relationship between food security and "desire fulfillment" (Sen 1985). Fidel Castro's sentiment that a supply and demand price policy "would have been nothing short of ruthless sacrifice on the part of the poor population with the lowest income," is reflected in Rafael's concept of food security; everyone is able to access what they need, but some end up sacrificing the ability to access luxury goods.

Both the narrative of Juan and that of Rafael reflect on historical periods in which things were better than they are today. Remembering or "misremembering" the past as utopia may be a part of the ways in which Santiagueros make sense of the difficulties of food acquisition today. As shown through Alex's reflections on the work involved in food acquisition today the process is exceedingly difficult, expensive, and inconvenient at least for some Santiagueros. In reflecting on Alex's narrative, I was fascinated by his quick calculation of his own energy expenditure versus the monetary costs of transportation.

Alex's focus on the monetary and nonmonetary costs of food acquisition are also illustrative of P. Sean Brotherton's focus on the difficulties faced by individual Cubans in the day-to-day work they must undertake to make the system work (Brotherton 2005:178). As food items have become less available and more difficult to access, as shown through the memories of Juan and Rafael, individuals must expend increased physical and emotional efforts to acquire food. Although relative to other countries with similar aggregate level data, such as GDP, Santiagueros have "extremely low" rates of hunger and food insecurity. Santiago households and individuals must devote a great deal of time and energy to food procurement.

CONCLUSIONS

In Cuba the national food rationing system guarantees all citizens access to minimum basic nutritional needs. These guaranteed basic needs also come with what some Santiagueros like Juan and Rafael perceive as a lack of variety or a lack of choice. The difficulties of acquiring food products legally may contribute to the expansion of black market food activity. Economic and political changes in Cuba have placed strain on the food distribution system; this in turn has necessitated increased efforts on the part of Cuban individuals to make the system work for themselves.

In considering Cuba's food distribution system as an example to be generalized and applied in other settings, it is essential to consider the fact that Cuba's food system is inextricably tied with many other systems at play in Cuba's socialist government infrastructure such as the free education and medical care provided to citizens. Additionally, country solutions to food scarcity must always take into account trade and other partnerships of that country with the rest of the world. Cuba's limited trade possibilities force the Cuban government to innovate solutions to food scarcity when other means are unavailable. As availability and access to food shifts, coupled with the dollarization of the Cuban economy, individuals must devote increasing amounts of time and energy to acquire food and remain within the designation of "extremely low" levels of hunger.

The dialectic of the two memories of past periods of food availability in Santiago presented here still leaves many questions regarding food security: How much is enough? Can everyone have what she or he wants? Do some need to sacrifice things they want so everyone can have what they need? Who determines what is necessary? What types of social needs must be accounted for with respect to nourishment?

Understanding the intricate workings of Cuba's food system at the level of individual and households in their daily lives provides insight into the complex linkages between Cuba's food system and other aspects of Cuban life. Additionally, the ethnographic examples presented here show the ways in which the same system can affect individuals in different ways. These Santiagueros present differing notions of needs and desires and how these needs and desires have shifted throughout time. Understanding local conceptualizations of need may be essential when considering solutions to food scarcity. By showing how individuals conceptualize food security and their ways of navigating the food system, this work shows the importance of ethnographic research in understanding how individuals use and experience food systems as a part of food security research.

ACKNOWLEDGMENTS

I would like to acknowledge my friends in Santiago who have made this project by sharing their stories with me, as well as Carole Browner, Linda Garro, Jason Throop, Akhil Gupta, Robin Derby, Paul Ryer, Jennifer Guzman, Ellen Sharp, Katja Antoine, and Christel Miller. I would also like to thank my editor David Himmelgreen and an anonymous reviewer for their comments, which greatly improved this article. This project was funded in part by: the UC Diversity Initiative for Graduate Study in the Social Sciences, the UC Cuba Initiative Travel Grant.

NOTES

1. Also, children up to seven years old get one liter of milk daily and children from seven to 14 get one liter of yogurt daily.
2. There are also food stalls that are more heavily subsidized by the Cuban government that people often prefer to buy food from, however these stalls are not usually very well supplied.
3. Note that after converting to CUC, a Cuban worker who receives 300 national pesos a month in salary has only 12 CUC a month.
4. Historically, detailed maps of Cuba were largely unavailable because of government efforts to limit knowledge of spatial information as a matter of national security. However, in recent years with the expansion of tourism and

particularly the use of rental cars by foreign clientele, maps have become more commonplace. Santiagueros and probably Cubans in general do not usually orient toward space through printed maps, nor do they write down or draw pictures to spatially orient themselves. This is in part because of a recent historical absence of maps and may also be indicative of forms of spatial logics in Cuba. Because of the fact that Santiagueros orient to their landscape in other ways, my attempt to use a community mapping exercise was somewhat difficult. I solicited people to draw a map of the various routes they use for daily food acquisition and to mark the locations of markets, ration stations and other food acquisition points on a map of Santiago that I purchased at a local tourist shop.

REFERENCES CITED

Alvarez, José (2004) Cuba's Agricultural Sector. Gainesville: University Press of Florida.

Benjamin, Medea, Joseph Collins, and Michael Scott (1984) No Free Lunch: Food and Revolution in Cuba Today. Princeton: Princeton University Press.

Brotherton, P. Sean (2005) Macroeconomic Change and the Biopolitics of Health in Cuba's Special Period. Journal of Latin American Anthropology 10(2):339–369.

Bruner, Jerome (1990) Acts of Meaning: Four Lectures on Mind and Culture. Cambridge, MA: Harvard University Press.

Centero, Miguel Angel, and Mauricio Font, eds. (1997) Toward a New Cuba? Legacies of a Revolution. Boulder, CO: Lynne Rienner.

Coveney, John, and Lisel A. O'Dwyer (2009) Effects of Mobility and Location on Food Access. Health and Place 15(1):45–55.

De La Fuente, Alejandro, and Laurence Glasco (1997) Are Blacks "Getting Out of Control"? Racial Attitudes, Revolution, and Political Transition in Cuba. In Toward A New Cuba? Legacies of a Revolution. Miguel Angel Centero and Mauricio Font, eds. Boulder, CO: Lynne Rienner.

Dominguez, Jorge I. (2005) Cuba's Economic Transition: Successes, Deficiencies, and Challenges. In Transforming Socialist Economies: Lessons for Cuba and Beyond. Shahid Javed Burki and Daniel P. Erikson, eds. New York: Palgrave.

Food and Agriculture Organization of the United Nations (2009) FAO and Emergencies: Cuba. Electronic document, www.fao.org/emergencies/country_information/list/latinamerica/cuba/en/, accessed July 22, 2009.

Garro, Linda C. (2000a) Cultural Knowledge as Resource in Illness Narrative: Remembering through Accounts of Illness. In Narrative and the

Cultural Construction of Illness and Healing. Cheryl Mattingly and Linda C. Garro, eds. Pp. 70–87. Berkeley: University of California Press.

—— (2000b) Remembering What One Knows and the Construction of the Past: A Comparison of Cultural Consensus Theory and Cultural Schema Theory. Ethos 28(3):275–319.

Gjelten, Tom (2008) Raul Castro's Reforms Raise Expectations in Cuba. All Things Considered. National Public Radio, May 9.

Hyman, Glenn, Carlos Larrea, and Andrew Farrow (2005) Methods, Results and Policy Implications of Poverty and Food Security Mapping Assessments. Food Policy 30:453–460.

Mesa-Lago, Carmelo (2005) The Cuban Economy Today: Salvation or Damnation? Miami: Institute for Cuban and Cuban American Studies, University of Miami.

Messina, William A. (2004) Cuban Agriculture in Transition: The Impacts of Policy Changes on Agriculture Production, Food Markets, and Trade. In The Cuban Economy. A. R. Ritter, ed. Pp. 106–117. Pittsburgh: University of Pittsburgh Press.

Phillips, Emma (2009) Dollarization, Distortion, and the Transformation of Work. Paper presented at A Changing Cuba in a Changing World conference, New York, March 12.

Pilcher, Jeffrey (1998) ¡Que vivan los tamales! Food and the Making of Mexican Identity. Albuquerque: University of New Mexico Press.

Powell, Kathy (2008) Neoliberalism, the Special Period and Solidarity in Cuba. Critique of Anthropology 28(2):177–197.

Prager, Jeffrey (1998) Presenting the Past: Psychoanalysis and the Sociology of Misremembering. Cambridge, MA: Harvard University Press.

Premat, Adriana (1998) Feeding the Self and Cultivation of Identities in Havana, Cuba. M.A. thesis, Department of Anthropology, York University.

Sahlins, Marshall (1990) Food as Symbolic Code. In Culture and Society: Contemporary Debates. S. Seidman, ed. Pp. 94–101. Cambridge: Cambridge University Press.

Sen, Amartya (1985) Weil-Being, Agency and Freedom: The Dewey Lectures 1984. Journal of Philosophy 82(4):169–221.

Sharkey, Joseph R. (2009) Measuring Potential Access to Food Stores and Food-Service Places in Rural Areas in the U.S. American Journal of Preventative Medicine 36(4S):S151–S155.

Stricker, Pamela (2007) Toward a Culture of Nature: Environmental Policy and Sustainable Development in Cuba. New York: Lexington.

Ver Ploeg, Michele, Vince Breneman, Tracy Farrigan, Karen Hamrick, David Hopkins, Phil Kaufman, Biing-Hwan Lin, Mark Nord, Travis Smith, Ryan Williams, Kelly Kinnison, Carol Olander, Anita Singh, and Elizabeth Tuckermanty (2009) Access to Affordable and Nutritious Food—Measuring and Understanding Food Deserts and Their Consequences: Report to Congress. USDA Administrative Publication, AP-036. Washington, DC: USDA.

World Food Program (WFP) (2009) Cuba: Country Overview. Electronic document, http://www.wfp.org/countries/cuba, accessed September 5, 2009.

6

Capitalism and Its Discontents: Back-to-the-Lander and Freegan Foodways in Rural Oregon

Joan Gross

The economic geographers who write under the appended surname Gibson-Graham argue that when people talk about "the economy," capitalism has trained us to only see the tip of the iceberg. Gibson-Graham urge people to not simply accept the hegemony of capitalocentrism, but to create a more inclusive discourse that recognizes the full complement of human economic activity (30–50% of which is accounted for by unpaid, household labor [2006: 57]). Applied to the food system, farmers are encouraged to grow for export, and economic statistics focus on crops sold. If people raise food to be eaten or traded, or if food is simply gathered, it doesn't warrant a place in the statistics. Neither does the time spent procuring, processing, and serving food in our homes. All of this food-related activity remains below the tip of the iceberg and yet it is what sustains us.

An increasing number of people are rebelling against the global industrial food system by expanding the non-capitalist aspects of our food system that are already present. Harvey argued that, at the turn of this century, opposition to capitalism and globalization was almost as widespread as global capitalism itself (2000). Dissatisfaction with the industrialized food-scape has become mainstream, as journalists and scholars with a gift for popular writing like Michael Pollan, Marion Nestle, Gary Nabhan, Carlo Petrini, Barbara Kingsolver, Eric Schlosser, and Bill McKibben have laid out the dystopic elements of industrial

farming and food processing and have written in defense of local foodsheds and healthier eating habits. Food has become the example of what is wrong with our environment and what is wrong with our economy. This is especially apparent in rural areas that used to produce more of the food they consume locally. Local and organic agrifood movements have come into their own and stories about farmers' markets and other forms of community-supported agriculture can be found in media venues around the world leaving the market racing to adjust.[2]

Alternative agrifood movements, such as back-to-the-landers and freegans, reacted against the global industrial food system before such complaints floated into the mainstream and they embellished non-capitalist food-ways that had fallen out of use. They resist the harm that is done to the earth and human health in the process of producing commodity food and work against the production of waste by buying bulk rather than packaged food, growing and gathering their own food, and rescuing items from the dumpster. Equally important, they resist the commodification of time, choosing to spend a good share of their time in unremunerated activities pertaining to food. However, they also recognize their inability to totally disconnect from the capitalist market and often the realities of feeding themselves and their families force them to compromise their ideals. This should not be seen as a failure, but as the evidence of multiple economic forms existing within capitalism.

Melucci defines the proliferation of social movements in contemporary society as group resistance to capitalist power. He notes that these types of identity movements are increasing as individuals lack the cultural bases for their self-identification (1996: 93). Melucci does not talk about the role of food in particular in these movements, but as Mintz and Du Bois state, "Like all culturally defined material substances used in the creation and maintenance of social relationships, food serves both to solidify group membership and to set groups apart" (2002: 109). Foodways definitely separate back-to-the-landers and freegans from the rural communities in which they are found.

In this article I describe the foodways of back-to-the-landers and freegans whom I met in rural Western Oregon. These rather extreme alternative agrifood movements elucidate many of the issues that have become central to more mainstream local food movements. Drawing on subsistence strategies that were dominant in pre-capitalist times, their foodways can help us envision post-capitalist food systems.

METHODOLOGY

The initial research for this article emerged out of a larger qualitative project on food insecurity in rural western Oregon, which is described in more detail in Gross and Rosenberger (2005; forthcoming). During the spring of 2004, I interviewed 39 low-income residents from around the Coast Range town of Alsea where, in a population of 1100, 36 households were on food stamps. I did not set out to focus on back-to-the-landers and freegans, but these two groups stood out from the larger sample in their openly anti-capitalist stance and non-mainstream food habits. They tended to prefer foods that were unprocessed by large corporations. They were not obese

and did not have diabetes, both of which were common in our larger sample. They identified with living "alternative lifestyles" in rural areas. Most of the back-to-the-landers moved out to the Coast Range in the 1970s when they were in their twenties, making them in their fifties at the time of the interview. The second group, who identified mostly as freegans though some were wary of all labels, were all in their twenties.[3] I met them at my colleague Margaret Mathewson's Ancient Arts Center where they were staying for free in exchange for doing some farm work. During the initial fieldwork phase, I recorded and transcribed lengthy interviews with two male and two female freegans who considered themselves a household, and three female back-to-the-landers in separate households. Subsequently, as an active member in the local food movement, I've had more informal conversations with four other freegans and several back-to-the-landers, both male and female. I also use published descriptions of back-to-the-lander foodways in order to compare the foodways of these two groups when they were at a similar stage in their lives.

PLACE

Detachment from place characterizes the global industrial food system, which is ready to do battle over labels of origin. For people who produce or forage for their own food, the particular place where their food comes from holds a lot of meaning. On the other hand, rural areas the world over have suffered from industrial food policies that reward agribusinesses for economies of scale and have caused massive emigration off the land to the cities. According to United Nations estimates, in 2007 the world became more urban than rural for the first time in history. Food has traditionally linked rural and urban populations, but today, despite the growth of farmers' markets, Americans who live in rural areas are dependent on grocery stores in the cities. In fact, much of "farm country" North America can be described as a "food desert" not unlike poor sections of big cities where grocery stores cannot be found (Morton and Blanchard 2007). Ken Meter and Jon Rosales (2001) explain how, in the richest farmland in the world in the American Midwest, people pay more to import food than they receive from growing and exporting it. And fewer people are involved in growing it. Most food secure rural residents own multiple freezers where they can store months of groceries bought during mega shopping trips to big box stores in the cities.[4]

The foodshed of western Oregon is bountiful. The Coast Range, an area of rain-drenched coniferous forests covering low mountains, is home to fish, elk, deer, mushrooms, and berries, all of which help feed the hills' human inhabitants. It is not difficult to imagine how the Alsea Indians sustained themselves on this land (Zenk 1990). The first white settlers arrived in Alsea in the 1850s and, besides hunting, fishing, and gathering, they made Alsea a thriving farming community. Polk's Classified Business Directory of 1913 reported that farming and dairying were the principal businesses of the valley. Apples, oats, and wheat were shipped out to Waldport on the coast. The wealth of the community was attested to by the founding of the Alsea state bank in the early 1920s.

Alsea, like rural towns all over the world, is a shadow of its former self.[5] After World War II many locals shifted away from farming and into logging where the money was better. When restrictions on logging began in the 1980s, mills closed and Alsea shrunk. In 2004, the town had one general store that carried basic groceries and one restaurant, but the other businesses had shut down. The owner of the general store drives into Corvallis to pick up the merchandise he sells in his store since the town has dropped off all distribution routes. Alsea residents consider themselves lucky that they have not lost their school like all the surrounding rural communities have, and they are pleased to have a rural health clinic and a new library that opened in 2006.

Alsea residents consist of a variety of people: descendents of early homesteaders, recent migrants from cities who telecommute, retirees, university professors, welfare recipients attracted by cheaper rents, government workers, and others attracted by the rural beauty of the area. The town lies about 25 miles from the county seat of Corvallis, but the route seems longer due to the winding road over Mary's Peak. There are times during the winter when Alsea is cut off from Corvallis and Philomath (which is closer, but smaller than Corvallis) due to mud slides or steep icy roads. A spirit of independence is shared by many of the residents, but they often do not always see eye to eye on issues. In this mix, we find back-to-the-landers and freegans. Jacob defined back-to-the-landers as people "who are interested in self-reliant living on their own land." He developed a typology of seven different types and of these; the ones who I talked with fall into the "purist" category or those who reduced their participation in the monetized economy while subsisting from the fruits of their own property and bartering with neighbors (1997: 28, 53). Some back-to-the-landers have lived around Alsea for over 30 years, but still might be considered newcomers by members of the old homestead families. They live on several acres of land and have large gardens. Freegans are not permanent residents and are not integrated into the community. Most Alsea residents do not even know that they are there. There are no dumpsters worth diving into in Alsea so their foraging range extends to cities, but they exploit what food the woods has to offer and butcher animals that are killed by passing vehicles.

TIME AND SLOW FOOD

One of the biggest social transformations brought in by capitalism concerns how we view time. The clock, not the steam engine, was the key machine of the industrial era (Thackara 2005). In other patterns of subsistence, biological time dominates since it is linked to the growth cycles of plants and animals. Looking through colonial documents, you can often find references to collisions between capitalist and biological time. For example, directors of Indian boarding schools in 19th century Oregon constantly complained how their students disappeared when it was time to hunt, dig roots, pick berries, or when the salmon were running (Gross 2007: 28).

The role of countercultural movements is to call into question behaviors that are taken for granted by mainstream society. Both freegans and back-to-the-landers rebel against selling their time to labor in the capitalist system. They prefer working for food instead of working to pay for food. They reject a lifestyle that requires spending the bulk of their time working for money in order to buy material goods. Many have read renditions of anthropological research in rural societies that lie outside of mainstream capitalism, societies that practice foraging and subsistence agriculture. Timing is far more important than generic clock time when hunting, gathering, or growing food. During certain periods of the year provisioning activities swallow up every waking hour and at other times of the year people, like the land, lie fallow. Marshall Sahlins (1966) described foragers as the original affluent society since they were able to cover all their needs with about 20 hours a week of work and could devote the rest of the time to leisure. Of course, even that division between leisure and work doesn't make sense to foragers. It's all life to them. John Zerzan, the Oregon anarcho-primitivist with devotees among the freegans, describes the life of

hunter-gatherers as the longest and most successful human adaptation to nature which was accompanied by gender equality, peacefulness, an egalitarian ethic of sharing, a lack of disease, and lots of leisure time (Zerzan 2002).

Post-Modern society is characterized by a speeding up of time. We constantly look for ways in which we can "save time" and new products are marketed on that basis. Growing food, finding food, preparing food, eating food; all these activities take time. That is why the appeal of fast food is overdetermined in advanced capitalism. Workers can quickly consume necessary calories, so that they can get back to work or spend more time doing other things. Employers benefit from the economies of scale and government subsidies that make fast food cheap, so that wages can remain low.

Fast food was anathema to both the back-to-the-landers and the freegans with whom I spoke. When I first arrived at the Ancient Arts Center to interview some freegans, four of them were making fire with a fire drill on a bed of thistle down. Each one took their turn rotating the drill between their hands, then seamlessly passing it to the next person until one spark finally ignited. They painstakingly coaxed it into a small flame using their breath. Then gradually they transferred the flame to larger tinder until an adequate cooking fire emerged. Rather than the contemporary focus on individuals working on multiple tasks simultaneously, this required the intense concentration and coordination of multiple individuals in order to perform a single task, the creation of fire, the means by which raw food is transformed into cooked food. To make acorn mush, they first gathered the nuts under oak trees, shelled them and ground them into flour. Then water was run continuously over the flour for quite awhile to leech out the bitter tannic acid. The leeched acorn flour was placed in a tightly woven and pitch-sealed basket filled with water. To cook it, they transferred a series of round fire-heated rocks into the basket. When one rock cooled, they would remove it and add a new hot one to the liquid. The water boiled and cooked the acorn flour into a thin porridge. This was really slow food and required group effort.

Even if back-to-the-landers didn't reach all the way back to a pre-agricultural era, they still searched for an alternative experience of time, one that was not divided up into equal units that fragment life's experiences. Belasco writes about how the counterculture of the late 1960s rebelled against the speed of the processed food business, preferring to spend hours baking bread and simmering stews over wood burning stoves (2007: 50–53). Jacob, in his study of back-to-the-landers, states that the central dilemma of simple living in the country is time versus money:

> In order to develop a self-reliant farmstead, a family or couple needs time to build fences, weed the garden, milk the goats, and cut and stack wood. But at the same time, back-to-the-landers must earn some kind of income to buy, if nothing else, garden seeds, a nanny goat, or the cast-iron stove that burns the wood to keep them warm through the winter. To the extent they sell their labor in the local economies, they lose valuable time to improve their property.
>
> (Jacob 1997: 47)

Unless someone is very wealthy to begin with or has a pension of some sort, land ownership generally means paying off a monthly mortgage. Even for people who want to disengage from the capitalist system, making money does take time. Most back-to-the-landers I have met envisioned spending the majority of their time on the homestead, but ended up spending it in waged labor. My friend Alison Clement wrote about this tension in her essay "On being wrong" in which she describes her family going back to the land in the Coast Range over the hill from Alsea:

> We each drove an hour to work and an hour home, every day. Evening and weekends, we split firewood, worked on the water system, fixed the truck, repaired leaks, drove the laundry to town, did endless chores. There was no time to visit friends, take walks in the forest, read to the kids, or go to the beach. We never quit working, but life only got harder.
>
> (Clement 1997)

Several of my back-to-the-land informants talked about the amount of time that they devoted to growing and processing food and how these activities had to be drastically curtailed once they joined the capitalist labor force. One back-to-the-lander talked about the farming and pig raising that she used to do before starting her own drywall business. Now, she explained that she makes her lunch while eating breakfast and is out of the door by 6 or 6:30. Then, she said, "I get home at night too tired to deal with anything." The freegans who are at an earlier stage of their lives have not succumbed to steady jobs. They agreed that if they had jobs or children, they would not have time to go dumpstering or to wait in line for a food box, let alone make fire and acorn mush.

BACK-TO-THE-LAND: "EVERY VEGETABLE WE GROW IS A BLOW AGAINST GLOBAL CAPITALISM"

In the late 1960s, but especially in the '70s, thousands of young Americans reversed the urbanization trend and migrated from the city to the country (Jacob 2003). They set out to construct a different kind of life from their parents, based on subsistence farming and home food processing. They were already part of the countercuisine movement. Belasco quotes the Underground Gourmet depiction of the movement as a "revolt against a plastic, money-centered, soulless culture and all its trappings" (Belasco

[1989]2007: 41). Dubisch points out the religious aspects of the movement with alimentation divided into "health foods" and "junk foods" ([1981] 2000). She also mentions how growing your own organic garden and grinding your own flour were seen as expressions of independence and self-reliance, which were characteristic of "an earlier 'golden age' when people lived natural lives" (2000: 217).[6] Belasco dates the entrance of food as a central component of the hippie movement to 1966 when "the Diggers" unloaded a scavenged feast in Haight Ashbury (2007: 17). By March 1967, they were gleaning apples, planting vegetables, and beginning a network of rural communes and urban co-ops (Belasco 2007: 19). The neo-Diggers disbanded, but by 1969 organic gardening was in and processed foods out (Belasco 2007: 25–27).

Since most back-to-the-landers escaped from suburban or city life, they needed manuals to learn how to be self-sufficient in the country. Starting perhaps with *The Whole Earth Catalog* at the end of the '60s, multiple books and magazines appeared with "Earth" in the title. The 1970s gave us both *Mother Earth News* and *Living on the Earth*, as well as the *Foxfire* books. Alicia Bay Laurel who began writing *Living on the Earth* when she was nineteen years old compared the back-to-the-land movement to other types of subsistence patterns in a recent entry on her webpage:

> We wanted intimacy—not a neighborhood where you didn't know anyone on the block, or you competed, kept up with the Joneses. A hunter-gatherer or early agricultural community meant that people lived, worked and sought deeper contact with the holy spirit as a group, and they all knew one another, from cradle to grave. I used to call my hippie friendships 'a horizontal extended family,' as opposed to the ancient tribal extended family, which was multigenerational, and therefore, vertical. . . .
>
> (Laurel 2009)

This sentiment was expressed by my informant Henry who said that alternative types stuck together. Just recently he needed a couple hundred dollars to help purchase some new farm equipment and an alternative group in town (who took over a fraternal organization) provided him the necessary cash. When describing the back-to-the-landers in the Willamette Valley, Henry said,

> [A] number of us felt the need to have a kind of extended family because we were no longer with extended families. In fact our families had pretty much blackballed us and rejected us. So, we built our own world, basically, of like-minded people and supported each other, still do.

Robert Houriet visited a couple of Oregon communes in 1971 and documented their lifestyle in his book, *Getting Back Together*. I rely on him to describe back-to-the-lander foodways when they were in their twenties, like the freegans today. I appreciate the level of detail he provides about foodways at High Ridge Farm in southwestern Oregon. Eleven adults and six children lived there and they had a two-acre garden, a greenhouse, and cold frames where they grew lettuce, spinach, Brussels sprouts, and kohlrabi through the winter. For breakfast they ate oatmeal with honey, raisins, brewer's yeast, and brown sugar. At other meals there were huge vegetable stews of potatoes, carrots, onions, turnips, and beets, and exotic salads, all out of their garden. Houriet claimed that the food mill seemed to be perpetually grinding. Five pounds of whole wheat flour took a half hour (1971: 37). They ate meat once or twice a week, usually commodities hash or a curry made from turkeys donated at Thanksgiving by the Welfare Department (1971: 38). Commune members, besides tending their own garden, made money picking fruit during the summer and the farmer often gave them extra food. The women spent most of September and October canning.[7] Houriet reports that by January half the stores had been used. They still had four dozen two-quart jars of tomatoes; a dozen quart jars each of peaches, apples, strawberries, cherries, blackberries, plums, squash, and onions; two dozen assorted jars of pickles; several bottles of mushroom catsup; a huge bag of dried mushrooms; bottles of home-brewed root beer and beer; a whole shelf of jams and blackberry syrup; and a bin of savory, marjoram, parsley, basil, spearmint, and sage. Two freezers were still nearly full of plastic bags of squash, corn, cherry tomatoes, beans, and other vegetables (1971: 39).

Oregon became a popular destination for rural communes and hippie farmers looking to develop traditional skills.[8] It was close to California and land was cheap. These people identified with the environmental movement and therefore did not always see eye to eye with the locals. One of my informants Catherine spent a good part of her time fighting with logging companies over their abundant use of defoliants. She documented how it was getting into the food system and poisoning people. Here is how she described her move to the Coast Range in 1974:

We originally started out in Berkeley, but Berkeley got too insane and Steve really wanted to grow things anyway. I mean, every inch of our whole yard had stuff growing in it. So, we first moved up the coast, but it was windy and we couldn't grow enough there. Then, we moved inland, but after a couple years all these rock stars and people like that started buying up all the land around us. The next thing you know they are bringing in electricity, putting in roads. I mean we were like a little island, you know. It was horrible. So that is when we decided to sell it and move up here, and, so far, no rock stars have moved in . . . We showed up with our chicken, donkey, pony, and a couple of goats. I even dug up my trees and brought them with us . . . I made our own cheese, I made our own butter, but I mean, it was a lot of work. I didn't do anything else

basically. With four kids we lived on $500 a month . . . After the divorce, I went on welfare for a couple months. Someone arranged for us to get a Christmas box, but basically it wasn't food that we really wanted anyway. You know, a canned ham that is probably 90% preservatives, some canned beans. Basically, we just redistributed it.

At the beginning, Catherine and her husband grew enough food to feed themselves and sell to others. The area was more populated then and people came by the house to buy food. Catherine got a reputation as a baker and the mill workers and truckers used to stop by to purchase baked goods from her. When the marriage dissolved and Steve sold the Caterpillar, Catherine had to reduce the amount of food she grew and find paid work. Traveling 90 miles round trip to get to work five days a week does not leave much time for food production, but she retains a distrust of industrially processed foods and keeps a small garden for herself. The apple trees produce excess on their own so, in the fall, she calls the gleaners to come and get them. Catherine said that it would be a lot harder to do what she did today. Land is a lot more expensive now and you can't pick up equipment like cream separators at garage sales like you used to be able to.

Social networks are important to all humans, and building social networks usually involves the sharing of food. When we asked low-income rural residents to describe a favorite meal, people from older settled families described large family gatherings (often Thanksgiving). At these dinners with extended family members, family recipes passed down from the last generation are likely to appear. Less-connected people in our sample often described meals in restaurants, focusing on the food, rather than the company. In contrast, both the freegans and the back-to-the-landers described either potlucks or communal cooking with groups of friends. Rather than a focus on traditional recipes, there was a focus on healthy, organic food. For the freegans it was food that they had gathered and shared with people whose paths they had crossed. The back-to-the-landers, on the other hand, had created a stable community over the years. One back-to-the-lander commented:

> We've all been friends for years and years and we like to get together every once in awhile and have everything in the meal stuff that we've either raised or made. It's great company and fun to do it and put it together.

While the back-to-the-landers did not share the same food habits or view of the environment as the earlier settlers, they did share an interest in independence and self-sufficiency. Because of this, many of them built a reputation over time. The first back-to-the-landers I met in Alsea were community leaders who we interviewed during the first stage of the research. When asked about poverty and food insecurity in the area, they spoke of their own poverty when they were young and contrasted their healthy diets with the unhealthy choices being made by poor people today. In the following passage you can see how Maria, a back-to-the-lander who eventually joined the work force, is torn between her deep empathy with having no money, and her rejection of what she considers bad diet choices of the poor people she knows.

> One of the main problems I see is that they get junk food from some of the stores in town and it's ghastly stuff that you really would not want to eat. And they're eating it because that's all they have. And so, some of the people have problems with weight. They're sick and I think part of it's because of the terrible food that they eat. And they don't have any choice, they're unemployed. Some of these people have had accidents and they can't work, or they're a single mom with some problems. The families

who are unemployed, they do seem to really have a great struggle in getting decent food. Why some of these people don't garden more than they do, I don't know.

The increasing price of gas affects rural residents far more than urban and suburban ones. People in Alsea commonly drove 25 to 40 miles to go to a grocery store. Maria continues the conversation, bringing up transportation problems of poor people, but then doubles back to stressing self-sufficiency as the route to a healthier diet.

> When I first moved out here I was in that same situation. I was extremely poor, had little kids, lived way out, 16 miles from Alsea, and sometimes didn't have enough money to drive to Corvallis, where I could buy good food. And so I understand where they're coming from . . . Yeah, it's first hand experience of robbing the kids' piggy banks to buy gas to go to town and then once you're in town, you don't have money to buy good food. I think people aren't taught how to be self-sufficient, in terms of if you can't buy it, grow it.

I then asked her what some of her strategies were when she didn't have much money. She answered,

> First thing we did was plant a garden. We actually got food stamps one time. My husband was working intermittently and we just lived very, very frugally. And that was good because we were eating a good diet and just mainly eating vegetables . . . I think our family was lucky because we were willing to not have a lot of stuff and we were willing to, to stay home and tend the garden and eat it. It was a pretty healthy life style really, in terms of actual health. We didn't have electricity and we didn't have running water, so we hauled the water. I mean it's kind of like Little House on the Prairie relived. We thought we were in heaven. I would buy 100 pounds of wheat from a local farmer and I would grind it up by hand and make my own bread. But people don't live like that now. I mean this was 30 years ago. I was willing to

do that. And grow my own corn and grind my own corn meal and so we ate really well.

Both Catherine and Marla moved away from agriculture into waged labor, though by keeping smaller gardens. Many hippie farmers in the greater area remained in agriculture and have plunged into the expanded market for organic produce. At a recent agricultural direct marketing conference held at Oregon State University, one audience member identified himself as a "hippie farmer" and part of the "back-to-the-land" movement before launching into a question about where the agricultural market was heading. He knew he wasn't alone in the audience and other farmers, some still sporting long pony tails behind their thinning pates, smiled and nodded.

One of my informants, Kim, has continued the lifestyle for over thirty years, feeding her family and others primarily from her land. She lives in an old wooden house at the end of a long dirt lane. During a visit last October, we walked past the chicken coop and the barn where the goats are kept. The year's harvest was gathered on the porch: peppers, apples, and grapes. As we stepped inside the kitchen, we noticed a large pot of goat milk being heated to make the day's cheese. Utensils hung above the wood counter; plastic bags stuck on twigs were drying in the corner. Multiple braids of garlic interspersed with sprays of quinoa hung from the rafters. The pantry off the kitchen was filled with home canned jars of fruit, pickles, and fermenting Kombucha (tea). On the wall hangs a sign saying, "Live like you'll die tomorrow. Farm like you'll live forever."

Lifestyles change as people grow older and especially if they commit themselves to raising children. Most of the back-to-the-landers talked about being far more mobile when they were younger and without children. Some of them, like the freegans, went dumpster diving, though for furnishings rather than for food. (The back-to-the-landers I grew up around referred to the county dump as the general store.) Once they had land and began growing food, their travels were curtailed and they became more rooted in a specific place. Parallel to constructing a more independent food system, back-to-the-landers commonly chose to homeschool their children. Both of these activities were considered integral parts of a holistic life, firmly rooted in a particular place.

FREEGANS: "WE'LL EAT YOUR SCRAP, BUT WE WON'T BUY YOUR CRAP"

When they are gathering wild foods, freegans are eating locally, but traveling defines their lifestyle so they do not have the same attachment to place as the back-to-the-landers. These modern-day foragers know where the best dumpsters are located in cities as far apart as Miami, Minneapolis, and Eugene and even local dumpsters carry food from all over the world. The freegans we interviewed had lived in from 4 to 15 places over the past year, not including cross-country trips where they slept where they could. Groups change membership and meet up from time to time either by chance or around particular events. Destinations are often chosen on the basis of food. They told me about a freegan from Quebec whom they met at the Turtle Mountain vegan ice cream dumpster in Eugene. He had heard about the dumpster and wanted to go to a warmer place for the winter, so he hitched rides to Oregon. He was trying to figure out how to get the ice cream while it was still frozen, and then would move to another dumpster destination in Seattle.

The freegan movement got started in the mid-1990s as an offshoot of the anti-globalization and environmental movements. They prefer to opt out of the economic system entirely, living "in the cracks of society" as they say, consuming only what society throws away, or what they can gather in other people's gardens, along roads, or in the wild. Small-scale shoplifting of items that are hard to find in dumpsters (like dental floss) is perfectly acceptable, though they prefer to steal from corporations, rather than small businesses.

The freegans I first interviewed had no regular jobs and paid no rent or mortgage. They belonged to the primitivist fringe, closer to what Edwards and Mercer call "forest ferals" in Australia (2007: 284). All of them had been to WTO protests and several had been tree sitters. I met them through my friend and fellow anthropologist, Margaret Mathewson. They were trading labor for a place to stay and access to the classes she was giving on techniques for identifying and using wild foods and fibers at her Ancient Arts Center. Even while learning these ancient arts, however, they said that they had to go to the city every 2 or 3 weeks to dumpster dive for food and the Center lies over an hour from the nearest city. In their trips to the city there is a logical progression to getting food. Ted described to me the routine:

> We get to Eugene maybe every two weeks or something. And when we go, we go to the dumpsters first. That gets us our produce and then anything else that we might find. Like if we find like a bunch of pasta, a bunch of eggs, bunch of dairy . . . Then we get grains that we're low on from the store with food stamps, and other things that we like to have around, you know like teas and spices and things like that.

There is a code to dumpstering, though not everyone complies. You only take what you can use, leave some for others and leave the area clean. The food is usually past its prime, so it must be consumed quickly, and some more quickly than others. Tomatoes and avocados need to be eaten immediately, while potatoes can be held onto longer. Occasionally they come across a windfall of a certain

product. That is a good time to have a large communal meal or to trade with someone who has a lot of something else.

Like the punk café in Seattle described by Clark, these freegans reject the commodification of food by refusing to pay for it and by using food that borders on rotten (2008: 412–413). In media interviews with freegans, non-dumpster divers always ask if they have ever gotten sick from eating food out of the dumpster. I asked that question too and got the same answer. No one had ever gotten sick from eating out of the dumpster. (One girl added that she had gotten sick from gorging herself on pastries more than once, but admitted that it was her own fault for having a sugar addiction.) Still, they admitted that they had to be careful because some people pour stuff on the food, like bleach and rat poison. It's pretty obvious from the smell and they don't take it. If it has just been in contact with other rotten stuff, they wash it before eating it. They all said that they ate food from time to time that they didn't like (mayonnaise on a hotdog bun, for example) because they were hungry. This especially happened when they were traveling. Lila described a time when she was hitchhiking and got dropped off at a truck stop with only a Burger King and she had to make do with what was in their dumpster. "If you're really hungry, any food is delicious," Lila said, "if you're not really that hungry, things become gross that aren't really, you know."[9]

The freegan household I first interviewed estimated that they got 60% of the food they consumed out of dumpsters, insisting that dumpsters provide a great variety of healthy food. Top on their list are the dumpsters of organic food processors and health food stores.[10] The goal is to eat a healthy varied diet, while not contributing to the production systems that treat food as commodities. Lila claimed that she increased the variety of food she ate when she began dumpster diving. She said that she would never have tasted the delicious tropical fruit, chirimoya, had she not found one in a dumpster. My informants preferred the dumpsters of health food stores because the quality of food was higher in their estimation and the people were nice to them, even sometimes making separate piles of edible food outside the dumpster.

"Table scoring" (eating unfinished meals at restaurants) is another way of getting food in big cities. Ted and Alvin explained to me how this works:

T: If you want a good adventure for the night, go to a large city like Chicago and find the food district, all the yummy cafés and such. Go into I those places and start eating the food.
A: You gotta look really crusty when you go in.
T: Yeah, look just really dirty. And go in and start eating food, leftover food. After people get up, they pay their bill, you go over and eat their leftover food until the workers come and they kick you out. Then you go to the next one down the block, you start eating there and they kick you out. You go to the next. It's fun. You can spend the whole night doing that.
A: And you can sneak into hotels and eat people's leftover room service that's sitting outside their door, and then sneak into the pool.

While cities provided a cornucopia of free food, they also told me that it was easy to have an unhealthy diet when eating out of dumpsters because lots of food is always available and most of it is bread, doughnuts, and pastries. One freegan went so far as to stop eating wheat because it forced him to have a healthier variety of food in his diet. Another one voiced his interest in learning primitive gathering skills after living near a pizza dumpster in Portland where complete, boxed pizzas were always available. The constant availability of food in city dumpsters was not considered in a positive light

by these freegans. While they felt good about preventing this food from going to landfills, they acknowledged that their health could suffer from the overconsumption of baked goods. One young woman felt like she was caught in a dilemma since she really liked to bake, following old traditions, but when she saw how many baked goods end up in the dumpster, she felt guilty about baking something from scratch. Several of the freegans I talked with voiced the opinion that it was healthier for them to be hungry sometimes and they alluded to fasting traditions. They told me about studies showing that people who didn't always have access to food lived longer and were healthier. "Fasting increases the lifespan," they said.

The freegans I spoke with are transitioning from gathering food from industrialized society to gathering food from nature. Nutrition was important to them. One of them remembered a chart on her mother's refrigerator that had the nutritional value of different greens. "Lettuce was like nothing. Spinach and kale were higher and dandelions were three times as high." She remembered her great grandmother eating dandelion greens, which the intervening generations had rejected and felt like she was recapturing some of the ways of her great grandmother. Foraging for wild foods means following the seasons and traveling to food sources. Zane always goes to Minnesota for the wild rice harvest in September (or "Ricetember" as he says). In October ("Octuber") he digs wapato roots. Then he moves on to the San Juan Islands and eats lots of shellfish and fish. In early spring he makes his way back to tap sugar maples. They claimed to feel better when they foraged in the wild. Some of the favorite foods they listed were hazelnuts, blackberries, burdock, chickweed, nettles, mushrooms, dandelion, lambs quarter, violets, and venison. One of them said she had heard that food thrown in the dumpster loses energy. When urban foragers shift to wild foraging, they often reserve dumpster diving for when they are on the road. Wild foraging also forces them to think more about preserving food since, unlike dumpsters, food will not always be available. Zane carried wild rice and maple syrup from Minnesota to Oregon to share with friends.

Like the back-to-the-landers, freegans extolled the virtues of sharing food, cooking and eating together. Cooking and preserving seem to be special interests among this group of primitivist foragers. Teeja talked about how working together makes the potential drudgery of preserving the harvest fun. Wilma offered us assorted vegetables that she had pickled. Cooking was shared by both men and women. Whoever wakes up earliest makes breakfast and then whoever gets hungry first cooks up a pot of something that everyone eats. Recent breakfasts had consisted of corn meal mush and couscous. They talked about the pleasure of getting food for nothing and sharing it with other people. Often with the dumpstering crowd, one person might have one ingredient and someone else might have another and they'll either combine food to make a meal or trade food if they're going separate ways. They raved about a big communal meal that they had recently prepared of wild salmon and acorn mush. They didn't want to take a salmon that hadn't spawned yet since they are endangered, so they grabbed one that had already spawned. They recognized that the taste had changed, but it was still good, smoked over an open fire. Other group meals they reminisced about included one in Saginaw with roadkill kabobs and dumpster vegetables and one in Wyoming:

We dumpstered this ridiculous amount of produce and I made this vegan pizza, made the sauce myself. I cooked it down from tomatoes in the sauce and invited our friends over. So there were four little kids and all these people around, and we're all eating vegan pizza and vegan apple pie. And everything in it was dumpstered, every single ingredient except, I think, a couple spices.

Two of the female freegans had gone through phases of vegetarianism. One had been a strict vegan for three years before becoming a freegan. Now she only consumes animal products that are "post-consumer," a term they use to describe food that has been discarded. The group prefers to eat wild game and has some reservations about grocery store dumpstered meat. They insist that roadkill meat is a lot fresher and more reliable than meat you find in the grocery store that comes from factory farms and is often filled with antibiotics and growth hormones. Freegan blogs talk about eating roadkill as having more political advantages than other forms of anti-capitalist food gathering. Unlike dumpster diving, it is entirely free of capitalist trappings, they say.[11] (This is debatable, of course, since driving fast in cars has a lot to do with saving time in our capitalist world.) These freegans had picked up three raccoons in that past few months, but one was "too far gone." Interestingly, trophy hunters are also a source of wild meat. Marvin told me that his favorite dumpster was near a popular hunting place in Minnesota. People chop the heads off the animals they killed so that they can mount them on the wall. They leave entire carcasses in a dumpster. Since it's so cold, the meat freezes quickly and freegans can use it during most of the winter. Everyone felt a little nervous about eating meat out of the dumpster during the hot months of summer.

Freegans do enter the mainstream low-income food network with their occasional use of food stamps and the emergency food system. Of the two, they prefer emergency food boxes since less invasive paperwork is required, but there is usually someone in the extended household group with food stamps. They are used to buy grain, oil, and spices in natural food co-ops. Since so much food is available in dumpsters, they often sell their food stamps for money to buy non-food stamp eligible things. Emergency food boxes require less invasion of privacy, and they seek out pantries where they can choose their own food and avoid commodity food:

> You can choose not to take the government food and 30-year-old canned food and stuff like that. A lot of times they'll have organic stuff . . . you can get just good food there, but you won't get as much food that way.

One freegan said that when she tells people at the food pantry that she is vegetarian, they give her "extra stuff because they think vegetarians are deprived of nutrients."

Freegans subsist on discarded food because they have made a choice not to participate in the capitalist system. They have a strong sense of self-reliance and independence which they share with back-to-the-landers and other rural Americans. But this does not include "waged labor." Paid work, in fact, was talked about as a kind of drug that sucked you in deeper and deeper, as can be seen in the following quote:

> Families where both parents have jobs, they're gonna have to have cars to drive them there, they're gonna have to have a house to pay rent, they're gonna have to have clean clothes, they're gonna have to have all these things that cost money. And once you get into that cycle, paying rent and paying insurance on your car, you need money to keep those things going. So you're dependent on your job, and you're dependent on your car and your house . . . and it's like you're constantly spending money and never have enough which ties into food. So then you have to put food in there somewhere. And you don't have time to go out and dumpster and wait on food boxes. (When you go there you don't just go and get food, you wait for an hour.) . . .

The point is they're probably 1 worse off than us.[12]

Our interviews with other low-income rural residents who followed a more conventional lifestyle seemed to support this point of view. Dual parents working for minimum wage, usually in fast food restaurants, ate both less nutritious and less enjoyable meals than the freegans. Nutrition was important to the freegans, but they realized that sometimes they had to fill themselves up 'with non-nutritious food.

The freegans I encountered are not yet reproducing, but they acknowledged that their lifestyle would be difficult to continue if they had children. A friend of theirs with a 9-month-old baby had to depend on food stamps because she could not be out nights dumpstering. Even waiting an hour for an emergency food box is difficult with young children, they conceded. A couple of the freegans talked about acquiring land at some point in the future so that they could grow their own food. A slightly older freegan woman I met later had, indeed, shifted into subsistence farming on communal land with six other people. She dug a root cellar to preserve winter vegetables and she cans and dries and also ferments mead from gleaned fruit. The only time she dumpster dives now is when she is traveling. She tans hides and makes buckskin clothing that she sells at primitive arts gatherings. She also works a couple days a week at an organic nursery to buy what she needs to farm.

CONCLUSION: RESISTING CAPITALIST FOODWAYS

Patricia Allen discusses the incompatibility between environmental sustain-ability and social justice on one hand (two issues that are central to alternative agrifood movements) and capitalist agriculture on the other (2004: 128–131). Food in the capitalist system is just another commodity wherein exchange value is privileged over use value and maximum profit drives the system. Back-to-the-landers, however, raise food primarily for its use value, not its exchange value. Even when they exchange food for money, they tend to favor direct sales where economic ties are socialized, not made anonymous. Under capitalism, economies of scale bring more profit, but they also force overproduction and waste. Both the exchange and the use value of the product is terminated once it ends up in the dumpster. Freegans, however, extend the use value of discarded goods, snatching edibles before their journey to landfills. Alternatively, they eat foods gathered directly from nature, outside of commodity circuits. By providing for their own food needs, either by growing or foraging, they lower the demand for commercial food and there-fore vote with their forks against the global capitalist agrifood system.

However, there is no escaping the webs of capitalism. Freegans and back-to-the-landers generally cannot sustain them-selves without the overproduction of the industrialized agrifood system that ends up both in dumpsters and in the emergency food system. The back-to-the-landers have been more likely to justify this as "ripping off the system," whereas freegans usually make more of an environmental argument. Nevertheless, their dependence on commodity foods does remind them that they are not as independent from the capitalist system as they would like to be. One of Robert Houriet's back-to-the-lander informants told him in 1970:

> Of course we're not self-sufficient. Economic self-sufficiency is a myth. We just don't want to be trapped by a system that makes you try to meet a standard of living that's too high; makes you eat food that's too rich; live in a house that's overheated in the winter and air-conditioned in the summer.
>
> (Houriet 1971: 38)

A generation later, freegans voice a similar opinion. Both groups demonstrate that diverse subsistence economies already exist within capitalist economic space.

Marx distinguished between the kind of labor in which humans feel productive and part of nature and wage labor in which work is not an end in itself, but rather a servant of the wage (Marx 1959 [1844]). People are alienated from their own labor as they perform repetitive tasks in order to bring capital to others (and to themselves). Alienated labor can be seen as one source of what Jameson referred to as "the waning of affect" that characterizes late capitalism (1991). In the realm of food, the waning of affect might translate as the consumption of calories to create human energy (fast food and nutritional supplements), rather than having a personal relationship with where your food comes from, how it tastes, and whom you share it with. Back-to-the-landers and freegans embrace labor when it means working hard to secure and process food. One young freegan told me that he turned to this lifestyle because he wanted to feel something. He was searching for authenticity in the same way that the Underground Gourmet from the 1960s quoted earlier rejected the "plastic, money-centered, soulless culture" (Belasco [1989]2007: 41). Back-to-the-landers and freegans seek out the intensity of feeling that comes when their access to food is unmediated by a series of middlemen and a capitalist system that substitutes simulacra for the "real thing." When a back-to-the-lander cuts the head off a chicken she or he has raised and puts it in the oven, or when a freegan climbs a tree in the middle of the night and clubs a raccoon that he roasts over a fire, both are resisting the alienation from our food sources that the global capitalist food system encourages. In so doing, they draw on knowledge that was important in past times that has become arcane in the present; how to make acorn mush, for instance. They accomplish what Gibson-Graham suggest we all should do, "cultivate ourselves as activists and subjects of noncapitalist economies" (2006: xxvii),

According to Melucci, contemporary movements announce a change that is already present (1996: 1). We all already participate in foodways that are distinctly non-capitalist, whether it be feeding family and friends or gathering mushrooms in the National Forest. Local food movements are bringing this to a new degree. Today, we can see alternative foodways slipping into the mainstream, especially in the face of contemporary crises. We see a renaissance of backyard, rooftop, and community gardening, farmers' markets, fair trade associations, recycling, and composting. We see a deepening concern with over-packaging, food miles, environmentally degrading agriculture, and nutritionally bereft foods. As the food crisis emerges, we see people reaching into past subsistence patterns to create new knowledge and foodways that are not dependent on global capital. This mirrors the way in which James Ferguson, in his ethnography of Zambia, drew attention to the ways in which older modes of economic and social organization never truly die out, but merely retreat into the background as relic forms that are overshadowed by more 'modern' modes of development. He shows how older ideas and practices resurge in times of economic and social crisis, when the 'main lines' that are supposed to lead to the future only lead to disappointment (Ferguson 1999: 251).

When we think about a "foodshed" or a "local food economy," we are necessarily acknowledging landscapes, and use value over exchange value. The local food movement also calls for the resocialization of the ties between producers and consumers (now envisioned as co-producers).[13] Capitalism has encouraged a disconnection from where our food comes from and where our waste goes, but pre-capitalist foodways never truly died out.[14] As global food insecurity increases and waste production reaches frightening levels, ideas embodied in the lifestyles of back-to-the-landers and freegans provide pathways to a postcapitalist future.

NOTES

1. I wish to thank Margaret Mathewson, Carole Counihan, and the anonymous reviewers of *Food and Foodways* for making this a better paper, and also the freegans and back-to-the-landers who shared their words and food with me. Oregon State University's Rural Studies Initiative, Center for the Humanities, and Department of Anthropology provided necessary support.

2. The evils of our industrialized food system have been portrayed in films such as "The Future of Food," "The Global Banquet," and "Our Daily Bread," just to mention a few. We can see the market adjusting in the advertising campaigns of global food industries. See, for example, Frito Lay's advertisement "We Grow the Best Snacks on Earth" depicting a small-scale potato farm where what looks like family members collect potatoes in baskets and place them in a burlap sack that is standing in the grass right next to the mounded rows of potato plants.

3. Freegans in NYC have gotten quite a bit of press over the past years, especially the group led by Adam Weissman. Interestingly, most of the publicity emphasized that these freegans held down regular jobs and had homes, but lived on food waste out of deep-seated ecological concerns (Bergot 2004; Weissman 2006). You can watch a video interview with him by Life and Style staff at http://www.youtube.com/watch?v=XqHhQGI-5KY.

4. This is the situation we found both in the rural Coast Range and in South Central Oregon where Nancy Rosenberger and I have been conducting ethnographic field schools centered on rural food systems. In both places there is still a lot of home-based provisioning of food, especially among families that have generational depth in the area. People without food-provisioning skills who moved to these rural areas because rents were cheap soon found out how difficult it was to put food on the table.

5. On the impoverishment of rural places, see Lyson and Falk (1993) and Sumner (2005). The Rural Families Speak project found that the rate of food insecurity among rural low-income families with children was five times greater than the national average (Olson 2006).

6. These ideas live on in the local food movement. At a recent Ten Rivers Food Web meeting focused on the revitalization of grain production in the Willamette Valley, one of the board members who has been fanning organically for 30 years turned to one of his age mates and said,

"We'll have to dig out the grinders we used to use in the 1970s."

7. I will not go into how the burden of food preparation fell on the shoulders of women in these so-called liberated communities.

8. Oregon has a history of communes dating back to the Aurora Colony of 1863, which prospered for two decades by marketing apples, pears, and pear butter, along with lumber and fine crafts. The most infamous commune of recent times in Oregon is Rajneeshpuram, where 5000–6000 people developed a nearly self-sufficient (discounting initial purchases of big farm equipment and inputs) spiritual community. It came to an end after one of the leaders infected a local salad bar in the Dalles with salmonella in 1984 (Kopp 2004).

9. Black found similar reactions in her research among urban foragers in France and Italy and questioned why throwing away edible food is socially acceptable but eating garbage is not (2008: 147–148).

10. This contrasts with the dumpster divers described by Edwards and Mercer who preferred the dumpsters of large supermarket chains because they support industrial farming, often importing foods from overseas to the detriment of local farmers (2007: 287). Since freegans are only accessing post-consumer goods, it does not affect the way in which the food was produced.

11. http://thetenoclockscholar.blogspot. com/2005/04/roadkill-is-yummy.html

12. This sentiment was echoed in the website, Welcome to Planet Freegan: Beg, wheel & deal, barter, serve those in need, but NEVER, EVER work too much for that dirty dog that is money worship—especially credit—lest it make you its financial inmate, a monetary serf—a wage slave to dead end wage slavery jobs, and credit debt, interest, economic & emotional servitude. Worse yet, U might become a slave taskmaster and be forced to oppress others, http://freegan. freeservers.com/

13. See, for example, Kirschenmann (2008) and Petrini (2007).

14. The British organization Waste Resources and Action Programme estimates that we throw away about one-third of all the food we buy and at least half of this is food that could have been eaten. They claim that we could make carbon savings equivalent to taking one fifth of the cars off the road if we avoided throwing useful food in the bin (2007).

REFERENCES

Allen, P. 2004. *Together at the Table*. University Park: The Pennsylvania State University Press.

Belasco, W. 2007. *Appetite for Change: How the Counterculture Took on the Food Industry*. Ithaca: Cornell University Press.

Bergot, N. 2004. *Newsday*, September 29. Accessed 1/6/08 in *Grist* at http://www.grist.org/news/ daily/2004/10/01/5/index.html

Benedict, R. 1934. *Patterns of Culture*. Boston: Houghton Mifflin.

Black, R. 2007. Eating garbage: Socially marginal provisioning practices. In *Consuming the Inedible: Neglected Dimensions of Food Choice*, eds. J. MacClancy, J. Henry, and H. Macbeth. Oxford: Berghahn Books, pp. 141–150.

Clark, D. 2008. The Raw and the Rotten: Punk Cuisine. In *Food and Culture: A Reader*, 2nd ed., eds. C. Counihan and P. Van Esterik, pp. 411–422. New York: Routledge.

Clement, A. 1997. On being wrong. *High Country News* 29:15.

Dirlik, A. and R. Prazniak. 2001. *Places and Politics in an Age of Globalization*. New York: Rowman and Littlefield.

Dubisch, J. 2000. You Are What You Eat: Religious Aspects of the Health Food Movement. In Goodman et al. *Nutritional Anthropology: Biocultural Perspectives on Food and Nutrition*. Mountain View, CA: Mayfield.

Edwards, F. and D. Mercer. 2007. Gleaning From Gluttony: An Australian Youth Subculture Confronts the Ethics of Waste. *Australian Geographer* 3:279–296.

Ferguson, J. 1999. *Expectations of Modernity: Myths and Meanings of Urban Life on the Zambian Copperbelt*. Berkeley: University of California Press.

Gibson-Graham, J. K. 1996. *The End of Capitalism (As We Knew It): A Feminist Critique of Political Economy*. Minneapolis: University of Minnesota Press.

Gibson-Graham, J. K. 2006. *A Postcapitalist Politics*. Minneapolis: University of Minnesota Press.

Gross, J., ed. 2007. *Teaching Oregon Native Languages*. Corvallis: Oregon State University Press.

Gross, J. and N. Rosenberger. 2005. Food Insecurity in Rural Benton County: An Ethnographic Study. *Rural Studies Working Paper* #05–02. Oregon State University. http://ruralstudies.oregonstate. edu/Publications/RSP05–02.pdf

Gross, J. and N. Rosenberger. Forthcoming. The Double Binds of Getting Food Among the Poor in Rural Oregon. *Food, Culture, and Society*.

Harvey, D. 2000. *Spaces of Hope*. Berkeley: University of California Press.

Houriet, R. 1971. *Getting Back Together*. New York: Coward, McCann and Geohegan.

Jacob, J. 1997. *New Pioneers: The Back to the Land Movement and the Search for a Sustainable*

Future. University Park: The Pennsylvania State University Press.

Jacob, J. 2003. Back-to-the-landers. In *Alternative Economic Spaces*, eds. A. Leyshon, R. Lee, and C. Williams. Thousand Oaks, CA: Sage, pp. 168–192.

Kirschenmann, F. 2008. Food as Relationship. *Journal of Hunger and Environmental Nutrition* 3(2–3):106–121.

Kopp, J. J. 2004. Documenting Utopia in Oregon: The Challenges of Tracking the Quest for Perfection. *Oregon Historical Quarterly* 105:308–319.

Laurel, A. B. http://www.aliciabaylaurel.com/ Accessed January 22, 2009.

Lyson, T., and W. Falk. 1993. *Forgotten Places: Uneven Development in Rural America*. University Press of Kansas.

Life and Style interview with Adam Weissman accessed at: http://www.youtube.com/ watch?v=XqHhQGI-5K 8/1/08

Marx, K. 1959 [1844]. Economic and Philosophical Manuscripts of 1844. Moscow: Progress Publishers. Accessed at http://www.marxists.org/ archive/marx/works/1844/manuscripts/labour. htm, January 14, 2009.

Melucci, A. 1996. *Challenging Codes: Collective Action in the Information Age*. Cambridge: University Press.

Meter, K. and J. Rosales. 2001. Finding Food in Farm Country: The Economics of Food and Farming in SE Minnesota http://www.crcworks. org/ff.pdf Accessed August 1, 2008.

Mintz, S. and C. Du Bois. 2002. The Anthropology of Food and Eating. *Annual Review of Anthropology*, 31:99–119.

Morton, L. W. and T. C. Blanchard. 2007. Starved for Access: Life in Rural America's Food Deserts.

Rural Realities 1:1–10. http://www.ruralsoci-ology.org/pubs/ruralrealities/RuralRealities1-4. pdf Accessed August 1, 2008.

Olson, C. 2006. Food Insecurity in Poor Rural Families with Children: A Human Capital Perspective. *Rural Families Speak Project Policy Brief*. March.

Petrini, C. 2007. *Slow Food Nation: Why Our Food Should Be Good, Clean, and Fair*. New York: Rizzoli.

Polk's Classified Business Directory, 1913. Portland, OR: R. L. Polk and Company.

Sumner, J. 2005. *Sustainability and the Civil Commons: Rural Communities in the Age of Globalization*. Toronto: University of Toronto Press.

Thackara, J. 2005. *In the Bubble: Designing in a Complex World*. Cambridge: The MIT Press.

Waste Resources and Action Programme. 2007. Understanding Food Waste. Oxford, UK. http:// www.wrap.org.uk/ Accessed July 31, 2008.

Weissman, A. 2006. It's not that Gross! Freeganism and the Art of Dumpster Diving: The *Satya* Interview with Adam Weissman. Accessed at http://www.satyamag.com/may06/weissman. html

Whorf, B. 1995. The Relation of Habitual Thought and Behavior to Language [1941]. In ed. Ben Blount, *Language, Culture and Society*. Prospect Heights, IL: Waveland.

Zenk, H. B. 1990. "Alseans," in *Handbook of North American Indians*, Vol. 7 Northwest Coast, ed. Wayne Suttles, pp. 568–571. Washington, DC: Smithsonian.

Zerzan, J. 2002. *Running on Emptiness: The Pathology of Civilization*. Los Angeles: Feral House.

7

Cultural Geographies in Practice. The South Central Farm: Dilemmas in Practicing the Public

Laura Lawson

Driving down Alameda Street in South Central Los Angeles in 2000, I knew I had reached my destination when warehouses, salvage yards, and truck transfer stations gave way to a large green space punctuated by banana trees and 12" high corn. The South Central Farm – also known as the South Los Angeles Community Garden and the Urban Gardening Program of the Los Angeles Regional Food Bank – was a 14-acre community garden that provided 350 primarily Latino households with space to garden.[1] As part of my research on community gardens, I had read articles that praised this garden since its inception in 1993. Fourteen years later, the Farm was again in the news, but this time for its contested closure and ultimate destruction. While unique in many ways, the South Central Farm illustrates the ambiguous public nature of community gardens that often puts the appeal of the idea at odds with its reality as a physical site. Even though community gardening garners widespread support as an activity that produces many personal and social benefits, as a land use it lacks value as a permanent resource. The case also underscores the tendency to consider gardening as a movable, replaceable resource, ignoring the labor and social networks necessary to create such spaces. Strategies to secure user-initiated spaces like community gardens require shifting public perception from appropriated space to validated public resource.

The idea to establish a community garden in South Central Los Angeles grew out of civic concerns about community health and well being. The garden was initially spearheaded by the Los Angeles Regional Food Bank as a way to heal the community in the aftermath of the 1992 Rodney King beating and subsequent civil disturbances that exposed the city's racial and economic disparities. At the same time, gardening fulfilled the Food Bank's mission to improve food access and nutrition to low-income households. A community garden would not only provide a place for people to grow food but also, as empirical research and anecdotal accounts suggested, it would expand social networks and provide opportunities for cultural expression, skill development, household income subsidy, and environmental restoration.[2] Credited with many positive outcomes, highly participatory, and relatively cheap to start compared to other community development initiatives, the Food Bank's proposal met with enthusiastic support that garnered land, volunteers, and funding. The city owned a vacant lot adjacent to the food bank that they donated for the project. Even though the lease stated that the City could give a 30-day notice to leave the site cleared of all vegetation, fencing, and use, the project proceeded with little attention to its temporary status. In addition to initial funding received from individuals, foundations, and public agencies, the garden also benefited from a United States

Figure 7.1 Aerial image of South Central (www.googleearth.com).

Department of Agriculture's Urban Resource Partnership Program Grant.

While anticipation of many beneficial outcomes catalyzed broad support for the project, the actual gardening and day-to-day interactions involved individuals who chose to participate for their own personal reasons. Initially, local residents were hesitant to invest their labor into the project but interest quickly grew so that after a few months all plots were assigned and there was a waiting list. Most participants were from Mexico, El Salvador, and other Central American countries along with some Caribbean and African American participants. While some came from nearby neighborhoods, the garden also drew participants from other areas in Los Angeles. After initial management by the Food Bank, the gardeners took over responsibility for its operation. Pragmatically laid out on a grid, the individual plots, enclosed by fences and locked gates, reflected the cultures of the gardeners through cultivation practices, crops, and social spaces. The driveway that ran through the center provided

parking as well as an informal marketplace for selling produce, CDs, and other goods.

Even as gardeners were busy planting corn, tomatoes, nopales, and other crops, the site became embroiled in a land struggle that set the claim of its public usefulness at odds with actual public ownership. The City of Los Angeles had initially acquired the site in the late 1980s through the process of eminent domain for the purpose of building a trash incinerator plant. Eminent domain grants certain governmental agencies the power to require a private landowner to accept just compensation for the sale of private property if it is needed for a public good. Amid public protest about the environmental injustice of locating such a contaminating facility in a low-income neighborhood, the plan for an incinerator was rejected. The site sat idle and shifted ownership to another public agency in search of a public purpose when it was proposed for the garden. However, while the garden was lauded as an important community resource, it was never validated as a 'public good' that justified its procurement through eminent domain.[3] As a result, when several of the site's original owners brought the City to court for not offering them the 'right of first refusal' to repurchase the property, as is required in eminent domain proceedings, the City, once so supportive, acquiesced. Negotiations between the City and one of the owners led to his repurchase for approximately $5 million, which is close to the price he had paid for the land 17 years prior. The owner then sent eviction notices to the gardeners.

To some of the gardeners, site possession meant that they were entitled to be part of the process. Arguing that the negotiations had not been public and that the garden was serving a public good worth protection, the gardeners organized into the South Central Farmers Feeding Families and used letter campaigns, speaking at city council meetings, marches, protests, and ultimately site occupation to publicize the conflict and gain support. The garden made national news when several famous activists and actors, including singer Joan Baez and actress Daryl Hannah, were arrested as part of the site occupation. Meanwhile the sympathetic Mayor's office worked with the Trust for Public Land and other foundations to purchase the property at the owner's asking price of $16 million. The battle became increasingly

contentious, to the point that the owner not only raised the price but also refused to release the land to the gardeners because of the personal insults he had received. Ultimately the sheriff's department enforced the eviction on 13 June 2006 and the garden was bulldozed. The City identified alternative gardening spaces under high-voltage power lines, to which some gardeners have since moved, reinvesting their sweat and energy into making a garden on untilled land.

While determining site ownership was largely a legal procedure, the Public debate that the conflict sparked centered on the public or private nature of the garden itself. News reports generally favored the gardeners and highlighted the economic, cultural, and social roles that the garden served. In an area of the city that lacked recreation facilities and open space, the garden provided food, nutrition, household income savings, recreation, social interaction, and a place to carry on agrarian cultural traditions for 350 households and their social and familial networks. In opposition, the owner argued that individuals were profiting from this use of city property and that gardening was not a valid form of public recreation. Instead, as part of his negotiations with the City, he offered 3 acres of the site to be developed as a soccer field, stating, 'A soccer field is open

Figure 7.2 View along one of the paths of the Farm. Photograph by author, 2000.

Figure 7.3 Many of the garden plots also included personalized spaces. Photograph by Lewis Watts, 2001.

to the whole community – anybody in the community can use that. The garden isn't. These little plots are used by them exclusively. If you or I wanted to take our rake or shovel or hoe and do a little gardening there, we can't.'[4] While advocates considered the larger public good derived from individual participation, critics focused on the private gain and loss of potential economic development through private development of the industrially zoned site.

Although the South Central Farm was unique in many ways, the fact that it was conceived opportunistically and without long-term planning and then had to struggle to justify its role as a permanent public resource is a far too common situation for community gardens, especially those on potentially developable urban sites. Nationwide, many community gardens that are started by local residents and organizations to address community concerns face tenuous land tenure on donated or leased properties. One might assume that a garden on public land is more secure than one on privately owned land; however, national trends indicate that these sites are just as likely to be developed for other public purposes or sold.[5] Furthermore, community garden sites tend to remain zoned according to the contiguous land uses even if serving as open space. As a result, garden sites

continue to be viewed as vacant land and therefore developable. A tended garden may have an aura of permanence, yet the determining factor is not use but potential land use and ownership. In the end, while most people like the idea of community gardening and applaud the resources the activity provides, a garden holds little power when pitted against potential development that might bring jobs or provide housing. To use a planning term, a community garden is rarely considered the 'highest and best use' of urban land. Furthermore, most public agencies do not acknowledge the site transformation – the site clearance, parceling plots and maintaining paths, soil development, cultivation, and ongoing maintenance – that participants contribute as volunteers. As a result, when faced with potential development of an existing garden, city officials often propose moving the activity to another site, granting the opportunity to continue gardening but ignoring the material and labor investments already made.

In light of this vulnerability to development, community gardening advocates are seeking new means to protect gardens. Interestingly, one option is to privately purchase the land thereby holding it in a semi-public manner, while another approach is to enhance its public role on par with parks. Obviously, the most effective way to secure a garden site is through

Figure 7.4 This man is preparing nopales, or prickly pear cactus, at his stand along the driveway of the Farm. Photograph by Lewis Watts, 2001.

ownership. In Boston, Chicago, and elsewhere, not-for-profit land trusts have been created to purchase and protect community gardens as well as other user-initiated spaces. In New York City, when the City prepared to auction off over 100 community gardens, a Supreme Court injunction and a $4.2 million purchase stopped the gardens from being destroyed.[6] However, while ownership would seem permanent, the New York purchase agreement included a clause that if a garden was not maintained then ownership would revert to the city, suggesting an ongoing consideration that gardens are temporary. Meanwhile the City benefits from a secondary open space system without being financially responsible.

Another approach is to enhance the garden's public role beyond the individual garden plot holders to the community at large. Establishing educational programs, hosting neighborhood events, and collaborating with local institutions (churches, schools, half-way houses, etc.) are examples of how garden groups have expanded public engagement. Design and site programming can also encourage non-gardening activities, such as the inclusion of walking paths, demonstration and education areas, active recreation, and public art. In Seattle, for instance, many

community gardens that are on publicly owned land are being developed as 'garden parks' that include individual gardening plots while also serving as neighborhood parks. In other cases, community gardens are included within public parks, in effect equating gardening as a recreational activity on par with soccer, tennis, and playgrounds.

The acknowledgment that social practices shape public space is well established through concepts of everyday life, as developed by Henri Lefebvre, and the 'everyday urbanism' approach promoted by some planners and designers.[7] However, while academics and advocates may celebrate this process of appropriation and transformation, the reality is that the user's investment remains undervalued by public officials. Created and shaped to meet important social and personal functions, the loss of user-initiated spaces like community gardens can be devastating to the people who rely on them. To acknowledge such spaces in terms of their public good justifies the public investment necessary for their sustainability. Flexibility is also necessary, however, to accommodate evolving uses and practices as determined by local participation. Interestingly, while the South Central Farm no longer exists, some of the farmers and activists have reorganized into the South Central

Farmers Health and Education Fund, a not-for-profit organization that promotes farmers' markets, gardens, and other community resources to assure healthier, culturally appropriate, and affordable food access. Thus, the pressure to transform the public landscape to meet the community's everyday needs persists.

BIOGRAPHICAL NOTE

Laura Lawson is Assistant Professor at the Department of Landscape Architecture, University of Illinois, Urbana-Champaign. She can be contacted at: Department of Landscape Architecture, University of Illinois, Urbana-Champaign, 101 Temple Buell Hall, MC-620, 611 E. Lorado Taft Drive, Champaign, IL 61820, USA; email: ljlawson@uiuc.edu

NOTES

1. A 1999 Los Angeles Regional Food Bank press packet included articles from the *New York Times, Los Angeles Times*, and *Tu Mundo*. The author visited the site several times and spoke with gardeners informally. Also see H. Becerra, M. Garvey and S. Hymon, 'L.A. garden shut down: 40 arrested', *Los Angles Times* (14 June 2006); J. Hoffman, 'L.A. urban farmers fight for community garden', *The News Standard* (5 April 2006), (http://newstandardnews.net/content/index.cfm/items/3027/printmode/true); 'Daryl Hanna arrested', (14 June 2006), http://www.cnn.com/CNN/PROTEST; 'South Central Farm', (21 December 2006), http://en.wikipedia.org/wiki/South_Central_Farm

2. D. Malakoff, 'What good is community greening?', *Community greening review* 5 (1995), pp. 4–11; L. Lawson, *City bountiful: a history of community gardening in America* (Berkeley, CA, University of California Press, 2005).

3. The scope of what is deemed public good has expanded with the recent Kelo v. City of New London Supreme Court case. The Dudley Street Initiative, a not-for-profit agency in Boston, has been granted eminent domain authority for local economic development through housing, community services, schools, community gardens, and public space.

4. J. Hoffman, C. Petit, *et al.*, '14 acres conversations across chasms in South Central Los Angeles', *Clamour* 36 (21 December 2006), http://www.clamormagazine.org/issues/36/people.php

5. American Community Gardening Association, *National community gardening survey* (ACGA Monograph, 1992, 1998).

6. R. Stapleton, 'Bringing peace to the garden of tranquility', *Land and people* 11(2) (1999), pp. 2–7.

7. H. Lefebvre, *Critiques of everyday life* (London, Verso, 1991); J. Chase, M. Crawford and J. Kaliski, *Everyday urbanism* (New York, Monacelli Press, 1999).

8

Charlas Culinarias: Mexican Women Speak from Their Public Kitchens

Meredith E. Abarca

"Honestly, I was afraid of cooking for the public. Yes, I would cook but only for my children," says María Luisa Gonzales, owner of Gorditas Cecy, a *puestecito* (food stand) in Ciudad Juárez, Chihuahua, Mexico.[1] I have heard aspects of Gonzales' story as a food entrepreneur as she and I have been sharing casual culinary conversations, or *charlas culinarias*, since October 2004. Usually our conversations take place while I sit at her *puestecito* savoring some *gorditas de picadillo*.[2] Gonzales' development as the owner of a food stand began once she was laid off from her job as a housekeeper in a hotel.[3] Luckily, someone came to her rescue: "an angel, who had worked in the same hotel years earlier, already had a restaurant and she opened another. She offered to pay me 500 pesos per week to work for her cooking *gorditas*." After three years, she left this job because it kept her from spending much time with her children. As she says, "I would go to work while the children were still sleeping; I would come back, the children were sleeping." Eventually, she balanced the financial necessity to support her children with the desire to spend time with them by opening her own food stand, Gorditas Cecy, in 1992. Gonzales' story of supporting her family by selling food is one that I have heard often while sharing *charlas culinarias* with working-class Mexican women.[4]

Such accounts of women beginning their own food business exemplify a practice where women call upon their domestic cooking skills and transform them into "commercialized housework" (quo. in Babb 1998:197). This tactic of relying on traditional female gender tasks to deal with life's economic challenges gives working-class women across national borders, ethnicities, and races the ability to empower themselves and become agents of social, cultural, and economic change despite the reality of their limited socio-economic status (Abarca 2006; Babb 1998; Pilcher 2004; Simon 2006). Lourdes Arizpe describes this action of poor working-class women as their way to "press the [economic] system for payment of their domestic services" since they transfer their skills to the public market (quo. in Babb 1998: 197). If women are consciously pressing the system, as Arizpe indicated in her study of Mexican village women twenty years ago, my study suggests that women's needs to meet immediate life circumstances grounds their motivation, and contributes to their empowerment.

In this article I explore how women's empowerment and agency comes not only from the status of owning their own business, but also, and perhaps more importantly, from the particular meanings and values they give to their entrepreneurial practices.[5] After three years of gathering and sharing *charlas culinarias* (culinary conversations) with women who own *puestecitos* in Cd. Juárez, Chihuahua, and El Paso, Texas, I coined the term "familial wealth" to capture the meanings and values women give to their own work.

Later on this study, through two ethnographic case studies, one based in El Paso and the other in Cd. Juárez, I highlight and analyze the reoccurring themes in the *charlas* that pertain to the concept of familial wealth, such as understanding a business's success beyond its economic capital gain. The women, who form part of this study, are not financially well off by any stretch of the imagination. Throbbing varicose veins in their legs, swollen feet, and aching back testify to the intense physical aspect of their labor. Yet the spirit and philosophy they bring to their public kitchens defines their businesses' profits in terms of the transformation these offer them, their families and others such as customers and acquaintances.[6]

The concept of familial wealth as an analytical model helps raise the following questions. First, in what ways can foodways researchers and feminist race/class scholars imagine and develop a socioeconomic paradigm that defines a business's success beyond its capital gain. Second, what lessons can one learn when the common spatial split of production and reproduction, with their specific gender labor value, one for capital profit the other for emotive gain, shift from a dichotomous structure to become a space that interconnects such ideological-spatial implications.[7] Finally, can the narratives of working-class women cooks and the function of their small public kitchens provide conceptual models that envision business' success in terms of collaboration and community gain?

FAMILIAL WEALTH AS A PARADIGM OF ANALYSIS

Familial wealth as a model that defines a business' success in terms other than capital gain undeniably requires a paradigm shift that moves beyond the principles of market economy. A market economy's main value accounts for an individual's self-interest, usually assumed to be the accumulation of capital. The concept of familial wealth does not ignore the importance of financial gain. However, the social as well as cultural advantages of owning a business can carry more weight, especially as the fruit of such profits are enjoyed not only by family members but also by other members of the community. In her analysis on how Third World women view the meaning of productive labor, Vandana Shiva explains how "productivity is a measure of producing life and sustenance." She goes on to assert that just because the "modern patriarchal economic categories" understand profits only as capital gain, life and sustenance as the benefits of productive labor are often "rendered invisible" (1992:338). Scott Simon concludes his study on Taipei women entrepreneurs by showing that the value a significant number of women see in owning a business is the space it gives them to create "social connections or explore their creative talents" (2003:214). These forms of social and personal gains become unnoticeable when analyses take into account only political-economic forces and ignore cultural-historical ones (Babb 1998). Familial wealth takes into account the social and cultural implications women attribute to their roles as entrepreneurs.

Applying the familial wealth model, this study analyzes productivity in terms of social networks of support. First a kinship network that at times extends a few generations is often the basic structure for a business work force. The different roles family members perform in the daily operations of a food stand changes according to age, gender, and other household and/or school responsibilities. These tasks range from working the morning or afternoon shift, serving soft drinks, cleaning tables, washing dishes, taking food orders, delivering food to owners of other businesses, organizing the distribution of supplies, putting down linoleum tile floors, budgeting, and, of course, cooking and baking. Frequently, family culinary heritage finds a place of honor in public kitchens, as family recipes become the source of signature dishes.[8] By working at a food stand, the women, their children, and in some cases grandchildren augment their cultural and social capital as they develop a work ethic based on communal effort. Business success is understood as an act of collaboration where ethics of community support, reciprocity, and citizenship get developed and strengthened.

Through familial wealth, the financial benefit that comes to the forefront carries long and short-term profits. Short-term gain translates into making enough income to support life's daily necessities, such as housing, food, clothes, and medical needs. Long-term profits are based on the hope and ability to invest in a son or daughter's future: i.e. education, personal, and professional development. For example, Severa Ochoa de Castaña, owner of Los Moros Burritos in Cd. Juárez, Chihuahua raised eleven children, primarily by selling burritos. Now some of her children make a living and serve their communities through careers as doctors, civil engineers, teachers, and food entrepreneurs.

The value of family-like relationships extends to customers as a home-like setting and atmosphere infuses the daily operation of business. The public kitchen becomes a "social device for community building" (Ferrero 2002: 194). For many customers public kitchens replace their home's breakfast, lunch or dinner tables. Their palate develops a loyalty to the seasonings of food cooked in such kitchens. This loyalty is not unlike the one we treasure when it comes to the flavors that reminds us of home. Customers also develop a loyalty to the cook's seasoning as most of us do to our mother's cooking. Eating out, therefore, carries the symbolic comfort of eating in by tapping into the sentiment of loyal palates.

Antojitos Mexicanos Noemy, in El Parque Borunda in Cd. Juárez, María Yañes sells a *gordita* (pita-like sandwich) that I have not seen in anywhere else, "Gorditas Light." What makes these *gorditas* "light" is that they are made with wheat flour, thus luring those interested in healthy eating. Considering the options for filling such *gorditas*, *chicharrón* (pork rind), *picadillo* (ground beef and potatoes stew), or *chile con queso* (a typical dish in the Cd. Juárez/El Paso area made simply of melted cheese mixed with hot chiles), the "gorditas light" are not necessarily ideal for those on a diet. This is specially the case if the billboard announcing them is correct in claiming that a person cannot simply just eat one: "*A que no puedes comer solo una!*" Yet, these *gorditas* have gained Yañes a steady follow of customers who come from different parts of the city to savor the familiar taste they have become accustomed to enjoying and to maintain their loyalty to Yañes' cooking.

Without a doubt those who can financially afford to eat at a public kitchen get fed. But in the case of Gorditas Cecy, discussed in greater detail below, I am aware of at least one regular *homeless* customer, often described as "*casi de la familia*" (almost like family), who always receives his daily meal at no cost. Furthermore, many patrons convert the public kitchen into a meeting hall where the current local politics are discussed or romances unfold. The latter scenario occurs so regularly at Los Moros Burritos that its owner Severa Ochoa de Castaña designated one out of the four tables in her food establishment as "the lover's table." Without a shift in the analytical process that investigates the values of market economy and productive labor to account for the kinds of social profits suggested in this article, such benefits will indeed remain invisible or rendered insignificant.

WORKING-CLASS MEXICAN WOMEN AND THEIR *PUESTECITOS* IN A BI-NATIONAL BORDER SETTING

The passion for gathering food stories by working-class Mexican women begins in my childhood, as I was raised in a public kitchen. The restaurants my mother and grandmother managed together were my first daycares, playgrounds, and schools. My own mother's food story is of a woman who raised seven children by selling food. The turning point that led her to become a self-sufficient woman capable of providing for her children came once she left a husband who used the little money he earned buying liquor for himself instead of food for the children.[9] As a child, I understood intuitively that in a public kitchen life is created, nourished, and maintained. In those restaurants, communities were simmered, loyalties kneaded, and families blended their unique qualities while building units of support. As a child, I understood the meaning and experience of familial wealth by living it.

I am also a child of the Mexican–U.S. border. I was born and raised in the border of Nuevo Laredo, Tamaulipas and Laredo, Texas, and now I live in El Paso, Texas, where I see the *colonias* of Cd. Juárez, Chihuahua from my office window. These geographies foster a border consciousness that motivates my life's politics and interests centered on food issues.[10] Border consciousness, for me, flavors the study of food with the complexity of cultural hybridity. Furthermore, a border consciousness represents a paradox: on the one hand, it gives the possibility of a constant flow of social and cultural intersections, while on the other hand, it never allows us to forget the reality of an asymmetrical economic relationship. Therefore, I am not oblivious to the ways the U.S.–Mexican border speaks volumes of cultural and racial inequalities, of privileges and limitations. However, I have chosen not to address these issues here.[11] Instead, I focus on how women build community for their families and others, on how they nourish others, their children and themselves. I write about how women make life happen from their food *puestecitos*.

CHARLAS CULINARIAS AS METHODOLOGY AND EPISTEMOLOGY

Charlas culinarias (culinary chats) represents a feminist methodology of gathering women's stories through the lens of food.[12] *Charlas* are free-flowing conversations informed by three basic principles. First, *charlas* offer a space to listen to "traditionally muted people," as anthropologist Carole Counihan says, who are not normally seen as "part of the political-economic or intellectual elite" (2004:2). Second, it recognizes the validity of what Linda T. Smith calls different fields of knowledge (1999). Since the women of the *charlas* are the experts of their own food knowledge, their culinary discourses represent a practice of theory making from the ground up, or theory born out of experience and necessity. Women speaking in these *charlas* are grassroots theoreticians whose culinary experiences ground their knowledge, power, and personal, as well as collective, sense of agency. Hearing women's stories not only prevents their realities from succumbing "to the alchemy of erasure," but also shows how their culinary philosophical practices can expand or redirect social paradigms created by the intellectual elite (*Telling to Live* 2001:2). *Charlas* capture women's philosophies of everyday life, of the "common sense," to echo Antonio Gramsci.[13] Finally, a successful *charla* is one based on *confianza* (trust). *Confianza* opens the door to means of keeping ourselves honest, informants and researchers. Only with such *confianza* do grassroots theoreticians express and theorize about the multiple layers of complexity surrounding their social, cultural, and economic milieu. Since women trust researchers with their stories, we owe it to them to conduct our research/ analysis with ethical integrity. With this in mind this study explores how working-class Mexican women use their cooking and management skills in their public kitchens as acts of empowerment by creating and defining the meanings and values of their own social *space*.[14]

TWO ETHNOGRAPHIC CASES

One: GG's Bakery: Mexican Style Breads and Pastries

The memory of my mother's sweet tamales led me to speak to the three founding women of GG's Bakery: Guillermina Gándara, Pilar Coral, and Rebecca Aguirre. In the summer of 2004 the El Paso Archeology Museum opened a six-month exhibit, "Mamá's Molca-jete: The Mestizaje of Mexican Cuisines." I was a guest co-curator for the exhibit and the guest speaker for the opening day, which included a reception after the lecture. Since Mexican food was the topic of the exhibit and the lecture dealt with my ongoing work on working-class Mexican women's foodways, it seems rather fitting that this event led me to GG's Bakery. Flor Moreno, the museum's janitor, was responsible for hiring GG's Bakery to cater for the event since she knew the women who work and manage GG's. The museum ordered twelve dozen tamales, some red, some green, and some sweet. With the first bite of the sweet *tamal*—the coconut, the raisins, and walnuts—my palate traveled from El Paso to my mother's kitchen in California. After visiting GG's Bakery and engaging in *charlas* with the three women who are its grounding force, I learned why I was able to savor the familiar tastes of my mother's sweet tamales. My mother learned the recipe for sweet tamales in her native state of Michoacan. At GG's, the recipe for the tamales comes from Gándara's mother who is also from Michoacan.

I was intrigued by GG's Bakery since I generally associate bakeries as a man's domain. On my first visit, for a short time such an assumption seemed confirmed. Located in a strip mall, Eastwood Village,

alongside a grocery store, a Mexican restaurant that specializes in *menudo* (beef tripe stew), and a beauty supply store, GG's Bakery's blue, red, and white billboard makes this business stand out from the rest. First of all, the billboard by illustrating the face of a male baker wearing a white hat reifies the popular notion of men as bakers. Besides this image, during my first visit and *charla* with Pilar Coral on September 13, 2004, she told me that Manny (Manuel) the baker has been working at GG's Bakery almost from the time of its inception.

ABARCA: He bakes all the bread.
CORAL: Yes, but we already learned how to make it too. My sister, Rebecca, is the one who learned. . . . She would just stand there observing, observing, observing till she learned. That she has learned to bake bread helps us a lot. Since, you know, there will always be reasons for the *panadero* (baker) to miss work. He is either sick or something happened in the family. So then we have to bake the bread.

Manny and the billboard image might establish men as bakers; however, once one enters the bakery—especially after establishing a relationship with Coral, Aguirre, and Gándara, it becomes clear that women run this business.

The above moment of the *charla* with Coral suggests two key issues regarding the network system embedded within familial wealth. First, it illustrates how at GG's Bakery family necessities are considered within the policies of managing the business. The baker's family responsibilities are highlighted as one of the reasons that keeps him from attending work, something I learned in subsequence *charlas* happens on a regular basis. Since Manny joined the bakery shortly after it opened, he obviously works in a setting where accommodations for family obligations are understood as one of life's basic necessities. Coral emphasizes this assessment by affirming that *"por fuerza"* (indubitably so) an employee would miss work to take care of family issues. Second, Coral's sister acquired knowledge of baking bread not only solves the pressure of providing goods to customers, but it also gives Rebecca Aguirre a crucial role in the operation of GG's Bakery by demonstrating her keen senses for baking and cooking.

During the first *charla* with Coral, she also shared a little of GG's Bakery's history. When GG's opened on October 22, 1997, Gándara and Aguirre ran the business.

CORAL: Guillermina and my other sister, Rebecca, began the business. I had my own job, so they worked here. Later I left my job and began working with my sister [Rebecca]. . . . Guillermina is like another sister. She lived with us many years. She is like a sister.

ABARCA: Then we can say this is a family business.

CORAL: Yes that is how we see it as a family business.

A sisterly entrepreneurial effort and unity forms the basic business force that makes GG's Bakery thrive day-by-day. Aguirre and Coral are the cooks of tamales and *menudo* as well as general managers, and on occasions Aguirre also functions as the baker. Gándara holds the status of the visionary, both to open a bakery and as the modifier of recipes.

The initials of GG's Bakery stand for Guillermina Gándara who had the vision to open a business. Gándara based her decision to open a food related business because as she says, *"la comida siempre deja porque todo mundo tiene que comer"* ("food always leaves a profit because

everyone has to eat"). In this particular moment of our *charla*, the word *"deja"* (to leave) refers to monetary profit. In Gándara's estimation a bakery offers greater financial gain since it requires less capital to operate, as compared to a restaurant. The bakery makes sufficient profits to pay the rent, utilities, supplies, Manny's salary, and allows the women who work there to afford a simple but modest living.

However, *"dejar"* which means to leave or to allow, has other implications that go beyond economic gain that the *charlas* with all three women demonstrate, and where implications of familial wealth are at work. GG's Bakery offers these three women much more than the financial means to make a living. For instance, the bakery feeds multiple necessities in Gándara's life. It serves as a connection to her paternal heritage. When I asked Gándara why she opened a bakery, she said that without her knowing, the decision was genetically based. She did not realize she carries a "baker's gene" until the day she told her father of her desire to open a bakery:

I told my father, 'I am going to open a business.' He said to me, 'What kind of business?' I told him, 'I am not sure, but I would like to open a bakery.' That is when he told me, 'Did you know that many years ago I worked for a long time as a baker [in Durango, Mexico]? . . . And do you know that your grandfather was also a baker for many years? I find it interesting that you want to open a bakery.'

According to Gándara's father, she had it in her blood to become a baker because of him and his father.

Without knowing this aspect of her family story, Gándara originally thought that her aspiration to open a business came from her desire to create art. A bakery would offer Gándara not only the space to create art, but also provide a receptive audience to affirm her culinary creativity.

I used to think [the desire to open a business] was because when I was younger [I would go] to the bakeries. I would always ask, 'How did you do this [bread] and that one?' All that bread captivated me. I would say, 'Not everyone can be a baker because this bread is an art.' This is art. You have to have a lot of imagination to come up with a form of decorating cakes. That is where I thought my interest in a bakery came, but my father says, 'No, it is in the blood.'

The opening the bakery offers a non-monetary sustenance that fulfills not only Gándara's desire for a setting to create art, but vicariously it also satisfies her father's dream of one day owning his own bakery. While her father and grandfather worked for many years as bakers, they never were proprietors of one.

Another benefit GG's Bakery le deja a (provides to) Gándara is a place to produce bread as art and a space where she can articulate her own ideas about the creative endeavors of baking bread. Gándara approaches this issue in our *charla* when we discussed the use of the word "style" as part of the bakery's name.

ABARCA: I ask about the word "style" because in other bakeries or restaurants I a word one often sees is—[Gándara finishes the sentence.]

GÁNDARA: Authentic.

ABARCA: Yes. But you decided to use the phrase "Mexican style bread" and not authentic Mexican bread. Why?

GÁNDARA: The main reason was because I like having Mexican style bread but with a different taste. People are going to say, "look they have Mexican style bread." This would make them come and buy it. But when they taste it, I want for it to have a distinct flavor.

Clearly, Gándara understands the importance of familiarity, particularly for a predominately Mexican area where GG's Bakery is located. Yet for Gándara the goal of achieving familiarity does not stifle her own desire for uniqueness. She expresses her sense of distinct flavor by a process of modifying traditional Mexican bread recipes as she asks the baker to add or change a few ingredients. For example, she adds vanilla to breads that normally do not require it. The recipe for the traditional Mexican bread, "*mantecadas*," as the name suggests asks for lard (*manteca*), but Gándara uses vegetable oil instead. Gándara's recipe modification comes from her easy affirmation that "everything advances." In the language of food anthropologists, such as E. N. Anderson, Gándara's actions reflect the internalization of culinary historical trade market (2005).

Thanks to Gándara's business skills, when she changes a recipe or creates an entirely new pastry or cake, she always offers free samples to her customers.

On one occasion I made many kinds of pastries and cakes that I like. I didn't sell them; I gave them to the customers. [I told them], 'I give you this cake that I made. I am going to sell it here.' For a number of days I make a lot of cakes and gave them away. Later people came [to the bakery saying], 'I want a cake like the one you gave me the other day.'

Through this practice, Gándara cultivates her customers' palates and in the process they become loyal patrons to her baking style— another key element of familial wealth.

Gándara's culinary practices demonstrate the internationalization of foodways, which undeniably reject any sense of culinary authenticity that "rest on static timelessness and false notions of purity" (Heldke 2003:186). For philosopher Lisa Heldke, if culinary authenticity is in fact definable, "it should emphasize 'adaptability' instead of or in addition to, 'replicability' " (31). Gándara embraces both forms of culinary practices—adaptability and replicability—which are both connected to her parents. While Gándara's "baker gene" comes from her patrilineal heritage, adaptability to feed her own creative needs carries more weight than strictly following a baking method that her father and grandfather might have used. Yet when it comes to the other two items sold at GG's Bakery, *menudo* and tamales, Gándara prefers to honor family tradition by following her own mother's recipes. The only things that have changed, of course, are the implementations of modern technology necessary to prepare and cook tamales in the hundred dozen and large quantities of *menudo*. The patriarchal genealogy of bakers running through Gándara's veins, therefore, does not overshadow the honor her mother receives by having her recipes remembered. Of particular significance is that a woman's family and home recipes are remembered and recreated in a public setting, thus preventing increasing the list of "the millions—billions—of unsung human beings who have created the food we eat and the foodways we love" (Anderson 2005:233).

Change and tradition within culinary practices overlap in the daily operation of GG's Bakery. With the modification of some traditional Mexican bread recipes and the affirmation of family recipes of *menudo* and tamales, GG's Bakery becomes a site that defies the binary notion that often tries to separate change as progressive and tradition as static and nostalgic, potentially, making change and tradition, antithetical. In the world of culinary history such debate has at times manifested itself by drawing distinctions between public and domestic cooking (Ravel 1982). In his historical study of cooks and cooking, Symons argues that "[p]rofessional cooks," assumed in this study to be men, "compete with and negate, but also emerge from and depend upon home cooks," assumed to be women, (2004:298). By incorporating home recipes at GG's Bakery, Gándara,

Coral, and Aguirre bridge such tensions that professional cooks might feel by eliminating the sense of competition from and negation of home cooking. Since the professional cooks at GG's Bakery are mainly women, they also overwrite the gender ideological distinction between professional (i.e., productive labor) and home cooks (i.e., reproductive labor) (Domosh and Seager 2001; Lamphere, Ragoné and Zavalla 1997; Hollins, Pershing and Yonge 1993).

From GG's Bakery's inauguration, Aguirre came up with the idea of including home cooking in the form of *menudo* and tamales as the regular staples one would *naturally* find in a Mexican bakery. Aguirre's professional decision has proven to be of tremendous success. Even with a sit-down restaurant that specializes in *menudo* next door to the bakery, it has been of no consequence to the sale of this traditional Mexican breakfast of beef tripe stew at GG's. When I spoke with Coral, she attributes the loyalty of their customers, and gaining more customers to her sister's and her skill at cleaning as well as preparing the *menudo*.

ABARCA: I see you have competition with the *menudo* next door.

CORAL: Yes, we do. Yet, even with the restaurant there we have not lost customers.

ABARCA: Great. It must be your *sazón*.[15]

CORAL: You know, what people have liked a lot is that our *menudo* is very clean.

ABARCA: It's not fatty.

CORAL: At the meat market they tell us, 'we have *menudo* ready to cook, ready to be placed in the pot.' But that is not true, since the *menudo* still has too much fat. And it comes in big chunks. We clean it [some more] and cut it in bite size pieces. That's why people like it; they say that the *menudo* is very clean. It's not fatty. That's why I tell you, the business next door has not taken our clients. On the contrary, more people have come.

The family recipes for making *menudo* as well as the tamales have become signature dishes at GG's Bakery.

In a *charla* with Aguirre, I learned that the original sources to make both the *menudo* and tamales came from a combination of family recipes. The basic recipe for *menudo* and the *masa* for the tamales comes from Gándara's mother, the method for preparing the meat for the tamales comes from Aguirre's ex-mother-in-law, and Aguirre's own modification. When I asked Aguirre for her source for making tamales, she said,

> I am good at eating tamales. Well, I learned with my mother-in-law. We visited her every Christmas. She lives in Santa Barbara, Chihuahua, near Parral. Boy did we make tamales! But when I first began visiting her, she would not strain the red chile sauce for the meat. The sauce had the skin of the chiles. One day I made the sauce and strained it. And my mother-in-law said, 'Why are you straining it?' And I told her, 'Because I don't like the chile's skin sticking to the roof of my mouth.' Honestly, it sticks. Since then, she also strains the sauce. The tamales taste a lot better.

Aguirre uses her *sazón*, the ability to season food guided by a sensory-logic, to recreate family recipes. The sensory-logic, or knowing through the senses, becomes extremely important for Aguirre's contribution to GG's Bakery success, and her own feelings of accomplishment, thus suggesting the act of agency embedded in the process of familial wealth. Since one of Aguirre's major responsibilities lays in the preparation of tamales, she must rely on her sensory memory to accomplish this task as her own mother has passed away, Gándara's mother is now an elderly lady whose own senses fail her in remembering recipes, and Aguirre's ex-mother-in-law is

no longer an accessible contact. The sensory skills Aguirre developed as she cooked with her mother and her mother-in-law are the same skills that give her the ability to recreate the process of making bread every time Manny cannot make it to work. Aguirre takes great pride not only in her talent to make tamales and *menudo*, but also in the fact that when she bakes the bread, customers cannot tell the difference between her bread and Manny's.

The last aspect regarding GG's Bakery in relation to familial wealth I would like to mention deals with community building, inside and outside the bakery through the annual ritual of the *tamalada*: a gathering of women to make tamales. Tamales and *tamaladas* hold a place of significant historical and cultural importance for Mexican and Mexican-American people. Jeffrey Pilcher, in *Que Vi-van Los Tamale*!, speaks of the importance of women making *masa* for tortillas and tamales as a culinary symbolic action that captures Mexicans' national and cultural sense of identity (Pilcher 1997). Other food scholars have written about the *convivencia* (co-living, co-sharing) the *tamalada* offers to a collective group of women (Blend 2001; Keremistis 1983; de la Peña Brown 1981). In the process of making tamales, women assert not only their own cultural identities, but also that of their family and friends who share in the consumption of the tamales.

Women gather at GG's Bakery to make a *tamalada* with the same spirit of *convivencia*. By employing only women to assists in the making of tamales, Aguirre and Coral assert the belief of ". . . tamale-making as a woman-centered, role-affirming communal ritual that empowers women as the carriers of tradition" (Blend 2001:44). Aguirre indicates that up to eight women work together to make tamales during the Christmas-New Year holiday season. They all gather around 5 pm and work often throughout the night to wrap the tamales customers have already ordered in the hundreds of dozens. The ambience serves as a time of socialization as women exchange advice regarding marriage, raising children, the latest political issues of the area, as well as the latest episodes of favorite Mexican soap operas.

The commercialized aspect of this *tamalada* does not take away the empowerment from women just because they are cooking a commodity for sale. On the contrary, this action shows a way to feminize, or better humanize, some of the principles of a market economy. One main goal of a market economy for those who embark as entrepreneurs in a large- or small-scale business, as mentioned earlier, is the opportunity it offers such individuals to pursue their own self-interests. Self-interest can represent the dark side of capitalism if it manifests only as a means to increase capital gain, thus reproducing and strengthening economic structures of inequality. However, making tamales carries an exchange-value promoting and maintaining cultural pride and spiritual unity to both the producers and consumers. This action "deviates from the behavior of the capitalist *homo economicus* who lives only for increasing [capital] profits" (Simon 2003:187). If the exchange-value of a particular product helps maintain and valorize a people's material and spiritual heritage, then such product helps instill a sense of personal, cultural, and historical pride, as these are symbolically inscribed in the product. In this case, tamales are the product.[16]

Finally, the *convivencia* and spirit of the *tamalada* experienced at GG's Bakery extends beyond the women making the tamales. Considering the cultural and historical implications wrapped within the husk of the tamales, the labor of the women at GG's is crucial in helping Mexican and Mexican American people maintain their own cultural heritage alive and vibrant. Bearing in mind that GG's receives on the average pre-orders of tamales that reach up to three hundred dozen, a significant majority of people do not make their own *tamaladas*. The consumers' form of *convivencia*, then, more likely than not takes place at the moment of eating tamales, especially during the holidays.

If the image of the male baker on the billboard and Manny, the employed baker, reifies the idea of men as bakers, I would argue then that the initials at GG's, which stand for Guillermina Gándara, act as a symbolic inscription of a woman's claim to a public space. Gándara not only uses her name's initials as the literal public identification for the bakery, but also she claims such public space as the site where she explores her baking artistic talent and ideas about it.[17] After reflecting on E. N. Anderson's suggestion that the "creators of bread [and] of lime-processed corn dough" were very probably women who will forever remain nameless in the accounts of culinary histories, I wonder if Gándara's baker gene as well as Aguirre's sensory culinary knowledge might not be connected to a long line of women who throughout history have fed millions and billions of people. If this is the case, then Guillermina Gándara, Pilar Coral, and Rebecca Aguirre will not remain nameless (2005:233).

Case Study Two: Gorditas Cecy

The model of familial wealth described above filters through political international borders. Gorditas Cecy is a *puestecito* located in El Mercado Solidaridad (Solidarity Market) in Cd. Juárez, Chihuahua. The market covers an entire block and within it there are twenty-two stalls, eleven of which are food stands, four that specialize in *gorditas*. The city provides gas and electric service to the market but no water facilities. Most booths are no larger than five by six feet; what makes some businesses bigger than others is that some owners, or renters, operate out of a few joined stalls. Customers usually sit on stools placed around the counter top that separates them from the cooks. Customers can also sit in small plastic or folding chairs placed around cardboard tables along the sidewalk, or order their food to go. Since El Mercado Solidaridad is located in a nontourist section of the city, it provides service mainly to local residents.

When Gorditas Cecy's opened in 1992, María Luisa Gonzales, its owner, began working out of just one market booth. Over the years, or as she says, "*poco a poco*" (little by little) the business has tripled in size, making it the biggest in the market. For the first few years, only Gonzales and her daughter Cecy ran the business. Gonzales explains this circumstance by saying, "Cecy has always been working with me; we have always been together." Perhaps this mother-daughter bond explains why Gonzales named her new *puestecito* Gorditas Cecy. When the department of public health inspection visited Gonzales' new business and asked for the establishment's name, she said to me: "Well the first thing it came to mind was to say 'Cecy.' And that was it. Gorditas Cecy."

Gonzales' journey to becoming an independent businesswoman goes back to the woman who offered her a job making *gorditas* in her new restaurant. Gonzales has never shared the name of this entrepreneur woman in our *charlas* referring to her simply as an "angel," which seems rather appropriate. After three years of working for this "angel," Gonzales told her that she was leaving. In an effort to keep her as an employee, particularly since this woman had just opened a third restaurant, she offered to double Gonzales' salary from 500 to 1,000 pesos (approximately a difference from $160 to $320 US dollars). But Gonzales' need and responsibility to spend more time with her children were more compelling than a weekly salary of 1,000 pesos. When Gonzales left, she received what she thought was a severance pay of 500 pesos.

For a short while, Gonzales felt depressed wondering what to do with her life. The supermarket, SMART, was soliciting a cook with the promise of good pay. After inquiring about this job, Gonzales felt even more depressed since they only offered 180 pesos per week (approximately $51 US). On her way home, she walked by El Mercado Solidaridad and in one of the market's booth she saw a sign: "for rent or sale; 250 per month and 250 deposit." The sign only made her feel, as she says, "*aguitada*" (sad). All she had was 500 pesos, where would she get the capital for supplies if she rented the market booth to open a business? A few days went by without a job and bills to pay, so she finally went to the bank to cash the 500 severance pay check. When the cashier gave her the money, Gonzales told her, "lady you have given me more money than the check is worth. 'No, the check is for 5,000 pesos. Look here." With such a delightful surprise, Gonzales returned to the market and the *puestecito* was still available. Considering that she only sold one *gordita* on opening day, I am sure the sadness did not dissipate. It took three months for business to pick up; now she has a rather strong and steady clientele. Thus, Gonzales began her life as a businesswoman, thanks to *her* "angel."

This story adds another social dynamic to the notion of familial wealth that goes beyond family networking. Gonzales' life as an entrepreneur became possible with the indirect assistance of another woman entrepreneur. Perhaps it is important to remember that this woman once made a living as housekeeper in a hotel but who "*poco a poco*" (little by little) became the owner of three restaurants. Gonzales made a statement suggesting that even with these restaurants her "angel" was not necessarily financially well off. Gonzales said, "The more money rich people have, the less they give you." From Gonzales' perspective 5,000 pesos (approximately $1,600 US) in severance pay in 1992 for an employee who only worked for three years making 500 (approximately $160 US) a week was a rather generous compensation. Even if this entrepreneurial female "angel" was not wealthy, her actions reflect a philanthropic spirit. Her access to some capital helped Gonzales begin her trajectory as a businesswoman.[18]

As mentioned earlier familial wealth does not ignore capital gain. Over the years, Gorditas Cecy's capital gain has become a source of financial support for multiple members of Gonzales' family. During out first *charla*, Gonzales mentioned that one of her sons, the oldest one living in New York, constantly asks her to stop working and that he will take care of her. She expresses her refusal of such generous offer by saying: "I'd keep working as long as I can. Besides my daughters make a living by working here too. And truly, they don't let me work that much anymore. As I long as I can, I will continue working because from here there is enough profit for all."

In addition to this family financial support, Gorditas Cecy also functions as a daycare for children and grandchildren, and as the nexus for community building. One example of collective support between different marketers that Gonzales has mentioned reflects their ability of caring for each other's children. "Here in the market we take care of each other's children. We keep on eye on them. If we see a stranger talking to a kid, we put a stop to it." This support between marketers expands to acting as consumers of each other's products. When Gonzales or her family feel like eating something other than *gorditas*, for example, they purchase food from other *puestecitos*. While this action might be simply one of convenience, Gonzales articulates this act as "*hacer el gasto.*" This expression conveys the notion of helping others make a profit—or in this case, make a living.

Another form of familial wealth's networking practice manifests itself in the different roles family members perform in Gorditas Cecy's daily operation. The distribution of labor usually consists of the following arrangement between Gonzales and her daughters. Belinda takes orders from customers and once they are ready, she wraps them in wax paper and places them in colorful plastic plates. Carmen takes a handful of flour dough, which she prepared early in the morning, rolls it in her hands into a small ball. After she has accumulated a number of them, she continues with the *palotiada*. Using a rolling pin, she turns the flour balls into perfectly rounded *gorditas*. Cecy does a combination of all these tasks. She also prepares and serves *caldo de res* (beef soup). Over the years, it has become clear to me that this is an independent side business that only Cecy controls. All women, except Gonzales, take turns washing dishes. During the summers, Cecy's teenage son is generally in charge of doing the prep work: peeling and dicing potatoes, cutting onions, chiles, and also washing dishes, which includes carrying buckets of water since the *puestecitos* have no running water. Cecy's younger daughter's job consists, as she says, "to serve the soft drinks." Gonzales mainly fills the gorditas with the *guiso*, the main meal, a customer wants, which are all displayed on the menu that hangs above the stove (Figure 8.1).

These *guisos* range from *barbacoa*, a stew like dish made with cow's cheek, to *mole* (chicken marinated in chocolate-chile sauce) to *wini* with beans (hotdogs with beans). While *barbacoa* is the most expensive *gordita* in the menu, it is also the most popular. Gonzales' *barbacoa* does not follow the traditional recipe, which calls only for the use of cow's cheek. While she has neither given me her actual recipe nor the process of making it, she has explained what let her to modify this dish. In one of our *charlas*, Gonzales said, "One day I noticed that this very polite man who has been eating here for a long time did not eat all of his *barbacoa*. The next day when he came, he also left some on the plate. But on this occasion, I

Figure 8.1 Gorditas Cecy's daily menu.

also noticed another costumer doing the same thing." These observations led Gonzales to the conclusion that her costumers were not eating their *gorditas* because the *barbacoa* was too fatty. "When I picked up the plates from these men, I noticed the plates were covered with puddles of oil oozing from the *barbacoa*. Since the meat from a cow's cheek is too fatty, from then on I have used two kinds of meat in my *barbacoa*, cheek and tongue. Now the first item we run out most days is my barbacoa." Thus Gonzales keen food critic eye led her to alter the recipe.

The fear Gonzales expressed, in the opening of this article, about cooking for a public audience has certainly dissipated. Yet such emotion does bring to the forefront ways that productive and reproductive labor have been historically conceptualized: production as the exchange of labor for capital gain in the public sector and reproduction as the use of women's *natural* domestic labor for subsistence and nourishment (Boydston 1990; Smith 1990; Engels 1942). Gonzales' feelings of fear are indicative of her awareness that home cooking for loved ones, even when rejected, does not involve the risk of financial failure. Gonzales' narrative, therefore, not only captures the general way in which production and reproduction are conceptualized as different labor forms, but also articulates in words and actions how they overlap blurring their spatial and ideological separation. Gonzales' home cooking, her family recipes, is what she literally cooks in her public kitchen—with the modification of her *barbacoa*. When Gorditas Cecy initially opened, the smallness of the stands the heat of the gas stove and the summer heat of the Chihuahua high desert made it extremely difficult to cook the *guisos* right on site. All the *guisos*, therefore, were prepared at home and transported to the market. Thus, this illustrates another form in which public and private spaces came together. As business has grown, now Cecy and Carmen arrive between 6:30 and 7:00 am to prepare the daily *guisos* right on site.

The sense of generosity that gets created between the food provider and the food consumer represents another aspect of familial wealth that speaks to how women's traditional reproductive family logic enters their public kitchen. The exchange between provider and consumer goes beyond the need to sell food for economic profit and the need to consume food just as fuel for the body. The giving and receiving of food in Gorditas Cecy embodies the basic belief that food provides substance that nourishes body and soul, and it builds community (Altman 1999; Khare 1992).

Only a few visits to Gorditas Cecy suffice to reveal that many customers are daily or weekly regulars. On one occasion a customer asked Cecy for a bowl of *caldo*, clear beef broth without any meat for her mother who had just returned home from the hospital. Cecy got the biggest container she could find and filled it to the top. When she gave it to the lady who had asked for it, Cecy refused to accept money saying, "No, no forget it; just take it to your mom. Hopefully she will get better soon." If a bowl of clear beef broth, like chicken soup, has medicinal qualities that help the healing process, Cecy's actions suggest that charging for it would take away such effect.

Another example of generosity is the story that Gonzales shared with me about one of her nephews. This particular nephew, then a high school student, one day took all of his classmates, "more then twenty," to have lunch at Gorditas Cecy. After they all had their *gorditas*, *tacos*, and *burritos*, Gonzales, just like Cecy, refused to take money from them. The fact that her nephew took more then twenty people to her *puestecito* meant more to her than the monetary profit such a sale implied. Gonzales, however, did gain something substantial from this visit. She recalls such benefit by saying, "They left very happy. Those are beautiful details in life that you do not forget. You remember them always." Her words expressed a sense of honor and gratitude for the recognition her nephew gave her culinary talent by taking his classmates to eat at Gorditas Cecy.

Besides supporting her children, providing some of them with a place of employment, and teaching them the value of reciprocity as the key to success, not just in business but life in general, Gonzales also uses Gorditas Cecy as a space for other socially directed services. She often shares part of her story as an entrepreneur with customers, and in the process she makes Gorditas Cecy a site to discuss local politics and history, and to give advice to potential new market food vendors. A reoccurring theme in our *charlas* is Gonzales's legal ownership of the land where Gorditas Cecy is located. Gonzales always speaks of this in conjunction with how other people throughout the city, particularly downtown, have lost their food stands due to corrupt government practices.

One story Gonzales often shares is about a city's governor who sold a number of "market booths located downtown but not the land where they were built. When the next governor came into office everyone lost their business because the only thing they actually owned was the material used for the structure of the booths." Since these people did not legally own the land, they had no recourses. Their loss was even more devastating, Gonzales, explains, because "they not only lost their business, but also the investment they made in getting electricity, gas, and some, even water." The deception came, as Gonzales makes clear, because "the governor never fully explained what he was selling. He got rich by the misfortune of working-class people, many of whom were women." But even while legally owning the land where Gorditas Cecy stands, Gonzales knows that if the government wants to take it one day, they could, perhaps in the name of city revitalization. The experience of dispossession goes beyond being anecdote for Gonzales. In 1968, her own mother's *gorditas* stand located downtown Cd. Juárez was demolished by garbage collectors who came and swept away all the food stalls. Hopefully Gorditas Cecy will not experience this fate and El Mercado Solidaridad (Solidarity Market) proves to be a place of unity and support that continues to build community among family members, co-marketers and customers.

CHANGING CONCEPTUAL PARADIGMS

Studying women's food stories in terms of their economic as well as social and cultural implications opens the door to engage in a dialogue for changing conceptual paradigms.[19] In this study through the ethnographic cases I have illustrated, I open a dialogue that specifically challenges two of the conclusions Scott Simon draws from his study on Taipei women entrepreneurs.

First Simon argues that in order for entrepreneurship "to become a tool of collective women's empowerment, it must be linked systematically to gender education and the feminist movement as a whole" (2003:217). However, where does the responsibility to create/affect structural social change rest? Does it rest on the shoulders of working-class women making a living in their small businesses? While familial wealth represents networks of collaboration, the women in my study are essentially in the business of supporting their children and feeding their customers. Their goal is not to generate a social network to engender official educational and social policies with the aim to promote ideological shifts on gender and economic views. However, lessons on these issues are not absent from the values embedded of familial wealth. Women teach each other the right to assert themselves within a public space. The principle of reciprocity represents the pedagogy women entrepreneurs use, at least within this study, to teach each other, their children and their community the basics for personal, social, cultural, and even economic capital gain. It seems to me that as scholars in the business of producing textual knowledge and with a broader access to social and political networks the responsibility for a larger (even global) systematic social and economic structural change must rest on our shoulders.

The second theme for conceptual dialogue exchange deals with Simon's lamenting the fact that "most women entrepreneurs are concentrated in fields traditionally seen to be female fields of endeavor: food, clothes, and childcare" (220). Personally, I do not see women

reliance's on traditional female social role, such as cooking, as a source of lamentation. To see it as such is to elide the self-empowerment and acts of agency women find within their work; it is to take away their self and collective affirmation and validation. Furthermore, working-class women with little to no formal education and many with the responsibility to raise children do have limited career choices. Perhaps we should recognize that the exploration of different possibilities of achieving a solid economic future based on career planning is a middle-class way of strategizing. For working-class women (and men), the small-scale business route is a result of poverty.

Exploring women's food endeavors within their public kitchens examines the knowledge found in the practical, concrete, and temporal aspects of everyday cooking.[20] It also acknowledges that historically those responsible for feeding the majority of the world's population are women. While women's food has a crucial role in shaping our cultural, political, and class identities, their contributions all too often go unrecognized— particularly in the case for working-class women (Abarca 2002, 2006; Anderson 2005; Cooper 1998; Pilcher 1997). For instance, Michael Symons in *A History of Cooks and Cooking*, recognizes, and rightly so, that without cooks, "we could not have survived" and that "cooks have not just made our meals, but have also made us" (2004:xi). Yet his study gives little attention to women commercial kitchens. In *Between Field and Cooking Pot: The Political Economy of Marketwomen in Peru*, Florence E. Babb points out how much of the work on the informal economy or small-scale business in Third World cities have not looked "at the principal participation of women as marketers" including in the realm of food (1998:52).

What explains this tendency is that most research on food and women centers within the principles of consumption and the ideological female gendered notions of reproduction.[21] Consumption ties to reproduction by framing women's social and cultural roles as homemakers and caretakers. Significant research on food and women deals with this particular interweaving (Inness 2001, 2005; Avakian 1997; Shapiro 2004). Women's connection to food, therefore, is often framed as part of their household responsibilities: what tactics do women use and what meaning they give to the task of feeding their family? My work does not differ in this respect since it explores how such principles of reproduction influence the work habits of working-class Mexican women within their public kitchens.[22]

By analyzing women's active participation in the market economy, via their food provider roles, we can examine how the principles of production as well as reproduction are affected by the way some working-class women value their food business. In this work I have offered the concept of familial wealth to highlight the values and meanings women give to their social functions as both producers and reproducers of life and sustenance. It also shows the overlapping, which I argue along with other scholars has always existed for working-class women, between public (productive) and private (reproductive) spaces (Williams-Forson 2006; Hooks 1990). The interlocking points of these spaces are the elements embedded in the concept of familial wealth: family networking, self-agency and empowerment, community building, reciprocity, generosity, collaboration, capital gain in terms of social, personal, and cultural profits not simply monetary.

NOTES

1. All conversations, or *charlas*, took place in Spanish. I have decided to offer translations in consideration of non-Spanish readers and constraint of space. However, in moments where word choices in Spanish are integral to the analysis, I am leaving sentences in the orig-

inal language, followed by an immediate translation. All translations are mine.

2. The *gorditas* served at Cecy's are particular to the region of Cd. Juárez, Chihuahua, Mexico. Generally they are made with flour, not corn tortillas; they are grilled, not deep-fried; they are as big as a typical corn tortilla, not as small as hamburger buns. They are as thick as pita bread. Once cooked, they are sliced in half, just like pita bread, and filled with a *guiso*. *Guisos* are a main Mexican meal such as *mole*, *picadillo*, *chile relleno*, red or green beef stew, *barbacoa*, of course all of this comes with either beans or rice, or both.

3. Oftentimes, ruptures as moments of anguish and suffering create the impetus that pulls women into opening small food related businesses. In Gonzales' case it was losing her job as a housekeeper in a hotel. Other examples of these turning points, in the case of married women with children, include a husband's death, a divorce, a husband walking out on the family, or a husband's inability to provide for the family. While my work focuses mainly on this group of women, there are other reasons women become food entrepreneurs. In the case of GG's Bakery: Mexican Style Bread and Pastries, following in a father's footsteps and the desire for a space for creative expression were the initial motivations in opening a bakery.

4. For over ten years, I have been engaging in *charlas culinarias* with working-class Mexican and Mexican-American women and many of them have helped support themselves and family by selling food at one period or another of their lives. See Abarca, 2001 and 2006.

5. Barbara Haber's *Cooking to Survive: The Careers of Alice Foote MacDougall and Cleora Butler* (2005) also addresses how these two women transformed their cooking skills into a means of surviving. Among the fundamental difference between Harber's work and one I am working on, is that Foote MacDougall and Butler left written records of their food stories.

6. Since this article forms part of a larger project, the comments I make about familial wealth are based on general observations from the seven groups of women with whom I have had *charlas culinarias* for the last few years.

7. I make no claims for this to be a groundbreaking question; other feminist scholars working on food studies explore such form of inquiry (Zafa 1996; Haber 2006; Williams-Forson 2006). Feminist critical race/class theory has done much to unveil patriarchal, capitalist ideological mechanism that aim to sustain the split of production and reproduction (Hooks 1990; Ruiz 1998). My work is one more voice to reinforce how concrete and ideological notions of production/reproduction have always been a

trenza (braid) for the majority of working-class women.

8. Women like Encarnacieón Pinedo, Fabiola Cabeza de Baca Gilbert, and Cleofas M. Jaramillo wrote down family and regional recipes with the intention that their cultural heritage remained in the memory of future generations. The women cooks of *puestecitos* who cook family recipes are engaged in the same practice, except they literally keep cultural heritage alive on people's palate.

9. In *Voices in the Kitchen*, (2006), Liduvina Velez's food voice and the stories she shares with it are central to the theoretical analysis of the entire book.

10. The combination of border consciousness and food studies solidify my commitment to become what Karon Olson and Linda Shopes call a "citizen-scholar-activist" who is rooted in her community (1991, 201). "By doing work where we have personal commitments," say Olson and Shopes, "our academic contributions are more likely to come out of a personal, creative, politically engaged self, one that has a social—and not simply academic—purpose" (201). My scholarship is based in the places and spaces I call home: the kitchen and the border.

11. The editors of *From Betty Crocker to Feminist Food Studies* (2006) argue that early food studies examined gender issues only in terms of women's pathologies. In resent border studies dealing with women, particular of Cd. Juárez, have focused on the disappearance and the deaths of women. While issues of women's pathological relationships with food and the epidemic of femicides demand much importance, we need to also address the ways women create and maintain life, community and a sense of personal social and cultural space.

12. The *charlas culinarias* joins other feminist ethnographic methodologies that gather women's stories through the lens of food as a powerful means of social and cultural expression: Carole M. Counihan's "food-centered life histories," Ramona Lee Perez's "kitchen table ethnographies," and Annie Hauck-Lawson's "food voice."

13. Concept quoted from Ashley, Hollows, Jones, and Taylor's analysis in *Food and Cultural Studies*, 16–18.

14. The work of Arlene Voski Avakian (1997) and Carole Counihan (2004) also examines numerous ways food can function as a source of empowerment for women.

15. *Sazón* refers the ability a cook has to create flavorful food using the senses as the guiding principles. In *Voices in the Kitchen*, I speak of the *sazón* as the epistemology of the senses, as an embodied sensory-logic.

16. In *Building Houses Out of Chicken Legs: Black Women, Food and Power* (2006) Williams-Forson studies a similar form of exchange-value for African American people as she explores the historical and cultural importance of fried chicken. She specifically studies women's significant role in this part of African Americans' culinary history.

17. The fact that Gándara (and a number of other women in my project) choose to inscribe her initials as the official name of the bakery, I see it as a public act of self-definition and self-validation. Women's names, bodies, or body parts often predominate in the realm of food business—this is certainly the case in many Mexican restaurants. In many cases these function to promote the nostalgic feeling of "mamá's coking" or "home cooking" or promoting food through sexualized images of women's bodies. Because of these gender stereotypes, the act of self-naming, of claiming ownership of a public space becomes a conscious or unconscious act that challenges the power dynamics that create gender, ethnic and, in this case, occupational stereotypes, Williams-Forson (2001) addresses this issue in regards to African-American people.

18. In his study of Taipei women entrepreneurs, Simon points out how the ability to helps others as a result of owning a business was a major motivating factor for many of the women he interviewed. For him this is an action that challenges the values of liberal economics, "which is based on the market economy of rational individuals pursuing their own self-interest" (2003: 214). What women highlight in Simon's case, and what is also evident in my work, is the social dimensions that businesses often afford them, which they manifest into their ability to help others, beyond their own children.

19. Correlation between my re-training as to how I see the meaning of knowledge, of theory making, within the context of the *charlas culinarias* echoes much of the critical challenging questions raised in the collection edited by Sharna Berger Gluck and Daphne Patai in *Women's Words: The Feminist Practice of Oral History* (1991).

20. Feminist and Buddhist principles significantly influence the theoretical and analytical process within my food studies research. *Cooking, Eating, Thinking: Transformative Philosophies of Food* (1992), edited by Deane W. Curtin and Lisa M. Heldke offer an excellent interconnection between these three concepts: food, feminism, and Buddhism.

21. Anthropologist E. N. Anderson sees the politics of academic institutions in the United States implicated in these consequences. First of all, he argues that the discipline of food studies was not only "dismissed as frivolous until the

1980s," but also "studies of food consumption, in particular, were relegated to the academic Siberia of 'women's field'." Academic men interested in food study focus their work in "food production—agricultural science—[which] was [and is] a 'men's field'." The result has been that academic departments where food production is studied receive much research funding (2005: 36).

22. The exploration of how women use the "home" appeal as the main promotional device in managing a restaurant is discussed and analyzed by Jan Whitaker in "Domesticating the Restaurant: Marketing the Anglo-American Home." Beside the obvious ethnic difference between the women in Whitaker and my own work, their socio-economic background is the most significant. Whitaker looks at middle-class women and their social values, my work is looking a working-class women.

REFERENCES

Abarca, E. M. 2001. "Los chilaquiles de mi 'amá: The Language of Everyday Cooking." In *Pilaf, Pozole, and Pad Thai: American Women and Ethnic Food*. ed. S. A. Inness. pp. 119–144. Amherst: UP Massachusetts.

———. 2006. *Voices in the Kitchen: Views on Food and the World by Working-Class Mexican and Mexican-American Women*. College Station: A&M University Press.

Altman, D. 1999. *Art of the Inner Meal: Eating as a Spiritual Path*. San Francisco: Harper.

Anderson, E. N. 2005. *Everyone Eats: Understanding Food and Culture*. New York: New York University Press.

Ashley, B., J. Hollows, S. Jones and B. Taylor, eds. 2004. *Food and Cultural Studies*. London: Routledge.

Avakian, V. A. ed. 1997. *Through the Kitchen Window: Women Explore the Intimate Meaning of Food and Cooking*. Boston: Beacon Press.

Babb, F. E. 1989. *Between Field and Cooking Pot: The Political Economy of Marketwomen in Peru*. (Revised Edition). Austin, TX: University of Texas Press.

Blend, B. 2001. " 'I Am an Act of Kneading': Food and the Making of Chicana Identity." In *Cooking Lessons: The Politics of Gender and Food*, ed. S. A. Inness. pp. 41–61. New York: Rowman & Littlefield Publishers, Inc.

Boydston, J. 1990. *Home and Work: Housework, Wages, and the Ideology of Labor in Early Republic*. New York: Oxford University Press.

Cabeza de Baca Gilbert, F. 2005. *The Good Life: New Mexico Traditions and Food*. New Mexico: Museum of New Mexico Press.

Cooper, A. 1998. *"A Woman's Place Is in the Kitchen": The Evolution of Women Chefs*. New York: Van Nostrand Reinhold.

Counihan, C. M. 2004. *Around the Tuscan Table: Food, Family and Gender in Twentieth-Century Florence*. New York: Routledge.

Curtin, W. D., and L. M. Heldke, eds. 1992. *Cooking, Eating, Thinking: Transformative Philosophies of Food*. Bloomington: Indiana University Press.

De la Peña Brown, M. H. 1981. Una Tamalada: The Special Event. *Western Folklore* 40:64–71.

Domosh, M. and J. Seager, eds. 2001. *Putting Women in Place: Feminist Geographers Make Sense of the World*. New York: The Guilford Press.

Engels, F. 1942. *The Origin of the Family, Private Property, and the State*. New York: International Publishers.

Ferrero, S. 2002. "Comida sin par: Consumption of Mexican Food in Los Angeles: Foodscapes in a Transnational Consumer Society." In *Food Nations: Selling Taste in Consumer Societies*, eds. W. Belasco and P. Scranton. pp. 194–219. New York: Routledge.

Hollins, S. T. L., Pershing, and M. J. Young, eds. 1993. *Feminist Theory and the Study of Folklore*. Urbana: University of Illinois Press.

Haber, B. 2005. "Cooking to Survive: The Careers of Alice Foote MacDougall and Cleora Butler." In *From Betty Crocker to Feminist Food Studies: Critical Perspectives on Women and Food*, eds. A. V. Avakian and B. Haber, pp. 89–105. Massachusetts: University of Massachusetts Press.

Hauck-Lawson, A. 1992. Hearing the Food Voice: An Epiphany for a Researcher. *Digest: An Interdisciplinary Study of Food and Foodways* 12 (1,2):6–7.

———. 1998. When Food Is the Voice: Case Study of a Polish-American Woman. *Journal of the Study of Food and Society* 2(10): 21–28.

Heldke, M. L. 2003. *Exotic Appetites: Ruminations of a Food Adventurer*. New York: Routledge.

Hooks, B. 1990. Yearning: Race, Gender, and Cultural Politics. Boston, MA: South End Press.

Inness, A. S. ed. 2001. *Kitchen Culture in America: Popular Representations of Food, Gender, and Race*. Philadelphia: UP Pennsylvania.

———. 2001. Ed. *Pilaf, Pozole, and Pad Thai: American Women and Ethnic Foods*. Amherst: UP Massachusetts.

Jaramillo, C. M. 1981. *The Genuine New Mexico Tasty Recipes*. Santa Fe, New Mexico: Ancient City Press.

Julier, P. A. 2004. Entangled in Our Meals: Guilt and Pleasure in Contemporary Food Discourses. *Food, Culture, & Society: An International Journal of Multidisciplinary Research* 7 (1): 13–21.

Kavasch, E. B. 1997. "My Grandmother's Hands." *Through the Kitchen Window: Women Explore* the Intimate Meanings of Food and Cooking, ed. A. V. Avakian. Boston: Beacon Press, pp. 104–108.

Keremitsis, D. 1983. "Del metate al molino: La mujer mexicana de 1910–1940." Historia Mexicana 33 (October–December): 385–302.

Khare, R. S. ed. 1992. The Eternal Fool: Gastronomic Ideas and Experiences of Hindu and Buddhists. New York: SUNY Press.

Lamphere, L., H. Ragoné, and P. Zavella. 1997. Situated Lives: Gender and Culture in Everyday Life. New York: Routledge.

Olson, K., and L. Shopes. 1991. "Crossing Boundaries, Building Bridges: Doing Oral History among Working-Class Women and Men." In Women's Words: The Feminist Practice of Oral History. Eds. Sherna Berger Gluck and Daphne Patai. New York: Routledge, pp. 189–204.

Pérez, L. R. 2004. "Kitchen Table Ethnography and Feminist Anthropology." Conference Paper. The Association for the Study and Food and Society (ASFS) and The Agriculture, Food, and Human Value Society (AFHVS). The Culinary Institute of America. Hype Park, New York.

Pilcher, J. 2005. "The Chili Queen of San Antonio, 1943." Conference Paper. Southwest/Texas Popular Culture and American Culture Association Conference Albuquerque, New Mexico.

——. 1998. Que Vivan los Tamales! Food and the Making of Mexican Identity. Albuquerque: University of New Mexico Press.

Pinedo, E. 2003. Encarnación's Kitchen: Mexican Recipes from Nineteenth-Century California. California: California University Press.

Ravel, J.-F. 1982. Culture and Cuisine: A Journey Through the History of Food. Trans., H. R. Lane. Garden City New York: Doubleday.

Ruiz, L. V. 1998. From Out of the Shadows: Mexican Women in Twentieth-Century America. New York: Oxford University Press.

Simon, S. 2003. Sweet and Sour: Life-Worlds of Taipei Women Entrepreneurs. New York: Rowman & Littlefield Publishers, Inc.

Shapiro, L. 2004. Something from the Oven: Reinventing Dinner in 1950s America. New York: Viking.

Shiva, V. 1992. "Development, Ecology, and Women." In Cooking, Eating, Thinking: Transformative Philosophies of Food. eds. D. W. Curtin and L. M. Heldke. Bloomington: Indiana University Press, pp. 336–346.

Smith, D. 1990. The Conceptual Practices of Power: A Feminist Sociology of Knowledge. Boston: Northeastern University Press.

Smith Tuhiwai, L. 1999. Decolonizing Methodologies: Research and Indigenous Peoples. New York: Zed Books Ltd.

Symons, M. 2004. A History of Cooks and Cooking. Chicago: University of Illinois Press.

The Latina Feminist Group. 2001. Telling to Live: Latina Feminist Testimonios. Durham: Duke University Press.

Voski Avakian, A., and B. Haber, eds. 2005. From Betty Crocker to Feminist Food Studies: Critical Prespectives on Women and Food. Boston, MA: University of Massachusetts Press.

Williams-Forson, P. A. 2006. Building House Out of Chicken Legs: Black Women, Food, & Power. Chapel Hill: University of North Carolina Press.

——. 2001. "Suckin' the Chicken Bone Dry': African American Women, Fried Chicken, and the Power of a National Narrative." In Cooking Lessons: The Politics of Gender and Food, ed. S. A. Inness. New York: Rowman & Littlefield Publishers, Inc., pp. 169–191.

Whitaker, J. 2005. "Domesticating the Restaurant: Marketing the Anglo-American Home." In From Betty Crocker to Feminist Food Studies: Critical Perspectives on Women and Food, eds. A. V. Avakian and B. Haber. Massachusetts: University of Massachusetts Press, pp. 89–105.

Zafar, R. 2002. "The Signifying Dish: Autobiography and History in Two Black Women's Cookbooks." In Food in the USA: A Reader, ed. C. M. Counihan. New York: Routledge, pp. 249–262.3

SECTION 2

Rethinking Food Consumption

9

Inequality in Obesigenic Environments: Fast Food Density in New York City

Naa Oyo A. Kwate, Chun-Yip Yau, Ji-Meng Loh, and
Donya Williams

INTRODUCTION

Public discourse and public health research on obesity have intensified in the wake of marked increases in US obesity rates, increases that have been particularly acute among the disadvantaged (Drewnowski and Specter, 2004). For African Americans, obesity is endemic—the National Health and Nutrition Examination Survey (NHANES) gave prevalence rates at 45% in 2003–2004 (Ogden et al., 2006). Given that many African Americans are obese, and that in most US cities, African Americans reside in segregated neighborhoods, it is not surprising that research has documented an association between residential segregation and obesity. However, this association is not purely compositional in nature. Although Blacks are 1.7 times as likely as Whites to be obese, they are 3.1 times as likely to reside in relatively obese communities, and individuals living in neighborhoods with high proportions of obese residents are more likely to be obese themselves, net of individual-level factors (Boardman et al., 2005). A positive association also exists between BMI and metropolitan area level segregation after adjusting for compositional differences in socioeconomic and other factors. Compared to a person living at the lowest level of segregation (isolation index = 0.25). the odds of being overweight increased by 77% for residents living in areas with the highest level of segregation (isolation index = 0.83) (Chang, 2006).

These studies point towards the role of social processes as mediators of associations between segregation and overweight/obesity, including institutional forces other than the concentration of poverty. A likely mediator is the food environment in Black neighborhoods. Environments that promote high energy intake and sedentary behavior have been described as obesogenic (Swinburn et al., 1999) (also termed obesigenic). Research on the food environment in Black neighborhoods has focused on access to resources that mitigate against obesity—supermarkets and high-quality produce. These studies show that access is often inadequate for African Americans (Horowitz et al., 2004; Inagami et al., 2006; Lewis et al., 2005; Morland et al., 2002; Schulz et al., 2005; Zenk et al., 2005). Less research has been conducted on disparities in the availability of fast food, despite its implication in overweight and obesity. Fast food is high in calories, fat, and cholesterol (French et al., 2000), has an extremely high energy-density profile (Prentice and Jebb, 2003), and is often served in large portion sizes (Brownell and Battle Horgen, 2003; Nestle, 2002). Some research has begun to investigate obesity-related correlates of fast food density and consumption, documenting associations with weight gain, insulin resistance, overweight/obesity, and acute coronary syndromes (Alter and Eny, 2005; Bowman and Vinyard, 2004; Jeffrey et al., 2006; Pereira et al., 2005).

Fast food consumption has been found to be a strong contributor of dietary fat among African American women (Daroszewski, 2004), and between 1985–1986 and 2000–2001, Blacks frequented fast food restaurants (FFR) significantly more often than Whites (Pereira et al., 2005). These consumption levels may stem from greater availability of fast food in neighborhoods rather than from greater intrinsic demand. As in international settings (Cummins et al., 2005; Macdonald et al., 2007; Reidpath et al., 2002), US research on disparities in fast food density has focused on area income. This research has tended to document the inverse relationships between income and fast food exposure that have been observed internationally (Burdette and Whitaker, 2004; Morland et al., 2002; Zenk and Powell, 2008). However, other studies have reported that middle- and high-income neighborhoods have greater numbers and proximity to fast food (Austin et al., 2005; Wang et al., 2007).

Anecdotal evidence of low diversity of dining options in African American neighborhoods has been borne out by empirical research (Lewis et al., 2005), but less research has investigated fast food prevalence as a function of neighborhood racial demographics. It has been argued that residential segregation works to increase the density of fast food in Black neighborhoods by creating localized geographic market areas, fostering economic, business, and land use characteristics that promote fast food, concentrating available labor pools, and weakening community political strength that would be deployed to oppose fast food siting (Kwate, 2008). Some research does show fast food to be more prevalent in Black neighborhoods. In New Orleans census tracts with at least 2000 people per square mile, fast food density (the number of restaurants per square mile in geographically described shopping areas) was predicted only by percent Black. On average, predominantly Black neighborhoods contained 2.4 FFR per square

mile, while White neighborhoods contained 1.5 (Block et al., 2004). In contrast, Zenk and Powell (2008) found that nationwide, Black neighborhoods had 30% less restaurants than White neighborhoods, and in the 20 largest cities. Black, neighborhoods had 44% less. Morland et al. (2002) and Powell et al. (2007a) found fast food to be more prevalent in racially mixed and predominantly White, rather than Black neighborhoods.

The mixed findings indicate the need for additional investigations of racial disparities in fast food density. There is also little available data on the distribution of fast food *within* predominantly Black neighborhoods that vary in income level. Fast food is inexpensive, takes less waiting time, and has a restricted menu, and thus should appeal to individuals with low income, those in a hurry, and people with simple and consistent food preferences (Brown, 1990). For that reason, it is often argued that the high densities of fast food in Black neighborhoods simply reflect the marketing of an inexpensive product in low-income areas. In this case, predominantly Black neighborhoods with higher incomes, should have lower densities of fast food than those with low incomes. However, if fast food density is driven primarily by neighborhood racial demographics, income should show less relative effect on the restaurant environment.

It also bears studying how density patterns map onto (multi)national chains compared to locally operated independent outlets. National supermarket chains are fewer in Black neighborhoods (Powell et al., 2007b; Sloane et al., 2003); the same may be true for national fast food outlets. One reason this might be so is because franchises of national chains require significant accumulated assets and expenditures for start-up. For example, though relatively few new franchisees obtain new stores, opening a new McDonald's store requires an initial fee of $45,000, plus equipment and pre-operating costs ranging from $685,750 to

$1,504,000 depending on such factors as the size of the restaurant, the area of the country, and the landscaping needed ("New Restaurants", 2007). After an initial outlay of 40% of the cost, the remainder may be financed through traditional means. Most franchisees purchase an existing restaurant, which requires a minimum 25% cash down payment, with the rest financed over a maximum of 7 years ("Existing Restaurants", 2007). In either case, all store owners must possess a minimum of $250,000 in personal, non-borrowed assets in order to open a restaurant ("Purchasing Your Restaurant", 2007). Given that franchisees in Black neighborhoods have often been African American or affiliated with African American institutions (Love, 1995; Roberts, 1987; Schlosser, 2001), but Blacks have significantly less wealth than Whites (Conley, 1999; Shapiro, 2005), the financial requirements for franchising may act as a barrier to their operation.

Thus, we sought to investigate inequalities in the density of fast food in New York City (NYC), the most populous, and a highly segregated US city. Our aims were fourfold. First, we investigated whether fast food density was positively associated with the percentage of Black residents in the city's census block groups, and whether an interaction with area income was evident. Second, we investigated whether predominantly Black block groups showed variability in fast food density by income. Third, we examined whether predominantly Black and White areas with similar income levels had similar densities of fast food. Fourth, we investigated whether predictors of restaurant density differed for national chains compared to local outlets. We hypothesized that fast food density would be positively associated with the proportion of Black residents; that there would be no relationship between area income and fast food density in predominantly Black areas; that Black areas would have higher fast food density than comparable White

areas; and that the relationship between percentage Black and fast food density would be strongest for local outlets.

METHOD

Geography

We examined fast food density in the 5730 census block groups comprising NYC's five boroughs; Manhattan, Brooklyn, Queens, The Bronx, and Staten Island. In 2000, NYC had 8,008,278 residents, of whom 24.5% were Black, 27% Latino, 35% White, and 9.8% Asian, and the median household income was $38,909 (New York City Department of City Planning, 2005). Although NYC is diverse in its racial/ethnic composition, it remains highly segregated. NYC's Black residents generally reside in large, clustered, racially concentrated neighborhoods in the Bronx (particularly the Northeast section), Central Harlem, Central Brooklyn, and Southeast Queens.

Data Sources

Fast Food Restaurants

FFRs were defined as national chains and local establishments that: (1) do not provide table service; (2) serve patrons at a cash register or drive-thru window; (3) require payment before eating (National Restaurant Association, 2005); and (4) whose primary menu items were hamburgers, hot dogs, and fried chicken. Restaurant addresses were obtained from The NYC Department of Health and Mental Hygiene's on-line directory of restaurant inspections (New York City Department of Health and Mental Hygiene, 2005). The Department conducts inspections of all food service establishments in the city, and the most recent results are posted by name, borough, and zip code. We searched the directory for the following national chains: McDonald's, Burger King, Kentucky Fried Chicken, Wendy's, White Castle, and Popeye's. We then searched for common local chains[1] (e.g.. Crown Fried Chicken, Kennedy Fried Chicken). Finally, restaurants that were neither national nor local chains were included if their names contained any of our target menu items (e.g., "Frankfurter House" or "Joe's Fried Chicken"). Chinese take-out is often viewed by community residents as fast food (Pierre, 1993), and research in Los Angeles found that for African American women, Chinese and Mexican take-out contributed a substantial portion of dietary fat (Daroszewski, 2004). Given the ubiquity of Chinese take-out in NYC, and the frequency with which these restaurants sell fast food items such as fried chicken wings and French fries, we could have considered these outlets as fast food as well. We did not, because although they may serve less nutritious foods, they still tend to have a greater variety of options that are healthier than fast food (e.g., rice with steamed vegetables). Additionally, because we obtained restaurant locations from online databases, we were not able to parse out which Chinese restaurants were "fast food-like", and which were formal sit-down restaurants with a greater variety of options.

City Infrastructure and Demographics

Data on zoning was obtained from NYC tax lot base map files. Data on consumer expenditures were based on a derivation of the US Bureau of Labor Statistic's Consumer Expenditure Survey (supplied by a commercial GIS firm). We used data on average household expenditures for food away from home (lunch and dinner) for the year 2006. Area income and racial composition were derived from the 2000 US Census Summary Files 1 (SF-1) and 3 (SF-3) and also supplied by the GIS firm.

A comparison of 2000 census data and estimates for the year 2006 revealed very high inter-correlations. Thus, we used 2000 data in order to allow comparison to other studies. Also, as previous research has defined "predominantly Black" areas as >70% and >80% Black (Morland et al., 2002; Zenk and Powell, 2008). we defined predominantly Black block groups as those with a percentage Black >70%. The commercial GIS firm completed geocoding of fast food data, assignation of zoning class to block groups, construction of fast food density (described below), and importation of census data.

Defining the Outcome Variable

One commonly used assessment of the density of neighborhood features (e.g., alcohol ads) is the number of points per 1000 residents at a particular geographic level (e.g., block group). However, simply adding the total number of sites in a given block group fails to take into account block group size and does not account for the fact that facilities affect residents in adjacent block groups (Downey, 2003). Thus, we employed a more inclusive method of quantifying exposure, which has previously been applied to mapping hazardous manufacturing facilities. After initial mapping, block groups were overlain with a custom grid demarcating smaller cells measuring 60 × 60 m^2 (approximately 1/2 of a NYC block). Next, we calculated the number of restaurants within a 300 m radius from the center of each cell in the grid and this count value was assigned to each cell. The sum of values for all cells in the block group were divided by the number of cells, yielding the average exposure for the block group (Downey, 2003). In our analyses of national vs. local outlets, average exposure for national chains was computed by taking the sum of average exposure values for Burger King, McDonald's, Wendy's, White Castle,

Kentucky Fried Chicken, and Popeye's. Average exposure for local outlets was computed by taking the sum of average exposure values for local chains and local individual outlets.

Analytic Plan

Our primary dependent variable was average exposure to FFR, as described above. We were interested in modeling FFR of each block as a function of block group characteristics (covariates). The primary covariate of interest was percent Black (BLK) and the remaining variables were: median age (AGE); population density, operationalized as persons per square mile (POP); percent White (WHT); median household income (MHI); average expenditures on lunch away from home (LUNCH); average expenditures on dinner away from home (DINNER); and zoning (ZONE). We modeled FFR by means of generalized additive models.

Generalized additive models can be described as non-parametric versions of generalized linear models (McCullagh and Nelder, 1989). In generalized linear models, a function of the mean of the dependent variable is expressed as a linear function of covariates, allowing for the possibility of non-Gaussian errors (e.g., Poisson or binomial). In generalized additive models, the relation between the dependent variable and the covariates is neither linear nor parametric, and thus allows for more flexibility. Fitting a generalized additive model involves estimating the non-parametric function linking each covariate to the dependent variable. Unlike generalized linear models, the dependence between response variables and covariates in generalized additive models are interpreted in terms of non-parametric functions rather than regression coefficients.

Specifically, define λ_k to be the expected value of FFR for the kth block group. With (x_k, y_k) representing the location of the block group and $COV1_k, \ldots, COVr_k$ representing the covariates, we fit the model

$$\begin{aligned} \log \lambda_k = {} & s_{xy}(x_k, y_k) + s_1(COV1_k) \\ & + s_2(COV2_k) + \ldots \\ & + s_r(COVr_k) \end{aligned} \tag{1}$$

using Poisson errors. We chose to model the errors as Poisson because FFR is essentially a measure of the number of restaurants. In Eq. (1) above, the s_i's are non-parametric smooth functions of individual covariates. Given data, these functions can be estimated, for example, using the *gam* function (Hastie and Tibshirani, 1990).

We selected the covariates that rendered the model (1) the best fit for the data by adding covariates in turn and testing at each step whether the new covariate was statistically significant. Specifically, let model 0 be the current model and model 1 be the model with a new covariate added, and let their deviances be D0 and D1, respectively. Then D0–D1 has an asymptotic χ^2 distribution. A large value of D0–D1 indicates that the new covariate is significant. For more details, see Hastie and Tibshirani (1990). Note that two-way interactions can be modeled by including functions of two covariates s_{ij} into Eq. (1).

Spatial information was included in the model in two ways. Firstly, the inclusion of the location of the block group as a covariate allows for modeling of any spatial trend that might be present in the data. Since we are modeling this non-parametrically, fairly complex spatial trends can be captured with very little prior assumptions about the actual structure. Secondly, some spatial correlation is captured through the covariates, which are themselves spatially correlated. It is possible that some residual spatial correlation that was not included in the covariates exists, and this would result in correlated errors. However, we expect the effect on our results to be small.

Furthermore, positive spatial correlation will tend to even out variations in FFR and reduce significance of estimates. Thus if residual spatial correlation is present, the estimates of the regression coefficients would be less efficient, making the estimates from model (1) more significant than we observed (Chatterjee et al., 2000). We are currently working on using an alternate method, using point process theory to model the actual locations of restaurants. Differences in results between these two models will better enable us to quantify the effect of correlated errors.

RESULTS

Descriptive Results

There were 802 fast food outlets across the five boroughs. Many block groups were not exposed to fast food, and exposure was highest in the areas of the city where the proportion of Black residents was high,[2] as well as in central business and commercial districts, transportation hubs and tourist areas (e.g., Wall Street, Port Authority, Times Square). Because these commercial areas have relatively few residents but many FFRs, we excluded them from our regression analyses. To do so, we excluded these areas based on zoning. NYC tax lots are zoned residential, commercial or manufacturing, with overlays among them to varying degrees. In order to quantify zoning at the block group level, we assigned each block group the zoning code of the tax lot closest to the block group centroid. Using NYC zoning codes, we excluded block groups that were zoned as central commercial districts (offices and retail that serve the entire metropolitan region), high-bulk commercial districts (e.g., corporate headquarters, large hotels, entertainment facilities), parks, amusement parks, and heavy manufacturing industry. Five thousand five hundred and

twelve block groups remained in the analyses, and were categorized into four zoning groups. The first three corresponded to the NYC Department of City Planning residential classifications of lower density (R-1 to R-5B), medium density (R6HF to R7x), and higher density (R8HF to R10x) (NYC Department of City Planning, 2006). We also included a fourth category that comprised manufacturing and the remaining commercial zones.

Aim 1: Relationship between percent Black and fast food density

To study the relationship between proportion of Black residents and density of FFRs, model (1) was fitted and the model

$$\log \lambda_k = s_{xy}(x_k, y_k) + s_1(\mathrm{BLK}_k) + s_2(\mathrm{MHI}_k) + s_3(\mathrm{POP}_k) \qquad (2)$$

produced the best fit, with the other covariates (median age, % White, and food expenditures) not statistically significant. This model accounted for 59.23% of the deviance in fast food density.

In terms of exposure to fast-food restaurants, median household income appeared to be non-significant except that there was a mild protective effect for the block groups with a median household income of $0–$40,000. Population density was not a significant factor in exposure to fast-food restaurants.

The expected exposure of FFRs increased with the proportion of Black residents in the block group. The strong positive effect of percent Black stood in marked contrast to the other covariates. Next, we investigated possible interactions between percent Black and area income. This can be done by comparing model (2) with

$$\log \lambda_k = s_{xy}(x_k, y_k) + s_1(\mathrm{BLK}_k) + s_2(\mathrm{MHI}_k) + s_3(\mathrm{POP}_k) + s_4(\mathrm{BLK}_k, \mathrm{MHI}) \qquad (3)$$

to test whether the additional interaction term $s_4(\text{BLK}_k, \text{MHI})$ is significant. Here $s_4(\text{BLK}_k, \text{MHI})$ is a two-dimensional smoothing surface for BLK and MHI which can describe a very general cross effect between these two variables.

Model (3) accounted for 72% of the deviance in fast food density. Nevertheless, a model comparison between model (3) and model (2) using deviance test shows that the additional interaction term of percent Black and median household income does not significantly improve model (2), ($p = 0.155$).

Aim 2: Median household income and fast food density in predominantly Black areas

To investigate whether fast food density was similar among predominantly Black block groups of varied area incomes, we restricted the analysis to block groups that were >70% Black, and fit a modified version of model (2), in which we omitted percent Black as a predictor. In addition, because the predominantly Black block groups with the highest median incomes (primarily Southeast Queens) are more suburban in nature, we added population density to control for this possible confound.

The final model was:

$$\log \lambda_k = s_{xy}(x_k, y_k) + s_1(\text{MHI}_k) + s_2(\text{POP}_k) \qquad (4)$$

This model accounted for 59.51% of the deviance in fast food density. All variables were statistically significant. As shown in Figure 9.4, the significant effect for income was a slight inverse relationship between median household income and fast food density at the lowest end of the income spectrum (approximately $0–$20,000). Otherwise there was no effect of median household income on fast food density in predominantly Black block groups. As before, the wide

confidence intervals at very high income levels are due to very few observations. Population density was positively correlated with fast food density, as expected.

Aim 3: Fast food density in Black and White areas with similar median household incomes

To investigate whether block groups that were predominantly White had the same exposure to fast food as predominantly Black block groups matched on median household income, we compared analyses in which we stratified all block groups into low (<$25,000), medium ($25,000–$550,000), or high (>$50,000) median household income, and considered the effects of percentage Black or percentage White within each. We fit model (2) with these three categories, giving

$$\log \lambda_k = s_{xy}(x_k, y_k) + s_1(\text{BLK}_{1,k}) \\ + s_1(\text{BLK}_{2,k}) + s_1(\text{BLK}_{3,k}) \\ + s_2(\text{MHI}_k) + s_3(\text{POP}_k) \qquad (5)$$

and

$$\log \lambda_k = s_{xy}(x_k), y_k + s_1(\text{WHT}_{1,k}) \\ + s_1(\text{WHT}_{2,k}) + s_1(\text{WHT}_{3,k}) \\ + s_2(\text{MHI}_k) + s_3(\text{POP}_k) \qquad (6)$$

At low- and medium-income groups, percent Black was always positively related to fast food density, and percent White was always negatively related. For both groups, there was no association between race and fast food density at high-income levels. Further, using the function predict.gam() in SPlus (version 7.0—Windows), we may predict the value of fast food density for a hypothetical situation. For example, a block group that is 80% White, with coordinates (–73.95, 40.85), a median household income of $20,000 and a population density of 50,000 persons per square mile yields a predicted fast food density of 0.055. On the other hand, if the percentage Black is 0.8, the predicted fast food density is 0.627. The same picture emerges in high-income areas. With the same location and population, but with an area income of \$80,000, the predicted fast food density will be 0.048 and 0.503 for block groups that are 80% White, and 80% Black, respectively. Both examples illustrate that percent Black and White have large and opposite effects on fast food density.

Aim 4: National chains and local outlets

To compare the national chains and local outlets, we fit model (1) two times, with the expected value of fast food density λk replaced with λ_k^L and λ_k^N, the expected values for local and national outlets, respectively. For local outlets, the best fit model is

$$\log \lambda_k^L = s_{xy}(x_k, y_k) + s_1(\text{BLK}_k) \\ + s_2(\text{MHI}_k) + s_3(\text{POP}_k) \qquad (7)$$

which is similar to that for the overall analysis (model (2)). This is to be expected because local FFRs constituted the majority of all FFRs. The effects were all significant and with p-values near 0. This model accounted for 77.58% of the deviance in local fast food density.

For national outlets, the best fitting model is

$$\log \lambda_k^N = s_{xy}(x_k, y_k) + s_1(\text{BLK}_k) \\ + \text{ZONE}_k \qquad (8)$$

Again, all effects were significant with p-values near 0. This model accounted for 4.10% of the deviance in national chain fast food density. The small proportion of deviance accounted for by the model is due to the relatively small number of national restaurants in the dataset. In contrast to model (3), median household income and population density were unrelated to fast food density, but zoning was significant, such that national chains were least dense in low-density

residential and most dense in commercial/manufacturing.

DISCUSSION

We found that percent Black in NYC's block groups was positively associated with fast food density, and this association was stronger than any other covariate, including median household income. We also found that with the exception of high-income block groups, in which no association was found between racial demographics and fast food density, the prevalence of fast food was always negatively related to percent White, and positively related to percent Black. Additionally, to our knowledge, this is the first study to report on the association between area income and fast food density within predominantly Black areas. Our results do not lend support to the idea that fast food is prevalent in Black neighborhoods simply because these areas are often low in income—more affluent predominantly Black areas had similar exposure to fast food as those of other income levels after controlling for relevant confounders. Taken together, these results starkly outline the role of racial segregation in shaping fast food exposure for Blacks and Whites in US cities.

We also found that national chains were least dense in low-density residential areas and most dense in commercial/manufacturing zones. Given that these areas are frequented by key target groups such as tourists, workers on lunch breaks, and shoppers, it is clear why national chains would be located in commercial districts. On the other hand, smaller, independent outlets would not be likely to operate in high-rent, business districts. Instead, "rickety fast-food joints" (Kleinenberg, 2002, p. 92) are often staples of the restaurant landscape in urban communities of color.

Our findings on percent Black as a predictor of fast food density are discrepant from some studies, with the exception of Block et al. (2004). Other research has found fast food to be more prevalent in racially mixed or predominantly White neighborhoods. The discrepant findings may be due in part to variation in fast food definitions across studies. For example, Block et al. (2004) examined only well-known national chains with two or more sites in the study area, and one local chain with five outlets. Food types included hamburgers, fried chicken, pizza and submarine sandwiches. Morland et al. (2002) used NAICS codes to extract business data on franchised fast food shops, pizza parlors and pizza delivery shops. Finally, Zenk and Powell (2008) and Powell et al. (2007a) obtained restaurant information from Dun & Bradstreet (D&B) for FFRs and stands. This category included fast food chains and independent outlets, but also a range of other restaurants, including delicatessens, sandwich and submarine shops, chili stands, grills, and carryout restaurants (not including pizza). Many of these restaurant types (e.g., pizza parlors, sandwich shops) are more likely to be located in predominantly White neighborhoods. For example, in NYC the sandwich chain Subway is most dense in predominantly White residential areas and commercial districts (map available upon request). Thus, the inclusion of such restaurants may skew associations between racial demographics and fast food prevalence. Business databases such as D&B may also contain more data for major chains than for the "rickety joints" often found in Black neighborhoods. For example, we searched D&B's "Million Dollar Database" and found McDonald's to be readily identified, but one local chain, Crown Fried Chicken, was not listed. Thus, in some studies, Black neighborhoods may appear to have fewer fast food outlets than is actually the case.

Some study limitations should be noted. First, because we obtained restaurant data from an online database of prior inspections, we are unable to determine whether all outlets continue to be in operation. There may also have been restaurants in operation that had not yet been inspected, and these would therefore not appear in our tallies. Second, in order to capture local outlets, we included restaurants that had specific menu items in the restaurant name. This may have resulted in under-inclusion if the target restaurants used names without reference to the menu (e.g., "Jane's Place"). It may also have resulted in over-inclusion, as sit-down restaurants such as grills, coffee shops, and fast-casuals may have included menu items in the store name (e.g., "Deluxe Burger"). However, because communities of color have fewer of these restaurants, over-inclusion would overestimate exposure in predominantly White areas, rendering our findings an underestimate of the observed relationships. Third, our measure of exposure is based purely on geographic location. Store fascias may be an important determinant of the relationship between density and area demographics (Macdonald et al., 2007), and also shape consumer access. Thus, if many of the locations in a given block group are primarily drive-thrus that serve few pedestrians, the effective exposure level for neighborhood residents may be lower. Relatedly, a block group's average exposure may include proximal restaurants that are not practically accessible (e.g., on the other side of train tracks or topographical barriers). However, in NYC, we do not anticipate this to be a significant limitation given the nature of the built environment and the characteristics of most fast food outlets.

We used a radius of 300m when computing the fast food exposure measure. We chose this because it was a reasonable walking distance. We did not explore the effects of changing this distance, although we suspect that changing the distance to 200 or 400m would make little difference to our findings. Finally, as mentioned before, we did not include correlated errors in our model. Unmodeled correlated errors would reduce the significance of estimates. Since our analysis already shows a clear relationship between percent Black and fast food exposure, introducing correlated errors in our models should not make significant changes to our findings. The non-significant relationship between fast food density and median income at the very high incomes, is due to the small number of block groups at these very high incomes. Introducing correlation in the errors might reduce the size of these confidence bands but probably not enough to make any observed relationship statistically significant.

Thus, despite some study limitations, our findings have important implications for public health. We showed that predominantly Black areas were dense in restaurant outlets serving menu items that increase the risk of overweight and obesity, and obesity rates in NYC's predominantly Black neighborhoods range from 21% to 34% (NYC and Department of Mental Health and Hygiene, 2003). The potential impact of restaurant dining on health is not trivial. In 2001, approximately 42% of total food expenditures were spent on food away from home (Bowman and Vinyard, 2004) and this figure continues to rise. The numbers of FFRs have also increased dramatically in recent years (Powell et al., 2007b).

Municipalities are beginning to consider legislative means through which to shape the restaurant landscape. In some cities, zoning codes have centered around concerns about planning and architectural character. For example, Warner, New Hampshire regulates the distance within which fast food outlets may locate from each other (Mair et al., 2005). While the codes are not meant to remediate obesity rates, they may have such an impact nonetheless. Other cities have actively addressed the role of fast food in population health. In NYC, a recent ruling requires chain restaurants to post information on calorie content

for menu items ("No More Dining", 2008). In Los Angeles, a moratorium on additional FFRs has been proposed for South L.A., a predominantly Black and Latino area with a high saturation of fast food and a high prevalence rate of obesity (Abdollah, 2007). Other interventions might include the use of conditional use permits to encourage restaurants to improve the nutritional quality of menu items, and to displace outlets that do not improve (Ashe et al., 2003). Our data highlight the need for attention to these, and other policy interventions as potential strategies to remediate disparities in food environments.

ACKNOWLEDGMENTS

Completion of the manuscript was supported in part by grants from the Department of Defense, The US Army Medical Research and Materiel Command (W81XWH-04-1-0829) and from the Robert Wood Johnson Foundation's Healthy Eating Research Program (63155). Dr. Kwate is an NIH National Center on Minority Health and Health Disparities Scholar. We would like to thank Sharneque Sylvester for her assistance in data collection.

NOTES

1. Although we use the word "chains", we do not mean to imply operations that are recognized franchising companies. These restaurants are outlets that have several locations in the city, but are likely sole proprietorships or partnerships.
2. Latinos also comprise much of the population in the Bronx.

REFERENCES

Abdollah, T., 2007. Limits proposed on fast-food restaurants. The Los Angeles Times, 10 September 2007.

Alter, D.A., Eny, K., 2005. The relationship between the supply of fast-food chains and cardiovascular outcomes. Canadian Journal of Public Health 96 (3), 173–177.

Ashe, M., Jernigan, D., Kline, R., Galaz, R., 2003. Land use planning and the control of alcohol, tobacco, firearms, and fast food restaurants. American Journal of Public Health 93, 1404–1408.

Austin, S.B., Melly, S.J., Sanchez, B.N., Patel, A., Buka, S., Gortmaker, S.L., 2005. Clustering of fast-food restaurants around schools: a novel application of spatial statistics to the study of food environments. American Journal of Public Health 95, 1575–1581.

Block, J., Scribner, R., DeSalvo, K., 2004. Fast food, race/ethnicity, and income: a geographic analysis. American Journal of Preventive Medicine 27 (3), 211–217.

Boardman, J.D., Saint Onge. J.M., Rogers, R.G., Denney, J.T., 2005. Race differentials in obesity: the impact of place. Journal of Health and Social Behavior 46, 229–243.

Bowman, S.A., Vinyard, B.T., 2004. Fast food consumption of US adults: impact on energy and nutrient intakes and overweight status. Journal of the American College of Nutrition 23 (2), 163–168.

Brown, D.M., 1990. The restaurant and fast food race: who's winning? Southern Economic Journal 56 (4), 969–983.

Brownell, K.D., Battle Horgen, K.B., 2003. Food Fight: The Inside Story or the Food Industry, America's Obesity Crisis, and What We Can Do About It McGraw-Hill, New York.

Burdette, H.L, Whitaker, R.C., 2004. Neighborhood playgrounds, fast food restaurants, and crime: relationships to overweight in low-income preschool children. Preventive Medicine 38, 57–63.

Chang, V.W., 2006. Racial residential segregation and weight status among US adults. Social Science and Medicine 63, 1289–1303.

Chatterjee, S., Hadi, A., Price, B., 2000. Regression Analysis and Example, third ed. Wiley, New York.

Conley, D., 1999. Being Black, Living in the Red: Race, Wealth, and Social Policy in America. University of California Press, Berkeley, CA.

Cummins. S.C.J., McKay, L., Macintyre, S., 2005. McDonald's restaurants and neighborhood deprivation in Scotland and England. American Journal of Preventive Medicine 29 (4), 308–310.

Daroszewski, E.B., 2004. Dietary fat consumption, readiness to change, and ethnocultural association to midlife African American women. Journal of Community Health Nursing 21 (2), 63–75.

Downey, L., 2003. Spatial measurement, geography, and urban racial inequality. Social Forces 81 (3), 937–952.

Drewnowski, A., Specter, S.E., 2004. Poverty and obesity: the role of energy density and energy costs. American Journal of Clinical Nutrition 79, 6–16.

Existing Restaurants. Retrieved 12 December 2007, from <http://www.mcdonalds.com/corp/franchise/purchasingYourFranchise/existingrestaurants.html>.

French, S.A., Harnack, L., Jeffrey. R.W., 2000. Fast food restaurant use among women in the Pound of Prevention study: dietary, behavioral, and demographic correlates. International Journal of Obesity 24, 1353–1359.

Hastie. T., Tibshirani, R., 1990. Generalized Additive Models. Chapman & Hall, London.

Horowitz, C.R., Colson, K.A., Herbert, P.L., Lancaster, K., 2004. Barriers to buying healthy foods for people with diabetes: evidence of environmental disparities. American Journal of Public Health 94, 1549–1554.

Inagami, S., Cohen, D.A., Finch, B.K., Asch, S.M., 2006. You are where you shop: grocery store locations, weight, and neighborhoods. American Journal of Preventive Medicine 31 (1), 10–17.

Jeffrey, R.W., Baxter, J., McGuire, M., Linde, J., 2006. Are fast food restaurants an environmental risk factor for obesity? International Journal of Behavioral Nutrition and Physical Activity 3 (2).

Kleinenberg, E., 2002. Heat Wave: A Social Autopsy of Disaster in Chicago. University of Chicago Press, Chicago, IL.

Kwate, N.O.A., 2008. Fried chicken and fresh apples: racial segregation as a fundamental cause of fast food density in Black neighborhoods. Health and Place 14 (1), 32–44.

Lewis, L.B., Sloane, D.C., Nascimento, L.M., Diamant, A.L., Guinyard, J.J., Yancey, A.K., et al., 2005. African Americans' access to healthy food options in South Los Angeles restaurants. American Journal of Public Health 95 (4), 668–673.

Love, J.F., 1995. McDonald's: Behind the Arches. Bantam, New York.

Macdonald, L., Cummins, S., Macintyre, S., 2007. Neighborhood fast food environment and area-deprivation—substitution or concentration? Appetite 49 (1), 251–254.

Mair, J.S., Pierce, M.W., Teret, S.P., 2005. The City Planner's Guide to the Obesity Epidemic: Zoning and Fast Food. The Center for Law and the Public's Health, Johns Hopkins & Georgetown Universities.

McCullagh, P., Nelder, J.A., 1989. Generalized Linear Models, second ed. Chapman & Hall, London.

Morland, K., Wing, S., Diez, R.A., Poole, C., 2002. Neighborhood characteristics associated with the location of food stores and food service places. American Journal of Preventive Medicine 22 (1), 23–29.

National Restaurant Association, 2005. Restaurant industry definitions. Retrieved 14 March 2005, from <http://www.restaurant.org/research/definitions.cfm>.

Nestle, M., 2002. Food Politics: How the Food Industry Influences Nutrition and Health. University of California Press, Berkeley and Los Angeles, CA.

New Restaurants. Retrieved 12 December 2007, from <http://www.mcdonalds.com/corp/franchise/purchasingYourFranchise/newRestaurants.html>.

NYC, & Department of Mental Health and Hygiene, 2003. One in 6 NYC adults is obese. NYC Vital Signs 2 (7).

NYC Department of City Planning, 2005. Census FactFinder.

NYC Department of City Planning, 2006. Zoning Handbook. Author, New York.

NYC Department of Health and Mental Hygiene, 2005. Restaurant Inspection Information.

No more dining in the dark (21 April 2008). The New York Times.

Ogden, C.L., Carroll, M.D., Curtin, L.R., McDowell, M.A., Tabak, C.J., Flegal, K.M., 2006. Prevalence of overweight and obesity in the United States, 1999–2004. Journal of American Medical Association 295 (13), 1549–1555.

Pierre, R.E., 1993. Some in Lake Arbor say carryout is unwelcome neighbor. The Washington Post, 6 May 1993.

Pereira, M.A., Kartashov, A.I., Ebbeling, C.B., Van Horn, L., Slattery, M.L., Jacobs, Jr., D.R., et al., 2005. Fast-food habits, weight gain, and insulin resistance (the CARDIA study): 15-year prospective analysis. The Lancet 365, 36–42.

Powell, L.M., Chaloupka, F.J., Bao, Y., 2007a. The availability of fast-food and full-service restaurants in the United States. American Journal of Preventive Medicine 33 (4S), S240–S245.

Powell, L.M., Slater, S., Mirtcheva, D., Bao, Y., Chaloupka, F.J., 2007b. Food store availability and neighborhood characteristics in the United States. Preventive Medicine 44, 189–195.

Prentice, A.M., Jebb, S.A., 2003. Fast foods, energy density and obesity: a possible mechanistic link. Obesity Reviews 4, 187–194.

Purchasing Your Franchise. Retrieved 12 December 2007, from <http://www.mcdonalds.com/corp/franchise/purchasingYourFranchise.html>.

Reidpath, D.D., Burns, C., Garrard, J., Mahoney, M., Townsend, M., 2002. An ecological study of the relationship between social and environmental determinants of obesity. Health and Place 8, 141–145.

Roberts, S., 1987. Brooklyn group serves up hope with fast food. The New York Times, 26 March. Retrieved on 28 April 2008. Available: LEXIS-NEXIS Academic Universe, News.

Schlosser, E., 2001. Fast Food Nation: The Dark Side of the Ail-American Meal. Houghton-Mifflin, Boston.

Schulz, A.J., Zenk, S., Odoms-Young, A., Hollis-Neely, T., Nwankwo, R., Lockert, M., et al., 2005. Healthy eating and exercising to reduce diabetes: exploring the potential of social determinants of health frameworks within the context of community-based participatory diabetes prevention. American Journal of Public Health 95 (4), 645–651.

Shapiro, T.M.M., 2005. The Hidden Cost of Being African American: How Wealth Perpetuates Inequality. Oxford University Press, New York.

Sloane, D.C., Diamant, A.L., Lewis, L.B., Yancey, A.K., Flynn, G., Nascimento, L.M., et al., 2003. Improving the Nutritional Resource Environment for Healthy Living Through Community-Based Participatory Research, vol. 18, pp. 568–575.

Swinburn, B., Egger, G., Raza, F., 1999. Dissecting obesogenic environments: the development and application of a framework for identifying and prioritizing environmental interventions for obesity. Preventive Medicine 29, 563–570.

Wang, M.C., Kim, S., Gonzalez, A.A., MacLeod, K.E., Winkleby, M.A., 2007. Socioeconomic and food-related physical characteristics of the neighbourhood environment are associated with body mass index. Journal of Epidemiology and Community Health 61, 491–498.

Zenk, S.N., Powell, L.M., 2008. US secondary schools and food outlets. Health and Place 14 (2), 336–346.

Zenk, S.N., Schulz, A.J., Hollis-Neely, T., Campbell, R.T., Holmes, N., Watkins, G., et al., 2005. Fruit and vegetable intake in African Americans: income and store characteristics. American Journal of Preventive Medicine 29 (1), 1–9.

10

Physical Disabilities and Food Access Among Limited Resource Households

Caroline B. Webber, Jeffery Sobal, and Jamie S. Dollahite

INTRODUCTION

Food is a basic need for all people, The degree to which people have access to food influences the quantity and quality of food choices they can make, and this has an impact on quality of life, health, and illness (Drewnowski & Specter, 2004; Eikenberry, 2003; Krebs-Smith & Kantor, 2001; Nord *et al.*, 2003; U.S. Department of Health and Human Services, 2000), A disability, as defined by the "Americans with Disabilities Act" ("Americans with Disabilities Act of 1990", 1990), means a physical or mental impairment (or being regarded as having such) that substantially limits one or more of the major life activities of such individuals. However, with the exception of the geriatrics literature (Lee & Frongilio, 2001; Roe, 1990; Smith, 1991; Wolfe *et al.*, 2003; Wylie *et al.*, 1999) and occasional international studies (Guilford *et al.*, 2003), the relationship between physical disabilities and food access, although acknowledged (Campbell, 1991; Olson *et al.*, 2004), has mostly received only cursory examination. Studies examining food access and health condition/status are more common. Stuff *et al.* (2004) found an association between household food insecurity and self-reported health status in adults in the Lower Mississippi Delta region. A Canadian study by Vozoris and Tarasuk (2003) found that individuals from food-insufficient households had significantly higher odds of reporting poor/fair health, of having poor functional health, restricted activity, poor social support, and higher likelihood of chronic diseases and major depression.

Food access is the extent to which consumers (individuals and households), as agents, are able to obtain food for an adequate and acceptable diet; the power to exercise this ability is dynamic and derives from the amount and type of household resources (personal health being a household resource), structural rules (e.g., imposed on those with disabilities), and food landscapes available (Webber, 2005). Food access is individual, variable, and subjective. Food access is an important component of food security, defined as "access by all people at all times to enough food for an active, healthy life and includes at a minimum: (a) the ready availability of nutritionally adequate and safe foods, and (b) the assured ability to acquire acceptable foods in socially acceptable ways e.g., without resorting to emergency food supplies, scavenging, stealing, and other coping strategies" (Anderson, 1990).

The concept of a food landscape is used in a variety of ways (Guptill & Wilkins, 2002; Sobal & Wansink, 2007) and is partly adapted from the geographical concept of landscape (Duncan, 2000). We use food landscape to represent the apparent set of sources of food available in a particular place. Thus a food landscape would include supermarkets, restaurants, vending machines, street vendors, farmers' markets, and other sources of food that a person knows about in a specific locale (Holloway & Kneafsey, 2000). A food landscape is not an objective condition that is uniformly perceived and interpreted by all individuals. It is a relative term, varying for each individual and influenced by their resources, which include health and physical capabilities. What may be an ample food landscape for one person, offering healthful foods like fruits and vegetables, as well as affordable foods, may provide more limited options for someone with disability-related or health problems that limit their mobility. The research reported here examined how low-income food shoppers with health and physical impairments managed food provisioning for their families, and the impact these impairments had on family food choice when resources were limited.

METHODS

This study was part of a larger project investigating relationships between low-income consumers and food retailers (Webber, 2005). In the work reported here, we examined food access and disabilities in an inductive, qualitative study that used ethnographic research methods and a grounded theory approach to capture the experience of grocery shopping. A pilot study and data from previously reported research about grocery shopping among low-income households (Crockett et al., 1992; Furey et al., 2001; MacIntyre et al., 1993; Morris et al., 1992; Travers, 1996) informed the research design and sampling. Sampling criteria and site selection were based on an interest in relationships between food acquisition activities of low-income households and the following; geographic location, seasonality, neighborhood characteristics, location of homes in relation to grocery stores, access to transportation; disparities in food access; and the influence of nutrition education and

consumer knowledge on food acquisition and food access, The project was reviewed and approved by the University Committee on Human Subjects (UCHS).

Twenty-eight low-income rural, village, and inner city households were selected from three research sites in upstate New York using purposive and theoretical sampling. Sites represented a mix of major retail food store formats. Household selection criteria included income (>185% of the U.S. federal poverty line), at least one child under 18 at home, and some proficiency in reading and writing English. We recruited participants to assure differences in car ownership status, household makeup, and exposure to formal nutrition education. Local nutrition agencies (i.e., Cooperative Extension, neighborhood centers, food pantries, family resource centers, a migrant education program, and a church-based outreach program) provided access to potential participants. We did not.seek disabled people or sample by health status. The interviewer communicated with participant households in person, by telephone, and mail two to ten times over two to eight months. All participants provided written informed consent.

The overall profile of household participants consisted of one male and 26 female household shoppers, as well as one married couple who shopped together; 22 white, 4 black, 1 Latino, and 1 black/ Latina shopper. Households were drawn equally from urban, village/small town and rural areas. Half of the participants (14 of 28) had at one time participated in a nutrition education program such as the Expanded Food and Nutrition Education Program (EFNEP) provided through Cooperative Extension. Participants' ages ranged from 19 to 35 with a median age of 36.

The primary researcher conducted semi-structured interviews in participants' homes and, in several instances, at community agencies. Topics covered shopping habits, especially for fruits and vegetables, barriers to acquiring food, and attitudes toward local food stores. Participants kept a weekly log of how they obtained fruits and vegetables during two seasons in order to triangulate the interview data and to learn more about food acquisition practices over time. Additionally, we asked participants to comment about how and where they would prefer to buy produce and their broader attitudes towards food shopping.

DATA ANALYSIS

Interviews were audio-taped, transcribed, checked for accuracy, and coded and analyzed using the constant comparative method of Strauss and Corbin (1998), Nvivo 2.0 (QSR, 2002) software was used to manage the data. Eighteen of the 28 participants were interviewed twice. For some, major changes occurred between the first and second interviews that were associated with how, when, or where participants procured food for the household. For instance, several households had moved, and several others had gained or lost a car. These households undergoing significant change were treated as two units (Time 1 and Time 2) that resulted in a total of 37 separate household profiles.

Analysis of the data produced categories of phenomena associated with the process of food procurement and related concepts (e.g., food choice), their properties and dimensions. We first examined the relationships among each of these categories within each household and then analyzed the categories looking for relationships across households. Finally, we developed a "metamatrix" (Miles & Huberman, 1994) that combined all households and major categories, and assigned values to subcategories (e.g., health and disability status) thus providing a way to conceptualize the gradations of food access across categories and households. Credibility and trustworthiness of the data were enhanced by multiple interviews and con tacts with participants throughout the study. In addition, the primary researcher discussed interpretation of early data with participants, triangulated shopping information from interviews with food acquisition records, and conducted periodic peer debriefing sessions with the research team. Negative cases were sought to provide validity to results (Mays & Pope, 2000; Patton, 1990).

RESULTS

Three kinds of resources emerged as important for low-income participants (Table 10.1): human/social, material, and contextual elements. Human/social resources consisted of (1) the physical health and capabilities of the primary food provider—e.g., locomotion, stamina, sensory acuity; (2) social support networks

Table 10.1 Household Resources to Access Food

Human/social resources:	• Physical capabilities of primary food provider
	• Social support networks
	• Knowledge-based skills
Material resources:	• Money, other financial resources
	• Transportation
	• Time
Contextual elements:	• Climate, season
	• Local physical environment
	• Local food landscape
	• Personal/household geography in relation to food

made up of family, friends, and neighbors; and (3) knowledge-based skills learned either formally, such as in school or adult education, or informally from parents or mentors (gardening or shopping skills, for example). Material resources included: (1) money and other financial resources (e.g., store discount cards and food assistance—such as WIC, FSP, NSLP); (2) transportation (car ownership, access to public transportation or dependable rides to the store); and (3) time. Contextual elements were dependent on participants' location in space and time: (1) climate and season; (2) local physical environment (density, demography, public safety); (3) local, food landscape—stores with accessible, appropriate and affordable food; and (4) location in relation to that food landscape.

Data suggested that these resources functioned as a hierarchy, with financial resources at the top. If adequate resources had been available, families reported they would have exercised more options to access foods of their choice, either paying more for local, more expensive foods where available or spending money on a car, gasoline, or a ride to take them elsewhere to meet their needs. However, financial resources were limited, and a second tier of resources then became critical; transportation (including walking), social support networks, and location (particularly in proximity to grocery stores). Many households did not possess all second-tier resources either. These households demonstrated adaptive qualities, combining what they had with advantageous contextual elements to acquire at least the minimum groceries needed to function.

Adaptation to limited resources was only successful when the food shopper was able-bodied and/or in good health or, if not, only when other allowances could be made to compensate. Participants without access to a car, public transportation, or a network of friends or family for dependable transportation relied on their ability to walk to a local store, often

walking home carrying groceries. These households reported purchasing more food during the summer or during good weather to stock up for wintertime when walking to and from a grocery store could be hazardous. Those whose physical health was compromised sometimes paid neighbors for rides to the store or had children take over many shopping duties.

Participants needed three characteristics of health and physical capability in order to access food without additional help. Stamina (walking to a store, walking through a superstore, or shopping several stores for the best buys), flexibility/ dexterity (bending into deep freezers, stretching or stooping to reach shelves to retrieve food items), and strength (lifting and carrying bags of groceries to the car) were necessary to successful grocery shopping, particularly for those with few other resources. The degree of participants' stamina, flexibility, and strength interacted with other factors to influence their level of food access. Taking public transportation generally required more stamina than the door-to-door service of a private car or taxi. A trip by public transportation in some cases involved up to four bus rides plus a walk carrying groceries from the bus stop home in heavy plastic bags that cut hands. Strength was often needed to take advantage of bargain-priced foods that had to be bought in large quantities, such as "buy one, get one free" promotions.

An unexpected finding emerged from the analysis of health and physical capabilities as resources for food procurement. A high level of functionality was found to be a core resource for acquiring food, and many of the participants—12 of 28—had one or more chronic or acute health conditions or physical impairments that limited their ability to get food, even though they were their household's primary grocery shopper. The primary shopper was often designated as such because they were the only adult member of the household or because another adult's functional status was even worse than their own. In some instances, poor physical health led to impaired ability to walk, drive, or lift. For others, impairments such as blindness, deafness, and epilepsy created additional socio-environmental barriers such as social stigma, social exclusion, and transportation issues. Table 10.2 lists specific health and impairment issues in this sample. Chronic conditions resulting in impairment included bone and joint problems, swollen legs, epilepsy (resulting in exclusion from driving), and difficulty breathing. One participant was blind; another was deaf. Two participants were recovering from recent hospitalizations.

For participants who had to compensate for poor health or a physical disability, using other resources became necessary. Otherwise, they risked jeopardizing their health further or compromising their household's food security. With limited financial resources, households frequently made use of social networks for assistance—family, neighbors, clergy, and in one case a migrant worker organization. However, reliance on a social network required some participants to relinquish a degree of independence. Extended family members or neighbors who did the driving often decided where and when to shop and how much time: to allow for a shopping trip. Some disabled

participants who lived within walking distance of a store selling food (though not usually a supermarket) or near a bus line often preferred to remain independent and make do with what they could get to on their own rather than ask for, and rely on, the help, of others. Sometimes they had little choice.

An urban participant who was not allowed to drive because of her epilepsy stated that she usually walked to a local grocery store. "Yes, we [epileptics] can get to the grocery store. But how do we get the stuff home? So that kind of limits where you can go, unless they're able to get a ride with someone."

One male participant with chronic back pain owned a car, but was not always able to drive. After remarking how much he missed the fresh produce of his native Puerto Rico he stated, "I'm trying to plan to go to farmers' market. But you know some days, me with this pain, I cannot plan . . . my pain around my day . . . 'Cause right now if I'm in pain, doesn't matter what's looking for me. I'm home in bed taking my pills." He reported that some days he could not bend to get into the car because of the pain. If he did drive on one of these days he said that he would choose a store for convenience rather than quality. "I like to go in and get out—the faster the better—where they've got

Table 10.2 Functional Status of Participants

Health and impairment status of participants (location)	Car	Age
spina bifida (small town)	No	25
severe asthma, hypertension, shortness of breath (urban)	No	35
blind (village)	No	36
bad back & hip (rural)	No	40
epilepsy (urban)	No	41
deaf pedal edema (village)	No	50
husband: heart bypass, diabetes, cellulitis; wife: arthritis (urban)	No	58
"bad legs" (urban)	No	59
automobile accident—hospitalized (rural)	Yes	29
recovering from major abdominal surgery (rural)	Yes	32
bad back, sometimes unable to drive (rural)	Yes	37
bad back, bad hip (urban)	Yes	40

everything that I need [snaps fingers], like this." He reported that some days were so bad that he stayed home and ordered pizza for the family.

A very independent, blind participant lived within walking distance of three grocery stores in a small village, a food landscape resource that made it possible for her to be self-reliant. However, the physical environment and the weather also influenced her choice of store. She stated that when she walked in one direction toward two stores, "It stinks because . . . about the next two-thirds of the way down there is no sidewalk and it's downhill and it's uphill and it's choppy and it's just nasty and in the winter with the snow and ice it's horrid, so I will tend to go [in the direction of the third store] just because it's got a better sidewalk."

Another village participant reported that the medicine prescribed by her doctor for stomach pain also made her retain water and caused her ankles to swell. "The doctor gave me the pills, but I shouldn't take them because my ankles swell right up. That bothers my feet. . . . So I have to stop [taking the medicine] until my feet are OK. . . . It's difficult to walk [to the store.]"

Poor health of a family member also influenced food access and choice among several participant households. One female farmer, mother to two teenaged boys and wife to a seriously ill husband, skipped planting the family garden in order to make time for other responsibilities. That year her family ate canned vegetables from the store and local food pantry in spite of a preference for the less expensive but more time-intensive produce fresh from their own garden: "I've been buying a lot of canned foods, I noticed, because it's a lot cheaper to buy it canned than it is fresh, . . . but I'm still trying to buy the fresh fruit for my kids." Two other mothers reported skipping grocery shopping for one or two weeks because they couldn't leave a sick child's bedside. As demonstrated in these examples, health of

the food shopper and other family members influenced where foods were procured and what kinds of foods were included in the family diet In most instances, poor health or disabilities led to limitations of food access and food choice.

Some adults with a disability or in poor health and with little visible social support or other resources reported relying on the help of their children. For instance, an urban participant with asthma, high blood pressure, and shortness of breath took her preadolescent children with her on the bus to a supermarket across town. She reported how she would find a seat in the store while the children retrieved the food items. She eventually became medically housebound, and the children would instead go to several neighborhood corner markets to shop.

> "My kids go to the corner store to get canned stuff—string beans, corn, peas, collard greens in the can. I usually go out to get the fresh ones, but I wasn't feeling up to all that walking, so they will go to different stores and get canned goods. . . . I'm eating more canned now since I'm unable to get out, but as soon as I do, I'll be back on the fresh."

Both store choice and food choice were greatly diminished, and the family now spent more of its food budget for their groceries, too. A blind participant explained that when she moved to town only one store agreed to have staff spend time helping her pick items and usher her through the line: "But the other stores said they just didn't have the personnel or the time or the interest." Despite this disability, with help from her two young teenage daughters, she made use of her consumer knowledge and awareness of local resources to provide a wide variety of fruits and vegetables for her family. Her main regret was that she was unable to take advantage of store ads or clip coupons in the papers. She considered asking her children to do this on top of the rest of their chores too much to ask:

"I wish I could use coupons. That's one thing I need help with desperately. . . . I could save, I have so many friends that will go and get a $100 worth of groceries for 45 bucks . . . you can perform miracles with coupons." She reported that some stores now have sale items recorded directly in the cash register rather than requiring paper coupons, "so that is one blessing."

While pregnancy is not a disability, a pregnant participant reported facing many physical challenges similar to those faced by the disabled participants. She may not have been expected to lift and carry heavy loads or bend and stretch with the same facility as able-bodied non-pregnant shoppers. Yet, as a non-driver she continued to walk to and from the bus stop with bags of groceries. She resorted to similar solutions as others in the study as exemplified by having her two preschoolers help her carry the groceries home.

All of these examples reveal how health and lack of major physical impairments are important resources in the provision of food. Those with both a disability and limited income reported the need to compromise the quality of diet in order to provide food of any kind for their family. Relying on other resources to access food—social networks, composition of local food landscape/proximity to home, time available—sometimes forced these shoppers to sacrifice greater food choice including healthier food choices and more affordable food.

In several cases, participants reported that the necessity of getting food, despite risk of bodily harm and lack of other resources, led to a decline in health. One woman who lived in the country without a car told of her common six-mile walk to the store. By her second interview she reported that the practice of carrying heavy groceries long distances had put so much stress on her back, legs, and hips that she was forced to go to the doctor and into physical therapy. At this point,

the family somehow found the means to get a car. She stated about the experience, "I got not even two miles up the road and I was all hunched over and just about in tears, 1 couldn't walk [any] more. I was just in so much pain from walking. So I won't walk that far again, not for anything."

DISCUSSION

For the households in this study, we found that food access was a dynamic process that involved (1) the ability or capacity of a household or individual to obtain adequate food for a healthy, personally acceptable diet; and (2) a level of consumer agency, which depended on human and material resources at a household's or individual's disposal (e.g., money, transportation, health and physical capability, social networks, time), and contextual factors, such as location, climate, and availability of local grocery stores and other food outlets (food landscapes). Participants with lower health capital made use of other resources, such as financial capital (when available), time, and social capital, as well as contextual factors such as proximity to nearby food stores. Food sources that may have been less acceptable when a household had more resources (e.g., food pantries, corner stores) became an acceptable way to provide food when the principal food shopper became less physically able to shop. The primary criteria on which food access decisions were made changed as primary food shoppers moved along the continuum ranging from fully able-bodied and good health to disabled or poor health. The level and duration of impairment was often fluid. Food landscapes that adequately served those without impairments did not prove sufficient for those who did have impairments.

Several questions raised by the findings of this study are whether and to what degree poor health, impairments, and disability may influence food access, and to what degree food access and food security affect health and impairments. Stuff *et al.* (2004) explored this in a survey of 1488 households throughout 36 counties in the Mississippi Delta region of Arkansas.

Participants reported their mental, physical, and general health status. Although they fell short of declaring that food insecurity causes poor health, the authors favored this hypothesis over the reverse causation hypothesis where poor health (especially involving disability) increases food insecurity. Data from the study reported here suggest that causality operates in both directions. As resources, including health, decline for ill and disabled low-income food shoppers, household food landscapes narrow as well. Participants' narratives illustrated how dietary quality may be traded for expediency when few viable options to access food appear to exist for them. What and where food was chosen reflected resources that were still available: walkable local corner shops rather than distant supermarkets, canned produce (or none) instead of fresh produce; home-delivered food (e.g., pizza)—or occasionally doing without—when shopping was too difficult or took them away from a dependent's bedside. It is easy to imagine how these and similar situations continue the cycle of poor nutrition that can lead to or exacerbate chronic disease and further disability.

It has been pointed out that understanding the context in which people live is essential in order to understand the origins of health disparities (Joint Center for Political and Economic Studies, 2004). Food access for those with disabilities can be understood in terms of community-level food landscapes as well as individual physical capabilities. Informants in this study saw different food landscapes, not only according to their particular health conditions and physical capabilities, but also in relationship to resources such as

transportation and social support. These additional resources expanded or constricted their interpretations of viable food landscapes. Disability and food access need to be examined as a spatial phenomenon (Gleeson, 1999) within the broad array of perspectives on disability (Albrecht *et al.*, 2001). Disability influences the ability of people to perform social roles (Verbrugge & Jette, 1994), and the acquiring, preparing, and consuming of food are among the most essential of personal and household tasks. Various indexes of ability, such as the Instrumental Activities of Daily Living (IADL's) (Lawton & Brody, 1969) consider shopping, cooking, and eating, and, to the extent that an individual or household is unable to perform these tasks, may be associated with food insecurity and hunger.

Of interest is that the research of both Stuff *et al.* (2004) and Vozoris and Tarasuk (Tarasuk, 2003) selected random members of participant households on which to assess health status. A strength of the research reported here is that all participants were purposively chosen because they held primary responsibility for acquiring food for their families. Yet even when charged with this responsibility, a large proportion reported health problems and physical impairments that limited their ability to carry out the task.

The findings of this analysis point out that coping with limitations in food access due to health and impairment lead some individuals to experience exclusion (and increased food insecurity) from their usual food landscape, others to develop techniques and networks for adapting to it, and still others to consider food choices beyond the "normal" (e.g., home-delivered restaurant meals and groceries), Coping styles may be connected to the types of barriers raised and the nature of a given impairment. The physical environment (transportation options, weather conditions) curbed those with physical impairments (difficulty walking, pain).

Socio-environmental factors (availability of sidewalks in good repair, grocery stores designed to accommodate all shoppers) forced others to cope in different ways. Based on one's physical abilities and resources, each individual in this study appeared to operate in a different food world. These differences in the match between health, coping, and food landscape required varying forms of "foodwork" (Bove & Sobal, 2006) to be performed by individuals with various capabilities. For example, the foodwork involved in getting more than the most basic ingredients for cooking was simple for some but virtually impossible for others.

Understanding the role of health and disability in food access also requires recognizing a medical condition or impairment may be chronic yet dynamic. A household's set of health resources may fall far short of the norm. Vozoris and Tarasuk (2003) counted a particular medical condition only if that person reported that it had lasted or was expected to last for six months or longer. Our study looked at functional ability to acquire groceries from week to week, Many interviewed in this study represented a group whose fluid membership changed depending on daily pain thresholds, medication side effects, accident proneness, and the medical condition of dependent household members. Moreover, inability to access food was linked not only to functional status but functional status in relation to household finances (how long until pay day?), the weather (will it be icy today?), social networks (are we speaking to the cousin with the car this week?), changes in the local food landscape (local grocery stores transformed into dollar stores?), and access to transportation (changes in bus routes, car reliability, gasoline prices?). These problems are interrelated, contextual, and not easily studied by reducing them to a few limited, objective criteria. We found that even temporary disabling conditions, accompanied by lack of other household resources and adverse contextual factors, could considerably decrease food access one week or one month but not necessarily the next.

A public policy dilemma that arises is how we acknowledge, and then address, the subjective, contextual relationship between disabilities, household resources, and local food landscapes, that results in poor access to food. Another policy dilemma is making connections between urban/regional planning, which studies the built environment, with public health, two fields that traditionally have not had much connection with one another (Corburn, 2004). It is commendable that discussion has begun on how to promote healthy communities that encourage walking and biking (Curtis & Rees Jones, 1998), although the majority of this work does not include people with disabilities as an explicit focus (Kirchner, Gerber, and Smith, 2007). Designers of these new communities need to keep in mind that future residents, young and old, will have a range of physical capabilities, and that their food security could be jeopardized if measures to improve access for them are not included.

The findings of this study are based on a small number of low-income households from one region of the U.S. early in the 21st century, and, therefore, care should be taken in extrapolation to other groups, places, and times. It focused only on physical health impairments and disabilities. However, the findings suggest public policy considerations as well as planning interventions that would improve food access for all. Future studies designed to examine food access impairments are needed including research in different locations and with different samples and compositions including those focusing on specific types of disabilities.

CONCLUSION

In conclusion, it appears than many forms of impairments and disabilities decrease capacity to access healthy and affordable food and increase reliance on other household, material and contextual resources to overcome these limitations. An impairment or disability may decrease consumer agency when faced with structural forces that affect food access and its availability. Overall, we need food to build good health, but also, our level of health and disability can play a critical role in acquiring food for a healthy diet.

REFERENCES

Albrecht, G. L, Seelman, K., & Bury, M. (Eds.). (2001), *Handbook of Disability Studies*. Thousand Oaks CA: Sage.

Americans with Disabilities Act of 1990. (1990). Washington DC: U.S. Congress.

Anderson, S. A. (1990). Core indicators of nutritional state for difficult to sample populations. *Journal of Nutrition, 120(11S),* 1557S–1600S.

Bove, C. F., & Sobal, J. (2006), Foodwork in newly married couples: Making family meals. *Food, Culture and Society, 9*(1), 69–89.

Campbell, C. (1991). Food insecurity: A nutritional outcome or a predictor variable? *Journal of Nutrition, 121*(3), 408–415.

Corburn, J. (2004). Confronting the challenges in reconnecting urban planning and public health. *American Journal of Public Health,* 94(4), 541–546.

Crockett, E. G., Clancy, K. L., & Bowering, J. (1992), Comparing the cost of a thrifty food plan market basket in three areas of New York State. *Journal of Nutrition Education, 24*(1), 71S–78S.

Curtis, S., & Rees Jones, I. (1998). Is there a place for geography in the analysis of health inequality? *Sociology of Health & Illness, 20*(5), 645–672.

Drewnowski, A., & Specter, S. E. (2004). Poverty and obesity: The role of energy density and energy costs. *American Journal of Clinical Nutrition, 79*(1), 6–16.

Duncan, J. (2000). Landscape. In R. J. Johnston, D. Gregory, G. Pratt & M. Watts (Eds.), *Dictionary of Human Geography* (4th ed., pp. 429–431). Malden, MA: Blackwell Publishing.

Eikenberry, N. (2003). *Access to food and healthy food choice for low-income Minnesotans: A literature review.* (Masters thesis, University of Minnesota, Minneapolis MN, 2003).

Furey, S., Strugnell, C., & Mcllveen, H. (2001). An investigation of the potential existence of "food deserts" in rural and urban areas of Northern Ireland, *Agriculture and Human Values, 18*(4), 447–457.

Gleeson, B. (1999). *Geographies of Disability*. New York: Routledge.

Guilford, M. C., Mahabir, D., & Rocke, B. (2003). Food insecurity, food choices, and body mass index in adults: Nutrition transition in Trinadad and Tobago. *International Journal of Epidemiology, 32,* 508–516.

Guptill, A., & Wilkins, J. L. (2002). Buying into the food system: Trends in food retailing in the us and implications for local foods. *Agriculture and Human Values, 19*(1), 39–51.

Holloway, J., & Kneafsey, M. (2000). Reading the space of the farmers' market: A preliminary investigation in the U.K. *Socioiogia Ruralis, 40*(3), 285–299.

Joint Center for Political and Economic Studies. (2004). *Making a Place for Healthier Living; Community Approaches to Improving Access to Healthy Foods and Physical Activity among People of Color.* Washington, DC: Policy Link, and the Joint Center for Political and Economic Studies.

Krebs-Smith, S. M., & Kantor, L. S. (2001). Choose a variety of fruits and vegetables daily: Understanding the complexities. *Journal of Nutrition, 131,* 487S–501S.

Kirchner, C.K., Gerber, E., and Smith, B.C. (2007). Designed to Deter: Community Barriers to Physical Activity for People with Visual or Motor Impairments. *American Journal of Preventative Medicine,* under review.

Lawton, M. P., & Brady, E. M. (1969). Assessment of older people: Self-maintaining and instrumental activities of daily living. *The Gerontologist, 9,* 179–188.

Lee, J. S., & Frongillo, E. A., Jr. (2001). Factors associated with food insecurity among U.S. elderly persons: Importance of functional impairments. *Journal of Gerontology: Social Sciences, 56B*(2), S94–S99.

MacIntyre, S., Maclver, S., & Sooman, A. (1993). Area, class and health: Should we be focusing on places or people? *Journal of Social Policy, 22*(2), 213–234.

Mays, N., & Pope, C. (2000). Assessing quality in qualitative research. *British Medical Journal, 320*(7226), 50–52.

Miles, M. B., & Huberman, A. M. (1994). *Qualitative Data Analysis: An Expanded Sourcebook* (2nd ed.). Thousand Oaks: Sage Publications.

Morris, P. M., Neuhauser, L., & Campbell, C. (1992). Food security in rural America: A study of the availability and costs of food. *Journal of Nutrition Education, 24*(1), 52S–58S.

Nord, M., Andrews, M., & Carlson, S. (2003). *Household Food Security in the United States, 2002.* Washington, DC: ERS, USDA.

Olson, C.M., Anderson, K., Kiss, E., Lawrence, F. C., & Selling, S. B. (2004). Factors protecting against and contributing to food insecurity among rural families. *Family Economics and Nutrition Review*, 16(1), 12–20.

Patton, M. Q. (1990), *Qualitative Evaluation and Research Methods* (2nd ed.). Newbury Park: Sage Publications.

QSR. (2002). Nvivo (Version 2.0). Doncaster, Australia: QSR International Pty Ltd.

Roe, D. (1990). In-home nutritional assessment of inner-city elderly. *Human Nutrition*, 120(Suppl 11), 1538–1543.

Smith, G. C. (1991). Grocery shopping patterns of the ambulatory urban elderly. *Environment and Behavior*, 23(1), 86–114.

Sobal, J., & Wansink, B. (2007). Kitchenscapes, tablescapes, platescapes, and foodscapes: Influences of microscale built environments on food intake. *Environment and Behavior*, 39(1), 124–142.

Strauss, A., & Corbin, J, (1998). *Basics of Qualitative Research* (2nd ed.). Thousand Oaks: Sage Publications.

Stuff, J. E., Casey, P. H., Szeto, K. L., Gossett, J. M., Robbins, J. M., Simpson, P. M., et at. (2004), Household food insecurity is associated with adult health status. *Journal of Nutrition, 134*(9), 2330–2335.

Travers, K. D. (1996). The social organization of nutritional inequities. *Social Science and Medicine, 43*(4), 543–553.

U.S. Department of Health and Human Services. (2000). Healthy people 2010: Understanding and improving health. Retrieved January 28, 2005, from http://www.healthypeople.gov/document/html/objectives/19–18.htm

Verbrugge, L. M., & Jette, A. M. (1994). The disablement process. *Social Science and Medicine, 38*, 1–14.

Vozoris, N. T., & Tarasuk, V. S. (2003). Household food insufficiency is associated with poorer health. *Journal of Nutrition, 133*, 120–126.

Webber, C. B. (2005). *Low-income households and grocery stores: Food access and availability in underserved areas.* (Doctoral dissertation, Cornell University, Ithaca, NY).

Wolfe, W. S., Frongillo, E. A., Jr., & Valois, P. (2003). Understanding the experience of food insecurity by elders suggests ways to improve its measurement *Journal of Nutrition, 133*(9), 2762–2769.

Wylie, C, Copeman, J., & Kirk, F. F. L. (1999). Health and social factors affecting the food choice and nutritional intake of elderly people with restricted mobility. *Journal of Human Nutrition & Dietetics, 12*(5), 375–380.

11

Other Women Cooked for My Husband: Negotiating Gender, Food, and Identities in an African American/Ghanaian Household

Psyche Williams-Forson

There are people who will say they haven't eaten the whole day, simply because they haven't had their soup and fufu. If you give them anything—bread sandwich, Caesar salad—they don't consider it as food, until they've sat down with their bowl of fufu and soup.
Dinah Ayensu, interview with
Fran Osseo-Asare

Other women used to cook for my husband. Or to state it more clearly, before and after we got married several women from within my husband's Ghanaian community would cook for him. I liken the experience to a communal collective—a tapestry of women's work that contributed to the physical, spiritual, and cultural nourishment of my household. Generally speaking, this culinary collective or relationship of plurality in planning, preparing, and presenting meals reinforced the complex nature of food and the ways in which the quotidian language of cooking performs as a crucial mode of communicating identities.

The field of food studies has witnessed the emergence of a significant body of scholarship on the importance of food in the production and shaping of gender identities in families, including *Through the Kitchen Window: Women Writers Explore the Intimate Meanings of Food and Cooking* and *From Betty Crocker to Feminist Food Studies: Critical Perspectives on Women and Food*. One of the most widely quoted studies is Marjorie DeVault's *Feeding the Family: The Social Organization of Caring as Gendered Work*, which argues that "part of the intention behind producing the meal is to produce 'home' and 'family.'" DeVault, as well as other anthropologists and sociologists, acknowledges the socially constructed nature of the efforts involved in orchestrating the daily task of feeding families. Among studies involving heterosexual couples, most of this "invisible" work falls heavily on the shoulders of women. Similarly, in same-gender loving or lesbian/gay households, Christopher Carrington makes the point that one person emerges as the clear food planner because she/he takes on the role of planning ahead, shopping, and often cooking. Others have found, however, that these tasks tend to be rotated between partners or assumed by the person with the most desire to perform the chore. What is clear, nonetheless, across lines of gender and sexuality is the considerable amount of work involved in planning and preparing meals.[1]

Yet, despite the diversity of the research on food, families, and households, with respect to gender, class, and sexuality little focus has been given to the issues of racial ethnicities. In their study on counseling married African American and African couples, Beth Durodoye and Angela Coker make the important point that the literature on mixed marriages generally focuses on whites marrying outside their ethnicity or race (Asian, Latino, American Indian, Jewish and Gentile, and so on). And despite the low intermarriage rates between black/

white couples, they too are persistently examined. Little research exists, however, concerning African American/African couples. According to Durodoye and Coker, this is most likely due to the racial politics in the United States that views people of African descent as a monolithic group.[2] Arguing against the myth of homogeneity among and between people of the African diaspora, this chapter recaptures experiences that took place during the first five to seven years of my relationship with my husband (who today not only cooks for himself but also for our family), in order to consider some of the complexities that inhere in the homes of those living together across ethnic borders and boundaries—specifically, African Americans and black immigrants from Africa. By examining my intercultural black household, I look at the home as a culinary landscape of gender, race, and ethnic negotiation, compromise, and accommodation. I bring to the fore critical cross-cultural challenges that can exist when couples negotiate the roles of domesticity and simultaneously try to create connections to a home-land—both real and imaginary. Finally, I contribute to the research exploring food and gender relationships among African Americans and Africans.

In any domestic relationship, procuring, preparing, eating, and cleaning up food are mundane, usually one-sided gendered tasks. The person with the most interests and/or abilities is usually the one in front of/or behind the pots and pans adorning the stove. But while mealtimes are powerful symbols of domesticity, they can also be fundamental sources of constant variation and frustration requiring versatility and compromise. More directly, food is instrumental in highlighting the ways that situated daily practices can reveal processes of identity formation and place making. Recognizing that food has a unifying power in helping us to construct our sense of belonging and nationality is not a new concept in itself. Neither is it novel to note that homes and kitchens are more than sites of consumption. They are, in fact, spaces where food and power intersect in the performance of identity negotiation, formation, and reformation. This discussion explores these notions and their significance, embracing a cultural investigation of my husband, members of his "family," and me.

FOOD AS A MARKER OF CULTURAL SIMILARITY AND DIFFERENCE

Food, including what it is, who prepares it, and sometimes how and when it is consumed, is intensely personal. Powerfully symbolic in its ability to communicate, food conveys messages about where we come from, who we are as individuals, and how we think and feel at any given moment. In the language of food, identity and place can become problematized. Because of this, food is a critical expression of cultural identity and an important marker of cultural borders. Women have a significant role in easing and complicating the symbolic relationships that people have between the foods they eat and their identities. Their responses to food situations can enable people to find spaces that nurture and sustain or reject and refuse. An example from my own life experiences illustrates this point.

Shortly after my husband and I started dating, I happened to call him while he was having dinner. When I asked him what he was eating, initially he became silent. After I pressed, however, he provided the generic descriptor "traditional Ghanaian foods." Realizing we had reached an impasse in our information exchange, I finally threw out the names of the few foods that I knew and explained that I study foods and food cultures. My response prompted him to assume a less defensive position. Later, he revealed that his hesitancy was the result of previous encounters with other African American women who had, in his experience, ridiculed and/or questioned his foods and his methods of eating. Because fallacies and stereotypes about the African continent and its peoples tend to dominate the few representations that exist, it is no wonder that when some African Americans (and Americans) learn that foods are eaten with the hands and not with implements, they associate the practice not with particularistic culinary habits but with primitivism. Although considered strange to most Americans, Fran Osseo-Asare describes the process of eating certain West African foods with the hands—specifically with the right hand because using the left hand is considered unclean—as an art form. She writes, "there is an art to neatly breaking off a small amount of the fufu with the thumb and first three fingers, making an indentation with the thumb to turn the portion into a kind of spoon, dipping it into the soup, and tossing it into the mouth. Fufu is not chewed, but swallowed whole, carried down the throat by a soothing peristaltic motion."[3]

Hindsight reveals that the response I gave to my husband's uncertainty about revealing his food choices and then his admission were as critical to the development of our relationship as anything else. His pause was a weighty one because it was filled with social and cultural importance. My reaction was of an equally serious nature because it not only reflected my social and cultural relationship to the African continent but also my intellectual training. Affirming his culinary practices and my interest in sharing them established a line of communication between us. This exchange of confidences and emotion was reassuring for both of us. My husband realized that he had found a place with me that he could consider home. I, in turn, was made to feel secure in my ability to provide comfort. I liken this experience to our having crossed a significant cultural borderland because the acceptance or rejection of certain meals is also a means of expressing and asserting a national, regional, or local identity. Food, then, is a metaphor for

diasporic continuity and cultural retention as my husband realized he could continue to eat the foods that satisfied him in a space that would be affirming.

My husband, Kwame, is Ghanaian. Specifically, he is from Asene, Akyem (Akom) Oda. Oda is part of the Ashanti region and is located south of Kumasi (the second largest city in Ghana) and north of Accra (the capital of the country). I, on the other hand, am a native of south central Virginia. According to the research, he and I, as an interculturally married couple, are part of the growing statistics that report an increased number of marriages between U.S.-born African American women and West African (Ghana, Nigeria, and Sierra Leone) men.

Similar to any couple that decides to join households we share similar and different cultural mores. Many of our similarities are the result of African retentions, values, and traditions that have been transmitted over generations, namely, a sense of community and connections to spirituality. Although both of us are characterized by the designation "Black," we do not share the same cultural realities. By holding weekly "Africa nights" where we would read, discuss, and mark up the *Encyclopedia Britannica* to highlight the inaccuracies written about African people from a 1960s–1970s' point of view, my politically Pan-African parents laid the foundations for much of what I learned about Africa early in life. Consequently, they helped to dispel misperceptions my sisters and I might have had about the continent, its people, and its cultures. My husband, on the other hand, has lived in the United States longer than he lived in his native land. His perceptions about African Americans come from direct experiences, as do many of his views on gender role expectations. They are informed first by his grandmother, mother, and sisters and then by U.S. culture. To this end, my husband believes more in degrees of gender equity, and therefore unlike some West African men he did not necessarily expect me to cook every meal. Durodoye and Coker indicate that there is a U.S. stereotype that believes African men are inflexible where gender issues in the home are concerned—childcare, housework, and meal preparation. In contrast, my husband did not have prescribed notions that asserted I should cook for him. At the same time, he did have expectations concerning "acceptable" foods (hot dogs, for example, were met with disdain). And even while I make this statement, most of these responsibilities are primarily assumed by me. Kwame initially saw his role in preparing meals as linked to romance and not as a central part of the household economy. Changing his way of thinking was one of the many places of understanding that came with the growth of our relationship.

Despite the length of time Kwame has lived in the United States, a strong memory of his homeland exists, most notably manifested by his overall preference for Ghanaian foods. While we were still dating and preparing to marry we were necessarily learning one another's likes and desires. I was made aware of his traditional favorites: *komi ke kenkey* (fried fish served with a starchy dough made of lightly fermented corn), *banku* (similar to *kenkey*, also made of fermented corn/cassava dough), pepper sauce (made of the tripartite chili peppers, tomatoes, and onions). Sundays usually brought with it a trip to the ethnic market where he showed me the various ingredients to purchase in preparation for making *Nkrakra* (light soup) or *Hkatenkwan* (peanut butter or groundnut stew), and *fufu* (a thick dough made by boiling and pounding a starchy vegetable such as cocoyam, plantain, potato, or cassava). My husband's penchant was toward root vegetables such as yam, starchy side dishes, and other foods such as plantains, okra, and goat meat. In contrast, my own Southern routes/roots led me to a preference for collard greens, string beans, macaroni and cheese, and chicken. But on a regular basis I ate much more lightly, these foods being

eaten, more or less, on Sundays and holidays. Consequently, the daily ingestion of starches like pasta and rice were not a part of my culinary repertoire. For my husband-to-be, however, this was quite the opposite, and it became crystal clear to me in a very happenstance way.

One Sunday I deviated from my normal dinner fare and made crab cakes as the main course. As we prepared to eat, Kwame asked, "What's my starch?" I was taken aback because I never thought twice that starches had to be included in the meal because they were not a major part of my mealtime experience. Later that day we visited Ghanaian friends. Upon entering the house we were immediately invited to have dinner. *Again*. Upon hearing what was being offered, Kwame remarked: "Now this is real food." Although relatively annoyed at the comment, I agreed that it was indeed *different* food and joined the others in eating the common combination of fried fish, pepper sauce, and the starchy kenkey. If my husband felt any discomfort over his inadvertent denouncement of my crab dinner, it did not show. This is less because he is callous and more because food encodes, as Brinda Mehta notes, "an entire semiotic system of political, cultural, and social significations." The smell of his home cooking instantly evoked a series of emotions and desires. Mehta reinforces this interpretation:

> The migrant's attitude to food unearths deep associations with what I call a "homeland imaginary." . . . [T]he sensory construction of the distant island home is a way of localizing space in the metropolis. Recreating the fragrances of "home" through the culinary occupation of space . . . symbolizes the act of creolizing dominant space whereby the familiarity of the birthland is both conjured and physically actualized through fragrant whiffs of memory. . . . [T]he recipes for these culinary performances [are where] home is imagined through associative ingredients, flavours, smells, tastes, and colours. In other words, food . . . delineate[s] recognizable mappings of home.[4]

Implicit in Kwame's offhand criticism is the claim provided by Dinah Ayensu in the quotation opening this article. For some Ghanaians, not having had their fufu and soup means they have not eaten at all. In this similar cultural context, the specific Ghanaian food was not necessarily the issue. Instead, on this occasion it was not having consumed some kind of native dish that left him feeling dissatisfied.

As one who studies the cultures of food and foodways I am aware that meals are political acts because they mark our identity and cultural location. Yet, on a personal level, this incident, coupled with others, left an indelible print on me as a person, as a woman, and as a wife. No cook wants to have her food rejected in favor of another's. And who wants to witness someone—especially her partner—being physically fulfilled by another after she feels she has been castigated? But the beautiful and dangerous power of food is that it gives full voice to the differences that separate us as well as the ties that bind. My husband's dismissal of the crab cakes was more about inclusion than exclusion, affirmation rather than negation. His offhand remark about "real food" was as much a statement to our Ghanaian hosts as it was to me. Parama Roy puts it this way: "Migrants preserve their ties to a homeland through their preservation of and participation in traditional customs and rituals of consumption." Quoting from Sara Suleri's memoir, *Meatless Days*, Roy further highlights the point that " 'expatriates are adamant, entirely passionate about such matters as the eating habits of the motherland.' Food, in the migrant/diasporic subject's cosmos, becomes—whatever it might have been at its place of putative origin—tenaciously tethered to economies simultaneously and irreducibly national and moral."[5] Kwame let it be known, albeit unintentionally perhaps, that even though he was marrying an African American woman he would always maintain certain cultural practices that located him first as a Ghanaian or a member of the in-group. While enjoying his kinfolk and reveling in the familiar smells and tastes with which he was accustomed, he was also working out the various social and cultural boundaries that inevitably accommodate marriage. These boundaries are heightened when facets of cultural differences emerge in bold.

Theoretically I am clear about how group identity is a natural component of self-identity and self-definition; my own research argues this point.[6] I am also aware that an act as mundane and everyday as eating can be the source of unwanted complications and tensions. When these issues are being worked out in a marriage they can become entangled in ways that render home a place of (dis)location. These tensions can result in households becoming the locus of gender, cultural, and political struggle, rather than havens from the snares of larger society. A point made by Carole Boyce Davies in another context is applicable here: "The mystified notions of home and family are removed from their romantic, idealized moorings, to speak of pain, movement, difficulty, learning and love in complex ways. Thus, the complicated notion of home mirrors the problematizing of community/nation/identity that one finds in Black women's writing from a variety of communities."[7] Food can and often does act as a conduit for conflict. Consequently, the myth of "home" as a romanticized narrative should be rejected here as well. From the direction that we were heading it was clear that our personal and collective agendas were going to collide on the culinary landscape if some kind of intercultural intervention did not take place. The answer, for us, came through a culinary collective.

CULINARY COOPERATIVE: A STRATEGY FOR SURVIVAL

As with most new marriages, routines that had developed while we were single carried over into our union. Needless to say, this made it difficult for a smooth culinary transition. We are hardly alone in having experienced this quandary. Married or not, living with others and working out meals always brings about relative amounts of discord. In her book, *Intercultural Marriage: Promises and Pitfalls*, Dugan Romero observes that food is often cited as the primary cultural source of difference between partners; however, she argues,

> the significance goes far beyond the digestive tract. The intercultural couple has to work out house rules, which satisfy them both, not only in terms of what is served but also how it is prepared and served and by whom and who cleans up. These seemingly minor issues often become bones of contention between spouses precisely because they contain so many underlying meanings and spring from so many unconscious sources.[8]

Before we lived together, most of my husband's foods had been cooked by one of his sisters or himself. In the course of preparing food for their own families his sisters would often share with their younger brother. I, on the other hand, would cook whatever was readily available in order to get back to the demands of being a graduate student. Blending our households, however, ushered in a multitude of similar and different culinary histories, cooking styles, and ingredients. And although we were not averse to fusing our menus, neither of us wanted to eat the other's foods consistently. Marriage meant that culinary negotiations would have to ensue. Because cooking is enjoyable to me, I was open to frequenting ethnic markets, but what I did not anticipate was the extra burden of time and resources needed to grocery shop at the specialty market in addition to the traditional stores—the invisible work of feeding my family.

In the initial year of our relationship, prior to getting married, we would go together to various African, Caribbean, and Latino markets where we would purchase a range of foods—smoked herring, smoked shrimp, yam, goat meat, and so on—in order for me to learn to cook various Ghanaian foods. Not only were we purchasing ingredients but also we were engaging in a bonding process by cooking together. Yet, despite these culinary forays, I was unsuccessful in learning to cook "correctly" the Ghanaian foods my husband desired. Even with him standing over my shoulder giving step-by-step instructions, the taste was never quite right for him—although it tasted perfectly fine to me. Amusingly, his own attempts to adequately duplicate the right tastes were equally futile, often leaving him frustrated and gastronomically unfulfilled. When the irritation proved too much, my husband sought other ways to satisfy himself and began seeking out women in what became our culinary collective—sisters, friends, and community grandmothers—to make his soups and sauces.

There are fundamental differences between the social organization of family and kinship networks in Ghana and those in the United States. But there are also consistencies in terms of working within extended family and community networks. Of particular relevance are the concepts of flexible gender relations, co-/Othermothering, and kinship networks. Writing from a Nigerian point of view, Ife Amadiume, in her oft-cited study, *Male Daughters, Female Husbands: Gender and Sex in an African Society*, argues that by using Western models of analysis, feminism, and social science, we have garnered flawed assumptions about the social conditions of African women. Prior to colonialism, Igbo women enjoyed certain elements of power under flexible gender systems. Under the institution of "female husbands" and "male daughters" women assumed male roles in the sense that they took on wives. As a result, they saw an increase in the workforce that consequently led to generational power, wealth, and authority, heretofore reserved for men under the strict gender guidelines of Eurocentric ideologies of masculinity.[9]

Patricia Hill Collins and Denise Segura discuss co- or Othermothering in African American and Chicana communities, respectively. Drawing on this work for applicability in a West African context, Oyeronke Oyewumi writes that

> the most profound sisterly relations are to be found in co-mothering, which is the essence of community building. Co-mothering as a communal ideal and social practice is not reducible to biological motherhood; it transcends it. . . . Furthermore, in many polygynous, multiple-generational households, the reality is that children experience many mothers. Notwithstanding the voluminous "co-wife" literature that Western anthropologists have used to define African polygamy, "co-mother" is the preferred idiom in many African cultures for expressing the relationship amongst women married into the same family. In Yoruba culture, for example, all women who have married into the family even when they are married to different brothers relate to each other as if they have one and the same husband, since marriage is a collective act contracted not between two individuals but two clans.[10]

From an African American point of view, the 1970s bore witness to a number of scholars writing against the grain of the Moynihan report and other studies that sought to demonize the diversity of black family structures. Carol Stack and others argued for the ways in which poor black urban families relied upon extensive women-centered networks for assistance. Harriette Pipes McAdoo expanded this discourse to consider upwardly mobile African Americans. Essentially, she found that even among those striving toward or safely ensconced in the middle class, utilizing kinship networks helped to foster and maintain a sense of well-being.[11] So then, while not unusual, the decision to engage our own women-centered extended network came about as part of a historical precedent, but it occurred deliberately and by happenstance.

Since the 1980s, the Washington, D.C., area, like many metropolises, has witnessed an explosion of specialized grocery stores serving African, Caribbean, Latino, and Asian customers. This is due in no small part to the interventions on the part of immigrant groups to provide necessary foodstuffs for their own communities as much as it is due to overt expansions in the global economy and culinary tourism. My sisters-in-law, as immigrants, own such a mini-market that caters to the foodways of African diasporic peoples.[12] On multiple occasions I would frequent the store for "kitchen-talk"—casual or serious family and business-related conversations—or to purchase items needed at home. Often, they would dole out motherly advice to me about "setting up house" or the idiosyncrasies of my husband. More often than not the conversations were idle but sometimes they became fraught with tension as lines were crossed and friendly advice turned to admonitions. During one of the less tense visits, our chatter turned to the subject of food and cooking. One of my sisters-in-law mentioned in passing that prior to our getting married, they would sometimes cook for their younger brother, stockpiling several of his favorite meals. It could have been missed, this subtle request/invitation to continue occasionally this practice. And while I recognized that such an arrangement could be loaded with all kinds of gender and family issues, not to mention power relations, the context and presentation of the request was understated enough that I agreed to its continuance. At that moment, a deal was struck that needed no additional clarification. Like seasoning without measuring, it was decided that my home, literally and figuratively, would be open to a certain amount of outside influence—culinary influence. So much went into that pact of gastronomy as we stood among jars of *shito* (a homemade hot pepper sauce), cans of Titus sardines, Maggi cubes, jewelry, and kente cloth. As spices and smells of foreign and homelands intermingled, we crisscrossed continents and once again married not just families but also food traditions. Consenting to the food arrangement proffered by the sisters made it clear that I was willing to engage in an act of culinary plurality. It was a befitting space—the ethnic market—in which to gel such an agreement because food would serve as an adhesive for binding our new family relationship. Opening myself and my home to participating in this kind of extended kinship network compelled me to focus on intercultural negotiations at the borders of gender, heritage, geography, and food even as my husband and I attempted to define our borders and boundaries as a couple.

This was not a decision made in haste even though it was made "on the spot." It was what Micaela di Leonardo describes as a "conscious strategy" on the part of my sisters-in-law and me. They knew that I was learning to negotiate and cope with the converging roles of wife, professor, and graduate student. They also knew the habits and peculiarities of their brother. They had long ago expressed as much concern for my welfare as for his. If I was happy then I would stay married and they (and he), in turn, would also be satisfied. Our agreement proved to be "crucial to the functioning of [our] kinship systems [as a source] of women's autonomous power . . . [a] primary site of emotional fulfillment and, at times . . . [the vehicle] for actual survival. . . ."[13] Embracing this kinship network around the vernacular tradition of cooking meant affirming certain cultural bonds between my husband and me. Equally, it meant welcoming into our family other Ghanaian women who we collectively regard as sisters, co-mothers, grandmothers, and aunts—most of whom transcended biology.

The nature of this communal effort cannot be underestimated nor is it unfamiliar. Foods and food habits are typically the last form of cultural expression that is relinquished because people will generally find ways to maintain the food and meal traditions with which they are accustomed.

Culinary historian VertaMae Grosvenor states that "although we may leave home, get rid of our accents, and change our names and diets, the aroma of certain foods will trigger warm memories and fill us with a longing and taste to return home."[14] For example, we would sometimes go on trips with a Ghanaian couple who would travel with a rice cooker and several thermoses filled with meat sauces to accommodate the grain. They would invite us for "rice," having brought with them the necessary accoutrements (bowls and spoons) to accommodate the meals. In an African American context, when black American migrants went West in the early 1940s they were unable to find basic dietary staples that they were accustomed to: cornmeal, okra, collard greens, black-eyed peas, and traditional seasonings like filé.[15] Similar to other migrants, organizations and mutual aid associations such as the Family Welfare Association were enlisted to help them make the necessary adaptations. Regardless of the assimilation processes that these migrants were forced to undergo and the changes that they were encouraged to make, they needed something solidly Southern to remain in place. Black women's work in helping to maintain these Southern traditions and mores was part of the process of self-definition and self-valuation or respect for their identity. In contrast to seeing community as "arbitrary" and "fragile," Collins argues that an Afrocentric worldview takes into consideration the aspects of connectedness, caring, and personal accountability inherent in such an approach.[16] Rearticulating black women's experiences using this framework not only challenges static notions of community but also makes elastic the intersections between race, gender, food, and power.

FOOD, CULTURAL WORK, AND POWER

In the 1940s, Kurt Lewin argued that women were essentially the "gatekeepers" of food consumption, because generally they are in charge of the flow of food in to (and out of) their household. W. Alex Mcintosh and Mary Zey countered with the view that although women are in charge of food flows, control is not necessarily a by-product of these consumption-producing activities. They reason that women may be responsible for procuring food and preparing meals, but they have little or no control over family finances. This, coupled with the pressure to produce a harmonious family life by deferring to their husbands' meal preferences, constitutes an actual lack of control over family food decisions. Marjorie DeVault, Nickie Charles and Marion Kerr, and others have staked out a similar position by maintaining that power for women is essentially absent from food provisioning. Rather, the power dynamic exists to favor men in that preparing meals for their spouses and families is equated to being in a position of subordination. In their experience, women serve primarily to satisfy the needs of their families, to the exclusion of self-consideration. Moreover, inasmuch as men economically provide the food and women merely prepare it, they lack any conceivable power other than that which comes from planning and cooking. Although a bit more complex, Carrington finds a similar amount of emotion management being performed in lesbigay households. While the power imbalance seems to manifest most overtly during dinner parties when one partner takes "frontstage" and the other "backstage," Carrington finds that these roles tend to be directly related to the occupations (female/male identified) held outside the home.[17]

It is not within the purview of this chapter to rehash or contest these arguments. Instead, I want to expand our thinking on the matter to consider ways that women in heterosexual families, in particular, may be empowered in their role as gatekeeper of the family food traditions. Theresa W. Devasahayam

states that "food [can be used] for a myriad of purposes, whether to resist, maneuver, change, express, and even reinforce the dominant gender ideology."[18] Part of this management or manipulation of household affairs involves recognizing the strategies that work for individual families. In the particular case of my family, it was a matter of doing the necessary cultural work that would not only help my husband and me each to maintain our cultural traditions but also to find the avenues for developing new practices that would sustain our family and reduce my personal workload.

In her article, "African Diaspora Women: The Making of Cultural Workers," Bernice Johnson Reagon uses the metaphor of mothering to describe the work of community gatekeepers of tradition. She asserts that

> their role was to resolve areas of conflict and to maintain, sometimes create, an identity that was independent of a society organized for the exploitation of natural resources, people, and land. There was a need to establish a structure and system with its own content that would allow an improved situation for survival . . . to work out ways to keep the traditions strong for the people.[19]

This kind of "creative power" is needed especially for community-bridging that uses American and African foods to form new, hybridized meals. Consider, for example, holidays such as Thanksgiving, Christmas, and Kwanzaa. Typically, these celebrations bring together cultural admixtures as our families and friends congregate. The natural flow of the evening means that those in attendance have an opportunity to sample everything from roast turkey to Ghanaian spinach stew, potato salad to Joll of rice.

But beyond these celebrations of creative power there are possibilities for seeing women as having other kinds of power vis-à-vis food. Feeding others is a major component of female identity, and it is here that women can have influence over others. The kitchen was and is my space because it represents the sociocultural demands feeding my family places on my time, primarily. I do all of the meal planning from deciding what foods come into my home (checking the cupboards, creating grocery lists, performing the shopping, putting away the food so I can find it) to determining how they enter (take-out, homemade, and so on), neither of which are trouble-free in terms of time and energy. This agency can be extended to accepting domestic cooperation and assistance. For example, my husband's sisters approached me, not him, to ask about continuing their cooking practices. Moreover, I was silent, but anger-free, when he brought home food cooked by other (Ghanaian) women. In all I exercised most of the power over the feeding work that occurred in our home, acquiescing mostly to those arrangements from which I too would benefit.

I have illustrated here the modicum of control I have and have always had in my home over food acquisition and consumption. But power is elusive. It manifests itself invisibly at times. But it should be clear, however, that Kwame also exercises elements of control. His power primarily manifests itself around the unstable, problematic concept of authenticity. As explained earlier in this chapter, some basic elements of preparing certain Ghanaian foods were learned from watching my husband. However, he made it clear that my version was usually not to his liking for one reason or another. Even boiling water for yams fostered some kind of corrective instruction—gently administered, but given nonetheless. Unless I ate the dish I prepared, it was rarely consumed. Although unspoken and certainly debatable, it seems that my ethnicity and not my cooking skills were called into question. Anything I cooked that was a non-native food was usually eaten without hesitation. This is not to say that all the kinfolk who participated in our culinary network

cooked to his liking—hardly—but the absence of my direct cultural knowledge in how to cook this cuisine was an issue. Conversations with African American and white women married to West African men elicited a range of similar responses. For example, as long as I can remember, my sister, who is married to a Liberian man, has always cooked his native foods. Refusing to be outdone by any of his kinfolk, she learned early on how to cook her version of cassava leaf and other foods, which are consumed readily by her family. In contrast, African American Theresa Kwakye, a Washington, D.C., native who is married to a Ghanaian and has lived in Ghana for over twenty years, explains that her husband prefers native foods only when cooked with "little oil." As with most families of a higher class, their cooking is performed by "the help." But because her husband likes to see her in the kitchen every now and then, she says, "I cook for him or at least am seen in the kitchen when he walks through the door." Osseo-Asare, a Caucasian American sociologist and West African food historian married to a Ghanaian professor, found my arrangement "interesting" and explained that she too insisted upon learning to cook the foods of her husband's native land. In one of her blog posts, "Recipe #6: Tom Brown Porridge," she writes about how she told a friend that her husband really loves *aprapransa* (a palm soup/stew dish with toasted corn flour), but every time she makes it he complains that it isn't as good as his grandmother's. Osseo-Asare says, "[my friend] assured me that no matter what I will do, it will NEVER be as good as he remembers hers, so I should 'just let go of that burden.' "[20] Similarly, I was willing to accept my husband's comfort eating some foods prepared by Ghanaian women because it seemed clear that his feelings were directly tied to issues of memory. By refusing to eat the Ghanaian foods cooked by me, however, my husband exerted a certain amount of emotional power and control in that he made it clear that when it came to Ghanaian cooking he preferred food cooked by Ghanaian hands.

This interplay of gender expectations and communications not only reveals the idiosyncrasies of my family but also the ways in which people—mostly women, of all races, classes, ethnicities, and regions—make adjustments in the household routine to accommodate others. DeVault refers to this phenomenon as deference, a situation she argues is not easily described in terms of control, power, or autonomy.[21] DeVault takes women to task for confusing acquiescence with equity. But in the absence of violence, sometimes deference may be fine if it means that balance and peace of mind is achieved and other agendas are fulfilled. My preference is to see this arrangement as one that provides an alternative to the binary formulation of cooking/not cooking. If we see this intercultural, intergenerational exchange of foods as part of a culinary continuum, then power and equity can return to the equation. There was a particular level of conjugal loyalty, trust, and intimacy that was being negotiated here, feelings that extended beyond my husband's thoughts, wants, and desires. This is not to idealize our situation or to represent the kitchen as a place of freedom and contentment. Far from it. Rather, the goal is to illustrate how primary food providers engage in survivalist techniques and strategies that assist in humanizing multiple environments. A couple of other examples lay bare my point.

CULTURAL RULES/CULTURAL VALUES

At times during the early phases of our marriage, my husband would make use of his extended cultural network by riding across town to the home of "the Ghanaian lady who makes *waakye*." Once there, he would disappear into an apartment complex and emerge ten minutes later having purchased the very popular Ghanaian rice and beans—waakye.[22] By inviting me to ride along he not only made me aware of the origins of the food but also privy to the underground network of women providing "food from home" (Ghana) to anxiously awaiting customers. Unable to afford the luxury of a formal restaurant, the kitchens in these women's homes became makeshift establishments for making money and transmitting culture. My husband likened these occasions to "taking a trip to McDonald's," attributing his actions to normal market exchanges of goods and services.

It is not unusual to find women and men who illegally prepare and sell ready-to-eat meals. This is especially the case in locales inhabited by various immigrant groups where formal restaurants catering to their gustatory needs and desires are few and far between. This underground trade is performed all the time by people in every social stratum to make ends meet and to garner a few additional funds. While illegal, it is an important occupation for women and men unable, otherwise, to find employment. This work not only contributes to their family's economic support but also to the cultural well-being of those who frequent their temporary eatery.

Like any kind of wage labor, cooking, whether for yourself or someone else, is not unproblematic. These women—strangers, friends, and family—engage in extra-labor so I can further my career and my husband's tastes can be satisfied. To be sure, the compensation Kwame gives these women is hardly comparable to the amount of physical labor we are extracting—planning, shopping, cooking, storing/presenting, and in some cases delivering the food before cleaning the kitchen and the dishes used to prepare the meals. In their article on the gendered politics of food, Patricia Allen and Carolyn Sachs describe the complexities of women nourishing family members and, in some instances, those outside their homes. As Allen and Sachs note, "male household members rarely step in" and, when they do, it is generally not fully to the extent that assistance is needed. Consequently, other women—usually poor, immigrant, women of color—are hired to assist in providing these services.[23] This was certainly the case for my family during the early years of our marriage, as I taught classes and wrote my dissertation. As my time at home to learn a new way of cooking was diminished, we aligned with kin and employed Ghanaian women, most of whom either worked solely in their own homes or in service positions, to aid in my career advancement and the overall functioning of our home, from the daily to the weekly or occasional. For example, when my husband got sick he would pay our godson's mother to make light soup or hot pepper soup.[24] Usually, this family friend would use the opportunity of cooking for her own family to simultaneously make enough to share with us.

Despite Kwame's dismissive explanation for how he sometimes acquired his evening meal, there were more weighty issues involved. Whether acknowledged by him or not, his decision to seek food prepared by other hands was directly tied to my inability to cook the foods he liked. For this and other reasons, there were entanglements and implications of great importance tied to the goods and services being produced and consumed. Gracia Clark puts it this way: "Domestic work, as unpaid production for immediate consumption, is dominated by the rules and values associated with the consumption of the goods and services it produces. . . . Cultural rules place values, for example, not only on the dishes produced by cooking, but on when to cook, who should cook for whom, and the consequences of specific deviations from these stipulations."[25]

Clark's observation is most salient in an experience we had when misconceptions entered into our food-sharing arrangement. Normally, the presence of Corning Ware containers indicates that one of the sisters has sent over spinach sauce for me or another dish for both of us. The container was usually accompanied by an explanation from Kwame of who made the food, the ingredients it contained, and so on. This particular occasion did not engender my husband's usual practice of telling me any of these details. I soon discovered the reason. The container held spaghetti, which had been prepared by one of his African American coworkers. Our very specialized arrangement allows for Ghanaian women (women who are known to me) to cook Ghanaian food. It is fine that Kwame enjoys Ghanaian prepared foods, but this does not mean that there are no boundaries that can be violated. In other words, it was a mistake for him to confuse gratification with rendering our kitchen a culinary free-for-all. Although unwritten, the rulebook did not allow for a sampling of non-Ghanaian foods cooked by random women. This is akin to culinary adultery because not only does it involve a kind of culinary intercourse between my husband and another woman, but also it moves into a realm where emotions and other affections can easily get entangled. Needless to say, it was necessary for a conversation to take place that emphasized spaghetti is not on the list of acceptable foods that can be imported into our kitchen. I can and often would make spaghetti, much to his liking. So if a red sauce and noodle combination would be consumed it would be by these African American hands.

In her article "Money, Sex, and Cooking: Manipulation of the Paid/Unpaid Boundary by Asante Market Women," Clark elaborates on this point. Writing about Ghanaian Asante market women, Clark explains that they face incredible hurdles managing their daily market responsibilities along with their domestic tasks. Because cooking is directly linked to the marital relationship in Ghanaian contexts the compromises they make are critical to their overall survival. In short, Clark argues that there is a direct correlation between cooking the evening meal and sex within marriage: "The exchange of his daily or weekly 'chop money,' or food money, for her cooking and other domestic services is the hallmark of marriage for urban Asante, distinguishing it from other less formal sexual relations even without the performance of customary or church rites." The chop money is used not only to feed an Asante woman's husband but also her family and to take care of the remaining household responsibilities. This is one of the many reasons women turn either to their children or to other kin for assistance when cooking obligations strain their personal and physical resources. Eating another woman's meal is akin to conjugal infidelity.[26]

MAKING PLACE, MAKING HOME—"IT IS MY DUTY TO COOK FOR YOU"

It was important to reconcile that the food practices in our home—I cook, we cook, others cook—would reinforce one another. In all, the cooking belonged to clusters of people, sometimes individually, sometimes collectively. Critical here is the element of home cooking that keeps us in touch with the basic social relationships that give form and meaning to our lives. The fact that others were willing to cook for us served a practical and cultural function, and it provided a context for maintaining certain personal relationships. In addition to being useful, the meal preparations were also acts of sociability and gender-specific acts of creative expression. My husband would often argue that, for him, food serves almost strictly as a function of staving off hunger. Left unconsidered is the fact that through the food preparation and consumption he too is

engaging in the very personal relationships that sustain his well-being. This form of sustenance is significant to his survival individually and our continuation as a couple. Nostalgic memories of home are imbricated here—as much fabricated as they appear to be real. They are, as Geneviève Fabre and Robert O'Meally suggest, "subject to the biases, quirks, and rhythms of the individual's mind."[27] Consequently, the connections between eating and memory are necessarily infused at times with plenty of disconnections. One contribution to this disconnect is the availability, or lack thereof, of certain ingredients. Culinary exchanges—like cream of wheat as a substitute for the starchy substances that must accommodate Ghanaian soups—are part of what fosters the creative side of adaptation.

I began this chapter with, "other women used to cook for my husband." Implicit in this is the understanding on my part that this is a privilege and not a right. It is born out of a particular consciousness that recognizes my liminal agency and power—economic, social, and cultural— as the primary planner, purchaser, and preparer of food in my home. It also recognizes the cultural status that my in-laws place upon me as a university professor. They see me as having "an important job that keeps me busy" and offered to help ease my burdens by preparing and providing meals. One last example brings home the importance of this observation.

Two years ago (and long after Kwame consistently started cooking the Ghanaian foods he likes), I received a call from my husband's niece announcing that she had arrived in the country. "Auntie," she said, "I am here; can you come get me?" Having no idea that she was coming to the United States, let alone that she would be coming to my house, I was taken aback by her fifteen-year-old mind that thought I was to drop everything and come get her right away. I was further shocked when she explained that she needed me to pick her up so she could babysit our daughter and cook for us. Somewhat bewildered, I arrived at my sister-in-law's store to pick her up, only to be confronted with "What do you want me to cook?" I had no idea. It was around three in the afternoon and my mind was on whatever project I was still completing. I had yet to make the mental transition to the evening meal. Stating as much, "our" niece and my sisters-in-law went about getting foodstuffs that would comprise some kind of dinner. As it was dictated to her from behind the checkout counter by her aunt and mother, Sara went about picking up this and that ingredient. When it was all said and done we had bags consisting of plantains, yams, tomatoes, mixed vegetables, canned corned beef, goat meat, and spices (one of the few times we were graced with food we did not have to buy). On our way home, Sara again brought up the subject of cooking for me. When I again protested and explained that I would cook with no problem, she said, "No, auntie . . . it is my duty to cook for you and my uncle." The concept hit me like a ton of bricks. Here was this young girl who was insisting that she prepare our food. On some level it seemed that to reject her offering would be more offensive than to accept. So I acquiesced—graciously.

When I shared what happened with Kwame later that evening he seemed less surprised than I, remarking, "These kids are raised to know what is expected of them. She's my niece, I'm the older one. She is expected to do her chores; that is part of her chore. That's a big difference between our kids; they are very, very, very respectful of what is expected of them. You wake up in the morning and clean the whole house, you cook. If you are a boy, you do the things that you are expected to do. She wasn't serving us. She was doing the things she is supposed to do in the household. It was a chore more than anything else." Steven J. Salm and Toyin Falola in "Gender Roles, Marriage, and Family," in their *Culture and Customs of*

Ghana, are less flexible in their explanation of why a fifteen-year-old could not only cook a full meal but also present it in such a way as to be restaurant ready. They suggest that domestic skills such as cooking, cleaning, and caring for children are "emphasized" because "women will need proficiency in these areas to attract a good husband."[28] The truth is no doubt somewhere between the two rationales. What was clear, however, is that ten years into our marriage I am still learning (and will continue to learn) and am amazed at the ways in which food culture shapes and impacts our identity as individuals and as a couple.

Some women, with whom I initially conferred about this chapter, thought my arrangement made little sense, especially since I am capable of cooking. From conversations over time I realized that they thought I was opening the door for all kinds of trouble. More to the point, they believed that I was merely shirking some of my familial responsibilities. These women, in effect, challenged my sense of "womanhood" and seemed relatively oblivious to the various ways that households can function. The fact that I am unwilling or unable to take the time to indulge in the labor-intensive preparations related to cooking my husband's native foods seems to somehow suggest a lack of nurturing. Left out of their thinking is the understanding that a carefully orchestrated culinary arrangement with numerous intricacies was set in motion. This decision was made with the same science and precision that is used in writing a recipe or cooking a nicely fashioned meal. Determining what foods get to my kitchen table and who prepares them is as much a part of the process of cooking as actually preparing the meal. Even more, establishing a sense of community and cultural relevancy is not static; it comes in all forms.

Freedom from some aspects of the cooking routine is liberating, but far more important for me is acknowledging and celebrating the unification of our family and the cultures of black diasporic peoples. As discussed here, food, in its ubiquity, is powerful, exciting, and dangerous for what it means and does to our bodies, minds, and souls. The adoption of this culinary lifestyle links present and past, Ghana and Maryland. We are a diasporic family unified by common foods such as tomatoes, onions, hot peppers, ginger, beans, okra, collards, kale, mustard greens, and rice (a lot of rice)—foods shared by many transatlantic peoples around the globe. Our form of food sharing has forced and encouraged some exciting and uncomfortable interactions. It has made it impossible for me to ignore and reject my husband's culinary traditions and him, mine. Kwame eats collard greens when they are cooked, and he will sometimes also eat *my version* of a spinach sauce. When he sees it necessary to comment on the taste of the sauce or what I should do "the next time," I gently remind him that this is my interpretation of the sauce and it is not meant to replicate the Ghanaian taste. Here again we are presented with a culinary boundary or what we might see as a bridge. What seems to be *Kontomereh* (spinach stew) is actually slow-cooked spinach with smoked turkey similar to a pot of collard greens but absent the "pot likker." When eaten with boiled yams and *Ampesi* (plantain) or *omor tuo* (rice balls), the taste might be different, but it is simply a matter of different mixtures and forms; the ingredients are the same. More to the point, it has encouraged him to do what he was clearly capable of doing all along—cook the foods he likes for himself and his family, a task he performs quite well every Sunday.

I am all too aware that for some of the women we employed cooking was an unwanted burden. But the kitchen space also can be synonymous with agency, self-definition, and self-awareness, given the social interactions that occur in and around it. It is a landscape that comes

with changing meanings and significance. These fragments of our life experiences speak as much to particularities in taste as to issues of group cultural identity. But they also speak to my own intimate meanings with food along with a willingness to provide a sense of social and cultural cohesion. By agreeing to the arrangement of sharing food, I opened up loci of commonality, creating a sense of community and simultaneously sanctioning different points of view. Aside from its personal usefulness, I was at home with these concepts because a womanist worldview encourages a commitment to the survival and wholeness of the entire people, female and male. This position sustained my connections to Africa and America, past and present. In these food events we can read strong connections to traditions informed by the rituals of preparation that mark time and place. These meals, and the hands that prepare them, bind my husband to his country, and by my sharing these foods with him they bind me to him. Having these women from home cook for him, and by extension, us, in ways that are familiar contribute to his sense of self. In turn, they help us create new cultural mores and hybridized forms of meal planning.

Placing food at the center of a gendered conversation allows for stories of feminist consciousness, community building, cultural work, and personal identity to emerge. Using the everyday domain of the kitchen, alliances were forged to help combat the stresses of this black woman's life, which remains inscribed by multiple jeopardies. Women's narratives around food reveal the intricate ways in which women influence the food and food habits of others but also illuminate the powerful ways in which food serves as a communicator of culture. Personal narratives also reveal how women—dependent and self-sufficient—engaged in strategies of individual and collective uplift. Using self-ethnography this article sought to highlight these issues as well as the translatability of food cultures by pointing to, rather than erasing, the differences between and among people of the African diaspora; to complicate further our understanding of blackness vis-à-vis the unstable signifier of food; and to interrogate how I, a womanist scholar of foodways, understood and participated in traversing the sometimes thorny terrains of power, food, identity, place, gender relations, and gender expectations in my home.

NOTES

1. Marjorie DeVault, *Feeding the Family: The Social Organization of Caring as Gendered Work* (Chicago: University of Chicago Press, 1991), 79; Christopher Carrington, "Feeding Lesbigay Families," in *Food and Culture: A Reader*, ed. Carole Counihan and Penny Van Esterik (New York: Routledge, 1997), 259–88, and *No Place Like Home: Relationships and Family Life among Lesbians and Gay Men* (Chicago: University of Chicago Press, 2002). See also Sarah Oerton, "Queer Housewives? Some Problems in Theorising the Division of Domestic Labour in Lesbian and Gay Households," *Women's Studies International Forum* 20, no. 3 (1997): 421–30; Maureen Sullivan, "Rozzie and Harriet? Gender and Family Patterns of Lesbian Coparents," *Gender and Society* 10 (December 1996): 747–67; M. Deborah Bialeschki and Kimberly Pearce, " 'I Don't Want a Lifestyle—I Want a Life': The Effect of Role Negotiations on the Leisure of Lesbian Mothers," *Journal of Leisure Research* 29, no. 1 (1997): 113–32.

2. Beth Durodoye and Angela Coker, "Crossing Cultures in Marriage: Implications for Counseling African American/African Couples," *International Journal for the Advancement of Counseling* 30 (March 2008): 25–26.

3. "We Eat First with Our Eyes: On Ghanaian Cuisine," *Gastronomica: The Journal of Food and Culture* 2 (Winter 2002): 50.

4. Brinda Mehta, "Culinary Diasporas: Identity and the Language of Food in Gisèle Pineau's *Un papillon dans la cité* and *L'exil selon Julia*," *International Journal of Francophone Studies* 8, no. 1 (2005): 35.

5. Parama Roy, "Reading Communities and Culinary Communities: The Gastropoetics of the South Asian Diaspora," *Positions: East Asia Cultures Critique* 10, no. 2 (2002): 471–502.

6. Psyche Williams-Forson, *Building Houses Out of Chicken Legs: Black Women, Food, and Power* (Chapel Hill: University of North Carolina Press, 2006).

7. Carole Boyce Davies, *Black Women, Writing, and Identity: Migrations of the Subject* (New York: Routledge, 1994), 21.

8. Dugan Romano, *Intercultural Marriage: Promises and Pitfalls* (London: Nicholas Brealey Publishing, 2001), 46.

9. The concept of the culinary collective draws from the idea of co-mothering or Othermothering. See Ifi Amadiume, *Male Daughters, Female Husbands: Gender and Sex in an African Society* (London: Zed, 1987); Akosua Adomako Ampofo, "Mothering among Black and White Non-Ghanaian Women in Ghana," *JENdA: A Journal of Culture and African Women Studies*, no. 5 (2004); on-line at http://www.africaknowledgeproject.org/index.php/jenda/article/view/96.

10. Oyeronke Oyewumi, "Ties That (Un)Bind: Feminism, Sisterhood, and Other Foreign Relations," *JENdA* 1, no. 1 (2001): 2–18; and Patricia Hill Collins, *Black Feminist Thought* (Boston: Unwin Hyman, 1990), 128–31.

11. The literature on kinship networks and mutual aid is extensive, including Carol Stack, *All Our Kin: Strategies for Survival in a Black Community* (New York: Basic Books, 1973); and Harriette Pipes McAdoo, "Factors Related to Stability in Upwardly Mobile Black Families," *Journal of Marriage and the Family* 40 (November 1978): 761–76.

12. Elisha Renne, "Mass Producing Food Traditions for West Africans Abroad," *American Anthropologist* 109 (December 2007): 616–25 and 624 n.4; Lynne Phillips, "Food and Globalization," *Annual Review of Anthropobgy* 35 (October 2006): 37–57; Fran Osseo-Asare, *Food Culture in Sub-Saharan Africa* (Westport, CT: Greenwood Press, 2005), and her BetumiBlog, www.betumiblog.blogspot.com.

13. Micaela di Leonardo, "The Female World of Cards and Holidays: Women, Families, and the Work of Kinship," *Signs* 12 (Spring 1987): 441–53.

14. VertaMae Grosvenor, "Forward," in Ntozake Shange's *If I Can Cook/You Know God Can* (Boston: Beacon Press, 1998), xii.

15. Gretchen Lemke-Santangelo discusses the problem of acquiring staples in *Abiding Courage: African American Migrant Women and the East Bay Community* (Chapel Hill: University of North Carolina Press, 1996), 133.

16. Collins, *Black Feminist Thought*, 223.

17. Kurt Lewin, *Forces behind Food Habits and Methods of Change, Bulletin of the National Research Council*, no. 108 (1943): 35–65; W. Alex McIntosh and Mary Zey, "Women as Gatekeepers of Food Consumption," in *Food and Gender, Identity and Power*, ed. Carole Counihan

and Stephen Kaplan (Newark, NJ: Harwood Academic Publishers, 1999), 125–41. See DeVault, *Feeding the Family*; Nickie Charles and Marion Kerr, *Women, Food, and Families* (Manchester, U.K.: Manchester University Press, 1988); and Carrington, *No Place Like Home*.

18. Theresa W. Devasahayam, "Power and Pleasure around the Stove: The Construction of Gendered Identity in Middle-Class South Indian Hindu Households in Urban Malaysia," *Women's Studies International Forum* 28 (January–February 2005): 1–20.

19. Bernice Johnson Reagon, "African Diaspora Women: The Making of Cultural Workers," *Feminist Studies* 12 (Spring 1986): 79, 84.

20. Theresa Kwakye, "African-Americans in Ghanaian Marriages," e-mail message to author, 24 Apr. 2008; Fran Osseo-Asare, "Recipe #6: 'Tom Brown Porridge,' " BetumiBlog, www.betumi.com/blog.html, 21 May 2009.

21. Marjorie DeVault, "Conflict and Deference," in *Food and Culture*, 180–99.

22. Waakye (pronounced waachay) or wanche, depending upon the person's ethnicity, is a well-known dish of rice and beans. It is so common that it is considered the equivalent of our fast foods. See Marian Shardow, *A Taste of Hospitality: Authentic Ghanaian Cookery* (Victoria, Canada: Trafford Publishing, 2002), 85; and David Otoo and Tamminay Otoo, *Authentic African Cuisine from Ghana* (Colorado Springs, CO: Sankofa, 1997), 55.

23. Patricia Allen and Carolyn Sachs, "Women and Food Chains: The Gendered Politics of Food," *International Journal of Sociology of Food and Agriculture* 15, no. 1 (2007): 1–23.

24. Light soup has as its base the three common ingredients of tomatoes, onion, and hot peppers. It is essentially a broth that might be seasoned with smoked fish and sometimes in our house it is cooked with smoked turkey. It is usually served with fufu, rice, or another starch.

25. Gracia Clark, "Money, Sex, and Cooking: Manipulation of the Paid/Unpaid Boundary by Asante Market Women," in *The Social Economy of Consumption*, ed. Henry Rutz and Benjamin Orlove (Lanham, MD: University Press of America, 1989), 323.

26. According to my husband, Asante/Ashanti, Akan, and Akuapem women of Ghana understand the practice of chop money exchanges. As such, it is familiar to him. So synonymous are sex and eating that both Kwame and Clark explain that in the Ghanaian language Twi, the verb (di) is used to mean both sex and food. Clark further clarifies that (di) must be reduplicated (didi) to directly refer to eating. See Clark's, "Money, Sex, and Cooking," 326–27. Also see, Gracia Clark, *Onions Are My Husband: Survival and Accumulation by West African Market Women* (Chicago: University of Chicago Press, 1995), esp. chap. 9.

27. Geneviève Fabre and Robert O'Meally, eds., *History and Memory in African-American Culture* (New York: Oxford University Press, 1994), 5.

28. Steven J. Salm and Toyin Falola, "Gender Roles, Marriage, and Family," in their *Culture and Customs of Ghana* (Westport, CT: Greenwood Publishing, 2002), 129.

12

Going Beyond the Normative White "Post-Racial" Vegan Epistemology

A. Breeze Harper

Popular definitions of who is and what defines veganism agree that in general it is a person (and a moment) that excludes meat, eggs, dairy products and all other animal-based ingredients. Many vegans also do not eat foods that are processed using animal products, and avoid the use of products tested on animals, and abstain from leather, fur and wool. In any case, one important fact to note is that plant-based living and eating has been around since time immemorial. Given the belief in ethical living and harmony with all animal life, why are so many voices excluded from mainstream thinking about the movement? Why, in fact, has the vegan movement been largely associated with and attributed to whiteness, the most popular book titles exemplifying race-neutral approaches to veganism? What does a race-consciousness approach look like in popular vegan writing? Taking up these and other questions of racialization, this essay will consider mainstream vegan media to argue that popular representations of veganism are far from race-neutral.

BRINGING IN RACE CONSCIOUSNESS INTO A "POST-RACIAL" MAINSTREAM VEGAN MOVEMENT

There is an underlying assumption amongst mainstream vegan media that racialization and the production of vegan spaces are disconnected. However, space, vegan or not, is raced/racialized (Dwyer and Jones III 2000; McKittrick 2006; McKittrick and Woods 2007; Price 2009) and simultaneously sexualized, gendered (Massey 1994; Moss and Al-Hindi 2008), and classed, directly affecting individual and place identities, including one's philosophy of what counts as a moral food system. Scholars engaged in critical geographies of race claim that the world is entirely racialized. How human beings develop their knowledge base is directly connected to the embodied experiences of the places and spaces we navigate through. David Delaney, a geographer employing critical race theory asks, "What does it mean for geographers to take this claim of a wholly racialized world seriously?" (Price 2009, 7).

Racialized places and spaces are at the foundation of how most of us in the USA develop our socio-spatial epistemological grid (Dwyer and Jones III 2000; Lee and Lutz 2005; McKittrick and Woods 2007). Hence, socio-spatial epistemologies are racialized. Socio-spatial epistemology is a concept that centers on how and why we know what we know, based on spatial relations and what our bodies mean in certain places. For example, collectively low-income urban black Americans in the USA *know* that a holistic plant-based diet is most often nearly impossible to achieve; simultaneously, the collectivity of white middle-class urban people in the USA *know* that a holistic plant-based diet generally is easy to achieve (Dubowitz et al. 2008). If you are the former, your relationship with healthier food options is influenced by a host of factors not the least of which might very well be environmental racism—lack of access to public transportation to get to healthier food sources, and the placement of fast food and liquor store chains in closer proximity to you than an affordable produce center (Baker et al. 2006; Cohen et al. 2010). If you are the latter, a combination of white and class privilege have socially and physically placed you in a location of environmental privilege, easy access to transportation to get to healthier options, and the placement of holistic health-oriented food locations (Community Supported Agriculture sites, farmers' markets, produce grocers, etc.) that exist in proximity to you in your town (Wilson et al. 2008). Racialization, of course, is linked to class, and class is linked to who gets to live in healthier environments more than others. The way vegans in the USA think about a moral food system cannot be separated from the places and spaces that they have been racialized within; hence, these epistemologies are racialized and vegan epistemologies are no exception. However, such reflections of intersections of racial privilege (or lack thereof), food knowledge, and place are thematically absent from most popular mainstream vegan literature, such as the top 100 bestselling books in the "vegan" category of online book store, Amazon. com. Using the search content tool to explore the content of the top 100 bestselling "vegan" categorized books on Amazon.com, I entered these keywords: "whiteness," "white privilege," "race," "racialization," or "racial." None of these concepts were found.[1]

What is Post-Racial?

Popular titles such as *Vegan: The New Ethics of Eating* (Marcus 2001), *The Vegan Sourcebook* (Stepaniak and Messina 2000), *Skinny Bitch* series, *The World Peace Diet* (Tuttle 2007) and *Becoming Vegan* (Davis and Vesanto 2000) are considered vegan literary essentials. Interestingly, these titles do not engage in any critical analysis of how one's racialized experience influences how and why one writes about, teaches, and engages in vegan praxis. Though it is not the intent of the aforementioned books to focus on racialized experience and its effects on vegan philosophy, the absence of *any* reflection on racialized consciousness cannot be ignored. Critical race theorists such as Zuberi and Bonilla-Silva (2008), Arnold Farr (2004), Charles W. Mills (1997), Shannon Sullivan and Nancy Tuana (2007) argue that even though ethical issues, such as veganism, are touted as "race-neutral" in the European tradition of philosophy, they are in fact raced. Such a critical observation is important to point out because such race-neutral popular titles assume that all people in the USA start from a *universal* social location/consciousness; however, *universal* is simply a coded phrase for assumed white middle-class experience. Such assumptions have created a rift between the collectivity of white middle class and women of color vegans[2] who must be 'race-conscious' to navigate and survive in what Bonilla-Silva calls a color-blind racist USA (Bonilla-Silva 2006). In her dissertation about the challenges of color-blind racism within grassroots social justice organizations, Dr. Beeman asserts:

> In contemporary society, the racist ideology of colorblindness helps to uphold the larger system of racism by denying its existence. I define color-blind ideology as a culturally sanctioned system of beliefs that justify and reinforce the larger system of racism. Unlike racist ideologies of the past, color-blind ideology rests on the seemingly positive belief that we should not judge one another by the color of our skin; we should treat everyone the same way. In fact, we should not notice skin color at all. These

ideologies, which are widely accepted by people in the U.S., conveniently ignore persisting racist discrimination. Political pundits have used color-blind ideology to argue against policies that take past and current racial discrimination into account. They attempt to explain away racial disparities in healthcare, educational attainment, wealth, etc. by arguing that other factors, such as income and cultural differences are to blame. It is through these racism-evasive attempts to deny the existence and significance of racism as the root cause of racial inequalities that keeps the larger system of racism intact.

(Beeman 2010, 4–5)

For the sake of not using ablest terminology, I have decided to use the phrases "race-neutral" or "post-racial" to describe the concept of color-blind racism for this essay. This essay will explore the consequences of race-neutral vegan writing, as well as discuss what race-conscious vegan writing projects look like.

What does it mean to be conscious of race when embarking on writing projects such as vegan-oriented research

There are two quite distinct issues in the study of race. One is a methodological matter: Who has access to what scene, and with what outcome? But in addition to the question of access, there is the less frequently examined question of the very building blocks of knowledge construction, namely, whose questions get raised for investigation?

(Twine and Warren 2000, xii)

I am the founder of *Sistah Vegan Project* (http://sistahvegan.wordpress.com/). Founded in 2005, this online project explores the black American female vegan experience, paying close attention to how race, legacies of colonialism, sexism, and classism manifest in American vegan praxis. With a combination of a blog and Yahoo listserv of 200 people, the black female vegan participants of this project engage in dialogues that make visible the

intersections of race-consciousness, socioeconomic class, problematics of normative whiteness, and First World and class privileged perspective within American veganism. The pinnacle of the project was the publication of my edited volume of narratives and critical essays called *Sistah Vegan: Black Female Vegans Speak on Food, Identity, Health, and Society* (Harper 2010). The themes that arise from the 25 black female vegan contributors, point to unique conceptualization and praxis of veganism that reflect the specific collective socio-historical and cultural experience of race (black) and sex (female). The narratives, essays, and poems in the *Sistah Vegan* book reveal that black females in the USA are more likely to be convinced of transitioning into a plant-based diet for the sake of combating racial health disparities (i.e. diabetes, fibroids, etc.) and decolonizing their bodies from the legacies of racialized colonialism, such as institutional and structural racism (Harper 2010).

The term health disparities refers to population-specific differences in the presence of disease, health outcomes, quality of health care and access to health care services—that exist across racial and ethnic groups. Many health and socio-economic factors contribute to health disparities, including inadequate access to care, poor quality of care, genetics, community features and personal behaviors. These factors are often associated with under-served racial and ethnic minority groups (often referred to as communities of color), individuals who have experienced economic obstacles, those with disabilities and individuals living within medically underserved communities. Consequently, individuals living in both urban and rural areas may experience health disparities.

("Disparities in Health" 2009)

However, to understand racial health disparities, one must also understand how and why it is a consequence of racism. Vernellia Rand defines individual, institutional, and systemic racism:

Individual racism consists of overt acts by individuals that cause death, injury, destruction of property, or denial of services or opportunity. Institutional racism is more subtle but no less destructive. Institutional racism involves policies, practices, and procedures of institutions that have a disproportionately negative effect on racial minorities' access to and quality of goods, services, and opportunities. Systemic racism is the basis of individual and institutional racism; it is the value system that is embedded in a society that supports and allows discrimination. Institutional and system racism establishes separate and independent barriers to access and quality of health care. Institutional racism does not have to result from human agency or intention. Thus, racial discrimination can occur in institutions even when the institution does not intend to make distinctions on the basis of race. In fact, institutional discrimination can occur without any awareness that it is happening.

(Randall 2006, 22)

The 25 women who contributed to *Sistah Vegan* collectively have a consciousness around practicing veganism within the context of the above quote. This is a significant contrast in comparison to my observation that white females who have written popularly selling mainstream vegan books promote the practice of veganism for animal rights or to become skinny as a conscious priority. The detriments of racialized colonialism, such as health inequities due to institutional racism, do not enter the conversation in the *New York Times* bestselling series *Skinny Bitch*, or in Alicia Silverstone's *The Kind Diet*. I argue that it simply does not enter their writings on vegan diets because their white privileged experiences with health and food in the USA mean they, and most of their constituency (70% of vegans in the USA are white females), do not have to make such considerations.[3]

In contrast, the *Sistah Vegan Project* is about observing how black female vegans perceive nutrition, food, health, and race. It asks: How does being racialized-sexualized in the USA as black female create a collectively different type of vegan praxis that is silenced in bestselling books such as *Skinny Bitch*, *Quantum Wellness*, and *The Kind Diet*, which cater to a post-racial white middle-class female audience? What does USA vegan epistemology look like through the eyes of race-conscious black females of *Sistah Vegan Project* and beyond?

Why Food Studies, Veganism, and Race?

Practitioners of veganism abstain from animal consumption (dietary and non-dietary). However, the culture of veganism itself is not a monolith and is composed of many different subcultures and philosophies throughout the world, ranging from punk strict vegans for animal rights, to people who are dietary vegans for personal health reasons, to people who practice veganism for religious and spiritual reasons (Cherry 2006; Iacobbo 2006). To provide a bit more context, more history of veganism in the U.S. is necessary here. According to one of the most popular information websites—The American Vegan Society (AVS) (founded in 1960 in Malaga, New Jersey)—veganism has been practiced "throughout recorded history." Accordingly, the first vegan society began in England in 1944 followed by the U.S. in California in 1948. Not surprisingly, the practice, more or less, reached its early peak in and throughout this country in the 1960s when most social movements, including the Civil Rights, Women's Rights and Gay Liberation struggles, were also in full force (Malesh 2005). Since this start, numerous books, magazines, journals, several of which have been published by AVS have emerged. This is in addition to the conferences and meetings, cooking classes and the like, and websites that have been spawned in dedication to the practice of vegan eating and living. According to the AVS website,

The present day vegan community in the U.S. involves many individuals and organizations. Besides the American Vegan Society, there are Gentle World, Vegan Outreach, Vegan Action, and vegan.com. A vegan diet is promoted by other organizations such as Physicians Committee for Responsible Medicine, the National Health Association (formerly American Natural Hygiene Society), Book Publishing (Tennessee), and Institute for Plant Based Nutrition. Increasingly, animal rights organizations, anti-vivisection societies, and farm animal reform and rescue groups have advocated the compassionate vegan lifestyle.

The overview on the website http://www.americanvegan.org/ goes on to explain notable contributions to the movement of veganism including the "the abundance of vegan information" supplied by the Vegetarian Resource Group since the mid-1980s. Marcia Pearson's contributions of "Fashion with Compassion"; Michael Klaper, MD an early practitioner who espoused the values of vegan lifestyle; William Harris, MD who presented "clear and compelling evidence of the superiority of vegan diet"; John Robbins, Howard Lyman and EarthSave who "have injected a note of urgency and marshaled facts demonstrating the folly of animal agriculture"; and, well-known author Joanne Stepaniak, "a contemporary teacher of compassion, and a prolific writer including many cookbooks." Of particular note and mentioned by the AVS are the number of stores that have emerged that now cater to vegan consumption, including Seventh Day Adventist stores.

Noticeably absent from this overview is anything that overtly reflects racial specificity, gender, or class. This is not necessarily surprising unless you are familiar with the practice of veganism/vegetarianism outside of white communities. In this vein, is the absence of any mention of long-time activist and politician Dick Gregory, who all but single-handedly brought the concept of raw food consumption to black communities, as early as the 1970s, after African American Dr. Alvenia Fulton introduced him to her plant-centered dietary regiment in Chicago, IL (Witt 2004). This is a noticeable contribution to say the least, especially since Gregory still advocates on behalf of people of color to adopt more healthy (indeed vegetarian if not vegan) lifestyles. Nor, of course, is there any mention of Rastafarianism (alongside Seventh Day Adventist) another religious group, but one that has its roots in Jamaica. These kinds of absences lead me to argue that veganism can have a plethora of sites from which vegan epistemologies are produced. However, popular media (such as AVS) only centralize white socio-spatial epistemologies of veganism, reflecting the collective history of white middle-class people's privileged relationship to consumption, spaces of power, and production of what is ethical. Food studies provides a useful platform for understanding socio-spatial epistemologies of consumption because

> Food habits—how we produce, procure, prepare, and consume food—represent powerful systems of symbols whose associations are closely held, in their own way, by nearly everyone. Looking at people's relationships with food can speak volumes about the people—their beliefs, their passions, their background knowledge and assumptions, and their personalities-all elements whose explorations can be strengthened by good research.
> (Miller and Deutsch 2009, 7)

Within my discipline of critical food geography with an emphasis in critical race feminism, I am intrigued by the phenomenon that veganism, in the United States of America, has the connotation of being a lifestyle of white socio-economic class privileged people. Despite this perception, there is a significant number of non-white vegans in the USA and there is little research that looks at how race (as well as class and geographical location) influence vegan praxis. I have particularly become concerned about the lack of representation of diverse epistemologies within mainstream vegan rhetoric and invisibility of epistemological contributions by black identified female vegans, especially since my earlier work shows that white vegans collectively believe that being racialized as white does not affect their vegan philosophy (Harper 2007; Harper 2010).

Black female vegans' experiences with food, let alone dietary veganism, are greatly influenced by class and by region. They are not monoliths. Family and social dynamics no doubt also affect their consumption. There are obvious differences in vegan philosophies amongst black female vegans across socio-economic class and regional locations. The working-class black woman practicing veganism in Mobile, Alabama will have a different relationship to food than the black middle-class vegan woman living in Harlem, New York. Factors such as access to transportation, restaurants, grocery stores, are all influenced by regional and class locations of black female vegans[4] throughout the USA. Most significantly, despite class and regional differences, an overwhelming majority of these black vegan women have a race-conscious approach to their vegan writing that is absent within the collective consciousness of the white middle-class popular mainstream vegan literature. Quite a few scholars of black women's food ways note that as black women rise up socioeconomically, they begin to engage in "racial uplift" that mimics the tastes of the white middle class. For example, Williams-Forson (2006) writes about how black middle-class women aspired to teach working-class black women how to cook and eat foods of the white middle class, in order to achieve racial uplift. Despite this obvious distinction amongst socio-economic classes, there is still a collective race-conscious understanding to these women's food empowerment philosophies; it may manifest

differently, but their race consciousness is clearly present. Black feminist theorist Patricia Hill Collins writes, "Despite difference created by historical era, age, social class, sexual orientation, skin color, or ethnicity, the legacy of struggle against violence that permeates U.S. social structure is a common thread binding African-American women" (Hill Collins 2000, 26). It is this observation of Black vegan women's race consciousness and survival against racialized violence (versus white middle-class vegan post-racial consciousness) that will be a central component of this essay with an understanding that gender, class, and *region* cannot be separated from the racialized experience.

Not all vegans are activists, however, for this essay I have intentionally focused on examples of black female vegan writers who consciously engage in social justice activism (i.e. food justice, environmental justice, and health activism) in response to the injustices that they themselves, and their communities struggle through due to ongoing and unresolved legacies of racialized colonialism, such as health disparities, racism, normative whiteness, socio-economic class struggle, and racialized sexism. Selecting these women was a strategic choice to make the case that the philosophy of veganism for individuals in the USA does not come from race-neutral consciousness. As the founder of the *Sistah Vegan Project*, I have received emails and read forum posts from white vegans who have defensively made the claim that explorations of race and criticisms of normative whiteness have no place within the vegan world (Harper 2007; Harper 2010). The black vegan women under analysis for this essay engage in a type of revolutionary black feminism. Hamer and Neville write:

> Articulations of Revolutionary Black Feminism (RBF) has increasingly become visible in the literature and has provided a radical analysis of these multiple systems of

oppression (e.g., Hamer & Neville, 1998; James, 1999); by radical analysis, we mean one that more explicitly outlines the impact of capitalism and class on Black women's lived experiences ... RBF is an evolving theory rooted in the traditions of Black feminisms, Black womanism, and revolutionary feminism ... We understand RBF as a set of systematically related principles designed to explain the lived experiences of Black women. The perspective is revolutionary in its underlying assumption that the dominant societal structures and ideologies must be transformed to eradicate oppression [. . . W]e delineate the following core RBF tenets: (a) Revolutionary vision is dynamic; (b) racial, gender, and sexual oppression are reconfigured within periods of capitalist restructuring; (c) Black women's oppression consists of two recursive components: structure and ideology; and (d) there is a dialectical link between theory and practice. An emphasis is placed on describing the current conditions of Black women and the interconnecting forces influencing these conditions as a way of contextualizing Black women's lived experiences and relevant areas of resistance.

(Neville and Hamer 2001, 437–38)

Before proceeding onto examples of black women engaged in a race-conscious approach to vegan activism, we will briefly explore what popular normative white and race-neutral vegan literature looks like, by examining the *New York Times* bestselling book, *Skinny Bitch*, as well as *Quantum Wellness*.

The Skinny on Race-neutral Veganism

In 2005, Rory Freedman and Kim Barnouin's vegan health book *Skinny Bitch* was published. Freedman and Barnouin's book became a *New York Times* bestseller, turning the book into a popular symbol for the mainstream vegan movement in the USA. It was a no holds barred guide to teaching women how to "stop eating crap and start looking fabulous." I have selected this text to provide an example of what I would call "white middle-upper-class" vegan literature written through race-neutral and class-neutral perspectives. Both Freedman and Barnouin are white women who are financially stable, and they seemingly write from such a social location without ever being cognizant of the implications of such privileges. Geared to *helping* women achieve a healthier and thinner body, never in the book do the authors reflect on how *easy* access to a whole foods vegan diet is directly connected to both race and class privilege in the USA (Gottlieb and Joshi 2010). Though the intent of the book is not to address the raced and classed aspects of "easy" access to vegan foods, I find it problematic that such a help guide leaves out these significant factors because, for me, this implies that it is a *universal* guide (versus white class First World and class privileged guide) to becoming a healthy vegan. Freedman and Barnouin have the privilege to suggest that *all* people in the USA have the same options that they had when they decided to transition into a vegan diet. This would suggest that the fourteen-year-old African American girl living in West Oakland, CA, in which access to a healthy lifestyle has overall been greatly impeded by food deserts, environmental racism, and gang violence (Cohen et al. 2010) is in the same position to "easily" go vegan as Freedman and Barnouin. Throughout the entire book, the authors yell at the readers, implying that they are lazy or moronic because they don't understand how to lose weight or eat healthier.

Give up the notion that you can be sedentary and still lose weight. You need to exercise, you lazy shit. Eating properly will dramatically improve your health, body, and all aspects of your life. But you've still gotta move your ass. Anyone with a brain can do the math: When done in conjunction with a good diet, exercise will make you lose weight faster than healthy eating alone.

(Freedman and Barnouin 2005, 20)

In addition, the authors "remind" us that going vegan is "easy" and that we shouldn't be "cheap assholes" about eating organic:

> Don't be a cheap asshole. Yeah, yeah, yeah, organic produce is usually more expensive than conventional produce. But we spent countless dollars on clothes, jewelry, manicures, magazines, rent or mortgages, car payments, and other bullshit. Surely your health and our bodies (we only get one body) are more important than anything else in our lives. Even if you are spending more on organic food, you'll save money in the long run if you're preparing more meals and snacks at home . . . Organic is worth the extra money, and you should aim to have everything you eat be organic. But especially when buying fruits or vegetables that you eat without peeling the skin.
>
> (Freedman and Barnouin 2005, 179)

Granted, the book is supposed to be a "no holds barred" take on dieting, but isn't it interesting that the reader never comes across passages like, "Going vegan and losing weight is easy. I make it look easy because I'm a white, class-privileged woman and our demographic collectively doesn't have to think about food deserts, environmental racism, or poverty"?

A few years later, the enormous success of the *Skinny Bitch* series helped to make Rory Freedman the winner of *VegNews's* 2008 "person of the year." Being the most popular vegan magazine in the USA, it is clear to me that their ideal candidate for such an honor is a white, class-privileged vegan woman whose books take a class- and race-neutral approach to veganism. Furthermore, *VegNews's 2008* pick for "book of the year" was Kathy Freston's *Quantum Wellness*, which sold over 200,000 copies. Like the authors of the *Skinny Bitch* series, Freston is a white, class-privileged vegan woman who offers a "practical and spiritual guide to health and happiness." She never reflects on how her race, First World and class privileges have led her to conclude why her guide is

"practical," or that even the concept of "practical" is not objective, but subjective. Though this was not the intent of her book, the lack of any reflection on this, coupled with she and Rory Freedman as the popular icons for "going vegan" in the most widely read vegan magazine in the USA, paint the picture that how one comes to and engages in veganism in the USA have nothing to do with racial or class locations. Despite the never-ending list of scholarly research that has been published to show that being of the white class privileged demographic is inextricably linked to easier access to healthier foods (Gottlieb and Joshi 2010), these factors continue to go unexamined in such popular race-neutral, white middle-class-oriented vegan books. In the next section, I will give several examples of what race-conscious popular vegan writing looks like, and how revolutionary black feminist vegan authors articulate what I find absent from Freston, Freedman, and Barnouin.

What Race-conscious Veganism Looks Like

Queen Afua is the author of *Heal Thyself for Life and Longevity, The Angry Vagina, City of Wellness*, and *Sacred Woman*. She is one of the most influential and famous African American vegan health activists within the black community in the USA. Afua is an example of a vegan who merges race-consciousness and anti-corporate capitalism within her paradigm of black female reproductive health and nutritional writing. In *Sacred Woman* and *City of Wellness*, Afua calls for people of the African diaspora to literally reorganize and rebuild their *home* spaces, turning these sites, especially the *kitchen space*, into spaces: of *self-love*, healthy *black nation-building* that challenge corporate capitalism and neocolonialism, and that heal the black female womb from fibroid tumors, ovarian cancer, endometriosis, etc., through whole foods veganism (Afua

2000; Afua 2008). In *City of Wellness*, Afua's socio-spatial epistemology manifests from seeing African Diasporic and Caribbean communities throughout the USA and beyond, suffer from nutritional related diseases over the course of 30 years:

> The City of Wellness grew out of the overwhelmingly positive response to the heal thyself national fasting crusades and my lifelong missions as a holistic health activist. During my thirty year watch from New York to Los Angeles, Detroit to Baton Rouge, Ghana to London, and countless communities in between, I have witnessed a common thread of disease that impacts most of my clients and many of the participants in my lectures and workshops. Today this life threatening health crisis is spreading through the African American community like a twenty-first century black plague.
>
> (Afua 2008, 3)

How plant-based diets can positively change the overall health of African Americans is an important topic to pursue, particularly since the benefits of a properly planned plant-based diet are proven to decrease nutritional related health disparities in the black community (Bailey 2006; Foster et al. 1998; Mangels 1994). Simultaneously, there is literature that points to the importance of considering that, collectively, the racial-sexual experiences of black females in the USA differ significantly, psychically and materially, from the white middle-class status quo (Bennett and Dickerson 2001; Hill Collins 2000; Hill Collins 2004; James 2002; White 1994; Williams-Forson 2006). Hence, popular mainstream (white middle-class) nutritional-health media (books, magazines, etc.) are not as culturally appropriate for a majority of the black female demographic as they are for its white middle-class American constituency (Bediako et al. 2004; Booth and Chilton 2007; James 2004; Montgomery 2005; Welcome 2004;

White 1994). However, as illustrated by my brief analysis of *Skinny Bitch* and *Quantum Wellness*, popular mainstream vegan books rarely, if ever, acknowledge such differing socio-historically racialized epistemologies between the white racial status quo and the collectivity of people of color in the USA. For example, the extremely powerful and most famous vegan-oriented organization in the USA, PETA, cater to white middle-class sociospatial epistemologies of consumption and have a clear message that animal rights should be the primary reason why one should become vegan (Deckha 2008). In contrast, Queen Afua's writing aims to take care of the racialized suffering of human beings *first*, as reason to become vegan.

In *City of Wellness*, Afua's orientation towards a vegan diet as liberation for people of African diaspora does not prioritize animal rights at all. I argue that because black people are still collectively dealing with *human rights* to health and food security, Queen Afua does not prioritize the animal rights motive the same way that popular race-neutral book series such as *Skinny Bitch* or Alicia Silverstone's *The Kind Diet* do (which we will explore in more depth further in this essay). I would argue that Afua is trying to meet the material realities of black people. Hence, skipping over the not yet fully attained human rights for animal rights, would not go over well with a constituency that, hooks and Hill Collins note, are also dealing with a collective colonial past that once equated black people as subhuman; as animals (Hill Collins 2006; hooks 1992). This is not to say that there are no black people who are convinced to 'go vegan' after reading about animal rights; for those who do, many still have a race-conscious and African American health-oriented approach to how they engage in animal rights which will be explored later in this essay. However, white middle and white upper class people collectively do not have to deal with *human rights* to health and food security, so it makes sense that this wouldn't be at the forefront of *Skinny Bitch, Quantum Wellness*, or *The Kind Diet*'s goals. Slow food movement, organic food, Farmers' Markets, CSAs, and nicely stocked whole foods grocery stores continue to be most accessible by white socio-economically stable people (Gottlieb and Joshi 2010; Slocum 2007). Furthermore, this demographic is not only less likely to have to worry about how their health is impeded by the *food they eat*, they are less likely to worry about the direct negative impacts of environmental racism on their bodies. For example, the placement of dumps, truck depots, or big industry farms next to their homes rarely happens at the astronomical rate that it does to communities of color (Bullard 1993; Sandler 2007). Specifically to black communities, Vernellia Randall writes that

> Of particular importance to Black health is the locating of environmental hazards and toxic dumps in Black communities as well as hazards in the workplace and the home.
>
> Studies have documented that hazardous waste landfills are disproportionately located in Black communities. In fact, such studies have concluded that race, more than poverty, land values, or home ownership, is a predictor as to the location of hazardous waste facilities. Race is independent of social-economic class in the distribution of air pollution, consumption of contaminated fish, location of municipal landfills and incinerators, abandoned toxic waste dumps, cleanup of superfund sites, lead poisoning in children, and asthma.
>
> (Randall 2006, 159)

Environmental racisms experienced by people of color create physical, emotional, and mental health ailments that are more than just a race-neutral whole foods vegan book guide can remedy, simply because racism also *induces socio-economic class inequality*, creating unequal access to *any* type of healthier lifestyle, vegan or not. In *City of Wellness* Afua is acutely aware of

how racism is classed, and how classism is raced. She explains how the health care system is so influenced by profit that nothing but production of illness in the black community results from this:

> Like many Americans, our people rely heavily on the "health care system" rather than on natural living to prevent and treat sickness of dis-ease. This profit-based system pays little attention to prevention and instead focuses on scientific "cures" and pharmaceutical mediations that often hide symptoms . . .
>
> The health care system that we so heavily depend on does not welcome us or treat us the same as it does White patients. Black are twice as likely not to have insurance to pay for health care, and even when we do have medical insurance we get a lower quality of care. . . .
>
> Yet the age-old problem of racism and profiteering in the health care system does not address the underlying conditions of our daily lives that give rise to poor health. Blacks are twice as likely to be unemployed and nearly three times as likely to live in poverty. This means that we are more likely to live in deteriorating neighborhoods, which promote higher chronic stress.
>
> (Afua 2008, 44)

What makes the above excerpt a unique *race-classed conscious* perception of food and wellness is that she directly writes that institutional white privilege operates in a way that consequently robs the black community of better health. This *obvious* element of how white privilege is linked to better access to living healthier is left absent in *Skinny Bitch* and *Quantum Wellness*. The reader is also introduced to Afua's race-conscious approach to eating problems.

When the topic of eating problems and weight gain arise in popular vegan race-neutral book series such as *Skinny Bitch*, the authors conclude that the reasons women eat junk foods that cause them to be overweight is because they are stupid and lazy; proper understanding of nutrition and motivation are the *easy* resolutions to all women's eating problems. Alternatively, Queen Afua takes a race-conscious approach to eating problems. In *City of Wellness*, she speaks of eating problems (food addictions, binge eating, etc.) within the context of collective black pain:

> When we use food as a drug, food as a substitute for sex, food as an anesthetic to mask our true feelings, we run the risk of heart attacks, stroke or cancer . . . Just as a child clings to its mother's breast, the child inside us clings to food as mother to hide us from the world, ease our pain and comfort us when challenged by external forces.
>
> The life experiences of African Americans that promote food as the drug of choice for numbing the pain is related to what Harvard psychiatrist Alvin Pouissant, M.D., calls "post traumatic slavery syndrome" and what we call "living while Black." Such dynamics are rarely accounted for in our health prescription.
>
> (Afua 2008, 8)

In *Skinny Bitch: Bun in the Oven*, the authors continuously blame personal laziness for the reason why pregnant women who learn about veganism still choose to eat junk food. Intersections of eating problems and racialized-sexualized violence never enter the conversation, let alone the ways environmental and nutritional racism, as well as issues of class struggle can impede a pregnant woman's access to food, period. The racialized trauma around "living while black" (or "living while any non-white racialized minority" in the USA) never enters the conversation. Such dynamics are rarely accounted for in race-neutral popular vegan books, and also within the most popular and powerful vegan-oriented organization, PETA, a staunch supporter of *Skinny Bitch*. This is not surprising, as PETA continues to rely heavily on promoting people to go vegan for animal rights by employing a plethora of popular famous white women entertainers as the poster children of "going vegan" (Deckha 2008). Similarly to *Skinny Bitch*, PETA constantly produces ads and literature with images of *skinny* and *conventionally beautiful* white, creamy skinned women to lure omnivores into veganism and vegetarianism. The *universal* assumption is that: 1) all straight men (regardless of race) would want to have sex with these "perfect 10s," but the caveat is that these types of women would only have sex with them if they were to go vegan and; 2) women should become vegan because it means they too can save animals and obtain the white racialized aesthetic of beauty which is becoming skinny and "modelesque," while simultaneously appealing to the hetero-normative white male gaze (Deckha 2008). I argue that *Skinny Bitch* and PETA complement each other quite well because they make *visible* the trauma of *non-human animal* suffering while making *invisible* the suffering and pain that privileging of *whiteness* causes to people like Queen Afua's audience. The trauma of racialized suffering and pain can manifest in a plethora of different ways. Queen Afua's *Sacred Woman* is a multifaceted version of veganism that employs plant-based dietary philosophy as a tool to fight the ravages of racialized colonialism on black women's womb health.

Afua is the number one womb health guru for black women willing to transition into a plant-based diet to achieve healthier reproductive health. In the introduction to her book, *Sacred Woman*, Queen Afua provides a clear example of a black female socio-spatial epistemology that makes *visible* the consequences of colonialism and chattel slavery on black women's womb health:

> *I cry a river of tears that heal for the Negro slave woman, my great-great-grandmother, who was forced to part her thighs for the entrance of a pale pink penis to fulfill her owner's demonic quest to force his way violently into her soft dark womb, leaving his . . . pardon me, I can't breathe,*

I'm still enraged two hundred years later. I still hurt. I still bleed. I'm outraged, feeling fear and helplessness for all my great-great-grandmothers who passed their self-hate, lack of self-esteem, their acceptance of abuse, their internal war down through the bloodline to me . . .

. . . I am the Afrakan Woman, crying out my pain, screaming and retching Rivers of Tears from generation to generation. My tears boil up from the bile of plantation slave life here in America the Beautiful. Here, where institutionalized sex factories were brutally imposed upon a stolen people for generations.

I cry for the soft wombs and damaged souls of my Mothers who were forced to bear babies of rage and incest. They were womb casualties in a four-hundred-year war that damaged them down to their DNA. The wounds go oh so deep within the wombs of the womenfolk of my tribe.

I'm praying . . . [to] wombs that carried on even after self-inflicted and societal womb violations; wombs that carried on with only one ovary left to fend for itself due to inner toxicity.

(Afua 2000, 57–58, original emphasis)

Afua is well aware of the social and physical placement of the collective Black body, since colonialism, in the USA. *Sacred Woman*, as well as her newer book *City of Wellness* persuades black females to understand veganism as a *decolonizing dietary tool* against the physical and psychic devastation of racialized colonialism, environmental racism-classism, and corporate capitalism. Queen Afua's embodied experiences of being a fifty-seven year old black American woman, born and raised in a New York city neighborhood as well as traveling to African Diasporic communities in America have led her to an ontological understanding that black people may eat unhealthier foods because they don't have what they need to properly heal from racialized trauma, as well as other legacies of racialized colonialism (environmental racism, class struggle, for example).

Unlike the *Skinny Bitch* series, Afua understands that eating problems have more to do with systemic oppression than being lazy, a "cheap asshole," or stupid. Afua's perspective is supported by many other black women (vegan or not) who know that most black females' relationships with food and their bodies are heavily influenced by racialization and racism. In *Hungry for More: A Keeping-It-Real Guide for Black Women on Weight and Body Image*, Robyn McGee dedicates narrative research on how black women "binge in the face of racism." One of her project participants says, " 'I believe internalized racism is at the core of the compulsive overeating in the black community,' says Octavia . . . She recalls how childhood fears of racism led her to find comfort in food" (McGee 2005, 66). In her recent dissertation, Dr. Connolly examines the role of racism, racial socialization, and stress in overeating among black American women (Connolly 2011). In *Breaking Bread*, bell hooks theorizes:

> We deal with White supremacist assault by buying something to compensate for feelings of wounded pride and self-esteem . . . We also don't talk enough about food addiction alone or as a prelude to drug and alcohol addiction. Yet, many of us are growing up daily in homes where food is another way in which we comfort ourselves.
>
> Think about the proliferation of junk food in Black communities. You can go to any Black community and see Black folks of all ages gobbling up junk food morning, noon, and night. I would like to suggest that the feeling those kids are getting when they're stuffing Big Macs, Pepsi, and barbecue potato chips down their throats is similar to the ecstatic, blissful moment of the narcotics addict.
>
> (hooks 1991)

These black women's understanding of food, health, and body are clearly defined by a *race-consciousness* that is crucial if they are to truly engage in any type of food-oriented guide to wellness for women of color. Black female vegan writers like Queen Afua, as well as Tracye McQuirter, Afya Ibomu, and contributors to *Sistah Vegan* (which I will explore further in this essay) know that an absence of critical reflection on the realities of racialization and racism on black America's wellness would make their literature less effective for African Americans. Afua transitioned into veganism to help herself and other African Americans achieve their *human rights* to food and healthy living that has been compromised by racism.

Alternatively, Alicia Silverstone's new 2009 vegan book, *The Kind Diet*, is currently at sales rank number 170 on Amazon.com as of August 22, 2010. She speaks about her reasons for why becoming vegan is important:

These days, it seems like there are a million and one problems in the world; global warming, droughts, rising food costs, toxic waterways, cancer, heart disease, diabetes, starvation . . . it's enough to make anyone want to crawl into a hole with a big bowl of ice cream!

Of course you know ice cream's not the solution. But what if I told you that the ice cream you're craving is actually one of the *causes* of every single one of those problems? What if I said that by choosing nondairy ice cream instead, you'd be taking a huge step toward solving them all?

And what about your health? Do you feel like your body is some mystery that only your doctor understands? Do you feel like getting older is just another way of saying 'falling apart'? What if I told you that, by eating a varied, plant-based diet, you will strengthen your immune system, beautify your skin, increase your energy, and reduce your risk (significantly) of cancer, heart disease, diabetes, arthritis, osteoporosis, allergies, asthma, and almost every other disease? What if I said that I feel myself getting younger, more powerful, and more beautiful as I age simply because of *what I eat?* Of course the food we choose is not the only factor in our health and well-being, but

it's definitely one of the most important- and, luckily, it's one we have control over. How does that nondairy ice cream sound now?

(Silverstone 2009, 1)

I argue that what makes her introduction a race-neutral (as well as class-neutral) explication of going vegan is that she assumes that *you* are just like her and have *control* over *your* food choices. As she shares her narrative for going vegan, not once does she mention what it means to reap the benefits of white class privilege that guarantee that she, and people of this demographic, have much more control over their food choices than others. In addition, not once does this Hollywood actress interrogate how white class privi- lege has shaped how she has developed her epistemologies around veganism. Rarely, if ever, do popular vegan 'race- neutral' books even have passages such as, "As a white woman. . . ." They are simply *vegan*, case closed.

Silverstone's, as well as Barnouin and Freedman's writing imply that they are deeply troubled by how much their *human* privilege has caused *non-human animals* to suffer. Absent from Silverstone's epiphany is any self-reflection on how possessive investments in white [class] privilege have collectively *protected* her demographic globally, while causing other *human beings* to suffer from these concerns stated in the first sentence of her introduction: rising food costs, toxic waterways, and starvation.

Alternatively, African American health activist and vegan, Tracye McQuirter's new book *By Any Greens Necessary: A Revolutionary Guide for Black Women Who Want to Eat Great, Get Healthy, Lose Weight, and Look Phat* (2010) is a dietary vegan book as well. Similarly to *Skinny Bitch* and *The Kind Diet*, McQuirter does convey the importance of understanding how animals suffer as one of the reasons to go vegan, however, a majority of her emphasis is on the need for African American women to go vegan for health reasons. Furthermore, it is quite evident in the title of the book alone that McQuirter is wholly conscious of how her racialized-gendered experience in the USA has shaped how she has come to vegan health activism. She was well aware of the white racialized association with plant-based diets and writes, "Honestly, I thought it was something that crazy white people did, and I had not given it a second thought since seventh grade" (McQuirter 2010, ix).

In her introduction, she speaks of how "By any greens necessary" mirrors Malcolm X's infamous phrase, "By any means necessary," in regards to liberating black Americans from the ills of white racism. She consciously chose to write a book about and for black women, acknowledging that black people have a unique racialized-sexualized experience with food and health. She writes that her major influence for becoming vegan came from African American health activist and vegan Dick Gregory who speaks frankly about how racially conscious black people in the USA cannot become fully liberated from a racist society until they change their eating habits. McQuirter quotes Dick Gregory's influence on her:

> In *Dick Gregory's Natural Diet for Folks Who Eat*, he states, "The quickest way to wipe out a group of people is to put them on a soul food diet." Addressing nationalists directly, he said, "The will lay down a heavy rap on genocide in America with regard to black folks, then walk into a soul food restaurant and help the genocide along."
>
> (Gregory in McQuirter 2010, 4)

This is an interesting contrast to *Skinny Bitch* and *Kind Diet* authors whose focuses are on changing one's diet to prevent the ongoing genocide of animals and a race/class-neutral approach to healthful eating. And unlike these aforementioned popular

vegan books, McQuirter understands that environmental racism influences black and low-income community food choices:

> Where we live influences our food choices. Walk through any black and low-income neighborhood in the United States, and what will you find on every corner? Liquor stores! And next to those you'll find greasy carryout. They're fast, cheap, convenient, and deadly. In contrast, ask yourself when was the last time you saw a café with an organic salad bar in a black neighborhood that wasn't being gentrified? What about a health food store or farmer's market? They are not there.
>
> (McQuirter 2010, 4)

Neighborhood gentrification is a racially classed, coded term, usually meaning that urban low-income people of color start seeing white middle-class people moving into their neighborhoods. What trails behind these new residents are options to healthier lifestyles, such as the establishment of a café with organic food options in the middle of what has been declared a food desert (Freeman 2006). Though subtle, the excerpt from above provides an example of how McQuirter is racially and class conscious about who has what healthy food options and why, and what happens when places such as the 'hood undergo gentrification. Furthermore, McQuirter also explains how her experience at Amherst College shaped her consciousness:

> My political science and African American studies classes had fostered in me a growing awareness around issues of racism, sexism, homophobia, classism, and imperialism. It was with this emerging consciousness that I digested Dick Gregory's words. I was open to questioning the way I had eaten all my life, as well.
>
> (McQuirter 2010, x)

Not once do the authors of *Skinny Bitch*, *Quantum Wellness*, or *The Kind Diet* even speak of how issues of racism had shaped their consciousness, let alone sexism, homophobia, classism, and imperialism. However, for McQuirter, this multi-faceted consciousness also comes through with her approach to African American women, eating, and weight management. She clearly has an understanding of the *raced-gender* aspect of body weight and image in the African American female community. Though subtle, the "phat" in the sub-title of this book: "A Revolutionary Guide for Black Women Who Want to Eat Great, Get Healthy, Lose Weight, and Look *Phat*," indicates that McQuirter has an awareness around the importance of maintaining "curves" as a standard of beauty in black America. She wants to assure her readers that on her diet, they can maintain a healthy weight but be curvaceous and keep the "booty." McQuirter isn't the only African American vegan aware of food and intersections of body image, gender, and race. In *Sistah Vegan*, the last chapter of the book is dedicated to exploring how African American female vegans speak of how their family members perceived "going vegan." The women speak about how the stereotypical perceptions of the vegan body (skinny white woman) coupled with stereotypical perceptions of the black female body (full sized woman) have given them multiple challenges with trying to practice a plant-based diet. Some women speak of being criticized by friends and work colleagues for being "too fat to be vegan" while others speak about being criticized by family members who think they are too skinny to be a true black woman (Harper 2010). Such consciousness around food, raced-gender experience, and body image, although present in McQuirter (2010) and Harper's (2010) books are absent in *Skinny Bitch*, *The Kind Diet*, and *Quantum Wellness*. However, this is not surprising, as Dr. Connolly notes in her 2011 dissertation that mainstream research and writing about intersections of body image, females, and eating still use the white

middle-class female experience as the *universal* lens to analyze *all* female relationships with food and body image in the USA (Connolly 2011).

In the *Sistah Vegan* book, I introduce to the readers how and why I decided to transition into veganism. Similarly to McQuirter and Afua, I explain to my audience that being racialized as "black" and having the gender experience of "girl/woman" in the USA greatly affected how I eventually decided to transition into a plant-based dietary philosophy.

> When I was twelve years old, I entered the halls of Lyman Memorial Junior High School for my first day of seventh grade. The first greeting I heard was, "Look at that skinny little nigger. Run, skinny little nigger, run." From this point on in my consciousness, I became very aware of my historically and socially constructed position in the United States through the unique fusion of Black/girl. Racially socialized and gendered through Eurocentric heteropatriarchal and capitalism-based society, my experiences differed drastically in comparison with my peers in our over-97-percent-white, rural town. Although whiteness was the "invisible" and comforting norm for this majority, it was the never ending and constantly visible, "in-your-face" foreign, and suffocating "norm" for me. It was expected that being teased for being "the Black girl" was what I'd have to accept, simply because none of my peers ever seemed to be reprimanded or chastised for being racist.
>
> (Harper 2010, xvii)

Further in the introduction, I explain to my readers that my exposure to Dick Gregory allowed me to make the types of connections to black liberation, anti-racism, *and* veganism that I had never encountered before. However, it was Queen Afua that would finally persuade me to fully consider how a plant-based diet was necessary for black women to cure reproductive health issues that she saw as legacies of unresolved trauma of slavery and racism:

It was with the help of these two critical thinkers that I finally saw the interconnectedness to my own "out of harmony" reproductive health (I had been diagnosed with a uterine fibroid and was seeking an alternative to allopathic medicine to address it) as a symptom of systematic racism, sexism, nonhuman animal exploitation (which I would later learn is called "speciesism"). Immediately, I made the transition to *ahimsa*-based veganism … Eventually, years after I started down my path on that first day of seventh grade, I made the connections between institutionalized oppression and unmindful consumption and what it *means* to be socialized as a Black female in a society in which I must navigate through racist legacies of slavery, while simultaneously being part of an economically "privileged" global northern nation in which overconsumption is the "norm." It is this type of unique experience—the social implications and historical context of being both Black and female in a neocolonial global society— that has led me to request voices from females of the African Diaspora living in the U.S.

(Harper 2010, xviii)

Earlier in this essay, I wrote that there are also African American women vegans who have made the animal rights component of veganism a very important part of their vegan activism. Tracye McQuirter spends a fair amount of time in her 2010 book talking about how horribly nonhuman animals are treated. *Skinny Bitch* and *The Kind Diet* also spend a significant amount of time teaching their readers about the ills of how animals are treated in the USA. The definitive difference between McQuirter's representation of animal rights and veganism and the latter authors' is that McQuirter is able to speak simultaneously from race-conscious and animal-conscious approaches to veganism. Similarly, Ain Drew, an African American woman vegan and contributor to *Sistah Vegan*, writes about her experience with PETA in the anthology. In 2006, Ain took what she described as a "dream job"

working with PETA. However, she explains that despite trying to get PETA to support her work around educating the African American community about the benefits of a vegan lifestyle, the organization showed a general lack of interest around the issues of racialized health disparities in the black community:

I was prepared and excited to teach my people about healthy eating and how to avoid the ailments that are prevalent among the Black community …

Unfortunately, after a few months, I found that PETA wasn't as concerned with helping Black folks overcome our health issues than they were about getting us to stop wearing mink coats or promoting dog-fighting. Apparently, Black folks wearing furs to the club was more of a problem than the health problems that plague us. In marketing meetings, there was a constant discussion about how to make fur "less hop," which celebrities to approach, and how we could come across as more "urban." After repeatedly being ignored when I mentioned tackling issues that were more pressing, I knew that my time with PETA was running out. This was not how I wanted to make a difference.

I am all too aware of the growing health disparities in the African-American community. While there is a disproportionate number of fast-food chains and liquor stores in neighborhoods where low- to middle-income families reside, the lack of health care and adequate insurance is even more alarming. Ongoing discussions about fur, among other albeit horrible animal atrocities, were taking away from relevant issues that would have made PETA more approachable to the Black community I'd been hired to represent.

(Drew, in Harper 2010, 63)

Drew is clearly able to understand and articulate how animal rights, health disparities due to environmental racism, and vegan educational outreach are integral elements for successful campaigning towards black America. Her essay is an excellent example of what *race-conscious* animal rights-oriented veganism can look like.

In *The Vegan Soul Food Guide to the Galaxy*, African American female vegan Afya Ibomu shares her vegan consciousness in the introduction of her book. After receiving many questions about her vegan lifestyle from non-vegans, she writes:

> These questions, coupled with the health crisis in the black and brown communities, helped me realize that there is a need for more ways to educate our selves about incorporating healthier food choices into our lives. Too many people in our communities are dying unnecessarily and living poor qualities of life just because of the foods they eat. No doubt, we are oppressed; this daily reality causes our communities to have higher incidences of disease. Poverty, police brutality, racism (housing, jobs, education, health care, grocery stores), jail, drugs, single parent homes and the multitude of other issues that plague our communities, are negatively affecting our mental, physical and spiritual health—our holistic health.
>
> (Ibomu 2008, i)

Ibomu is cognizant of how racial profiling ("police brutality"), *racism*, and *classism* ("poverty") affect black and brown communities' access to healthier lifestyles and knows that it will take more than a vegan diet to heal black and brown communities. This is indicative slightly further into her introduction when she writes, "Being a vegan is not the only answer to healthy living but it is one" (Ibomu 2008, i). Ultimately, though *race consciousness* manifests differently among them, and they may not all agree, Afua, McQuirter, the contributors to *Sistah Vegan*, and Ibomu intersect their black racialized female consciousness with a vegan writing style that clearly expresses the significance of the legacies of racialized colonialism on the collective black experience in the USA. This is fundamentally different from the popular vegan books *Skinny Bitch* series, *The Kind Diet*, and *Quantum Wellness, which* completely ignore how the author's own white racialized consciousness—and

lack of reflection on legacies of racialized colonialism—shape their vegan epistemologies.

CONCLUSION

Even though *By Any Greens Necessary* is clearly race conscious, I finished the guide feeling that McQuirter did not address the needs of African American women whose food access is greatly affected by both environmental racism and class struggle when it comes to transitioning to whole foods veganism. In her section "How to Eat Healthy on a Budget," she guides her readers through eating healthy without spending a lot of money, and guarantees that it is easier than they think. For someone who spoke of their race-class consciousness around food access at the beginning of the book, it was surprising that this was missing from the book. Perhaps if McQuirter were to update her edition of the book, she could include a section guiding African American women on how to engage in food justice activism to get to the point that they can access what is on McQuirter's vegan food list. This has led me to conclude that though the book is *race-gender conscious* on approaches to veganism, this missing section on accessing healthy vegan food for African American women who live in food deserts implies that this book's targeted readers are African American women with similar residential living and socio-economic status to McQuirter.

Similarly, though Queen Afua is incredibly conscious of how racism and classism have created health disparities and unequal access to food in the black community, both *Sacred Woman* and *The City of Wellness* include recipes and ingredient lists for healthier eating that are quite challenging to achieve if you are one of many brown and black people in the USA who live in a food desert or are on a very limited budget. For example, Afua feels strongly that one is at their healthiest when they are practicing a raw foods diet. If you do not have access to growing your own food and/or produce center, farmers' market, or a holistic health supplements store that sells sun foods such as hemp seeds, chlorella, spirulina, raw kale, etc., then Afua's regiment is nearly impossible to implement.

Also, even though Queen Afua's text provides superb examples of what race-conscious veganism can look like, hers is also an example of what heteronormative race-conscious veganism looks like in the African American community. *Sacred Woman* makes the assumption that all the African American females who read the book are heterosexual as well as in (or want to be in) a romantic relationship with a man of African descent. Such an approach can presumably be uncomfortable to African Diasporic women who are queer and/or in relationships with men who are not of African descent. Despite these weaknesses of Afua and McQuirter's work, they, along with Afya Ibomu and myself are engaged in revolutionary black feminist and race-conscious vegan activist writing. We collectively understand that there are material consequences of racialized colonialism on the lives of African American women and that our writing must start from that social location.

The Kind Diet, Skinny Bitch, and *Quantum Wellness*, have sold thousands of copies, indicating that there is a growing popularity amongst the population to investigate the potential benefits of a vegan-oriented lifestyle. Despite the race- and class-neutral approach to veganism in these books, the authors have helped many of their readers transition into a dietary lifestyle that they may have never considered. It is understandable that one vegan book *cannot* cover all topics—nor should the author be expected to take on such an unrealistic task. However, the purpose of this essay was to interrogate the consequences of popular vegan literature that does not reflect on an author's racial and class privileges, and also provide examples and reasons for why non-mainstream vegan authors would want to bring a race- and class-conscious approach to veganism. Such examples provide a starting point for people to begin to seriously start thinking about why and how their own privileges shape their conceptions of food, justice, and consumption and ethics in general. Popular mainstream vegan literature should be about *justice* and not simply "just us [white middle class]" epistemologies of consumption.

NOTES

1. I conducted an analysis of popular vegan literature because popular media are a barometer of how the status quo deals with (or silences) race and its discontents. Furthermore, the results of my keyword search imply that publishers who take "vegan" categorized books are interested in those books whose content does not mention how race privilege (or lack thereof) shapes who gets to create vegan epistemologies and why.
2. One can observe this rift on Vegans of Color *http://vegansofcolor.wordpress.com/*, the most popular site for critical race analysis of veganism from non-white identified vegans throughout the world.
3. In fall of 2009, I conducted an online survey to gather information about American vegans' race and gender. The results of the survey found that 1100 of the participants identified as white females. http://www.lulu.com/product/ebook/ vegans-by-racialethnic-identification-in-the-usa/ 5592689
4. This essay will only be referring to vegans and not vegetarians.

WORKS CITED

Afua, Queen. *Sacred Woman: A Guide to Healing the Feminine Body, Mind, and Spirit*. New York: Ballantine Publishing Group, 2000.

Afua, Queen. *The City of Wellness: Restoring Your Health through the Seven Kitchens of Consciousness*. Brooklyn: Queen Afua Wellness Institute Press, 2008.

Bailey, Eric J. *Food Choice and Obesity in Black America: Creating a New Cultural Diet*. Westport, CT: Praeger, 2006.

Baker, Elizabeth A., Mario Schootman, Ellen Barnidge, and Cheryl Kelly. "The Role of Race and Poverty in Access to Foos That Enable Individuals to Adhere to Dietary Guidelines." *Preventing Chronic Disease: Public Health Research, Practice, and Policy* 3, no. 3 (July 2006): 1–11.

Bediako, Shawn M., Naa Oyo Kwate, and Reggie A. Rucker. "Dietary Behavior among African Americans: Assessing Cultural Identity and Health Consciousness." *Ethnicity and Disease* 14 (2004): 527–32.

Beeman, Angie K. "Grassroots Organizing and 'Post-Civil Rights' Racism: The Dilemma of Negotiating Interracial Solidarity in a 'Color-Blind' Society." Dissertation, University of Connecticut, 2010.

Bennett, Michael, and Vanessa D. Dickerson. *Recovering the Black Female Body: Self-Representations by African American Women.* New Brunswick, NJ: Rutgers University Press, 2001.

Bonilla-Silva, Eduardo. *Racism without Racists: Color-Blind Racism and the Persistence of Racial Inequality in the United States.* 2nd ed. Lanham, MD: Rowman & Littlefield Publishers, 2006.

Bullard, Robert D. *Confronting Environmental Racism: Voices from the Grassroots.* 1st ed. Boston, MA: South End Press, 1993.

Cherry, Elizabeth. "Veganism as a Cultural Movement: A Relational Approach." *Social Movement Studies* 5, no. 2 (2006): 155–70.

Cohen, Larry, Rachel Davis, Virginia Lee, and Eric Valdonvinos. "Addressing the Intersection: Preventing Violence and Promoting Healthy Eating and Active Living." Oakland: Prevention Institute, 2010.

Connolly, Margaret Kassakian. "Overeating among Black American Women: The Role of Racism, Racial Socialization, and Stress." Dissertation, Boston College, 2011.

Deckha, Maneesha. "Disturbing Images: Peta and the Feminist Ethics of Animal Advocacy." *Ethics & the Environment* 13, no. 2 (Autumn 2008): 35–76.

"Disparities in Health." National Conference of State Legislatures, http://www.ncsl.org/?tabid=14494. August 2009.

Dubowitz, Tamara, Melonie Heron, Chloe E. Bird, Nicole Lurie, Brian K. Finch, Ricardo Basurto-Dávila, Lauren Hale, and José J. Escarce. "Neighborhood Socioeconomic Status and Fruit and Vegetable Intake among White, Black, and Mexican Americans in the United States." *The American Journal of Clinical Nutrition* 87 (2008): 1883–91.

Farr, Arnold. "Whiteness Visible: Enlightenment Racism and the Structure of Racialized Consciousness." In *What White Looks Like: African-American Philosophers on the Whiteness Question*, edited by George Yancy, 143–57. New York: Routledge, 2004.

Foster, Gwen, Dr. Mary A. Harris, Dr. Christopher L. Melby, Dr. W. Daniel Schmidt, Dr. M. Lynn Toohey, and Dr. DeWitt Williams. "Cardiovascular Disease Risk Factors Are Lower in African-American Vegans Compared to Lacto-Ovo-Vegetarians." *Journal of the American College of Nutrition* 17, no. 5 (1998): 425–34.

Freeman, Lance, and ebrary Inc. *There Goes the Hood: Views of Gentrification from the Ground Up.* Philadelphia, PA: Temple University Press, 2006.

Freston, Kathy. *Quantum Wellness: A Practical Guide to Health and Happiness*: Weinsten Books, 2009.

Gottlieb, Robert, and Anupama Joshi. *Food Justice.* Cambridge, MA: MIT Press, 2010.

Harper, Amie Breeze. "Cyber-Territories of Whiteness: Language, 'Colorblind' Utopias, and 'Sistah Vegan' Consciousness." Masters in Educational Technologies, Harvard University, 2007.

Harper, Amie Breeze. *Sistah Vegan: Black Female Vegans Speak on Food, Identity, Health and Society.* New York: Lantern Books, 2010.

Harper, Amie Breeze. "Whiteness and 'Post-Racial' Vegan Praxis." *Journal of Critical Animal Studies* VIII, no. 3 (2010): 7–32.

Hill Collins, Patricia. *Black Feminist Thought, Knowledge, Consciousness, and the Politics of Empowerment.* Rev. 10th anniversary ed. New York: Routledge, 2000.

Hill Collins, Patricia. *Black Sexual Politics: African Americans, Gender, and the New Racism.* New York: Routledge, 2004.

Hill Collins, Patricia, and ebrary Inc. *From Black Power to Hip Hop Racism, Nationalism, and Feminism.* Philadelphia: Temple University Press, 2006.

hooks, bell, and Cornel West. *Breaking Bread: Insurgent Black Intellectual Life.* Boston, MA: South End Press, 1991.

hooks, bell. *Black Looks: Race and Representation.* Boston, MA: South End Press, 1992.

Ibomu, Afya. *The Vegan Soulfood Guide to the Galaxy.* Atlanta, Georgia: Nattral Unlimited, 2008.

James, Joy. *Shadowboxing: Representations of Black Feminist Politics.* 1st Palgrave paperback ed. New York: St. Martin's Press, 2002.

Lee, Jo-Anne, and John S. Lutz. *Situating "Race" And Racisms in Time, Space, and Theory: Critical Essays for Activists and Scholars.* Montréal: McGill-Queen's University Press, 2005.

Malesh, Patricia Marie. "Rhetorics of Consumption: Identity, Confrontation, and Corporatization in the American Vegetarian Movement." Dissertation, University of Arizona, 2005.

Mangels, Reed. "A Vegetarian Diet Helps to Protect Older African Americans from Hypertension." *Vegetarian Journal* 13, no. 2 (1994): 347–56.

McGee, Robyn. *Hungry for More: A Keeping-It-Real Guide for Black Women on Weight and Body Image.* Emeryville, CA: Seal Press, 2005.

McKittrick, Katherine. *Demonic Grounds: Black Women and the Cartographies of Struggle*. Minneapolis: University of Minnesota Press, 2006.

McKittrick, Katherine, and Clyde Adrian Woods. *Black Geographies and the Politics of Place*. Toronto, Ont. Cambridge, MA: Between the Lines; South End Press, 2007.

McQuirter, and Tracye Lynn. *By Any Greens Necessary: A Revolutionary Guide for Black Women Who Want to Eat Great, Get Healthy, Lose Weight, and Look Phat*: Chicago: Lawrence Hill Books, 2010.

Miller, Jeff, and Jonathan Deutsch. Food Studies: An Introduction to Research Methods. New York: Berg, 2009.

Mills, Charles W. *The Racial Contract*. Ithaca, NY; London: Cornell University Press, 1997.

Neville, Helen A., and Jennifer Hamer. " 'We Make Freedom': An Exploration of Revolutionary Black Feminism." *Journal of Black Studies* 31, no. 4 (2001): 437–61.

Randall, Vernellia. *Dying While Black: An Indepth Look at a Crisis in the American Healthcare System*. 1st ed. Dayton: Seven Principles Press, Inc., 2006.

Sandler, Ronald, and Phaedra C. Pezzullo, Eds. *Environmental Justice and Environmentalism the Social Justice Challenge to the Environmental Movement*. Cambridge, MA: MIT Press, 2007.

Silverstone, Alicia. *The Kind Diet: A Simple Guide to Feeling Great, Losing Weight, and Saving the Planet*. New York: Rodale Books, 2009.

Slocum, Rachel. "Whiteness, Space and Alternative Food Practice." *Geoforum* 38, no. 3 (2007): 520–33.

Sullivan, Shannon, and Nancy Tuana. *Race and Epistemologies of Ignorance*, Suny Series, Philosophy and Race. Albany: State University of New York Press, 2007.

Twine, Frances Winddance, and Jonathan Warren. *Racing Research, Researching Race: Methodological Dilemmas in Critical Race Studies*. Edited by Frances Winddance Twine and Jonathan Warren. New York: New York University Press, 2000.

White, Evelyn C. *The Black Women's Health Book: Speaking for Ourselves*. New, expanded ed. Seattle, WA: Seal, 1994.

Williams-Forson, Psyche. *Building Houses out of Chicken Legs: Black Women, Food, & Power*. Chapel Hill: The University of North Carolina Press, 2006.

Wilson, Sacoby, Malo Hutson, and Mahasin Mujahid. "How Planning and Zoning Contribute to Inequitable Development, Neighborhood Health, and Environmental Injustice." *Environmental Justice* 1, no. 4 (2008): 211–17.

Witt, Doris. *Black Hunger: Soul Food and America*. Minneapolis: University of Minnesota Press, 2004.

Zuberi, Tukufu, and Eduardo Bonilla-Silva. *White Logic, White Methods: Racism and Methodology*. Lanham, MD: Rowman & Littlefield Publishers, 2008.

13

Purity, Soul Food, and Sunni Islam: Explorations at the Intersection of Consumption and Resistance

Carolyn Rouse and Janet Hoskins

No other fundamental aspect of our behavior as a species except sexuality is so encumbered by *ideas* as eating; the entanglements of food with religion, with both belief and sociality, are particularly striking.
—Sidney Mintz, *Tasting Food. Tasting Freedom: Excursions into Eating, Culture and the Past*

Paul Robeson Park in Los Angeles County was often the designated location for Eid al-Fitr, the obligatory group prayer and celebration following Ramadan, the Islamic month of fasting.[1] Families, predominantly African American, would begin arriving around 7:00 am dressed in their best Eid clothing. Well before the crowd began to trickle in, plastic tarps would be positioned in straight rows so that the *salat* (prayer) could be performed facing the Ka'aba in Mecca.[2] Following the prayer and *khutbah* (lecture), the community would hold a celebration that included music, kiosks, and food. While the prayer and lecture usually lasted an hour, the gatherings on the blankets, which included talking and eating, would last up to five hours. At one Eid, I was situated among three cowives who were enjoying one another's company on several large blankets.[3] Also within the group were Safa, Hafiza, one of the few women who veils, and Fatima, a single mother and engineering student at a local state college. The picnic area was clearly a gendered space, although occasionally

a husband would wander by and eat a piece of chicken or a plate of salad. The exchange between husband and wife, or wives, would usually last no longer than five minutes at which point he would find his way back to his group of male cohorts.

One of the best and most generous cooks was Safa who brought enough fried chicken to feed five large families. Safa, who often entertained this community of women at her house with large quantities of southern fare, had "come into al-Islam" at the same time she was conquering alcoholism. In terms of consumption, the excesses of alcohol were replaced with the excesses of food, but while the former distanced her from friends and family, the latter drew her closer to her large circle of Muslim friends: "Sisters." As a form of exchange, southern cooking strengthened Safa's bonds with African American converts to Islam whose personal and social histories mirrored her own. Macaroni, and cheese, collard greens, fried chicken, potatoes, okra, curried lamb, corn bread, black-eyed peas, hot links, beef kabobs, barbecued beef (not pork) ribs. In every sense, the preceding list represents African American Sunni Muslim "soul food." Most of the list references the community's social history, but the eager adoption of a Middle Eastern cuisine alongside southern fare references yet another set of cultural linkages and histories. At one level, eating was an expression of social, personal, and religious communion, and as such, food was not prepared to simply fill one's stomach. Cooking was an expression of religious duty, love of community, and love of Allah. The choice of what to eat and how to prepare and serve it, in this respect, could be understood as an expression of resistance or personal agency. At another level, these desires were entangled in historically informed perceptions of subjectivity, citizenship, race, and *habitus* and therefore mired in structural forms that made food and food taboos as structurally predetermined as they were potentially transformative (Bourdieu 1977; Douglas 1966; Harris 1995; Kondo 1997; Mauss 1979).

Our focus on food taboos looks at them as part of a communicative process of social action, in which pragmatic and social dimensions are fused to comment on a particular historical moment. We argue, following Comaroff (1985:5), that practices of the body such as eating can give a cultural form to the principles governing objective orders of power relations. To do this, we look at structural and semiotic entanglements of food and African American social history during three different periods: before Black Muslim leader Elijah Muhammad's death in 1975, during the rise of the African American Sunni movement 1975–2001, and after the September 11 attack on the World Trade Center. Each period is marked by a different understanding of African American citizenship: In the earliest period of African American Islam, the religion was seen as a way of differentiating black Muslims from other Americans, and marking those differences with defiance. In the second period, there was a movement toward making a more "American" version of Islam, represented most profoundly by the placement of the American flag on top of the front page of the Muslim community's journal. Finally, as a result of the demonization of "Muslim terrorists" following the events of September 11, 2001, a new guardedness has emerged with respect to

understandings of citizenship and Islam and with it a new set of signifying practices in the Los Angeles Muslim community. Heightened government suspicions regarding African American Muslim links to terrorists have forced the leaders to defend their patriotism, and women converts have had to defend their choices in the context of new attention being paid to practices like veiling.

The semiotic use of the body, in this case, has been as liberating as it has been an act of resignation to a number of powerful discursive and material structures. Performing race, gender, and citizenship through food and consumption while determined in part by structures of power nevertheless offers opportunities for symbolic critique. As Kondo argues, "Meaning is never fully closed, and in those moments of instability, ambiguity, and contradiction may lie the potential for interventions that might destabilize a field, ultimately exposing and throwing into question its constitutive logic" (1997:151). Particularly for the African American Muslim community, the potential for bodily resignification occurred alongside the civil rights movement, affirmative action, and second and third wave feminism.

With respect to agency, the fact that some of the women at the picnic had chosen to be cowives, coupled with the fact that they performed the domestic tasks of child rearing and food preparation, begs the question: Is conversion a reinstantiation of patriarchy? Using the example of food and food taboos, we assert that female converts are not simply acquiescing to male domination. Rather, through food, female converts articulate their relationship to a number of ideological domains including race, class, gender, nation, and Islam. As a signifying practice associated with issues of race, authenticity, and group membership including citizenship; food preparation and exchange are vital communicative processes. Women who are generous with food and who understand the dietary requirements of the community, have extensive social networks and are credited with having a greater understanding of the faith. It is through food that women gain membership into various overlapping social networks, and it is through these social networks that women developed organized systems of exchange. Without these exchange networks, many of the women would not have sufficient incomes to pay their rent. The relationship between food preparation and patriarchy is understood by the women to be indirect because the meaning of food extends well beyond the borders of male/female relationships. The quality and preparation of food is about faith, ideology, community, and securing resources. Embodied in the production and eating of food is the performance of an agency owned not so much by individuals, but by a community intent on authoring new social configurations.

This study reaffirms that concepts of polluted and clean should not be understood as binaries, but rather define particular relationships between objects and ideas within particular cultural, social, spatial, and temporal contexts. With respect to this community, the practice of food production, distribution, and consumption clarified each members' relationship to the group and to the intellectual and spiritual project of self-purification. Who brought what food? How much? Was the meat *halal* (in accordance with Islamic law)? Who was eating from whose picnic spread? Who made the best soul food? We argue that for African American Muslim women perceptions of food act as metaphor for an evolving gender, race, class, and citizenship identity politics.

The issue of "politically correct eating" surfaced in the course of ethnographic research on conversion to Sunni Islam in Los Angeles County. Rouse began her study of conversion in 1991, when she taught math, reading, and video production at an Islamic elementary and junior

high school. Since then, she has interviewed over 100 women and men; continues to attend community events including *Jumah* (Friday prayer); and has followed 12 women closely for the past 11 years. During almost all of these interviews and encounters, food was served. After Friday prayer, for example, hot food (e.g., barbecued meats, bean pies, and red beans and rice) was often sold outside the *masjid* (mosque). At larger gatherings, particularly during the month of Ramadan when people break their fast together, southern cooking was typically the cuisine of choice (e.g., collard greens, biscuits, hot links, macaroni and cheese). At people's homes, Rouse would often find herself eating a combination of southern-American, Caribbean, and Middle-Eastern cuisine attesting to the emergence of new race and religious diasporic linkages.

Islam is now one of the fastest growing religions in the United States, and a large proportion of Muslims in America, an estimated 30–40 percent, are African American. African American Sunni Muslims now number some 1.6 million, in contrast to the better known (but much smaller) group called the Nation of Islam led by Louis Farrakhan.[4] While the focus of the study was on issues of gender and politics, a lot of time was spent in kitchens and at feasts. Food was found to be a central medium for expressing religious commitment, and for positioning oneself in relation to a history of slavery and new forms of liberation. During the initial stages of fieldwork, food was taken for granted: The everyday mundaneness of eating seemed *under*whelming in light of an ethnographer's search for the extraordinary. Over time, however, efforts to understand the relationship between the Nation of Islam and Sunni Islam, forced a recognition of changing perceptions of lawful and unlawful foods, particularly in light of the community's newly emerging desires for historical relevance.

THE SOUL OF THE NATION

Referring to Elijah Muhammad, the founder of the Nation of Islam, Doris Witt argues:

> Muhammad used food as part of his effort to formulate a model of black male selfhood in which "filth" was displaced onto not white but black femininity as articulated within African American culture via discourses of gender and sexuality rather than class. He adopted the traditional Islamic ban on pork to pursue this rearticulation, while supplementing it with numerous other dietary recommendations which, through their stigmatization of the foods associated with "soul," seem to have been intended to purify the black male self of black female contamination.
>
> [Witt 1999:104]

Witt is not the only one to characterize the Nation of Islam, and by extension the African American Sunni Muslim community, as the producers of new oppressive gendered tropes (Lubiano 1998; Sizemore 1973). Witt in particular argues that, within the Nation of Islam, soul food signified the role of women in the pollution of the black physical, intellectual, and spiritual body. Witt's thesis fits neatly into a "second wave" feminist paradigm that male and female are a binary opposition parallel to oppositions between public and private, culture and nature, and (according to Witt) sacred and profane (Ortner 1974; Rubin 1975). In these models, relations between men and women are points of contestation and competition rather than uniquely situated at the intersections of race, class, nation, and gender (see Collins 1990, 1998; Mohanty 1991; Moraga and Anzaldua 1981). Rather than assuming that conversion to Islam is an instantiation of patriarchy, we argue it is more productive to explore how African American Muslim women make sense of their gender.

In pursuit of this goal, discourses about food and food taboos offer an entrée into the various ways in which race and gender are understood in the African American community. The anthropology of food taboos is a long-established field of study, but it has been characterized by a preoccupation with classification, anomaly, and disorder that is usually divorced from concerns with power, history, and social change. Philosophers (Ricoeur 1969), classicists (Dodds 1951; Moulinier 1952; Parker 1990; Vernant 1980), and anthropologists (Douglas 1966; Leach 1964; Tambiah 1985) have long embraced a tradition that identifies the dangerous with "matter out of place" (Douglas 1966), things that do not fit into existing schemes, as if these schemes remained constant, and the only possible response to confusion was ostracism from the system and fear of contagion. As Valeri notes, "the whole field of taboo is characterized by the blending of the physical and the moral" (2000:43) and a position that "taboo" is a characteristic of "primitive" societies, which exist in stark opposition to modern, complex historical societies.

Food is, however, an obsession in contemporary America, the main subject of best-selling books and articles and a key location for the articulation of notions of goodness, purity, and wellbeing. Dieting is highly politicized, opposing the moral arguments of vegetarians to those of high protein advocates, calorie counters to carbohydrate addicts, fusing notions of health with those of virtue. American cuisine, while highly commercialized, is also amazingly diverse, combining eating traditions from all over the world—apparently the opposite of a homogeneous society preoccupied with anomaly at its borders and labeling these anomalies as taboo.

And yet we propose to argue that food taboos are very much alive in contemporary American society and deserve attention precisely because they bring together a series of political and historical controversies. The study of African Americans who are self-consciously articulating a form of eating that they see as liberating them from the heritage of slavery can show us how a classic anthropological concern with food taboos can be opened up to history and how the experience of the past can be reinterpreted in terms of the struggles of the present. It can also show us how complex societies and contemporary religious movements are not immune to processes of classification but incorporate them into new visions of purity imbued, in this case, with nostalgia for a time before slavery combined with utopian aspirations for transnational religious community.

THEORIES OF TABOO: FROM CLASSIFICATION TO THE EMBODIED SUBJECT

The most influential anthropological theories of taboo have emphasized ideas of classification and order rather than history and struggle. While we can gain some insight from them, they need to be reformulated to address the dynamics of changing African American attitudes toward the foods of slavery. Durkheim (1915:337) saw taboo as a form of social control, a religious prohibition that divided the world into the sacred and the profane. Radcliffe-Brown (1948:402–403) developed this point by analyzing taboo as the manipulation of sentiments, particularly fear, which was given prominence in ritual. He explained the dangerousness of food by saying that eating furnishes the most intense and primordial experience of the moral power of society over the individual. However, he neglected to examine the motivations for considering certain foods as dangerous, and the cosmological ideas that lie behind taboos.

Leach refined Radcliffe-Brown's ideas by arguing that "taboo serves to discriminate categories in men's social universe . . . in so doing it reduces the ambiguities of reality to clear-cut ideal types" (1971: 44). Sacred powers are seen as both

contaminating and ambiguous; therefore taboos teach us to avoid the sacred and keep the destructive powers of confusion at bay. Unambiguous categorization is required for successful communication, therefore taboos are necessary to cognitive notions of order. Douglas carried this idea further, seeing ideas of taboo and pollution as ways of "imposing system" in the face of "an inherently untidy experience" (1966:4): "Where there is dirt there is system. Dirt is the by-product of a systematic ordering and classification of matter, in so far as ordering involves rejecting inappropriate elements" (Douglas 1966:36).

Recent critics have noted that this tends to reify both order and disorder to an extent that is at odds with the essentially relational nature of taboo:

> To give just one obvious example, the claim that only the dirty dirties conflicts with the belief that pollution may be induced by *inappropriate* contact with eminently clean sources of order, such as gods, sanctuaries, sacred objects, and, in many parts of the world, rulers or priests. The reason is not that notions of purity and impurity are confused in the notion of sacredness, but that pollution is a much more relational notion than Douglas makes out.
> [Valeri 2000:68–69]

Douglas's most novel contribution is in her associating pollution with taxonomy: "A hierarchical classification in which at each level of the hierarchy all the categories are mutually exclusive" (Sperber 1975:12). Her famous analysis of the abominations of Leviticus argued that pigs and other animals were taboo for the ancient Hebrews because they were anomalous in terms of a taxonomic order that was viewed as an expression of divine order. Pigs, who "part the hoof" but do not "chew the cud," do not fit into the usual divisions of domestic animals, and so they were excluded.

Soler, reanalyzing the same material, countered that what made pigs ritually taboo was that they would also eat meat and were predators, while animals that "chew the cud" are clearly vegetarian (1973:944). In Paradise, both humans and animals ate only herbs and fruits, but after the Flood, humans were allowed to eat meat as long as they killed animals in a ritual fashion that reserved the blood containing the essence of life for God.

The Old Testament rules for eating derive, then, not from a decontextualized taxonomic impulse, but from a mythical historical development of ideas of sacrifice to compensate for the loss of vegetarianism: Taxonomy came into play not as an autonomous principle or an ideal of classificatory order but as a way to identify whether an animal was herbivorous or not (Valeri 2000:76). The change in food taboos was prompted by changes in the ways of eating and their historical circumstances.

Julia Kristeva has attempted to combine Douglas and Soler with Freud in a study of pollution (which she calls "abjection") as a progressive historical reinforcement of the "male" principle of symbolic differentiation and order as against the "female" principle of indifferentiation (1983:79–80). The Old Testament is dominated by a God, the father who excludes phenomena related to motherhood such as menstruation and childbirth from his cult as polluting, perhaps because this activity might rival his power as the one and only creator. Since taboos are about food and dirt, Kristeva sees them as about the relationship with the mother as feeder and toilet trainer. In the usual process of constituting the subject, the separation from the mother is a fundamental but never fully completed stage. So she interprets food taboos and other taboos as ultimately modeled after the incest taboo. Kristeva traces an evolutionary sequence from a "primitive" notion of external pollution through the Levitican notion of tabooed foods to the internalized pollution of Christianity. By grounding the experience of pollution in the body and the precultural experience of threats to the subject, Kristeva brings a subjective

and developmental dimension into what had been an exclusively classificatory perspective.

Valeri further extends this notion of the embodied subject as resisting the inarticulate by focusing on the constantly moving and transforming body experienced by us in its processes of ingestion, excretion, reproduction, transformation, and decay:

> The body is not only a substance to be legislated upon, to be turned into grist for the symbolic mill, but also a constant source of nonsense undermining the affirmation of sense. . . . A subject symbolically constituted, but necessarily located in the body, must be haunted by the fear of its disintegration through the body, since it constantly experiences the body's resistance to the subject's symbolic ordering of itself. The embodied subject's fear of disintegration through the body and by the body is the ultimate basis for the notion of pollution.
> [2000:109]

RESISTING BODIES: BRINGING HISTORY INTO THE STUDY OF FOOD TABOOS

Disease is metaphoric of social disorder and anthropologists have paid significant attention to the ways in which people resist state-sponsored control by resisting diagnoses and/or treatments (Lock and Kaufert 1998; Rapp 2000; Scheper-Hughes and Lock 1987). The relationship between disease and resistance is, however, as indeterminate as the relationship between health and acquiescence. Preoccupation with health enlists the body in a struggle over social value and meaning. Technologies of health (e.g., psychoanalysis, eating) discipline the body while simultaneously providing a conceptual platform on which one can author novel subversive practices and desires (Foucault 1990). Applying Valeri's reformulation of the problem of taboo to contemporary American cultural politics, we can see how subjective experience, especially the experience of subjugation and exclusion, can be transformed into a historical approach to food taboos. Fears of bodily disintegration can also express a historical experience of social disintegration, and efforts to "reform the body" through new eating habits can also be aimed at revitalizing the community.

The groundwork for this has been laid by Sidney Mintz's work on food and its relationship to power. Focusing on the history of Caribbean slavery and its links to the emergence of a new Caribbean cuisine, he writes:

> Eating is not merely a biological activity, but a vibrantly cultural activity as well. Under slavery, this activity, like all else in slave life, had to be rebuilt and endowed anew with structure and meaning, by the slaves themselves. Slavery shredded the whole of the material life of its victims, penetrating the very cell of the family, tearing people loose from their cultures, lands, and kin groups. But in the New World the slaves remade their lives culturally. They drew upon their ultimate resources as human beings, and they succeeded by struggle in keeping their humanity intact. They did so, as human beings have always done, by giving meaning to their achievements,
>
> [1996:49]

As everyday forms of resistance, Caribbean slaves kept small gardens where a combination of New and Old World plants were cultivated, finding new ways to cook discarded parts of animals that their masters did not want, and developing foods suited to the climate of the region. "Created at the insistence of the masters to reduce the cost of feeding slaves, the plots and then the markets were to become training grounds for freedom, a basis for the eventual rise of a free peasantry" (Mintz 1996:41). A new cuisine emerged from a situation of great adversity and came to be seen as a regional way of eating that included its own repertoire of meats, starches, vegetables, and preparation techniques.

Mintz goes on to consider various regional cuisines in America (1996:92–124), but not the question of a specifically "ethnic" or even "racial" cuisine. However, the foods developed in slavery *were* specifically marketed in the 1960s and 1970s as "soul food," and at that time they became entangled in a complex political struggle over the legitimacy of a menu dictated by poverty and exclusion. Are foods such as pig's feet, collard greens, black-eyed peas, and hominy grits simply "southern home cooking," or should they be identified as the food of slaves? Should they be embraced as part of a lost cultural heritage or banished as contaminated by the shadow of the chains that once bound the cooks? Mintz's argument does not include the 20th-century debates within the African American community—especially among those who were converting to Islam—about what historical significance should be given to the "foods of slavery."

Taboos normally mark events or situations that may threaten bodily integrity and thereby the integrity of the subject. Slaves, who were treated as food producing machines, had to reestablish their identities as moral beings. Sidney Mintz argues that they did this partially through productive activity—through growing and preparing their own foods, an activity that gave them some dimension of autonomy in a world where they were heavily constrained. After emancipation, the descendants of slaves continued to produce these same foods, but these became controversial when African Americans found in Islam a non-Western tradition in which the dream of a free subject could be realized. As Islam became associated with a turning away from the historical experience of slavery, African American foods became linked to a legacy of suffering.

THE HISTORICAL SIGNIFICANCE OF "SOUL FOOD"

Food is tied to emotional and sociopolitical processes that shape what we eat and how we eat it (Becker 1995; Counihan 1999; Kahn 1986; Witt 1999). In Tracy Poe's (1999) article on the origins of soul food, she traces the emergence of what has come to be understood as "authentic" black cuisine to inter-and intra-racial antagonisms. African American migrants to the Northeast who came during and after the Great Migration were often scorned by a black middle class that was both established and integrationist. Southern cooking was a symbol of the "backwardness" of the new migrants, and it threatened what middle-class blacks perceived as their hard-earned acceptance by some of the white establishment. For example, *The Chicago Defender*, a widely circulated African American newspaper, had a number of articles denigrating southern cuisine. The articles written in the 1920s and 1930s associated southern food with poor health and ultimately reinforced binary divisions between north and south: white and black, civilized and uncivilized, educated and uneducated, good and bad. The fact that African Americans were saying this to and about other African Americans meant that food situated itself squarely within the ambivalent terrain of black identity politics. Eighty years after the Great Migration, and forty years after the coining of the term "soul food," what does southern cooking mean to Muslim converts such as Safa? This history is marked by many switchbacks and dead ends, and the fact that today Sunni Muslims eat southern cooking is the result of overlapping historical processes that have changed the way African American Muslims understand and appropriate their history.

To a large extent, the African American Sunni community grew out of what is called "the transition," which occurred two years after the death of Elijah Muhammad in 1975. Debates over food taboos and eating rituals developed early in the Nation of Islam and occurred at about the same time that the black middle class was rejecting southern cuisine. In

his books and in his column "How to Eat to Live," a regular feature in *Muhammad Speaks*, Elijah Muhammad made the rejection of traditional black southern cooking a practice of faith. Unlike the black middle class who associated eating southern cuisine with a lack of sophistication, Elijah Muhammad argued that southern cuisine was a tool used by whites to physically, morally, and intellectually weaken blacks. While these two arguments differed in character, both were linked to ambivalence toward an inherited racial identity, and confusion over what constitutes liberation. In 1977, the Nation of Islam split into two factions: one side was eager to adopt Sunni Islam and the other determined to continue the teachings of Elijah Muhammad. The transition marks the period when many converts began to adopt the practices and religious beliefs of what can be described as orthodox Islam. It was during this critical period in the movement that changes in political, religious, and personal identification with Islam and America changed how food taboos were articulated. These changes demonstrate a historical dimension to ideas of purity that argues that relational metaphors of pure and impure are profoundly contextual and temporal.

THE NATION AND UNDERSTANDINGS OF PURITY

The mysterious and charismatic Wallace D. Fard founded the Lost-Found Nation of Islam in Detroit in 1930 (Clegg 1997; Evanzz 1999; Lincoln 1961).[5] The Nation was based on black self-determinism modeled by the separatist philosophy of the Marcus Garvey movement; as well as the ritual and religious ideology of Nobel Drew Ali's Moorish-American Science Temple. The early Nation borrowed quite openly from these two organizations, including the adoption of Marcus Garvey's slogan, "One God, One Aim, One

Destiny." Soon after the movement began, it gained a reputation as a subversive and potentially destabilizing organization. The movement attracted poor migrants who had fled the state-supported violence and economic disenfranchisement endemic to the South. The organization had the quality of a secret club with mysterious rituals of initiation and mythologies about the evil white race. Following a bizarre sacrificial murder performed by a Fard disciple, W. D. Fard was forced by law enforcement to leave Detroit on December 7, 1932 (Evanzz 1999:86–91).

By June 1934 when Fard disappeared for good, the Nation had already lost many members who were attracted perhaps more to Fard's charisma than to his ideology (Clegg 1997:34–35). It was a difficult transition as members left and Elijah Muhammad was forced to defend his title as Messenger. It was not until Elijah Muhammad began to reframe much of Fard's message in ways comprehensible to large audiences of African Americans that the Nation began to take shape and grow in terms of membership and ideology. Elijah Muhammad's success can be traced to his creation of a racially charged agenda for black revitalization that struck a chord with many residents of Chicago's South Side, the location of the Nation's new headquarters following Fard's disappearance (Clegg 1997; Evanzz 1999).

Through the institutionalization of the Nation by means of the establishment of black-owned businesses and the dissemination of the Nation's ideology through various forms of media, Elijah Muhammad successfully transformed the Nation into one of the most important religious movements of the 20th century. Appearing regularly in *Muhammad Speaks* was the column "How to Eat to Live." The most striking feature of "How to Eat to Live" is the recategorization of foods as healthy, dangerous, sacred, tainted, or polluted, according to the physiological and spiritual

needs of Black and Asiatic people. The Nation's origin myth stated that whites were created by the evil god-scientist Yacub through the removal of genetic materials from black and brown "germs." Clegg describes the supposed physiological outcomes of this genetic alteration:

> Their bones were fragile and their blood thin, resulting in an overall physical strength one-third that of blacks. Weak bodies made Yacub's man susceptible to disease, and most future aliments, 'from social diseases to cancer,' would be attributable to his presence on earth. . . . Actually, the grafting process had made the white race both incapable of righteousness and biologically subordinate to the black people.
> [Clegg 1997:51]

A corollary of these physiological differences marked by disease and moral pollution was the urgent need for members of the Nation to construct behavioral barriers to potential physical decay and weakened immunity to white "tricknology" or treachery. Limiting ingestion of particular foods, of course, represented one of the most important methods against disease of the physical and social body. In a published collection of food edicts, Elijah Muhammad warned: "Peas, collard greens, turnip greens, sweet potatoes and white potatoes are very cheaply raised foods. The Southern slave masters used them to feed the slaves, and still advise the consumption of them. Most white people of the middle and upper class do not eat this lot of cheap food, which is unfit for human consumption" (Muhammad 1967:6). Articulating his disdain for another slave food, catfish, Muhammad wrote, "The catfish is a very filthy fish. He loves filth and is the pig of the water" (Muhammad 1972:64). Also rejected were foods used as animal feed, such as sweet potatoes, collard greens, and corn, which would put blacks in the same category with beasts of burden. Refined sugars and flours, scavenger fish, inexpensive meats such as chitterlings, corn bread, cabbage sprouts, mustard salads, beet-top salads, and kale were all on the list of foods to avoid. Alternatively, members were encouraged to eat brown rice, milk, butter, fresh vegetables, the best and most expensive cuts of beef and lamb, but only twice a week, fish weighing between eight ounces and ten pounds, white and red navy beans, asparagus, eggplant, okra, squash, and rhubarb (Muhammad 1967, 1972). By cleansing their bodies through the avoidance of traditional "slave" foods, Nation followers cleansed their minds of the ideological poisons that made them participants in their own degradation (Kepel 1997:29–32).

What ideological shift took place enabling the African American Sunni Muslim community to once again enjoy southern cooking with collard greens, fried chicken, black-eyed peas, and corn bread? This question has more than one answer because looking historically at the transition of food categories within the Nation, one recognizes that food taboos exist simultaneously as a method for blending the physical and the moral (Valeri 2000); as a form of social control or a way of delineating order (Douglas 1966; Durkheim 1915); as a way of reducing ambiguities (Leach 1971); as a way of embodying resistance to disintegration (personal and social), and as a method for ascribing sacredness (Valeri 2000). In the movement's transition in the 1970s from Nation of Islam to Sunni Islam, the dynamic and changing character of food taboos demonstrates that food taboos are mired in a dialectical relationship between historical memory and identity versus social and ideological change. As a result, most foods occupy more than one category allowing fluidity for constantly shifting subject positions.

In one clear example, Elijah Muhammad, who earlier in the text warns that the hog is a polluted animal, takes the old adage "you are what you eat" to a new level:

Allah taught me that this grafted animal [hog] was *made for medical purposes*—not for a food for the people—and that *this animal destroys the beautiful appearance of* its eaters. It *takes away the shyness* of those who eat this brazen flesh. Nature did not give the hog anything like shyness.

Take a look at their immoral dress and actions; their worship of filthy songs and dances that an uncivilized animal or savage human being of the jungle cannot even imitate. Yet *average black people who want to be loved by their enemies*, regardless of what God thinks of them, have gone to the extreme in *trying to imitate* the children of their slave masters in all of their wickedness, filthiness and evil.

[Muhammad 1967:14, emphases added]

In this excerpt the hog shifts from a polluted object to a medicine from Allah to an active agent causing evil behavior and a loss of control. So what does this taboo represent? The hog stands in for itself, for history, for oppression, for negatively valued modes of behavior, for a liberated consciousness, and for poor health. In other words, the taboo on eating hog organizes multiple political, social, and personal locations, and these food categories shift in priority based upon changing spatial and ideological contexts.

While we argue that rejecting soul food was, for the Nation of Islam, ideologically tied to racial empowerment, Witt argues that rejecting soul food is tied to patriarchy and the association of women with filth and moral decay. Witt contends that the iconic figure of Aunt Jemima, the black slave woman, has come to represent soul food and therefore "the perception that blackness itself is irrevocably inscribed . . . by women" (1999:99). Quoting the line that Spike Lee gives to his own character in the film Malcolm X, "My trouble is—I ain't had enough stuff yet, I ain't et all the ribs I want and I sure ain't had enough white tail yet" (1999:103), Witt argues that the temptations of pork and white women are often identified as dangerous and threatening to black men. As evidence, Witt cites Elijah Muhammad's *Message to the Blackman:* "The woman is man's field to produce his nation." From this, she concludes:

> By reducing all black women to the status of womb-in-waiting and literalizing the equation of womb and dirt, Muhammad's dictum stands as pervasive evidence for the validity of Kristeva's argument that the maternal body provides the paradigm for that which must be abjected because it threatens the boundaries of the self. African American women were necessary to give birth to this social order of original black men, but they were also the "filth" that had to be othered, lest the purity of that order be undermined.
>
> [1999:108]

Witt argues that Elijah Muhammad deliberately demonized all the foods of "Mama's kitchen" because "Muhammad's goal seems to have been not just to insert the black father into view but to render invisible the legacy of black women in generational continuity" (1999:114).

This reading lacks an appreciation for the discursive context of the 1950s and 1960s. For Elijah Muhammad, the enemy that needed to be vanquished was the discourse of white supremacy that described the black body as filthy, ugly, and unable to control corporeal desires. At the end of *Message to the Blackman*, Muhammad includes a letter written by J. B. Stoner, an imperial wizard of the Ku Klux Klan, which was addressed to a gathering of Muslims in Chicago in 1957:

> Islam is a dark religion for dark people. . . . There are several reasons why niggers should oppose it. One reason is that the Qur'an forbids Muslims to drink intoxicating drinks, whereas most niggers like to get drunk. It says also that thieves should have their hands cut off. How many niggers would be left with hands? . . . One of the main purposes of Mohammedan invasion of white Europe was to capture white

women. Only white women are beautiful. . . . They didn't like their own dark women. The African race has never produced a beautiful woman. . . . If the Africans were as good as whites, they would be happy with their own women instead of lusting for our white women. Your desire for white women is an admission of your own racial inferiority. One reason why we whites will never accept you into our white society is because a nigger's chief ambition in life is to sleep with a white woman, thereby polluting her. . . . Africans in America are ashamed of their own race. . . . As proof, look at the nigger newspaper that advertise skin whiteners, and so-called hair straighteners
> [Muhammad 1965:331-332]

Elijah Muhammad did not simply dismiss the Klu Klux Klan's characterizations of blacks. He agreed that black men sometimes prefer white women, and that black men and women are altering their bodies out of shame. However, while Stoner attributes these behaviors to an essential moral poverty and racial inferiority, Elijah Muhammad attributes these behaviors to the ingesting of racism both materially and ideologically. Women in the Nation of Islam read Elijah Muhammad's message to avoid soul food as a warning to the "so-called Negro" to either break from dominant ideologies instilled by the "white man" or suffer continued degradation. Therefore, in opposition to Witt, we argue that the debates about Islamic foods are connected to the particular history of slavery, Jim Crow laws, and unstable citizenship, rather than to the development of the trope of black womanhood as filth.

Theories of taboo require the element of history to understand how practices become meaningful to embodied subjects. As Valeri says,

> The strong embodiment of the subject implies that it is intrinsically difficult to differentiate sharply between bodies that are

subjects and bodies that are mere objects. . . . More generally, if subject and object are not radically distinguished, being invaded by external agencies must acquire the significa- tion of a potential I shattering of one's subjective identity. One loses more than one's health: one loses one's distinct being.

[2000: 110]

In order to understand how food has been used to return a sense of subjectivity and historical agency to a people who had long been deprived of such notions, we will describe the religious practices of two Muslim women: Afaf, who moved from the Nation of Islam to Sunni Islam, and Hudah, who converted directly to Sunni Islam.[6] For Sunni Muslims, the recasting of the African American in history from object to creative subject meant that southern "slave" food was reappropriated to signify the hopeful embrace of American citizenship.

Afaf's story articulates how her reli- gious "transition" altered her conscious- ness or sense of self in relationship to society and inspired her to follow new religious practices. Hudah's story demon- strates new ways in which consumption choices are linked to African American social history. Whereas Afaf describes general ideological shifts in Muslim consciousness since the death of Elijah Muhammad, Hudah represents at a personal level how food and consumption are tied to understandings of empower- ment and agency.

CONVERSION THROUGH THE TRANSITION: WOMEN'S EXPERIENCES

Afaf lives in a lower-middle class neigh- borhood in Los Angeles. The neighbor- hood is made up of well-maintained single-family homes and belies a pervasive assumption by outsiders that black fami- lies living in South Central are impover- ished, dysfunctional, and victimized by

chronic crime. Afaf is a tall woman who dresses in flowing print fabrics accented by ethnic jewelry.

Afaf heard about the Nation of Islam through her brother. She had become disillusioned by what she describes as the hypocrisy of the Church but nevertheless maintained a strong belief in God. Having little patience for the 1970s counter- culture of drugs and individualism, Afaf searched for a spiritual community that embodied her values. The Nation, with its focus on hard work, discipline, and community empowerment, fulfilled that need and she joined in 1975. In 1977, she chose to follow Elijah Muhammad's son, W. D. Mohammed, into the practice of Sunni, or traditional, Islam.

When I came, there was a whole lot of glitter to attract people. So when I see people come in now, I say, Wow! I wonder what attracts them. I say there must be something to this religion that makes people want to come to it, although that glitter that was out there, those flashy cars, and those nice fezzes, and those white out- fits, and those suits, and that military disci- pline, and that type of thing, and the stores and the restaurants that was there when I came [are gone]. But I think what made me stay was I just liked it. Even after all the other stuff started breaking down, I just like the fact of Allah being the true God, the sense that it made.

Afaf asserted the importance of con- necting consciousness with practice. When she joined, for example, a member's consumption practices, both spending and eating, were considered expressions of personal empowerment. Both the Nation of Islam prior to 1975 and the emerging Sunni community of the late 1970s recog- nized that embodying faith was a neces- sary prerequisite to staying "on the job" and "living right," but as new understand- ings of African American empowerment developed after the death of Elijah Muhammad, "the job" changed. Notably, during Elijah Muhammad's tenure, black nationalism was the ideological foundation on which a spiritual movement was built; but for Sunni Muslims, Islam has become a spiritual quest within which a radical political, economic, and social agenda for the inner city has found legitimacy.

Elijah Muhammad reasoned that the development of a future nation must be preceded by the establishment of a black moral citizenry. To become a moral citizen meant only one thing for Elijah Muhammad, and that was the reclaiming of an authentic Asiatic essence lost in slavery and Jim Crow. Muhammad thought that this essence, which included race consciousness, industriousness, dignity, and resistance to white domination was obscured by the figurative and literal digestion of white supremacy. By linking consumption to liberation and social order, a seeming contradiction, Elijah Muhammad naturalized the need for whites and blacks to have a separate nation. Within a separate nation, blacks could live free from the polluting foods (and ideas) of whites and therefore in a state of purity as ordained by God.

Given how entrenched people can be in the eating rituals and foods of childhood, it is remarkable that Elijah Muhammad was able to encourage an entire community to change their eating habits (Farb and Armelagos 1980), even though the permitted foods were often costlier and harder to obtain in white neighborhoods. After Elijah's death in 1975, Elijah Muhammad's son, in an effort to move the community toward orthodox Sunni Islam, slowly replaced Nation of Islam food taboos with Islamic decrees. Afaf describes these changes:

AFAF: At that time when I came in, before I came in like the book *How to Eat to Live* you didn't eat certain foods like you didn't eat greens and sweet potatoes a lot of . . . . Carolyn: He made them taboo because they were all associated with slavery.

A: Right. So you couldn't eat certain kind of foods, so like this is what I'd heard, so now I'm telling you, "I can't eat that, I can't eat that." And then some people say, "You can eat that." I'm like, "No the book said . . ." Well, they said, "You can." So you really didn't know what to do. So I was going kind of confused, but I was hanging in there you know, and then they started talking in Arabic [laughs]. You know you had to learn your prayers in Arabic.

Clifford Geertz asks, "How do men of religious sensibility react when the machinery of faith begins to wear out? What do they do when traditions falter?" (Geertz 1968:3). For African American Muslims, the machinery of their faith had gradually worn out, and as African Americans began to make their way into spaces closed to them under segregation, black nationalism and Muslim separatism seemed less appealing. After winning institutional reforms in the 1970s, many African Americans moved away from seeing themselves as unique victims of racism and instead situated themselves universally as victims of a racist, capitalist-industrial complex (Wilson 1980).

Given African Americans' increasing access to power and social status during the 1970s, W. D. Mohammed encouraged his followers to assume some responsibility for their continued marginal economic and social status. The movement's journal, which underwent several name changes from *Muhammad Speaks* to *Bilalian News* to *The Muslim Journal*, began to introduce Islam as a tool for interpreting social problems and authorizing solutions. This shift meant that Islamic ideals of food consumption and purity still challenged Western norms and engendered self-control, but instead of being used as a symbolic marker of race essentialism, these taboos literally went by the Qur'an. Afaf recalls:

I said I was going to hang on in there and see what's going to happen, because like I said, I liked the atmosphere. Then I started learning things. I don't know how I finally learned how to [pray]. I'm trying to remember. I guess what I did was I went home, because I like to read. I had this little book called *The Muslim Prayer Book* Matter of fact here it is now. Sitting here. This is my second copy, because I gave the other one away to somebody. So I took this little book, and that's how I learned a lot of my Arabic.

The transition for African American Muslims moving toward Sunni Islam involved changes in both language and in symbolic expression. In Afaf's interview she describes the change from English to Arabic in naming and prayers; ritual ablutions; designation of sacred spaces; the elimination of certain food taboos; observance of Ramadan; and the use of the Qur'an as the sacred text. At a deeper level, these changes issued from a new structural relationship between black and white America. The Muslims wanted to reposition themselves as citizens with an ethnic, rather than a raced, identity with a unique set of claims about work ethic, cultural authenticity, and ability to submit to authority (Omi and Winant 1994). Perceptions of the community as "ethnically" Sunni Muslim opened up a set of propositions about social place unavailable when the community was perceived to be a racial project (i.e., as Black Muslims). The replacement of Elijah Muhammad's food taboos with the generalized Islamic concepts of *haram* and *halal* did not reject the marriage between social empowerment and religious practice, but they did resituate notions of citizenship and entitlement.

While the community was developing these new edicts and identities, outsiders, including Muslims from other ethnic and racial groups, continued to identify African American Muslims in terms of race. In response to the stubbornness of race as a predetermining structural object,

W. D. Mohammed introduced an Islam that was not entirely lacking in race consciousness, but defined race in nonessentialist ways. Often referring to the Prophet Muhammad's last speech in which the Prophet describes race equality, the Sunni Muslims have created a community that is color-blind but not culture blind. What makes African American Islam unique is the way the ideology is discussed in the context of African American social history and consciousness. Islamic religious festivals and feasts in the African American community now include fried chicken, sweet potato pie, black-eyed peas, and collard greens; all of which are foods formerly forbidden by Elijah Muhammad. What happened to the earlier consciousness equating traditional black cooking with slave foods and slave mentality? We contend that the elimination of certain food taboos is related to changes in understandings of self and society.

The criticisms lodged at African American leaders of nationalist movements in the late 1960s and early 1970s opened up a discursive space in which members reevaluated the subjectivity of blacks during slavery and Jim Crow. Many followers of Elijah Muhammad eventually came to the realization that there were a number of philosophical and social contradictions within the Nation of Islam that needed to be resolved. One of the most important of these was the idea that individuals can have agency, and even feel empowered, even when they are living in conditions of oppression. The binaries black and white, good and evil, object and subject did not always line up with each other to reflect the social reality of the Nation of Islam in which blacks sometimes treated each other poorly. The acknowledgment of social complexity by women such as Afaf opened up a space for Muslims to view slaves and blacks under Jim Crow as subjects who created a culture to sustain them despite the oppressive conditions in which they were forced to live.

Food taboos therefore reflect the evolution of African American Muslim economic, social, and personal consciousness. Importantly, this shift occurred as African Americans were slowly being ushered from partial to full citizenship with the enforcement of antidiscrimination laws and affirmative action. While Sunni Muslims continue to appreciate the semiotic entanglements of food and oppression and the link between avoidance of certain substances and spiritual and physical strength, purity now is orchestrated around themes of religious orthodoxy and community empowerment. The Sunni Muslims now embrace southern black culture, and accordingly, African American cuisine has been reappropriated as a point of cultural pride. This change accompanies the adoption of American patriotism. As mentioned earlier, African American Sunni Muslims represent their national allegiance by placing an American flag at the top of *The Muslim Journal*; a gesture directed inward to the community as well as outwardly to American society as a whole. When Muslims give *dawah*, or teach Islam to non-Muslims, Islam is represented as complementary to mainstream America. Eating halal is described as not very different from the traditional American diet. The Islamic movement now asks African Americans to try to change the American political landscape from within. This means that their identity as African Americans, as opposed to so-called Negroes, is a point of pride and not shame, and the reappropriation of southern cooking represents that shift in identity.

Unlike Afaf, Hudah converted directly to Sunni Islam in the late 1970s and therefore had no prior involvement with the Nation of Islam. In the 1990s, Hudah ran a marriage class for single and married Muslims, teaching individuals and couples how to work out problems and divide responsibilities according to the teachings in the Qur'an and *sunnah* (deeds and sayings of the Prophet Muhammad). Hudah thought that faith, gender roles, food, and discipline were necessary tools in the struggle against social and personal decay. In the fall of 1995, I met Hudah at her home on two occasions when we talked for hours about her perspective on Islam. Hudah was a cancer survivor, and while her health was extremely fragile, she said that a combination of prayer, herbal, and alternative medicines, as well as following the Prophet's advice for eating as outlined in *hadith* (sayings and deeds of the Prophet) and the Qur'an, was keeping her healthy. Her diet requirements were stringent, and during each of our interviews, we would have to break every two hours for a meal. Ultimately, our discussions were always peppered with Hudah advising me to eat lamb, honey, meat in moderation, fresh vegetables, shitake mushrooms, and an assortment of food regimens. Hudah, who has since died, was representative of the newer convert in the way she related to her southern identity and food consumption—not as a source of shame but of pride. As she remembers her childhood: "We were too poor to have a lot of meat. We were raised mostly on beans, and I would eat the vegetables coming up. As a result of that, having gotten the potassium I need, when I developed colon cancer, that brought me through." Unlike Elijah Muhammad, who argued that southern cooking destroys the black community from the inside out, Hudah saw her early diet as the source of her physical resilience. Avoiding the entanglement of food with ideas of race purity, Hudah's eating restrictions literally went by the book:

The Prophet Muhammad, peace be upon him, told us to practice preventive medicine. In other words we should eat the proper foods, so that we don't get sick. He tells us in the 45th chapter and the 13th verse, Bismillah. . . . "He has subjected to you from himself all that is in the heavens and all that is on the earth." And then in the 20th chapter and the 81st verse, he says,

"Eat of the good things we have provided for your sustenance, but commit no excess therein." Then in the 2nd chapter and 158th verse, he says, "Ye people eat of what is on earth lawful and good." So there are laws that we have to follow in eating.

Although she never claimed that American food is designed to weaken a specific population of Americans, she did say:

I had a friend that went to the Sudan, drank the milk, and did not get gas. They put some pork products in the milk [in America] that's why it makes people sick. God said he made milk pure and agreeable. God does not lie so it's not milk, it's ilk in many cases as we say. *Halal* milk you can get from the *halal* market and it doesn't have all those chemicals in it and it won't make you sick.

Hudah's sentiment is tied to her critique of the American capitalist system, which, she believes, allows food to be tainted in order for businesses to increase their profit margins. As we closed our discussion Hudah added:

Cancers and tumors are a result of blood stagnation and not having proper circulation. God said he subjected the whole creation to us. If we know the foods that we should eat, the laws we should practice in dealing with our children and our marriage, we will have peace, because Islam means peace. . . . This is holistic medicine, submission to the will of God, to the laws that he left us.

GENDER AND FOOD

Now that African Americans have embraced Sunni Islam, one might mistakenly assume that current food taboos and consumption practices are doctrinal and therefore fixed. Data from interviews conducted in the summer of 2002 indicate that the community's relationship to food continues to shift. In the Nation of Islam

prior to 1975, consumption practices were a symbolic expression of race consciousness and a rejection of American citizenship. In the Sunni community in the 1980s and 1990s, eating practices expressed a sense of personal and social empowerment and an attempt to balance Islam, race consciousness, and patriotism. Current consumption practices, especially after September 11, are expressions of religious individualism which emerge from an even deeper embrace of democratic principles. Many women in the community currently express the view that each Muslim's spiritual journey is unique and should not be judged by others. In addition, many women believe that the Qur'an and sunnah must be subjected to feminist rereadings that stress the spirit of Islam. As a consequence, many women who once believed in the importance of wearing *hijab* (woman's covering) no longer do so. Similarly, many who bought and ate only halal meats, avoided refined flours and sugars, and purchased food in Muslim- and black-owned establishments have eliminated many of their former restrictions and expanded the repertoire of foods they consume.

These changes are related to the fact that African Americans are now recognized as Sunni (orthodox) Muslims in mediascapes and interfaith relations. The use of Islam by terrorists to justify violence opened up a space for African American Muslims to demonstrate the compatibility between American neo-liberalism (individualism and capitalism) and Islam. At a Los Angeles masjid in 2002, I heard Abdul, a man assigned to give the Sunday lecture, express great joy about being asked to speak as an expert on Islam rather than being asked to represent "Black Muslims." He was ecstatic that his opinions were being given as much weight in interfaith meetings as were immigrants from the Middle East. The recognition from outside the community that individuals can be simultaneously African

American, Muslim, and patriotic has had the effect of quelling any uncertainty or insecurity about how the community should position itself in contemporary American constructions of citizenship and belonging.

Returning to the issue of patriarchy, clearly within the Nation there was a desire to resituate men as the head of household and of the community. Rejecting slave foods was, however, not an association of women with filth so much as an association of southern black cooking with white supremacy, internalized racism (pollution), and partial citizenship. Members of the emerging Sunni community have tried to resolve a number of philosophical and social contradictions and, in this ideological context, southern cooking was reappropriated as a tribute to African American agency during slavery and Jim Crow. Within the current community, it is important to remember that because food is generally situated in the domestic sphere, consumption taboos continue to have relevance to issues of gender and the division of labor within marriage. For many women, particularly those who work, the pragmatic issues of feeding children and shopping for food have inspired many women to look more closely at men and women's specific gender roles as outlined in the Qur'an and sunnah. These edicts outline the rights and responsibilities of men and women to one another. Many women view these edicts as empowering because they encourage African American men to practice their family obligations that for many include joining their wives and children in healthy eating.

The current state of food taboos within the African American Sunni community speaks to a desire to make Islam more compatible with living in mainstream America. There is currently no consensus about the relationship between the body and empowerment, only that a relationship exists. Being "on the job" now means intellectual engagement with *tafsir* (Islamic exegesis). As the community attempts to build bridges to other Muslim populations and defend the faith against antagonists, African American social history has new relevance and the African American body finds itself awash in new meanings.

CONCLUSION: HOW FOOD TABOOS REPRESENT GENDERED STRUGGLE

Controversies about the "right" form of Islamic diet are not yet resolved. Most African American Muslims in the Sunni tradition now follow a relatively conventional set of food taboos, but they combine elements of traditional "soul food," while excluding pork and other foods incompatible with orthodox Islam. They are part of a social effort to reform eating habits, decrease the use of alcohol and drugs, and establish healthier patterns that can be maintained throughout life. Our argument is not only that food taboos are articulated in an historical—rather than simply a classificatory—framework, but also that women's agency in cooking and preparing food is particularly marked in this arena. Witt's (1999) analysis of conflicts about renouncing both "pork and women" in the Nation of Islam intersects in interesting ways with this ethnographic material, but her conclusions are markedly different.

Whatever they might write and say in public speeches, the leaders of African American Islam left the work of buying and preparing food to women. While Afaf remembers her efforts to conform to Islamic taboos as initially confusing, she soon began to feel that this was an arena where she could gain control and even take command. Hudah reported that she learned to heal her own body by buying halal products untainted by capitalist greed. In each case, these women felt that their actions in the kitchen were part of a larger emancipatory movement in which food helped define a new subjectivity that had agency at the community rather than the individual level. In each case, Muslim identity, while marked by taboos such as the ban on pork, was also reconciled with family traditions for sharing certain kinds of foods. If Elijah Muhammad's initial aim was to discredit the black slave mother as well as her "soul food," this is not the way in which the message has been understood by female converts.

Contemporary practitioners of Sunni Islam see food taboos as a way of reaffirming their heritage within a much wider religious tradition. African American Muslims who worship in this tradition do not preach a politics of racial separation, and neither do they accept a politics of female subjugation. For them the dinner table is a place to practice an everyday form of purity and religious discipline, in which women play a central role. The disproportionate attention paid to Farrakhan by mass media has given African American Islam a "phallic" face that serves all too easily to confirm practices of discrimination and condemnation for all Muslims. Women such as Afaf, Hudah, and Safa show us how the selection and preparation of foods can also be an empowering religious practice.

Food is always about more than simply what fills the stomach. "An embodied subject necessarily tends to embody itself beyond the limits of its body. This is particularly true of powerful people, but every subject participates in objective correlatives, analogues, or metonoymies of itself on whose integrity its integrity depends" (Valeri 2000:110). Eating is one form of creative activity in which subjects are allowed to make choices about what will come to constitute their very being, both corporeally and symbolically. It should come as no surprise that these decisions are politically charged and that they cannot escape the weight of history in their articulations.

NOTES

1. Paul Robeson Park is a pseudonym. This article grew out of a chapter of Rouse's dissertation that is now a book (Rouse 2004). This article examines some of the same ethnographic material but with greater attention to the theoretical issues of taboos.

2. The Ka'aba was built by the Prophets Ishmael and Abraham and is considered God's sacred house. The Prophet Muhammad destroyed idols that had been built on the same grounds where the Ka'aba now stands, thus "purifying" it for the worship of God alone.

3. The idea for this article was developed in conversations about food taboos and Islam between the authors. Rouse did all of the ethnographic fieldwork, as part of a long-term study of Islamic conversions among Sunni African American women in Los Angeles. Hoskins felt these materials also had relevance for the comparative study of food taboos and drafted the treatment of theories of taboo, as well as sections of the conclusion. We have worked on this piece together, merging two different field perspectives into a single argument.

4. These figures come from *Time* magazine, "As American As ... Although Scape-goated, Muslims, Sikhs and Arabs are Patriotic, Integrated—and Growing," October 1, 2001:5. For a comprehensive list of relevant demographic data see http://www.adherents.com/Na/Na_347.html#2067.

5. After W. D. Fard disappeared, Elijah Muhammad began to refer to him as Master Farad Muhammad.

6. Both names are pseudonyms and the stories of these two women were collected through oral interviews by Carolyn Rouse in March 1993 and October 1995, respectively, in Los Angeles County.

REFERENCES CITED

Becker, Anne (1995) Body, Self, and Society: Review from Fiji. Philadelphia: University of Pennsylvania Press.

Bourdieu, Pierre (1977) Outline of a Theory of Practice. Richard Nice, trans. Cambridge: Cambridge University Press.

Clegg, Claude Andrew, III (1997) An Original Man: The Life and Times of Elijah Muhammad. New York: St. Martin's Press.

Collins, Patricia Hill (1990) Black Feminist Thought: Knowledge, Consciousness, and the Politics of Empowerment. Boston: Unwin Human.

—— (1998) Fighting Words: Black Women and the Search for Justice. Minneapolis: University of Minnesota Press.

Comaroff, Jean (1985) Body of Power, Spirit of Resistance: The Culture and History of a South African People. Chicago: University of Chicago Press.

Counihan, Carole (1999) Anthropology of Food and Body: Gender, Meaning and Power. New York: Routledge.

Dodds, Eric Robertson (1951) The Greeks and the Irrational. Berkeley: University of California Press.

Douglas, Mary (1966) Purity and Danger: An Analysis of Purity and Taboo. London: Routledge and Kegan Paul.

Durkheim, Emile (1915) The Elementary Forms of Religious Life. Joseph Ward Swain, trans. New York: The Free Press.

Evanzz, Karl (1999) The Messenger: The Rise and Fall of Elijah Muhammad. New York: Pantheon Books.

Farb, Peter, and George Armelagos (1980) Consuming Passions: The Anthropology of Eating. Boston: Houghton Mifflin.

Geertz, Clifford (1968) Islam Observed: Religious Development in Morocco and Indonesia. New Haven: Yale University Press.

Harris, Cheryl (1995) Whiteness as Property and Legal Doctrine. In Critical Race Theory. Kimberle Crenshaw, Neil Gotanda, Gary Peller, and Kendall Thomas, eds. Pp. 276–291. New York: The New Press.

Kahn, Miriam (1986) Always Hungry, Never Greedy: Food and the Expression of Gender Relations in a Melanesian Society. Cambridge: Cambridge University Press.

Kepel, Gilles (1997) Allah in the West: Islamic Movements in America and Europe. Susan Milner, trans. Stanford: Stanford University Press.

Kristeva, Julia (1983) Powers of Horror: An Essay on Abjection. New York: Columbia University Press.

Kondo, Dorinne (1997) About Face: Performing Race in Pashion and Theater. New York: Routledge.

Leach, Edmund (1964) Anthropological Aspects of Language: Animal Categories and Verbal Abuse. In New Directions in the Study of Language. E. H. Lenneberg, ed. Cambridge, MA: MIT Press.

—— (1971) Kimil: A Category of Andamese Thought. In Structural Analysis of Oral Tradition. P. Maranda and K. E. Maranda, eds. Pp. 22–48. Philadelphia: University of Pennsylvania Press.

Lincoln, C. Eric (1961) The Black Muslims in America. Boston: Beacon Press.

Lubiano, Waheema (1998) Black Nationalism and Black Common Sense: Policing Ourselves and Others. In The House That Race Built. Waheema Lubiano, ed. Pp. 232–252. New York: Vintage Books.

Mauss, Marcel (1979) Sociology and Psychology: Essays. London: Routledge and Kegan Paul.

Mintz, Sidney (1996) Tasting Food, Tasting Freedom: Excursions into Eating, Culture and the Past. Boston: Beacon Press.

Mohanty, Chandra (1991) Under Western Eyes: Feminist Scholarship and Colonial Discourses. In Third World Women and the Politics of Feminism. Chandra Mohanty, Anna Russo, and Lourdes Torres, eds. Pp. 51–80. Bloomington: Indiana University Press.

Moraga, Cherrie, and Gloria Anzaldua, eds. (1981) This Bridge Called My Back: Writings by Radical Women of Color. New York: Kitchen Table: Women of Color Press.

Moulinier, Louis (1952) Le Pur et l'Impur dans la Pensee des Grecs d'Homere a Aristote. Paris: Klincksieck.

Muhammad, Elijah (1961–75) How to Eat to Live. Muhammad Speaks. Chicago: Muhammad's Mosque of Islam No. 2.

—— (1965) Message to the Blackman in America. Chicago: Muhammad Mosque of Islam No. 2.

Omi, Michael, and Howard Winant (1994) Racial Formation in the United States from the 1960s to the 1990s. New York: Routledge.

Ortner, Sherry (1974) Is Female to Male as Nature Is to Culture? In Women, Culture and Society. Michelle Rosaldo and Louise Lamphere, eds. Pp. 67–87. Stanford: Stanford University Press.

Parker, Robert (1990) Miasma: Pollution and Purification in early Greek Religion. Oxford: Clarendon Press.

Radcliffe-Brown, A. R. (1948) The Andaman Islanders. Glencoe, IL: The Free Press.

Rapp, Rayna (2000) Testing Women, Testing the Fetus: The Social Impact of Amniocentesis in America. New York: Routledge.

Ricoeur, Paul (1969) The Symbolism of Evil. Emerson Buchanan, trans. Boston: Beacon Press.

Rouse, Carolyn (2004) Engaged Surrender: African American Women and Islam. Berkeley: University of California Press.

Rubin, Gayle (1975) The Traffic of Women. In Toward an Anthropology of Women. Rayna R. Reiter, ed. Pp. 157–210. New York: Monthly Review Press.

Scheper-Hughes, Nancy, and Margaret Lock (1987) The Mindful Body: A Prolegomenon to Future Work in Medical Anthropology. Medical Anthropology Quarterly 1(1):6–41.

Sizemore, Barbara (1973) Sexism and the Black Male. Black Scholar (March–April).

Soler, Jean (1973) Semiotique de la nourriture dans la Bible. Annales 28:943–955.

Sperber, Dan (1975) Rethinking Symbolism. Cambridge: Cambridge University Press.

Tambiah, Stanley J. (1985) Animals are Good to Think and Good to Prohibit. In Culture, Thought and Social Action. Pp. 169–211. Cambridge, MA: Harvard University Press.

Valeri, Valeria (2000) Forest of Taboos: Morality, Hunting and Identity among the Huaulu of the Moluccas. Madison: University of Wisconsin Press.

Vernant, Jean-Paul (1980) The Pure and the Impure. *In* Myth and Society in Ancient Greece. Janet Lloyd, trans. Pp. 110–129. Brighton, U.K.: Harvester Press.

Wilson, William Julius (1980) The Declining Significance of Race: Blacks and Changing American Institutions. Chicago: University of Chicago Press.

Witt, Doris (1999) Black Hunger: Food and the Politics of U.S. Identity. Oxford: Oxford University Press.

14

Gleaning from Gluttony: An Australian Youth Subculture Confronts the Ethics of Waste

Ferne Edwards and David Mercer

INTRODUCTION

And when ye reap the harvest of your land, thou shalt not make clean riddance of the corners of thy field when thou reapest, neither shalt thou gather any gleaning of thy harvest: thou shalt leave them unto the poor, and to the stranger.

Leviticus 23: 22

Recent years in the more affluent countries have witnessed an explosion of interest—both in academic circles and more widely—in the ethics of food consumption and production, in differential access to quality food in retail outlets, and in the analysis of different food economies (Norberg-Hodge *et al.* 2002; Wrigley 2002; Singer & Mason 2006). Geographers have played a leading role in this resurgence. In part, research interest has accelerated because of various 'food scares' that have shaken public confidence in agricultural production and distribution systems in the UK, in particular (Lyons *et al.* 2004; Scrinis 2007). In part, it is also a response to concerns over escalating greenhouse gas emissions associated with expanded 'food miles' as well as growing recognition of the enormous global divide separating the majority, who are undernourished, and those in the affluent world who often exhibit obesity and attendant health problems associated with overeating. In many cases, too, as the "food deserts" research has highlighted, there are often pockets of serious disadvantage in affluent countries where there is only limited access to healthy and nutritious food (Whelan *et al.* 2002). The most recent of the regular, population health surveys conducted in Victoria, for example, revealed the disturbing finding that 1 in 20 of those surveyed ran out of food in the previous year. Moreover, almost 25 per cent reported that this happened on a regular basis (Department of Human Services 2005).[1] At the other extreme, farmers' markets are becoming increasingly popular with more affluent consumers willing to pay higher prices for good-quality, fresh farm produce.

The issue of *food security* is becoming increasingly important at both the national and local scales in all countries. Adapted from California's Community Food Security Coalition (www.foodsecurity.org), this has been defined in Australia by VicHealth (2005, p. 2) as:

> . . . the state in which all persons obtain nutritionally adequate, culturally acceptable, safe foods regularly through local non-emergency sources. Food security broadens the traditional conception of hunger, embracing a systemic view of the causes of hunger and poor nutrition within a community while identifying the changes necessary to prevent their occurrence. Food security programs confront hunger and poverty.

In Victoria, the State government agency, VicHealth, has taken a lead role in promoting research into identifying those groups most vulnerable to food insecurity and—through its Food For All program—encouraging action at the grassroots level. Certain local municipalities, especially in inner-city Melbourne, have been active in addressing the food insecurity question. With the highest level of public housing rental tenancy in Victoria, the City of Yarra has been particularly proactive.

Another related issue that has captured both public and academic attention—and is the main focus of this paper—is that of *waste* (Chappell & Shove 1999; Bulkeley *et al.* 2005). Waste in general, and food waste in particular, challenge our environmental integrity and the recklessness of overproduction and the attendant over-consumptive lifestyles. It also raises issues of value and social inequality (Thompson 1979; Hawkins & Muecke 2002; Scanlan 2005; Hawkins 2006). It has been estimated, for example, that Australians waste nearly 3.3 million tonnes of food each year (Smith 2005), and a more recent study in the UK has found that around 33 per cent of all food purchased by households is thrown away (or 15 pence for every pound spent) (Waste and Resources Action Programme 2007). This excess garbage places undue pressure on landfill sites, contributing to environmental degradation and greenhouse gas emissions. Food waste occurs at all stages along the food chain from field to market to landfill, with Australian research finding that the most wasteful consumers are young people aged between 18 and 24 years (Hamilton & Mail 2003a). Interestingly, this Australian 'demographic' also reflects the largest decline in environmental concern over the years, falling from 57 per cent in 2001 to 49 per cent in 2004 (ABS 2004; Bentley *et al.* 2004).

However, notwithstanding this disturbing trend, two international youth subcultures have emerged to confront the scandal of food waste produced within over-consuming capitalist societies. Individuals within the subcultures of 'Dumpster Divers' (DD)[2] and 'Food Not

Bombs' (FNB)[3] live their environmental and social justice beliefs by practising alternative consumption choices. These lifestyle choices go beyond 'sustainable consumption' options, such as green or ethical consumption, to participate in 'anti-consumerist' activities, choosing to reduce their consumption by transforming their housing, transport, work practices and social values, rather than simply purchasing 'environmentally friendly' products. These 'anti-consumerist' lifestyles are often coupled with political and environmental activism that can span the globe through the actions of what have been termed highly mobile *flaneur* activists (Leontidou 2006).

Consisting mainly of young people, individuals who DD and participate in FNB procure their food in accordance with the philosophy of 'freeganism'. This is a term first coined around the year 2000, but the concept has much in common with the earlier 'voluntary simplicity' movement (Elgin 1981). It is defined as the belief in 'minimising impact on the environment by consuming food that has literally been thrown away' (*Macmillan English Dictionary Online 2002*).[4] DD and FNB represent freegan subcultures as DD procure food from supermarket dumpster bins for individual consumption, while FNB possesses the characteristics of an urban social movement comprised of a globally spanning group who redistribute organic food donated by markets and shops to feed the urban poor at no cost. FNB, for example, have been particularly active in New Orleans in the aftermath of Hurricane Katrina. Another Australian equivalent charity organisation is SecondBite. Each Sunday, after trading has ceased at one of Melbourne's largest fruit and vegetable markets—the South Melbourne Market—some 500 kg of unsold produce is sorted by 85 volunteers and distributed to the needy (*Port Phillip Leader* 2007).

Little academic research has been conducted into these forms of political gleaning (Lack 1995; Clark 2004; Rush 2006), though as the quotation from the Bible at the start of this article clearly demonstrates, the principle of gleaning has a very long heritage. In more recent times (in 2000) the practice was publicised in Agnes Varda's French documentary film *The Gleaners and I*.

The research presented in this paper bridges the divide between the broad research areas of *food production-consumption* (Holloway *et al.* 2007) and *urban social movements* demanding a right to the city (Lefebvre 1968; Pickvance 2003; Massey 2005). It also links in strongly with Gibson-Graham's (2006) important project on post-capitalist politics and provides an important alternative interpretation of Australian youths' consumption patterns, documenting how subcultures use anti-consumption practices to ascribe alternative identities to oppose mainstream Western societal norms, while negotiating inequalities within a neoliberal framework.

Based on ethnographic research, we document and analyse how young people in Australian cities are drawn to these subcultures and the ethics embedded within their alternative consumption diets. These findings are analysed in terms of the creation of their alternative identities performed on temporal–spatial terrains to exemplify the role of the contemporary activist's use of space, place and culture in relation to social issues.

BACKGROUND TO DD AND FNB

DD (or 'dumpstering', 'dumping', 'binning', 'bin scaben', 'trashing', 'scabbing' or 'skip-dipping') has existed for as long as there have been dumpsters and excessive waste. The practice of DD also extends to 'diving' for non-food items and scavenging materials. In the USA the term 'dumpster diving' is also used in relation to identity theft, the stealing of sensitive information from rubbish bins. DD and FNB often have a strong political connotation, with members of these subcultures gleaning food as a symbolic, political act against capitalist overproduction and waste. This 'political gleaning' contrasts with the foraging of wild foods (such as is a legal entitlement in Scandinavia), the scavenging of recyclable materials, or food scavenging as practised by the homeless. For this study, we focus on people who choose to glean food for a blend of economic, political and environmental reasons within these subcultures.

Food Not Bomb's history is documented from its political origins in the USA in 1980 when a group of friends were protesting against the Seabrook nuclear power station project in Cambridge, Massachusetts. FNB originally formed as the Cambridge Collective, evolving through the Affinity Group and the National Organising Period stages to number over 214 autonomous Chapters in the present international era (Butler & McHenry 2000; Food Not Bombs Seattle 2004). These groups share a common praxis endorsed by shared experiences and ideas gained from working together at servings, through participation at fund-raising events, and from representation on international websites, and from participation at annual international FNB convergences (Food Not Bombs 2005; Food Not Bombs News 2005).

METHODOLOGY

The main source of information for this study was provided by interviews with 30 participants who were involved in freegan activities mainly within Australia, although some had also participated in freegan activities in the USA, the UK and Mexico. The interviews were qualitative and semi-structured, and predominantly conducted individually. In addition, we undertook ethnographic research of associated freegan activities such as FNB food collection, preparation, serving and fundraising, 'dumpster dinners', ware-house parties, gleaning co-operatives, and activist events such as Critical Mass and Reclaim the Streets, both of which seek to reclaim the streets from cars.

Respondents were selected from attend-ance at such events or recommended by participating friends. The sample consisted of 20 men and 10 women, ranging in age from 18 to 58 years, with the majority in their early 20s. Two Australian capital cities served as the research bases for the study, allowing site comparisons. This sample provided a useful overview of contemporary political gleaners as it represented people who: (i) practised either DD or FNB, (ii) prac-tised both activities, and (iii) one person who exclusively collected 'wasted' food put aside by supermarket and bakery staff in separate boxes and bags. While most of the people interviewed moved within similar subcultures, the sample also included people who practised gleaning activities outside of these subgroups. Also, seven people interviewed no longer parti-cipated in either DD or FNB, providing insights as to why participants discon-tinue these activities.

WHO PARTICIPATES, AND WHY?

The people drawn to Dumpster Divers and Food Not Bombs are predominantly male, in their mid-20s, and from well-educated middle-class backgrounds. They have strong ideological beliefs, basing their lifestyle choices, such as diet and career choices, on ethical bases. For instance, freegans consider where and how their food is produced in terms of environmental and humanitarian concerns and many respondents devoted much of their time to activism. As also found in Fincham's (2007) recent study of the bicycle courier subculture in the UK, 'fun' and 'socialising' are two, additional, major motivators for people who dump-ster dive and participate in FNB alike. The

sociality of gleaned food is evident in the way people first became aware of food 'waste', methods of appropriation of food, and its incorporation within associ-ated activities and activist subcultures. For example, people often became aware of DD and FNB through friends, eating at FNB servings, and through participation in the vegan network or participating in street protests. Associated activities included dumpster dinners, the establish-ment of dumpster households and the redistribution of DD food to DD-friendly households. People often dumpster dive with their friends, while some FNB members will travel over an hour on public transport to attend a FNB prepara-tion and serving.

Although DD food is generally shared with only DD-friendly people, FNB extends this reach to redistribute gleaned food within the public domain, often drawing together 'punk' subcultures, the disadvantaged, the mentally ill and Indigenous and war veteran communities; These people do not all participate for purely social reasons, but all end up socialising just the same. An FNB partici-pant describes this communion:

> . . . and the socialising that happens on the street with everyone, all the different people who are brought together for it. Like you've got all your crusties who go and eat there or who cook there, and are into activism and that and come there because it's FNB and its ethical and cool. Then you've got all the people in the commission flats who love it because it's the best and healthiest meal you can get for free on the streets . . . It's really, really good and you know it—people say it all the time, the regulars who come . . .
> (Mas FNB/DD5)[5]

FNB contributes not only to the individu-al's personal gratification but also the wider community, extending its public outreach to provide regular food drop-offs to various community groups and by feeding people who attend environmental, social and Indigenous justice events.

ASSOCIATED FREEGAN ACTIVITIES

The freegan philosophy to minimise the impact on the environment by using fewer resources also extends to other anti-consumerist activities. These activities can be defined as the DIY-punk (or 'do-it-yourself' punk) movement. This movement correlates with freegan philosophy, activities and politics by advocating for people to live outside the capitalist system and hence not support environmental exploitation or social injustices embedded within capitalist power structures. Associated DIY-punk activities include squatting, scavenging, living in community warehouses, cycling, second-hand clothes' shopping, fare evasion, 'zine' (magazine) production and making one's own clothes or music. It also complements more conventional ideas of sustainable gardening and housing design—yet materials used to make these gardens ideally would be scavenged rather than purchased (Hoffman 1993). As one FNB participant explains:

> Yep, that's basically really what anarchists do, and it's what FNB started on really. 'X' is a perfect example of that—it's a warehouse set up by people who are within the scene, open to people who want to go to that scene. People can practice there, they have their own recording rooms, they printed their own cds, t-shirts and everything. It was like, you know, no involvement of corporations whatsoever, that's what it really is—an avoidance of corporations ... Yep, definitely. Capitalism is the opposite of Punk.
>
> (Fem FNB2)

As another FNB participant elaborates:

> DIY is taking something into your own hands and out of other peoples' hands ... With dumpster diving you're taking that back in your own hands, your own life back in your own hands. That's your DIY— if I do it myself and spend less, essentially the more of my life I'm able spend doing what I'd love to do ... Stuff that's

beneficial to myself and to the community ... It could be about putting out a record that's not a label ... I would really like to try and get my own sustainable vegie garden. I make my own clothes; I listen to mainly DIY music.

> (Mas FNB/ DD6)

Aside from dumpster diving, squatting— the occupation of privately owned buildings that are not being used (Labourlawtalk n.d.)—is another key example of a DIY-punk activity.[6] A dumpster diver comments:

> Yep, [there's] definitely a correlation between dumpster diving and squatting— they've basically let the house become a bin ... Thrown it away ... We used to have a joke that the house was just a big dumpster ... We had all these appliances we DD as well, like sandwich grills, grinders, juicers and stuff. We used to joke that we'd get this garbage and spread it with this garbage, put some garbage in it, stick in the hot garbage ... All the ingredients in the toasted sandwich were dumpstered including the appliance.
>
> (Mas FNB/DD5)

This freegan form of 'DIY-punk' demonstrates the acceptance of an 'informal economy' within an alternative economic space, allowing freegans to decrease their dependence on the capitalist economy whilst proving that alternative lifestyles are possible. However, as acknowledged on the Crimethlnc. Workers' Collective website, 'being a one-person economy is extremely difficult' (D.B. n.d.). To counter alienation, they advocate for the creation of a DIY-punk community with people who share similar values and practices working together for mutual support (D.B. n.d.).

ACTIVIST SUBCULTURES

In addition to the overarching DIY-punk theme, there exist overlapping activist subcultures. Each of these has slightly different discourses and practices, yet are involved in Dumpster Divers or Food Not Bombs to different degrees. Members can be identified loosely according to dress, their lifestyle politics and whom they socialise with, yet much overlap and socialisation occurs between the groups. For this reason, and given that people are hesitant to be 'boxed' into static identities, most people are reticent to identify with a particular subgroup. However, according to a dumpster diver (Mas DD5), activist subgroups can be roughly delineated along the following lines:[7]

(1) *Purist (university) food co-op hippies.* The diver elucidates:

> So they'll all do lots of work at [an environmental park] and plant big beautiful gardens [and] wear really flowing pretty dresses ... Most of them won't DD largely because they'll be more into organic food and being healthy and good to your body, but there's edges of that community that will also be into squatting and DD.
>
> (Mas DD5)

(2) The *anarcho-punk community* (also known as 'pc-punks'). The anarcho-punks are generally politically aware and 'intellectual'. They are heavily involved in FNB and moderately involved in DD (Mas DD5).

(3) The *autonomistas* represent a smaller activist subculture that arose in Australia out of protests such as at the World Economic Forum in Melbourne on 11 September 2000, and at the Woomera detention centre in South Australia in 2002. Autonomistas are generally well-educated and '... they're all into being really intellectual about their politics and they're autonomist socialists and all ...' (Mas DD5). Autonomistas are also often involved in independent media projects.

(4) The *forest ferals*. They are described as sporting 'a shaved head with crusty hair out the back, kinda anti-intellectual' (Mas DD5) who

originated in the Jabiluka protests against the mining of uranium in Kakadu National Park since 1998. According to the dumpster diver (who identifies as an autonomista), ferals are central to DD, yet it would be rare to see a feral doing FNB, although they may come to eat at FNB.

Our research found that gleaned food predominates in anarcho-punk and forest feral subcultures, with FNB generally favoured by anarcho-punks and DD by forest ferals. However, these affiliations change over time, with one FNB site which was originally dominated by 'hippies' having since been appropriated by 'punk-ravers',[8] then to become run almost exclusively by 'anarcho-punks' (Fem FNB/DD1; Fem FNB/DD4; Mas FNB/DD8). Furthermore, from the ethnographic research, associated activities such as Reclaim the Streets (a street protest to reclaim street space for pedestrians rather than cars) tended to be dominated by 'crusty-' and 'anarcho-punks', whereas the Students for Sustain-ability Conference, a national conference held since 1991 for students pursuing environmental and social justice causes, traditionally had a majority of forest ferals in attendance.

THE ETHICS OF EATING 'GARBAGE'

The selection of gleaned food by participants of DD and FNB depends upon factors such as the potential health risks, personal preference and the source. General foods collected by DD (in declining order of popularity) include vegetables and fruit, damaged packaged goods (such as rice and canned food), bread, eggs and cheese. The range of food available from DD is best explained by a diver:

> Basically, when it comes to food, anything you can think of that the supermarket stocks, you can get it in the bin from

organic macadamia nuts to apples to laundry detergent to fertiliser to jars of olives to fetta cheese . . .

[(Mas FNB/DD5)

The main FNB site in the study collected fruit and vegetables directly from an organic market. This produce—generally highly priced—is donated by stallholders at the end of the day when no market is to be held on the following day. Food donors in New South Wales and Victoria[9] are protected from liability by the Good Samaritan Law (see Victorian Government 2002), which allows edible, safe food to be given away.

POTENTIAL HEALTH RISKS

Although they consume 'garbage', every participant in the study claimed that they had never been aware of falling ill from food either dumpstered or prepared by FNB, except for a single person who ate dumpstered mushrooms wrapped in plastic found in a warm climate (Fem FNB/DD4). These health standards are upheld while keeping within an environmental ethos, by boiling the cutlery frequently and following standard food safety precautions. For dumpstered food, the negotiation of health is ensured through the wide selection of food available, a vegan or vegetarian diet and food preparation knowledge. The condition of the gleaned food is explained by a previous FNB participant:

> There's no high risk food [because there's no meat or dairy] and the food's at its point where it's at its height in ripeness and it's the most nutritionally good when the shops would throw it away . . . It's because of its shelf life—you can't have something there that would be rotten by the end of the next day . . .
>
> (Fem FNB2)

The Food Not Bombs soup kitchen menu considers the nutritional content of the food, the physical state of its clients (nothing too spicy and providing a variety of dishes for anyone with allergies), and their established food tastes (for example, baked potatoes are offered as a healthy alternative to hot chips). Excess organic produce is also given away at the serving, so people attending can cook their own food during the week.

PERSONAL FOOD PREFERENCES

The study revealed that all participants were aware of the ethics of food consumption and related their consumption practices to their beliefs and identity. These dietary preferences reflected predominant environmental and vegan discourses, with participants' diets including alternative forms of freegan diets such as the vegetarian 'dumpsterian' or 'frego' diets, and diets such as 'raw foodism' (a diet consisting of fruit, vegetables, nuts and sprouts), 'veganic' (vegan organic foods), and the consumption of roadkill.

Participants' motivations for dietary preferences include not contributing to demand for products that are ethically unacceptable, such as industrial agriculture which promotes 'chemical, pesticide, industrial waste-ridden food' (Mas FNB/DD3) and animal cruelty. Meat consumption was sometimes considered acceptable to some if farmed sustainably or if found in a dumpster bin or killed by cars. In the latter example, roadkill would be consumed 'to show [animals] the dignity they deserve' (Mas FNB/DD6) by placing value on meat that would otherwise go wasted.

The ethical implications of food consumption were taken to the extreme by one FNB participant who supported the dietary preference of vegan 'raw foodism', defined as 'you don't eat anything that is cooked or manufactured' (Mas FNB1), due to a combination of animal rights ethics, waste and nutrition. Furthermore, many participants raised the issue of fossil fuels and food consumption, favouring locally-based diets as they used '. . . less transport, energy, refrigeration, packaging' (Mas

FNB1). These beliefs in supporting local, sustainable food production were further endorsed by some participants who complemented dumpstered food by purchasing organic food from local independent stores.

This ethical consideration of diet was upheld by the practice of FNB which served either vegan, vegetarian or often organic food. The denomination of the FNB menu emerged from the preference and physical environment of each local chapter, illustrating FNB's capacity to adjust to different circumstances and promote its message and function throughout the world.

However, the central issues of the redistribution of waste and the issue of maintaining strict vegan food came into conflict in 2005 at a second FNB site. As one FNB participant explains:

> This one time we cooked up this incredible meal but then we put in some breadcrumbs. And this guy found that the breadcrumbs had very small traces of an additive that was made from fish oil. And this guy was adamant that we couldn't serve this food and there was tons of it and it was really good.
>
> (Fem FNB/DD1)

She continues to explain that—as they had to respect everyone's opinion because of FNB's consensus decision-making process—they chose not to serve the food. Instead, FNB participants who were not strict vegans took the food home.

FREEGAN FOOD SOURCES

Ethical factors for choosing Dumpster Diver locations often take priority over other considerations such as the quality and quantity of food, proximity to food collection locations and the degree of ease. These ethical factors consider issues such as the company's history, labour conditions, the environmental and social background of the products

they sell, and the sheer volume of waste they generate that contributes towards environmental degradation. Although people can DD from almost any source, big supermarket chains are favoured over smaller independent stores because they generally support large-scale industrial farming, often importing foods from overseas to the detriment of local farmers, while endorsing the unequal distribution of wealth between the poor and affluent worlds.[10] Multinational chains are also chosen on account of their impersonal nature and their use of micro-management techniques within the stores to induce citizens to consume more (Mas FNB/DD3). The latter was a particular point of criticism in the recent UK study mentioned above (Waste and Resources Action Programme (WRAP) 2007). The WRAP report was strongly critical of supermarket chains for packaging up too many items in pre-packaged packs of fruit, vegetables and meat.

By targeting these large corporations, dumpster divers may be perceived as modern day 'Robin Hoods', redistributing wealth to people who need it, choosing to spend their money and time on products and activities that endorse their politics. A dumpster diver recalls a fine example of this style of behaviour:

> When we found thirty frypans in the dumpster . . . [we felt] that the public should have those frypans . . . We put them all in a trolley and took them all down to the Brotherhood [a local charity store]
>
> (Mas DD9)

People also dumpster dive from small stores but for different reasons. These stores' bins often provide gourmet- or health-related produce, highly valued by those who dive. Given the shops' smaller size, they are often more resourceful with their stock than larger stores, producing less waste overall and investing more time in shop details. As one participant explains the difference in practice:

The bigger the stores, the less likely they are to have these policies—like smaller organic bakeries will give food . . . Whereas bigger ones will say it's too much of an effort and chuck it out.

(Mas DD9)

Hence, through their alternative consumption, freegans consider and act upon the long-term social and environmental ethics embedded within the food chains of their diets. This freegan consumption often takes place within a social setting, ascribing a sense of collective identity. Thus, the individual and collective identity of freegans and their opposition to mainstream capitalist economy are physically and symbolically ascribed. The next section discusses how freegans choose to construct themselves as 'other'.

FREEGANS AS 'OTHER'

Freegans' ability to construct their identity in order to oppose mainstream Western societal norms through the consumption of food 'waste' occurs in terms of their anarchist discourse, practice and structure, and

through their performance of these alternative identities on temporal-spatial terrains. These opposite characteristics are listed in Table 14.1.

FREEGANS' ANARCHISTIC DISCOURSE AND PRACTICE

Freegans' political discourse of anarchism rejects capitalism in terms of anti-consumerism, anti-corporatism and anti-bureaucracy. As one respondent describes:

It's set up so that if you don't consume, you're identity-less and you don't exist, so you find yourself consuming just to feel like you're still here. And especially when travelling, you find yourself quite lonely sometimes and you'll just go to a cafe and drink a coffee just so you're doing something legitimate and that's how people validate their existence on mass scales . . .

(Mas DD9)

This 'othering' has been described by theorists Douglas (1970) and Clark (2004). Douglas (1970) explores the issue of cultural demarcation using the categories of purity and danger. Applying

Table 14.1 Characteristics of gleaners *vs* 'mainstream' capitalist culture

Gleaning culture	Mainstream capitalist culture
Informal economy	Capitalist economy
Free food	Commodified food
No hierarchy nor organised structure	Hierarchy/organised structure
Chaos/anarchy—order relies on internal control	External control exercised by government and corporations
Food found dumped in bin	Food found stacked neatly on supermarket shelves
Eat 'raw' or 'rotten' foods	Eat 'cooked' foods
'Dirty'	'Hygienically clean'
No label—rely on senses to determine food safety	Rely on label to dictate food state
Slow food/lifestyle	Fast food/lifestyle
Eat food on footpath	Eat food within contained, regulated and often commodified spaces
Social collection, distribution and consumption of food	Greater individualization of food collection, i.e. less social interaction in supermarkets

Douglas's theory to the consumption of 'wasted' food, it would be considered 'repulsive and disgusting' by mainstream society as it transcends societal norms by re-appropriating food that has been set aside as 'untouchable'. Clark (2004) further examines 'othering' by applying Levi-Strauss's categories of the raw, cooked and rotten to the related topic of punk subculture's ideologies and identities with relation to DD cuisine. He finds that punks generally identify industrially processed (or 'cooked') food as corporate-capitalist 'junk food' which supports cash cropping, causing cancer and leading to the objectification of nature. Punks wishing to break free from the fetishism of products choose to eat 'raw' (unprocessed) or 'rotten' meals (such as stolen natural foods from health shops or groceries from dumpster bins) rather than 'cooked' foods. Clark (2004) explains that by appropriating their provisions outside of the marketplace, punks maintain their anti-consumerist identity by symbolically returning blemished 'cooked' food to a 'raw' status, rendering it acceptable for anarcho-punk consumption. The freegan appropriation of waste can also be viewed as transforming tainted products (including meat) into 'pure' acceptable raw foods, as it places value on products that have been socially devalued as 'waste'.

Freegans' appropriation of 'wasted' food from a bin also sets them apart as an 'other' contrasted to modern consumer culture's preoccupation with domestic cleanliness. The issue of gleaning healthy food from 'garbage' confronts the modern Western concept of cleanliness and hygiene. Notions of cleanliness have altered throughout history and are closely associated with changing concepts of the body. Historically we can identify three distinctive health discourses: humours, miasmas and germs. The former refers to the infiltration of disease though the porous human body by heat or water, while miasmas associate disease with decay and smell. The modern discourse of disease is germ based, which calls for responsible individual behaviour to ensure self-protection (Vigarello 1998; Shove 2003). All three discourses are challenged by the behaviour of gleaners, and especially dumpster divers, who experience the physical proximity of mixed rubbish, strong odours and invisible germs. This changing cultural perception of hygiene illustrates the importance of the socio-political context in defining garbage (see also Hawkins 2006).

The germ-based theory is countered by the 'Hygiene Hypothesis'—the hypothesis that living in an overly clean environment makes us sick. Using this hypothesis, epidemiologist David Strachan attempted to explain how the 'allergy epidemic' rose dramatically in industrialised countries due to cleaner living standards and smaller family sizes over the last 30 years. As a consequence, individuals received less exposure to infection during childhood, thus weakening their immune systems (see Stanwell-Smith & Bloomfield 2004). The sentiments of this hypothesis are often raised by freegans. As expressed by one respondent:

> I've done some travelling . . . And I really know that we have a super-high standard of food, and we don't expect to eat things that have a blemish on them or little weevils in them. Does that really affect your health? I don't believe it does . . . [I recently read an] article about diabetes and the high level of cleanliness—that the immune system hasn't got enough to deal with so it's attacking itself . . . I think you can maintain a reasonable standard and still be a gleaner . . .
>
> (Fem Gleaner)

And a joking remark that also attacks the mainstream understanding of hygiene: 'Yes, definitely . . . me and my friend used to have this joke: for a healthier immune system, lick the walls of a dumpster . . .' (Mas FNB/DD5). Another participant further questions this notion of cleanliness in relation to the generally accepted practice of chemical 'hygiene':

Modern health inspectors are so fastidious about germs that they don't stop to consider chemicals . . . How many industrial chemicals are used in cleaning stuff that are not beneficial to your health?

(Mas FNB/DD2)

Rather than relying on use-by dates to tell them what food is edible and safe, freegans use their innate senses of touch, taste and smell. This attitude marks a conscious shift away from corporate control enabling the diver to reclaim a connection to their senses and to the natural world.

FREEGAN ANARCHIST STRUCTURE

The discourse of anarchy among the subcultures is also apparent as a lack of organised or formalised structure. For example, FNB has no hierarchy or single person in control. Delight in anarchy is also symbolised by the jumbled collection of food from the bin found among the squashed, rotten and discarded. Gleaning as an informal economy also challenges the Western assumption that neoliberalism is the only viable global economic option. Ironmonger (1996, cited in Gibson-Graham 2003, p. 55) acknowledges that 30–50 per cent of the total economic output of the developed and developing worlds takes place within the non-commodity sector. The act of gleaning, and thus DIY-punk, reaffirms freegans' identities as 'citizens' rather than 'consumers', illustrating that (albeit partial) alternative economies do exist and are viable. Gibson-Graham (1996, pp. x–xi) claims that the diversity of 'noncapitalist ones had been relatively "invisible" because the concepts and discourses that could make them "visible" have themselves been marginalised and suppressed'. A more recent text (Gibson-Graham 2006) provides many concrete examples of 'community economies' and challenges the hegemony of an undifferentiated capitalist economy. In addition,

Clode (2007) has provided a useful guide to the rich diversity of alternative economies that now exist and are expanding rapidly in the UK.

PERFORMING DIFFERENCE THROUGH THE USE OF TIME

Increased time is required to collect and prepare gleaned meals in contrast to corporate fast food consumption, as many dumpster divers (after the initial thrill) choose to take fruit and vegetables home to wash and cook, rather than consuming processed foods. This anti-consumerist stance is further endorsed by the freegans' choice to work as little as possible in low-paying, low-skilled employment, preferring to spend their time on activities that they personally value, such as activist campaigns, creative projects or social occasions. This chosen time allocation parallels a preference for a 'slow' lifestyle, reconstructing temporality to their personal values rather than endorsing capitalist values of modernisation and speed (see Parkins 2004). The alternative 'work ethic' perspective is expressed online by CrimethInc. Workers' Collective, which unites unhappiness with low-skilled work, as it is repetitive, there is little choice in activities and because it often does not directly benefit humanity. Happiness, instead, is associated with creativity, working actively on projects that people value (CrimethInc. Workers' Collective n.d.). This work trend is reflected in freegans' career choices, often choosing studies that will lead to social justice causes rather than money-based careers (for example, one participant changed their course from neurosurgeon to social worker).

In a sense, this freegan lifestyle pattern represents an extension of Hamilton and Mail's (2003b, p. 8) concept of 'downshifting': 'people who make a voluntary long-term lifestyle change that involves accepting significantly less income and consuming less'. Downshifting is often used to describe an older and wealthier demographic, while the freegan case study broadens this term by representing a younger population who have the opportunities to earn money, but choose instead to live out their social beliefs.

PERFORMING DIFFERENCE THROUGH THE USE OF SPACE

The freegans' consumption of food on the public footpath also feeds into the anarchistic 'other' in the public presentation of an alternative economic space. While many respondents would like to present DD as a public political statement to highlight the waste and inequalities present within the capitalist system, they felt that it should remain a private (or hidden) activity due to the threat of heightened security and potential loss of food supply.

The private behaviour of Dumpster Divers contrasts sharply with the public nature of Food Not Bombs. FNB is seen as a public vehicle to educate people about the extent of food waste resulting from Western over-consumption of resources and to visualise and partially address social inequalities existing within the heart of the city. FNB serving locations often reflect the permaculture concept of the 'edge' (Crabtree 1999) located at the interface or overlap between two ecosystems, on street corners shouldering poor and affluent communities. These fringe territories convey the activists' identity and message to a range of social 'bodies' within this communicative zone. From the FNB sites in the study, a broad spectrum of people ranging from business commuters, people going out to dinner or art exhibitions, to university students and travellers witnessed FNB feeding a blend of punks, 'ferals' and the homeless and hungry. Hetherington (2004, p. 170) expresses the public reappearance of 'unfinished disposal' as 'haunting': where the act of second burial, such as disposal

at the end of the market day, has failed (see also Gordon 1997). According to Hetherington (2004), 'haunting' represents an unacknowledged lingering of guilt, such as the wasting of food while people are hungry. The reappropriation of food by members of FNB conveys the public message of capitalist impotence, with its mismanagement of resources and inability to protect its citizens from hunger. As such, the urban streetscape represents a key 'haunting' site to contest the capitalist erosion of the realms of common provision, the commodification of resources and rights, and social inequalities (Burgmann 2003).

However, the occupation of this public space sometimes needs to be negotiated with other communities that are often 'invisible' to the general public. Some friction has occurred at FNB serving sites where the predominance of punk youth attending the serving encroached on an Indigenous place, intimidating the homeless and disrespecting the site. This conflict raises the issue of the exclusivity of punk members and ferals who adopt distinct dress codes and behaviours. This community's 'othering' makes them unapproachable to some, compromising their ability to project their message to the general public. As one participant explained:

> Yeah—I just don't think the people who do it have a public persona that would let a broad demographic of people understand the issues . . . I think the general public are kind of scared . . . whereas the homeless people are just jolly people who are happy that they're getting fed.
>
> (Fem FNB2)

This use of space as an opposition to mainstream behaviours is also illustrated by the activities of Food Not Bombs and its relationship to other soup kitchens. One key difference between FNB and other soup vans is that after serving, FNB participants serve themselves and sit down on the street kerb to eat their dinner with whoever attended. This action dissolves any symbolic and physical boundaries that normally exist between those who serve and those who are served by people at other soup kitchens. As one FNB participant explains:

> The other thing that amazed me is that they [the people at other soup vans] never ate the food . . . And we'd offer them food . . . and the guy would say that he'd try not to eat on these days so I can identify with the cause, and we're like, the hunger cause? I find it really patronising for these people to come and serve people food and not eat it themselves, as if it's not good enough for them . . . Whereas FNB is completely different because you've got all these students and activists and just bums . . . And we sit down and have a meal together and it's this big social occasion where everyone is on the same level and there's no 'I'm the server, I'm the pious server'.
>
> (Mas FNB/DD5)

Food Not Bombs also provides an alternative 'ideological space' to the environment of many religious-based soup kitchens. Studies by Sager and Stephens (2005, p. 297) identify that people eating at proselytising soup kitchens find them 'coercive, hypocritical, condescending, and conflicting with their beliefs'. One post-FNB member outlines the differences between her father's church soup van and FNB:

> [My dad] . . . does free brekkies like FNB but they preach to homeless people . . . How it's not free at all as it comes with a price of Christianity, like preaching, which is what's so beautiful about FNB because in an anarchistic way there's no political view that's being forced onto people like religion or dogma.
>
> (Fem FNB/DD3)

CONCLUSION

In this study, we have described and analysed a subculture that defies and provides an alternative to Western mainstream culture's consumption practices. The people drawn to this Australian freegan subculture are primarily young, male, well-educated, politically motivated, from the middle-class and are involved in activism. Through their shared consumption of food 'waste' they construct themselves as a social 'other', working alongside other activist groups to contribute towards greater environmental and social justice.

In a period dominated by a succession of Australian governments espousing a neoliberal ethic, these groups strive to bridge the gap between the rich and those the welfare system fails. Freegans, and more specifically participants of FNB, do this through the creation of a communitarian 'third space' between the public and private sectors. Through their alternative consumption practices, participants within freegan subcultures challenge Western mainstream societal norms by contesting conventional notions of hygiene, the use of public space, and temporality in the form of downshifting. Ultimately, they represent anti-consumerist subcultures that broaden the ethics of responsibility from the individual to consider the long-term and far-reaching consequences of conventional industrial agricultural practices both within the West and developing worlds. This ethnographic study provides a fuller understanding of contemporary Australian youth's attitudes towards consumer culture, whilst contributing to social theory in the fields of youth identity construction and anti-consumerism. It also adds an additional 'food economy' category to the classificatory scheme recently produced by Holloway et al. (2007).

This study has raised many more questions than could be addressed within this article. Further research could be conducted into other forms of freegan practices such as squatting, links to international anti-consumerist movements and the effectiveness of government vs grassroots charity. The future of freeganism could also be explored with the international increase of Food Not Bombs Chapters and freegan web- and blog-sites. One interesting recent development has been heightened media interest in Dumpster Divers, in particular. What until recently was an activity known to relatively few has now become much more widely discussed in the print and electronic media, leading some supermarkets (perhaps fearful of legal action) to constrain this activity by locking dumpster bins and/or donating 'waste' food to central collection agencies such as VicRelief for later distribution to charity outlets.

Freegans are more than 'kids playing in bins for fun'. Freeganism has emerged within a rapidly changing world bombarded with growing incidences of terrorism, global warming-related disasters and recently introduced work casualisation and anti-terrorism laws, which together threaten free speech, the physical environment and social equality. The freegan counter-community shows that a commitment towards finding alternatives for greater social equality and environmental sustain-ability persists among youth in Australian society. Eating 'garbage' may not be the answer for all, but it is actively seeking change whilst symbolically illustrating the excesses of the West.

ACKNOWLEDGEMENTS

In addition to one anonymous referee especially, the authors would like to thank the following for their comments on an earlier draft of this paper: Dr Anitra Nelson, RMIT University, Melbourne, and Professor Lily Kong, National University of Singapore. The authors would also like to thank all who participated in the interviews as well as Dr Ruth Lane and Pam Morgan, RMIT University, for ongoing debate and information sharing around issues of waste and food security in contemporary urban Australia.

NOTES

1. By contrast, a recent survey of low-income diets and nutrition in the UK (the LIDNS study) came up with the perhaps surprising finding that there is little difference in the nutritional value of the diets of the poorest 15 per cent of the population than the average for that country (see Nelson *et al.* 2007).
2. See www.dumpsterdiving.net
3. See www.foodnotbombs.net
4. See www.freegan.info
5. The respondents are coded to protect their identities. 'Mas' is male respondent, 'Fem' is female respondent, 'FNB' is participates in FNB, 'DD' is participates in DD, and 'FNB/DD' is participates in both FNB and DD activities.
6. The perception and legalities of 'squatting' vary according to where it is practised. For example, squatting is sanctioned by the state in the Netherlands.
7. Please note that these observations are based on the respondent's opinions and do not serve as an authoritative definition of each of these subcultures.
8. Punk-raver scene: this scene refers to a youth culture that participates in outdoor parties, which are often arranged outside mainstream societal procedures and are often associated with party drugs (Fem FNB/DD4).
9. Also present in national legislation in the USA.
10. One DD participant noted this discrepancy of wealth and its consequences for the developing world when she established a FNB at Cancun, Mexico, in defiance of the World Trade Organisation's conference (Fem FNB/DD3).

REFERENCES

Australian Bureau of Statistics (ABS) (2004) *Environmental issues: people's views and practices*, ABS, Canberra.

Bentley, M., Fien, J. & Neil, C. (2004) *Sustainable consumption: young Australians as agents of change*, report, National Youth Affairs Research Scheme, Canberra.

Bulkeley, H., Watson, M., Hudson, R. & Weaver, P. (2005) 'Governing municipal waste: towards a new analytical framework', *Journal of Environmental Policy & Planning* 7, pp. 1–23.

Burgmann, V. (2003) *Power, profit and protest: Australian social movements and globalisation*, Allen & Unwin, Sydney.

Butler, C. & McKenry, K. (2000) *Food Not Bombs*, Sharp Press, Tucson.

Chappell, H. & Shove, E. (1999) 'The dustbin: a study of domestic waste, household practices and utility services', *International Planning Studies* 4, pp. 267–80.

Clark, D. (2004) 'The raw and the rotten: punk cuisine', *Ethnology* 43, pp. 19–31.

Clode, R. (2007) 'Another life is possible', *The Ecologist* 37, pp. 38–9.

Crabtree, L. (1999) 'Sustainability as seen from a vegetable garden', unpublished Honours thesis. Department of Human Geography, Macquarie University, Sydney.

CrimethInc. Workers' Collective (n.d.) 'How ethical is the work "ethic"? Reconsidering work and "leisure time" ', available at: www.crimethinc.com/library/english/howethic.html (accessed 29 March 2007).

D.B. (n.d.) 'How I spent my permanent vacation', CrimethInc. Workers' Collective website, available at: www.crimethinc.com/library/english/vaction.html (accessed 29 March 2007).

Department of Human Services (2005) *Victorian population health survey*, DHS, Melbourne.

Douglas, M. (1970) *Purity and danger: an analysis of concepts of pollution and taboo*, Routledge & Kegan Paul, London.

Elgin, D. (1981) *Voluntary simplicity*, Morrow, New York.

Fincham, B. (2007) ' "Generally speaking people are in it for the cycling and the beer": bicycle couriers, subculture and enjoyment', *Sociological Review* 55, pp. 189–202.

Food Not Bombs (2005) Food Not Bombs website, available at: www.foodnotbombs.net (accessed 29 March 2007).

Food Not Bombs News (2005) Food Not Bombs News website, available at: www.fhbnews.org (accessed 29 March 2007).

Food Not Bombs Seattle (2004) Seattle Food Not Bombs website, available at: www.scn.org/activism/foodnotbombs (accessed 29 March 2007).

Gibson-Graham, J.K. (1996) *The end of capitalism (as we knew it): a feminist critique of political economy*, Blackwell, Oxford.

Gibson-Graham, J.K. (2003) An ethics of the local, *Rethinking Marxism* 15, pp. 49–74.

Gibson-Graham, J.K. (2006) *Post-capitalist politics*, University of Minnesota Press, Minneapolis.

Gordon, A. (1997) *Ghostly matters*, University of Minnesota Press, Minneapolis.

Hamilton, C. & Mail, E. (2003a) *Overconsumption in Australia: a seachange in pursuit of happiness*, Australia Institute, Canberra.

Hamilton, C. & Mail, E. (2003b) *Downshifting in Australia*, Australia Institute, Canberra.

Hawkins, G. (2006) *The ethics of waste*, University of New South Wales Press, Sydney.

Hawkins, G. & Muecke, S. (eds) (2002) *Culture and waste: the creation and destruction of value*, Rowman & Littlefield, Lanham, MD.

Hetherington, K. (2004) 'Secondhandedness: consumption, disposal, and absent presence', *Environment and Planning D: Society and Space* 22, pp. 157–73.

Hoffman, J. (1993) *The art and science of dumpster diving*, Loompanics Unlimited, Washington, DC.

Holloway, L., Kneafsey, M., Venn, L., Cox, R, Dowler, E. & Tuomainen, H. (2007) 'Possible food economies: a methodological framework for exploring food production–consumption relationships', *Sociologia Ruralis* 47, pp. 1–19.

Labourlawtalk (n.d.) Labour Law Talk Dictionary webpage, available at: http://encyclopedia.laborlawtalk.com/Squatter (accessed 29 March 2007).

Lack, T. (1995) 'Consumer society and authenticity: the (il)logic of punk practices', *Undercurrent* 3, available at: www.uoregon.edu/uc3/3-lack.html (accessed 29 March 2007).

Lefebvre, H. (1968) *Le droit a la ville*, Anthropos, Paris.

Leontidou, L. (2006) 'Urban social movements: from the "right to the city" to transnational spatialities and *flaneur* activists', *City* 10, pp. 259–68.

Lyons, K., Burch, D., Lawrence, G. & Lockie, S. (2004) 'Contrasting paths of corporate greening in antipodean agriculture: organics and green production', in Jansen, K. & Vellema, A. (eds) *Agribusiness and society: corporate responses to environmentalism, market opportunities and public regulation*, Zed Books, London, pp. 91–113.

Macmillan English Dictionary Online (2002) 'Freegan', available at: www.macmillandictionary.com/New-Words/040213-freegan.htm (accessed 29 March 2007).

Massey, D. (2005) *For space*, Sage, London.

Nelson, M., Erens, B., Bates, B., Church, S. & Boshier, T. (2007) *Low income diet and nutrition survey*, Food Standards Agency, London.

Norberg-Hodge, H., Merrifield, T. & Gorelick, S. (2002) *Bringing the food economy home: local alternatives to global agribusiness*, Zed Books, London.

Parkins, W. (2004) 'Out of time: fast subjects and slow living', *Time & Society* 13, pp. 363–82.

Pickvance, C. (2003) 'From urban social movements to urban movements: a review and introduction to a symposium on urban movements'. *International Journal of Urban and Regional Research* 27, pp. 102–9.

Port Phillip Leader (2007) 'Appetite for good deeds sways market', 3 July.

Rush, E. (2006) *Skip dipping in Australia*, Australia Institute, Canberra.

Sager, R. & Stephens, L. (2005) 'Serving up sermons: clients' reactions to religious elements at congregation-run feeding establishments', *Nonprofit and Voluntary Sector Quarterly* 34, pp. 297–310.

Scanlan, J. (2005) *On garbage*, Reaktion Books, London.

Scrinis, G. (2007) 'From techno-corporate food to alternative agri-food movements', *Local–Global: Studies in Community Sustainability* 4, pp. 112–40.

Shove, E. (2003) *Comfort, cleanliness and convenience: the social organization of normality*, Berg, Oxford and New York.

Singer, P. & Mason, J. (2006) *The way we eat: why our food choices matter*, Rodale, Emmaus, PA.

Smith, B. (2005) 'Australia wastes three million tonnes of food', *The Age* (Melbourne) 6 May.

Stanwell-Smith, R. & Bloomfield, S. (2004) *The hygiene hypothesis and implications for home hygiene*, report commissioned by the International Scientific Forum on Home Hygiene, Nexthealth SRC, Milan.

Thompson, M. (1979) *Rubbish theory: the creation and destruction of value*, Oxford University Press, Oxford.

VicHealth (2005) *Healthy eating—food security investment plan 2005–2010*, Melbourne.

Victorian Government (2002) *Wrongs and other acts (Public Liability Insurance Reform) Act 2002*.

Vigarello, G. (1998) *Concepts of cleanliness: changing attitudes in France since the middle ages*, Cambridge University Press, Cambridge.

Waste and Resources Action Programme (WRAP) (2007) *Packaging innovation to reduce food waste*, WRAP, London.

Whelan, A., Wrigley, N., Warm, D. & Cannings, E. (2002) 'Life in a "food desert" ', *Urban Studies* 39, pp. 2083–100.

Wrigley, N. (2002) ' "Food deserts" in British cities: policy context and research priorities', *Urban Studies* 39, pp. 2029–40.

15

"If They Only Knew": Color Blindness and Universalism in California Alternative Food Institutions

Julie Guthman

"If people only knew where their food came from. . . ." This phrase resounds in alternative food movements. My students voice it in the classroom, and it is often the first sentence of papers they write. It undergirds many of the efforts of local food system activists, who focus a good deal of effort on encouraging more personalized relationships between producers and consumers. It is the end goal for a new round of muckraking led by the likes of Eric Schlosser and Michael Pollan, who seek to unveil existing food production practices. It animates the long list of ingredients on upscale restaurant menus.

The phrase warrants additional parsing. Who is the speaker? Who are those that do not know? What would they do if they only knew? Do they not know now? When pushed, the subjects of this rhetoric argue that such an unveiling of the American food supply would necessarily trigger a desire for local, organic food and people would be willing to pay for it (cf. DuPuis 2001). Then, so the logic goes, the food system would be magically transformed into one that is ecologically sustainable and socially just. To be sure, many U.S. alternative food advocates see lack of knowledge as the most proximate obstacle to a transformed food system, and in their elevated esteem for farmers—and chefs—relative to others who make their living in the provision of food, think that consumers should be willing to pay the "full cost" of food (Allen et al. 2003).

This assertion is made with respect to the growing sense that food in the United States is artificially cheap due to both direct and indirect subsidies to agriculture, which include not only crop payments, but also water, university research and extension, and even immigration policy. It then follows that food produced in more ecologically sustainable and socially just ways would necessarily cost more. On its face, the solution clearly runs up against the goals of food security for low-income people. However, if we consider nutritional quality in addition to food cost and access in our definition of food security, as does the community food security movement, many low-income people are food insecure despite the ubiquity of cheap food (Community Food Security Coalition 2006). For that reason, even the community food security movement, with its focus on linking up producers and consumers at the local level, rarely challenges this rhetoric (Allen 2004).

Although there is much to say about the perverse ecological, social, and health-related effects of U.S. agricultural subsidies (Magdoff, Foster, and Buttel 2000; Kimbrell 2002; Pollan 2006), this article takes on the cultural politics of "if they only knew" as it relates to alternative food practice. Following Stuart Hall, I define cultural politics as the relationship between signifying practices and power and am particularly concerned with how racialized representations and structural inequities are mutually reinforcing (Chen 1996, 395; Hall 1996). In this vein, I argue that rhetoric such as "if they only knew" is illustrative of the color-blind mentalities and universalizing impulses often associated with whiteness. Moreover, much alternative food discourse hails a white subject to these spaces of alternative food practice and thus codes them as white. Insofar as this has a chilling effect on people of color, it not only works as an exclusionary practice, but it also colors the character of food politics more broadly. My objective in raising this issue, therefore, is not to condemn, but to remark on the importance of a less messianic approach to food politics, and even the need to do something different than "invite others to the table"—an increasingly common phrase in considering ways to address diversity in alternative food movements. (Who sets the table?)

To make this argument, I report on heretofore unpublished results from a study I led on the convergences and contradictions of food security and farm security in two kinds of alternative food institutions: farmers' markets and community-supported agriculture (CSA). My discussion of managers' responses to survey questions and interviews regarding the dearth of participation of people of color in their markets (particularly CSA) reveals not only the pervasiveness of rhetoric of "if they only knew" and its cognates; it also shows how they reflect a problematic kind of color blindness. I entertain the possibility of their chilling effect by connecting several unrelated observations that I and others have made. First, however, I present a prima facie case that there is disproportionately low participation of people of color in these institutions.

MARKET PLACES AS WHITE SPACES

Farmers' markets and CSAs, the latter being arrangements where consumers sign up in advance for a regular weekly or biweekly box of food from a specific farm or group of farms, are frequently heralded as ideal spaces by alternative food advocates. Their presumptions are that these institutions shorten the social and economic distance between producers and consumers, build community and participatory democracy, and otherwise serve as sites of contestation against a globalized food system (Kloppenberg, Henrickson, and Stevenson 1996; Feenstra 1997; Hendrickson and Heffernan 2002; Hassanein 2003; Lyson 2004). Thus far, existing research suggests that people of color, and African Americans especially, do not participate in these markets proportionate to the population. It may also be the case that working-class or, more likely, less formally educated whites do not participate equal to their numbers either, but neither have they been subject to the same sort of scrutiny regarding their food provisioning practices, including attempts to enroll them in alternative food practice.

Unfortunately, most scholarly studies of these institutions have paid more attention to class than race in ascertaining their demographic composition. This tendency no doubt reflects the relative ease of establishing class composition. For example, many markets accept food stamps, now in the form of Electronic Benefit Payment cards. Measuring the use of this program can provide a reasonable proxy for low-income participation. So, for example, a series of studies in the late 1990s determined that less than 25 percent of food stamp recipients reported shopping at a farmers' market at all, and food stamp redemptions at farmers' markets accounted for only 0.02 percent of overall redemptions (Kantor 2001).

A study of farmers' markets conducted by the Agricultural Marketing Service of the United States Department of Agriculture (USDA) is the only comprehensive study that directly attempted to ascertain the ethnic composition of farmers' market customers. Based on the observations of farmers' market managers, it reported that 74 percent were white, 14 percent African American, 5 percent Asian, and 6 percent Hispanic. In the far west, though, the region discussed in this article, African American participation was considerably less at 5 percent, whereas Asian and Hispanic participation was higher, at 10 percent and 13 percent, respectively (Payne 2002).[1] This latter distribution in part reflects the ethnic makeup of the far west, but is still not proportionate to population. Although a comprehensive study of CSA has yet to be done, a number of highly localized studies have found that CSA primarily serves members with high incomes and include general observations that clienteles are white (Cohen et al. 1997; Festing 1997; Lawson 1997; Cone and Myhre 2000; Hinrichs and Kremer 2002; Perez, Allen, and Brown 2003).

This point must not be construed as a claim that African Americans do not participate in these markets (which surely varies by region) or, worse, a blanket indictment of African American food provisioning practices. A study of a farmers' market in a working-class predominantly African American neighborhood in Chicago found that shoppers at that market were much happier with the food at the farmers' market relative to that at nearby stores (Suarez-Balcazar et al. 2006). Still, the study did not suggest much breadth in participation. In fact, only sixty-four residents out of a community of 117,000 were interviewed in the study despite a methodology that was designed to capture a large sample. In addition, 80 percent of the respondents were regular shoppers at the market. In the last several years, I have visited eight different farmers' markets in California at least a half a dozen times each, four of which are in neighborhoods with a large percentage of African American residents (two in Berkeley, two in Oakland). In my

observations, I, too, have noted that African Americans frequent these markets, but not nearly to the extent of reflecting neighborhood demographics or, for that matter, in numbers near the supermarkets in the area. In the markets with which I am most intimately familiar, I have come to know or recognize many of the African Americans who shop there, suggesting they are dedicated but few in number, echoing the results of the earlier study. This speaks to my overarching point: The "whiteness" of these spaces is something that regular shoppers have in some sense had to overcome. Further research could shed more light on this particular phenomenon.

In any case, the problem I am addressing is not negated by the presence of a few black bodies in these alternative food institutions. Indeed, to the extent that studies only count bodies as a way of determining if all phenotypes are adequately represented, they in certain ways contribute to the problem. They not only reinforce notions of race that are based in stabilized categories (cf. Moore, Pandian, and Kosek 2003; Reardon 2005), they bow to the conceit that racism is solved merely by attention to distributional outcomes. As Shrader-Frechette (2005) has argued in regards to environmental justice, fair distribution of environmental burdens and benefits is a necessary but not sufficient condition of justice. In her view, justice can only be achieved with substantive participation in defining the terms and conditions by which those burdens and benefits exist in the first place. In keeping with her concern, mine is not just the numbers, but the ways in which the space itself is coded in ways that create immediate discomforts, which, in the long run, may reinforce broader exclusion. As geographers of race have noted, no space is race neutral; there is an iterative coding of race and space (Thomas 2005; Saldanha 2006; Schein 2006). The question is to what extent these marketplaces are coded as "white space," not only through the bodies that tend to inhabit them, but also the discourses that circulate through them. That many advocates and admirers of these institutions are blind to this coding suggests that whiteness is at work in these institutions. To this, I now turn.

THE DOUBLE-EDGED SWORD OF WHITENESS: COLOR BLINDNESS AND UNIVERSALISM

At the outset it needs to be said that whiteness is a messy and controversial concept with which to work, variably referred to as the phenotype of pale bodies, an attribute of particular (privileged) people, a result of historical and social processes of racialization, a set of structural privileges, a standpoint of normalcy, or particular cultural politics and practices (Frankenberg 1993; Kobayashi and Peake 2000). My interest in using whiteness is to make the invisible visible, to decenter white as "normal" or unmarked. I do so cognizant of the critique that the prominence given to whiteness scholarship has effectively recentered whiteness, as noted by McKinney (2005) and Sullivan (2006). Nevertheless, in agro-food scholarship and practice, concerns about race and whiteness are notable for their absence (cf. Slocum 2006, 2007), suggesting there is more work to be done.

For some scholars of whiteness, the point is to encourage more reflexivity among whites as to their privileged social position. Building on the work of Frankenberg, whose point was to bring into view the "social geography of race," several scholars have highlighted the presumptions and effects of those who inhabit white bodies. So, according to McKinney (2005), the purpose of an engagement with whiteness is not to determine who is racist or not, but to uncover what whites think about being white and what effects that has on a racial system. Her position is that one can be nominally nonracist and still contribute to a racial society. Further augmenting this line of argument, Sullivan (2006) makes the point that the unconscious habits of white privilege are in some respects more pernicious than the explicit racism of white supremacy because it is not examined. She draws particular attention to how nonrecognition of being the beneficiaries of privilege allows whites to retain a sense of being morally good. These insights, along with those drawn from a growing body of literature, particularly sociological, as to how whites experience their whiteness are important, but they also tend to personalize whiteness (Perry 2002; Bettie 2003). When I teach Wendell Berry, a poet of agrarianism much beloved by the sustainable agriculture movement, I do so to show the racial underpinnings of modern-day agrarianism. I am not interested in having students depict Berry as a racist because of his skin color. My goal instead is to show how a romanticized American agrarian imaginary erases the explicitly racist ways in which American land has been distributed historically, erasures that ramify today in more subtle cultural codings of small farming.

In this argument, I am drawing, then, from geographers of whiteness who as a whole seem less concerned with white personhood and instead focus on the work that whiteness does as an unmarked category in shaping social relations and, hence, space (Holloway 2000; Dwyer and Jones 2003; Schein 2006; Shaw 2006). Kobayashi and Peake (2000, 394) capture the subtle distinctions in this possibly more geographic approach when they state that "whiteness is indicated less by its explicit racism than by the fact that it ignores, or even denies, racist implications." It is not only a matter of making white people, those inhabiting pale-skinned bodies, accountable as to their effects on others (Frankenberg 1993; Lipsitz 1998; McKinney 2005), although that is an important project in its own right. Rather it is to show how discourses associated with whiteness touch down practically and spatially. In addition, focusing on the discursive aspects of whiteness opens the door to understanding how the doctrine of color blindness, for example, can be embraced by all kinds of people, whites and nonwhites alike.

With this concern in mind, two related manifestations of whiteness are particularly important for how they define alternative food practice and space. One is color blindness. For many, color blindness or the absence of racial identifiers in language are seen as nonracist (Frankenberg 1993; McKinney 2005). Refusing to see (or refusing to admit) race difference for fear of being deemed racist has its origins in liberal thought, yet as many have remarked regarding the doctrine of color blindness, it does its own violence by erasing the violence that the social construct of race has wrought in the form of racism (Holloway 2000; Brown et al. 2003). Inversely, color blindness erases the privilege that whiteness has brought. This is the point made by various scholars who have considered how whiteness acts as property, a set of expectations and institutional benefits historically derived from white supremacy that in their contemporary invisibility work to naturalize inequalities (Roediger 1991; Harris 1993; Lipsitz 1998).

The other manifestation of whiteness is universalism, or the assumption that values held primarily by whites are normal and widely shared. Sometimes this takes the form of an aesthetic ideal that is not obviously raced but is predicated on whitened cultural practices (Kobayashi and Peake 2000, 394). This move erases difference in another way, by refusing to acknowledge the experience, aesthetics, and ideals of others, with the pernicious effect that those who do not conform to white ideals are justifiably marginalized (Moore, Pandian, and Kosek 2003). In other words, when particular, seemingly universal ideals do not resonate, it is assumed that those for whom they do not

resonate must be educated to these ideals or be forever marked as different. It is in this classic missionary impulse that universalism works to reinscribe difference (Hall 1992; Stoler 1995).

Within geography, the only scholar who has engaged concerns at the nexus of whiteness, space, and alternative food practice has been Rachel Slocum. In her first article on this topic (Slocum 2006), she notes how community food movements have been slow to address issues of white privilege in the movement. She attributes this failing both to the persistent invisibility of whiteness as a racial category and to resistance within the movement to embrace an antiracist practice for fear of offending allies. In a more recent exploration (Slocum 2007), she works to see the possible affective affinities of whites and others in spaces of alternative food practice. There is much to be said for this position in regard to the need for an empathetic politics. Still, she is quite sanguine about white efforts "to bring this good food to others" (Slocum 2007, 523). In what follows, I want to suggest that this construction may be part of the problem.

EVIDENCE OF WHITENESS IN ALTERNATIVE FOOD INSTITUTIONS

In 2004–2005, I led a study of farmers' markets and CSA in California. The purpose of the study was to examine to what extent these market forms meet the twin goals of farm security and food security, goals that have been championed as synergistic by the community food security movement. Overall, we found that managers of these institutions generally support the idea of improving the affordability of the food they provide, and most have made an effort to do so, although these efforts vary with institutional capacity. Still, some hedged their interest in supporting food security goals with countervailing concerns such as the need to support farmers first (Guthman, Morris, and Allen 2006).

This article reports on some heretofore unpublished results of the study, specifically those that queried managers' inclinations to implement practices that might encourage participation of people of color in these markets. The majority of data were gathered through surveys sent to all California CSA and farmers' market managers for whom we could find accurate mailing addresses. The response rate for the CSA survey was 37 percent of 111 surveys sent out. For farmers' markets the response rate was 35.4 percent of 443 surveys sent to 294 managers. Both questionnaires addressed background information about farmers' markets and CSA (e.g., years in operation, organization type, profitability), and farmers and customers (e.g., income level, ethnicity). We also asked managers how important they considered addressing food access issues and how willing they were to employ tactics that other markets or CSA farms had adopted to encourage participation among low-income and "non-European-American" populations. Both surveys included short-answer, multiple-choice, and Likert-scaled questions.[2] In addition, the study involved interviews with a directed sample of CSA and farmers' market managers to explore some of these issues in more depth. We analyzed quantitative responses with descriptive statistics, tested for significance. We analyzed qualitative answers by coding them thematically. For example, an open-ended question regarding the reasons that more affluent people participate in these markets included answers grouped into emergent categories such as "better education," "more concern about food quality," "more health consciousness," "more time," or "neighboring demographics." However, some of the responses cited in this article are not necessarily representative, but tend toward the strongly put. Because we had stated the normative purpose of the study, namely to improve access to low-income

people and people of color, many respondents were clearly conscious that they would be judged on their answers and so provided quite timid and limited responses. Therefore, I contend that these responses are the tip of the iceberg, given the lukewarm response to our questions among the less strident. Even if they only represent a minority of respondents, they still bear relevance because of their potential chilling effect.

In indirect ways, this research did provide additional evidence about what is already widely felt to be true: These institutions disproportionately serve white and middle to upper income populations, although it almost goes without saying that farmers' markets are more racially and class diverse than CSAs. Most CSA managers reported that the vast majority of their customers were white. In response to a survey question as to why European Americans appeared to be the dominant ethnic group, one CSA manager wrote, "cause unfortunately we are in honky heaven! And the only people who seem to be able to afford to live here are people of this race." Farmers' market managers reported having more ethnic diversity at their markets, mainly because farmers' markets more closely mirror the demographics of the area in which they are located, as many managers noted. Still, few are located in communities of color, especially those that are primarily African American, and those that exist in African American neighborhoods tend to be very small. As one farmers' market manager noted on the survey form,

> Farmers' markets are good for everyone, but many of them are being located in "high-end" areas. The farmers may make more money there, and the higher income communities are "entertained" by outdoor markets.

To be sure, as the primary purpose of such markets is to serve farmers by providing a regular source of income, most markets are set up in areas where palpable demand exists for them (which also includes many Asian immigrant communities), unless market charters require otherwise.

Putting these important demographic issues aside, it is worth considering why these institutions tend to be disproportionately white even in communities with a more racially mixed population (like my own). I posit that managers' qualitative responses can shed a great deal of light on participation of people of color in these alternative food institutions. Following various scholars of whiteness, they serve as a reminder that attention to the subjects rather than objects of racializing discourses is a compelling way to understand the work that representational practices do (Morrison 1992; Frankenberg 1993; McKinney 2005). In this case, they illustrate the whitened cultural politics that operate in these institutions.

At one level, most respondents were sympathetic to a project that would make their markets more inclusive. Seventy-four percent of farmers' market managers and 69 percent of CSA managers thought it important to address the ethnic diversity of their markets, although the enthusiasm among CSA managers dropped to 59 percent when asked if they would consider strategies that increase the ethnic diversity of their customers. The inconsistencies between these responses and those expressed in open-ended written comments and interviews revealed the deeper discomforts invoked by the survey and, hence, the discursive issues.

Most of the managers surveyed and interviewed in this study believed their market spaces are universal spaces that speak to universal values. As one CSA manager stated, the purpose of CSA is to "have people eat real food and understand where it comes from." For some, that entails rejecting the very idea of having strategies to reach out to particular communities of color. When asked how to improve diversity at the market,

one manager responded, "We always hope for more people and do not focus on ethnic—what we present attracts all!" Likewise, a CSA manager said,

> Targeting those in our communities that are ethnic or low income would show a prejudice we don't work within. We do outreach programs to reach everyone interested in eating locally, healthily, and organically.

Some managers explicitly invoked the language of color blindness. Aversion to questions regarding the ethnicity of customers was founded on the presumption that the questions themselves were racist. As one farmers' market manager put it,

> Some of your questions are pretty intrusive—I also found some to be racist. I left these questions blank. This was intentional, not accidental.

Echoed the CSA respondent mentioned earlier,

> Difference is wrong; it is better to try to become color blind in how we do things. . . . Your questioning has a slant of political correctness. . . . We are set up for our community.

Yet, another CSA manager responded:

> I think it is an admirable goal to try to get our customers to be more diverse, but I feel a bit troubled by all of this. I sometimes feel pressure to be perfectly politically correct. . . . I wish we could elevate the farmers first, then it might be easier to bring the rest of the world along.

Whereas in one register managers rejected the idea of difference, in another they invoked it. Importantly, this last comment was followed immediately by one in which the manager said "the [CSA] concept needs to be taken on by low-income and ethnic folks." Indeed, another recurring theme throughout the responses was that healthy, local, sustainable eating is a "lifestyle choice" and one to which people of color apparently do not adhere. For example, in responding to the question "What do you think are some of the reasons that it is primarily European-American people who seem to participate in CSAs?," respondents consistently imputed personal characteristics and motives rather than structural problems with access and affordability. In the qualitative analysis, phrases such as "better education," "more concern about food quality," "more health consciousness," and even "more time" were mentioned repeatedly. One manager portrayed white people as "more aware and willing to do something with food for socio-political reasons rather than other reasons and involved in the social component of CSAs and what they represent." Another simply said, "Hispanics aren't into fresh, local, and organic products."

Farmers' market managers named some of these same issues, but also tended to include additional factors regarding neighborhood demographics, location, and cost as obstacles to participation. Even attributing behavior to cost, though, makes presumptions about difference in values. For example, in reference to a question about expanding entitlement programs to make farmers' markets more affordable to all, one manager responded,

> I'm not sure that I agree that subsidy is the best route. In my experience, the subsidy customers are the least committed and reliable. I believe that the food is affordable to all; it's just a matter of different values and priorities. Education and outreach are the only hope I have of interesting more low-income people.

One respondent characterized his market as one that "caters to high-income consumers seeking quality and freshness" and said that "low-income people shop elsewhere unless they are given freebies like WIC." He further said he would not want

to use strategies to attract low-income consumers because those strategies "may discourage the high-end consumers that we cater to."

In short, these responses represent various ways in which lack of knowledge or the "right" values is seen as the barrier to broader participation in alternative food institutions. As Nash (2007) subtly shows in respect to the horrific pesticide exposures that farm workers have been subject to, it is an old trope to attribute structural inequalities to cultural differences or lack of education. What I hope I have shown in addition is that this position involves certain significations: Specifically, managers portray their own values and aesthetics to be so obviously universal that those who do not share them are marked as other. These sorts of sensibilities are hallmarks of whiteness. So, in assuming the universal goodness of fresh, local, and organic food, the authors of these quotes ask those who appear to reject this food to either be subject to conversion efforts or simply be deemed as other. If they only knew.

THE WHITE CHILL: IS IT LACK OF KNOWLEDGE?

In her unpublished dissertation, "Black Faces, White Spaces: African Americans and the Great Outdoors," Carolyn Finney (2006) found a tendency among whites to attribute the lack of participation of African Americans in U.S. national parks to such things as different values, lack of interest, or the costs of getting there. When she queried African Americans on the same issue, many rejected those sorts of prompts and responded to an open-ended prompt of "exclusionary practices." Not all respondents specified these practices, but those that did pointed to issues such as cultural competency, white privilege, and varying levels of commitment by environmental groups. I want to argue for a similar phenomenon with these spaces of alternative food provision, and the exclusionary practices I want to point to are a pervasive set of idioms in alternative food practice that are insensitive to or ignorant of the ways in which they reflect whitened cultural histories and practices (Kobayashi and Peake 2000). "Getting your hands dirty in the soil," "if they only knew," and "looking the farmer in the eye" all point to an agrarian past that is far more easily romanticized by whites than others (Guthman 2004).

In particular, the rhetoric of paying the full cost illustrates not only a lack of cultural competency, but also what Lipsitz (1998) has called "the possessive investment in whiteness." It seems to be asking people who might have historical connections to those who have more than paid the cost with their bodies and livelihoods in U.S. agricultural development—who in certain respects have themselves subsidized the production of cheap food—to pay even more. At the very least, full cost presumes that all else is equal, even though U.S. agricultural land and labor relations are fundamentally predicated on white privilege. As elucidated by Romm (2001), land was virtually given away to whites at the same time that reconstruction failed in the South, Native American lands were (appropriated, Chinese and Japanese were precluded from land ownership, and the Spanish-speaking Californios were disenfranchised of their ranches. Given this history, it is certainly conceivable that for some people knowing where your food comes from and paying the full cost would not have the same aesthetic appeal that it does for white, middle-class alternative food aficionados. For similar reasons, the broader rhetoric of sustainability must be brought under scrutiny. As Finney (2007) asks, "Exactly who and what are being sustained?"

Although the study discussed in this article did not ask nonwhite clients of these institutions why they participate or, more aptly, non-clients why they do not, there is evidence that these discourses and

the way they hail a particular subject is read as exclusionary by people of color. For example, Tattenham (2006) conducted a long-term participant observation study of an organization that delivers below-market organic food to an African American neighborhood without conventional supermarkets. One day, she asked one of her neighbors why she did not shop from the truck. The neighbor's response was, "Because they don't sell no food! All they got is birdseed. . . . Who are they to tell me how to eat? I don't want that stuff. It's not food. I need to be able to feed my family." Stowe (2007) conducted a survey of organizations in California that work on social justice issues as they relate to agriculture and food. The purpose of the survey was to ascertain whether the Ecological Farming Association could do more to encourage low-income and nonwhite constituents attend its annual conference. One question was whether having more Spanish language translation at the conference would encourage more participation among Spanish-speaking farmers. An advocate for such farmers was unsure that translation would make a difference, saying "Yeah those hippies freak them out." Finally, I have also had several discussions with my campus diversity trainer who works with interns at the university-run organic farm to teach cultural competency. She has heard consistent feedback from the few people of color who attend the program. Many of them feel isolated, not only because of the language employed, but also in their fear of challenging it.

IF WHO ONLY KNEW

The data presented in this article say much more about the subjectivities of managers of CSA and farmers' markets than those who are the objects of conversion—or dismissal—in the context of alternative food efforts. Still, I have also tried to suggest some of the reasons that these institutions do not seem to resonate among people of color as much as they do for whites. Clearly more research is needed to understand how and to what degree people of color experience exclusionary practices in the spaces of alternative food provision. It is research I hope to pursue.

Yet, my underlying concern is that because these spaces tend to hail white subjects, whites continue to define the rhetoric, spaces, and broader projects of agrofood transformation. As I have argued elsewhere (Guthman forthcoming), the current menu reflects a fairly delimited conception of the politics of the possible. This is an enormous problem given how race intersects with agriculture and food in myriad ways, yet many substantial health and livelihood inequalities are barely addressed through existing social movement activity. Insofar as people of color see their deaths earlier due to such lack of attention, the problem in its totality surely meets Gilmore's (2002) criterion of racism. In other words the implications of these perhaps minor exclusions are far-reaching.

The problem I describe has not gone unnoticed by movement activists. I have attended many public meetings of the sustainable agriculture and alternative food movements where people of color and whites working in communities of color insist that the messages of these movements are, simply put, "too white." Groups such as the Community Food Security Coalition are keenly aware that they have a race problem and conduct antiracism training workshops for their staff and volunteers. There are also a growing number of organizations that are actively attempting to reframe their messages to attract people of color, from Mo' Betta Foods and the Peoples' Grocery in Oakland, to Food from the Hood in Los Angeles, to Growing Power in Milwaukee, to Just Foods in New York. That said, their success has been mixed on this objective, for many of the reasons discussed in this article.

Therefore, I want to conclude by returning to the missionary impulses enacted in alternative food spaces and practices. In the absence of other raced bodies in alternative food spaces, and perhaps in the absence of other explanations that might render indifference to alternative food practice understandable, the rhetoric of "if they only knew" tends to be reinforced. Meanwhile, the subject positions of the proselytizers, as well as the goodness of the food, continues to go without saying. This is the hallmark of whiteness and its presumption of normativity; it goes to the deeper way in which color blindness and acts of doing good can work to separate and scold others. My point, however, is not to disable activists and advocates who have good intentions, out them for being overtly racist, or even to claim the important counterfactual: that without whiteness food activism would take a substantially different course and be wildly successful. My immediate goal for this article is to encourage much deeper reflection on the cultural politics of food activism. Saldanha (2006, 11) is surely right that "the embodiment of race . . . encompasses certain ethical stances and political choices. It informs what one can do, what one should do, in certain spaces and situations." Following Sullivan (2006), whites need to think about how to use the privileges of whiteness in an antiracist practice. In the realm of food politics, this might mean turning away from proselytizing based on universal assumptions about good food. Perhaps a place to start would be for whites to state how much they do not know to open up the space that might allow others to define the spaces and projects that will help spurn the transformation to a more just and ecological way of providing food.

ACKNOWLEDGEMENTS

Much of the research reported herein was funded by the Social Sciences Division and the Committee on Research at the University of California, Santa Cruz. I am deeply indebted to Mike Goodman and Amy Morris for research assistance and to Patricia Allen for her efforts and ideas in project development. I would also like to thank the three anonymous reviewers who provided extremely useful comments on an earlier draft.

NOTES

1. Because the survey asked respondents to make eye-ball guesses—certainly a problematic starting place in matters of race—descriptions of ethnicity were necessarily coarse. This explains the conflation of Asian and Asian Americans into one category, for example.
2. Likert-scaled questions ask responders to state the strength and direction of their agreement with a given proposition on a five-point scale (e.g., strongly agree, somewhat agree, neutral, etc.)

LITERATURE CITED

Allen, Patricia. 2004. *Together at the table: Sustainability and sustenance in the American agrifood system.* State College: Pennsylvania State University Press.

Allen, Patricia, Margaret FitzSimmons, Michael Goodman, and Keith Warner. 2003. Shifting plates in the agrifood landscape: The tectonics of alternative agrifood initiatives in California. *Journal of Rural Studies* 19 (1): 61–75.

Bettie, Julie. 2003. *Women without class: Girls, race, and identity.* Berkeley: University of California Press.

Brown, Michael K., Martin Carnoy, Elliott Currie, Troy Duster, David B. Oppenheimer, Marjorie M. Shultz, and David Wellman. 2003. Of fish and water: Perspectives on racism and privilege. In *Whitewashing race: The myth of a color-blind society*, ed. M. K. Brown, M. Carnoy, E. Currie, T. Duster, D. B. Oppenheimer, M. M. Shultz, and D. Wellman, 34–65. Berkeley: University of California Press.

Chen, Kuan-Hsing. 1996. Cultural studies and the politics of internationalization: An interview with Stuart Hall. In *Stuart Hall: Critical dialogues in cultural studies*, ed. D. Morley and K.-H. Chen, 392–408. London: Routledge.

Cohen, N. L., J. P. Cooley, R. B. Hall, and A. M. Stoddard. 1997. Community supported agriculture: A study of shareholders' dietary patterns and food practices. Paper presented at the International Conference on Agricultural Production and Nutrition, Tufts University, Boston.

Community Food Security Coalition. 2006. What is community food security? http://www.

foodsecurity.org/views_cfs_faq.html (last accessed 13 September 2006).

Cone, Cynthia Abbott, and Andrea Myhre. 2000. Community supported agriculture: A sustainable alternative to industrial agriculture. *Human Organization* 59 (2): 187–97.

DuPuis, E. Melanie. 2001. *Nature's perfect food.* New York: New York University Press.

Dwyer, Owen J., and John Paul Jones. 2003. White socio-spatial epistemology. *Social and Culture Geography* 1 (2): 209–22.

Feenstra, Gail. 1997. Local food systems and sustainable communities. *American Journal of Alternative Agriculture* 12 (1): 28–36.

Festing, H. 1997. Community supported agriculture and vegetable box schemes. Paper presented at the International Conference on Agricultural Production and Nutrition, Tufts University, Boston.

Finney, Carolyn. 2006. Black faces, white spaces: African Americans and the great outdoors. PhD dissertation, Clark University.

———. 2007. Commentary on paper session on Race and food: Bodies and spaces. Annual meeting of the Association of American Geographers, San Francisco.

Frankenberg, Ruth. 1993. *White women, race matters: The social construction of whiteness.* Minneapolis: University of Minnesota Press.

Gilmore, Ruth Wilson. 2002. Fatal couplings of power and difference: Notes on racism and geography. *The Professional Geographer* 54 (1): 15–24.

Guthman, Julie. 2004. *Agrarian dreams? The paradox of organic farming in California.* Berkeley: University of California Press.

———. Forthcoming. Neoliberalism and the making of food politics in California. *Geoforum.*

Guthman, Julie, Amy W. Morris, and Patricia Allen. 2006. Squaring farm security and food security in two types of alternative food institutions. *Rural Sociology* 71 (4): 662–84.

Hall, Stuart. 1992. The West and the rest: Discourse and power. In *Formations of modernity*, ed. S. Hall and B. Gieben, 275–320. Cambridge, U.K.: Polity Press.

———. 1996. New ethnicities. In *Stuart Hall: Critical dialogues in cultural studies*, ed. D. Morley and K.-H. Chen, 441–49. London: Routledge.

Harris, Cheryl I. 1993. Whiteness as property. *Harvard Law Review* 106 (8): 1709–91.

Hassanein, Neva. 2003. Practicing food democracy: A pragmatic politics of transformation. *Journal of Rural Studies* 19 (1): 77–86.

Hendrickson, Mary, and Wiliam Heffernan. 2002. Opening spaces through relocalization: Locating potential resistance in the weaknesses of the global food system. *Sociologia Ruralis* 42 (4): 347–69.

Hinrichs, Claire G., and K. S. Kremer. 2002. Social inclusion in a Midwest local food system. *Journal of Poverty* 6 (1): 65–90.

Holloway, S. R. 2000. Identity, contingency and the urban geography of "race." *Social & Cultural Geography* 1 (2): 197–208.

Kantor, L. S. 2001. Community food security programs improve food access. *Food Review* 24 (1): 20–26.

Kimbrell, Andrew, ed. 2002. *The fatal harvest reader*. Washington, DC: Island Press.

Kloppenberg, J., Jr., J. Henrickson, and G. W. Stevenson. 1996. Coming into the foodshed. *Agriculture and Human Values* 13 (3): 33–42.

Kobayashi, Audrey, and Linda Peake. 2000. Racism out of place: Thoughts on whiteness and an anti-racist geography in the new millennium. *Annals of the Association of American Geographers* 90 (2): 392–403.

Lawson, Jared. 1997. New challenges for CSAs: Beyond yuppie chow. *Food Security News*, 3–4, 6.

Lipsitz, George. 1998. *The possessive investment in whiteness*. Philadelphia: Temple University Press.

Lyson, Thomas A. 2004. *Civic agriculture: Reconnecting farm, food, and community*. Lebanon, NH: Tufts University Press.

Magdoff, Fred, John Bellamy Foster, and Frederick H. Buttel, eds. 2000. *Hungry for profit*. New York: Monthly Review Press.

McKinney, Karyn D. 2005. *Being white: Stories of race and racism*. New York: Routledge.

Moore, Donald S., Anand Pandian, and Jake Kosek. 2003. Introduction: The cultural politics of race and nature: Terrains of power and practice. In *Race, nature, and the politics of difference*, eds. D.S. Moore, J. Kosek, and A. Pandian, 1–70. Durham, NC: Duke University Press.

Morrison, Toni. 1992. *Playing in the dark: Whiteness and the literary imagination*. Cambridge, MA: Harvard University Press.

Nash, Linda. 2007. *Inescapable ecologies: A history of environment, disease, and knowledge*. Berkeley: University of California Press.

Payne, Tim. 2002. U.S. farmers' markets 2000: A study of emerging trends. Washington, DC: USDA, Agricultural Marketing Service.

Perez, Jan, Patricia Allen, and Martha Brown. 2003. Community supported agriculture on the central coast: The CSA member experience. Santa Cruz: Center for Agroecology and Sustainable Food Systems, University of California.

Perry, Pamela. 2002. *Shades of white: White kids and racial identity in high school*. Durham, NC: Duke University Press.

Pollan, Michael. 2006. *The omnivore's dilemma: A natural history of four meals*. New York: Penguin.

Reardon, Jenny. 2005. *Race to the finish: Identity and governance in an age of genomics*. Princeton, NJ: Princeton University Press.

Roediger, David R. 1991. *The wages of whiteness: Race and the making of the American working class*. New York: Verso.

Romm, Jeff. 2001. The coincidental order of environmental injustice, In *Justice and natural resources: Concepts, strategies, and applications*, ed. K. M. Mutz, G. C. Bryner, and D.S. Kennedy, 117–37. Covelo, CA: Island Press.

Saldanha, Aran. 2006. Reontologising race: The machinic geography of phenotype. *Environment and Planning D: Society and Space* 24 (1): 9–24.

Schein, Richard H. 2006. Race and landscape in the United States. In *Landscape and race in the United States*, ed. R. H. Schein, 1–21. New York: Routledge.

Shaw, Wendy S. 2006. Decolonizing geographies of whiteness. *Antipode* 38 (4): 851–69.

Shrader-Frechette, Kristen. 2005. *Environmental justice: Creating equality, reclaiming democracy*. New York: Oxford University Press.

Slocum, Rachel. 2006. Anti-racist practice and the work of community food organizations. *Antipode* 38 (2): 327–49.

——. 2007. Whiteness, space, and alternative food practice. *Geoforum* 38 (3): 520–33.

Stoler, Ann Laura. 1995. *Race and the education of desire*. Durham, NC: Duke University Press.

Stowe, Dorothy. 2007. Neoliberalism and rhetoric in the sustainable agriculture movement. Senior thesis, Univeristy of California, Santa Cruz.

Suarez-Balcazar, Yolanda, Louise I. Martinez, Ginnefer Cox, and Anita Jayraj. 2006. African-Americans' views on access to healthy foods: What a farmers' market provides. *Journal of Extension* 44 (2): 2FEA2. http://www.joe.org/joe/2006april/a2.shtml (last accessed 17 March 2008).

Sullivan, Shannon. 2006. *Revealing whiteness: The unconscious habits of racial privilege*. Indianapolis: Indiana University Press.

Tattenham, Katrina. 2006. Food politics and the food justice movement. Senior thesis, University of California, Santa Cruz.

Thomas, Mary. 2005. "I think it's just natural": The spatiality of racial segregation at a US high school. *Environment and Planning A* 37: 1233–48.

16

Feeding Desire: Food, Domesticity, and Challenges to Hetero-Patriarchy

Anita Mannur

In her short story, "A Lesbian Appetite," Dorothy Allison writes, "I remember women by what we ate together, what they dug out of the freezer after we'd made love for hours. I've only had one lover who didn't want to eat at all. We didn't last long" (276). By recalling past lovers and remembering what they ate together, Dorothy Allison's autobiographical story offers an alternative way to conceptualize food preparation within the domestic sphere. While Allison's text severs the seamless link between heterosexuality and food preparation, it is not enjoined to any particular definition of nationhood. She tells a story of love and desire mediated through food that transgresses the logic of the domestic space, but her story does not place sexuality within a national or transnational framework. Nevertheless, I begin with this story because it radically reconfigures the relationship between food and desire within the domestic space. Allison's story suggests that food consumption and preparation in the domestic space is not circumscribed by compulsory heterosexuality. Instead, her story sutures food and sexuality, engendering affiliations that necessarily transgress the implicit heteronormative logic of the home.[1]

As postcolonial critics of nationalism in South Asian contexts including Partha Chatterjee and Rosemary Marangoly George point out, the home is never a neutral space divested of ideological constructions of gendered nationhood; rather it is a site that produces gendered citizens of the nation. But the home, as queer theorists also point out, is a sexualized space. It is a space that demands an isomorphic alignment between sex and gender within a heterosexual matrix; such logic portends that male bodies are necessarily heterosexual "men," and female bodies are necessarily heterosexual "women."[2] Within a rigidly patriarchal vision of nationhood women in particular are exhorted to maintain and uphold traditional domestic familial structures. But such monolithic edicts rarely reproduce standard modes of subject positioning within the household economy. Instead, the attendant fissures within the domestic space become productive spaces from which to alter the very nature of affiliative links within the home. It is this question, in particular, that this article pursues. Specifically, if the home is a gendered and sexualized space, what happens when members of the house hold use food to express queer desire? Moreover, if we follow the lead of Paul Gilroy in viewing the family as microcosm of the nation, how do we negotiate the contours of postcolonial fiction that reframe food preparation and consumption within the home by exploring the possibilities that inhere in anti-normative relationships that develop within the domestic space?

The fictional works I analyze in this article are implicitly in dialogue with the logic that seamlessly aligns the project of nation-building and culinary practices in the domestic space. I stage a conversation between the novel *Reef* (1994) by Sri Lankan British author Romesh Gunesekera with Indo Canadian director Deepa Mehta's film *Fire* (1996) in order to explore how the consumption and preparation of food in each text becomes an important, perhaps even over-determined activity for the protagonists within the home, closely aligned with the expression of queer desire. In *Fire*, the female characters cook with one another and in *Reef* the male character cooks for another man. *Reef* and *Fire* are particularly well suited to a discussion of how culinary relationships can buttress non-heterosexual or queer relationships, particularly within domestic settings.

EATING AND CLASS: HOME AND NATION

In her work on home and belonging, Dorinne Kondo argues that the "home" is a sexualized space that is often hostile to non-straight bodies, or queer bodies. She points out that people who have been marginalized, such as gays and lesbians, rarely experience "home" as a safe space (97). David L. Eng adds, "issues of home are particularly vexing" ("Out Here" 31) for queer diasporic subjects, as many are literally ejected from such spaces. Eng's argument centers on Asian-American experiences, but his observation rings true for the characters in *Reef* and *Fire*— Triton, Sita and Radha—who enjoy, at best, a tenuous relationship with their home space. Such subjects experience deep ambivalence towards the notion of home, experiencing it both as a safe space of refuge or shelter that nurtures their desire for a person of the same sex, and as a space that is implicitly heteronormative. But what happens when characters use food to forge a queer relationship that works both with and against the regulatory heteronormative logic of the home site?

José Esteban Muñoz's work on disidentification locates multiple strategies that queer subjects use to find alternative modes of (un)belonging in the domestic space. Muñoz explains,

> . . . the first mode is understood as 'identification,' where a 'Good Subject' chooses the path of identification with discursive and ideological forms. 'Bad Subjects' resist and attempt to reject the images and identificatory sites offered by dominant ideology and proceed to rebel, to 'counteridentify' and turn against this symbolic system. (11)

Disidentification, Muñoz concludes, is "the third mode of dealing with dominant ideology, one that neither opts to assimilate within such a structure nor strictly oppose it; rather disidentification is a strategy that works on and against dominant ideology" (11). Mira Nair's *Monsoon Wedding* (2002) relays one such tale about a disidentifying subject whose relationship to food complicates a simple logic of assimilating to the dominant system. The wedding between the daughter of a Delhi-based family and an Indian American from Houston, Texas, is the central story of the film's narrative. The film also includes a sub-plot that hints at the threat posed to heteronormative familial structures by Varun (Ishaan Nair), the flamboyant, dance-loving and food-loving younger brother of the bride-to-be, Aditi (Vasundhara Das). When he makes his first appearance, Varun is watching culinary personality Sanjeev Kapoor, host of the popular cooking show *Khana Khazana* ("treasured cuisine") prepare coconut chicken curry. He is gently wrenched away from the television set by his mother Pimmi (Lilette Dubey) and asked to get dressed for pre-wedding festivities instead of wasting time watching a cooking show.

Later in the film, when familial tensions are running high, his father, Lalit Verma (Naseruddin Shah) enters into a discussion about his son's "future," raising the question whether Varun should be sent to boarding school to discipline him into being more "masculine." Questioning why his son prefers cooking to cricket, Lalit blames his wife, Pimmi for "spoiling" their son and for not disciplining him into performing his masculinity within the home. In mock seriousness, laced with palpable homophobia, he asks Pimmi what will become of their son and his love for cooking and *Khana Khazana*. Will he become a "khansama" (cook), the next Sanjeev Kapoor? Should they try and find a "nice boy" for him to marry? Read alongside Varun's penchant for dancing—he is supposed to dance with his cousin Ayesha (Neha Dubey) at Aditi and Hemant's wedding to the Bollywood style dance number, "Chunari, Chunari" from David Dhawan's *Biwi No 1*—Varun's love of "India" cooking hints at his queerness. The film refuses to provide a simple answer to the question of his sexuality: Is he straight? Is he gay? Varun's queerness emerges, instead, through his interest in cooking and dancing against the backdrop of the celebration of heterosexual Hindu familial life. Varun's dancing and cooking may be viewed with suspicion, but by marking its emergence within the Verma home in Delhi, the film complicates the notion that queerness is a "Western" phenomenon with no roots in South Asian domestic structures.

'A LADY COMES TO TEA': FEEDING DESIRE IN *REEF*

Like *Monsoon Wedding*, *Reef* tells a tale of queerness that is born within the South Asian domestic space.[3] Set in the 1960s against the backdrop of escalating inter-ethnic conflict between Sinhalas and Tamils in Sri Lanka, *Reef* is a coming-of-age story pivoting around the cenral character, eleven year-old Triton. Constructed as a long flashback, the story begins in London in the 1980s. A chance encounter with a fellow Sri Lankan at a gas station prompts the narrator, Triton, to recall his childhood and his twenty-year

affiliation with his employer Ranjan Salgado, an unmarried Sri Lankan man with a penchant for marine ecology. In Triton's words, it "begins in 1962: the year of the bungled coup" (Gunesekera 15). While the political upheaval brought on by ethnic conflicts between the Sinhala and Tamil populations in Sri Lanka resulting in the mass dispersal of Sri Lankans to Australia, Britain, Canada, and the United States is a constant presence, it never enters into the foreground of the story, serving instead as a yardstick marking the passage of time as Triton passes from childhood to adolescence and finally into adulthood, as well as marking his passage from house-hold servant to a business entrepreneur who owns a restaurant. Through the course of the narrative, we see how Triton forms a bond with Mr. Salgado that culminates in their eventual emigration from Sri Lanka to England.

As readers, everything we learn about the goings on in the Salgado household comes through Triton. In addition to being the primary filter of all goings on in the household, by virtue of his position as the always-present, yet always-invisible servant, he is often privy to private conversations and intimate encounters between persons in the house. While the text continually alludes to the world "out there," Triton is wholly immersed in his new world within the walls of Ranjan Salgado's home. For Triton, "Mister Salgado's house was the center of the universe, and everything else in the world took place within its enclosure" (27). From an early stage, it becomes a matter of paramount importance for Triton to please Mr. Salgado. To this end, Triton spends much of his time preparing intricate and sumptuous feasts as a way to earn a few good words from his employer and the object of his affection.

Initially he is not accorded much importance in the house, but following the dismissal of Joseph, another servant in Mr. Salgado's house, Triton is given more responsibility. Triton's ascent from general household help to central household figure and cook is cast in typically hyperbolic terms. He downplays the importance of global upheaval in light of the purportedly monumental shifts happening in his own life within the Salgado home: "All over the globe, revolutions erupted, dominoes tottered and guerilla war came of age; the world's first woman prime minister—Mrs. Bandaranaike—lost her spectacular premiership on our island, and I learned the art of good housekeeping" (55). Although Triton's lessons in good housekeeping are relegated to the end of the sentence, it is clear that this is the most important "global" shift in his universe. It matters less that the world is in a state of flux; what is important is that he is one step closer towards having reign over the household.

Despite Triton's insularity, the novel as a whole speaks to contemporary culinary-political history as it emerges from the pages of a popular Sri Lankan cookbook of the time. In the front matter for Hilda Deutrom's *Ceylon Daily News Cookery Book* (1964), a cookbook that was first published in 1929, an unnamed reviewer notes, "good cooks thrive best in the wholesome atmosphere of good homes" (i). The book was subsequently reprinted nine times in five different editions and catalogues the nation's history, and the impact of Arab, Malay, Moorish, Portuguese, Dutch, and British occupation on the native Sinhala and Tamil cuisines. The *Ceylon Daily News Cookery Book* contains a "representative list of the recipes handed from generation to generation of Ceylon's housewives, reflect[ing] the march of the Island's history" (ii). It responds to the dual need of building an archive of national (culinary) history and reminding women of their "duties" to nurture happy families who are clean, well fed, and well nourished in the "wholesome atmosphere of good homes" (i).

Indeed, the chapter focusing on Triton's coming-of-age, "Cook's Joy," places Triton squarely at the center of narratival development, but its title also references a brand of cooking oil, produced by the British Ceylon Corporation. Marketed as a brand of cooking oil that "improves the flavor of food," "Cook's Joy" is prominently advertised in the *Ceylon Daily News Cook Book* along with other household foods of the time such as Ovaltine, a chocolate malted milk for children. The advertisement for "Cook's Joy" cooking oil from the 1960s is an important interlocutor to this chapter narrating Triton's culinary prowess insofar as it underscores how Gunesekera's novel reimagines the terms under which Triton fits into a domestic structure. As the advertisement boasts, "clever cooks choose Cooks Joy because it makes all the difference to a meal. It is pleasant to use and economical." Behind the bottle of "Cook's Joy" are three sari-clad women waving to the implied consumer. To the right of the bottle of oil is a woman wearing an apron looking at a fish in a life-size frying pan. Using "Cooks Joy," the advertisement seems to suggest, is a way for women of the household to improve the taste of home cooked food. Because it appears within the pages of a cookbook intended for "housewives," the advertisement is probably directed at female consumers. The joy of cooking is implicitly coded as being a female activity. It is the female cook—the housewife—who can and should relish in being able to prepare foods. Triton, as a male servant, is clearly not the intended audience of the advertisement. Nor for that matter is he expected to carry the burden of upholding Sri Lanka's culinary traditions. To thus name the chapter after the popular brand of cooking oil is to reimagine the terms of culinary national discourse. The chapter, "Cook's Joy," is not merely about maintaining the fabric of Sri Lankan culinary home life; rather the term "cook's joy" comes to stand in for the pleasure that Triton derives from cooking for Ranjan Salgado.

While it is not transgressive to think of a male in the role of household domestic servant—in *Fire*, for instance, the household domestic, Mundu is also male—it is significant that he is described as a "housekeeper." While other forms of labor may participate in the general upkeep of the house, the work of "housekeeping" is often positioned as female labor. It is the wife who must toil to keep the house looking good for the master, and this is also reinforced in the *Ceylon Daily News Cookbook*. Here, Triton toils for his master, but for the housewives who read the *Ceylon Daily News Cookbook*, it is the wife who works for the "master." Triton's presence as the flamboyant and solipsistic household domestic servant, by contrast, disrupts the gendered and sexualized structure of household management.

Gunesekera's novel is not traditionally queer in the sense that it does not foreground gay sexual practices between the male characters, but as Asian-American critics David L. Eng and Alice Hom write in reference to their project centered on recovering gay histories and stories, "we use 'queer' to refer to a political practice based on transgressions of the norm and normativity rather than a straight/gay binary of heterosexual/homosexual identity" (1). In keeping with Eng and Hom's strategic use of the term queer to reference non-normative disidentificatory practices, I use the term "queer" to name Triton's presence as one that disrupts the home space in a way that results in a queering of that space. As Eng suggests, the actual number of groups and individuals that are branded deviant in Asian-American history and culture is not limited to subjects who "readily self-define as queer, gay or lesbian"; instead, a historically disavowed status renders them "queer as such" (*Racial Castration* 18.) Eng's definition usefully illumines how queering can take on different significations speaking to the multiple ways in which subjects with a disavowed status might use

disidentificatory strategies rendering them "queer as such." While Eng's comments reference a specific history that is not coeval with Triton's history within the walls of the Salgado home in Sri Lanka, it is a useful point of entry into Gunesekera's novel. At this stage in the narrative, *Reef* espouses a politics of non-normativity, or perhaps even anti-normativity, that can be coded as homosocial or homophilic insofar as it marks how a non-consummated form of same-sex desire emerges within the heterosexual structuring of the domestic space.

Despite the emergence of a nascent homophilia, the relationship between Triton and Mr. Salgado is not egalitarian; Triton is, after all, employed in Mr. Salgado's house as his cook. Mr. Salgado is highly educated, Triton has only completed schooling up to the fifth standard. Several class-based distinctions differentiate the two, but an affinity develops between Mr. Salgado and Triton that endures longer than any of Mr. Salgado's relationships. Friends come and go, but as long as they live within the domestic space, Triton remains the constant presence in his life, providing Salgado with both alimentary and emotional nurturance.

Triton's desire for Salgado is rarely coded as being exclusively about the promise of sexual satisfaction. In part, the master-servant dynamics between Salgado and Triton suggest that a sexual relation between the two is taboo; Triton desires Salgado and admires his stoic masculinity and reticence, but must always keep his desire at bay. While the text remains resolutely ambiguous about naming the nature of Triton's desire, it strategically articulates how Salgado's appreciation of Triton's culinary prowess invigorates Triton.

In the following scene, Triton overhears a conversation between Mr. Salgado and his new girlfriend, Miss Nili, in which the latter inquires where Mr. Salgado obtained the *love cake*, Triton's confectionery creation of eggs, cream and *cadju* (cashews):

"Where did you get this, this cake?"

"Triton made it," my Mister Salgado said. *Triton made it*. It was the one phrase he would say with my name again and again like a refrain through those months, giving me such happiness. *Triton made it*. Clear, pure and unstinting. His voice at those moments would be a channel cut from heaven to earth right through the petrified morass of all our lives, releasing a blessing like waters springing from a river-head, from a god's head. It was bliss. My coming of age.

"Your cook?"

"*Your life, your everything*," I wanted to sing pinned up on the rafters, heaven between my legs.

(Gunesekera 74–75)

Mr. Salgado and Miss Nili's flirtation is routed through the exchange of love cake, but Triton also participates in this wooing game, albeit obliquely, by routing his sexual desire through food. The sexually charged image of "heaven between [Triton's] legs" is a candid account of Salgado's effect on Triton. Salgado's words are profoundly affective and create more than mental or emotional pleasure: Triton is sexually aroused. Thus, while Triton plays a part in helping Mr. Salgado woo Miss Nili by baking a cake, which he describes as a love cake, the act of sharing love cake cannot be understood solely in terms of desire between Mr. Salgado and Miss Nili. Rather, Triton emerges as a vital actor in this bizarre love triangle. Hanging on to Mr. Salgado's every word, it is less important for Triton to think about whether or not Miss Nili enjoys the cake. What matters at this juncture is how Mr. Salgado speaks about *him*. Triton's hyperbolic asides to the reader clearly spell out his desire for Mr. Salgado. His pleasure and joy is heightened by Mr. Salgado's praise, climaxing at the moment that he imagines Ranjan Salgado proclaiming Triton to be his "everything."

While Miss Nili continues to be a presence in Ranjan Salgado's life, eventually moving into the house, her presence cannot be read as an affirmation of compulsory heterosexuality. Whenever Miss Nili visits Mr. Salgado, Triton prepares ever more complex and elaborate dishes designed to satisfy her voracious appetite. At the same time that he derives satisfaction from seeing Miss Nili's appreciation for his food, he is equally attuned to the way that the reticent Ranjan Salgado seems invigorated by Miss Nili's appetite. Triton's observation, "he seemed so radiant when she was there with him that I wished she would come more often and lift the monkishness from our monastic house," (79) acknowledges Ranjan Salgado's desire for Miss Nili, but also allows for the possibility that Triton comes alive when Miss Nili is present because she enlivens Mr. Salgado in a way that makes him more attentive and appreciative of Triton. While it is never made clear whether Triton's feelings are reciprocated, a triangulated form of desire emerges between Triton, Miss Nili, and Mr. Salgado. He can receive much coveted praise from Salgado only through his interactions with Nili; in this sense, Triton and Salgado's relationship queers the text insofar as Triton's ability to effect gustatory pleasure in Miss Nili—ironically—nourishes and nurtures his relationship with Mr. Salgado.

But in spite of the obvious specular pleasure that Salgado derives from watching Miss Nili eat, he rarely eats in front of her. Miss Nili's remark to Triton, "Your Mister Salgado never seems to eat . . . What is it about this house that makes it hard for you to eat?" (108) is met with an uncomfortable silence. Triton's inner thoughts, unheard by Miss Nili, explain why Ranjan Salgado can only eat in Triton's company:

He needed his privacy to feel comfortable . . . there was no security in eating in the company of a lot of people; attention always got divided. Only the intimate could eat together and be happy. It was like making love. It revealed too much. Food was the ultimate seducer. But I could not tell that to Miss Nili. I had not even thought it through at the time. (108)

This passage reveals a closeness between the two men that does not, indeed cannot, exist between Miss Nili and Mr. Salgado. When it comes to eating, an activity deemed intensely personal and sexual, Mr. Salgado can only eat alone, or in Triton's presence, thereby altering the traditional hierarchy between master and servant, where the two will generally eat separately and in different spaces. While Triton is sexually aroused by Ranjan Salgado's praise for his cooking, it never translates into a sex act.

But, we might ask, is eating together a substitute for sex? Like Dorothy Allison's story, food in *Reef* engenders queer desire. Triton describes food as the "ultimate seducer," suggesting that his culinary skills allow him to seduce Ranjan Salgado. As the narrative unravels it becomes clear that Triton continues to serve as Mr. Salgado's cook, feeding and nurturing him, long after Miss Nili and Ranjan Salgado part. Through a complex relationship with food, then, Mr. Salgado and Triton develop a powerfully affective bond. Triton may not ever be able to consummate his desire, but the seductive potential of food suggests that Triton can route his desire for Salgado in non-physical terms, transgressing traditional borders between persons of different class statuses within the same household. Eating together becomes a partial substitute for sexual gratification. Thus, by preparing food with an eye toward pleasing and seducing Mr. Salgado, Triton gives "voice" to a desire that can escape detection, even by Miss Nili, Mr. Salgado's girlfriend. In effect, it is through his culinarily disidentificatory acts within the household that Triton is ultimately able to let his affection for Ranjan Salgado develop into a form of love that brings him pleasure within the domestic space.

'PRACTICES OF EVERYDAY LIFE': SAME-SEX DESIRE AND FOOD IN *FIRE*

Deepa Mehta's successful and controversial film, *Fire*, offers a somewhat different example of same-sex desire emerging within a domestic household. Following its release in 1998, *Fire* has become an important film within branches of academic study that seek to explore mechanisms by which "non-Western" queer sexualities attain legibility within "Western" cultural production. While many articles offer strategies for reading how queer sexuality emerges within the practice of domestic everyday life in the film, food is never discussed at great length in critical material on *Fire*. My reading of *Fire* builds on this existing criticism to suggest that food has been overlooked and needs to be reintegrated into analyses of this film. Though the absence of critical attention on the place of food in this film may be explained by the fact that food is by no means the primary axis along which the narrative of the film develops, it would be an oversight to ignore how and where food figures into the film's narrative. In her work on queerness in South Asian cultural production, Gayatri Gopinath explores how practices of everyday life are re-signified in this film, allowing for a form of female homoeroticism that emerges at the interstices of heterosexuality and homosociality in the Kapur household:

> [T]he articulation of female same-sex desire within the space of the domestic directly confronts and disrupts contemporary nationalist constructions of the bourgeois Hindu home as the reservoir of essential national cultural values, embodied in the figure of the Hindu woman as chaste, demure, and self-sacrificing.
>
> ("Nostalgia" 480–81)

Gopinath's analysis astutely considers how various homosocial rites that occur within the parameters of daily life for Radha and Sita can be considered as acts of disidentification, but is curiously silent about how interactions with food allow for the articulation of desire between the two lead female characters in Mehta's film.

Set in the middle-class neighborhood of Lajpat Nagar in New Delhi, India, *Fire* tells the story of two women, Radha (Shabana Azmi) and Sita (Nandita Das) who are trapped in emotionally and sexually unfulfilling relationships and gradually fall in love with one another. Radha and Sita are married to two brothers, Ashok (Khulbushan Kharbanda) and Jatin Kapur (Jaaved Jaafri). As the narrative develops, so too does the bond between the two female lead characters. The film culminates when Radha and Sita leave the Kapur family home under considerably fraught circumstances. It should also be noted that the characters' names are important. Within Hindu mythology, "Radha" and "Sita" are important female deities; Sita is best known as the self-sacrificing and loyal wife of Rama, and Radha is the devoted consort of the philandering Krishna. In fact, Bal Thackeray, the reactionary leader of the *Shiv Sena*, the Hindu fundamentalist party in Bombay that most vociferously opposed the public screening of *Fire* in Bombay theaters, critiqued the film on these grounds: that the names of revered Hindu goddesses were being "defiled."

Initially, the women bond out of necessity more than desire; Radha's husband Ashok has chosen a life of monkish celibacy, because, as the doctor tells Radha she has "no eggs in ovaries" and is therefore unable to bear children, and thereby produce citizens for the nation. Once she ceases to be useful in a reproductive sense, Ashok has no use for her. It is only when Sita enters her life that other aspects of her labored existence acquire an immediate urgency. Working in the family business alongside Sita eventually provides Radha with the means and desire to exit the fraught home space. Indeed, Radha spends her time working in the kitchen of the family business, a take-out food establishment, and when Sita marries into the family, she too begins working alongside Radha in the family catering and take-out business. As the relationship between

Radha and Sita develops, the kitchen becomes subtly but significantly transformed into a space where the women can spend time together under the watchful eye of the men of the house. At the same time, the routinized nature of their work in the kitchen makes it possible for their affections to remain virtually unnoticed by Ashok and Jatin.

At a critical juncture in the film, when the women are clearly beginning to desire one another, they playfully use food to mark their feelings. While preparing food in the kitchen, Radha mentions to Sita, "Certain spices are good for some occasions and some for others. Did you know that black pepper gives you energy which is why it is given in such abundance to newly-wed husbands. For better or for worse!" When Sita asks what spices are given to brides, Radha responds, "Green cardamoms, to make the breath fragrant," simultaneously placing a green cardamom pod in Sita's mouth. Sita provocatively exhales, asking Radha if her breath is indeed fragrant, to which Radha answers with affirmative appreciation. By using food to mark their desire for one another, the female characters transform the mundane signification of food. By placing the cardamom pod suggestively in Sita's mouth, not only are the women able to playfully flirt with one another, but under the auspices of a "traditional" exchange that might take place between a bride and a groom; here however, cardamom is exchanged between the women, allowing for the emergence of same-sex desire within activities that are coded as heterosexual. Similarly, the women transform another ritual of heterosexual marriage to mark their desire for one another. On Karva Chauth, a day when married Hindu women ritually fast to ensure their husbands long lives, the women deny themselves food, but the rest of the day is spent in each other's company.[4] The absence of food in this case becomes the vehicle that brings them closer together, highlighting ways that "female same-sex desire and pleasure [emerge] firmly within the confines of the home and 'the domestic' rather than occurring safely 'elsewhere' " (Gopinath, "Nostalgia" 481). The transformation of Karva Chauth into a ritual marking female same-sex desire can also be read in conjunction with Kirin Narayan's argument that "in Hindu traditions, it is important to think of multiple, perhaps even contradictory versions rather than [emphasizing] a single correct and authoritative one" (30). Mehta's evocation of this important ritual within the film reaffirms that "multiplicity is inherent to Indian traditions, both Hindu and non-Hindu" (Narayan 38). Karva Chauth, by this estimation cannot be contained by heterosexual normativity, nor is it solely within the cultural jurisdiction of heterosexual Hindu culture. Instead it is part of a Hindu tradition that Kirin Narayan, quoting Indian folklorist A.K. Ramanujan, describes as " 'indissolubly plural and often conflicting' with texts often acting in dynamic interplay as 'contexts, pretexts and subtexts' to other texts" (38).

Indian feminist scholar and activist Madhur Kishwar has critiqued the film precisely because it reinterprets female-female homosocial intimacy as a pretext for queer desire. Her criticism of *Fire* is based on the fact that expressions of female homosociality in the film, including providing massages to an older sister-in-law, hugging, and oiling one another's hair, are acts of female-female intimacy that have widespread acceptance in India and, therefore, can not be considered not homoerotic or homosexual. Thus, where Gopinath identifies the potential for homoeroticism to emerge through homosocial rituals, Kishwar's objections are grounded in her refusal to see how female-female intimacy might buttress the expression of homoerotic desire. Responding to Madhu Kishwar's controversial critique of *Fire*, Monica Bachmann conjectures, "Kishwar sees the open expression of female homoeroticism as a threat to

Indian women's ability freely to express physical affection" (236). While neither Kishwar nor Gopinath mention the trips to the market, food preparation in the take-out kitchen, or even the ritual fasting associated with Karva Chauth, they fall within the broader regimen of everyday homosociality among Indian women as defined by both Kishwar and Gopinath.

Even when Radha and Sita are outside of the kitchen and outside the home, food allows them to fashion a language to express mutual desire. As they meander through the local market purchasing vegetables—presumably for meals that will be prepared in the Kapur home—Sita and Radha exchange stories passed on to them from their mothers. In response to Radha's comment, "My mother used to say that the way to a man's heart is through his stomach. Apparently it's a great English saying," Sita mentions, "my mother says that a woman without a husband is like boiled rice. Bland and unappetizing—useless. This must be an Indian saying!" Going beyond a merely anecdotal level, each saying places food squarely within a heterosexual framework, establishing a continuum between English colonial and Indian postcolonial patriarchy. The clichés differ, but both idiomatic expressions route patriarchal expectations through food. For Radha's mother, cooking is a tool to woo men; for Sita's mother, a woman has no depth or interest value without a husband. Not only is she unappetizing, but she is also useless. Interestingly, however, Radha's response to the "Indian" saying challenges the idea that a woman needs a man to make her useful or interesting. Her apparently innocuous response, "I like plain boiled rice," is double edged; she at once rejects the idea that a woman needs a man to be interesting and hints that a woman without a man holds a certain allure for her.

The scene in the market, as well as the scene in which the two women exchange cardamom pods, complicates a queer reading of the text that casts the relation-ship within a butch / femme, seducer / seduced dyad. In the scenes involving food, Radha is the seducer. She places the cardamom pod in Sita's, mouth, and she subtly flirts with Sita by telling her that she finds "plain boiled rice" more inter-esting. Read against the other scenes in which Sita is seen to be the "seducer" who initiates physical love-making as well as the pivotal first kiss, these two scenes involving food disrupt a simple seducer / seduced dynamic. Both women seduce one another, creatively marking their desire for one another in slightly different ways. Radha, the woman who has been a paragon of wifely devotion in the film, begins to chart an alternative path for herself using food as her means of expres-sion. Up until this point in the narrative, she dutifully feeds her mother-in-law, indulges her husband's "need" to be celi-bate, prepares meals for the family, and works in the family business. Eventually, she refuses to feed her mother-in-law, asking Ashok to feed her instead, at the same time that she gradually begins to use food to "voice" her desire for Sita. Thus, food serves as an important index of desire between the women. Where same-sex desire might be frowned on if it were to be expressed overtly, the film captures the way that mundane everyday activities associated with food preparation are imbued with subversive potential.

Rosemary George suggests that the notion of "home" is built around a logic of "select inclusions and exclusions" (2). In the case of *Fire*, the women are part of the home, but they are woefully neglected by their respective spouses. Sita's husband, Jatin, alternates between spending time with his Chinese Indian girlfriend, Julie, and managing his pornography video store that fronts as a Hong Kong action and Bollywood *masala* video rental store. Ashok, Radha's husband, spends most of his time with Swamiji, a holy man who has been instrumental in teaching Ashok how to control desire. In the scenes

leading up to her departure, Radha and Ashok are in the throes of a passionate argument. When Ashok tries to "remind" Radha of the ways in which she has neglected her duties as a wife, the ends of Radha's sari catch on fire.

Radha's "trial by fire" cannot be discussed without a brief reference to Sita's plight in the Hindu epic, *Ramayana*. A truncated version of the *Ramayana* enters into the film's narrative when Ashok attends a theatrical performance of the *Ramayana* that pivots around the goddess Sita's trial by fire and eventual expulsion from her royal community. The televised version of *Ramayana* also enters the film in important ways. When Mundu, the household domestic servant, is asked to look after Biji, he often substitutes the televised serial version of the *Ramayana* for bootleg pornographic videos procured from Jatin's business. When he is asked why the mute Biji seems upset, and why he appears to be in a sweat, he explains that the *Ramayana*—particularly the scene where the goddess Sita has been captured by Rama's nemesis, Ravana—is "very emotional," covering up the fact that Biji has been an unwilling audience to the pornographic video to which Mundu masturbates. Later, when he is caught masturbating, he is punished by the family and asked to watch episodes of the serialized version of *Ramayana* as a means of inculcating basic "family values" that he has overlooked by seeking self-gratification.[5]

At the level of character development, Radha bears a striking resemblance to the goddess Sita, rather than her namesake. Like the goddess Sita, Radha has followed her husband into a version of exile. For the goddess Sita it is physical exile into the forest, whereas for Radha it is an exis-tential and sexual exile. Like the goddess Sita, Radha dared to cross the invisible boundaries set for her by patriarchal society. For Sita, crossing the "Lakshman Rekha," a line drawn by her brother-in-law Lakshmana to "protect" her leads her into danger; for Radha, crossing the invisible borders laid out by society leads her into "danger." Finally, the goddess Sita has to undergo *agni pariksha*, a "trial by fire," testing her purity. Radha's "trial by fire" is also a "test," but it is not to "test" her devotion to her husband. Rather it is a "test" that questions whether Radha should necessarily subvert her own desires to maintain her "duties" as a wife.

In keeping with the overall thematic trajectory that sees culinary practices transformed in order to speak of, and to, non-normative forms of desire—cardamom pods are exchanged between women rather than between a bride and groom, women express desire for one another while shopping, patriarchal idioms become imbued with the language of flirtation—it is fitting that the fire originates from the gas burner, a household appliance used to cook food, in the home kitchen, rather than in the "take-out" kitchen. The gas burner ignites Radha's sari literally ejecting her from the home space and marking her passage from the role of a wife who performs her duty to her husband to that of a woman who unites with the woman with whom she can be true to herself. In sum, Radha and Sita find ways to live together, rejecting the terms of their exclusion. Through their negotiations with food they are able to imagine ways that they can belong with one another, disidentifying with the narrative available to them.

HOME AND AWAY: TAKE-AWAYS AND RESTAURANTS

For Radha and Sita, the world out there is constructed somewhat utopically as the space that will free them from their confining roles within the Kapur household if they learn to look at the world through different lenses. The film intersperses the present with scenes of Radha as a child sitting with her parents in a field of mustard-yellow flowers. Radha speaks about wanting to see the ocean, and her mother advises her not to look so hard, but to close her eyes and imagine the ocean. At the moment when Radha finally leaves her husband of fourteen years, the film flashes back to the moment when Radha the child looks at the same scene in front of her and is finally able to see the ocean. Taking a closer look implies learning to look anew at the same scene and imagining how the horizon can capture the essence of one's desires. The ocean is not tangibly present from the fields of rural northern India; instead, by allowing her imagination to guide what she sees, Radha the child is using a different mode of seeing. The ocean is there for her to see in the geography of her mind's imagination.

For Radha, the more pragmatic of the two women, leaving the home is not a simple matter of looking at things anew. But for Sita, leaving the Kapur household is a distinct and viable option. At the moment when Sita and Radha are contemplating leaving to embark on a new life for themselves, Sita surmises, "I wish we could be together forever. I'm serious. Let's leave. See Jatin has Julie, Ashok Bhaiya has Swamiji and Biji has Mundu. They won't even miss us!" When Radha's voice of reason intervenes asking, "And how will we survive?" Sita assertively responds, "we'll start our own take-away of course," emphasizing the vital role that the women have played in the Kapur family business, the video store and food take-out. The addition of the phrase "of course" naturalizes Sita's statement; in her mind, it is the logical way that things will play out between them. To envision a place where, as Gayatri Gopinath aptly phrases it, "an alternative queer logic [emerges] that allows for two brides in bed together" (485), an emotional link is not enough. The two brides also need to be able to imagine how they will survive "out there."

The film ends with Sita and Radha reunited at the Nizamuddin Shrine, glossing over class issues, thereby evading a discussion of whether Radha and Sita are able to successfully transact an independent life. The film utopically suggests that Sita and Radha's relationship to food allows them to imagine a way out of their present realities. Sita's famous tag line in the film, "we can find choices," is an important one, but submerges a potentially useful discussion about how certain choices might be available to them because of their class status as middle-class women. In part, their relationship to food allows them to find the choice and to not be afraid of rejecting their gendered roles within the household. Their combined ability to imagine a world where food can be put to a use other than to support a repressive patriarchal familial structure that refuses to acknowledge their desires and needs is not merely a function of their emotional strength. If Radha and Sita will be able to survive together in a world that Jatin describes as "hell for a divorced woman" it is not solely because they can use food to "find choices," but because they have access to means of production that allows them to "find choices" and to find the ocean amid a field of yellow flowers.

Sita's logic, the inevitability of opening a "take-away" after quitting the domestic space, invites comparison with *Reef*. Now in his adult phase, Triton has relocated to England with Mr. Salgado and has successfully opened a restaurant. Eliding questions about how the migration takes place, and only briefly suggesting that the political unrest of the 1960s precipitates their departure, the narrative remains largely silent about the intervening years between Triton's departure from Sri Lanka and his arrival in England. However, it evocatively narrates how the two men find comfort in one another's company. Triton continues to cook for Mr. Salgado who reciprocally introduces Triton to his world of ocean ecology and literature. Imagining a fusion of their two passions, Mr. Salgado recalls,

> I used to plan it in my head: how I'd build a jetty, a safe marina for little blue bottomed boats, some outriggers with red sails and then a sort of floating restaurant at one end. You could have produced your finest chilli crab there, you know, and the best stuffed sea-cucumbers . . . It would have been a temple to your gastronomic god, no?
> (Gunesekera 187)

But when Triton suggests opening a restaurant together, Mr. Salgado insists that Triton needs to accomplish this on his own, for himself, and eventually resolves to leave England to join Miss Nili, or Tippy as he calls her, thus forcing Triton to live on his own for the first time in twenty years.

In the closing pages of the novel, Triton realizes what is about to happen and reflects,

> I knew he was going to leave me and he would never come back. I would remain and finally have to live on my own . . . I would learn to talk and joke and entertain, to perfect the swagger of one who has found his vocation, and, at last, a place to call his own. It was the only way I could succeed: without a past, without a name, without Ranjan Salgado standing by my side. (190)

While it is troubling that Triton's entry into adulthood, as well as his ability to imagine himself on an even footing with Ranjan Salgado coincides with the end of the queer narrative, it would be a gross oversimplification to negate the importance of Mr. Salgado or to suggest that the text's apparent return to compulsory heterosexuality invalidates a queer reading of the entire text. By not framing departure as a precondition for sexual liberation, the text demands a rethinking of the connection between queer desire and the home site. In the typical queer bildungsroman, the outside world typically looms large as the site of liberation and freedom. The outside world holds a certain promise for Radha and Sita's dream of opening a take-away and

Triton's dream of opening a restaurant, but it is the domestic space that gives birth to queer desire. As such, both of these narratives usefully intervene into discussions that position the South Asian domestic space as a repressive site that refuses to nurture anti-normative relationships. For in these texts, it is through relationships with culinary practices and food that queer subjects produce anti-normative, non-reproductive relations between men, and between women in the domestic space, a space that is typically configured to be hostile to queer desire. The worlds created by these works highlight the powerfully affective potential of food, and its ability to engender anti-normative forms of desire that challenge the notion that the home, as microcosm of the nation, is a necessarily heterosexual formation designed to reproduce citizens that will uphold tradition and its concomitant values. In her important work on the relationship between food, sex, and gender, Elspeth Probyn asks whether food has "replaced sex as the ground of identities, be they gendered, national, post-colonial, collective or individual?" (69). Food does not necessarily replace sex, nor does it de-legitimize any of the approaches that take on the task of exploring dimensions of identity. But as these texts suggest, a reading of food and sex, outside an economy of compulsory heterosexuality, makes it possible to mark the emergence of queer desire, thus suggesting that food is an equally important vector of critical analysis in negotiating the gendered, sexualized, and classed bases of collective and individual identity.

ACKNOWLEDGMENT

I would like to thank the two anonymous reviewers for their feedback as well as my colleagues in the Program in South Asian and Middle Eastern Studies at the University of Illinois at Urbana-Champaign, especially Ken Cuno, Suvir Kaul, Simona Sawhney and Amita Sinha for their helpful comments on this piece.

NOTES

1. For an interesting reading of the relationship between food and sex in Allison's story, see Elspeth Probyn's "Eating Sex" in *Carnal Appetites: FoodSexIdentities*.
2. See Karin Aguilar San-Juan's "Going Home: Enacting Justice in Queer Asian America," Gayatri Gopinath's "Funny Boys and Girls: Notes on A Queer South Asian Planet," and "Homo-Economics: Queer Sexualities in a Transnational Frame."
3. My heading, " 'Lady Comes to Tea': Feeding Desire in *Reef*," references a comment made by one of the two main characters, Ranjan Salgado. As the protagonist Triton phrases it, "Before Miss Nili came to our house on the *poya*-holiday of April, 1969, Mister Salgado only said to me, 'A lady is coming to tea.' As if a lady came to tea every week" (Gunesekera 74).
4. It is also worth noting that in response to Ashok's devotion to Swamiji, Sita observes, with mock seriousness, "I think Ashok bhaiya should keep this fast for Swamiji," highlighting the ways that Ashok is more devoted to this holy man than his own wife, Radha.
5. For useful discussions on the politics of Hindu nationalism and the presence of the *Ramayana* in public circuits of Indian culture, see Purnima Mankekar's *Screening Culture, Viewing Politics: An Ethnography of Television, Womanhood and Nation in Postcolonial India*, Arvind Rajagopal's, *Politics After Television: Religious Nationalism and the Reshaping of the Indian Public*, and Usha Zacharias' "Trial By Fire: Gender, Power, and Citizenship in Narratives of the Nation."

WORKS CITED

Allison, Dorothy. "A Lesbian Appetite." *Trash: Stories by Dorothy Allison*. Ithaca: Firebrand Books, 1988.

Bachmann, Monica. "After the Fire." *Queering India: Same Sex Love and Eroticism in Indian Culture and Society*. Ed. Ruth Vanita. London and New York: Routledge, 2002. 234–43.

Chatterjee, Partha. "The Nationalist Resolution of the Women's Question." *Recasting Women: Essays in Indian Colonial History*. Ed. Kumkum Sangari and Sudesh Vaid. New Brunswick: Rutgers University Press, 1989. 233–53.

Deutrom, Hilda, ed. *Ceylon Daily News Cookery Book*. Colombo: Associated Newspapers of Sri Lanka, 1964.

Eng, David L. "Out Here and Over There: Queerness and Diaspora in Asian American Studies." *Social Text* 52/53 (1997): 31–52.

—. *Racial Castration: Managing Masculinity in Asian America*. Durham and London: Duke UP, 2001.

Eng, David L., and Alice Hom. "Introduction Q&A: Notes on a Queer Asian America." *Q&A: Queer in Asian America*. Ed. David L. Eng and Alice Hom. Philadelphia: Temple University Press, 1998. 1–21.

George, Rosemary. *The Politics of Home: Postcolonial Relocations and Twentieth Century Fiction*. Berkeley: University of California Press, 1999.

Gopinath, Gayatri. "Funny Boys and Girls: Notes on A Queer South Asian Planet." *Asian American Sexualities: Dimensions of the Gay and Lesbian Experience*. Ed. Russell Leong. New York and London: Routledge, 1996. 119–27.

—. "Homo-Economics: Queer Sexualities in a Transnational Frame." *Burning Down The House: Recycling Domesticity*. Ed. Rosemary Marangoly George. Boulder, CO: Westview, 1998. 102–24.

—. "Nostalgia, Desire, Diaspora: South Asian Sexualities in Motion." *Positions: East Asia Cultural Critiques* 5.2 (1997): 467–89.

Gunesekera, Romesh. *Reef*. New York: Riverhead Books, 1994.

Kishwar, Madhu. "Naïve Outpourings of a Self-Hating Indian: Deepa Mehta's Fire." *Manushi* 109 (1999).

Kondo, Dorinne. "The Narrative Production of 'Home' Community and Political Identity in Asian American Theater." *Displacement, Diaspora and Geographies of Identity*. Ed. Smadar Lavie and Ted Swedenburg. Durham and London: Duke University Press, 1996. 97–117.

Mankekar, Purnima. *Screening Culture, Viewing Politics: An Ethnography of Television, Womanhood and Nation in Postcolonial India*. Durham and London: Duke University Press, 1999.

Mehta, Deepa. *Fire*. Zeitgeist Films. 104 mins, 1996.

Muñoz, José Esteban. *Disidentifications: Queers of Color and the Performance of Politics*. Minneapolis: University of Minnesota Press, 1999.

Nair, Mira. *Monsoon Wedding*. Mirabai Films. 114 mins, 2001.

Narayan, Kirin. "Sprouting and Uprooting of Saili: The Story of the Sacred Tulsi in Kangra." *Manushi: A Journal about Women and Society* 102 (1997): 30–38.

Probyn, Elspeth. *Carnal Appetites: Food Sex Identities*. New York and London: Routledge, 2000.

Rajagopal, Arvind. *Politics After Television: Religious Nationalism and the Reshaping of the Indian Public*. Cambridge and New York: Cambridge University Press, 2001.

San-Juan, Karin Aguilar. "Going Home: Enacting Justice in Queer Asian America." *Q&A: Queer in Asian America*. Ed. David Eng and Alice Hom. Philadelphia, PA: Temple University Press, 1998. 25–40.

Zacharias, Usha. "Trial By Fire: Gender, Power, and Citizenship in Narratives of the Nation." *Social Text* 19.4 (2001): 29–51.

17

Towards Queering Food Studies: Foodways, Heteronormativity, and Hungry Women in Chicana Lesbian Writing

Julia C. Ehrhardt

I had known for years that I was a lesbian, had felt it in my bones, had ached with the knowledge, gone crazed with the knowledge, wallowed in the silence of it. Silence *is* like starvation. Don't be fooled. It's nothing short of that, and felt most sharply when one has had a full belly most of her life.

In this passage from her volume of essays and poetry entitled *Loving in the War Years*, Chicana lesbian writer Cherríe Moraga uses the metaphor of starvation to describe her life as a closeted lesbian struggling to keep her sexual identity a secret (44).[1] Though Moraga did not write these words for a food studies audience, her provocative linkage of lesbianism, hunger, and silence invites a consideration of how queer people, bodies, and appetites figure in the discipline of food studies. Anthropologist Carole M. Counihan has contended that the study of foodways—the social beliefs and behaviors associated with the production, distribution, and consumption of food—provides powerful evidence about cultural conceptions of sex and gender (6). As she states, "In many cultures, eating is a sexual and gendered experience throughout life" (9). Writing in the introduction to the essays collected in *Cooking Lessons: The Politics of Gender and Food*, Sherrie A. Inness concurs, maintaining, "Every aspect of food is intermingled with issues of gender." Inness then goes on to explain that an analysis of the gendered messages in food can teach us much about societal gender differences and inequities (xv).

The study of gender has indeed emerged as one of the most exciting topics in food studies. However, when investigating what foodways can tell us about "the relations between the sexes, their gender definitions, and their sexuality" (Counihan 1999: 9), we tend not to specify that we are usually investigating heterosexual gender relations between women and men. In the words of queer theorist Michael Warner, this discursive phenomenon reflects a heteronormative analytic framework: one in which heterosexuality is presumed to be the "elemental form of human association . . . [and] the very model of intergender relations" (xxi). The new discipline of queer studies invites scholars to consider that "heteronormativity (or heterosexuality as an institution) is never absolutely coherent and stable" (Sullivan 132), and to examine the ways in which its power is both reinforced and resisted. As the nascent field of food studies takes shape, insights from queer studies have the potential to enrich our understandings of the interrelationships among food, gender and sexuality by encouraging us to rethink and refine our conceptions of these connections. For example, how food and foodways shape the gender and sexual identities of people who are not heterosexual in addition to those who are has not been extensively investigated by food studies scholars working on gender. Nor has there been a great deal of discussion about how our analyses of foodways and gender may unintentionally reflect heteronormative biases.

As Ruth Goldman explains, to "queer" an academic discipline means to alter its "discourses about sexuality and gender" in order "to problematize identity and challenge the normative." Goldman further stresses that "queer theory is theoretically structured around the concept of intersecting identities" (173), such as race, class, and ethnicity in addition to sexual orientation and gender identity. In this essay, I make a foray into queering food studies by analyzing contemporary Chicana lesbian writings about food, examining texts that illustrate the cultural endurance of heteronormative gender and sexual culinary ideologies even as they demonstrate how queer Chicanas in literary kitchens disrupt, destabilize, and transform these beliefs. After summarizing the culinary models that have structured recent interpretations of Chicana literary foodways, I analyze several lesbian texts that challenge these dominant interpretive paradigms, focusing specifically on writings that employ the figure of the hungry lesbian to question heteronormative cultural assumptions about food, sex, and identity. I highlight Carla Trujillo's *What Night Brings*, a novel that documents the struggles of a young Chicana lesbian to assert her queer appetites in the midst of an oppressive culinary culture that seeks to subdue them. I conclude by suggesting the ways in which the insightful perspectives that Chicana lesbian writers bring to gender, sexuality, and food might be applied to the endeavor of queering food studies more generally.

In her groundbreaking 1995 study of Chicana literature, Tey Diana Rebolledo devotes a chapter to a mode of authorship she terms "the writer as cook." She explains, "Women are imagined as nourishers both physically and symbolically; therefore, it is only natural that Chicana writers have seized that nourishing space and have linked writing and cooking" (Rebolledo 1995: 130). Noting the ubiquitous presence of women preparing food in Chicana texts, Rebolledo summarizes that female authors use cooking metaphors to depict "work, sexuality, and women's spiritual and cultural hunger" (Rebolledo 1995: 133). Benay Blend extends Rebolledo's argument, stating that the kitchen serves as a "safe refuge" for Chicana writers oppressed by a racist, imperialist, and sexist culture (Blend 2001: 58). By writing about food and cooking, Blend declares, these authors imaginatively create "a world where there are no politics of oppression" (Blend 2001: 57). Ellen M. Gil-Gomez finds weaknesses in Rebolledo's claims, suggesting the metaphor of the writer as cook may "actually re-inscribe women's subordination rather than articulating women's agency, freedom, or power" (Gil-Gomez 2001: 70). Debra Castillo concurs, proposing that while the figure of the female cook may symbolize "female creative power," in reality "her own work and her hunger, both physical and textual, go too often unrecognized" (xiv). Though compelling, the debate about the "writer as cook" does not address if or how the perspectives of nonheterosexual women might affect this gendered paradigm; even though Re-bolledo and Blend do briefly mention works by lesbian writers, the critical discussion about the Chicana kitchen implicitly establishes it as a heterosexual female space.

The provocative food symbolism and metaphors in recent Chicana lesbian poetry challenge both the heteronormative construction of the Chicana kitchen and the limitations Castillo and Gomez see in the literary figure of the female cook. By celebrating the kitchen as a place where lesbians eagerly and lovingly prepare food for their female partners, these poets assert that queer as well as straight Chicanas regard cooking as a vital source of female identity and pride. Furthermore, by figuring lesbians not only as cooks but also as hungry women who deserve to have their physical and sexual appetites fulfilled, these poets break the cultural silence imposed on the expression of lesbian desire. In her poem, "Making Tortillas," Alicia Gaspar de Alba erotically venerates lesbians as both cooks and lovers by punning on the word "tortillera" ("tortilla maker"), a derogatory term used to refer to queer Chicana women (de Alba 1993). As Catrióna Rueda Esquibel explains, the insult actually references the time-honored female tradition since the sound of tortilla making—slapping the hands together back and forth—can also be interpreted as a "representation of tribadism" (Esquibel 2003: 272). Lines from Gaspar de Alba's poem erase the distinction between the heterosexual female cook who sustains her family with food and the lesbian who satisfies her sexual needs by making love with women. Blurring the culinary boundaries between straight and queer women, de Alba writes:

My body remembers
the feel of the griddle
beads of grease sizzling
under the skin, a cry gathering
like an air bubble in the belly
of the unleavened cake. Smell
of baked tortillas all over the house,
all over the hands still
hot from clapping, cooking.
Tortilleras, we are called,
grinders of maíz, makers, bakers,
slow lovers of women.
The secret is starting from scratch.
　　(de Alba 1993: 355–356)

This poem insists that by "starting from scratch," the tortillera initiates new understandings of Chicana culinary tradition by queering the meanings food and foodways usually signify in Chicano culture. Several poets anthologized in *Chicana Lesbians: The Girls Our Mothers Warned Us About* appropriate this power by employing traditional Chicano foods to depict lesbian sexual desire, to refer to female body parts, and to metaphorize lesbian sex. In E. D. Hernández' poem, 'You as a Public Turn On," the speaker compares her lover's taste to that of

"salsita de chile en mi lengua" (a little chile sauce on my tongue) (56). In "untitled," Angela Arellano queers the cultural significance of biscochitos, die Mexican anise-flavored cookies traditionally served at wedding receptions. Using a metaphor that legitimates her sexual hunger and validates the sanctity of her relationship, the speaker likens the passionate intensity of her lover's kiss to the crumbling of "biscochitos dunked in hot creamy coffee" (Arellano 1991: 62). In addition to legitimating lesbian desire, the delectable image of the crumbling cookie ironically alludes to the fragility of the heterosexual bonds supposedly rendered unbreakable when couples speak their wedding vows. In the erotic fantasy poem "La enchilada," M. Álvarez imagines her potential female lovers as chile peppers. Though the speaker craves the "green ones/vine ripened, ready for salsa," the "tiny red ones" are undeniably her "favorite," for these "little red bullets of fire" always bring her to the brink of orgasm:

They're sooo good!
I can't get enough
bite after bite
gasping for breath
"Yes, yes, more, more!"
. . . .
Piquín/Jalapeño
Manzano/Serrano
What magnificent lovers you are!
　　(Alvarez 1991: 71–72)

These writers turn the tables on heteronormative food practices not only by appropriating foods that represent the cornerstones of the Chicano diet and its most sacred heterosexual rituals to represent queer sexuality, but also by perverting the Chicana's traditional culinary gender role. In contrast to heteronormative constructions of the Chicana cook, these poems configure the lesbian as food eater in addition to food preparer. They present the tortillera as a woman with appetites that deserve to be satisfied rather than as one who must deny her own hunger so that she may feed others first.

Cherríe Moraga identifies a literary ancestor for this queer female in the Aztec creation myth entitled "the Hungry Woman." According to Moraga, the body of the eponymous character is covered with mouths: "She had mouths in her wrists, mouths in her elbows, and mouths in her ankles and knees." The woman's mouths cry incessantly for food; in an attempt to silence them, the spirits divide her body and use it to create the earth. But her voracious appetite cannot be satisfied. "Her mouths were everywhere, biting and moaning. . . . but they were never filled. Sometimes at night, when the wind blows, you can hear her crying for food" (Morega 2000: 146). Moraga embraces this hungry woman as the essence of Chicana lesbian narrative. "She is the story that has never been told truly, the story of that hungry Mexican woman who is called puta/bruja/jota/loca ["whore, witch, dyke, crazy"] because she refuses to forget that her half-life is not a natural-born fact" (Morega 2000: 147).

Carla Trujillo's 2003 novel *What Night Brings* presents a contemporary retelling of the myth of the hungry woman. The plot depicts the struggles of eleven-year-old Marci Cruz, a hungry Chicana lesbian who must reconcile her queer sexual appetites, her desires to escape her abusive father, and her quest for social acceptance with the ideals of femininity that her heteronormative culture expects her to embrace. Trujillo's text documents Marci's efforts to resist through foodways the three most powerful social institutions that define and control her sexuality: her patriarchal family, in which heterosexual male and female gender roles are clearly demarcated and women's subservience to men is mandated; the Catholic church, which enforces these heterosexual gender roles; and the homophobia of the Chicano community, which emerges from cultural gender and religious beliefs as well as the racist, classist, and imperialist oppression Chicanos/as have historically experienced in America.

Though the novel takes place in California in 1967, before either the Chicano or gay civil rights movements gain national prominence, Marci Cruz is already well aware that her nonnormative sexual identity will not be tolerated in any area of her life. But rather than succumbing to her culture's dominant ideas about proper female gender identity, Marci bravely decides to confront them, using her relationships with food to assert her queer sexuality.

The Cruz family's foodways exemplify Counihan's observation that "power relations around food mirror the power of the sexes in general" (Counihan 1999: 11). Marci's mother, Delia, does not work outside the home because her husband Eddie "won't let her" (Trujillo 2003: 3), nor does she drive. Her primary responsibilities, according to Marci, include planning "every dime we spend on food" (10) and having dinner ready for Eddie when he gets home from the Chevy plant where he works. But though Delia purchases and prepares the family's food, Eddie decides who eats what. As Marci ruefully relates, there is a double standard in the household when it comes to her father and food. Delia purchases Hostess cupcakes and deli ham for Eddie's lunch that her daughters are forbidden to eat (185, 186); yet despite the energy Delia devotes to satisfying her husband's hunger, he regularly indulges his insatiable sexual appetites by sleeping with other women. "My dad likes looking at girls—all kinds, all the time. If a girl he likes has big chiches ["breasts"], he smiles and looks at her like he's about to eat pudding" (1). Unfortunately for Marci and her sister, Corin, Delia immerses herself in her culinary responsibilities so that she will not have to confront her husband's alcoholism or his infidelities. Whenever Marci complains about her father's behavior, Delia ignores her and "keeps cooking" (9).

Delia's refusal to stand up to Eddie's cruelty frustrates Marci, as does her mother's silence when Eddie complains about the food she fixes. According to

Counihan, men can wield domestic power over women by disparaging the food females prepare or by demanding certain dishes (11). When meals do not meet Eddie's expectations, he regularly erupts into temper tantrums, throwing his food with a " 'this makes me sick' " scowl. Marci angrily relates, "I hated that look. I wanted to tell her to tell him to 'eat shit' or 'get up and fix it yourself' " (11). But Delia never speaks up. Rather, she meekly follows her husband's orders, preparing only the dishes Eddie likes. Marci despises the "frijoles guisados"—beans cooked with onions and oil thickened with flour—that Delia prepares almost every night at Eddie's insistence. But as Marci explains, "Mom fixes them this way because the king of the castle likes them like that. Since the king says, 'I pay the bills,' I have to eat them the way he likes them" (57).

As opposed to Chicana literary cooks who use "traditional Mexicano/Chicano/Indian foods" to symbolize their ethnic identity (Rebolledo 1995: 133), Trujillo uses Marci's food preferences to reinforce her queer sexuality. Though Marci looks forward to the delicious fresh tortillas her mother makes on Saturday mornings, eating them hot off the *comal* like a "happy pig" (46), she refuses to eat the beans "guisados" that represent her father's power over the family and her mother's subservience to his culinary demands. By rejecting this particular dish, Marci symbolically refuses to ingest the subservient culinary role her culture expects her to embody. In addition to her mother's tortillas, Marci favorite foods include candy, McDonald's hamburgers, and ice cream—foods not traditionally associated with Chicano culture. As well, her mother does not have to cook these foods; Marci can procure them for herself when she has spending money.

The family's precarious finances coupled with Eddie's draconian control limit Marci's access to the foods she enjoys, however, and consequently, she is always starving. There is never enough food in the Cruz kitchen to satisfy Marci's rumbling stomach, nor can she resolve her growing sexual desire for girls with the heterosexual culture that surrounds her. "I don't know when or how it happened. Maybe I was born this way, but the second I saw chiches, I wanted them. I couldn't stop thinking of girls, during the day at school, at night in my dreams, and especially when I watched TV" (9). Because Delia forbids Marci from asking questions about sex, she turns to a higher authority for help. Every evening, in addition to asking God to make Eddie vanish (1), Marci also asks Him to turn her into a boy (9). As she reasons, if granted a sex change she could beat Eddie up when he hits her; as well, she knows that her culture only tolerates romantic relationships between men and women. "*I* know you can't be with a girl if you *are* a girl. So that's why I have to change into a boy" (9).

Marci comes to see a heavenly miracle as the only way her desires will be granted because violence almost always erupts when she attempts to satisfy her appetites on her own. One evening when the family is visiting relatives, Marci helps herself to leftovers from their supper table because she has not been able to stomach the beans her mother had prepared for dinner. When Eddie sees Marci take the food, he erupts into a rage, and his anger increases exponentially when his relatives remark that the stick-thin Marci "looks hungry" (58). Here, Marci's appetite blatantly calls Eddie's masculine authority into question: her action implies that her father cannot afford to feed his family, nor can her control her. As punishment for these offenses, he whips her with a belt.

This is the first of several chilling episodes in the novel when Eddie beats his daughters for breaking the food rules he forces the subjects of his familial empire to follow. Counihan has observed that husbands often justify abusing their wives because of meal failures (Counihan 1999: 11); using similar reasoning, on Easter morning Eddie claims the right to beat

Marci and Corin due to their failure to eat properly. After the girls sit down to eat the hardboiled eggs they have colored, Corin eats the yolk of hers but gives the white part to Marci to finish. Furious, Eddie, starts screaming: "Mira, in this house nothing gets wasted. Everything costs me money and it's money I have to bust my ass for. You peel an egg, you eat it. The whole thing, not just the parts you like" (84). Though Marci tries to explain that the sisters have worked out their own system of egg consumption—each eats only the parts she wants—Eddie brutally force-feeds Corin the egg while explaining: "When your daddy was little we never had enough to eat. We were starving, all of us, your grandma and my brothers. Sometimes all we had to eat were a few beans. . . . Now do you see why I get so upset when you waste food?" (87). Even though the girls have planned to eat all of the egg, in Eddie's eyes they are guilty of assuming the power that rightfully belongs to him as the person with the "huevos" (balls) in the family. (Here Trujillo pointedly employs a culinary double-entendre, since "huevos" also means "eggs" in Spanish). Eddie's words imply that because he is a man with the parts to prove it his daughters will never succeed in defying his rules.

Though Eddie presides over the Cruz kitchen with patriarchal authority, Marci finds a place to indulge her queer appetites when she decides to grow food in the family's backyard. As she confides to the reader, "I wanted corn. I liked the way it looked. Its smell. And how fast it grew" (40). As Jeffrey Pilcher documents, in Mexico this indigenous food has been associated with female sexuality since pre-Columbian times and has been used for centuries in art to symbolize male desire for nubile women (58 Pilcher 1998: 17). In this case, the corn Marci plants helps her to cultivate a relationship with Raquel, the beautiful sixteen-year-old girl next door who gives the young lesbian gardening tips. "I felt all melty and good

when I looked at her, like I'd just eaten two packs of Reese's Peanut Butter Cups" (26). By expressing her lesbian sexual longings though chocolate and corn, Marci queers the heterosexual meanings associated with both foods, challenging both the heteronormative and Chicano ideologies that "love and desire are constituted in relation to heterosexuality" (Esquibel 1998: 678). In addition to helping Marci to grow her own food, Raquel shares extra produce from her own garden with the younger girl. The beautiful teenager's generosity supplements Marci's meager diet and assuages the brutality that accompanies mealtimes in the Cruz household. "Each time she put something in my arms, I wanted to grab her and kiss her just like the people on TV. . . . I felt good because I got to be with her" (43).

Over the course of the novel, the Catholic church also emerges as a place where Marci can express her queer appetites. Initially, Marci finds this traditional cornerstone of Chicano heteronormativity alienating, since the catechism teacher dissuades her from asking questions and she finds the literal sustenance the Church offers unappetizing. In her opinion, communion wafers taste "exactly like store-bought tortillas" (66) and the flavorless bread discourages her from accepting the doctrine that "eating a body and drinking some blood was holy" (65). She instead prefers the message—and the refreshments—distributed at the Baptist church: a building painted "the same color as bubblegum" (50) where a youth minister bribes children with candy to listen to her message. But when Delia discovers that Marci has "accepted Jesus" at a prayer meeting in exchange for some stale red licorice (55), she insists that her daughter renounce her sin at the family's own church.

Though Trujillo has maintained elsewhere that "lesbians and gay men are not given sanction by the largely Chicano Catholic community" (Trujillo 1991: 190), Marci does receive a queer sort of sanctification for her sexuality when she makes her first confession. After she discloses her sins—wishing that Eddie would leave, liking girls, and "wanting to squeeze chiches [breasts]" (71)—to the priest, he surprises her by sympathizing with her: "Life isn't easy, even if you don't like your dad. . . . We must try to forgive those who hurt us. . . . And as for liking girls and squeezing chiches. I don't see a problem with this, except it seems you're still a little young to be squeezing chiches. I don't think this is a sin either, unless the girl doesn't want them squeezed" (71–72). After receiving absolution, Marci deduces that her confessor has mistaken her for a boy. But when she realizes that the priest is Father Chacón, she is not so sure, since her father derisively refers to him as a "jotito" (little queer) (75).

Marci does not know what the word "jotito" means, but she realizes that there is something different about Father Chacón when she attends the church "spaghetti feed" he has organized to benefit starving refugees in Biafra.[2] Her curiosity as well as her appetite is whetted when she glimpses him in the hot church kitchen "with an apron on and his shirt sleeves rolled up" working with women to prepare the meal: "The pots of boiling water were so big they looked like bathtubs. The spaghetti sauce smelled good, and so did the garlic bread. . . . Father Chacón was sweating so much his hair was wet" (76). This moment of culinary cross-dressing coupled with the enormous quantity of food makes Marci ravenous, and she returns to the kitchen for second and third helpings of spaghetti. Marci's Uncle Tommy, a restaurant cook, then leaves the table. Ostensibly he has gone to help Father Chacón, but when she tries to find the men later they are not in the kitchen. While wandering through the church, she hears laughter; then she spies her uncle walking out of a confessional "tucking in his shirt" (78). Marci cannot believe her eyes when she sees Father Chacón emerge from the same door. Having watched the men come out of a closet together, Marci is certain that something

besides a confession has occurred, but she cannot imagine what. Weeks pass, but Marci cannot stop thinking about the incident, especially when Eddie calls Tommy a "queer" during an argument. After hearing the insult, Tommy's wife Arlene's grimaces "like she was eating something awful" (131). Thus Marci decides not to ask her uncle about his dalliance with the priest. "I didn't know what queer meant, but I could tell it was bad" (131).

Just as she cannot comprehend why Eddie beats her for eating when she is hungry, Marci does not understand why her father and her aunt seem so perturbed by Uncle Tommy and Father Chacón, nor why people react in shock when Eddie refers to them with a word that, to her, merely means "being different" (133). Marci identifies with the men not only because one is a family member and the other a priest who assures her that she is "normal" (73), but because these jotitos are cooks. Because these men take pleasure in the quintessential women's work—preparing food for others to eat—Marci reasons that she too can resist the dominant gender order. More important, Marci deduces that if Uncle Tommy and Father Chacón like each other, there may be nothing wrong with her desire for girls. After consulting the dictionary to learn what "queer" means, Marci deduces that the word "queer" indeed applies to her: "I'm a girl. I like Raquel. That makes me a girl liking a girl, which is a homosexual queer" (137). Notably, Marci's newfound security with her sexuality is accompanied by significant improvements in the family's food situation. When Eddie leaves his wife and daughters and moves in with his girlfriend, Delia finds work at Woolworth's and befriends the lunch cook, who gives her leftovers to take home. As Marci reports, in addition to the hotdogs, macaroni and cheese, fried chicken, and fish sticks that diversify her diet, she and Corin also frequently eat "grilled-cheese sandwiches, spaghetti, cold cereal, or weenies wrapped in bacon. This made us happy because we didn't have to eat beans so much anymore" (100).

In addition to giving Marci increased access to the kinds of food she prefers in amounts sufficient to satisfy her hunger, Eddie's absence gives her more freedom to decide what she will eat. While Delia is working, Marci takes control of the kitchen on her own initiative and teaches herself to cook meatloaf, hamburgers, and spaghetti. As a result of these dietary and domestic changes, Marci gains a few pounds and remarks that she is "finally happy" at home (107). When Eddie surprises the family by returning to Delia, Marci does not surrender the power she has claimed for herself. She gleefully prepare foods her father hates the most and also deliberately ruins dinners by cooking "bad on purpose": "I would always burn the meat, cook the green beans too long, or put garlic in everything, which Eddie hated" (123–124). According to Counihan, women have long resisted gendered power relations in the kitchen by refusing to cook or by cooking foods men dislike (Counihan 1999: 11), but Marci also disrupts the normal order of dinner by refusing to remain silent when Eddie complains about the new supper routine. When he belligerently asks Marci, "Where the hell is your goddamn mother and why isn't there any food on the table?" she retorts, "If you want food, why don't you ask that girlfriend of yours to come over and cook it?" (107).

Marci's queering of her household's foodways and her refusal to adopt a proper Chicana culinary gender role emerge as even more poignant because her transgressions always result in brutal beatings. It is clear that when Eddie punishes Marci for cooking improperly he is also violently responding to his daughter's gender queerness. (Though Eddie always complains about Delia's cooking, he never raises a hand to his wife.) One evening when Marci is preparing spaghetti, Eddie picks up the pot and throws it on the floor, spattering hot sauce on her arms and legs while he screams, "If you have to cook, you'd better cook me some goddamn beans and chile. And learn to make tortillas, too. I ain't eating none of this shit you cook anymore. It's about time you started learning things that's gonna do you some good, and that's learning how to cook food a man will eat ... Don't fix this crap again, Marci" (126). Eddie's diatribe indicates that he perceives Marci's queering of gastronomy and gender as an insult to his masculine authority and, worse, as behavior that jeopardizes her desirability as a potential wife. His insistence that Marci yield to the authority of Chicano foodways betrays the unspoken demand that she assume a heterosexual female identity.

However, even when Marci attempts to play the role of dutiful Chicana cook, she cannot satisfy Eddie's expectations. The next time she prepares supper, Marci fixes beans and chile and tries to make tortillas. Blend maintains that the literary depiction of tortilla-making in Chicana literature "empowers women as the carriers of tradition" (Blend 2001: 44) but Marci has not inherited Delia's skill with the *comal*. As opposed to her mother's round, "thick and puffy" productions (46), Marci's tortillas instead resemble "a map of California." While Eddie concedes that her mistakes "taste pretty good" (143), he ultimately regards her culinary shortcomings as indicative of her failure as a female. During a drunken rant, he insults her by calling her a "hombrecito" (little man): "Hell, that's what you are. I'm not gonna lie to you. . . . Your mother and I made a big mistake when we named you. We should have called you Mauricio . . . Pero, how did we know you'd be a boy when we saw your little bizcocho?" (144)

Though Eddie acknowledges Marci's queerness here by suggesting that she is at once a boy with a "bizcocho,"[3] he stops short of calling her a "tortillera" because the possibility that his daughter really is queer is too frightening for him to imagine. Marci herself remains silent about her sexual identity during the scene (insisting only that her father call her "Marci," not the masculine "Mauricio" that Eddie decides is a more appropriate name for his daughter), but she scores a symbolic victory by implicitly daring him to use the word and then witnessing his cowardice. Unable to think of more insults, Eddie only repeats the tired refrain about his "huevos": "I'll tell you one thing . . . you ain't never gonna be man enough to take on your father. . . . Your daddy here's the one with the balls" (144). Nevertheless, Marci is still wounded by the force of Eddie's words. By referring to her as a boy, as opposed to a lesbian, Eddie implies that Marci is not only a failed tortillera literally, but queerly as well.

After this episode, Marci's gnawing desire to confide her sexuality to anyone poignantly echoes the silent starvation Moraga describes. When Uncle Tommy volunteers to cook Thanksgiving dinner for his extended family, the invitation apparently promises Marci a perfect opportunity to break her silence about her lesbianism, especially when she sees Father Chacón helping her uncle in the kitchen. Free from her father's scrutiny—Eddie has refused to spend the day at a "house that had 'a bunch of queers in it' " (164)—Marci watches the couple as they cook together:

> Both of them had on big, white aprons. Uncle Tommy was wearing a white shirt with rolled-up sleeves and as usual, looked really handsome. On top of the stove cooling off was a giant turkey that he'd cooked with some kind of stuffing in it. He made mashed potatoes—well, he cooked them and told Father Chacón to mash them. Father Chacón ('Diego, Diego' he kept telling me) was sweating a little. He took the electric beater and added butter, salt, and heated-up milk to the potatoes and whipped them till they were super creamy. Whenever one of them got in the way, they used their hands to steer around each other so they wouldn't bump together . . .
>
> I saw how they looked at one another when they talked, and I thought I could see

something different than how regular men talk. I don't know exactly what it was, but the closest thing I could think of was how I might have looked when I talked to Raquel (166–167).

The queer culinary bliss that Marci witnesses here initially promises to end her hunger for acceptance and understanding. Trujillo's description of the gay men cooking for their lesbian guest provocatively perverts the heteronormative iconography of the Thanksgiving meal as immortalized in Norman Rockwell's painting "Freedom from Want."[4] Father Chacón's friendly overtures, the sensual mood in the kitchen, and the surfeit of food on the stove give Marci her first taste of what a loving homosexual relationship might be like. Seeing these queer cooks in action encourages her to consider the men as potential confidantes in her silent struggle, but when she attempts to come out to the couple by alluding to their queer behavior in the kitchen—"You don't usually see men cooking" (167)—the men ignore her innuendo. Tommy tersely replies, "No you don't . . . and for sure not in our family" (167), while, like Delia, Father Chacón turns from Marci's eyes and concentrates on buttering the potatoes. The disappointed Marci leaves the kitchen still hungry; pointedly, Trujillo does not depict her heroine eating anything the men have prepared for the family feast.

After this rejection by the only queers she knows, Marci struggles to accept the possibility that her starvation will never end. Comparing her futile struggles to her father's frequent food tantrums, she concedes, "Nothing else changes when you throw food against walls" (137). Despite her efforts to resist the heterosexual role her culture foists on her, signs abound that she will ultimately be forced to surrender to it. Her potential girlfriend, Raquel, elopes; Eddie continues to date his mistress, Wanda; and Uncle Tommy, sensing that Marci knows his secret, refuses to protect her and Corin from Eddie's fists. As her twelfth birthday nears, Marci's prayers for a sex change grow more desperate: "God, I hope you're paying attention now because I'm not talking about little baby wishes like wanting candy or a new bike for Christmas. This is almost the same as people starving in Biafra . . . Start paying attention to me, will you?" (172).

By equating her own experience as a queer Chicana to that of Nigerian refugees physically perishing from famine, Marci, like Moraga, realizes that she is slowly starving to death, and makes one last-ditch culinary attempt to subdue Eddie. After consulting her great aunt, Marci obtains a polvo to sprinkle on Eddie's beans, hoping that the mixture, as its label promises, will magically enable her to "dominate" her father (206). Here, Marci follows Mexican culinary folk wisdom; as Pilcher documents, in colonial Mexico it was commonly believed that a woman could bewitch an abusive husband by putting herbs in his food (Pilcher 1998: 59). But the eager Marci uses so much of the powder that Eddie complains about his beans "tasting funny" (212) and then insists that Delia change her work hours so that she can cook the family meals. Reading the figurative writing on the kitchen walls, Marci's resolve to resist her cultural destiny begins to dissipate. "No matter how hard I pray, or how good I try to be, I'll always be a girl . . . What do you do, God? What do you do with people like me?" (223).

Though the trajectory of Trujillo's novel suggests otherwise, it does end happily for the queer heroine. Significantly, however, the only way the kitchen ultimately assists Marci on her quest to assert her queer identity is as a literal, not symbolic, escape route. During a family argument in the dining room, Corin grabs Eddie's gun and shoots him. While the police and Delia tend to his wounds, Marci silently leads Corin out the kitchen's back door to the bus station. After the girls arrive at Delia's mother's house in New Mexico, Marci befriends a girl named Robbie, whose mother owns a grocery store. As they fall in love, Marci's references to hunger noticeably vanish from the novel, and on the last page of the book she revels in the joy of coming out of the closet and the taste of her first lesbian kiss. Marci's repeated failure to find a place for her queer sexuality in the kitchens Trujillo describes, as well as her inability to nourish herself when she tries to adopt the heteronormative gender role her culture's foodways force upon her, suggest that the culinary strategies available to straight female cooks who wish to "subvert feminine gender roles" (Blend 2001: 48) may not work for queer women. In this case, the only way the hungry lesbian avoids starving to death is by leaving the kitchen and the deference to heterosexual gender ideologies demanded of the cooks who enter it.

In their literary depictions of hungry women who queer gendered foodways (albeit with different measures of success), Chicana lesbian writers undertake the two most vital endeavors of queer studies: to challenge heteronormativity and to question the systems that sustain it (Goldman 1996: 174). As Chicana lesbian literature attests, foodways indubitably comprise one of the most powerful such systems. Though I have focused primarily on literary depictions of foodways in this essay, the project of queering food studies has the potential to enrich other arenas of food studies in myriad ways. The following lines from Cherríe Moraga's poem "Open Invitation to a Meal" are instructive here:

> I am
> you tell me
> *a piece of cake.*
>
> I wonder about your eating habits
> which make me dessert
> instead of staple
> a delicacy, like some chocolate mousse
> teasing your taste buds, melting
> in your mouth—stopping there (16).

Moraga's poem metaphorically warns that the endeavor of queering food studies should not be considered a proverbial piece of cake. Nor can it be accomplished merely through supplemental footnotes or superficial treatments; we must avoid the temptation of employing queer perspectives as decorative garnishes that hide entrenched epistemologies. How might our academic investigations of food and gender roles as they reflect power relationships in the kitchen and in the home, access to food and nutrition, and the very acts of cooking and consuming food benefit from a queer studies approach? How might an increased attentiveness to heteronormativity change scholarly assumptions about what practices constitute culturally representative or deviant foodways? How might perspectives from queer studies influence academic analyses of food and social justice, food and ethics, and food policy? These are just a few of the questions that arise when we queer food studies; undoubtedly many more will arise as the discipline grows. As the writings of Chicana lesbians assert, is time to hear what queer voices can bring to the table of food studies, starting from scratch to develop new recipes for inquiry.

I thank Robert Con Davis-Undiano, Jane Park, Carole Counihan, and the three anonymous readers for *Food and Foodways* for their helpful comments and suggestions for revision.

NOTES

1. A note on terminology: I use the term "Chicana" to refer to Mexican American women of mixed Spanish, Indian, and Anglo descent living in the United States.
2. The African state of Biafra was established by the Igbo people of Nigeria who seceded from that country on May 30, 1967. Nigeria refused to recognize the sovereignty of the state and a brutal civil war broke out in July of that year. As part of its military strategy, the Nigerian government set up blockades around Biafra, cutting off its food supplies. When news of the resultant famine spread worldwide, the plight of the starving Biafrans attracted the attention of international humanitarian and religious groups worldwide, who raised funds for relief. By the time Biafra surrendered to Nigeria in 1970, it is estimated that severe malnutrition had claimed the lives of 1 million people (Goetz 2001).
3. Literally translated, the word "biscocho" means "cookie" or "pound cake." Here Eddie is using it as a crude reference to female genitalia.
4. Norman Rockwell's' painting "Freedom from Want" was part of a series of works intended to depict the ideas in Franklin D. Roosevelt's "Four Freedoms" speech before Congress. It appeared in *The Saturday Evening Post* on March 6, 1943.

REFERENCES

Álvarez, M. 1991. La enchilada. In *Chicana Lesbians: The Girls Our Mothers Warned Us About*, ed. C. Trujillo, p. 71. Berkeley: Third Woman Press.

Arellano, A. 1991. untitled. In *Chicana Lesbians: The Girls Our Mothers Warned Us About*, ed. C. Trujillo, p. 62. Berkeley: Third Woman Press.

Blend, B. 2001. I Am an Act of Kneading: Food and the Making of Chicana Identity. In *Cooking Lessons: The Politics of Gender and Food*, ed. S. A. Inness, pp. 41–61. Lanham: Rowman and Littlefield.

Castillo, D. A. 1992. *Talking Back: Toward a Latin American Feminist Literary Criticism*. Ithaca: Cornell University Press.

Counihan, C. M. 1999. *The Anthropology of Food and Body: Gender, Meaning, and Power*. New York: Routledge.

de Alba, A. G. 1993. Making Tortillas. In *Infinite, Divisions: An Anthology of Chicana Literature*, eds. Tey Diana Rebolledo and Eliana S. Rivero, pp. 355–356. Tucson: University of Arizona Press.

Esquibel, C. R. 1998. Memories of Girlhood: Chicana Lesbian Fiction. *Signs: Journal of Women in Culture and Society* 23:645–682.

Esquibel, C. R. 2003. Shameless Histories: Chicana Lesbian Fictions Talking Race/Talking Sex. In *Tortilleras: Hispanic and U.S. Latina Lesbian Expression*, pp. 258–275. Philadelphia: Temple University Press.

Gil-Gomez, E. M. 2001. Salpicando La Salsa and Spicing Up the Text: Power and Consumption in Latina Food Culture. *Voces: a Journal of Chicana/ Latina Studies* 3:68–93.

Goetz, N. October 7, 2001. Humanitarian Issues in the Biafra Conflict. *The Journal of Humanitarian Assistance*. Accessed May 15, 2005. http://www. jha/ac/articles/u036/htm

Goldman, R. 1996. Who Is That *Queer* Queer?: Exploring Norms Around Sexuality, Race, and Class in Queer Theory. In *Queer Studies: A Lesbian,*

Gay, Bisexual, and Transgender Anthology, eds. Brett Beemyn and Mickey Eliason, pp. 169–182. New York: New York University Press.

Hernández, E. D. 1991. "You as a Public Turn On." In *Chicana Lesbians: The Girls Our Mothers Warned Us About*, ed. C. Trujillo, p. 56. Berkeley: Third Woman Press.

Inness, S. A. 2001. Introduction: Of Meatloaf and Jell-O. . . . *Cooking Lessons: The Politics of Gender and Food*, pp. xi–xvii. Lanham: Rowman and Littlefield.

Moraga, C. L. 2000. *Loving in the War Years: lo que nunca pasó por sus labios*. Cambridge, MA: South End Press.

Pilcher, J. 1998. *Que Vivan los Tamales! Food and the Making of Mexican Identity*. Albuquerque: University of New Mexico Press.

Rebolledo, T. D. 1995. *Women Singing in the Snow: A Cultural Analysis of Chicana Literature*. Tucson: University of Arizona Press.

Sullivan, Nikki. 2003. *A Critical Introduction to Queer Theory*. New York: New York University Press.

Trujillo, C. 1991. Chicana Lesbians: Fear and Loathing in the Chicano Community. In *Chicana Lesbians: The Girls Our Mothers Warned Us About*, ed. Carla Trujillo, pp. 186–194. Berkeley: Third Woman Press.

Trujillo, C. 2003. *What Night Brings*. Willimantic, CT: Curbstone Press.

Warner, M. 1993. Introduction. In *Fear of a Queer Planet: Queer Politics and Social Theory*, ed. Michael Warner, pp. vii–xxxi. Minneapolis: University of Minnesota Press.

18

Metrosexuality Can Stuff It: Beef Consumption as (Heteromasculine) Fortification

C. Wesley Buerkle

My father once recounted to me that some acquaintances of his felt the need to drive off gay-male clientele from their family-style restaurant. The restaurateurs in question changed their establishment to a steak house because, as my father explained to me, "they [homosexuals] don't eat meat." He spoke as though he were citing the 1975 *World Book* encyclopedias we had as children: "Homosexual: . . . non-carnivorous." To my father, the assumed lack of meat consumption was simply one more sign that homosexuals—especially, gay men—defied normality. In his understanding of the world, gay men had senselessly denounced their God-given right to social dominance by allowing themselves to become effeminized; as a matter of course, they also refused to eat beef products, if not all animal flesh.

Though, clearly, my father held—what can charitably be described as—anachronistic principles on gender and sexual politics, his brash assessment provides an overt statement of otherwise submerged cultural practices and beliefs. Where it may seem "un-ladylike" to eat much, consuming large quantities of food seems expected from men. In western culture, consuming animal flesh, especially beef, has a long association with traditional masculinity. The image of men as hunters with hearty appetites eating their kill cooked over an open flame haunts our cultural conceptions of gender.[1] Despite changes in conceptions of masculinity that include a broader acceptance of men's participation in the home and of equality with women, men's eating behaviors remain a characteristic assumed to be biologically driven, a point of gender distinction beyond cultural change. Harry Brod observes that western culture accepts as a given that there exists a natural essence to masculinity as opposed to feminine performance, which openly discusses changes in social fashions and politics (13). The cultural recognition that men too perform their gender began with the emergence of "metrosexuality," a masculinity concerned with aesthetics and other heretofore interests classed as feminine. Against such a trend, recent burger franchise advertising markets beef consumption as a fundamental masculine activity and a means to resist metrosexuality's effeminizing influence and defeat the suggestion that the "real" man is itself a fiction. In this essay, I explore the performance of beef consumption in hamburger advertising as a means to fortify a retrograde masculinity against the alternatives represented by metrosexuality.

For the last three decades, discussions within masculinity studies have primarily focused on traditional performance and representations of heteromasculinity and gay men's exclusion from heteronormative culture (Brod and Kaufman; Buchbinder; Craig; Kaufman; Kimmel *Changing*; Kimmel *Manhood*; Kimmel and Messmer; Levine; Messmer; Messmer and Sabo; Pleck and Pleck; Pronger). Two studies even outline fundamental elements of dominant US masculinity, emphasizing men's physical strength and social dominance (Brannon; Trujillo).[2] Across all research comes the understanding that heterosexuality is implicit to traditional, dominant US masculinity. In recent years, cultural studies has given more attention to the rise of the metrosexual, a masculinity that challenges heteronormativity by incorporating gender performances heretofore deemed feminine and, thereby, queer (Clarkson; Miller; Ramsey and Santiago; Simpson). Mark Simpson officially introduces the concept of metrosexuality in 2002, pointing to British soccer star David Beckham as a metrosexual *par excellence*, emphasizing the narcissism of culture industry obsession mixed with the heteromasculine assets of desire from straight women and admiration from straight men.

To understand metrosexuality's function in dominant US culture, much critical attention has gone to Bravo's popular series *Queer Eye for the Straight Guy* and its service to heteronormative culture. *Queer Eye* provides shining examples of how to create metrosexuals by showing five gay men transform stereotypically messy, slovenly, uncultured straight men—those resembling Oscar Madison from Neil Simon's *The Odd Couple*—into neat, well-groomed and dressed men-about-town—like Felix Unger. Similar to Felix, the metrosexual has an appreciation for the arts, can cook, keeps a tidy home, displays warm human emotions, and dresses dapperly. Unlike Felix, the metrosexual engages in a public performance that invites a gaze upon his body and uses his kinder, gentler masculinity for the purpose of heterosexual conquest. This latter point often serves as the issue around which feminist and queer critics debate metrosexuality's political potential. Jay Clarkson, for one, observes that components of traditional masculinity merely undergo a makeover in *Queer Eye* (e.g., physical perfection

replacing physical force) to improve men's heterosexual desirability (252). Similarly, Robert Westerfelhaus and Celeste Lacroix find that *Queer Eye's* episodes purge "potential homoerotic contamination" by concluding with the remade man engaging in a heteronormative performance (e.g., a heterosexual date). Thus, the metrosexual transformation remains a decidedly heterosexual performance.

Because metrosexuality blurs the distinction between masculine and feminine activities, inviting the perception of sexual malleability, we can expect heteromasculine hegemony, as a self-preserving structure, to re-assert traditional masculinity against any challenges to its dominance. This study's interest in the relationship between masculine performance and food consumption contemplates the ways that men eating—especially beef—asserts a retrograde masculinity, one that returns to an undomesticated performance driven by biological desire. I argue, as Judith Butler says, that these performances disguise their fictitiousness as naturalness, thereby "[concealing] gender's performative character and the performative possibilities for proliferating gender configurations outside the restricting frames of masculinist domination and compulsory heterosexuality" (140). To begin the discussion, I demonstrate the link between masculinity and meat ingrained in dominant US culture, relying upon both social-scientific and cultural analyses. Looking to key examples of hamburger franchise advertising, I consider the depiction of burger consumption as a means for men to anchor ever-broadening masculine definitions to a physical compulsion of the body equated to sexual appetite. I focus primary attention on Burger King's commercial, "Manthem," as a literal protest of men against perceived effeminization. Other advertisements similarly promote and prove the fixity of a retrograde masculinity through hamburger consumption.

EATING LIKE A MAN

Considerable academic research and discussion gives attention to women's experiences with food, their bodies, and weight (e.g., Spitzack; Basow and Kobrynowicz; Martz et al.; Mooney, DeTore, and Malloy; Thompson and Heinberg). Discussing men's relationship to food seems unusual in that we typically focus our attention on women's negotiation of eating and body image concerns. In *Unbearable Weight* Bordo provides careful analysis of women's bodies as cultural products always related to food. Bordo's later book, *The Male Body*, says nothing of men's food consumption, yet eating remains a central, if unspoken, element in men's masculine performance. As research indicates, men's eating goes largely unnoticed, whereas women often feel the social norms for proper consumption weighing down upon them (Saukko; Scott; Spitzack). The social-scientific research on food consumption demonstrates exactly that point. Likewise, cultural analyses of food reveal the significance of meat consumption for successful masculine performance. In the following I discuss social-scientific literature to reveal the ways in which masculinity claims for itself the right to consume. Turning to cultural analyses, I then review ways in which meat consumption serves as a masculine performance, supposedly innate to the heteromale experience. By bringing into conversation the literature from divergent research perspectives, I mean to create a broad, cultural understanding of the relations between men and food.

Men Eating, Women Wanting

The social scientific literature pertaining to the gendered perceptions of men and women as they eat often directs attention and implications to the perceptions of women, which seems logical in light of eating disorders' prevalence among women.[3] Within that research, however, lie gendered meanings of food that serve important functions in the performance of masculinity. Studies consistently show that men and women subject women's eating behaviors to harsh criticism (Basow and Kobrynowicz; Chaiken and Pliner; Mooney et al.; Mori et al.; Pliner and Chaiken). When asked to compare the eating behaviors of men and women, a pattern emerges in which others perceive men as more masculine by merely eating. Beth Bock and Robin Kanarek and Susan Basow and Diane Kobrynowicz find that as meal size increases women are perceived by others as less feminine whereas men are seen as just as masculine if not more so. This suggests that at the very least men enjoy eating as a value free behavior, whereas women never escape scrutiny. Compounding these findings, Kim Mooney and Erica Lorenz show that when men and women eat identical meals, the males are perceived as both consuming more calories and as possessing more favorable social traits (e.g., emotional, conscientious, self-control, strong, and intelligent). Against any hope that a double standard does not exist, their study indicates that observers seemingly root for a man to better perform his masculinity.

Compounding the differences between men and women's experiences with food, young men voice a sense of entitlement to unrestrictive eating entirely absent when women discuss their experiences. Representing this contrast, Annette Levi and associates report anecdotal findings from their study of college men and women: men reported, "I don't care what I eat, as long as there's a lot of it and it's cheap," and, "I eat *what* I want *when* I want" (respondent's emphasis) (94). In contrast, one woman noted, "I usually wonder what I will look like after eating this" (95). The drastic differences embody the sense of entitlement men bring to the table against women's fear of social rejection for daring to enjoy a meal. As Bordo says, "It is a mark of the manly to eat spontaneously and expansively" (*Unbearable* 108). The spontaneity and expansiveness of men's eating behavior mimics the reality that men enjoy greater social freedoms with few restrictions, whereas women must heed public expectations to restrain themselves.

The division between men and women's relation to food widens as the performance of meal preparation further differentiates gendered expectations. In the common scenarios of men grilling outside and women cooking in the kitchen, men employ fire, whereas women surround themselves with technology that distances them from men's primordial methods (Mechling 81). As a response to having to be in the kitchen, Jonathan Deutsch records that the language among firefighters involved in communal cooking only becomes regularly coarse and sexualized (e.g., "you liked my cock-slaw") when in the kitchen," [seeming] to use language to 'masculinize' the 'women's' work that they do in the kitchen" (105). Even *Queer Eye*'s food "make-over" segment acknowledges the fact that men typically have poor culinary skills, which often change very little on follow-up visits (Julier and Lindenfeld 2). The collective picture tells the story that men do not belong in the kitchen and should maintain a place as the consumer, not the laborer.

From social-scientific research we see men and women engage in drastically different gendered performances of food. Men participate in a performance of privilege in which they may eat expansively and without concern for social repercussions, whereas women must constantly regulate themselves under a scrutinizing social gaze. Sandra Bartky recounts everyday gender performances that demonstrate women's subjection to heteromasculine norms and the demand that they carefully regulate their bodies to those ideals. Though men have largely enjoyed freedom in eating, the appearance of metrosexual masculinity has brought

about a new sensibility for men's relationship with food. Just as beauty and consumer cultures' expanded capture of men creates a wider market for high-end blue jeans and hair-care products, metrosexual sensibilities teach men to watch calories and more carefully choose the foods they eat. Fabio Parasecoli says that with men's increased participation in consumer culture, they eat to improve their bodies' beauty and health, not to enjoy themselves (26). In this way, metrosexuality introduces men to the heretofore feminine concern for how food directly affects one's appearance and thus one's sexual appeal, for Katherine O'Doherty Jensen and Lotte Holm document healthy eating habits associated with women, not men (358). Looking at research on gendered perceptions of eating, metrosexuality feminizes men's relationship with food by restricting men's access to pleasure-by-food-consumption. As I will show later, recent hamburger advertising responds to men's perceived effeminization at the dining table by punctuating their desire and capacity to consume despite any effort to place on them gendered expectations similar to women's.

I'm Not a Vegetarian . . . Not that There's Anything Wrong with that

In western culture meat often represents the centerpiece and fullness of a meal. If eating presents an activity reserved for men, then meat, the ideal food, represents the epitome of masculine consumption. Feminist critique and media texts bear out this point. In what follows, I discuss the ways in which men eating meat, especially beef, constitutes a masculine performance that specifically excludes and rejects femininity. Drawing from cultural critique, I invoke the history and arguments that connect male meat consumption and the deprivileging of women and feminine culture. Meat's importance in masculine culture ultimately plays a role in a resurgence of traditional masculinity against metrosexual effeminization by re-asserting an innate link between males and animal flesh.

Both social-scientific studies and cultural critiques demonstrate a clear pattern of men associated with meat consumption, an act itself often seen as more ideal than a meat-free diet. Reviewing literature on European eating behaviors, O'Doherty Jensen and Holm argue that a food's status relates to its gender association, with men associated with the highest status foods (357). Carol Adams similarly finds a privileging of masculine food in anglophile countries that centers specifically on meat. As a case in point, Adams cites a nineteenth-century British study's findings that in working-class homes, where the budget allowed only limited meat purchases, the husband/father consumed meat on a daily basis, whereas his wife and children could have it only once a week (29). By the twentieth century, when most have access to meat as a regular dietary component, carving—not cooking—the meat becomes a duty and privilege for men that women access only by usurping it from their husbands (Mechling 74).

Within the compulsion toward valuing meat and the predisposition to viewing meat as men's food, we see the perpetuation of dichotomous gender images. The social logic behind presenting meat as a masculine food of choice assumes that by consuming meat men gain strength, whereas vegetables and other nonmeat products provide nothing to the body in the way of substance. The anthropologist James Frazer documents the cross-cultural assumption that consuming animal meat, actual muscle, translates into the acquisition of strength and power, noting many nonindustrialized cultures' belief "that by eating the flesh of an animal or man [sic] he [sic] acquires not only the physical, but even the moral and intellectual qualities which were characteristic of that animal or man" (463). Likewise, in "Eating Muscle," Patrick McGann recounts his experiences as a teenager in West Texas playing football where the young men equate consuming meat with gaining muscle (90). Bettina Heinz and Ronald Lee state the point plainly: "The symbolic linkages among masculinity, strength, and power maintain meat's dominant place in the US diet" (95).

In contrast, vegetable-rich diets in US culture symbolize the lack of aggression and marginal substance associated with feminine ideals. Adams offers the most vivid example of vegetables as powerlessness, citing the adjective "vegetable" when applied to humans in a coma or suffering severe brain damage (36). Furthermore, McGann notes the rhetorical relationships between food and sexuality when "fruit" serves as a homophobic slur against men, which "[denigrates] women since it is gay men's identification with the feminine that is a negative marking" (88). One study even finds that respondents reliably match dietary preferences and personality traits, connecting vegetarianism to noncompetitive pacifists and burgers and fried chicken eaters with logic and competition (Sadalla and Burroughs).

The relationships between dietary behavior and personal and political identities mirror binary gender images of women as docile and men as active. The assumptions that women prefer salads and men prefer meat instantiates beliefs that women would rather lead a life of peace and men a life of action. The cultural tradition of saving meat for men grows from beliefs about meat's effect on the body as emboldening and empowering. Associations between men and meat seen in both social behavior research and cultural critiques solidify underlying notions that men naturally hold strength and power, while women merely stand by watching. Metrosexual food practices, which seek to either refine men's choices in terms of sophistication or health rationale, challenge distinctions between masculinity and femininity that food use in western culture has for so long helped to define and maintain. Examples of recent hamburger advertising discussed below reify the perception that men's new food choices effeminize them. As my primary case in point, I examine Burger King's commercial "Manthem" as a protestation of the heteromasculine belief that desiring beef emanates from a supposed instinctive masculine desire rather than as a function of their gender role performance. In the advertisement, burger consumption serves as a resistance to the fear that metrosexuality seeks to rob men of their social privilege through linkages with feminine performances.

A FEAST FIT FOR A KING

Against shifting norms of male food consumption, recent hamburger franchise advertising depicts eating beef as a heteromasculine activity done in the absence and at the expense of women. Burger King's commercial, "Manthem," provides an especially powerful example of beef consumption represented as a means for men to reassert a traditional masculinity, which occurs through rejecting femininity. Other advertisements by Burger King and Hardee's further meat's use as a means for men to re-affirm social dominance by symbolically consuming women. Elisabeth Badinter asserts that dominant US masculinity constitutes itself through a series of rejections, specifically, men refusing subordination and dependence, avoiding those things considered feminine, and denouncing any appearance of homosexuality (54, 115). Metrosexuality creates some obvious conflicts with this image. The advertisements I discuss here seek to restore an innate and traditional masculinity, as described by Badinter and others, against metrosexuality's influence.

Appropriating Helen Reddy's 1972 feminist liberation anthem, "I Am Woman," Burger King's "Manthem"—a *man's anthem*—engages in a parodic

emancipation of men from feminine domestication made material in diet. Promoting their Texas Double Whopper—a burger with two beef patties, bacon, jalapenos, and other burger fixings—Burger King suggests that eating a large burger defies efforts to domesticate and feminize men through their diet. Using the imagery of mass protest the commercial creates scenes of men renouncing both women and the foods women eat as an act of rebellion from oppressive and unnatural ways for men. That men eat meat as a rejection of feminine influence renders beef consumption a male activity that revels in a retrograde masculinity, one that celebrates more traditional gender performances over emerging images like that of the metrosexual.

The series of rejections in "Manthem" begins with the simultaneous rejection of women and feminine cuisine. In the opening scene a waiter in an elegant restaurant sets a plate with a single small shrimp, presented in the manner of an *amuse bouche*, before an attractive 20-something male-female couple. The young, trim man with a five-o'clock shadow looks up from his plate to begin singing, "I am man, hear me roar/In numbers too big to ignore/And I'm way too hungry to settle for chick food!" While singing, the man jilts his assumed date, abruptly leaving the table and storming out of the restaurant, tossing another piece of "chick food" from a plate a server carries past him. As the commercial progresses, we learn more about what constitutes amasculine food: "I'll admit I've been fed quiche!/Wave tofu bye-bye!/Now it's for Whopper beef I reach." Adams defines the relation between male-dominated ideology and meat consumption: "According to the mythology of patriarchal culture, meat promotes strength; the attributes of masculinity are achieved through eating these masculine foods" (33). Thus, the men wave "bye-bye" to nonmeat foods that deny them their social dominance. More shots of men pushing away plates of—we can presume—quiche makes clear the idea that women's feminine influence on men is embodied in the feminine foods women encourage men to eat.[4]

The justifications for rejecting women's food elaborate on the supposed innate differences between men and women. "Manthem" defines a masculinity associated with an animalistic, carnivorous instinct that requires fully satiating meals. Georg Hegel writes of the differences assumed between men and women as analogous to elements of nature: "The difference between men and women is like that between animals and plants. Men correspond to animals, while women correspond to plants because their development is more placid" (263). Likewise, one of the men of "Manthem" declares, "my stomach's starting to growl/And I'm going on the prowl." Where both Helen Reddy and the "Manthem" men want you to "hear me roar," Burger King reminds its consumers that men, not women, "growl" and "prowl," as do predatory carnivores of the wild seeking satiation from animal meat:

> I will eat this meat / ([Chorus] Eat this meat) /
> 'Til my innie turns into an outie. / I am starved! /
> I am incorrigible! / And I need to scarf a big burger, beef, bacon, jalapeño, good thing down!

The men explain that their desire to "scarf. . . . down" beef until their navels invert ("innie turns into an outie") comes from both their deep hunger ("starved") and their inability to become domesticated ("incorrigible"). Subsequently, men's desire for eating equates to a wild animal uncontrollably gorging on its kill. Such an image stands entirely opposite to common ideals for feminine behavior and metrosexuality. Having left women and feminine foods behind, the men can glory in a rapacious consumption all their own.

The flight from the feminine in "Manthem" stresses the desire for a retrograde masculinity to denounce women and their influences upon masculinity. Against recent images of masculinity, especially the metrosexual, that challenge traditional heteromasculine assumptions, the commercial uses beef eating as an opportunity to enliven supposedly fading masculine performances that emphasize men's difference from women. Badinter writes that "To be a man signifies *not* to be feminine, . . . *not* to be effeminate in one's physical appearance or manners" (115, emphasis in original). Though the metrosexual does not necessarily deny carnivorous inclinations, the refinement associated with metrosexuality curbs what is otherwise seen as a base, biological masculine desire. As *Queer Eye* shows us, men with polished tastes eat bluefish from cedar planks, not burgers from wax-paper wrappers.

Against the attempts to be domesticated and refined, Burger King's men publicly protest for freedom to perform a retrograde masculinity. The public demonstration in "Manthem" engages in a parody of liberation that borrows from imagery of struggles for equality, which simultaneously undercuts the signified images' importance. Denouncing an effeminized masculinity, the men in Burger King's commercial take to the streets in mass protest. As a mob of men marches through the streets others rush away from women to join the manly crowd of young men. One man running into the scene wears a moisturizing mud mask, symbolizing the aesthetic influence of feminine culture upon men that "Manthem" means to reject through eating a burger. In the mostly white crowd, some men carry signs that read plainly, "I Am Man." The reference to the 1968 Memphis sanitation-workers strike—when Black men wore sandwich boards reading, "I AM A MAN"—parodies and thereby detracts from more serious fights for equality. In another shot we see men tearing their underwear from under their clothes and tossing them into a burning barrel, both mimicking and mocking 1968 Miss America pageant when women symbolically—not literally—burned their brassieres. As Bonnie Dow says of the bra-burning myth itself, the parody belittles and dismisses women's very serious struggle for social equality (130). Rather than protesting treatment as second-class citizens, the men in "Manthem" are merely "way too hungry to settle for chick food." Even still, "Manthem" expresses the sense that men have endured oppression, here at the hands of women and feminine culture, from which they now wish to escape.

The fullness of the commercial's association between males' meat consumption and championing a retrograde masculinity arrives when the men literally discard a symbol of their familial domestication, the minivan. For the last two decades the minivan, replacing the station wagon, has symbolized utter domestication for men and women, bespeaking familial commitment over personal desires represented by the sporty two-seat automobile. Amidst the mob of men congregating to protest their right to meat, the minivan screeches in, and from it emerges the only man easily visible in the mob that does not have a trim body and only the second man in the commercial to wear glasses. As such, he represents men who have "softened" from domestic life. His slightly zaftig form suggests a man who no longer has the time for the personal indulgences of playing sports or going to the gym in light of familial responsibilities. Stepping away from his vehicle, the minivan driver slams the door behind him to seize a burger and hoist it proudly above his head with both hands in an act of triumphal rebellion. As the mob cheers, they move in on the minivan, which they proceed to pick up and throw from the elevated roadway onto a dump truck below. In so doing, the men physically reject the trappings of domestication as an act concurrent and equitable

with claiming their desire for beef consumption.

As the discarded minivan falls from the bridge, the scene below creates the hyper image of an idealized masculinity and femininity that bares no resemblance to the world the "Manthem" men reject. The minivan discarded from above falls into an oversized dump truck, which when then see linked by chains to a circus strong-man. The large man, valued only for his girth and physical strength, lurches forward with the dump truck and minivan in tow. Before the hulking man stands a slender young blonde woman in a tight, pink top and pant set smiling at the strong man as she holds a shining snow shovel before him on which rests Burger King's Texas Double Whopper. The man pulling the dump truck represents a hypermasculinity, beyond most men's actual desire, based strictly in the value of musculature and strength. As an excessive figure of masculinity, merely a body, he represents the end of the spectrum toward which the "Manthem" men run as they flee a feminine diet and a subsequently more delicate frame. By placing the attractive woman holding out a juicy burger before the strong man, we see a man as a carnivorous animal trudging forward in pursuit of his reward, meat. It remains unclear, however, which reward the man craves more, the burger or the woman. Of course, within the retrograde masculinity depicted, women and meat are one in the same. They are both prizes: they both represent dominant masculinity's goals, and they both emphasize men's consumptive impulses (both sexual and dietetic) as essential to their maleness.

By relying upon the cultural relationships between men, meat, and masculinity, Burger King sells its oversized hamburger as men's opportunity to seize a retrograde masculinity, which has supposedly been eroded by the appearance of the metrosexual and men's increased involvement in the home. The repeated rejections in "Manthem" of women, femininity, and domesticity reiterate the compulsion for a masculinity that places men and men's concerns as preeminent. Within the laughter the commercial means to provoke, a discourse for supporting men's social privilege finds new life. Parasecoli's analysis of men's health magazines includes the example from one article that encourages men to perform cunnilingus (i.e., *eat* her out) on the kitchen table while snacking on foods to add better flavor to the experience (32). The interchangeability of sexual engagement with women and consuming food further demonstrates the unity of both activities in a misogynistic heteromasculinity. Two other recent hamburger advertisements also fuse men's beef consumption with their heteromasculine desire.

Burger King's 2006 Super Bowl commercial collapses men's food and women's bodies into one and the same idea. In the style of an elaborate 1950s stage show, women dressed as burger patties, hamburger buns, lettuce, tomatoes, and other burger fixings dance and smile prettily, some of whom wear skintight clothing cleverly covering their breasts and genital region. Looking into the camera, smiling and winking as appropriate, they sing, "Yes, we're tasty and eye popping/We don't blame your jaw for dropping. . . . Ask away, we're always willing to make one your way." As the women sing these lines, a woman in a close-fitting, open-back red dress with tomato slices as a wide hat and skirt leads the camera behind her, glancing seductively over her shoulder as she continues on. The words and sexual teasing mix together heteromasculine desire for food and women's bodies as the food-clad women describe themselves as "tasty," "eye popping," and "jaw dropping." At the commercial's climax the women are thrown in a pile of human flesh to create a living hamburger as the words "Have it your way" drone on. The commercial's completion presents the women as malleable to men's desires and ready for

consumption. The 1950s fantasy—a somewhat literal return to a retrograde gender relations—presents men's burger consumption as an escape to their earlier, unrefined ways, when gender relations held a stronger dualism than the vagaries encouraged by metrosexuality.

Hardee's also relates eating burgers to consuming women, but in a more naked celebration of heteromasculine desires. In "Cheater," we see an attractive 20-something man eating a burger as an autobody crew attempts to buff out from the side of his car the spray-painted word, "CHEATER." As the young man smirks at the scene, the voiceover adds, "Sometimes having three girlfriends is great. Other times it's just expensive." The man's meat intake and the smirking pride of dating three women at once demonstrates his consumptive desires. In both instances we see the frightening reality of meat as a metonym for women's bodies. Against cultural changes seeking gender egalitarianism, the young man in question still enjoys consuming freely unrestrained, whether meat or women.

The images of men and women in the burger advertising discussed above present a world in which men enjoy beef consumption as an extension and performance of their rights to independence, resistance to metrosexual effeminization, and heterosexual desire. Butler contends that binary gender roles, like those perpetuated in the commercials here, maintain a "compulsory and naturalized heterosexuality" (22). In "Manthem," especially, we see young men rejecting a newly popularized masculine image, the metrosexual, in favor of a "true," traditional masculinity based in biological essence rather than a learned gender role. The masculinity "Manthem" embraces suggests men have a primal nature as carnivores that feminine influence seeks to squelch, emblematic of men's natural dominance women likewise wish to tame. Kenneth Burke describes the power of metonymy as its ability to reduce complex relations into something more basic, thus, enabling humans to "to convey some incorporeal or intangible state in terms of the corporeal or tangible" (506). Here, burgers and burger consumption subsume a complex set of changing gender and sexual relations into a statement of men's perpetual right to take what they will as their own. Burger King's 2006 Super Bowl commercial and Hardee's "Cheater" emphasize that women, like the burgers men prefer to eat, exist for men's pleasure. Just as the commercials forgo questioning the assumption that men have a God-given need for beef over any other food, the advertisements accept without question that men also have the right to women's bodies. Richard Nate explains that metonyms, over metaphors, often illustrate social conditions through closely related expressions (496). Put another way, critics need not look far to find the thing represented by a metonym, for it is the placeholder of an object close at hand rather than highly abstract. The utter collapse of women with food, especially in Burger King's Super Bowl ad, speaks to a conflation of sexual and culinary desires, men having the absolute right to enjoy both at their will and without restraint.

CONCLUSION: BIG BOYS, BIG BURGERS, AND BIG CARS

Masculinity, as much as femininity, exists in a state of flux without any single definition able to capture either cultural ideals or practices. Retrograde masculinity denies such an assertion about itself, perpetuating the myth that within men lies an essential masculinity corrupted by the likes of metrosexuality. Despite such a protest R. W. Connell stresses that we must speak of masculinities as existing in relation to one another, whether competing or supporting (37). Metrosexuality as a masculinity popularized in recent years, offers but

one definition for masculinity, whereas traditional masculinity, as described by Badinter, constitutes itself by fleeing from anything that approaches femininity, signals weakness, or suggests homosexuality. The link between masculinity and meat, suggesting the consumption of strength and muscle, emanates from traditions surpassing those found in the contemporary US. A seeming anthropological imperative of a patriarchal culture, meat connotes men's assumed dominance and thereby women's disassociation from both the food and the privilege. The heterosexist assumption that gay men mimic women, including their dietary behaviors and corporeal discipline, suggests that gay men refrain from eating meat or large quantities of any food for fear of spoiling their "girlish figure." Against homophobic disdain for gay men as necessarily effeminate, metrosexuality accepts those things previously considered too feminine for men and thereby queer. As I have argued here, some recent hamburger franchise advertising seeks to capitalize on the anxieties resulting from ever broadening masculine ideals. The use of beef eating as an evocation of a retrograde masculinity, one celebrating masculine norms challenged by metrosexuality and domestic participation, speaks to the vitality of existing cultural beliefs about meat as a proper male food that attains its virility through the exclusion of women.

Badinter foreshadows metrosexuality in 1992, writing of changes to masculinity in dominant US culture in which "young men do not identify either with the caricatured virility of the past or with a total rejection of masculinity" (183). It is worth noting that protagonist males in the commercials described here all occupy the age group of men whom Badinter describes as "Sons of more virile women and more feminine men" (183). The flux within accepted heteromasculine performances and an increasing—though never fully realized—gender egalitarianism questions, however subtly, men's presumed privilege and produces anxiety for some men as their status changes. The hamburger commercials discussed above demonstrate a response to these changes and anxieties. Burger King and Hardee's both suggest that by enjoying hamburgers men can seize a supposedly stable component to masculinity, their natural desire for animal flesh. By extension, eating a burger also allows men to engage in a cultural performance of sexual domination. The allusions to a retrograde masculinity fortifies men's sense of self amidst masculinities fluctuating more rapidly than before.

Obviously, the anxieties and tensions resulting from diversifying masculinities play themselves out in venues other than the dinner table. Hummer's "Restore the Balance" commercial promotes men driving a sports utility vehicle as an assertion of masculinity against "feminized" lifestyle choices represented by a health-conscious diet. "Restore the Balance" opens with the mundane scene of an attractive, 20-something white male at the grocery store checkout counter. As the checker rings up his clearly-labeled tofu—which the "Manthem" men "wave bye-bye"—and vegetables, the young man in question looks in the direction of the attractive, 20-something male behind him in line. The second man's items include a rack of ribs, a package of steaks, and bag of charcoal. The look on the first man's face registers self-consciousness about his purchase. The shot of them side-by-side at the checkout counter, facing forward, mimics men's posture at a urinal, with the first man disappointed in himself when he sees what "meat" the second man boasts.[5] Upon noticing a Hummer advertisement on the magazine rack, the self-doubting man leaves with his groceries and proceeds posthaste in his small, yellow sedan to a Hummer dealership, where he quickly and assertively buys a Hummer off the showroom floor, throwing his groceries in the rear-storage compartment before heading out. As the man drives home, projecting self-assured

masculinity, he takes a vigorous bite from a carrot, while the words, "RESTORE THE BALANCE" occupy the screen's lower half.

The question, of course, is "What balance does the Hummer restore?" It would seem that for the commercial's protagonist, it restores the balance in his life between the feminine foods he purchases after leaving his home and the masculinity he buys on his way back. In fact, the commercial's original tagline read, "RESTORE YOUR MANHOOD," but quickly became "RESTORE THE BALANCE" after negative market response (Lavrinc). The idea that the men who select nonmeat foods have lost their manhood, which they can restore by purchasing a large, military-repurposed vehicle, makes it clear that men who eat tofu, vegetables, and the like lose the strength and power crucial to most masculine definitions. General Motor's choice to call for restoring "balance" in place of "manhood" suggests more than the original message concerning meat, strength, and manhood. The emphasis on "balance" also indicates that new ideals of masculinity have become out of balance. The commercial both expresses and responds to an anxiety that men have become too influenced by an effeminizing culture and must grasp at aspects of traditional masculinity to remain stable. The dangers of equating eating meat with successful masculinity need little explanation. The Physicians Committee for Responsible Medicine specifically criticizes "Manthem" and "Restore the Balance" for encouraging men to court heart disease and other life-threatening illnesses: "This new genre of TV ads is tantamount to daring men to smoke or abuse alcohol" (Physicians). Sadly, men have also followed just such dares in efforts to prove their manhood.

The need to prove and maintain manhood motivates the celebrations of a retrograde masculinity present in some hamburger advertising. These overtures to a traditional masculinity attempt to fortify manhood as a given against indicators to the contrary. The "Manthem" men predicate their protests on the belief in an essential, biologically determined masculinity. Such an assumption drives the vernacular notion that men are "uncomplicated" because they act on natural inclinations unlike women who perform their gender, overtly contemplating their choices and practices (e.g., diet and physical appearance). The white, middle-class, able-bodied, straight men depicted in hamburger advertising largely enjoy a social privilege they can take for granted. Men's cognizance of their food choices and appearance—their gender performances—jeopardizes heteromasculine hegemony by questioning the presumption that "men are men" and have a natural right to their privilege. To mediate the crisis "Manthem" depicts metrosexuality as a masquerade, a fiction masking truth (Brod 17). Celebrating a retrograde masculinity eschews the suggestion that men have a gender rather than a sex, presupposing that they—unlike women—act merely on the intrinsic impulses of a "real man" rather than out of concern for social prescription. Advertising that attempts to "restore the balance" by re-asserting men's social position over women ensconces heteromasculinity as prediscursive, thereby fixing heterosexuality itself as natural to the human experience (Butler 148). Certainly men eating meat does not directly correlate to masculine anxiety. The commercials discussed here, however, do signify, one, some men's anxieties as "what it means to be man" diversifies, two, the importance of framing a retrograde masculinity as natural to maintain heteronormativity, and, three, the potential to capitalize on male disquietude. Food has long played a role in instantiating a gender hierarchy: the attempts described here to imply that beef consumption anchors masculinity present only the latest examples.

ACKNOWLEDGEMENT

An earlier version of this essay was presented at the 2007 meeting of the Mid-Atlantic Popular/American Culture Association. Philadelphia, PA.

NOTES

1. Deutsch notes this assumption as well, drawing from popular press imagery of male-only Neanderthals cooking meat over fire (109–10).
2. Robert Brannon defines traditional masculinity's core elements as the edicts "no sissy stuff," "be a big wheel," "be a sturdy oak," and "give 'em hell." Similarly, Nick Trujillo finds that idealized masculinity includes physical force and control, occupational achievement, familial patriarchy, frontiersmanship, and heterosexuality.
3. Though the numbers suggested vary, the National Eating Disorders Association (NEDA) finds that in the US as many as 10 million women suffer from bulimia or anorexia. Though equally serious in nature but less so in occurrence, the NEDA also estimates one tenth as many US men as women struggle with those same eating disorders. The National Institute of Mental Health, a division of the National Institute of Health, reports similar statistics regarding the number and prevalence of eating disorders among women over men. The Academy for Eating Disorders underscores the frequency of eating disorders among women, noting that beyond the number of women diagnosed, as many as "10 percent or more of late adolescent and adult women report symptoms of eating disorders."
4. Research shows that some men assimilate their eating behaviors to be more like their wives, which often includes reducing the amount of meat consumed (Sobal 146–17).
5. My thanks to John Suits for bringing this reading to my attention.

REFERENCES

Academy for Eating Disorders. "Prevalence of Eating Disorders." 11 Feb. 2007 <http:drwww.aedweb.org/eating_disorders/prevalence.cfm>.
Adams, Carol J. The Sexual Politics of Meat: A Feminist-Vegetarian Critical Theory. New York: Continuum, 1990.
Badinter, Elisabeth. XY: On Masculine Identity. Trans. Lydia Davis. New York: Columbia UP, 1995.
Bartky, Sandra. "Foucault, Femininity, and the Modernization of Patriarchal Power." Free

Spirits: Feminist Philosophers on Culture. Ed. Kate Mehuron and Gary Percesepe. Englewood Cliffs, NJ: Prentice Hall, 1995. 240–56.

Basow, Susan A., and Diane Kobrynowicz. "The Effects of Meal Size on Impressions of a Female Eater." *Sex Roles* 28 (1993): 335—41.

Bock, Beth C., and Robin B Kanarek. "Women and Men are What They Eat: The Effects of Gender and Reported Meal Size on Perceived Characteristics." *Sex Roles* 33 (1995): 109–19.

Bordo, Susan. *The Male Body: A New Look at Men in Public and in Private.* New York: Farrar, Straus, and Giroux, 1999.

——. *Unbearable Weight: Feminism, Western Culture, and the Body.* Berkeley: U of California P, 1993.

Brannon, Robert. "The Male Sex Role: Our Culture's Blueprint of Manhood and What it's Done for Us Lately." *The Forty-Nine Percent Majority: The Male Sex Role.* Ed. Deborah David and Robert Brannon. Reading, MA: Addison-Wesley, 1976. 1–14.

Brod, Harry. "Masculinity as Masquerade." *The Masculine Masquerade: Masculinity and Representation.* Ed. Andrew Perchuk and Helaine Posner. Cambridge: MIT P, 1995. 13–19.

Brod, Harry, and Michael Kaufman, eds. *Theorizing Masculinities.* Thousand Oaks, CA: Sage, 1994.

Buchbinder, David. *Performance Anxieties: Re-producing Masculinity.* Malaysia: Allen and Unwin, 1998.

Burke, Kenneth. *A Grammar of Motives.* 1945. Berkeley: U of California P, 1969.

Butler, Judith. *Gender Trouble: Feminism and the Subversion of Identity.* New York: Routledge, 1990.

Chaiken, Shelly, and Patricia Pliner. "Women, but Not Men, are What They Eat: The Effect of Meal Size and Gender on Perceived Femininity and Masculinity." *Personality and Social Psychology Bulletin* 13 (1987): 166–76.

Clarkson, Jay. "Contesting Masculinity's Makeover: Queer Eye, Consumer Masculinity, and 'Straight Acting' Gays." *Journal of Communication Inquiry* 29 (2005): 235–55.

Connell, R. W. *Masculinities.* Berkeley: U of California P, 1995.

Craig, Steven, ed. *Men, Masculinity and the Media.* Newbury Park, CA: Sage, 1992. 9–22.

Deutsch, Jonathan. " 'Please Pass the Chicken Tits': Rethinking Men and Cooking at an Urban Firehouse." *Food and Foodways* 13 (2005): 91–114.

Dow, Bonnie J. "Feminism, Miss America, and Media Mythology." *Rhetoric and Public Affairs* 6 (2003): 127–49.

Frazer, James George. *The New Golden Bough: A New Abridgement of the Classic Work.* Ed. Theodor H. Gaster. New York: Criterion, 1959.

Hegel, Georg Wilhelm Friedrich. *Philosophy of Right.* Trans. Thomas M. Knox. London: Oxford UP, 1952.

Heinz, Bettina, and Roland Lee. "Getting Down to the Meat: The Symbolic Construction of Meat Consumption." *Communication Studies* 49 (1998): 86–99.

Julier, Alice, and Laura Lindenfeld. "Mapping Men onto the Menu: Masculinities and Food." *Food and Foodways* 13 (2005): 1–16.

Kaufman, Michael, ed. *Beyond Patriarchy: Essays by Men on Pleasure, Power, and Change.* Toronto: Oxford UP, 1987. 195–215.

Kimmel, Michael S., ed. *Changing Men: New Directions in Research on Men and Masculinity.* Newbury Park, CA: Sage, 1987.

——. *Manhood in America: A Cultural History.* New York: Free, 1996.

Kimmel, Michael S., and Michael A. Messner, eds. *Men's Lives.* 3rd ed. Boston: Allyn and Bacon, 1995.

Lavrinc, Damon. "Restore Your Manhood: Hummer Ad Revised." *Autoblog.com.* 7 Aug. 2006. 18 Aug. 2007 <http:drwww.autoblog.com/2006/08/07/restore-your-manhood-hummer-ad-revised/>.

Levi, Annette, Kenny K. Chan, and Dan Pence. "Real Men Do Not Read Labels: The Effects of Masculinity and Involvement on College Students' Food Decisions." *Journal of American College Health* 55.2 (2006): 91–98.

Levine, Martin P. *Gay Macho: The Life and Death of the Homosexual Clone.* Ed. Michael S. Kimmel. New York: New York UP, 1998.

Martz, Denise M., Kevin B. Handley, and Richard M Eisler. "The Relationship between Feminine Gender Role Stress, Body Image, and Eating Disorders." *Psychology of Women Quarterly* 19 (1995): 493–508.

McGann, Patrick. "Eating Muscle: Material-Semiotics and a Manly Appetite." *Revealing Male Bodies.* Ed. Nancy Tuana, William Cowling, Maurice Hamington, Greg Johnson, and Terrance Macmullan. Bloomington: Indiana UP, 2002. 83–99.

Mechling, Jay. "Boy Scouts and the Manly Art of Cooking." *Food and Foodways* 12 (2005): 67–89.

Messner, Michael A. *Power at Play: Sports and the Problem of Masculinity.* Boston: Beacon, 1992.

Messner, Michael A., and Donald F. Sabo, eds. *Sport, Men and the Gender Order: Critical Feminist Perspectives.* Champaign, IL: Human Kinetics, 1990.

Miller, Toby. "A Metrosexual Eye on *Queer Guy.*" *GLQ: A Journal of Lesbian and Gay Studies* 11 (2005): 112–17.

Mooney, Kim M., and Erica Lorenz. "The Effects of Food and Gender on Interpersonal Perceptions." *Sex Roles* 36 (1997): 639–53.

Mooney, Kim M., Joanne DeTore, and Kristin A Malloy. "Perceptions of Women Related to Food Choice." *Sex Roles* 31 (1994): 433–2.

Mori, DeAnna, Shelly Chaiken, and Patricia Pliner.
"'Eating Lightly' and the Self-Presentation of
Femininity." *Journal of Personality and Social
Psychology* 53 (1987): 693–702.

Nate, Richard. "Metonymy." *Encyclopedia of
Rhetoric*. Ed. Thomas O. Sloane. Oxford: Oxford
UP, 2001.

National Eating Disorders Association. "Statistics:
Eating Disorders and their Precursors." 11 Feb.
2007 <http://www.nationaleatingdisorders.org/p.
asp?WebPage_ID=286&Profile_ID=41138>.

National Institute of Mental Health. "The Numbers
Count: Mental Disorders in America." Rev. 2006.
11 Feb. 2007 <http://www.nimh.nih.gov/publicat/
numbers.cfm>.

O'Doherty Jensen, Katherine, and Lotte Holm..
"Preferences, Quantities and Concerns: Socio-
cultural   Perspectives   on   the   Gendered
Consumption of Foods." *European Journal of
Clinical Nutrition* 53 (1999): 351–59.

Parasecoli, Fabio. "Feeding Hard Bodies: Food and
Masculinities in Men's Fitness Magazines." *Food
and Foodways* 12 (2005): 17–37.

Physicians Committee for Responsible Medicine.
What's the Worst "Badvertisement"? 7 Dec. 2006.
18   Aug.   2007   <http://www.pcrm.org/news/
release061207.html>.

Pleck, Elizabeth H., and Joseph H. Pleck, eds. *The
American Man*. Englewood Cliffs, NJ: Prentice
Hall, 1980.

Pliner, Patricia, and Shelly Chaiken. "Eating, Social
Motives, and Self-Presentation in Women and
Men." *Journal of Experimental Social Psychology*
26 (1990): 240–54.

Pronger, Brian. *The Arena of Masculinity: Sports
Homosexuality, and the Meaning of Sex*. New
York: St. Martin's, 1990.

Ramsey, E. Michele, and Gladys Santiago. "The
Conflation of Male Homosexuality and Femininity

in *Queer Eye for the Straight Guy.*" *Feminist
Media Studies* 4 (2004): 353–55.

Sadalla, Edward, and Jeffrey Burroughs. "Profiles in
Eating: Sexy Vegetarians and Other Diet-based
Social Stereotypes." *Psychology Today* (Oct.
1981): 51–57.

Saukko, Paula. "Rereading Media and Eating
Disorders: Karen Carpenter, Princess Diana, and
the Healthy Female Self." *Critical Studies in
Media Communication* 23 (2006): 152–69.

Scott, JulieAnn. "Performing Unfeminine Femininity:
A Performance of Identity Analysis of Bulimic
Women's   Personal   Narratives."   *Text   and
Performance Quarterly* 28 (2008): 116–38.

Simpson, Mark. "Meet the Metrosexual." *Salon.
com* 22 July 2002. 1 Mar. 2007 <http:drdir.salon.
com/story/ent/feature/2002/07/22/metrosexual/
index.html>.

Sobal, Jeffrey. "Men, Meat, and Marriage: Models
of Masculinity." *Food and Foodways* 12 (2005):
135–58.

Spitzack, Carole. "The Spectacle of Anorexia
Nervosa." *Text and Performance Quarterly* 13
(1993): 1–20.

Thompson, Kevin, and Leslie J. Heinberg. "The
Media's Influence on Body Image Disturbance and
Eating Disorders: We've Reviled Them, Now Can
We Rehabilitate Them?" *Journal of Social Issues*
55 (1999): 339–53.

Trujillo,   Nick.   "Hegemonic   Masculinity   on
the Mound: Media Representations of Nolan
Ryan and American Sports Culture." *Critical
Studies   in   Mass   Communication* 8 (1991):
290–308.

Westerfelhaus, Robert, and Celeste Lacroix. "Seeing
'Straight' Through *Queer Eye*: Exposing the
Strategic Rhetoric of Heteronormativity in a
Mediated Ritual of Gay Rebellion." *Critical Studies
in Media Communication* 23 (2006): 426–44.

19

"Please Pass the Chicken Tits": Rethinking Men and Cooking at an Urban Firehouse

Jonathan Deutsch

"... Feeding others is women's work. Women collect, prepare, and serve our daily bread. So doing, they care for us. The acts of feeding and caring, as connected to each other as earth to water, maintain and sustain the family."
–Catharine R. Stimpson (in DeVault 1991, viii)

The above quotation from Stimpson solidifies much of our thinking about women, food, and family. Women, for centuries, have been the primary cooks and nurturers in most cultures. They have filled this role with great success amidst careers, household management, child raising and eldercare, social demands, and a host of other obligations and obstacles (DeVault 1991; Ellis 1983; Murcott 1983). Men, on the other hand, rarely represent family primary food providers (Warde and Hetherington 1994; DeVault 1991; Ekstrom 1991; Charles and Kerr 1988).

Of course, it is hardly unusual to see a man in the professional food sphere. A quick check of the food network line-up (foodtv.com) will help to reveal where the gender balance lies, at least in the professional sphere: Emeril Lagasse, Mario Batali, Ming Tsai, Alton Brown, David Rosengarten, Jamie Oliver, and the Iron Chef's dwarf Sara Moulton, Rachel Ray, and the Two Fat Ladies. The titles "Iron Chef" and "Two Fat Ladies" work to emphasize this disparity even further. On the other side of the continuum, we have also accepted and embraced the idea of

men cooking recreationally. Backyard barbecues complete with "kiss the cook" aprons are as masculine a phenomenon as mowing the lawn or scowling under the hood of a car in suburban Middle America. Adler (1981) helps to codify the idea that an important part of fatherhood in the United States is preparing a festal signature dish. But between these extremes of cooking men, from professional chef to recreational "burgermeister," is another important, and often neglected group of male cooks—men who are domestic cooks, who feel a need to and choose to cook.

My interest lies in what happens when men who are not food professionals take on this role as primary cook for a group of people. I recently spent a year doing qualitative fieldwork with one such group, the men of an urban firehouse, Engine 3000 (a pseudonym). These are men— and they are all men—who choose to shop and cook two-to-three times daily to feed their group.

Men in this scenario perform in roles typically ascribed to both men and women, and when a woman is involved, her presence is mitigated, as she is an outsider, a dinner guest, or "exception to the norm" (McCarl 1985). I found that the men created a unique food system, and while each brings intact a value system and ethnic heritage to the table, these packages become negotiated, in many ways most powerfully in the kitchen and at the table, as when an African-American Muslim and

Irish-American Catholic need to make food decisions to feed the firehouse.

I was interested in how these men perform in roles that, in popular culture, we often ascribe to women. How do they shop, cook, and eat? How do they feel about what they are doing? How and why do they choose to cook? What issues do they face with regard to their identity as men, and how does this influence their food choices, cooking, and eating? By observing and interviewing men in the role of amateur cook as primary food provider for a group, I was challenged to rethink many of my preconceived ideas about men and cooking. Specifically, I was surprised that what the literature and popular culture agreed was largely a manly or masculine way of cooking—huge chunks of greasy meat, signature dishes, and high status items—was almost entirely at odds with the cooking I observed among these men, whose cooking gravitated more toward being what both the literature and popular culture consider to be domestic, even feminine. But the tension between machismo in an all-male setting and the nurturing, domestic aspects of everyday cooking for a "family" of "brothers" brought with it some fascinating permutations.

As Sobal suggests (in this issue), gendered foodways, rather than being a singular behavior set, are more likely a pluralistic set of scripts, where actors draw on the script that works for their setting in place and time. The data from this study reinforce Sobal's iteration. Consistent with Coltrane's (1989) work on household labor, the men of Engine 3000, faced with "feminine" or "motherly" tasks, embrace their performance, but in this case, they do so in a decidedly self-conscious way, a proverbial winking over one's shoulder. Observing these men's activities and descriptions of cooking for each other, we can uncover a nuanced performance of domesticity that allows men to draw upon multiple versions of masculinity in their everyday lives.

FIREHOUSE COOKING

Firehouse cooking has become entrenched in American popular culture. Firefighters conspicuously shop en masse, author cookbooks (cf. Bonanno 1995; Adams 1993; DePasquale 1993; Sineno 1986), and demonstrate their recipes on television. Excluding foodservice professionals, no other occupation is so deeply and publicly involved in shopping, cooking, and eating as part of their work lives.

It is notable that firehouse cooking has come to figure so prominently in popular culture, since there are many obstacles associated with it. Perhaps the most important obstacle materially is that most fire departments have never financially supported fire-house cooking. Firefighters, both in Engine 3000 and elsewhere, negotiate the menu among themselves, shop together for food with the fire truck, so that if they receive a call, they will be ready to abandon their carts at the market and go to the emergency, and divide the cost for each meal among those present. Moreover, the firefighters contribute to a commissary fund to provide staple ingredients and to fund necessary maintenance on their kitchen equipment.

Another obstacle to firehouse cooking is the obviously unpredictable nature of firehouse life. Smith (1972), a New York City firefighter writes, "I once kept a running account of how many meals I could eat in the firehouse without interruption. It went for three and a half months, and in that time, I never ate one uninterrupted meal." Furthermore, firefighters in the department where my fieldwork was done received no formal training with regard to food and cooking. Indeed, nutritional information was couched within larger training sessions on health and wellness. This lack of knowledge can produce some unsavory results among the new recruits, such as raw hamburgers cooked in their buns in the oven (Sineno 1986).

Though the obstacles to firehouse cooking may be significant from a materialist standpoint, firehouse meals have important social functions that go unacknowledged by department administrators and training materials. In a corporate environment, these functions might be called "acculturation," "diversity training," and "feedback sessions." Chetkovich (1997), in a study of a firefighter training class and subsequent placement in the field, notes that housework, and especially cooking, serve as "proving grounds" for the new recruits. In the urban fire department, it is not sufficient to perform well at the fire ground or to master the book knowledge, but one has to prove oneself competent and active in firehouse culture. This may include learning one another's cultural tastes and experiences, adapting to each firehouse's meal system, and debriefing from the day, done most typically in the kitchen and at table (McCarl 1985). Working together smoothly in the relaxed atmosphere of the firehouse kitchen may be seen, at least unofficially, as insurance that the group will be able to work well in the stressful emergency environment.

While firehouse cooking may endure as a pop culture icon, it also has value behind the closed doors of the firehouse. The firefighter never knows which meal will be his or her last, and may feel this more saliently than most people do (Smith 1972). Firefighters tend to celebrate the everyday and, negotiating the intricacies of the meal, cook elaborate meals together. The raucous and convivial atmosphere at meals can be explained by this underlying sense of urgency.

INSIDE ENGINE 3000

Engine 3000 in many ways, could be considered a typical urban firehouse in the U.S.[1] It is a double house, consisting of a ladder company and an engine company that work together. While both respond to fires, the ladder company also handles incidents such as gas leaks and elevator emergencies, while the engine company firefighters have additional training to respond to medical calls.

All of the house's firefighters on the roster are men and most are white. Fourteen men work at a time, in varying shifts. Of the core group of twenty-two men that I studied, four were African-American. The rest were white, largely Italian-American and Irish-American, with a few other European-Americans among them. Twenty of the twenty-two lived in the suburbs. Eighteen were married, and one divorced. None was openly gay, bisexual, or transgender. Ages ranged from twenty-five to fifty-four, with most in their late-thirties to mid-forties. The men largely self-identify themselves as "working class," regardless of actual household income. The firehouse was located in a relatively affluent area of the city with somewhat of a suburban feel. This was considered desirable among the firefighters, and many had been on waiting lists to transfer to this house from poorer areas of the city. The neighborhood's affluence makes this house desirable among the men for its slower pace, access to good shopping, safe parking, and lower incidence of false alarms. Located near major highways, the house is also considered desirable for its easy commute from the suburbs.

COOKING IN ENGINE 3000

The timeline for a typical Engine 3000 evening meal is typically as represented in the Table 19.1. Lunch follows approximately the same pattern, but begins around eleven o'clock in the morning. Edited log notes to give context to the timeline follow:

Toward the end of the evening news, the struck arrives with food. Everyone mobilizes once the food arrives. Barney explains, for my benefit, that every-one cooks. Cliff

Table 19.1 Engine 3000 meal timeline

Times (all are approximate)	Typical activity
5:30 PM–6:30 PM	Discuss, Negotiate and Decide on Meal. The night tour begins work at 6 PM, with many firefighters arriving early to socialize. Deciding the evening's menu is among the first orders of business.
6:30 PM–7:30 PM	Cooks shop. The company that will be cooking for the evening shops at the local supermarket, approximately a ten-minute drive away. The men go together and drive in the fire truck. There is a closer market of the same brand across the street from the firehouse but the men only shop there if they forget something.
7:30 PM–9:00 PM	Cooking. The cook for the meal assigns prep work and the men sit around the large dining room table with knives and cutting boards to prepare the ingredients. When they finish, the men take their ingredients to the kitchen where the cook, usually with one or two self-selected assistants prepares the rest of the meal.
8:30 PM–9:00 PM	"Nosh." Men eat an appetizer and begin to set the table for dinner. Plates are laid out along one end of the dining table where the cooks distribute the food.
9:00 PM–9:45 PM	Meal is served. The men take their plates pre-filled with the main dishes from one end of the table and add additional ingredients.
9:45 PM–10:45 PM	Cleanup. The company that does not cook cleans up after the meal.
11:00 PM	Dessert. Self-service, typically store-bought ice cream, cake, or pastries.

takes charge and tells everyone what to do. Cliff tells me that they're having Chicken Cacciatore. He asks Barney to slice peppers, Dave to cut onions, Eddie to peel garlic, while Gary goes to work cutting jarred roasted peppers (he does this on his own, without direction from Cliff). Gary precisely cuts the peppers in half to make translucent sheets. These sheets will later be tossed with garlic and olive oil, and served on toasted bread for the "nosh." [I think it is funny that these largely Italian, Irish, and African American men throw the word "nosh" around. It is a word I associate with my [Jewish] grandmother and sounds cacophonie when used in a sentence like "Yo assholes, come in for nosh," as it was said over the intercom at the firehouse]. The vegetable prep was done in the dining room, sitting at the tables, and as the vegetables were cut, the men would bring them into the kitchen to Cliff, who was doing the cooking. I asked how they decided to make Chicken Cacciatore, and I was told it was by committee. Cliff was in the mood for "sauce," Gary was in the mood for chicken, and when they put their heads together, this

is what they got. After the prep is done, the dining room clears out. Four men try to get a dart game together and go upstairs to play. Others exercise, watch TV, or sleep until dinner.

Despite the work involved, the position of "cook" seems a desirable role within the firehouse, especially since conflicts about who *will* cook are resolved by seniority. I ask Barney why this is the case:

When you're the cook
You're
I don't know
You're the *man*
You're the *dog*
You say *hey*
Like it or not, this is the *meal*
This is what I'm cooking, and this is what you're eating
You want chicken tonight, you're making chicken
Feel like pasta?
It's pasta
Well
But then
You know

Everyone with their own requirements
You can't really make *anything*
But pretty much you can.

The fact that regardless of who the appointed "cook" for the meal is, everyone is involved, seems to contribute to the desirability of the cook's position. Since everyone will be doing *something*, it is more desirable to tell the other men what to do then to be told to do something undesirable, such as chopping onions or peeling garlic.

Spending time observing and talking about firehouse cooking yielded a richer set of ideas, issues, problems, and meanings than I could have imagined. However, there are some guiding themes and categories of interest that can serve as an entry point to this world. These categories and larger themes were culled from coded log notes, analyzed, and presented to some of the participants for comments and collaborative revision. Two major areas of meaning that emerged were the importance of family and the expression of masculinities.

FAMILY

The first and largest theme is the metaphor of "family." Family permeates many aspects of firehouse life (Farrell 1994)—masculinity issues, nostalgia, language, and, of course, food, to name a few. This theme divides itself into two major groups, first, valuing the "family atmosphere" within the firehouse, and second, placing high importance on one's own, that is, biological and/or legal family. In an interview with Matt, I asked what he thinks is the draw to become a firefighter, he replies expressly, "I think the draw is because of the family atmosphere here."

This sentiment is reinforced by a number of instances. Increasingly, scholars note the reversals between work and home life for both men and women, where work becomes a place of refuge from chaotic home life, or minimally, a place to debrief and commiserate on family life (Hochschild 2001). But the firehouse "family" seemed to go beyond serving as a refuge, in many ways, serving as a surrogate family. Perhaps most graphic is the importance ascribed to the division between "family" members and non-members in the firehouse, "Self" versus "Other." For example, when firefighters from other companies are asked to fill in "on detail" at Engine 3000, they are not allowed to cook. In one instance, a visitor, Biff, tries to lend a hand by snapping green beans at the dining room table, and the evening's cook, Quinn, snatches the beans away and puts a men's magazine into his hands instead saying, "Check out the blond in the boots." Cooking, even more than eating, is a family act for the firehouse "family," and by not allowing outsiders to participate in the cooking process and inviting them to eat as guests, preserves the integrity of this workplace family. Each house has its own nicknames, symbols, outings, and traditions, all making the firehouse a distinctly bounded group.

Like a large family, many firefighters experience a lack of privacy when dressing, sleeping, or talking on the phone, but don't seem overly embarrassed or upset about this. On one occasion, a four-by-six inch snapshot of a firefighter wearing only his open jacket was passed around the dining room table, as everyone commented on his endowment. Or Larry having what might, in another setting, necessarily be a private conversation on his cell phone in the middle of the kitchen, and then reporting the details of the conversation to those around, an intense discussion with his mother about whether his daughter had been picked up from school on time, and whether she was being properly tended to in general. Also, like any family, the firehouse family is fraught with tensions between "brothers," partly based on personality clashes, but also likely influenced by the structure of a self-defined family with a boundary that is officially occupational rather than familial, where cultures come together, clash, as well as complement one another. Thus Matt's statement,

> Whatever you do on the outside
> And when it comes into the firehouse
> It's all
> It's all relative, because this is like
> A family in itself
> So what you do with your own family, you bring here this is another family!
> You know and everybody's bringing bits and pieces from what they do, and it all has to come together here
> You know
> And hopefully it's a harmonious type of thing
> Sometimes it is
> Most of the time it is
> But sometimes it gets a little out of hand, but because everybody has their problems
>   Quinn: [yelling from across the room] Oh, Really?
> You know but what are you gonna do
>   Quinn: Shit, man.
> But we try our best

In fact, I often sensed tension between the men's competing families—occupational and legal/biological—and food is perhaps the way it is most powerfully manifested within the firehouse. For example, Barney indicates that it is standard practice to lie to one's spouse on the phone about what the firefighters are eating for dinner, for fear that "she becomes jealous about our filet mignon or shrimp, while she eats a hotdog." In fact, I hear examples of this sort of minimizing firehouse cooking to a family member twice during my observations. Once, when Quinn does it, the effect seems to be to reduce the celebratory, high-cost (fourteen dollars per person) aspect of a steak dinner, prepared with much anticipation and excitement by the men, telling her, "We're just having a barbecue and shit." A second instance also minimizes what was happening in the firehouse kitchen, but the purpose seems to be more nutrition-than finance-motivated, in reducing a family member's perception of decadence. In this second case, Matt, a thirty-one

year veteran of the firehouse, tells his daughter-in-law that that evening's chicken Parmesan, ziti, salad, and garlic bread dinner is to be, "Some pasta with chicken." After he gets off the phone he says, "[She's] always on my case about fat. No fried this, no buttered that."

There are also times where a meal is elaborately and perhaps even exaggeratedly described, especially when speaking with off-duty firefighters or firefighters from another company, which, in a sense, says to colleagues, "This is how well my [firehouse] family is taken care of." One afternoon, Jerome calls the firehouse to ask if someone could swap an upcoming shift with him and Kevin regales him with the dinner menu that had just been agreed upon, "Turkey breast roasted till golden brown, garlic mashed potatoes, green beans, *bruschetta* for nosh, and, of course, warm golden rolls. You don't know what you're missing!" Similarly, after an article in the local newspaper is printed about Burt's firehouse cooking talents, firefighters visiting on detail are told nostalgic stories of the seafood feasts he prepared for them, reinforcing the idea that this firehouse is a unique bounded group.

While "brother" and "sister" are terms used within many constructs of life—religious groups, ethnic groups, fraternal organizations, friendships—the brotherhood of the firehouse, in many ways, can resemble a familial brotherhood. Jimmy speaks to this particularly well, I think, when he says, "Just like real life, you'd die for your brother, but usually, you want to kick his friggin' ass too." The situation is further complicated because, unlike brothers in a "traditional" family, the firehouse fraternity is composed of men from a variety of ethnic, family, and personal backgrounds. A heated discussion about the edibility of the trim from a chicken among an African-American and Italian-American firefighter, for example, is just one of many manifestations of differences in individual and ethnic orientation, causing misunderstanding, tension, disagreement, or outright fights that comes up during my fieldwork—when to add the basil in tomato sauce, whether Kevin's honey-mustard sauce for "nosh" of chicken tenders more resembled diarrhea or vomit, which pans are most appropriate for various applications, whether quantities of ingredients are adequate both in the store and in the kitchen, where equipment is when needed, which foods are "healthy," or whether it is sanitary to spit in oil to determine its temperature.

The other major aspect to this family theme concerns the importance the firefighters place on their own (that is, their legal and/or biological) families. The firehouse serves as a virtual clearinghouse for home and family advice. When I share this observation with Barney, he tells me, "You can bring your family to work here with you, but you don't bring the problems of the firehouse home." He elaborates by saying that it is appropriate, even expected, that firefighters discuss their home life with their "brothers" at work—"kids, money, sex, vacations, whatever." But work, Barney emphasizes, and the men's spouses confirm, is seldom, if ever, discussed at home, "Unless someone dies or something," he said. "But otherwise you don't talk about what happens here—guys not getting along, or the details of a job."

Another element of the family theme is that many of the firefighters express ideas that are often collectively identified as "conservative family values," and connote a nostalgic nuclear-family type existence:

Years ago my wife stayed home to watch my kids
Now *these* guys
Their wives can't stay home they have to
They don't have the luxury of having their wives at home
With their kids
Now they got
They're babysitting
When the wife's working *they're* home

When they're here the wife's
You know
It's a funny thing
Everybody's running in different directions
[coughing]
We used to do a lot more
A lot more
Here at the firehouse
With off-time activities
We used to get together a lot more with people because
People were used to
It was a more home
Homey type atmosphere
Now nobody has the *time* to do that
We can't get together as much as you can, because nobody has the time
And I think it hurts
The fire department as well as their family life
I mean
You know
It's
The perfect thing would be
Have the mothers stay home with their kids
You know
They're their kids
But that just can't happen anymore
You know it's a shame
And it's happening with my kids the same way
You know
I'm sitting home watching grandchildren now because not to let them
    leave them with uh
You know
Day care or something else like that
So I stay home
[long pause]
That's what it is
It all
Whatever you do on the outside
And when it comes into the firehouse
It's all
It's all relative, because this is like
A family in itself

It is fascinating how Matt weaves what many would label "conservative values," such as strict gender roles, mothers as homemakers, family leisure time, and suburban life, with the metaphor of the firehouse as a family (Coontz 2000). This worldview, with its emphasis on the family in a very traditional sense, while typically not so emphatically expressed, seems to pervade the firehouse. Of the twenty-two core firefighters for whom I made note, twenty owned or rented suburban homes, and all commuted to work by car, despite frequent complaints about the costs of housing, car maintenance, and commuting. When I ask John and Jimmy why more of the firefighters don't live in more affordable city apartments, in light of their frequent complaints about debt and the high cost of living, Jimmy says, "It's the whole package—you gotta do what's right for your family, and it's good to live where you have people to help out. Jimmy is referring to extended family members, who assist with child care, and the other firefighters, who often help one another with things like home repairs.

The firefighters in Engine 3000 complain often of financial and other stressors stemming from their high-stress low-paying job, their families, and their commutes from the suburbs. I ask Matt what he thinks the draw to firefighting is, in light of all these problems. I wondered if it was status, excitement, a sense of tradition or family obligation (many of the firefighters' fathers were also in the fire service or other uniformed service), the desire to help the community, or some other factors. I should not have been surprised by his answer:

> Well I'll tell you what
> I think ahh
> um
> the draw is because of the
>   family
>   atmosphere here
> You know it's
> it's not like the police department
> you know
> it's not like any of these other jobs where
> you're more or less
> you're by yourself
> You're alone
> You're this
> You're ahh you you know you do have
> partners in the police department
>   but this you have more than one partner
> you're here with twelve guys tonight
> Your bosses are not sitting in the station
> house like in the police department
>   and you're out on the street

> You have a fire
> your boss is in there with you
> It's more of that type of a uh
> a family type thing
> It's not
> Nobody's sending you in there by yourself
> You're in a fire situation
> if anybody's gonna get hurt or anybody's
> gonna die the boss is gonna die
>   with you
> So you know you have that camaraderie
> that closeness
> That's the only thing
> And also the time off

MASCULINITY

Inextricably linked to the metaphor of family is the construction and expression of masculinity, which figure highly in the kitchen and at the table. Defining masculinity is always problematic in that, as Connell (1995) suggests, " 'Masculinity,' to the extent the term can be briefly defined at all, is simultaneously a place in gender relations, the practices through which men and women engage that place in gender, and the effects of these practices in bodily experience, personality, and culture" (p. 71). There is simply no singular "way" that men do—or should do—things. Rather, there are situations in which activities are done that invoke their sense of masculinity. Here, I rely on what Leach (1994) identifies as the ideology of masculinity, the collectively shared popular conception that, "presents a set of cultural ideals that define appropriate roles, values, and expectations for and of men" (p. 36). This conception is useful in allowing the men themselves to articulate what is culturally "masculine," even as that encompasses widely-held stereotypes.

The discussion of family focused heavily on men's roles in their homes and firehouse families. The kitchen and dining room, much more than other areas of the firehouse, such as the bunks, gym, garage, or office space, form a stage for an exchange of thoughts on being a man, as well as for words and actions that reinforce or challenge these thoughts. Throughout my field log, language is peppered by phrases such as "What a man [or *real* man] would do . . . "or, "Be a man." Discussions of the roles of men and fathers are also pervasive. Almost every time I met a new firefighter at the firehouse he would ask, "Are you married?" or, more often, "You have kids?" What I find interesting is that in most aspects of my daily life—school, work, social groups—new acquaintances rarely ask about children, unless it otherwise comes up in conversation. In the firehouse, though, it was asked of me as a prelude to many other conversations.

Some actions by firefighters explicitly reinforce their identities as men. Interestingly, these behaviors seem to surface more among the firefighters who are involved in cooking. Especially prominent during cooking is the use of what most would label foul or misogynist language and behaviors, where the language during other activities, such as exercising, washing the trucks, watching television, playing cards, or doing paperwork, seem milder, even professional. While profanity has been an element of note in many male-dominated or male-only workplaces, and especially those labeled or self-identified as blue-collar (Metcalfe 1990; Greebler 1982), in the general atmosphere of the firehouse, it seems somewhat subdued, with occasional profanity used for emphasis. But when the topic concerns food and cooking, my field log and transcripts are full of glaring uses of such language, like "please pass the chicken 'tits,' " "you liked my cock-slaw?" or "throw those fuckers on the pan." I heard relatively little of such language outside of the kitchen. In many ways, the Engine 3000 firefighters seem to use language to "masculinize" the "women's" work that they do in the kitchen. I ask Barney for his thoughts:

Is a woman's presence missed in the firehouse kitchen? Or do you have to make up for it in some way?

Well there *are* women firefighters I mean
They're none here
But
You know
No
I mean
We do our own thing
We don't need women to do it or anything

But Barney tells a partial story. While the firefighters may not "need" a woman in the kitchen, her absence seems noted and compensated for, in some ways, by firefighters who self-consciously assume her role in thought or action. At times a woman, typically a wife, but sometimes a mother or, more rarely, once during my fieldwork, a daughter, has a presence in the firehouse in the form of food brought from home, usually a dessert or other baked good. But only rarely during my fieldwork were women physically present in the firehouse at all. These were most often low-level department administrators, there to collect or convey specific information, and they tended to be given the same politeness offered to their male counterparts. They, like most outsiders, were typically invited to stay for a meal and always declined.

At other times, a woman is absent in both the corporal and culinary senses, but aspects of an imaginary woman's presence in the kitchen are embodied by the firefighters. Food and cooking brought about highly sexualized, heterosexual, and homosexual talk and play, with food, about food, and around food. My log yields many examples of firefighters using food and other kitchen items to "dress" in drag, from making and posing with breasts made from eggplants, tomatoes, zucchini, peppers, and mozzarella cheese; pubic hair from a mop head; buttocks from a packaged turkey breast; as well as, to be equitable, penises from zucchini and cucumber; testicles from avocados, tomatoes, limes, onions, and lemons. Meals are almost always announced in a voice impersonating a female's, "OK, boys, time for the meal!" and at other times, in the same sexualized female-like voice, "Eat me up. I'm so hot!" or "Dig in. It's *so* tasty." The men also assume this voice and sexually-suggestive behavior at other times during the cooking process. Jimmy, hands dirty, tastes sauce from a spoon proffered by Quinn, squealing "Oh, put it in my *mouth*!" More of this type of banter occurs among men doing what they label as more "domestic" or "feminine" task, such as cleaning, preparing vegetables, or grating cheese and peeling garlic, which rank as more feminine than cooking with heat and handling main meat items.

RETHINKING MEN AND COOKING AT ENGINE 3000

Firehouse cooking is everyday, private cooking. Meals are planned, prepared, served, eaten, and cleaned-up two to three times daily and shopped for twice daily. The men add the costs for each meal and divide them evenly, rounding up and contributing extra money to the commissary fund that provides for staple ingredients and supplies. The needs of the entire firehouse must be met with some degree of accommodation for individual tastes and preferences, nutritional goals and perceptions, dietary restrictions and food intolerances, and allergies, as well as the group's needs for variety, value, ease of preparation and clean-up, and taste. It is done by the men, with the men, and for the men, with very little regard to what others think about their food. Their food is private, to the point that the firefighters tell outsiders, such as family members, different versions of their meals than from those they are actually eating. The firehouse kitchen is a stage for the adaptation of this domestic cooking, allowing for the invention of family, providing a forum for expressions and exchanges of power and status, and assisting in the definition of identity.

Firefighters have a popular culture characterization as macho, virile men, popularized by fundraising calendars,

television appearances, and their roles as lifesaving everymen. Their jobs require them to be physically fit, and popular culture perceptions often equate this fitness with sexiness. 'Body,' for them, represents not only their paycheck, but also their most important asset as a life-saver. What I found is that there is a large disconnect between the popular culture characterization of this group, and how that image might accordingly suggest that they should cook. Popular culture associates firehouse cooking, macho five alarm firehouse chili, and competent male cooks as firehouse cookbook authors and television demonstrators. What I observed at Engine 3000 was quite different than this image of macho men unafraid to flex their muscles in the kitchen. Instead, it appears that these supposedly macho, virile firefighters cook very much in a way that is often identified as domestic, feminine, or womanly. Consider this excerpt from an interview with Quinn:

Why do you shop there [at that particular supermarket]?
We like it
You know
We're used to it

There's a guy there
The meat guy
He'll say "Hey guys I got something special for you today"
And he'll tell us what to do with it
You know
So it's friendly
Neighborhoody

Plus, they have a lot of the things in bulk, you know, so that helps
Oil
Canned shit
And some of the guys are really good about bringing in coupons on stuff
    we use all the time
You know pasta, ice cream, tomatoes, whatever
And they do double coupons
What days?

Tuesdays, I think
Yeah, Tuesdays

To someone whose perception of firefighters stems more from their virile image on the television show *Sex and the City* than from first-hand experience, the thought of such a domestic discussion—friendly and instructive butchers, double coupons, and buying in bulk to save money—may seem unusual, even when presented through the use of language like "canned shit." But as cooks who must deal with a variety of constraints in preparing and providing two or three meals a day, these are real concerns. As men, the firefighters construct a kind of masculinity together, where private everyday cooking becomes men's work in the firehouse.

Each meal in the firehouse begins with a discussion hours earlier about what to prepare at the forthcoming meal that will appeal to the largest number of men working on a given shift. While there is no requirement that this be done, the men consider it bad form for the cooks of the meal to knowingly prepare something that will not "go over big with some of the guys." This sentiment mirrors data on women's domestic food work, evoking mothers who strive to prepare meals that please and nurture the largest number of family members and meet the least resistance (DeVault 1991; Ellis 1983; Murcott 1983).

At Engine 3000, there is an explicit attempt to provide "home cooking" for the firehouse "family:"

We try you know
I mean sure
Some guys would be happy if we just did steak this and meat that
I mean
We have guys that only eat that stuff
But it's important you know
We sit down as a family
You need to have a family type meal
Now we do it differently of course
But still.

To Matt, in the quote above, a "family type" meal is one eaten communally, starting and ending together around the table, representing a balanced proportion of major food groups, and culminating in a sweet. By including vegetables or other side dishes, dessert, and multiple dishes, the men recreate a nostalgic conception of the American family meal, even if the men themselves might prefer a sandwich or stand-alone combination dish like pizza. One of the important functions of this balanced meal is that those who will not eat one or more foods can still eat. There is an unwritten rule in this firehouse, and in many others (cf. McCarl 1985; Smith 1972), that anyone who does not want to eat the meal can be "counted out," and provide his or her own food or simply not eat. Being "counted out" is alluded to often. For example, "If you don't like the way I cook this just go count yourself out," but during my fieldwork, I have never seen it happen. Once, even when Kevin announces that he won't be eating because he has "the runs" and ends up just nibbling on some bread, he still pays his share at the end of the meal, and no one objects to his doing so. Even though he is sick, he doesn't exclude himself from table but rather sits, noticeably uncomfortably, with the "family" and engages in the conversations. The balanced meal has something for everyone, nutritionally and socially.

Many invoke an almost *a priori* relationship between men and cooking meat when speaking of men's cooking:

Barbecue's appeal isn 't hard to fathom and may explain why barbecue cookery seems such a Neanderthal corner of modern gastronomy. It elegantly I embraces several stereotypically Guy Things: fire building, beast slaughtering, fiddling with grubby mechanical objects, expensive gear fetishes, afternoon-long beer drinking, and, of course, great heaps of greasy meat at the end of the day. Top this off with the frisson of ritual tribal warfare and you've got the mother of all male pastimes.

(Dudley 2000).

It's the caveman in us. I think that's why you see more and more men barbecuing.

It's a macho thing. Playing with fire and being outdoors, bragging I about how good you cook, it's got all the macho rush to it without any of the violence.

(Elie 1997).

Though I find it hard to accept that the early Neanderthal or cave woman *did not* barbecue while her early counterpart did, the literature on men and cooking is fairly consistent with this popular culture stereotype; men cook over flame, women cook in vessels. Warde and Hetherington (1994), in a survey of household cooking practices, found, not surprisingly, that women did the majority of the cooking in the households surveyed, and that when men cooked, it was primarily grilling out of doors. Neustadt (1988) finds that in a festival setting, women tend the food while men tend the fire.

Engine 3000 does have a grill, and the men talk often about grilling steaks or barbecuing ribs. Interestingly, it seldom happened during my fieldwork. The men cook almost entirely indoors in pots and pans. Pasta, lasagna, baked chicken, pan-fried chicken cutlets, potatoes, and salad were the norm; barbecued or grilled ribs, steaks, or chicken were nearly absent. Citing the inconvenience of lighting the grill, cleaning the coals out after they have cooled, and standing outside, the men grilled steaks only once during my time with them. All of the men, however, spoke of grilling at home on at least one occasion. Curious about this disconnect, I called Barney for his perspective:

I don't know
It's kind of something we do more at home you know
Like at home you have the family
Hot dogs on the grill burgers, whatever
Here, we have guys that can cook
So it's just easier
You don't need to go outside
Away from everyone
Light fhe grill
Keep the fire right
Run in and out with meat
Time it with the stuff in the kitchen

Worry about this guy's rare this guy's medium-rare this guy's medium
It's just easier

The men of Engine 3000 have a strong interest in health and a fit body, probably stemming, at least in part, from very practical purposes. They have physically demanding jobs, where being fit can literally represent life or death differences in their workplace success, both for them and for the people they will be rescuing. The intersection of fitness and food raises questions about what is "healthy." Indeed, this uncertainty is not unique to Engine 3000. Popular confusion about food and health is endemic to the United States, if not to the entire world (Nestle 2003). In an interview with a department administrator tasked with improving firefighter health and fitness, I learn that firefighters in the department are given no official training with regard to cooking, though his office's newsletter includes nutrition tips, such as "Avoid red meat for cardio health." This lack of training and abundance of snippets of nutrition wisdom that I heard during my fieldwork—"Chocolate can reduce risk of heart attack," "Omega 3s are in fish, and they're good for you," "Carbs make you fat," or "Rice is healthy"—together comprised a babel of discussion related to food and health.

Discussions of food and health were constant fixtures in fire-house conversation, as were frank appraisals of body and fitness. The rubric of fitness invites discussions of food and the body similar to those well-documented in the literature on women, food, and the body (cf. Brumberg 1998; Bordo 1995). The men's close proximity, in and out of clothes, and frequency of seeing one another, produced discussions unthinkable in other workplaces:

"Does my ass look fatter since last weekend? I always gain a ton of weight over the holidays."

"Do my triceps look flabby? No amount of working them seems to make a difference. I feel the burn, but they always look the same to me in the mirror."

"What do you do for your abs? I want abs like that."

In all, the absence of women and the presence of everyday home-style cooking in Engine 3000 creates an interesting tension. The frequency and practical issues associated with the cooking process demand concern with domestic cooking attributes—economy, health, pleasing the group, and cooking with efficiency. But at the same time, these are men who self-identify as largely conservative, working-class men who enact distinct gender roles at home. In the firehouse, they move between these roles, at times, relaxing into appraisal of another's body or offering heartfelt advice; at other times, self-consciously making more masculine the task at hand, through language, action, or humor.

CONCLUSION

Firehouse cooks engage in an activity that has been ideologically and materially assigned to women, relying on both shifts and re-assertions of what it means to be a man who cooks domestically. As Sobal suggests, gendered foodways are more likely a pluralistic set of scripts, where actors draw on the script that works for their setting in place and time, cooking functionally and situationally. The experiences of firehouse men are consistent with the kind of work/home transitions among factory workers that Halle (1984) documented. Firehouse cooks who, at home, may be (as one participant defined himself in conversation) a "working class man's man," doing the things out of the kitchen that men do, may, when in the firehouse setting, need to draw from a different gender script to achieve respect when constructing their workplace family of firefighters. This multiplicity suggests that the relationship between gender and cooking is complicated by particular contexts where people construct their work identities and their domestic lives.

ACKNOWLEDGMENT

Deepest thanks to the editors, Alice Julier, Laura Lindenfeld, and Carole Counihan, the reviewers, and my dissertation committee, Amy Bentley, Krishnendu Ray, and Margot Ely, for their thoughtfulness, patience, and humor.

NOTE

1. Data for this study were collected and analyzed using qualitative methods, specifically participant observation and interview, recorded in a thick log, and analyzed recursively through a variety of tools (Bogdan and Biklen 1998; Ely, Vinz, Downing and Anzul 1997; Ely et al. 1991). Consistent with the research paradigm, the field site was selected by convenience sample (Creswell 1994), and a signature of informed consent was obtained from all participants. All names in the field log and this document are pseudonyms, and other identifying markers have been changed as well. Under federal guidelines, this study qualified as "exempt" from supervision by the University Committee on Activities Involving Human Subjects. The transcription format I used throughout the fieldwork and in this document is a variation of one coined by Patai (1988) in her interview study of impoverished Brazilian women. Patai's contention is that to transcribe speech into neat and fluid blocks of prose is not a realistic or trustworthy way to represent the data. Rather, she allows a line for every group of words spoken by her participants, with a line break allowed for pauses.

REFERENCES

Adams, R. G. 1993. *Firehouse Cooking: Food from North America's Bravest*. New York: Gramercy.
Adler, T. 1981. "Making pancakes on Sunday: The male cook in family tradition." In M.O. Jones, B. Giuliano, and R. Krell (eds.), *Foodways and Eating Habits: Directions for Research*, pp. 45–54.
Bogdan, R. C., and Biklen, S. K. 1998. *Qualitative Research for Education: An Introduction to Theory and Methods*. Boston: Allyn and Bacon.

Bonanno, J. T. 1995. *The Healthy Firehouse Cookbook: Low-Fat Recipes from America's Firefighters*. New York: Hearst.

Bordo, S. 1995. *Unbearable Weight: Feminism, Western Culture, and the Body*. Berkeley, CA: University of California Press.

Brumberg, J. J. 1998. *The Body Project: An Intimate History of American Girls*. New York: Vintage.

Charles, N., and Kerr, M. 1988. *Women, Food and Families*. Manchester: Manchester University Press.

Chetkovich, C. 1997. *Real Heat: Gender and Race in the Urban Fire Service*. New Brunswick: Rutgers University Press.

Coltrane, S. 1989. Household labor and the routine production of gender. *Social Problems*, 36:473–490.

Connell, R. W. 1995. *Masculinities*. Berkeley, CA: University of California Press.

Coontz, S. 2000. *The Way We Never Were: American Families and the Nostalgia Trap*. Basic Books.

Creswell, J. W. 1994. *Research Design: Qualitative and Quantitative Approaches*. Thousand Oaks, CA: Sage.

DePasquale, L. A. 1993. *The National Firefighters Recipe Book*. Phoenix: All Hands.

DeVault, M. 1991. *Feeding the Family*. Chicago: University of Chicago.

Dudley, D. 2000. Taking the low slow road to perfect barbecue. *Baltimore Magazine* (July).

Ekstrom, M. 1991. "Class and Gender in the Kitchen." In E. L. Furst, R. Prattala, M. Ekstrom, L. Holm, and U. Kjaernes (eds.), *Palatable Words: Sociocultural Food Studies*. Oslo: Solum Forlag.

Elie, L. E. 1997. The Tao of barbecue. *Forbes*. 125–127 (Summer).

Ellis, R. 1983. "The Way to a Man's Heart: Food in the Violent Home." In A. Murcott (ed.), *The Sociology of Food and Eating*. pp. 164–171. Aldershot: Gower.

Ely, M., Anzul, M., Friedman, T., Garner, D., and Steinmetz, A. M. 1991. *Doing Qualitative Research: Circles Within Circles*. Philadelphia: Falmer.

Ely, M., Vinz, R., Downing, M., and Anzul, M. 1997. *On Writing Qualitative Research: Living by Words*. Philadelphia: Falmer.

Farrell, B. A. G. 1994. *Gender Integration of the FDNY Firefighting Force: An Organizational Case Study*. PhD. Dissertation, Colombia University.

Greebler, C. 1982. Men and Women in Ships: Preconceptions of the Crews. ERIC Report NPRDC-TR-82-57.

Halle, D. 1984. *America's Working Man: Work, Home, and Politics Among Blue-Collar Property Owners*. Chicago: University of Chicago.

Hochschild, A. R. 2001. *The Time Bind: When Work Becomes Home and Home Becomes Work*. Owl Books.

Leach, M. 1994. The politics of masculinity: An overview of contemporary theory. *Social Alternatives*, 12(4):36–37.

McCarl, R. 1985. *The District of Columbia Firefighters' Project: A Case Study in Occupational Folklife*. Washington, DC: Smithsonian Institution Press.

Metcalfe, A. W. 1990. The demonology of class: The iconography of the coalminer and the symbol construction of political boundaries. *Critique of Anthropology* 10(l):39–63.

Murcott, A. (1983). "It's a Pleasure to Cook for Him: Food, Mealtimes and Gender in Some South Wales Households." In E. Garamarnikow et al. (eds.). *The Public and the Private*. London: Heinemann, pp. 78–90.

Nestle, M. 2003. *Food Politics: How the Food Industry Influences Nutrition and Health*. Berkeley, CA: University of California

Neustadt, K. 1988. "Born Among the Shells': The Quakers of Allen's Neck and Their Clambake." In Humphrey, T. C, and Humphrey, L. T. (eds.), *We Gather Together: Food and Festival in American Life*. Logan, Utah: Utah State University Press.

Patai, D. 1988. Constructing a self: A Brazialian life story. *Feminist Studies*, 14:143–166.

Sineno, J. 1986. *The Firefighter's Cookbook*. New York: Vintage.

Smith, D. 1972. *Report from Engine Co. 82*. New York: McCall.

Warde, A., and Hetherington, K. 1994. English households and routine food practices: A research note. *The Sociological Review*, 42(4):758–778.

20

The Magic Metabolisms of Competitive Eating

Adrienne Rose Johnson

Professional competitive eaters, or "gurgitators," can rattle off an encyclopedic record of their stats. 66 hot dogs, 12 minutes. 3 lbs. bologna, 6 minutes. 49 donuts, 8 minutes. Men like Badlands Booker, a 400-pound competitive eater who suffers from high blood pressure, often risk the soundness of their health and the stability of their families to compete professionally. Gurgitators have died from this passion – some indirectly, from heart disease and stroke, others on stage, coughing, choking, asphyxiating themselves to death.

What motivates them? What provokes them? And what do we get from watching them eat? What does eating nine pounds of deep-fried asparagus say about our culture, the needs of our bodies, the anxieties in our lives?

Competitive eating is often seen as a trash sport, well below the status of even professional wrestling or Monster Trucks. Called the "junkiest part of America's junk culture," competitive eating is often dismissed as meaningless by critics and gurgitators alike (Fagone 2006, 304). Joey Chestnut, the current reigning champion, told me in one interview that "we can overanalyze it and there could be tons of theories, but it really doesn't amount to much." Undoubtedly, competitive eating is neither viewed by its insiders nor American culture as a viable outlet for political and social expression in the United States.

However, ideas of the carnival, masculinity, consumerism, and the spectacle demonstrate that, like the cockfight, competitive eating can be read as a story that we tell ourselves about ourselves. By drawing together these ideas with ethnographic research of gurgitators, it becomes clear that competitive eating is a deeply meaningful performance of American culture that harnesses the communicative functions of body and food to articulate deep-seated anxiety and serve as grounds for societal rebirth. By applying Bakhtin's ideas of the material bodily principle and the collective body, we can see that eating contests' focus on the degrading apertures of the body—the open, gaping mouth, the buggy, sweaty eyes, the bulging stomach— challenges the power of the self and society. The "rotten babies" or bloated stomachs of the male gurgitators, in particular, use the degrading aspects of the body to direct the eating contest towards rebirth and rejuvenation. Ultimately, the societal rejuvenation emblematized in the gurgitator's "pregnancies" uses the alterity of the carnival to expose everyday constructions of power as similarly ephemeral and arbitrary.

Unlike the medieval carnival, however, competitive eating attends to very modern ideas of consumerism, assimilation, and American abundance. Women like Sonya Thomas and Juliet Lee engage these ideas through the performances of their very thin bodies—often bodies that weigh less than 100 pounds but consume spectacularly large quantities, such as Lee's 13 pounds of cranberry sauce in 8 minutes. Lee, Thomas, and others actively participate in the mythopoeia of the magic metabolisms and the public fascination with these slim eaters speaks to an embedded cultural desire—the fantasy to consume without consequence. The performing body of the competitive eater is only one text this research draws from; a series of interviews with gurgitators, fat activists, and audience members have offered personal understanding and contributed to a richer view of this spectacle.

For the purposes of this study, competitive eating is limited to the public, highly structured events in which contestants qualify to compete against each other to eat as much of one food-stuff as they can in a short period of time. While state fair pie-eating contests have always been popular in the United States, the last few decades have seen a surge in professional, highly publicized eating contests run by the International Federation of Competitive Eating (IFOCE). By their own account, IFOCE is responsible for more than a billion consumer impressions each year, 300 million of which derive from the hugely popular Nathan's International July Fourth Hot Dog Eating Contest which counts its physical attendance at 40,000 and its ESPN broadcast reach in the hundreds of millions. Outside of the events themselves, competitive eating features prominently in American popular culture; ever since Jughead Jones first triumphed in a pie-eating contest, television shows and documentaries such as *The Simpsons* or *Gut Busters* and a spate of newspaper and magazine articles attest to public fascination with the topic.

IDENTITY AND THE IMPURE BODY

While they do diverge in significant ways, the points of alignment between the eating contest and the carnival run deep. To Bakhtin, the carnival offers an "extrapolitical aspect of the world" to the common people in which they build a "second world and second life outside of officialdom" in order to rejuvenate traditional society (Bakhtin 1984, 6). As the "least scrutinized sphere of the people's creation," laughter, merriment, and nonsense offered a true freedom by which medieval people were most able to express political belief (1984, 4).

Just as Bakhtin interprets the performance of carnival to be actually more meaningful for its lack of self-awareness, competitive eating bypasses traditional loci for self-reflection to directly represent us to ourselves. The vast majority of gurgitator interviews demonstrate that, while competitive eating figures prominently into the individual's sense of pride and accomplishment, gurgitators hesitate to attach larger symbolic weight to their actions. Pete "Pretty Boy" Davekos told me that he "does it to hang out with my buddies" and Nathan "Nasty Nate" Biller said, "I eat [competitively] just because it's fun."

The popular press follows suit, dismissing competitive eating as meaningless and juvenile. Newspaper articles are rife with kitschy puns, degrading metaphors, and condescension that often uses a bestial vocabulary to describe the "monkeys," "dogs," or "apes" who participate in such debased entertainment (see Fischler 2002; Hesser 2002; Fagone 2006, 24). In light of the Bakhtinian carnival, these themes of inconsequentiality can be read not as an indication of competitive eating's triviality, but of its significance.

Unlike traditional athleticism, the eating contest is premised on the universality of eating. Eating's capacity to transcend cultural and linguistic barriers is directly linked to competitive eatings' claims to be an empathetic and democratic endeavor which, in turn, both aids and masks the serious cultural work of establishing group identity. By creating a sport premised on shared need, competitive eating smuggles serious ideas about nation-building and American identity in an approachable rhetoric of frivolity.

The language of the gurgitators themselves supports these claims explicitly: Crazy Legs Conti told me that unlike "the experience of dunking a basketball or scoring a touchdown," eating is universally relatable and "always causes a visceral response" in the audience via the physical empathy of shared experience. Patrick "Deep Dish" Bertoletti told me because "people all eat, so it amazes them [the audience] how many pounds of food we eat." The structure of professional eating supports the democratized nature of professional eating; as Lawrence Rubin notes, because eaters are not "drawn from a rarified farm system that grooms the professional athlete," the "gorger is us, and we are the gorger" (2008, 254). World-champion Joey Chestnut echoed this in plain language, reassuring me that he is "as normal as they come."

To Bakhtin, the primary distinction between carnival and art is that the carnival, which belongs to the "borderline between art and life" does not distinguish "between actors and spectators" (1984, 7). In exact accord with Bakhtin's description of the carnival as "not a spectacle seen by the people; they live in it, and everyone participates because its very idea embraces all the people," competitive eating audience members frequently expressed their feelings of participation within and influence upon the spectacle on stage (p. 7). Likewise, gurgitators also expressed how the distinction between audience and actor blurred when they credit audience enthusiasm for their abilities, as Joey Chestnut did for his 2008 Nathan's Famous Hot Dog victory. Bakhtin's language echoes gurgitator Pete "Pretty Boy" Davekos when he told me, "But we all eat. If you order a slice of pizza, three or four larges—that's why I think it's so interesting because *everyone participates* without even knowing."

By creating a direct, bodily link between the food consumed on stage and their own feelings of revulsion or nausea, audience members tie their own bodies not only with the gurgitators on stage but also the surrounding crowd. This bodily empathy, combined with the physical closeness of the packed audience, creates a situation where spectators become "a member of the people's mass body" where the individual is subsumed in the "sensual, material bodily unity and community" (Bakhtin 1984, 255). Impressions gathered from audience members support this claim; as one 14-year-old girl attending the Stockton Asparagus Fest said, she began to feel "sick to her stomach and gross" as she watched the contest. Her father reiterated this by saying he was so "blown away" by the amount of food consumed that he felt "queasy." Popular descriptions of eating contests also reflect on shared bodily experience: one writer relays that seeing the contest "left a bad taste in my wife's mouth" (Rubin 2008, v).

By looking at the nature of shared bodily experience through the anthropological lens of ritual, it becomes clear that the body of the gurgitator morphs into a social body linking the bodies of the spectators to the body politic via shared corporeal experience. On stage, the eating, spewing, body clearly violates American social sanctions of decorum and control; it is a living definition of bodily impurity that, as contrast, re-establishes an American definition of bodily purity. The material definition of bodily purity reinstates both a "clear distinction between insiders and outsiders, [and] a stress on loyalty" (Bell 1997, 184). In this sense, the eating may reflect and reinforce not only group ties, but also key ideological projects of nation-building.

An analysis of early American eating contest newspaper coverage reveals how the eating contest's empathetic and participatory nature built national identity. By communicating through the common language of eating, early American eating contests may have inspired unity and built patriotism through the evocative social symbol of the performative body—a body which transcended the barriers of a multi-lingual, multi-ethnic society. A survey of one hundred news articles from prominent U.S. newspapers such as the *New York Times*, the *Chicago Daily*

Tribune, and the *Washington Post* has suggested a distinct feature of the pre-1900s eating contests. In contrast to today's contests, the vast majority of these contests used blandly generic, instantly relatable foods. These foods— onions, watermelon, eggs—can be linked to many cuisines but tied to none. Unlike foods such as corn or sauerkraut (which generated their own eating contests in the last hundred years), these foods hold little in common with Native American and even less with Old World foods. While this might simply reflect the restrictions of a pre-industrialized food system, it might also be indicative of an attempt to homogenize immigrant diet, inspire patriotism, and create unity in new Americans.[1]

In this light, we see how competitive eating draws from the individual's knowledge of his own body to create an understanding of the body politic. As Mary Douglas notes, the body is often used in ritual as a "symbolic medium" by which "work upon the body politic" is accomplished; in rituals, the body gives social relations "visible expression" and "they enable people to know their own society" (1966, 129). In this way, the bodies of competitive eaters speak even as their mouths remain full; they literalize and confirm key tenets of the American belief system—classlessness, consumerism, and assimilation. Classlessness finds expression in the athleticization of eating and public binging, in a display of desire, literalizes consumerism. Assimilation takes shape in the evasion of language barriers and ethnic cuisines via the communicative medium of the body and culturally indefinite foods and, perhaps, more elementally, in the assimilatory processes of digestion by which difference is crushed and processed into sameness. Further, the public nature of these early contests, usually held in street fairs, created a situation where casual passers-by were interpellated as Americans who, even if they did not share the same cuisine or language, shared the same bodily frame of reference by which they could judge the enormity of the feat before them.

News coverage of early eating contests demonstrates that, in the meritocracy of the eating contest, the results of the contest often trump the ethnicities or class of the contestants. While most articles never refer to ethnicity or class, the few that do privilege contest results against personal detail. For example, an 1886 *Chicago Daily Tribune* article only mentions that it was an "Italian who won the match by an orange and two bananas" after laboriously chronicling the results and methods of the greased-pig chasing, melon-seed guessing, and fruit-eating contests. By using a common set of instantly relatable referents, competitive eating capitalizes on our visceral understanding of our bodies to teach an understanding of the values of classlessness, consumerism, and assimilation in the American body politic.[2]

However, Bakhtin differentiates between the collective "material bodily principle" and the "biological individual or bourgeois ego" (1984, 19). The biological individual or bourgeois ego limits the expression of the material bodily principle just as the experiences of one person limit the expression of the collective experience of the human race. Drawing from early American contests, we see that, in competitive eating, the biological individual's expression is not subsumed by the collective human body but by the collective *American* body. As a common set of bodily rules, the material bodily principle transcends and subsumes the biological individual, hyperbolizing the group's collective experiences until it becomes "grandiose and exaggerated" (Bakhtin 1984, 19). These exaggerated symbols center around the greatest anxiety-producing parts of the body: apertures of anus, genitals, eyes, and mouth.

Competitive eating's most representative symbols lie in the human body: the wide, gaping, yawning mouth; the lines of trickling saliva; the rivers of sweat; the bulging, buggy eyes; the sight of half-chewed food in an open mouth; and, of course, the threat of vomit. The open, chewing, wet mouth is the key visual symbol of the American competitive eater. The mouth dominates, even appears to subsume, the face, the body, and, perhaps, the individuality of the person. Bakhtin assigns the gaping mouth "the leading role" of the lower stratum (1984, 325).[3] The mouth, he writes, "is the open gate leading downward into the bodily under-world" and is closely related to "swallowing, the most ancient symbol of death and destruction" (p. 325).[4] Much like medieval gargoyles, competitive eaters serve to represent the collective, living body that emphasizes "the apertures or the convexities, the open mouth . . . the potbelly" (p. 26). This eating body literally "swallows the world and is itself swallowed by the world" and is "continually growing and renewed" (pp. 18–35).

Unsurprisingly, the body parts which produce great anxiety are also the "parts of the body that are open to the outside world," which blur the boundaries of the body and, consequently, the power of the self and society (Bakhtin 1984, 26). Douglas advances the idea that "strong social control demands strong bodily control" and, by extension, the loosening of bodily control implies a loosening of social control (1996, 76). A step further, Bakhtin argues that loose bodily control, in the exhibition of the "bodily lower stratum," is the degradation necessary for metaphoric renewal. "The purely bodily aspect" of degradation is "not clearly distinct from the cosmic," Bakhtin writes, defining degrading body parts as the "life of the belly and the reproductive organs" which "swallows up and gives birth at the same time" (1984, 21). By linking regenerative, ambivalent, and growing body parts to societal regeneration, the loosening of bodily control in the eating contest might ultimately result in societal rejuvenation.

If we consider societal rejuvenation as simply the re-instantiation of social order, the impure body would work paradoxically to re-establish the repressive society which limits its expression. However, the impure body and the carnival more broadly can be viewed as more than a short-lived aberration to the dominant social order—more than a release valve for the engine of late capitalism—if we apply David Carroll's notion that the carnival reveals both its own power and larger society's as similarly irrational and constructed (Carroll 1983, 82). Societal rejuvenation, found in all carnivals, is clearly articulated in the grotesque figure of the male gurgitator's bloated "pregnancy."

At first glance, an American eating contest only upholds the first half of Bakhtin's definition of the lower bodily stratum as the "life of the belly and the reproductive organs" which "swallows up and gives birth at the same time" (Bakhtin 1984, 21). Surprisingly, however, the "life of the reproductive organs" is similarly emphasized in competitive eating (p. 21). Over the course of my research, I have found that often after a contest ends, the victor is asked to pull up the front of his shirt. Bloated and bulging, the belly is showcased for the crowd.

Invariably, the sight produces a strong audience reaction—cat-calls, yelling, and astonished applause. A woman watching Kobayashi's display told me, "He looks pregnant! A little guy like that with such a giant belly." This sentiment was repeated elsewhere; another young woman said: "he's got a rotten baby," while a man told me "he almost looks like a pregnant girl." Of the other contests I have attended, all ritualistically display the extended belly of the victor. Additionally, emcees commonly ask the contestants to lift their shirts to the crowd before the contest. The flat and muscular "before-belly" is later contrasted against the swollen distension of the "after-belly."

The Bakhtinian carnival is defined by its ability to "swallow up and give birth at the same time" and competitive eating combines gorging with growth, eating with pregnancy, consumption with distension, effectively swallowing new life and then, due to the constraints of their sex, miscarrying this "rotten baby" (1984, 21). Gluttony and pregnancy are made more grotesque by the fact that only men have been asked to display their bulging "pregnant" stomachs. Bakhtin explicitly references male pregnancy when he writes that the image of masculine childbirth "is a miniature satirical drama of the word, of its material birth, or the drama of the body giving birth to the word."

Bakhtin cites figurines in the Kerch terracotta collection of "senile pregnant hags" to epitomize "grotesque concept of the body" (1984, 23–24). He writes:

> It is pregnant death, a death that gives birth ... combines a senile, decaying, deformed flesh with the flesh of new life, conceived but as yet unformed. Life is shown in its two-fold contradictory process.

The "rotten babies" of male competitive eaters are much like senile pregnant hags; both combine decay with new life, both are metaphorically conceived but will remain unformed due to constraints of sex and age.[5]

The grotesque tropes, however, realize the carnival's ultimate regenerative purposes. As we have seen, the eating body is an expressive, performative, representative body, yet it is a silent body, a body whose chewing, bursting mouth leaves no room for language. Although the expressions of the performative body speak through embodiment, this body also gives birth to the very vocabulary it eludes. Bakhtin argues that language is birthed by this silent body; explicitly referring to imagery of male pregnancy, Bakhtin writes that the typical symptoms of grotesque life—the "gaping mouth, the protruding eyes, sweat, trembling, suffocation, the swollen face"—are cathected

with the meaning of childbirth and, in particular, the birth of the word (1984, 308). In this way, the entire "mechanism of the word is transferred from the apparatus of speech to the abdomen" which acts out a "miniature satyrical drama of the word, of its material birth, or the drama of the body giving birth to the world" (p. 309). Even with their mouths full, these bodies not only talk, but also birth the words which evade their grasp in an extraordinary realism (p. 309).

HIERARCHY AND LANGUAGE

While the body figures principally in Bakhtin's discussion of the carnivalesque, he also cites "comic verbal compositions" to be central to the suspension of hierarchy and, consequently, a carnival's regenerative spirit (1984, p. 15). In the chapter, "Language of the Marketplace," Bakhtin likens the carnival's comic language to that of the "advertising spirit of a barker at a show" which dialectically combines praise and abuse, the elevated and the lowly, and death and life in an active, changing process that resists and re-imagines officialdom (p. 160). Full of laughter and irony, this language combines the "exalted and the lowly, the sacred and the profane" until they are "leveled and drawn" together (p. 160).

Drawing from the narratives of the eating contests emcees, we can see the language of competitive eating shares its language of comic, spirited irony with carnivalesque speech. Dressed in three-piece suits, emcees such as Ryan Nerz and George Shea engage the audience before the contest in a non-stop dialogical barrage of nonsensical falsehoods and extravagant exaggerations that situates gurgitators within and against traditional American themes. The tall-tale biographies of contestants, which often position the eater as hero in the drama of their lives, are most emblematic of the emcee's style. Clear themes of class and hierarchy upheaval thread through these mock biographies which allows for a multiplicity of voices, a dialogism that assimilates the languages of high and popular cultures in order to invigorate them both.

For example, Pete "Pretty Boy" Davekos was introduced at Nathan's Famous in 2008 as a lower- or middle-class young man "who spent his summers chasing well-bred girls whose families summered in Cape Ann." Following ample precedent set by authors like F. Scott Fitzgerald, Davekos transcends class barriers to win the heart of "a fair-haired co-ed" by dint of his eating capabilities. In testament to the generative power of carnivalesque language, Davekos internalized his mythic mock history to the extent that, in an author interview, he linked his compulsive dieting, binging, and body-building partly to the pressures to uphold his IFOCE persona. He said, "My nickname is 'Pretty Boy'. You can't be pretty if you're fat. I need to be the best looking guy up there."

Davekos' biography is representative of nearly all competitive eater introductions. Often, the emcee uses both the characters and the form of traditional narratives to introduce eaters to the stage. In an overt comparison, Dale Boone, costumed in overalls and a coonskin cap, rings a wooden liberty bell as he is introduced as Daniel Boone's direct descendant. With mock-scholarly language, Tim "Eater X" is described as an anguished artist, a Heathcliff-like "man of mystery" who disguises both his inner torment and valuable eating secrets beneath his painted mask.

Often, the eater will be situated in a mock-history that parodies not only the eater but also the historical events to which he is compared. This is bellied by bombastic academic language which reveals the very silliness it purports to elevate. Sonya Thomas' biography follows, excerpted from the Major League Eating's website, which I have heard repeated at contests in which she participates:

There is a century-old prophesy within the competitive eating community, dismissed by most, that foretells the rise of the One Eater, a woman who will electrify America's gurgitators and lead them to international victory once again. Like Joan of Arc before her, this eater will be slender of stature, but mighty in strength.

This "highbrow" language does not simply mock the upper classes but uses its themes to dialectically situate competitive eaters within and against the established traditions of officialdom, to use Bakhtin's word. By creating a dialogue with tradition, emcees are proving the power of dialogic language to affect both the high and popular cultures in which it is deployed.[6]

These class-challenging relationships support what one literary theorist defines as the "basic principle of the carnivalesque" in which "a reversal in fortune is achieved by an individual of low position removed to one that is high" (Danow 1995, 13). Bakhtin names the carnival's main function to present an alternate reality, a second world where the rules of society no longer apply; it was not merely outside the rule of law, but rule-less (Bakhtin 1984, 9). In this second world of the eating contest, we see the suspension of class hierarchy in the juxtapositional mingling of the themes and heroes of high- and popular-culture. By comparing dissimilarities (e.g. Sonya Thomas and Joan of Arc), the language of competitive eating works to suspend hierarchy, allow for multiplicity, and rejuvenate the society in which it was produced.

CLASSICIZING THE GROTESQUE: A STUDY OF THE SLIM EATER

At first glance, competitive eating's celebration of the grotesque, focus on bodily display, and suspension of class hierarchy imply a wholly carnivalesque show of the big-bellied eater. However, contrary to stereotype, the top ten American gurgitators, ranked by the IFOCE are far from obese. Although official estimates are difficult to attain and rankings change from contest to contest, the top ten eaters range from extraordinarily thin (Sonya Thomas, ranked #4, weighs 105 pounds) to average build.

The stereotype of obese gurgitator persists from an earlier era of competitive eating—the so-called "big man" or "trophy" era which featured large men like Eric "Badlands" Booker or Ed "Cookie" Jarvis who, via the medium of competitive eating, equated size with masculine power.[7] Over the last few decades, however, younger, more athletic eaters have unseated these older, larger eaters. Chestnut, a young, fit eater, voiced his disdain to me in commenting that larger eaters are "lacking discipline and they don't control their diet—they're not real competitive eaters" in contrast to the real gurgitators who are "pretty healthy." Crazy Legs Conti similarly compared older and contemporary eaters as he reflects that he "came out in an era where there wasn't a lot of science, where there wasn't a lot of body knowledge. Today's eaters are much more in tune."

The popular press has similarly noted this trend: in reference to a cannoli-eating contest, reporter Chris Hardesty notes that, unlike most eating contests today, this championship offered no prize money or ESPN broadcast in an effort to "recapture a more innocent era—a time when eaters were mostly rotund fellows who enjoyed a pile of free food, not self-styled athletes with season stats and endorsement contracts" (Hardesty 2010). This trend has not been sudden or dramatic and, contrary to the common idea repeated in even scholarly works that all "American gurgitators are overwhelmingly large, weighing in at or above 300 lbs" all of the top ten competitive eaters have been glorified for their average or noticeably fit builds (Halloran 2004, 3).

While the stereotypical body of the overweight and big-bellied competitive eater exhibits all the Bakhtinian traits of the grotesque, the idolized slim competitive eater defies the easy alignment between grotesqueness and public gorging. The slim eater's body exhibits all the symbols of the grotesque yet does so within the archetype of the classical body. The contradiction between the grotesqueries of the open, gorging mouth and the closed, classical body ruptures easy assumptions, and, as interviews with audience members and gurgitators have demonstrated, constitute much of the allure of modern competitive eating. By reframing the grotesque within the classical, the slim eater's body demonstrates its imperviousness even as it literalizes the glut of American consumerism.

Like all spectacles, the body of the slim eater literalizes a worldview that has always already been established in American culture—that of the ideal citizen who can consume without consequence.[8] The public acknowledgment and adoration of the slim body, alongside its widespread exhibition on stage and in broadcast to millions, demonstrates the full re-conceptualization of the ideal embodiment of an American consumer and citizen. Neither the grotesque nor the classical, the slim eater's body can be considered to constitute a differently embodied ideal—a body that could be termed the American grotesque.

The slim, eating body does not simply literalize a fantasy; it transmutes this fantasy into a performing dreamwork that distorts and condenses its content into a living body. As a breathing embodiment of an ideal, this body directly contrasts to the "ready-made and completed" hierarchy and finds expression only in the "ever unfinished and ever creating body" which stands in for "all-people" (Bakhtin 1984, 9–26). By contextualizing the slim eating body in the rhetoric and activities which produce its myth, the active, living forces that inscribe meaning onto the slim body are brought to light.

Slim eaters often actively participate in the myth-making of their "magic metabolisms." Sonya Thomas claims she manages a Burger King solely for its employee discount while Juliet Lee said, in an author interview, that "I always knew I was special." A common publicity stunt is the before and after weigh-in: before a contest, the audience will watch eaters weighed on a doctor's scale and, after the contest, the eater will be weighed once more. In Thomas' case, her weight never varies from its set point at 105 pounds—even after eleven pounds of cheesecake in nine minutes.

Sonya Thomas is repeatedly referred to as "petite," "super-skinny," or "bulimic" (Wexler 2008, 4). The visual richness of the contrast between a 105-pound woman who "downs 173 buffalo wings to beat a dozen large men" recurs in almost every article about this "skinny superwoman" who out-eats men four times her weight (Wexler 2008, 5). George Shea, one of the few Major League Eating emcees, regularly introduces Sonya to eating contest crowds by emphasizing her slenderness; for example, "Sonya Thomas, she's so small, it looks as though she could not eat a tin of cottage cheese" (Shea, qtd. in Fagone 2006, 124).

Thomas is now one of a few petite women who belong to the new group of "slim superwomen" who dramatize their slenderness, claim to eat large quantities of high-calorie foods, and have been celebritized on the competitive eating circuit. I cannot overstate the fascination both competitive eating fans and the general public have with Thomas' ability to "eat and eat and never show a thing" (Wexler 2008, 3). Patrick "Deep Dish" Bertoletti even notes that many fans see competitive eating as "some sort of diet, eating like we do and never gaining a pound." One competitive eating fan has even speculated if Sonya Thomas' "superhuman control over her own stomach" could be capitalized on by pharmaceutical companies to "make a pill to make you skinny" (Fagone 2006, 103). In nearly all of my gurgitator interviews, Thomas'

colleagues expressed considerable awe, appreciation, and even resentment of what many condsidered her "natural talent."

Thin eaters like Sonya Thomas and Joey Chestnut directly contradict Bakhtin's grouping of both the "yawning mouth" and the "potbelly" in the material lower bodily strata. In the introduction to *Rabelais and his World,* Bakhtin considers "a fat belly" to be a necessary and direct consequence to "appetite and thirst" (1984, 22). Popular opinion and medical dogma holds that a hearty appetite inevitably leads to a "fat belly," but the bodies of slim gurgitators like Sonya Thomas weaken this argument. These bodies not only do not corporealize the effects of appetite, but, in fact, the slim eater's extraordinary slenderness can be argued to materialize its polarity: the more they eat, the thinner they appear.

As a material contradiction of medical dogma, the slim, eating body also works to symbolically destroy the authority of officialdom; since the Great Depression, American medical views of obesity have simply blamed the obese for consuming too many calories (Levenstein 2003, 10). Harvey Levenstein, American food historian, writes that, since the discovery of vitamins in the 1910s, American diet has been enormously influenced by the restrictive and prohibitive measures of American nutritionists, dieticians, and the medical health establishment. As Halloran has pointed out in her study of extreme eating, "the rebellious disregard of manners, propriety, and moderation involved in the consumption of large amounts of food" allows the public "to project its own guilt about habitual overindulgence in food," or, more broadly, any diet that conflicts with the dominant nutritional tenets outlined by the medical health industry (2004).[9]

Joey Chestnut related to me that, as a competitive eater, he often feels "ashamed" during an eating contest because he is disobeying American diet restrictions. He said that, during an eating contest, he is "up on stage doing something we're not supposed to do—eating that much food. We've been told and believe that eating that much is really unhealthy, very bad."

However, slim gurgitators like Chestnut do not appear to corporealize any of the effects predicted by the vigilant medical health establishment: no flaccid belly, no rotting teeth, no strained joints. In fact, many eaters pride themselves on their health: Davekos told me that he had just received a sound bill of health from his life insurance company with "perfect blood pressure, perfect cholesterol, perfect everything—I'm in great health." Photos taken of eaters like Davekos outside of the eating contest depict this healthy, muscular classical form; the belly does not protrude, the breasts do not sag, and the posture is erect. Photos of slim eaters show that their forms share more in common with classical sculpture, such as the Venus de Milo, than they do with the artistic emblem of the grotesque: the gargoyle. Juliet Lee, for example, wears tight, flattering clothes and attractive makeup and champion eater Hall Hunt is a muscular and well-groomed young man. However, during the contest, these bodies exhibit all of the characteristics of the grotesque; their open, yawning, spewing mouths contradict the classic form of their bodies. The tight, classical body displays itself in grotesque hyperbole and, as typical to carnival regeneration, destroys an old societal order—in this case, of diet restrictiveness and classical body form—to create a new ideal.

In this instance, the contestant embodies a differently idealized human form: one that exhibits the life-affirming grotesque but within the discipline of the classical. Slim eaters, as representative of the new idealized form, can consume without fearing symbolic repercussions or literal corporealization of fat. American audiences, suffering from the ill effects of both metaphoric and literal consumption themselves, are eager to idolize slim eaters for their "superhuman abilities."

Competitive eating is an exaggeration of the performance of everyday American capitalism much like Bakhtin's medieval festivals exaggerated the everyday medieval European hierarchy. As literary theorist David Danow comments, "The literatures of carnival heaven and carnival hell spring from what is, or had been mundane experience" (1995, 7). Americans have had a long, anxiety-ridden relationship with consumerism that doesn't bear repeating in detail; however, American's anxious relationship to their consumerism stretches back to the country's inception. In one of the first accounts of American life, Alexis de Tocqueville warns new Americans in the early 19th century that democracies are particularly susceptible to materialism, which he calls a "dangerous disease of the human mind," and these anxieties persist throughout American history—from Thorstein Veblen to Naomi Klein (Tocqueville 2004, 631).

Given a history that often applies the economic language to diet and, vice versa, nutritional vocabulary to economic conditions, competitive eating effortlessly appears as a literalization of economic consumption. Hillel Schwartz's cultural history of dieting links an American fear of economic overabundance in form of monetary treasury surplus to the "menace of 'overnutrition' " in the early 1900s.[10] Early 20th-century Americans considered fatness to be "uneconomical" and Schwartz writes, "The crusade against fatness arose from . . . fashions in [economic] consumption" (1986, 88). Economic rhetoric is rife in diet literature: calorie budgets, bargains, and splurges are popular ways to think of weight loss plans and even the official U.S. Department of Agriculture site advises Americans to "Think of the calories you need for energy like money you have to spend" (MyPyramid). Similarly, we find themes of economic efficiency in the language of competitive eating; Crazy Legs Conti reflects on his experiences as a professional gurgitator by saying, "It's about turning your body into a human processing machine." The act of consuming food in an eating contest literalizes and hyperbolizes everyday American consumerist behavior.

By charting competitive eating's popularity via media coverage over the last hundred years, I have found evidence that may suggest a pattern: the greatest spikes in eating contest popularity occur in periods of heightened consumerist behavior and economic prosperity. If correct, the correlation between competitive eating popularity and economic prosperity would support my argument that the myth of the slim eater drives competitive eating. Drawing from this correlation, we see that during periods of economic prosperity, when American people are most apprehensive about abundance, the slim eater speaks most strongly in the language of consumerism.

During the economic boom of the Roaring Twenties, eating contest popularity was more than double that of the period of wartime economic control. From 1923–1927, 145 references to eating contests appear in major newspapers; from 1941–1947, only 87 contests are chronicled. Likewise, eating contest popularity during the prosperous 1980s is almost triple the popularity of eating contests after the dotcom bubble burst in 2000. While patterns in popularity are difficult to find and even harder to interpret, a correlation between economic prosperity and competitive eating popularity is in keeping with Hillel Schwartz's theory that "thin people are capitalism's ideal consumers" (1986, 329).

Schwartz writes that "thin people are capitalism's ideal consumers for they can devour without seeming gluttonous; they have morality on their side;" likewise, slim competitive eaters appear to be morally good and classically formed yet they, like all good American consumers, can "eat much, eat often, eat sweetly," and yet remain slender (1986, 329–330).

From Veblen to de Tocqueville, Americans have had a long and anxious relationship with consumerism. Rising levels of debt, growing health concerns about nutrition, the threat of impending ecological collapse, and the rising popularity of anti-consumerist movements all point to an American anxiety about the nature of our country and its consumerist habits. Alongside the body of the slim gurgitator, the narratives which extol the consumerist habits of the ultra-wealthy articulate the conditions that necessitate their production; the debt, clutter, anxiety, and dependence which besiege American consumers.

Reading the myth of the slim competitive eater as a national fairy tale, we see the American desire to consume without consequence, eat food without becoming fat. Slim competitive eaters flawlessly represent the collective consumerist fantasy of consuming and consuming without fear of repercussion. Individuals like Sonya Thomas and Joey Chestnut are, in Hillel Schwartz's words, the "ideal consumers" of Late Capitalism; they are "never satisfied" and may follow "society's urgings to eat much, eat often, eat sweetly, and be slender" (1986, 329–331).

FINAL THOUGHTS ON AN UNFINISHED TOPIC

Over the course of my research, I have held certain standards of respect for both the competitive eaters and the eating contest audience—I believe they are essentially intelligent, thoughtful, and sincere people participating in a sport that speaks to them and the world in which they live. For this reason, I do not believe the eaters when they say they eat competitively because it's entertaining, because it's cool, because it's a shot at fifteen minutes of fame or five minutes of fun.

I cannot believe these statements because I cannot believe these people—these thoughtful and intelligent people—could sincerely dedicate their lives to eating pounds of apple pie or gallons of macaroni without it meaning something to them and the thousands who watch them eat. And, as my research indicates, competitive eating does articulate deep-seated ideas about identity, consumerism, and the role of the American body.

While competitive eating appears to affirm all the principles of the carnivalesque, it also adapts to communicate specific meaning about American culture. The forms of the body exhibited and extolled in the American eating contest are markedly different from the traditional bodily forms of the Bakhtinian grotesque: the slender body exhibits traits of the grotesque—the open, wet, gorging mouth—but does so in the form of the closed classical thin body. This paradoxical body performs a national fairy tale, articulating both our fantasy to consume without consequence and the underlying anxieties which necessitate the production of such fantasy. Neither the grotesque nor the classical, the slim eater's body constitutes a differently idealized American body that articulates common fantasies and pervasive anxieties.

NOTES

1. In contrast to the patriotic and assimilatory goals of 18th- and 19th-century eating contests, modern eating contests often differentiate Americans by their regional and ethnic backgrounds. Tiramisu, jalepeños, and kloches contests are now found in ethnic food festivals for Italian-Americans, Mexican-Americans, and Czech-Americans, respectively. For example, Sheboygan, Wisconsin's annual Brat-Eating Contest is rife with German pride. Dressed in lederhosen and dirndle, men and women are encouraged to speak with German accents and a quotation from their website demonstrates this: "Dis heres Fritz an on behaf a da Sheboygan Jaycees me an my lovely lil mustard cup Helga." Additionally, one of the greatest upsets in competitive eating's history was when gentile Hungry Charles Hardy overthrew Don "Moses" Lerman, the longtime Jewish matzoh ball champion, in New York City in 2001.

2. Themes of assimilation and patriotism thread through to contemporary competitive eating, as well. As Sonya Thomas, the Korean-born 105-pound world champion in cheesecake and chicken nuggets, eloquently put it, "and beneath what you may see on the surface, know this: My Yankee Doodle Dandy heart proudly pumps red, white, and blue blood to the beat of "God Bless America."

3. A visual analysis of Japanese and Korean eating contests reveals that bodily emphases are culturally specific. I have found that Asian eating contests place less emphasis on the mouth than American contests and more on the hands; the hands often serve as a covering for the mouth. See a super-sized Japanese gyoza contest, found at http://www.youtube.com/watch?v=hMGpFUHuym4

4. It is interesting to compare similarities in vocabulary between the Bakhtinian language of the grotesque and the language competitive eaters themselves use to describe their participation: while Bakhtin considers the open mouth the "gate leading downward into the bodily underworld," Pete "Pretty Boy" Davekos describes his hunger and eating habits by saying, "If I open the floodgate, it's like a crack in the dam, open the floodgate, open my mouth. If I allow myself to have one slice of pizza, I'm going to have probably two large pizzas."

5. In popular culture, the image of the pregnant man recurs as a grotesque trope; in April 2008, Thomas Beattie, a woman who lived and looked like a man, made national headlines when "he" became pregnant and agreed to be photographed shirtless, depicting a graphic image that contrasted his 5 o'clock shadow and pregnant stomach. Beattie appeared on the Oprah television show, was featured in the popular press such as *People Magazine* and quickly rose to celebrity in the United States. Further, movies such as *Junior*, starring a pregnant, gruffly effeminate Arnold Schwarzenegger and an episode of Star Trek featuring an interspecies male pregnancy all elaborate on the grotesque theme.

6. Joey Chestnut, the world's #1 champion eater, explicitly insisted upon the class-less nature of competitive eating when he said, "There's a lot of people here who are just working class people. I think that's what's cool to people about competitive eaters. If they look at me they see that I'm just a normal guy. I'm as normal as they come, I'm as normal as everyone else" (Author interview, April 24, 2008).

7. In Booker's case, his career as a rap artist, rapping mainly about the largeness of his body and the strength of his eating skills, makes this movement clear. As Fagone notes, Booker follows in the tradition of large, often African-American, rappers like Biggie Smalls or The Fat Boys, as he recontextualized his fatness as power to "make people see it in a different way" (Fagone 2006, 131). The other very prominent overweight eater, Ed "Cookie" Jarvis, has similarly used his fatness to explore ideas of discipline and power: his

website features Jarvis' dramatic weight loss via two photos contrasting a younger, muscular Jarvis and a photo depicting his overweight body today. In tight spandex shorts and a tank top, Jarvis proudly demonstrated the girth of his large biceps in the first photo and the second, contemporary photo is accompanied by the text declaring that "It's time for me to show some self discipline by eating better" (Janvis 2007). To date, Jarvis has dropped 170 lbs from his originally 525 lbs body in an effort to regain his bodybuilder's physique. His slimmer, post-weight loss self, at 354 lbs, is consequently re-read as a triumph of discipline over fat and not viewed simply as an overweight body.

8. While competitive eating presents the strongest example of this American fantasy, I have found many instances in which fashion models are treated similarly. For example, when supermodel and Victoria's Secret "Angel" Adriana Lima was quizzed on her diet and exercise habits in an interview, the reporter was astonished when Lima "confessed" that she eats "anything [she] wants to" such as "meat, chocolate, cakes." Similarly, FoodNetwork star Paula Deen, in her preface to *Lady & Sons Just Desserts* cookbook retells the story of the very slender "cute little" woman who, after eating 24 pieces of chicken, ate both her peach cobbler and her husband's pound cake. Deen writes, "if only I could eat that way and look that good!" (Deen 2002, xi).

9. The origins of these strict, often confusing, nutritional guidelines are more often rooted in social and political ideas than they are physiological. Journalist Frederick Kauffman has argued that, in the American climate of irreligiousness, strict diet restrictions have come to stand in for religious practices. Similarly, feminist historian Rosalyn Meadow has argued that, for American women, modern food conflicts such as dieting "have taken over the sexual conflicts of yesteryear" (Meadow 1992, 4).

10. The treasury surplus of the 1880s led many Americans to cite "overproduction" and overabundance as the cause for the economic sluggishness of the late 19th century. In 1877, American economist David Wells credited American economic stagnancy to, "not because we have not, but because we have; not from scarcity, but from abundance" (Wells, qtd. in Schwartz 2008, 84).

WORKS CITED

"10,000 Expected to Feast and Frolic at Fair: Italian Festival is in 7th Year." (1962, June 21). *Chicago Daily Tribune (1872–1963),* Retrieved October 30, 2008, from ProQuest Historical Newspapers (1849–1986) database.

Anderson, E. N. *Everyone Eats: Understanding Food and Culture.* New York: New York University Press, 2005.

Bell, Catherine. *Ritual: Perspectives and Dimensions.* New York: Oxford University Press, 1997.

Bakhtin, Mikhail. *Rabelais and His World.* Bloomington: Indiana University Press, 1984.

Bertoletti, Patrick "Deep Dish." Personal interview. 23 April 2008.

Biller, Nathan "Nasty Nate." Personal interview. 24 April 2008.

Carroll, David. "The Alterity of Discourse: Form, History, and the Question of the Political in M. M. Bakhtin." *Diacritics*, Vol. 13, No. 2 (Summer, 1983), pp. 65–83. The Johns Hopkins University Press. http://www.jstor.org/stable/464660

Chestnut, Joey. Personal interview. 24 April 2008.

Conley, Robert. (1958, May 19). *The New York Times* "U.S. and Russia Tie in Platelifting: Steaks Too High for Two Weightlifters in Eating Contest Contestants Dispose of 4 Lobsters, but Halt at 6 Squab." Retrieved October 29, 2008, from ProQuest Historical Newspapers The New York Times (1851–2005) database.

Conti, Jason "Crazy Legs." Personal interview. 3 July 2008.

Danow, David. *The Spirit of Carnival: Magical Realism and the Grotesque.* Louisville: University Press of Kentucky, 1995.

Davekos, Pete "Pretty Boy." Personal interview. 2 July 2008.

Deen, Paula H. *The Lady & Sons Just Desserts: More Than 120 Sweet Temptations from Savannah's Favorite Restaurant.* New York: Simon and Schuster, 2002.

Douglas, Mary. *Natural Symbols: Explorations in Cosmology.* 1970. New York: Routledge, 1996.

—— *Purity and Danger: An Analysis of Concepts of Pollution and Taboo.* 1966. New York: Routledge, 2002.

Fagone, Jason. *Horsemen of the Esophagus: Competitive Eating and the Big Fat American Dream.* New York, Crown Publishers, Inc., 2006.

Fischler, Marcelle. (2002, January 27). *Long Island Journal*: "Champion Overeaters, and Proud of It." Retrieved October 1, 2008, from ProQuest Historical Newspapers The New York Times (1851–2005) database.

Halloran, Vivian Nun. "Biting Reality: Extreme Eating and the Fascination with the Gustatory Abject." *Iowa Journal of Cultural Studies* 4 (2004): n. pag. Web. 05 June 2010.

Hardesty, Chris. (2010, September 17). "Cannoli Binge Brings Back Simpler Era" htpp://blog.wsj.com/metropolis/2010/09/17/in-little-italy-cannoli-binge-brings-back-a-simpler-era/. The Wall Street Journal Blog: Metropolis.

Hesser, Amanda. (2002, October 30). *New York Times:* "Big Eaters, Sure, But This Is Absurd." Retrieved November 1, 2008, from ProQuest Historical Newspapers The New York Times (1851–2005) database.

"Inside the Pyramid: What Are Discretionary Calories?" MyPyramid. United States Department of Agriculture, 23 Sept. 2009. Web. 05 Sept. 2010. <http://www.mypyramid.gov/pyramid/discretionary_calories.html >

Jarvis, Ed. "Welcome to Ed Cookie Jarvis: Coming Soon to a Dining Table Near You." Entertainmentli.com 2007. Web. 12 februrary 2009.

Kauffman, Frederick. *A Short History of the American Stomach.* New York: Harcourt, Inc., 2008.

Khan, Kim. "How Does Your Debt Compare?" 2008. *Money Central MSN:* <http://moneycentral.msn.com/content/SavingandDebt/P70741.asp>.

Lee, Juliet. Personal interview. 3 July 2008.

Levenstein, Harry. *Paradox of Plenty: A Social History of Eating in Modern America.* Berkeley: UC Press, 2003, Print.

Lloyd, Carol. "Status Quo: Retail Therapy—Shopocalypse Now!" *San Francisco Chronicle* October 31, 2008: 6.

Meadow, Rosalyn M., and Lillie Weiss. *Women's Conflicts about Eating and Sexuality: The Relationship between Food and Sex.* Philadelphia: Haworth Press, 1992.

Rubin, Lawrence. "Beyond Bread and Circuses: Professional Competitive Eating." *Food for Thought: Essays on Eating and Culture.* Ed. Lawrence Rubin. North Carolina: McFarland & Company, Inc. 2008: 248–265. Print.

Schwartz, Hillel. *Never Satisfied: A Cultural History of Diets, Fantasies, and Fat.* New York: Doubleday, 1986.

Thomas, Sonya. Personal interview. 5 July 2008.

Tocqueville, Alexis de. *Democracy in America*, trans. Arthur Goldhammer. New York: Library of America, 2004.

Wexler, Sarah. "America's Hungriest Woman." *Marie Claire.* June 2008.

21

Vintage Breast Milk: Exploring the Discursive Limits of Feminine Fluids

Penny Van Esterik

What are feminine fluids – fluids consumed by women or fluids produced by women? Fluids that enter female bodies or fluids that exit female bodies? Breast milk is clearly a fluid that leaves one body and enters another. No fluid is more feminine than breast milk. No fluid carries with it as much complex symbolic baggage surrounding what it means to be female. This article explores the material and symbolic dimensions of breast milk in North America, building on the provocations of a Toronto performance artist whose work has transformed breast milk from a fluid produced by women to a fluid consumed by women.

The Lactation Station Breast Milk Bar was performed in July 2006 by Toronto-based performance artist Jess Dobkin in a beautiful studio space at the Ontario College of Art and Design (Professional Gallery). The performance was presented as part of FADO's show, Five Holes: Matters of Taste, curated by Paul Couillard. The press release for the show invited audience members to "quench [their] curiosity" at the breast milk bar during the cocktail hour, 5 to 8 p.m. (Dobkin). Tastings of pasteurised breast milk, donated by six women in the local community, were offered at a softly lit white wine bar decorated with coasters, bar snacks (Cheerios), a bar menu listing six flavours of breast milk, and a sign reading, "We can't serve minors." On a tray, Dobkin placed a unique set of serving vessels made to order for the donors, based

on the kind of containers they envisioned their milk being served in. These included vessels reminiscent of pink plastic nipples, earthenware chalices, a teacup, and a champagne glass filled with curdled milk and a submerged Lact-Aid tube (a nursing aid). As in a vintage wine tasting, Dobkin arranged and paired tastings of pasteurised breast milk, each vintage sample named provocatively: *passion's legacy* and *sweet fall harvest; temple of the goddess* paired with *truth serum number nine.*

A server took names and called people when there was a seat available at the bar. Dobkin, the bartender, introduced the tasting samples and listened to the intimate stories of the bar patrons as they sampled the beverages. Videotaped interviews with the donors were screened on the wall at the other end of the room and played throughout in the background. Breastfeeding support pillows were scattered around the space for comfort. Some people "dropped into the bar for a drink" and left quickly, followed by curious murmurs of, "How was it?" after the tastings. As the artist–bartender observed, "Not everyone will be comfortable at the milk bar" (Dobkin, Interview with CBC).

THE TASTING

I was one of the first called to taste the vintage brews, and I did so along with

Figure 21.1 *The Lactation Station Breast Milk Bar*, Jess Dobkin, 2006
Photo by David Hawe

several other young women. The first sample was called *passion's legacy*; we were asked to smell, swirl the product, and sip. Jess led us through the tasting, telling us that the donor of this sample had craved chocolate during and after pregnancy, accounting for the milk's sweet taste. From the video, we learned that the donor's baby was eight months old when she gave the samples. The donor spoke of the emotional and physical pleasures of breastfeeding and the release that she experienced when milk was removed. The tasters differed in their reactions to the small cups of breast milk. I was relieved to have no feelings of disgust when drinking the milk; I just tasted a light, mildly nutty fluid. Others thought it tasted like almond milk, honey or ice cream.

The second sample, *sweet fall harvest*, tasted quite different: fruitier and heavier. The donor was a vegetarian who began craving and eating meat during her pregnancy but was concerned that meat would alter the flavour of her breast milk. An articulate animal rights activist, she spoke in the video of her dismay that we, as humans, claim that a child has a right to its mothers' milk while at the same time denying the calf's right to its mother's

milk. We take the calf's milk for ourselves with no hesitation, she said. Why should we hesitate at drinking human milk? Of course, standard infant formulas are made with cow's milk and chemical additives, a fact unknown to many users, who rarely think about the source of the milk in the can. The conversation on the video revealed the difficulties that emerge from drawing inappropriate analogies and false equivalences between breast milk and cow's milk, products that are in no way commensurate.

Straight up with a twist, the third sample, was considered sweet by some tasters, while *truth serum number nine* was reported as sour. *Temple of the goddess* left "an angry aftertaste" as the donor mother had a penchant for highly spiced foods. Others felt the sample tasted medicinal. We searched for analogies, but since so few people had ever tasted breast milk, our comparisons were inadequate, fumbling, imprecise.

Differences of opinion at the bar reinforced the artist's argument about the diversity of the taste of breast milk. Each donor's experience is embodied in the taste of her milk and its unique place of production: the mother's body as terroir.

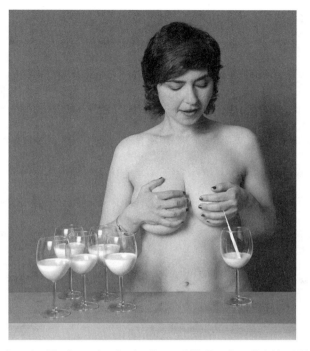

Figure 21.2 Publicity photo for *The Lactation Station Breast Milk Bar*, Jess Dobkin, 2006
Photo by David Hawe

The artist's intentions were clearly to celebrate but unsettle the intimate act of breastfeeding in motherhood and project a playful, non-judgemental gaze onto breast milk. This sense of play was obvious on Jess's flyer advertising the event. Here, she stands against a hot pink background; she gazes into the camera, nude, squirting breast milk into a wine glass.

But Jess's own experience with breastfeeding her daughter was anything but playful. On the bar in a cowhide frame, we encounter a photograph of the artist grimacing in pain while she was nursing her daughter. During the performance, Dobkin spoke of the feelings of shame that overtook her when she failed at breastfeeding as a new mother. In an interview that I conducted following the show, Jess revealed some of the motivations for developing the performance. Denaturalizing the romantic relationship between mothers and their milk, she

lamented, "The things I thought would be easy were so hard and the things I thought would be so hard were easy" (Personal interview). Breastfeeding was supposed to be the easy part, but without adequate support, it was a real challenge. After trying everything she could to breastfeed successfully and after being told just to try harder, she was later criticized for (eventually) bottle-feeding her daughter. The Lactation Station was, in this sense, more than food for thought; it was also a ritual of healing for the artist. By recording and listening to the stories of the breast-milk donors, Dobkin realized that she did do her job as a mother, just with a different kind of feminine fluid.

Analogies

Anthropologist Mary Douglas once wrote, "The meal is a kind of poem, but by a very limited analogy. The cook may not be able to express the powerful things poets can say" (*Implicit* 240). Analogies matter, particularly when it comes to food. And this was especially the case at the Lactation Station, as few people had tasted breast milk and even fewer had been to a milk bar. Analogies can intensify meaning and draw mind and memory back to past traditions and experiences. But how do we develop analogies for products like breast milk that are unique? Tea is quite like coffee. Fruit juices can be compared to soda pop. But what is an appropriate analogy for breast milk? What is breast milk really like? Is it a food? A drug? Or perhaps like a vaccination, as it provides an infant with its first immunity against disease.

As anthropologists and psychoanalysts remind us, analogies also set up new and paradigmatic opportunities to explore basic natural processes. The dominant analogy for breastfeeding in North America is urination, something best done in a bathroom. This is especially true for those who grew up without the experience of seeing a mother breastfeeding her child. Urination is an inappropriate and insulting analogy, meant to humiliate women and devalue the production of this precious fluid. And very effective it is, as any woman who is banished to the bathroom to breastfeed knows.

But human milk is secreted not excreted, in spite of the spate of analogies to the contrary. And more importantly, as performance theorist Rebecca Schneider might say, it is "secret-ed" – it is the repressed that the male gaze fears to see (57). What Dobkin has done in Lactation Station is force us to confront this secreted/secret-ed fluid by thinking through an additional analogy, an improbable one perhaps. Her work moves us away from using a private excretory act as an analogy for breastfeeding by developing, with the audience, another unique analogy: wine making and tasting. The analogy connects a fluid secreted by a body to another culturally valued fluid that is squeezed from grapes, an analogy that elevates taste, discrimination, nuance and pleasure, as experienced at the Lactation Station Breast Milk Bar.

Figure 21.3 Dobkin nursing daughter; presented in a cow print frame on the milk bar

INTIMACY AND DISGUST

Mary Douglas makes an important distinction between food and drinks, and suggests that the consumption of drinks is generally a less intimate event. Drinks may be shared with relative strangers, as compared with, say, food shared at dinner parties with close friends (*Deciphering* 40). Not so, when breast milk is on tap. Drinks flow and shift – are difficult to pin down – because they take the shape of what contains them, a point captured by Dobkin in the set of vessels created for each sample of donor milk. (This reminds me of my collection of breast beer mugs, perhaps designed for frisky frat boys, which are considered slightly obscene. But are the plastic, breast-shaped containers designed to hold expressed breast milk any less so?) Certainly, several critics, and even spectators, responding to the performance, have used the term obscenity to describe the show (women's explicit body art routinely attracts this label). Having drinks at the Lactation Station Milk Bar means participating in an exceptionally intimate consumptive act, one likely to evoke feelings of disgust as so many boundaries are being transgressed. Disgust arises from the loss or removal of distance. Elspeth Probyn writes, "[I]n disgust, things, categories, people are just too close for comfort" (133), and you cannot get much closer to the other than by consuming milk from its breast.

Perhaps the most successful aspect of the show was its ability to bring to light the intense revulsion that surrounds breast milk, a substance that is inextricably linked to the feminine body. This was particularly obvious in the disgust expressed by men writing about the show. Several male reporters simply dismissed the art performance as a waste of taxpayers' money. One particularly offensive report by John Strobel in the *Toronto Sun*, published prior to the opening, made fun of the show by proposing his own Fluids pest: "I would bring heaping platters of phlegm sandwiches and eye gunk pies . . . Care for a mixed drink? Blood, sweat and tears." But strangely, he made no jokes about semen. Strobel also expressed surprise that the Tories had "held their fire" about the Canada Council's support for the project and, accordingly, the taxpayers' support of the performance through a grant to Dobkin.

Partly in response to the performance, Health Canada issued a press release on the day of the show, warning against buying or consuming breast milk from strangers. The press release, published in papers across the country, warned of the possibility of Hepatitis B, HIV, bacteria and legal or illegal drugs passing through the breast milk. They warned that cross-nursing and purchasing breast milk online is not controlled in any way. This lack of regulation may be due to the fact that authorities can't decide whether to regulate it as a bodily fluid or as a food. Maybe they need a new category: feminine fluids.

Mary Douglas would have loved the show. Consuming an intimate bodily product like breast milk, she would say, arouses a feeling of disgust as it breaks down differences between self and other, inside and outside, pure and impure. One female reporter got it. She saw the performance as a critique of cultural discourses that present the "mother as untouchable," lauding Dobkin for highhghting the "complexities of breastfeeding by openly and creatively recognizing the sensual, ordinary and even comical aspects of this act" (Sasha). Of course, the humour elicited by this performance is very different from the cheap laughs extracted from mainstream audiences in movies like *Meet the Fockers* or *Little Men*, when a male character accidentally drinks breast milk stored in the refrigerator.

In *Alice in Wonderland*, Alice complains that "it is impolite to eat food that you've been introduced to" (Probyn 135). This might explain the discomfort I felt when speaking to a donor mother whose milk I had just consumed at the milk bar. And this might also explain why another donor mother spoke of feeling strange to be breastfeeding her own child while she was also drinking her own breast milk at the bar, rather like sneaking out and having a glass of wine when she should be abstaining during breastfeeding. Much like Annie Sprinkle's signature perform-ance, *Public Cervix Announcement*, where she invited the audience to view her cervix through a speculum while she sat spread-eagled onstage, Dobkin's perform-ance forces us to confront the judge-mental, suspicious gaze that we project on women's bodies, particularly the bodies of breastfeeding women.

WORKS CITED

Dobkin, Jess. Press release for *Lactation Station Breast Milk Bar*. 11 July 2006. 27 Aug. 2008 <http://www.myocad.com/talk_view.php?topicID =5720>.

——. Personal interview. Aug. 2006.

——. Interview. *Toronto at Six*. CBC Television. 13 July 2006.

Douglas, Mary. *Deciphering a Meal. Food and Culture: A Reader*. Ed. C. Counihan and P. Van Esterik. New York: Routledge, 1997.

——. *Implicit Meanings*. London: Routledge, 1975.

Probyn, Elspeth. *Carnal Appetites: Food Sex Identities*. New York: Routledge, 2000.

Sasha. "Love Bites." *Eye Weekly* 13 July 2006: 70.

Schneider, Rebecca. *The Explicit Body in Performance*. London: Routledge, 1997.

Strobel, John. "Lactation Smacktation. A Phlegm-Filled Fluids Fest – Complete with Boogers 'n' Mash and Eye Gunk Pies – Is a Much Better Idea." 21 June 2006. 28 August 2008 <http://www. torontosun.com/News/TorontoAndGTA/2006/06 /21/pf-1644704.html>.

22

Do the Hands That Feed Us Hold Us Back? Implications of Assisted Eating

G. Denise Lance

INTRODUCTION

When I was in third grade, school officials decided that it was unacceptable for my mother and aide still to be feeding me. The seven years I spent in occupational therapy and the numerous utensils with built-up handles and plates with raised edges and suction cups on the bottom had not proved helpful in bringing me to a point at which more food would be in my mouth than on the floor. Still, how was I ever going to be an accepted member of society if I could not feed myself?

The day before the feeding experts came to evaluate me and pass down their learned suggestions, the speech therapists asked me a question that foreshadowed the fate of this next self-feeding trial: "What kind of Jell-O do you like?" I requested lime, since that was what I always had when my family ate at the local steakhouse. Not a fan of Jell-O otherwise, the presentation in glass parfait glasses topped with a glob of whipped cream always enticed me. Even in my third grade mind, I knew that Jell-O was just about the toughest food they could have selected, a food that is promoted based on wiggling and jiggling. Yes, that was the perfect choice for someone with unsteady hand control from cerebral palsy to prove her self-feeding ability.

Needless to say, I failed the test. I am not sure which moved more, the Jell-O or my hand. From then on, I was no longer pressured to learn to feed myself, and I have relied on family members and personal assistants ever since. I did not dwell on the need to be fed or let it ruin my self-image.

As I grew older, I encountered more events involving food and the social implications of having to be fed became apparent. It wasn't just about satiating hunger anymore: there were definite social disadvantages to having to be fed.

Food and socializing are inextricably bonded in our culture. As Mintz and Du Bois (2002) point out: "Next to breathing, eating is perhaps the most essential of all human activities, and one with which much of social life is entwined" (100). Going out to lunch or dinner, attending informal and formal receptions, and inviting people to our homes for meals are all ways in which we build social capital.

Social capital refers to the potential benefit we achieve from establishing a network of friends, acquaintances, and business associates. The concept was first theorized by Bourdieu, applied to education by Colman, and popularized by Putnam (Field, 2003). A multidimensional concept, social capital depends upon our everyday interactions with others (Dekker & Uslaner, 2001). While 'bridging social capital' refers to one's involvement in groups of people with diverse opinions and backgrounds, 'bonding social capital' refers to belonging to groups whose members are more similar to one's own.

Putnam saw social capital as the reciprocity and trust built through networking with others through civic involvement. Putnam argued that Americans lack of involvement in groups was responsible for an overall decline in society, as manifested in a lack of connectedness and concern for others (Field, 2003). Accordingly, I suggest that people who need assistance eating are more likely to be disadvantaged in building the bridging type of social capital, but experience the bonding capital in a significant way with others. Therefore, building on Putnam's ideas, building "bonding capital" helps to strengthen society; engaging people with feeding assistance could offer benefits to society as a whole.

The purpose of this article is to investigate the implications of needing assistance in eating through analysis of the responses of people with disabilities to an email interview and from my own experiences as a person with cerebral palsy who must be fed. Because so many potential networking events involve food, I was curious if others felt, as I sometimes do, that their ability to build social capital was hampered by their need for eating assistance.

Studies of eating in public, such as Martens and Warde's (1997) study of the experiences of people in Northern England, have neglected the perspective of people with disabilities. In fact, there are very few articles addressing the issues associated with public eating for people who need assistance to do so. In articles dealing with aftereffects of stroke and surgery for essential tremor, eating in public is only mentioned in passing (Perry & McLaren, 2003; Hariz, Lindberg, & Bergenheim, 2002). The pilot research presented in this article begins to address that gap.

METHOD

To investigate the issue of assisted eating, I posted messages on three disability related discussion lists asking for people who needed assistance eating to participate in email interviews about their experiences. List members were also asked to forward my request to any other people who might be willing to be interviewed. Seven people responded to the call for participants and received a list of questions in return. Respondents included two women and four men, ranging from 17 years old to middle age, who require assistance eating and one mother of a teenager with physical disabilities (whose son was also a participant). Their impairments included spinal cord injury, polio, brain hemorrhage, spinal muscular atrophy, and a type of brain damage called kernicterus.

In this exploratory research, I asked the respondents their views on the following topics: eating with assistance in public settings, both business and social; whether they avoided eating events because of their need to be fed; whether being fed interfered with conversations; whether they felt that they had been left out of events; whether they had sensed uneasiness with eating partners; whether being fed affected romantic meals or dating, and whether etiquette or the stares of other people concerned them.

Responses were analyzed using standard qualitative methods to determine common themes and variation in experiences. Despite the limited number of participants, the answers of most were quite similar. Again, the purpose of this study was to determine the range of experiences in negotiating public eating and to document how the use of eating assistance in American culture limits the building of social capital. Further studies should investigate how generalizable these experiences are, and whether there are differences based on gender, length of time using feeding assistance, or other variables.

LIMITATIONS

Time constraints limited the soliciting of interviewees to those connected with disability listservs, thus limiting the generalizability of the results. Centers for independent living and other disability organizations could be contacted in order to locate more people who require assistance eating. In addition, finding people through non-electronic sources would allow for the opinions of those without internet access to be included. More in-depth interviews and perhaps observations could also expand our knowledge in this area.

EXPERIENCES OF ASSISTED EATING

All the interviewees reported avoiding events that involved food, at one time or another, on the basis of having to be fed. Another popular tactic was to attend, but not to eat in public, opting to eat before or after the event.

There are instances in which feeding ourselves in public is not an attractive option. While many use any means necessary to eat in private, they realize that unconventional methods of eating would not be well accepted in public. As a man with polio explained:

> Though I can do it at home alone, I never bend down and pick up something with my mouth in public. Left to my own devices, when no one is around, I can do a piece of fruit, bread, or nuts, etc. but not in public.

The people with whom one eats and the nature of the event make a difference in how individuals negotiate eating situations. A college man with physical disabilities points out: "I'm very picky at where I'll allow myself to be fed. I allow myself to be fed around close friends or family members, or at disability conferences where I won't be the only one." A study by Miller, Rozin, and Fiske (1998) revealed that American college students associated feeding with romantic relationships but not with casual friendships or coworker relationships. Notions concerning the intimacy of feeding another person may not only interfere with our comfort with being fed in public but also complicate others' comfort with our being fed or feeding someone who is not a romantic partner.

In situations where we are in the company of friends and family, most did not have difficulty being fed. In the company of unfamiliar people, however, the risk of being stigmatized or stared at increases. Those who have acquired disabilities in adulthood report that they had to become accustomed to public reactions to being fed. As one woman told me:

> I got angry at the "walkie-talkies" for staring and started to be a smart-mouth, saying, "What the f*** are you staring at???" After a while, that got old, and I just ignored the funny looks from the *vox populi* and started to enjoy myself again. Now, I go out every week with my mom, sister, or friends and am oblivious to the people.

A mother of a teenager with physical disabilities stipulated that even disability-related gatherings are not always easy to negotiate in terms of eating:

> When he went to wheelchair basketball camp, he made sure he had extra food that he could eat in case they had things that would be difficult for him. Even activities that cater to people with disabilities don't always get it right.

For those who have speech disabilities, speaking and eating are not necessarily compatible activities. A teenager with physical disabilities shared: "It's hard enough doing one of those things let alone both at the same time, if there is a conversation, and I want to contribute, I have to stop eating in order to respond." As the teenager's mother added, talking and eating also lengthens the meal.

> My husband and I always talk a lot at the table, and for [my son] to participate he has

to stop doing everything else. It does make dinner longer because he is a slower eater and when he spends time talking it takes even longer. We try to think about that, but sometimes we have to tell him to stop talking and eat because he is running late.

In time, most said that they had learned to ignore the stares cast their way. For most, the curious looks of children provide an opportunity to teach about disabilities. As one woman with a disability from a brain hemorrhage admits: "I'm oblivious to the people — except for the children, whom I adore. For them, I smile, say Hi, and patiently answer their honest questions about me and my wheelchair."

Although conclusions cannot be generalized due to the small number of interviewees, for those in this study, concern about public perception of assisted eating seems to be influenced by factors such as onset of disability and gender. For example, the male respondents indicated either that etiquette issues had never concerned them or that they had experienced disability long enough that they no longer worried over it. One man with quadriplegia said that he used to worry about public reaction to his being fed, but now, "I'm too busy with friends to even notice other people staring." In contrast, a woman with spinal muscular atrophy, for whom having a disability is fairly new, affirmed:

I often worry about etiquette. In public places, I'm a very careful eater and try to do everything to minimize effects of disability. Sometimes, I even get a little obsessive about etiquette to a point that appearing graceful takes precedence over filling my tummy!

These interviews demonstrate that most people with eating disabilities have strategies with which to handle public eating events by eating at another time, selecting foods, that they can feed themselves, or joining the festivities by bringing an

assistant. Nonetheless, there are additional social, economic, and political consequences of sometimes choosing not to attend events involving food.

According to Warde, Tampubolon, and Savage (2005), eating, events are important to networking and building social capital, which involves our use of social relationships to advance our positions in life. As Potts (2005) explains, social connections often serve as venues through which people, both those with and without disabilities, find employment. Therefore, having to be fed may be a disadvantage if it causes people to avoid opportunities in which social capital may be gained. Gaining leadership positions and employment opportunities frequently involve meeting and socializing at conferences and other meetings.

Those who use attendants reported that they are comfortable talking about business or work-related topics with attendants present, but personal, family issues and sex were identified as problematic topics. Additionally, having another person around can hamper socializing. Some people may assume that a person who has an assistant already has a conversation partner, and some just do not know how or want to approach someone with an assistant.

Lin (2001) suggests that the traditional means of building social capital are being replaced by "cybernetworks," although the extent to which this is happening remains understudied. While increasing use of online communication for social networking may benefit those who have difficulty socializing while dining, some argue that electronic networks are helpful in sustaining contacts already made in person but not necessarily the best means of building new social capital (Wellman, Haas, Witte, and Hampton, 2001). Although online communications may help people with disabilities build social capital, those in my interviews stress that hiding behind our computer screens should never be a sole, resort. In order to increase society's awareness and comfort with disabilities and strengthen our advocacy efforts, we must be seen doing as much as possible in public venues.

Not only does having to be fed present potential exclusion from some employment and social opportunities, but it can also make romantic relationships more difficult to establish. Eating is often a part of dating in North American culture. A person needing assistance must insure that his or her date is prepared to offer assistance or not mind that a personal care attendant comes along. The later option lacks appeal to many, who envision dating as becoming familiar with another person on a one-on-one basis. Having someone along seems as if it would hinder this intimacy, or at least make it more awkward. As one young woman with spinal muscular atrophy explained:

> I would not make going out to a restaurant the first date. In fact, I probably would not eat with my date until (if even) the relationship was more serious. Then, I would start by making sure that he was aware of the fact that I needed assistance and have a meal in private with him first.

However, she also pointed out:

> I think it's important to note that having someone help you to eat is not always a negative thing in a serious romantic relationship. For example, I know of a pretty high class and very romantic fondue restaurant in which feeding one another is not uncommon. Patrons have semi-private booths, so it isn't right out in public, and "assisted eating" is sort of the norm.

A man with polio also shared an experience that illustrated that feeding someone might not quash "the mood" for some after all:

> When I was in my 20's, I used an orthotic setup sometimes called a BFO (balanced forearm orthesis). It worked pretty well for me then on a level surface at the level of functioning I had then. But I only hooked it up for eating . . . I remember a particular young woman about my age, a kind of poetic, literary grad student. We had shared some pleasant experiences and eaten together a few times (she doing it all for both of us) when I showed up one day with my eating equipment in a case. I explained what it was and that I needed her to set it up including the hand-splint. It was always a bit of an ordeal, especially the first time. But she complied. The meal went well. It was at a mutual friend's house. But then she said, obviously not impressed by my "independence" with my contraption, "You made me do all that just to deprive me of the intimacy of feeding you?

These comments are consistent with the connection between feeding and romantic relationships found by Miller, Rozin, and Fiske (1998).

Thus, it seems as if having to be fed may or may not be an obstacle to romance, depending on the other person, the setting, the closeness of the relationship, etc., and many still have concerns. A mother of a teenage boy with physical disabilities commented: "I worry about how he will come across on a date. I don't expect that he'll start out with dinner dates but he could surprise me!"

A PERSONAL PERSPECTIVE

Like the respondents, I have avoided social situations that involved eating because of my need for assistance. I have also used the tactic of going to events but not eating. I first realized the difficult social position of needing assistance eating in high school, when I attended extracurricular activities without assistance. If a meeting had snacks, my strategy was just not to eat, but take a straw so I could drink. Surprisingly, none of my friends ever offered to help me, just letting me sit and watch them eat. I admit that I never asked for their assistance either, so they probably thought that if I wanted to eat, I would have asked for help.

One Saturday, I went to a journalism conference with friends from the newspaper staff. Afterwards, we stopped at a fast food place for lunch. My strategy that day was to order finger food that I thought I could eat without too much mess, so I told my friend to order chicken nuggets. He asked if I wanted fries too, but I said, "No, they're too hard for me to feed myself." I knew this from an unsuccessful attempt at getting the long, limp potatoes into my mouth. To my shock, he said, "Don't worry. I'll help you." That day, sitting with my friends, eating, talking, and laughing, I felt more accepted than I had in 11 years of being included.

I have declined several invitations to "get acquainted" lunches because I need to focus my attention on eating or speaking. Switching between the two increases my chances of choking, which does not make a great first impression! Unlike those I surveyed, I do believe that other colleagues may have excluded me from eating events such as impromptu lunch outings. I am unsure whether I am not asked because people do not want to assist me or are uncomfortable eating with me, or if they realize that visiting and eating are difficult for me and do not want to place me in an uncomfortable situation. Nonetheless, I can see instances in which needing assistance eating might hamper my ability to build social capital, especially if I needed to network in order to advance my professional status. For example, I have avoided receptions that are common in academic settings, even while noting that this might hurt my chances at forging new connections and placing me in mind when colleagues are looking for collaborators.

For me, writing is the most comfortable form of communication, so electronic networking works well. However, I am sure that when I avoid live events in which eating is expected, I miss opportunity for gaining social capital.

DISCUSSION

In their analysis of Northern Englander's reasons for eating out, Martens and Warde (1997) argue against Finkelstein's notion that eating in restaurants is detrimental to society in that these settings do not encourage the self-reflection necessary for civility. According to Finkelstein; "Civility is not the respecting of conventions which facilitate peaceful interaction and exchange of views, but engagement in dialogue without restriction of topic or constraint: by authority, rules or orchestration" (qtd. in Martens and Warde, 1997, 133), Finkelstein argues that restaurant eating encourages people to engage in ritualized exchanges without giving much thought to the social condition, and as such, fosters incivility. However, Martens and Warde's interviews demonstrated that "Diners are discerning people, who actively participate in and shape the event, rather than being confused, blinded or de-sensitized by the regime of the establishment in which they find themselves" (146). Participants noted several reasons for eating out, including wanting to eat good food, to spend time with friends and family, to avoid cooking, and to add variety to their lives. Although Finkelstein suggests that eating in private is preferable because private places encourage unobstructed, genuine social interactions, Martens and Warde disagree, charging their colleague with misunderstanding public spaces:

> If Finkelstein's utopia is the private, domestic, introspective episode of self-examination, others hold contrary views, expecting positive social benefits from participation and interaction in public space. However, neither of these alternative aspirations are apparently realised in the restaurant. One observable trait of behaviour in restaurants is that people at different tables rarely engage in conversation with one another. The restaurant is not exactly a public place, rather it is a quasi-public place. The restaurant is a space containing a number of private reservations (tables),

from which mutual inspection of the tenants of other reservations is permitted, and where one's own behaviour is restrained by the gaze (and power) of others. So, eating out is not necessarily commendable for its encouragement of public conviviality and coexistence. Rather it is private behaviour in a public place. To that extent, it has limited potential for encouraging a public sphere or civil society. However, it does have some other, if less elevated, functions for customers. (147).

In the above discussion, I have outlined several implications of having to be fed in public. This initial investigation integrated my personal experiences with the responses of seven other people to a brief e-mail interview. I hope that the issues raised spark further research, especially concerning how assisted eaters build social capital and the impact of assisted eating on romantic relationships. The nature of restaurants as quasi-public spaces, relating that with public acceptance of disabilities, would also prove an interesting and important topic for disability studies.

CONCLUSION

Those who need eating assistance and others with disabilities should view eating in public as a venue for education and advocacy, as well as opportunities for building social capital. If we only eat in private, as Finkelstein suggests, dialogue concerning disability would be stifled, as would the civility of society.

REFERENCES

Dekker, P. & Uslaner, E. M. (Eds.). (2001). *Social Capital and Participation in Everyday Life*. London: Routledge.

Field, J. (2003). *Social Capital*. New York: Routledge.

Hariz, G-M, Lindberg, M., and A. T. Bergenheim. (2002). Impact of thalamic deep brain stimulation on disability and health-related quality of life in patients with essential tremor. *Journal of Neurology, Neurosurgery and Psychiatry*, 72(1); 47–53,

Lin, N. (2001). *Social Capital: A Theory of Social Structure and Action*. Cambridge, England: Cambridge University Press.

Martens, L. & Warde, A. (2005), Urban pleasure? On the meaning of eating out in a northern city. In P. Caplan, (Ed.) *Food, Health, and Identity* (131–150). London: Routledge.

Miller, L, Rozin, P., & Fiske, A. P. (1998). Food sharing and feeding another person suggest intimacy; two studies of American college students. *European Journal of Social Psychology*. 28(3), 423–436.

Mintz, S. W. & Du Bois, C. (2002). The Anthropology of Food and Eating. *Annual Review of Anthropology*, 31, 99–119.

Perry, Lin & McLaren, Susan (2003), Eating difficulties after stroke. *Journal of Advanced Nursing*, 43(4), 380–369.

Potts, B. (2005). Disability and Employment: Considering the Importance of Social Capital. *The Journal of Rehabilitation*, 71(3), 20+. Retrieved November 1, 2006, from Questia database: http://www.questia.com /PM.qst?a=o&d=5010939023

Warde, A. Tampubolon. G., & Savage, M. (2005). Recreation, Informal Social Networks and Social Capital. *Journal of Leisure Research* 37(4), 402–25.

Wellman, B., Haase, A., Witte, J, and Hampton, K. (2001) 'Does the Internet increase, decrease or supplement social capital?: Social networks, participation and community commitment', *American Behavioral Scientist*, 45(3): 436–455.

23

Will Tweet for Food: Microblogging Mobile Food Trucks—Online, Offline, and In Line

Alison Caldwell

Walking through Midtown Manhattan at lunchtime, Union Square in the early evening, or the West Village late at night, it is difficult not to notice a subtle yet stirring culinary uprising in the streets of New York City. There is a collective clamor, online and offline, about a new street food trend with an elevated artisanal design—the microblogging mobile food truck. The fact that it's not always there when you want it, unless you *know* exactly how to get it, is what makes this phenomenon stand out. Occupying the intersection of food and technology, this latest public event has adopted online social networking, and in doing so, creates an innovative and shifting trend in street food culture. In 2008 and 2009, New York City saw a major influx in these modern and distinctive specialty mobile food trucks. At the heart of each start up is an elevated culinary style not typical of street food, combined with the popular internet marketing platform, Twitter. Compared to the traditional New York street food carts or trucks, this operation is one of the most animated events to happen to street food since the 1950s when the Mister Softee ice cream truck emerged with its classic musical draw.[1] Though ice cream, taco, and catering trucks are not new to the city, this novel wave in mobile food trucks stands out as separate for many reasons.

Today, New York City street food carts and mobile food trucks line sidewalks of nearly every avenue. The culinary landscape is generally saturated with Middle Eastern style food carts, American hot dogs and pretzel stands, Mexican style food trucks, and fruit and vegetable vendors. On the fringe is a marginal number of street food vendors selling additional cuisine like Asian, Caribbean, and other ethnic fare. In all, these are today's traditional vendors of New York City. That said, this chapter focuses on a new version, or wave, of street food vendors. They arrive on a city block with their artisanal brand, and stand out as separate from the traditional culture of street food vending. Unlike the typical street food cart and truck, they cry out business plan and graphic designer along with hip vendors, chic food, and savvy technology. Each is armed with its own unorthodox variety of menu items that stand out as gourmet and diverse by street food standards. From local hand-made ginger ice cream, to hand-pounded cod schnitzel, the cuisine is more reminiscent of restaurant fare than what most would consider street food to be. Most significant, the vendor/entrepreneur ventures into the business of street food with a strategy to brand their business through utilizing the online social networking (OSN) platform, Twitter. This new generation of vending has embraced the culture of internet marketing media, distinguishing themselves from the traditional food vendor on the street whose main form of promotion depends on repeat customers, word of mouth, tourist traffic, and location. In fact, the use of Twitter is a prerequisite for defining this modern mobile food truck that emerged as a result of the available technology. This relationship between food and OSN technology has created an emerging subculture that exists because of its response to the Twitter phenomenon. It represents a group of food trucks that collectively stand out as one emerging event, each with its own style of food and individual brand.

While this new way in street food has a significant presence in other urban centers, including Washington D.C. and Los Angeles, the focus here is New York City. Street food and New York City have a historic relationship that has long shaped its urban character. Food cart vending in the street has been a fundamental part of New York City's local culture since the late nineteenth century when compact and crowded immigrant neighborhoods looked to pushcarts for fresh, affordable, and familiar provisions.[2] First generation Irish, Italian, and Jewish peddlers sold items like fruits, vegetables, hot corn, chestnuts, and knishes.[3] Today, street food in New York can be constituted as any food sold on the street via licensed or unlicensed vendors. It can range from an organic grass-fed burger off a nouveau food truck of topic here, to an Italian icee at a simple one-man push-cart, to a mango on stick sold from a grocery store shopping cart.

Street food vending has provided a foothold into the American dream for the immigrant worker who arrives in a culture with less access to credit, education, or cultural capital. Today, traditional New York City street food remains largely a business of immigrants, many first generation. The majority of these food vendors are not chefs or entrepreneurs by trade. They are mainly lower-skilled businessmen and women investing in a business with little capital risk.[4] On the contrary, the emerging micro-blogging food truck vendor population is predominantly non-immigrant, and where they are not, class and status usually sets them apart. Hence, the status of the emerging street food vendor's fare, combined with the use of internet technology, becomes an immediate remark on class and access. The vendor, menu, the marketing, and even the customer look different. Unlike traditional street food start ups, entrepreneurs in the form of lawyers, chefs, and corporate professionals have recognized a business that could be generated through branding a culinary experience using a mobile food truck and Twitter.

It is important to note, however, that while this trend is drawing significant attention and creating a new public interest in New York City street food, it only represents a small burgeoning sub-industry in the street vendor culture as a whole. While only a few dozen of these new food trucks populate the city, their following is considerable. Of the current 4,100 licensed street food vendors in New York City, the new Twitter-based mobile food truck makes up between 25–40 units operating during a given time, less than 1%.[5] Even so, this new crossroad of artisanal street food and OSN technology creates nothing short of a virtual-meets-actual social food phenomenon. Driven by a savvy breed of vendors and customers, it speaks of a modern day culinary obsessed landscape, where "food is the new black."

This essay examines the emerging phenomenon of the online social-networking mobile food truck in New York City and explores events under way at the cross-section of microblogging and street food. Questions include: Does the food truck phenomenon influence a shift in the way people communicate, consume, and socialize around street food, offline, online, and in-line? What does this explain about actual and virtual communication around OSN and food? What is the actual and virtual experience of the new food truck consumer? How do elevated marketing and novel street food provoke change in the street food scene of New York City? How is this new street food formula a comment on class, technology, and consumption?

My ethnographic research offered a significant look into this particular street food trend where food vendors use Twitter to sell their upscale street cuisine. A subscription to Twitter was necessary, as well as a downloaded Twitter application for my mobile PDA phone. This provided for instant status updates from the trucks as they tweeted. The main food trucks I followed were the Wafels [sic] & Dinges truck, the SweeteryNYC truck, the Rickshaw Dumpling truck, and the Cravings truck. Selling Liege waffles, hand-made brownies, savory pork dumplings, and Taiwanese-style fried chicken, they each have followers numbering well into the thousands.[6] Fieldwork included spending time in line talking to customers and conducting additional interviews with truck owners and vendors. Time was also spent on board the SweeteryNYC Truck, observing operations from the vendor perspective.[7] Additionally, I "followed" a popular New York City food truck fan on Twitter, and ultimately interviewed her. Because both Twitter and the tweeting mobile food trucks are so recent, no scholarly literature exists at this intersection.

THE MICROBLOGGING FOOD TRUCK

Twitter is considered a microblogging OSN platform. Microblogging is a type of blogging that facilitates sharing short forms of information, such as messages and small image files either publicly or within a social network. Microblogging encourages faster and more frequent communication compared to a blog.[8] Twitter is a free service that permits its users to answer the question, "What are you doing?" by sending messages of 140 characters in length, called "tweets," to your friends or "followers." These messages are posted to a user's Twitter profile or blog and sent to their followers.[9] Users can send, receive, or re-post tweets via the Twitter website, or any filter, to any group he or she is following or being followed by. Filters include mobile phone devices or websites, such as Facebook and food blogs. In the case for users who follow mobile food trucks, they can search, or Google, tweeted information, go to the purveyor's website, or go to a truck's Facebook page and see the Twitter update that has been filtered. For this reason it is not necessary to subscribe to Twitter to find a truck. However, you will need to look up the truck's website, or search for a site that filters their Twitter feed to find the truck's most updated status. The mobile food trucks change their location from day to day, and often within that day. They travel to and from different neighborhoods to reach a broader clientele. Twitter allows the vendor to tweet their latest location as well as daily specials, promotions, and last minute menu changes to followers.

For the emerging microblogging mobile food truck vendor, Twitter serves as a simple and rewarding marketing tool. It is a free and direct line of communication from business to customer. Because a user chooses to follow, she is instantly willing to receive information in the form of status updates or tweets from that food truck vendor. As users compose and forward tweets, they create their own social networks and personal brands. The truck's online-generated clientele is, in fact, a small percent of sales in comparison to walk-ups from locals and tourists. Yet, the small group of loyal customers committed to following the trucks, online via Twitter and its filters, plays an integral part in shaping the allure and character of the truck on the street. What defines this phenomenon is the sum of its parts: the vendor with savvy food, the virtual marketing, and the street food enthusiasts with an online edge.

The tweeting mobile food trucks are capitalizing on the technological advantages of instant and direct communication with their customer base. In doing so, they are creating a subtle yet significant shift at the cross-section of online social-networking and street food. Where the food curious typically blog, review, and converse online *about* street food and food trucks, a food truck Twitter feed *is* the truck, creating real-time direct conversation between trucks and followers. As a result, there is an instant and engaging online-generated back and forth of communication to and about the specialized fare. The microblogging mobile food truck is instigating a distinctive real-world interaction within OSN communities. In essence, they are directing social communication from online to offline, and ultimately, to the mobile food truck where people collect and wait in line. Crafted in between, is a food forward community of belonging that lives in both online and offline spaces.

This new event takes street food public in novel ways. The microblog becomes a viral vehicle of communication for the newest fashion in street food, pushing it to the forefront of popular food culture in New York City. That said, the actors utilizing these tools, the microblogging patrons and vendors, represent a group with technological know-how. But along with their abilities comes access to technology and the devices utilized to drive this new trend forward into the public sphere. In his work on class and the information age, Manuel Castells points out that early adopters of new internet technology are generally those with more affluence and access.[10] While Twitter is becoming more popular, it could be debatable whether a new user today would be considered an early adopter. Castells classifies the gap that separates the new technological haves and have-nots as the "digital divide."[11] As discussed later, the class divide not only speaks to notions of technological access, but to issues

provoked by the haute-like cuisine being introduced to the street.

THE ACTUAL AND THE VIRTUAL

Microblogging mobile street food vendors merge the actual and the virtual through their novel use of Twitter, creating a genuine interaction amongst the online social-networking food truck follower. Traditionally, OSN is an introverted activity that lives and sustains itself by remaining in a virtual arena. Its ultimate goal is to drive people back to the social network, or website, to create more virtual socializing. Like Facebook, MySpace, or Twitter, online social networks are ultimately geared to keep people socially connected in cyber time and space. Alternatively, mobile food trucks use Twitter to collect, persuade, and direct followers to the street food they provide.

Twitter functions to keep people engaged online in the vast messaging realm of the microblogging world. Popular perceptions toward Twitter have been met with criticism by those who find it lacking significance. It's often perceived less about authentically connecting with others than it is about being heard, in 140 characters or less, and letting others know who you are by who you follow while collecting followers for social gain.[12] Miller, with a more serious critique, says that time spent on Twitter is an irrelevant waste saturated in "phatic-culture . . . pointless messages . . . devoid of substantive content."[13] That is, the context of microblogging serves no greater purpose and remains fragmented in hyper-communication contained in cyberspace. Browsing through numerous tweets, it is fair to say that Twitter is a place for members to gather and communicate around to collect social capital. More often than not, time spent on Twitter remains solely in the online environment. That said, the food truck vendor who has adopted the use of Twitter as a marketing tool seems to successfully fracture the superficial use of the social application and, in the process, contradicts claims of empty rhetoric. In fact, the raw and virtual back and forth chatting around street food creates a communication that invokes subjective conversation around a substantive object, food, that will be sought after for actual consumption while straddling the virtual world. This behavior renders the characteristics of this internet communication, shared by tweeters and bloggers, more subjective, honest, and credible. Appealing to physical and social consumption of food and information, tweeting food trucks are contributing towards a culture of relevant, content-rich information exchange, online, offline, and in line.

In a few short words, vendors and followers alike communicate about food and status with, what appears, sincere enthusiasm in real time. Maybe it's the subtext, rich with sensory meaning around cravings, hunger, and instant satisfaction, that lends this virtual space sincerity. With actual supply and demand for foodstuff in mind, perhaps honest chat is generated by information that is relied upon by both the follower and business owner, perpetuating a genuine actual/virtual supply and demand of information unique to this concept.

The oscillating from the virtual realm to the actual (Figure 23.1) creates a highly original experience. The tweeter can go from following, receiving, and re-tweeting

others in a virtual online space (a), and then exit that space and go offline (b) to find, locate, order, and eat her food in an actual space. In between the two realms enter the phenomena happening amongst mobile food truck tweeters. That is, they can at once occupy the actual and the virtual (c), communicating and tweeting information while at the actual/physical mobile food truck site. At the truck, they can tweet updates about its location, how many people are in front of them in line, or what they have decided to order. They can even tweet requests to their followers for a menu recommendation as they wait in line deciding what to eat. They can even tweet a review about the service or food. In doing so, a follower instantly publicizes messages to his food truck community and any other Twitter circles he is a part of, reaching a broad audience. Essentially, the food truck patron can be online tweeting what they are going to eat while in line waiting to order their meal, only to go offline (or not) to sit and eat their lunch. This, in part, is what separates this particular use of Twitter from a perceived immaterial use, rendering it worldly and uniquely concrete. Connected to followers, or patrons, vendors instantly tweet messages that actually serve to remove the online social networker from their virtual space and bring them into the actual/physical world, to the truck, where vendors and customers make an online-generated connection, in person.

"@Jesuisjuba," that's her Twitter name, is very much the face of New York City mobile food truck tweets. Her profile photo is a bright, red-masked, voracious looking eater that can't be missed. She follows most of the food trucks that use Twitter in the city and has a following of her own as a result. After tweeting a request for an interview, she responded (by email) with first hand insight. When asked how often she tweets for food, she replied, "Daily! It makes me get outside for a few minutes a day instead of glued to my desk, which was what I was doing

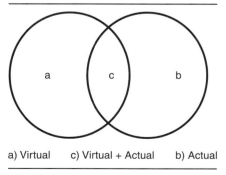

a) Virtual   c) Virtual + Actual   b) Actual

Figure 23.1

before I started tweeting my adventures. Kind of an added bonus."[14] By "adventures" "@Jesuisjuba" infers the chase that begins online searching for a truck to eat from, and then offline, or not, on foot into the streets to track down her mapped out cravings. As observed through research, finding lunch or dinner often becomes a scavenger hunt of sorts. Risk is a factor. Often a truck may sell out of the specialty or switch to another location before she gets there, increasing the level of intrigue and anticipation. But as "@Jesuisjuba's" experience quantifies, tweeting cyber food trucks can have considerable influence on actual daily lives, the culture of OSN, and how we are eating street food. Most significantly, she is an example born out of the new mobile food truck subculture that has created Twitter followers who uniquely go between and within the actual and virtual as they maintain engagement on their quest for consumption.

As the novel street food alternative embraces the information technology age, through OSN, it creates substantial connections and experiences in its wake. For the microblogging mobile food truck scenario, Twitter delivers itself useful to our senses and cravings. In doing so, it introduces us to one another in both actual and virtual spaces. Imbedded in the food forward tweets, often with a social agenda, is a complex web of meaning. While these can be deemed honest tweets for food, it cannot be lost, and fair to argue, that Twitter's lure plays on status and recognition that comes along with an active following. As people emotionally tweet, like "@Jesuisjuba," they are acknowledged as trendy authorities who collect social cache inherently attractive in OSN. Hence, the tweeting food truck vendor/follower interaction is a provoking interchange, influencing the relationship of personal identity and status within OSN.

Once a follower travels from online to in line at a truck, the tweeter is transformed from virtual pseudonym to actual subjective person in line. True physical identity becomes revealed, even if remaining socially anonymous. The mobile food truck breaks the virtual fourth wall, the cyber/real world barrier, and engages and entices people's senses into an actual physical culinary location. Within this context, through virtual extensions, Twitter guides people to actual social places in the street. In the process, virtual food truck followers come out from behind their digital profile, exposing their physical identity once at the truck. Gary Alan Fine states that the "connection between identity and consumption makes food the central role in the creation of community."[15] Among endless online social networks today, personal identity can be created and recreated to no end.[16] Only do we show who we really are, physically, when we break away from the microblogging interaction and make real face-to-face connections. While the consumption of digital information and food in one is not new, the relationship that OSN is manufacturing via the microblog and the food truck between vendors and patrons is unique. All this exposes an experience that creates multiple layers of community, consumption, and interaction through street food.

EXPERIENCE

On the street and online, microblogging mobile food trucks are creating a lively, atypical experience outside the traditional street food culture of New York City. Thomas DeGeest, owner and head of tweeting for Wafels & Dinges Truck, insists he is creating an overall experience for his customer base. He claims that he started to use Twitter purely as a function so customers could find them upon opening. After, he realized he could shape a brand and communicate the spirit and message of his business to the masses, which led him to the observation that what he was actually creating was a "very emotional experience."[17] Online, his tweets are often full of play. On top of multiple daily location updates, DeGeest consistently tweets challenges for free waffle toppings. Followers/customers answer them when they arrive at the truck. For example, it's not uncommon for a challenge to ask you to sing a song or do an impersonation (Figure 23.2). The tone of the Wafels & Dinges tweets are stylized, fun, and appear to make the tweeting customer feel like he is a part of the quirky and hip Wafels & Dinges family while online or physically at the truck. Mr. DeGeest often engages in tweets about his fare, and partakes in the conversations with followers both tweeting with him and each other.

Between the food, the truck, and the tweets, character is superimposed in the total experience, or brand, while crafting an identity for the whole. DeGeest's intention is to rally and market a certain feel and wanting associated with his waffles and Twitter circle. This brand loyalty, motivated by tweets and communicated through conversation about food, moves tweeters to the street to satisfy their cravings on many levels. As a result, the loyal customer is rewarded with a sense of belonging to a hi-tech and hip virtual and physical community.

Arjun Appadurai says that one of the fundamentals of food is "its capacity to mobilize strong emotions."[18] For many Americans, the first street food experience most often includes the classic ice cream truck. To recall this image is to summon a slew of feelings. The impulse to run outside and catch the truck whose amplified jingle could be heard a block away, creates an anticipation and wanting in a child that, for many, remains intact whenever memory serves. An approaching ice truck is often an iconic sense memory in time that has been culturally imbedded in the mind. With a Pavlovian response, perhaps nostalgia and recall superimposes the same response or excitement when a follower receives a tweet from a food truck. The truck rings its bell in virtual space and, perhaps, instigates excitement and wonder with energetic appeal. The tweet serves as the signal to crave and salivate. In a modern landscape like New York City, the food truck tweet becomes a substitute for the Pavlovian bell, translated into a familiar contemporary tone, partaking in a highly marketed culture of consumption.

Figure 23.2 Example of a waffle truck requesting a song or an impersonation from Twitter followers.

After reviewing tweets, it is clear that the new mobile food truck is a constructive mobilizing author of emotions on the web and in the streets. As a whole, this translates into a genuine interactive experience. Examples of tweets from vendors to followers include: "Come on out . . . we are here for you,"[19] "Happy Fantabulous Friday! Order with an attitude today for 1 free dinges."[20] Conversely, tweets from passionate and pleading followers to trucks look like: "@Street Sweet, I just died in their arms tonight . . . musta been something I ate."[21] "Crossing my fingers so hard for @Rickshaw Truck at Hudson and Houston today."[22] These tweets suggest a playful form of entertainment between mobile restaurateur and connoisseur. Customers tweet and re-tweet with elation, critique, upset, and sometimes rejoice in response to a mobile food truck's status. The tweeting street food vendors offer engagement and community, and food truck followers appear to crave the experience as much as the fare (Figure 23.3).

From online to in line, the microblogging mobile food truck is creating a wide experience that encompasses this particular relationship between vendor and customer. Appadurai's claim that food is a "highly condensed social fact" speaks to this specific and fast interaction, saturated in dialogue, and creating instant social food-centric communities.[23] Food's role here is both intermediary and material, unifying conversation and creating community amongst consumers and the market, online and offline. OSN, specifically Twitter, creates the potential to impose such meaningful exchange through food and new media.

The food, style, and interaction of this elevated mobile food truck is professional, contemporary, and vibrant. These retrofitted ice cream trucks of old scream hip and sub-cultural compared to the standard street food experience available in New York City. They stand out as separate, if not foreign, compared to the traditional "offline" street carts selling hot dogs,

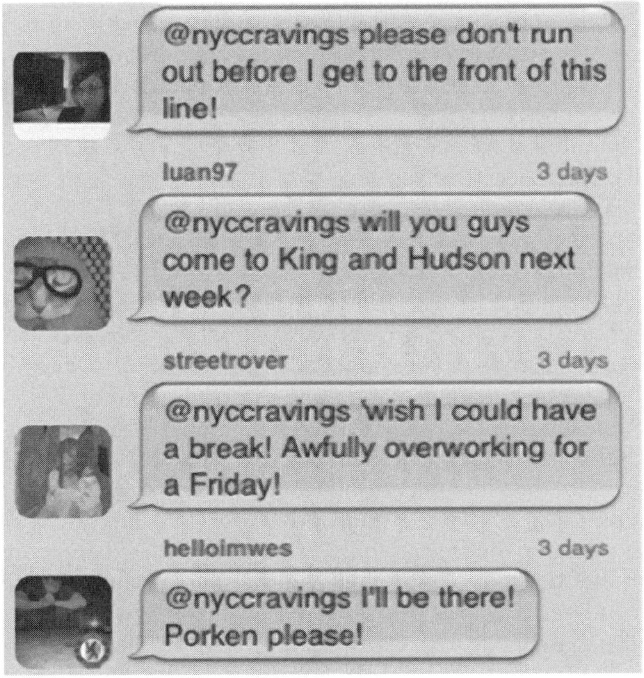

Figure 23.3 Examples of food truck followers sending tweets to nyccravings.

pretzels, and even falafels, on the streets of New York City. In the process, they have taken on an entire life of their own, embodied with charm, wit, and play. Unlike the typical street food experience, walking up to one of these trucks is, at times, like walking into a dramatic and stimulating arena, a traveling troupe of sorts. Bold and vivid, they appear unusual on any city block.

To encounter an eccentric tweeting food truck on the street is like walking into a theatrical and sometimes carnivalesque experience. If the person in charge of tweeting, usually the owner, is the director, then the often charismatic vendor serving up food on the truck is the actor. The mesmerized food enthusiast, much like a theater groundling, looks up at the stage from below, or in this case, from the street up to the counter. True to Shakespearian form, the customer is always engaged, if not charmed, and sometimes even heckled in jest by the totality of the physical experience. The scenes vary, but all are typically dynamic with color, art, digital media, humor, and lines for food filled with anticipation. Grant Di Mille, owner of the SweeteryNYC truck, commented how "women are skipping arm in arm up to the truck." The viral form of communication combined with the overall experience that vendors project seem to have a genuine and infectious effect. When asked what her favorite truck was, "@Jesuisjuba" said, "Probably the Rickshaw Dumpling Truck, they always remember me—it's nice. If your food is good, you remember me, and are nice? Sold." "@Jesuisjuba" demands good food, friendly service, and personal recognition in exchange for her online/in line loyalty. Through this identification, she is cast amongst the characters that heighten the overall experience for anyone who may follow the Rickshaw Dumpling Truck, online or in line.

Pierre Bourdieu explains that the working-class café is a "site of companionship," where the "focus is the counter,"

and "free rein is given to the typically popular art of the joke."[24] With its casual, jovial, and pedestrian setting, the microblogging food truck is very much a street café built upon this relationship and environment Bourdieu is describing. At the same time, it's debatable how working class the new mobile food truck may be, especially in light of its elevated fare and social media platform. After all, the full hi-tech experience of the food truck portrayed above may, in fact, be unattainable to those without access to OSN tools. All this, ultimately, speaks to a not so black and white class distinction. Like traditional carts that are predominantly working class, food is served in to-go containers, and seating is never provided. Patrons exit the food line in search of public seating, or like many, they walk and eat. But unlike typical street food vendors, some new food trucks accept credit cards, pointing to a clientele and vendor with greater means. Finally, items may range anywhere from $3 to $7 for a food item, and rarely exceed $9, where as a traditional New York City street food generally ranges from $2 to $6.[25] In comparing prices of the new and familiar street food, the gap is not so great. The same cannot be said, however, for the difference in cuisine.

STREET FOOD 2.0

If Twitter is the first ingredient, and the experience at the truck is the second, then the third and most integral component is the untraditional and eclectic street food, itself. Lucy Long writes of a constant shifting model from the exotic to the familiar when it comes to the market of new food.[26] The way tweeting mobile food trucks are using contemporary viral marketing mirrors and encourages a shift, or evolution, in the style of food being marketed in contemporary street food culture. With its perpetual cycle from online to in line, virtual to actual, and all the tweeting and eating in between, this event begins to reclassify street food culture, while expressing a novel change that echoes the effects of an equally enterprising predecessor.

Beginning in the late 1990s, emerging Middle Eastern street food began to expand and divert culinary attention in the street away from, what was deemed then, traditional fare of hot dogs, pretzels, and the like. It appealed to demands for the foreign, exotic, or different with much success.[27] Since this time, it has saturated New York City and has become extremely prevalent, today. In essence, the exotic has transformed into the familiar. Perhaps we are now turning to new modes of street food to, as Long puts it, "satisfy our curiosity about otherness," "confront the impulse to explore the unknown," and "to climb the mountain because it's there."[28]

For many, the challenge of the initial ascent is figuring out how to tweet, a sometimes foreign and overwhelming task for the food aficionado, determined to track down a particular new style of artisan street food. Once virtually connected and clear about where to hunt and how to find a particular mobile food truck, the challenge becomes downhill and the interaction and play, specific to this style of street food begins. Based in new media marketing, it is an elevated food experience that heightens curiosity. What makes this food different from the hot dog, pretzel, or kebab in the streets today, are the new choices in cuisine that come packaged with the actual and virtual experience. Menu items from various trucks include: red velvet cupcakes, locally procured Hudson Valley duck dumplings, Belgian waffles with imported Spekuloos spread, Taiwanese style fried chicken over rice with green chili pork sauce, or the infamous Macarella, a thin macaroon cookie sandwich with Nutella on the inside. Ultimately, these new alternatives are as novel to street food as Twitter is to vending.

New advertising strategies within OSN are allowing food vendors an opportunity to spark a change in cuisine with widespread reception on the street. Even with the small number of tweeting mobile food truck vendors compared to thousands of typical vendors on the street, this evolution in street food is receiving significant notice by the media and the press. The style of food, combined with an uncommon marketing platform like Twitter, makes these few street vendors celebrities in the blogosphere, magazines, newspapers, and even television programming.[29] The attention seems to arise from a combination of trend, new food genre, and an unorthodox approach to OSN marketing that, together, sell an interesting story. Between the food, the offline and online following, and the media coverage, these trucks have been catapulted into a subculture of their own, perhaps foreshadowing greater shifts to come in New York City street food.

It seems eaters who had yet to venture to street food are doing so, and in the process, expanding their range of taste as more options emerge. The handmade quiche at the SweeteryNYC truck became so alluring to one woman interviewed that she said, "This is the third time I bought the quiche this week . . . I've been going to Au Bon Pain (the restaurant bakery chain directly across the street) for twelve years . . . I'm coming here because the people are nice and it's excellent."[30] This is an example of the specialized cuisine, with its engaging novel experience, that is making waves in the culture of street food. Another woman interviewed in line at the SweeteryNYC truck commented, "There's like a new type of food that's more interesting than the other chicken and rice place . . . I wish there was more variety of the food carts you see offered."[31]

The irony here is that ten years ago the Middle Eastern chicken and rice carts, to which she refers, once were considered untraditional and foreign compared to today's interpretation. In 2000, Taylor, et al. claimed, "New York City is known for its all-American hot dog stands which abound many street corners ... Middle Eastern selections also appeal to those seeking a change from the typical."[32] In a mere ten years the landscape of street food has significantly shifted. Yesterday, the Middle Eastern chicken and rice cart was in fact adventurous, if not different and elevated; and yet today, they saturate the street where the hot dog stands are slightly harder to find amidst the Middle Eastern street food fare. Like in the past, the specialty food of the tweeting mobile food truck stands out as separate and as *other*, perhaps pushing a shift in the culture of street food. This suggests that another evolution in New York City street food is under way. The internet's constant changing and evolving technology is finding its way into the culture of consumption, influencing change and constructing new habits as they relate to food. This emerging cuisine, with its relationship to OSN strategies, is a complex component in the constant change contemporary culture invites.

As seen above, there is a new appeal for street food by some who may have never typically eaten it before; and perhaps conversely, people familiar with traditional street food may be venturing towards the more haute fare that the microblogging food truck provides. In the same context, we can ask questions around OSN culture: Are street food fans, who have never used an OSN platform like Twitter, being introduced to new technology when they are confronted with the challenge to find a food truck? Are people who are active in OSN, and who wouldn't typically eat street food, doing so as a result of the social attention it is receiving in OSN circles? In essence, does the tweeter find out about the food or does the food curious find out about Twitter? Or possibly, do they occur simultaneously?

Whatever initiates the interaction, the motivation is a social interest for food that assembles itself in the streets, creating

a significant following in the micro-blogosphere. Grant Di Mille says, "In order to be successful we have to have a menu that evolves. That will keep us in front of Twitter. It makes people want to check tweets about us like, 'Oh you have a new product? I want to try it.' " As seen in the blogosphere, the internet has created an arena that permits the transformation from average eater into self-proclaimed food critic. Official or not, the internet has created a platform where anyone may qualify themselves as an authority, and like any restaurant, reviews happen. Nonetheless, the broad, instantaneous and public fashion here leaves a microblogging mobile food truck vendor slightly more vulnerable and accountable to criticism. Therefore, microblogging vendors have the pressure to keep abreast of the tweets and blogs and react accordingly. As such, Mr. DeGeest considers Twitter a risk management tool. He claims the transparency of the tweets helps him manage the good and the bad in an expedited manner.[33] Mr. Di Mille's strategy was confirmed when one of his customers declared, "I think it's a great way to find new food."[34] In this regard, Twitter has elevated and shifted the design and strategy affiliated with vending and eating street food. Culturally, it exposes an innovative interaction that is responsible for changing street foodways, and the reception these changes are receiving.

CLASS, TASTE, AND TECHNOLOGY

These latest mobile food trucks, practically leaping off the pages of *Gourmet Magazine*, could easily be interpreted as traveling containers of cultural capital. In adopting Twitter to broaden appeal for their specialized fare, they acculturate themselves into a local community of consumption that reasserts itself upon followers of higher cuisine with common social (networking) roots.[35] Food and technology, here, influence and separate this emerging street food from traditional vending, clearly exposing larger issues related to class.

Castells states there is a universal pattern associated with affluence and wireless users that "adds a peculiar dimension to the processes of social appropriation."[36] Likewise, it can be argued that today's traditional street food in New York City is being co-opted by gourmet-like menu items and a culturally affluent community with more overall access compared to the average street food eater and vendor. Yet, like Castell's claim, the formula here is equally peculiar. Mainly under $10 for any item, specialty food is being disseminated in the streets and made attainable cross class with affordability, especially compared to the inflated price it would bear in a New York City sit-down restaurant.

At the same time an argument can be made that the fresh catalogue of menu items is a democratization of consumption as affordable, indulgent, artisan food becomes available to the consumer through a working-class model of street food. Bourdieu writes that consumption is a "stage in a process of communication" deciphering taste through a mastery of codes.[37] New York City's haute cuisine, traditionally encoded in class and access, is disseminating downward into the streets, while being made more public, and breaking cultural models of class distinction.[38] Sidney Mintz claims that "if one way of eating is considered lower than another, then there is hierarchy," and out of this, haute cuisine is classified as privileged.[39] While it can be argued that hierarchies of taste have imposed themselves onto the street, it can also be said that the unique distribution of such fare influences greater access to the types of cuisine once unattainable for most.

Hence, the microblogging mobile food truck appears to be straddling the class line. Castells claims that because broadband internet is becoming more accessible to consumers cross class, the "digital

divide" of access is shrinking.[40] In the same way, as more specialty cuisine is introduced to the street, perhaps the cuisine/class division of who eats what may be shrinking here as well. Similarly, it is possible that new vendors may begin to influence traditional vendors to create more specialized food alternatives, closing another gap. Ultimately, what might appear a cultural appropriation by the emerging high-end street food today may actually be another evolving shift in the historically adapting street food of tomorrow.

Numerous issues are provoked by this most recent street food trend that this chapter does not permit time and space for. As seen here, the microblogging mobile food truck with its artisanal fare introduces a range of class issues related to access, taste and cultural capital. For example, the politics of territory, permitting, and policy could be further teased out to answer many questions this new phenomenon brings up. Inquiry around the timing of the nation-wide emergence of these food trucks is equally relevant, as it was born during the same period as the economic downturn of 2008. What financial factors have influenced the culinary street entrepreneur in such a recession period; and how does this occurrence superimpose itself onto street food and class issues? Likewise, it is also important for future study to raise questions about the dominant street food culture, the 4,100 plus licensed and unlicensed food vendors in New York City who are predominantly immigrant and people of color.[41] Through the lens of class and access, how does this emerging trend affect these populations both directly and indirectly? With respect to this majority, questions may include researching the relationships and divisions between the modern and traditional vendor. Will the new combination of communication, technology, and consumption drive the old, low-tech, immigrant vendor out of business? Will these traditional vendors begin to reach out to OSN platforms to compete? Or, do they even feel an impact, and if not, does it matter? Finally, in the frequent debate on urban authenticity, is the tweeting gourmet mobile food truck influencing homogenization; or do they provide a progressive alternative by resisting norms and rules, countering current tradition on the street?[42] These questions are worthy to consider, extending the conversation into the socio-political sphere of this modern street food event.

CONCLUSION

Through food, street vendors and patrons are creating virtual and actual mobile venues to socialize in. Sylvia Ferrero states "the market becomes the arena where individuals build up new social spaces for themselves."[43] As new social communities form within online social networks around the mobile food truck phenom-enon, physical spaces with communal appeal are being built up in response. These new social spaces exist within the realm of the internet, online, as much as they do in the actual world. The combina-tion of consuming artisan street food, the communication it manufactures in a virtual world, and the actual and virtual experience of the food truck appears to be transforming contemporary foodways and how people respond and interact with food on the street. At the same time, it is forming community and identity in both spheres while gaining notoriety and unprecedented attention, launching them into a subculture of their own.

Microblogging food trucks are emerging from coast to coast. Los Angeles, traditionally known for its history of taco and catering trucks, has scores of artisan mobile food truck vendors on the street.[44] Similar food trucks can be found in smaller spaces such as Bloomington, Indiana and Boulder, Colorado, where street food culture is considerably less

imbedded as a whole. Through media, new and old, word is spreading and this OSN food truck is expanding. Trucks are emerging by the score across the country with a variety of cuisine that sets no standard for this model. Online and offline eaters are being pulled into the realm of OSN to partake in the virtual conversation surrounding a mobile culi-nary phenomenon.

The microblogging mobile food truck with its haute-like fare is a comment on the evolution of space and food in an urban setting. In a post-modern context, these spaces extend not just to the phys-ical reality, but also to the virtual realm, where people are socializing and consuming information. As a result, new life is given to actual experience through the innovation of new technologies, and new conversation and communities are being designed through new foodways. Street food has never before been so glam-orized in the United States as it is today. Microblogging and the internet play a central role as a go-between connecting real-world cravings for the new, be it food or technology. Because stationary street food vendors in New York City typically inhabit the same location, the latest mobile trend allows for, ideally, the addi-tion of, rather than replacement of, vendors. For a landscape like New York City, where a culture rich in street food already exists, perhaps this departure towards the new OSN street cuisine is a market signal of change to come.

Social directors, actors, patrons, and critics are engaging and embracing an innovative script with different ingredi-ents, packaged with a contemporary style that's capable of a modern day delivery. The niche vendors, with their boutique cuisine and unusual display in actual and virtual space, are a remark on an acceler-ated change that may be coming in the following years. People are sharing in relevant and real-time communication over food. As explained here, an alluring and theatrical experience around street food has become a key player via the microblogging mobile food truck, creating a successful life of its own within and outside the virtual social arena.

In 1904, thousands of peddlers in New York City were arrested for standing in one place for too long.[45] Vendors were forced to adapt by changing locations. The latest and most untraditional wave in mobile vending has arrived on the street food scene and, in some ways, appears a reflection of the traveling sellers of old as they alternate from location to location with, ideally, followers in tow. It seems clear today, that vendors, patrons, and cuisine are on the move. Through progressive 21st-century strategies, a small group of food vendors is influencing the culinary style on the street, emerging as a subculture, and merging with its greater culture-sharing group. With it comes an atypical range of variety from BBQ Mexican brisket sliders to curry dusted ice cream. Like food, it can be said that tweeting carries its own set of semiotic devices, which in this case, has married with food to create a new kind of interactive social experience not common in the street.

Through actual and virtual identities, people are collecting around new food markets, and the cultural and class boundaries of these social spaces are becoming blurred. Claude Levi-Strauss said things should be "not only good to eat, but also good to think."[46] In the case of the Twitter and the food truck phenomenon of New York City, I would add, "good to feel." The trucks, complete with the total experience, from online, offline, and in line, are feel-good mobiles that have virally captured the attention of the street food public and the online social networker in one. In both these spaces, they have introduced an alternative consumption of communication and taste. Instigated by a handful of food entrepreneurs who embraced a viral technology like Twitter, this subculture on the street speaks to a scenario that just may be the beginning of how we shape food dialogue,

communities, and venues in the future. As Twitter is replaced by the next hi-tech trend, we are sure to see food assisting the progress under way, creating greater shifts that merge and transform culture within the sociology of food.

NOTES

1. http://www.mistersoftee.com/about-us.
2. Suzanne Wasserman, "Hawkers and Gawkers." In Annie Hauk-Lawson and Jonathan Deutsch eds., *Gastropolis*. (NY: Columbia University Press, 2009), 155.
3. Ibid.; 156; Diner, Hasia R. Hungering for America: Italian, Irish, and Jewish Foodways in the Age of Migration. (Cambridge, MA: Harvard University Press, 2001), 126.
4. *New York Times*. "Ask About New York's Street Vendors." Retrieved from: http://city-room.blogs.nytimes.com/2009/10/05/ask-about-new-yorks-street-vendors/
5. New York City Independent Budget Office Fiscal Brief. "Sidewalk Standoff: Street Vendor Regulations Are Costly, Confusing, and Leave Many Disgruntled." November 2010.
6. Retrieved from Twitter website. www.twitter.com
7. SweeteryNYC was formerly known as StreetSweets, a changed that occurred during the course of this research.
8. Akshay Java, Tim Finin et al., Song, X., Finin, T. and Tseng, B. "Why We Twitter: Understanding Microblogging Usage and Communities." (Proceedings of the Joint 9th WEBKDD and 1st SNA-KDD Workshop 2007), 2007.
9. Crystal. Frequently asked Questions. *Twitter.com*. Retrieved from http://help.twitter.com/entries/13920-frequently-asked-questions, Anonymous. Retrieved from http://tweeternet.com/
10. Manuel Castells, et al., Mobile Communication and Society: A Global Perspective. (Massachusetts Institute of Technology, 2007), 106.
11. Manuel Castells, The Internet Galaxy: Reflections on the Internet, Business and Society. (London: Oxford University Press, 2001), 248.
12. For example, the television news network CNN and celebrity Ashton Kutcher raced each other in an attempt to be the first to collect one million followers. Albeit that it was for charity, much publicity for each party was attained.
13. Vincent Miller, "New Media, Networking and Phatic Culture." (Sage Publications, 2008), 394–396.
14. "@Jesuisjuba." Personal Interview. December 8, 2009.

15. Gary Alan Fine. The Kitchens: The Culture of Restaurant Work. (Berkley and Los Angeles, CA: University California Press, 1996), 1.

16. One unique identifying factor is a newer web OSN application called foursquare.com. It, too, represents that place where the actual and the virtual collide. It is a platform/marketing tool that rewards users for reporting their location status at a particular venue. The more places you visit, the greater your Four Square ranking for that venue. In the case of "@Jesuisjuba," she was elected the official mayor of the Rickshaw Dumpling Truck. For now she holds this title, a manufactured cyber achievement, along with bragging rights in both actual and virtual space.

17. Thomas DeGeest. Phone Interview. December 5, 2009.

18. Arjun Appadurai, "Gastro-Politics in Hindu South Asia." American Ethnologist. Vol. 8 (1981): 494.

19. @StreetSweets. Retrieved from Twit Bird Pro. December 2009.

20. @Waffletruck. Retrieved from http://twitter.com/waffletruck. September 15, 2010.

21. Unknown. TwitBirdPro application. Twitter filter. September 18, 2010.

22. Unknown. TwitBirdPro application. Twitter filter. September 18, 2010.

23. Arjun Appadurai, "Gastro-Politics in Hindu South Asia." American Ethnologist. Vol. 8 (1981): 494.

24. Pierre Bourdieu, Distinction: A Social Critique of the Judgment of Taste. (Cambridge, MA: Harvard University Press, 1984), 183.

25. Traditional food carts sell hot dogs for $1.50 to $2.00 and lamb and rice entrées in the $5 to $7 range. The NYC Cravings truck sells a main entrée for $7.00 where the Rickshaw Dumpling truck sells their main for $6.00. Smaller items on both trucks start at $3.00.

26. Lucy Long, Culinary Tourism. (Lexington: The University Press of Kentucky, 2004), 34.

27. Denise S. Taylor et al., "Street Food in America—A True Melting Pot." (Switzerland: Karger Publishers, 2000), 7, 11.

28. Lucy Long, Culinary Tourism. (Lexington: The University Press of Kentucky, 2004), 22.

29. The Food Network's "Great Food Truck Race" is a nationwide primetime competitive reality TV program.

30. Anonymous Sweet Street Customer 1. Personal interview. December 12, 2009.

31. Anonymous Sweet Street Customer 2. Personal interview. December 12, 2009.

32. Denise S. Taylor et al., "Street Food in America—A True Melting Pot." (Switzerland: Karger Publishers, 2000), 10.

33. Thomas De Geest. Personal interview. November 22, 2010.

34. Anonymous Sweet Street Customer 3. Personal interview. December 12, 2009.

35. Sidney Mintz. Tasting Food, Tasting Freedom: Excursions into Eating, Power, and the Past. (Boston, MA: Beacon Press, 1996), 101.

36. Manuel Castells et al. The Mobile Communication Society: A cross-cultural analysis of available evidence on the social use of wireless communication technology. Annenberg Research Network on International Communication. (University of Southern California, 2007), 56.

37. Pierre Bourdieu. Distinction: A Social Critique of the Judgment of Taste. (Cambridge, MA: Harvard University Press, 1984), 2.

38. Susan J. Terrio. "Crafting Grand Cru Chocolates in Contemporary France." American Anthropologists. Vol. 98 (1996): 67–79.

39. Sidney Mintz. Tasting Food, Tasting Freedom. Excursions into Eating, Power, and the Past. (Boston, MA: Beacon Press, 1996), 100.

40. Manuel Castells. The Rise of the Network Society. The Information Age: Economy, Society, and Culture, Volume I. (Blackwell, 1996), xxv.

41. Retrieved from http://www.urbanjustice.org/ujc/projects/street.html

42. Sharon Zukin. Naked City: The Death and Life of Authentic Urban Places. (Oxford University Press, 2009), 20.

43. Sylvia Ferrero, "Comida Sin Par: Consumption of Mexican Food in Los Angeles 'Foodscapes' in a Transnational Consumer Society." In W. Belasco and P. Scranton eds. Food Nations. (New York: Routledge, 2002), 195.

44. http://www.findlafoodtrucks.com/

45. Suzanne Wasserman, "Hawkers and Gawkers." In Annie Hauk-Lawson and Jonathan Deutsch eds., Gastropolis. (NY: Columbia University Press, 2009), 157.

46. Claude Levi-Strauss, as cited in Joan Jacobs Brumberg "The Appetite as Voice." In Carole Counihan and Penny Van Esterik eds., Food And Culture: A Reader. 2nd edition (New York: Routledge, 1997), 150.

WORKS CITED

Appadurai, A., "Gastro-Politics in Hindu South Asia." American Ethnologist 8. 1981. 494

Brumberg J.J. "The Appetite as Voice." Counihan C. & Van Esterik P. Food And Culture: A Reader 2nd edition. NY: Routledge. 1997. 150

Bourdieu P. Distinction: a social critique of the judgment of taste. Cambridge: Harvard University Press, 1984. 2, 183

Castells, M., Fernandez-Ardevol, M., Qiu, J., & Sey, A. Mobile communication and society: a global perspective. MA: Massachusetts Institute of Technology. 2007. 106

Castells, M. The Internet Galaxy: Reflections on the Internet, Business and Society. Oxford: Oxford University Press, 2001. 248

Castells M., Fernandez, Ardevol, JL Qiu, A Sey., The Mobile Communication Society A cross-cultural analysis of available evidence on the social use of wireless communication technology. Annenberg Research Network on International Communication. University of Southern California, 2007. 56

Castells, M. The Rise of the Network Society: The Information Age: Economy, Society, and Culture Volume I. Cambridge, MA, Oxford, UK: Blackwell, 1996. xxv

Crystal. (Nov 4, 2008). Frequently asked Questions. *Twitter.com*. Retrieved from http://help.twitter.com/entries/13920-frequently-asked-questions

Diner, H.R. Hungering for America: Italian, Irish, and Jewish Foodways in the Age of Migration. Cambridge, MA: Harvard University Press. 2001. 126

Ferrero, S. "Comida Sin Par: Consumption of Mexican Food in Los Angeles 'Foodscapes' in a Transnational Consumer Society." Belasco & Scranton, Food Nations. NY: Routledge. 2002

Fisher, C., "Food, Self and Identity." Social science information [0539–0184] (1988) vol.27 iss.2

Fine, G.A., The Kitchens: The Culture of Restaurant Work. Berkley and Los Angeles, CA: University California Press, 1996.1

Iglis, Gimlin, Thorpe. Food: Critical Concepts in the Social Changes. London, NY: Routledge, 2008. V1.

Java, A., Song, X., Finin, T. and Tseng, B. "Why We Twitter: Understanding Microblogging Usage and Communities." Proceedings of the Joint 9th WEBKDD and 1st SNA-KDD Workshop 2007. August 2007.

Long, Lucy. Culinary Tourism. Lexington: The University Press of Kentucky, 2004. 24, 34

Mintz S. Tasting Food, Tasting Freedom excursion Excursions into Eating, Power, and the Past Boston, Massachusetts: Beacon Press, 1996. 100

Miller V. "New Media, Networking and Phatic Culture." Sage Publications, 2008. 394–396

Taylor, D. S., et al. "Street Foods in America-A True Melting Pot." *Street Foods* 86, 2000. 7,10, 11.

Terrio S. J., "Crafting *Grand Cru* Chocolates in Contemporary France." *American Anthropologists;* Mar 1996; Vol.98. 67–79

Wasserman S. "Hawkers and Gawkers." Annie Hauk-Lawson, Jonathan Deutsch. *Gastropolis*. NY: Columbia University Press, 2009. 155,157

Zukin S.. Naked City: The Death and Life of Authentic Urban Places. Oxford: Oxford University Press. 2009. 20

24

Visualizing 21st-Century Foodscapes: Using Photographs and New Media in Food Studies

Melissa L. Salazar

The use of visual media as a rigorous ethnographic data collection method has yet to be fully accepted by the anthropological research community (Prosser 1998; Ruby 1996). Ethnographic research textbooks mention photographs and video, but often treat them as secondary sources of information, to be used as teaching aids or as illustrations of research findings. A growing number of visual anthropologists, however, see value in moving photographs and other visual media from the sidelines to center stage, where photographs *become* data, rather than illustrate it. Visual methods, they argue, capitalize on our visual preferences, as we are drawn naturally to understand and make sense of concepts and ideas through drawings, videos, and photographs (Pink 2007; Ruby 1991).

Food studies, with its interdisciplinary and (to some) mundane subject matter, is already pushing the boundaries of what constitutes as "proper" research. And while food studies certainly does not have limitless options of research methods (this volume is just one that helps begin to characterize what "doing food studies" means methodologically) the flexibility that characterizes this growing field means that food studies might be a place where visually based methodologies can make significant contributions and gain acceptance. In fact, the development of image-based methodologies seems natural in food studies, as food itself has a strong visual dimension. Consider that visual appearance is one of the most important factors infants use in deciding what might be tasty to eat (Birch et al. 1987) and how visuals are often used in nutritional studies, to help participants recall food dishes and portion sizes (Williamson et al. 2004; 2003).

Another reason for us to consider image-based methods for food research is that, as we exit the first decade of the 21st century, the sharing and storing of images and text is now an important part of our daily lives and the overall cultural landscape. The Internet and the rise of so-called "new media"[1]—interactive software such as email, Instant Messenger, as well as information-sharing websites like Facebook and MySpace—is at the heart of this new market place of text and visuals.

While cell phone manufacturers, Internet website creators and social media software designers were probably not thinking about food research when they created their products, the same interactivity in image-making, sharing, and text communication that makes new media devices and websites so popular is exactly what makes them also useful for conducting food-related research in the 21st century. The global sharing of information and images that occurs when users interact with new media in many ways mirrors the ways we now "take food public" through the sharing of our eating habits and "food images." Consider a few examples (none of which existed even two years ago): a "new media" user can upload to their followers in the Twittersphere, or to their Facebook network, a short text and photo of what they ate for lunch, and even where they ate it by including a GPS link to the restaurant's location on Google Maps. At the same instant (and maybe even in the same restaurant) another person might be typing in the details of their meal on their Blackberry, perhaps to post on their online diet diary that automatically tracks their daily caloric intake. Across town, at the same moment, a teenager in the high school lunchroom might be snapping a shot of their friends eating lunch with their "cameraphone" (a word that has emerged into our vocabulary in the last few years) and uploading it to their Facebook or MySpace account. According to Nancy Van House (2007), a communications scholar whose work explores the meanings of the interactions between people, photos, and the Internet, new media users are *image-makers*, both figuratively and literally. New media tools are popular because they tap into our desire to create and re-create an image, and then take it public. Users do this by chronicling not only the highlights of their lives but also the mundane events such as what they had for lunch. By doing this they, at the same time, build narratives of identity and self-representation, as well as reinforce relationships with others in their social community.

All of these types of food image-making are ripe areas of study for food scholars, especially in light of how they reflect 21st-century consumption. Rick Dolphijn (2004) uses a concept of *foodscape*[2] as a way to describe the modern food landscape as unpredictable and dynamic, a reflection of an increasingly global foodshed, and an increasingly public ecology of ideas and foods. Constant changes to the network mark not only our physical environments but also what goods are available to eat; both people and objects move through spaces more quickly than ever before due to quicker and cheaper

transportation, share more food information through an ever-widening and accessible public arena. Personal food blogs, recipe sharing websites, and the popularity of Food Network television programs are just a few examples of the crosslinking of public displays of images and food.

Rather than studying what people eat, it is the *changes* in what we eat that is the new pattern for us to examine as food scholars. Doing research with immigrants in Sacramento, California, over the past ten years, I've seen several examples of this changing foodscape. A rural Ukrainian family I knew that had recently immigrated to the U.S. bought American breakfast cereal at the supermarket, not because they wanted to be more American, but because their relatives from the U.S. had already been using United Postal Service to send breakfast cereal to their rural Ukraine village for years. In another instance, I met a Laotian woman who was growing traditional South Asian vegetables in her community garden through seeds she carried in her pocket (illegally) through U.S. Customs. In a public twist, her daughter's teacher asked her to run a school garden and sell them to the school lunch program. And in a third case, an adolescent girl I knew who had recently immigrated from Vietnam refused to eat her mother's homemade Vietnamese dinners of chicken feet and rice because she thought "Viet" foods with meat and fish were too fattening now that she was in the U.S. Instead she was trying to drink more cows' milk, even though she did not like the taste at first, since she heard in Nutrition class at her high school that it would make her grow taller.

In this 21st-century foodscape, it becomes harder and harder for food researchers to generalize about consumption patterns, as well as find theories to describe humans' food behavior. Where consumers get ideas about what to eat, and where their food comes from, is increasingly difficult to trace. However, while what they eat and how they eat it has been, and remains, deeply personal. With new global information networks, eating is less and less private, and more accessible through images. While tape recorders, paper-and-pencil surveys, and participant interviews will surely continue to have their place, for food researchers, now is the time to use image-based interactive tools to capture these dynamic food relationships. For example, if lunches are eaten mainly while working or in cars, is it accurate for researchers to observe lunch cafés during the lunch hour? Or is it better to simply assign participants to take pictures of their lunch with their cameraphones and upload them to a website where both parties can view and discuss the photos? If we want to study these foodscapes characterized by shifting intersections of people, places, and food, then perhaps researchers need to think more innovatively about the tools they use, and include image-based research in their methodologies.

For the remainder of this essay I will present some examples from my own journey into using images and, then, new media, as a way of "visualizing" food-scapes of a specific population—young people. In these stories I've attempted to capture both the benefits and challenges of using new media and also show that new media can be used from different disciplinary dimensions. My own background approaches food studies first as a nutrition/consumer scientist, and second from a cultural anthropology perspective. I hope that by showing examples from these relatively different dimensions I can show how the intersection of images and new media is useful for a broad range of research projects and questions, especially if the research is conducted with young populations who are already heavy users of both.

Through specific examples, I'll discuss how new media tools change the generation and analysis of food and culture data, as well as how new media tools can spark deeper conversations between researchers and their participants about participants' food habits and attitudes. At the same time, I will provide some cautionary and practical notes about the ethical issues that arise when using web-enabled tools for food documentary work. This essay is not meant to be an authoritative or exhaustive list of the many new media tools at researchers' disposal since anything I specifically recommend here will likely be outdated before the publication of this book. But sharing the details of this work will hopefully encourage others to consider present tools, as well as forthcoming ones, as important to the future of food studies, not only because they make communicating with certain participants easier, but because new media might be key to uncovering and exploring the modern foodscape.

CASE #1: NUTRITIONAL EVALUATION OF SCHOOL LUNCHES

My own journey into visualizing food-scapes began with digital photography. I had the fortune to be presented with an image-focused research project at the same time I was taking a visual studies class in graduate school. School district officials in a nearby school district were curious about the use of a new salad bar that had been recently installed in an elementary school. Anecdotal information from the school's teachers indicated that the children were eating more fruits and vegetables (and were enjoying their lunches more), but due to grant pressures, the district officials wanted quantitative data in order to support the continued financing of the salad bar. Our research team, made up of nutritionists and consumer scientists considered doing what nutrition research often uses in situations like this: a food-weighing study where we would weigh the amount of produce before and after lunch (and assume that the difference was the food consumed). As we discussed our options, we realized that we wanted more information than simply grams of produce eaten, however; we wanted to know *why* children were choosing the foods they were, and as consultants to the district, help school nutrition staff use this information to gear the salad bar offerings towards the produce children preferred and eliminate what was unpopular.

As a consumer scientist, I had done previous work in evaluating and quantifying children's dietary intakes, and knew that asking the children for information about what they eat would be tough. Although interested in the topic of food, children are less aware of abstract principles that guide their eating habits, and less apt to see patterns or generalities. Moreover, their food habits can be fickle and haphazard compared to adults (Birch et al. 1987). According to food psychologist Paul Rozin, when it comes to children's food behaviors, "we only know a small amount of what is to be known, and still cannot advise a parent about how to make his/her child like vegetables" (1999: 257).

While taking photographs-as-data was, perhaps, an unusual path for us as nutritionists, my research in visual studies led me to believe that we could use photographs as ways to "visualize" cultural behaviors, especially how they occur in specific environments. In recommending the value of this kind of analysis, sociologist Howard Becker (1986) notes that photographs can provide insight into a certain existence or "a way of life . . . by detailing major forms of association among group's members and placing them in relation to some set of environing forces" (p. 279). For other researchers, photographic records shot over a particular period of time have provided insights about cultural and social changes, and made behavior patterns more visible (Chalfen et al. 2000). As photographic historian Anna Pegler-Gordon notes, photos can "make[s] the past seem more accessible, giving concrete shape to a world that sometimes seems intangible" (2006: 28).

The unpacking of food habits into its everyday details by using a series of systematic photographs was particularly useful for us as nutritionists. We figured that the photographs could help participants to discuss their food behaviors in the past tense, and aid students' memories of past meals. Food itself, and especially a rushed lunch, is ephemeral and prone to be forgotten soon after it is eaten, particularly among young participants. Students as participants could analyze concrete behaviors at a particular time (*What did I eat today?*) as well as transfer their behavior into general terms (*How does this compare to how I generally eat?*). It was unlikely that we would be present every time that a student chose to select something in a cafeteria filled with nearly 100 children going through a quickly moving serving line. But a camera, particularly a cheap and portable one, could act as an additional "eye" and capture something as fleeting as a lunch plate before a hungry child.

With this latter purpose in mind, our research team took over 800 photographs of students' lunch plates and eating places, not only to determine nutrient intake but also document any plate patterns children had when making salads with their salad bar choices. We were pleasantly surprised with the photographic data we collected, for several reasons. Not only did the photographs provide us with the nutritional information we desired (and we painstakingly counted every single crouton in all 800 photos), it turned out that the photographs revealed unexpected cultural data. We discovered that children were mainly using the salad bar not to build "salads" in the adult sense (lettuce on bottom, toppings on top, covered with dressing) but instead the vast majority of the children used the salad bar as a way to collect piles of finger foods. The children did not see the salad bar as an encouragement to eat salad, but to eat small distinct piles of fruits, vegetables, and proteins for lunch. Subsequent interviews with some of the children proved that the small piles of food on their plate were being eaten much like an adult would eat *tapas*, or small plates of various dishes (Salazar et al. 2008).

There were limitations to this type of digital data collection, however. Due to the volume of photographs produced in such a short period of time (often we would snap 100 photographs in the span of 15 minutes) it was nearly impossible to match photographs with specific children. Due to ethical limitations from our university Institutional Review Board as well as our own concerns about protecting the identity of the students in our research, our school lunch photographs showed only food, and never the students' faces. As a result, we were unable to generalize about our results based on children's age, gender, and out of school eating habits. Ironically, students were less bothered by us taking their lunch pictures than by the fact that we were not interested in

photographing their faces with their school lunch plates—evidence, perhaps, that they felt their lunches were only part of their at-school identities (Salazar 2008).

CASE #2: THE SECRET FOOD LIVES OF ADOLESCENTS

After that project was completed, I joined a graduate program in educational anthropology and began to study ethnography in earnest in order to continue my studies of youth food culture. Encouraged by my earlier project, I wondered how I could use photographs more deeply to study children's eating habits, in a less intrusive way than I had in my nutrition studies.

At this time I shifted my thinking about photographs and objectivity. As a social rather than nutritional scientist, I began to see that photographs were not simple recordings of what appeared in front of the camera, but also evidence about the photographer who made them (Wagner

Figure 24.1 Unusual food combinations a child made at their school lunch salad bar. The systematic photographing of students' lunch plates as they came away from the self-serve salad bar helped us analyze patterns in student lunch plates, as well as giving us excellent visuals to use in photo-elicitation interviews with students later (Salazar et al. 2008).

2004). As visual researchers have argued, what to frame in the camera, and when to take the picture, are all decisions about what is important to the photographer. Photographs viewed in this light can still have documentary value, but they are also of interest to social scientists for what they reveal about how visual information is produced and distributed. The foundation for this approach is summarized in what John Grady (1996) calls *doing sociology visually*. The act of taking a photograph, he notes, is "an intentional process, articulated culturally and located in space and time" (p. 14).

In order to include children's food culture into my research, therefore, it seemed that the research participants were the ones who should be holding the camera. In my preliminary study I was working with a group of adolescent middle school children, and as a result decided to loan each of them a digital camera. I gave them few instructions other than that I was interested in how they thought about food, including some of the things they ate. By doing this, I hoped that I would minimize my own photographic "voice" and maximize theirs. I was not the first to use participant-produced photography as a way of producing ethnographic data. The theorizing of sharing image-making with others in research is an expansive and growing field of visual anthropology, pioneered by Sol Worth's (1972) participant videos, and pushed further theoretically by visual anthropologists Jay Ruby (1991) and Peter Biella (2008). Closer to my own goals of working with young people, Burris and Wang's PhotoVoice methodology (1997) and Richard Chalfen's Video Intervention Assessment (2007) tools also promote image-making by those in underrepresented social positions, (especially women and children) as a way to forefront the participant's voice, or, to construct and produce their own "image." Ruby argues that balanced research collaborations, ones that include both researchers' and participants' voices in a way that neither dominates, create new opportunities for true co-authorship (Ruby 1991).

I gave digital cameras to immigrant youth for this reason, but also so I could deepen my own understanding of their lives. The technology of digital cameras (both still and video, although now cameras have both functions so I will use them interchangeably here) allows all participants in research, and especially young ones, the ability to carry documentary devices with them, without being burdened by equipment or needing extensive training. While film cameras, especially the disposable kind, could also serve this purpose, the digital format makes it much easier for participants to document more events. The large memory capacity of these cameras also removes the problem of having to think carefully about what 24 or 32 snapshots participants can take before filling their roll. Now participants (and researchers) can snap away to the order of 2 Gigabytes (600 pictures or 15 minutes of video) before filling their cameras to capacity.

My co-participants were adolescents, and recent immigrants besides, and in those senses I found that their home lives were relatively inaccessible to me. I was their classroom aide at the time, and going to certain students' homes seemed like a good way to draw cries of favoritism from the other students in the class. I also wanted this particular group of children, English Language Learners, to experience the power of photography, and give them as much agency as possible. Because adult voices have dominated the discourse over understanding children's diets, it was important for me to foreground these children's own perspectives and "insider" meanings attached to foods and their eating acts. Since language was a barrier for them, I hoped that the photographs they took would serve as accessible information supplementing text or oral conversations.

As students brought their cameras back filled with images, there were again surprising benefits as well as limitations to the digital cameras as a methodological tool. When I reviewed images with the students one-on-one, they were more engaged in the photos, and recalled much about the context of the images they took. But I found that many (and in fact, the majority) of the images they returned were not related to food in any way (themselves in dressed up clothes, at the mall with friends, watching TV, etc.) and that the camera was more focused on people than food if there was an eating event. But the participant-produced photographs captured some things that I might not have noticed or thought important—so the lack of food showed me that food was indeed not the "main event" for this age group. Instead friends were. In addition, some photos showed food events that I would not have known about. They took pictures of passing gum, Tic-Tacs, and other snacks during class that I was teaching (Figure 24.2), as well as of communal lunches where they and their friends pooled all their food to eat one large, family style meal. Finally, some photos showed strange concoctions that mixed elements of school lunch and home foods (Figure 24.3).

During this time I became aware that even though these youths had been in the U.S. a few years or less, most used MySpace accounts and had large stockpiles of photos and slideshows in MySpace as well as in photo sharing websites like Photobucket. To capitalize on their interest in the Internet, I asked youth participants in my dissertation project to take their digital camera and make photo-diaries of everything they ate within a 7-day period. I had tried written diet diaries with adolescents in a previous study, and had been frustrated with the small amount of information I could get. Digital cameras, I hoped, would help me get a wider selection of foods.

One of the participants, Phoebe, a 14-year-old Vietnamese immigrant, took her hundred or so food diary photographs and put them in a slideshow format, complete with her favorite rap music as background music. She added captions such as "So good!" and "Yum!" to her pictures, and her finished product looked more like a music video than a diet diary (my feelings about it confirmed when she excitedly posted the video to her MySpace page, titling it *My Foods*). But when she showed me what she had done we could both see patterns in her eating that she had not realized before. This type of review beat the self-report questionnaires I had used previously that asked youth to generalize their food habits over a week or month because they left out details like amounts, places, and tastes that this project included.

When Phoebe and I watched her video over and over it became obvious to both of us that in her life the mixture of two, or even three cultures (American, Vietnamese, and teen) blended together in a single day, even coexisting in a single place (her home). Below is an excerpt from the audio of an interview we did together after she completed her video. The brackets show what image was playing on the screen as she spoke about the snapshot.

Day 1
[Fruit loops cereal photo] "I just eat them like that, no milk. I eat them out of the box."
[Mug of milk photo] "Milk is healthy for you. I try drinking it to get taller."
[Ice cream photo] "In the afternoon."
[Snack photo] "Steamed rice in banana leaf: it has meat inside. It's kind of like Mexican food. My mom made these too."
[Fish for dinner photo] "With the sauce and stuff. And then rice, Asian [she laughs]."
"I had a more quail egg after dinner."
[Sun Chip photo] "While I was watching TV with my sister."

Figure 24.2 A photo showing a pack of gum on a student's backpack. While initially I thought this was not very interesting, after spending more time with this student, and carefully watching his behavior during class I realized that this photo was important in showing cultural value of certain foods at school. Students like this one secretly passed gum to other students by pressing sticks of gum into books and notebooks and then putting the books on other students' desks. When the recipient opened up the school book or notebook they would find a gum "present." Without the ethnographic field observations I would not have discerned this from the photograph or from the explanation the student gave me during the interview about his photo set. All he said was that he "liked gum."

Figure 24.3 A photo taken by a middle school student during his school lunch. When I first saw the photograph, I couldn't identify what I was looking at, but during an interview with the photographer he explained that it was Hot Cheetos he brought from home (they were not allowed to be sold at school) covered with nacho cheese sauce (purchased at school). The construction of this lunch showed some prior planning on the student's part as it mixed school and home foods.

[Junior Mints photo] "It was at night like in the movies and then I shared them with my sister. Yeah I usually eat candy at night. I get too hyper and can't go to sleep. I'm like lying on the bed, and looking at the sky, and think *I'm too hyper and how can I go to sleep?*"

Day 2
[Cereal photo] "Special K at home."
[A photo of her school lunch, a rice bowl] "I had school lunch that day."
[Candy photo] "Nerds and Twizzler . . . I ate in school."
"After school, I have noodle with spring roll and vegetable and peanut sauce.
At night I had rice and broccoli, and tomatoes at home when my uncle came over and made it. I also had strawberries smoothie, my uncle made it. I think he put orange juice in there too. It's kind of like a Jamba Juice."

While this project did not perfectly capture every eating event (Phoebe told me that she had forgotten to photograph a few drinks or sticks of chewing gum) it was obvious to me that the photographs gave us something from which to launch a deeper conversation. Phoebe was more at ease as the creator of the photographs, and reacted more positively to these discussions than interviews where I showed her photographs I had taken. Giving her control of the camera, while relinquishing control of what photos would eventually be shown to me, was an overall benefit to me as I was shown food events I was not privy to as an outsider.

CASE STUDY #3: DIGITAL FOODSCAPES: FOOD PHOTOGRAPHS AND GEO-SPATIAL DATA

During the initial stages of my research with my teenage participants, I often

asked them to sketch maps of places where the photos were taken, to get a better sense of what might have been going on outside of the frame of the photo. The geographical context helped me to understand the socio-cultural context of the things they were eating in the photo.

At the same time, I was constantly being text messaged and Instant Messaged by my youth co-researchers, who, while English Language Learners at school, were quite versatile in "textspeak." I also noted that although they had limited English writing abilities, they were not shy in using the "comment" boxes of social media websites. Many of them commented on each other's photographs. It was at this time I realized the power of the new media tools for not just keeping in communication with my participants, but also in sharing food images and conducting interviews about themselves on a more informal level.

I was interested not only in what my participants could say about the content of their photographs, but also where they took them. This coding of photographs with location would allow me to look more deeply at the intersections between food and place, and how these recent immigrants experienced food in a new place, both culturally and geographically. I searched for a suitable program that would allow my participants to "map" their eating to the location, or contexts, within which they ate. At this time I was introduced to similar work being done by Lidia Marte who studied the spatial and cultural aspects of immigrants' food lives through participant-drawn "memory maps," as well as conducted participant observation "go-alongs" as her participants shopped and cooked in their neighborhoods. Marte was the first to introduce me to the term *foodmapping*, which she defines as

 . . . an image-based approach to research that pays attention to the way people relate to food in the interaction of senses, emotions, and environments ... As thematic ethnographic maps, foodmaps can be used to research actual places, but also spaces (social/racial relations, community networks, local food paths, etc) and place-memory (sense of place and home, relations to homeland, linguistic landscapes, etc). Food mappings can also be produced by tracing food relations to states, institutions, organizations, local neighborhoods, social networks, and family histories, paying special attention to how and where individuals earn their "bread."

(2007: 263).

I was drawn to Marte's research practices since they connect food and place, something I was deeply interested in exploring as a theme in these immigrant adolescents' lives. But since my participants were young, and interested in technology, I wanted to also find a way to use computers to make food maps. After some searching, I came upon a method called *geotagging*. Flickr, a free photo storage and sharing website (www.flickr.com) had recently offered this new feature for users. With geotagging users who created a set of personal photos on Flickr could then link their photos to a Yahoo map, by dragging them onto a particular place on a Yahoo map that indicated where the photo was taken. While the feature was intended for the creation of travel photo-diaries, I was interested in having the children use the geotagging feature to combine *what* they ate with *where* they ate it. I hoped that the geotagging feature would give both me and the children more information about their spatial movement without me having to follow them around or ask them where they were when they took their photos. Their work with cameras, and then uploading the photos to the Yahoo map, would therefore "make visible" to me the geography of their everyday food habits.

Figures 24.4 and 24.7 show the results of foodmaps that two of the 14-year-old participants produced with photographs

they took over a seven-day period. It is impossible to present statically the food-maps themselves as their power is in their interactivity. What the students created was an online clickable map that featured their photos and any text that they included as a description. As a way to express parts of their maps for this chapter, I selected key photos and took screenshots of the maps and their embedded photos.

These interactive foodmaps were effective tools for both me and the children to visualize the contexts of time and space with their eating habits. It became clear through analyzing these maps with them that the maps made visible, and public, the ways they were developing a "mixed adolescent identity" as they transitioned from child to adult, and from immigrant to American.

Figure 24.4 belonged to Phoebe (mentioned in Case Study #2). Although she had been living in the United States less than two years Phoebe, like many American adolescents and "digital natives", was a heavy user of MySpace and Yahoo Instant Messenger and spent a lot of her time at home on her personal computer. When I met her she already had several hundred images stored in her own Photobucket account, swapped her profile image every hour or so, and, as a result, it was a relatively easy task for her to learn how to geotag.

Phoebe spent considerable time constructing her foodmap and taking pictures of her food life. We had not just one, several follow-up interviews to talk through her foodmap, and in all I recorded more than six hours of interviews to go through all the components of her food map. To display pieces of her map, I took screenshots of her final foodmap at varying degrees of zoom. I also used the satellite rather than the roadmap function of Yahoo Maps as I wanted to keep the identity of my participants' locations confidential.

The numbered circles in Figure 24.4 indicate the three main places where

Figure 24.4 Phoebe, a 14-year-old immigrant girl from Vietnam created this geotagged foodmap using Flickr and Yahoo Maps. I could see from her map that there were three main locations where she consumed food: her home (labeled "22"), her high school school (labeled "10"), and her aunt's house where she sometimes ate dinner (labeled "3").

Phoebe had "located" each of her photos (she took more than 50). The numbers in the circles indicate how many photos were taken at each location.

From this particular view, I could quickly make a general observation that Phoebe took the majority, 35, of her photos within about a 10-mile radius of her home. From this perspective it was easier to see how Phoebe's food life was strongly influenced by her and her mother's lack of transportation (her mother did not know how to drive). The majority of the time it appeared that Phoebe ate food in only three locales, all of them very close to her home. Twenty-two pictures were from her home (the number 22), ten were taken at her high school (the number 10), and three were taken at her other aunt's house who lived within walking distance from her home. Her mother and sister would walk over for dinner or bring dinner Phoebe's mother prepared over there to eat. It was interesting to note how the decisions the family made about Phoebe's safety were not based solely on geography—even though her second aunt lived a few blocks away, Phoebe was allowed to walk there for dinner, but not allowed to go and "hang out" at the public park, which was just across the street from her house.

Besides having the geographical data for her photographs, through the geotagging software on Yahoo Maps, I was able to "click" open each set of Phoebe's photographs that she had placed in a single location, and view a slideshow of Phoebe's photographs from each place. I had asked her to write a comment about

NERDS!

NERDS! nerds are heller AWESOME! I forgot who I got this from. I think that was Phan or Dana that gave it to me. It tastes good and fun to play with too

Milk

I drink milk in the morning and sometimes in the day. I used to be unable to drink whole milk, but for awhile of trying and putting sugar less and less, now I am able to drink them and trying to get taller... :]

Figures 24.5 (above) and 24.6 (below) Detail of Phoebe's individual foodmap photos, which could be accessed by clicking on one of the numbered locations. Each photograph had a caption/comment box where she could write down any information she wanted about the photograph.

each photo, exactly as she did for her MySpace photos. Figures 24.5 and 24.6 show what this looked like.

Sitting down with my participants, I realized that the maps were excellent interview prompts. With this interactive combination of images, captions, and geo-spatial data, I had at my disposal both quantitative and qualitative food data. By clicking on each data point, the participants could talk through each photo and help me "visualize" their food experiences there, and with the captions there to jog their memory, they could more easily discuss what they had to eat. As a researcher, I could also compare participants' distance between their eating spaces and the area of their consumption (as well as food sources) and quantitatively measure. For example, Phoebe's clustered foodmap (Figure 24.4) revealed her lack of adult transportation and how limited her food environment was. Rugiya, another 14-year-old participant in the foodmap study, produced a foodmap that covered nearly double the area of Phoebe's (Figure 24.7). Curious to find out why Rugiya's map covered so much of the city compared to Phoebe's, I spent more time asking her how she got from place to place. She described how a large network of adults from her Baptist church took her and her friends to eat snacks and sometimes dinner before and after their daily afterschool church programs. This conversation led us to a broader discussion of how religion played a large role in her immigration to the U.S., and her out of school life.

The youth participants' foodmaps were also interesting visualizations of their material ecology—particularly how these immigrant children were learning to deal with the cartography of space, time, and the institutional systems of home, school, peers, and family—in a sense, both the physical and cultural "architecture" of their city, and what it meant to adjust to life there. Taken together, these foodmap projects were visualizations of the connections between people, places, and foods for my participants, and revealed to me the importance of "place" within my youth research studies. According to Bell and Valentine's *Consuming Geographies* (1991), place-based eating is an important component to food studies as "at different geographical locations—at home, school and work—we learn how to present, maintain, and reproduce our bodies over space and time" (1991: 31), and eating can be an important part of how we, as people, experience the physical spaces and materials that make up our institutions of city, home, and school.

MAKING IMAGES AND NEW MEDIA: WHO, WHEN AND FOR WHAT?

The interactivity of images and text available with new media tools make them promising for inclusion in food research. In each of the cases, I described I found digital photographs in particular to be useful in revealing changing eating habits that might be difficult to otherwise study. New media tools and web-enabled devices have made their way into everyday life, and videos and photos can be taken anywhere and anytime. Participants can now document their own travel and location (GoogleMaps have an "upload photo" function), text their minute-to-minute thoughts and feelings through status updates on Facebook or Twitter, and photograph and videotape themselves as well as others. These technologies bring new opportunities for researchers in two ways—both in the way we co-construct and the ways we share knowledge with our participants.

There are challenges, however. With these new tools come responsibilities to use them ethically. Even as both participants and researchers become more accustomed to sharing our private lives publicly, to be videotaped or photographed and

Figure 24.7 Another teenage participant, Rugiya's, "foodmap" was quite a large geographic area compared to Phoebe's in Figure 24.4. While both her parents had cars, they both worked during the day and on weekends, so adults from her church drove her to church-related afterschool programs (the right-hand data points). Her eating clusters were her home (#16) and school (#2, left side), the two clusters on the left side. The right side shows the Ukrainian/Russian grocery store her family frequented (#34) and her church (#2, right side) and a Chinese restaurant she often visited after church (#5).

then have our likenesses and geographic information broadcast by others is a scary proposition. In my own work, I had to find ways to address this—through using password-protected websites, and promising to destroy passwords of my individual participants' websites after the project concluded. Since my participants were minors, I also went through several iterations of reviews with them and their parents, and asked them to sort photographs we had collected into three categories: (1) photos that should not be used and needed to be deleted from my project archives (in which case I handed them a CD-ROM with these photographs and deleted them from my own computer), (2) photos that could be used by me for my research but not used in any displays of the research (conferences, publications, etc.); and (3) photos that were allowable for research and also could be used for publication purposes. This was a time consuming as my participants were prolific photo takers but a crucial element to gain trust as my participants were minors. In the end I used only several hundred out of the more than 3,000 photos the participants and I collected over the two years we worked together, and due to the embedded geographical data, I was unable to ever present their foodmaps as interactive sites during conferences and meetings with other scholars.

Due to the difficulties I encountered in protecting my participants' privacy, I was asked several times by my peers in the research community if I felt these photo-sharing methods were worth the trouble. My short answer was and continues to be yes. These youth-produced photographs allowed me to access events that were inaccessible to me otherwise—the digital cameras and cameraphones used by my participants served as research partners and a surrogate set of eyes.

But, giving these young participants the cameras meant that I also gave them the ultimate power to decide what was important to photograph and what would remain hidden. Each photograph shared with me had before it a series of decisions the participants made. In this respect, I had to always consider what was outside the camera lens, and 'fill in' the gaps through more traditional participant observation and discussions with my participants. Piper and Frankham (2006) discuss this limiting nature of photographs, and caution researchers to not limit "the research story" to simply photos:

> [There is a] tendency to use visual images as if these represent the truth. We would argue it is just as likely that a photograph acts as a "trap". In other words, the still image is made to mean something because it has been made significant through its fixing in photographic form. It could also be argued that photographs, because of their mimetic quality, encourage us to tell singular truths about them, in contrast to interview transcripts where people move unconsciously between positions, writing and re-writing themselves as they talk. Rather than providing access to an "essential" self, one could equally argue that photographs make us stand apart from the self when providing interpretation or commentary . . . the truths that are elicited need to be interrogated in relation to the medium and method, and not accepted independently from them (p. 38).

Visual sociologist Howard Becker has also written extensively about the limitations as well as benefits of photos as data. When it comes to photographs, he notes, the question of whether or not photos tell the truth is actually the wrong question to ask (1986). Instead, it is more appropriate for researchers to ask themselves what do these photos tell the truth about? For my own projects, I had many layers of truth-telling that I had to make explicit in my analysis. It was important for me to remember that the students only shared photos with me that they felt safe in sharing. Many photos were deleted, they admitted, before they returned the cameras to me, either because they didn't like the way they looked, or they thought the photo would "get them in trouble." This latter point was a particularly important one—in showing me the photos, the children continually raised concerns about whether or not these photos would be seen by others—peers, teachers, and their families. This showed the tensions students felt between showing me the truth about their lives, and this truth being used later against them.

These are cautionary notes not just for work with minors. Any images contain this tension, perhaps in a stronger way than words that have noreal image and are less powerful in that regard. Handing out cameras brings up for participants a range of feelings about what the photos will be used for (some may feel important, others might feel anxious). But in either case these issues need to be discussed between researcher and the participant in order to have a project that truly can be called "co-participatory."

There are other lessons I learned that may be of value to a food researcher using photographs and other digital data that participants will collect. First, I found it helpful to, discuss what it was exactly that I wanted participants to photograph: in food research what qualifies as a "food event" might be very different for the researcher and the participant, and should be discussed explicitly so there is no confusion later on. In my own work, for example, I instructed teenage participants to photograph "school lunch," thinking that it was obvious I wanted them to take pictures of food. However, I received, at first, very few photographs about food. Instead, I learned a significant amount about their friends, the types of clothes their friends wore, and where they sat at lunch, rather than the things they ate. As it turned out, school lunch, for these teenagers, was not about the food.

A second important conversation to have is to discuss how to photograph or capture behavior in public settings. Many people, both children and adults, find it embarrassing to pull out large cameras and use flash photography in public eating spaces, and as a result, I found that a photo taken with a cameraphone, or perhaps even a sketch drawing yielded more success in showing what happened in places such as restaurants or the classroom. At home, however, when participants were more likely to have more control over their setting, photographs were more prolific, clearly focussed, and well described. At home, the teenagers using my cameras were even able to pose with their meals, by using siblings and parents to take the pictures.

A final discussion should be one concerning authorship. *Who will see the picture after it is taken?* was an important question for both children and adult participants, whether or not they voiced it to me directly. While food is an engaging topic, it is also one laden with emotions. If participants think they are being evaluated on their "food image" or dietary habits they might be less inclined to show all the details of what they eat, or where they eat. But making sure that photographs do not contain identifying markers like their faces or addresses (removing the street names in geotagged maps, for example) made a large difference in whether or not a participant wholly embraced the idea of handing over a set of photographs of something as personal as what they eat.

Despite these many tensions, using portable new media devices for photography and data collection allowed for a more fluid and dynamic type of data collection than a data collection system dominated completely by the researcher. I found that my participants that used new media devices like their phones or the internet to collect and analyze their food data enjoyed viewing and re-viewing their photographs. Often the teenagers commented on their own food activities on their own, without my urging or direction. Rather than having to wait for me to upload photos to a website, they did it themselves, and then labeled and analyzed their habits before I viewed it. New media, therefore, provided my participants ways to reflect on their own food culture, as they were constructing it. An important aspect for researchers to consider, therefore, is how to find ways for participants to review and comment on their own new media produced food documents *as the research progresses*, rather than seeing the data in a more traditional fashion (after the researcher has produced it for them).

As new media rapidly grows and develops, food researchers should consider the potential of web-enabled devices and collaborative software for doing research on food culture. New media devices can make it easier for both researchers and participants to collect data, and involve our participants in their own food research as well. In this sense new media is not about being flashy, but about tapping into our need for visual understanding. In addition, by using new media devices and skills that participants already use, cultural food researchers can more easily co-construct knowledge with their participants. Anthropologist Michael Wesch highlights this potential in his article *Web 2.0 and What Does it Mean for Anthropology?*:

> . . . if we focus on the media alone we are missing the bigger picture. It is not just the mediascape that is transforming, it is human relationships, and anthropologists are increasingly being called upon to explain this. Understanding human relationships within this new mediascape will require us to embrace our anthropological mainstay, participant observation. We know the value of participant observation in understanding social worlds. Now we need to participate in the new media in order to understand the new forms of sociality emerging in this quickly changing mediated world.
>
> (2007: 30)

In conclusion, using new media in food studies is as much about studying our relationships with each other, as it is about food. To borrow from the *Web 2.0* lexicon, it is a "mash-up"—a rich and complex display of relationships. Of how people now relate to themselves, to others, and to their changing foodscapes. While it remains to be seen all the ways new media can help us get close to the truth, thoughtful use of these tools may indeed help us not only uncover our dynamic relationship with food but also to continually "refine the image of the thing we are studying" (Becker 1998: 12).

NOTES

1. What sets new media apart from merely digital media is that new media can be accessed any time, anywhere, on any digital device, and is characterized by a participatory community around its content. In other words, what is collected and sent on new media is meant to be shared with other people.

2. Arjun Appadurai (1991) uses the suffix *-scape* as a way to describe the concept of postmodern globalization in its complexity. His theoretical framework is often referred to as a way to characterize the cultural power networks that result from an uneven, fluid, and irregular flow of goods, people within a globalized system. *Mediascape*, for example, refers to the ways images and text are transmitted and shared and used in both local and global contexts.

REFERENCES

Appadurai, A. (1991). Global Ethnoscapes: notes and queries for a transnational anthropology. In *Recapturing Anthropology* (pp. 191–210). Santa Fe: School of American Research.

Becker, H. (1986). *Doing Things Together*. Evanston, IL: Northwestern University Press.

——. (1998). *Tricks of the Trade*. Chicago: University of Chicago Press.

Bell, D. and Valentine, G. (1991). *Consuming Geographies: We Are Where We Eat*. London: Routledge.

Biella, P. (2008). Elementary Forms of the Digital Media: tools for applied action research in visual anthropology. In Mary Strong and Laena Wilder, eds. *Viewpoints: Visual Anthropologists at Work*. Austin: University of Texas Press.

Birch, L.L., McPhee, L., Shoba, B.C., Pirok, E., and Steinberg, L. (1987). What kind of exposure reduces children's food neophobia? Looking vs. tasting. *Appetite* 9, 171–178.

Burris, M. and Wang, C. (1997). Photovoice: concept, methodology, and use for participatory needs assessment. *Health Education & Behavior*, 24, 369–387.

Chalfen, R. (2007). *Variations of bio-documentary representation: kids make pictures*. Paper presentation at the 2007 International Visual Sociology Association Conference, New York University, NY.

Chalfen, R., Rich, M., Lamola, S., and Gordon, J. (2000). Video Intervention/Prevention Assessment (VIA): a patient-centered methodology for understanding the adolescence illness experience. *Journal of Adolescent Health*, 27, 155–165.

Dolphijn, R. (2004). *Foodscapes: Towards a Deleuzian Ethics of Consumption*. Delft: Eburon Publishers.

Grady, J. (1996). The scope of visual sociology. *Visual Sociology*, 11, 10–24.

Marte, L. (2007). Foodmaps: tracing boundaries of "home" through food relations'. *Food and Foodways*, 15: 3, 261–289.

Pegler-Gordon, A. (2006). Seeing images in history. *Perspectives*, February, 28–31.

Pink, S. (2007). *Doing Visual Ethnography: Images, Media and Representation in Research*. London: Sage Publications.

Piper, H. and Frankham, J. (2006). Seeing voices and hearing pictures: image as discourse and the framing of image-based research. *Discourse: studies in the cultural politics of education*, 28, 373–387.

Prosser, J. (1998). The Status of Image-based Research. In *Image Based Research: A Sourcebook for Qualitative Researchers* (pp. 97–113). London: RoutledgeFalmer.

Rozin, P. (1999). Food is fundamental, fun, frightening, and far-reaching. *Social Research*, 66, 9–30.

Ruby, J. (1991). Speaking for, speaking about, speaking with, or speaking alongside—an anthropological and documentary dilemma. *Visual Anthropology Review, 7*, 50–67.

——. (1996). Visual Anthropology. In *Encyclopedia of Cultural Anthropology. Vol. 4* (pp. 1345–1351). New York: Henry Holt & Co.

Salazar, M. (2007). Public schools, private foods: *Mexicano* memories of taste and conflict in American school cafeterias. *Food & Foodways*, 15, 153–181.

——, Feenstra, G. and Ohmart, J. (2008). Salad Days: using visual methods to study children's food culture. In Carole Counihan and Penny Van Esterik, eds. *Food and Culture: A Reader, 2nd Edition*, pp. 423–437. Florence, KY: Routledge. Taylor & Francis Group.

Van House, N. (2007). Flickr and Public Image-Sharing: Distant Closeness and Photo Exhibition. *Ext. Abstracts CHI 2007*. ACM Press.

Wagner, J. (2004). Constructing credible images: documentary studies, social research, and visual studies. *American Behavioral Scientist*, 47, 1477–1506.

Wesch, M. (2007). What is Web 2.0? What does it mean for anthropology? Lessons from an accidental viral video. *Anthropology News*, 48, 5, 30–31.

Williamson, D.A., Allen, H.R., Martin, P.D., Alfonso, A., Gerald, B., and Hunt, A. (2004). Digital photography: a new method for estimating food intake in cafeteria settings. *Eating and Weight Disorders*, 9, 1, 24–28.

Williamson, D.A., Allen, H.R., Martin, P.D., Alfonso, A.J., Gerald, B., and Hunt, A. (2003). Comparison of digital photography to weighed and visual estimation of portion sizes. *Journal of the American Dietetic Association*, 103, 9, 1139–1145.

Worth, S. (1972). *Through Navajo Eyes: An Exploration in Film Communication and Anthropology*. Bloomington: Indiana University Press.

SECTION 4

*F*ood Diasporas: Taking Food Global

25

Justice at a Price: Regulation and Alienation in the Global Economy

Daniel Reichman

For more than a century, governments in advanced capitalist countries have used regulatory law to "domesticate" pure market forces in the interest of national societies. In recent years, the realities of the global division of labor have outgrown the regulatory structures of nation-states, and no supranational agency enforces standards of economic justice at the global level. The imbalance between high normative standards of justice and weak institutional structures produces discomfort among citizens of advanced countries who rely on mass-produced commodities for their livelihood, but who have grown accustomed to the idea that "fair capitalism" is not a contradiction in terms: Who knows what nefarious forms of exploitation are happening on the other side of the world? And, even if one did know, what could be done? In an environment where existing political institutions seem incapable of adapting the standards of the modern class compromise to the global division of labor, concerned citizens formulate and enforce normative principles of economic justice outside the boundaries of the nation-state.

The rising popularity of "fair trade" is the best example of this phenomenon. Fair trade is a non-governmental process that certifies and labels commodities that have been produced under "socially just" conditions, according to the standards of an international auditing agency, the International Fairtrade Labeling Organization (IFLO). Through the fair trade system, consumers enforce a transnational standard of economic justice by paying a premium for products that have been certified as "fair." Consumers intend to effect political change by consumer choice, using a non-governmental auditing body and market decisions, rather than legal mechanisms, to enforce standards of justice. In effect, "fair trade" is a voluntary form of market regulation, in which a transnational group of consumer-citizens enforces a price floor for a commodity and maintains labor standards by choice. In this sense, they perform the regulatory function of nation-states in an essentially stateless environment.[1]

In general, "fair" certification for coffee guarantees that farmers (or grower cooperatives) have been paid a minimum price of $1.26 per pound of unroasted coffee ($1.41 for certified organic coffee) and that workers are treated fairly on farms. The standards of fairness are developed by unelected experts, and are published in handbooks that read like legal codes, albeit without a state-based system of law enforcement.[2] Some fair trade coffee roasters buy directly from farmer cooperatives, while others buy from large-scale import/export operations that have purchased coffee already certified and labeled as "fair trade" by a third-party auditing agency.[3] This process is similar to organic certification, although instead of certifying ecologically healthy practices, they are auditing social health, as it were.

With the addition of a "fair trade certi-fied" label, "fairness" becomes an attribute of the commodity, similar to its country of origin, flavor characteristics, or caffeine content. In the past five years, fair trade has undergone phenomenal growth. In 2005, 44 million pounds of fair trade coffee were imported into the United States alone, 75 percent from Latin American countries. This constitutes about 2 percent of the total coffee sold in the United States, and fair trade's market share has grown by 1,000 percent since 2000.[4] While still on the fringes, fair trade is moving toward the mainstream.

The current popularity of fair trade is especially significant because coffee, the commodity upon which the fair trade movement has focused, was among the world's most heavily regulated commodi-ties markets from 1962 to 1989. During that time, the global coffee trade was controlled by the International Coffee Agreement (ICA), an international treaty that established national production quotas and price controls for all countries that exported or imported coffee.[5] Coffee thus provides an instructive example of the shift from international market regu-lation to transnational market regulation. In the former, the nation-state remains the basic unit of political activity. In the later, the nation-state disappears from view, replaced by transnational NGOs and the buying practices of individual consumers.

In this essay, I will focus on the forms of political subjectivity that underlie contemporary attempts to regulate the global coffee market.[6] I use the term regu-lation in an unusually broad sense, refening to the ways in which a defined social group controls economic behavior in the name of collective principles. In this sense, regulation could include both customary and legal precepts—practices as diverse as cultural prohibitions against usury (Nelson 1969), forms of alternative finance (Maurer 2005), cultural ideas of the "moral economy" (Scott 1976), or leveling mechanisms like "image of the

limited good" (Foster 1965). In this discussion I focus on three forms of regu-lation: local-level violence against coffee farmers, fair trade consumerism, and international regulatory treaties like the ICA. The specific normative principles that underlie regulatory strategies vary greatly, but a comparative analysis of these principles enables a critical under-standing of contemporary forms of polit-ical subjectivity in relation to global political economic forces. Through ethno-graphic description, I will draw an analogy between attempts to regulate the coffee market at different points in the global division of labor. I suggest that different social groups face similar ideological struggles in their attempts to conceptualize and enforce "economic justice" in the contemporary global economy, which seems too complex and indeterminate to regulate or control.[7]

COFFEE UNDER THE RADAR

Building 45 in the cargo area of JFK Airport is, aesthetically, about as far as one can get from a Starbucks.[8] It looks like a warehouse on the outside, and the inside has the feel of a decrepit public school—lots of fluorescent lights, tiled walls, and squeaky floors obsessively buffed by bored-looking janitors. The building houses Port Authority Police and U.S. Customs officials, and holstered pistols far outnumber laptops. A yellow sign outside the building advertises Warm Winds Coffee, a glorified break-room on the building's first floor, where Tony Chan sells some of the world's most interesting coffee.

Behind a door simply marked "Coffee," Tony sells his product for $1.25 per cup, one size only. The coffee is grown on Tony's farm in La Quebrada, Honduras, a small town of 4,000 people in the moun-tainous center of the country.[9] A Taiwanese immigrant to the United States who became a coffee farmer after being fired from McDonalds, Tony grows his coffee in Honduras, ships his coffee to the United States, roasts it himself in the JFK cargo area, and sells it to airport workers from three small outposts, one of which is managed by his wife. Tony's coffee is specialty-grade, grown at high altitude and under shade, and meticulously managed at all stages of the production process. He has one paid employee in the United States, a full time field boss in Honduras, and serves the coffee to customers himself, seven days a week.

I first met Tony in La Quebrada late in my fieldwork. Beginning in 2001, I had heard rumors about a "Chinese" coffee farmer (called *el chino*) living up in the mountains who had supposedly made millions selling his product in the United States. Given the fact that this rumor was told amidst the most severe coffee crisis in the past half-century, I doubted its veracity. It was unlikely that anyone was getting rich off coffee, because the market price was below the production cost of coffee. At first, I chalked the rumor up to small-town jealousy and the myth of easy money in the United States.[10] There was clearly an element of xenophobia or racism to the rumors, blaming one of the community's only ethnic outsiders for exploitative business practices.

I also doubted the rumor that Tony exported his own coffee; it is rather difficult for a coffee farmer to obtain an export license from the Honduran government. They usually must work through several established companies, selling to a miller-processor or an exporter. Later, I learned that the story was not entirely false. Tony did grow, transport, roast, and retail his own coffee, but he was not getting rich. Far from it. He barely broke even.

Tony is a hardened entrepreneur. He became a coffee farmer after being fired from McDonalds in 1993 after 18 years of employment. He began working at the restaurant at 16, making minimum wage. He worked his way up the ladder at McDonalds, eventually becoming a regional supervisor in Queens. He hoped to one day own a branch of the franchise himself, but he was fired, replaced by a younger employee as a way of cutting costs. As he puts it,

> I was making too much money for them. I had been to Hamburger University [a McDonalds training center] twice. I knew everything. How many napkins to order, how many ketchup packets we needed. I had it down to a science. But I made too much money, man. They threw me out and hired some kid out of college making 20 thousand a year.

Tony's wife, a Honduran woman he had met at McDonalds, heard about a coffee farm for sale in her home country. Out of work but fueled by a mix of ambition and bitterness, Tony used all of the family's savings and much of his pension to buy the property. At first, Tony knew nothing about coffee, and viewed his farm merely as a way to turn a profit. He now seems to make a constant effort to repress his sentimentality and view his livelihood with the cold objectivity of a shrewd businessman, but the romantic side often shows through. He tells me, "You don't know what being a farmer is like until you do it. You live and die with your plants. If they die, my family dies. I didn't know anything about coffee, but now I love my farm. It's my life." But then he catches himself, and says, "Man, I just want to grow this stuff, bring it to the States, and sell it. That's it."

The romantic side takes over while we walk through his farm, early one morning during the harvest. Set in a beautiful cloud forest where the temperature rarely rises above 75 degrees, Tony's farm is twenty miles from a telephone, and about ten miles from the electrical grid. His fields are filled with tropical fruit trees, birds, and snakes. Pure spring water bubbles out of the ground near his mill, and he has built a house with beautiful views in a clearing at the high point of his farm. In every sense, it is the opposite of his bustling, workaday life in Queens. Families walk up the dirt roads with their picking baskets, on the way to work. Schools are closed during the harvest, and people come from nearby towns to participate. He describes his property as "paradise" and tells me how he wants to move here permanently with his family and lead a pastoral farmer's life.

Tony would do so, if only people did not want to kill him so badly. In the past few years, his home has been burned down three times, his crop has been stolen out of his barn, and he has been attacked by a family of machete-wielding thugs in the central plaza of a nearby town. While I was in Honduras, his field boss was attacked by two men while driving through the farm. They shot at him with pistols, leaving bullet holes in the driver side door of his pickup. Fortunately, Tony's right-hand man was unscathed, but the next time Tony goes to visit his farm, he will wear a bulletproof vest. The causes of the violence against Tony are complex. From 1994 to 1999, coffee prices were consistently over $1 per pound, but they dropped below 60 cents from 2000 to 2003, which is less than the cost of production. Tony pays his pickers slightly above the going rate of about $2.50 per hundred pounds of coffee cherries, but he is singled out as an exploitative outsider while other coffee growers are not. This is due to the fact that he is an absentee landlord who does not speak Spanish, and the belief that he makes millions selling his coffee in New York. It is important to note that there are few strong social bonds between landowners and peasants in La Quebrada, as is often the case in the "moral economy" model of peasant life (Foster 1965; Scott 1976).[11] Although, in a general sense, landless people depended on landholders economically, the particular families that were "up" or "down" at a given moment were constantly changing (Reichman 2006).[12] Therefore, people hated Tony not because he was an outsider, but because they believed he was making enormous profits in New York that were far greater than the amounts earned by "normal" farmers.

One night I naively asked a man who lived on the outskirts of Tony's farm what he thought of him. He launched into a racist tirade about how Tony could not speak Spanish, barely ever visits his farm, and lives a life of luxury in New York while his neighbors suffer. Adding to the problem, Tony's field boss is not from the adjoining hamlet. He is the owner of a medium-sized coffee farm who lives in town and who formerly worked as a migrant in New Jersey, where he learned to speak English, enabling him to communicate with Tony. Therefore, Tony's only full time employee is, by local standards, a member of the upper class—a returned migrant and coffee farmer, who also happens to make a steady income managing Tony's farm and running an electrical supply store in town.

Due to the class inversions that occur on Tony's farm, workers have to confront their place in a productive system in a far different way then they would if Tony were a typical local farmer who sold his coffee to a *coyote* (intermediary) or local miller-processor. The fact that people are "out of place" according to local social structure, coupled with Tony's foreignness, force people to reflect upon the nature of the system. Tony, who is supposedly a wealthy New York businessman, becomes the symbol of exploitation in the coffee trade, a metaphor for the relationship between poor Honduran workers and the wealthy people at the centers of the capitalist world.[13]

Tony balks at the idea that he is exploiting workers, since he is losing money himself. How can he pay them any more when he is not making a profit? He arrived in the United States as an unskilled immigrant worker, and he sympathizes with his employees, but feels the violence against him is motivated by a misunderstanding of the system, for which he is unjustly singled out. He says to me,

"Picking coffee all day, carrying sacks on your back up and down hills, that's no life, man. . . . And then they got nothing to do for the rest of the year, it's no wonder they hate us."[14] I sense some tinges of guilt and ask him if he feels any. "I feel *nothing*. I'm just trying to run a business and support my family. I don't want to live like a dog. I've done it before. It's the system we live in."

Tony dreams of expanding his business to the JFK passenger terminal, but concessions for spots in the terminal are only open to national brands. He currently is only roasting about 10,000 of the 100,000 pounds he produces each year, and the rest is sold to a Honduran exporter for the market price of about 35 cents a pound (2002 price).[15] This puts him in a bizarre position. He imagines that the coffee he grows—but cannot roast himself—is sold on the commodities market and then roasted, brewed, and sold by a national chain, while he languishes in Building 45, frustrated by his inability to expand the business.

Tony's case is especially interesting because he has participated in the global division of labor from almost every conceivable angle. He was both a worker and manager at a major international company, but he was ultimately fired for reasons beyond his control. He became an entrepreneur, hoping for more control over his life, but ultimately, his success in the coffee business is limited by the power of international corporations to dictate the terms of the coffee trade. He is seen as an exploitative capitalist by his employees in Honduras, and has been robbed and physically attacked, but he is a struggling small-businessman in the United States. He lives in a crowded home in Queens, hoping to send his daughters to college one day, but barely scraping by.

One would expect Tony to have an interesting perspective on global capitalism and fairness. He is an example of what Michael Kearney (1996) has called "polybians," in an attempt to theorize class in the global economy. Polybians—a play on the word "plebian"—are people who occupy a polymorphous place in the global class structure, and cannot rightly be called peasants, workers, or capitalists according to their relationship to the means of production. Tony, a *señor* (somebody, landlord) in Honduras and a *peon* (peasant, peon) in the States, certainly fits the bill.[16] Despite this unique perspective, Tony locates injustice at the most immediate level. He accepts the basic facts of capitalist life, and this is most apparent in his resigned acceptance of the violence directed against him. He understands what is like to be an exploited worker, and he understands the hopelessness the pickers on his farm face. Yet he feels powerless to change anything.

He directs his anger toward national chains. He is especially frustrated by advertisers and marketers who, as he sees it, hype inferior coffee made by major brands. He is also frustrated by the political clout of the major companies, which keeps him from relocating to the JFK passenger terminal. The symbolic and the political aspects of the coffee value chain are the elements that he does not understand or control. He is frustrated by the fact that he grows, transports, roasts, and sells his own coffee yet still loses out to the Starbucks of the world, who claim to have close relationships with coffee farmers, yet rely on "hype" to sell their coffee. If people really cared about coffee farmers, he reasons, they would avoid the flashy brands altogether, because farmers play a relatively small role in their business, compared to small-scale operations like his.

In this case, people at various points in the division of labor locate injustice at the proximate level. Tony's pickers blame him for their low wages, and he blames the national brands for limiting the growth of his business. No one has a systemic picture of the totality of the coffee market, even Tony, who perhaps more than anyone else has participated within it from multiple positions and can therefore transcend the segmentation of knowledge that occurs in any complex division of labor, let alone the contemporary global economy.

FAIR TRADE'S ETHICAL PHILOSOPHY

In the cases of Tony and his angry employees–neighbors, a social relationship that was previously hidden was brought into consciousness, forcing the subjects to reconsider their place in a total social system. Tony's workers resorted to violence when they thought of the coffee they harvested being shipped off to New York to be sold for millions of dollars. Tony lashed out against the national brands that seemed to limit his success in the coffee business by dominating the passenger terminal at JFK. In each case, coffee becomes a medium through which people imagine and reflect upon their place in a system of production and exchange.

In their own way, Tony and his workers are thinking in ways that are analogous to those of fair trade coffee buyers. Both groups reflect upon their own relationship to distant others to whom they are connected through trade (Silk 2004). Fair trade's rhetoric rests upon affective bonds between producers and consumers in the global division of labor, mediated by cash and coffee beans. Through the purchase of coffee, consumers seek to establish a social relationship between producers and consumers.

To create a conscious impression of this relationship, fair trade emphasizes the simplification of the commodity chain— removing the intermediaries that separate coffee growers and drinkers (Barham 2002). As its marketing material says, "fair trade enables cooperatives to bypass middlemen and sell directly to U.S. importers at fair prices."[17] The middlemen that are removed from the fair trade process are local *coyotes*, small-time

coffee buyers who process or transport coffee prior to export. In fair-trade's rhetoric of directness, the mediating role of importers, fair trade auditors, or the roaster/retailers is downplayed to create a dyadic relationship between farmer and coffee drinker. By simplifying the commodity chain ideologically, coffee drinkers can comprehend their place in a total productive system.

Robert Foster (2005:285) has suggested that "renewed interest in the sociospatial life of stuff . . . has emerged as a therapeutic defense against the alienating specters of globalization." He argues that scholars and citizens come to terms with their place in a productive system by tracking objects across time and space; he thereby draws a connection between the academic study of commodity chains and popular movements like fair trade. Implicitly, the study of global commodity chains is set against the notion of totalities. Because the totality (the global economy) cannot be understood in abstract terms, it can be approached empirically by tracking the movement of particular commodities through various points in the system.[18] The new interest in "where stuff comes from" is a response to the alienating aspects of participation in the global division of labor.

This leads one to ask why the "stories" of certain commodities, like coffee, resonate so well with popular experience, given the fact that globalization has transformed virtually all aspects of international trade. Why is coffee the symbol through which consumers reflect on their position in the global system, and why has the plight of the world's coffee farmers become a key symbol of the injustices of global capitalism? Coffee has always been a volatile industry, with exploitation at various links of the supply chain, from agriculture, to distribution, to retail, yet only recently has it become a key symbol in public culture. Coffee's place in the popular mindset is certainly disproportionate to its actual significance in the global capitalist system (compared to, say, petroleum).

Since the 1980s, coffee has shifted from a staple commodity to a highly symbolic expression of social identity (Roseberry 1996). Increased prosperity and consumer choice have created new possibilities for people to fashion themselves according to their own values, but tying one's identity to the fruits of the capitalist market can lead to profound contradictions. In a world where individuality is valued, how does one simultaneously depend on mass-produced goods *and* assert individual creative autonomy? Relying on commodities to express oneself can provoke ambivalence if the objects of desire are contradictory to the values people use to define themselves. Due to coffee's new symbolic power, it is an especially appropriate commodity through which people imagine their social position.

The ambivalence over commodity dependence is especially common among the professional classes, who tend not to be directly involved in the material production of commodities. Coffee has become such a powerful symbol of the contemporary upper-middle class, schooled in the countercultural values of the sixties, that American journalist David Brooks famously referred to highly educated suburban communities in the so-called "blue states" as "latté towns" (Brooks 2000:104). Brooks struck a nerve by coining the term "Bobo" or "bourgeois bohemian." The "bobo" ideology is rooted in a value of the "particular," "the unique," and "the authentic," but, contradictorily, boboism is based on the consumption of mass commodities.

The result of these processes has been an ever-expanding search for "authentic" commodities in a homogenized world (Kopytoff 1986). Food and clothing are important elements of the creation of one's social identity, so consumer brands like McDonalds, The Gap, Nike, and Starbucks are the most targeted symbols of homogenization. Educated,

cosmopolitan people are especially ambivalent about their coffee—it is an addictive necessity for the professional lifestyle. Addiction is bad enough, but addiction to a product that compromises one's sense of justice is even worse—a physical and moral vice. This is especially true now that tobacco use has become uncommon in offices, and strong coffee and caffeinated soft drinks have become the stimulants of choice for the professional class.[19]

Compared to other tropical food products, the "story" of coffee is easy to tell. Sugar provides a useful comparison, since it is also a mild stimulant mainly grown in the tropics. Sugar is a relatively undifferentiated product. There are only a few brands of sugar on the supermarket shelves, and no brand carries any symbolic message about status or lifestyle. Unlike coffee, sugar is used as an ingredient in hundreds of processed foods like soft drinks and candy. Coffee is consumed in relatively unadulterated form, and is not used in many processed foods. It would be almost impossible to try to know the origin of the sugar we consume, since it is found in so many products and in so many forms (fructose, glucose, dextrose, sucrose, etc.), and is produced all over the world, including the United States. Coffee is easy to follow from plantation to cup because it is purchased as a whole or ground bean with relatively little modification.

For fifty years, the image of the coffee farmer in the United States has been Juan Valdez, the trademark of Colombia's National Federation of Coffee Growers (FNC). As an idealized version of the rural producer, this image is a nostalgic nod to the Jeffersonian rural tradition, a man and his mule. In an age where industrialization and the global expansion of corporate food production make the small farmer into a valued nostalgic category, this image of the small coffee farmer is appealing. Some of the most famous U.S. ad campaigns, such as Uncle Ben's rice, the Cream of Wheat man, Aunt Jemima, and the Corn Flakes girl, have all used nostalgic depictions of rural life to sell industrial food products (Lears 1994). The relatively unadulterated form in which we consume coffee, coupled with an idealized version of the small farmers who grow it, make it easy to put a "face" behind coffee, especially when compared to commodities like sugar (or tea and bananas) that are associated with plantation agriculture rather than yeoman farmers.

In this context, fair trade coffee becomes the ultimate unmediated commodity, even though the ideological vision of a direct consumer-producer link is entirely dependent upon marketing and branding. Small-scale production can only obtain its nostalgic value under advanced capitalism, in which mass-produced goods are the norm.[20] Although this valorization of "simplicity" is founded on principles of social justice and progressive politics, it has an inherently conservative component, in that it requires coffee farmers to fit within a nostalgic cultural category derived from contemporary ideological trends in the developed West.

As a form of political subjectivity, fair trade is based on the elimination or negation of mediating institutions—be they *coyotes*, states, marketing boards, or international corporations. It is especially easy for consumers to erase the state from view with regard to coffee, because the centers of demand for fair trade are western Europe and the United States, places where coffee is not produced (with the exceptions of Hawaii and Puerto Rico). Therefore, consumers can avoid tough political questions about the role of national politics in market regulation (the debate over protectionism, for example) that would not be possible if applied to domestic industries like sugar, corn, or wheat.

I would suggest that the alienation experienced by Tony and his workers is, in many ways, parallel to that felt by fair trade coffee consumers. Through the medium of coffee, people begin to consciously re-imagine their roles as citizens in the global economy. In the absence of a systematic theory or frame through which they can comprehend this structure, people resort to individual behavior as the source of political transformation, locating injustice (and the potential for justice) at the most immediate level possible.

GLOBALIZATION AND THE (IM) POSSIBILITY OF REGULATION

Earlier in this essay, I mentioned that coffee was one of the world's most heavily regulated commodities for almost thirty years (1962–89), and the failure of fair trade's proponents to recognize the ICA's significance shows the degree to which political institutions have been erased from contemporary ideas of economic justice. The ICA was a treaty that established a quota system, restricting the coffee supply when international prices dropped to levels that threatened farmers' survival. It involved stakeholders from all sectors of the coffee trade in its organization, which allowed it to grasp the industry at a relatively high level.[21] Its standards were legally enforceable; individuals or groups could face fines or punishment if they exchanged coffee that had not been handled under the rules of the ICA.

It is not a coincidence that the ICA system basically followed the chronology of the Cold War. The ICA was passed in 1962, after the Cuban Revolution led the United States to take the fate of rural Latin America seriously. The United States saw the agreement as a way of warding off social revolution by guaranteeing a fair price for coffee. Because coffee-producing countries were mostly in the centers of the post-colonial world— Africa, Latin America, and Southeast Asia—the United States had a strategic interest in promoting economic stability in rural parts of these countries. Fittingly, the ICA collapsed in 1989, after the demise of the Soviet Bloc and the Central American peace accords ended the threat of Soviet-style communism in those regions. Fair trade began to grow in popularity immediately after the ICA's demise, and it maintains the exact same price floor that was maintained by the ICA. Surprisingly, fair trade's proponents never mention its functional similarity to the ICA, or the fact that it developed after the international treaty fell apart.

Given the fact that contemporary globalization is based on the existence of a single social system, it is surprising that the possibility of international regulation has systematically disappeared from political discourse. Even fair trade, a movement that is ideologically concerned with social justice and the well-being of commodity producers in the developing world, negates the power of collective institutions to regulate or transform society in the interest of the public good.

Returning to Foster's suggestion that movements like fair trade are responses to the alienating effects of globalization, I would ask what the concrete form of this response says about contemporary political subjectivity. When people begin to consider their place in the global economy, why does this lead to responses that are basically private or personal? After all, one can imagine many possible ways that individuals could be integrated into wider social groups to combat these alienating forces. This was exactly the problem that Durkheim set out to solve in *The Division of Labor in Society* (1984[1893]): How can solidarity be created in a society with a highly fragmented division of labor?

For Durkheim, the answer was "occupational groups," institutionalized bonds formed by people at all points in the division of labor. He believed that institutionalized communication between occupational groups would enable individuals to see their place in a collectivity, leading to utopian collective effervescence. Like fair trade, occupational groups would create a social relationship between distant others, connected by the division of labor; unlike fair trade, this relationship would be based on institutionalized communication, rather than advertising, marketing, and private consumer practice.

I would suggest that the narrow forms of political subjectivity I have described are the products of systematic changes in the relationship between nation and state. For much of modern history, the nation-state functioned as the framing principle of social identity (Anderson 1982). Turner (2002:64) has argued that economic globalization has eroded popular identification with states, a process that he calls the "de-hyphenization" of the nation-state. As a result of this process, citizens identify with shared participation in the global market, rather than membership in a national community. Akhil Gupta (1998:314–320) describes a similar process, by which nation and state are "un-bundled" in India as a response to the demands of global markets. As a result of the erosion of the ideological bond between nation and state, alienated citizens see no collective institution that mediates between their personal needs and the global market. Thus, private action becomes the only outlet for their dissatisfaction. In the case described by Gupta, Indian peasant groups attack the fast food chain KFC as a response to their declining political power in a newly liberalized marketplace.

This basic contradiction—the recognition of participation in a single, global society, with no means of transformation beyond individual acts—is symptomatic of trends in contemporary theory, including the anthropology of globalization. Most anthropologists are critical of neoliberal globalization, but few have any hope in the state's ability to regulate the economy. Post-1968 intellectuals have tended to see the state as an agent of oppression, following in the legacy of Foucault. The realities of globalization are usually seen as challenges to the power of nation-states, but few see global integration as presenting the possibility for greater transnational regulation of the economy.

It is surprising that globalization is tended to be seen as complex, indeterminate, and unstructured (e.g., Appadurai 1996), while the concept itself is based upon the existence of a single, integrated system. Writers like Michael Hardt and Antonio Negri, for example, have tried to develop a collective political platform to reform the global economy, but they explicitly deny the power of states or international institutions, arguing that new "multitudinous" de-centered social formations must develop in the place of modern nation-states for true reform to take place (Hardt and Negri 2004). They see the source of potential reform in "the common," a transnational group linked through technology and shared participation in a global sociocultural whole. David Graeber (2001) has argued in favor of anarchism, the establishment of new social bonds outside of authoritarian state structures.

Returning to the story of Tony Chan and his workers, recall that Tony's frustration came from two sources—his inablilty to access the JFK terminal, and the low price paid for his coffee on the open market. According to Talbot (1997a,b), five transnational corporations—Nestle Foods, Procter and Gamble, Kraft (Altria/ Phillip Morris), Coca Cola, and Sara Lee—control over 60 percent of the world coffee market. Tony sells the coffee he cannot roast himself to an exporter that is a subsidiary of Volcafe, the world's third-largest green coffee trader. Volcafe sells to the major coffee roasters mentioned above, and is a subsidiary of London-based ED&F Man Holdings, one of the world's largest corporations and operator of a hedge fund worth tens of billions of dollars.

Faced with this consolidation of trade, the fact that transnational consumer groups have come to re-imagine their place in the global division of labor is an important development. Renewed interest in global commodities systems can make social relationships explicit across time and space. However, this recognition has produced forms of political subjectivity that are inadequate to the task at hand, regulating the global economy in the interest of social solidarity. Alienated citizens comprehend their role through the metaphor of coffee, and struggle to formulate principles of justice in a seemingly incomprehensible system. I would suggest that the integration of the economy into a single global market should be seen as an opportunity for the type of transnational regulation accomplished by the ICA. After all, the WTO has been remarkably effective in regulating capital transnationally, while social concerns are left to fragmented or private movements like fair trade. Fair trade demonstrates that there is popular will for this sort of program, but, in the absence of any guiding theory, it is channeled toward private behavior.

ACKNOWLEDGEMENTS

An earlier version of this paper was presented at the session "Fair Trade/Free Trade: Alternatives and Realities in Cross-Cultural Perspective" at the 2005 Annual Meeting of the American Anthropological Association. I thank the organizer, Sarah Lyon, and the other panelists for their comments and insightful criticism. Other versions of this paper were read at Cornell University and the University of Massachusetts, Boston. I am grateful to many people who suggested ways to expand and improve this work, especially Elizabeth Ferry, Terry Turner, Dominic Boyer, Robert Foster, Hiro Miyazaki, Annelise Riles, Ted Fischer, and one anonymous reviewer. The fieldwork upon which this study is based was conducted while I was a NSF Graduate Research Fellow, and was assisted by grants from the Cornell

International Institute for Food and Development and the Mario Einaudi Center for International Studies. I also thank the Instituto Hondureño de Antropología e Historia (IHAH) for their support during my field research in Honduras.

NOTES

1. I recognize that fair trade is not stateless, in the sense that its practices are still covered by the laws of the individual nations in which it exists. In theory, fair trade's claims could be regulated by laws against consumer fraud or truth-in-advertising if disputes over its auditing practices arose. To my knowledge, this has not occurred anywhere in the world.

2. The particular standards vary by country, based on the average wage and size of land holdings in a given country. See: http://www.transfairusa.org/pdfs/Coffee%20SP%20versionJune04.pdf for more details.

3. Recently, there has been considerable scholarly work on fair trade. Early studies looked at the potential of fair trade as a corrective to mainstream global capitalism, written from the point of view of fair trade activists (Barham 2002; Renard 1993; Raynolds 2000, 2002; Raynolds et al. 2004). Recent empirical studies by Lyon (2007) and others have taken a local-level approach, studying the effects of participation in fair trade markets in particular cooperatives in Central America, and then contrasting the actual material benefits to coffee farmers with the rhetoric of the fair trade establishment.

4. See the 2005 Fair Trade Almanac, Section II Exhibit III, for the exact figures. http://www.transfairusa.org/pdfs/2005FTAlmanac3.17.06.pdf

5. The ICA technically still exists, but it no longer contains any regulatory provisions. Instead, the current ICA provides funding for the International Coffee Organization, which publishes price data and conducts studies to improve efficiency in coffee production. See Bates (1997) for a comprehensive account of the rise and fall of the ICA.

6. I use the term "forms of political subjectivity" rather than Foucault's concept of "governmentality" to avoid the state-determinism implied by the latter. "Governmentality" is based on a view of political agency in which the state ultimately disciplines its subjects to consolidate control. Although I certainly see contemporary fair trade as an effect of neo-liberal regimes, I do not see its rise as the consequence of state-led discipline, given the fact that the importance of the state has weakened under neo-liberalism.

7. Miller (2001) asserts that the anthropology of global commodity chains can provide the empirical grounds upon which consumers can judge the impact of behavior on the wider society, leading to new forms of political engagement.

8. The specific names and places described here are pseudonyms.

9. *La Quebrada* is a pseudonym that I use to protect the identities of local people involved in illegal activity, especially human smuggling. It was the site of field research I conducted between 2001 and 2004.

10. The coffee crash coincided with a major boom in emigration to the United States, so these "easy money" myths were quite common. See Reichman (2006) for more information about the relationship between coffee and migration.

11. Eric Wolf's early work on coffee communities in Puerto Rico (1956) showed that the international coffee market was too volatile for such stable bonds to exist, and this was certainly the case in La Quebrada.

12. Wolf referred to this process as "the circulation of elites." The class structure itself remained constant, but the particular members of each class changed due to luck in the market.

13. Workers are also forced to confront the wealth of the United States due to the pervasive presence of returned migrants and families that live on migrant remittances. Although few migrants from La Quebrada actually live in the New York area, it is still considered to be the center of American capitalism.

14. The coffee harvest generally lasts from late-October to mid-February.

15. Note that this price is far lower than the spot price of 65 cents that I mentioned above. The spot price is the average price paid for imported coffee at the New York Board of Trade. The price paid to producers is far lower.

16. Kearney's description of "polybians" was based on the experience of Oaxacan peasants, most of whom do not own significant land or capital, in contrast to Tony. In this sense, he is closer to the bourgeoisie than the subjects of Kearney's study, but the core of Kearney's argument about class still holds: categories like "peasant" and "capitalist" are hard to sustain in the contemporary global economy.

17. Brochure available at www.transfairusa.org/pdfs/wrk_croptocup.pdf.

18. Appadurai's (1996) landmark essay on "flows" made the anti-structural basis of this argument explicit.

19. As if to prove that coffee is now literally seen as a fuel for capitalist work, the American chain Dunkin' Donuts has, as its slogan, "America Runs on Dunkin."

20. This is analogous to the valorization of nature during the Industrial Revolution in England, described by Raymond Williams in his classic book, *The Country and the City* (1973).
21. The ICA's demise was largely due to the fact that its most powerful member states placed their own national political interests over the interests of the industry as a whole, and it became dominated by internal conflicts and the hegemonic interests of the two largest coffee-producing nations, Brazil and Colombia (Bates 1997).

REFERENCES CITED

Anderson, Benedict, (1982) Imagined Communities: Reflections on the Origin and Spread of Nationalism. London: Verso.

Appadurai, Arjun (1996) Modernity At Large: Cultural Dimensions Of Globalization. Minneapolis: University Of Minnesota Press.

Barham, Elizabeth (2002) Towards a Theory of Values-based Labeling. Agriculture and Human Values 19:349–360.

Barnett, Clive, et al (2005) Consuming Ethics: Articulating the Subjects and Spaces of Ethical Capitalism. Antipode 37(1):23–45.

Bates, Robert (1997) Open-Economy Politics: The Political Economy of the World Coffee Trade. Princeton, NJ: Princeton University Press.

Brooks, David (2000) Bobos in Paradise: The New Upper Class and How They Got There. New York: Simon and Schuster.

Cook, Ian, and Phillip Crang (1996) The World on a Plate: Culinary Culture, Displacement, and Geographical Knowledges. Journal of Material Culture 1(2):131–153.

Durkheim, Emile (1984)[1893] The Division of Labor in Society. W.D. Halls, trans. New York: Free Press.

Foster, George (1965) Peasant Society and the Image of Limited Good. American Anthropologist 67:293–315.

Foster, Robert J. (2005) Tracking Globalization: Commodities and Value in Motion. In The Sage Handbook of Material Culture. Christopher Tilley et al., eds. London: Sage.

Graeber, David (2001) Toward An Anthropological Theory Of Value: The False Coin Of Our Own Dreams. New York: Palgrave.

—— (2004) Fragments Of An Anarchist Anthropology. Chicago: Prickly Paradigm Press.

Gupta, Akhil (1998) Postcolonial Developments: Agriculture in the Making of Modern India. Durham, NC: Duke University Press.

Hardt, Michael, and Antonio Negri (2004) Multitude: War And Democracy In The Age Of Empire. New York: The Penguin Press.

Kearney, Michael (1996) Reconceptualizing the Peasantry: Anthropology in Global Perspective. Boulder, CO: Westview Press.

Kopytoff, Igor (1986) The Cultural Biography of Things: Commoditization as Process. In The Social Life of Things. Arjun Appadurai, ed. Cambridge, UK: Cambridge University Press.

Lears, T. Jackson (1994) Fables of Abundance: A Cultural History of Advertising in America. New York: Basic Books.

Lyon, Sarah (2007) Maya Coffee Farmers and Fair Trade: Assessing the Benefits and Limitations of Alternative Markets, Culture & Agriculture 29(2):100–112.

Maurer, Bill (2005) Mutual Life, Limited: Islamic Banking, Alternative Currencies, Lateral Reason. Princeton, NJ: Princeton University Press.

Miller, Daniel (2001) The Dialectics of Shopping. Chicago: University of Chicago Press.

Nelson, Benjamin (1969) The Idea of Usury: From Tribal Brotherhood to Universal Otherhood. Chicago: University of Chicago Press.

Raynolds, Laura T. (2000) Re-Embedding Global Agriculture: The International Organic and Fair Trade Movements. Agriculture and Human Values 17:297–309.

—— (2002) Consumer/Producer Links In Fair Trade Coffee Networks. Sociologia Ruralis 42(4):404–424.

Raynolds, Laura T., Douglas Murray, and Peter Leigh Taylor (2004) Fair Trade Coffee: Building Producer Capacity Via Global Networks. Journal of International Development 16(8): 1109–1121.

Reichman, Daniel (2006) Broken Idols: Migration, Globalization, and Cultural Change in Honduras. Ph.D. dissertation, Department of Anthropology, Cornell University.

Renard, Marie-Christine (1993) The Interstices of Globalization: The Example of Fair Coffee. So-ciologia Ruralis 39(4):484–500.

Roseberry, William (1996) The Rise of Yuppie Coffees and the Reimagination of Class in the United States. American Anthropologist 98(4):762–775.

Scott, James C. (1976) The Moral Economy of the Peasant: Rebellion and Subsistence in Southeast Asia. New Haven, CT: Yale University Press.

Silk, John (2004) Caring at a distance: Gift Theory, Aid Chains, and Social Movements. Social and Cultural Geography 5(2):229–251.

Talbot, John M. (1995) Regulating the Coffee Commodity Chain: Internationalization and the Coffee Cartel. Berkeley Journal of Sociology 40:113–149.

—— (1997a) The Struggle for Control of a Commodity Chain: Instant Coffee from Latin America. Latin American Research Review 32(2):117–135.

—— (1997b) Where Does Your Coffee Dollar Go?: The Division of Income and Surplus Along the

Coffee Commodity Chain. Studies in Comparative International Development 32(1):56–91.

Turner, Terence (2002) Shifting the Frame From Nation-State to Global Market: Class and Social Consciousness in the Advanced Capitalist Countries. Social Analysis 46(2):56–80.

Wolf, Eric R. (1956) San José: Subcultures of a "Traditional" Coffee Municipality. *In* The People of Puerto Rico. Julian Steward, ed. Urbana, IL: University of Illinois Press.

Williams, Raymond (1973) The Country and the City. New York: Oxford University Press.

26

From the Bottom Up: The Global Expansion of Chinese Vegetable Trade for New York City Markets

Valerie Imbruce

New York City presents an enormous and ever-changing market for a vast diversity of food products. In New York you can indulge your senses in sticky Jordanian pastries made with pistachios imported from Afghanistan, Amazonian *açaí* whipped into shakes, and a steaming bowl of Vietnamese *pho* with a fresh sprig of Thai basil floating atop. New York City prides itself on the ability to offer authentic tastes from distant cornets of the world. This joy of urban life depends on a global order of trade. Traditional food products increasingly come from nontraditional places.[1] Chinese okra is grown in Honduras, rambutan in Guatemala, and longan in Mexico. New York, like most other cities, contributes to a supposedly efficient, industrial, and corporately controlled food system. Such agribusiness developed in part to feed burgeoning urban populations. Yet within the same cities that support industrial, agriculture, other systems are defined and redefined every day. The many spaces of New York City offer opportunities for alternatives to the seemingly dominant political economic reality of corporate globalization. Multilingual, transnational peoples find ways to use spaces not appropriated by corporate interests to create their own international systems of capital exchange.

Immigrant populations develop alternative food systems, yet they have not been adequately analyzed, empirically or theoretically, in the food system literature. Studies have analyzed the ethnicities of farm workers highlighting otherwise invisible aspects of production systems (Wells 1996). Ethnicity, however, has not been considered in studies of marketing and distribution (Friedland 2001). Researchers are finding that the activities of once seemingly ephemeral immigrant communities are playing an important and unnoticed role in global political and economic restructuring, particularly in New York City (Stoller 2002; Guest 2003), and that global circulation is not just the rhetoric of corporate expansion (Tsing 2000). The complexities and dynamism of cities in particular present a multitude of opportunities for activities alternative to dominant structures (Harvey 2001).

In this chapter I begin to sketch what I see as an alternative food system in New York City, the Chinatown food system. The Chinese control their own distribution networks, moving thousands of boxes of fruits and vegetables a day through warehouses in Manhattan and Brooklyn to be sold by independent greengrocers and street vendors in the city's multiple Chinatowns. While some Chinese merchants use Hunt's Point Terminal Market, the city's main distribution point and the country's largest terminal, market for conventional fruits and vegetables, the vast majority of Asian products are traded by Chinese brokers outside of Hunt's Point.

The practice of fruit and vegetable exchange in Chinatown has historical, roots. Since the development of a Chinese enclave in lower Manhattan, over one hundred years ago, the Chinese have created their own networks of exchange. Local farms in New Jersey and Long Island operated by Chinese families grew and trucked fruits and vegetables preferred by the urban Chinese to be, sold in Chinatown markets.

Currently Chinatown's fresh fruit and vegetable markets are part of a highly complex, global system of production and distribution. Fresh food products now come from New York state, New Jersey, Florida, California, Mexico, Honduras, and the Dominican Republic as well as Taiwan, mainland China, and other places Although Chinatown's food system is undergoing rapid geographic expansion, it does not display the hegemonic tendencies of global agro-food systems (McMichael 1994; Lyson and Raymer 2000; Goodman and Watts 1997; Bonnano et al. 1994; Barndt 2002). The industry is neither vertically not horizontally integrated, nor has it been subject, to corporate appropriation. From farm to retail level, businesses are individually owned and operated. Transport: is contracted by independent trucking companies, and as many as three brokers may be involved in international commodity chains. Individuals who grow, sell, import, and export Chinese fruits and vegetables employ their cultural knowledge about food preferences, language skills, and kin and ethnic ties to develop a food system to meet the demands of Chinese, other East Asian, and Southeast Asian ethnic groups.

CAN A GLOBAL FOOD SYSTEM MEET THE GOALS OF "ALTERNATIVE" FOOD SYSTEMS?

Food systems that contest, resist, and oppose global agro-food systems share a political agenda for ecological sustainability economic viability, and social justice.

Alternatives are united in the practice of reconstructing a locally situated, decentralized food system (Kloppenburg et al. 1996; Hinrichs 2000), or in the commodification of ecologically and socially responsible food production and trade (Guthman 2000; Murray and Raynolds 2000). Tensions between local and global processes are constantly negotiated and it is clear that the local-global binary is problematic. Although it has been recognized that the ideology of alternative food systems has been better theorized than the practice itself (Allen et al. 2003), the tensions; between the local and global have not been reconsidered in theory or in practice. The commitment to the relocalization of agriculture is indeed an important one, but I am afraid, that it may obscure merits of other systems, particularly systems that feed people across class boundaries. We cannot ignore that farmers' markets, artisan slow foods, organic, and fairly traded foods can often be prohibitively expensive, and they may only appeal, to certain demographics as well as class sensibilities. We continue to face the challenge of defining the many manifestations of "alternativeness" (Watts et al. 2005).

If we compare part of the mission of slow food and its sister alternatives—to conserve agricultural diversity and protect traditional foods—to Chinatown's food system, there is a clear commonality. Supplying a market with over one hundred types of fresh, culturally specific ingredients year round, as Chinatown's food system does, can very much help conserve biodiversity as well as gastronomic traditions. *Cittaslow* (slow cities), according to their website, seek to promote something "less frantic, yielding, and fast—no doubt more human, environmentally correct and sensible." Chinatown at any given moment is often frantic, but when you step back and think about how the community has retained, so much of its cultural tradition while the city is constantly changing and hybrid cultures are constantly forming, you recognize the "slowness" of New York's Chinese community. The pace of immigration and trade may deliver change, but it can also slow change. New immigrants sustain old habits, and old habits are sustained by trade.

This chapter seeks to bring the global into the alternative food system discussion by exploring what Chinatown's food system looks like. While the Chinatown food system *in practice* displays part of the vision of alternative food systems, it does not share in its political agenda. The global expansion of the food system follows processes outside of the dominant industrial and corporately controlled food system, but not by consciously resisting it. I argue that Chinatown's food system constitutes an alternative global food system in which individual entrepreneurs are making new spatial connections through their lived experiences, and that this system contributes biological diversity to produce stands of the city, as well as helping sustain, cultural practices of new and old urban inhabitants.

THE DEVELOPMENT OF CHINATOWN'S FOOD SYSTEM

The development of Chinatowns food system is intertwined with the history of Chinese immigration and the development of the Chinese enclave in lower Manhattan. The first major wave of Chinese immigration to the United States was from Canton Province (now Guangdong) and began over one hundred years ago. Until this migration, only small populations of Chinese sailors, cooks, and others involved in U.S.-China trade were living in lower Manhattan in the mid-1800s in the multiethnic Five Points area. After the British forced open the ports of south-eastern China in the Opium War (1839–1842), Chinese laborers from the port city of Canton (now Guanzhou) were transported to California to mine in the Gold Rush. They later went on to build the western spur of the transcontinental railroad At this time Chinese "coolies" were also sent to the Caribbean and South America, and many Chinese immigrated to locations through Southeast Asia initiating the Chinese diaspora. As a result, of these labor migrations, New York's Chinese population expanded, steadily in the late 1870s.

An economic recession heightened, antipathy toward the Chinese. Many Chinese departed from California back to China or to the East Coast to escape California's racially charged environment. Anti-Chinese sentiments were codified with the passage of the Exclusion Act in 1882, Chinatowns along the East Coast grew both involuntarily and voluntarily. Because they were denied structural assimilation, the Chinese developed enclaves for self-protection as well as social and economic improvement (Zhou 1992).

The food system arose out of the desire to preferentially feed the enclave. Like much of Chinatown's social and economic activity, the food system operated outside of the mainstream food system in New York. Restaurants were one of the first business sectors to develop in Chinatown, Restaurants catered to Chinatown's bachelor society. Tea houses and "chop suey" houses were places where men could get hot, homemade meals and socialize with others. Typical Cantonese dishes (which would come to be known as Chinese-American food) like chop suey, lo mein, chow mein, and fried rice were served because they were quick and inexpensive mixtures of meats and vegetables (Zhou 1992). The demand for basic Chinese vegetables like bok choy, *lo bak* (Chinese radish), *ong choy* (water spinach), and *dau mui* (snow pea shoots) encouraged Chinese farms to develop in the agricultural areas outside of New York City,

Much like the dominant food systems of the time, Chinese fruits and vegetables were grown in New Jersey and Long

Island and trucked into Manhattan. It was also reported that greens for winter trade and some subtropical items were supplied from gardens in Florida and even Cuba (Porterfield 1951). Records of Chinese crops in the United. States date back to the nineteenth century. The prominent American horticulturalist Liberty Hyde Bailey wrote about Chinese crops in the United States in 1894 and their great potential for assimilation into the American diet. Mainstreaming "ethnic" crops is a preoccupation of those interested in the economic potential of new crops. The Chinese cabbages (*Brassica spp.*) were among the earliest cultivated Chinese crops in the United States, possibly because they were regarded in this way. It is no wonder that bok choy and napa cabbage are seen on almost every supermarket shelf today. There were many more food items of less interest to agronomists but regularly sold in Chinatown. In 1937 over forty types of plant foods were available in Chinatown, including dried items like fungus, fruits, and lily flowers in addition to fresh roots, tubers, fruits, and leafy vegetables (Porterfield 1937).

THE FIRST CHINESE FARMERS

A few of the vegetables sold, such as cabbage, found their way into Chinese markets in the United States many years ago, but a large number, because they do not appeal to American palates, because of difficulties raising them as agricultural crops or perhaps merely because they are as yet unknown to the American farmer, are cultivated for Chinese use, that is for their own benefit or for Chinese-American restaurants.

(Porterfield 1951:5)

In Porterfield's musings over why many Chinese plants were not more popular crops there is affirmation that the Chinese were not only selling and buying a wealth of crops but growing them as well. The

first Chinese farm on Long Island, Sang Lee Farms, was founded by the Lee family in 1948.[2] The Lees were part of the Cantonese migration to New York City in the early 1900s. They ran a laundry business in which their son helped after school. After returning from World War II, George Lee, father of the current owner of Sang Lee Farms, went to the State University of New York at Farmingdale to study agronomy. His parents, immigrants from Canton, approved of his career choice. In an interview with the *New York Times*, George Lee's wife said, "In those days, being a farmer was different than in China, where it was considered low. Here, they knew you had to have an education and know what you're doing" (Toy 2003). George Lee and his cousin began Sang Lee Farms. At this point Chinese farms were well established in southern New Jersey, but the Lees preferred Long Island because of its extensive underground aquifer. Southern Jersey has a longer growing season, but the aquifer promised a competitive advantage during dry periods.

The Lees' intuition was right. Sang Lee Farms quickly became the main supplier of Chinese vegetables for New York, Philadelphia, and Boston, as far north as Montreal, west as Detroit, and south as Miami. They established a reputation in Chinatown among wholesalers as well as market shoppers. The farm expanded to Hobe Sound, Florida, to produce during winter months in the late 1950s. At the peak of production the farm was double cropping six hundred acres in East Moriches, Long Island, and several hundred in Florida during the winter. Half of their acreage was bok choy, and the other half was a mix of about two dozen types of vegetables.

The farm grew alongside the immigration rates of the Chinese, The mid-1960s saw a boom in Chinese immigration. Although sixty years of Chinese exclusion ended in 1943 when China became allied with the United States in World War II, it was not until the year 1965 that there was a turning point in. U.S. immigration history. In 1965 the United States government abolished nation-of-origin quotas that had favored immigration from northwestern Europe for eighty years. Whereas the first half of the twentieth century saw 85 percent of its immigrants from. Europe, the second half saw the reverse; 85 percent from Asia, Latin America, and the Caribbean. Between 1961 and 1970, the number of Chinese immigrants to the United States was just over 100,000, more than, four times that of the previous decade, and from 1971 to 1980 the number, jumped to roughly 240,000 (INS Statistical Yearbook 1950–1988).

Chinese growers followed the Lees to Florida. Tommy Yee, the son of a New Jersey farmer, established a 110-acre farm in Loxahatchee in 1974,[3] His father farmed in Warren County, New Jersey, during the summer and bought vegetables from Florida in the winter to hold over their New York and Boston customers until the next season (Snyder 2004). Prior to the establishment of his farm, Tommy drove a truck between Florida and New York for his father. During this time he gained a valuable insight. He noticed a broken link in the commodity chain. Brokers (wholesalers, also called jobbers) in New York could not supply a steady product, and farmers in Florida didn't have consistent buyers. He wondered why there was no stability, so he developed a business solution to this problem. Tommy found that "as long as I could supply an above average product, it didn't have to be superior, and the market was good, the wholesalers would consistently buy." He used independent truckers since they were fairly priced and reliable. Now 95 percent of his business is repeat business. He has worked with the same two wholesalers in New York since 1978. He attributes the longevity of his success to his business philosophy. He believes that "one hand, washes the other."

ONE HAND WASHES THE OTHER: THE BUSINESS OF EXPANSION

Tommy's attitude, toward the business of agriculture is one I have heard espoused numerous times from, other successful farmers in Chinatown's food system. Trust and mutual respect in addition to a quality product (from the farmer) and a good price (from the broker) are necessary ingredients for long-term success. Getting paid, of course, is also crucial. Farmers are very vulnerable to market conditions because they sell highly perishable goods. Chinatown brokers in New York City work on consignment, which means they don't pay until after shipment is received. Farmers have to ship their product in good faith that they will get paid. From the brokers' perspective, they don't want to pay for a product, that they haven't yet seen. If it is of poor quality, they lose, plus they have to pay for disposal. Just about everyone has a story about how they were never paid by so-and-so, with whom they never worked again. The only way to survive in this type of market is to find buyers and sellers that can be trusted.

Some who have achieved stable business relations have done so by trial and error, taking risks and taking losses, but most have tried to preempt this gamble by partnering with trusted friends or family members. As agriculture in general has become a global system, and imports from Mexico, Latin America, and the Caribbean have challenged American farmers throughout the 1980s and 1990s, actors in Chinatown's food system have used social networks and practiced the philosophy of give and take to become global players.

Double Green

Double Green,[4] for example, began with international ambitions. Double Green Farm, Inc.; Double Green Produce, Inc., in Florida City; and Double Green

Wholesales, Inc., in New York City, were born out of the same idea: to supply the rapidly growing Chinese population in Flushing, Queens. From 1980 to 2000, the number of Chinese inhabitants in New York City grew by almost 250 percent (New York City Department of City Planning, 2000 Census). The rapid growth led to the development of satellite Chinatowns in the outer boroughs of New York City, the largest located in Flushing, Queens. Flushing was economically depressed in the 1970s and offered many opportunities for those with the capital to start their own businesses. Chinese investment turned the community around. Laura Huang, a Taiwanese immigrant and resident of Flushing, seized a rather serendipitous business opportunity to co-found Double Green.

Laura Huang's family fell from high society to the farming peasantry under wartime suspicions in Taiwan. Laura worked on her family's farm until she immigrated to New York in the 1970s. Through her church Laura met a Taiwanese family living in Haiti who was looking for a good school for their children in New York. Laura took it upon herself to help them. Laura took Mrs. Li and her children to get the appropriate forms for student visas, which must be acquired at the school one intends to attend. She also found, them an apartment. The Lis were so appreciative that Mr. Li flew from Haiti himself to thank Laura. When they met, Laura and Li discovered that they were both interested in going into business. Li suggested importing fish from Haiti because it was plentiful. Laura saw the need for vegetables for the growing Taiwanese population in Flushing. Since Li had expertise in agriculture (at the time he was an agronomist in Haiti), Li and Laura decided that they could open a production and distribution business. Li would, run the farm and Laura would run the wholesale warehouse in Chinatown's distribution hub of lower Manhattan.

Li scouted locations where he could establish a farm and packing operation. He decided on southern Florida because it has the humid climate he likes and is accustomed to in Taiwan and Haiti. He drew confidence about his choice of location from seeing the other successful Chinese farms in Florida. Li, however, decided to go further south in Florida than the other farmers, like Yee, where more subtropical and tropical fruits and vegetables could be grown. He believed that he would have an advantage that way.

Li and Laura, opened Double Green in 1985. They decided on a name that means "very lucky" in Chinese, yet they were quite unlucky in the beginning. The first year they lost money. The second year they also lost on many crops but made some money on papaya and bitter melon. However, it was not enough to keep them together. It was more difficult than Li expected to farm Chinese vegetables under Florida's ecological and economic conditions. In China, agriculture is very labor intensive. In Florida, however, it is too expensive to use the same labor dependant methods Li knew from China. He was forced to develop new techniques and needed time to learn how to farm in Florida City. Laura felt that she could not wait, so she went on to find new farmers. Although the partnership dissolved, Li and Laura helped one another realize their goals of opening a business. They both went on to build successful businesses.

Li used his experience and contacts in Haiti and Honduras to develop export agriculture. He was chief agronomist of the Taiwanese Mission to Agriculture in Haiti. There is also a Taiwanese Mission in Honduras. These missions began with the sole purpose to aid in rice production but have since diversified their interests. In Honduras, the mission is a key part of the Chinese vegetable industry: Haiti has more infrastructural challenges to exporting goods than Honduras, and Li's production there has waned. Production in Honduras, on the other hand, is growing. Li remains in close contact with both missions. Since he has established himself as a successful businessman and farmer in Florida he has been recommended as an importer and a consultant. The Honduran mission put a new exporter of Chinese vegetables in contact with Li. Now Li is importing three to four container loads of produce per week from Honduras. Li was recently invited to Honduras in October of 2004 to give a workshop to agronomists from all over Central America on growing Chinese vegetables for U.S. markets. Li also hosts his colleagues at his house in Florida and shows them his business. One Taiwanese colleague who was visiting while I was interviewing Li was interested in retiring from the mission in Haiti and beginning his own farm in Florida. Perhaps he will represent a new generation of Chinese agriculture in Florida.

After Laura left Li she took extraordinary risks to find new growers. She believes that it is important to take a chance with new growers. She looks for potential business partners through her social networks. Friends would go into partnership with her, or introduce others to her. If the grower turned, out to be good, then she would take care of them. By taking care, Laura means giving her farmers a good price and keeping them aware of exactly what the market wants. Both of these aspects are critical to a farmer's and wholesaler's success. Ironically while Laura has a wonderful reputation with "her" farmers, she has a terrible reputation with other farmers. Those who have tight relationships get paid, those who do not experience a cutthroat, perhaps unethical way of doing business. The famous line in Chinatown upon the receipt of a shipment is, "quality no good!" Farmers know that this means they are going to get paid poorly. Even if the quality is good, unless the farmer can get on a plane and fly to New York that minute (and that does sometimes happen), there is nothing they can do to prove it.

One of the growers with whom Laura took an extraordinary risk is Jack. Jack was up from Florida visiting his New Jersey farmer friend Johnny. Jack was a conventional grower.[5] He had a good contract to grow chili peppers for Pace foods. Johnny, on the other hand, grew Chinese vegetables for a woman in Chinatown. Jack had no interest in this, although he did have experience with Chinese growers. Besides Johnny, Jack was also a friend and neighbor of Tommy Yee in Florida. Jack spent a lot of time hanging around Yee's packing house because he borrowed the vacuum cooler to pack his peppers. Inadvertently, he was learning about farming Chinese vegetables at the time.

Johnny worked with Laura. Laura was looking for a new grower, and requested to meet Jack. Jack, being a courteous fellow, agreed to the meeting, but his immediate reaction to Laura's request was "No way!" He knew nothing about Chinese vegetables and could not afford to take the risk, not did he have the capital to expand. He gave Laura his ear until he could not listen anymore. He said straight out, "Laura, I am absolutely not interested. I don't know these vegetables and frankly I don't trust Chinese people." Laura, calmly replied, "What would it take for you to trust a Chinese person?" Jack sarcastically said, "Laura, in America we have an old saying. Shit walks and money talks." Laura reached into her pocketbook and asked, "How much do you want?" Jack left that meeting with a $25,000 check and a verbal agreement that he would learn to grow Chinese vegetables for Laura. Now he owns seventeen hundred acres on the south banks of Lake Okeechobee and packs a semi-truckload a day for Laura. He is the largest and only farmer of European descent to farm Chinese vegetables in Florida and it is because of Laura's leap of faith.

In Jack's opinion the advantage of working with Laura is that she really knows the market, what people do and do not like. She is an avid cook and high-quality produce is of paramount importance to her. Jack says, "Laura taught me about the place of vegetables in the Chinese diet. If I can understand that, then I can understand how to grow and sell them." Once, she was complaining about a little sand on the cut end of the bok choy. She wanted to be able to open a box and see perfectly neat and clean bok choy ends. The Chinese pick many of their thick-stemmed vegetables by the quality of the cut end. The cleanliness of the cut that Laura was demanding was impossible, given the price the market was willing to pay for the vegetable. Laura did not understand the real production cost; she thought it was simple to change the harvest technique. She flew clown to the farm to show Jack her idea. Jack recalls, "She opened a box of bok choy and started furiously pulling the vegetables out of the box, pulling off old leaves and cutting the butts. She cleaned off one-third of the box." Laura said, "For this type of packing job I would give you double the previous price, $18 a box." Laura thought that sounded like a very attractive offer. Jack was still skeptical. He said, "Laura, that is still not worth it for me. Let me show you how we pack."

Jack took Laura out to the field, where his workers harvest and pack the bok choy. It took them one labor hour ($6.00) to pack one box the way Laura wanted it. "Maybe my good pickers can do it in less time, for $4.00, about two-thirds an hour of labor." Jack broke down the math on this new procedure for Laura. With all other costs the same (cost of the crate, postharvest cooling and shipping), the labor cost for the new approach increases from $1.75 per box to $5.00 per box, almost by three. The sales price doubles per box and the profit margin increases from $4.65 to $10.40. However, with the new procedure, fewer boxes are harvested per acre. In the end, the new way made only a little bit more per acre, much less than what Laura first perceived to be

doubling Jack's profit. Jack would not honor Laura's request. He does not make agreements he does not believe in, but he does believe in open communication, as illustrated by this story. Because Jack and Laura have been able to have detailed interchanges like this, it has benefited both of their businesses. They keep each other aware of their strengths and shortcomings.

Yi Jen

The relationships I continue to find within Chinatown's Food System never cease to amaze me. In part it may be because the ominous term *globalization* once seemed so nameless and faceless. Or it may be that the environmental destruction and human exploitation associated with the globalization of agriculture has been so well documented. One of the most inspirational stories I was told comes from a now successful distributor in Homestead, Florida, who sells locally grown produce and imports produce from Honduras. Yi Jen[6] used to be a farmer herself, so she understands its hardships, the insecurity of the harvest and the exhaustion that comes with the work. However, she was not a farmer by choice. Yi Jen was forced to work on a farm in China during the Cultural Revolution. Someone in her family had to, and she was not going to permit her younger sister to do it. So she went, and she persevered. She found a way to study and get out of an imprisoned farm life. She left China when her grandfather gave her the chance to immigrate to the Dominican Republic, and she helped him open a hardware store. Yi Jen became familiar with business and recalls that she learned "mainly how to fight and not be afraid of people," Aspiring to open her own business, she got her grandfather's permission and moved to Florida.

Yi Jen worked for Li at his packing house, where she learned the ins and outs of the business. When she was ready to go out on her own, she raised $70,000 in cash from friends and family and went into business packing and shipping produce. She had a friend in the Dominican Republic who had moved to Honduras to export vegetables. She began to work with him. They have been working together for over ten years, and they have the most stable export business in Honduras.

Yi Jen does not work with many people. Rather, she builds strong relationships with the few she does work with. Yi Jen treats her business relationships like long-term investments. She says, "one penny today is worth ten tomorrow." She has even gone so far as to take a loss so that her farmers could turn a profit. She has a handful of growers in Florida, one that credits her as the only reason he makes money on his longan harvest. Last summer there was a glut of longan on the market from Florida and prices bottomed out. Yi Jen took a smaller cut on her share of the longan sales so that her farmer, who depends on longan for his primary income, could make a more respectable profit. Yi Jen says, "after all, what was one season's loss on one crop with one farmer, when you have had that farmer working with you for many seasons and you will have them for many more?" Yi Jen has not only built a stable business, she has the best reputation for quality products in Chinatown.

CHANGING TIMES, CHANGING PRACTICES OF CHINATOWN'S FARMERS

These examples show how entrepreneurs in Chinatown's food system have established and expanded their businesses. Through social networks they meet potential partners, and they strengthen and expand relations that prove to be mutually beneficial. These stories bring out the human side of trade relations. But I do not want to mislead you into thinking that

relations never change and trust is never broken. Some observers perceive Chinatown's food system as insular and difficult to penetrate. This may be true in some cases; however, it is not a niche system immune to the challenges of international competition. There are many farmers and distributors who have sought to duplicate the business success achieved by entrepreneurs in the system, but who have failed. There are constantly new farmers and brokers coming in and out of the system, and at some points there are more than the market can bear. This pressure can cause once stable businesses and business relations to crack.

Sang Lee Goes Chi-Chi

Sang Lee Farms has a new shingle outside the farm gate. It announces Sang Lee's positioning in the farm-chic rurality of the north fork of Long Island. On their website they boast "over 250 varieties of naturally grown produce"; *naturally* meaning "utilizing sustainable agricultural practices and integrated pest management." Their competitive advantage is their Chinese twist. On-line or at the farm stand you can buy premium baby greens like mini bok choy and shanghai choy for premium prices ($4.50 for 12 ounces and $5.99 for 24 ounces, respectively). Bok choy is usually $1.00 per pound in Chinatown! Or how about purple opal microbasil for $6.99 a quarter ounce? They claim that: it will add intense flavor to any recipe! The farm, and its image, has drastically changed since its inception as the first Chinese farm on Long Island in 1948. But of course, agriculture on Long Island has changed. Now it is an industry that fosters agrotourism and caters to the elite summer lifestyles of Long Island's East End.

Fred Lee, son the founder of Sang Lee Farms and current proprietor, just gave up their last account in Chinatown. It was a hard decision, he says, but he could not emotionally or financially stand having truckloads of harvest returned, unpaid. This practice became more and more frequent when Fred's wholesaler could not sell his produce; it was simply too expensive in the face of Mexican-grown products. Fred's long-time associate offered him the chance to go to Mexico and set up a farm, but it was against Fred's own idea of farming. He wanted to stay on Long Island, so he did what the other farms around him were doing. He began to diversify his product line and market directly to restaurants, consumers, and caterers. He went into baby vegetables, herbs, cut flowers, and heirloom tomatoes. He kept his array of Chinese vegetables, and now assembles bags of ready-to-cook stir fry greens and sauce. He set up a farm stand and began to advertise his own organic philosophy (he did not want to bother with certification; too much bureaucracy). Maybe Fred and his wholesaler no longer shared the same goals or vision of agriculture. But one thing was definitely true: internationally grown produce was undercutting Fred's business, and he had to change.

Losing Faith in Chinatown Markets

Jack was also getting restless. His relationship with Laura lasted for ten years, but it has come to a close. When I last visited him Jack told me the news. He said, "I had a divorce with my Chinese broker!" In Jack's opinion, Laura lost her aggressiveness in the market. It may be because she has realized that her son will not take over the business. Without Laura fighting for a good price for him, working closely with him to understand his needs, and keeping him informed about market demands, Jack could not continue to work with her. Jack clearly emphasizes that the Chinese vegetable market is not a niche market. There is no added value in growing Chinese vegetables, and competition is growing every

day, particularly from Mexico, where high-quality vegetables can be grown at a fraction of the cost. If he does not have a broker working for him, pushing his product and demanding the prices that he needs to make a profit, then he will not continue growing Chinese vegetables. In fact, in the 2003–2004 growing season Jack lost money on his Chinese vegetables. The other vegetables he grew carried his farm. Jack's divorce with Laura, however, did not end his tenure as a grower of Chinese vegetables. Jack's decision to leave Laura was provoked by a common event in Chinatown markets: Jack was offered better prices by another broker. Because Jack had been growing tired of working with Laura, the offer helped him make up his mind to leave her. As Jack believes in honesty and integrity, instead of deceiving Laura and selling to another broker behind her back (a more frequent practice), Jack flew to New York to settle the divorce in person.

CONCLUSION

There are over one hundred fresh fruits and vegetables for sale in New York City's Chinatown year-round. Old and new Chinese immigrants, as well as Vietnamese, Thai, Malaysian, Cambodian, and Laotian immigrants make a living within Chinatown's food system. Countless other first-, second-, and multi-generation Americans patronize Chinatown's shops and street vendors. The cultural heterogeneity of the system is iconic of New York City. The abundance, freshness, and cost of produce in Chinatown are unrivaled in the city. Where else can you get a pound of baby bok choy or Chinese eggplant for a dollar?

The marketing channels that deliver the great diversity of products to Chinatown are constantly growing and changing. Entrepreneurs continually enter and leave the system and continually look for new suppliers as well as new products. Thai guava is the new popular fruit among Florida growers, and longan, available practically year round, was once only available in July. The shift in product availability is as much a result of international competition as it is inter-regional competition. When a product grows well in an area, others also want to grow it. Because of this dynamism and competition, the successful farmers as well as brokers are always experimenting with new items and new places. Brokers do not shy away from global trade but use their social networks to develop new trade relations. The globalization of Chinatown's food system has happened like a groundswell, in a bottom-up rather than a top-down fashion.

Chinatown's food system exemplifies an alternative globalization that some scholars call globalization or transnationalism from below (Glick Schiller 1999; Basch et al. 1994), globalization from the margins (Appadurai 1996), or transnational urbanism (Smith 2001). As a process it is not something extrinsic to daily life, or imposed by regulatory bodies, but rather it is a result of mew spatial arrangements made by individuals. Globalization, in this sense, is the means of conducting business over widening distances and distended social relations (Flusty 2004). As Smith (2001) points out:

> Specific collectivities—local households, kin networks, elite fractions, and other emergent local formations—actively pursue such strategies as transnational migration, transnational social movements or transnational economic or cultural entrepreneurship to sustain or transform resources, including cultural resources, in the face of the neoliberal storm. (167)

Chinese immigrant entrepreneurs have indeed transformed their cultural as well as economic resources in a way that has led to globally distended networks of trade. What remains exceptional is that they have done so in a way that *remains* outside of the dominant modes of food trade.

There is no single explanation for this; rather, there are several contributing factors that begin to explain Chinatown's food system as it exists today. The people who control access to the markets are the wholesalers based in urban Chinatowns. As Chinese people they fully understand the food preferences of their community. Some non-Chinese people have told me they would like to deal in Chinese vegetables but are unknowledgeable about them. The wholesalers also largely do business in Chinese. Of course many are multilingual, but I have often seen Chinese wholesalers hide behind feigned language difficulties as a way to protect themselves from people to whom they are not interested in talking. The closed ethnic character of the entrepreneurs, whether created or real, may have protected the food system from appropriation, by American and European food giants.

Extreme competition, particularly on the retail end, keeps companies within the system from getting too big. It also keeps quality high but prices low. In Manhattan's Chinatown alone there are eighty-five small vendors (greengrocers and street vendors) and eight wholesalers. An informal system of apprenticeship serves to sustain this tradition of doing business. Many "new" entrepreneurs have gotten their start by working for others in the system, are family members sent to open an independent branch of the business at another point in the commodity chain, or are children who inherited the family business. Finally, Chinatown wholesalers and Florida brokers, as we have seen, drive expansion of the system by networking, rather than through buy-out and consolidation. They have set an example that is in perpetuation.

The global, fast-food systems that most slow food advocates oppose are not the only global food systems in existence. Far from leading to simplification and loss of diversity, global trade can help preserve traditions as well as foster innovation. New business ambitions can thrive without inevitable cooptation of appropriation by larger, more powerful global giants. Variety and diversity can exist in a food system at competitive prices, and without the sophisticated rhetoric that many people are unaware of, disenfranchised from, or completely skeptical about.

ACKNOWLEDGEMENTS

This research has been completed through the support of the New York Botanical Garden and the NSF Doctoral Dissertation Research Improvement Award 0425734. Fieldwork could not have been undertaken without the help of Louis Putzel, Andrew Roberts, and Karen Jiron, who not only assisted in interviews but helped in the conceptualization of the project. Most invaluable has been the academic advice of Christine Padoch, Charles Peters, and Roberta Balstad, and the editorial advice of Richard Wilk.

NOTES

1. The production of nontraditional agricultural exports (NTAEs), also known as high-value exports, is an economic development strategy prevalent in Latin America. NTAE refers to those products that (1) were not traditionally produced in a particular country for export (traditional exports are soybeans, sugar, bananas, and coffee); (2) were traditionally produced for domestic consumption but are now exported; (3) are traditional products now exported to a new market. NTAEs are generally high-value or niche products. Fresh fruits and vegetables and fair trade coffee are examples of NTAEs (Thrupp 1995).

2. I conducted an interview with Karen Lee in July 2003. She is the wife of George Lee, the son of the founder of Sang Lee farm. Karen now works full-time with her husband on the farm. About a month after the interview an article on the farm came out in the Long Island section of *New York Times*, covering much of what Karen had told me in addition to other things. I use my interview data supplemented with the *New York Times* article, in this chapter.

3. I had the fortunate experience of visiting Tommy, his wife, and most of his nine fields in February 2004 with Ken Schuler. Ken used to be the vegetable specialist at the Palm Beach County Agricultural Extension Office and was especially active with the Chinese vegetable growers. Although he is now retired, he works as a pest scout for Tommy, visiting his fields once a week. He invited me along and shared much of his expertise about Chinese vegetable farming in Florida. He also created a very comfortable interview atmosphere for Tommy, who needed reassurance of the validity of my study.

4. All of the individuals discussed in this section are protected by the use of pseudonyms. They were interviewed between August 2003 and October 2004. Li was interviewed on two occasions, once in Florida and once in Honduras. I also interviewed his son, who now runs the packing house. In addition to Laura, I interviewed her long-time employee. Because all of these people have worked together and remain in contact, it was very easy to cross-reference data.

5. Laura put me in contact with Jack. On my second trip to Florida in February 2004 I visited his farm and interviewed him.

6. Yi Jen is also a pseudonym. My first try at interviewing her in August 2003 failed: she flat out refused. Fortunately I subsequently interviewed her friend, a fruit grower who had been supplying her for several years and largely attributes his financial success to her. When I told him that Yi Jen refused to speak with me, he called her and told her I was harmless. That afternoon I had a four-hour interview with her.

REFERENCES

Allen, Patricia, Margaret Fitzsimmons, Michael Goodman, and Keith Warner 2003. Shifting Plates in the Agrifood Landscape: The Tectonics of Alternative Agrifood Initiatives in California. Journal or Rural Studies 19:61–75.

Appadurai, Arjun. 1996. Modernity at Large. Minneapolis: University of Minnesota Press.

Bailey, L. H. 1894. Some Recent Chinese Vegetables. Cornell University Agricultural Experiment Station, Horticulture Division Bulletin 67:177–201.

Barndt, Deborah. 2002. Tangled Routes: Women, Work, and Globalization on the Tomato Trail. Boulder, CO: Westview Press.

Basch, Linda, Nina Glick Schiller, and Cristina Szanton-Blanc. 1994. Nationals Unbound: Transnational Projects and the Deterritorialized Nation-State. New York: Gordon and Breach.

Bonnano, A., L. Busch, W. Friedland, L. Gouvia, and E. Mingione. 1994. From Columbus to Con-Agra: The Globalization of Agriculture and Food. Lawrence, KS: University of Kansas Press.

Flusty, Steven. 2004. De-Coca-Colonization: Making the Globe from the Inside Out. New York: Routledge.

Friedland, William H. 2001. Reprise on Commodity Systems Methodology. International Journal of Sociology of Agriculture and Food 9:82–103.

Glick Schiller, Nina. 1999. Who Are These Guys? A Transnational Reading of the U.S. Immigrant Experience in Identities on the Move. In Transnational Processes in North America and the Caribbean Basin, L. Goldin ed. New York: Institute for Mesoamerican Studies.

Goodman, David, and Michael Watts, eds. 1997. Globalizing Food, Agrarian Questions and Global Restructuring, New York: Routledge.

Guest, Kenneth J. 2003. God in Chinatown: Religion and Survival in New York's Evolving Immigrant Community. New York: New York University Press.

Guthman, Julie Harriet. 2000. Agrarian Dreams? The Paradox or Organic Farming. PhD Dissertation. Department of Geography, University of California, Berkeley.

Harvey, David. 2001. Spaces of Capital: Towards a Critical Geography. New York: Routledge.

Hinrichs, C. 2000. Embeddedness and Local Food Systems: Notes on Two Types of Direct Agricultural Markets. Journal of Rural Studies 16(3): 295–303.

INS Statistical Yearbook. 1950 to 1988. Statistical Yearbook of the Immigration and Naturalization Service. U.S. Department of Justice.

Kloppenburg, Jack, J. Hendrickson, and G. W. Stevenson, 1996. Coming into the Foodshed. Agriculture and Human Values 13:33–42.

Lyson, Thomas A., and Annalisa Lewis Raymer. 2000. Stalking the Wily Multinational: Power and Control in the US Food System. Agriculture and Human Values 17:199–208.

McMichael, Philip, ed. 1994. The Global Restructuring of Agro-Food Systems. Ithaca, NY: Cornell University Press.

Murray, D., and L. Raynolds. 2000. Alternative Trade in Bananas: Obstacles and Opportunities for Progressive Social Change in the Global Economy. Agriculture and Human Values 17:65–74.

New York City Department of City Planning. 2000. Census, Demographic Profile of New York 1990–2000.

Porterfield, W. M. 1937. Chinese Vegetable Foods in New York. Journal of the New York Botanical Garden 38:254–57.

——. 1951. The Principle Chinese Vegetable Foods and Food Plants of Chinatown Markets, Economic Botany 1(5):3–37.

Smith, Michael. 2001. Transnational Urbanism, Location Globalization. Malden, MA: Blackwell Publishers.

Snyder, James. 2004. Black Gold and Silver Sands: A Pictorial History of Agriculture in Palm Beach County. Historical Society of Palm Beach County.

Stoller, Paul. 2002. Money Has No Smell: The Africanization of New York City. Chicago: University of Chicago Press.

Thrupp, Lori Ann. 1995. Bittersweet Harvests for Global Supermarkets: Challenges in Latin America's Agricultural Export Boom. Washington D.C.: World Resources Institute.

Toy, Vivian. 2003. East End's Lost Link to Agriculture. New York Times, August 31: Long Island Weekly Desk.

Tsing, Anna. 2000. The Global Situation. Cultural Anthropology 15:327–60.

Watts, D. C. H., B. Ilbery, and D. Maye. 2005. Making Reconnections in Agro-Food Geography; Alternative Systems of Food Provision. Progress in Human Geography 29:22–40.

Wells, Miriam. 1996. Strawberry Fields; Politics, Class, and Work in California Agriculture. Ithaca, NY: Cornell University Press.

Zhou, Min. 1992. Chinatown: The Socioeconomic Potential of an Urban Enclave. Philadelphia: Temple University Press.

27

SPAM and Fast-food "Glocalization" in the Philippines

Ty Matejowsky

Few US products have captured the imaginations and appetites of Filipinos in quite the same way as SPAM.[1] The canned meat enjoys an intense culinary following in the Philippines and throughout the Asia-Pacific that leaves many Westerners pleasantly baffled. This article explores the popularity of SPAM in the Philippines within the context of "glocalization" (Robertson 1995; Yamashita 2003: 6).[2] Specifically, it considers the ways in which this ham and pork-shoulder blend is utilized by Filipinos as both a commodity and a cultural symbol. Of particular interest is the emergence of SPAM within the country's burgeoning fast-food scene. As global chain restaurants have become more and more influential in shaping local lifestyles and nutritional regimes, SPAM's appeal to Filipinos has taken on increased significance by adapting to changing market conditions.

SPAM AS PRODUCT

SPAM is arguably one of the most successful manufactured foods of modern times. The 12-ounce rectangular tin with its blue and yellow color scheme is a familiar icon to millions the world over. The canned meat's affordability, storability and versatility have a mass appeal that transcends national, cultural, and socioeconomic boundaries. SPAM's durability and long shelf life makes it an ideal protein source for those living without refrigeration or electricity. Its simple ingredients give it an adaptability that translates well to almost any cooking style. Like other tinned foods, SPAM can be cooked inside its container or served cold directly from the can. The fact that SPAM can be prepared as a main dish, a side item, or an ingredient in more elaborate recipes adds to its consumer allure. Likewise, SPAM is an all-day food. It can be eaten for breakfast, lunch, dinner, or as a snack with only minimal preparation. While often derided by Western tastemakers as nothing more than culinary kitsch, SPAM has a staying power that is indisputable (Stern and Stern 1991).

SPAM was launched by the Hormel Food Corporation (headquartered in Austin, Minnesota) in 1937 as a moderately priced blend of ham and compressed pork shoulder. As a processed meat it contains several additives including salt, sugar, water, and sodium nitrate (Schroeder 2001).[3] This mishmash of ingredients is reflected in the product's name which is a portmanteau derived from the words "spiced" and "ham."[4] SPAM's consistency is that of a firm gelatinous loaf. It is encased in a viscous jelly that clings to the meat when expelled from the can. This oily residue gives SPAM its distinctive outer glaze. In terms of flavor, the pink luncheon meat is noted for a bland taste that is more salty than sweet. Like other processed foods, SPAM is high in sodium and fat.

Hormel has produced billions of cans of SPAM over the past seven decades. The company recently hit the 6 billion mark and is rapidly moving towards its next major milestone of 7 billion. Hormel has also introduced several variations of the original SPAM flavor. Newer incarnations reflect not only changing culinary tastes but also growing concerns about health and nutrition. Recent additions to the SPAM line-up include Smoke-Flavored SPAM (1971), Low-salt/sodium SPAM (1986), SPAM Lite (1992), and SPAM Oven Roasted Turkey (1999) (Schroeder 2001).

Besides its Minnesota headquarters,[5] SPAM production facilities are also found in seven other countries: Australia, Denmark, UK, Japan, Philippines, South Korea, and Taiwan. At present, the luncheon meat is distributed in more than fifty countries and is trademarked in over 100 (Patten 2001: 47).

SPAM AS HISTORY

If any one event thrust SPAM into the global consciousness, it was the World War II. Although some 20,000 tons of SPAM were sold prior to the war's outbreak, the conflict sparked a renewed surge in SPAM's national and international popularity. In the United States, the mobilization of resources to support the war effort prompted a series of home front austerity measures. Meat, among other valued commodities, was rationed by the federal government so that the choicest cuts would go to troops overseas. SPAM became the meat substitute of choice for civilians during these lean years as few other protein sources were available. In many ways, mainland America's love-hate relationship with SPAM was born out of this period of national sacrifice.[6] For some, SPAM grew from an acquired taste into a lifelong craving; for others, it was and will always remain an unappetizing reminder of the widespread deprivation brought on by the Great Depression and World War II.

Either way, SPAM's popularity suffered no real setback once government restrictions were lifted and quality meats were again made available.

SPAM's inclusion in US military canned field rations (C-rations) further solidified its historical importance. The luncheon meat has remained a battlefield staple in every major US combat operation since World War II. In fact, it was SPAM's space-saving rectangular can that influenced the US government's decision to abandon unwieldy round field tins in favor of more efficient packaging. Provisions of SPAM are also credited as playing a critical role in the Allied victory over Axis Forces. In his memoir *Khrushchev Remembers* (1970), the late Soviet Premier credits the Red Army's survival to SPAM. He fondly recalls that "there were many jokes going around in the army some of them off-color, about American Spam (sic); it tasted good nonetheless. Without Spam (sic), we wouldn't have been able to feed our army" (Khrushchev 1970: 226).

Notably, besides helping tip the war's balance in the Allies' favor, SPAM also gained a foothold in previously untapped markets as combat operations drew to a close. SPAM's unrivaled popularity in the Asia-Pacific owes much to the efforts of the US Armed Forces during World War II and the Cold War. It is probably of little coincidence that many of the largest markets for SPAM today—Guam,[7] South Korea,[8] Okinawa, and the Philippines—are found in regions where the American military has maintained a major presence. The US military played a key role in introducing and supplying SPAM to local populations, Whether obtained as pilfered goods on the black market or as food relief in times of need, SPAM quickly established itself as a local favorite despite the ambivalences and resentments felt by indigenous populations towards the US military.[9] Consequently, a strong consumer base for the luncheon meat was already in place among civilians across the Asia-Pacific when Hormel Foods went global in the 1950s.[10]

SPAM AS POPULAR CULTURE

SPAM's reputation as a consumer product extends well beyond culinary matters. SPAM has developed, a life of its own as a mainstay of Western popular culture. No other processed food holds this iconic status within the public imagination except possibly Cheez Whiz or Wonder Bread. SPAM references appear in virtually all genres of entertainment. Whether cited in film, song, literature, or television, the product is invariably portrayed in a humorous or satirical light. The entertainment value of a low-priced canned meat with a funny name clearly strikes a chord with Western audiences; so much so, in fact, that SPAM has served as a rich source of comic fodder for generations of humorists and satirists.

Doubtless the most famous and successful purveyors of SPAM humor are the British comedy troupe Monty Python. From the famous "Green Midget Café" sketch on their popular 1970s television program *Monty Python's Flying Circus*, to the more recent musical comedy smash *Monty Python's Spamalot*, the group has undoubtedly done more than anyone else to shape public perception about SPAM's shortcomings as wholesome fare. Doubtless taking a cue from Monty Python. "Weird Al" Yankovic recorded a song called "Spam" (which spoofs the R.E.M. song "Stand") for the soundtrack of his 1989 film *UHF*. There is also mention of SPAM in the last line of the Captain Beefheart song "The Dust Blows Forward 'N the Dust Blows Back" from the seminal 1970 album *Trout Mask Replica*.[11]

Nowadays, SPAM's comic saliency in the United States and Europe is almost completely played out, SPAM has become a hackneyed concept like pink flamingos, mullets, and velvet Elvis paintings. Nevertheless, it is notable that SPAM humor never really took off in other parts of the world. Even as SPAM humor wears thin in the West, the canned meat is still pretty much taken at face-value elsewhere. Overseas, it is essentially viewed as a convenience food with wide culinary applications. If other symbolic associations have emerged around SPAM outside of the West, they are usually not satirical in nature.

SPAM ATTITUDES: UNITED STATES

SPAM holds a paradoxical position in the United States as a cultural commodity. Americans appear to be of two minds when it comes to assessing the product's symbolic value. On the one hand, SPAM is associated with a lack of cultural sophistication and refinement due to its mass appeal and affordability. On the other hand, SPAM is celebrated as a definitive piece of Americana that resonates with society's populist inclinations. In many ways, the latter view is born out of the former. SPAM has carved out a special niche in that strain of popular culture that extols the campy aspects of modern life (Stern and Stern 1991); Shrewdly Hormel taps into this fascination with American kitsch by portraying their product in a whimsical light and offering a vast array of SPAM-inspired memorabilia (Schroeder 2001).

Ambivalence towards SPAM manifests itself in other ways. SPAM is regarded with increasing nostalgia by those born after World War II as a reminder of childhood. While this quasi-sentimental view may evoke fond memories, it does little to influence the dietary choices of most middle-class Americans. SPAM is generally considered children's fare like Jell-O, Chef Boyardee, and Kraft's Macaroni and Cheese because of its bland taste and easy preparation (ibid.). An implicit assumption of this view, therefore, is that the canned meat does not befit the discerning tastes of grown-ups. Adults who do eat SPAM—so the logic goes—must do so because they are either on a budget or never developed a sophisticated palate.

The impression that SPAM is a poor person's food places it alongside Ramen Noodles and Kool-Aid as a lowbrow dietary staple. For better or worse, SPAM has been stereotyped as the culinary domain of America's children and less affluent.[12]

The conflicting views many Americans feel towards SPAM are rooted in considerations beyond class or age. Matters of authenticity also exert a significant if not subtle influence on how SPAM is perceived. As a processed food, SPAM is not a "real" meat but rather a compressed loaf of chipped pork shoulder and other ingredients. The fact that it closely resembles cooked ham in both form and flavor gives it an air of "genuineness" that belies its origins. Most Americans grasp that SPAM is not real ham just as they know that Cheez Whiz is not real cheese. This awareness contributes to the view that SPAM is somehow not bona fide: that is to say. it is counterfeit because it aspires to be something it is not. While Hormel Foods neither suggests nor implies that SPAM is anything other than canned luncheon meat, it is hard for consumers to disassociate SPAM from suspicions that it is dubiously manufactured as a ham substitute. The fact that it is commonly used in recipes and other preparations calling for ham only reinforces this notion. In a very real sense, part of SPAM's lowbrow reputation among many Americans is the belief that it is an unconvincing facsimile of a more "genuine" food.

SPAM IN THE PHILIPPINES

SPAM's mixed reputation in the mainland United States and Europe, while pervasive, does not really extend to other parts of the world. As a global product, SPAM is subject to new and varied meanings when consumed in different cultural contexts. Nowhere has SPAM's public meaning been more radically reconfigured

from conventional Western views than the Asia-Pacific. Culinary followings centering on the tinned meat have emerged in diverse settings such as South Korea, Japan, Guam, and the Philippines (Stern and Stern 1991). Consumers in these countries are so taken with SPAM, in fact, that Western criticisms of the product are rendered all but irrelevant. As it so happens, SPAM's considerable fan base in the Asia-Pacific reveals both the nuanced character of local tastes and the complex range of historical, political, and socioeconomic processes that links the region to the United States.

In the Philippines there is an intense affection for SPAM as both a commodity and cultural symbol. SPAM enjoys a widespread popularity across the archipelago even in the predominately Muslim area of Mindanao to the south. There consumers opt for Turkey SPAM instead of the original pork flavor. SPAM's appeal transcends social class so that wealthy, middle-class, and working-class Filipinos all regularly consume it. That SPAM is viewed more as a dietary staple of the affluent and moderately affluent than that of the poor says a lot about its negotiated meaning outside of the West. SPAM's versatility is something Filipinos capitalize upon to create an array of dishes that complement their staple food of steamed rice. SPAM provides a rich source of protein that can be served practically anytime. Even the traditional afternoon snack of *merienda* is an appropriate time for the canned meat. Whether dipped in condiments like vinegar or banana ketchup or stuffed between two slices of bread and slathered with mayonnaise, SPAM is usually enough to tide over appetites until supper. In most cases, SPAM is pan fried on a gas range, as stovetop cooking remains the primary mode of food preparation in the Philippines.

SPAM's popularity in the Philippines dates back at least three generations to the end of World War II when it was distributed as C-rations by American GIs. Since this time SPAM has developed a special cachet amongst Filipinos that it sets it apart from other canned meats. Unlike more widely available brands of sardines and corned beef, SPAM is considered as something of a delicacy. This choiceness is reflected in both its price and market exclusivity. In the Philippines, a 12-ounce can (340 grams) costs roughly P110 (US$2) which is considered slightly expensive, since a kilo of pork goes for about P150 ($2.70).[13] Given the choice, most low-income families will opt for fresh pork because it can feed more mouths. For this reason much of the SPAM consumed by ordinary Filipinos is not bought locally but instead comes from friends and relatives returning from abroad. The tinned meat is customarily brought as *pasalúbong* (homecoming gifts) by the millions of overseas contract workers and *balikbayans* who live and work outside of the Philippines.[14] Whether purchased abroad or at one of the hundreds of duty-free shops that cater to overseas Filipinos, SPAM is a product thoroughly steeped in global associations for local consumers.

SPAM's allure is further enhanced by the fact that it faces no real competition from other canned pork products. In terms of both selection and quality, SPAM effectively stands alone in the Philippines. Its closest competition comes from various brands of tinned Vienna sausages which many Filipinos find cheap and unsavory. Presently, there are nine SPAM varieties available locally: (1) SPAM Classic, (2) Turkey SPAM, (3) SPAM Lite, (4) Low-sodium SPAM, (5) SPAM with Cheese, (6) Barbecue Flavored SPAM, (7) SPAM Oven Roasted Turkey, (8) Burger SPAM, and (9) Hot and Spicy SPAM. All are manufactured and distributed in the Philippines through a joint partnership between. Hormel Foods International and the locally owned San Miguel Pure Foods.[15] To adhere to laws barring majority foreign ownership, the US-based Hormel partnered up with San Miguel in a 60/40 shared venture known as the Purefoods Hormel Corporation (PHC). The company's primary processing plant is in Marikina, an eastern municipality of Metro-Manila. PHC reports sales of some 1.25 million kilos of SPAM in the Philippines each year (Chee Kee 2005).

In many ways SPAM is a product ideally suited to contemporary Filipino lifeways. Its pork taste and fatty texture are in keeping with local cooking styles where *lechon* (roasted pork) is highly valued and meat dishes invariably retain their animal fat. Its long shelf life gives it a storability that accords well with households lacking electricity or refrigerators.[16] Its simple preparation makes it convenient for working families in search of a quick and wholesome meal. Its investment with local meaning creates an emotional attachment that evokes positive associations with family and home. This is particularly significant for the millions of Filipinos living and working abroad. With few exceptions, overseas Filipinos will always have a comfort food in which to take solace, given SPAM's worldwide availability. When considered all together, it is not surprising that SPAM maintains such a significant and lasting appeal in the Philippines.

SPAM AS A SYMBOL OF AMERICA

SPAM's popularity in the Philippines reveals a great deal about Filipinos and their general penchant for all things American. To a significant degree, SPAM is steeped in the "Americanism" that continues to fascinate most Filipinos. It is not an exaggeration to suggest that Filipinos are seriously preoccupied with America. Indeed, the ultimate aspiration of many is to immigrate to the United States and become naturalized citizens. This is commonly considered the surest route to material success and well-being (Espiritu 2003).[17] As both former American colonial subjects and fluent

English speakers, Filipinos are very much attuned to happenings in the United States. Among other things, this awareness contributes to the widespread belief that American products, trends, and lifeways are superior to their local counterparts (Strobel 2001).

Against this backdrop, it is easy to see how SPAM assumes symbolic meaning as a representation of America. The product was introduced locally through the US military during World War II. Its historical relevance underscores both the shared struggle against the Japanese and the almost ninety-year presence of the US Armed Forces on Philippine soil. Similarly, SPAM reflects the US military's assistance during times of national crisis. SPAM C-rations were a staple item of relief packages distributed by the US military during the postwar years. Food aid was provided in the aftermath of floods, typhoons, earthquakes, and other natural disasters that regularly impacted the Philippines.

No less significant is the fact that SPAM's efficient packaging and convenient format represents the quality that Filipinos have come to expect from US brands. Local consumers take it for granted that they are getting a high value product when they "buy American" (ibid.). Much of the SPAM brought over by overseas Filipinos comes directly from the United States. This not only enhances SPAM's status as a luxury item, it also reinforces the idea that America is a land of abundance. Families have come to expect *pasalúbong* from relatives and friends visiting from the United States. Besides chocolate and whiskey, no other consumable is as popular as SPAM. For the millions of Filipinos who will never make it to the United States, SPAM provides a small taste of the "America" that looms large over Philippine life.

Speaking as an American, it is interesting to see firsthand just how SPAM reflects Filipino perceptions about the United States. Oftentimes when invited to local households for dinner, I am served fried SPAM as a side dish of more traditional fare. Serving SPAM to an American is clearly a point of pride for my hosts. Not only is it offered to make me feel like an honored guest (i.e. SPAM as a luxury item) but also to ensure that I have something familiar to eat. The underlying assumption is, of course, that all Americans enjoy SPAM since it is a US product.

If I mention how SPAM is commonly viewed in the United States, the standard response is one of surprise and curiosity. My Filipino friends find it puzzling that SPAM could have humorous qualities, much less a lowbrow reputation. For them, it is very much a wholesome food along the lines of how most middle-class Americans regard steak: something eaten periodically, usually on special occasions. Questions of authenticity or tastefulness do not really resonate with them either. SPAM's reputation in the Philippines is that of a "genuine" food consumed by those with some level of affluence. So far, I have been unsuccessful in conveying the nuanced US view of SPAM to these friends. Without the same cultural reference points, our distinct interpretations of SPAM will likely persist. Suffice it to say, the common Filipino view that SPAM embodies all that is desirable about the United States remains strong.

SPAMJAM CAFÉ

SPAM's brand recognition in the Philippines increased dramatically following the opening of the world's first ever SPAMJAM Café in February 2004. This unique concept restaurant merges two distinctly American culinary icons—SPAM and fast-food[18]—in a decidedly "glocal" way. SPAMJAM offers Filipinos a diverse selection of menu options based around the popular luncheon meat. All food items are comprised of low-sodium SPAM with the exception of French fries, hot dogs, and desserts. Top sellers include the SPAM Burger, SPAM Hero, SPAMJAM Club, SPAM Spaghetti, SPAM Baked Macaroni, SPAM Nuggets, and SPAM Caesar Salad.

SPAM lends itself quite well to the fast-food format in the Philippines. Its versatility makes it the ideal foodstuff for an array of innovative menu items. Its simple preparation jibes well with the rapid pace of quick-serve eateries where consumers expect a speedy turn-around on their orders. It is easily marketed to fast-food consumers who are already aware of the product as a household brand name. Considering that SPAM holds such a special place for Filipinos, it is surprising that the luncheon meat has not played a more significant role in the country's fast-food scene until only recently.

By 2005, two SPAMJAM branches were operating in and around Makati City, the country's main center of finance and cosmopolitan culture. Both are located in exclusive shopping centers and feature sleek modern designs that cater to affluent urban professionals and brand-conscious college/high-school types. Both include large statues of the SPAMJAM Café mascot—a smiling cartoon SPAM can—to greet arriving customers. Tourists, mall walkers, and curious passers-by often pose for pictures around these shoulder-high fiberglass figures.

SPAMJAM Café Background and Operations

SPAMJAM Café is the brainchild of Philip Abadilla, a forty-something entrepreneur from Metro-Manila who previously dealt in retail footwear and shoe exporting. While fast-food chains centering on already established products are nothing new—A&W Restaurants based around the famous root beer have been in the Philippines since the 1990s—few have developed this concept as successfully and single mindedly as Abadilla has with SPAMJAM. A seasoned businessman with

connections in Manila's shopping mall trade, SPAMJAM represents his first foray into fast-food.

In many ways, Abadilla's concept came along at the right time as chain restaurants began to pervade the commercial landscape of the Philippines. The 1990s witnessed accelerated growth in the country's fast-food industry as international brands like McDonald's, Wendy's, Burger King, Kentucky Fried Chicken (KFC), Pizza Hut, and their Philippine counterparts Jollibee (hamburgers, French fries, fried chicken), Chow King (Chinese fast-food), Goldilocks (bakery), and Greenwich Pizza proliferated in Metro-Manila and beyond. By 2000, there were approximately 2,000 chain fast-food eateries operating nationwide with some 60 million regular patrons. Significantly these consumers spent considerable amounts on fast-food even when they have little discretionary income (Business Asia 2000).

If any one firm dominates the Philippines' fast-food scene, it is Jollibee. The company's phenomenal rise approaches the stuff of national legend. The fast-food giant was founded by Chinese-Filipino entrepreneur Tony Tan Caktiong in the mid-1970s. Over the course of three decades, Jollibee established hundreds of outlets across the Philippines. By the 1990s, thanks to an aggressive marketing plan and, more importantly an intimate understanding of the Filipino palate, Jollibee emerged as the top fast-food brand in the Philippines. More remarkably, it also became one of Southeast Asia's most successful corporations. Jollibee maintains a commanding 55 percent share of the Philippines' fast-food market. For 2002, the company posted upwards of P27 billion in corporate earnings, exceeding the previous year's high of some P24 billion. Notably, the Philippines is one of the few countries where McDonald's does not control the largest share of the fast-food market (Economist 2002). In many ways, Jollibee provides an important model for local entrepreneurs like Abadilla looking to tap into the Philippines' burgeoning fast-food scene. Start-up enterprises like the SPAMJAM Café have a viable reference in terms of effective operational techniques and gearing menu items towards Filipino tastes.

A confessed SPAM lover since childhood, Abadilla came up with the idea for an all-SPAM restaurant while scuba diving in 2002. A casual conversation with a dive buddy who also worked for Hormel was all it took to spark his entrepreneurial imagination. A SPAM-based eatery targeting well-to-do Filipinos seemed viable given the country's huge appetite for SPAM and fast-food. Convinced of its profitability Abadilla pitched the concept to Purefoods Hormel Corporation (PHC) who, as it so happened, were contemplating a SPAM restaurant of their own (Food Pacific 2005).

After some deliberation, PHC opted to shelve their plans and allow Abadilla to spearhead the café's development. His spirited entrepreneurship and shopping-mall pedigree convinced the company that he was ideally suited for the project. As part of the deal, the SPAM and SPAMJAM trademarks were licensed to Abadilla's newly formed Store Café Enterprises for exclusive use in the Philippines. Letting someone else take on SPAMJAM not only mitigated PHC's financial risk, it also provided a test case should Hormel ever launch their own version of SPAMJAM elsewhere. To what extent Abadilla would be involved or compensated in the future start-up of overseas SPAM eateries remains unclear.

The basic arrangement between Store Café and PHC leaves Abadilla in charge of restaurant operations, promotion, and development, while PHC serves mainly as a product supplier with some oversight responsibilities. To ensure freshness, PHC furnishes SPAMJAM with an uncanned and preservative-free version of its luncheon meat. The company not only has final say over product presentation and recipes, it also employs a special menu development team that works closely with Abadilla to come up with new products. All selections are crafted to meet PHC's rigorous quality standards and conform to the general Filipino preference for sweet-tasting foods.

With an agreement intact, Abadilla quickly began working out the logistics of SPAMJAM. Focus groups, taste tests, and market surveys all provided valuable input during this planning phase. Initially, he considered selling only a few takeout items from kiosks resembling hotdog stands. This idea was scratched in favor of more sophisticated outlets offering an expanded menu within the fast-casual, dine-in atmosphere of upscale shopping malls. Abadilla planned three different sized SPAMJAM Cafés—a showcase restaurant, a medium-scale outlet, and a food court kiosk—all featuring a red, yellow, and blue color scheme mirroring the classic SPAM look. After securing a 70 sq. m. space in Glorietta Four, a sprawling shopping mall in Makati's posh Ayala Center, the inaugural SPAMJAM Café was quickly outfitted with a galley kitchen, flashy signage, and seating for forty customers. The mid-sized outlet was established on the mall's second floor away from the crowded food court but adjacent to other national and international eateries like Pancake House and Starbuck's. Remarkably, it took only a year and a half for Abadilla's original concept to become a reality (Fucanan 2004).

The SPAMJAM Café featured only five dishes at the time of its soft opening in December 2003. This number increased incrementally over subsequent weeks so that by the restaurant's official start two months later some fifteen items were available. These core products currently comprise SPAMJAM's stationary menu. Each quarter seasonal favorites like SPAM Maki (sushi) and SPAM Chowder are added to this signature bill of fare. Bringing in special selections provides both opportunities for repeat business and the testing of new products. Although the SPAMJAM Café is by Western standards inexpensive, it is slightly more costly than the Philippines' most popular fast-food chains of Jollibee and McDonald's. SPAMJAM is able to compete with these brands by offering Lunch Box combination meals that include a main dish, side item, and soft drink for a discounted price. By March 2004, the entire SPAMJAM Café operation was capitalized at P7.5 million ($136,000) with the majority of funds utilized for developing and implementing the first SPAMJAM outlet (ibid.).

SPAMJAM's grand opening at the Glorietta Four Mall made a big media splash in the Philippines. Ribbon-cutting ceremonies were attended by Abadilla and Hormel representatives. National television personalities were also on hand to help in the festivities. A few of these celebrities worked behind the counter taking orders, while others signed autographs or posed for pictures. Segments about the opening were aired on evening newscasts across the Philippines over the next few days. National newspapers printed features on the restaurant. For the most part, these straightforward accounts profiled Abadilla and his efforts to get SPAMJAM up and running.

International news agencies quickly picked up the story and ran brief pieces on SPAMJAM. The restaurant garnered mention on news programs from the BBC, Fox News, CBS, and CNN. In contrast to the way SPAMJAM was portrayed in the Philippines, the general tone of this overseas coverage was decidedly tongue in cheek. That the Western press focused mainly on the novelty value of an all-SPAM eatery is not surprising given SPAM's mixed reputation in the United States and Europe. If anything, the different story angles employed by overseas journalists and their local

counterparts speak volumes about the ways in which SPAM is variously regarded in different cultural contexts.

The original SPAMJAM Café proved very successful in its first few months of operation. The eatery averaged at least 300 consumers per weekday, with a higher customer turnout on the weekends. Many diners returned to SPAMJAM as repeat business (Food Pacific 2005). So thriving was SPAMJAM, that less than a year later a second branch was opened in the Robinsons' Galleria, a four-story shopping mall in the neighboring district of Ortigas. This outlet was established as a large showcase restaurant with more seating and kitchen space than its mid-sized counterpart. Besides sharing an identical menu and glossy décor as the smaller venture, the newer SPAMJAM also attracts pretty much the same clientele. During the week brand-savvy professionals generally frequent the café, while families with school-age children are the main weekend customers.

The showcase SPAMJAM is distinctive in that it also doubles as a concession counter for the adjacent mall Cineplex. SPAMJAM takes advantage of this ready-made customer pool of movie patrons by offering alternatives to the typical fare of popcorn and candy. Filmgoers have the option of several SPAM-based snack meals conveniently served on paper trays. Additionally, the larger outlet features a glass display case of SPAMJAM merchandise for consumers, such as T-shirts, caps, and flip-flops.

The few times I dined at the showcase SPAMJAM Café in August 2005, I was struck by how I did not feel like I was in the Philippines. Ensconced in the upscale Robinsons' Galleria, the restaurant is insulated from the harsh realities of urban life in Metro-Manila. This detachment created for me a skewed sense of place. My surroundings felt more akin to that of a US shopping mall than what I had come to associate with traditional consumer life in the Philippines. The showcase restaurant has all the trappings of a US fast-food outlet—trendy design, durable furnishings, uniformed employees, clean surroundings, disposable dinnerware, and an easy to understand menu board. This SPAMJAM could easily pass as a quick-service eatery in the United States if not for its Filipino personnel and distinctive menu.

Incidentally, I found the food to be quite good and the atmosphere and staff more than welcoming. It was clear that store employees had undergone training for efficient and friendly service. Their smiles and red cap/apron combos personified fast-food professionalism. Most of the dishes I tried did not have the bland-to-salty taste for which SPAM is known. Rather, they conveyed a more unassuming and blended quality. The luncheon meat was flavorful without overpowering the other ingredients of a dish. So the "SPAM Spaghetti" tasted more like fast-food spaghetti than simply spaghetti with SPAM. To be sure, there was nothing in the dishes that really hinted at traditional Philippine cuisine. The emphasis on rice and gristly meats was all but absent at SPAMJAM. As such, there was little to convince Filipino diners that they are eating anything other than American fast-food.

The symbolic relationship for Filipinos between SPAM and the United States clearly finds expression in the SPAMJAM Café. This association was something Abadilla intentionally cultivated when designing the restaurant. As he recently pointed out, "the layout was designed to make diners experience the American treat in an American like setting" (Burgos 2004). In nearly all ways, the café resembles the classic US fast-casual mall eatery with notable exception of its bill of fare. It is hard to imagine an all-SPAM restaurant chain operating in the United States, much less having a broad appeal. Given SPAM's lowbrow status and limited popularity among Americans, it is notable that the luncheon meat is viewed as a US delicacy

by Abadilla and his fast-food clientele. The common Western belief that SPAM is a poor person's food holds little resonance within the context of SPAMJAM. Not only is the chain located in and around Makati, one of the Philippines' most exclusive areas, but its prices are effectively out of reach of most ordinary Filipinos as well. In a very real sense, SPAMJAM takes a distinctly global product and redefines it into something largely divorced from its US roots.

SPAMJAM Café: Implications and Future

The successful launch of SPAMJAM in 2004 led to several important developments for PHC and Store Café Enterprises. Most notably, it spurred SPAM consumption in the Philippines. SPAM sales grew remarkably in the wake of the restaurant's first few months of operation. Thanks in part to the intense media coverage, SPAMJAM reinvigorated Filipino appetites for the processed meat. In fact, PHC noted record sales for its signature product. The months of February and March 2004 registered an incredible 274 percent increase in SPAM sales from the same period in 2003. Figures from April and May 2004 reveal a no less impressive 173 percent increase from the same two months a year before (Chee Kee 2005).

So extraordinary were SPAM sales, in fact, that PHC constructed another production facility in General Trias, Cavite, to complement their existing plant in Marikina. The newer $40 million factory became operational in May 2004. It produces some 500,000 metric tons of PHC chilled products for the Philippines and the South East Asia region. Notably, it also serves as the main supplier of the luncheon meat to SPAMJAM Café (Philippine Business Report 2004).

The success of SPAMJAM generated considerable buzz about Store Café Enterprises for outside investors. Following the grand opening, Abadilla was approached by several parties interested in establishing SPAMJAM franchises in other parts of the Philippines and South East Asia. SPAMJAM's preliminary success coupled with the luncheon meat's regional appeal seemed a lucrative combination for potential backers. With franchising a vital aspect of fast-food operations in the Philippines, the start-up of new SPAMJAM. Cafés elsewhere certainly would be more feasible if only under different circumstances. Store Café was not yet equipped to enter into franchise partnerships at this stage of SPAMJAM's development. The firm had yet to streamline its business model to take advantage of franchise demands. Centralizing its base of operations and establishing a commissary were steps Abadilla deemed essential before moving into franchising (Food Pacific 2005).

By 2005, the main issue confronting Store Café Enterprises was locating premium retail space in Manila's other mega-malls. Finding sites large enough to accommodate SPAMJAM customers at peak business hours was proving problematic. It was necessary to secure spaces anywhere from 150 to 200 sq. m. in order to seat the 100 or so diners who frequented the café during these busy times. The firm had its sights set on two additional showcase branches in Metro-Manila by the year's end. Negotiations for these possible outlets seemed to be moving along favorably by mid-2005. After issues of retail space have been resolved, the development of a franchise system will begin. Once again, the extent of Abadilla's involvement in SPAMJAM franchising outside of the Philippines is a matter that remains undetermined (ibid.).

SPAM AND GLOCALIZATION

Glocalization creates a compelling framework for those in the social sciences interested in addressing the complexities brought on by increased global/local interfaces. The blurring of global and local distinctions causes established meanings and authenticities to be no longer broadly defined but rather expressed through myriad interpretations. Obviously, foodways prove particularly susceptible to this process of cultural borrowing.

SPAM consumption in the Philippines, as this work makes clear, illustrates how global foods can be reimagined and reinvigorated by local populations in new and surprising ways. SPAM is a US product thoroughly steeped in global associations. Its universal availability and iconic status gives it a basic character that is subject to local interpretations. Indeed, few manufactured foods have been as indigenized the world over as SPAM. For Filipinos, the canned meat holds varied meanings. These views oppose conventional American perceptions of SPAM in key ways. In the United States, the convenience food is considered a lowbrow staple of children and the poor with distinctly comic overtones. In the Philippines, SPAM is something of a delicacy consumed by those with at least a moderate level of affluence. Of particular significance is the prevailing Filipino view that SPAM personifies America in all of its perceived grandeur. By virtue of its associations with the US military, its efficient packaging, and use as *pasalúbong* (homecoming gifts). SPAM reflects an idealized version of America that many everyday Filipinos hold to be true. This view was something Abadilla capitalized upon when developing the SPAMJAM Café. Restaurant patrons can dine on an "all-American" food in a genuine "American" setting. So, while SPAM is rooted in United States, its meaning within the context of SPAMJAM has been indigenized to create a much more distinctive interpretation.

The intermeshing of global and local features to create new forms or processes that suit the needs of specific localities finds clear expression in the SPAMJAM

Café. Without question, the restaurant owes as much to US influences as it does to those Filipino. The melding together of these different elements brings about a result that does not fit neatly into one particular cultural domain. What emerges is neither a homogenized manifestation of global culture nor a radical subversion of transnational processes but rather a simultaneous blending of Filipino and US practices, styles, preferences, and attitudes. Arguably, most Filipinos would consider SPAMJAM to be preponderantly American, while most Americans would define the restaurant, especially its bill of fare, in terms almost exclusively Filipino.

Beyond the product itself, SPAMJAM also adheres to a quick-service format that originated in the United States some fifty years ago. The fast-food model, with its emphasis on regimentation, standardization, predictability and cleanliness, transfers easily to diverse cultural contexts despite differences in local tastes and cuisine (Watson 1997). US fast-food eateries have become commonplace in the Philippines over the last twenty-five years. Their success rests largely on an ability to adapt to local palates and preferences. For example, McDonald's in the Philippines famously serves "McSpaghetti"—a dish geared towards the Filipino penchant for sweet pasta sauce (Ritzer 2000: 173). By the time Abadilla came up with the idea for SPAMJAM, national chains such as Jollibee and Chow King were using the US fast-food set-up to compete against international brands like McDonald's and KFC. SPAMJAM stands apart from other indigenous fast-food companies in that it was the first Filipino chain to apply the US production model to a well-known US product for a customer base comprised almost exclusively of Filipinos.

CONCLUSION

In short, the SPAMJAM Café illustrates the dynamics of glocalization, since it weds the global with the local to produce something new. On the global side is a US/global product, SPAM, served within the context of a US/global production model, the fast-food format. On the local side is Abadilla's original concept, an ail-SPAM restaurant, which capitalizes on established cultural preferences (Filipinos' deep fondness for SPAM and continuing fascination with the United States) and aims to serve a particular segment of the country's consumer market (affluent urban Filipinos). What emerges from this confluence of elements is an enterprise that is partly American and partly Filipino but, more significantly, something entirely "glocal."

ACKNOWLEDGMENTS

The author wishes to thank Elaine Cruz, josie Gonzalez, Mario Granada, Martha Heine, Leslie Lieberman, Brigette Maramba, and Elayne Zorn for their valued contributions to this work. Moreover, gratitude is extended to the University of Central Florida (UCF)'s Department of Anthropology and the UCF Southern Region for their support during this research endeavor.

NOTES

1. The Hormel Food Corporation promotes the formal spelling of "SPAM" (all capital letters) to refer to their trademarked canned luncheon meat. This usage has been formalized by the company to draw a distinction from the more recent usage of the term "spam" in reference to unwanted email.

2. As its name suggests, "glocalization" is a fusion of the terms "globalization" and "localization" (Tulloch 1991). These root words hold varied meanings within and across academic disciplines. Although details of the two processes are still debated by scholars (Lewellen 2002: 7–27), there is general consensus about their core aspects. By and large, globalization refers to the rapid integration of transnational linkages arising from increased trade, technological advances, and cultural flows. This process is usually characterized as unidirectional and

hegemonic with few positive outcomes for global cultural diversity. Localization, by contrast, is commonly associated with grass-roots responses to globalization's homogenizing tendencies.

3. Salt is used for binding, flavor, and firmness, while water facilitates the mixing during production. Sugar is included for flavor and sodium nitrate is added for color and as a preservative.

4. SPAM was originally launched as "Hormel Spiced Ham." There is some discrepancy about exactly how the "SPAM" name emerged. One story suggests Hormel held a contest for consumers to come up with a new product name and the winning suggestion received $100. Another is that a brother of the Hormel vice-president recommended the name which is a play on "shoulder of pork and ham" (Patten 2001: 11).

5. SPAM is manufactured in only one other US location—Fremont, NE.

6. SPAM is extremely popular in both Hawaii and Alaska (Wyman 1999: 41–47). In fact, some Hawaiian fast-food chains serve dishes made from SPAM. As such, any negative US associations about SPAM are primarily harbored by mainlanders rather than Hawaiians or Alaskans.

7. Guam is the world's largest market for SPAM, Each year, the average Guamaoian consumes eight cans of the product (Patten 2001:8).

8. SPAM's status in South Korea approaches an almost exalted state. Besides the traditional 12 ounce tin, SPAM also comes in fashionable gift boxes that hold up to nine individual cans. The traditional Korean fare of *kimchi* (pickled cabbage) is often combined with vinegared rice and seaweed to produce a SPAM sushi roll known as *kimpap*. There is even a cheaper SPAM knock-off with a name that borders on trademark infringement—Lo-Spam (Stern and Stern 1991).

9. In most cases, this fondness for SPAM was rooted in a pre-war appetite for pork and canned goods.

10. Many countries have laws restricting foreign participation in manufacturing and retailing. Hormel Food's ability to sell and distribute SPAM overseas is made possible through negotiated joint agreements with local partners.

11. This section really only scratches the surface of SPAM popular culture references. For a more comprehensive overview see Chapter Seven of Carolyn Wyrnan's "SPAM: A Biography. The Amazing True Story of America's 'Miracle Meat'!" (1999: 86–104).

12. Curiously, SPAM is not all that different from pâté in terms of ingredients, taste, and consistency. Varieties of the spreadable meat paste are considered something of a continental delicacy by Westerners while SPAM is almost certainly not.

13. Prices were collected from three different supermarket chains in Dagupan City, Pangasinan during the summer of 2005.

14. Roughly ten per cent of the Philippines' 85 million citizens live and work abroad. *Balikbayans* refers to Filipinos who live overseas on a more or less permanent basis and return periodically to their communities of origin in the Philippines.

15. San Miguel Pure Foods is a subsidiary of the San Miguel Corporation: the Philippines' top brewery and one of the country's most profitable companies.

16. Filipino pantries are stocked with numerous instant and ready-made foods that preserve well at room temperature or above. Perishable items like meat or vegetables are typically bought on a daily basis to compensate for a lack of refrigeration.

17. So pervasive is this dream, in fact, that Filipinos often take drastic steps to achieve it. In 2005, Philippine newspapers reported that the number of physicians practicing medicine nationwide was rapidly dwindling. Many doctors were returning to school to get their nursing certifications so that they could find more lucrative employment in the United States as healthcare assistants.

18. McDonald's in the Philippines also offers fried SPAM as a side item for their breakfast meals.

REFERENCES

Burgos, R.C. 2004. A Pinoy Favorite gets Exclusive Treatment. *Philippine Daily Inquirer*, March 3: D1.

Business Asia, 2000. Cashed-up Filipinos Feast on Fast Food. *Business Asia*, February 11: 8.

Chee Kee, R.J. 2005. SPAMJAM Opens 2nd Branch. *Businessworld*.

Economist. 2002. A Busy Bee in the Hamburger Hive. If McDonald's is the Goliath of Fast Food, Tony Tan's Jollibee is its Filipino David. *Economist*, February 28.

Espiritu, Y.L. 2003. *Home Bound: Filipino American Lives across Cultures, Communities, and Countries*. Berkeley, CA: University of California Press.

Food Pacific. 2005. Meatloaf Mania in Manila. Retrieved September 5, 2005 from Food Pacific Web site: http://www.foodpacific.com.

Fucanan, T.B. 2004. The Spam Story. *Manila Times*, November 13: B1.

Khrushchev, N.S. 1970. *Khrushchev Remembers*. Boston: Little Brown.

Lewellen, T. C. 2002. *The Anthropology of Globalization. Cultural Anthropology Enters the 21st Century*. Westport, CT: Bergin and Garvey.

Patten, M. 2001. *SPAM: The Cookbook*. London: Hamlyn.

Philippine Business Report. 2004. Purefoods Builds New Facility. *Philippine Business Report* 15(4): 8. Department of Trade and Industry. Quezon City, Philippines.

Ritzer, G. 2000. *The McDonaldization of Society*. Thousand Oaks, CA: Pine Forge Press.

Robertson, R. 1995. Glocalization: Time-Space and Homogeneity-Heterogeneity. In M. Featherstone *et al.* (eds), *Global Modernities*. London: Sage Publications, pp. 25–44.

Schroeder, F.E.H. 2001. SPAM. In R.B. Browne and P. Browne (eds). *The Guide to United States Popular Culture*. Bowling Green, OH: Bowling Green State University Popular Press, p. 762.

Stern, J. and Stern, M. 1991. *Encyclopedia of Bad Taste*. New York: Harper Collins.

Strobel, L.M. 2001. *Coming Full Circle: The Process of Decolonization Among Post-1965 Filipino Americans*. Quezon City, Philippines: Giraffe Books.

Tulloch, S. (ed.) 1991. *The Oxford Dictionary to New Words*. New York: Oxford University Press.

Watson, J, (ed.) 1997. *Golden Arches East: McDonald's in East Asia*. Stanford: Stanford University Press.

Wyman C. 1999. SPAM: A *Biography. The Amazing True Story of America's "Miracle Meat"!* New York: Harvest Brace and Company.

Yamashita, S. 2003. Introduction: "Glocalizing" Southeast Asia. In S. Yamashita and J.S. Eades (eds), *Globalization in Southeast Asia. Local, National, and Transnational Perspectives*. New York: Berghahm Books, pp. 1–20.

28

The Envios of San Pablo Huixtepec, Oaxaca: Food, Home, and Transnationalism

James I. Grieshop

On the northern perimeter of the San Pablo Huixtepec municipal plaza stands an impressive fifteen meters tall, square, red brick clock tower. Although the clock itself is less than reliable in telling the hour, the plaque affixed to the face of the tower tells several stories. The words on the plaque (translated) say: "This clock was donated by citizens of this community located in the cities of San Jose, Milpitas, Morgan Hill, Santa Cruz, Devenport (sic), Half Moon Bay, La Selva Beach and Seaside, all in the state of California, U.S.A., in coordination with the Honorable City Council and the Committee for Moral Civic, and Material Improvement. San Pablo Huixtepec, Oaxaca, Sept, 1988." The plaque's words communicate significant messages about both the municipality's immigration history, and the long-standing value of giving back to the community. Engraved within these words are other messages about importance of maintaining connections with the home community even while working and living far away in the United States, as well as the history and civic importance of financial support by immigrants.

The message of the plaque creates the framework for the following case study focused on previously undocumented transnational migration links between the Oaxacan community of San Pablo Huixtepec and the Seaside-Monterey, California area. The study uncovers some new realities of transnational migration and transnational entrepreneurs. The unique system of envios (or small scale, international but family level, package services) that operates in the unexpected direction of South to North (in contrast to the North to South remittances) provides the basis for the following story.

In the past decade the topic of transnational migration has attracted significant academic attention among researchers. This attention has not been limited to Mexico but has been world-wide (Vertovec 1999; Kearney and Besserer 2004). Hundreds of studies, reports, and papers have been produced adding to the understanding and application of the concept of transnationalism and transnational migration. The transnational paradigm, in contrast to the assimilation model, advances the idea that immigrants do not break their home country ties although they often are re-defined. In spite of the extensive body of literature, this concept is not universally or unquestionably accepted.

In 1999 Portes, Guarnizo, and Landolt (1999:218) proposed that if transnational migration studies were to go beyond being a "highly fragmented, emergent field" and to develop a "well-defined theoretical framework," a set of conceptual guidelines had to be defined, created and tested. Conway (2000) raised similar concerns and questions, arguing for the need of clarification on what is meant by transnational migration. Although this study does not answer the questions raised by these and others, it does add to the understanding of the realities of transnational migration, the power of home, the power of cultural remittances, and dimensions of transnational economies.

Transnationalism, whether from Mexico to California or from Ecuador to Spain, involves a number of activities that play out between the immigrant and the place or origin. Portes, et al. (1999) originally proposed that transnationalism must include economic, political, and sociocultural activities, all of which can be expressed in different levels of institutionalization—from high to low. In addressing questions related to transnational economics and entrepreneurship, Portes, et al. (2002) further acknowledge the continuing debate, while others (cf. Itzigsohn and Saucedo 2002; Guarnizo 2003; Levitt 2003; Conway 2005) expand the discussion on the paradigm.

For example, Guarnizo (2003), using a perspective that stresses the idea of "transnational living" rather than simply transnational migration, argues that transnational living provides a more holistic (and thereby more realistic) and inclusive perspective that can capture the economic implications "generated by the migrants multifaceted transnational engagement" (Guarnizo 2003:669). Conway's (2005) discussion of transnational migration also resonates. He suggests that too often in the transnational migration literature and research the idea of transnational communities is viewed as a new phenomenon, whereas in reality such communities have been around for as long as migration has occurred. Conway questions the view that transnational migration too often separates migrant peoples from their home communities. He argues that "home" is not just a symbol, but a powerful force in the lives of the immigrants who carry with them "the memories of childhood" and the "lasting power of attachments to birthplaces" (Conway 2005:265). Home is an anchor for the transnational migrant composed of an influential set of forces acting in their lives—and in the lives of the family at home.

In reality migration undoubtedly has multiple effects on the individual. The individual migrant becomes separated from his family, home, and/or community and all mat the family, home, and community contain. Migration also impacts the individual's identities, often leading to the assignment of new and undesirable ones. Despite the arguments from the assimilation model (Portes and Rumbaut 1996), when the individual lives in the new setting, separate and with altered identities, the tendency may be to attempt to reduce these changes, to live in a familiar way and system and with familiar cultural objects. In effect the reality is to create a life that is nearly as like that left at home, while those at home may attempt to help reinforce that tie to home through whatever means they can use. For example, in recent years phone, computer, and audiovisual technologies have expanded the tools available for transnational immigrants (Richman 2005; Levitt 2003).

In cases of Mexican transnational migration research, attention has been directed to the nature of this migration and types of political, economic, and sociocultural actions and outcomes. Studies have detailed the connection between transnational migration and civic participation via home-town associations (Fox and Rivera-Salgado 2004) as well as political participation in both Mexican and United States settings (Kearney and Besserer 2004; Martinez-Saldaña 2004). Increasingly attention has been focused on the flows of people from Mexico to the United States (or from South to North) and the flow of money in the form of remittances from the United States to Mexico (from North to South) (Massey and Parrado 1994; Cohen 2001; 2005; Cohen and Rodriguez 2005). This latter flow, now estimated to exceed $16 billion per year, has also attracted the attention of the Mexican government (Banco de Mexico 2004; Thompson 2005).

Others have expanded the ideas related to transnational entrepreneurship and remittances. In the case of remittances from "north to south," Levitt (1998) documents examples of social remittances, or those that go beyond the emphasis on financial or economic, by providing evidence of the importance of the flow of ideas, behaviors, identities, and social capital within the Dominican transnational immigrant communities. Itzigsohn et al. (1999) documented the flow of food, music, and other goods moved by couriers from the other direction from the Dominican Republic to New York, providing evidence of what has been referred to as "return migrant enterprises" (Portes et al. 2002).

This study contributes to the focusing of the lens for viewing transnational migration, particularly as it relates to sociocultural activities and specific related economic/entrepreneur activities. In the case study presented here, transnational migration is not just the movement of people from South to North. Nor is it only limited to money moving from North to South. The movement is not solely financial capital but social and cultural capital in the form of food and other goods. Such movements also include the movement of ideas, the impacts on identities, and the maintenance of home in the new setting. These more inclusive views provide the framework for this study.

This case study focused on the village of San Pablo Huixtepec (SPH), Oaxaca, Mexico to examine specific socio-cultural activities inherent to the local forms of transnational migration. While the study focuses on San Pablo, no doubt similar cases can be found in other areas of Mexico. This case study also portrays the roles that technologies, specifically telephones and computer internet, play in the maintenance of family, community, and cultural identities in a transnational living situation.

Central to this study is the description of small, family level systems of *envios* (shipments) between Mexico and California. The system of envios services found in San Pablo Huixtepec are on the surface similar to the package shipping services exemplified by DHL or FedEx. For a fee paid in California, these envios

provide the delivery of goods from Oaxaca to receiving families in California and other states. Corporate style envios services are found in the city of Oaxaca, with branches in Puebla and some smaller municipalities in Oaxaca. However, more unique are the purely community based (or family or "mom and pop") businesses in SPH. These latter varieties of envios are also in contrast, both in size and direction, to the highly visible and more often studied system of money remittances from North to South.

The research for this study was carried out in Oaxaca from March through July 2004. During that time the author was involved in other work in SPH related to a collaborative educational project on cultural traditions and which provided entry into the local system of envios. Research used observation, interview, and questionnaire procedures to gather information and data on the envios. Seven of the 11 operators of envios were interviewed and home and store level observations carried out. In addition six of the seven telephone caseta businesses were interviewed, along with four of the existing five computer center businesses.

During late 2004 and in 2005, fieldwork on the envios was also conducted in San Jose and Seaside, California, where the largest number of San Pablo immigrants live and work. Observations and interviews of envios operators (some of whom were originally contacted and interviewed in San Pablo) took place in Seaside. Contact, in person, by phone and by computer, with two of the envios operators has been maintained to date. The latter has included providing advice on dealing with entry issues into the United States (see below for more details).

THE SETTING

SPH is an agricultural community situated in the District of Zimatlan, approximately 40 kilometers from the capital of

Oaxaca. Although nearby communities such as Santa Ines Yatzeche are indigenous Zapotec communities, SPH exhibits little evidence of its original Zapotec roots. In 2000 SPH had a population of 8,500 inhabitants (INEGI 2000), a figure that does not include the estimated 2,000 to 5,000 residents living in the United States. The majority of these immigrants are found in California and concentrated in and near Seaside, California. Migration from SPH has been a reality since the 1980s and continues at a high level today. Many nearby communities such as Santa Ines Yatzeche, San Bernardo Mixtepec, and Santa Maria Ayoquezco also send a large percentage of their population to California and other states.[1]

While estimates of the number of persons from SPH and the surrounding communities in the Monterey, California area range from 1,500 to 4,000, the real number of migrants is unknown. Also, the flow of undocumented immigrants continues. For those who are documented and even citizens of the United States, contact with families in SPH is spoken of as essential. Some residents of Seaside make yearly and even more frequent return visits to SPH. At the same time communication via phone and internet/e-mail has increased.

In the past few years the number of telephone *casetas* or public phone services in SPH has grown to seven, most with three to five lines each. These casetas provide a relatively inexpensive means for family members in Seaside to communicate with family in SPH. A person in Seaside will call the caseta closest to their family in SPH where a message is taken for the family member to be at the caseta at a specific hour in order to talk with their family member in Seaside. The Seaside (or other US) caller pays for the call and the local caseta charges a small fee (usually ten pesos per hour) for the use of the phone. Casetas' owners report anywhere from three to ten calls on a weekday from the United States, a number that increases on the weekend and during holidays and fiestas.

The increase in computer facilities has enhanced the communication from the United States to SPH. Currently five computer centers, some with satellite connections, permit regular e-mail and even chat services. In January 2004 a webpage and site for SPH was created (www.huixtepec.com) with the support of the local municipality. This webpage receives on a daily average between 100 and 125 "visitors," the vast majority from immigrants from SPH living in California. This web site also now includes a chat room that attracts hundreds of visitors from California and other settings.[2]

The history of migration from SPH to California can be traced back to the 1980s, a fact important for understanding the creation and operation of the envios systems. While many migrants began their work in the agricultural fields of the Salinas (California) Valley area, over time they began to obtain employment in the large hotel, restaurant and service industry of the Monterey area. Also in the late 1980s with the signing of the Immigration Reform and Control Act (IRCA), many then undocumented immigrants became documented. As the number of immigrants continued to grow, so did the demand for regular contact and connections with families and friends in SPH.

The appearance of organized envios in SPH is relatively recent. According to two of the envios operators, the first organized envios were started by chance in 2000. These individuals, like many other envios operators, had originally entered California illegaly in the 1980s but gained legal immigrant status with the passage of IRCA. Subsequently they could travel relatively easily between California and Oaxaca. While some family members stayed in California, others returned to live and work in Oaxaca. In one case the wife returned to live in SPH but periodically traveled to California to visit her husband. On such trips she would be asked by others in SPH to carry food items to their own relatives in Seaside. She was also offered a "tip" (propina in Spanish) for the service. According to this informant, the idea for a regular envios system was catalyzed by this coincidence. From that point it has grown to include local advertising, regular trips, and the delivery of multiple remittances in reverse via the envios, sometimes two or three times per week.

Of the 11 envios businesses operating in SPH in 2004 the largest counts on five individuals including family members in Seaside, California. The smallest consist of two persons—one in SPH and one in Seaside. Since the original interviews, several of the envios businesses have added couriers whose function is to move the items from SPH to the United States. The overwhelming percentage of goods sent to Seaside (and elsewhere in California and the United States) consists of food. The variety of food shipped includes chile peppers, *mole* (a chocolate based cooking sauce), *tlayudas* (a tortilla unique to Oaxaca), cheese, *mezcal*, grasshoppers (or *chapulines*, a Oaxacan and SPH delicacy), pumpkin seeds, meat, and other food items. For family-provided items, the majority of this food is produced in homes of the senders in SPH and nearby villages. Other items such as letters, videotapes, jewelry, and artisan goods are also sent. To send a package, the sender drops off the item at a local store or at the home of the envios owner. Food is wrapped in a plastic bag with the intended recipient's name and phone number in California and their own name taped to the bag. A log of items received and personal identification is kept. Dates for drop-off of items and departure are posted throughout SPH on flyers attached to light poles or on signs in front of stores. Prior to departure, the items are packed in either cardboard boxes or suitcases. Due to airline restrictions, each container cannot weigh over 70 pounds. On the day of departure, the

courier takes the containers/suitcases to the airport in Oaxaca. Most envios operations fly to San Jose, California where, once they pass through customs and immigration, they are driven to Seaside by the local contact. Upon arrival in Seaside, the containers are opened, the packages are set out and organized by last name, and telephone calls are made to the persons who are to receive them. When recipients come to the local house to pick up their items, they are required to pay for the delivery. "Delivery" charges for food are usually $3.50 per pound but vary for other items such as letters, jewelry, or artisan goods. The costs for delivery are all the responsibility of the recipients; senders from SPH do not pay for the charges. In addition to transporting food and other items to California, envios "couriers" return to SPH with items, mainly clothes, shoes, letters, and money (with a five percent charge). Costs for sending these items are also paid by the person sending the items.

Changes, both minor and major, have occurred in the system. The rapid and resourceful responses of the owners to these changes illustrate their resiliency and creativity. For example, the importation of meat and cheese was slowed and then halted due to U.S. Customs requirements. In fact the restrictions were unevenly applied in 2003 in that the Customs officers in the San Francisco airport stopped the importation resulting in a re-direction of the envios to the San Jose, California airport where, for a period, they could pass. In the latter part of 2004 family operations began to face more serious challenges in the San Jose entry port. Since 2003 the U.S. Food and Drug Administration (FDA) required anyone bringing in food from a foreign country to file a Prior Notice (cf. www.fda.gov). This requirement specified that the person physically transporting food items must identify, prior to arrival, what food is being imported, its source, its manufacturer, all arrival information, and the persons responsible, among other information. A Prior Notice must be submitted via the FDA website on the internet and in English, thus requiring computer access and knowledge, as well as English literacy. None of the SPH envios operations was prepared or equipped to file the required information. None had the computer/internet equipment to submit the Prior Notice or the computer skills or the English literacy to complete the forms. As a result, with the 2004 enforcement of the Prior Notice requirement, San Jose couriers were allowed to enter but the containers were not and were sent back to Mexico. Their return resulted in high cost and major losses to the businesses as well as a loss of confidence by the senders.

To overcome this obstacle envios owners had to rapidly (within a matter of weeks) and creatively find ways to complete and to submit via the internet the Prior Notice forms prior to leaving Mexico. For the first few weeks, the response was for the envios couriers to fly into Tijuana and also into Los Angeles where the Prior Notice requirement was less stringently enforced. However, significant added costs for transportation resulted, as well as added time. These added costs were too much for the system to continue in this fashion. The two person operations stopped operating. Responses on the part of other operators indicated their resourcefulness. In two cases the author himself was contacted by long distance phone calls to California from envios owners in SPH seeking advice and computer assistance to complete the required Prior Notice forms. Also, as a result of this requirement, one of the computer center operators in San Pablo Huixtepec responded by providing a fee based service to complete the required Prior Notice forms, thereby ensuring and expanding the movement of the goods. He now provides Prior Notice filing services for eight different envios operators.

FREQUENCY AND SIZE OF ENVIOS

Interviews conducted with the SPH envios operators provided other important information. In regards to the frequency of trips, during most of the year most owners indicated that one trip was made every three or four weeks. At holiday times such as Mother's Day, Semana Santa (Holy Week), and other holidays, trips were more frequent. For one enterprise, trips have been increased to twice, and sometimes three times, a week. Reasons for this increase were that more people send more items. But, more important was the fact that the food items being carried often are for commercial use in restaurants in the Seaside, Santa Cruz, and San Jose areas. In the California homes where packages were received it was not unusual to see dozen of bundles of tlayudas with over a 100 tlayudas in each, With more frequent trips, other changes have been made. Owner/operators of the envios now hire for a fee couriers to ferry the containers to San Jose, paying them around $300 per trip. In this situation, the couriers, be they family members or not, are ferrying up to eight containers each.

The increase in number of containers is the result of several factors. One is the increased demand for food items from the San Pableños living in California. As well, another source of demand beyond the family has occurred. In the case of tlayudas, a unique Oaxacan tortilla, a constant demand exists, such that now multiple packages of tlayudas are sent for sale to restaurants and stores in communities beyond Seaside. As the entrepreneurial aspect of the envios has expanded, so too has the reach of the operations. Couriers, upon arrival to Seaside, now make regular trips to towns in the Central Valley of California to deliver packages to immigrants from San Pablo and other communities. Packages are also delivered to small stores and restaurants in these smaller towns. Tlayudas, one of the popular items, normally sell for $1 or more per tlayuda.

THE ECONOMICS OF THE ENVIOS

In one sense the business of envios is just that—a transnational economic enterprise. It is a capital-based, entrepreneurial operation with expenses and income. To illustrate: a round trip plane fare from Oaxaca to San Jose usually costs from $650 to $700 per courier. In addition airline shipping charges must be paid for additional containers beyond the first two. Specifically, Mexicana Airlines charges $75 for each of the third and fourth containers, $100 each for the next five containers and $200 for any additional containers. Costs to the operators to transport eight containers total $1,200 and are as follows: $650 for the plane ticket and $550 for eight containers (first two 'free,' second two $150 and next four $400). This figure does not include other costs of local transportation, food, or lodging.

On the "income" side, fees charged are $3.50 per pound of food. Each container weighs 70 pounds for a total of 560 pounds: 560 lbs × $3.50 totals $2,000. Without considering other costs, a "profit" of $800 could result. Even with a courier fee of $300, a positive balance still results. Such "mom and pop" businesses are indeed the products of the transnational entrepreneurs. Other factors impact and increase the "bottom line." These include the fees charged for other items including jewelry, artisan goods, and letters. In addition, couriers returning to Oaxaca transport items such as shoes and clothing that generate additional fees and income, as well as carry money remittances which carry a five percent fee.

This system of small-scale, family-operated envios, as it has evolved, has become an economic enterprise. However, these operations are much more than businesses concerned with capital. The innovators who organized the first envios operations were explicit: the desire was to provide a means to connect those at "home" with the immigrant "away" in California (cf. Conway 2005). The service,

certainly from the points of view of both the recipient and the sender, provides connections, links, and nostalgic reminders to those who are at "home" and who are "away." The movement of the food, cultural items, letters, pictures and other objects appears to carry the power to re-attach the immigrant to his or her family and community. On the home side, items sent can serve as reminders of obligations to stay connected and to reciprocate (cf. Mauss 1955).

Comments from those receiving food and other items in the Seaside community, as well as those senders in SPH, provide insight into the sociocultural significance of the envios, especially food. Recipients would commonly talk about the "authenticity" of the food, both in regards to the taste and the fact that it came from their homes and was made by their mother. Similarly, recipients would talk about the feeling of obligation to call or communicate or send money, in other words how to reciprocate. In SPH, conversations with those sending food also revealed the themes of the "need" or "obligation" to send items and to provide support for the family member in Seaside. Such comments and actions suggest that family obligation was central to the sending of envios from SPH and in turn the sending of goods, letters and money from Seaside back home (cf. Conway and Cohen 2003).

The idea of "home" is central to the reality of the envios at the sociocultural level. "Home-places" (Conway 2005:266) provide the anchors for the experiences of the transnational migrant. The drive is to avoid homelessness and to maintain the ties to home. However, while the "home" may be the anchor, the food, be it tlayudas or grasshoppers, is the chain connected to the anchor.

The anchor and the chain are symbols of the networks, and the particular items that flow from SPH to Seaside serve to solidify and reinforce the networks. These networks are also reinforced and expanded by technologies such as telephones, computers, and internet messaging. In different cultural settings (i.e., Haiti and Virginia) and with a different technology (i.e., audio-cassettes), Richman (2005) documents in a similar fashion the use of tools of technology for maintaining family and community networks between immigrants and the home. Technology can create networks and connections, and can ensure the ties to the anchor.

The concept of cultural capital (as differentiated from economic capital and social capital) applies to this case. For example, Coleman (1988) and Putnam (2000) refer to social capital as that pertaining to connections, relationships, and roles that help shape the social interactions of a system. Social capital consists of non-material concepts such as trust, understanding, and shared values and practices that bind the members of a network and a community. Cultural capital, according to Bourdieu (1986), represents non-economic forces including family background and class. He differentiates three forms: the embodied state, the objectified state, and the institutionalized state of cultural capital. Of importance here is the objectified state represented by "cultural goods and material objects which is a type of cultural capital transmissible in its materiality" (Bourdieu 1986:246). Although he speaks principally of such material objects as writings, paintings, and musical instruments and their transferability, food may also be considered a form of cultural capital. And, it is in this sense that food sent via the envios system becomes a form of cultural capital.

The receipt of the food and other goods also has an instrumental effect (VanWey et al. 2005). From comments of recipients, foods received are valued as much for their sociocultural significance as their nutritional value. They often commented that the food, be it tlayudas, mole, grasshoppers, or mezcal, was important to them and their identity as a person from San Pablo. They mentioned the authenticity (i.e., "it tasted better") of the food as a highly valued quality. Food takes on a function far beyond the nutritional one, fulfilling cultural and psychological ones (cf. Brown and Mussell 1984; Counihan and Van Esterik 1997).

Observations and interviews of recipients in Seaside originally from SPH and nearby communities confirm the meaning of the food to them: food represents "home," the family, the household, and the local community of SPH. The food received is the real thing and is accepted as culturally authentic. It signifies a person's identity as being a resident of San Pablo Huixtepec. As one respondent said "The food we get here is not the same. The real food comes from home."

An intriguing but unanswered question about home and away, transnational immigrants, and the power of food lies within those who are members of the second and third generations of San Pableños living in the Seaside area. It is unclear and undetermined how youth view the importance of the food to their identities as San Pableños. Similarly, it is not known how or if they view the home as the anchor. Evidence, in this case, remains to be gathered as to how second generation individuals view these cultural remittances or even whether they are considered as such. This question is part of the much larger question Foner (2002) raises: is transnationalism only a first generation phenomenon?

The system of envios and their operation go beyond that of economic capital into the realms of social capital and cultural capital. As well, the food and other material goods that are physically transmitted from family members to family members illustrate the reality of cultural remittances. The direction of these remittances is one of the fascinating aspects of this system, be it economic or sociocultural. Their flow is from South to North, whereas with other capital or social remittances, the flow is the reverse— from North to South.

The existence, influence, and power of the envios system also speak to the reality of transnational migration. To migrate requires great flexibility, resourcefulness, and creativity. These are qualities also exhibited by the entrepreneurs who have organized, managed, and adjusted the system of envios. Their ability to be entre-preneurial, not just in economic activities but in sociocultural ones, in the face of constant change is an under-appreciated dimension of transnational migration. The reality of these transnational migrants is far more than migrating from Mexico to California and working, saving, and sending money back to family in SPH. They are living in a transnational context, one that is a dynamic field of social inter-actions and practices that connect the migrants with their communities of origin. But those connections are not one-way but two-way and affect not only the indi-viduals, but their families, local groups, and institutions.

EPILOGUE

In late 2005 the construction of a new, modern municipal building (or city hall) for San Pablo Huixtepec was completed. Built on the western side of the municipal plaza, at right angles to the 1980s clock tower, this structure was a product of community efforts. Thousands of San Pableños from both the local community and returning immigrants from California contributed their labor through commu-nity *tequios* (or communal work parties) to tear down the original municipal building, to lay the foundation for the new one and to build the three-story modern building. Each tequio involved men, women, youth, and children. Men carried buckets filled with cement to lay the foundation and to create the three-story structure. Women prepared and served drinks and food for all the workers. Youth provided music and entertainment and children offered their enthusiasm and support. Participating community members were not only from San Pablo,

but some came from San Jose and Seaside, California to help. Others sent money to support the effort. As the construction progressed, pictures were taken and posted on the internet for all San Pableños whether in San Pablo or in Seaside. At the conclusion of the Sunday tequios, everyone sat down to eat the food prepared by the women of San Pablo—mole, res (beef), tlayudas, cheese, grass-hoppers, mescal, and more. The food also confirmed for all there that they were members of the community of San Pablo Huixtepec.

NOTES

1. One case, uncovered in late summer 2005, was an envios operator from San Pablo Huixtepec who contracted with two couriers from San Pablo to carry 16 packages from San Bernardo Mixtepec to the immigrant community in Columbus, Ohio.
2. As of April 2006, the webpage www.huixtepec.com no longer is accessible. A new webpage www.huixtepec.org is now accessible. It includes a chat room and an extensive photo section.

REFERENCES

Banco de Mexico (2004) Remesas familiares 2003–2004 de Banco de Mexico. URL:<http://www.banxico.org.mx/CuadrosAnalitiicos/>.

Bourdieu, Pierre (1986) The Forms of Capital. *In* Handbook of Theory and Research for the Sociology of Education. John G. Richardson, ed. Pp. 241–258. New York: Greenwood Press.

Brown, Linda K. and K. Mussell, eds. (1984) Ethnic and Regional Foodways in the United States: The Performance of Group Identity. Knoxville: University of Tennessee Press.

Cohen, Jeffrey H. (2001) Transnational Migration in Rural Oaxaca, Mexico: Dependency, Development, and the Household. American Anthropologist 103(4):954–967.

——— (2005) The Oaxaca-US Connection and Remittances. URL:<http://www.migrationinfor-mation.org> (January 1, 2005).

Cohen, Jeffrey H. and L. Rodriguez (2005) Remittance Outcomes in Rural Oaxaca, Mexico: Challenges, Options and Opportunities for Migrant Households. Population, Space and Place 11:49–63.

Coleman, James (1988) Social Capital in the Creation of Human Capital. American Journal of Sociology 94:S95–S120.

Conway, Dennis (2000) Notions Unbounded: A Critical (Re)read of Transnationalism Suggests that U.S.-Caribbean Circuits Tell the Story Better. *In* Theoretical and Methodological Issues in Migration Research: Interdisciplinary, Intergenerational and International Perspectives. B. Agozino, ed. Pp. 3–226. Brookfield, Vt: Ashgate Publishers.

—— (2005) Transnationalism and Return: "Home" as an Enduring Fixture and "Anchor." *In* The Experience of Return Migration: Caribbean Perspectives. R. B. Potter, D. Conway, and J. Phillips, eds. Pp. 263–282. Burlington, Vt.: Ashgate Publishing.

Conway, Dennis and J.H. Cohen (2003) Local Dynamics in Multi-local Transnational Spaces of Rural Mexico: Oaxacan Experiences. International Journal of Population Geography 9:141–161.

Counihan, Carole and P. Van Esterik, eds. (1997) Food and Culture: A Reader. New York: Routledge.

Foner, Nancy (2002) Second-Generation Transnationalism, Then and Now. *In* The Changing Face of Home: The Transnational Lives of Second Generation. P. Levitt and M.C. Waters, eds. Pp. 242–254.

Fox, Jonathan and G. Rivera-Salgado, eds. (2004) Indigeneous Mexican Migrants in the United States. La Jolla, Calif.: Center for U.S. Mexican Studies (UCSD).

Guarnizo, Luis E. (2003) The Economics of Transnational Living. International Migration Review 3(3):666–699.

Instituto Nacional de Estadística Geografía e Informática (INEGI) (2000) XII Censo de Poblacion y Vivienda 2000. Oaxaca: Instituto Nacional de Estadística Geografía e Informática.

Itzigsohn, Jose, C. Dore, E. Hernandez, and O. Vazquez (1999) Mapping Dominican Transnationalism. Ethnic and Racial Studies 22:316–339.

Itzigsohn, Jose and S. G. Saucedo (2002) Immigrant Incorporation and Sociocultural Transnationalism. International Migration Review 36(3):766–798.

Kearney, M. and F. Besserer (2004) Oaxacan Municipal Governance in Transnational Context. *In* Indigenous Mexican Migrants in the United States. J. Fox and G. Rivera-Salgado, eds.

Pp, 449–466. La Jolla, Calif.: Center for US Mexican Studies (UCSD).

Levitt, Peggy (1998) Social Remittances: Migration Driven Local-Level Forms of Cultural Diffusion. International Migration Review 32(4):926–948.

—— (2003) Keeping Feet in Both Worlds: Transnational Practices and Immigrant Incorporation in the United States. *In* Toward Assimilation and Citizenship. C. Joppke and E. Morawsha, eds. New York: Palgrave MacMillan.

Martinez-Saldaña, Jesus (2004) Building the Future: The FIOB and Civic Participation of Mexican Immigrants in Fresno, California. *In* Indigenous Mexican Migrants in the United States. J. Fox and G. Rivera-Salgado, eds. Pp. 125–144. La Jolla, Calif: Center for US Mexican Studies (UCSD).

Massey, D. L. and F. Parrado (1994) Migradollars: The Remittances and Savings of Mexican Migrants to the USA. Population Research and Policy Review 13:3–30.

Mauss, Marcel (1967) The Gift: Forms and Functions of Exchange in Archaic Societies. New York: The Norton Library.

Portes, Alejandro, L. E. Guarnizo, and P. Landolt (1999) The Study of Transnationalism: Pitfalls and Promise of an Emergent Research Field. Ethnic and Racial Studies 22(2):218–237.

Portes, Alejandro, W. J. Haller, and L. E. Guarnizo (2002) Transnational Entrepreneurs: An Alternative Form of Immigrant Economic Adaptation. American Sociological Review 67:278–298.

Portes, Alejandro and R. G. Rumbaut (1996) Immigrant America. Berkeley: University of California Press.

Putnam, Robert (2000) Bowling Alone: The Collapse and Revival of American Community. New York: Simon and Schuster.

Richman, Karen (2005) Migration and Vodou. Gainesville: University Press of Florida.

Thompson, Ginger (2005) Mexico's Migrants Profit from Dollars Sent Home. The New York Times, February 23.

VanWey, L. K., C. M. Tucker, and E. Diaz McConnel (2005) Community Organization, Migration, and Remittances in Oaxaca. Latin American Research Review 40(1):83–107.

Vertovec, S. (1999) Conceiving and Researching Transnationalism. Ethnic and Racial Studies 22(2):447–462.

29

Consuming Interests: Water, Rum, and Coca-Cola from Ritual Propitiation to Corporate Expropriation in Highland Chiapas

June Nash

A growing demand for water that exceeds scarce resources is changing political and social alignments and provoking the emergence of water wars. The scarcity of water is a result of deforestation, the contamination of existing water sources, and the diversion of groundwater to commercial enterprises. These commercial enterprises include irrigation agriculture and, increasingly, consumer beverage production, especially of bottled water, now sold to people who face growing water scarcity. A natural resource once considered a blessing for all people granted by the rain gods is now a contested commodity exacerbating the growing divide between classes.

In this article, I examine ways in which a consuming interest in water that once promoted community integration in early civilizations in Mesoamerica has become a multibillion-dollar industry with sales throughout the world, based on a commodity that many local people cannot afford. The concern of preconquest civilizations to ensure the water supply was transformed by the Spanish conquerors, who drained and diverted the abundant waters in the Aztec capital and then introduced commercialized cane and maguey used in the production of rum and tequila. Adopted by indigenous pueblos as a libation in ceremonies offered to the saints and divine powers during colonial and independence times, the demand was finally diverted to the consumption of Coca-Cola and other soft drinks imported by local concessionaires responding to corporate inducements. Today the major extraction of groundwater in San Cristobal de Las Casas, Chiapas is done by the Coca-Cola Company. The company now bottles the water and sells it throughout the world and to the people from whom it was expropriated.[1]

The transformation of water from a deified resource to a commodified multibillion dollar industry reveals how a public interest can be distorted by unregulated privatized expropriation. It is a morality tale that applies equally to other resources such as gold, silver, oil, and tin. Unlike these other resources, however, water has a human rights dimension; without water, humans cannot live. I have concentrated on water as a consumption product in this article because it is intrinsic to the social relations linking indigenous pueblos to their environment.[2] I include in my critique of privatized exploitation of water resources the failure of national and local governments to reach consensus on policies to address the growing shortages.

WATER IN PRECONQUEST CITY STATES

The availability of drinking water was a significant factor in the location of populations throughout Mesoamerica from the earliest known settlements hundreds of years before the Christian era to the present. In prehispanic times, growing concentrations of populations that depended on a communally controlled water supply propitiated deities who were believed to ensure a continuous flow. The confidence gained by fulfilling their obligations to the gods in ritual cycles encouraged people of early empires to perform spectacular engineering feats to control rivers and contain springs.

Possibly at the same time or even before the great ceremonial center of Teotihuácan near Mexico City developed their water control cultivation system about 500 B.C.E., precursors of the Mesoamerican civilizations in the central valleys of the state of Jalisco in western Mexico were developing chinampas, or cultivated islands anchored in lakes connected by canals that became the leading edge of horticultural activities in Mexico's central plateau. Archeological research over the past three decades by Phil Weigand and Acelia Garcia, who have examined the ecosystems of the Guachimontones site in Teuchitla, indicates that cultivators in this fragile environment were knowledgeable and concerned about soil fertility and water resources.

When I toured the site with Phil Weigand in April 2006, he pointed out the monumental lagoon where the chinampas were built and remain as islands grouped in regular blocks in canals that connected lakes. The extensive hydraulic engineering ensured the flow of water and capture of eroded topsoil in constantly enriched sites for sustained farming by inhabitants of over 2000 villages. It also provided a habitat for a variety of fish and animal species. These chinampas are, according to the site brochure "among the earliest, most extensive and best designed cultivation fields within swamps in the whole of Mesoamerica" (Weigand and Esparza Lopez 2004:31).

Massive ritual mounds built at ceremonial sites near the springs and other sources of water, and the presence of a 2,200 meter square ball court, reveal the prosperity of the people who also developed fine pottery and sculpture. Sculptured figurines depicting dances and domestic life found in this early site and displayed in the Teuchitla museum suggest the collective basis for social organization. The widespread distribution of tools from more than 150 obsidian mines at the Guachi-monton site attests to the part these people played in the circulation of ideas and techniques throughout Mesoamerica.

In the centuries after the Christian era, images of the rain god Tlaloc in Teotihuácan, and those of the Mayan rain god Chac in Palenque and Chichenitza, give further evidence of the power accorded to deities worshipped as the givers of water. This power extended to the gods of maguey and corn that produced fermented liquor that enabled humans to communicate with spiritual beings. Among the Aztecs, the goddess Mayahuel was venerated as the deity who gave pulque, the fermented juice of maguey, to humans.[3] The corn god, Ixim, was venerated not only as the provider of the main dietary staple but also as the very source of human life among Mayas throughout the Yucatan, Chiapas, and the western highlands of Guatemala. Rituals in their honor solidified the social group dedicated to maintenance of the environment, but failure in cases of drought, often led ruling elites to exact human sacrifices for the gods that promoted conflicts and even cultural collapse.

The Aztecs left their homeland in Aztlan, whose geographic location is not known, about C.E. 820, arriving in the Central Plateau about three centuries later. There they introduced chinampa cultivation into the densely populated centers where they served as mercenaries for the Culhuacán and other kingdoms. Within two centuries they were able to use their military skills to forge powerful alliances; and by the mid-13th century they established a kingdom of their own, known as Tenochtitlán. Located in a river basin encompassing 70–80 thousand hectares, the capital city was set on an island in a lake surrounded by a chain of lakes, including the marshy sweet waters of Chalco-Xochimilco, the salty bitter waters of Texcoco, and the sweet waters of Zumpango verging into the salty lake Xaltocan (Tortolero Villaseñor 2000:23).

The setting for the major Aztec temple, the templo mayor, is that of a chinampa rising out of the lake that surrounds the ceremonial center. Tlaloc, the rain god, was enthroned in the vertex of the pyramid, and four of the 18 months in the ceremonial calendar were dedicated to the gods of rain. Like all powers of nature, the Aztecs conceived of water in the form of rains, floods and storms as potentially destructive as well as beneficial to humankind (Tortolero Villaseñor 2000:24). The lakes provided fish, turtles, frogs, toads, mollusks, and algae, and supported ducks and birds and many species of animals. Highly developed hydraulic systems made up of dykes, locks, and water transport all attest to the engineering skills of the Aztec administration, enabling them to take advantage of an abundant supply of food in areas that had been abandoned by the enemies they had defeated.

Undoubtedly, the Aztec mastery of chinampa cultivation contributed to their power in the central plateau, offering them sustained irrigated lands that were replenished with rich fertilizers from the lake bottom. They fortified this material base with an ideological and ritual structure honoring the power of rain and water deities that were related to the moon, Coyolxauki; but they placed the tribal god of war Huitzilopochtli at the apex. A gigantic image of Tlaloc, the god of water, found in the biggest chinampa site of Lake Texcoco, has recently been removed to the entrance of the National Museum in Chapultepec Park. The population density of the area—hundreds of thousands in the Valley

of Mexico at the height of Aztec civilization—attests to the success of hydraulic cultivation (Sanders and Price 1968:202). But the increasingly onerous demands for sacrificial offerings of human captives to their gods engendered the hostility of neighbors and even their own population so that the Spaniards found ready allies in their invasion.

Until recently, Mayas who inhabited areas to the south in Mexico and Guatemala were thought to have relied on swidden cultivation, an extensive slash and burn process requiring that large land areas be left fallow for future use. Certain of the classic sites in Chiapas seem to be chosen for the proximity of still lakes, particularly characteristic of Ch'inkultik, just south of Palenque where the dominant ceremonial site rises about 200 meters above a series of still freshwater lakes. In the streams that flow between them one can still find lilies growing. Linda Schele and Peter Mathews (1998) hypothesize that the recurrence of the lily as an emblem of kingship in Mayan glyphs may have related to the kings' responsibility to maintain chinampas that were sustained by the tuberous roots of the lily. As yet this hypothesis has not been substantiated by any archeological dig.

In these preconquest city states, hydraulic systems reveal economic and social integration extending over large regions that were strongly focused on the control and conservation of water resources. The importance granted to water and the responsibility taken to guarantee its continued abundance contrasts with the culture introduced by the Spaniards and even more so with intensive commercial crop cultivation promoted after 1960s. Where these practices dominate the landscape, the valuation of nature and the commitment to balance in the cosmos found in the Mesoamerican formative era are violated, just as they were by warring elites before the conquest when deforestation caused the collapse of lowland civilizations. Today for example, the Teuchitla area in western Mexico is environmentally devastated, and the river and lakes have shrunk or disappeared. The national government subsidizes extensive irrigation systems for the production of cane sugar and maguey that divert water from subsistence cultivation. Tequila, the chief product made from maguey, is a product identified not only with the town from which the name is derived but also with Mexico as a nation, yet it was recently sold to a foreign corporation, along with the water rights that sustain its production.[4] Mexico City is experiencing a water shortage, and water supplies in most large urban centers are threatened with contamination or scarcity.

I now turn to the logic and practices of the Spanish invaders and conclude by highlighting the attempts now being made by Mayas to pursue an autonomous course of development reinstating small plot cultivators and craftspeople.

THE SPANISH CONQUEST AND THE DRIVE TO DESICCATE WATERLANDS

Spaniards expressed awe and admiration for the beauty of the Aztec capital, overflowing with vegetation, flora, and birds. Fountains and canals connected lakes from which rose the artificial islands or chinampas capped with flowers and fruits. Yet coming from the arid lands of Asturias, Andalusia, and Madrid the colonial bureaucrats were bent on draining the water that impeded their plans to replace the temples and palaces of Tenochtitlan with replicas of the quarried stone cathedral and government offices that still stand in Mexico City's zocalo. They are a testament not only to the dominance and control exercised by the conquerors but also to their insensitivity to the knowledge and artistry of the people and to the environment.

In the century following their conquest of the Aztecs, the Spaniards proceeded to carry out what Tortolero Villaseñor (2000:33 et seq.) calls "an ecological destruction without parallel" in the world. They diverted waters from the lakes and canals, constructing dams in ways that caused the waters to stagnate and the fish and plants to die. They burned woodlands to make pasture for cattle, introduced plow cultivation so deep that it caused erosion, and brutally disrupted the marshy lake bottom. The soft subsoil could not support the weight of their stone buildings. Lacking the constant flow of waters through canals that kept the lake waters oxygenated, the dead waters no longer maintain the life of plants and fish.

Given their own failure to dry out the landscape, the Spaniards hired a Dutchman, De Boot, because Dutch engineers had recovered 80-thousand hectares of land from the sea between 1540 and 1615. His plan to dig a ditch around the city, expel the surplus waters with hydraulic pumps as they did in Holland, and connect the lakes with canals was rejected because it too closely replicated what the Indians had had. He was denounced as a Dutchman and a Calvinist, a spy and a heretic, and condemned to death by the Inquisition in 1636. Although the sentence was suspended, he died, apparently of natural causes, in 1638 (Tortolero Villaseñor 2000:37).

Colonial government policies were guided by the attempt to dry out the urban environment of the capital city they replaced, in effect replicating the arid environment from which the Spaniards had come. Subsequent projects spread the Spaniard's ecological disaster with the advance of hacienda cultivation in the north and in the flatlands to the east and south. The destruction that followed the conquest was accelerated through the ineptitude of bureaucrats and the rejection of often-superior techniques and practices of the Indians, setting the stage for local rebellions that ultimately brought down Spanish rule. This insensitivity to the environment persisted after independence when buildings such as the Palacio de Bellas Artes and the interrupted Benito Juarez monument meant to celebrate the power of the state sank several meters. Floods resulting from the destruction of the intricately engineered canals continue to plague the population, with Lake Texcoco periodically disgorging its waters on the Mexican capital.

CHIAPAS AND THE DELAYED REVOLUTION

The highlands of the state of Chiapas did not attract many Spaniards during the colonial period. Without the participation of indigenous people, the decision to join forces with Mexico rather than Guatemala was made by the few land barons who dominated the state in 1824, three years after Mexico had gained its independence. Promoted by liberal policies in the last quarter of the 19th century, the descendants of these elites and immigrant Europeans seized coastal lands and the better lands of Indian pueblos in highland valleys. There they established a racially divided society that maintained an impoverished, geographically isolated majority of Indians in the highlands, reduced to a subordinated status, deprived of education, and dispirited by alcoholism. Mexico's independence from Spain did not bring freedom for the indigenous people, but, rather, greater freedom for the descendants of Spaniards, deculturated and mixed blood Indians, or ladinos, to exploit Indians in feudal institutions of work. The relative isolation of indigenous townships allowed some precolonial practices to survive until the mid-19th century when the attrition of restricted lands previously granted to Indian pueblos by the crown forced many to migrate temporarily or become peons in coastal plantations. The vision that fostered the growth of empires dedicated to cosmological forces

was further attenuated by commercial activities dominated by Europeans and a growing population of ladinos.

Throughout pre-Colombian Mexico, consumption of fermented beverages was an intrinsic part of religious and secular celebrations. Powerful seers *(iloletic)* or shamans imbibed these intoxicating beverages and smoked strong tobacco cheroots to enhance their communication with the animal spirit of the patients and their malefactors to carry out a cure or intercept witchcraft. After the conquest the fermentation and distillation of sugarcane liquor, or rum, became a monopoly of religious *cargo* (lit. "burden") holders who required the drinking of *posh*, or home brewed cane liquor, in all celebrations in the calendar cycle of saints, and in curing ceremonies, betrothal rites, and in funerals. In some towns, such as Chamula, a Tzotzil speaking municipality contiguous with San Cristobal de La Casas, both the production and distribution of posh was monopolized by the elders themselves. In other towns such as Amatenango liquor production became a cottage industry with rudimentary stills discretely located in hamlets surrounding the town center.

When I was living in Amatenango during the 1960s, drinking was institutionalized in every celebration within the home as well as in the church and town hall. Civil and religious officials addressed prayers, called pat'otan (behind the heart), to the ancestors *(me'iltatil)*, asking permission to swallow the drink. Liquor was considered to be the gift of our Lord Jesus Christ, derived from the bath water of the crucified Christ when he was taken down from the Cross *(s'mahtan sapilyok, sapilsk'aab yu'un tatik Jesu Kristo)*. During civil and religious celebrations, officials tested each other's manliness, equated with the ability to drink a great deal without staggering. When they reached their limit of tolerance, they could not refuse it but were allowed to pour the offering into bottles carried by young boys who accompanied each official.

Every young man produced his first batch of posh when he started his campaign to win a wife, a long drawn out series of visits to her parents in which gifts of liquor along with bread, chocolate, and brown sugar, played an important part. When the parents of the girl accepted the drink, due troth was announced, and then the big production of liquor for the wedding began (Nash 1973). The worth of a woman was measured in the number of liters of posh given by a youth in the betrothal match, and years after the marriage the quantity was remembered and remarked on.

In 1957, Pedrero, one of the largest cane growers who owned the sugar refinery of Pujiltic on the lower slopes of the central Chiapas plateau, used his political connections throughout the state to make home distilled beverages illegal. Soon afterward, state police were dispatched to the towns and proceeded to flush out the moonshiners in the hill towns. I was told after the campaign that there were two killed on each side of the fight. Sensing the futility of the military campaign, the state government called in the National Indigenist Institute (INI). They proposed a reward for anyone who brought in their equipment, in exchange for which they received ancient copper coils and metal drums. These items, including pottery tinajas (or water carriers) used to capture the evaporation of the boiling sugar, made for a fine museum collection, but in the following weeks the stills were back in operation with updated copper tubing. The owners of the 41 stills operating when I was there resisted attempts by federal police to locate them, broadcasting warnings in Tzeltal of the impending raid on loudspeakers that played popular songs to attract young men to the bars they operated in town.

Given the prevalence of this consuming interest in liquor, anthropologists were attracted to the subject, resulting in a large-scale research project and extended computer analysis during the 1960s, when this technology was not much in use. The book that resulted from the investigation in three towns, Amatenango del Valle, Chamula, and Oxchuk, was entitled *Drinking Patterns in Highland Chiapas: A teamwork Approach to the Study of Semantics through Ethnography* (Siverts 1973). It was a triumph of structural functional investigation, showing minutely the functioning of the civil religious hierarchy based on age, gender, and rank as this was played out in drinking order. In the process, a great deal of liquor was imbibed, both by anthropologists and "informants," possibly promoting what was called rapport in those days. The requisite drinking in ceremonial occasions may have promoted conviviality, as the authors claimed (and I was one of them), but it also promoted a compulsive addictive behavior that was ruining the health of local people and promoting domestic violence. The interpretations generated by the research ignored both the overarching structures of inequality that held Indians in bondage and the way in which drinking behavior reproduced the relations of subordination.[5]

The high consumption of liquor not only increased the brutalizing impoverishment of indigenous people who expended so much of their labor and land on cane sugar liquor but also succeeded in anesthetizing Indians to the injustice in which they were held captive. Those who became conscious of this, especially women who were not so engaged in the ceremonial life requiring that they imbibe copious amounts of liquor, chose to convert to Protestantism because it absolved them of participating in the civil religious hierarchy. This strategy was notable, especially in Oxchuk where in the late 1940s over 5,000 adults had converted to escape the required drinking in civil and religious ceremonies, and particularly in curing rituals where drinking was considered an essential part of the cure (Villa Rojas 1990). Women were among the first to convert and made up the majority of the converts that Villa Rojas recorded during his field work in the 1940s. The women, who were the first to accept the new faith, often converted their husbands because drinking was prohibited in the congregation, a pattern that Christine Eber (1995) recorded over two decades later in Chenalhó.

Aware of growing concern about alcohol, traditional religious leaders began to substitute soft drinks for the liquor, establishing concessions with the Coca-Cola Company or PepsiCo that were making inroads in indigenous markets during the 1980s. In Chamula, leaders of the hierarchy reinstated their monopoly with the new product replacing posh. The Coca-Cola Company advertised the beneficial health effects of the nonalcoholic drink, and the religious brotherhoods provided the infrastructure for the promotion of Coca-Cola in local celebrations that had previously served locally distilled cane liquor. The monopoly of this sale was granted by elders of the civil religious hierarchy to the Coca-Cola Company. In Amatenango, the concessions were granted through party allegiance, with Institutional Revolutionary Party (PRI) officials purchasing Coca-Cola and Party of the Democratic Revolution (PRD) officials favoring Pepsi. When I returned to Amatenango in 1987 after a 20-year absence, I found that these soft drinks were dispersed with the same ceremonial practices and prayers that had accompanied the distribution of posh during celebrations in the past. Soft drinks, including national brands as well as the U.S. brands that tended to be distributed in accord with monopolized markets, have even replaced the gift of posh in the elaborate household ceremonies of betrothal and death.[6]

The consumption of both posh and soft drinks opened indigenous society to wealth opportunities for a few, engendering a class system that divided the town between those who were part of the cacicazgo—political leaders dependent on the ruling party—and those who were

not. The cacicazgo fostered political alliances between indigenous leaders and the state that debilitated indigenous autonomy more than any previous colonial or independence institutions. It became a key factor in the extreme marginalization of Chiapas after the Revolution of 1910–17, in which it perpetuated the rule of feudal land barons long after they had been superseded by modernizing agents in ouher states. Government services, including education, health clinics, electricity, and piped water, came late or not at all. Indigenous villages did not have any piped water service when I arrived in Amatenango in 1957, and it was not available even to residents in the center of town until a decade later. When it was finally introduced in the late 1960s and 1970s, it was given out preferentially; those who lived in outlying hamlets or were marginalized from the government largess were the last to receive piped water, and often the hamlets that were opposed to the party in power never gained it.

Piped water has created another basis for partisan discrimination and conflict within communities. When piped water was first proposed by the INI, the curers in Amatenango did not want to have the spring waters covered and tapped with pipes because this was the site of curing rituals where patients were bathed. It was only after a year's negotiation that INI reached a compromise and diverted a stream for curing purposes. In the spring of 2004, Zinacantán's PRD officials who occupied the town offices refused to grant water to nonparty members. The resulting conflict caused two deaths. In Chamula, residents in the hamlet of Petet were discriminated against when potable water was first introduced in 1995 because they voted for the party opposed to that of incumbent PRIistas. Remote hamlets of Amatenango have never received running water.

These local conflicts are not caused by the corporations that enter into market relations with indigenous communities, yet the concession granted to soft drink companies have aggravated deep-seated conflicts based on religious and political party schisms by promoting access to privatized gains. To resist the influence of corporations requires more than a boycott of the product, as the people of Mitzitón learned in 2004 when they opposed the order of a township official who demanded that they purchase twenty cases of Coca-Cola per week for meetings so that he could retain his concession with the company. Faced with expulsions and even death threats for refusing to buy Coca-Cola from the incumbent official, the dissidents had to leave their community and colonize a new settlement in Teopisca on the basis of Catholic Word of God principles (CIEPAC 2004:3).

Many indigenous communities are beginning to reject the authoritarian rule of traditional leaders and the increasing threat to land and water resources by foreign private enterprises. Some seek autonomy, following the path of Lacandon communities that support the Zapatista Army of National Liberation that constituted themselves as Regional Autonomous Pluriethnic Pueblos on October 12, 1993. This group drafted the demands that were later codified in the San Andrés Agreement signed but never implemented in 1996 by President Zedillo.[7]

This course is being pursued by Chamula residents who have settled on the slopes of Huitepec, the volcanic peak where the major springs that supply water for the department of San Cristobal and many of its surrounding indigenous communities are found. During the presidency of Vicente Fox, who had served as the chief executive officer of Mexico's Coca-Cola Company prior to his taking office, the federal water agency gave permission to the company to tap deep groundwater resources. The water is not metered, and the municipality does not receive reimbursement. Perhaps to confirm the concession of this precious

resource, the newly installed Partido Acción Nacional president Felipe Calderon declared Huitepec a national environmental reserve. This step, which allows the federal government to abrogate land and water rights of localities, has been taken in many of the water rich environments throughout the state. Following this preemptive act, the new paramilitary organization that has been active in prime Lacandon sites since Calderon's inauguration arrived in the area and threatened the long-term settlers, claiming that they were cutting down trees in the new reserve. The settlers claim that they have not done any more than cut small trees for firewood as they have done for the past six or seven decades of residence, and that the large-scale cutting was done by the intruders. Meanwhile, Maderos del Pueblo, an activist NGO of Great Britain, supports the residents and has called environmental and human rights organizations in the area to rally around the threatened residents. When I visited the encampments of volunteers on April 12, 2007, they reported a lull in hostilities but were maintaining daily tours to ensure that no new cutting of trees occurred.

The Coca-Cola Company, which moved its headquarters from the state capital of Tuxtla Gutierrez a few years ago to take advantage of the excellent water supply in San Cristobal, has expanded its fleets of trucks that canvass the neighborhoods of the city, proclaiming their presence with a happy jingle that draws adults and children to purchase their soft drinks and the increasingly popular bottled water. The company claims to be trying to recruit indigenous workers, but the manager complained to me in an interview (March 2006) that the level of education is too low for the jobs they need to fill. As a result, he said, they are giving grants to communities such as Chamula to upgrade the educational level. When I visited the town soon after, officials told me that, to their knowledge, Coca-Cola has not invested in any educational program in town.

PRIVATIZED APPROPRIATION OF WATER IN A NEOLIBERAL ECONOMY

In global markets, the links between resource bases and consumption needs have changed. Instead of rendering liquor, candles, tobacco, and incense to the gods in thanks for their gift of water, public officials now grant concessions to foreign firms that allow them to extract unlimited quantities of an increasingly valuable resource. In the new exchange relationship the ritual responsibilities that promoted communal integration are waived, and in their place class differences have created the basis for growing conflicts among indigenous people.

The demand for commoditized bottled water has grown as a result both of contamination of existing water supplies and new industrial uses, particularly in agroindustry. It has also grown because of the diversion of groundwater and springs to the companies that sell bottled water. During 2004, more than 154-billion liters of bottled water were consumed worldwide. The United States is a foremost consumer with 26-billion liters and Mexico is the second highest consumer with 18-billion liters.[8] The biggest gains in the sale of bottled water are in Third World countries, which face growing scarcity of clean water along with rising populations. Companies like Coca-Cola, PepsiCo, and Nestle that have always drawn on world water resources for their beverages, now use their water rights to exploit groundwater for sale. In countries that are experiencing the greatest growth in the world economy, bottled water conduces to the scarcity of potable water: in India Coca-Cola's export sales of water called Dasani have reduced the capacity of 50 cities to meet the needs of the people.

Although not always healthier than tap water in countries that purify piped water, bottled water is 10,000 times more costly if one takes into account the energy expended in bottling, commercialization, and recycling. Bottled water is also highly costly for the environment. There are few government regulations on the production of bottled waters, and some bottling companies simply take tap water and add minerals, a practice that has not always proved healthful (*La Jornada* 2006: 6a).

Investment in water services has low return when the server does not hold monopoly control of water. The Mexican government had hardly begun to provide water services to indigenous areas when the transfer of water services to the municipality began to be privatized illegally in 1982. Privatization was then legalized by the reform of Article 27 of the Constitution in 1992 during Salinas's presidency. The drive to privatize rights to exploit groundwater and make it available to foreign private companies surged during Vicente Fox's presidential term. As former president of Mexico's Coca-Cola Company, Fox was instrumental in assessing the wealth of subsoil waters and asserting the need of foreign capital with the perforation technology to dig deep wells. It was no surprise when he introduced the new Law of National Waters in 2004 that authorizes the privatization of the entire hydraulic infrastructure of federal property—dams, canals, and irrigation ditches—and prioritizes the rights of extraction of water by corporations. These resources had been considered the patrimony of the nation. The new Law of National Waters expands the creation of markets of water, taking advantage of the small farmers who can sell their right of extracting water. During his presidency the Fox administration has granted rights to exploit more groundwater in a country than ever before. The country now faces water shortages owing principally to the use of subterranean water, by large-scale agribusiness.[9]

The water hunters are now actively entering the new markets opened up by the Fox administration's reforms. Carlos Slim, a man who made his multibillion-dollar fortune in the privatization of telecommunications rights over a decade ago, has now offered to assist Mexico City with its water supply. The reform in the law at the federal level has enabled the Coca-Cola company to exploit deep wells in San Cristobal de Las Casas. Although the municipality of San Cristobal does not receive any rent or payments for the rights of exploitation of the wells, Coca-Cola Company is now selling not only their signature soft drink but also 400 product lines that now include bottled water for this increasingly scarce resource. The corporation's new distribution center in San Cristobal consolidates its market gains in consumption of Coca-Cola in indigenous territory while taking advantage of low prices for clear water in territory that was known for abundant water supplies. The market has expanded with the demands of a growing tourist industry and also of low income ladinos and Indians who have no access to groundwater. Consumption of bottled water in Mexico has doubled from 1999 to 2004 as a result of increasingly contaminated waters, and the buyers are not just tourists or young urban professionals. Indigenous entrepreneurs use the corporate frame to enhance political party goals internally at the same time that the corporation uses the local concessions to promote sales and secure their position in a sovereign nation on their own terms.

THE WORLD RESOURCE WAR IN WATER

The tenuous link between consumer and producer, stretched in the western expansion and consolidation of the capitalist market system in the 20th century, is now being severed in the third millennium. Privatization had already been legislated in the North American Free Trade Agreement, railroaded through Congress during the Clinton administration and ratified by Carlos Salinas in 1993. That agreement defines water as a tradable good, obliging all parties to sell their water resources to the highest bidder under threat of being sued by private companies that want it. These parties will be strengthened by the proposed Free Trade Area of the Americas (FTAA), which would allow foreign investors to sue and demand compensation from governments for any law or rule that affects their profits, even when these laws are motivated by environmental considerations (Americas Program 2004). The World Bank is now making its loans to countries conditional on the privatization of water services and resources.

We are on the brink of a new resource war that will divide the populations of the world into the haves and have-nots of water. The first major water war grew out of Bolivian popular resistance to the privatization of the Cochabamba water system. It was set off when Aguas del Tunari and Abengoa Corporations, subsidiaries of Bechtel's operations in Bolivia acquired the rights to manage the water service of Cochabamba in 1999. This concession was a response to the IMF offer of a development loan to Bolivia's government on the condition that Bolivia would sell to private corporations the municipal water system of Cochabamba and the national oil refineries. The offer was cunningly related to a World Bank report advising that no relief be granted to ameliorate the increase in water tariffs that took place (Albro 2004:235 et seq.) Massive popular mobilizations ensued, involving large segments of both indigenous and chola or mestizo populations. In the process, they generated what Albro calls a "plural popular" subject that was neither Indian nor elite and that became the base for the political success of the indigenous leader, Evo Morales in the presidential elections of 2006.

Other countries in Latin America have followed the example set by Bolivia's popular resistance to privatization. In Uruguay a 2004 plebiscite limited private participation in water services, and in

Argentina the government restricted the benefits that had been customary in water contracts to private companies. This could happen in Colombia, too. Costa Rica is one of the few Latin American countries that provides public water services for all, whereas in Haiti only 50 percent are served. Water has become yet another measure of the poverty index, and investments in water services for Latin America are considered a poor market risk.

The Fourth World Water Forum, held in Mexico City in March 2006, differed markedly from the First World Forum on Water held in Marrakech. The First World Forum was organized by civil society with groups such as the Coalition of Mexican Organizations for the Right to Water and the movement for an alternative to privatization and for recognition of water as a human right setting the agenda. The agenda for the Fourth World Forum was set by financial organizations that now support it, including the Interamerican Development Bank and the World Bank. (As I have mentioned, the World Bank financing for installing water service is in fact conditional on privatizing water.) These organizations prevailed on the assembled groups not to proclaim water as a human right (Galan et al. 2006: 43). The watered down (no pun intended) declaration, simply says that water is important for health and for the poor.

Local initiatives and community-level projects to supply, conserve, and treat water were overshadowed by very different neoconservative concerns. As a result, the NGOs and indigenous dissenters held an alternative Water Forum outside in the streets of Mexico City. An estimated 10,000 demonstrators were blocked from marching to the meeting site. They included members of communities threatened with sewage contamination, Indians whose water is being diverted to supply big cities, and farmers whose lands are scheduled to be flooded by hydroelectric projects. Mazahuas carried out a ritual asking for protection of water. Representatives of Pueblos Indígenas of Latin America announced that water is not merchandise, but life, and it ought not to be sold. "We know that some chiefs of State have not accepted satisfactorily that the liquid of the indigenous pueblos is like blood for the land; it is sacred, and therefore we respect it and for it we demand that the agenda of agreements of this forum establish actions that include us." As the most threatened consumers, they were the most forceful in protesting the threatened scarcity of water. Capitalist providers might take note that the break between consumption and production will also terminate their survival.

CONCLUSION

This brief-review of transformations in the social organization of water systems from preconquest to colonial to independence to modern times reveals the need for a holistic analysis to ensure sustainable development and equitable distribution of such a basic necessity. The imposition of Spanish rule interrupted well-established adaptations to fragile environments and in so doing aggravated the scarcity of water in heavily populated areas and contributed to the concentration of power and wealth. In the early colonial period, the conquerors were able to reach water with wells of nine meters, now they have to dig 450 meters to find water.

The transformation from ritual propitiation of the gods that engaged entire populations in collective action to the private expropriation of water resources is having a profound impact on the indigenous pueblos that are now major consumers of these costly products. The shift from rum to Coca-Cola or Pepsi Cola is not entirely negative; the devastating effects of alcoholism are not nearly as apparent today as when I worked in the highlands during the 1960s. Yet the immediate effects are the dental caries that afflict the population coming of age in the 1970s, and the dehydration of infants and elders with parasites that sometimes causes death. The delayed effects are environmental changes that are already becoming apparent, along with the increasing scarcity of a gift of the gods that is becoming too costly for the poor. The alliances made between corporate and government leaders to secure water rights without redistribution of profits to the consumers remain the most pernicious effect of privatization and monopolization of this precious resource.

The magnitude of the water crisis is made clear by the indigenous people who live on the frontiers of capitalist expansion. They are the most forceful in addressing the values that are threatened in the new resource wars for water. They remind us of a culture that promoted collective rights through practices that enhanced the environment, and the will of those who were the "keepers of water and earth" (Enge and Whiteford 1989) in earlier epochs. The privatization of a resource once considered to be the gift of gods and nature threatens universal access to a primary resource that many think should be protected by human rights covenants.

ACKNOWLEDGEMENTS

I have benefited from the many helpful suggestions of David Barkin, Robert Benfer, and Frank Reynolds in clarifying this article. I am grateful for the assistance of Elizabeth Story for her web search that netted some of the global stories cited.

NOTES

1. Federal permits to the Coca-Cola Company were granted during the presidency of Vicente Fox, who was formerly chief executive officer of the Coca-Cola Company in Mexico. The municipality does not receive compensation for the unmetered pumping from deep groundwater reserves.

2. Intensive agricultural exploitation uses far more of the country's water supply than does bottled water, as studies to the north of Chiapas amply demonstrate. Enge and Whiteford (1989) have noted the remarkable feats accomplished by small plot farmers in the Tehuacán Valley who retain a collective organization and control of the irrigation system they devised. Roberto J. Gonzalez (2001) also indicates the scientific acuity of Zapotec farmers who have adapted the new coffee crops without abandoning their cultivation of subsistence crops. Although the impact of privatization is emphasized here, I do not overlook the dangers of government programs that ignore or reject the solutions that indigenous people make.

3. Eloise Quiñones Keher (1995), traces the roots of worship of Maguey through the goddess Mayahuel in her book *Codex Telleriano, Remenses: Ritual, Divination, and History in a Pictorial Aztec Manuscript*. Like pulque, made from maguey, mushrooms and tobacco were used by Aztec shamans to conjure up demons and the devil himself. Yucatec Mayan shamans could send diseases inflicted by underworld rulers back to the realm of the dead.

4. Researchers in the Latin America Data Base (vol. 17, no. 35, September 2006): Source Mex, Economic and Political News on Mexico. Latin American and Iberian Institute, University of New Mexico) reported the sale of Casa Herradura, on August 28, 2006, to U. S.-based Brown-Forman Corp. Other firms have recently been acquired by U.K.- and U.S.-based brands. The sale that occurred during the month for celebration of Mexican independence was usually toasted with tequila, now a bitter potion for Mexicans.

5. Sergio Navarro Pellicer's (1988) incisive analysis of aguardiente examines the way in which aguardiente reproduces the relations of subordination in Chenalhó. Eber (1995) analyzes the double subordination of women as victims of domestic abuse and ethnic subordination aggravated by alcohol.

6. Another variation in this party alliance was played out in Mitzitón where the Coca-Cola Company gave the town's storekeeper a refrigerator, chairs, tables, and free gifts in a contract that required him to sell 20 cases of soft drink a week. The storekeeper used his links with the PRI-controlled community council to force the sale of the drink on all members. When the people refused to buy the costly drinks, the PRI monopoly threatened them, and they were forced into exile (Centro de Investigaciones Económicas y Políticas de Acción Comunitaria [CIEPAC] n.d.).

7. On October 12, 1994, the Lacandon communities that supported the Zapatista Army of

National Liberation constituted them as Regional Autonomous Pluriethnic Pueblos and drafted the demands that were later codified in the San Andreas Agreement signed by President Zedillo. The state has failed to implement the policies.

8. See *La Jornada* (2006: 6a) and the anthology prepared for the Fourth World Forum on Water.

9. Felix Hernández Gamundi, an engineer working with indigenous communities, spoke in Taller Popular en Defensa del Agua, April 2005, printed in *La Jornada* (Gamundi 2006). He has been chipping away at the nationalized enterprises of Pemex and the Federal Commission of Electricity, permitting foreign exploitation of natural gas, illegal contracts to Repsol, Petrobras, Techint, Teikoku, and Lewis Energy Group.

Editor's Note: Other *Cultural Anthropology* articles have examined ways capitalism reorients desire and consumption. See, for example, Debra Curtis's "Commodities and Sexual Subjectivities: A Look at Capitalism and Its Desires" (2004), Nickola Pazderic's "Recovering True Selves in the Electro-Spiritual Field of Universal Love" (2004), and Adeline Masquelier's "Of Headhunters and Cannibals: Migrancy, Labor, and Consumption in the Mawri Imagination" (2000).

REFERENCES CITED

Albro, Robert, (2004) "The Water Is Ours, Carajo!" Deep Citizenship in Bolivia's Water War. *In* Social Movements: A Reader. June Nash, ed. Pp. 249–271. Oxford: Blackwell.

Americas Program (2004) Free Trade and Water Privatization. Electronic document, http://www.americaspolicy.org/articles/2004/0412water_bodyhtnl, accessed March 29, 2005.

Centro De Investigaciones Económicas y Politicas de Acción Comunitaria (CIEPAC) (2004) Chiapas al Dia 437(October 27):3.

N.d. October 17, (2004) Coca-Cola vs. Indigenous Peoples in Chiapas. Electronic document, http://www.laneta.apc.org/ciepac/boletines/chiapas_en.php?id=437, accessed June 1, 2007.

Curtis, Debra (2004) Commodities and Sexual Subjectivities: A Look at Capitalism and Its Desires. Cultural Anthropology 19(1):95–121.

Eber, Christine (1995) Women and Alcohol in a Highland Maya Township. Austin: University of Texas Press.

Enge, Kjell I., and Scott Whiteford (1989) The Keepers of Water and Earth: Mexican Social Organization and Irrigation. Austin: University of Texas Press.

Galan, José, José Antonio Roman, Angelica Enciso, and Matilde Perez (2006) Se perfila declaracíon final que no proclama derecho humano al recurso. La Jornada, March 21: 43.

Gamundi, Felix Hernández (2006) El agua en México y su crisis, Ojarasca, from talk in Taller Popular en Defensa de Agua. La Jornada, April: 7.

Gonzalez, Roberto J. (2001) Zapotec Science: Farming and Food in the Northern Sierra of Oaxaca. Austin: University of Texas Press.

La Jornada (2006) El agua embotellada, altamente costosa para el medio ambiente. La Jornada, February 7: 6a.

Latin America Data Base (2006) Mex-Economic and Political News on Mexico 17(35). Albuquerque: Latin American and Iberian Institute, University of New Mexico.

Masquelier, Adeline (2000) Of Headhunters and Cannibals: Migrancy, Labor, and Consumption in the Mawri Imagination. Cultural Anthropology 15(1): 84–126.

Nash, June (1973) The Betrothal: A Study of Ideology and Behavior in a Maya Community. *In* Drinking Patterns in Highland Chiapas: A Teamwork Approach to the Study of Semantics through Ethnography. Henning Siverts, ed. Pp. 89–120. Bergen: Universitetsforleget.

Navarro Pellicer, Sergio (1988) El Aguardiente en una Comunidad Maya de los Altos de Chiapas. Mexico, DF: Instituto Nacional de Antropología e Historia.

Pazderic, Nickola (2004) Recovering True Selves in the Electro-Spiritual Field of Universal Love. Cultural Anthropology 19(2):196–225.

Quiñones Keher, Eloise (1995) Codex Telleriano, Remenses: Ritual, Divination, and History in a Pictorial Aztec Manuscript. Austin: University of Texas Press.

Sanders, William T., and Barbara J. Price (1968) Mesoamerica: The Evolution of a Civilization. New York: Random House.

Scheie, Linda, and Peter Mathews (1998) The Code of Kings: The Language of Seven Sacred Maya Temples and Tombs. New York: Scribner.

Siverts, Henning (1973) Drinking Patterns in Highland Chiapas: A Fieldwork Approach to the Study of Semantics through Ethnography. Bergen: Universitetsforleget.

Tortolero Villaseñor, Alejandro (2000) El Agua y su Historia: México y sus desafios hacía el silo 21. México DF: Siglo 21.

Villa Rojas, Alfonso (1990) Etnografía Tzeltal de Chiapas: Modalidades de una Cosmovisión Prehispanica. Tuxtla Gutierrez: Gobierno del Estado, Secretaría para el Fomento de la Investigación y Difusión de la Cultura.

Weigand, Phil M., and Rodrigo Esparza López (2004) Guía del Sitio Arqueólogica de Los Guachimontones. Guadalajara: Gobierno de Jalisco.

30

Feeding the Jewish Soul in the Delta Diaspora

Marcie Cohen Ferris

Mention "The Delta" and vivid images come to mind of a dramatic, flat landscape etched by rows of cotton and bounded by the Mississippi River. One imagines catfish, juke joints, barbecue, and pick-up trucks in a world inhabited by white planters, poor white sharecroppers, and black blues musicians. Although the Mississippi and Arkansas Delta is largely populated by black and white working-class laborers and upper-class white land-owners, the region is also shaped by a small group of Jewish southerners, now numbering no more than three hundred, whose families first arrived in the Delta in the late nineteenth century as peddlers and fledgling merchants.[1] Between the Mississippi River levee and Highway 61, amidst the shotgun houses, cotton fields, and Baptist churches of the Delta, are a handful of synagogues, Jewish cemeteries, Jewish-owned clothing stores, and businesses that were central to the economies of small Delta towns prior to the coming of discount stores like Wal-Mart. Less visible but nonetheless present are the adapted folklore and foodways of a transplanted culture, for feeding the Jewish soul, both spiritually and physically, has challenged Delta Jews from their first arrival in the region through today.

In the town of Blytheville in the Arkansas Delta, my family's Jewish identity separated us from our white and black Gentile neighbors. Contrary to popular belief, this division was more respectful than mean-spirited. Biblical identification

of Jews as the "chosen people" carries weight in the South; because of our distant lineage to Moses, Jewish families had a special status in the Delta. Although there were violent incidents of antisemitism such as the 1960s temple bombings in Jackson and Meridian, Mississippi, most antisemitic expressions were far more benign actions such as exclusion from debutante parties, garden clubs, country clubs, and occasional comments about Jewish tightfistedness. My family attended synagogue—known to non-Jewish locals as "the Jewish church"—and offered up prayers to a deity, which helped to secure our acceptance in town. More than Judaism, it was the fact that we had not *always* lived in the community that separated us from the Gentiles. Because generations of history did not intimately link "our people" with "their people," our place in the local hierarchy of white society was never clear.[2]

My Jewish ancestors arrived in the Delta in the early 1920s. We lived within the Delta world of cotton planting, fall ginning, church socials, and football and the Jewish world of weekly Sabbath services, visiting rabbis, and preparation for the Passover seder in the spring and the High Holy Days of Rosh Hashanah and Yom Kippur in the fall. We ate *between* these two worlds in a complicated culinary negotiation of regional, ethnic, and religious identity. Within Jewish homes in the Delta, African American cooks and domestic workers set bountiful tables and prepared the cuisine for which the region is famous. Their meals featured elegant dinners of standing rib roast, as well as down-home southern Gentile meals of barbecue and fried catfish. Less familiar dishes served at Jewish tables in the Delta included matzah balls, kugels (dairy casserole), tortes, and tzimmes (baked sweetened vegetables and fruits), foods that tied Jewish worlds to central and eastern Europe.

Food writer Craig Claiborne was "initiated into the joys" of Jewish foods in the home of Sadie Wolf, who lived across the street from the Claiborne family in Indianola, Mississippi. Claiborne recalls visiting the Wolfs' home one Passover when daughter Anita had eaten her fill of traditional holiday foods. "If somebody feeds me one more matzah ball I'm going to kill them," protested Wolf. As Claiborne recalls in his memoir, it was the "talent and palate" of African American cooks who blended "soul food"—a mix of African and American Indian flavors—with creole cuisine that made the southern kitchen unique. Although separated by a gulf of race and class, African Americans and Jews in the Mississippi and Arkansas Delta were brought together by a culinary exchange that has existed since the late nineteenth century.[3]

Throughout the nation food strongly defines ethnic and regional identity. But in the South, and especially in the Delta, a region scarred by war, slavery, and the aftermath of Reconstruction and segregation, food is especially important. Historian David Blight suggests that the South was conquered during the Civil War, and afterwards the slow process of rebuilding and "re-imagining" the South began. Blight contends that while the South is no richer in history and memory than any other region, more of its collective energy is devoted to defining the past through literature, storytelling, and monument-making.[4] We should add food traditions to this list, because southerners also use food to define the history of their

region. For generations, southerners, including southern Jews, have struggled to understand their experience through memory-making, and much of that struggle takes place at the dinner table. In this tradition Delta Jews connect to family and regional history at every meal, Oneg Shabbat, and Sisterhood luncheon.

Food historian Joan Nathan argues that because of their "wandering history" Jews always adapted their lifestyles and foodways to local cultures. Apart from matzah (the Passover unleavened bread), haroset (the Passover apple and nut spread), and cholent (a traditional slow-cooked Sabbath stew), she argues that there are no specifically Jewish foods; rather, foods are associated with Jewish countries of origin. Since more than two-thirds of American Jews trace their roots to eastern Europe, Polish and Russian foods such as rye bread, borscht, and herring in sour cream became known as Jewish foods in America.[5] Eastern European Jews were not the only Jews to learn to "make do or do without" while adjusting their tastes to regional food traditions and local ingredients. Earlier waves of Sephardic and Ashkenazic Jews left many culinary traditions in the Old World, but not all. After arriving in the South, Jewish immigrants revived their memories of stewed fish dishes flavored with lemon, olive oil, and almonds, bean soups, roasted goose, duck, chicken, kugels, challahs, kuchens (coffee cake), and tortes. Jewish women gave these recipes to African American cooks, who integrated these dishes into the culinary tradition of the South.

From the handful of Conservative and Orthodox Jews in the Delta, who closely adhere to the Jewish dietary rules, or *kashrut*, to the most liberal Reform Jews, who do not recognize these culinary restrictions, eating is inseparable from religion. Anthropologists, folklorists, and food historians agree that food is invested with symbolic meaning and that any food-related activity—from a simple meal at home to the most elaborate public cele-bration—is an act of communication.[6] In Judaism, food is both communication and communion. This concept is central to understanding the power of food in ethnic and regional communities like the Delta.

For observant Jews, eating is an act of divine law dictated from the Bible and expanded in the Talmud, the ancient rabbinic commentaries related to the Torah, the first five books of the Bible. As Blu Greenberg, an orthodox *rebbetzin* (wife of a rabbi) and an authority on the precepts of traditional Jewish life, explains, "Kashrut is not simply a set of rules about permitted and forbidden foods; kashrut is a way of life."[7] This way of life determines which foods are prohibited, how certain foods should be prepared, and how animals should be slaughtered. For example, Jews are allowed to eat meat only from animals that chew their cud and have cloven hooves, fish that have both fins and scales, and no combinations of dairy and meat dishes. Even this rudimentary explanation of kashrut hints at the predicament of Jews in the Delta, who are surrounded by a cuisine that celebrates *treyfe* (nonko-sher) foods like pork, catfish, shrimp, crawfish, and wild game such as rabbit, squirrel, and deer. (Catfish is not kosher because it has no scales and is a nocturnal scavenger.)

Less observant Jews in the Delta ignore kashrut and eat Jewish foods like bagel and lox on Sunday morning as their only expression of Jewishness, a practice referred to as "kitchen Judaism."[8] For Delta Jews who position themselves between these two poles of observance, daily choices about food either connect them to or distance them from their Jewish identity. Thus, one encounters Jews who enjoy a pork barbecue sandwich at restau-rants but avoid serving or eating pork at home. Some Jewish families keep separate dishes at home for serving nonkosher foods like shrimp and pork barbecue so that the "regular" dishes are not tainted by these forbidden foods—a "south-ernism" of kashrut that requires separate sets of dishes for meat and dairy items.

Sylvia Klumok Goodman and her sister Ann Klumok Bennett grew up in the Delta town of Moorhead, Mississippi, where their African American cook, Eva-lina Smith, prepared Jewish foods under the tutelage of their mother, Fannie Klumok. Smith created her own names for these foreign-sounding dishes. Gefilte fish was "filthy fish," chremslach (fried Passover fritter) became "himself," and haroset was "roses." "She might not have pronounced all these dishes correctly," said Sylvia, "but she could cook them as well as any Jewish *yenta* from the old country, actually better."[9]

The world of Delta families like the Klumoks, who lived "Jewishly" in a world dominated by the Mississippi River, cotton, churches, and the blues, reveals a unique expression of American Judaism. Although they were far removed from Jewish butcher shops, bakeries, grocery stores, and even synagogues, Delta Jews frequently drove to Greenville, Greenwood, Clarksdale, Vicksburg, and Blythe-ville to socialize and worship. Regular trips were made to Memphis to buy kosher meat and "kosher-style" and Jewish foods like bagels, rye bread, pastrami, and corn beef.[10]

Jewish foodways in small towns throughout the Delta illustrate how "country Jewish" life was distinctive from that of "city Jews" in Memphis, where it was possible to socialize almost exclusively with other Jews. Strong Jewish social ties in the Delta created a sense of Jewish community through monthly dinner clubs, Sisterhood and B'nai B'rith activities, deli lunches, seders, Jewish golf tournaments, dances, and youth activities that reinforced Jewish identity. Foodways of Delta Jews reveal a regional Jewish culture shaped by a deep sense of place, isolation, kinship ties, agricultural occupations, the influence of white and black Protestant cultures, and a long history of racial and class divisions.

"COTTON HAS BEEN GOOD TO THE JEWISH PEOPLE"

Morris Grundfest was born in Russia in 1869. He came to New York in the late 1890s, married Mollie Bernstein, and after the birth of their two children, the couple came to the Mississippi Delta. They were drawn by family already settled in the South and their belief that the South was an "open place" that presented opportunity with its many farms and plantations. Like so many southern Jewish immigrants, Morris Grundfest began as a pack peddler, walking between farms and plantations to sell goods to white and black families. Eventually, the Grundfests opened M. Grundfest's, a dry goods store in the nearby town of Cary. Later, stepping outside the retail sphere, Morris Grundfest purchased two hundred and twenty acres of Delta farmland and established himself as both a shopkeeper and a cotton planter.[11]

Betty Grundfest Lamensdorf, the great granddaughter of Mollie and Morris, and her husband, Ben, farm the original acreage known as "the Grundfest place." "People are surprised you're Jewish and a farmer," said Ben Lamensdorf, who has raised cotton in the Delta for over forty years, "but we were farming a long time ago in Israel. We just went from sheep herders to raising cotton. Cotton has been good to the Jewish people who came to the Mississippi Delta."[12]

Morris's son Ike raised cotton in the Delta, ran his father's store after his death in 1925, and married June Flanagan, an Episcopalian. Their store was open six days each week, except for Rosh Hashanah and Yom Kippur, when Ike Grundfest closed it for half a day. Betty and her sister, Ann Grundfest Gerache, worked in the store after school and on Saturdays, the busiest shopping day of the week. "The labor would come in on Saturday to receive their pay, and then they'd buy their week's groceries. They usually ran about fifteen dollars," said Betty. "That would hold you for a whole week. And then, when everyone had gotten their groceries and visited and everything, we'd take the people and their groceries back to their houses."[13]

Despite the racial and class divisions that separated them, African Americans in the Delta found that Jews like the Grundfests were fair employers and shopkeepers. African Americans could try on clothes and shoes in Jewish-owned stores, and they were often employed as sales clerks. The Grundfests also provided transportation and housing for the black laborers who worked for them, an arrangement shaped by long-held Delta rules of race and class. "We knew that there was something different about them [Jewish southerners]," said writer Cliff Taulbert, an African American who grew up in nearby Glen Allan. "You didn't really expect them to do the same types of things that you'd expect a white person to do. And I guess, in our minds, we divided the two—there were white people in Glen Allan and there were Jewish people in Glen Allan. They may have felt they were white, but we never did."[14]

Some white gentile southerners may have questioned the racial status of their Jewish neighbors as well. Historian Leonard Rogoff argues that although southern Jews were accepted as white, their "precise racial place was not fixed," especially after Reconstruction with the arrival of thousands of eastern European Jews whose "swarthy" complexions concerned white southerners. The newly arrived Jews quickly realized that skin color in the South determined where they fell in the socioeconomic order. Jews in the Delta were accepted as white, and many joined local White Citizens' Councils during the 1950s and 1960s. Journalist Jack Nelson argues that the few resident Jews who became members of the councils did so either out of fear of antisemitism or because they too were "hard-rock segregationists."[15]

With their own racial identity questioned in a region plagued by nativism and growing antisemitism, Jews bridged the chasm between white and black cultures in their roles as merchants, cotton brokers, and music agents. A less visible but equally compelling source of identity was associated with food—at the Jewish dinner table, in the synagogue kitchen, and in Jewish-owned grocery stores and dry goods stores throughout the Delta. Here Jews encountered white and black Gentile neighbors, customers, domestic workers, cooks, and caterers, and southern and Jewish foods mixed. At times, the food choices emphasized Jews' "southerness," and at other times, the selections emphasized their "otherness."

With income from farming and their store, the Grundfests could afford to hire African Americans as cooks and domestic workers. Having full-time household help in the Delta—even with the meager salaries African American women were paid weekly—was often only possible for families where the wife worked in the family store and could not do the housework herself. In their Delta home, June Flanagan Grundfest supervised the work of African American employees, including Alice Watson, the family's cook, and Edna Davis, the housekeeper and the children's nurse.

Ann Grundfest Gerache described the family's daily meals as "southern country food." The Grundfest home was next door to the family store, and any ingredients Alice Watson needed were either found in the store or grown in the family's garden. "Mother didn't like to cook," said Ann. "She loved to garden. She did not like being inside cooking, because you worked half a day for every meal, and then it was gone in thirty minutes." Not allowed the luxury of "likes and dislikes," and limited to few options for work, African American cooks like Watson prepared three meals a day for white families like the Grundfests every day except Sunday. Watson worked a "double day," caring for the Grundfests during the day and beginning another round of labor

with her own family when she returned home at night.[16]

In addition to her vegetable and flower gardens, June Grundfest raised squabs and chickens and tended a strawberry patch, plum and pear trees, and a fig tree from which she made delicious jams and jellies. The foods that Ann and Betty associate with their mother are a southern and Jewish mix of homemade jams and pickles, salted pecans, and blintzes, topped with June's homemade strawberry jelly, which their father, Ike, ate each Sunday evening. "If she put salted pecans on the table," said Ann, "it meant a celebration."[17] The pecans were grown locally on the place and were buttered, salted, toasted in the oven, and then put away for "company" and special occasions.

As Hortense Powdermaker observed in her sociological studies of Indianola in the 1930s, black domestic workers like Alice Watson were "the chief liaison agent between the races." The Grundfest girls were not allowed to help with the cooking, work considered inappropriate for well-to-do southern white women and girls, but after school they would slip into Watson's kitchen at the Grundfest home, where they sat on the kitchen counter and visited with Watson while she cooked. On occasion, Watson slipped the girls a forbidden cigarette. Ann and Betty recalled the cooking of "Ma Mary," who lived nearby and weighed cotton that the laborers picked in their cotton sacks during the fall harvest. "Ann and I used to walk down there and eat," said Betty. "She'd go out into her garden and pick the butter beans, peas, and okra. We'd sit at this little table and she'd bring the bread in a skillet from the wood-heated oven. That was the best food. It just stuck in my memory how good it tasted." Powdermaker collected a similar story from one of her female informants in the 1930s who said that the "happiest memory of her childhood" was when the family's black cook took her home, "across the tracks," to play with her children and eat turnip greens.[18] The narrative confirmed Powdermaker's belief that whites long cared for by black workers sentimentalized those relationships in their memories of nurturance and caring, often centered at the table.

The ample meals at the Grundfest table included several meats, bowls of fresh vegetables, rice and gravy, hot biscuits and cornbread, preserves, and two or three desserts. Ann found oppressive the amount of food and the ritual associated with their meals. "I'm not going to put all this food on my table," she brashly told her mother when she married. "We're going to have one meat, two vegetables, and I don't know if I'm going to have dessert."[19] In the Delta in the 1950s, Ann's declaration was considered a radical act.

Holidays were divided between June's Episcopal family in Blanton, Mississippi, where they celebrated Thanksgiving and Christmas, and Ike's Jewish family in Greenville and Clarksdale, where they visited on Sunday afternoons and at Passover and High Holy Days to attend religious services. The Grundfests belonged to temples in both Greenville and Vicksburg, which were fifty miles and thirty-seven miles respectively from Cary. At Christmas, June's aunt, Elizabeth Darden, oversaw an elegant dinner prepared by three African American cooks who were expected to work on the holiday. The feast included a turkey and all the trimmings, a coconut cake and ambrosia for dessert. Ike's sisters, Kate Grundfest Sebulsky and Hattie Grundfest Brownstein, worked in "ladies' ready-to-wear." During market trips to Memphis and St. Louis they bought kosher salamis, pastramis, and rye bread, treats that were served with home-made chopped liver when the family visited on Sundays.[20]

Beyond June's Sunday evening blintzes and the aunts' deli foods, Jewish foods were rarely eaten by the Grundfest family until they began to participate in the local community Passover seder, which was organized by Jewish families in the Rolling Fork area in the 1950s. Gefilte fish was bought in Jackson, and other dishes for the seder were prepared by Jewish women in Rolling Fork, Cary, and Anguilla. June always contributed a 1950s-style congealed salad. The dessert was individual "sham tarts," a Delta version of the German-Jewish shaum torte, a meringue served with fresh strawberries and whipped cream. Ann Gerache continues to serve the same dessert at family seders, where it has become known as "Mamaw's Slip and Slide Cake" because of its tendency to melt and slip on warm spring seder evenings.[21]

LIVING JEWISHLY IN A GENTILE WORLD OF CATFISH AND PORK BARBECUE

Food traditions in the Grundfest family tell us much about the defining issue faced by Jews in the Delta since the late nineteenth century: the tension between the pull of assimilation as Jews began to make the Delta their home and the religious imperative to follow Jewish laws and foodways that by definition serve to set Jews apart from their Gentile neighbors. This tension touched all Jews in the Delta, regardless of their expression of Judaism and level of observance.

In the 1950s writer David Cohn, a native of Greenville, where his eastern European immigrant parents had opened a dry goods store, wrote that the Jews of the Delta had conformed so completely to the way of life of their Gentile neighbors that "they had not even clung to the many items of cookery gathered by their forebears during their peregrinations through Russia, Rumania, Hungary, Poland, Germany, and the Baltic States." Cohn underestimated the tenacity of food and the strength of food memories even in situations of great duress. In the Mississippi Delta Jews preserved food memories passed down by Jewish grandmothers and African American cooks alike. Despite intermarriage, a deep attachment to the South, and the strong influence of the white and black Protestant world in which they lived, Delta Jews preserved Jewish foodways in "the most southern place on earth."[22]

As with Ike Grundfest and June Flanagan, there was a high rate of inter-marriage among Jewish families in the Delta because of the limited number of potential Jewish mates for young adults who chose to remain in the region. When Ike and June married in the 1930s, they had a tacit understanding that they would respect both their Jewish and Episcopal religious upbringings and would not influ-ence their children's decisions about reli-gion. "We observed everything," their daughter Ann explained.[23] For Ike, this amounted to little or no participation in formal Jewish life, but he was conscious of his Jewish identity. Being with his Jewish sisters on Sunday afternoons and enjoying the deli foods they served him and his family was Ike's weekly expres-sion of Jewishness.

When Ann Grundfest married her first husband, Robert Emmich, a Vicksburg Jew, in the early 1950s, they agreed that a decision had to be made about their chil-dren's religion. "You can't have Christmas *and* Hanukkah," Robert told Ann. "You have to decide how you want to raise your children, and you must do one or the other."[24] They chose Judaism for their children, and with this choice came Jewish food. Ann learned to prepare Jewish foods rarely seen in her childhood home as she turned to Jewish cookbooks, in-laws, Sisterhood friends, and the rabbi for advice and their recipes.

Families like the Emmichs encouraged their high-school-age children to attend regional Jewish summer camps, like the Henry S. Jacobs camp in Utica, Mississippi, and supported the creation of Jewish youth organizations like the Mississippi Federation of Temple Youth, which later became the Southern Federation of Temple Youth or SOFTY. Jacobs Camp and similar programs across the nation

were evidence of a revitalization of Jewish education beginning in the 1970s. An attempt to counter rising rates of inter-marriage and assimilation, Jewish summer camps, adult education weekends, and retreats emphasized spirituality, ritual, and a sense of community in nontradi-tional settings outside the synagogue. Jewish parents in the Delta pushed their college-age children to enroll at a college or university with a significant Jewish population like the University of Alabama or the University of Texas. When Ann Grundfest joined a Jewish sorority at the University of Alabama, her "preference" for Judaism was set. "I remember one Shabbos dinner, the hostess, a mother of one of my sorority sisters, had a whole baked fish with a creole sauce over it," she recalled. "It was the first time I'd ever seen anything like that." Ann was used to fried chicken or roast beef at special dinners. If fish was eaten, it was either shrimp prepared in a creole fashion, such as jamba-laya or étouffée, or fried fish such as catfish or crappie (a local white fish) served often at outdoor fish fries. From the colonial era to the present, Jewish families of central European and Sephardic descent frequently served baked or stewed fish dishes with a sauce for Sabbath meals.[25]

Whether or not one found Jewish life at college, what mattered most in the Delta was having a religion and a place to pray. Denomination was less important than demonstrating one's attachment to a reli-gious community and a belief in God. "The South is not known as the Bible Belt for nothing," explained David Orlansky, a native of Greenville. "People probably take religion more seriously here than many other areas. It's important for people to belong to something, not neces-sarily to any particular church or religious affiliation, but just to be affiliated with something." Gene Dattel, raised in the Mississippi Delta communities of Sunflower and Ruleville, observed that "100 percent of Jews belonged to congregations in the Delta."[26] Their smaller numbers required a visible demonstration of religious commitment.

This concern was raised when in May of 1889 a small group of Jewish men in Port Gibson, thirty miles south of Vicksburg, sought financial support from congregations around the country to help them build a synagogue. "Our Christian fellow citizens often ask why the Israelites have no church," they explained. "They think we Jews care for nothing but business. For our children's sake, and in order to command the proper respect, we must have a Temple."[27] In 1892 Temple Gemiluth Chassed was dedicated in Port Gibson. Its Moorish architectural style is unique in the state. Jews throughout the Delta organized congregations during this same period. Vicksburg's Anshe Chesed Congregation was founded in 1841, Greenville's Congregation B'nai Israel, now Hebrew Union Congregation, was founded in 1880, Greenwood's Ahavath Rayim in 1893, and Clarkdale's Temple Beth Israel was founded in 1896.

An article published in 1870 in *The Israelite* by Rabbi Max Lilienthal, who officiated at the dedication of Vicksburg's Anshe Chesed Synagogue, described the gala affair attended by both Jewish and Gentile citizens from the city, as well as guests from Natchez, New Orleans, Baton Rouge, Mobile, Montgomery, and Jackson. Lilienthal, a German-ordained rabbi, was a distinguished leader of Reform Judaism in both New York and Cincinnati and traveled to officiate at many American congregations throughout the nineteenth century. Notable figures such as the governor of Mississippi, the mayor of Vicksburg, and most of Vicksburg's clergy also attended. "With true genuine southern hospitality and Jewish sociability no effort was spared to make me feel quite at home," wrote Lilienthal. "I have attended at many a consecration of larger temples in larger cities and congregations, but I have found nowhere more sincere enthusiasm, more

deep felt interest in our holy cause, than among our good brethren of Vicksburg."[28]

Yeager's Brass Band from New Orleans, plus a midnight banquet aboard the steamboat, the *Frank Pargond*, convinced Lilienthal that a congregation in the Delta was unique. They understood that the two unspoken rules in the Delta were to demonstrate your respect for "the Lord" and to show everyone a good time, which meant foot-stomping music, free-flowing alcohol, and abundant food. Although the ball lasted until three o'clock in the morning, the new synagogue was filled at nine o'clock by all "the Israelites living or staying in Vicksburg."[29] Vicksburg's Jewish merchants honored the occasion by closing their businesses from Friday noon until the following Monday morning, an unprecedented act in an agricultural community where retailers did most of their business on Saturdays.

The prosperity that made possible the new synagogues, as well as the lavish parties attending their openings, had its basis in the cotton economy, which affected everyone in the Delta, including Jewish merchants, their families, and rabbis. In 1874 Rabbi Aaron Norden of Natchez received a letter from temple officers informing him that his promised annual salary of $2,500 would have to be reduced to $2,000 due to a poor cotton season. The letter declared that the proposed salary of $2,500 was made "when the prospects for a good crop were very flattering and indications for a good business season was then thought more than likely to follow such a crop." Rabbi Norden replied to the Temple officers: "I have assurances from several of the members, and from appearances in general, [that] commercial affairs in this community are much more flourishing this year than they were last year."[30] The rabbi informed his congregants that he knew as much about the financial circumstances of the cotton economy in Natchez as they did.

In Jackson and Canton, Mississippi, the Wiener family paid close attention to the cotton market. Every year at the Passover seder, the family appointed one member to record seder "statistics" on the inside covers of the family *haggadahs* (the small book of prayers and songs used at the Passover seder). The names of seder guests, those who were away at college, illnesses, and recent births and deaths were recorded, along with a description of the seder highlights and praise for tasty dishes, such as "Sally's matzo balls, Thelma's Haroses, and Tinka's ice cream and meringues." A summary of local as well as national and international events, including the market price of cotton and soybeans, was also a part of each haggadah entry. At the April 12, 1912, seder, a participant recorded, "July cotton closed today: 11.06; low for season, 8.66. Last year of Boll Weevil and Vardaman." (James K. Vardaman, elected governor of Mississippi in 1904, ran a campaign steeped in racism.) From the late 1890s to the present, each entry also included the weather, flood conditions on the Mississippi River, whether the azaleas had bloomed early or late, and the market price of cotton and soybeans. "If there was too much rain or it was too cold, it could be devastating for cotton," said Kathryn Loeb Wiener, who came from a family of cotton factors in Montgomery, Alabama. "Cotton was currency, cotton was still king."[31]

Practicing Judaism in an overwhelmingly gentile world like the Delta was challenging, and for most Jews in the region, it meant adjusting religious practices to live in a farming society that conformed to both a southern and Protestant time table. For Jewish merchants like those in Vicksburg in the 1870s, this meant keeping their stores open on Saturdays—the Sabbath and holiest day of the Jewish calendar. In the 1940s and 1950s, Jewish retailers were overwhelmed with business from both white and black families that began early on Saturday morning and continued late into the evening. "This street on Saturday

night when I was growing up," said Joe Erber of Greenwood's downtown, " 'till one thirty, two o'clock in the morning would be packed with people. The Mississippi Delta was an agricultural-based economy, ... and the farmers all paid off on Saturdays."[32] Jewish merchants did what they had to do to make a living, and those who kept their stores open on the Sabbath hoped that God might understand the business cycles of the Delta.

Many stores were owned by Jewish families who were either close friends or relatives, and children of these merchants spent Saturday visiting from store to store and assisting with sales and other chores. "You ran from aunt to uncle, because our father had a brother who had a store a few doors down," said Shirley Fleischer Solomon, describing the scene in Shaw, Mississippi, where her parents had a small dry goods store.[33] This scene of family togetherness was repeated throughout the Delta on Sabbath mornings and was a common experience shared by Delta Jews.

Although most opened their stores on Saturdays, Jews in Greenwood observed the Sabbath by going to Friday evening services at Orthodox Congregation Ahavath Rayim. "We've tried to honor our forefathers, our ancestors," explained Joe Erber, whose grandfather was a charter member of the congregation. "We've never been perfect. We've done the best we can with what we've got." Erber, a postal worker and part-time police officer, continues to serve as a lay leader at the synagogue. Harold and Lucille Hart of Eudora, Arkansas, located across the river from Greenville, also tried to do their best "Jewishly." With little access to Jewish institutional life, the Harts' religion focused on the basic tenets of Judaism. "You don't have to know a whole lot about tradition in order to get to heaven," said Mr. Hart. "Just live right."[34] In Clarksdale, Temple Beth Israel changed the time of their Friday night services to six o'clock to allow the congregation to attend services as well as the local football games. In the Delta, football was a religion.

Such examples of Jewish "self-sufficiency" allowed the isolated Jews of the Delta to maintain their religious beliefs without adhering to the letter of the law. Jews faced special challenges in the Delta regarding their burial practices. Local Protestant funeral directors knew little about Jewish ritual, and usually one or two Sisterhood and Brotherhood members constituted the *hevra kaddisha*, or burial society, that stepped in on such occasions. Abe Barkovitz drove seventy miles from Hayti, Missouri, to attend Temple Israel in Blytheville each week and depended on a visiting student rabbi to instruct him in preparing a Jewish body for burial. "The Rabbi did a prayer, 'Excuse us, Oh Lord, for we know not what we do,' " said Barkovitz. "And then we would proceed with the directions that he had brought with him."[35]

Congregants frequently led services because hiring a permanent rabbi or even securing the services of a visiting student rabbi from Hebrew Union College in Cincinnati was too expensive for small Jewish communities. Assuming this responsibility forced congregants to assume leadership roles and become personally active in Judaism in ways they would never have done had there been a rabbi to lead the congregation. "I think some of us come more since we don't have a rabbi," said Marion Metzger about attendance at Vicksburg's Congregation Anshe Chesed. "I didn't mean that because we didn't like the rabbi, because whoever happens to be saying the service, we all try to support them."[36] In Vicksburg a rabbi is hired only for the High Holy Days season and stays in a local bed and breakfast for that twelve-day period. During other times of the year, three or four congregants take turns reading the services. In a modernization of the worship service, an organist and her daughter from the Baptist church provide the music.

(American Reform congregations have had organs since 1841 at Congregation Beth Elohim in Charleston.) Thelma Havard and Sophie Smith, African American housekeepers who work for Anshe Chesed, unlock the temple, put out the books, the wine, the candles, and prepare the sanctuary for the Sabbath.

Isolated Jews in small Delta communities made lengthy road trips to the nearest synagogue for services and religious school, to purchase Jewish foods, and to visit Jewish family and friends. Traveling thirty to seventy miles each week was a common fact of life for Delta Jews. "We grew up, and my parents grew up, traveling somewhere to go to Sunday school or temple," said Leanne Lipnick Silverblatt of Indianola. "You know you have to do it, and you just do it." Food and visiting eased the burden of such trips, which could mean enjoying bagels and lox, strudel, and pound cake with family or, just as likely, stopping at the Dixie Pig, a favorite barbecue restaurant in Blytheville, or a café like the Resthaven in Clarksdale, owned by the Chamouns, a Lebanese family known regionally for their kibbe, stuffed grape leaves, and baklava. "We do not ride on the High Holiday, so our family, as well as a number of other families from small Delta towns, would spend the High Holy Days in Greenwood with our relatives," says Ann Klumok Bennett, who grew up in Moorhead. With Jewish food supplies brought in from Memphis and Birmingham, "meals were very festive with many family members and close friends participating."[37]

Obtaining Jewish food supplies in the Delta was one of the biggest challenges of being far from a center of Jewish population. Jewish women in the Delta never traveled without an ice cooler in the trunk of their cars to keep their foods fresh. No traveler went to Jackson, Memphis, St. Louis, Birmingham, New Orleans, and especially to New York, without promising to return with bagels, lox, corned beef, and dark loaves of pumpernickel. Women charged relatives and friends traveling outside the region with this task, and returning empty-handed required a good explanation. Cecile Gudelsky remembered her grandfather bringing Jewish foods with him on the train when he returned from St. Louis to Paragould, Arkansas. He sat with friends on the way to St. Louis, but on the return trip he sat alone because the smell of salami and pastrami was too much for his companions.[38]

Delicatessens and kosher butcher shops like the Old Tyme Delicatessen in Jackson and Rosen's, Segal's, and Halpern's in Memphis were known in the Delta by word of mouth as well as through advertisements in Jewish newspapers like the *Hebrew Watchman* and the *Jewish Spectator*. Advertisements guaranteeing "prompt attention given out-of-town orders" encouraged Delta Jews to mail-order foods that would be delivered by bus and train. Gilbert Halpern, the son of Thelma and Louis Halpern, who opened their Memphis delicatessen in 1946, remembered their busy mail-order business at Passover time.[39] After the restaurant closed at the end of the day, the building turned into a packing business at night. Gilbert personally delivered food supplies to families in the Delta and Arkansas, and he remembered the warm reunions when those same families visited his deli in Memphis.

Preparing for Passover posed challenging logistics for Jewish homemakers in the Delta. In Shaw, Bess Seligman did the trips to Memphis. "I was the 'delivery boy'," said Seligman. "I went to Memphis and took everybody's order and brought back the meat and the perishable foods. The matzah, the flour, the potato starch, and all that, we would ship by bus or by train, because we couldn't put it all in a car." In Moorhead, Fannie Klumok ordered her kosher meats and other Passover foods from Rosen's Delicatessen in Memphis. The primary Passover order arrived several days before Passover.

"Each day as she assessed our needs," said Sylvia Klumok Goodman, mother "called Rosen's and they would send us the current day's request by Greyhound bus." Fannie Klumok hired two African American men and three additional African American women to help with the Passover cleaning and preparations. "Nonkosher and non-Passover foods were either given to the black workers or stored at a gentile's house until after Passover," said Sylvia.[40] Passover was the one week a year when the Klumok family observed the dietary laws of kashrut.

Because she worked at the family's store in Indianola and could not be home to oversee the kosher-keeping skills of her domestic workers, Fannie Klumok outlawed any dairy products in the home for that week. Relying on African American cooks to prepare daily southern fare was acceptable to her, but their involvement in Jewish tradition and dietary laws was another matter. Race and class shaped the Klumoks' daily decisions, including preparations for a southern Jewish Passover. "We had kosher meats and no dairy on Passover as my mother was afraid that our cook and maid wouldn't be able to keep the dishes separate. I never knew that you could eat matzah with butter until I went to college and learned that dairy wasn't prohibited during Passover."[41] Fifty Jews and Gentile friends attended the Klumok seder, for which Fannie annually prepared three hundred pieces of gefilte fish made from a mixture of locally available carp and buffalo fish.

In Chatham, Mississippi, Rabbi Fred Davidow described his Lithuanian great-grandmother Sarah Stein and her oldest child, Fannie Stein Schwartz, his maternal grandmother, as an "island of kashrut" in the Delta. Stein and Schwartz kept kosher themselves but did not prepare kosher food for their families. Davidow explained that the problem of obtaining meat for Stein was "solved not by importing kosher meat, but by importing *shohets* (Jewish butchers)." Her husband, V. A. Stein, made sure his wife could keep kosher by paying for a shohet's passage from Europe to Mississippi. When it became difficult to keep shohets in Chatham, V. A. Stein went to Cincinnati to confer with an Orthodox rabbi about his dilemma. The rabbi gave him permission to slaughter poultry only for his wife, and he returned home with a *halif* (a kosher butcher's knife) and the rabbi's instructions on kosher slaughtering.[42]

Sarah Stein and her daughter Fannie created their own interpretation of kashrut. Allowing no pork or shellfish in the home, observing kashrut during the week of Passover, and ignoring treyf eaten outside the home enabled the Stein women to make peace with their religion while accepting the fact that they lived in a Gentile world of catfish and pork barbecue.

In Ruleville, Flo Silverblatt Selber's mother, Eva, tried to keep kosher by salting the family's meat to remove any traces of blood and keeping a kosher home during the week of Passover.[43] Eva Silverblatt taught her African American cook Georgia Lee to make strudel, blintzes, kreplach (noodle dumplings filled with meat or vegetables), stuffed cabbage, mandelbread (sweet bread), and matzah kugel. Lee and Silverblatt also prepared turnip greens, black-eyed peas (flavored with kosher salami), and fried chicken for the family's Sunday noon dinner. Eva Silverblatt drew the line on certain nonkosher southern dishes like ham and bacon, and other foods associated with poor whites and blacks, such as biscuits with white gravy flavored with bacon fat. These foods were forbidden according to Eva's personal rules of kashrut.

Fannie Klumok maintained a similar system of kashrut at her home in Moorhead. Evalina Smith, her African American cook, prepared two batches of vegetables at every meal, one without pork for Fannie and one with pork for her husband,

Sol, and their four children. Kosher pots and pans and glass plates were set aside for visiting Orthodox salesmen and the rabbi. When Fannie's father visited, the pork mysteriously disappeared from everybody's food.[44]

Evalina Smith prepared the Sunday noon meal at the Klumok home, at which there might be ten to twenty-five guests, including salesmen and visiting relatives. Her menu illustrates the family's complete acceptance and celebration of Delta cuisine. Smith made homemade rolls to go with the shrimp cocktail, followed by a green salad, fried and broiled chicken, roast beef, tomato sandwiches, butter beans, fried corn or corn on the cob (sometimes both), crowder peas, lady peas, mashed potatoes, sweet potatoes with marshmallows, and asparagus or cauliflower with béchamel sauce and melted cheddar cheese. She also served two desserts, such as rice pudding, homemade ice cream, strawberry shortcake, and fresh watermelon when it was in season.[45]

Sol Klumok picked up Smith at 6:00 a.m. and drove her home each night at about 8:30. She received fourteen dollars a week in salary. Sylvia Klumok explained the system of "deputy motherhood" that occurred each day at the Klumok home. Evalina Smith "ordered us around and was the boss of the house while my mother was working at our store in Indianola," said Sylvia. "She always had black gospel music or blues playing in the kitchen. Sometimes she'd grab my hand, and we'd dance together."[46]

Pearl and William "Bill" Borowsky of Manila, Arkansas, who had immigrated from Russia and Poland, were among a small number of families in the Delta who kept an absolutely kosher home with no allowances for family preferences or for the difficulties of obtaining kosher supplies. The Borowskys' daily food "would have to be described as Jewish," said their daughter Fruma Borowsky Kane. "There was very little southern influence." In the 1920s Bill Borowsky came to visit an uncle who owned, the Tiger-Levine Store, a local dry goods business in Manila.[47] Bill met Pearl while traveling through Oklahoma City as a young salesman. They married, returned to Manila, and eventually bought the business, which they operated for the rest of their lives.

As observant Jews, the Borowskys followed Orthodox practices as much as possible given the restrictions of life in Manila, where even a *minyan* (the ten men necessary for worship according to Jewish law) was impossible. The family's kosher meat and other food supplies were delivered from Memphis, St. Louis, and Chicago. Founding members of Temple Israel in Blytheville in the late 1940s, the Borowskys were active participants in the Sisterhood and Brotherhood. Huddy Cohen of Blytheville recalled a "close call" with Pearl that illustrated her commitment to Jewish law. After driving together to the funeral of an old friend in Helena, Cohen realized that they might not make it back to Manila before the Sabbath began at sunset. "Won't God forgive you if we're just a few minutes late?" asked Cohen. "After all, we were doing a mitzvah." "No, I have to be home," replied Borowsky. "That's the law."[48] They arrived just in time for Pearl to light her Sabbath candles.

"Mother cooked from her head and her heart," said Fruma Kane.[49] She was known for elegant kosher holiday meals that she prepared at home, since the family did not travel on the Sabbath and on other holidays. Pearl prepared all her family's meals, including traditional European delicacies such as sweet and sour tongue, candied fruit peel (which required seven days of preparation), and lighter-than-air sponge cakes and angel food cakes. She allowed her African American housekeeper to assist only with washing and chopping vegetables so that kashrut was never breached. Although both shared experiences of

marginalization, African American and Jewish women were not equal players. Judaism did nothing to erase the long-standing racial division between white and black women, and at times, particularly during the Jewish holidays and concerning matters of kashrut, Judaism reinforced the division.

In less observant southern Jewish homes, Jewish women cooked the family's meals instead of hiring African American cooks due to cost, personal preference, or sometimes regional experience. In my home in Blytheville, a division of labor in the kitchen existed that was based on state of origin. My mother, Huddy Horowitz Cohen, a native of Connecticut, prepared Jewish holiday dishes and the family's daily meals, which rarely featured anything southern because of her Connecticut upbringing. "I thought it was my job to do the cooking," says Cohen. "I was at home, and could handle it, but I did need help with the cleaning."[50] Cohen left one aspect of cooking—southern food—to "an expert," and that expert was Richie Lee King, an African American housekeeper born in Arkansas who worked for my family from 1955 to the early 1980s. King did the household cleaning, and on special occasions she prepared southern specialties like fried chicken, cornbread, vegetable stew, and sweet potato pie and also helped serve at the family's annual Rosh Hashanah and Yom Kippur dinners.

Alfred and Rebecca Fendler, natives of Krakow, Poland, came to Manila in 1910 and opened a cleaning and pressing business. "They could not keep kosher in a town like Manila, but they did their best," said Oscar Fendler, their son, who practiced law in Blytheville for over sixty years. "We never had any pork in our home during all of the time Dad and Mother lived." Rebecca Fendler slaughtered her own chickens, salted beef that she bought from the local butcher, and prepared European-inspired dishes such as gedempte (well-stewed) meat, goulash, tongue, roast goose, liver, blintzes, knish, latkes (potato or matzah meal pancakes), and borscht. Unlike Pearl Borowsky, Rebecca Fendler included southern foods in the family's diet, foods such as locally caught perch and crappie, fried chicken, homemade fruit preserves, but no catfish. "That food was not considered proper," said Oscar Fendler.[51] Catfish was treyf and before it was farm-raised was considered a "trash" fish eaten primarily by African Americans.

As Rebecca Fendler's decision about catfish reveals, the foods Jews chose to eat positioned them in Delta society, and these choices were not limited to the broader categories of "southern" and "Jewish." There were subcategories. Delta Jews could eat southern food, but it was important to eat only those foods associated with their own race and class, including foods prepared by African American cooks, who understood what was appropriate fare in a white home. Fried chicken was appropriate, chitterlings ("chitlins") were not.

A similar hierarchy existed for the Jewish foods a Delta Jewish woman would serve to her family and her gentile guests. Foods associated with higher class, German-Jewish tastes—roast chicken, tortes, sponge cakes, and kuchens—were acceptable to serve for family and Gentile company. Heavier foods of eastern European cuisine—kugels, kiskha, tzimmes, and cholents—were more questionable. Some Delta Jews avoided foods associated with Jews from the *shtetl*, the small villages of eastern Europe. Although outwardly accepted by the white society around them, Delta Jews were mindful of their "otherness" and vigilantly strove to maintain status in the community, even at the dinner table.

Because of their small numbers and the lengthy drives between home and synagogue, Jews in the Delta often gathered together at holiday time for community seders, Rosh Hashanah dinners, Yom Kippur break-the-fasts, and Hanukkah

latke parties. Depending on the number of participants, these events might be held in private homes, at the synagogue, in a Jewish social club like Vicksburg's B.B. (B'nai B'rith) Literary Association, the Olympia Club in Greenville, or at a local restaurant. Jennifer Stollman observes that the annual Sisterhood-sponsored "deli lunch," still held in Greenville, not only raises money for the synagogue and brings members together but helps to "demystify" the Jewish community to the hundreds of Gentiles who come to purchase cornbeef sandwiches.[52]

The minutes of Jewish women's groups in the Delta reveal the importance of these food events and social activities for small congregations. Throughout the 1950s the Annie Weinberg chapter of B'nai B'rith women in Blytheville sponsored a constant round of congregational pot luck suppers, community seders, Oneg Shabbats, Hanukkah suppers, dinners for the rabbi, and meals associated with Sisterhood and Brotherhood meetings. Jewish women participated in the chapter's activities from Blytheville, a center for buying and selling cotton, as well as the nearby Arkansas communities of Osceola, Manila, Luxora, and Joiner, and Hayti and Caruthersville in Missouri. The organizational minutes' frequent mention of the "kitchen fund" and needed kitchen supplies like refrigerators and steam tables, donations of serving dishes, and redecoration of the recreation hall suggests that significant money and time were dedicated to these activities.[53]

The B'nai B'rith Literary Association, or "B.B. Club," as it was known in Vicksburg, was organized in the 1880s by the Jewish community. Architect William Stanton designed its elegant building standing at the corner of Clay and Walnut Streets, which was completed in 1887. The club included a banquet hall for five hundred guests, which was frequently filled to capacity for balls, banquets, lectures, and wedding receptions. In the 1890s the club's eighty members reflected the size and affluence of Vicksburg's Jewish community at that time. "The club and club house is known all over this part of the Mississippi valley as the center of the most lavish, yet refined, hospitality, while its cuisine under the direction of its accomplished caterers, past and present, is no less celebrated," wrote the authors of *Picturesque Vicksburg* in 1891.[54] Local Jewish grocers and butchers like D. J. Shlenker, Sol Fried, and A.A. Ehrman supplied the club's caterers with food and drink for all occasions. Due to the decline in congregational membership, the building was sold in 1967 to the Vicksburg Police Department. Recently, this historic property was purchased by Laurence Leyens, the mayor of Vicksburg and a descendant of an early Vicksburg Jewish family. Leyens has restored the B.B. Club to its 1890s grandeur, and it is once again a popular location for community social functions.

Living in small communities where there were few other Jews—in some cases only a single family—Delta Jews developed networks to sustain their social and spiritual worlds. From formal dances at the B.B. Club in Vicksburg in the 1950s where Jewish youth were entertained by the music of the Red Tops, a popular African American band, to monthly dinner clubs and Sunday afternoon family visits, the dispersed Delta Jewish community gathered for friendship and courtship. The active calendar of Jewish social life reflected the lifestyle of the Gentile community in the Delta where both blacks and whites are known for their hospitality, high standards of entertaining, and love of a good time. Delta people have a sense of space and distance that distinguishes them from people in the city, and they willingly travel an hour or more on lonely Delta roads to attend a good party. Harry Ball describes the social life of Washington County in the Delta from the 1880s to the early decades of the twentieth century in his diary. Ball recalls a "full-dress ball" at the Jewish social club in Greenville, which was attended by two hundred people, "the

largest public ball we have ever had."[55] Decades later during the Civil Rights movement of the 1960s, such hospitality was not extended to Jewish "freedom riders" from the Midwest and Northeast who threatened the Jewish community's tenuous position in the racially charged, violent state of Mississippi.

Folklorist Carolyn Lipson-Walker argues that the experience of Jews in the South was defined by mobility, and larger towns like Greenville, Vicksburg, Clarksdale, and Blytheville served as "magnets" for Jews who lived in the smaller towns. Lipson-Walker suggests that unlike Jewish ghettos and neighborhoods in the Northeast, in the South there is a "temporary recurring community" that Jews re-create each time they gather for a social function, a meal, or holiday worship. Today Delta Jews view their parents' generation in the 1940s and 1950s and their ancestors as models of Delta Jewish sociability. "People from Clarksdale, Greenwood, Greenville, Vicksburg, they would get together once or twice a month for dances and so forth," said Earl Solomon Jr. "And they still talk about all the parties they used to have." Leanne Lipnick Silverblatt of Indianola remembers the Young People's Jewish League, or the YPJL as it was called by her parents, which sponsored a monthly supper club. "They met every month or so to eat—Jewish couples from all over the Delta belonged," said Silverblatt.[56]

The biggest Jewish social event in the Delta now takes place each year in October. Begun fifteen years ago as a fundraiser for the Henry S. Jacobs Camp in Utica, the Delta Jewish Open Golf Tournament draws over one hundred participants from communities throughout the Delta and from other parts of Mississippi. "The fact that they're so scattered, there's a real bond among them," said Macy Hart, former director of Jacobs Camp. "Here's a chance for them to come together, have some fun, do something for a good cause that they created to begin with." After the sun has set and the Sabbath is officially concluded, the festivities begin with a Saturday evening social hour at Greenville's Hebrew Union Temple and hors d'oeuvres prepared by the congregation. Fred Miller, whose family were long-time members of a small synagogue in Rolling Fork that has now closed, operates the grill for the dinner. The tournament begins Sunday morning with a blessing, "*lahdlik ner shel* golf balls," said by congregant Barry Piltz. (The Hebrew phrase means "to light the candle," or in this version "to light [or drive] the golf balls.") After the blessing, Piltz blows the tournament's opening *shofar* (ram's horn).[57] More food and partying follow a full day of golfing and visiting.

As Jewish population has diminished in the Delta, social functions have become even more important in sustaining Jewish life in the region. Delta Jews were hit particularly hard by the decline in the overall population of the Delta. This decline is associated with the arrival of the boll weevil in the early 1900s, the mechanization of cotton picking in the 1940s, the "great migration" of black laborers out of the Delta to industrial cities like Chicago, and the movement after World War II of veterans and young adults from their rural communities to cities like Memphis and Chicago. These changes, accompanied by the decline of downtown business districts and the growth of regional discount stores like Wal-Mart, pushed third and fourth generation Jews out of their small mercantile businesses in the Delta and into professions located in cities.

In the 1930s there were over two dozen Jewish-owned businesses in Blytheville.[58] Today there are no Jewish-owned businesses downtown. Temple Israel held its last service in the fall of 2004. Congregants donated the sanctuary's stained glass windows and a Torah to Congregation Beth Sholom in Memphis, a vital synagogue of 325 families, where several Blytheville residents now worship.

Jews who remain in Delta communities—older adults and sons and daughters who work with family businesses and farms—are bound together by kinship and the challenge of maintaining Judaism in their region. While their Judaism is different from that of Jews outside the South, for Delta Jews it is the "real thing" despite their different ritual practices, accents, and food traditions. Judaism in the South is not defined by "faith, theological principles, or affiliation only," says Carolyn Lipson-Walker, who argues that in the South "the criterion for who and what is Jewish is more visceral than rational." Lipson-Walker believes that southern Judaism is a mix of "loyalties, historical memories, beliefs, and cultural expressions," and chief among those cultural expressions is food.[59] Although Delta Jews share the same religious heritage as urban Jews in the Northeast, they are bound to their gentile Delta neighbors by fried chicken, cornbread, and field peas.

Eli Evans, the unofficial dean of the Jewish South, grew up in Durham, North Carolina, where his father, E. J. "Mutt" Evans was the first Jewish mayor in the 1950s. Eli Evans became the first Jewish student-body president at the University of North Carolina at Chapel Hill in 1958. In his personal biography of growing up Jewish in the South, *The Provincials*, Evans writes about the complicated negotiation of regional and religious identity:

> I am not certain what it means to be both a Jew and a Southerner—to have inherited the Jewish longing for a homeland while being raised with the Southerner's sense of home. The conflict is deep in me—the Jew's involvement in history, his deep roots in the drama of man's struggle to understand deity and creation. But I respond to the Southerner's commitment to place, his loyalty to I the land, to his own tortured history, to the strange bond beyond color that Southern blacks and whites discover when they come to know one another.[60]

Evans's words eloquently capture the spirit of Jewish life in the Delta. Delta

Jews value their own expression of religion and ethnicity, yet their world is defined by the region's rules of race, class, intermarriage, strong family ties, social activities, deep sense of place, intimate ties to Gentile white and black neighbors, and the agricultural economy. They are also defined by a sense of Jewish self-sufficiency and by the inventiveness required to obtain Jewish foods, supplies, and educational and cultural resources for their Jewish community. The rich cultural world of the Delta that is expressed in the region's music and food is an equally important part of the region's Jewish life. Delta Jews are southerners, and this allegiance to region profoundly influences their Judaism. "I love the South. I can't imagine living anywhere besides the South," said Fred Miller of Anguilla. "We believe in our Jewish heritage for sure, but I think that there's no one who was born in this area who doesn't feel a real kinship with the South—and with the history of the South. Right or wrong, we are and were part of it."[61]

ACKNOWLEDGEMENT

I would like to thank Dr. Stuart Rockoff, director, history department, Goldring/Woldenberg Institute of Southern Jewish Life, Jackson, Mississippi, for his review of earlier versions of this article. I am indebted to Mike DeWitt for his interviews of Jewish southerners in the Delta.

NOTES

1. Interview with Stuart Rockoff, director, history department, Goldring/Woldenberg Institute of Southern Jewish Life, Jackson, Mississippi, 3 September 2003.
2. See David Goldfield's theory of social "place" in "A Sense of Place: Jews, Blacks, and White Gentiles in the American South," *Southern Cultures* 3.1(1997): 58.
3. Craig Claiborne, *A Feast Made for Laughter* (Double Day and Co., Inc., 1982) 47, 31.
4. David W Blight, "Southerners Don't Lie; They Just Remember Big," *Where These Memories*

Grow: History, Memory, and Southern Identity, ed. W. Fitzhugh Brundage (University of North Carolina Press, 2000) 348–49; W. Fitzhugh Brundage, "No Deed but Memory," *Ibid.*, 2, 7.
5. Joan Nathan, *Jewish Cooking in America* (Alfred A. Knopf, 1994), 3, 4.
6. See Frederik Barth, *Ethnic Groups and Boundaries: The Social Organisation of Culture Difference* (1969; Waveland Press, Inc., 1998), 15; Mary Douglas, *Implicit Meanings: Selected Essays in Anthropology* (1975; Routledge, 1999), 231–51; Claude Levi-Strauss, "The Culinary Triangle," *Food and Culture: A Reader*, ed. Carole Counihan and Penny Van Esterik (Routledge, 1997), 28; Sidney W. Mintz, *Tasting Food, Tasting Freedom: Excursions into Eating, Culture, and the Past* (Beacon Press, 1996), 7. See also Susan Kalcik, "Ethnic Foodways in America: Symbol and the Performance of Identity," *Ethnic and Regional Foodways in the United States: The Performance of Group Identity*, ed. Linda Keller Brown and Kay Mussell (University of Tennessee Press, 1984), 37–65.
7. Blu Greenberg, *How to Run a Traditional Jewish Household* (Simon and Schuster, 1983), 95.
8. Jenna Weissman Joselit, *The Wonders of America: Reinventing Jewish Culture, 1880–1950* (Hill and Wang, 1994), 171, 293–94; see also Barbara Kirshenblatt-Gimblett's article, "Kitchen Judaism," *Getting Comfortable in New York: The American Jewish Home, 1880–1950*, ed. Susan Braunstein and Jenna Weissman Joselit (The Jewish Museum, 1990), 77, for a discussion of the term "kitchen Judaism."
9. Sylvia Klumok Goodman, email to the author, 4 June 2001.
10. "Kosher-style," explains historian Jenna Joselit, was an American invention that allowed Jews to ignore the rigor of the Jewish dietary laws by choosing which rules of kashrut they wished to observe and which they chose to ignore. Jenna Weissman Joselit, *The Wonders of America*, 173–74.
11. Betty G. Lamensdorf, interview with Marcie C. Ferris, Cary, Mississippi, 28 June 2001; Betty G. Lamensdorf, telephone conversation with Marcie C. Ferris, Cary, Mississippi, 21 October 2003.
12. Ben Lamensdorf, Cary, Mississippi, *Delta Jews*, dir. Mike DeWitt, 1999, Mike DeWitt Productions.
13. Betty G. Lamensdorf, interview.
14. Cliff Taulbert, *Delta Jem*, dir. DeWitt.
15. Leonard Rogoff, "Is the Jew White? The Racial Place of the Southern Jew," *American Jewish History* 85.3 (September 1997): 195; see also, Jennifer Stollman, "Building up a House of Israel in a 'Land of Christ': Jewish Women in the

Antebellum and Civil War South," (Ph.D. diss., Michigan State University, 2001), 275. Jack Nelson, *Terror in the Night. The Klan's Campaign Against the Jews* (Simon and Schuster, 1993), 41.

16. Ann G. Gerache, interview with Marcie C. Ferris, Vicksburg, Mississippi, 27 June 2001; see Jacqueline Jones, *Tabor of Love, Labor of Sorrow: Black Women, Work, and the Family, from Slavery to the Present* (Vintage Books, 1985) 127–30, 325, for a discussion of the daily lives of African American female domestic workers and what she describes as the "double day."

17. Ann G. Gerache, interview.
18. Betty G. Lamensdorf, interview; Hortense Powdermaker, *After Freedom: A Cultural Study in the Deep South* (1939; Atheneum, 1968), 118, 31–32.
19. Ann G. Gerache, interview.
20. Ann G. Gerache, interview.
21. Ann G. Gerache, Vicksburg, Mississippi, Southern Jewish Foodways Survey, 3 October 1998.
22. James C. Cobb, *The Mississippi Delta and the World: The Memoirs of David L. Cohn* (Louisiana State University Press, 1995), xii, 171.
23. Ann G. Gerache, interview.
24. Ibid.
25. Jonathan D. Sarna, *American Judaism: A History* (Yale University Press, 2004), 323; Gertrude Philippsborn, *The History of the Jewish Community of Vicksburg from 1820 to 1968* (Vicksburg, Mississippi, 1969), 56; Ann G. Gerache, interview; Claudia Roden, *The Book of Jewish Food* (Alfred A. Knopf, 1997), 28, 326.
26. David Orlansky, Greenville, Mississippi, *Delta Jews*, dir. DeWitt; Gene Dattel, "Growing Up Jewish and Black in Mississippi," lecture, Southern Jewish Historical Society Annual Conference, Memphis, Tennessee, 1 November 2003.
27. Kenneth Hoffman, "The Jews of Port Gibson, Mississippi," *100th Anniversary Celebration Program*, Gemiluth Chassed Synagogue, 20 October 1991, Museum of the Southern Jewish Experience.
28. "Consecration of the new Temple in Vicksburg, Miss." *The Israelite*, 3 June 1870, 9–10, Vicksburg, Mississippi—Anshe Chesed file, collection of American Jewish Archives, Cincinnati, Ohio.
29. *Ibid.*
30. Letter from Samuel Ullman and Temple B'nai Israel committee to Rabbi A. Norden and his reply, July 1874, Natchez, Mississippi, Temple B'nai Israel Archives, Natchez, Mississippi.
31. Passover Haggadah, 17 April 1992, 1 April 1912, collection of Kathryn L. Wiener, Jackson,

Mississippi; Kathryn L. and Julian Wiener, interview with Marcie C. Ferris, Jackson, Mississippi, 1992, Museum of the Southern Jewish Experience; Kathryn L. Wiener, interview with Marcie C. Ferris, Jackson, Mississippi, 26 June 2001.

32. Joe Erber, Greenwood, Mississippi, *Delta Jews*, dir. DeWitt.
33. Shirley Fleischer Solomon, Shaw, Mississippi, interview with Marcie C. Ferris, 1993, Museum of the Southern Jewish Experience, Jackson, Mississippi.
34. Erber, *Delta Jews*, dir. DeWitt; Harold Hart, interview with Marcie C. Ferris, Eudora, Arkansas, October 1991, Museum of the Southern Jewish Experience, Jackson, Mississippi.
35. Abe Barkovitz, interview with Marcie C. Ferris, Hayti, Missouri, April 1991, Museum of the Southern Jewish Experience, Jackson, Mississippi.
36. Marion Metzger, Vicksburg, Mississippi, *Delta Jews*, dir. DeWitt.
37. Leanne Silverblatt, Indianola, Mississippi, *Delta Jews*, dir. DeWitt; Ann Klumok Bennett, New Orleans, Louisiana, Southern Jewish Foodways Survey, July 2001.
38. Cecile Gudelsky, email to author, 17 July 2001.
39. Segal's Kosher Delicatessen advertisement, *The Hebrew Watchman*, Memphis, Tennessee, 30 March 1928; Halpern's Kosher Snack Shop advertisement, *The Hebrew Watchman*, Memphis, Tennessee, 12 December 1946; Rosen's Kosher Delicatessen; advertisements for Dalsheimer's Brothers, Albert Seessel and Son, *The Jewish Spectator*, Memphis, Tennessee, 1908, 23rd Anniversary Edition, Temple Israel Archives, Memphis, Tennessee; Gilbert Halpern, interview with Marcie C. Ferris, Memphis, Tennessee, 20 December 2001.
40. Bess Seligman, interview with Marcie C. Ferris, Shaw, Mississippi, April 1991, Museum of the Southern Jewish Experience, Jackson, Mississippi; Sylvia Klumok Goodman, email to author, 25 May 2001, 25 August 2003.
41. Ibid.
42. Rabbi Fred Victor Davidow, "Greenville, Mississippi," *Jews in Small Towns: Legends and Legacies*, ed. Howard V. Epstein (VisionBooks International, 1997), 244, 245
43. Florence Silverblatt Selber, Shreveport, Louisiana, Southern Jewish Foodways Survey, October 1998—June 2001.
44. Sylvia Klumok Goodman, email to author, 25 August 2003.
45. Sylvia Klumok Goodman, email to author, 4 June 2001.
46. Ibid.
47. Fruma Borowsky Kane, Port Jefferson, New York, Southern Jewish Foodways Survey,

26 September 1998; Carolyn Grey LeMaster, *A Corner of the Tapestry,: A History of the Jewish Experience in Arkansas, 1820s–1990s* (University of Arkansas Press, 1994), 98.

48. Huddy Horowitz Cohen, interview with Marcie C. Ferris, Memphis, Tennessee, 22 December 2001.

49. Kane, Southern Jewish Foodways Survey.

50. Hulda H. Cohen, telephone conversation with Marcie C. Ferris, 13 October 2003.

51. Oscar Fendler, interview with Marcie C. Ferris, Blytheville, Arkansas, April 1991, Museum of the Southern Jewish Experience, Jackson, Mississippi; Oscar Fendler, Blytheville, Arkansas, Southern Jewish Foodways Survey, 22 September 1998.

52. Jennifer Stollman, "We're Still Here: Delta Jewish Women in the Twentieth Century," lecture, Southern Jewish Historical Society Annual Conference, 1 November 2003, Memphis, Tennessee.

53. Temple Israel Sisterhood minutes, Blytheville, Arkansas, 12 October 1955, 11 March 1956, 26 August 1956, 23 September 1956, 11 November 1956, 10 March 1957, Box 418, Collection of American Jewish Archives, Cincinnati, Ohio; "Temple Israel Fiftieth Anniversary Pamphlet and History," 11 May 1997, Blytheville, Arkansas, collection of author; LeMaster, *Corner of the Tapestry*, 255.

54. H. P. Chapman and J. F. Batde, *Picturesque Vicksburg* (Vicksburg Printing and Publishing Co., 1891), 105–107, manuscript collection 10, American Jewish Archives, Cincinnati, Ohio.

55. James C. Cobb, *The Most Southern Place on Earth: The Mississippi Delta and the Roots of Regional Identity* (Oxford University Press, 1992), 138.

56. Carolyn Lipson-Walker, "Shalom Y'all: The Folklore and Culture of Southern Jews" (Ph.D. diss., Indiana University, 1986), 99, 98; Earl Solomon Jr., Greenville, Mississippi, *Delta Jews*, dir. DeWitt, 1999; Leanne Lipnick Silverblatt, Indianola, Mississippi, Southern Jewish Foodways Survey, November 1998.

57. "Delta Jewish Open Scheduled for October 7," *Deep South Jewish Voice* (August 2001), 3; Macy B. Hart, Jackson, Mississippi, *Delta Jews*, dir. DeWitt, 1999.

58. LeMaster, *A Corner of the Tapestry*, 255.

59. Lipson-Walker, "Shalom Y'all," 43–44.

60. Eli N. Evans, *The Provincials: A Personal History of Jews in the South* (1973; Free Press Paperbacks, 1997), 22.

61. Fred Miller, Anguilla, Mississippi, *Delta Jews*, dir. DeWitt.

31

Yoruba-Nigerians, Cosmopolitan Food Cultures and Identity Practices on a London Market[1]

Julie Botticello

INTRODUCTION

"Have a look, have a look" beckons Mrs Williams[2], a Yoruba vendor who trades in household goods of toilet paper, soap and laundry detergent, from the warm sanctuary at the back of her semi-enclosed wooden market stall. Next to her, David, a Jewish-English shoe vendor, who had his eye poked out by the mobile phone aerial of a disgruntled customer a few years back, shouts and curses from the back of his stall at the hoards in front, who, ignoring his venom, rummage and jostle for the latest bargain. Across from him, another English vendor, Tom, sits quietly at the back of his barrow, reading the *Sun*, a daily tabloid, waiting patiently for battery replacement requests or buyers of new watches to approach and ask for his attention. Nearby, a family of Turkish Kurds run a lively stall, offering apples, oranges, pears, and bananas for better prices per kilo than the more established English vendors situated at the entrance to the market. Across from them, another Yoruba vendor, Jo, standing at the front of her barrow, is engaged in a hard sell of her herbs and bottled tonics to two women. She is detailing how they are to take her products and what benefits these will bring, while a small crowd of market passers-through hovers loosely nearby to listen and consider if these products will suit their own health care needs. Next to her, an English couple, whose stall space is so crammed with rails of hanging clothes – bras, t-shirts, skirts and trousers – that they have to sit on chairs at the front, their abundance of goods leaving them no space inside or behind. Not far off, a Jamaican vendor of tropical fruits and vegetables chops up a melon, tempting customers with a sweet taster of his Caribbean garden selection. Wafting over from slightly further away, High Life, a pan West African musical genre which fuses African roots music with Western music, blares out from a television monitor playing sensual and sensational Video Compact Discs (VCDs). Aurally and visually these sounds entice customers to stop and look at this collection of music and films imported from Nigeria. They mingle with Christian hymns billowing forth from a Charismatic Christian bible, book and tambourine stall; the Yoruba Pastor of the Pentecostal church it supports sometimes present to sell his goods and his faith to anyone expressing interest.

Such is one picture of Valley Market, a street market in London situated south of the river Thames, which caters to a diverse and relatively low-income local population. The sounds and smells of different wares jumbling and overlapping in this public space are representative of the variety of peoples and cultures whose lives intersect both in the market and in London, more generally. I have written previously (Botticello, 2007) about this market and the way in which the area at the back of the stall can be understood as home-like. This happens because the stall serves as a physical interface between its front and back areas, suggesting public and private spaces, respectively, and the relative depths of connection between the stallholders and their customers. In this chapter, I focus on the public space of interaction, that which is situated out in front of the stalls. Here I will consider how the identities of persons of different nationalities and ethnicities who come together in this street market through their common interest in particular foods, are both conflated and separated, depending on context of sale and the interests of the vendors or customers at a given time. Specifically, it will focus on the transactions occurring at the stall of a Yoruba woman, named Jo, who sells health granting herb-based tonics. My work builds on Keeler's research amongst Kurdish immigrants in Hackney, East London and their food cultures, where she focused not on the actual compositions of their foodstuffs, but on how these are "perceived and utilized through social interactions within [the] processes of identity construction and negotiation" (Keeler, 2007: 167). Similarly, the concern in this chapter centers on the negotiation of complex cosmopolitan identities arising in the discourses and practices surrounding particular herbal health foods, as these occur in the public space of the street market.

Before continuing with the description and analysis of this intercultural and transnational encounter of both peoples and foods, the scene needs to be set; for one important aspect of this is the specificity of the site, not just of the market, but more generally of London, the capital city of the United Kingdom (hereafter UK) and former center of the British colonial empire. The placing of London (Eade, 2000) is an important feature of this cosmopolitan interchange. The relocation of diverse peoples from the peripheries of this former empire into its capital city precipitates these new encounters in London's public places. An understanding of London as a particular place geographically and historically helps to make sense of the expansion and contraction of

personal and social identities taking place there.

LONDON, FROM HUB OF COLONIAL EMPIRE TO COSMOPOLITAN GLOBAL CITY

London holds a unique place in Britain. Although this capital is located in England, its significance extends to all four nations that comprise the UK. It also affects members of its former colonies, in which the site of remote rule has transformed into a destination for global migration. Its significance in the past as the center of Imperial Britain is attested to by "its wealth of heritage monuments and institutions, and its international links" (Young, 2002: 6). London First, an agency commissioned to report on the necessity of redevelopment of London's Heathrow Airport, states that "the strength and future of London's economy, and the United Kingdom's, depends on the capital's success as a world city. London's international links have always been one of its greatest assets" (anon., 2008: 4). These international links have a long historical presence, with traceable waves of migrations coming in from Ireland and Europe for the past 200 years (Eade, 2004: 13). Amongst these earlier migrations were also people from Africa and the African diasporas, whose presence in Britain can be traced back to Roman times; indeed, to "before the English came" (Fryer, 1984: 1).

The forced migrations of the transatlantic slave trade in the 16th century escalated the frequency and number of African peoples in Britain. Post slavery, labour migrations of Africans and Caribbeans into Britain started in the early 19th century. According to Fraser, from the end of the 19th century to the late 1940s many of the Africans born and educated in London were occupying elevated positions in society as doctors, business professionals, ministers and students (Fraser, 1993: 53). These migrations were not as significant numerically as those taking place in the 20th century, from 1948 onwards, when a new wave of Caribbeans and Africans came to London, the former to work and the latter to study (Fraser, 1993: 57). Eade notes that the demise of Empire has been to the advantage of its capital city. He further states that the black and Asian workers arriving into London post-independence "have played a major part in creating London's multicultural society" (Eade, 2000: 2). These migrations show the "long term trajectory" (Grillo and Mazzucato, 2008: 178) of Africans and Caribbeans in London and their ongoing significance in its development. Migrations from the peripheries of Empire were encouraged, to maintain London as a city of global economic importance, yet through the diverse peopling of the city and their various "ethnicities, subcultures, alternative cosmopolitanisms, representations of center and periphery," the city has undergone not only economic restructuring, but also restructuring on the nature of "culture and identity" (King, 1990: 150). In becoming a world city of central importance post-Empire, London has itself been transformed into a space where many representatives of the globe meet and intersect.

London remains a palimpsest of migratory traces. As London cannot be defined as singular or coherent, neither can its people. The "multiplicity and ambiguity" (Eade, 2000: 6) of London's inhabitants is something which arises not only between different groups, but also within them. The different communities associated specifically with the south London street market, as noted in the introductory description, of English, Turkish, Caribbean, and Nigerian descent, can be refined further in some cases into Jewish, Kurdish, Jamaican, and Yoruba, expressing shades of difference glossed through the former generalizations. Because of this, the market is a local place and a transnational forum, as well as a space in which finer shades of

difference are articulated. As Keeler notes, "in a cosmopolitan context such as London [. . .] we cannot conceive of a simple dichotomy of host/migrant cultures, but must take into consideration interactions across and within minority groups as well as the internal diversity of migrant populations and the often subversive manifestations of overarching power relations that exist within supposedly homogeneous 'groups' " (Keeler, 2007: 168). In the case discussed here, of the health granting food products sold in a south London street market and their primary uses, by African and Caribbean peoples (though not exclusively), the generality and specificity of local, racial, national, ethnic and gendered identities impinge on our understanding of how and why particular products may or may not suit them. As will be seen, depending on particular contexts, identification shifts between different kinds of association.

AN INTRODUCTION TO THE FIELD SITE AND VALLEY MARKET

Given that different migrations come in waves, and that settlement does not necessarily displace the existing populations, settlement areas in London do not become absolute enclaves for particular ethnicities, but remain a mix of people from different races, ethnicities, nationalities and religions, albeit with a distinctive flavor of the dominant group. The area in which I undertook my research, in the London borough of Southwark, remains faithful to this model. A range of people lives there: working-class English, Jamaicans, Western and Eastern Europeans, and more recently, West and East Africans. Whereas the nearby Borough of Lambeth maintains a high concentration of African and Caribbean settlers from the post-independence migrations of the 1950s and 1960s (Eade, 2004: 14; Newman, 2002: 7), the settlement of African peoples in

Southwark is more recent and on the rise. Local census data confirm this, in which the Black African[3] population has more than doubled between the two census years of 1991 and 2001 (McDonnell, 2001: 11), giving Southwark the highest percentage of Black Africans of any London borough. A significant sending country to Britain is Nigeria. Data collected by the UK Home Office from the years 1991 to 2006 show that Nigeria consistently remains one of the top ten sending countries, with Nigerians accounting for roughly 5% of total immigrations during that period.

This increase is reflected in this local area, with Nigerian restaurants, dressmaking studios, churches, barber shops, and nail and hair salons, appearing in increasing numbers. The BBC news website declared that one area of Southwark, due to the influence of Yoruba-Nigerians living there, "looks very [much] like Lagos. [. . .] Over the past 10 years it has been transformed into a Yoruba heartland. Many of the shops are Yoruba owned and you can buy any Nigerian food you want, and it's fresh from a farm near Lagos" (White, 2005: 1). This specificity within diversity is similarly reflected in the local street market. As one of the older markets in London, dating back to the 1700s, Valley Market has changed in keeping with the demographic changes undergoing in the area. A walk through the market will reveal both its influences and its potential customers, with a range of inexpensive essential goods available on the stalls, including fruit and vegetables, clothes and shoes, bedding, towels and kitchenware. These are intermixed with wares intended for more particular ethnic or national groups, such as the VCDs, tonics and exotic fruits mentioned earlier, along with wax print and other cloths, fresh food items like yams and plantains, and dried items such as fish and vegetable powders.

Picking up on the ideas about foods suggested by some of the above examples,

food in migration often brings to the forefront notions of authenticity, particularly with regard to constructions of foods from home as unique, special, and geographically indicative of an area and the people who come from there. There may be particular food items which pertain to one's "own culture" whose real or imagined trajectories become important for providing "minimal reminders of who they are and where they come from" (Parkin, 1999: 313). Taking note of the cosmopolitan contexts of a city like London, however, in which the transnational movements of food-items and people intersect, equally important are the encounters with new food items and the ways in which people situate themselves with respect to the diversity of foodstuffs available. On the street market, encounters with foods from outside one's immediate familiarity shift the discourses away from notions of authenticity and origins, and toward the different positionings people negotiate in response to the increased accessibility of items from the "global supermarket" (Mathews, 2000). As Cook and Crang argue, the "issue becomes not [. . .] the authenticity or accuracy of commodity surfaces, but rather the spatial settings and social itineraries that are established through their usage" (Cook and Crang, 1996: 148). Significant is the social space of the encounter, and how food items are re-constructed in that space as having potential uses for different groups and how people from those various groups, in turn, position themselves in relation to those food items and each other.

From the market sketch related earlier, I will now return to the Yoruba stallholder, Jo, whose vignette opened this essay and whose herbal tonics are said to offer potential health benefits for passersby. I worked on Jo's stall at least once a week for a year, as part of my PhD research on Yoruba-Nigerians in London and their quests for physical, social and spiritual well-being in migration. At first, my involvement at the market was to gain access to diverse populations, in particular the local Yoruba people. I subsequently realized that the street market, and Jo's stall within it, were significant spaces for both intra- and inter-cultural interaction, where people and products from different parts of the world intersected. This essay is concerned with detailing aspects of these interactions from my observations of Jo and how she situates herself and her products to different market publics. I will proceed with two scenarios relating to the health granting herbal tonics she sells, predominantly to Yoruba-Nigerian and Jamaican customers, and the expressions of general and specific collective identities these food items articulate in this public space. The first scenario addresses the palatability of products designed for cleansing one's system to generate better health, while the second scenario concerns an alternative marketing of products designed for increasing virility and libido. The aim of this discussion is to show that varying degrees of similarity and difference in identity are articulated through ideologies of the food's palatability (literal and metaphorical) and the ways in which "foreign" foods can become useful to populations beyond their expected scope.

HERBAL TONICS AND THE (DE) LIMITATIONS OF FORMS

Jo covers the display space of her street market barrow with a white tablecloth, and pegs a blue and white striped tarpaulin to the wooden struts above to protect herself and her goods from the sun and rain. She arranges a selection of Jamaican herbal tonic infusions in long rows on top of the tablecloth, the sealed wine-style bottles clustered together by variety, labels facing outwards towards the customers, with the prices penned on the plastic screw lids in black marker. The names of the products give some indication to

their potential uses: Bitters, Vitality, and Stamina. Other health products, such as packages of flax seed, cartons of soya milk and boxes of redbush tea, are positioned to either side of the bottle rows. Above the products, clipped to the struts, hang handwritten signs made from cardboard sheets, which aim to intrigue the passersby with some information about the products: "Natural herbs for fat burning/weight control, energy, allergies, skin, blood thinner, cholesterol/diabetes, fibroid/fertility, high/low blood pressure, general well being, whatever you need, just ask" and "Weight loss program: detox, burn the fat: repair and re-fuel, keep your weight forever." These signs give information about what Jo's products are—natural herbs—and what they can do—burn fat, reduce blood pressure, blood sugar and cholesterol, and increase energy. The products themselves also give information, in which ingredient labels mark the global reach of their ingredients, and through their packaging, mark them as legitimate products that are commercially produced and distributed.

The stallholder, Jo, is a Yoruba woman who came to England in the early 1990s. A qualified aromatherapist, she has taken to selling herbal tonics for the health care needs of "her people," as she calls them, for she is concerned about the ill-effects on health that come from living in England. Recent medical investigation in Europe has revealed that people of sub-Saharan African descent have a high prevalence of hypertension, Type II diabetes, and obesity (Agyemang et al., 2009), indicating that Jo's concerns are not unfounded. Early on in my research, I asked Jo what would be most important for Nigerians living in London; she answered that food would be first, followed by "medicines," like the herbal tonics she sells. On the importance of food, one informant I met in Nigeria, an Igbo man, who came to Britain in the 1970s to study, tells of his difficulties finding Nigerian foods at that time:

"When I was in the UK in the late 70s and 80s, we did not have a very large Nigerian population, it was very difficult to get Nigerian foodstuff. So we had to go to Indian shops and kind of improvise. Nigerians love what we call pounded yam and now you can get it in powdered form, exported from [Nigeria] to [the UK]. When I was [in the UK back then], you had to put powdered potatoes together with ground rice [instead]. You had to improvise."

Since then, more Nigerian foods have become available, many of which can be bought at Valley Market or in shops nearby, but the freshness is now called into question. One reason Jo cites for the ill health of Africans abroad is that the food is "not fresh enough." Her brother-in-law, Yinka, who sometimes helps on the stall, agrees. He illustrates the significance of fresh food by saying that at home he can just go out into the bush and harvest a vegetable and that it will taste so much nicer than anything in London, in large part due to its absolute freshness. The herbal tonics as food aim, in part, to capture that freshness. Morris, a producer of the Jamaican drinks Jo sells, explains: "What we try and do is convey the effects of the fresh foods into the drinks. So you might not be able to get the freshness from the fruits anymore, but if you were to use the tonics, you get some value from the food preserved in the tonics." In this way, the tonics are able to bridge a gap between fresh food "back home" and what is available in London.

With regard to Jo's second point, on the importance of herbs as medicine, Ogoye-Ndegwa and Aagaard-Hansen note "the use of herbs both as food and medicine is widespread among African communities" (Ogoye-Ndegwa and Aagaard-Hansen, 2006: 323). One of Jo's regular customers, Wumi, who is an elderly Yoruba widow, told me that when she is back in Nigeria, where she lives for nine months of the year, she will go to the market in Lagos to seek advice and fresh herbs when she feels her health to fall below par. When I was preparing to work alone on the market stall one day and I expressed my concern about being able to sell the tonics successfully, Yinka assured me that I would because Nigerians, Ghanaians, and Sierra Leoneans are familiar with the herbs, and will come for them. Taking herbs for well being, as food or as medicine, is not an unusual practice.

The most common request and the one for which most products are sold is to lose fat, particularly among women. The weight issues are often combined with other health problems, such as high blood pressure and cholesterol levels, but it seems to be the main reason women stop at the stall and look at the goods on offer. When working on the market, static in a street of movement, there is ample opportunity to people watch. Jo often comments on women's physiques as they pass by, criticizing the bad ones and complimenting better ones. Skinny is not the order of the day, but well proportioned and round in the right places—though preferably not on the stomach. The women who stop at the stall are generally concerned about their figures as too much fat has settled on their bodies, especially since having children, and they are keen to lose a fair portion of it.

When in London, Wumi, the elderly widow, comes to Valley Market regularly as part of her weekly shopping routine. Intrigued by Jo's "Natural Weight Loss Program" sign, she approaches the stall to know how she can reduce her stomach. After a dialogue about the problem: constipation and bloating, and the solutions: one bottle of Bitters to clean out and one bottle of Vitality to burn fat and give energy, she makes her purchases. Later, she returns to confirm the dosages and usage instructions, and comes back the following week to be advised of her progress and seek further advice on her care.

An Indian woman, and mother to four children, stops at the stall, saying she is concerned about her stomach. She wants to reduce its size, and she is looking to Jo's drinks as a means to do this. Another woman, this time Jamaican, who has more fat on her than the previous woman, comes along and immediately buys two bottles of bitters only. She chats with Jo about being fatter in the stomach post-child birth, with Jo commenting that it is natural to be so. On another occasion, two women, one English and one African, come over together, and Jo spends a long time explaining to them about the products she sells. Jo selects different bottles from their neat rows and brings them forward, putting the bottles together in different combinations as she explains which of the drinks would be best for their needs and how much this would cost. After a lengthy discussion, the two women each buy a bottle of Bitters and a bottle of Vitality, the cocktail for general cleansing and weight reduction. On another occasion, an African woman approaches and says she too wants to lose weight. Jo tells her that she is not fat, but the woman points to and presses on the fat on the top of her back, below her shoulders, and insists that she is. She also comes away with the fat burning Vitality. In spite of being quite slim and well proportioned herself, Jo also complains about the fat she has accumulated around her own waist and her wish to lose it. These are just a few cases where women stop at the stall, physically grab hold of their excess flesh, and plea for its reduction.

There are two main herbal tonics, which can deal with these requests: Bitters, followed by Vitality. The bottled herbs can be classified into two categories: there are those that take away and those that restore. In the first category are the Bitters, whose purpose is to cleanse. When encouraging her customers to use bitters, which clean you out, Jo has no shame in telling them what it will do and advises them to get in "lots of air freshener." Made from a blend of ash, aloes, barks and bitters, this tonic works by purging the colon of its contents, cleansing through this action. The second category of tonics restores. The Vitality falls into this category. This "fat burner," as Jo calls it, is a red drink that comprises sarsaparilla, dandelion roots, Korean ginseng, and other herbs. It works as a stimulant, contains iron, gives energy, has anti-inflammatory properties, boosts the immune system and cleanses the blood. Although it has no sugar in it, making it acceptable for diabetics, it is not a bitter drink. Many people are keen to buy it as it will burn their fat and its taste is mild. Eager to reap the benefits of the restoratives, many of Jo's African customers are reluctant to take the bitters first, as they do not like the taste. Jo has to surmount this resistance. To drive home the importance of cleansing prior to restoring, she often employs the metaphor of a house in her sales pitch, saying: "When you move into a house, before you put in all the furniture, first you have to sweep it out," giving the analogy of Bitters as broom and Vitality as furniture to help her customers appreciate the value of the bitter drink.

The palatability and use of bitters is a point of distinction between the Jamaican customers and the African and other customers to whom Jo sells. When Jamaican customers approach Jo's stall, it is to buy either one of two products, the Bitters or the Stamina, the former by both women and men, and the latter, only by men, for their libido. For the purposes of weight and health, amongst the Jamaican users, the Bitters are considered essential, and do not need to be used in conjunction with a restorative tonic. The herbal drink producer, Morris, explains: Jamaicans "cleanse with the bitters as a routine and then [follow up with] a food. The tonics are used specifically for energy purposes or for libido. As you feel you may need [the tonics] you take those. But they are not as essential as would be say, the bitters." For Jamaicans, Bitters constitutes a complete remedy in itself. Their general lack of interest in the other tonics (apart from the Stamina tonic discussed in the next section) reflects this ideology of cleansing as an essential practice. Furthermore, the effectiveness of the cleanser is testified through its bitter taste (Sobo, 1993: 36). Although bitter is considered efficacious in other contexts (for West Africa, see Etkin and Ross, 1982; for China, see Farquhar, 2002), there remains unwillingness in some of Jo's customers to appreciate the effects of this attribute.

In light of this general reluctance, about halfway through my year working with her, Jo branched out to selling flax seed as an alternative cleanser with a more pleasant taste. This is a complementary food product found in most conventional health food shops. It is high in Omega 3 fatty acids and works for a host of ailments: from strengthening the cardiovascular system, boosting the immune system, assisting in cell formation, circulation, digestion, and weight loss, to giving increased energy, improving hair, skin and nails, and aiding in sexual reproduction (Smith Jones: n.d.). The one Jo sells is organic and is grown in Canada. Not quite a herb, it nevertheless espouses some profound healing qualities and, as such, takes its place alongside the herbal tonics. Generally, Jo does not highlight its vast array of uses, but markets its function as a colonic cleanser, and with the added values of mopping fat in its movement, clearing skin and growing hair, thus contributing to the weight loss agenda when used in conjunction with the Vitality. Most of her African customers are unfamiliar with flax seed, as it is more of a Western mainstream health food. When they witness Jo selling its merits to other customers, however, some are intrigued and wish to experience how it may work for them. For instance, one African woman watched with interest as Jo made a sale of flax to two other women, listening to its merits and considering how it may help her. When Jo had finished her primary

sale, the woman on the side grabbed hold of a bag of flax seed, came to the front and said, "Now, tell me how to use it!" Jo then proceeded to give her the full instructions on what she would need for her own regimen. Given the relative success of flax as a marketable product, Jo considered relinquishing the Bitters altogether, as it is readily available elsewhere near the market. Yet, to meet the needs of her diverse clientele, she continued to stock it while I worked with her.

I will stop here to consider these products for cleansing and weight loss, as there are a few conjunctions and distinctions I wish to highlight. One connection is that between a variety of women from different backgrounds who, upon coming across Jo's market stall offering alternative weight loss and general healthcare programs, decide to stop, make inquiries, and buy. Without delving into perceptions of fatness among women, it is noteworthy that this is a cross-cultural, unifying link among women. In the public space of the market, where different peoples and "traditions" meet, alternative solutions can be encountered and experimented with. Another connection exists between the African and Caribbean populations, on the use of herbs as remedial for health and well being, with an understanding of the efficaciousness of the herbs to act in the body. In their research in Northern Nigeria, Etkin and Ross note that the Hausa "wish to see evidence that the disease leaves the body" (Etkin and Ross, 1982: 1559–1560), and use purgatives in their preparations to comply with this expectation of having visible effects. Similarly, Sobo notes that amongst her Jamaican informants "every household medicinal supply includes, if nothing more, a purgative of some sort, such as Epsom salts, cathartic herbs or castor oil" (Sobo, 1993: 41–42), which will wash out one's system.

In terms of differences, it has been noted already that what is essential for health is different between the different populations. Jamaicans consider Bitters to be essential, while Jo (and her other customers) see Bitters or flax working best when in collaboration with restorative tonics. A further difference could be linked to form—whether liquid or powder. Morris, the herbal drink producer, notes that medicines in the Caribbean and West Africa have a "totally different [. . .] presentation. You find that in the West African tradition, they tend not to boil things; they tend to use the herbs in a fresh way as they are, maybe by grinding or pounding. [. . .] There's a technology difference, because in the Caribbean, [. . .] they extract and boil. [This is because] a lot of the [latter's] development [is based on] the sugar style production." While the swapping of a bitter, boiled liquid for a milled seed may be a coincidence, it could also suggest that in addition to the taste, it is also the form which makes something easier to "digest." These preferences may objectify subtler differences between people, revealing in material form where they position their social identities.

This section focussed on physical aspects of the products, the different forms taken by the foodstuff, and how these impinge on where people see themselves both in relation to the food and to one another. In the next section, the focus shifts from food form to user group, this time repositioning the product so that its reach extends beyond the limited user base for which it was developed, thus also changing the alignment of those relating to it.

WIDENING THE APPLICABILITY OF HERBAL TONICS

As noted earlier, amongst the assorted bottles on Jo's tablecloth-topped barrow are other tonics that restore. One of particular note, at least as far as significance in volumes of sales, is the Stamina Conqueror Tonic, whose ingredients are blended to optimize virility and libido stimulation. If there is a tendency for women to approach the stall to address issues relating to weight and beauty, then there is a similar tendency for men to approach the stall to address issues of virility.

Sales are often made based on Jo's "Va Va Voom" catch phrase. Jo advertises "Va Va Voom" on her signs and through her spoken words. When asked what this is, she answers that these tonics give "Va Va Voom": energy and drive in sex. Although many laugh, some choose to buy. Many African, Caribbean and black British men come along looking for stamina products to help them "get up and stay up." Some men are interested in this product primarily because they have sexual problems. One older Caribbean man approached the stall and wanted to know if the Stamina would help him get an erection. He was quite plain about his question. As this was early on in my fieldwork, I was not able to assure him that the Stamina product would produce this result, and as Jo was not present at that moment, he did not buy anything. His candidness, however, was insightful. This concern with getting strong and remaining there does not just lie among older men, the target Viagra audience in the West, but among young men too. Even those in their twenties stop and buy the tonic more often than their elders. Two black British men stop at the stall, and one effectively makes the sale to his friend. He tells the other about the merits of Stamina, remarking on the power it gives to their "members" to stay strong all night, please their girlfriends and keep them happy with their virility. Having caught conversations about Stamina and its benefits to libido stimulation, David, the Jewish-English shoe seller, whose stall is often situated across from Jo's, sometimes picks up a bottle for himself in preparation for a night in with his wife at the end of the market day. Not all men passing by are interested in building up their sexual stamina. A different market colleague, a Sikh man who works in one of the shops framing the street market, stops to see if there is something to help him with his endurance, as he has recently started going to the gym to build himself up. After a conversation with Jo, he buys a bottle of the Stamina tonic for this purpose, rather than for sexual performance. Others declare their complete lack of use for the product. Two young black men walking past the stall notice the Stamina products and laugh out loud, repeating the name "Stamina" in their chuckle. Two young women also pass the stall, and as Jo tries to sell them Stamina for their men, one replies that if her partner had any more stamina, it would kill her; he was quite "strong" enough.

On the practice of taking herbal drinks to increase libido, Sobo finds that men in rural Jamaica build up their sexual stamina by drinking a locally made herb drink, referred to as "roots tonic," which energizes the body "by building, cleansing, and mobilizing the blood" (Sobo, 1993: 56–57). Energizing the blood and making it healthy, "means a strong libido" (Sobo, 1993: 221) and by association, increased sexual potency. Like the Vitality, Stamina has a base of sarsaparilla, and so is also a red drink, into which more specific herbs, such as strong back, chaney roots, kola nuts, and donkey weed, are blended to create the desired effects: cleanse the blood, stimulate, strengthen the back muscles and reproductive organs, and from a folk medicine point of view, act as aphrodisiacs. Resorting to the ingestion of natural herbs for the improvement of virility is not something confined to African or African Diasporic folk medicine practices. In a small town in Shandong province, China, Farquhar discovered a restaurant which served "medicinal meals" to cater for the physiological needs of middle-aged men. When trying to understand how these meals benefited the customers, Farquhar (2002, 2007) proposed that the herbs work on two levels, the physical and the emotional. Once ingested, the herbs act on

the body, where their physical effects can be felt and seen. The emotional benefits, she noted, are more difficult to define, but she suggests that the physical boost received would impinge positively on their outlook about their lives and their masculinity. This can be related to the older man who approached Jo's stall to inquire whether her products would enable him to get an erection, as this ability impinges on his sense of self as a man who is physically capable of reproduction. Thus, the masculinity "boost" derived is beyond personal, and relates also to the realms of both biological and social reproduction. Men's concerns with performance and stamina, although appearing to have a macho rather than paternal intention, are grounded in the ability to procreate and to fulfil male cultural expectations. Sobo states, "Having children affirms one's link into a consubstantial social network and is required for full adult status [. . .] Procreation and birth confirm male and female virility and fecundity, demonstrating that one has life inside to give and that one's vital essence of life blood will persist" (Sobo, 1993: 128–129). The herbs aim to assist with this, to increase a user's energy and strength, but also to enable the conception and subsequent birth of children.

Having said this, more women come down to the market than men. As such, making sales of the Stamina tonic must also be woman centered. The "Va Va Voom" approach adopted for men is translated into "sperm count increaser" for women. Although the products are geared toward the workings of men's bodies, the social pressure to bear children lies with women, and as such, it becomes their responsibility to take care of this situation. Wumi, the elderly Yoruba widow, once declared, "If you have no children, you have nothing," which clearly underlines the social significance of procreation. In my training for selling, Jo told me that the Stamina tonic can be sold to women who want to get pregnant, not to take themselves, but for their husbands to drink, in order to raise their sperm count. Jo explains that she is quite graphic about what the product will do, so that even if the women customers are shy, once that have heard its merits, they will send someone else along to come and buy it for them later. Not that many women do buy the product, though some do and apparently to good effect. One Yoruba customer, Remi, who lives in London with her husband, commented on her pregnancy, stating that she had waited a long time to get pregnant and thought it never would happen. Taking Jo's advice, she decided to buy Stamina for her husband to take and the month that he was drinking it, she fell pregnant—thus attesting to Jo's statement that it improves sperm count. Successfully selling this Jamaican tonic to appeal to the social and reproductive aspirations of Yoruba women suggests that in the global marketplace, self reproduction—both literal and social—can be achieved, both within a normative expectation of what is appropriate, which sits alongside a "certain degree of freedom" (Mathews, 2000: 23) from that norm.

This section focussed on the wider applicability a particular foodstuff could hold for cultural and gender diverse consumers. Two different senses of familiarity are at play here: one with a product and the other with a person. Whereas Jamaican men would buy the Stamina tonic based on a familiarity with it, Jo's female Yoruba customers would buy the tonic based on their familiarity with Jo, a fellow Yoruba woman in this London market. Through her social positioning, Jo is able to "transform" a product designed for a particular user group into something relevant and desirable to another one. This suggests that the intermixing of different people and products in the street market allows for and reveals degrees of familiarity between both people and things. It also shows how different people mix and at the same time retain particular social positions about themselves, and in relation to others.

COSMOPOLITAN CONCLUSIONS

This chapter considers the relationships between African immigrants, Caribbean immigrants and global foodstuffs in London, with a view to understanding the subtle shifts in self-positioning that occur as people negotiate their identities and affiliations in the global marketplace. As geographers, Cook and Crang offer a metaphor of displacement as useful to discern how people find themselves positioned *and* position themselves in relation to food (Cook and Crang, 1996: 138, italics original) in a cosmopolitan setting such as London. Taking multiple displacements as the starting point for the interactions on the market, a location where displacements intersect, an anthropological focus on food, and its taste, form, character, and potency, reveals how different people position themselves in relation to their own senses of identity, and to that of others. These different African and Caribbean peoples have both intersecting and divergent identities, revealed through their states of health, places of origin, current sites of residence, cultural expectations, and gender responsibilities. A focus on how global foodstuffs are marketed, perceived, "transformed" and used reveals that within the contexts of multiple displacements of both people and food items, different alliances emerge depending on degrees of familiarity with people and/or the products.

In terms of the African and Caribbean peoples who meet in Valley Market, in particular the overlap of Jamaicans and Yoruba-Nigerians, which takes place at Jo's stall, there is both conflation and separation of identities. Certain health concerns and the recourse to herbal tonics remain a point of similarity for these two populations, but the form, taste and potential uses of the products provide a lens through which to see their differences. While Jamaican and other customers from the Caribbean shop with Jo because of the familiarity with certain goods she sells, namely Bitters and Stamina, others from Nigeria and West Africa shop with her because of the role she plays, as someone "familiar" in a city where everyone is displaced, who can broker (Luedke and West, 2006) more distant goods. This is the case whether it is Jamaican boiled herbs or Canadian flax seed. Jo makes each accessible and appropriate for the outcomes she feels are desired by her customers. This social familiarity evidenced through tonic consumption further extends to new relationships created in the market space with people whose connections are based on this shared local space, such as those developed between Jo and her fellow traders, for example, David the shoe seller.

According to James, neither the movement of foodstuffs between nations, nor the acquisition of new cuisines encompasses the globalization of food. She argues instead that the globalization of food is better defined as "a complex interplay of meanings and intentions which individuals employ subjectively to make statements about who they are, and where and how their Selves are to be located in the world" (James, 1996: 92). In this market space, these "selves" are in a constant process of positioning and repositioning, depending on context and familiarity with place, product or person. This case study shows how groups of African, Caribbean and other London communities located around the market see themselves in relation to one another and particular food stuffs, and make respective associations and dissociations based on different (and changeable) conceptions of physical, social, gender, racial or cultural proximity.

NOTES

1. This chapter is based on my PhD in anthropology at University College London, the research for which was undertaken in London and in Nigeria, from 2005 to 2007.
2. All names of people and places have been changed to offer anonymity.

3. For the 1991 and 2001 censuses, "Black African" was the classification offered, with no further distinction on nationality or ethnicity.

REFERENCES

Agyemang, C., Addo, J., Bhopal, R., de Graft Aikins, A. and Stronks, K. 2009. "Cardiovascular Disease, Diabetes and Established Risk Factors among Populations of Sub-Saharan African Descent in Europe: A Literature Review." Globalization and Health 5(7): 1–17.

Anon. 2008. "Imagine a World Class Heathrow." Report commissioned by London First.

Botticello, J. 2007. "Lagos in London: Finding the Space of Home." Home Cultures 4(1): 7–24.

Cook, I. and Crang, P. 1996. "The World on a Plate: Culinary Culture, Displacement and Geographical Knowledges." Journal of Material Culture 1(2): 131–153.

Eade, J. 2000. Placing London, from Imperial Capital to Global City. London and New York: Berghahn Books.

Eade, J. 2004. "Rather than Making Upset," in Identities on the Move. Edited by J. Eade, D. A. Jahjah, and S. Sassen. London: British Council.

Etkin, N. L. and Ross, P. J. 1982. "Food as Medicine and Medicine as Food: An Adaptive Framework for the Interpretation of Plant Utilization among the Hausa of Northern Nigeria." Social Science and Medicine 16.

Farquhar, J. 2002. Appetites: Food and Sex in Postsocialist China. Durham and London: Duke University Press.

Farquhar, J. 2007. "Medicinal Meals," in Beyond the Body Proper: Reading the Anthropology of Material Life. Edited by M. Lock and J. Farquhar. Durham and London: Duke University Press.

Fraser, P. 1993. "Africans and Caribbeans in London," in The Peopling of London, Fifteen Thousand Years of Settlement from Overseas. Edited by N. Merriman. London: The Museum of London.

Fryer, P. 1984. Staying Power: The History of Black People in Britain. London: Pluto.

Grillo, R. and Mazzucato, V. 2008. "Africa <> Europe: A Double Engagement." Journal of Ethnic and Migration Studies 34(2): 175–198.

James, A. 1996. "Cooking the Books, Global or Local Identities in Contemporary British Food Cultures?" in Cross-Cultural Consumption, Global Markets, Local Realities. Edited by D. Howes. London and New York: Routledge.

Keeler, S. 2007. "Hackney's 'Ethnic Economy' Revisited: Local Food Culture, Ethnic 'Purity' and the Politico-Historical Articulation of Kurdish Identity," in Travelling Culture and Plants. Edited by A. Pieroni. New York and London: Berghahn Books.

King, A. D. 1990. Global Cities: Post-imperialism and the Internationalization of London. London and New York: Routledge.

Krause, K. 2008. "Transnational Therapy Networks among Ghanaians in London." Journal of Ethnic and Migration Studies 34: 235–251.

Luedke, T. J. and West, H. G. 2006. Introduction: Healing Divides: Therapeutic Border Work in Southeast Africa. Borders and Healers: Brokering Therapeutic Resources in Southeast Africa. Bloomington and Indianapolis: Indiana University Press.

Mathews, G. 2000. Global Culture, Individual Identity: Searching for Home in the Cultural Supermarket. London: Routledge.

McDonnell, B. 2001. "2001 National Census: Key Statistics for Southwark." Retrieved 26/02/2005, from http://www.southwark.gov.uk.

Newman, J. 2002. Windrush Forbears: Black People in Lambeth, 1700–1900. London: Lambeth Archives.

Ogoye-Ndegwa, C. and Aagaard-Hansen, J. 2006. "Dietary and Medicinal Use of Traditional Herbs among the Luo of Western Kenya," in Eating and Healing: Traditional Food as Medicine. Edited by A. Pieroni and L. L. Price. New York, London and Oxford: Food Products Press.

Parkin, D. 1999. "Mementoes as Transitional Objects in Human Displacement." Journal of Material Culture 4(3): 303–320.

Smith Jones, Susan (n.d.) "The proven benefits of flaxseed and LNA," Flax facts, promotional leaflet.

Sobo, E. J. 1993. One Blood: The Jamaican Body. Albany: State University of New York Press.

White, R. 2005. "Little Lagos in South London." Retrieved 03/03/2005 from http://news.bbc.co.uk/2/hi/africa/4182341.stm.

Young, Lola. 2002. "Foreword: Making History," in Windrush Forbears: Black People in Lambeth, 1700–1900. J. Newman. London: Lambeth Archives.

32

Tequila Shots

Marie Sarita Gaytán

Please visit the companion website at to see photos for this chapter.

The town of Tequila, Mexico, lies about an hour's drive from Guadalajara. Along with a population of fifty-one thousand, it boasts roughly twenty tequila factories, which is hardly surprising when you consider that nearly all tequila today originates from Tequila, its neighboring town, Amatitán, and the Los Altos region of Jalisco two hours to the north. In 2005 and 2006, I conducted fieldwork in this region. What made tequila so special, I wondered, and how did it come to be regarded as Mexico's national drink?[1] After all, across the border in the United States, drinkers and nondrinkers alike associate tequila with rowdiness and fiesta-fueled excess. In its native Mexico, however, tequila symbolizes collective national identity and pride. Nowhere is this truer than in Tequila itself, where the drink embodies both traditional and modern means of production, bespeaks the Mexican countryside, and celebrates life even as it commemorates its passing. A potent symbol indeed.

Ever since the sixteenth century, when Spanish settlers introduced the process of distillation, Tequila has been known for the manufacture of *mezcal*, an early incarnation of tequila (tequila is to mezcal as cognac is to brandy, the proprietary form). However, long before its official founding in 1530, Tequila was inhabited by various indigenous groups—the Chichimecas, Otomíes, Toltecas, and Nahuatlacas—who produced *pulque*, a beverage fermented from the agave (maguey) plant and similar to beer in its low alcohol content and high number of nutrients. Like *pulque*, tequila is fermented from agave, but then it is distilled. Therefore, tequila is among the earliest *mestizo* products to have emerged from the encounter between colonizers and native inhabitants. This venerable history no doubt influenced UNESCO's (United Nations Educational, Scientific and Cultural Organization) decision in 2006 to add the Tequila region to its list of World Heritage sites.

With its rolling hills, ancient *guachimontones* (rounded pyramids), stunning fields of blue agave (*Agave Tequila Weber*), and state-of-the-art factories, the Tequila region represents a uniquely Mexican blend of indigenous traditions and European technology. As the UNESCO proposal affirms, "the cultural profundity of the agave landscape and the production of tequila hearkens back to the very foundation of our nationality—for it fuses the closeness to nature and the land of the indigenous populations with the transforming and fundamental spirit of the Spanish settlers. From this union the spirit of a new culture was born giving rise to the traditions and values that now characterize the Mexican people."[2] Despite such flowery language, this statement captures the way Jalisco's landscape and industry combine to link Mexico's indigenous past with its *mestizo* present.

In a similar way, tequila symbolizes the balance of the traditional and contemporary in its production techniques. After harvesting, the *piña* (the agave's heart or root) is either slowly roasted in a traditional stone or brick oven (*horno*) or cooked more quickly in a steam autoclave. The *piñas* are then crushed, either by a large stone wheel known as a *tahona* or by a modern mechanical chipper. The resulting must (*mosto*) is strained and left to ferment. Fermentation takes place either naturally (thanks to a yeast that occurs on the agave plant) or through the help of commercial brewer's yeast. As with the roasting, modern methods accelerate the fermentation process. The resulting liquid is then distilled twice, either in traditional copper pot stills or in stainless-steel column stills. Traditional tequila makers are skilled enough to stop the distillation at 40 percent alcohol; but more often than not, after the tequila has aged in wooden barrels to develop its flavor, water is added to the distilled spirit to bring it down to 80 proof (40 percent alcohol) before bottling. Only three types of tequila (reposado, añejo, and extra añejo) are actually aged in wooden barrels—tequila blanco (or silver, as it is known in the United States) is bottled immediately following distillation.

Although most tequila is now mass-produced using modern machinery, some small-scale producers continue to rely on artisanal methods, including the use of *tahones*, *hornos*, and rustic fermentation tanks. Ironically, even though they use these time-honored procedures, some artisanal producers, such as those illustrated here, do not conform to the standards enforced by the Tequila Regulatory Council. Therefore, their products cannot legally be called "tequila." Instead, the beverage they manufacture is typically called *aguardiente de agave* (agave firewater) or *vino de mezcal* (mezcal wine).

No rituals better reflect the central role of tequila in Mexican culture than those associated with *Día de los Muertos*, the Day of the Dead. Predating the conversion of Mesoamerican populations to Christianity by roughly two thousand years, Day of the Dead rituals (which now coincide with the Catholic feasts of All Saints' Day and All Souls' Day on November 1 and 2) commemorate the continuation of life after death. People erect *altares* (altars) to the departed and decorate gravesites with *ofrendas* (offerings) of the deceased's favorite food and drink. At the historic Panteón de Belén cemetery in Guadalajara, altars are adorned with incense, flowers, candles, and *papel picado* (paper cutouts) ornamented with skulls. Tequila is also frequently part of the offering. As family members tell stories of the dear departed, they place tequila on the grave—and often drink it—as a symbol of the good times in that person's life.

The elaborate decorations on the altar for famed Mexican actress Maria Félix include *pan de muerto* (bread of the dead) and candied *calaveras* (skulls), as well as a range of other foods (*carnitas*, corn, and jicama) and drinks (cups of hot chocolate, a bottle of tequila). The graves of less celebrated individuals can hold candles, a bowl of *chicharrón* (pork rind), flower petals in the form of a cross, and a bottle of tequila—that ubiquitous image of Mexico so vital to all rituals of passage.

In every country, national identity both emerges from and creates material culture. In Mexico, tequila represents a unique national product that binds the country's diverse inhabitants and expresses the dynamism of Mexican culture, a culture that, as many *Jaliscienses* (Jaliscans) told me, should not be swallowed in a single gulp but should be appreciated in flavorful sips.

NOTES

1. As early as 1974, tequila became the first Mexican product to receive a Denomination of Controlled Origin (DOC) from the World International Property Organization, meaning that any product bearing the name tequila must be produced in accordance with a specified process in one of five Mexican states

(Guanajuato, Jalisco, Michoacán, Nayarit, and Tamaulipas). The DOC safeguards against misuse of the product's name and protects consumer interests by ensuring quality production.

2. Sofia González-Luna, "Introduction," in Ignacio Gómez-Arriola, *The Agave Landscape and the Ancient Industrial Facilities of Tequila* (Guadalajara: Instituto Nacional de Antropología e Historia, 2004), 13.

33

The Political Uses of Culture: Maize Production and the GM Corn Debates in Mexico

Elizabeth Fitting

When evidence of genetically modified (GM) corn was found among the corn-fields of highland Oaxaca and the Tehuacán Valley of Mexico the debate over whether, and to what extent, such corn poses a risk to local maize varieties (or landraces and creolized varieties, called *criollos* in Spanish)[1] intensified. The likely source of such GM corn is maize imported from the United States for use as animal feed, grain for *tortillas*, or industrial processing, which made its way to regional markets and rural stores where small-scale Mexican cultivators unknowingly purchased and then planted the grain.[2]

In this article, I want to examine the political uses to which the concept of a culture of corn is put in the recent Mexican debates about importing, testing, and planting GM corn. The Mexican anti-GM corn campaign has enrolled a broad spectrum of anti-GM focused organizations by portraying maize as a symbol of Mexican culture now under attack by neo-liberalist, corporate-led globaliza-tion. Maize is represented as quintessen-tially Mexican—originally domesticated in the area—and at the heart of Mexican culture as the most cultivated crop, the mainstay of most diets, rural or urban, and the cornerstone of ancient Aztec and Mayan cosmologies. Indeed, as one recent slogan and book collection put it, "Without corn, there is no country" *(Sin maíz, no hay país)*.[3] This 'pro-maize' and anti-GM coalition significantly challenges

the official perspective, articulated by government and industry spokespeople, which assumes the inefficiency of small-scale corn agriculture based on low yields and the use of 'traditional' technology, primarily non-breeder improved seed. The coalition also challenges the single focus on the risks of gene flow between GM corn and *criollos* and the privileging of scientific expertise in the evaluation of such risks.

Elsewhere I have drawn on the work of such critics to make the case that GM corn is not the only challenge facing maize-based livelihoods, agriculture, or in-situ biodiversity in Mexico (Fitting 2006). A neo-liberal corn regime or a series of policy changes which prioritize market liberalization, corn imports, and a notion of agricultural 'efficiency' also threaten such agriculture.[4] My aim here is to present a 'political economy of meaning' of the GM corn controversy to explore how certain claims about culture and expertise are used to frame, reject, or defend these policies (Murcott 2001). In order to do this, I situate the GM corn controversy in the context of these policy changes and how they have affected small-scale farmers.

I suggest that while the pro-maize coalition draws our attention to the wider policies which exacerbate the difficult conditions for small producers, in some cases, it shares with the official perspective a reified notion of corn culture that tends to portray maize agriculture as part of tradition, distinct from the capitalist economy of modern Mexico. The official perspective posits the production of corn as inefficient precisely because it is deemed a culture of use-values untouched by the market. Critics counter that such use-values are an alternative to the market and its processes of commodification. Both narrative strategies thus rely on a conceptual binary between the 'market' and the 'local community' (Hayden 2003).[5] When critics employ the notion of corn culture to generate support for their anti-GM campaign, they misrepresent some of the changes in the Mexican countryside. Additionally, this notion of a culture of corn is not unequivocally used or adopted by rural communities themselves.

My research in the Tehuacán Valley of Puebla (2001–2002, 2005), one of the regions where GM corn was discovered, found that rural households have adapted to the neo-liberal corn regime and water shortages by combining small-scale maize production with migrant labor. Their reliance on corn agriculture does not represent isolation from the market, but interaction with it. Valley households adjust their cultivation of maize in response to, or in anticipation of, fluctuations in the price of corn and the availability of paid employment. Maize-based agriculture and livelihoods are shaped by the practices of state and capital, and are increasingly monetized—a detail about rural change that the narrative about corn culture overlooks.

While these valley producers are by no means representative of the Mexican countryside—which is far too regionally diverse for such a generalization—they do represent a particular type of small producer. Unlike their neighbors to the south in the Oaxacan sierra who have garnered much media and activist attention, valley residents are not politicized around, nor cognizant of, the GM debates raging outside their community. They articulate concerns about the future of their livelihood and community, but such concerns do not fit easily into the main narratives of the GM corn controversy.

BACKGROUND TO A CONTROVERSY: DEFINING RISK AND ITS EXPERTS

The debate over GM corn began in the scientific and government regulatory community after the General Directorate of Plant Health (DGSV) of the Ministry of Agriculture began to grant permits in 1988 for scientific field trials of GM crops in Mexico. The directorate was advised by an ad hoc committee consisting of scientists from various disciplines and government agencies, which became the National Agricultural Biosafety Committee (CNBA) in 1992. This advisory committee is now known as the Specialized Agricultural Subcommittee of the newly created Committee on Biosafety (CIBIOGEM). The bulk of requests to plant experimental plots were made by universities and corporations like Monsanto, the single most frequent applicant between 1988 and 1999 (Alvarez-Morales 2000: 91). Maize was the most tested GM crop in Mexico (CONACYT-CONABIO 1999). However, in late 1998, the directorate decided to impose a de facto moratorium on GM corn trials because the traits most commonly tested were not of any particular benefit to Mexico (Alvarez-Morales 1999: 91). Members of the committee were also concerned about the possibility of GM corn mixing with and displacing *criollos* and teosinte, maize's wild relative.

As the center of maize biological diversity, Mexico is home to more than forty racial complexes, many landraces, and teosinte (Nadal 2000: 4; Turrent Fernández 2005: 51). There is little known about the effects of GM corn on maize landrace diversity. Like modern varieties or cultivars (those varieties developed by plant breeders), GM corn can displace or mix with landraces if widely adopted.

However, the potential risks of GM varieties also include the development or intensification of weeds tolerant to herbicides, and pests resistant to transgenic plants (Serratos 1996: 69).

While the moratorium on field trials was in place, environmentalist groups began to suspect that GM corn was making its way into Mexico in shipments of imported corn from Canada and the United States, where at the time somewhere between 20 to 30 percent of cultivated corn was genetically modified. Although Mexico's dependence on grain imports such as corn had been increasing since the 1980s, with the implementation of NAFTA there was a notable rise in this dependency. This rise in imports is the result of various factors including the dismantling of the long-running public program for the purchase and distribution of Mexican-grown maize. The market for maize in Mexico is now dominated by a few multinational corporations who prefer to import inexpensive corn from the United States, where the crop is subsidized by the government, rather than purchase corn grown in Mexico.[6]

Between 1994 and 2000, imports from the United States went from 14 to 24 percent of the total consumption of corn in Mexico. In the year 2000, Mexico was the second largest importer of US corn. At the time, Bt corn comprised over 20 percent of corn grown in the United States. Bt corn is a transgenic variety with genes from the soil bacterium *Bacillus thuringiensis*, which produces insecticide toxins that kill the European and Southwestern corn borers (Ackerman et al. 2003: 11). Mexico now imports roughly six million metric tons of US corn annually, a third of which is transgenic (Dyer and Yúnez-Naude 2003: 24). Under regulations implemented in October 2003, up to 5 percent of such imports can be transgenic without requiring identification as such.[7]

In 1999, Greenpeace Mexico (2000) tested samples taken from ships in the port of Veracruz carrying US corn and found GM corn among the grain. They launched an anti-GM corn campaign, along with, among others, the Environmental Studies Group (Grupo de Estudios Ambientales or GEA), also based in Mexico City, and the Canadian based environmental and farmers' rights organization, the ETC group (formerly called RAFI). Simultaneously with this nascent anti-GM corn campaign, other researchers not affiliated with these environmental or food rights groups were studying in situ maize biodiversity in Mexico, the effects of NAFTA imports on domestic corn production, and the regulation of GM corn. They would later enter the public stage to weigh in on the controversy.

In late 2001, Dr. Ignacio Chapela and David Quist from the University of California at Berkeley reported they had found the cauliflower mosaic virus (CaMV 35S) among the maize fields of the Sierra Norte de Oaxaca (Chapela and Quist 2001). CaMV 35S is a gene promoter, a DNA sequence used to incorporate transgenic DNA into plants. Another study co-authored by two branches of the Mexican government, the Mexican National Ecology Institute (INE) and the Biodiversity Commission (CONABIO), tested samples from different localities in the states of Oaxaca and Puebla and confirmed the presence of CaMV 35S, a promoter used in commercially planted or sold GM crops. These studies were initially dismissed by the Mexican Ministry of Agriculture and biotech industry representatives who questioned the studies' scientific procedures and argued that the gene flow between GM varieties and *criollos* is part of a natural and even beneficial process of hybridization. In contrast, critics have argued that the finding of GM corn in Mexico was not benign hybridization, but rather a form of genetic pollution or contamination (Soleri et al. 2005). Because Mexico is the crop's center of origin, this pollution was also considered the first of its kind to occur anywhere.

Chapela and Quist published their findings in the scientific, peer-reviewed journal *Nature* setting off an international debate not only about the risks of gene flow between such modified corn and native varieties, but also about the reliability of the researchers' methods. In a rare turn, which GM critics view as the result of pressure from the biotech industry, *Nature* rescinded its editorial support for the study in April 2002. The lingering debate about the scientific validity of these results has been given new life recently with the publication of a study in the same area that found little evidence of GM corn (Ortiz-García et al. 2005). My concern here, however, is not which studies conform to rigorous scientific standards for testing corn for evidence of transgenes, but how particular forms of expertise about maize have been validated or disqualified.

One of the key turning points in the anti-GM corn campaign was the *En defensa del maíz* (In defense of maize) forum in Mexico City in January 2002 precisely because it presented an alternative account to the dominant government and industry's focus on gene flow. At the forum, over three hundred academics, activists, farmers, and NGOs (ANEC, CECCAM, CENAMI, ETC group, Food First, GEA, Global Exchange, GRAIN, UNORCA, *La Via Campesina*, among others) concluded that the risks facing Mexican corn were much larger and more complex than the issue of GM contamination. So while this controversy has garnered much media and activist attention, it is not, as the emergent *En defensa del maíz* coalition has pointed out, the only challenge faced by maize producers or maize biodiversity in Mexico. At this forum and similar venues to follow, a broader campaign and a list-serve[8] emerged. Peasant groups, academics, scientists, environmental NGOs, and indigenous rights groups strengthened existing networks explicitly around the question of corn and

all that corn symbolizes: the fate of the Mexican countryside, rural subsidy cuts, increased dependency on food and grain imports, enormous levels of out-migration, and the biological diversity of the most cultivated and consumed crop in Mexico.[9]

The campaign has widened the focus beyond GM corn to include the challenges facing maize biodiversity, agriculture, knowledge, and cuisine. In so doing, the campaign argues that 'Mexican culture' itself is at risk. The privileged experts at such forums are not biotechnologists but the activists, academics, and environmentalists who consume maize, and the *campesinos* (peasants or small-scale farmers) who cultivate, process, prepare, and select maize. Much like anthropologist Chaia Heller's (2002) finding that the anti-GM campaign in France portrays French small-scale farmers as artisans central to the survival of the national cuisine and culture, in the Mexican campaign maize farmers are portrayed as the producers and guardians not just of traditional corn varieties, but of *national cultural practices and traditions*. This sentiment is reflected in much of the writing by *En defensa del maíz* supporters. Take the following excerpt from public intellectual and anthropologist Armando Bartra:

"*El Popol Vuh* and *la Suave Patria*, emblematic texts[10] of indigenous and mestizo Mexico, emphatically suggest that the Mexican countryside is much more than a great producer of foods and primary materials for industry. Peasants not only cultivate maize, beans, chile, or coffee, they also cultivate clean air, pure water, and fertile land; biological, social and cultural diversity; a plurality of landscapes, smells, textures and tastes; a variety of dishes, hairstyles, and attire; a great many prayers, sonnets *[sones]*, songs, and dances; peasants cultivate the inexhaustible multiplicity of uses and customs that make us the Mexicans we are"

(Bartra, "What purpose does agriculture serve?" in *La Jornada*, 21 January 2003; translation by the author)

Another reason this forum represents a turning point in the campaign is because it was the platform used to present the results from INE-CONABIO study,[11] that I mentioned before. This prompted the then director of INE to call for a reconsideration of biosafety measures in Mexico (Enciso in *La Jornada*, 12 August 2002; see also INE-CONABIO 2002; McAfee 2003). The INE-CONABIO study also found GM corn among the grain from some of the government's own rural DICONSA supply stores. As a consequence, DICONSA claims to have restricted its purchase of corn to domestic grain only. In late 2003, a coalition of Mexican NGOs presented their own study which suggested that the presence of GM corn was not confined to the states of Oaxaca and Puebla but was much more widespread.[12] In some areas, they had even found evidence of Starlink corn (Bt Cry9c) made by Aventis, which had been recalled for human consumption in the United States.[13] Representatives of the agro-biotechnology industry, the Ministry of Agriculture, and some members of the scientific community were quick to disqualify these test results as they had those of Chapela and Quist.

Biotechnologists and regulators, and at times agronomists and activists, evaluate GM crops by using a framework of risk and asking about the likelihood and effects of gene flow between GM crops and non-GM plants. As researchers on the social construction of environmental risk have pointed out, this focus on evaluating risk relies on the expert knowledge of scientists and often trivializes non-risk concerns and frameworks like those that focus on ethics, food quality or taste, and livelihoods (Beck [1986] 1992; Heller 2002; Wynne 1996). It reproduces the notion that only scientifically trained experts are qualified to determine the potential harm of GM crops. GM regulatory bodies often focus on gene flow as the main risk factor for evaluation and regulation when it is just one unknown

out of many. As Heller (2002: 8) explains referring to the French anti-GM movement:

> Despite the often subjective and conditional nature of the risk construction process, actors within these networks tend to assume risk definition and management to be an objective endeavor, falling within the jurisdiction of risk experts, thus marginalizing 'non-experts' from the process of agenda setting.

But, as Heller points out, when the anti-GM movement challenges the discourse of risk as the central frame for evaluating and debating GM crops, it also questions the boundary between scientific 'experts' and 'publics'. This boundary is also at issue in Mexico.

In the Mexican case, official accounts of the GM corn scandal tend to disqualify the concerns and expertise of maize farmers, activists, environmentalists, and agronomists critical of GM corn imports and tests in several different ways. First, as previously mentioned, the focus on gene flow renders other concerns less relevant. Second, some experts minimize the concerns of non-scientists about GM corn by suggesting that the possible gene flow between GM corn and native varieties may actually be *beneficial* for Mexican maize biodiversity and for *criollos*. They argue this despite the fact that Mexico does not suffer from the European corn borer which Bt corn, the most common type of GM corn, is designed to combat. This suggestion that GM corn can be beneficial for native varieties is based on the assumption that traditional or 'indigenous' technology and knowledge is inefficient and distinct from (rather than interactive with) modern technology, in this case, breeder or biotech-improved seed.[14] In other words, the problem of traditional agriculture and maize varieties is that they *have not interacted enough* with improved seeds and other technologies. Third, when non-scientists have used commercially available kits to test for the presence of GM corn, their results have been discounted. In an interview with Antonio Serratos, a biologist who has been involved in the corn debates since the government first regulated experimental field tests in the late 1990s, he explains his own perspective in contrast to that of other Mexican scientists:

> The NGOs used enzyme tests to detect protein in plants and found positive results [in 2003]. For me, this study to detect protein was reliable and the measures were adequate for a preliminary evaluation. But we need a more profound study. However, the Mexican scientific community has largely rejected these studies because they are not conducted by scientists. This includes CINVESTAV [The Center for Research and Advanced Studies of the National Polytechnic Institute]. It's not that these scientists are insulting. They don't trust the results of NGOs for various reasons; 'It's not in a lab, it's without *técnicos*, without controls . . .' But if the NGOs followed protocol, then we cannot reject these results—whoever conducted the tests. We cannot negate the ability of *campesinos* to use these kits. The scientific community has rejected the results because they believe the people do not have the capacity to conduct the tests—the scientific rigor and so on . . . We cannot exclude results because X or Y person did the test. I would not take their results as *certification* that there is GM corn [*transgénicos*] but they are useful as preliminary findings.
>
> (Mexico City, 30 April 2005)

In contrast, during a group interview, several employees of one government agency involved in the debates about regulation and the new bio-safety law, explained that the controversy over GM corn has been fuelled by misinformation because non-experts are dominating the discussion:

> "The debate should be among agronomists in academic circles, rather than among

ecologists and activists or civil society [as it is now]. The debate should be among peasant organizations rather than conservationists. This is a serious absence in the debate . . . The focus on GM is a smokescreen. It just clouds the issues. We need non-ideological investigations into gene flow".
>
> (Mexico City, 11 May 2005)

By associating civil society with ideology and agronomists (or science) with neutrality, these officials de-legitimize the voices and concerns of non-scientists, with the notable exception of peasants. There has been a strong counter-tradition in Mexico among agronomists and anthropologists which validates peasant agricultural knowledge despite the dominant trend within the Ministry of Agriculture and other government ministries to consider peasant practices and knowledge as backward and inefficient.[15] This counter-tradition emerged as part of post-revolutionary narratives of the early twentieth century which celebrated the peasantry. Additionally, many anthropologists outside the Mexican tradition have also sought to validate the knowledge practices of indigenous and peasant groups, along with their folk taxonomies and classifications (Gupta 1998; Nader 1996; Richards 1985). These two traditions, along with the transnational slow food movement and other anti-corporate globalization movements, contribute to the narratives about the expertise and values of peasants in the corn debates today. They are mobilized to counter official, industry, and scientific attempts to disqualify non-scientific expertise and priorities such as food quality, the ability of peasants to maintain a rural livelihood, and sustainable agriculture.

Even as controversy began over the findings of Chapela and Quist's now famous study and the disqualification of lay people from using commercially available kits to test for GM corn, there have been debates within the scientific community itself over *which scientific experts* should be represented on regulatory bodies. The inclusion of an agro-biotechnology industry representative on the government's Biosafety Committee (CIBIOGEM) has been viewed as a conflict of interest by activists and some academics and plant scientists.[16] Others have argued that industry representatives are members of civil society and their inclusion in regulatory bodies helps promote a diversity of opinion. There is little consensus about who is qualified to measure risk. Selecting experts for representation on regulatory bodies is a particularly contentious process in Mexico because of the country's difficult history of government corruption and political clientelism. Many members of the *En defensa del maiz* coalition argue that the voices of transnational corporations are already heard in the halls of the Mexican senate, and do not need representation on regulatory bodies as well.

OUT-DATED CULTURE, INEFFICIENT PRODUCTION

Neo-liberal government policy and rhetoric has framed peasant maize-centered agriculture as archaic and inefficient, particularly when compared to US producers whose corn yields are generally much higher than Mexican yields.[17] There are, of course, differences in the rural policies of the administrations of presidents Miguel de la Madrid, Carlos Salinas de Gotari, Ernesto Zedillo, and Vicente Fox, but all share certain assumptions about corn production, in particular the notion that such production, as Kirsten Appendini (1998) has pointed out, is a drain on scarce government resources and as such needs to 'modernize' or 'globalize'. Corn production thus needs to become more efficient through technology (improved seeds, fertilizer, pesticides, tractors, etc.) or be replaced with crops that have a comparative advantage for Mexico in the global market, such as fruits and vegetables.

From the perspective of free trade proponents, corn production is inefficient. In this market-oriented logic, small-scale maize production is viewed as dominated by the use values of subsistence rather than those of profit and exchange. The Minister of Agriculture (SAGARPA) under the Fox administration, Javier Usabiaga, articulated this perspective in a newspaper interview. He explained that, for rural producers today, it is more important to know how to sell agricultural goods than it is to know how to grow them.

"We need to teach the agriculturalist how to sell. They should do things well *[las cosas se deben hacer como Dios manda]*. We cannot resolve the problem with speeches nor with subsidies. We are going to solve the problem with actions that provide the producer with access to the market. Today it is more important to know how to sell than it is to grow."

Journalist: "Is it possible to make corn, beans, and coffee viable when they are grown for cultural reasons?"

Minister Usabiaga: "This is a very serious problem that we need to change. We are fighting against a culture. But there are situations in which the grower has been convinced that he cannot continue to do the same thing . . . because even with subsidies it is difficult to earn or cover his costs of production."

(*La Jornada*, 17 January 2001; translation by the author)

The Ministry of Agriculture has promoted rural development through modern, commercial agriculture, improved seeds, the import of grains, and the displacement of inefficient *campesinos* or peasants.[18] These policy initiatives tend to devalue the cultivation and in situ diversity of *criollos*—despite the important counter-tendency in Mexico that values peasant knowledge—and rely on the assumption that agro-biotechnology and transgenic seeds are 'scale-neutral'. Critics have demonstrated that such improved seeds are not, in fact, scale-neutral since the often costly inputs necessary for increased yields are only available to resource-rich farmers. High yielding modern varieties depend on expensive irrigation, chemical pesticides, tractors, etc. Indeed, this criticism emerged in Mexico and elsewhere after the Green Revolution (Barkin and Suarez 1983; Hewitt de Alcantara 1976; Shiva 1991).[19] One state agency has even argued that national self-sufficiency in maize could be possible, even under free trade, with the right, scale-appropriate technology (INIFAP cited in Appendini 1994: 153). Additionally, the argument that small-scale corn production is inefficient overlooks the role of producers in maintaining and modifying the biological diversity of maize and other crops.

While most observers and participants in the corn debates would agree that maize-based agriculture and cuisine is a central feature of the Mexican countryside, and even would agree on what it means to be Mexican, the official position views corn production as part of a *cultural* barrier to economic development. The notion of a culture of corn is used to promote policies which attempt to modernize or displace small rural producers. It also obscures the ways in which indigeneity and peasantries are socially and historically constituted. The anti-GM movement challenges this official portrayal of corn agriculture as inefficient by also drawing upon the long-standing symbolic associations between maize and the Mexican nation (Pilcher 1998; Warman 1988). But in so doing, some anti-globalization spokespeople portray corn agriculture as a cultural alternative to modernity that is now threatened with extinction or in the throes of resistance against the forces of neo-liberal globalization. Let us look at this position a little closer.

CORN AS CULTURAL ALTERITY?

In late 2002, a coalition of fourteen peasant groups and 100,000 protesters opposed to NAFTA and neo-liberal policy came together under the banner of *El campo no aguanta más* (the countryside can't take it anymore)[20] and organized an impressive series of protests that took over the center of Mexico City. Included in the coalition's list of demands was not only the renegotiation of NAFTA, but the immediate halt of GM corn imports.[21] These December protests were preceded by years of organizing among various camps against IMF-led economic restructuring, trade liberalization, cuts to rural subsidies, and the plight of Mexicans who migrate to the United States in search of work. While corn production was often an issue in these campaigns as a feature of the Mexican countryside, the *En defensa del maíz* forums united the various groups and issues around the rubric of corn. By joining forces under the symbol of corn, the campaign resonated with a broad range of Mexicans and the international anti- or alter-globalization networks.

This campaign tends to portray corn-based livelihoods as a culture distinct from urban, market, or modern cultures. Informed by transnational environmentalist discourses about small-scale agriculture, Mexican peasant studies, and popular discourse, some critics of GM crops represent corn-based livelihoods as a millennial culture of subsistence that is protective of the natural environment. This was the case, for instance, at a press conference held in Mexico City in March 2001 by the international coalition *La Via Campesina* when Mexican representatives welcomed the French union leader, farmer, and anti-McDonalds activist José Bové to Mexico. Bové explained his visit by saying that because of the EZLN (Ejército Zapatista de Liberación National) uprising against NAFTA and the movement for a GM-free agriculture, Mexico was at the center of anti-globalization struggles. A panelist from *La Via Campesina* then juxtaposed industrial, commercial agriculture to that of small-scale producers, explaining that Mexican indigenous producers and peasants have "always existed in harmony with nature."

Statements about living "in harmony with nature" are often made to highlight the dependency of rural farmers on their environment or to foreground the uncompensated contributions of rural people to crop biodiversity and in situ conservation. Such portrayals of rural people can be an important political gesture in emphasizing their unpaid and uncompensated labor in the adaptation, selection, and modification of landraces and the related production of potential economic value.[22] Such portrayals can also reify small-scale corn production as an authentic, millennial tradition of 'deep Mexico'.[23] Gustavo Esteva, one of the editors of the recent pro-corn collection, *Sin maíz, no hay país*, employs the notion of a deep and authentic Mexico to talk about the modern nation as "the coexistence of two distinct civilizations: the Mesoamerican and the occidental" (2003; 297). The former involves a worldview dominated by the values of community and use rather than those of the market or exchange. In this way, the use of the idiom of deep Mexico or a culture of corn obscures the ways indigeneity and peasantries are made and remade in interaction with larger forces and processes—as is also the case in the official, neo-liberal narrative on corn.

During the peasant debates of earlier decades, indigenous or rural culture was often seen as a 'natural economy' (Roseberry 1993). Such natural economies were characterized as isolated, millennial, and self-provisioning rather than as profit-seeking, embodying use-value over exchange-value, and beyond the reach of external markets and state policies. While certain peasantries may indeed be isolated and subsistence-based, such peasantries are *always* historically and socially produced (Roseberry 1989).

Oppositions between the natural economy and the exchange values of commodity-based systems often romanticize the former and can slip into a notion of primary and original cultural alterity (O'Brien and Roseberry 1991: 3). The concept of the natural economy has crept back into contemporary discussions of rural resistance and corn culture. As primary and original, this natural economy is seen as morally superior.

A related problem is the reliance on a classic anthropological notion of culture as a bounded, autonomous entity with an internally coherent system, pattern, or logic, as found in Esteva's quote. Just as rural culture is viewed in some anti-GM narratives as a slow-changing tradition, maize-based knowledge and practices are seen as passed down through the millennia, unchanged and unchallenged. Yet, many anthropological studies have shown that when agricultural knowledge is handed down from generation to generation, it is a dynamic process in which both subaltern and dominant knowledge systems and practices are transformed (Brush 1996; Gonzalez 2001; Richards 1985). Such studies emphasize the fluidity between different scientific and knowledge traditions. Forms of subaltern knowledge interact with, and adopt, aspects of science-based agriculture. As Stephen Brush (1996: 5) has argued, "This give and take among cultures has long been recognized by anthropologists (e.g., Redfield 1962), but the urge persists to reify knowledge systems and set artificial boundaries around culture where none exist in everyday life."

Rather than approaching culture as an entity in and of itself, anthropologist Kate Crehan suggests an examination of the relationships of power between the dominant and the dominated "and how these create fluid and shifting social entities" (2002:66). Following Crehan and others, I view maize agriculture in the valley as a framework of meaning and shared practices that are embedded in wider economic and political structures and relationships of power. Rural residents share some ideas and practices about corn. But these ideas and practices need to be explored as a process and set of relations, *not as the already* existing entities ('cultures' or 'natural economies') that now confront the Mexican neo-liberal project and the global economy. Rather than relying on a notion of corn culture that is insulated from wider economic, political, and social processes, we might ask in what ways corn agriculture is a cultural practice and how such practices and meanings are transformed by trade liberalization, GM imports, and cuts to rural funding. I cannot fully answer these questions here, but only provide a brief example from one community where the meanings and practices of corn are indeed changing in their ongoing engagement with larger forces.

CORN AS RURAL LIVELIHOOD STRATEGY

As argued by the pro-maize coalition, the neo-liberal corn regime has exacerbated the difficulties faced by small-scale farmers. But rather than interpreting maize production as a millennial culture or unchanging tradition, we can see the complex ways rural Mexicans are adapting to state policy and economic crisis by approaching such agriculture as a dynamic practice and set of social relations. In the southern Tehuacán Valley town of San José Miahuatlán (pop. 8,700; INEGI 2000), an older generation of residents cultivates corn despite rising costs. However, my interviews and household surveys also found that this has coincided with an overall decline in the town's agricultural production, an increased preference for non-agricultural work among younger residents, and the monetization of maize production.

Rural Mexicans now migrate in record levels to cities and to the United States. But the remittances migrants send home help finance rural households and local agriculture. Such remittances help offset the rising costs of agricultural inputs which may include mules, tractors, fertilizer, pesticides, irrigation water, and labor. After the implementation of NAFTA, and despite these rising costs, the domestic production of Mexican corn actually increased, particularly in rain-fed areas (Barkin 2003; Nadal 2000). In other words, export-friendly crops have not displaced corn, as the Mexican neo-liberal position had hoped. Rather than abandoning maize agriculture, many rural households have adapted to the import of inexpensive US corn and economic crises by using migrant remittances to supplement small-scale maize production (de Janvry, Gordillo, and Sadoulet 1997; Dyer 2000).

My own research in the Tehuacán Valley also found that the key to household maintenance or survival was this combination of corn production with wage labor. Most of the *campesinos* to whom I spoke described increased difficulty in affording agricultural inputs faced with a continuing economic crisis and a shortage of irrigation water. While state reforms have introduced new subsidies in order to cushion the abrupt transition to free trade, residents expect little help from the government. For instance, Procampo grants, a transitional rural subsidy designed to soften the impact of NAFTA, tends to be insufficient to make up for the overall effect of inflation and the cuts to corn price supports and other rural subsidies (Myhre 1998; Nadal 2000).

Since the 1980s, corn cultivation in San José has become a more important share of agricultural production. This reliance on maize, however, is not the resurgence of a millennial tradition of use values, as suggested by some voices of the *En defensa del maíz* coalition. Rather, as other researchers have argued, corn is a particularly adaptable crop, a mainstay of the Mexican diet, and its cultivation provides a safety net for rural Mexicans.

The crop can be eaten or sold in small quantities when there is little available income. In San José, an older generation of male residents practices maize agriculture as a way of reducing the risks of an unstable income or employment and the variable price of maize. In the valley, maize is grown for both household consumption and for sale as fresh corn called *elote*.[24] When the price of *elote* is not profitable or when there is no buyer for the crop, it is dried and consumed by the household in the form of *tortillas*, a dietary staple. In this way, residents expand or reduce their production of corn in response to wider socio-economic forces and the situation of the household within those forces (Macip 1998; Otero 1999; Warman 1980). The adaptation to such forces is not a recent phenomenon. Valley residents and their agricultural practices have long been affected by, and have negotiated, state policies and economic processes.[25]

It is important to point out that corn is not merely a form of rural insurance for valley residents. Interviewees also prefer to buy and grow local varieties *(criollos)* for their taste and texture in the making of *tortillas*. In post-NAFTA Mexico, it is more expensive to purchase locally grown, white *criollo* corn than to buy imported yellow corn. Yet, when residents run out of their own supply of harvested maize, they are often willing to pay extra for better quality local corn even when household funds are strained.

In the southern valley, household members perform different tasks according to gender and generation. Many households combine maize cultivation, a male task, with various forms of remunerative employment. Most particularly, they combine corn production with migrant labor and valley *maquiladora* (assembly plant or factory) work. Migrant labor to the United States is largely undertaken by young men in their teens and early twenties, and slightly older men in their mid-twenties and thirties.

Maquiladora work is undertaken largely by young women. Young migrants and *maquiladora* workers contribute funds to their parents' household in order to cover the costs of household maintenance, subsidize corn agriculture, or to build a house of their own. Together these tasks form an inter-generational, transnational household strategy to weather local water shortages, neo-liberal reforms and national economic crisis. The social relations of valley production are changing in particular ways. But the increasingly necessary inflow of migrant remittances does not contribute to the *long-term* reproduction of maize agriculture. Rather, this strategy contributes to a shortage of local agricultural labor, increases the monetization of corn production, and engenders or strengthens an aversion to agriculture among the young (Fitting 2004).

With work experience in the United States or urban Mexico, a young labor force has become accustomed to an hourly wage or at least to thinking in terms of one. In contrast, most agricultural production a generation ago relied on sharecropping arrangements between producers of different means. Most commonly, one *campesino* would contribute the land and water (if growing an irrigated crop), while the other would contribute his labor. The resulting harvest would be divided equally. According to residents this practice has been on the decline since the 1980s largely because returned migrants prefer wages over sharecropping. Many households now pay day laborers *(peones* or *mozos)* in cash for *elote* production. Moreover, households with high rates of male out-migration may hire laborers to farm corn for household consumption. In other words, maize production, *even for household consumption*, is increasingly monetized.

According to one older *campesino*, not all men in San José can devote their time to agriculture because there is not enough land for every child to inherit a parcel.

Additionally, he complained about the shift from sharecropping to the expectation of a wage when working the cornfields: "We [the older generation] used to work like mules when we worked the fields. Now the young ones want to be paid by the hour." This interviewee, like many other maize growers in San José, is in his fifties. When I asked residents about maize production, invariably they would direct me to men in their forties or older as the most knowledgeable on the matter. This is to say that corn cultivation is increasingly the domain of older men. Perhaps the younger generation will take up maize agriculture as they age, but various factors are making this increasingly unlikely. There has been a decline in agricultural production *overall* due to rising costs, the need for migrant remittances, population pressure on available land, soil fatigue, pests, and water shortages.

One interviewee, a returned migrant in his thirties, also suggested that there is a generational difference in the residents' perspective on maize. On the one hand, older men cultivate corn and migrants in their thirties send money home to work the land and work the cornfields themselves when in town. On the other hand, there is a younger generation of migrants and residents who do not know how to work the land nor want to return to it. My interviewee felt that this was a worrisome trend: "What's going to happen to this town if no one wants to work the land?" (San José, 21 November 2001). His perception of the generational difference in attitude toward a maize-based livelihood was confirmed in my interviews with younger migrants and residents.

Migrants in their teens and twenties overwhelming told me that there is no future in corn production because, "you can't make any money in the countryside! There is no money in the cornfield" (San José, 30 November 2001). They consider corn agriculture an old-fashioned, unprofitable dead end. It represents part of the problem faced by the town, not part of making a better future. When back in San José, these migrants prefer to work temporarily in valley factories and in regional construction until they trek north again for work in the US service sector. Moreover, I found that young migrants had little knowledge of local corn varieties. When asked, these interviewees were unable to name the local varieties in regular use, despite the fact that they were fluent in the local dialect of Nahuatl (Fitting 2004). The insight made by anthropologists that transnational migration and globalization pose particular challenges to the reproduction of cultural practices and knowledges across generations is applicable here (Appadurai 1996).

Despite the fact that the INE-CONABIO study found GM corn among valley cornfields, none of the residents I spoke to between 2001 and 2005 had ever heard of GM corn *(maíz transgénic)*, with the exception of a university educated teacher and an agronomist. This stands in stark contrast to indigenous communities and NGOs who are politicized around corn politics and indigenous identity and who employ a notion of a millennial culture of corn to represent themselves as the traditional 'people of maize'.[26] A coalition of indigenous farmers and environmental groups in the neighboring state of Oaxaca, for instance, recently petitioned the Commission on Environmental Cooperation (CEC) of NAFTA to investigate the effects of imported GM corn on their communities. In response, the CEC organized a series of consultations and wrote a report (2004) that was submitted to, and criticized by, the environment ministers of all three NAFTA signatory countries. In some regions, the narrative strategy of the pro-maize coalition resonates with rural producers themselves. But this is not the rule in rural Mexico.

Residents of the southern Tehuacán valley, like other communities who are not politicized or organized around the issue of GM corn, discuss their livelihoods in terms of a different set of risks and challenges. In San José interviewees frequently mentioned the risks and challenges posed by the recent cuts to rural subsidies, the lack of employment opportunities, crop pests, local agricultural labor shortages, and environmental problems such as declining levels of spring water for irrigation. At a meeting of communal land holders in San José, one *campesino* in his late twenties complained that, "We used to grow crops that were sold in Mexico City and elsewhere. But free trade is screwing us over. Products from the other side [of the border] are already here" (San José, May 2001). Similarly, older residents and migrants tend not to frame corn production as backward or inefficient but question the government's agricultural policies. In this sense, they share some of the concerns raised by the *En defensa del maíz* and *El campo no aguanta más* coalitions. But they do not take up a notion of corn culture. The narrative about maize as a link to the past, as a tradition handed down from generation to generation, as a fundamental element of their indigenous identity and heritage, does not resonate here. Moreover, a younger generation rejects this narrative outright. As previously mentioned, younger migrants often discussed maize agriculture as part of the town's problems.

Valley maize producers and migrants of different generations discuss the future of maize distinctly. But even as residents turn to corn as a way to cope with the insecurity of the job market, economic crisis and restructuring have rendered the conditions for corn agriculture and the related in situ maintenance of different traditional varieties more difficult. In other words, this process of semi-proletarianization through migration reinforces corn agriculture in the short and medium term. But the conditions for sustainable corn agriculture are deteriorating for complex reasons including out-migration, a growing dependency on

non-agricultural work, high inflation, and environmental problems such as water scarcity.

CONCLUSION

In an era of late capital and an increasingly interconnected world, political claims to culture have become all the more strident and pressing. One of the challenges faced by anthropologists is not only to continue the critique of our own traditions in conceptualizing culture, but to investigate the ways culture is used to make political claims. In Mexico, the struggles over and narratives about the fate of the countryside, and indeed the nation, frequently draw upon a notion of authentic Mexico and its culture of corn.

This article has demonstrated that the anti-GM corn coalition shifted the terms of the debate away from the official focus on the risks of gene flow toward wider concerns about the future of the Mexican countryside in a globalized world. In so doing, the pro-maize, anti-GM coalition contends that the appropriate 'experts' for evaluating the potential harm to Mexican culture and the countryside are not (or not only) bio-technologists, agronomists, and other scientists, but corn consumers and producers themselves. In effect, the coalition is calling for nothing less than a democratization of the decision-making process on GM regulation, NAFTA, and rural policy. But in arguing that rural funding and trade policies should reflect the concerns and interests of consumers and small-scale Mexican producers, the coalition has also, at times, reified corn culture. It portrays maize agriculture as steeped in millennial practices and dominated by subsistence values. Such reifications can downplay rather than foreground the dynamic and interactive aspects of maize-based livelihoods and agriculture.

In the southern Tehuacán Valley, maize agriculture is not (and never was) insulated from state policies and economic processes, but is shaped through engagement with them. The cultivation of local maize provides residents a form of rural insurance. Residents have taken up a transnational household strategy which uses migrant remittances in part to fund small-scale maize production. But this strategy also contributes to the monetization of agriculture and a disinterest and lack of knowledge about maize agriculture among a younger generation. Such agriculture is not the basis of a politicized identity, as it is elsewhere, and the narratives about millennial culture have little resonance here.

I have suggested that while any culture of corn is a historical product—as the practices and values of peasants are historically constituted through dynamic engagement with wider processes—its conceptualization is also an ideological project of the late capitalist, neo-liberal present (Roseberry 1989:223). The official government and pro-GM position also employs a reified notion of corn culture, but in support of a neo-liberal agenda. The Mexican government frames small-scale corn production as a distinct culture characterized by inefficiency in its efforts to legitimize market liberalization and the end to post-revolutionary rural commitments. Precisely because this notion of corn culture is part of the ideology of Mexican neo-liberalism, we need to interrogate its use and attendant assumptions, even when it appears among critics of neo-liberal policy and GM corn.

ACKNOWLEDGMENTS

I would like to thank David Barkin, María Mercedes Gómez, Regino Melchor Jiménez Escamilla, Ricardo F. Macip, Gerardo Otero, and Antonio Serratos for their input at various stages of this project. The shortcomings of this article are my own. My dissertation research was funded by the generous support of the Wenner Gren Foundation for Anthropological Research. This essay is based on this research and reworks the ideas from two pieces published in Spanish (Fitting 2004 and forthcoming).

NOTES

1. In Spanish, both landraces and creolized varieties are referred to as *criollos* but the latter are the outcome of an intentional or accidental mix of landraces with improved varieties. I use the words maize and corn interchangeably here.
2. On a smaller scale, there are two other possible sources of such corn: returned migrants from the United States who wanted to cultivate a northern variety and the monitored field trials of GM corn that were conducted in Mexico between 1988 and 1998.
3. This slogan emerged out of the anti-GM corn movement. It was the title of a museum exhibit at the Museum of Popular Culture in Mexico City (2003) as well as the title of an edited collection from Mexico (Esteva and Marielle 2003).
4. Due to space limitations, I do not discuss the specific policies of the neo-liberal corn regime here. For more thorough discussions of the policy shift from national self-sufficiency in maize to import dependency, see Barkin (2002, 2003), Bartra (2004), Fitting (2006), or Nadal (2000).
5. In her work on bioprospecting projects in Mexico, anthropologist Cori Hayden (2003) found that in framing the redistribution of corporate returns from such projects, the binary between the idiom of the market and community were reproduced. In the case of GM corn, we can see such boundaries at work between liberalized corn imports (read: the market) versus subsistence corn agriculture (read: the community).
6. In her article, Kathleen McAfee (2003) analyzes. the GM corn debates in relation to how agricultural policies and the agro-food industry affect rural Mexico. She provides an excellent discussion of recent agro-food restructuring at the international level.
7. The trilateral "Documentation requirements for living modified organisms for food or feed or for processing" signed by Victor Villalobos, Coordinator of International Affairs for the Ministry of Agriculture (SAGARPA) is available online at: http://www.cibiogem.gob.mx/norma-tividad /Documento%20Trilateral/acuerdo.htm.
8. At http://maiceros_l@laneta.apc.org.
9. In terms of area of land use, maize is the most cultivated crop in Mexico. Maize ranks second

in terms of volume of production (Alvarez-Buylla 2003; Nadal 2000).

10. "Their flesh was formed of yellow corn and of white corn; of cornmeal the arms and legs of man were formed. Only cornmeal became the flesh of our fathers, the four men who were created" (*El Popol Vuh*, Mayan Book of Counsel). "My country: Your surface is corn" (Ramón López Velarde, *Sauve Patria*). Both works cited in Armando Bartra's (2004) "Rebellious cornfields" in Gerardo Otero's edited collection.

11. The corn samples were sent to two Mexican institutions, Centro de Investigaciones y Estudios Avanzado del Instituto Politécnico Nacional (CINVESTAV) of the Irapuato Campus and el Institute de Ecología de la UNAM, but the report presents only the results from the former institution.

12. CECCAM, CENAMI, ETC Group, CASIFOP, UNOSJO, and AJAGI. 2003. *Contaminación transgénica del maíz en México: Mucho más grave*. Collective Press Release, 9 October. Mexico City, Mexico. http://www.etcgroup.org/article.asp?newsid=408.

13. Starlink has been found to cause allergic reactions in humans. As the US recall of taco shells containing Starlink in 2001 illustrates, the regulatory system is not perfect. One type of GM corn that was approved as animal feed and may cause allergic reactions in humans, made its way into the US food system. It is safe for animals but "may trigger allergic reactions in humans, including fever, rashes or diarrhea, according to government scientists" ("Corn woes prompt Kellogg to shut down plant," *The Washington Post*, 21 October 2000).

14. Plant scientist Luis Herrera-Estrella at CINVESTAV in Irapuato has downplayed the risks associated with gene flow between *criollos* and biotech crops. In a published interview, he argued that "for decades the Creole [*criollo*, see note 1] varieties have lived together with commercial varieties, included the hybrid varieties from the multinational companies without causing their disappearance and in most of the cases not even their substitution by the small farmers … [D]uring all this time our creole materials and the materials improved through conventional techniques have had the opportunity to interchange genes, and this not only has not eliminated the biodiversity of our creole materials but has enriched them and the small farmers have incorporated the genes which allow them to obtain enough for their consumption" (interview available at: http://www.check-biotech.org/root/index.cfm?fuseaction=newsletter&topic_id=3&subtoc_id=14&doc_id=2310).

15. The work of Ephraim Hernandez Xolocotzi during the 1940s onward in collecting native maize varieties is a notable case. See M. A. Díaz León's (1998) *Nueve mil años de agricultura en México: Homenaje a Efraím Hernández Xolocotzi*. For a recent ethnography of Mexican small-scale agriculture as scientific knowledge, see Roberto González's (2001) *Zapotec science*.

16. In addition to being a member of CIBIOGEM, Dr. José Luis Solleiro is also General Director of AgroBio Mexico, which was founded by the biotech corporate giants DuPont, Monsanto, Sygenta, Bayer and Dow.

17. While regionally variable, the average Mexican corn yield is around two tons per hectare, whereas US yields can reach between ten and twelve tons per hectare (Nadal 2000).

18. When Salinas and his administration of technocrats implemented a 'modernization' program whose stated goals were to allocate resources more efficiently to the countryside and to increase agricultural competitiveness and productivity, a high-ranking official of the Ministry of Agriculture articulated how such a modernization program envisioned rural displacement: "It is the policy of this government to remove half of the population from rural Mexico during the next five years" (Dr. Luis Tellez in 1991, cited in Barkin 2002: note 13).

19. Agronomist, maize collector, and teacher, Efraim Hernández Xolocotzi was an early critic of the notion that Mexican peasant/indigenous agriculture was inefficient (Díaz León and Cruz León 1998; see also Nadal 2000).

20. The organizations involved were the Asociación Mexicana de Uniones de Crédito del Sector Social, Asociación Nacional de Empresas Comercializadoras de Productores del Campo (ANEC), Coordinadora Estatal de Productores Cafetaleros, Coalición de Organizaciones Democráticas Urbanas y Campesinas, Central Independiente de Obreros Agrícolas y Campesinos, Coordinadora Nacional de Organizaciones Cafetaleras, Coordinadora Nacional Plan de Ayala, Frente Democrático Campesino de Chihuahua, Frente Nacional en Defensa del Campo Mexicano, Red Mexicana de Organizaciones Campesinas Forestales, Unión Nacional de Organizaciones en Forestería Comunitaria, Unión Nacional de Trabajadores y El Barzón Nacional. UNORCA (Unión Nacional de Organizaciones Regionales Campesinas Autónomas) was also involved in the protests, among others. The National Confederation of Peasants (or CNC) of the Institutional Revolutionary Party (or PRI) was initially part of the protests but broke off their affiliation with *El campo no aguanta más* in January. The Left press argued that the Ministry of Agriculture (SAGARPA) was trying to divide the movement by negotiating an National Agreement on agriculture with PRI member organizations like the

CNC ("El Campo ante la TLCAN", *La Jornada*, 30 January 2003). The PRI ruled Mexico from 1929 to the end of the twentieth century. Mexico was dominated by one-party rule for more than seventy years which involved both political stability and widespread corruption. The National Confederation of Peasants (or CNC) was founded to represent the large peasant population during the early years of PRI rule.

21. The position against transgenic crops was one of the six demands made by UNORCA (among other groups) in their call for the December protests ("Movilizaciones campesinas" e-mail from unorcalistas@laneta.apc.org, 29 November 2002). Other platforms that came out of the demonstrations, like "Six proposals for the salvation and reevaluation of the Mexican countryside" did not include specific reference to GM corn, but did include a call for a moratorium on the agricultural chapter of NAFTA (see Bartra 2004:21).

22. Of course, some indigenous people themselves have claimed an affinity with nature as a strategy for making claims on political and economic resources. An indigenous identity articulated in relationship to collective resources and territory can be an important strategy in claiming such resources (Muehlebach 2001). At the National Indigenous Congress in March 2001, for example, indigenous representatives produced a declaration calling for the constitutional recognition of indigenous collective rights, an issue that garnered national and international attention because of the EZLN campaign for a law recognizing collective rights. Biodiversity figured prominently in the National Indigenous Congress' declaration: "For us, Indian people, the true people, our Mother Earth is sacred, as is all those that live on her, the animals, the plants, the rivers, the mountains, the caves, the valleys, the biological resources, and the knowledge that our people have of them. They are not merchandise that can be bought or sold . . . We demand a moratorium on all prospecting projects and explorations into biodiversity, minerals, water, and so on" (Reprint of NIC declaration in *Cuadernos Agrarios* 2001 (21): 203). However, while these issues inform and overlap with the corn debates, the problems related to corn biodiversity and production differ in significant ways from the question of indigenous rights. Corn agriculture is not a resource in the same way that other collective resources are, such as water, minerals, or wild plants subject to bio-prospecting (Brush 1996; Brush and Stabinsky 1996).

23. Deep Mexico is an expression taken from anthropologist Guillermo Bonfil Batalla's ([1987] 1996) *México profundo*.

24. While maize and beans are the most widely grown crops in the region, other commercial crops include alfalfa, tomato, squash, garlic, melon, flowers, and sugarcane. Prior to the 1980s, the region was also an important wheat producer.

25. Elsewhere, I explain the twentieth century remaking of social relations in interaction with wider forces (2004). For an excellent historical account of how the valley peasantry was shaped through the projects of state and capital see Henao (1980).

26. For examples of how indigenous Mexicans represent themselves as the people of maize, see the articles by Silvia Ribeiro (2004) or Rámon Vera Herrera (2004). For instance, Zapotec Indian from Oaxaca, Aldo González Rojas, said at the Second Forum of *En defensa del maíz*, "we have recently found out that native maize varieties have been contaminated with transgenic seeds. This means that what our indigenous peoples took thousands of years to develop can be destroyed in no time at all by companies that trade in life" (quoted in Ribeiro 2004:1).

REFERENCES

Ackerman, Frank, Timothy A. Wise, Kevin P. Gallagher, Luke Ney, and Regina Flores. 2003. *Free trade, corn, and the environment: Environmental impacts of US-Mexico corn trade under NAFTA*. Medford, MA: Tufts University.

Alvarez-Buylla, Elena. 2003. *Ecological and biological aspects of the impacts of transgenic maize, including agro-biodiversity*. Secretariat report prepared for Commission for Environmental Cooperation. http://www.cec.org/pubs_docs/ documents/index.cfm?varlan=english&ID=988.

Alvarez-Morales, Ariel. 2000. Mexico: Ensuring environmental safety while benefiting from biotechnology. In *Agricultural biotechnology and the poor*, ed. Gabrielle J. Persley and Manuel M. Lantin, 90–196. Washington, DC: Consultative Group on International Agricultural Research, http://www.cgiar.org/biotech/repO100/Morales.pdf.

Appadurai, Arjun. 1996. *Modernity at large: Cultural dimensions of globalization*. Minneapolis: University of Minnesota Press.

Appendini, Kirsten. 1994. Transforming food policy for over a decade: The balance for Mexican corn farmers in 1993. In *Economic restructuring and rural subsistence in Mexico*, ed. Cynthia Hewitt de Alcántara, 145–57. San Diego: United Nations Research Institute for Social Development and *Ejido* Reform Research Project, Center for US-Mexican Studies, University of California.

———. 1998. Changing agrarian institutions: Interpreting the contradictions. In *The transformation of rural Mexico: Reforming the* ejido *sector*, ed. Wayne Cornelius and David Myhre, 25–38. San Diego: Center for US-Mexican Studies, University of California.

Barkin, David. 2002. The reconstruction of the modern Mexican peasantry. *Journal of Peasant Studies* 30 (1): 73–90.

———. 2003. El maíz y la economía. In ed. Gustavo Esteva and Catherine Marielle, 155–76.

Barkin, David, and Blanca Suárez. 1983. *El fin del principio: Las semillas y la seguridad alimentaria*. Mexico City: Centro de Ecología y Desarrollo.

Bartra, Armando. 2004. Rebellious cornfields: Towards food and labour self-sufficiency. In *Mexico in transition*, ed. Gerardo Otero, 18–36. London: Zed Press.

Beck, Ulrich. [1986] 1992. *Risk society: Towards a new modernity*. London: SAGE Publications.

Bonfil Batalla, Guillermo. [1987] 1996. *México profundo: Reclaiming a civilization*. Austin: University of Texas Press.

Brush, Stephen. 1996. Whose knowledge, whose genes, whose rights? In *Valuing local knowledge: Indigenous people and their intellectual property rights*, ed. Stephen Brush and Doreen Stabinsky, 1–21. Washington, DC: Island Press.

Brush, Stephen, and Doreen Stabinsky, eds. 1996. *Valuing local knowledge: Indigenous people and their intellectual property rights*. Washington, DC: Island Press.

CEC. 2004. *Maize and biodiversity: The effects of transgenic maize in Mexico*. Secretariat report. Montreal: North American Commission for Environmental Cooperation.

Chapela, Ignacio, and David Quist. 2001. Trangenic DNA introgressed into traditional maize landraces in Oaxaca, Mexico. *Nature* (414): 541–43.

CONACYT-CONABIO. 1999. Organismos vivos modificados en la agricultura mexicana. *Biotecnología* 4 (2): 47–60.

Crehan, Kate. 2002. *Gramsci, culture, and anthropology*. Berkeley: University of California Press.

de Janvry, Alain, Gustavo Gordillo, and Elisabeth Sadoulet. 1997. *Mexico's second agrarian reform: Household and community responses, 1990–1994*. San Diego and La Jolla: Center for US-Mexican Studies, University of California.

Díaz León, Marco Antonio, and Artemio Cruz León, eds. 1998. *Nueve mil años de agricultura en México: Homenaje a Efraím Hernández Xolocotzi*. Mexico City: Grupo de Estudios Ambientales, Universidad Autónoma Chapingo.

Dyer, George. 2000. In situ conservation in the Sierra Norte de Puebla, Mexico. Paper presented at the Scientific basis of participatory plant breeding and conservation of genetic resources conference, Oaxtepec, Mexico, 8–14 October.

Dyer, George, and Antonio Yúnez-Naude. 2003. NAFTA and conservation of maize diversity in Mexico. Report prepared for the Second North American Symposium on Assessing the Environmental Effects of Trade, Commission for Environmental Cooperation (CEC), 25–26 March 2003. http://www.cec.org/files/PDF/ECONOMY/Dyer-Yunez_en.pdf.

Esteva, Gustavo. 2003. El maiz como opcion de vida. In ed. Gustavo Esteva and Catherine Marielle, 285–322.

Esteva, Gustavo, and Catherine Marielle, eds. 2003. *Sin maíz, no hay país*. Mexico City: CONACULTA and Museo Nacional de Culturas Populares.

Fitting, Elizabeth. 2004. 'No hay dinero en la milpa': El maíz y el hogar transnacional del Sur del Valle de Tehuacan. In *La economía política de la migración acelerada internacional de Puebla y Veracruz: Siete estudios de caso*, ed. Leigh Binford, 61–101. Mexico City: Editorial Luna Arena.

———. 2006. Importing corn, exporting labor: The neoliberal corn regime, GMOs, and the erosion of Mexican biodiversity. *Agriculture and Human Values* 23: 15–26.

———. Forthcoming. La economía natural enfrente al global? Desafíos a los debates sobre el maíz mexicano. *Bajo el volcán: la revista de BUAP*.

Gonzalez, Roberto. 2001. *Zapotec science: Farming and food in the northern sierra of Oaxaca*. Austin: University of Texas Press.

Greenpeace Mexico. 2000. *Maíz transgénico*. Documentos de campana. Mexico: Greenpeace.

Gupta, Akhil. 1998. *Postcolonial development: Agriculture and the making of modern India*. Durham: Duke University Press.

Hayden, Cori. 2003. From market to market: Bio-prospecting's idioms of inclusion. *American Anthropologist* 30 (3): 359–71.

Heller, Chaia. 2002. From scientific risk to paysan savoir-faire: Peasant expertise in the French and global debate over GM crops. *Science as Culture* 11 (1): 5–37.

Henao, Luis E. 1980. *Tehuacán: Campesinado e irrigación*. Mexico City: Edicol.

Hewitt de Alcantara, Cynthia. 1976. *Modernizing Mexico's agriculture: Socioeconomic implications of technological change, 1940–1970*. Geneva: United Nations Research Institute for Social Development.

INE-CONABIO. 2002. Evidencias del flujo genético desde fuentes de maíz transgénico hacia variedades criollas. Findings presented by E. Huerta at the *En defensa del maíz* conference, Mexico City, 23 January.

INEGI. 2000. *Instituto Nacional de Estadística, Geografia, e Informatica: Anuario Estadístico del Estado de Puebla*. Mexico City: INEGI.

Macip, Ricardo F. 1998. The politics of identity and internal colonialism in the Sierra Negra of Mexico. MA Thesis, New School for Social Research.

McAfee, Kathleen. 2003. Corn culture and dangerous DNA: Real and imagined consequences of maize transgene flow in Oaxaca. *Journal of Latin American Geography* 2 (1): 18–42.

Muehlebach, Andrea. 2001. 'Making place' at the United Nations: Indigenous cultural politics at the UN. *Cultural Anthropology* 16 (3): 415–48.

Murcott, Anne. 2001. Public beliefs about GM foods: More on the makings of a considered sociology. *Medical Anthropology Quarterly* 15(1): 9–19.

Myhre, David. 1998. The Achilles' heel of the reforms: The rural finance system. In *The transformation of rural Mexico*, ed. Wayne Cornelius and David Myhre, 39–65. San Diego: Center for US-Mexican Studies, University of California.

Nadal, Alejandro. 2000. *The environmental and social impacts of economic liberalization on corn production in Mexico*. Oxford: Oxfam GB and WWF.

Nader, Laura, ed. 1996. *Naked science: Anthropological inquiry into boundaries, power, and knowledge*. New York: Routledge.

O'Brien, Jay, and William Roseberry. 1991. Introduction. In *Golden ages, dark ages: Imagining the past in anthropology and history*, ed. Jay O'Brien and William Roseberry, 1–18. Berkeley: University of California Press.

Ortiz-García, S., E. Ezcurra, B. Schoel, F. Acevedo, J. Soberón, and A. A. Snow. 2005. Absence of detectable transgenes in local landraces of maize in Oaxaca, Mexico, 2003–2004. *Proceedings of the National Academy of Sciences* 102 (35): 12338–43. http://www.pnas.org/cgi/doi/10.1073/pnas.0503356102.

Otero, Gerardo. 1999. *Farewell to the peasantry? Political class formation in rural Mexico*. Boulder: Westview Press.

Pilcher, Jeffrey. 1998. *Que vivan los tamales! Food and the making of Mexican identity*. Albuquerque: University of New Mexico Press.

Ribeiro, Silvia. 2004. The day the sun dies: Contamination and resistance in Mexico. *Seedling*, July: 5–10. http://www.grain.org/seedling_files/seed-04-07-02.pdf

Richards, Paul. 1985. *Indigenous agricultural revolution*. London: Hutchinson.

Roseberry, William. 1989. *Anthropologies and histories*. New Brunswick: Rutgers University Press.

——. 1993. The agrarian question. In *Confronting historical paradigms: Peasants, labor, and the capitalist world system in Africa and Latin America*, ed. Frederick Cooper, Allen F. Isaacman, Florencia C. Mallon, William Roseberry, and

Steve J. Stern, 318–68. Madison: Wisconsin University Press.

Serratos, Antonio. 1996. Evaluation of novel crop varieties in their center of origin and diversity: The case of maize in Mexico. In *Turning priorities into feasible programs*. Proceedings of a policy seminar on agricultural biotechnology for Latin America, Peru, 6–10 October 1996, ed. John Komen, Cesar Falconi, and Hilda Fernandez, 68–73. The Hague / Mexico City: Intermediary Biotechnology Service / CamBioTec.

Shiva, Vandana. 1991. *The violence of the green revolution*. London: Zed Press.

Soleri, Daniela, David A. Cleveland, Flavio Aragón, Mario R. Fuentes, Humberto Ríos, and Stuart H. Sweeney. 2005. Understanding the potential impact of transgenic crops in traditional agriculture: Maize farmers' perspectives in Cuba, Guatemala, and Mexico. *Environmental Biosafety Research* 4 (3): 141–66.

Turrent Fernández, Antonio. 2005. La diversidad genética del maíz y del teocinte de México debe ser protegida contra la contiminación irreversible del maíz transgénico. In *Transgénics, quien los necesita?*, ed. Armando Bartra, José Luis Cabrera Padilla, Ana Maria Calderón de la Barca, Ignacio Chapela, Mária Colin, María del Rosario Herrera Ascencio, Fidel Márquez Sánchez, José Óscar Mascorro Gallardo, Yolanda Cristina Massieu Trigo, Adelita San Vicente Tello, Percy Schmeiser, Antonio Turrent Fernández, and Pablo Uribe Malagamba, 51–60. Mexico City: Grupo parlamentario del PRD den la LIX Legislatura, Centro de Producción Editorial.

Vera Herrera, Ramón. 2004. En defensa del maíz (y el futuro). *Citizen Action in the Americas* 13 (August): 1–10. Programa de las Américas, Interhemispheric Resource Center (IRC), http://www.americaspolicy.org.

Warman, Arturo. 1980. *We come to object: The peasants of Morelos and the national state*. Baltimore: Johns Hopkins University Press.

——. 1988. *La historia de un bastardo: Maíz y capitalismo*. Mexico City: Instituto de Investigations Sociales, UNAM. Fondo de Cultura Economica.

Wynne, Bruce. 1996. May the sheep safely graze? A reflexive view of the expert-lay knowledge divide. In *Risk, environment and modernity*, ed. Scott Lash, Bron Szerszynski, and Brian Wynne, 44–83. London: SAGE publications.

SECTION 5

*F*ood Activism

34

Practicing Food Democracy: A Pragmatic Politics of Transformation

Neva Hassanein

1. INTRODUCTION

In *Hungry for Profit*, an edited collection of essays, contributor Henderson (2000) examines some of the current social activity opposing the excesses of industrialization, economic concentration, and globalization of agriculture and food systems. Henderson gives us a glimpse of organizations in the United States developing alternative farm practices, of farmers and eaters engaged in community supported agriculture, of groups working to guarantee the right to a nutritious and sufficient diet, and of policy advocates operating at the national and international levels. From this vista of the organizational landscape, Henderson (2000, p. 175) observes that: "sustainable agriculture is swelling into a significant social movement with a national network and an effective policy wing". She sees rich potential in the ability of people to organize and build local food systems from the grassroots up. In this context, she concludes, "food becomes political," and even a backyard garden becomes "a small piece of liberated territory in the struggle for a just and sustainable society" (Henderson, 2000, pp. 187–188).

The editors of *Hungry for Profit* apparently felt compelled to respond to Henderson in a note following her essay, the only such note in the volume (Magdoff et al., 2000, p. 188). The editors comment that most people "on the left" might resonate with the vision for an alternative agro-food system that Henderson paints, but those same people "may think that the key tactics chosen by activists at the grassroots are insufficient to mount a systematic critique of corporate agriculture and liberal capitalist economics as a whole" (Magdoff et al., 2000, p. 188). The editors concede that strategies such as farmers' adding value to their produce by direct marketing and efforts to improve the access to nutritious food by the poor can help people confront immediate problems in their everyday lives. The editors maintain, however, that "a left analysis would question whether this pathway is really a solution to the problems or rather something that will produce only a minor irritant to corporate dominance of the food system. A complete transformation of the agriculture and food system, it might be argued, requires a complete transformation of the society" (Magdoff et al., 2000, p. 188).

The above exchange points to a tension regarding the potential of the alternative agro-food movement to create meaningful change. From one perspective, individual and organizational actors working to change the dominant agro-food system need to be engaged on a daily basis in political and social struggles and accomplish what is presently possible given existing opportunities and barriers. From an alternate view, such incrementalism and pragmatism are woefully inadequate for achieving the complete transformation of the food and agriculture system that many movement actors and academic analysts see as necessary.

Can pragmatic, incremental steps transform the dominant agro-food system so that it will be more sustainable in the long term? Of course, there are no easy answers to that question. In my attempt—both as an activist and as a student of social movements—to think about it, I find useful the emerging concept of "food democracy". It is the purpose of this essay to discuss that concept and to elaborate upon its practical utility with respect to collective action within the alternative agro-food movement, with a primary focus on the United States.

If it is the job of a critical social scientist to go beyond surface impressions and uncover underlying social structures and conflicts as a way to empower people to improve society, it is the job of activists to execute strategies for social change and anchor that work in hope for a better world. I identify and have experience with both of these projects. As a result, I appreciate the value of an on-going cycle of inquiry—of action and reflection and then adjustment based on knowledge gained through experience. Such reflection suggests to me that the thoughtful practice of pragmatic politics and the development of a strong food democracy will be keys to transformation of agro-food systems in the long run.

2. THE IMPERATIVE OF FOOD DEMOCRACY

In the 1980s, "sustainability" emerged as a powerful symbol and the goal of a social movement focused on food and agriculture in the United States. Ever since, the concept has been contested, and the term has eluded a consensus on its definition. In part, the question of definition results from the wide variety of interests—such as environmentalists, alternative farmers, food security advocates, farm worker unions, and consumer groups—that have

a stake in building more sustainable agriculture and food systems. Although these actors are not unified on a political agenda and they pursue different strategies and approaches to change, there is a general sense of being on the same side of the social conflict over food and agriculture. Definitions of sustainability that are broad and inclusive are therefore useful because they can encompass this range of individual and organizational actors. For instance, Allen et al. (1991, p. 37) defined a sustainable agro-food system as "one that equitably balances concerns for environmental soundness, economic viability, and social justice among all sectors of society".

While the above definition is useful because it embraces the range of interests that should be included in a vision for sustainability, it is difficult to apply this—or any—definition as a practical guide for action. What does it really mean *in practice* to equitably balance concerns for environmental soundness, economic viability, and social justice among all sectors of society? How should each dimension be evaluated in relation to the others? How should society weigh, for example, the protection of water quality from agricultural runoff against the possibility that additional regulation of farming practices might make it even more difficult for small agricultural producers to operate in an economically viable manner? What should be done in the many cases where there is considerable scientific uncertainty and incomplete ecological and social data, such as in the realms of pesticides and genetic engineering? How do we make judgments about the needs, wants, and rights of current generations in light of considerations for future generations? Perhaps most importantly, who gets to decide where the "equitable balance" lies?

Definitions of sustainability cannot fully anticipate responses to these kinds of questions because at their core these matters are about conflicts over values.

When values clash, there is no independent authority that society can *meaningfully* appeal to for a definitive resolution of disputes. For example, most proponents of sustainability would argue that agricultural science is incapable of guiding decisions about the food production and distribution system. Indeed, sustainability advocates have long challenged many of the knowledge claims generated by the dominant institutions of agricultural research and the privileged role of science in shaping agriculture (Hassanein, 1999). And, many of the technologies generated by public and private agricultural science are precisely at issue in contemporary food politics (e.g., genetically engineered crops). Surely, agronomists, geneticists, agricultural economists, and other scientists can and should contribute to the discussions; but ultimately "experts" cannot by themselves fairly make the decisions that impact the sustainability of agricultural production and the food system because those decisions involve choosing among values. In a pluralistic society, agreement on science (or religion) as an independent authority for making decisions about values is not likely, nor desirable.

If the very real disputes over the consequences and direction of the agro-food system cannot be resolved by appealing to an independent authority for an objective answer, how then should they be resolved? Drawing heavily on Barber's (1984) exploration of "strong democracy," Prugh et al. (2000, p. 7) suggest an answer to this question about sustainability more generally, and their observations certainly apply to food and agriculture as well. They argue that: "Because the conflict is about values, sustainability must be socially and politically defined". Furthermore, solutions to the ecological, social, and economic problems associated with the excesses of industrialized, corporate-dominated, and globalized agriculture cannot all be prescribed in advance. Natural and social systems are neither static nor predictable. Because decision-making is usually shrouded in uncertainty, society must assume and plan for the reality that the agro-food system is temporally and geographically variable, that we cannot have complete knowledge in advance of the consequences of the choices that are made, and that notions of what is sustainable will evolve over time. Selecting sustainable solutions from various options means making choices that affect everyone, and in that context, conflict is inevitable. Politics is the arena in which we deal with disagreements over values. Such conflict is not something to shy away from; conflict leads to change. As the well-known organizer Alinsky (1972, p. 21) wrote: "Change means movement. Movement means friction. Only in the frictionless vacuum of a nonexistent abstract world can movement or change occur without that abrasive friction of conflict". The best hope for finding workable solutions to conflicts about the character and direction of the agro-food system is through the active participation of the citizenry (in the broad, denizen sense of the word) and political engagement to work out our differences.

If solutions to problems in the agro-food system depend in a very fundamental way on participation, the emerging concept of food democracy serves as a constructive method for political practice because participation is a key feature of democracy. Lang (1999) has popularized the term food democracy and begun to develop it conceptually. He argues that the agro-food system is ultimately "both a symptom and a symbol of how we organize ourselves and our societies," and it represents "a microcosm of wider social realities" (Lang, 1999, p. 218). Food reflects "a titanic struggle between the forces of control and the pressure to democratize". The recognition that the agro-food system has been and continues to be contested terrain acknowledges an important space for individual and collective agency. Accordingly, Lang argues that, historically as well as today, "a set of demands from below" has bubbled up in many areas of the world. Specifically, he refers to political pressure to ensure "greater access and collective benefit from the food system" so that it provides "the means to eat adequately, affordably, safely, humanely, and in ways one considers civil and culturally appropriate" (Lang, 1999, p. 218). At the core of food democracy is the idea that people can and should be actively participating in shaping the food system, rather than remaining passive spectators on the sidelines. In other words, food democracy is about citizens having the power to determine agro-food policies and practices locally, regionally, nationally, and globally.

The force for food democracy confronts the control that powerful and highly concentrated economic interests exert on food and agriculture today (see McMichael, 2000). Significantly, the industrialization, concentration of economic power, and globalization of the agro-food sector are not immutable processes with a foregone conclusion. Whatmore and Thorne (1997, p. 289) have applied actor network theory to call for greater attention to social agency and the struggle to create alternative food networks, and to demonstrate that globalization is not a logical but "a socially contested process in which many spaces of resistance, alterity, and possibility become analytically discernible and politically meaningful". Similarly, Gottlieb (2001, p. 258) argues that: "...the dominant food system, embedded as it may be in influencing how food is produced as well as consumed, is not immovable; its outcomes are not inevitable". To speak of the pressure to democratize the food system is to recognize that there are spaces of resistance and creativity in which people themselves attempt to govern and shape their relationships with food and agriculture.

Food policy councils offer a concrete example of a deliberate attempt to develop the practice of food democracy.

Established by a few North American cities and counties over the last decade, food policy councils dedicate resources and give validity to an arena that has not traditionally been part of local government: community food security and local, sustainable agriculture (Feenstra, 1997). Unlike most hunger intervention models, community food security puts emphasis on the community rather than individual level, looks for strategies for empowerment and food self-reliance, and stresses prevention with a focus on nutrition and sustainable food production (Gottlieb, 2001). Successfully implementing this integrated and coordinated approach requires bringing together representatives of a range of local food-system stakeholder groups from both the public and private sectors, groups that do not otherwise engage in regular dialogue and constructive, collaborative action.

Welsh and MacRae (1998) have drawn on their involvement with the Toronto Food Policy Council (TFPC) to further elaborate the concept of food democracy and the associated idea of food citizenship. Formed in 1990, the TFPC challenged the traditional assumption that hunger, poor nutrition, and environmental problems associated with agriculture can be adequately addressed without significant redesign of the food system. The TFPC recognized that long-lasting, local solutions necessitate moving beyond the limiting notions of food as commodity, people as consumers, and society as marketplace. Instead, Welsh and MacRae (1998, p. 241) stress that advocates need to focus on food citizenship and the recognition of both the rights and responsibilities that the term implies: "Food, like no other commodity, allows for a political reawakening, as it touches our lives in so many ways. . . . Food citizenship suggests both belonging and participating, at all levels of relationship from the intimacy of breastfeeding to the discussions at the World Trade Organization".

Accordingly, the TFPC has pursued hundreds of community food projects and advocated for reinforcing policies that encourage food democracy. For example, rather than the disempowering charity model typical of anti-hunger advocacy, their Field to Table program sells food produced by area farmers at wholesale prices to organized groups of primarily low-income people, and trains these groups in food-related skills that have been lost with the food industry's emphasis on convenience and the consequent "de-skilling" of consumers. In turn, trainees work in different parts of the Field to Table program, and some have started microbusinesses that sell products back into the distribution program. These and other innovative structures emerge from a holistic critique of the food system, and simultaneously unearth and celebrate the social and cultural role of food. For Welsh and MacRae, the transformative potential of food democracy lies in its significant challenge to the structures of capital because food democracy contests the commodification of food and transforms people from passive consumers into active, educated citizens.

3. SOCIAL MOVEMENTS AND THE PRESSURE TO DEMOCRATIZE

The main source of the pressure to democratize the food system comes from the constellation of organizations in the alternative agro-food movement. By alternative agro-food movement, I refer to the social activity of sustainable agriculturalists, local food advocates, environmentalists, food security activists, and others who are working to bring about changes at a variety of different levels of the agro-food system. Buttel (1997, p. 352) observes that social movements are "the most important social forces that could provide a countervailing tide to global integration of the agro-food system, to the decline of household forms of agricultural

commodity production, and to structural blockages to achievement of sustainability". He maintains that environmental and related agricultural sustainability movements will most likely be the primary mechanism for bringing about significant, positive change in the agro-food system if it is to occur. Similarly, Gottlieb (2001) appreciates the numerous local efforts at building an alternative food regime because they provide valuable and rich examples of the potential for change. He maintains that the "new food movements" have begun to build a pathway for necessary environmental and social change by "challenging the ways we think and talk about food" (Gottlieb, 2001, p. 271).

While recognizing the power and promise of social movements, both Buttel (1997) and Gottlieb (2001) raise important concerns that they feel must be addressed if a movement is to realize its full potential. Specifically, these analysts point out that the alternative agro-food movement is very diverse in terms of its organizational forms and strategies, and in terms of the locus of action. Buttel (1997, p. 353) states that there is no "underlying notion or strategy that can serve as a singular unifying focus for the movement," and he worries that the divisions among the groups in terms of interests and worldviews limit the effectiveness of the movement. Similarly, Gottlieb (2001) is concerned that movement actors remain too disconnected from one another, their source of power is too dispersed, and their visions too focused on specific issues and goals. "The challenge to the movement itself," he maintains, "is the need to shift the arguments about discourse to the arena of action where the sum of different actions, policy initiatives, and movement building activities—whether environmentally or socially defined—can become greater than any one of its individual parts" (Gottlieb, 2001, pp. 271–272). While the diverse organizational forms and strategies within the movement are potentially problematic in ways Buttel and Gottlieb identify, there are also positive aspects of this diversity that should be appreciated.

3.1. Diverse Organizational Forms and Strategies

In considering the diversity of approaches to social change that exists within the alternative agro-food movement, it is important to acknowledge that diversity is a feature of the so-called "new social movements." The "new" movements (like feminism, ecology, and peace) are often contrasted with the "old" (workers') movements which tended to be more coherent forces for change. New social movement theory stresses that what distinguishes the new movements is that their actors struggle to create new social identities, to open up democratic spaces for autonomous social action in civil society, and to reinterpret norms and develop new institutions (Scott, 1990). The new movements are understood to be trying to bring about changes in civil society by transforming values, lifestyles, and symbols (Melucci, 1985). The alternative agro-food movement—as a kind of new social movement—is dynamic and multi-dimensional, involving various groups of people situated in particular places, who create and implement assorted strategies, participate in diverse forms of action, and encounter a variety of obstacles and opportunities.

There are at least three positive aspects of this diversity of organizational approaches that should be acknowledged. First, different social movement organizations address specific problems and thereby fill different functions within the movement. For example, I served from 1997 to 2000 as coordinator of a statewide coalition campaign, the goal of which was to establish a law requiring the comprehensive reporting of pesticide use in the state of Oregon, US. Although this pesticide right-to-know campaign involved a broad coalition (discussed in more detail below), three organizations had significant resources in terms of staff time, member mobilization, and money dedicated to the achievement of very specific, achievable, and measurable objectives designed to meet our goal over a 3-year period. There were other pesticide or agricultural issues we *might* have chosen to work on during that time, but we had to leave those issues to others to address and instead fulfill our particular niche in the movement. To be effective, an organization must focus its resources. A powerful social movement can result from multiple organizations each effectively filling specific niches.

A second reason the diversity of organizational approaches can be seen as a strength of the movement is that different groups give their members an opportunity to participate in different ways. There are many people who have real or potential grievances with the agro-food system, and their participation in social movements is crucial if meaningful change is going to occur. These grievances, however, do not automatically translate into action, as social scientists using resource mobilization theory to understand social movements have long recognized (Zald, 1992). An individual or organization may care about an issue, but lack the capacity to act. A major challenge for organizers is how to effectively mobilize people out of their routines of social life, work, and leisure, and get people to participate in social change activities. The reality for the organizer is that people will choose to participate in particular ways; the existence of a variety of organizations allows for that choice.

Opportunities for movement participation are crucial because a high level of mobilization needs to occur if the alternative agro-food movement is going to effect transformational change. The *organizing* processes that lead to greater mobilization must be well understood and implemented by movement activists. Organizing is about understanding a community's resources, and working on issues that people care about and that are easily understood and communicated. An issue is a solution or partial solution to a particular problem. A problem may exist for a long time, but it is the work of organizations to make it into an issue to be solved. For instance, in the pesticide right-to-know campaign referred to above, the problems created by the lack of reliable and accurate data about which pesticides are used, where, when, and in what amounts had been recognized for a long time (e.g., National Research Council, 1975). But it was not until the 1990s that activists in Oregon made the problem into a public issue that decision makers had to address by calling for a comprehensive and mandatory pesticide use reporting law. This required a series of steps to frame the issue such that large numbers of people agreed that the policy proposal was a solution to a real problem—a problem that had, for instance, hampered society's ability to understand how pesticides affect children's health or to develop meaningful remedies to the problems of non-point source water pollution. The campaign also focused on the basic democratic right to know about the use of toxic chemicals. Having a variety of organizations involved in the campaign made it easier to articulate multiple reasons why the issue needed to be solved and thus to attract a greater number of supporters.

Third, the different organizational approaches foster an essential vitality that can lead to new insights and practices, as is characteristic of the so-called new social movements. Actors in social movements often articulate ideas that challenge not only established arrangements, but also the ideas of others in the movement. This ongoing struggle to integrate goals, beliefs and strategies *within movements* is part of the process of social change (Melucci, 1985). Through struggles among individual and organizational movement actors, new social movements can be understood as social laboratories in which people experiment with new practices, ideas, and organizational principles (Eyerman and Jamison, 1991; Wainwright, 1994). In short, movements move.

Within the alternative agro-food movement, this kind of contestation that leads to innovation is evident in the recent debates about organic food. Over the last decade, the organic industry has grown tremendously in terms of volume, variety of products, and sales (Klonsky, 2000). The US Department of Agriculture released the final National Organic Standards in extensively revised form after it received a record number of over 275,000 public comments opposing the agency's draft rules that would have implemented weak organic standards (Allen and Kovach, 2000). By most measures the above observations are all signs of movement success. Within the movement, however, some groups are raising critical questions about the meaning of this success and exploring new avenues that they hope will achieve broader goals. For example, the Land Stewardship Project is developing a labeling program called the Midwest Food Alliance. The group's associate director Dana Jackson says: "The new National Organic Standards will essentially be a list of do's and don'ts for production, but they will not necessarily address the social context: Did family sized farms produce this? Were people paid well? Do the farmers have a connection to their community? How far did this food travel? What we're promoting is beyond organic, it's a regional food system" (quoted in Maas, 2001, p. 24). Thus, the Midwest Food Alliance label tries to unmask the social context of agricultural production. The proliferation of such eco-labels is the result of debates that are occurring within the movement, and that is because the actors are diverse and they challenge one another in ways that at least potentially can lead to further positive change.

3.2. Coalition Building

Even if one recognizes the value of the multiplicity of interests, organizations, and strategies within the alternative agro-food movement, there are still important opportunities for a greater level of convergence and the creation of strategic alliances among various groups. Building coalitions to work on particular issues increases citizen power and enables organizations to effect change that they could not achieve on their own. These are usually temporary alliances built around a particular issue. For example, in the pesticide right-to-know campaign referred to above, the creation of a broad coalition made a tremendous difference in increasing our power to move legislation in a tough political climate. Initially, three organizations essentially designed and coordinated the overall strategy, and each group brought different and complementary strengths to the effort. One group has expertise in the scientific and policy aspects of pesticides and a membership dedicated to the issue; another group has a strong legislative presence and access to key decision makers; and a third group has a strong ability to mobilize large numbers of people at the grassroots through their canvass. In turn, these environmental and public interest organizations made a deliberate attempt to reach out to a broad range of organizations that conceivably had an interest in securing better data on pesticides. Our coalition building targeted non-traditional allies who would be effective messengers with the public and policy makers, such as public health advocates, public drinking water providers, commercial fishing organizations, watershed councils, children's advocates, and labor unions. Of course, coalition building required a variety of approaches to appeal to the varying interests of the groups of potential allies. Eventually over 70 groups endorsed the policy proposal, and the broad-based coalition strengthened the effort considerably.

Buttel (1997, p. 352) argues for the creation of an "omnibus coalitional agro-food system movement that contests deregulation, globalization, and agro-ecosystem degradation". While an omnibus coalition that functions on a permanent basis may remain elusive, there are signs of important coalition-building efforts among organizations protesting unbridled globalization at international trade meetings. In an unprecedented move, the Institute for Agriculture and Trade Policy (IATP) recently called for the creation of a "civil-society delegation" to the ministerial meeting of the World Trade Organization held in Qatar in November of 2001 (Longworth, 2001). After the battle in Seattle in 1999, the WTO selected the isolated peninsula as the site for the next meeting in hopes of thwarting protestors. As a result of Qatar's limited facilities, the WTO severely cut the number of unofficial observers, and restricted each nongovernmental organization (NGO) seeking accreditation to one delegate, for a total of 647. The number stands in stark contrast to the tens of thousands who showed up at Seattle and subsequent anti-globalization protests. Mark Ritchie of IATP was concerned that the 647 delegates could amount to as many different versions of ineffectiveness. Therefore, he issued a plea to the NGOs that they pool their individual accreditations and that each group get a vote to elect a committee of trusted leaders who would then pick a technical support staff and a unified, balanced delegation that would represent the many interests of the organizations, including food and agriculture issues. While this creative approach is borne out of necessity, it may signal a transcendence of single-issue advocacy and a move toward the implementation of a joint, cooperative strategy that Ritchie and others hope will be "the wave of the future" (Longworth, 2001, p. Al). This practical obstacle created by the WTO thus turns into an opportunity for coalition building on a scale hitherto unseen.

Coalitions not only increase citizen power to effect change on a particular issue, but also serve as important mechanisms by which groups can learn about one another and facilitate the broadening of participation of larger numbers of people. As Rose (2000, pp. 213–214) observes:

> Movements are schools for democracy where citizens learn what they can never understand from formal civics classes or from armchair infusions of media sound bites. But movements working in isolation are not enough. They require coalitions, democratic schools for community building, to bring people another critical step closer to a democratic society.

In this way, coalition building among groups working to transform the agro-food system—and even globalization and trade liberalization overall—is a step toward food democracy.

4. THE PRAGMATICS OF FOOD DEMOCRACY

Several scholars have argued that democracy—especially a stronger form than is practiced today in the United States—offers the best chance for achieving sustainability (Morrison, 1995; Prugh et al., 2000). Certainly, an oligarchy ruled by a handful of multinational corporations—the obvious tendency in the agro-food system that dominates at present—does not engender much hope for achieving sustainability. Food democracy seeks to expose and challenge the antidemocratic forces of control, and claims the rights and responsibilities of citizens to participate in decision-making. Food democracy ideally means that all members of an agro-food system have equal and effective opportunities for participation in shaping that system, as well as knowledge about the relevant alternative ways of designing and operating the system.

Conceived of in this way, food democracy is a *method* for making choices when values and interests come into conflict and

when the consequences of decisions are uncertain. Therefore, food democracy is essentially a pragmatic device for moving toward sustainability of agriculture and food systems. If food democracy is pragmatic, it is important to recognize that pragmatism has two sets of meanings—politically and philosophically. Both connotations can inform our understanding of the practice of food democracy.

4.1. Political Pragmatism

Commonly understood by the proverbial phrase, politics is the art of the possible, pragmatism is considered to be at the heart of democratic politics in the United States. Narrowly construed, political pragmatism refers to a willingness to negotiate differences—that is, to compromise—and to be satisfied with the achievement of incremental results rather than standing firm for inflexible absolutes. Those who take a pragmatic approach to policy—by crafting legislation or striking political deals—pride themselves on being goal-oriented and able to get something done.

Others criticize this approach as lacking a moral anchor. Consider, for instance, the comments of Michael Colby (1997, p. 9) of Food & Water, an organization that he describes as "radical" in the sense that it approaches the problems of our culture by "trying to get at the root of the problem and not settling for anything short of fundamental change". The root he identifies is "corporate control of a centralized and industrialized food supply". Colby (1997, p. 9) is frustrated with "a movement far too often fixated on legislative or regulatory gimmicks and far too willing to accept health-threatening compromises that do little other than merely tinker with a rotten system . . . When the issues we're working on involve life-and-death decisions, how can we accept crumbs when we deserve the full loaf of bread?"

Perhaps sustainability advocates need not be limited to crumbs if they recognize that creating social change, like making bread, requires the right ingredients, the proper skills, and sufficient patience for the bread to rise and bake. Perhaps a pragmatic approach to change need not mean that actions are based on expediency and lack integrity. Perhaps with the right ingredients and skills, our actions can move us in incremental steps toward true transformation. I emphasize the importance of having the right ingredients and skills because not every compromise leads down a transformative path. Citizen power and the skills to use one's power are especially crucial.

In the Oregon pesticide right-to-know campaign discussed above, our coalition came face-to-face with the question of when and whether to compromise. After building political power and considerable public support for comprehensive, mandatory pesticide use reporting through a multi-faceted campaign, the coalition had a bill introduced into the state legislature. If the legislative effort failed, we were prepared to use Oregon's ballot initiative process, which allows for passage of laws through an electoral vote. Governor John Kitzhaber, a popular Democrat, was an important ally, but his support alone was insufficient. A Republican and anti-environmental majority has controlled the state legislature for most of the last decade, and one of the most powerful lobby groups in Oregon represents pesticide users, sellers, and manufacturers. However, polls indicated strong voter support for mandatory pesticide use reporting, which was essential if the question was to go to a ballot measure. The coalition's preference was to pass the bill through the legislature because of the tremendous costs of a ballot initiative campaign. Working in our favor was the fact that the chemical and agricultural industry groups opposing the legislation had recently spent millions of dollars fighting (and crushing) other environmental ballot measures, and they were wary of spending even more, especially

when the majority of voters believes they have a right to know about pesticide use. Eventually, these dynamics more or less equalized the power of both the proponents and opponents of the pesticide reporting legislation. Each side confronted and weighed strategic questions about the risks and benefits of compromise in the legislative arena and about the possibility of winning or losing completely in a ballot initiative campaign. The result was that, after months of opposition from the chemical and agricultural industries, the coalition negotiated and passed compromise legislation, which achieved many but not all of our policy goals.

The story is like many others in the adversarial political system, where competing interests face the possibility of compromise, a word that wrongly carries with it shades of weakness and surrender. As Alinsky (1972, p. 59), one of the foremost architects of "radical pragmatism," wrote in his *Rules for Radicals*: ". . . to the organizer, compromise is a key and beautiful word. It is always present in the pragmatics of operation. It is making the deal, getting that vital breather, usually the victory. If you start with nothing, demand 100%, then compromise for 30%, you're 30% ahead." Carter (1996) argues that a compromise can possess integrity if it moves you toward your goal rather than away from it, and integrity *requires* that at times we take what we can get because achieving our moral ends perfectly or all at once is extremely rare, if not impossible. In other words, a compromise must "be part of the strategy for attaining the end that discernment has taught to be good and right . . . And the individual of integrity, having agreed to compromise, must not pretend that the compromise is itself the end. Instead he or she must be forthright in announcing that this is but one step along the road and that the journey will continue" (Carter, 1996, p. 46). Accordingly, while the 1999 passage of Oregon's pesticide use reporting law constituted a "victory," it was admittedly partial, marking the conclusion of one campaign and the start of another (i.e., achieving strong implementation of the new law). In the case of food democracy, the "end" toward which any incremental steps must move us is the vision of an ecologically sound, economically viable, and socially just system of food and agriculture.

4.2. Philosophical Pragmatism

At first blush, the political pragmatism described above does not seem to share much with the branch of philosophy known as pragmatism. Originally developed from the 1890s through the 1930s by William James, John Dewey and others, pragmatism has recently sparked a revival of interest and debate among contemporary philosophers. Pragmatist philosophy emerged as a critique of theoretical abstractions and absolutes, and embraced the idea that theory must ultimately be tested by practical experience (Dickstein, 1998). Practical experience refers to critical reflection on our experience and then modification of our subsequent actions accordingly (Dickstein, 1998; Hilde and Thompson, 2000). In the spirit of James and Dewey, pragmatism emphasizes open-ended inquiry into particular real-life problems, and is thus contextual and dynamic.

Hickman (2000) has suggested one link between pragmatism and contemporary efforts to revitalize local food systems. Specifically, he observes that the edible schoolyard recently created by Alice Waters—the restaurateur and advocate of local, organic foods—at the King Junior High School in Oakland shares a close resemblance to John Dewey's experiments in education at the University of Chicago's Primary School a century earlier. Both Dewey and Waters sought to engage students in terms of their own needs and interests, and to do so with gardening and the preparation of foods. Dewey's edible schoolyard was a tool to encourage

students to explore a whole range of related subjects that involved increasing levels of abstraction. Waters uses gardening to introduce students to an appetizing and nutritious diet that can enhance their ability to learn and their pride in the school that might serve as a springboard for further improvements. Despite the century that spans the two promoters of the edible schoolyard, the growing and preparing of food is "a kind of metaphor for the cultivation of intelligence" (Hickman, 2000, p. 205).

Although philosophers debate the relationship between traditional pragmatist epistemology and democracy, a number of scholars emphasize that democracy is the form of social life most consistent with pragmatism, which in turn suggests that it is consistent with the idea of food democracy as discussed here (Kloppenberg, 1998). Dewey envisioned democracy or "experimental politics" as an ongoing method requiring gradual, participatory, intelligent action on the part of educated and informed publics (Hickman, 2000; Prugh et al., 2000). Like food democracy, a pragmatist perspective calls for a deeper engagement by ordinary citizens, including recognizing and identifying social problems in need of attention, setting the agenda, and staging the debate. This kind of pragmatism runs through the food democracy created by the Toronto Food Policy Council, as described by Welsh and MacRae (1998). Sustainable farming networks where farmers share their own personal, local knowledge in their attempts to adopt alternative farming practices are another example (Hassanein, 1999). The pragmatic practice that is food democracy seems ideally suited to the pursuit of agro-food sustainability, because we cannot answer with certainty the question "how should we live sustainably?" Therefore, continuing inquiry and engagement are needed. Food democracy facilitates and encourages making choices that creatively and constructively involve all the voices of a food system.

5. CONCLUSION

Coming full circle to the question I raised at the beginning: Can pragmatic, incremental steps truly transform the dominant agro-food system so that it will be more sustainable in the long term? An option for answering the question is simply to declare it a ruse; after all, the outcomes of collective action around agro-food sustainability are not assured or predictable— whether we are conjecturing about the prospects for success or for failure. My inclination, however, is to answer in the affirmative. One reason, of course, is that there are no clear, practical alternatives to incremental change at this time. Calls for fundamental change and complete transformation of the agro-food system are rarely—if ever—accompanied by specific suggestions on how to achieve such a total makeover. But I see a more important reason for embracing pragmatic, incremental change, and that is because in the form of food democracy it could result in transformative change.

The above analysis suggests that food democracy is necessary because achieving sustainability involves conflicts over values, and there is no independent authority, such as science or religion, to which we can appeal for resolution of these conflicts. Therefore, sustainability *must* be defined socially and politically, and our collective understanding of it will evolve over time as conditions change. In turn, active participation and political engagement—broadly defined—are prerequisites, if solutions to the ecological, economic, and social justice consequences of the dominant food system are to be achieved. The concept of food democracy rests on the belief that every citizen has a contribution to make to the solution of our common problems.

Food citizenship eschews the passive and confining roles of "consumer" or "producer" or "worker." By contesting the commodification of food in this way, the pressure by social movements to democratize the dominant food system challenges the forces seeking control of the system and the very structure of capital itself. Therein lies the transformative potential of the alternative agro-food movement. The consequences of collective action are not only the product of strategic interactions between movements and their targets, however. The outcomes are also a product of movement actors' negotiations with one another and their integration of aims, beliefs, and strategic decisions. In the contemporary movement, actors pursue a wide range of approaches to social change and operate at various levels—from the local to the global. This diversity is a source of power in that different organizations can fill different niches, there are increased opportunities for citizen participation, and the multiplicity of thought and activism creates a vibrancy that leads to new forms of innovation and new ideas. Still, there are times when organizations must enter into strategic coalitions to build citizen power that they cannot achieve on their own. Thankfully, the prospects for and attention to forming such alliances now appear to be greater than ever before. Coalitions create new democratic spaces in which different social groups can learn about one another, broadening both participation and understanding. Analysis of the interactions (1) within movements, (2) among allied movements, and (3) between movements and their opponents can inform theory and action, and deserves more critical attention.

Food democracy is a method for making choices when values come into conflict and when the consequences of decisions are uncertain. That method embraces the pragmatic, that is, the achievement of what is presently possible coupled with ongoing inquiry by an active and informed citizenry. Of course, food democracy is not *only* a method; establishing a strong food democracy will itself constitute a genuine transformation of societal values and practices. Food democracy thus appears to offer some hope for achieving the transformation many seek to a sustainable agro-food system. As such, food democracy provides fertile ground for further work by both theoreticians and activists.

ACKNOWLEDGEMENTS

I am grateful to Jill Belsky, Bill Chaloupka, Lita Furby, David Goodman, and three anonymous reviewers for their invaluable comments on drafts of this paper. I also thank the UCSC Institute of Agro-Food Studies and Rural Change for organizing the workshop on International Perspectives on Alternative Agro-Food Networks, where I presented an earlier version of this manuscript.

REFERENCES

Alinsky, S., 1972. Rules for Radicals: A Pragmatic Primer for Realistic Radicals. Vintage Books/ Random House, New York.

Allen, P., Kovach, M., 2000. The capitalist composition of organic: the potential of markets in fulfilling the promise of organic agriculture. Agriculture and Human Values 17 (3), 221–232.

Allen, P., Van Dusen, D., Lundy, L., Gliessman, S., 1991. Integrating social, environmental, and economic issues in sustainable agriculture. American Journal of Alternative Agriculture 6 (1), 34–39.

Barber, B., 1984. Strong Democracy: Participatory Politics for a New Age. University of California Press, Berkeley.

Buttel, F.H., 1997. Some observations on agro-food change and the future of agricultural sustainability movements. In: Goodman, D., Watts, M.J. (Eds.), Globalising Food: Agrarian Questions and Global Restructuring. Routledge, London, pp. 344–365.

Carter, S.L., 1996. Integrity. Harper Collins, New York.

Colby, M., 1997. Going local in the age of globalism. Food & Water Journal, 8–11.

Dickstein, M., 1998. Introduction: pragmatism then and now. In: Dickstein, M. (Ed.), The Revival of Pragmatism: New Essays on Social Thought, Law and Culture. Duke University Press, Durham, pp. 1–18.

Eyerman, R., Jamison, A., 1991. Social Movements: A Cognitive Approach. Pennsylvania State University Press, University Park.

Feenstra, G.W., 1997. Local food systems and sustainable communities. American Journal of Alternative Agriculture 12 (1), 28–36.

Gottlieb, R., 2001. Environmentalism Unbound: Exploring New Pathways for Change. The MIT Press, Cambridge, MA.

Hassanein, N., 1999. Changing the Way America Farms: Knowledge and Community in the Sustainable Agriculture Movement. University of Nebraska Press, Lincoln.

Henderson, E., 2000. Rebuilding local food systems from the grassroots up. In: Magdoff, F., Bellamy Foster, J., Buttel, F.H. (Eds.), Hungry for Profit: The Agribusiness Threat to Farmers, Food, and the Environment. Monthly Review Press, New York, pp. 175–188.

Hickman, L.A., 2000. The edible schoolyard: agrarian ideals and our industrial milieu. In: Thompson, P.B., Hilde, T.C. (Eds.), The Agrarian Roots of Pragmatism. Vanderbilt University Press, Nashville, pp. 195–205.

Hilde, T.C., Thompson, P.B., 2000. Introduction: agrarianism and pragmatism. In: Thompson, P.B., Hilde, T.C. (Eds.), The Agrarian Roots of Pragmatism. Vanderbilt University Press, Nashville, pp. 1–21.

Klonsky, K., 2000. Forces impacting the production of organic foods. Agriculture and Human Values 17 (3), 233–243.

Kloppenberg, J.T., 1998. Pragmatism: an old name for some new ways of thinking. In: Dickstein, M. (Ed.), The Revival of Pragmatism: New Essays on Social Thought, Law and Culture. Duke University Press, Durham, pp. 83–127.

Lang, T., 1999. Food policy for the 21st century: can it be both radical and reasonable? In: Koc, M., MacRae, R., Mougeot, L.J.A., Welsh, J. (Eds.), For Hunger-proof Cities: Sustainable Urban Food Systems. International Development Research Centre, Ottawa, pp. 216–224.

Longworth, R.C., 2001. Protest groups consider WTO 'all-star' team. Missoulian 20, A1, A10.

Maas, S., 2001. Putting a face on your food: an interview with Dana Jackson and Brian Devore of the Land Stewardship Project. Orion A field 5 (3), 22–25.

Magdoff, F., Bellamy Foster, J., Buttel, F.H. (Eds.), 2000. Hungry for Profit: The Agribusiness Threat to Farmers, Food, and the Environment. Monthly Review Press, New York.

McMichael, P., 2000. Global food politics. In: Magdoff, F., Bellamy Foster, J., Buttel, F.H. (Eds.), Hungry for Profit: The Agribusiness Threat to

Farmers, Food, and the Environment. Monthly Review Press, New York, pp. 125–143.

Melucci, A., 1985. The symbolic challenge of contemporary movements. Social Research 52 (4), 789–816.

Morrison, R., 1995. Ecological Democracy. South End Press, Boston.

National Research Council, Environmental Studies Board, 1975. Contemporary Pest Control Practices and Prospects: The Report of the Executive Committee. National Academy of Sciences, Washington, DC.

Prugh, T., Costanza, R., Daly, H., 2000. The Local Politics of Global Sustainability. Island Press, Washington, DC.

Rose, F., 2000. Coalitions Across the Class Divide: Lessons from the Labor, Peace, and Environmental Movements. Cornell University Press, Ithaca.

Scott, A., 1990. Ideology and the New Social Movements. Unwin Hyman, London.

Wainwright, H., 1994. Arguments for a New Left: Answering the Free Market Right. Blackwell, Oxford.

Welsh, J., MacRae, R., 1998. Food citizenship and community food security: lessons from Toronto, Canada. Canadian Journal of Development Studies 19, 237–255.

Whatmore, S., Thorne, L., 1997. Nourishing networks: alternative geographies of food. In: Goodman, D., Watts, M.J. (Eds.), Globalising Food: Agrarian Questions and Global Restructuring. Routledge, London, pp. 287–304.

Zald, M.N., 1992. Looking backward to look forward: reflections on the past and future of the resource mobilization research program. In: Morris, A.D., McClurg, C. (Eds.), Frontiers in Social Movement Theory. Yale University Press, New Haven, pp. 326–348.

35

Food, Place and Authenticity: Local Food and the Sustainable Tourism Experience

Rebecca Sims

INTRODUCTION

Tourism researchers now acknowledge that there is more to tourism than the visual aspects of the visitor experience epitomised by Urry's "tourist gaze" (1990). A growing body of work is beginning to pay testament to the role that sensations of taste, touch, sound and smell can play within the holiday (Boniface, 2003; Davidson, Bondi, & Smith, 2005; Eastham, 2003; Mitchell & Hall, 2003; Urry, 1995), with holiday food becoming of particular importance to researchers (Cohen & Avieli, 2004; Germann Molz, 2004; Long, 2004b; Torres, 2002). More specifically, it is recognised that the kind of foods and drinks on offer for tourists can have major implications for the economic, cultural and environmental sustainability of tourism destinations, with researchers arguing that a focus on locally sourced products can result in benefits for both hosts and guests (Boniface, 2003; Clark & Chabrel, 2007; Enteleca Research and Consultancy, 2001; Ilbery, Kneafsey, Bowler, & Clark, 2003; Torres, 2002; Woodland & Acott, 2007). Similar debates are also taking place in agriculture, where a focus upon "local" food and drink products sold through "alternative" outlets such as farmers' markets and organic box schemes are being championed as a way to boost the sustainability of "traditional" farming, and the landscapes and communities sustained by that farming (Boniface, 2003; Ilbery & Kneafsey, 2000; Marsden, 2004;

National Farmers' Retail and Markets Association, 2007; Parrot, Wilson, & Murdoch, 2002; Policy Commission on the Future of Farming and Food, 2002; Tregear, Arfini, Belletti, & Marescotti, 2007).

Despite such developments, the precise nature of the links between food and tourism remains unexplored (Bessière, 1998; Germann Molz, 2004; Long, 2004a). There is therefore a need to investigate whether the growth of the "alternative" food sector and the renewed interest in "local" food can provide a boost to rural destinations looking to develop a sustainable domestic tourism industry within the United Kingdom.

The results presented in this paper are taken from a qualitative study of the local food and tourism industries of two national parks – the Lake District and Exmoor. Located in the North West and South West of England, respectively, both are popular tourist destinations where the attraction is the beauty of the upland landscape and the chance to take part in outdoor activities such as walking and cycling, with Cumbria receiving 5 million overnight visitors in 2007 (Cumbria Tourism, 2007), while equivalent figures for Exmoor show that 1.1 million visitor nights were spent in the park in 2003 (Exmoor National Park Authority, 2003). Both destinations also have a thriving local food industry that is based around a number of iconic food products, with the Lake District being famous for specialities such as Cumberland sausage, Kendal Mint Cake and Grasmere Gingerbread, while Exmoor is part of a region well known for cream teas, cider and Cheddar cheese.

This paper argues that "local" food and drink products can improve the economic and environmental sustainability of both tourism and the rural host community through encouraging sustainable agricultural practices, supporting local businesses and building a "brand" that can benefit the region by attracting more visitors and investment. In this way, developing a thriving "local" food industry can generate the kind of all-round benefits for hosts and guests that are sought as part of the drive to promote Integrated Rural Tourism in peripheral areas of Europe (Clark & Chabrel, 2007; Ilbery, Saxena, & Kneafsey, 2007). The research presented here shows that local food initiatives are able to achieve these benefits because they offer an enhanced visitor experience that can connect the consumer with the people and places involved in food production. By telling the "story" of food production in this way, it is possible to use the tourist's desire for authenticity to encourage the development of products and services that will boost sustainability and benefit rural regions for visitors and residents alike.

SUSTAINABLE TOURISM AND FOOD

Research has shown that food is important to sustainable tourism on a number of levels. Firstly, it is argued that increasing tourist consumption of local foods can generate a multiplier effect that will benefit the local economy (Enteleca Research and Consultancy, 2001; Torres, 2002). Secondly, concerns about the environmental consequences of transporting food across the globe have led researchers to argue that "buying local" is vital if the tourism industry is to reduce its carbon footprint (Boniface, 2003; Mitchell & Hall, 2003). Thirdly, there is a growing

recognition that tourism destinations throughout the world are competing with each other in a bid to attract visitors. Successful tourist destinations must, therefore, exhibit what Urry (1995) terms "tourism reflexivity" whereby every destination must develop a range of goods and services that will distinguish it from other destinations and attract a steady stream of visitors. Promoting high-quality cuisine or distinctive local food products is one way of achieving this (Hage, 1997; Hashimoto & Telfer, 2006; Ilbery et al., 2003; Woodland & Acott, 2007). Indeed, local foods may be particularly popular with tourists because they are considered "iconic" products that capture the "typical" nature of a particular place (Bessière, 1998; Urry, 1990).

The link between food and drink and sustainability can also be understood in terms of the recent research agenda which explores the concept of "Integrated Rural Tourism" (IRT). Often described as "all-round sustainable tourism" (Clark & Chabrel, 2007; Ilbery et al., 2007), IRT is focused upon achieving all-round social, economic and environmental benefits on the understanding that "the best form of tourism would be one which achieves gains on all dimensions and for all groups. It would not, for example, protect the environment by disadvantaging businesses, or benefit businesses at the expense of the host communities" (Clark & Chabrel, 2007, p. 372). Therefore, IRT is not just concerned with the sustainability of the tourist industry; it is about creating thriving rural communities and enhancing the local environment, economy and culture in ways that can be enjoyed by hosts as well as guests. Local food and drink projects can play an important role in the IRT agenda because they can embrace all these concerns simultaneously. This idea of "all-round sustainability" is also integral to the aims of the Slow Food movement – a worldwide initiative which is concerned about the environmental and social consequences of a fast-paced, heavily industrialised food system. In its place, the Slow Food campaign "envisions a future food system that is based on the principles of high quality and taste, environmental sustainability, and social justice-in essence, a food system that is good clean and fair" (Slow Food USA, 2008).

"LOCAL FOOD"

Similar approaches to sustainability are evident in the rural research agenda where concerns have centred upon falling farm incomes (Ilbery, Morris, Buller, Maye, & Kneafsey, 2005; Morris & Buller, 2003) with Pretty (2001, cited in Ilbery et al., 2005) claiming that, in the United Kingdom, only around 7.5% of the final retail price of food returns to farmers, as opposed to a figure of 50% more than 60 years ago. Such developments have been accompanied by a loss of consumer confidence in what Morgan, Marsden, and Murdoch (2006) have termed the "conventional" food sector as a result of food scares such as BSE and the Foot and Mouth Crisis (Blay-Palmer & Donald 2007; Boniface, 2003; Kneafsey et al., 2004). Ilbery et al. (2005) have also claimed that the expansion of industrial agriculture has led to consumers becoming alienated from contemporary food production. In response to these problems, it has been argued that we are seeing the development of an "alternative" food sector (Morgan et al., 2006), which is associated with a more ecological approach to production, and where smaller companies are involved in producing food for localised markets. It is claimed that participation in these networks can enable food producers to escape the spiral of declining prices and add value to their sales (Boniface, 2003; Policy Commission on the Future of Farming and Food, 2002; Tregear et al., 2007).

However, recent work has criticised the notion that a discrete and coherent "alternative" food sector exists in opposition to a discrete and coherent "conventional" food sector (Holloway et al., 2007a, 2007b; Morris & Kirwan, 2007; Watts, Ilbery, & Maye, 2005; Watts, Ilbery, & Jones, 2007) with Ilbery and Maye (2005) arguing that most producers show a more hybridised approach to production, which is characterised by a tendency to "dip in and out" of conventional and alternative modes at different times. Similar arguments have been made by Watts et al. (2005) who suggest that a spectrum exists from weaker to stronger versions of "alternativeness". At the weaker end of the spectrum are projects that emphasise particular "quality" aspects of the food products themselves – for example, better taste or freshness – but which do not necessarily say anything about the networks through which such products circulate. By contrast, projects with a stronger understanding of "alternative" will be more explicit about the avenues via which products are produced and sold – for example, they may emphasise that products have reduced food miles and provided more jobs for local people.

Other arguments have focused upon the ambiguity which surrounds the concept of "local" food, with Morris and Buller (2003) explaining that "local" can be understood either in terms of a bounded region within which products are produced and sold, or in terms of "speciality" or "locality" foods which are intended as value-added products for export to other countries or regions. Following Watts et al. (2005), the latter approach could be interpreted as a weaker version of localism on the basis that such speciality products may be sold beyond the region through more "conventional" networks. Allen and Hinrichs (2007) also argue that the many benefits attributed to "local" products – for example, a better environment, healthier food, greater social justice – can contradict each other. They highlight the conflicts that surround the meaning of "local" before concluding that: "the ambiguity about what local means... allows it to be about anything and, at the margin, perhaps very little at all" (Allen & Hinrichs, 2007, p. 269).

As Holloway et al. (2007a) have argued, such critiques are not intended to dispute the potential benefits that "alternative" food systems can yield, as many researchers support the rationale that exists for improving the sustainability of food systems. However, in view of the problems associated with an alternative/conventional dualism, Holloway et al. recommend abandoning such distinctions in favour of an approach where we can 'recognise the relational contingency of what is regarded as alternative at any one time and in any one place . . ." (Holloway et al., 2007b, p. 5). This "relational" approach is echoed by Maxey (2007) who suggests that a sustainability framework could provide a solution to the problems inherent in the alternative/conventional discourse. In contrast to those who want the certainty of a defined and measurable concept, Maxey argues that sustainability is socially constructed and that this is one of its greatest strengths as an analytical concept because "sustainability encourages us all to consider what we want to sustain and to assess the ways we wish to go about this" (Maxey, 2007, p. 59).

AUTHENTICITY

Consumer demands for foods perceived to be "traditional" and "local" can also be viewed as linked to a quest for authenticity. Debates about the meaning and validity of authenticity have played a central role in the tourism literature with Taylor claiming that "there are at least as many definitions of authenticity as there are those who write about it" (Taylor, 2001, p. 8). Today, accounts such as those presented by Boorstin (1964) are criticised for theorising authenticity as an "objective" concept that is based upon a

static understanding of place and culture. By contrast, contemporary researchers argue that all cultures change and there are therefore no examples of "pure" societies upon which concepts of authenticity can be based (Bell & Valentine, 1997; Germann Molz, 2004; Jackson, 1999; Meethan, 2001). Consequently, it is argued that authenticity should be viewed as a social construct (Hughes, 1995). Jackson's (1999) work on the commodification of cultural artefacts also suggests that, instead of talking about "authenticity", we should focus upon "authentification", which is the process whereby people make claims for authenticity and the interests that those claims serve.

Recent developments have extended such discussions by arguing for a third kind of authenticity. According to Wang (1999), objective and constructivist accounts of authenticity are limited by the fact that both relate to the nature of the attractions being visited by the tourists. Objective understandings thus depend upon whether something can be "proved" authentic with reference to external criteria, while constructivist understandings focus on the ways in which particular attractions are "staged" by tourism operators (MacCannell, 1989). By contrast, Wang argues that we need to develop an "existential" understanding of authenticity that relates – not to the objects or attractions themselves – but to the response that a particular tourism experience generates in the tourist. Existential authenticity thus describes the way in which tourists, by participating in holiday activities, can construct their identity to experience a more authentic sense of self. Therefore, "tourists are not merely searching for authenticity of the Other. They also search for the authenticity of, and between, themselves" (Wang, 1999, p. 364).

The concept of existential authenticity as linked to identity formation is important in relation to the provision of tourist products and services – including food and drink – because tourists may look to develop an authentic sense of self through the purchase of particular products. For example, Yeoman, Brass, and McMahon-Beattie (2006) talk about the importance of "authenti-seeking" – a process which describes "consumers searching for authenticity from a range of products, services and experiences, and looking for it within themselves" (Yeoman et al., 2006, p. 1128). Just as explanations for the emergence of alternative food networks have revolved around increasing consumer resistance to the industrialisation of agriculture, so discussions of authenticity have focused upon society's need for meaning in the face of the increasing commodification of culture. For example, Taylor (2001) sees the tourist's desire for authenticity as a result of a world where people feel they have become alienated from nature, and where everyday life is viewed as increasingly inauthentic.

> Authenticity is valuable only where there is perceived inauthenticity. Such is the "plastic" world of the consumer. Enamoured by the distance of authenticity, the modern consciousness is instilled with a simultaneous feeling of lack and desire erupting from a sense of loss felt within "our" world of mass culture and industrialisation and giving rise to possibilities of redemption through contact with the naturally, spiritually and culturally "unspoilt".
>
> (Taylor, 2001, p.10)

Kate Soper's work on "alternative hedonism" also reflects consumer concerns with the "inauthentic" nature of modern life (Soper, 2007). Soper argues that many people are changing their consumption practices, not just to limit what they see as the undesirable side effects of modern lifestyles, but also because they have become dissatisfied with the supposed "pleasures" that come from consuming in this way. Consequently, they are choosing different forms of consumption that they consider both more ethically sound and more personally pleasurable. Similar themes have also been explored by many authors (Barnett, Cloke, Clarke, & Malpass, 2005; Clarke, Cloke, Barnett, & Malpass, 2007) who argue that the rise of ethical consumerism associated with the Slow Food and Fair Trade campaigns challenges the popular view of the consumer as an entirely self-interested and egotistical person. Instead, they argue that such behaviour involves "new forms of citizenly action . . . being configured through creative redeployment of the repertoires of consumerism" (Clarke et al., 2007, p. 233).

In response to the debate that such differing accounts of authenticity have created, Cohen (2002) offers a way forward by arguing that, if we are to understand the motivations for tourist behaviour we must focus, not on academic debates about authenticity, but on the ways in which the concept is understood by the tourists themselves. According to Cohen, contemporary tourists seek both objective and existential authenticity in their holidays because, while some tourists are spending more, travelling further and experiencing more discomfort in order to experience encounters with "untouched" environments and cultures, others are happy to simply relax, have a good time and experience the existential authenticity that comes from "being themselves".

A further explication of Cohen's arguments can be found in his research into the Naga fireballs on the Mekong River in Thailand (Cohen, 2007). The fireballs, which are said to be produced by a mythical serpent, became a major tourist attraction and this resulted in widespread public debate over their origins (Were they supernatural? Manmade? Or a natural phenomenon?). The answer to this dilemma proved to be what Cohen described as a "postmodern" account where all three interpretations of the fireballs could coexist, leading to new insights into how authenticity can be theorised. According to Cohen, "The concept of 'staged authenticity' proves inadequate to deal with alleged supernatural phenomena, which are ingrained in a local tradition, and attract potential believers. Such phenomena could be 'staged' from one perspective, but nevertheless 'authentic' from another" (Cohen, 2007, p. 180). Therefore, in Cohen's account, the focus of authenticity is not on the fireballs themselves, but on the multiple meanings that the tourists bring to the event.

From this discussion of the literature, it can be seen that "local" food has the potential to play a central role within the sustainable tourism agenda, by encompassing everything from concerns about food safety and the impacts of agriculture on the rural environment to visitor demands for more "authentic" tourist experiences. However, despite the apparent synergy between debates around local food, sustainable tourism and authenticity, few studies have attempted to bridge the gap between the literatures (Bessière, 1998). Using a qualitative approach based around interviews in the Lake District and Exmoor, this study unites these themes by exploring how the link between local food and perceived authenticity can facilitate the development of sustainable tourism in rural areas.

METHODOLOGY

In order to explore the values and motivations behind tourists' holiday food choices, a qualitative approach based upon semi-structured interviews was chosen (Mason, 2002). In total, 78 tourists were interviewed across the Lake District (42) and Exmoor (36) during a four-month period from July to October 2005. Interviews were carried out with available tourists across a range of locations, from popular picnic spots in "honeypot" villages through to "residents' only" facilities such as the lounge areas of youth hostels and the bar areas of top hotels. This strategy had two advantages: firstly, it allowed the researcher to access tourists from a wide

range of backgrounds and, secondly, by interviewing tourists while they were relaxing, it ensured that respondents were able to talk in greater depth than would have been possible had they been engaging in other activities. During interviews, respondents were asked to describe the kinds of foods and drinks that they had encountered on their current holiday, and to explain why they had – or had not – chosen to eat them. They were also asked which foods or drinks – if any – they associated with being "typical" of their destination, and were encouraged to reflect on how these foods and drinks differed from those encountered on previous holidays and with the home setting. In this way, it was possible to explore how food was related to place in the case study areas, and to look at how this compared to respondents' past experiences of food at other destinations.

These conversations with tourists were supplemented by interviews with 24 café, pub and restaurant owners (13 from the Lake District and 11 from Exmoor) and 17 local food and drinks producers (8 from the Lake District and 9 from Exmoor). This was essential because, as consumers, tourists can select only from the kinds of foods and drinks available at their destination, and it was therefore necessary to talk to those supplying food products in order to establish how their attitudes towards food, place and authenticity compared to those of their customers. Café, pub and restaurant owners were selected according to price and apparent policy on local sourcing (see Table 35.1), while food producers were selected to represent the principal types of product available in each region (see Tables 35.2 and 35.3). In both cases, the aim was not to produce a statistically representative sample but to reflect the range of businesses encountered in both regions. Interviews were conducted by the original researcher and were carried out during a three-month period from January to March 2006.

Table 35.1 Café, pub and restaurant interviewees by type and study area

Type of establishment	Number of Lake District interviewees	Number of Exmoor interviewees
Traditional English country house restaurant offering luxury fine dining	1	1
Mid- to upper-price-range restaurant that was innovative (as opposed to traditional) in style, but which was passionate about local sourcing	2	1
Mid- to upper-price-range restaurant that was innovative but which did not appear to make a feature of local sourcing.	1	1
Foreign or speciality restaurant	1	1
Café/tea room that was passionate about local sourcing	1	1
Upmarket modern café that did not appear to make a feature of local sourcing	1	1
Inexpensive tourist café	1	1
Café attached to popular visitor attraction	2	1
Fish and chip takeaway	1	1
"Gastro-pub" with a reputation for good-quality food and beer	1	1
Standard pub offering typical pub fare at accessible prices	1	1
Total	13	11

Table 35.2 Lake District food producer interviewees

Product type	Number of interviewees
Bakery products	2
Meat and dairy products	2
Drinks	2
Jams and preserves	2

Table 35.3 Exmoor food producer interviewees

Product type	Number of interviewees
Confectionery	1
Meat and dairy products	3
Drinks	2
Jams, preserves and honey	2
Fish	1

SOUVENIR PURCHASE: LOCAL FOOD AS A SYMBOL OF PLACE AND CULTURE

In order to understand why local food is important to sustainable tourism, it is vital to investigate how tourists interact with particular food products during their holiday, and a good example of this is the purchase of food souvenirs. Over 50% of the tourists interviewed said that they had bought, or were definitely planning to buy, food and drink souvenirs of their holiday, with less than 10% saying that they were not interested in doing so. The souvenir purchasers varied in their levels of enthusiasm, from "reluctant" buyers who felt compelled to buy small gifts for family or colleagues, to one enthusiastic couple who, while visiting Exmoor, had spent £60 on specialist tea and coffee by a renowned local tea merchant in addition to "the usual stuff like fudge." Interviews also showed that ideas about the food identity of certain regions can frequently precede the holiday itself:

INTERVIEWER: Will you take back any food or drink as souvenirs, at all, do you think?

RESPONDENT: Oh yes! I've heard fudge is quite a good thing to take back, and I'm hoping to get something in the

Scrumpy cider line for my neighbour who is doing little jobs – you know, gardening.

Urry (1990) and Wang (1999) have argued that tourists look for "typical" signs of place that accord with their own perceptions, and foods and drinks are good examples of these signs (Ilbery et al., 2003). As a result, visitors are likely to want to try these "typical" products during their holiday because there is a sense that, if you want to be a "good traveller", as opposed to an "irresponsible tourist" (Rojek, 1993), you must engage with these regional specialities. This notion of being a "good traveller" is important to sustainability because previous research has shown that "local" foods are popular because they are associated with a host of values, such as being better for the environment, conserving "traditional" rural landscapes and supporting the local economy, and there is, therefore, a "feel-good" factor associated with consuming them (Allen & Hinrichs, 2007; Boniface, 2003; Enteleca Research and Consultancy, 2001). Soper's ideas of "alternative hedonism" are helpful here because it could be argued that, by selecting "local" foods on holiday, visitors can experience the moral satisfaction of choosing what they consider to be a more ethical form of consumption *and* the personal pleasures of eating and shopping differently (Soper, 2007).

It can also be argued that "local" food aims to "reconnect" consumers with the people and places that produce their food (Kneafsey et al., 2004) and that this connection is a powerful part of an integrated tourism experience (Clark & Chabrel, 2007). Unlike other popular souvenirs, such as a decorative key-ring or craft item, foods and drinks engage all the senses and have stronger connections with place because we have personal, sensory memories of consuming them in that setting. This ability of food to recall emotions was described by one Lake District interviewee who owned a delicatessen.

> I think food evokes a memory . . . You know, you eat something, not just because it feels good, but because it evokes that memory of the good time – whether it's the Cornish pasty or a cream tea, or a Cumberland sausage – and it doesn't matter where in the world you eat it. The time when you first ate it is what the memory relates back to, and it's very unifying.

Thus, local food can be an asset to integrated tourism development as a result of its ability to symbolise place and culture, provide a moral "feel-good" factor associated with its consumption and enable visitors to experience a sense of connection to their destination – both during and after their visit. These links between food and place become more apparent when we analyse what lands of food experience tourists are seeking during their holiday. The following section argues that local foods and drinks are an asset to integrated and sustainable tourism because they enable host communities to capitalise on visitors' desire for some form of "authentic" experience that will enable them to connect with the place and culture of their destination.

THE SEARCH FOR "AUTHENTIC" FOOD EXPERIENCES

Local food is not only valuable as a souvenir of a holiday. Over 60% of the tourists interviewed said that they had deliberately chosen to consume foods or drinks that they considered "local" while on holiday which suggests that, rather than just looking for something "different", tourists are seeking products that they feel will give them an insight into the nature of a place and its people. As one interviewee explained, "I think you need to try the local food because it's part of the culture really, isn't it?" Another said, "You want to try the local food wherever you are, and get a taste of the place".

Visitors often rationalised this desire for "genuine" food experiences by explaining that it formed part of a search for some kind of authenticity on holiday.

> I do think, yes, if you go and stay somewhere, then obviously you could get an Italian meal anywhere – it feels fake and not quite right . . . And so it's nice to have something that purports to be local.

This example indicates two things: firstly that, for tourists, local food is about the search for products that are not "fake" and which appear to say something about the place and culture that created them. Secondly, this demand for a "local, authentic" experience can persist even where there is a degree of scepticism about the "local" claims being made for the product (as indicated by the use of "purports"). This theme will be explored in more depth later in the paper. However, the key question is why it is that *local* food experiences come to be seen as "authentic" events that represent place and culture while other kinds of food experience do not. To understand why this is so, it is important to examine the ways in which food and place relationships are constructed by visitors. As discussed previously, tourists may have their own ideas about what a "typical" food experience of that place might look like, and anything that fits this image – including the setting, the ambience and the food itself – is more likely to be identified as "authentic". For example, when asked what kind of establishment they would look for if they wanted to stop for lunch while out touring around the Lake District, several respondents explained that they would prefer something that appeared traditional and English:

> It's either got a charm to it, or it's got a sort of look that's authentic. Not the fast-food

type place – that's not us. It's got to be authentic and 'olde tea shoppy' for me.

> We tend to avoid loud and plastic! You know, I think if we're going to eat, we'd rather be in a cosy little real-ale pub that looks like it is home cooking, you know? Rather than something that's been zapped in a microwave.

These comments can be said to reflect concerns about food quality, on the grounds that home-cooked food should be tastier than its microwaved equivalent. However, the choice of a "cosy little real-ale pub" above anything "loud and plastic" also indicates a desire for a more authentic, traditional, Lakeland eating experience.

The preceding examples illustrate three ways in which the tourist socially constructs authentic relationships between local food and place. Firstly, an occasion is more likely to be considered authentic if it corresponds with our preconceptions about what a typical food experience for that place will look like. A second – and related – factor is that a food experience can seem more authentic if it takes place in a sympathetic surrounding environment. Finally, authentic experiences tend to emphasise some element of tradition or naturalness. For example, Yeoman et al. (2006) has argued that tourist attractions must not appear too contemporary or manufactured because "authentic" implies origins in the distant past – the idea that a certain activity has been going on for generations adds a sense of legitimacy to an experience. Here, this is reflected in the preference for "olde worlde" Lake District charm over anything too modern. Therefore, the concept of heritage is relevant here as it appears that tourists value local foods, not just because they are perceived to be local but also because they are seen to be "traditional" products with a long history of production in that location.

This is important for the development of an integrated and sustainable tourism agenda because it shows that there are market opportunities for local products that can satisfy the visitor's desire for experiences that promote a connection with place, culture and heritage (Bessière, 1998; Boniface, 2003; Buller & Morris, 2004; Clark & Chabrel, 2007; Kneafsey et al., 2004). It also allows destinations to use "iconic" products to build a "brand" that can be used to distinguish the region from its competitors (Urry, 1995). However, this account assumes two things: an unproblematic understanding of "local food" and an unproblematic understanding of authenticity. Neither can be assumed.

"LOCAL FOOD" AND "AUTHENTICITY": TWO CONTESTED CONCEPTS

Any study which attempts to understand the relationship between food and place must first consider the question of what is meant by the term "local food". In accordance with Allen and Hinrichs (2007), this study revealed extensive debate about the meaning of the term "local", with tourists, food producers and restaurateurs adopting a range of definitions in accordance with their own interests.

For example, tourists tended to associate local food with particular speciality products. Of the 36 Exmoor tourists interviewed, 32 were able to name specific examples of foods and drinks that they associated with the area, with a similar trend being observed in the Lake District, where 38 of the 42 tourists identified at least one food or drink product with the area. Figures 35.1 and 35.2 show how both destinations were conceptualised through food and, although there is some overlap (meat, cheese and beer appear on both graphs), it is clear that both regions have distinct food identities, with cream teas, pasties, fudge and cider being seen as characteristic products for Exmoor, and Cumberland sausage, Kendal Mint Cake and Grasmere Gingerbread performing this role for the Lake District.

However, interviews with food producers and café and restaurant owners revealed different understandings. For example, 10 interviewees favoured a geographical definition, where "local" referred to products from within a defined area. There was, however, considerable disagreement over the extent of this area. In the case of the Lake District, one

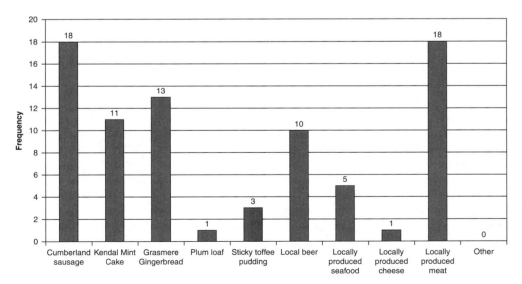

Figure 35.1 Local specialities identified by visitors to the Lake District.

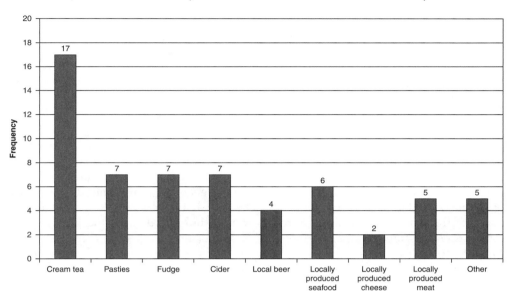

Figure 35.2 Local specialities identified by visitors to Exmoor.

producer felt that "local" should mean products from the county of Cumbria, whereas another thought the definition should extend to the whole of the North West of England.

There was also debate about the relative importance of local ingredients and local manufacture. Interviews revealed that a spectrum similar to that described by Watts et al. (2005) was operating, which ranged from strong definitions of locality based upon the use of local ingredients, at one end, to weaker definitions based upon local manufacture of imported ingredients – or even the use of local supply companies – at the other. For example, one Lake District jam producer felt that the concept of "local" would be too limiting if it could be applied only to local ingredients. He felt that his company should be considered local because, by manufacturing locally and employing local people, he was helping the Cumbrian economy.

> I always get quoted the thing about adding value to the product, which I think is a very good way, because you couldn't possibly

make apricot chutney in Cumbria and call it local . . . So if you went along the lines of saying it's got to be reared or grown locally and then produced locally . . . you're limiting yourself. We couldn't make chilli jam. Even red onion marmalade – the onions aren't produced within Cumbria . . . So, especially on ours, you can't have anything that you can say is really local, local.

However, other respondents argued for a stronger definition of locality, including a jam producer from Exmoor who made her preserves by handpicking local fruit, before peeling and chopping all the ingredients in her kitchen. She was angered by rival producers who used preprepared, frozen fruits from abroad to make their "local" jam.

> Their whortleberry jam, the fruit comes from America! Personally I think that's misselling, because everybody thinks they are eating Exmoor whortleberries and they're not . . . An awful lot of product comes from abroad and yet, because they are processed here, it's called a local product. And, in my view, that isn't a local product. It's a local product if it's grown here.

Such a diversity of opinion illustrates how the concept of local is socially constructed according to a person's beliefs and circumstances. These examples show that, by concentrating on the ingredients and manufacturing processes involved producers are using an "objective" understanding of authenticity. By contrast, tourists focus less on the origins of the products, preferring, instead to concentrate on their symbolic attributes – thus reflecting more of the "constructed" aspects of authenticity. However, producers were aware of the symbolic importance of food for tourists and some were attempting to "stage" the authenticity of their products accordingly, as this Lake District bakery owner described:

> We had a product which was a very nice sultana cake . . . We made that as Devon Fruit Cake for years, and it did nothing – it just stayed on the shelf knocking around. I changed it to Cumbrian Fruit Cake, and it's one of our better-selling products . . . It's like our Dundee Cake – we made a Dundee Cake, and we can't sell that here. We now call our version of the Dundee Cake a Westmorland Cake.[1] And it's not a big seller – it's not like the Cumbrian. But it still does better than Dundee.

Such differing interpretations of the "local" and the "authentic" might appear to present a serious challenge for those wishing to use food and drink as part of a sustainable, integrated tourism offering: how can we develop an "authentic local food industry" if the concepts behind it are so contested? However, this research shows that, if we focus on tourist understandings of authenticity and ask *why* visitors are seeking it from their holiday food experiences, we are able to interpret their decisions in a different light.

FINDING MEANING IN FOOD

To re-establish the meaning and value behind local food it is necessary to begin

with Cohen's (2007) analysis which shows that different understandings of authenticity can coexist within tourism. This study shows that similar claims can be applied to holiday food because, while some descriptions – such as that relating to the "olde worlde tea shop" – reflect an enjoyment resulting from what felt like a "typical" experience of local culture, other stories show visitors having a good time despite knowing that an experience is not "genuine" in this way, as illustrated by the diner who enjoyed trying things which "purported" to be local. Existential accounts may also be present on occasions where the enjoyment of the meal is less about the foods being consumed and more about the feelings provoked in the individual – for example, the sense of personal satisfaction and wholeness that comes from sharing food in a relaxed holiday setting, as this interviewee described: "It's spending time with people that's important and I think part of that, when you're relaxing, is eating and drinking, and I think that's part of the social occasion and food and drink are important in that context, you know? It's that shared experience that's important for me".

By recognising that holiday food experiences can involve different kinds of authenticity it can be seen that "local" food is important to the sustainable tourism experience in several ways. Firstly, it allows those with objective or socially constructed understandings of authenticity to try foods that they may consider to be related to the landscape, culture and heritage of their destination – hence, the attraction of Cumberland sausage and Kendal Mint Cake in the Lake District, and cream teas, fudge and cider on Exmoor.

However, local food can also contribute to the experience of existential authenticity. As described by Wang (1999), existential authenticity is about identity formation and the chance to experience a more intense feeling of connection with ourselves and the world around us. It could therefore be argued that a greater sense of existential authenticity can result from the consumption of local foods because the imagery surrounding these foods can help us feel that we are connecting more deeply with the people and places that produced them (Clark & Chabrel, 2007; Kneafsey et al., 2004). This is particularly important for those who may be dissatisfied by what they perceive as the "inauthentic" nature of contemporary consumerism (Soper, 2007). For example, when describing the attraction of farm shops, one interviewee, who worked for a regional food group on Exmoor, explained, "A lot of this is about the story of the food, which you don't get if you buy in the supermarket. And that's what people are getting from coming to a farm shop – they're getting a bit more of an experience, really."

Similar comments were made by a Lake District bakery owner when describing the popularity of her Victorian-themed shop:

> You've got the smell, you've got the atmosphere of the shop, you've got the tradition . . . it's really like hand to mouth, isn't it? It goes all the way through a little production system and then you literally get it in a bag, walk out and eat it, and it can still actually sometimes be warm. And people aren't just buying that – they're buying the whole package.

Of course, not all tourists will have such an encounter because, as Yeoman et al. (2006) describe, there must be a personal desire to engage in this process of "authenti-seeking" first. However, for visitors who may be disillusioned with consumerism (Soper, 2007; Taylor, 2001) or anxious about the growing industrialisation of agriculture (Boniface, 2003), "local" food products can offer a way to achieve a more authentic sense of self and a more satisfying form of engagement with the people and places around them. This is because "local" products have a

story – and a meaning – behind them that can be related to place and culture. This meaning is particularly important for tourists, because the search for existential authenticity can also be interpreted as a search for meaning. Thus, tourists choosing to consume local products may not just be enjoying the physical taste of the food. Instead, they are also consuming the meaning behind it. Eating and drinking thus becomes a three-dimensional experience that enables the visitor to connect with the place and culture of their destination.

CONCLUSION

Despite extensive disagreement about the precise meaning of "local" food, the idea of a link between food and place remains a powerful one and the evidence presented here shows that offering visitors a way to experience some form of authenticity through food can assist the development of sustainable tourism in a number of ways. Firstly, and most obviously, the promotion of iconic food and drink products can help to create an "image" for a particular destination that will help it attract new visitors and boost its economic sustainability in the long term (Ilbery et al., 2003). Food and drink products are a particularly effective means of creating such an image because they can be linked to the kind of "traditional" landscapes and farming methods that tourists will "gaze" upon during their holiday (Enteleca Research and Consultancy, 2001; Urry, 1990).

Secondly, in contrast to some of the more "traditional" discourses surrounding sustainability where "trade-offs" are involved, "local" products promise the kind of all-round social, economic and environmental benefits for hosts and guests that have been sought as part of IRT initiatives throughout Europe (Clark & Chabrel, 2007; Ilbery et al., 2007). For example, tourist consumption of local foods creates a market opportunity that can encourage the development of sustainable agriculture, help conserve traditional farming landscapes and assist the local economy (Buller & Morris, 2004). The results of this study thus accord with previous research which shows that the appeal of local food lies in its ability to encompass everything from a concern for environmental and social sustainability, through to consumer demands for foods that are safe, distinctive and traceable (Boniface, 2003; Ilbery et al., 2005; Marsden, 2004).

Local food is able to achieve all these things because of its ability to appeal to the visitor's desire for authenticity within the holiday. This study shows that "local" products can appeal to tourists on a number of levels, from the simple demand for "typical" products that can be purchased and consumed as a symbol of place, through to the complex and deep-seated quest for a more authentic sense of self. In this way, those who are worried about the environmental consequences of contemporary agriculture or disillusioned with what they perceive to be the "inauthentic" nature of modern life (Soper, 2007; Taylor, 2001) can choose to engage with "local" food and drink products on holiday as a way of restoring a more meaningful sense of connection between themselves, as consumers, and the people and places that produce their food. For these consumers, the fact that local products are equated with economically and socially sustainable behaviour acts as a further attraction because it enables them to cast themselves in the role of the "good" and "responsible" tourists who care about the destinations they are visiting (Barnett et al., 2005; Clarke et al., 2007; Enteleca Research and Consultancy, 2001; Rojek, 1993; Soper, 2007). In short, it is the meaning behind food that many tourists are seeking and, by harnessing this meaning through the foods and drinks on offer at particular destinations, sustainable initiatives can have a better chance of success.

ACKNOWLEDGEMENTS

This research was funded by a Lancaster University 40th Anniversary Studentship, for which I am very grateful. I would also like to thank the editor and the four anonymous reviewers who provided valuable comments on an earlier version of the paper.

NOTES ON CONTRIBUTOR/S

Rebecca Sims is a post-doctoral Researcher in Lancaster University's Department of Geography. Her research interests centre around alternative food networks, sustainable consumption and rural tourism in addition to the social impacts of flooding. She also has a particular interest in qualitative methods and participatory research.

NOTE

1. Westmorland was a small ancient county subsumed into the county of Cumbria in 1974.

REFERENCES

Allen, P., & Hinrichs, C. (2007). Buying into "buy local": Engagements of United States local food initiatives. In D. Maye, L. Holloway, & M. Kneafsey (Eds.), *Alternative food geographies*. London: Elsevier.

Barnett, C., Cloke, P., Clarke, N., & Malpass, A. (2005). Consuming ethics: Articulating the subjects and spaces of ethical consumption. *Antipode, 37*, 23–45.

Bell, D., & Valentine, G. (1997). *Consuming geographies: We are what we eat*. London: Routledge.

Bessière, J. (1998). Local development and heritage: Traditional food and cuisine as tourist attractions in rural areas. *Sociologia Ruralis, 38*, 21–34.

Blay-Palmer, P., & Donald, B. (2007). Manufacturing fear: The role of food processors and retailers in constructing alternative food geographies in Toronto, Canada. In D. Maye, L. Holloway, & M. Kneafsey (Eds.), *Alternative food geographies*. London: Elsevier.

Boniface, P. (2003). *Tasting tourism: Travelling for food and drink*. Burlington, VT: Ashgate.

Boorstin, D. (1964). *The image: A guide to pseudo-events in America*. New York: Harper.

Buller, H., & Morris, C. (2004). Growing goods: The market, state and sustainable food production. *Environment and Planning, A 36*, 1065–1084.

Clark, G., & Chabrel, M. (2007). Measuring integrated rural tourism. *Tourism Geographies, 9*, 371–386.

Clarke, N., Cloke, P., Barnett, C, & Malpass, A. (2007). Globalising the consumer: Doing politics in an ethical register. *Political Geography, 26*, 231–249.

Cohen, E. (2002). Authenticity, equity and sustainability in tourism. *Journal of Sustainable Tourism, 10*, 267–276.

Cohen, E. (2007). The "postmodernization" of a mythical event: Naga fireballs on the Mekong River. *Tourism, Culture and Communication, 7*, 169–181.

Cohen, E., & Avieli, N. (2004). Food in tourism: Attraction and impediment. *Annals of Tourism Research, 31*, 755–778.

Cumbria Tourism. (2007). STEAM model: Tourism volume and value 2007. Cumbria Tourism, Staveley, Cumbria.

Davidson, J., Bondi, L., & Smith, M. (Eds.). (2005). *Emotional geographies*. Aldershot: Ashgate.

Eastham, J. (2003). Valorizing through tourism in rural areas: Moving towards regional partnerships. In C. Hall, L. Sharpies, R. Mitchell, N. Macionis, & B. Cambourne (Eds.), *Food tourism around the world: Development, management and markets*. Oxford: Butterworth-Heinemann.

Enteleca Research and Consultancy. (2001). *Tourist attitudes towards regional and local food*. Richmond upon Thames, Enteleca Research and Consultancy.

Exmoor National Park Authority. (2003). *The value of tourism to Exmoor 2003*. Retrieved June 9, 2008, from http://www.exmoor-nationalpark.gov.uk/the_value_of_tourism_to_exmoor_2003.pdf

Germann Molz, J. (2004). Tasting an imaginary Thailand: Authenticity and culinary tourism in Thai restaurants. In L. Long (Ed.), *Culinary tourism*. Kentucky: The University Press of Kentucky.

Hage, G. (1997). At home in the entrails of the West. In H. Grace (Ed.), *Home/world: Space, community and marginality in Sydney's west*. Annandale, NSW: Pluto.

Hashimoto, A., & Telfer, D. (2006). Selling Canadian culinary tourism: Branding the global and the regional product. *Tourism Geographies, 81*, 31–55.

Holloway, L., Kneafsey, M., Cox, R., Venn, L., Dowler, E., & Tuomainen, H. (2007a). Beyond the "alternative"-"conventional" divide? Thinking differently about food production-consumption relationships. In D. Maye, L. Holloway, & M. Kneafsey (Eds.), *Alternative food geographies*. Oxford: Elsevier.

Holloway, L., Kneafsey, M., Venn, L., Cox, R., Dowler, E., & Tuomainen, H. (2007b). Possible food economies: A methodological framework for exploring food production-consumption relationships. *Sociologia Ruralis, 47*, 1–19.

Hughes, G. (1995). Authenticity in tourism. *Annals of Tourism Research, 22*, 781–803.

Ilbery, B., & Kneafsey, M. (2000). Producer constructions of quality in regional speciality food production: A case study from South West England. *Journal of Rural Studies, 16*, 217–230.

Ilbery, B., Kneafsey, M., Bowler, I., & Clark, G. (2003). Quality products and services in the lagging rural regions of the European Union: A producer perspective. In K. Beesley, H. Millward, B. Ilbery, & L. Harrington (Eds.), *The new countryside: Geographic perspectives on rural change*. Manitoba, Canada: Brandon University.

Ilbery, B., & Maye, D. (2005). Alternative (shorter) food supply chains and specialist livestock products in the Scottish-English borders. *Environment and Planning, A 37*, 823–844.

Ilbery, B., Morris, C, Buller, H., Maye, D., & Kneafsey, M. (2005). Product, process and place: An examination of food marketing and labelling schemes in Europe and North America. *European Urban and Regional Studies, 12*, 116–132.

Ilbery, B., Saxena, G., & Kneafsey, M. (2007). Exploring tourists and gatekeepers' attitudes towards integrated rural tourism in the England-Wales border region. *Tourism Geographies, 9*, 441–68.

Jackson, P. (1999). Commodity cultures: The traffic in things. *Transactions of the Institute of British Geographers, 24*, 95–108.

Kneafsey, M., Holloway, L., Venn, L., Cox, R., Dowler, E., & Tuomainen, H. (2004). Consumers and producers: Coping with food anxieties through "reconnection"? Cultures of Consumption, Working Paper no.19.

Long, L. (2004a). Culinary tourism: A folkloristic perspective on eating and otherness. In L. Long (Ed.), *Culinary tourism*. Kentucky: The University Press of Kentucky.

Long, L. (2004b). Introduction. In L. Long (Ed.), *Culinary tourism*. Kentucky: The University Press of Kentucky.

MacCannell, D. (1989). *The tourist: A new theory of the leisure class*. New York: Schocken Books.

Marsden, T. (2004). Theorising food quality: Some key issues in understanding its competitive production and regulation. In M. Harvey, A. Mcmeekin, & A. Warde (Eds.), *Qualities of food*. Manchester: Manchester University Press.

Mason, J. (2002). *Qualitative researching*. London: Sage.

Maxey, L. (2007). From "alternative" to "sustainable" food. In D. Maye, L. Holloway, &

M. Kneafsey (Eds.), *Alternative food geographies*. London: Elsevier.

Meethan, K. (2001). *Tourism in global society: Place, culture, consumption*. Basingstoke: Palgrave.

Mitchell, R., & Hall, C. (2003). Consuming tourists: Food tourism consumer behaviour. In C. Hall (Ed.), *Food tourism around the world: Development, management and markets*. Oxford: Butterworth-Heinemann.

Morgan, K., Marsden, T., & Murdoch, J. (2006). *Worlds of food*. Oxford: Oxford University Press.

Morris, C., & Buller, H. (2003). The local food sector: A preliminary assessment of its form and impact in Gloucestershire. *British Food Journal, 105*, 559–566.

Morris, C, & Kirwan, J. (2007). Is meat the new militancy? Locating vegetarianism within the alternative food economy. In D. Maye, L. Holloway, & M. Kneafsey (Eds.), *Alternative food geographies*. London: Elsevier.

National Farmers' Retail and Markets Association. (2007). *Certification-abridged rules*. Retrieved June 9, 2008, http://www.farmersmarkets.net//certification2.htm

Parrot, N., Wilson, N., & Murdoch, J. (2002). Spatializing quality: Regional protection and the alternative geography of food. *European Urban and Regional Studies, 9*, 241–261.

Policy Commission on the Future of Farming and Food. (2002). Farming and food: A sustainable future. London: DEFRA, Department of Environment, Food and Rural Affairs.

Rojek, C. (1993). *Ways of escape: Modern transformations in leisure and travel*. Basingstoke: Macmillan Press.

Slow Food USA. (2008). *About us – Slow food USA*. Retrieved June 9, 2008, from http://www.slowfoodusa.org/about/index.html

Soper, K. (2007). Re-thinking the good life. *Journal of Consumer Culture, 7*, 205–224.

Taylor, J. (2001). Authenticity and sincerity in tourism. *Annals of Tourism Research, 28*, 7–26.

Torres, R. (2002). Towards a better understanding of tourism and agriculture linkages in the Yucatan: Tourist food consumption and preferences. *Tourism Geographies, 4*, 282–307.

Tregear, A., Arfini, F., Belletti, G., & Marescotti, A. (2007). Regional foods and rural development: The role of product qualification. *Journal of Rural Studies, 23*, 12–22.

Urry, J. (1990). *The tourist gaze: Leisure and travel in contemporary societies*. London: Sage.

Urry, J. (1995). *Consuming places*. London: Routledge.

Wang, N. (1999). Rethinking authenticity in the tourist experience. *Annals of Tourism Research, 26*, 349–370.

Watts, D., Ilbery, B., & Jones, G. (2007). Networking practices among "alternative" food producers in England's West Midlands region. In D. Maye, L. Holloway, & M. Kneafsey (Eds.), *Alternative food geographies*. London: Elsevier.

Watts, D., Ilbery, B., & Maye, D. (2005). Making reconnections in agro-food geography: Alternative systems of food provision. *Progress in Human Geography, 29*, 22–40.

Woodland, M., & Acott, T. (2007). Sustainability and local tourism branding in England's South Downs. *Journal of Sustainable Tourism, 15*, 715–734.

Yeoman, I., Brass, D., & McMahon-Beattie, U. (2006). Current issues in tourism: The authentic tourist. *Tourism Management, 28*, 1128–1138.

36

Mexicanas Taking Food Public: The Power of the Kitchen in the San Luis Valley

Carole Counihan

PROLOGUE: PHOTOGRAPHY IN ANTHROPOLOGY/ ETHNOGRAPHY

Ethnography has always engaged with photography. Ethnographers, or cultural anthropologists, study human beings through cultural immersion, interviewing, participant-observation, and visual documentation. We study what makes people tick. We compare diverse groups across the globe, explore the influence of culture on human behavior, and explain cultural differences. Photography plays an important role in fulfilling our goals.

Anthropologists have used photos to frame, to tell, to illustrate, and to contradict. Some use photos as illustration of words; others tell the story with photos and make words secondary; still others have the photos stand alone. In this essay I have tried to weave words and images into a conversation with each other to enable the images to illustrate and enrich the text and vice-versa. The essay is comprised of several pages of words and images followed by a bibliography of sources for the key issues expressed in the essay organized by topic. The goal of the interweaving is to bring to public view the experiences and perspectives of people long absent from history.

THE RESEARCH—ETHNOGRAPHY OF WOMEN AND FOOD IN THE SAN LUIS VALLEY OF COLORADO

I went to Antonito, Colorado—a poor, rural, Hispanic community in the southwestern United States—in 1996 with my husband, anthropologist Jim Taggart, and our two sons Ben and Will, then aged 6 and 9. My husband wanted to collect oral narratives and explore men's experiences while I planned to document the ways that women used food to express identity, to forge family and community, and to survive. We chose Antonito because it exemplified an understudied segment of the Latino population in the USA—impoverished rural Mexicanos with longstanding roots in the Upper Rio Grande region who were once independent farmer-ranchers raising cattle and sheep and growing food in large irrigated gardens. I wanted to study the women of these communities to give them a public hearing and to expand understanding of the diversity and contributions of US Latinas. I collected food-centered life histories from Mexicanas in Antonito, wrote fieldnotes based on observations of events and activities, and took photographs.

When I began the research in 1996 I was using a 35 mm single-lens reflex camera with wide angle and telephoto zoom lenses and photographing with kodachrome color slide and black and white film. Around 2000 I switched to a digital camera because of its ease and diverse uses. It was easy to catalogue and use the photographs in multiple formats—color prints, sharing photos, PowerPoint presentations, publication, and so on. Over ten summers of fieldwork I took hundreds of photos with the goals of documenting and communicating Antonito culture—to have a visual record for myself as well as to use the photos to inform others, especially my students, about the people, places, and events of the Hispanics in the Upper Rio Grande region.

THE SETTING

Figure 36.1 shows the western United States, and the arrow points to the location of Antonito, Colorado, the town I studied for ten summers from 1996–2006, in the southern San Luis Valley. The encircled area on the map belonged to Mexico until 1848 when the Mexican-American War and Treaty of Guadalupe Hidalgo ceded almost half of Mexico's Territory to the USA. Antonito is near the northern edge of what some call "greater Mexico," that area of North America with a longstanding Mexican cultural presence. People in town refer to themselves with the Spanish word Mexicana/o or with English terms Spanish, Spanish American, and/or Chicana/o, and on the 2000 census, 90% of Antonito's population self-identified as Hispanic.

The town is located in Conejos County, in between the Sangre de Cristo and the San Juan Mountains. In 1852 Hispanics moved north from Rio Arriba County, New Mexico, to practice small-scale ranching and farming in an area populated by Ute, Apache, and Navajo Indians. Figure 36.2, a map of the Antonito area

Figure 36.1 Map of the western United States.

Figure 36.2 Map of the Antonito area, the cover of a 1985 high school project.

made by a local student in 1985, reveals the community's cultural roots in the Upper Rio Grande Hispano culture in the names of the earliest towns scattered at intervals along the rivers. Antonito was founded as a railroad town in 1881 by the Denver and Rio Grande Railroad at the junction of two lines (Figure 36.3). It became a commercial and trade center relying on sheep and cattle ranching, lumbering, saw mills, perlite mines, and agriculture, and the population grew slowly to a peak of 1255 in 1950. But at the turn of the millennium, the population had dwindled to 872 and these traditional activities had petered out except for large-scale farming of alfalfa for hay. In 2010, the town was among the poorest in Colorado and had few jobs, with some people working in the public sector or in the service economy in Alamosa, thirty miles north, and others getting by on pensions, public assistance, home or car repair, trading in used goods, doing hair, or selling local food products.

MEXICANAS AND THE KITCHEN: A COMPLICATED STORY

Janice DeHerrera (born 1955) and Helen Ruybal (born 1906) were among the 19 Mexicanas aged 34 to 94 whom I interviewed in Antonito, Colorado between 1996 and 2006. I used a food-centered life history methodology—recording interviews about everything to do with food in their lives: food production, distribution, preservation, preparation, and consumption; meals, recipes, and child and infant

Figure 36.3 Train depot built in 1881, Antonito, Colorado, looking south toward San Antonio mountain.

Figure 36.4 Claudine and Janice DeHerrera, cooking enchiladas in Janice's kitchen.

Figure 36.5 Helen Ruybal in her kitchen.

feeding; men's and women's roles around food; beliefs, rituals, and lore surrounding feeding and eating; and so on. Many of the interviews centered on women's experiences with food *inside* the home, but what I did not expect was the extent to which women used food *outside* the home; to describe those activities I came up with the term "taking food public."

My goal was to use food-centered life histories to gather the verbatim accounts of women and give them a public forum. Women generally talked about food willingly and felt confident about their command of the topic. In the food-centered life histories I collected in Antonito—just like those in my earlier book on food in Florence, Italy—I found that food was central to many women's lives, fraught with conflict and meaning, a truly complicated relationship. Cultural expectations that they manage food in the home posed a challenge of how to do so and still maintain agency and efficacy. Some resented food work, some embraced it, some

passed it onto others, and some accrued economic benefits and status by taking food public.

Forty-five-year-old Janice DeHerrera (Figure 36.4) said she loved to cook when she could experiment with new ingredients or flavors, but felt burdened by cooking while she was raising seven children and struggling to plan, budget, produce, and clean up after three huge, economical, and nutritious meals day after day. During those years, Janice shouldered cooking and domestic chores while her husband worked outside the home for money. As her children grew up and moved away, Janice returned to paid work as an elementary school reading specialist, but she still did all the cooking and clean-up and felt overburdened.

Somewhat different was the story of 94-year-old Helen Ruybal (Figure 36.5) who said to me, "I'm not really a kitchen guy, if you know what I mean." Her kitchen showed no signs of cooking except for the coffee pot on the stove. Helen had turned her kitchen into a space for what she called "pencil work"—paying bills, writing letters, clipping newspapers, and opening mail—work that was essential to her identity as a teacher and more important to her than cooking. She sent her children to boarding school, enlisted her husband's help at home, and relied heavily on her sister Lila for assistance with reproductive labor. Lila babysat Helen's children and often gave Helen gifts of cooked food, especially her delicious pies. Helen made monetary gifts to Lila in return, and treated her to meals out and gifts of clothes.

Across cultures and history, how women managed their relationship to reproductive food work—producing, preserving, and cooking food for their families—has been a central determinant of their lives. This work has taken place in all kinds of circumstances and involved power and oppression, creativity and drudgery, and agency and deference.

EXPANDING THE KITCHEN

In *The Origin of the Family: Private Property and the State* (1972), Frederick Engels pointed out that with the development of capitalism, women's reproductive labor was privatized, isolated in the home, and devalued. Scholars who have studied only the reproductive dimension of women's food work have found much oppression, however, researchers are increasingly looking at ways that women gain power by taking food public, i.e. by using food to cross the boundaries between the home and the outside world, and between reproduction and production. By doing so, they become public actors and create social value for their work. The two photos (Figures 36.6 and 36.7) show occasions where women expanded their cooking and feeding beyond the home at birthday parties and team picnics, and thus simultaneously forged community and honored their children.

Figure 36.6 Shanaya's birthday party, near Antonito. On the far right in the foreground, Shanaya peeks at the camera, framed by her kneeling uncle and many assembled extended family members and friends in her maternal grandparents' backyard at her fifth birthday party.

Figure 36.7 Baseball Picnic, Antonito. Antonito mothers celebrate the end of the little league baseball season with a picnic for the players and families at the town park.

EXCHANGING FOOD AND BUILDING COMMUNITY

Antonito women throughout the twentieth century have taken food public and sometimes made money from it. Giving food, like the sopaipillas Cordi Ornelas gave me (Figure 36.8) was an important way to be actors in the public sphere and build social alliances. At least one woman, Pat Gallegos, still made cheese for sale in Antonito in 2000. Ramona Valdez purchased cheese from her and gave it to my husband and me (Figure 36.9). Ramona herself had made and sold *queso* at her family ranch along the Conejos River in Guadalupe in the 1930s and 40s, as did Helen Ruybal in the nearby hamlet of Lobatos in the same period. Although Helen eschewed cooking, she embraced remunerative food work and said, "For ten years, I made cheese, white cheese, *queso* ... As long as I had the milk, instead of throwing it away, I made cheese ... I loved to get the money that I got from my work." In addition to selling *queso* women sold tortillas, tamales, burritos, cheese, eggs, and empanadas—small fried mincemeat and raisin filled tortilla dough dumplings made especially for Christmas. Some women made and sold food at school basketball and football games to raise money for the teams. Yvonne Sisneros (Figure 36.10) sold homemade tamales to raise money to help her sister-in-law. She said,

> At Christmas ... we always do tamales and we've gotten to the point that people like our tamales so last year we made almost seventy dozen ... We use chile molido, we use chile caribe, and if we want it hotter we use chile pequin ... We add our meat in there, cook it, and then we use masa harina to make our dough, put it in corn husks, roll them, boil them, cook them ... We did them for a whole entire weekend—Friday, Saturday, Sunday we did tamales ... Me and Frances did it and my other

Figure 36.8 Sopaipillas—a gift from Cordi Ornelas.

Figure 36.9 Queso—a gift from Ramona Valdez.

sister-in-law helped a little bit . . . We had the kids helping, doing little things here and there. We had my husband Anthony helping. But I had to tie every single one because the others didn't know how to tie them . . . That was when Kathy was having problems with her baby . . . so all the money we made, we gave it to Kathy.

Women's control of food exchanges allowed them to help friends, have an influence on the community, and earn money, which in turn gave them some economic power. Many women who earned money through food used it to buy groceries, clothes for the children, home furnishings, or household items, thereby contributing to family wellbeing.

TAKING FOOD PUBLIC AND MAKING MONEY

Dos Hermanas (Two Sisters) restaurant on Main St., Antonito, is a good example of how women used their reproductive skills

Figure 36.10 Yvonne Sisneros and son Dustin.

Figure 36.11 Dos Hermanas Restaurant, Main St. Antonito.

learned at home to start a business and make a living (Figure 36.11). Budgeting, meal-planning, shopping, cooking, serving, and cleaning up were all useful skills in the restaurant trade. A Mexicana also owned and ran The Dutch Mill Café (Figure 36.12) with help from her large extended family. While more formal than the "public kitchens" described by Abarca (this volume), these two restaurants had a similar function of enabling women to earn a living and create "family wealth," both material and emotional, that rippled throughout the community.

Figure 36.12 Dutch Mill Café and Virgin of Guadalupe mural, Main St., Antonito.

Figure 36.13 Woman selling home-grown peas at La Jara Farmers' Market, near Antonito, 2009.

Working in the vegetable fields or maintaining gardens was traditionally an important activity for women and men in Antonito but suffered a gradual decline after World War II. Recent resurgence of farmers' markets in La Jara (15 miles north of Antonito) and Alamosa (30 miles north) may stimulate small-scale food production of honey, grass-fed beef, vegetables, potatoes, and local fruits (Figure 36.13). This could boost the faltering local economy and provide jobs for both men and women. All over the US and Europe, farmers' markets are a growing part of the

Figure 36.14 Food bank entrance.

Figure 36.15 St. Augustine Catholic Church, food bank entrance at left.

alternative food movement seeking to provide fresh local food for consumers and markets for struggling family farmers.

STOCKING THE PUBLIC KITCHEN: THE ANTONITO FOOD BANK

In the 2000 Census and still today, poverty and food insecurity have been severe in Antonito and Conejos County. In 2004, the percentage of people below poverty was a staggering 19.1% vs. 10.2% in Colorado and 12.7% in the U.S. But in Antonito poor people benefitted from the fact that food sharing was normative in their culture. This was not only demonstrated in informal food gifts and frequent community dinners for funerals or anniversaries, but also in the Antonito food bank

Figure 36.16 Church basement, food bank at end on right.

Figure 36.17 Antonito food bank door.

in the basement of the St. Augustine Church (Figures 36.14, 36.15, 36.16, 36.17).

Access to the food bank was straightforward and immediate—clients had to be residents of southern Conejos County and fill out a short application, whereupon they could immediately walk down to the basement and through the church hall to the door on the far right end where they could fill several shopping bags with food—how many depending on family size. Antonito women played a key role in the food bank, administering it and organizing food drives through the churches. Janice DeHerrera, a member of the Catholic Church, said: "The Church has a food bank and has drives for food all the time. They ask people to bring in canned food or pasta or anything people have." Teddy Madrid, a lifetime member of

Antonito's longstanding Presbyterian congregation, said: "At the Presbyterian Church we support the food bank . . . It gives us satisfaction, spiritual satisfaction, that we can help someone else."

Women's work on behalf of the food bank promoted public food sharing, combated hunger, and maintained values of mutual aid.

CLAIMING PUBLIC FEEDING: POWER IN RESISTANCE

But a new priest came in and tried to change things. Janice De Herrera (Figure 36.18) described what happened:

> We had this priest that came in and he says, "The only people that are going to get free

Figure 36.18 Janice De Herrera.

Figure 36.19 Antonito Food Bank shelves.

food from the food bank are people that get food stamps." He put a requirement and that got everybody mad, a lot of people mad. It got me mad because some people won't go for food stamps because they don't want the government to know anything about them . . . Sometimes somebody's husband . . . used the food budget for the liquor and they're still within the income where they wouldn't qualify for food stamps . . . There's people that are barely making it and something else came up. They've got to go to the doctor or something and then they don't have money now for food. So I don't believe they should have restrictions.

Janice continued:

Our conscience is stronger than the law . . . Nobody that has food will deny somebody that is hungry that asks for food.

The women believed so fully in the food bank that they defied an effort by the priest to change it. Rather than allow him to impose a bureaucratic restriction on who would be fed, the Antonito women insisted on food sharing and resisted the priest's efforts to impose what they considered an unjust value system on the community. They used their control of the public collection and redistribution of free food at the food bank to foster a pragmatic ethic of community care and the belief that "The needy are honest," as Tina Casias, the food bank administrator put it.

Even though it was in the church, the women's actions asserted that the food bank belonged to them (Figure 36.19).

CONCLUSION: EXPANDING THE KITCHEN: SUSTAINING SELF, FAMILY, AND COMMUNITY

In women's public feeding, the personal becomes political. When they take

Figure 36.20 Women selling organic beef at the Alamosa Farmers' Market, 2010.

Figure 36.21 Women conducting nutrition education at the Alamosa Farmers' Market, 2006.

practices from the home out into the broader community, they take family values with them—values of mutual responsibility and sharing so beautifully encapsulated by former mayor of Antonito, Carla Lucero, in an interview, "The thing that the elderly people used to say is this, 'Give because it multiplies.' "

Taking food public is an important way women sustain themselves, their families, and their communities. Increasingly in the new millennium, women and men both are taking food public by practicing food activism—working to make the food system more democratic, sustainable, and healthy. Women appear to be playing key

Figure 36.22 Community garden stand at the Alamosa Farmers' Market, 2010.

roles in establishing community supported agriculture, food education programs, school and urban gardens, community kitchens, food banks, soup kitchens, and farmers' markets (Figures 36.20, 36.21, 36.22). An important question for future research is: does gender matter in food activism? How do men's and women's food roles in the home affect how, where, and why they take food public?

EPILOGUE: PHOTOGRAPHY TAKES FOOD PUBLIC

Rural Hispanic women's using food outside the home to promote personal and community well-being is a step toward food activism. Photography can bring their stories into the public, enrich understanding of their food work, and launch further thinking about the role of visual ethnography in the digital age, when photography has changed radically. Gone are the 35 mm slides and carousels; gone are the darkrooms and the black and white photos; gone is 8 mm film—all key tools of anthropology up until the mid-1990s. Those technologies were slower and they generated far fewer images. Today digital cameras and new media technologies have transformed the visual landscape. With the increasing e-publishing and web-based dissemination of research, we have a growing ability to illustrate, expand, and transform our work with images.

Exemplifying the complexity and embeddedness of digital photography, Figure 36.23 is a screen-shot of a web page showing a digital film of a live conference where I used digital photos in a PowerPoint presentation. The web page is part of Harvard University's open access digital video archive of university events. It depicts my presentation in a Food and Gender conference at the Radcliffe Institute for Advanced Study. I used photographs taken in Antonito to illustrate how studying food illuminates gender. In the screen-shot the PowerPoint slide uses the image of Teddy Madrid in her kitchen to address the questions "Why food? Why women?" It manifests the centrality of food in women's lives by showing Teddy in the center of her kitchen, between her old wood stove and her new gas stove.

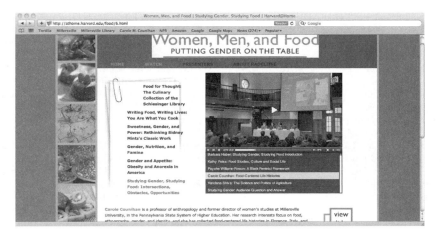

Figure 36.23 A screen-shot of a web page http://athome.harvard.edu/food/6.html showing the author at the podium taking food public in a presentation on "Studying Gender, Studying Food," at the Radcliffe Institute for Advanced Study conference on "Women, Men, and Food: Putting Gender on the Table," April 2007.

As digital photography offers us the chance to use photos in public lectures, on web pages, in podcasts, on blogs, and in myriad other ways, we face an ever-greater responsibility to photograph ethically: asking permission to photograph and to publish, ideally securing a signed consent form. The issue of using someone else's photo is complicated because what the anthropologist sees in the photo may not be what the person depicted sees nor what the reader sees. Ambiguity is inherent in ethnographic photography and we need to tread softly as we use photos to take food public in the information age where images are infinitely replicable and very powerful.

BIBLIOGRAPHY

On Photography in Anthropology/Ethnography

Agee, James and Walker Evans. 1960. *Let Us Now Praise Famous Men*. New York: Ballantine.

Bateson, Gregory and Margaret Mead. 1942. *Balinese Character: a Photographic Analysis*. New York: New York Academy of Sciences.

Berger, John. 1972. *Ways of Seeing*. New York: Penguin.

Berger, John. 1975. *A Seventh Man: Migrant Workers in Europe*. New York: Viking.

Collier, John Jr. and Malcolm Collier. 1986. *Visual Anthropology: Photography as Research Method*. Albuquerque: University of New Mexico Press.

Counihan, Carole. 1980. La fotografia come metodo antropologico. *La Ricerca Folklorica* 2:27–32.

Hockings, Paul. 1995. *Principles of Visual Anthropology*, 2nd ed. New York: Mouton De Gruyter.

Mead, Margaret and Ken Heyman. 1965. *Family*. New York: MacMillan.

Pink, Sarah. 2006. *Doing Visual Ethnography*, 2nd ed. New York: Sage.

Sontag, Susan. 1977. *On Photography*. New York: Farrar, Straus and Giroux.

On the History and Culture of Mexicanos in Antonito and the San Luis Valley

Counihan, Carole. 2009. *A Tortilla Is Like Life: Food and Culture in the San Luis Valley of Colorado*. Austin: University of Texas Press.

Counihan, Carole. 2008. Mexicanas' Public Food Sharing in Colorado's San Luis Valley. *Caderno Espaço Feminino*, special issue on "Comida e Gênero [Food and Gender]" eds. Mônica Chaves Abdala and Renata Menasche. 19, 1: 31–56.

Peña, Devon G., ed. 1998. *Chicano Culture, Ecology, Politics: Subversive Kin*. Tucson: University of Arizona Press.

Simmons, Virginia McConnell. 1979. *The San Luis Valley: Land of the Six-Armed Cross*. Boulder, CO: Pruett.

Stoller, Marianne L. 1982. The Setting and Historical Background of the Conejos Area. In *Diary of the Jesuit Residence of Our Lady of Guadalupe*

Parish. Conejos. Colorado. December 1871–December 1875. Eds. M. L. Stoller and T. J. Steele. Colorado Springs: Colorado College, pp. xvii–xxviii.

Swadesh, Frances León. 1974. *Los Primeros Pobladores: Hispanic Americans of the Ute Frontier.* Notre Dame: University of Notre Dame Press.

Taggart, James. 2002. Food, Masculinity and Place in the Hispanic Southwest. In *Food in the USA: A Reader,* ed. Carole M. Counihan. New York: Routledge, pp. 305–313.

Taylor, José Inez and James M. Taggart. 2003. *Alex and the Hobo: A Chicano Life and Story.* Austin: University of Texas Press.

Tushar, Olibama López. 1992. *The People of El Valle: a History of the Spanish Colonials in the San Luis Valley.* Pueblo, CO: El Escritorio.

Valdez, Olivama Salazar de and Dolores Valdez de Pong. 2005. *Life in Los Sauces.* Monte Vista, CO: Adobe Village Press.

On Greater Mexico

Limón, José E. 1998. *American Encounters: Greater Mexico, the United States, and the Erotics of Culture.* Boston, MA: Beacon Press.

Paredes, Américo. 1993. *Folklore and Culture on the Texas-Mexican Border.* Edited by Richard Bauman. Austin, TX: CMAS Books.

On Food-Centered Life Histories and Other Methodologies Exploring Women's Food Voice

Abarca, Meredith. 2001. Los Chilaquiles de mi' ama: the Language of Everyday Cooking. In *Pilaf, Pozole and Pad Thai: American Women and Ethnic Food,* ed. Sherrie A. Inness. Amherst: University of Massachusetts Press, pp. 119–144.

Abarca, Meredith. 2006. *Voices in the Kitchen: Views of Food and the World from Working-Class Mexican and Mexican American Women.* College Station: Texas A & M University Press.

Counihan, Carole. 2002. Food as Women's Voice in the San Luis Valley of Colorado. In *Food in the USA: A Reader,* ed. Carole M. Counihan. New York: Routledge, pp. 295–304.

Counihan, Carole. 2004. *Around the Tuscan Table: Food, Family and Gender in Twentieth Century Florence.* New York: Routledge.

Counihan, Carole. 2007. *Mexicanas'* Food Voice and Differential Consciousness in the San Luis Valley of Colorado. *Food and Culture: A Reader* revised edition. Eds. Carole Counihan and Penny Van Esterik. New York: Routledge, pp. 354–368.

Hauck-Lawson, Annie. 1992. Hearing the Food Voice: An Epiphany for a Researcher. *The Digest: An Interdisciplinary Study of Food and Foodways* 12, 1–2: 6–7.

Hauck-Lawson, Annie. 1998. When Food is the Voice: A Case Study of a Polish-American Woman. *Journal for the Study of Food and Society* 2, 1: 21–28.

Perez, Ramona Lee. 2009. Tasting Culture: Food, Family and Flavor in Greater Mexico. PhD Dissertation, Anthropology, New York University.

On Cooking and Gender Relations Among Mexican Americans and Mexicans in the US

Abarca, Meredith. 2006. *Voices in the Kitchen: Views of Food and the World from Working-Class Mexican and Mexican American Women.* College Station: Texas A & M University Press.

Blend, Benay. 2001a. "I am the Act of Kneading": Food and the making of Chicana Identity. In *Cooking Lessons: The Politics of Gender and Food,* ed. Sherrie A. Inness. New York: Rowman and Littlefield, pp. 41–61.

Blend, Benay. 2001b. "In the Kitchen Family Bread is Always Rising!" Women's Culture and the Politics of Food. In *Pilaf, Pozole and Pad Thai: American Women and Ethnic Food,* ed. Sherrie A. Inness. Amherst: University of Massachusetts Press, pp. 119–144.

Counihan, Carole. 2005. The Border as Barrier and Bridge: Food, Gender, and Ethnicity in the San Luis Valley of Colorado. In *From Betty Crocker to Feminist Food Studies: Critical Perspectives on Women and Food,* eds. A. Avakian and B. Haber. Amherst: University of Massachusetts Press, pp. 200–217.

Counihan, Carole. 2006a. Food as Mediating Voice and Oppositional Consciousness for Chicanas in Colorado's San Luis Valley. In *Mediating Chicana/o Culture: Multicultural American Vernacular,* ed. Scott Baugh. Cambridge: Cambridge Scholars Press, pp. 72–84.

Pesquera, Beatríz M. 1993. "In the Beginning, He Wouldn't Lift Even a Spoon": The Division of Household Labor. In *Building with Our Hands: New Directions in Chicana Studies,* eds. A. Torre and B. M. Pesquera. Berkeley: University of California Press, pp. 181–195.

Williams, Brett. 1985. Why Migrant Women Feed Their Husbands Tamales: Foodways as a Basis for a Revisionist View of Tejano Family Life. In *Ethnic and Regional Foodways in the United States,* eds. Linda Keller Bown and Kay Mussell. Knoxville: University of Tennessee Press, pp. 113–126.

On Women's Home and Family Food Work

Avakian, Arlene Voski, ed. 1997. *Through the Kitchen Window: Women Explore the Intimate Meanings of Food and Cooking.* Boston, MA: Beacon Press.

Avakian, Arlene Voski and Barbara Haber, eds. 2005. *From Betty Crocker to Feminist Food Studies: Critical Perspectives on Women and Food.* Amherst: University of Massachusetts Press.

Charles, Nicki and Marion Kerr. 1988. *Women, Food and Families.* Manchester: Manchester University Press.

Counihan, Carole. 1999. *The Anthropology of Food and Body: Gender, Meaning and Power*. New York: Routledge.

Counihan, Carole. 2004. *Around the Tuscan Table: Food, Family and Gender in Twentieth Century Florence*. NY: Routledge.

DeVault, Marjorie L. 1991. *Feeding the Family: The Social Organization of Caring as Gendered Work*. Chicago: University of Chicago Press.

Inness, Sherrie. 2001a. *Cooking Lessons: The Politics of Gender and Food*. Lanham, MD: Rowman & Littlefield.

Inness, Sherrie. 2001b. *Kitchen Culture in America: Popular Representations of Food, Gender and Race*. Philadelphia: University of Pennsylvania Press.

Inness, Sherrie. 2006. *Secret Ingredients: Race, Gender, and Class at the Dinner Table*. New York: Palgrave Macmillan.

On Women's Status and the Public/Private Constitution of their Labor

Engels, Frederick. 1972. *The Origin of the Family. Private Property and the State* by Frederick Engels. New York: International.

Lamphere, Louise. 2000. The Domestic Sphere of Women and the Public World of Men: the Strengths and Limitations of an Anthropological Dichotomy. In *Gender in Cross-Cultural Perspective*, eds. Caroline B. Brettell and Carolyn F. Sargent. Upper Saddle River, NJ: Prentice Hall, pp. 100–109.

Leacock, Eleanor Burke. 1972. "Introduction" to *The Origin of the Family, Private Property and the State* by Frederick Engels. New York: International, pp. 7–67.

Sacks, Karen. 1974. Engels Revisited: Women, the Organization of Production, and Private Property. In *Women, Culture and Society*, eds. M. Z. Rosaldo and L. Lamphere. Stanford, CA: Stanford University Press, pp. 207–222.

Sargent, Lydia, ed. 1981. *Women and Revolution: The Unhappy Marriage between Marxism and Feminism*. Boston, MA: South End Press.

On Women Taking Food Public

Abarca, Meredith. 2007. *Charlas Culinarias*: Mexican Women Speak from the Public Kitchens. *Food and Foodways* 15, 3–4: 183–212.

Barndt, Deborah, ed. 1999. *Women Working the NAFTA Food Chain: Women, Food and Globalization*. Toronto: Sumach Press.

Barndt, Deborah, 2001. On the Move for Food: Three Women Behind the Tomato's Journey. *Women's Studies Quarterly* 1&2: 131–143

Barndt, Deborah, 2002. Fruits of Injustice: Women in the Post NAFTA Food System. *Canadian Women's Studies* 21, 4: 82–88.

Barndt, Deborah. 2010. *Tangled Routes: Women, Work, and Globalization on the Tomato Trail*, 2nd ed. Lanham, MD: Rowman and Littlefield.

Pardo, Mary. 2000. Creating Community: Mexican American Women in Eastside Los Angeles. In *Las Obreras: Chicana Politics of Work and Family*, ed. Vicki L. Ruiz. Los Angeles: UCLA Chicano Studies Research Center Publications, pp. 107–135.

Wardrop, Joan. 2006. Private Cooking, Public Eating: Women Street Vendors in South Durban. *Gender, Place and Culture*, 13, 6: 677–683.

Williams-Forson, Psyche A. 2006. *Building Houses out of Chicken Legs: Black Women, Food, and Power*. The University of North Carolina Press.

Yasmeen, Gisèle. 2008. "Plastic-bag Housewives" and Postmodern Restaurants? Public and Private in Bangkok's Foodscape. In *Food and Culture: A Reader*, eds. Carole Counihan and Penny Van Esterik, 2nd ed. New York: Routledge, pp. 523–538.

On Food Banks, Soup Kitchens, and Other Forms of Food Charity

Glasser, Irene. 1988. *More than Bread: Ethnography of a Soup Kitchen*. Tuscaloosa: University of Alabama Press.

Poppendieck, Janet. 1998. *Sweet Charity? Emergency Food and the End of Entitlement*. New York: Penguin.

On Women and Food Activism

Allen, Patricia and Carolyn Sachs. 2007. Women and Food Chains: The Gendered Politics of Food. *Journal of Sociology of Food and Agriculture*, 15, 1: 1–23.

Field, Debbie. 1999. Putting Food First: Women's Role in Creating a Grassroots Food System Outside the Marketplace. In *Women Working the NAFTA Food Chain: Women, Food and Globalization*, ed. Deborah Barndt. Toronto: Sumach Press, pp. 193–208.

Hayes-Conroy, Allison and Jessica Hayes-Conroy. 2008. Taking Back Taste: Feminism, Food, and Visceral Politics. *Gender, Place and Culture: A Journal of Feminist Geography*, 15, 5: 461–473.

Moffett, Deborah and Mary Lou Morgan. 1999. Women as Organizers: Building Confidence and Community through Food. In *Women Working the NAFTA Food Chain: Women, Food and Globalization*, ed. Deborah Barndt. Toronto: Sumach Press, pp. 221–236.

Schroeder, Kathleen. 2006. A Feminist Examination of Community Kitchens in Peru and Bolivia. *Gender, Place & Culture*, 13.6: 663–668.

Villagomez, Maria Dolores. 1999. Grassroots Responses to Globalization: Mexican Rural and Urban Women's Collective Alternatives. In *Women Working the NAFTA Food Chain: Women, Food and Globalization*, ed. Deborah Barndt. Toronto: Sumach Press, pp. 209–219.

37

A Feminist Examination of Community Kitchens in Peru and Bolivia

Kathleen Schroeder

INTRODUCTION

Kitchens are universal and configured in a wide variety of ways. In the western world, we usually think of kitchens as private spaces but public, or community kitchens, are common in many low-income countries. In the Andean countries of Peru and Bolivia, community kitchens tap into women's unpaid kitchen labor and have become a vital part of many families' strategies for surviving economic crisis. Soup kitchens, or community kitchens, in Peru and Bolivia have received a great deal of scholarly attention in the development literature and they provide an excellent example of how kitchens can be spaces of both women's autonomy and women's oppression. Community kitchens in the Andes are both public and private spaces. They are ostensibly open to all, but usually run by a fairly small group of powerful women. They are showcases of women's entrepreneurial abilities and an indication that the state has abdicated its responsibility to the poor as it adopts neo-liberal policies. This essay will examine communal soup kitchens in the Andean countries of Peru and Bolivia to demonstrate the complexities of these spaces and their potential to empower and subjugate women.

A NOTE ON METHODS

I have been interested in kitchens in the Andes since my first fieldwork experience in the 1980s in Peru (Schroeder, 1990). Since that time, I have kept my hands in the kitchen both figuratively and literally. During dissertation research in marginal barrios in Bolivia in 1993, I spent a great deal of time as a participant observer in community kitchens. Since 1993, I have continued to be involved with soup kitchen research on repeated trips to both Bolivia and Peru, including four months living in Bolivia in 2005. My comments here are based on 15 years of observation and are supported by the current literature, discussions with development experts and participant observation with women in community kitchens.

SOUP KITCHENS IN THE US AND HOW THEY DIFFER FROM THOSE IN PERU AND BOLIVIA

Before I began working in soup kitchens (better described as community kitchens) in the Andes, my preconceived notion of these spaces was predicated on my experiences with similar institutions in the United States. Irene Glasser (1988) provides an excellent ethnographic portrayal of a soup kitchen in the United States, which can be contrasted with kitchens in Peru and Bolivia. In her description, soup kitchens are typically hidden. They are established in church basements or community centers and the patrons ('guests' in her language) are hidden from society's gaze. Many of the people she describes are profoundly isolated and alone in the world. Many have emotional and physical disabilities and, for them, the soup kitchen is a safe place to pass the morning hours while they wait for someone to prepare their lunch. Lunch is usually provided for free, and the patrons have no responsibility to the kitchen other than to be respectful of the space.

Community kitchens in Latin America are different places in many ways. They share the objective with US institutions of providing a nutritious meal to economically disadvantaged people. They also share the characteristic of being safe places where people can meet. A major difference, however, is that in Latin America these places are not hidden. They have prominent places in communities and are usually a source of civic pride. Many different types of community kitchens exist in Latin America. Some are run by the state, but many more are considered autonomous, or self-help, establishments. In an autonomous community kitchen, the women running the program also receive the food. Officials from donor agencies may provide some guidance and oversight, but on a daily basis the women are in charge. These types of kitchens in particular have been lauded as training grounds for entrepreneurial women in Latin America. Women who learn the skills needed to run a community kitchen, it is argued, can apply those skills in other settings.

One very telling difference between Latin American and US soup kitchens is that in Latin America politicians visit community kitchens looking for votes. Community kitchens are places where community formation and consolidation can happen, and politicians are quick to seize the opportunity to address this important constituency. During any given election cycle, political leaders from a variety of parties will court the community kitchen vote. Politicians understand the power of these women as community activists and will aim their political stump speeches towards wooing these voters.

Finally, community kitchens in Latin America just feel different from those in the US. These are not places where people pass the time because they have nothing to do. The women there are not bored and lonely. They are very likely to be community leaders. The women participating in community kitchens are frequently the best connected and most involved in community activities. Significantly, these are the same women whom Moser (1992) discussed as facing a 'triple role' because of their responsibilities to their families, employers and projects sponsored by well-meaning non-governmental organizations.

KITCHENS, HYGIENE AND THE NEO-LIBERAL AGENDA

Community kitchens are depicted as spaces where women's empowerment is nurtured and women can find their voices for the first time (Mujica, 1994). Women of indigenous origin are frequently associated with the community kitchen model of economic and social empowerment. However, during times of economic crisis women of all ethnic backgrounds in Peru and Bolivia have relied upon community kitchens. UNICEF has been an important funder and supporter of community kitchens and their literature makes a link between community kitchens and women's empowerment (UNICEF, 2004). Development experts argue that women can learn community organization skills, nutrition, and hygiene and at the same time provide an inexpensive meal for their families. The Catholic organization, Sisters of the Holy Cross, shares this commitment to community kitchens and has taken its work a step further by also establishing 'tambos', or stores, where community kitchens can purchase supplies. They are helping women to broaden their skills by providing training in wholesale and retail store management (CSCSISTERS, 2004).

A training manual on the organization and function of community kitchens (CECYCAP, 1989) reads more as a primer on participatory democracy than a guide for cooking for large numbers of people. Clearly, the kitchens are viewed as places where women's capacity is built and women become more empowered. The kitchen is only the starting place to gain access to these women and teach them about hygiene, health, and the importance of literacy. Community kitchens can serve a wide variety of functions by simply providing a space for women to come together and conduct socially sanctioned gendered activities such as cooking.

During the off hours, these same buildings can house meetings of Mother's Clubs. In Peru and Bolivia, Mother's Clubs are popular organizations that bring women together to address issues of special concern to women. The issues can and will vary according to the needs of the group. Participants in Clubs might learn about child development, or participate in a literacy program, or engage in an income-generating activity. These weekly meetings always have an objective, but often the meetings become focused on other issues that concern the women. The women can get sidetracked and end up discussing a situation where a woman in the community is facing domestic violence or debating the progress of a community water project. Frequently, women exchange information about the retail prices of different foods or products. This informal networking provides support and concrete information that women can use to better their material wellbeing.

Feminist scholars working in the Andes have outlined the dialectic between the empowerment of women and the control of women as demonstrated in various improvement projects sponsored by the state and non-governmental organizations. For example, Stephenson (1999) examines the formation of the modern state in Bolivia and its explicit prioritization of indigenous women who, according to the state, are dirty. Improving the hygiene of the indigenous population has long been a focus of development projects. Implicit in much of the materials about community kitchens is an expectation that indigenous women were not concerned with cleanliness. Not only are indigenous women considered dirty, according to much of the literature, these women also need the basic organizational skills that running a community kitchen can provide. If indigenous women can learn to manage an efficient kitchen, this will have spillovers to other aspects of their lives. This strategy mirrors much of the post-World War II literature that tried to train women in the United States in the efficient use of kitchen resources (MATRIX, 1984).

The economic collapse of the 1980s that spawned the growth of community kitchens (particularly in Peru) has been well documented (Blondet & Montero, 1995; Boggio et al., 1990; Kogan, 1998; PRODIA, 1989). The growth of community kitchens emerged from the social and economic morass of the 1980s in Latin America. Women could survive economic crisis by binding together in a shared strategy of community labor. By pooling resources, women could buy food in bulk, thereby saving money. As the state and non-governmental organizations began to grasp the power of the kitchens, they started to help out through food subsidies or donations. The community kitchen model flourished and was even promoted as an opportunity for women's empowerment. Women's daily struggle to feed themselves and their families is repackaged as a wonderful opportunity that benefits women.

Hays-Mitchell (2002) argues that communal kitchens are premised on the volunteer labor of women with already demanding work and family obligations. One study found that about 80% of women participating in community kitchens spent between three and eight hours a day working in those kitchens (Immink, 2001). In addition to the hours spent shopping, cooking and cleaning up, women active in community kitchens must also endure an endless number of meetings (Mujica, 1994). These kitchens expand women's reproductive tasks, always assuming that poor women have an endless supply of time and energy.

AGENTS OF CHANGE?

For all the discussion of community kitchens as places where women gain valuable experience, what evidence exists that women active in soup kitchens can actually transfer these skills into income generation? Although the health, status and living conditions of families that participate in community kitchens has been documented (Fernández et al., 1994) the long term effects of participation remain questionable. It appears that autonomous kitchens (ones not run by the state) are most likely to foster women's empowerment (Lenten, 1993), but no compelling evidence exists that women in fact can use the organizational skills they gain through their unpaid kitchen labor to substantially increase their earnings. Women spend considerable time and energy in these enterprises and have very little to show for it but a cheap bowl of soup. This helps to explain why 'burnout' and 'turnover' are such big issues when it comes to staffing community kitchens.

Community kitchens are not egalitarian. Women with better social connections, more supportive spouses, and other family members able to contribute reproductive labor, are much more likely to be in leadership roles in the community kitchen. Women already on the fringes of society may not feel welcome to participate, or might not be permitted to by their husbands. It is questionable if community kitchens have been effective in meeting the nutritional needs of the poorest of the poor in the Andes. If these kitchens survive

over a long period of time, they can divide a community.

Not all poor neighborhoods have community kitchens, but those that do tend to attract other development projects. Women in the kitchens can provide the needed structure to support other community-based projects. Women's role as unpaid community monitors is reinforced. A barrio with a well-established kitchen has proven itself as a community that can work together, and is better able to assure development workers that they will live up to their end of an agreement in a project. Communities that have kitchens also attract the attention of political leaders who are always on the lookout for potential constituents.

Twelve years after conducting research in a marginal barrio in Bolivia and acting as a participant observer in a soup kitchen established there, I was able to return in 2005. Although the kitchen no longer operates, the women who were in charge of its daily operation continue their involvement in the neighborhood. Over the years, development projects and funding from international agencies has come and gone. They have had medical clinics established and disappeared, training sessions for women's income generation, dietary supplement programs for children and most recently a project that provides academic tutoring and after-school care for barrio children. The projects and funding sources have changed, but the key neighborhood players have not. The same core group of women has been involved in every project. This neighborhood has a reputation with development workers as a likely place for success, because of the involvement of certain key women.

IMPLICATIONS: SELF-HELP AND THE ABANDONMENT OF THE POOR

Community kitchens are the perfect neoliberal tool. They ostensibly teach indigenous women skills that are useful in a

capitalist economic system such as entrepreneurial skills and record keeping
and they allow the state to abdicate
its responsibility to the poor (Gill, 2000).
Women who are struggling to feed
their families benefit by learning basic
accounting and time management skills.
If hardworking women can rally and
manage to feed their families under even
the most adverse economic situations, the
state can further reduce its support for the
poor. Community kitchens in the Andes
emerged in the 1980s during a time
of profound economic and social crises.
Since that time, community kitchens have
received substantial scholarly attention
and are now a common feature of development plans. Although substantial benefits to particular women can be traced to
their involvement in community kitchens,
their long-term benefits for most women
are questionable.

ACKNOWLEDGEMENTS

I would like to thank the editors and three
anonymous reviewers for their constructive comments.

REFERENCES

Blondet, Cecilia & Montero, Carmen (1995) *Hoy:
Menu Popular—Comedores en Lima* (Lima,
IEP—UNICEF).
Boggio, A., Boggio, Z., De La Cruz, H., Florez, A. &
Raffo, E. (1990) *La Organization de la Mujer en
Torno al Problema Alimentario: Una proximación
socio-analítica sobre los comedores populäres de
Lima Metropolitana—Década del '80* (Lima,
CELATS).
CSCSISTERS (2004) Available at: < http://www.
cscsisters.org/development/development_south
america.asp > (accessed 28 May 2004).
CECYCAP—Centro de Estudios Cristianos y
Capacitacion Popular (1989) *Comedores
Familiares: Manual de Organización Roles y
Funciones* (Peru, Arequipa).

Fernández, M., Munita, F, Crovetto, M. & Medioli,
A. M. (1994) *Participation Comunitaria en
Programas Alimentarios: El Programa de
Colaciones a Niños y Ancianos a través de Ollas
Comunes—Evaluación de la Experiencia 1990–
1994* (Santiago, PET-PROSAN).
Gill, Lesley (2000) *Teetering on the Rim: Global
restructuring, daily life, and the armed retreat of
the Bolivian state* (New York, Columbia
University Press).
Glasser, Irene (1988) *More than Bread: Ethnology of
a soup kitchen* (Tuscaloosa, University of Alabama
Press).
Hays-Mitchell, Maureen (2002) Resisting austerity:
a gendered perspective on neo-liberal restruc-
turing in Peru, *Gender and Development*, 10, pp.
71–81.
Immink, Maarten D. C. (2001) People's community
kitchens in Peru: women's activism pro urban
food security, *Ecology of Food and Nutrition*, 40,
pp. 699–705.
Kogan, Luiba (1998) Soup kitchens, women and
social policy: studies from Peru, *Development in
Practice*, 8, pp. 471–478.
Lenten, Roelie (1993) *Cooking under the Volcanoes*
(Amsterdam, Centro de Estudios y Documentación
Latinoamericanos).
MATRIX—Boys, J., Bradshaw, F., Darke, J., Foo, B.,
Francis, S., McFarlane, B. & Roberts, M. (1984)
*Making Space: Women and the man made envi-
ronment* (Leichhardt, Pluto Press).
Moser, Caroline (1992) Adjustment from below:
low income women, time and the triple role in
Guayaquil, Ecuador, in: Haleh Afshar & Carolyne
Dennis (Eds) *Women and Adjustment Policies in
the Third World* (New York, St. Martin's Press).
Mujica, María-Elena (1994) *Meals, Solidarity, and
Empowerment: Communal kitchens in Lima,
Peru* (East Lansing, Michigan State University
Working Paper).
PRODIA—Programa de Desarrollo Integral con Apoyo
Alimentario (1989) *Módulo para la Capacitaión de
Dirigentes de Comedores Comunales* (Lima,
PRODIA).
Schroeder, Kathleen (1990) Senora Camino's
kitchen: cuisine as strategy in the Sierra of Piura,
Peru (Master's thesis, University of Texas at
Austin).
Stephenson, Marcia (1999) *Gender and Modernity
in Andean Bolivia* (Austin, University of Texas
Press).
UNICEF (2004) Available at: <http://www.unicef.
org/sowc01/countries/peru.htm> (accessed 28
May 2004).

38

Visceral Difference: Variations in Feeling (Slow) Food

Allison Hayes-Conroy and Jessica Hayes-Conroy

INTRODUCTION

"Slow Food has spread in the US through a certain gastronomic society, which is basically white. It has only spread in one category, white and wealthy, and has done so through volunteers. We have never made a selection of volunteers ... it was just whomever asked to be part of the movement, and so the message reached only those who were there and ready to hear it. This [process] revealed the organization, and [being] organized this way organically generates problems. It doesn't guarantee diversity."

Slow Food leader (personal interview)

As the above quote indicates, many alternative food activists—people dedicated to securing alternatives to conventional means of food production/distribution—purport to want to increase membership diversity in alternative food movement organizations. At least this seems to be the case for the Slow Food movement (SF), whose leaders have suggested that inadequate racial and economic diversity may be an impediment to strengthening the US faction of the global movement. As movement leaders in the US begin to ask the tough and laudable question of how to increase membership diversity, they find themselves attempting to recruit across difference. Recent research has examined how structural/economic and discursive/rhetorical processes work to maintain alternative food movements like SF in the US as largely liberal, white (European-American), upper-middle-class

groups (eg Allen, 2008; Guthman, 2008a; Hinrichs, 2000; Jarosz, 2008; Slocum, 2007). Particularly intriguing here is Guthman's (2008a) insistence that alternative food discourse codes spaces of alternative food practice as white, having a "chilling effect on people of color" (page 388). This paper enriches such work by questioning whether visceral processes may also be relevant to understanding difference in alternative food.

While this paper speaks through empirical example, more than an assessment of 'gathered' data, what we attempt to advance here is a particular approach to understanding difference that takes into account what we call the visceral body. Throughout the paper, *visceral* is defined as the bodily realm in/through which feelings, sensations, moods, and so on are experienced (similar to Connolly, 1999; Hayes-Conroy and Hayes-Conroy, 2008; Hayes-Conroy and Martin, 2010; Longhurst et al, 2009; Probyn, 2001). Necessarily, visceral includes the cognitive mind; the visceral body is an internal relation of mind/body. Thus, we do not seek to circumvent so-called 'cognitive' and 'representational' aspects of identity/ difference, but rather we seek to rework concepts of identity/difference to include both bodily sensation and mental conceptualizing. Addressing difference viscerally, we ask: how do various relations between bodies and their social and material environments manifest as feelings/sensations/ moods which can encourage or inhibit participation in food-based social groups such as SF? We use SF in Bay Area, California as a working illustration that allows us to interrogate how differences in feeling/sensation/mood surrounding food can be seen to both emerge from and help to construct boundaries in alternative food.

This paper is thus premised upon the suggestion that recruiting a diverse membership in alternative food movement organizations demands an understanding of how different bodies differentially feel food, food environments (restaurants, markets, farm fields), and food practices (buying local/organic, culinary customs, gardening). We pay attention to cases of feeling to offer a moving picture of the catalytic potential(s) of visceral experience: how feelings can work to *charge* or to *chill* membership and participation in alternative food groups like SF. The picture we offer while focused on SF is one of many potential pictures that might have been given. We do not try to make claims about SF as a social movement organization through this paper; the paper is about the *possibilities of understanding* that emerge from our engagement with SF.

We use data cocreated through participatory fieldwork in order to track some visceral mechanisms through which movements may (often unwittingly) generate or reinforce boundaries along various lines of difference. Fieldwork tended to involve people whose local versions of SF were permeated by an existing culture of anxiety in the Bay Area over class and racial privilege. Our cocreated data echo this undertone and help us to illuminate difference as a visceral phenomenon. In the coming section we discuss recent literature that explores the materiality— specifically the molecularity—of feeling, and this helps us to understand difference in terms of the visceral body. Then, after explaining our methodology, we draw on empirical examples to explore the viscerality of difference—one focused on tangible food ingestions and another

focused on intangible (food-based) ingestions. Throughout these examples, we often use the term Slow Food (SF) in reference to all material and immaterial aspects of SF (foods, events, environments, claims, ideologies, missions, and members). We also use the lexicon 'feeling' as shorthand for all sensations, moods, and states experienced in the visceral body. Importantly, we understand bodily feeling to result not from purely individual sensations or intrinsic qualities of the self, but rather from different(ly situated) bodies' capacities to affect and be affected by other bodies [including non-human bodies, like food or music, as in Anderson (2005)].[1]

UNDERSTANDING DIFFERENCE AS VISCERAL

Difference, particularly social difference, has been a common theme in social research for over two decades. Scholarly interest in how to sensitively theorize difference intensified throughout the late 1980s and 1990s (Calhoun, 1995; Fincher and Jacobs, 1998; West and Fenstermaker, 1995; Young, 1990). An important agenda in this work was to replace boxed or static understandings of classic social differences, including race, class, gender, and sexual difference, with more fluid and dynamic understandings of these categories by pointing out the processes through which they are continually socially produced. Meanwhile work on bodies and embodiment reacted and responded to discursive approaches by trying to express the real, material impact that cultural representations of difference have on bodies (Butler, 1993; Jacobs and Nash, 2003; Weiss, 1999). Within this work there has been much dispute over the role of bodies themselves in the creation of difference; maintaining distance from biological determinism as well as (total) social constructivism, scholars have tried to eke out a way to adequately depict difference as it relates to the body. Today, many find feminist theories and relational philosophies helpful in theorizing cultural representations of difference alongside the 'fleshy realities' of the human body (Beasley and Bacchi, 2007; Colls, 2007; Longhurst, 2005). Specifically, corporeal feminist scholarship is cross-pollinating work on affect, emotion, and sensation to demonstrate a need to attend to *visceral difference*—singularities and variations of experience that emerge as sensations/moods/states of the human body [eg, Knights and Thanem (2005). Markula (2006), Probyn (2001; 2005). Saldanha (2006), and see Grosz (1994) on corporeal feminism].

Particularly relevant for thinking through visceral difference is the notion of 'biosocial', which invites us to understand biological and social forces as internally combined. The term has been used as a disruption to the nature/society binary, and thus effectively to the mind/body binary (Pollard and Hyatt 1999). Notions of 'biosocial' have penetrated a handful of geographic subdisciplines—eg health geography [Mansfield (2008); and differently, Hall (2000)]; resource geography (Bakker and Bridge, 2006); social and cultural geography (Anderson and Tolia-Kelly, 2004); and urban geography (Latham and McCormack, 2004). In a valuable illustration, Mansfield (2008), inspired by various relational theorists (Castree and Braun, 2001; Whatmore, 2002), uses the term 'biosocial' to complicate understandings of bodily health. She explains how the wellbeing of the body is "about the 'physiological' translation of . . . 'social' practices, even as these [social practices] react to physiological processes. The social [becomes] the biological, while the biological [does] not exist on its own, without the social" (page 1018). Drawing from this account, we similarly suggest that feeling is more than either biological response or socialized reaction to situations/surroundings—feelings are visceral judgments that are simultaneously biological and social in a way that is irreducible to either/or.

Yet, if visceral experience is an ever-shifting biosocial process, how are we to 'get at' feeling as social science researchers? McCormack's (2007) work on 'molecular affects' reminds us that 'lay' intervention into the visceral realm of mood and emotion has become increasingly commonplace. McCormack describes how various scientific and industrial advances have offered working maps of the molecular body by attending to biochemical movements in the brain and body. With this new cartography, affective experiences are increasingly rendered available for manipulation, as various drugs, techniques, and practices are presented and sold to the public as molecular self-help technologies. It is now commonplace to take an active role in manipulating one's biochemical exchanges—from the ingestion of Prozac or St John's Wort to the practice of exercise or meditation. Of course, many pharmaceutical interventions for altering brain/body chemistry are marketed in bioreductionist ways, claiming to produce specific and certain results, and ultimately eschewing the more holistic, biosocial conception of bodily wellbeing described above by Mansfield. Yet, as McCormack's work illustrates, this focus on the biochemical has also opened the door for envisioning other ways of intervening in corporeal/affective economies that admit and allow a great deal more uncertainty.

For our interest in the visceral, these advances are important because they make affective relationships both imaginable and palpable. Once we accede that drugs can alter one's mood, sensations, or state of being ('bodily feeling' for short), other ingestions—like food and drink—are not far behind. Nor, we would add, is the leap so great between these tangible ingestions and more intangible ones—things like ideas, representations, or theories. Certainly if meditation and yoga have been used to alter bodily feeling, so too could other mind-body activities: learning, reading, discussing, labeling.

More accurately, tangible and intangible ingestions happen concurrently: eg food-stuffs being eaten along with food ideas, food rhetoric, food labels. Part of our goal as researchers in this project was thus to witness and to critically discuss the production of different states or feelings through participants' engagement in food-based activities (tasting, growing, creating, describing, etc). A bit later, we hope to describe how food produces feelings that serve to differentiate bodies in/around SF.

An important point to reiterate first is that whether we are talking about tangible food ingestions (sugars, fats, spices) or intangible food ingestions (ideas, beliefs, values) we cannot reduce bodily state or feeling to chemical composition. Foods and food-based activities could help to produce certain moods, or might get certain feeling chemicals moving (McCormack, 2007), but the molecular economies of bodies are much too complex—and unique—to claim guaranteed, universal results. Instead, we take McCormack's view that, "bodies emerge as nonreducible, relational rhythmic orderings, the affective capacities of which can be transformed through various techniques and practices" (page 370). For McCormack the value of biochemical mappings of the body lies not so much in providing scientifically objective explanations for feeling but rather in proposing one potential means through which the 'barely sensed' micro-spaces of the body might be surveyed and discussed in their biosocial complexity (page 369). Biochemical or molecular processes offer 'material consistency' to all kinds of affective relations, without needing to draw watertight causal equations about them. Moving in the realm between biological and social sciences, we can begin to see the visceral body as an active and translational space in which constantly mixing and merging molecules interpret and convert (various 'ingested' parts of) the rest of the world.

A second and related point to make clear here is that, again whether talking about tangible or intangible ingestions, different bodies will interpret and convert differently. Such difference may seem obvious when discussing seemingly imma-terial/cultural things that a body might take in: for instance, the idea of local eating might translate to a rousing feeling in one body as a singular blend of chemicals spill out and move within the body upon hearing, viewing, and/or mulling over the idea, while in another body the same idea might translate into quite different chemical mixtures and movements. But, we insist that such visceral difference can also exist in regard to mate-rial ingestions: ingredients like sugar, fats, or spices also inspire different molecular movements in different bodies, and ulti-mately differences in feeling. To be clear, these visceral differences are not simply a product of social variation, but instead result from the particular interactions of bodily molecules themselves, translating ingestions, releasing and reacting in a wider climate of biosocial variability, and building upon previous interactions and bodily memories to produce variation in moments of feeling.

Therefore, contrary to colloquial depic-tions of viscerality as knee-jerk response, we understand visceral differences (or, variations in bodily feeling) as develop-mental in their immediacy. That is, an in-the-moment feeling builds from a seem-ingly chaotic intersection of new(er) and old(er) factors influencing that moment's unique molecular mixing and moving in the body: things like a smell, a comment, weather, prior moods, a new theory, a recurrent idea, a headache, a memory, or a pat on the back. Herein we might also add structures like race, gender, and class; these can be seen as key factors in forming visceral difference both because they influ-ence how bodies can and do develop on a chemical/molecular level and because the social categories themselves can be 'ingested', generating mixings and movings of molecules, and ultimately shaping bodily feeling. It is for this reason that we insist a visceral approach is a way to see social difference operating *in* the body alongside and interconnected to other processes more often recognized as chemical, molecular, or bodily. Issues of race, gender, and class are not outside the visceral (for instance, see Saldanha, 2006).

Below, after summarizing our methods, we offer a background to some of the anxieties (about difference) that seem to be present in/around SF. We then venture into the visceral, detailing two conversations about particular ingestions, which serve as illustrations of how differences in feeling are produced in relation to SF.

EXPLORATIONS IN SLOW FOOD

The data discussed in this paper reflect our contention as researchers that it is possible to get at visceral experience through intentional dialogue and conscious bodily/sensory action. The research activities we discuss come from the California-based portion of a larger research project on visceralities of food activism that took place in Nova Scotia, Canada, and Bay Area, California. To be clear, viscerality in this project worked as both method and theory in a fully participatory sense; that is, we found that an attentiveness to the visceral body both centered our/participants' bodily capacities of feeling (in order to make feeling available in research encounters) and proved valuable for *thinking* about food—body relations (and more broadly food—environment relations). Our project directly engaged past and present SF members as well as food activists and professionals on the edges of SF; participants (forty in total in California) and researchers cocreated data through a series of research events that allowed for verbal and nonverbal communications, of which participants had overall control. Events included 'intentionally designed experiences' of SF created by participants, as well as in-depth conversations and group discussions, which often included further

sensory exchanges (meals, gardening, marketing, or outings to food-production sites). During fieldwork stays in California and Nova Scotia, we also immersed ourselves ethnographically in the regions, talking with adults and school-age children met in day-to-day activities and while volunteering. The second author was engaged in a related project regarding school garden and cooking programs, which greatly enhanced our understanding of food activism in both sites. All communications loosely addressed the question, what does food and/or SF *feel* like?

The theme of difference, while playing a lesser role in Nova Scotia, emerged as a particularly powerful theme in California, most likely because difference—particularly issues of race and class—has intensified as a pressing issue among Californian food activists and academics in recent years. Evidently, to be politically correct in alternative food circles in California is to be aware of multiple intersections of race, class, and food. The work of Alkon (2008), Allen (2004; 2008), Guthman (2004; 2008a), and Slocum (2007) parallel this increasing awareness in the academic world, and indicate persistent inequity in California alternative food, particularly along class, race, and occupational lines. Appropriately, in a project such as ours, where data are created in collaboration with participants, it is unsurprising to have generated much *discussion* on difference. We emphasize discussion because the theme of difference emerged more in verbal communications than in nonverbal communications. We attribute this to two related factors: first, the fact that participants had total control over nonverbal, sensory experiences usually meant that they designed experiences that resonated with them viscerally and thus did not tend to recall differences in feeling between themselves and an 'SF other'; second, as activists working within particular political repertoires, many of our participants found that the topic of difference was something easier to insist upon verbally than to show/share through sensory engagement with food. Hence, we use mostly verbal data below to offer an illustration of how SF/alternative food *is being felt* (by some) and *might be felt differently* (by many).

Before doing so, however, it seems crucial to note that SF, in the context of Bay Area food politics, is unique. SF began in Italy in the 1980s as a resistance to food-system standardization/corporatization (Pietrykowski, 2004). Today, as an internationally organized, member-supported movement, SF seeks to shape the future of food systems and culture worldwide, focusing on the protection and enjoyment of 'good' (tasty), 'clean' (environmentally friendly), and 'fair' (socially just) foods. SF has many branches, working through grower communities, 'presidia' projects aimed at agro-biodiversity preservation, global and regional conventions, and local chapters called 'convivia'. Internationally, SF is quite diverse, including food producers and consumers, wealthy and poor, from over 100 countries in the Global North and South.

In contrast, as previously indicated, SF's US membership (particularly the convivia) is not as diverse. In California specifically, spaces and networks of SF often appear to be divided across racial and economic lines. Lack of diversity has been suggested in critiques of food elitism leveled on the region, such as that made by SF founder Carlo Petrini himself (Petrini et al, 2007), as well as by the voiced concerns of numerous local food activists (including SF), and by a survey conducted as part of this project: consider that, in the Bay Area over 90% of approximately 100 SF members responding to our survey were white (only 7% were Asian, 3% other, and 0% black, also 2% Hispanic of any race), while the Bay Area statistics at large are considerably more diverse: 47.3% white, nearly 20% Asian, 9.5% other, 7.3% black, and nearly 20% Hispanic of any race. Rates of education were similarly skewed. Of those responding to our survey

nearly 90% boast undergraduate degrees or higher, while in the Bay Area, 41% of the population has an undergraduate degree or higher.[2] We cite this apparent lack of diversity in Bay Area SF not to critique the organization, but rather to point out why race-based and class-based difference seemed imperative to our participating group of California food activists. (For more on our methods see Hayes-Conroy, 2010).

FEELING CHEETOS, DIFFERENTLY

One of us has explored elsewhere the emergence of pleasurable feelings via social and material aspects of SF (Hayes-Conroy and Martin, 2010). We understand such sensations as indicative of particular body—food and body—environment relationships that catalyze forms of alternative food practice (eg organizing workshops or public events, supporting local farmers, participating in community gardening). For instance, one food activist described her relationship with a box of apples that sat next to us during a conversation:

> "These apples give me physical pleasure and an emotional response. My friend's mother grew them on their cherished family farm. They are an heirloom variety. It is really raising an emotional response to smell them and that galvanizes me in a way that is much stronger than any intellectual or abstract or ideology could" (Cecily).[3]

As we hope to have made clear already, one critical matter that arises in accounting for such motivating is: how do some bodies become inspired or charged through SF—activated towards alternative food practices—while others are chilled or turned off? Before delving into the visceral body to answer this question, we use this section to set the stage—to illustrate (one version of) the background of food—body politics and political anxieties and ambivalences in/around Berkeley-area SF.

SF's eco-gastronomic projects have often focused on the goal of *taste education*—the cultivation and appreciation of particular tastes like heirloom varieties, seasonal organic produce, and free-range heritage poultry—for the purposes of protecting these species and upholding agro-biodiversity (Petrini et al, 2007). The predictable flipside of such appreciation of tastes is a disapproval of other tastes. In conversations and during shared meals and other activities, many SF members reported negative feelings and sensations in relation to products like Coca Cola, microwave oatmeal, and Sysco chicken, or upon entering chain supermarkets. Others referenced bad meals—eg McDonalds or Jack in The Box[4]—in comparison with better meals, usually at nonchain local restaurants or cooked at home. Such visceral appraisal of bad taste, negative feelings, or other adverse sensations can be easily problematized, as they were in numerous conversations with activists in this project. A number of participants recognized that such feelings not only trigger a rejection of certain foods, activities, ambiances, or experiences but also set up a dynamic of judgment against others for their own food enjoyments.

Yet, while some food activists take issue with the potential dynamic of judgment that comes linked with the rejection of fast/processed foods, many hold firm to the value of tasting what they consider to be 'real' food. One social-justice-oriented food activist insisted:

> "The allure of Jack In The Box is everything tastes so over the top. It's like Extreme Cheetos. That's what everyone in my neighborhood eats. . . . If you grow up eating. . . . I mean, I ate tons of junk food when I was little and somehow I got out of eating that way but when I see people eating Extreme Cheetos I think how are you ever going to enjoy a peach or whatever?".
>
> (Thea)

Another activist, equally spirited towards justice was even more adamant about what 'good food' is:

CECILY: "Everyone can enjoy good food. I mean, I am not wealthy. . . . I just ate at Chez Panisse today and man it is good. . . . I think that everyone is redeemable, everyone can experience and enjoy good food if they have a chance to taste it. Even little black kids who live in Oakland and eat cheese puffs, they are redeemable."

AHC: "Is good food always universal? I mean doesn't goodness depend on what some people like the taste of?"

CECILY: "Goodness in food differs, yes, but good food is never Cheetos, never!"

Such comments demonstrate an ambivalent kind of attention to feelings engendered through food. On the one hand, activists are uncomfortable with the scenario of ostensibly training bodies to feel negatively about what many others ('the masses') eat, do, or find pleasure in; such a scenario quickly begins to seem either elite, colonialist, inequitable, or otherwise unacceptable (eg see Guthman, 2008a; 2008b). Yet, many are also unwilling to accede that all tastes, feelings, and sensations engendered by foods are equally acceptable; some foods—like the highly processed foods produced by the corporate industrial system—are not good.

The political challenge entangled in this ambivalence becomes ever more complex if we insist on a biosocial understanding of bodily feeling. The 'feel' of food experiences, including quite emphatically the 'taste' of food itself, cannot be separated from each event of feeling or tasting; the taste of a meal or the feel of an environment includes the social relationships embedded in it, the cultural representations it brings up, the spiritual keys, imagery, a body's past experiences with flavors, hunger sensations in the stomach, and so on. Hence, included in one's in-the-moment 'taste' for Cheetos or Jack in the

Box is a variety of factors that become intertwined (whether unintentionally or intentionally) with SF commentary on fast/junk/processed foods. As one Berkeley food professional explained:

> "It's not just the food. It could be, I go to Jack In The Box on my own, or with my friends, or [maybe] it's my family ritual. So there are these other parts of the experience. . . . Food is deep, so deep, and people have so many issues around it . . . you don't want to judge them on that".
>
> (Cindy)

Indeed, food is one way in which bodies connect to innumerable aspects of the social world. Thus, by criticizing popular 'tastes' for fast or processed foods as uninformed or false, alternative food movements can end up denying the biosocial mechanisms through which fast food actually comes to taste good to some people. In opting for a simpler, fixed explanation of bodily tastes and pleasures, a taste for fast food may be read as a symptom of a passive, incapable, or malfunctioning body that should be 'redeemed' to its 'true' state of being/tasting. In rejecting the notion that fast food can really taste good to some people, alternative food movements end up overlooking the possibility that people's taste for fast food could indeed be a result of an *active* and *capable* body responding to a particular social and physical environment. Most importantly, as a few participants insisted, this kind of a rejection also can *feel bad*. In the next section we unpack what we mean by 'feeling bad' by using some participants' reflections to imagine what might be happening in the body at a microlevel when different bodies encounter SF.

VARIATIONS IN FEELING FOOD

As we previously insisted, the data revealed through this project reflect our contention that it is possible to get at visceral experience through intentional dialogue and conscious bodily/sensory action. Much of what we draw upon in this section comes from participants and researchers' collective attempts to think through and to verbalize, as well as demonstrate, how food/activities propel molecular or biochemical changes in their bodies. Our intentional dialogue often progressed through the vernacular of feeling, which served as a common point of entry to visceral matters. We used dialogue on feeling to collectively imagine—more accurately to *glimpse* in bits and pieces—the molecular, visceral body. Below, we use our collective imaginations to discuss some processes through which 'difference' is constituted between SF and 'the rest'.

Jorge (and Beyond)

We begin, strategically, with Jorge, a non-SF food activist, who, when we met him, had recently begun to think about food activism in terms of the body. Our dialogue with Jorge not only helped us to imagine what SF and fast food each *do* to different bodies, but it also specifically addressed how race and heritage might be ingested along with food. Jorge, himself a Mexican-American who represents a variety of communities of color through his Bay Area activism, began by expressing how SF rouses him at the same time that it repels:

JORGE: "I think I am warmed up [to SF] because it's very romantic and I do have my dream of seeing our communities of color . . . participate in . . . our own [kind of SF], our own way of slowing down and having sacred relationships with our food . . . redefining [it] in our own, with our own flavor. So in a sense it does inspire me to recreate it for us."

AHC: "So why does it need re-creation? What about it doesn't feel right?"

JORGE: "I don't see us joining that movement, nothing against the movement, or the people, but they don't reflect us and they have never really tried to incorporate us in any way. So, I just see that as a natural, I don't want to say process. It just hasn't happened so it's not natural; it hasn't been natural for them, it hasn't been natural for us to gravitate towards it, so that's alright."

While Jorge seems to judge SF positively, citing it as a source of inspiration, he goes on to express dissatisfaction with SF's approach to body-food relations, particularly its failure to encourage a sense of bodily wisdom coming from one's own lineage. In a similar vein to the postmodern critique of expert knowledge, Jorge implies that much of the alternative food movement sees food knowledge as something that connoisseurs, food professionals, or educated and refined individuals have, and that others, often the uneducated, minorities, and the poor, need to be provided or taught. Instead, the food initiative that Jorge leads is about giving people of color a sense of wisdom in relation to food that is not simply about intellect but rather about the cultural and biological ways in which intelligence has been embodied in them:

"I want to reinforce that what their culture eats, that is intelligent, that is wise, a part of their evolution . . . they still exist because they knew to eat [such and such] foods and spice them with this, and make these certain combinations that maybe killed this bacteria or had this enzyme to break down this protein and make it available, that kind of stuff . . . [I want] to begin [alternative food practice] there . . ."

(Jorge)

As Jorge talks, he describes his hopes for a different way to *feel* alternative food, which SF could be creating/tapping into/

transforming. This alternative 'visceral imaginary,' or feeling potential, has to do with an inclusive and biosocial rather than reductive and intellectual view of food wisdom. Jorge suggests that SF is not encouraging affective relationships with food in which bodies are activated in/ through the feeling that people *already have* wisdom in their minded bodies. He further suggests that by not tapping into or, worse, eliminating the validity of already existing wisdom(s) in many bodies of color, SF physically turns off many of these bodies to the possibility of feeling alternative foods in empowering ways.

Jorge's comments also imply that, by not acknowledging already existing capacities of bodies of color, alternative food movements may be relinquishing the opportunity to better understand why and how processed/fast foods come to be desired within his community. More specifically, in not allowing for the possibility that desire for fast food could signal a functioning and capable body, movements may fail to account for the often inequitable social and physical circumstances in which such bodily desires develop. For example, Jorge gives an illuminating explanation of why he thinks that communities of color may be gravitating towards certain kinds of (not so 'good') foods:

"[I think] that we are filling voids— emotional, social, psychological voids— with certain foods and behaviors . . . [We] find ways to try to feel connected or a part of something . . . and we find that we *do* get the right chemicals moving when we eat certain junk. . . . It will fulfill certain feelings that our people are sometimes looking for in these unjust times and environments. Whether it's a sense of sweetness that we might not be feeling; it's easy to fill us up with other sweetness, pan dulce Mexicano . . . you really experience that sweetness and that rush in your blood and your whole chemistry changes and for a moment you really feel good."

He continues later:

"We are not gravitating towards [junk foods] saying, '[these people are treating me badly], so I am going to go eat this to protect me from them,' but there is a part of our intelligence that starts to realize, 'Hey, I feel like this when I eat this and either, I want to feel like that right now, or I might want that [food] in me before something like this.' . . . This is what's new for [our activist community], in bringing to the . . . bigger analysis of our food system issues and [in figuring out] our community's health, that not only is [junk] food strategically situated and placed in our environments but now, psychologically we are more inclined to eat it. We might even go a little bit further to find it; it's our refuge at times . . . a short way, a quick easy way to feel a way that we are kind of desiring."

We emphasize Jorge's statement about feeling in order to draw attention to the visceral mechanism he posits behind actions of eating; there is a bodily *charge* there, an impetus to eat something in order to *feel* a particular way. Jorge refers to this as a psychological phenomenon, but clearly makes the connection to the visceral/biosocial in recognizing that such psychological tendencies arise out of his community's desire for sensations that particular foods offer. Moreover, Jorge implies that this visceral drive makes sense within the context of a disadvantaged community; it is a sign of a functioning and capable body that is coping with economic inequities and emotional voids. In this example the question of how food feels in the viscera therefore becomes a matter of a whole host of factors including race/heritage, but also cultural longing, social inequity, and perhaps personal healing. Jorge helps us to imagine how social relations involving food in various settings—home, community, school—may encourage people to develop or nurture visceral associations (specific molecular tendencies of mixing/moving) between particular types of food and particular social identities, groups, cultural ideas, and discourses. According to Jorge,

social inequities may indeed heighten and reify these associations.

In our work within the Bay Area we were told numerous times about associations between being 'black' and enjoying fast and other processed foods. Likewise, what has come to be known as common 'California' cuisine—like local arugula and goat cheese salads—were perceived as 'white' or 'hippie' foods. As a middle school student from Berkeley commented:

"If you look around Berkeley you'll see that the people who are all about organic [food] happen to be white hippies, not African Americans or Latinos . . . it's just what they are used to, what they grew up with."

Considering the commonness of these associations (according to research participants), it is not surprising that SF does not *feel* equally 'good' or 'right' to all racial/ethnic groups. While the outcomes of SF's food politics are certainly not predetermined, by encouraging the trendy, expensive, organic kinds of food to be posited as simply 'better' or more 'wise' than the 'inferior' cheap, easily accessed, processed foods, SF and other food movements can encourage certain visceral feelings about food to adhere to other tendencies of feeling about race, economic capacity, and social status (eg tending to feel biochemical 'heat' of anger with the way that 'they' call 'my' food inferior). Without acknowledging and countering such associations, even the most well-intentioned and socially conscious food activists can end up reinforcing such visceral difference.

At times over the course of our research, such associations did indeed seem to be deeply embedded in the social networks and structures we were studying. Yet, as we engaged our participants in discussion about these associations we also came to understand them as fluid biosocial propositions (as in Latour, 2004), rather than just definitive statements. In other words, at each moment of experiencing goat cheese or arugula these foods can feel more or less black or white, good or bad, fitting or not; there is always an opportunity for small shifts, or even large jumps. Differences in the *feel* of food result from the heterogeneous ways in which memories, ideas, discourses, moods, tastes, and so forth come together in the body; they are unpredictable, but also not completely beyond our control. It was for this reason that several of the nonwhite food activists that talked with us indicated that being visibly nonwhite played an important role in their work, not only in re-presenting alternative food to nonwhite consumers but, in so doing, encouraging new visceral experiences of alternative food within Berkeley's communities of color. These activists felt as though their visible appearance created new visceral opportunities for nonwhites to experience alternative food as something that feels 'good', 'fitting', or other-than-white.

From such examples, then, we begin to expand our repertoire for imagining how difference might be constituted viscerally. Jorge's discussion invoked tangible ingestions, like pan dulce (sweet bread), with which certain bodies have developed particular affective relationships. Yet, as we can quickly realize, it is not just ingredients—eg sugar—that get 'feel good' chemicals moving. Intangibles such as values, ideas, and labels, as well as things like prior experiences with a food are part of the irreducible biosocial production of feeling. Indeed, not everyone would 'feel good' eating pan dulce (eg, we have encountered many an organic foodie that seems repulsed by refined sugar). Body-food relationships are emphatically not reducible to either biological or social explanations; yet, as we attempted to do in a small way with Jorge, by calling attention to and imagining how specific foods work in specific bodies, we begin to appreciate the biosocial nature of these relationships. To further advance this project, we now turn to a second example from our empirical work, focusing on our dialogue with an SF activist, Missy.

Missy (and Beyond)

If the above subsection highlighted the tangible ingestion of food, slowly illuminating the intangibles that come to be ingested therein, this subsection works on the contrary, focusing on intangible ingestions, which circle back to and play into the tangible ingestion of food. Our conversations and shared sensorial experiences with Missy, a young food professional and SF member, often detailed how values, discourses, and practices of SF were 'taken in' and judged by the visceral body as feelings.

For instance, as we shared a green salad at her workplace, Missy scrunched up her nose to describe how she came to 'feel bad' eating lettuce in the SF context:

"[In SF] it's always called lettuces, not lettuce . . . you will notice that people [who aren't food professionals or activists] call it lettuce and that's what it was growing up and all of a sudden it's, 'Oh those were delicious lettuces,' and I am like, 'Oh really? Were they?' You couldn't just say lettuce?" (Missy, Berkeley, CA, with a sarcastic tone).

Missy went on to hypothesize that similar discourses make others in SF 'feel good.' In other words, some members may have developed affective relationships with the ways in which food is discussed and valued in particular alternative food circles that 'charge' them viscerally, offering bodily sensations that inspire continued SF interaction/participation. Indeed, many of our research conversations in California explored how alternative food tends to attract bodies that can use various intangibles of 'slow' food (values, discourses, and so on), as well as those of associated food-based spaces, to access positive feelings, which 'charge' the body or 'physically inspire' continued SF actions. For instance, a professional woman and single mother in her late thirties commented:

> "In Berkeley [SF/alternative food practice] to me is a scene, a hip thing . . . it's part of the little Berkeley club. It's about being 'in' in Berkeley. Like, you know that Friday night is going to Cheeseboard Pizza. You hear the Berkeley kids play jazz.
> You see people in line and all of it. It's a good feeling".
>
> (Brynn)

In Brynn's case, daily acts of SF practice, like going out to eat at alternative restaurants, allow her to access (self-defined) 'good' feelings that charge her, or encourage her continued presence at these establishments as well as her continued attempts to inform herself about food system issues. While Brynn is indicative of many, certainly not all SF members have the same affective relationships with the intangibles of Berkeley-area alternative food. The quote below exemplifies a contrary trend in which a man encounters the SF movement through convivia events and comes to feel a series of 'bad' feelings (narrated as feeling 'blue collar' or inexperienced) that deactivate or *chill* him towards continued attendance at SF events:

> "Although I support the ideals of Slow Food, belong to a CSA, shop at farmer's markets . . . I do find the local events to be mostly 'Foodie' events, with prices that are out of many of my friends' reach. I grew up on a working farm, growing most of our vegetables, fruit, and nuts, trading for eggs and butter, contracting with another local farmer for a side of beef and a side of pork, and supplementing our meals through hunting for squirrel, deer, wild turkey, rabbit and possum (I don't recommend possum). So . . . I was raised in a slow food culture. But at events, I feel a little 'blue collar' since I'm not a wine expert, and have limited international travel experience".
>
> (anonymous male)

In keeping with our collective research task we want to insist how this quote, as well as the others above, do more than narrate participants depictions of what SF *feels* like in a colloquial sense; they edge toward a molecular imagination of what is going on in the body during SF events by indicating that feelings are (bodily) judgments, which encourage or discourage action. Throughout the research, participants discussed 'good' or 'positive' feelings, feelings that charged them towards continued SF actions, as well as 'bad' or 'negative' feelings, that chilled them. To be clear, 'good' and 'bad' here are stand-ins for highly complex and subjective visceral judgments defined by each body in the moment of action. While we explore elsewhere the distinction of good and bad feelings in SF (Hayes-Conroy and Martin, 2010), the point to understand here is that a kind of visceral resonance (or lack thereof) serves to offer physical rationales for various kinds of food-based acting.

Thus, through such commentary we can begin to envision the production of difference as a visceral process: varied affective relationships between minded bodies and social/material environments manifest as different feelings about SF. These differences in feeling engender diverse 'needs' of action—going out to an SF-type restaurant or separating oneself from an SF event. While each time-space moment of encounter with SF is unique (eg some days Brynn might feel less 'charged' through dining out), over time, the way that bodily feelings come to correlate with actions can influence future tendencies of visceral judging and acting. We can imagine how through SF events and activities, feelings of the minded body can become viscerally associated with acting, speaking, or thinking in certain ways. For instance, Missy explained:

> "New behaviors come up and the in-crowd knows it. . . . Like, people in this scene love to eat salad with their hands. I asked [my peer] about it, saying, I felt [that] it was this

in-crowd thing to do, like once you learn you are in, and he said that it's true. It's supposedly a way of being with your food in a more sensual way because lettuce is so crunchy and sort of slimy and all".

(Missy)

Here the act of touching/eating the lettuce couples with particular SF intangibles—perhaps the theory that this is the best way to eat lettuce or the thought that one belongs to a group of food enthusiasts who really understand how to eat. These intangibles act molecularly in a similar way to the tangible foods discussed with Jorge above; in certain bodies they help to produce certain moods, or they might get certain feeling chemicals moving. They are feeling-producing, mood-altering ingestions.

Of course, as Missy recognized and explained, these ingestions do different things to different bodies. Missy expressed disillusionment with SF as a result of the mood she feels in/through various SF practices, including eating salad with one's fingers. Such practices create physical feelings, coupled with a clearly articulated intellectual response, that have come to differentiate her minded body from an 'SF other':

"All of it feels really snobby and exclusive. I am not intimidated by it; I just am not interested in being in that little microcosm. There are things that are much more important to me. I mean, if there is [a hypothetical] African American woman with three children and two jobs, you can't tell her that [enjoying salad with your fingers] is [so] important . . . that disconnect will always exist and I am becoming bitter about it. The more I work in this community the more I see the intense irony and I intense conflict in that and I want to move away from it".

(Missy)

We once more want to stress the importance of a visceral reading of the above quote. In Missy's words, SF *feels* at times snobby, elite, and trivial, and, in comparison with her previous enthusiasm for SF, she feels bitter and conflicted. Her use of the term *feeling* here importantly works as more than just a colloquial epithet; Missy is also talking about sensations in her body, which she associated in the particular time – space of our research conversation with the words 'snobby', 'elite', and 'trivial.' Without denying the content behind these words that Missy chose for narrating the experienced sensations, our research task was to focus on presence of these feelings in her body and what they make her capable of doing or not doing. Participating in this project through several in-depth conversations and two sensory-led experiences (mostly meals), Missy came to express how her minded body began to feel SF as 'bad' and how this shift in bodily judgment has deactivated her urge to participate in the movement, separating her from others for whom SF still engenders mostly 'positive' feelings. Thus importantly, the terms Missy uses to describe SF are not simply adjectives—cognitive categories through which she organizes an understanding of where she fits in the world; we can also see these terms as verbs—words describing the actual *motion* of bodily feelings that allow her to do, act, and be in specific ways (similar to Thien 2005).

Complementing our dialogue with Jorge, narrations such as Missy's help us to appreciate and imagine difference in alternative food as a function of visceral feelings engendered in/through various 'intangible' elements of slow foods or SF events. As we insisted at the beginning of this paper when we claimed that mind – body practices and even ideas, theories, or beliefs could have mood-altering (perhaps biochemical) effects, these intangibles of food are 'ingested' (often alongside the actual food) and do become molecular, catalyzing different feelings in different bodies. These differences in feeling indicate powerfully divisive mechanisms through which boundaries may be created and upheld within alternative food activism. Yet, unlike the fixed categories revealed by our above-mentioned survey (race and education), these differences in feeling seem to be constantly shifting. Many participants insisted that the way SF feels is not 'black and white'. Some days, SF feels 'better', more resonant, offering more 'charge'. Other days it may feel 'worse', less resonant, more 'chilling'. More often contradictory feelings may be experienced concurrently. Thus, without denying the fact of persistent social categorizing that undoubtedly permeates many alternative food circles, by focusing on feelings we emphasize the variable ways in which bodies meet up with and become these groupings. Each encounter with food and SF brings a new mixture of categories, memories, friends or strangers, flavors, information, and so on. People come to feel alternative food through this mixture, thus *feeling out* difference and identity in relation to food as they come to be knowable in the minded body.

CONCLUSIONS

This paper has illustrated a means of understanding difference in alternative food as visceral. In presenting this illustration we have suggested that alternative food movements like Slow Food could benefit from assessing how various foods and food environs come to *feel differently* in different bodies. Such assessment might involve, alongside a critique of the structural constraints and discourses that shape alternative food movement organizations, an acknowledgement of the varied ways in which food enters into the body to shape feeling. Together with our participants, we have imagined how food is 'ingested' in both tangible and intangible ways that amount to interventions in the molecular realm of mood, state, or feeling. Such ingestions are irreducible to mere biological or chemical equations,

and instead might be understood as biosocial phenomena, producing variable (albeit somewhat directable) results. Through intentional dialogue on bodily feeling (as well as through shared sensory experience), our project worked to detail specific instances of ingestion in order to describe some processes through which 'difference' is constituted between SF and 'the rest'.

In insisting on the need to attend to the viscerality of difference in food systems, we do not seek to deny real and formidable societal forces—institutionalized discrimination, organizational procedures, economic disparities—that are unquestionably powerful in solidifying social difference and creating social boundaries. Certainly these forces have much impact on the way that food movements and systems operate. The visceral approach we advance attempts to understand these forces, as well as many others, from the perspective of the visceral, minded body. Thus through empirical example we have sought to show, in a small way, how we might imagine the body taking in, embodying, and acting upon the tensions of these broader societal forces. We used food, and specifically Slow Food, to do this.

Our two brief but revealing empirical examples help us to grasp not only how certain foods become powerful forces in certain bodies, but also how imagining and tracing the differential feelings engendered through foods could help food movements to understand and ultimately recruit across difference. Attending to the visceral seems valuable in at least two ways: first, in the sense that alternative food projects could find more support if organizers began to attempt to understand and perhaps tap into the myriad ways in which foods and food environs come to feel differently to people who identify as 'other than SF,' specifically to those nonwhites and working-class communities who feel 'other than SF'. And, second, in the sense that minority and disadvantaged groups could work to develop new ways of *feeling* alternative food projects/practices by recognizing the evolution of feelings and bodily wisdom that they have inherited as part of their own racial, ethnic, or cultural heritage. Attending to difference *viscerally* thus seems to be a potentially fundamental way to break down some of the barriers that academics and activists have noted in alternative food. Our participatory work not only details the power of visceral feeling, but it also models some kinds of dialogue and shared experiences that make accessing the visceral a little bit more possible.

ACKNOWLEDGEMENTS

We are indebted to our research participants for their involvement. Also, special thanks to Deborah Martin for her valuable advising, as well as to Susan Hanson, Jody Emel, and Ben Anderson for their comments on earlier versions of this paper.

NOTES

1. For a clear explanation of the relationship between affect, feeling, and emotion see Anderson (2006).
2. Statistics come from an online survey answered by ninety-six members in the San Francisco I Bay Area and from the US Census Bureau 2006 data for the defined area referred to as the 'San Francisco Bay Area'.
3. All names have been changed.
4. A major fast food chain.

REFERENCES

Alkon A, 2008 *Black White and Green: A Study of Farmers Markets* PhD dissertation, Department of Sociology, University of California

Allen P, 2004 *Together at the Table: Sustainability and Sustenance in the American Agrifood System* (Pennsylvania State University Press, University Park, PA)

Allen P, 2008, "Mining for justice in the food system" *Agriculture and Human Values* 25 157–161

Anderson B, 2005, "Practices of judgment and domestic geographies of affect" *Social and Cultural Geography* 6 645–659

Anderson B, 2006, "Becoming and being hopeful: towards a theory of affect" *Environment and Planning D: Society and Space* 24 733–752

Anderson B, Tolia-Kelly D, 2004, "Matter(s) in social and cultural geography" *Geoforum* 35 669–674

Bakker K, Bridge G, 2006, "Material worlds? Resource geographies and the 'matter of nature' " *Progress in Human Geography* 30 5–27

Beasley C, Bacci C, 2007, "Envisaging a new politics for an ethnical future: beyond trust, care and generosity—towards an ethic of 'social flesh' " *Feminish Theory* 8 279–298

Butler J, 1993 *Bodies that Matter: On the Discursive Limits of 'Sex'* (Routledge, New York)

Calhoun C, 1995 *Critical Social Theory: Culture, History, and the Challenge of Difference* (Wiley Blackwell, Malden, MA)

Castree N, Braun B, 2001 *Social Nature: Theory, Practice, and Politics* (Blackwell, Maiden, MA)

Colls R, 2007, "Materialising bodily matter: intra-action and the embodiment of 'fat' " *Geoforum* 38 353–365

Connolly W E, 1999 *Why I Am Not a Secularist* (University of Minnesota Press, Minneapolis, MN)

Fincher R, Jacobs J, 1998 *Cities of Difference* (Guilford Press, New York)

Grosz E, 1994 *Volatile Bodies: Toward a Corporeal Feminism* (Indiana University Press, Bloomington, IN)

Guthman J, 2004 *Agrarian Dreams: The Paradox of Organic Farming in California* (University of California Press, Berkeley, CA)

Guthman J, 2008a " 'If they only knew': color blindness and universalism in California alternative food institutions" *The Professional Geographer* 60 387–397

Guthman J, 2008b, "Bringing good food to others: investigating the subjects of alternative food practice" *Cultural Geographies* 15 431–447

Hall E, 2000, " 'Blood, brain and bones': taking the body seriously in the geography of health and impairment" *Area* 32 21–29

Hayes-Conroy A, 2010, "Feeling Slow Food: visceral fieldwork and empathetic research relations in the alternative food movement" *Geoforum* 41 734–742

Hayes-Conroy A, Deborah M, 2010, "Mobilizing bodies: visceral identification in the slow food movement" *Transactions of the Association of British Geographers* 35 269–281

Hayes-Conroy A, Hayes-Conroy J, 2008, "Taking back taste: feminism, food and visceral politics" *Gender, Place and Culture* 15 461–473

Hayes-Conroy A, Martin D G, 2010, "Mobilizing bodies: visceral identification in the slow food movement" *Transactions of the Institute of British Geographers, New Series* 35 269–281

Hinrichs C C, 2000, "Embeddedness and local food systems: notes on two types of direct agricultural market" *Journal of Rural Studies* **16** 295–303

Jacobs J M, Nash C, 2003, "Too little, too much: cultural feminist geographies" *Gender, Place, and Culture* **10** 265–279

Jarosz L, 2008, "The city in the country: growing alternative food networks in metropolitan areas" *Journal of Rural Studies* **24** 231–244

Knights D, Thanem T, 2005, "Embodying emotional labour", in *Gender, Bodies and Work* Eds D H J Morgan, B Brandth, E Kvande (Ashgate, Aldershot, Hants) pp 31–59

Latham A, McCormack D, 2004, "Moving cities: rethinking the materialities of urban geographies" *Progress in Human Geography* **28** 701–724

Latour B, 2004, "How to talk about the body? The normative dimension of science studies" *Body and Society* **10** (2/3) 205–229

Longhurst R, 2005, "Fat bodies: developing geographical research agendas" *Progress in Human Geography* **29** 247–269

Longhurst R, Johnston L, Ho E, 2009 "A visceral approach: cooking 'at home' with migrant women in Hamilton New Zealand" *Transactions of the Institute of British Geographers, New Series* **34** 333–345

McCormack D P, 2007, "Molecular affects in human geographies" *Environment and Planning A* **39** 359–377

Mansfield B, 2008, "Health as a nature – society question" *Environment and Planning A* **40** 1015–1019

Markula P, 2006, "Deleuze and the body without organs: disreading the fit feminine identity" *Journal of Sport and Social Issues* **30**(1) 29–44

Petrini C, Furlan C, Hunt J, 2007 *Slow Food Nation: Why Our Food Should Be Good, Clean and Fair* (Rizzoli, New York)

Pietrykowski B, 2004, "You are what you eat: the social economy of the slow food movement" *Review of Social Economy* **62** 307–322

Pollard T M, Hyatt S B (Eds), 1999 *Sex, Gender and Health* (Cambridge University Press, Cambridge)

Probyn E, 2001 *Carnal Appetites: Food Sex Identities* (Routledge, New York)

Probyn E, 2005 *Blush: Faces of Shame* (University of Minnesota Press, Minneapolis, MN)

Saldanha A, 2006, "Reontologising race: the machinic geography of phenotype" *Environment and Planning D: Society and Space* **24** 9–24

Slocum R, 2007, "Whiteness, space, and alternative food practice" *Geoforum* **38** 520–533

Thien D, 2005, "After or beyond feeling? A consideration of affect and emotion in geography" *Area* **37**(4) 450–454

Weiss G, 1999 *Body Images: Embodiment as Intercorporeality* (Routledge, New York)

West C, Fenstermaker S, 1995, "Doing difference" *Gender and Society* **9**(1) 8–37

Whatmore S, 2002 *Hybrid Geographies: Natures, Cultures, Spaces* (Sage, London)

Young I M, 1990 *Justice and the Politics of Difference* (Princeton University Press, Princeton, NJ)

39

Expanding Access and Alternatives: Building Farmers' Markets in Low-Income Communities

Lisa Markowitz

It's probably safe to say that the pleasures of farmers' markets are familiar to most readers of this journal. Fans of food and farmers relish their weekly visits to church parking lots or town centers to peruse rare radishes, sample fresh berries, and stock up on corn, tomatoes, and cucumbers. We enjoy chatting with producers and knowing that these markets help small farmers to get by, or even to prosper. We also look forward to meeting up with friends, snacking, hearing music, and even, as one Louisville shopper commented, "seeing other people's dogs." Although this enactment of community occurs on weekend mornings in nearly every American city, inequalities of class and geography preclude many. In this essay, I examine the problems and prospects of establishing farmers' markets that serve low-income customers.

Over the past three decades, farmers' markets have blossomed across the United States. According to the latest count from the United States Department of Agriculture (USDA), there are now 5,274 in operation (USDA/AMS 2009). Participating farmers report that they can make 40 to 60 percent more (Egan 2002), or even 80 percent (Myers 1991:3, cited in Andreatta and Wickliffe 2002) more, for their commodities through direct sales than they can selling to wholesalers. Nonetheless, only a small percentage of the nation's two million farmers sell their products directly to consumers (Egan 2002); in 2000, just over

77 thousand farmers participated in farmers' markets, collectively grossing $888 million in sales (USDA/AMS 2006), whereas overall farm revenue came to over $200 billion (Egan 2002). Although by 2005 sales reached above one billion, and the number of farmers had increased significantly (Ragland and Tropp 2009:1), farmers' markets, in strictly numerical terms, appear to feed a small, if rapidly expanding, niche appetite. But the combination of pleasure and produce portends something more as the physical marketplace restores the largely severed connections between farmers and eaters.

Farmers' markets are perhaps the most visible of a variety of new food-farm initiatives that have emerged since the 1970s through the swelling of variegated social movements aiming to create a healthier, environmentally and economically sustainable, and more equitable agrifood system. These alternative agrifood institutions (Allen 2004:64) include, to name a few examples, community gardens, local food councils, farm-to-school-projects, and Community Supported Agriculture. Especially over the past decade, as disenchantment with the scale and production practices of organic agriculture has spread, agrifood activists have become increasingly oriented toward encouraging people to eat closer to home and building the social and economic relationships and institutions that will make this possible. Different rubrics embrace this constellation of efforts toward creating locally based food systems: terms such as civic agriculture (Lyson 2004), food democracy (Hassanein 2003), and food sovereignty (Rosset 2003) allude to the animating vision of widespread participation and responsibility in casting the organization and outcomes of systems of food production and distribution. Alternative agrifood institutions are spaces where this already occurs; as such, they beckon and promote further popular engagement in shaping farm and food politics. If, as it is reasonable to propose, farmers' markets—given their ubiquity, social appeal, and economic benefits—are the "flagship" of civic agriculture (Hinrichs et al. 2004:32), then it is worth asking, Who is on board? In what ways is this alternative institution available and accessible to economically vulnerable populations?

These questions redound to concerns about the class problem or class bias (Berg 2008) within alternative food movements that have emerged among movement participants and observers in the United States. In engaging this discussion, I emphasize the policies and political protagonism that have contributed—and have the potential to contribute further—to enhancing food access. Relatively few markets, for reasons elaborated below, are oriented toward low-income customers, and, accordingly, this account diverges from more localized market studies by highlighting the importance of public subsidies and social activism. In this article, I trace the connections among policies (some alarmingly attenuated), community organizing, and the trajectories of two small markets, part of the story of alternative institution-building in Louisville, Kentucky. There, the creation of farmers' markets in low-income neighborhoods has been central in efforts to create a more equitable local food economy. The Louisville experience illustrates the necessary interplay between community-based efforts and government (local, state, and/or federal) policy in

creating the possibilities for sustainable rural and urban improvement.

MARKETS BLOOM, POLICIES SPROUT, BUT WHO GETS TO EAT?

Responding to the interests of small farmers unwilling or unable to compete in conventional markets, federal and state policies have facilitated the expansion of farmers' markets. From a historic low of 342 in 1970, market numbers begin to mount quickly through the decade and into the next, reaching nearly 1700 by 1986, a spurt associated with the 1976 passage of the Farmer-to-Consumer Direct Marketing Act, which authorized cooperative extension agents to work on behalf of markets and enabled local governments and nonprofits to foster farmers' market development and promotion (Brown 2001). Subsequent support to producers has been primarily administered via various programs under the aegis of the USDA's Agricultural Marketing Service and its Farmers' Market Promotion Program (Becker 2006).

A second set of USDA programs addresses the needs of low-income consumers. It is worth taking a step back to review the genesis of these programs since their emergence highlights the innovative anti-hunger/community development work, which, in the 1990s, developed into the movement for Community Food Security. Urban organizers, dissatisfied with welfarist and individually based forms of food assistance, coalesced to formulate a broad vision of food security, one based on strengthening community self-reliance and embedded in sustainable regional and local agriculture (Bellows and Hamm 2002; Allen 2004).

A principle concern of Community Food Security activists has been improving poor people's access to high-quality, fresh food. The dearth of grocery stores in low-income urban neighborhoods (Curtis and McClellan 1995; Eisenhauer 2001; Winne

2007) poses myriad barriers to obtaining nutritious, desirable food. Urban organizers have employed various strategies to increase food options: community gardens, public–private partnerships to attract supermarket chains, and nonprofit linkages with CSAs, among others (Winne 2007). Farmers' markets appear to be an obvious means for increasing the flow of fresh foods to urban shoppers while expanding markets for regional producers, an ostensible win–win solution. Establishing markets in low-income neighborhoods, however, presents many challenges (Fisher 1999; Guthman et al. 2006; Winne 2007). As Mark Winne, former director of the Hartford Food System asks, "How do you make farmers' markets work for low-income shoppers— offering them affordable fresh produce at convenient locations—and also develop the market as viable business opportunities?" (2007:41). Similarly, Guthman et al. (2006:663–664) worry about how farmers are to be paid for the real costs of their production, "a decent return"—as opposed to those for artificially cheap industrialized food—while selling their products at prices manageable for the growing ranks of low-income consumers. Both conclude that meeting these twin goals usually requires some sort of public or private subsidy.

Public subsidies come largely through a pair of USDA programs that have furnished limited, if often instrumental, support to the development and operation of low-income markets.[1] One such subsidy is the Women Infant and Children's Farmers' Market Nutrition Program (WIC FMNP), a component of a federal program to protect the health of low-income women and their small children. In the late 1980s, community activists and state agencies had successfully experimented with providing WIC participants with coupons redeemable at farmers' markets, and went on to lobby Congress to implement a national program (Winne 2007). In 1992, Congress established the WIC FMNP, which, administered by the USDA's Food and Nutrition Services, allocates funds via state governments. Federal benefits are limited to $30 annually, to be used at authorized markets for the purchase of unprepared fruits and vegetables. In 2005, a reported 59 percent of markets in the participating 46 states accepted WIC vouchers (USDA 2006). In 2008, some 2.3 million individuals received coupons, and 16,016 farmers and 3,367 farmers' markets and 2,398 roadside stands had been authorized to accept them; FMNP coupon redemptions tallied over $20 million in revenue to farmers (USDA/FNS WIC 2009). A second coupon-based national subsidy program was authorized under the 2002 Farm Bill: the Senior Farmers' Market Nutrition Program (Becker 2006). In 2008, this program provided 963,685 low-income (defined as not more than 185 percent of the federal poverty level) seniors with vouchers to purchase fresh fruits and vegetables from 17,156 farmers, selling at 3,159 farmers' markets, 2,512 roadside stands, and 199 CSAs (USDA/FNS SFMNP 2009). In 2005, 44 percent of reporting farmers' markets in 46 states accepted senior coupons (USDA 2006).

Table 39.1 Farmers' Market Nutrition Programs (FMNP)

	WIC FMNP 2008	Senior FMNP 2008
Voucher Recipients	2,300,000	963,685
Participating Farmers	16,016	17,156
Authorized Farmers' Markets	3,367	3,159
Authorized Roadside Stands	2,398	2,512

USDA/FNS WIC FMNP 2009; USDA/FNS SFMNP 2009.

Seniors receive \$16–24 a month through the growing season (Table 39.1).

The FMNP appears to provide a salutary nutritional supplement to some program participants (Dollahite et al., 2005; Herman et al. 2008) and affords a critical economic support to many low-income markets (Fisher 1999; Ragland and Tropp 2009; Tessman and Fisher 2009; Winne 2007). Guthman et al. (2007:675–76), drawing on a statewide study of California farmers' markets, find, however, that "because they are limited in both season and amount, FMNP vouchers may serve to introduce low-income families and seniors to farmers' markets, but they are not a substantial or consistent source of subsidy."

The principal federal nutritional subsidy for the poor is the food stamp program, or, as it was renamed in October of 2008, the Supplemental Nutrition Assistance Program (SNAP), which served nearly 34 million people in 2009 (USDA/FNS 2010). Since the mid-1990s, the use of food stamps at farmers' markets has been substantially constrained by the adoption of the system of Electronic Benefit Transfer (EBT). Under this system, instituted as part of the 1996 Welfare Reform to reduce paperwork and potential fraud, each recipient's benefits are deposited into an account and the funds are applied to a plastic card, which functions like a bank card. Since farmers' markets frequently lack telephone lines and electricity, accepting electronic benefits cards has posed many technical challenges that regularly frustrate, if not infuriate, market organizers. (Indeed, Fisher [1999] devotes an entire section of his review of low-income farmers' markets to describing technological options for conducting transactions.) Although Fisher also observes that at some markets, food stamp redemptions make up a majority of sales, their use, overall, at farmers' markets has been modest. In 1998, farmers' market purchases accounted for just .02 percent of redemptions nation-wide, and fewer

than a fourth of food stamp users reported shopping at farmers' markets (Kantor 2001:22). The transition to EBT is linked to a drop in food stamp spending at farmers' markets, which fell, between 1994 and 1998, from \$6.4 to \$3.8 million (ibid., p. 23). Guthman et al. (2006:675) note that in California at one time, 150 markets took paper food stamps, but by 2005 only 65 markets redeemed electronic benefits. Nationally, in 2005, only 6.8 percent of markets reported accepting food stamps, likely reflecting the high costs (\$1,000–1,500) of investing in a wireless EBT terminal and those involved in its maintenance and use (Ragland and Tropp 2009:69). Recognition of this obstacle to fresh food access is found under Title X of the new Farm Bill: ten percent of funds for the Farmers' Market Promotion Program will be allocated to assisting markets with electronic benefits acceptance (USDA/ERS 2008).

Beyond the complications of accommodating public subsidies, a successful market, including even those in upscale settings, requires careful Organization and planning. Farmers' markets may be alternative institutions, but they are, in practice if not always at heart, business undertakings. In November of 2007, at the National Farmers' Market Summit, a predominant theme of discussion among the assembled stakeholders was "the importance of *establishing a minimum standard of technical experience in business planning and marketing* for farmers market participants" (Tropp and Barham 2008:5 italics in original). The demands confronting markets in low-income communities are greater still, given the contradiction between the needs of farmers and of customers. Farmers, already skeptical about the sales potential of low-income markets, may have additional concerns about parking and safety, and hesitate to drive to those in inner-city neighborhoods (Tropp and Barham 2008). Fisher (1999) notes a series of considerations regarding the shopping habits of the prospective clientele. The fact that residents frequently lack vehicles, which may limit market attendance, points up the importance of location and availability of public transportation. Connected to this are multiple job schedules and limited temporal flexibility, which may preclude weekday or daytime markets. Monthly cash flow is variable, and spending declines toward the end of the month. Product mix and pricing need to reflect eating preferences and resources. Fisher concludes by stressing the importance of generating a sense that a market belongs to the community, and encourages organizers to develop a broad base of support by reaching out to local institutions. Winne (2007) echoes this view, noting the inclusive organizing strategy that led to the booming Crescent City Market in New Orleans. More broadly, Feenstra (2002) argues that public participation and decision-making power are central to the creation of new spaces of local food system projects.

FROM BURLEY TOBACCO TO BENIGN TOMATOES: MARKET BUILDING IN LOUISVILLE

"It's the tomatoes," Karyn explained one afternoon in June of 2008. "People are freaking out and want local food. We're getting three times as many phone calls and the media coverage of the work is amazing." Karyn was a lead organizer of low-income farmers' markets in Louisville. Fears of killer tomatoes and contaminated spinach, coupled with the popular writings of Michael Pollan and Barbara Kingsolver, spurred a demand for local food, challenging the city's young alternative agrifood institutions. The creation of low-income farmers' markets in Louisville emerged from the ongoing efforts of rural producers and urban consumers to discover and act upon their common interests. The particular circumstances of agriculture in the state,

which I summarize below, and the existence of food deserts in its largest city, point to the logic of developing direct supply chains as that putative win–win for farmers and consumers. Gillespie et al. (2007) have noted that creating markets that foster development of the local food system requires concerted, strategic efforts, but often, celebratory depictions of farmers' markets slight the details of the hard work and frustrations involved. In practice, as this account reveals, the process of building markets in Louisville has manifested most of the challenges and complications enumerated above, along with some hard-won successes and the cultivation of new social connections and collaborations.

Until the past decade, farmers in Kentucky had been able to rely on a steady, if limited, cash flow from the cultivation of Burley tobacco. This remuneration, provided though the tobacco price support system, buffered many Kentucky farmers from the farm crisis of the 1980s (van Willigen and Eastwood 1998). As a result, there are about 86,500 farms in Kentucky, which puts the state fourth in the number of farms nationally (NASS 2004a). However, the decline in the demand for tobacco has led to a reconfiguration of the sector and the loss of a major, high-value-per-acre crop. Consequently, in recent years, Kentucky's agriculture has been at something of a crossroads as farmers explore alternative crops and commercial outlets, including direct sales to consumers. These have exceeded the national trend, doubling in reported value between 1997 and 2002 (NASS 2004b). Farmers' markets now number 108 and can be found in every formerly tobacco-dependent county in the state (CFA 2003). The potential to expand in-state markets, especially for fruits and vegetables, is high since most of these consumed in Kentucky are produced somewhere else (ibid.).

Kentucky is unusual in that state support exists for pursuing diversified agriculture. Under a singular piece of legislation, House Bill 611, half the funds the state is receiving from the Tobacco Master Settlement Agreement, a total of 1.75 billion dollars over 20 years, are directed to the development and diversification of the state's agriculture. Thus funds, through grants to individuals and organizations, are available for a range of initiatives supporting new production endeavors and marketing approaches. The state-wide grassroots organization instrumental in the design and passage of H.B.611, the Community Farm Alliance (CFA), has directed it energies to developing a locally integrated food economy, particularly to creating and strengthening rural–urban commercial channels. To this end, CFA, with its 25 years of organizing experience, took on the role of catalyst for instigating some of the more difficult economic development strategies in Louisville's low-income neighborhoods.

The West Louisville and East Downtown sections of Louisville are home to about 65,000 people, with median household income levels of 1/2 and 3/8 those found in the metro area as a whole.[2] Like many other predominantly African-American urban areas, these can be characterized as "food deserts," with limited access to shops, high prices, poor quality, and a narrow variety of food items, especially fresh produce.[3] In West Louisville, the ratio of customers to full-service supermarkets is 25,000 to one, whereas the city-wide average is about 13,000 (CFA 2007:6). Existing shops, mostly convenience outlets, charge about fifty percent more than do supermarkets for basic grocery items, and fresh produce is notably absent on their shelves (Raskin 2006; Thurman 2005). An additional barrier to grocery shopping is the low rate of household vehicle access (CFA 2007).

City health professionals and activists have linked the difficulties of obtaining food with poor health outcomes. Health indicators state-wide and city-wide are distressing: Kentucky ranks among the states with the highest rates for cancer deaths, smoking, lack of exercise, cardiovascular diseases, and obesity. In Louisville, mortality rates for heart disease, stroke, and diabetes are higher for African-Americans than for whites, and nutritionists comment that the difficulty and expense of eating fruits and vegetable contributes to these health problems (Halbach 2006). Additionally, Louisville ranks second nationally for fast food consumption as measured by the number of visits per person per month to fast food restaurants (Davis 2006). Indeed, the main boulevard connecting West Louisville with East Downtown also happens to be the single most concentrated strip of fast food outlets in the state: 24 in 2.8 miles (Raskin, 2007). In the insidious geography of food deserts, procuring healthy food at reasonable prices is most difficult for those in most need.

A TALE OF TWO MARKETS

In 2003, the Community Farm Alliance began working with city business people and community leaders, set up an office in a West Louisville neighborhood, and formed a chapter, with a membership that by 2008 had grown to about 250.[4] CFA members and community residents (who over the years would become increasingly one and the same), their efforts spearheaded by a talented, young African-American CFA organizer, laid the groundwork for Portland-Shawnee, the first explicitly low-income market in the state. It failed.

Despite the work of a second dedicated organizer, recruiting farmers proved a challenge. As the former executive director of CFA explained (Webb 2007), farmers seek, at minimum, to replace the income formerly generated by tobacco; an acre of tobacco cleared about $2,500 and, statewide, a conservative earnings estimate for a market season is $3,000 to $5,000; some producers take in much more. However, most farmers (who are mostly white) were generally unfamiliar with Louisville, especially its African-American neighborhoods. Farmers had to adjust pricing and volume to their new customers, who could spend much less that those in more affluent areas. Daily purchases tallied only five dollars at Portland-Shawnee in contrast to twenty dollars at the city's best known middle-class market (Markowitz 2005). Also, the market, although located in a block of businesses (selected to bolster as well as benefit from the shops), drew little foot traffic and spending remained low, despite the availability of electronic benefits acceptance. Over the next two seasons, market organizers tried to overcome these difficulties by partnering with community groups and city agencies to sponsor special events and festivals, and ultimately moved the market to a better-traveled West Louisville location provided by a Baptist church. In spite of the congregation's promotional assistance, a sufficient customer base never materialized.

The second market established in 2004, in East Downtown has fared much better.[5] The Smoketown/Shelby Park Market, open Saturday mornings from June through October, sits in the parking lot of Meyzeek Middle School. Neighborhood leaders had expressed interest in establishing a market there, and middle school staff were supportive. The principal speaks enthusiastically of the market, and the former community-school coordinator serves on the market's governing board (Rosenblum 2007). Shoppers, vendors, and observers praise the market atmosphere. As one student commented on his research experience there, "By the end of the season, I had become a regular, recognized by the farmers and organizers, treated with the same respect and kindness that I observed other market regulars receiving" (Rosenblum 2007:6). The market manager, a long-time neighborhood resident, knows and greets the regulars, who she estimates make up about 80 percent of the market clientele.

Attendance ranges from around 70 to upwards of 100 in peak season or on special event days. Although the market is situated in one of the city's poorest neighborhoods, within a block of a large housing project, it is an easy drive or bike ride from more affluent areas and attracts customers (including me) from different parts of the city. This location renders it what Fisher (1999:38) calls a "fringe market," able to draw "customers from diverse income levels."

The market's five or six farmers offer an appealing variety of items. In addition to produce, priced favorably in comparison with upscale markets, they sell meat, including hard-to-find rabbit, eggs, baked goods, and honey. The political convictions of some of the farmers play a role in their presence—at least three are CFA members—but all the vendors like the market and seem to feel appreciated there. Selling at Smoketown is not lucrative; although no data on sales are available, the market manager reported that $125 would be considered a good day's take.[6] In 2007, the market augmented farmer receipts with a $25 "buyout" of unsold produce, for donation to a local shelter.

Funds for this producer subsidy and those to customers come from an array of collaborations among community groups, public agencies, and the private sector. Though the CFA continues to be a key promoter of the market, it has successfully initiated partnerships that support both the market and related community activities. For example, a local bank purchased the EBT machine. The market manager estimated that about half the customers used food stamps, which accounted for five to ten percent of total sales. The machine, however, functioned properly only in 2004 and 2006. The lower-technology, independent WIC voucher program generates about the same percentage of sales. The nearly 15,000 WIC participants in the Louisville metro area do not receive the USDA/FNS WIC FMNP coupons via the state of

Kentucky, since current funding levels for the program can support it in only 43 of the state's 120 counties (Halbach 2006: 11–12). In 2005, CFA, along with a Robert Wood Johnson-supported health program, ACTIVE Louisville, and the Metro Health Department initiated a voucher project for WIC-eligible women and children. The project receives further support from Making Connections, a local organization, which also pays the market buyout. Making Connections is, in turn, funded by the Annie E. Casey Foundation. Under the market's independent voucher project, each week WIC participants may receive tokens valuing ten dollars to purchase fruits and vegetables. The farmers redeem the tokens with the manager, who writes them a check at the end of each market day. On a typical Saturday, these total sixty or seventy dollars. The manager would like to see more women take advantage of the voucher project and, more generally, engage along with their children in learning more about food and cooking.

The activities undertaken to encourage this engagement and to promote the market highlight additional collaborations. A volunteer Friends of the Market committee has helped orchestrate special events. Chefs from the County Extension Service and from a local community college, together with local businesses, participate in frequent cooking demonstrations, taste tests, and handing out of recipe cards. The market also serves neighborhood children via the Presbyterian Community Center, which runs a summer Kid's Café for nutritionally vulnerable children. The Café relies on donated food—ironically, mostly fast food. In 2005, the Center began to use the market as a resource to acquire and promote fresh food for their young clientele. The market's location on school grounds provides another point of engagement with youth. Students painted a glorious mural on the school wall, which has since been transformed into billboards, publicity underwritten by

a local telecommunications company. The middle school science teacher is an avid gardener who, on his own time, has worked with students to create an attractive community garden that is situated between the school and a historic church—after the Metro Health Department paid for the land's remediation. In the fall of 2007, the garden was inaugurated with a visit from Alice Waters, who was interviewed outside by a local public radio affiliate, while in the church an independent filmmaker screened the movie she had just completed about foodwork in the neighborhood.

POLICIES FOR A BETTER MARKET

This brief tale of two markets illustrates a number of points I presented in the review of market policies and experiences. Leaving aside such critical practical aspects of market operation as location, ambience, and pricing and product mix, I want to conclude with a discussion of policy-related issues.

First, local governments can provide both legitimation and material support to farmers' markets. Officials of the Louisville Metro Department of Health and Wellness have been outspoken in recognizing inequities of food access in the city and have underwritten market activities as well as other programs to rectify health disparities. The offices of agencies that serve the poor are obvious places to publicize low-income markets. City and town governments can assist low-income markets in other ways, including reconfiguring public transportation routes to accommodate shoppers and extending facilities such as parking lots, meeting rooms, water, restrooms, and electricity.

Second, as Community Food Security researchers have emphasized, community outreach and broad participation are key to making markets work and, more broadly, to stimulating the creation of other alternative institutions, which will expand and enhance people's access to food. Shawnee-Portland seems to have lacked the key community-based support that has anchored and animated Smoketown-Shelby Park Market. Although the latter is, in financial terms, a poor market, the current spate of food-related activities in the neighborhood suggest that the marketplace is becoming, as well, a space of social engagement. At the national level, increased funding to initiatives such as those supported by the Community Food Project grants (CFSC et al. 2007) would further such social, nutritional, and educational synergies while reinforcing the viability and impact of the market. Related to this is a need for additional support for conducting local research that can provide a basis for the sound planning and expansion of projects (see Lev et al. 2007). This task too often falls to already overextended community organizers.

Finally, subsidies are critical to both establishing the market infrastructure and making products affordable to low-income shoppers. Examples include the salary of the Smoketown/Shelby Park manager who sets the market's pleasant tone, the colorful billboards that advertise the market, and the EBT machine, which *should be* boosting buying power and farmer revenues. For several years, Smoketown/ Shelby Park customers effectively received no federal support, although half the shoppers are food stamp-eligible and, based on earlier patterns, would likely be purchasing more food if the machine worked. In view of the USDA's recent commitment to upgrade EBT use, Michael Pollan's suggestion (2008) that the value of food stamps redeemed at farmers' markets be doubled deserves consideration. Thanks to arduous nonprofit efforts, WIC participants there actually enjoy more generous support than the FNS program provides, although a handful of tokens, however warmly dispensed, should not have to substitute for a federally legislated benefit. The 2008 Farm Bill (Title IV) increased support of the Senior FMNP by over twenty-five percent, but offers no additional funding for WIC FMNP (USDA/ERS 2008). In a more promising vein, recent reconfiguration of the WIC program includes a new provision, cash value vouchers (CVV), for purchase of fresh fruits and vegetables, which states may authorize for redemption at farmers' markets and farmstands. (Tessman and Fisher 2009). The CVV annual individual allocation ($72 to $120) far exceeds that of the FMNP ($20–30). Implementing widespread use of the vouchers at markets rests with state governments, and evidently will require significant streamlining of redemption procedures. With the total new allocation of $500 million, "the potential impact on farmers' markets and consequently the improvements in food access in low-income communities is enormous" (ibid.:2).

Thanks to grassroots efforts to mobilize existing modest resources, farmers' markets in low-income areas serve, falteringly and valiantly, to extend access to fresh foods. The abiding contradictions in the capacity of markets to simultaneously support producers and to play a role in advancing food equity both complicate these aims and call into question their feasibility. Nonetheless, farmers' markets, with their vibrancy and visibility, not only engender wider public awareness of food and farming but are central to civic efforts to relocalize agrifood systems (Gillespie et al. 2007). The work of market-building draws upon, stimulates, and requires active participation in shaping the food system, which lies at the core of food democracy (Hassanein 2003). As the Louisville experience illustrates, participation occurs on multiple levels, from the immediacy of community organizing at middle schools to the national scope of advocacy for food security and redistributive justice. It also encompasses individuals and groups with differing interests and perspectives collaborating to recraft the city's food system. To flourish, markets in Louisville, like alternative agrifood institutions elsewhere, will likely need to embrace or at least negotiate this diversity of engagements and actors, as part of the larger, and still uncharted, process of building a more sustainable and equitable food economy. In the meantime, expanding access to pleasure and produce brings us a little closer to that day.

NOTES

1. A more comprehensive suite of projects, conceived explicitly toward strengthening community food security, have come via the Community Food Projects Competitive Grants Program. Authorized in 1996, the Program has supported some 240 innovative projects, including development of farmers' markets (CFSC et al. 2007).
2. In 2003 Louisville and the surrounding Jefferson County merged, and the resulting entity is now referred to as Louisville Metro or simply Louisville.
3. See Jones (1988) for more on the political-economy of West Louisville.
4. Disclosure: I joined CFA in 1996 and my Louisville membership has comprised the role of activist–researcher. I participated with the organization's Community Food Assessment, have carried out fieldwork on local farmers' markets and other food system initiatives, and served on the Louisville Food Security Task Force.
5. In the summer of 2007, another West Louisville farmers' market was established, with organizational support from CFA. This was run by a new food business, Urban Fresh, composed of a small group of young African Americans. At the market and other venues, they sold local produce bulked by the city's new farmer-owned distribution business, Grasshoppers, Inc. (see Markowitz 2008).
6. Although this figure sounds distressingly low, nation-wide, about a quarter of markets surveyed in 2005 generated average monthly sales of less than $2,500 (Ragland and Tropp 2009: Table 46.2, p. 26).

REFERENCES

Allen, P. 2004. *Together at the Table: Sustainability and Sustenance in the American Agrifood System*. University Park, PA: Pennsylvania State University Press.

Andreatta, S. and W. Wickliffe, II. 2002. Managing Farmer and Consumer Expectations: A Study of a North Carolina Farmers Market. *Human Organization* 61(2):167–176.

Barham, J. 2008 (March). *Assessing Alternative Food Distribution Models: Improving Marketing Opportunities for Small-Scale and Limited-Resource Producers*. Paper presented at the Meetings of the Society for Applied Anthropology, Memphis, TN.

Becker, G. S. 2006. "Farmers' Markets: The USDA Role." CRS Report for Congress.

Berg, J. 2008. *All You Can Eat: How Hungry Is America?* New York: Seven Stories Press.

Brown, A. 2001. Counting Farmers Markets. *Geographical Review* 91(4):655–674.

Community Farm Alliance. 2003. "Bringing Kentucky's Food and Farm Economy Home." CFA Report, Frankfort, KY.

——. 2007. "Bridging the Divide: Growing Self-Sufficiency in Our Food Supply." CFA Report, Louisville, KY.

CFSC, USDA, CSREES, and WHY. 2007. "Healthy Food, Healthy Communities: A Decade of Community Food Projects in Action." Report.

Curtis, K. and S. McClellan. 1995. Falling Through the Safety Net: Poverty, Food Assistance and Shopping Constraints in an American City. *Urban Anthropology*, 24(1–2):93–133.

Davis, A. 2006. "Fast Food Fanatics." *Louisville Courier Journal*, p. D1. November 19.

Egan, T. 2002. "Growers and Shoppers Crowd Farmers' Markets." *New York Times*. September 29. Available at www.nytimes.com/2002/09/29/national/29FARM

Eisenhauer, E. 2001. In Poor Health: Supermarket Redlining and Urban Nutrition. *GeoJournal*, 53(2):125–133.

Feenstra, G. W. 2002. Creating Space for Sustainable Food Systems: Lessons From the Field. *Agriculture and Human Values* 19(2):99–106.

Fisher, A. 1999. *Hot Peppers and Parking Lot Peaches: Evaluating Farmers' Markets in Low-Income Communities*. Venice, CA: Community Food Security Coalition.

Gillespie, G., D. Hilchey, C. Hinrichs, and G. Feenstra. 2007. Farmers' Markets as Keystones in Rebuilding Local and Regional Food Systems. In *Remaking the North American Food System*. (eds. C. Hinrichs and T. Lyson), pp. 65–83. Lincoln, NE: University of Nebraska Press.

Guthman, J., A. Morris, and P. Allen. 2006. Squaring Farm Security and Food Security in Two Types of Alternative Food Institutions. *Rural Sociology* 71(4):662–684.

Halbach, N. A. 2006. "Building Health and Wealth: Assessing Potential Benefits and Raising Awareness of the WIC FMNP in Louisville Metro, KY." CFA Report, Frankfort, KY.

Hassanein, N. 2003. Practicing Food Democracy: A Pragmatic Politics of Transformation. *Journal of Rural Studies* 19:77–86.

Herman, D.R., G.G. Harrison, A.A. Afifi, and E. Jenks. 2008. Effect of a targeted subsidy on intake of fruits and vegetables among low-income women in the Special Supplemental Nutrition Program for Women, Infants, and Children. *American Journal of Public Health* 98(1): 98–105.

Hinrichs, C., G. Gillespie, and G. Feenstra. 2004. Social Learning and Innovation at Retail Farmers' Markets. *Rural Sociology* 69(1):31–58.

Jones, Y. 1988. Street Peddlers as Entrepreneurs: Economic Adaptation to an Urban Area. *Urban Anthropology*, 17(2–3):143–170.

Kantor, L. S. 2001. Community Food Security Programs Improve Food Access. *Food Review* 24:20–26.

Lev, L., G. Stephenson, and L. Brewer. 2007. Practical Research Methods to Enhance Farmers' Markets. In *Remaking the North American Food System* (eds. C. Hinrichs and T. Lyson), pp. 84–98. Lincoln, NE: University of Nebraska Press.

Lyson, T. 2004. *Civic Agriculture: Reconnecting Farm, Food, and Community*. Medford, MA: Tufts University Press.

Markowitz, L. 2008. Produce(ing) Equity: Creating Fresh Markets in a Food Desert. In Geert de Neve et al. (eds.) *Hidden Hands in the Market: Ethnographies of Fair Trade, Ethical Consumption, and Corporate Social Responsibility. Research in Economic Anthropology*, Volume 28, 195–211.

———. 2005. "Sure Beats Krogers: Shopping for Change at Farmers' Markets." Paper presented at the 104th Meeting of American Anthropological Association, Washington, DC.

National Agricultural Statistics Service (NASS). 2004a. *2002 Census of Agriculture*. Volume 1, Chapter 2. Table 46.1: State Summary Highlights. USDA.

National Agricultural Statistics Service (NASS). 2004b. *2002 Census of Agriculture*. Volume 1, Chapter 1: Kentucky State Level Data. Table 46.2: Market Value of Agricultural Products Sold. USDA.

Pollan, M. 2008. "Farmer in Chief." *New York Times Magazine*. October 9.

Raskin, S. 2006. "Why It's Easier to Get a Burger Than Broccoli on West Broadway: The Geography of Food Insecurity in Louisville, With a Focus on the West End and East Downtown." CFA Report, Frankfort, KY.

Rosenblum, A. 2007. "Kentucky Farmers at a Low-Income Louisville Farmers' Market."

Research Paper, Department of Anthropology, University of Louisville.

Rosset, P. 2003. Food Sovereignty: Global Rallying Cry of Farmer Movements. *Food First Backgrounder* 9(4). Oakland, CA: Food First.

Ragland, E. and D. Tropp. 2009. *National Farmers Market Managers Survey, 2006*. Marketing Services Division, USDA Agricultural Marketing Service.

Tessman, N. and A. Fisher. 2009. "State implementation of the New WIC Produce Package: Opportunities and Barriers for WCI Clinets to Use Their Benefits at Farmers' Markets." Community Food Security Coalition. Available at http://www.foodsecurity.org/pub/WIC-FarmersMarket Report.pdf

Thurman, S. 2005. *Optimal Location of A Regional Marketing Center in West Louisville, KY*. Senior Thesis. Department of Geography and Geosciences, University of Louisville, Louisville, KY.

Tropp, D. and J. Barham. 2008. "National Farmers Market Summit Proceedings Report." Marketing Services Division, USDA Agricultural Marketing Service.

USDA/AMS. 2006. *USDA Releases New Farmers Market Statistics*. AMS No. 281–06. December.

USDA/AMS. 2007. *Farmers Market Growth*. Available at www.ams.usda.gov/farmersmarkets/FarmersMarketGrowth.htm

USDA/AMS. 2009. *Farmers Market Program*. Available at http://www.ams.usda.gov/AMSv1.0/getfile?dDocName=STELPRDC5080175&acct=frmrdirmkt

USDA/ERS. 2008. *Farm Bill Side-by-Side*. Available at http://www.ers.usda.gov/FarmBill/2008/

USDA/FNS. 2008. *A Short History of the Food Stamp Program*. Available at www.fns.usda.gov/fsp/rules/Legislation/about_fsp.htm

USDA/FNS SFMNP. 2009. *Senior Farmers' Market Nutrition Factsheet*. Available at www.fns.usda.gov/wic/SFMNP-Fact-Sheet.pdf

USDA/FNS WIC FMNP. 2009. *WIC Farmers' Market Nutrition Program Factsheet*. Available at www.fns.usda.gov/wic/WIC-FMNP-Fact-Sheet.pdf

USDA/FNS. 2010. *SNAP Monthly Data*. Available at http://www.fns.usda.gov/pd/34SNAPmonthly.htm

Van Willigen, J. and S. C. Eastwood. 1998. *Tobacco Culture: Farming Kentucky's Burley Belt*. Lexington, KY: University Press of Kentucky.

Webb, D. 2007. Personal communication.

Winne, M. 2008. *Closing the Food Gap: Resetting the Table in the Land of Plenty*. Boston: Beacon Press.

40

Vegetarians: Uninvited, Uncomfortable or Special Guests at the Table of the Alternative Food Economy?

Carol Morris and James Kirwan

INTRODUCTION

Over the last decade, in rural sociology and cognate disciplines, considerable interest has developed in what have been variously labelled as 'alternative food strategies' (Kirwan 2003), 'alternative food initiatives' (Allen *et al.* 2003), 'alternative food supply chains' (Renting *et al.* 2003), 'alternative consumption practices' (Bryant and Goodman 2004), 'alternative food networks' (Whatmore *et al.* 2003) and the 'alternative food economy'[1] (Morris 2002). These labels are used to describe a number of diverse initiatives and developments that have recently risen to prominence in the agro-food system. Examples include organic and other forms of ecological agriculture, direct marketing such as farm shops, farmers' markets and box schemes and fairly traded goods and produce which comes from locally unique and distinctive places of production. The appellation, 'alternative' points to the oppositional character of these phenomena, which have often been developed in an attempt to counteract and offer sustainable solutions to some of the environmental, social and economic problems that have come to be associated with the mainstream or conventional agro-food system. More specifically, alternative food networks embody relations between their constituent actors that are somehow different from the conventional industrial food supply chain model. These differences may be environmental, social or economic, but what they

have in common is an intention to make more explicit the connectedness between the production of food and its eventual consumption. They have been defined by Renting *et al.* (2003, p. 394) as being 'newly emerging networks of producers, consumers, and other actors that embody alternatives to the more standardised industrial mode of food supply'.

Whereas in a North American context interest in alternative food networks has tended to focus on their political ability 'to wrest control from corporate agribusinesses and create a domestic, sustainable and egalitarian food system' (Goodman 2003, p. 2), in Europe the focus has been more towards the ability of these initiatives to benefit the rural economy and contribute towards endogenous development. Thus, Marsden *et al.* (2002) describe them as being part of 'economies of scope' or 'synergy', in contrast to the dominant post-war 'economies of scale'; similarly, Goodman (2004) talks of alternative food networks as creating 'new spaces of possibility' for rural development. Through re-embedding the production and consumption of food in specific places and relationships and facilitating adding and retaining value at a local level, they are recognised as being able to 'create positive "defences" for rural regions against the prevailing trends of globalisation and further industrialisation of markets' (Marsden *et al.* 1999, p. 295). Within a European context, therefore, the alternative food economy is seen as a critical element of emerging rural development patterns and perhaps even of a rural development paradigm (Marsden *et al.* 2000; Renting *et al.* 2003). As this snapshot suggests, much of the discussion surrounding alternative food has been of a positive and optimistic nature. Nevertheless, Goodman (2004, p. 13) has recently voiced concern about the missing guests at the table of the alternative food economy. For him, these are the consumers who are unable to buy into alternative food networks through their limited purchasing power and/or lack of cultural capital. While this is undoubtedly a significant issue, it is possible to identify other types of potential guests who appear to have been neglected in the discussion of the alternative food economy to date. One notable example is people who exercise particular dietary choices and preferences, and specifically those who practice a vegetarian diet. In this article we explore whether vegetarians deserve a place at the table of the alternative food economy, through an examination of the tensions and contradictions in the cognitive praxis (after Eyerman and Jamison 1991) of the vegetarian movement. In essence, we are concerned to elucidate the congruence between vegetarianism and the alternative food system. A secondary objective is to consider, albeit in a preliminary and speculative manner, whether this invitation is justified on the basis of any rural development potentialities that might be associated with people choosing a vegetarian diet.

It is, of course, the case that vegetarianism has been the focus of some scholarly enquiry (e.g. Twigg 1983; Adams 1990; Beardsworth and Keil 1992; Spencer 1993; Eder 1996; Maurer 2002; Smart 2004), but not, on the whole, among those interested in the operation of the agro-food system and the reconfiguration of this system along more sustainable lines through the development of alternative production–consumption relationships, with all that

this might imply for rural development (a couple of notable exceptions are McManus 1999, and Miele 2001). A number of reasons for this neglect can be posited. Firstly, vegetarianism is a dietary practice of ancient origin, albeit one that has expanded in popularity in recent years. In contrast, most of the phenomena currently conceptualised as 'alternative' are relatively new to the agro-food scene, at least in terms of their public and policy interest. Secondly, much of the social science scholarship on vegetarianism to date has been undertaken by sociologists, historians and anthropologists of food, rather than those scholars concerned with agriculture and the food system, and it is the latter who have been significant in theorising the emergence of, and investigating empirically, agro-food system alternatives. This illustrates the divide between the work of rural sociologists – who focus on agricultural organisation and production – and sociologists of food – who focus on diet, culture and consumption (Tovey 1997). Although recent years have witnessed the emergence of attempts by agro-food scholars to bridge this divide (e.g. Lockie and Collie 1999; Lockie and Kitto 2000; Goodman 2002; Goodman and Dupuis 2002), there remains considerable scope for further work. Thirdly, vegetarianism is arguably a predominantly consumer-oriented movement, albeit one that is built upon a set of concerns about production and production practices, which may reduce its immediate relevance to those scholars interested in bridging the consumption–production divide, specifically where this interest has a rural focus.

There are, however, good reasons why an exploration of the relationship between vegetarianism and the alternative food economy is a relevant, interesting and fruitful exercise. Characterised as representing a rejection or inversion of the 'conventional hierarchy of foods' (Beardsworth and Keil 1992, p. 258), vegetarianism emphasises animal rights and welfare, and a variety of environmental, societal and health benefits over meat-based dietary norms. In its efforts to create more ethical relationships within the food system, vegetarianism therefore appears to reflect, even embody, much of the contemporary interest among policymakers, rural development practitioners and agro-food scholars in alternative food initiatives. Indeed, in their analysis of Californian alternative food initiatives Allen *et al.* (2003) point to the publication, in the 1960s, of vegetarian advocacy books such as *Diet for a small planet* as being part of the broader movement for social justice and environmental regulation that stimulated the emergence of alternative food initiatives as we know them today. Meanwhile, the oppositional and alternative nature of vegetarianism (as opposed to mainstream dietary patterns) is a recurrent theme throughout the history of this ancient consumption practice, dating back to its earliest recorded proponents, most notably Pythagoras in the sixth century BC (Spencer 1993). The leitmotif of the vegetarian creed was originally one of strong-minded individuals looking askance at the morals of mainstream society. More recently, vegetarianism has occupied (and perhaps continues to do so) a position in the popular imagination as an alternative practice, not only on the grounds of it rejecting the consumption of meat (i.e., the dietary norm), and thereby challenging the dominant food ideology of western culture, but also through its association with alternative cultures, such as hippy culture. Finally, it is estimated that up to 7 per cent of the UK population practices a vegetarian diet in some form or another (Ashley *et al.* 2004) and as Dietz *et al.* (1995) have stated, a major shift towards vegetarianism could have profound implications for rural areas and the organisation of agriculture in particular.

In order to undertake our analysis, vegetarianism is understood as a social movement with the potential to effect change within the food system and, ultimately (perhaps), bring about rural development benefits. In adopting this approach, we draw on Hilary Tovey's (2002) recent examination of the alternative agriculture movement in Ireland and its rural development potential. Her use of Eyerman and Jamison's (1991) cognitive approach to social movements enables contradictions and tensions to be revealed within social movements, and between social movements and other institutions, as well as enabling an understanding of how the knowledge that defines these movements is the result of an ongoing and dynamic process. This is seen as particularly pertinent to the vegetarian case, and to the assessment of the place of vegetarianism within the alternative food economy. However, the focus of our analysis is not social movements *per se*; rather, a social movement framework provides a vehicle for, or means of making sense of vegetarianism in relation to the wider food system and the alternative food system in particular. In the remainder of the article we briefly outline the key characteristics of the cognitive approach to social movements as adapted by Tovey, before applying the framework to the vegetarian movement. We then move on to reveal how contradictions and tensions in the cognitive praxis of vegetarianism (together with tensions between vegetarianism and other, largely private-sector institutions) may be making it an uninvited, or at best uncomfortable, guest at the table of the alternative food economy. In conclusion, we suggest ways in which the vegetarian movement might reclaim a place at the table of the alternative food economy and in the process make a contribution to rural development. We do this through a discussion of the extant academic literature on vegetarianism and the agro-food system, together with an analysis of a variety of secondary sources including websites and promotional materials. While the analysis draws on research from the UK, the US and Europe, where vegetarianism is very much a product of individual choice as opposed to being socially or religiously prescribed, such as in India (Twigg 1983), ultimately interest is oriented towards the UK and European situation where research on alternative food networks has been particularly concerned with rural development.

SOCIAL MOVEMENTS, THE FOOD SYSTEM AND RURAL DEVELOPMENT

Social movements can be seen as challenging the *status quo* in some way. They are about more than simply individuals exercising personal choice, even though they may emerge from individual action. Over time, if individual action is to become a social movement it must necessarily become political, promoting lifestyle change and subsequently engendering a broader cultural change within society. How this happens is central to the role that particular movements have to play in influencing the dominant culture. It is also the case that social movements do not exist in isolation and inevitably there will be a degree of overlap between different movements. Indeed, Maurer (2002) suggests that there is potential overlap between the environmental movement and the vegetarian movement, and in the context of this article our intention is to explore the degree of overlap and synergy between vegetarianism and the alternative food economy.

Although largely neglected by rural sociologists, social movements perspectives 'can yield some insights into the dilemmas and contradictions embedded in projects for sustainable development' (Tovey 2002, p. 2). In the context of alternative agriculture movements, which are the focus of Tovey's analysis, these have tended to be seen as movements for technical change, that is, change in the forces

and means of production and consumption to make them less damaging to nature. However, Tovey asks whether in fact they should be understood as movements for rural regeneration and the recreation of community within rural spaces. Potentially of course, social movements can be about both of these concerns which, in Habermasian terms, respectively articulate 'instrumental-strategic' or 'communicative' forms of reason as the basis for social and society-nature relationships. In reviewing the extensive literature on social movements, Tovey seeks to identify a framework that uncovers the extent to which social movements like organic farming, and other movements for sustainable development, confront and struggle with a duality of aims and values that constantly place problematic choices before the actors concerned. This duality refers to the political/instrumental orientation of social movements, on the one hand, and cultural orientations on the other. The former may be understood in more formal organisational terms (polity/economy), and the latter as the development of more informal networks of actors (civil society). Some scholars have regarded this as an either/or focus, while others such as Cohen (1996) have argued that both may be a feature of any one social movement, although one or the other may be more significant at particular times.

Tovey combines some of the insights from 'cultural' approaches to social movements (notably Cohen 1996) with Eyerman and Jamison's (1991) 'social movements as cognitive praxis'. This is an approach, as the label suggests, which focuses on the cognitive dimension, conceptualising social movements as collective knowledge innovators or producers of knowledge; an aspect neglected by both the political and identity-oriented analyses of social movements. Eyerman and Jamison attribute much of their thinking to Habermas and, in particular, to his conception of 'knowledge constituting interests', enabling them to identify three distinct dimensions of cognitive praxis. The first dimension, the *cosmological*, refers to the basic assumptions and beliefs of a social movement which come to be taken for granted by movement participants. The *technological* dimension concerns the specific topics of protest and, in particular, the techniques and artefacts against which movement actors are protesting, together with the (alternative) techniques they are proposing or trying to develop in order to realise movement goals. The third dimension is *organisational* and describes the manner in which knowledge should be produced and disseminated, or as a means of 'organising social relations to put technological innovations into practice' (Tovey 2002, p. 5). In Eyerman and Jamison's case study of the environmental movement, the organisational dimension referred to the calls by environmentalists for the de-professionalising of expertise and more democratic forms of knowledge production. Meanwhile, in Tovey's analysis of the organic agriculture movement in Ireland, she argues that movement actors are interested in non-technical as well as technical forms of innovation, particularly as these manifest themselves around alternative social relationships with on-farm employees and/or with consumers. This organisational dimension of the alternative agriculture movement is the key to bringing about the rural community development that is Tovey's principal interest.

Social movements coalesce individual interest into organisational concerns and their identity is dynamic. Critical to this identity is a movement's cognitive praxis that is actively articulated and discussed. Eyerman and Jamison argue that a movement can only be called a social movement if its three knowledge interests are combined into an active, integrative force that results in a living

cognitive praxis among activists. It is this cognitive praxis that defines the social movement, rather than any organisational structures it may have. What is of interest in this framework, for our analysis of vegetarianism and the alternative food economy, is that social movements face problems in trying to maintain the integration of all three dimensions of knowledge over time. This is not to suggest that their cognitive praxis should be seen as reified in any sense, but that other social actors or institutions, from the state or private sector, will bring strong pressures to bear on movements, trying to single out those elements of the cognitive praxis that most interest them, leading to the disintegration of the whole. Typically, these are innovations in technical knowledge. Other institutions take certain elements of the cognitive praxis and incorporate them within their own knowledge sets, discarding the rest:

> It is thus inevitable that social movements are impermanent and transient sources of what may be permanent and far-reaching political and cultural change. Social movements define themselves in the process of creating, articulating and formulating new knowledge, but once this knowledge has been accepted and formalised, whether within the scientific world or the established political culture, then it has left the space of the movement behind.
>
> (Tovey 2002, p. 5)

The development and innovation that Tovey brings to Eyerman and Jamison's framework is a questioning of the assumption that tension and confrontation only occurs between the social movement and outside institutions, but not within the movement itself. Thus, Tovey emphasises instead how the relationships between the three dimensions of knowledge may be/become incoherent or contradictory within a single given movement, and that there may be a constant tension between the cognitive praxis which actors develop around one dimension and the praxes manifest in the other two. This is not to suggest that change is necessarily detrimental to a social movement; indeed, cognitive praxis actively involves 'the social shaping of knowledge' (Eyerman and Jamison 1991, p. 47); simply that it may result in certain contradictions at certain times, which may or may not be resolvable within the context of the social movement concerned. In applying this to the organic agriculture movement, Tovey (2002, p. 8) reveals significant tensions between the desire of movement participants to innovate technologically and their desire to innovate socially/organisationally. The latter is important because 'this is the way in which civil society can check the proliferation of instrumental rationality associated with the technology'. It is the technological dimension of the organic movement which is most under threat of 'capture' by institutions outside the movement (as work by Buck *et al.* 1997, and Guthman 1998 have revealed), but this is also the aspect of cognitive praxis that many movement participants tend to emphasise, recognising that in so doing they may produce dilemmas for the movement. However

> . . . the cosmological commitments of Irish organic producers are what prevent their passion for technique from undermining their concern with interpersonal interaction, community and the development of new forms of rural social organisation.
>
> (Tovey 2002a, p. 8).

Hence, the ability of this social movement to make a positive contribution to rural development.

While the alternative agriculture movement, as analysed by Tovey, and vegetarianism are acknowledged to be somewhat different types of social movement (emerging as they do from within different parts of the food system), a cognitive approach to their analysis is relevant to our concerns for the following reasons. Firstly, the framework as adapted by

Tovey concerns the relationship between social movements and the sustainable development of the food system and rural areas in particular. Likewise, we are interested in exploring the relationship between vegetarianism and its potential for shaping a more sustainable agro-food system and rural development. Secondly, the framework pays particular attention to the contradictions and tensions that social movements have to negotiate, both those that are internal to themselves and external forces and institutions. This, we believe, provides a useful means of making sense of the ambiguities and tensions that we observe in the context of vegetarianism, and how these impact on its agro-food system sustainability and rural development potential. In the next section we outline the cognitive praxis of vegetarianism before moving on to discuss the contradictions in the movement and between the movement and external institutions.

THE COGNITIVE PRAXIS OF VEGETARIANISM

Vegetarianism involves the exclusion of certain food products from the diet. These are, most notably, flesh foods – meat, poultry, game, fish and sea food – but also, for other vegetarians, dairy products and eggs, or the by-products of slaughtering such as gelatin and animal fat. Concomitantly, vegetarian diets entail the relatively greater use (compared with a conventional omnivorous diet) of other food products such as seeds, fruits, pulses, nuts and grains. Underpinning the daily practice of vegetarianism (whatever the individual motivations of those involved)

> exists a structured set of organisations, ideas and related phenomena: a movement that includes local and national organisations, a body of movement literature, a set of relatively coherent arguments and a wide range of products and services. A vegetarian

ideology – vegetarianism – provides both a critique of meat eating and the vision of a vegetarian world.

(Maurer 2002, p. 2)

Likewise, Twigg (1983) characterises vegetarianism as a rare example, in the west, of an 'explicit food ideology', as distinct from the 'more pervasive yet implicit ideology of meat culture'. Key to Twigg's analysis is the notion that vegetarianism requires a step 'outside the culturally prescribed forms of eating' (Twigg 1983, p. 19), representing an oppositional or alternative mode of eating, and indeed way of relating to the world. Both of these authors are making the point that vegetarianism is a social rather than an individual phenomenon, and in Maurer's case, a social movement[2]

In cognitive terms, the vegetarian movement (as it has evolved since the mid-nineteenth century) represents a collective effort to produce knowledge which will enable and subsequently persuade people to make the transition to a vegetarian diet. The three dimensions of knowledge (or cognitive praxis) of vegetarianism as a social movement can be identified as follows (after Tovey [2002] and Eyerman and Jamison [1991]). At the core of the cosmological dimension of vegetarianism's cognitive praxis is a set of moral beliefs and values relating to the use of animals by humans. Thus, a number of philosophical and spiritual arguments are deployed which oppose the killing of animals for food as both cruel and unnecessary (e.g. Singer 1983; Regan 1984; Shafer-Landau 1994; Alward 2000; Benatar 2001; Zuzworksky 2001). In the vegan case, it is argued that animals should not be kept for food, or other human uses, at all. Surrounding this core belief and value in the rights and welfare of animals is a belief in 'natural' or 'whole' foods and the healthiness and vitality of the diet, as well as a broader concern for the well-being of the environment.

Vegetarianism can be said to embrace the concepts of 'nature' and 'natural', because it values 'rawness', in comparison with a meat culture which emphasises cooking (Twigg 1983). Lévi-Strauss argued that the process of cooking effectively mediates between raw food (seen to represent nature), and cooked food (seen to represent culture), even if this is an unconscious dichotomy at an individual level (Ashley et al. 2004). While acknowledging that organisations which promote whole/health/natural foods do not necessarily espouse vegetarianism, Maurer (2002) suggests that the health-food movement is a closely related social movement which has contributed to an increase in the health-related aspect of vegetarian diets and an increasing sensitivity about eating meat. Moreover, vegetarians, she observes, frequently shop at natural food stores. In other words, there are complementarities between the cognitive praxes of these two social movements.

With respect to the technological dimension of vegetarianism's cognitive praxis, it is possible to identify a set of concerns underpinning this particular knowledge-constituting interest. Vegetarianism's specific topic of protest is meat eating, and its espoused alternative is for a plant-based diet and agriculture: entirely plant based in the case of veganism, and largely so in the case of lacto-/ovo-/demi-vegetarianism. We interpret this as an argument which is for the most part technological and scientific and it is a position advanced by vegetarian organisations not only because of what it implies for animal rights and welfare, but also because of the implications for human welfare, the environment and human health. Each of these latter three aspects of the philosophy of vegetarianism is worth a brief elaboration at this point, in that although they can be identified as part of its cosmological praxis, they are perhaps less widely appreciated than the animal rights and welfare concerns of the movement; and yet speak directly to the growing sustainability concerns within the agro-food system.

Concerning human welfare in a global sense, vegetarianism asserts a morally superior position to meat eating because feeding grain to animals is less efficient than feeding it directly to humans: 'Grain-fattened animals take more energy and protein from their feed than they return in the form of food for humans' (Compassion in World Farming Trust 2004, p. 22). Adopting a vegetarian diet, therefore, is seen as an important step towards alleviating some of the problems of the world food shortage and starvation that are likely to be exacerbated by the predicted livestock revolution in the developing world, in which meat consumption is projected to rise by 3 per cent per annum until 2020 (Compassion in World Farming Trust 2004, p. 22).[3] More specific ecological arguments are also used to justify the adoption of a plant-based diet, although these tend to 'get less than [their] fair share of publicity', according to the President of the Australian Vegetarian Society, in his address to the 33rd World Vegetarian Congress (Fraser, 1999). The ecological argument for vegetarianism encompasses a number of environmental concerns about livestock farming, including the production of greenhouse gases,[4] losses of tropical rainforest to cattle ranching, the collapse of global fisheries, water pollution from intensive livestock holdings and the inefficient use of land and water resources. Taking the last two of these issues for illustration, it is argued that a vegetarian diet is a more efficient user of both land and water (e.g. Goodland 1997; Leitzmann 2003; Pimentel and Pimentel 2003). For example, research in the US has shown that 0.5 ha of land is required for a meat-based diet, compared with 0.4 ha for a vegetarian-based diet (Pimentel and Pimentel 2003).[5] Similarly, in terms of water usage, there is a growing concern that water scarcity will become at least as important a constraint on future food

production as a lack of available land. The argument advanced for vegetarianism in this context is that 'by moving down the food chain, Americans could get twice as much nutritional benefit out of each litre of water consumed in food production' (Sandra Postel, quoted in Compassion in World Farming Trust 2004, p. 25).

Human health concerns also emerge as an important reason why a plant-based diet should be pursued. These concerns are often couched in terms of 'meat is bad for you', although the benefits of vegetable staples are also emphasised. Indeed, various recent scientific studies have suggested that a vegetarian diet is associated with, although not necessarily causally related to, a reduced risk of certain diseases. For example, a 12-year study of 6,000 vegetarians and 5,000 meat eaters published in 1994 showed that vegetarians have 30 per cent less heart disease and a reduced risk of various types of cancer by up to 40 per cent (Compassion in World Farming Trust 2004). While the sustainability implications of this aspect of vegetarianism are perhaps less clear than those arising from the human welfare and ecological arguments, it appears that vegetarianism is being advocated as a more socially sustainable form of consumption through the reduced costs of healthcare associated with the widespread adoption of a vegetarian diet.

Finally, an important subset of the opposition within vegetarianism to animal-based agricultures and diets is the protest against the factory farming of livestock, that is, a specific type of technological development in agriculture. In the US, Maurer (2002) points to FARM as an example of a vegetarian organisation that focuses on the reform of the farm animal industry as well as attempting to change consumer preferences. Meanwhile, Viva is an organisation that has been particularly critical of factory farming in the UK (Viva n.d.). It is clear, therefore, that there are a number of strands to the technological dimension of vegetarianism's cognitive praxis, aspects of which may not necessarily be complementary to one another or to other dimensions of the movement's cognitive praxis; something we will return to later.

Turning to the organisational dimension of the vegetarian movement's cognitive praxis, it is helpful to draw on Donna Maurer's (2002) analysis of North American vegetarianism as it provides a full length account of the movement and the manner of its organisation. Maurer argues that the vegetarian movement is more than the formal national and local organisations which promote vegetarianism (membership of which is relatively small compared to animal rights organisations), identifying many groups[6] and individuals that support vegetarian principles and are therefore constitutive of a much broader vegetarian movement than the relatively small number of explicitly vegetarian organisations might suggest. She sees the primary concerns of this broadly conceived vegetarian movement as motivating individuals to become vegetarian, increasing the cultural acceptance of vegetarianism and making vegetarian foods more readily available. In turn, these activities can be characterised as promoting and entailing personal, cultural and political change. Perhaps more significant here than the details of the structure and activities of national and local vegetarian organisations is Maurer's characterisation of how the North American vegetarian movement goes about recruiting participants. This illustrates how knowledge about vegetarianism is produced. Drawing on Weberian ideas, Maurer distinguishes between social movements that call for participants to change for the benefit of a collective good ('ethical' movements) and those that encourage change for the individual's own benefit ('exemplary' movements). Ethical movements are seen as offering prescriptions for moral attitudes, while exemplary movements provide suggestions and general direction.

'In an ethical movement, adherence to prescribed rules is viewed as a duty, a moral obligation; in an exemplary movement this adherence is a more processual, less absolute path' (Maurer 2002, p. 19). Acknowledging that a social movement may include characteristics of both types, or can evolve from one type to the other, Maurer suggests that in the North American context, vegetarian organisations often pursue an exemplary line at first, motivating people to change for their own self benefit (i.e. health reasons), and then, once recruitment is achieved the organisations adopt a more ethical approach; that is, promoting concern for animals, human welfare and the environment.

Viewing the vegetarian movement through the lens of cognitive praxis, it is possible to argue that vegetarians are worthy guests, perhaps even deserving of special guest status, at the table of the alternative food economy. This is because the cosmological, technological and organisational dimensions of the vegetarian movement collectively represent an attempt to counteract, and offer sustainable solutions to, some of the environmental, social and economic problems that have come to be associated with the mainstream or conventional agrofood system. Furthermore, they offer a challenge to conventional relations between agro-food production and consumption, particularly as these concern making consumers aware of the implication for the sites of production (in terms of fanned animals and the farmed environment, less so perhaps for the producers themselves) of their purchasing and consumption decisions. Nevertheless, as will be revealed in the following section, there are a number of ambiguities, tensions and contradictions both within the vegetarian movement (i.e. between the three dimensions of knowledge), and between particular dimensions of the movement's cognitive praxis and external forces and institutions which undermine its position as a special guest at the table of the alternative food economy.

THE CONTRADICTIONS AND TENSIONS WITHIN THE COGNITIVE PRAXIS OF VEGETARIANISM

Social movements, according to Eyerman and Jamison (1991), face problems in trying to maintain the integration of all three dimensions of knowledge over time, as other social actors or institutions (particularly state or corporate groups) focus on the particular elements of a movement's cognitive praxis that most interest them and incorporate them within their own knowledge sets. In the case of the vegetarian movement, as in other social movements, it is possible to identify a number of ways in which the technological dimension of the movement's cognitive praxis has either been appropriated by external forces and institutions, or show how significant contradictions appear to be emerging between aspects of vegetarianism's technical knowledge and the arguments advanced by external bodies (including other social movements).

Perhaps the most obvious way in which this is occurring is in the human health argument for eating less meat and more plant-based alternatives. This dimension of vegetarian movement knowledge has proved particularly attractive to food processors and retailers in the conventional and industrialised food system:

> In recent years, the vegetarian food industry has flourished. Concern about fat intake, the desire to consume more natural, less processed foods, and interest in the potential health benefits of soy foods all contribute to this trend.
>
> (Maurer, 2002, p. 132)

Scares about the safety of meat (particularly in a UK context following the bovine spongiform encephalopathy [BSE] scandal) can also be added to this list. As a result, UK companies producing Quorn[7] and other similar products such as Quinova[8] boast that the UK market for vegetarian and meat-free foods is growing and is now estimated to be worth between £500 and £600 million per annum.[9] Likewise, in the US, the manufacture and retail of 'vegetarian friendly' foods such as vegetarian burgers and sausages is becoming increasingly lucrative, with Maurer reporting sales of these products rising by 13 per cent between 1996 and 1997. Alongside this trend, food processors increasingly label a wide range of manufactured goods as 'suitable for vegetarians', once again playing to the health concerns of the movement; that is, if it is vegetarian it must be somehow more natural and better for you. Vegetarian organisations, such as the UK's Vegetarian Society, have played an active role in this process by endorsing numerous (typically highly processed) food products that appear on the shelves of the major supermarkets.

These developments, which entail the incorporation of aspects of vegetarianism's cognitive praxis within the mainstream, industrialised agro-food system could not be further from a non-industrialised, locally based and natural alternative food system. Indeed, this is supported by Smart's (2004) study of the UK Vegetarian Society which he suggests is now 'adrift in the mainstream' (2004, p. 1), even though its strategy (of persuading the food processors and retailers to label foods as suitable for vegetarians or by endorsing particular products) has successfully recruited many more people to vegetarianism:[10]

> The commercialisation of vegetarian foods, which suggests that the food industry has co-opted vegetarianism as a menu choice, can have both positive and negative consequences for the vegetarian movement. It presents a strong opportunity for the vegetarian movement to capitalize on a cultural

environment in which vegetarian menu choices are acceptable. But it may also serve to further dilute the vegetarian collective identity.

(Maurer 2002, p. 133)

While private interests have clearly been significant in the capture of vegetarianism's technological knowledge, Maurer also identifies how the 'mainstreaming of vegetarianism has been facilitated by the endorsement of the diet by health professionals' (pp. 45–46) in the public sector, particularly in the case of the US by government regulations that favour non-meat protein sources. This pressure on the cognitive praxis of the vegetarian movement is largely the result of external bodies seeking to benefit from relating to (and arguably appropriating) certain elements of its underlying philosophy.

Alongside this incorporation by private and public institutions of aspects of the vegetarian movement's technological praxis, contradictions can be identified between the environmental knowledge produced by the movement and the environmental arguments deployed by other institutions. One of these concerns the role of livestock in the creation of sustainable farming systems. According to some recent commentaries, extensive systems of livestock production may ultimately be more sustainable than purely plant-based agricultures[11] (e.g. Schiere et al. 2002). This suggests that meat and animal, rather than plant-based, foods may be more at home in the alternative food economy. Indeed, the Food Ethics Council (2001), for example, has recently rejected vegetarianism as the basis of a more ethical and sustainable approach to food production systems.[12] Furthermore, while the evidence presented above suggests that a reduction in farm animals would produce environmental benefits, such an approach is also likely to generate environmental disbenefits, for example, where animal husbandry and pasturing practices are key to the maintenance, enhancement or recreation of

valuable habitats and landscape features such as biodiverse grasslands. This is evident within the context of European agri-environmental policy. Take, for example, UK environmentally sensitive areas which, in spite of their diversity in terms of landscape characteristics and habitats, all seek to maintain extensive livestock grazing and the conversion of arable to grassland.

The link is also made clear in work on high natural value farming systems (Hellegers and Godeschalk 1998), upland farming (Bignall and McCracken 1993), low intensity farming systems (Beaufroy et al. 1994) and sensitive environmental area management (Evans 2000). In short

> when livestock are raised according to the tenets of good husbandry . . . they hugely increase the overall economy of farming. Agriculture that includes the appropriate number of animals judiciously deployed is *more* efficient, not less, than all-plant agriculture
>
> (Tudge, quoted in Porritt 2004, p. 5)

Even Compassion in World Farming Trust (2004), in advance of pointing out that livestock farming in general is both energy and land-use inefficient when compared to growing crops, acknowledges that in areas where animals are fattened predominantly on grazing land that could not easily grow food crops for direct human consumption, or else where they eat primarily crop residues or other waste products, livestock farming can have a part to play. Likewise, the life-cycle impact assessments reviewed by Reijnders and Soret (2003 p. 667s) for vegetarian and meat products reveals how 'long distance air transport, deep-freezing and some horticultural practices for producing fresh vegetables may lead to environmental burdens for vegetarian foods exceeding those of locally produced organic meat'.

Furthermore, research suggests that the contemporary practice of vegetarianism is actually highly dependent on a *global* agro-food system. Thus, Beardsworth and Keil (1992, pp. 289–290) note that

> the conditions in which contemporary vegetarianism can flourish are located not only in a cultural climate of national (menu) pluralism, they also rest on the economic foundations of an affluent, consumer-oriented economy which can draw on a variety of food items, freed by the channels of international trade from the narrow limits of locality, climate and season.

This is supported by Lockie and Collie (1999) in their assertion that the decline in red-meat eating in Australia may be attributed to an increased access to a range of alternatives (both meat and non-meat based), supplied by the globalised agro-food system, rather than increased unease about red meat and its violent origins. Likewise, in an analysis of the rise of veganism in the UK, Leneman (1999) points to the increased availability of ethnic foods from around the world, in which dairy products have never been a key feature, as offering an important means of moving to an all-plant based diet. Situating contemporary vegetarianism within the alternative food economy, which is often intent on relocalising the agro-food system agenda, may therefore represent a significant challenge for its proponents and practitioners, and points to a growing contradiction *within* the cognitive praxis of vegetarianism. It is to these internal tensions that the discussion now turns.

Tovey (2002) argues that the relations between the three dimensions of knowledge may be incoherent or contradictory within a single given movement, and that there may be a constant tension between the cognitive praxis which actors develop around one dimension and the praxes manifest in the other two. To this, we add that there is also potential for tension (or at least incoherence) within any one of the dimensions of cognitive praxis, which also present challenges to movement practitioners and to the ability of the movement to effect social change (in this case, effecting change within the agro-food system to create a more sustainable system and to provide rural development benefits). Tensions and contradictions are particularly apparent within the cosmological dimension of the vegetarian movement's cognitive praxis.

At the heart of the vegetarian cosmology is a moral concern about the consumption of meat. This core concern disguises, however, the considerable diversity in the practices and motivations of vegetarians, which in turn raises questions about the 'moral elegance' attributed to the practice of vegetarianism by some (Porritt 2004). Beardsworth and Keil (1992), for example, have identified six general types of vegetarianism. These are suggested as being on a spectrum of animal product use ranging from least restrictive, where some meat is still consumed, to most restrictive, where only vegetable-derived products are consumed, that is, veganism. It is clear that in its most popular – lacto-ovo and lacto-forms (Beardsworth and Keil 1992), vegetarianism remains highly dependent on animal husbandry. In other words, it requires the keeping of animals for dairy and egg production, not to mention their killing at the end of their productive lives and, in the case of dairying, the selling off (often into veal production) of male calves (Penman 1996). This in itself does not represent a contradiction, except that dairy and egg production systems are often highly intensive and there are serious animal welfare and environmental concerns associated with them (Evans 2000). Moreover, some vegetarians, while refusing to consume meat and other flesh foods, continue to wear animal products in the form of leather and wool and in doing so, 'occupy a somewhat precarious moral position' (Beardsworth and Keil 1992, p. 283). The impracticality of excluding all animal-derived items is acknowledged by some vegetarians, but for others the moral ambiguity implicit in the consumption of animal products is a position they 'deliberately avoid subjecting to too careful scrutiny' (Beardsworth and Keil 1992, p. 283).

Even a shift to a vegan diet, based on an all-plant based agriculture, has been shown to present ethical dilemmas, as recently illustrated by Davis (2003). His analysis begins with the argument that we should seek to feed ourselves through production systems that produce the 'least harm', a position that usually leads to the conclusion that a plant-based diet is necessary. Nevertheless, he goes on to demonstrate that a diet based on large herbivores might in fact involve fewer animal deaths overall than an all-plant based diet, whereby numerous animals that live in and around agricultural fields (e.g. voles and rabbits) are killed during the multiple field activities that are required in the production of most crops (ploughing, harrowing and planting, as well as harvesting). While his calculations have been disputed (Matheny 2003), they do raise questions about the coherence of the vegetarian movement's cognitive praxis and, in particular, highlight an apparent contradiction between its cosmological dimensions (i.e. its concern about the killing of animals) and technological ones (i.e. the assertion that a plant-based diet is the means of achieving a vegetarian, and environmentally better, future).

Finally, we observe some discordance between the cosmological and organisational dimensions of vegetarianism's cognitive praxis. As outlined earlier, the vegetarian movement has tended to adopt an exemplary, as opposed to an ethical, approach to participant recruitment, emphasising the health benefits of vegetarianism in advance of ethical dimensions. This has tended to encourage the emergence of a group of 'lifestyle vegetarians' (Tester 1999). Although the consequences for the food system of a lifestyle approach may be the same as those brought about by the ethically motivated vegetarian, the sustainability gains may be superficial and short-lived, as lifestyle vegetarianism may not represent a permanent shift in dietary practice, being susceptible, like other lifestyle choices, to the vagaries of fashion. As Maurer observes:

> Promoting concern for animals and the environment is essential to the advancement of the vegetarian movement because people motivated to become vegetarian for health reasons are more likely to switch back to animal products when lower fat/lower calorie products become available. The role of committed, strongly motivated advocates must increase significantly if the movement is to confront . . . [the meat and dairy interests] . . . in any meaningful way.
> (Maurer 2002 p. 45)

Parallels can be drawn between lifestyle vegetarians and those consumers of organic foods (and other foods from the alternative systems of production) who consume them because they perceive benefits to themselves, either in terms of their own health, or from the improved social status associated with the accumulation of cultural capital (Lockie *et al.* 2002).

Taken together, these factors suggest that vegetarianism occupies an uneasy, paradoxical and contradictory position in relation to the emergence of oppositional and alternative food networks that seek to improve the sustainability of the agrofood system and to benefit rural development through the relocalisation and/or valorisation of their local food production assets. What this implies for our understanding and explanation of contemporary vegetarianism, and for the future direction and role of empirical research, is explored in the final section of this article.

(RE)SITUATING VEGETARIANISM IN THE ALTERNATIVE FOOD ECONOMY

In this article we have explored, through the use of a social movement framework, the place and relevance of vegetarianism in the alternative food economy. Understanding social movements as cognitive praxes implies that ongoing debate and the creation of knowledge is central to the development of these movements, and that although change might be accommodated within the existing movement's identity, this is by no means inevitable. As we have highlighted in the previous section, it is clear that the modern-day vegetarian movement's cognitive praxis exhibits a number of contradictions, tensions and incoherency both within the movement, and between it and other institutions. In turn, these tensions may prove significant in determining the ability of vegetarianism to claim a place at the table of the alternative food economy and, in particular, whether it has anything to contribute towards rural development. In this final section we consider how the cognitive praxis of vegetarianism might accommodate those aspects of the alternative food economy that are currently a cause of tension within the movement. In addition, we begin to raise some questions about what the apparent dilemmas associated with vegetarianism might mean for current debates around rural development and its links with agro-food alternatives.

In envisaging the vegetarian movement's position in relation to the alternative food economy, it is worth considering Maurer's (2002, p. 45) reflection that 'many vegetarian organisations find themselves in a difficult position of wanting to promote the ethical reasons for adopting veganism without alienating their health-motivated ovo-lacto-vegetarians'. In other words, there is a balance to be drawn between philosophical absolutism and the practicalities of increasing adherents to a diet that utilises less meat, or as Tovey (2002, p. 4) puts it, a 'constant need to manage and balance instrumental and cultural goals'. Social movements develop from individual actions which then coalesce into 'packages of ideas' that form

the cognitive praxis of the movement concerned (Eyerman and Jamison 1991). Nevertheless, 'packages of ideas' do not exist in a vacuum and are constantly exposed to a wide range of individual, institutional and other social movement inputs. In discussing the emergence of the environmental movement in western Europe from the 1970s, Eyerman and Jamison (1991) point to the importance of other previous and contemporary movements to the formation of its cognitive praxis, most notably the women's movement and the peace movement. In much the same way as Maurer (2002) talks of other movements' ideas impacting on vegetarianism in the 1960s (such as the hippy and health-food movements), we argue that the ongoing shaping of the package of ideas that define vegetarianism as cognitive praxis is influenced by other organisations in modern-day society, whether they be social movements for change, the growth of globalised networks of food supply, or the development of the alternative food economy. As Tovey (2002) argues, in the context of the organic movement in Ireland, this may then lead to incoherent or contradictory relations between the three dimensions of knowledge – cosmological, technological and organisational.

It is clear from the arguments put forward in this article that vegetarianism is being jostled cosmologically, technologically and organisationally, not least because much of the alternative knowledge in the current food supply chain is concerned to make more explicit the connection between the production and consumption of food, and to create initiatives which valorise local food assets for rural developmental purposes. However, vegetarian food is increasingly globally and amorphously sourced and processed. In addition, meat and animal-derived products (such as cheese) from particular grazing regimes or artisan-production practices are being suggested as offering the best environmental and rural development potential in certain instances. This is creating tensions between the vegetarian cosmology of abstaining from meat eating and its technological concern for the environment. Demi-vegetarians are already in a somewhat 'morally inelegant' position in this respect, but so, too, are those who use other animal products. It is possible, however, that these latter groups may be influenced to choose products that can be identified with particular production practices or places of production. Similarly, in the technological dimension, concern for the use of global resources in a diet based on meat would seem to conflict with an increasingly global sourcing of vegetarian foods. Again, a greater cognisance of food provenance might help to overcome this tension. Finally, in organisational terms there is clearly a tension between increasing the cultural acceptance of vegetarianism and making its produce more widely available (which includes not scaring off potential converts), and ensuring that over time these converts will be encouraged to engage with its underlying philosophy. Perhaps in the future this could include a specific encouragement for adherents to question more closely the origins of the vegetarian food they purchase.

It may be that the cognitive praxis of vegetarianism engages with, and is able to accommodate, these emerging ideas, some of which may help to connect it more closely and less ambiguously to the alternative food economy. However, on the other hand, it may be that the movement is due for another schism, the last one (in the UK) having occurred in 1944, when tensions surrounding the inclusion of lacto-/ovo-/demi-vegetarians in the movement's cognitive praxis, and indeed the acceptance of using animal products at all (such as shoes and clothing), proved to be too much of a knowledge shift for some, and the vegan movement broke away to create a separate, although related, social movement (Spencer 1993). Cosmologically, vegans perceived the inclusion of meat

and animal products in the diet as too much of a shift in the underlying value of compassion for all living beings; techno-logically, it involved a dilution of the benefits a vegetarian diet could bring in terms of human health, the environment and animal exploitation and organisation-ally, it confused the message that the movement was trying to propagate. A new form, or further offshoot, of vegetari-anism could, therefore, emerge from the current situation; one which still values a reduction in the quantity of animal products eaten, but one which also gives a relatively higher priority to issues of food provenance. If so, there is a strong argument for this form of vegetarianism (and its adherents) to be seated at the table of the alternative food economy and to be recognised as a potentially significant contributor to rural development.

In order to establish this, empirical research is required which 'ground truths' the arguments made in this article. The focus of this research may be individual vegetarians and how they understand their praxis: do they themselves identify the kinds of tensions and contradictions highlighted in this article? In particular, investigation is needed of how they view their practices in relation to debates about more sustainable agricultures and forms of rural development through, for example, expressed concern about the provenance of their food: or, whether they are eating at a quite different, but for them just as satisfying, table.[13] Furthermore, how are these issues balanced against the seemingly more mundane, but no less significant issues of price, conven-ience and accessibility? As Weatherell et al. (2003, p. 241) assert:

> . . . although fair levels of awareness and concern for wider food-related issues may exist within the population . . . in practice many will only act upon these concerns if the offerings meet their normal, food-intrinsic and practical needs.

Alternatively, research might examine the governance of vegetarian food, and in particular whether its standards and labelling addresses its supply origins and 'natural' credentials: together with the vegetarian commodity system and the way in which vegetarian food is being processed, distributed and retailed. All of these research endeavours would help to shed further light on the ongoing cognitive praxis of vegetarianism, its place within the alternative food economy and its potential to contribute to rural development.

However, all these suggestions approach the issue of the relationship between vegetarianism and the alternative food economy essentially from one perspective: that vegetarianism needs to adapt to the alternative food economy (if it wants to be a guest at its table), and not the other way around. It might therefore be interesting to also explore the implications of being unable to accommodate vegetarian consumption trends within sustainable rural development impulses built on an alternative food economy. Perhaps inviting vegetarians to eat at the table of the alternative food economy actually begins to reveal some of the contradictions, not just in vegetarianism, but also in discussions of 'sustainable' and 'alternative' food systems where the emphasis of concern (both in policy and academic debates) tends to lie with, first and foremost, production and producers rather than consumers. Recently, a consensus has begun to emerge in agro-food studies of a need to bring together food-producer and food-consumer perspectives through revised analytical frameworks (e.g. Tovey 1997; Lockie and Kitto 2000; Goodman 2002). However, the analysis of vegetarian praxis within this article suggests that such efforts may actually reveal fundamental cleavages and conflicts in these perspectives which may be very difficult to resolve. This does not mean that these efforts are not worthwhile, rather, that we need to be alert to

the possibility that analysing producer and consumer perspectives together will raise new sets of issues which may, in turn, challenge these new analytical frameworks. Similarly, a number of authors have started to unpack the notion that the re-localisation of food systems (an underlying tenet of much of the alternative food economy) necessarily results in more sustainable outcomes, or maximises the rural development potential of a particular area (e.g. Hinrichs 2003; Winter 2003). Indeed, Ilbery and Maye (2005) argue that in many instances initiatives operating with the alternative food economy (such as specialised regional food products) are in fact better understood as hybrids, in that they rarely operate exclusively as alternative forms. This apparent incongruity may help explain the ambiguities and contradictions between vegetarianism and the alternative food economy. By the same token, it also suggests that analyses (and proponents) of the alternative food economy need to be more aware of how it relates to other actors, initiatives and philosophies in the food supply system. It may be that inviting vegetarians to the table of the alternative food economy has provided a useful opportunity to reflect further upon the nature and values of the alternative food economy menu that is on offer.

NOTES

1. To a large extent these various terminologies are addressing the same issues, albeit within different conceptual contexts, but what they have in common, we suggest, is a concern with alternatives to the norm, or mainstream. As such, when discussing 'alternatives' in relation to the 'mainstream' (food) economy it is appropriate to use the term alternative (food) economy; likewise, in the context of (food) network development, alternative (food) networks and so on.

2. Indeed, until the mid-nineteenth century, when the British Vegetarian Society was formed, vegetarianism was largely practiced by individuals motivated by a variety of philosophical and ideological concerns. At its inception, the Vegetarian

Society was an intensely ideological organisation intent on addressing what it saw as the moral depravation of eating meat, as well as espousing the health benefits of excluding meat from the diet (Spencer 1993).

3. These arguments also have resonance in, and for, the west. In the US, for example, the current livestock population consumes more than seven times as much grain as is consumed directly by the entire US human population. According to Pimentel and Pimentel (2003) the amount of grain fed to US livestock is sufficient to feed approximately 840 million people existing on a plant-based diet (the current population is 285 million which is predicted to rise to 570 million in the next 70 years).

4. According to the Compassion in World Farming Trust, who refer to a number of sources, a little under one-quarter of all methane emissions (an important global-warming gas) globally come from livestock. Livestock farming is also a major contributor of other atmospheric pollutants such as ammonia, nitrous oxide and carbon dioxide (which contribute to soil acidification and global warming). It is estimated that 10 per cent of total global greenhouse gases are derived from animal manure.

5. For an older articulation of this argument, see Keith Mellanby's book, *Can Britain feed itself?* (1973).

6. For example, parts of the environmental movement, the health food movement and animal rights organisations.

7. Quorn is described on the manufacturer's website as a 'myco-protein' being derived from a type of fungus, and is sold in a variety of forms, including as a 'mince' which can be made into various dishes using other ingredients, and in pre-prepared foods such as pies and sausages.

8. Quinova, according to the manufacturer, is a meat-free product derived from the quinoa grain, which is a traditional food source in the Andes. It is described by its manufacturer, Anglesey Natural Foods, as 'gluten free, low in saturated fat, provides a rich source of carbohydrates and minerals and has an ideal balance of amino acids . . . Quinova is also Soil Association Approved, Vegetarian Society Approved, Vegan Society Approved, Gluten Free, GM Free and it qualifies as one of the 5 daily portions of fruit & vegetables'.

9. It is interesting also to note that meat substitute products are derived from highly industrialised processing systems (Quorn, for example, is produced in factories in two locations in the UK). While they may be able to be promoted as healthy meat free alternatives, any claims to 'naturalness' could not be further from the truth.

10. Maurer presents contradictory evidence, suggesting that the overwhelming majority of people (80 per cent, according to one study) who consume meat alternatives are not vegetarians, neither are the many people who eat vegetarian options at restaurants. As such, she concludes, the food industry's impact on the vegetarian movement has not had a significant impact on the number of vegetarians.

11. If universally adopted, this would necessarily entail dietary shifts in the form of significantly reduced meat consumption because extensive livestock systems tend to yield less output.

12. A co-evolutionary perspective on the relationship between humans and animals is used to arrive at this position:

> Domesticated animals have undergone marked evolutionary changes which, in many cases, makes them totally dependent on human care, having largely lost their adaptation to the wild. Their instincts of dominance and territoriality have become greatly diminished and their physical defence mechanisms atrophied. . . . So it would be a totally perverse act, resulting from a misguided sense of compassion, to attempt to return such domesticated animals to 'the wild', even assuming such territory could be found. They simply could not survive. (Food Ethics Council 2001, p. 6)

13. We are grateful to one anonymous referee for suggesting this point.

REFERENCES

Adams, C.J. (1990) *The sexual politics of meat* (Cambridge: Polity Press)

Allen, P., M. FitzSimmons, M. Goodman and K. Warner (2003) Shifting plates in the agrifood landscape: the tectonics of alternative agrifood initiatives in California. *Journal of Rural Studies* 19 (1) pp. 61–75

Alward, P. (2000) The naïve argument against moral vegetarianism. *Environmental Values* 9 (1) pp. 81–89

Ashley, B., J. Hollows, S. Jones and B. Taylor (2004) *Food and cultural studies* (London: Routledge)

Beardsworth, A. and T. Keil (1992) The vegetarian option: varieties, conversions, motives and careers. *Sociological Review* 40 (2) pp. 253–293

Beaufroy, G., D. Baldock and J. Clark eds (1994) *The nature of farming: low intensity farming systems in nine European countries.* (London: Institute for European Environmental Policy)

Benatar, D. (2001) Why the naïve argument against moral vegetarianism really is naïve. *Environmental Values* 10 (1) pp. 103–112

Bignal, E. and D. McCracken (1993) Nature conservation and pastoral farming in the British uplands. *British Wildlife* 4 pp. 367–376

Bryant, R.L. and M.K. Goodman (2004) Consuming narratives: the political ecology of 'alternative' consumption. *Transactions of the Institute of British Geographers* 29 (3) pp. 344–366

Buck, D., C. Getz and J. Guthman (1997) From farm to table: the organic v vegetable commodity chain of northern California. *Sociologia Ruralis* 37 (1) pp. 1–20

Cohen, J.L. (1996) Mobilisation, politics and civil society: social movements. Pp. 173–204 in J. Clark and M. Diani eds, *Alain Touraine* (London: Farmer Press)

Compassion in World Farming Trust (CIWF) (2004) *The global benefits of eating less meat*. A report prepared for CIWF Trust, Petersfield

Davis, S.L. (2003) The least harm principle may require that humans consume a diet containing large herbivores, not a vegan diet. *Journal of Agricultural and Environmental Ethics* 16 (4) pp. 387–394

Dietz, T., A. Frisch, L. Kalof, P. Stern and G. Guagnano (1995) Values and vegetarianism: an exploratory analysis. *Rural Sociology* 60 (3) pp. 533–542

Eder, K. (1996) *The social construction of nature* (London: Sage)

Evans, N. (2000) The impact of BSE in cattle on high nature value conservation sites in England. Pp. 92–110 in H. Millward, K. Beesley, B. Ilbery and L. Harrington eds, *Agricultural and environmental sustainability in the new countryside* (Nova Scotia Agricultural College: Truro)

Eyerman, R. and A. Jamison (1991) *Social movements: a cognitive approach* (Cambridge: Polity Press)

Food Ethics Council (2001) *Farming animals for food: towards a moral menu*. A report. (London: Food Ethics Council)

Fraser, R. (1999) Environmental aspects of vegetarianism: the Australian experience. A talk at the 33rd World Vegetarian Congress, Thailand, 4–10 January available online at: http://www.ivu.org/congress/thai99/texts/ozenviron.html Accessed 13 June 2006

Goodland, R. (1997) Environmental sustainability in agriculture: diet matters. *Ecological Economics* 23 (3) pp. 189–200

Goodman, D. (2002) Rethinking food production-consumption: integrative perspectives. *Sociologia Ruralis* 42 (4) pp. 271–277

Goodman, D. (2003) The quality 'turn' and alternative food practices: reflections and agenda. *Journal of Rural Studies* 19 (1) pp. 1–7

Goodman, D. (2004) Rural Europe redux? Reflections on alternative agro-food networks and paradigm change. *Sociologia Ruralis* 44 (1) pp. 3–16

Goodman, D. and E.M. DuPuis (2002) Knowing food and growing food: beyond the production-consumption debate in the sociology of agriculture. *Sociologia Ruralis* 42 (1) pp. 5–22

Guthman, J. (1998) Regulating meaning, appropriating nature: the codification of California organic agriculture. *Antipode* 30 (2) pp. 135–154

Hellegers, P. and F. Godeschalk (1998) Farming in high nature value regions; the role of agricultural policy in maintaining HNV farming systems in Europe. *Onderzoekverslag* 165, Agricultural Economics Research Institute, The Hague

Hinrichs, C. (2003) The practice and politics of food system localisation. *Journal of Rural Studies* 19 (1) 33–45

Ilbery, B. and D. Maye (2005) Alternative (shorter) food supply chains and specialist livestock products in the Scottish-English Borders. *Environment and Planning* A 37, 823–844

Kirwan, J. (2003) The reconfiguration of producer-consumer relations within alternative strategies in the UK agro-food system: the case of farmers' markets. Unpublished Ph.D. thesis. Cheltenham: Countryside and Community Research Unit, University of Gloucestershire

Leitzmann, C. (2003) Nutrition ecology: the contribution of vegetarian diets. *The American Journal of Clinical Nutrition* 78 (3) pp. 657–659

Leneman, L. (1999) No animal food: the road to veganism in Britain, 1909–1944. *Society and Animals* 7 (3) pp. 219–228

Lockie, S. and L. Collie (1999) 'Feed the man meat': gendered food and theories of consumption. Pp. 255–273 in D. Burch, J. Goss, and G. Lawrence eds, *Restructuring global and regional agricultures: transformations in Australasian agri-food economies and space*. (Aldershot: Ashgate)

Lockie, S. and S. Kitto (2000) Beyond the farm gate: production-consumption networks and agri-food research. *Sociologia Ruralis* 40 (1) pp. 3–19

Lockie, S., K. Lyons, G. Lawrence and K. Mummery (2002) Eating green: motivations behind organic food consumption in Australia. *Sociologia Ruralis* 42 (1) pp. 23–40

McManus, P. (1999) Geographies of competing food networks: meat and vegetarian sausages. Paper presented to the annual conference, Royal Geographical Society, Institute of British Geographers, Leicester University, 4–7 January

Marsden, T., J. Banks and G. Bristow (2000) Food supply chain approaches: exploring their role in rural development. *Sociologia Ruralis* 40 (4) pp. 424–438

Marsden, T., J. Banks and G. Bristow (2002) The social management of rural nature: understanding agrarian-based rural development. *Environment and Planning* A 34 (5) pp. 809–825

Marsden, T., J. Murdoch and K. Morgan (1999) Sustainable agriculture, food supply chains and regional development. Editorial introduction. *International Planning Studies* 4 (3) pp. 295–301

Matheny, G. (2003) Least harm: a defense of vegetarianism from Steven Davis's omnivorous proposal. *Journal of Agricultural and Environmental Ethics* 16 (5) pp. 505–511

Maurer, D. (2002) *Vegetarianism: movement or moment?* (Philadelphia, PA: Temple University Press)

Mellanby, K. (1973) *Can Britain feed itself?* (Monmouth: Merlin Press)

Miele, M. (2001) Changing passions for food in Europe. Pp. 29–50 in. H. Buller and K. Hoggart eds, *Agricultural transformation, food and environment. Perspectives on European rural policy and planning.* Vol. 1 (Aldershot: Ashgate)

Morris, C. (2002) Exploring food-environment linkages within the alternative food economy: the case of food labeling initiatives. Paper presented at 'The Alternative Food Economy: Myths, Realities, Potential' conference, Institute of British Geographers, 6 March

Penman, D. (1996) *The price of meat* (London: Gollancz)

Pimentel, D. and M. Pimentel (2003) Sustainability of meat-based and plant-based diets and the environment. *The American Journal of Clinical Nutrition* 78 (3) pp. 660–663

Porritt, J. (2004) Foreword. Pp. 4–7 in CIWF Trust, *The global benefits of eating less meat.* CIWF Trust: Hampshire

Regan, T. (1984) *The case for animal rights* (London: Routledge)

Reijnders, L. and S. Soret (2003) Quantification of the environmental impact of different dietary protein choices. *The American Journal of Clinical Nutrition* 78 (3) pp. 664–668

Renting, H., T. Marsden and J. Banks, (2003) Understanding alternative food networks: exploring the role of short food supply chains in rural development. *Environment and Planning* A 35 pp. 393–411

Schiere, J.B., M.N.M. Ibrahim and H. van Keulen (2002) The role of livestock for sustainability in mixed farming: criteria and scenario studies under varying resource allocation. *Agriculture, Ecosystems & Environment* 90 (2) pp. 139–153

Shafer-Landau, R. (1994) Vegetarianism, causation and ethical theory. *Public Affairs Quarterly* 8 (1) pp. 85–100

Singer, P. (1983) *Animal liberation* (Cape: London)

Smart, A. (2004) Adrift in the mainstream: challenges facing the UK vegetarian movement. *British Food Journal* 106 (2) pp. 79–92

Spencer, C. (1993) *The heretic's feast: a history of vegetarianism* (London: Fourth Estate Limited)

Tester, K. (1999) The moral malaise of McDonaldization: the values of vegetarianism. Pp. 207–221 in B. Smart ed, *Re-visiting McDonaldization* (London: Sage)

Tovey, H. (1997) Food, environmentalism and rural sociology: on the organic farming movement in Ireland. *Sociologia Ruralis* 37 (1) pp. 21–37

Tovey, H. (2002) Alternative agriculture movements and rural development cosmologies. *International Journal of Sociology of Agriculture and Food* 10 (1) pp.1–11

Twigg, S. (1983) Vegetarianism and the meanings of meat. Pp. 18–30 in A. Murcott ed, *The sociology of food and eating* (Aldershot: Gower)

Viva (n.d.) You don't have to gobble, gobble, gobble. Pamphlet encouraging readers to avoid turkey at Christmas (Bristol: Viva)

Weatherell, C., A. Tregear and J. Allinson (2003) In search of the concerned consumer: UK public perceptions of food, farming and buying local. *Journal of Rural Studies* 19 (2) pp. 233–244

Whatmore, S., P. Stassart and H. Renting (2003) What's alternative about alternative food networks? Guest editorial. *Environment and Planning A* 35 pp. 389–391

Winter, M. (2003). Embeddedness, the new food economy and defensive localism. *Journal of Rural Studies* 19 (1) 23–32

Zuzworksky, R. (2001) From the marketplace to the dinner plate: the economy, theology, and factory farming. *Journal of Business Ethics* 29 (1–2) pp. 177–188

41

Advocacy and Everyday Health Activism Among Persons with Celiac Disease: A Comparison of Eager, Reluctant, and Non-Activists

Denise Copelton

INTRODUCTION

When people come together to share a meal, they are fulfilling a basic biological need as well as a social one (Lupton 1996). Families are constituted and friendships strengthened through the social act of eating. Preparing a meal for others is an act of caring that cements and strengthens relationships (DeVault 1991). Yet the social act of eating can also create friction, as people bring tensions to the table along with food. At times, food itself is the source of conflict, such as when a child refuses to eat her vegetables or a family member adopts vegetarianism. Both disrupt established foodways, the social patterns and meanings of eating. Medical restrictions on eating may also challenge foodways both in- and outside of the home (Olsson et al. 2009; Walker 2005). Foodways must be adapted to the particular dietary restriction, which often requires education and advocacy via social movements (Maurer 2002). Support from friends and family is a key determinant of compliance with medical regimens, including those involving dietary changes (Gallant 2003; Levy 1983; van Dama et al. 2005). While dietary modifications can create new opportunities for family and friends to demonstrate care and affection, change can also create frustration and resentment, particularly when it involves staple ingredients and cooking techniques, and requires strict adherence. While most studies on medically restricted diets focus on diabetes, this study examines the education and advocacy work necessary to follow a gluten-free diet required by celiac disease.

Celiac disease (CD) is an auto-immune disorder triggered by gluten, a protein in wheat, barley, and rye. When persons with CD consume gluten or products containing gluten-derivatives (e.g., malt, malt flavoring, triticale), the immune response damages villi in the small intestine, causing gastrointestinal (GI) symptoms and malabsorption of nutrients and calories.[1] Untreated CD is linked to other auto-immune diseases, intestinal cancer, and malabsorption disorders (i.e., iron-deficiency anemia, osteopenia/osteoporosis). Treatment is lifelong adherence to a gluten-free (GF) diet, which entails eliminating glutenous breads, cereals, and pastas; foods with hidden gluten; and all foods cross-contaminated through contact with glutenous foods (Green & Jones 2006; Thompson 2008).

Persons with CD must be on guard when dining out, including dining at restaurants and friends' or family members' homes. To ensure that foods are safe, persons with CD must educate hosts and food service workers about CD and the GF diet. Putting their otherwise invisible illness on display in social settings brings the personal into full public view. I explore the social movement centered on CD and GF eating, and the everyday health advocacy necessary for dining successfully outside the home. Drawing on field research with CD support groups, national CD conferences, and interviews, I explore the determinants of everyday activism and compare those who embrace their role as everyday activists with those who resent and reject it.

CD AND THE GF DIET

Because small amounts of gluten trigger an autoimmune response, persons with CD must be vigilant to remain healthy. Cross-contamination is a problem and GF dining requires that chefs scrutinize ingredients and use clean equipment uncontaminated by gluten. Workers cannot pick croutons off a salad, cook steak on a grill used to brown breaded items, or plate foods using a ladle previously dipped in glutenous sauce, as these practices will contaminate the food. Clear communication with chefs and other food workers about safe ingredients and cooking techniques is therefore necessary to remain GF.

Reading and understanding product labels and knowing what to look for on a label, is also necessary for ensuring that foods are GF. The Food Allergen Labeling and Consumer Protection Act of 2004 (FALCPA) mandates that packaged products containing any of the top eight allergens, including wheat, be labeled in clear language. Because wheat is a primary source of gluten, CD movement leaders credit FALCPA with easing the burdens of following a GF diet. However, they argue that FALCPA did not go far enough because it did not identify *gluten* as a top allergen. Thus, rye and barley, two sources of gluten not among the top allergens, do not need to be declared on package labels, and are persistent sources of confusion. Malt and malt syrup (used in many cereals and processed foods) are glutenous ingredients derived from barley and persons with CD must commit these and other non-wheat glutenous ingredients to memory. While products labeled for institutional use must comply with FALCPA, customers must rely

on food service personnel to read labels correctly and accurately convey this information, making it difficult to guarantee the GF status of restaurant meals.

Although FALCPA mandated the development of a "gluten-free" labeling standard by 2008, it has not been finalized as of July 2010. Products voluntarily labeled "gluten-free" use varying cutoffs, although most follow the CODEX standard of less than 20 parts per million. Some labels warn that a product was manufactured in a facility that processes wheat. Because such advisories are voluntary, it is impossible to compare two similar products, one with the advisory, one without, as both may have been produced under similar conditions. This leads to additional confusion concerning the safety of products with advisory labels.

In addition to labeling flaws, persons with CD are confused by science and production processes. Some incorrectly think gluten is destroyed when heated or burned. Others incorrectly believe all alcoholic beverages are off-limits, even though distillation removes gluten. The use of shared equipment to produce glutenous and GF products is controversial, with some believing strongly that GF products must be made on dedicated lines (used only to produce GF foods) and others advocating that thorough cleaning between production runs will ensure safety.

The need to remain GF amid ambiguous labeling and misinformation makes dining outside the home difficult. Dining out requires educating others about gluten (both obvious and hidden sources), safe preparation and cooking methods, and advocating for gluten-free options. In short, dining out with CD requires engaging in everyday activism.

THE CD MOVEMENT AS AN EMBODIED HEALTH MOVEMENT

Health social movements (HSMs) have become more common over the past three decades, as individuals sharing a medical condition identify core experiences and forge cooperative problem-solving strategies (Allsop, Jones and Baggott 2004; Brown et al. 2004). HSM organizations collectively form a health consumer movement, with members and leaders relying on scientific and lay knowledge to press for structural change (Allsop, Jones and Baggott 2004; Brown et al. 2004). Centered on the social experience of disability and illness, the CD movement represents a specific type of HSM, an embodied health movement (EHM), in which the lived experience of illness is a central factor (Brown et al. 2004: 52–3). The stigmatizing nature of GI symptoms (with 50% suffering chronic diarrhea and gas) (Green and Jabri 2006; Weinberg and Williams 2005), the invisibility of the disease in asymptomatic forms (Green and Jones 2006), and the impact of the dietary treatment on social interactions involving food (Olsson et al. 2009) create a strong collective identity among persons with CD.

The U.S. CD movement consists of national advocacy groups such as the Celiac Disease Foundation, the Celiac Sprue Association, the Gluten Intolerance Group of North America (GIG), and the National Foundation for Celiac Awareness (NFCA); local and regional support groups; and university research centers. Movement leaders include elected officers and professional staff of national, regional, and local organizations, and physicians and dieticians working at academic and healthcare institutions associated with CD. Specific movement goals include increasing public awareness of CD, its symptoms, and diagnosis; expanding research on alternative treatments; improving food labels, including mandating declaration of gluten and supporting a uniform definition of gluten-free; promoting more varied, palatable, and healthful GF products; expanding GF restaurant offerings; and educating restaurant staff. Movement participants want food companies and restaurateurs to market GF products to them, making the movement's relationship with biomedicine and corporate America highly complex.

My focus is on individuals and the loosely arranged social movement communities they form, rather than the formal organizations to which they sometimes also belong. Buechler (1993: 223–4) argues that "formal organization[s] cannot be assumed to be the predominant or even the most common form for mobilizing." Within the CD movement, individual action has played a large role in facilitating growth in the number of establishments accommodating GF dining. While social movement organizations such as NFCA and GIG advocate for GF options via training and awareness programs, the everyday advocacy of rank and file members plays a more immediate, if less visible, role in communities across the U.S.

I examine rank and file members, those comprising the general membership of support groups, rather than movement leaders. In their study of feminist activism, Dauphinais, Barkan and Cohn (1992) operationalized rank and file activism as joining or giving money to an advocacy organization, or writing a letter to a public official expressing pro-movement views. They argue that these "low-risk activities" are a better representation of rank and file activism than the "more intense and structured involvement" typical of demonstrations and high-risk activities on which most social movement scholars focus (Dauphinais, Barkan and Cohn 1992: 336). While movement leaders visibly and actively pursue movement goals, rank and file members pursue an equally important form of everyday activism. Everyday activism includes health advocacy work required to engage in normal and mundane activities, including eating. In the context of CD, everyday activism includes advocating for GF menu options and educating others about CD and the GF diet. However, some everyday activists are more eager than others. While some persons adopt a GF diet for reasons other than celiac (e.g., treatment for autism, weight loss, or because they believe it is healthier), my focus is not on these "lifestyle" followers, but on those who follow the diet out of medical necessity.

METHODS

This chapter is based on a large ethnographic study of CD and GF eating. I attended monthly meetings and social gatherings (dinners, cooking classes, fund raisers, etc.) of four celiac support groups in the Northeastern United States, from September 2007 through July 2010, taking detailed field notes before, during, and after gatherings, and speaking informally with members. Groups hold regular meetings featuring a medical practitioner or other person knowledgeable about CD and the GF diet, or business that caters to the GF community. The two largest groups, each with approximately 60–100 monthly attendees, host a newcomer orientation before or after the meeting, at which detailed dietary information and bags of GF food donated by a large grocery store are shared. These two groups, and a third (with approximately 30–50 attendees), are formally structured, with a president and other elected positions, and each hosts an annual fund-raising walk, designating the proceeds to a university CD research center. The fourth and smallest group (with no more than 25 attendees) lacks a formal structure and does not hold fund-raising events. All four groups are affiliated with a national support group, although most rank and file members are inactive at the national level.

I also participated in web-based education seminars on CD, attended regional lectures and four education conferences of national CD organizations, and spoke informally with celiac experts (physicians, dieticians, and self-help authors) and persons with CD in attendance. I formally interviewed fifteen adult men and fifty-six adult women with CD, and nine family members of persons with CD, for a total of eighty interviews.

Participants' ages ranged from 19 to 79 years, with educational attainments spanning high school to completing a Ph.D. Two interviewees identified as Hispanic, while the remainder identified as white. Because CD is three times more common among women than men (Green and Jabri 2006; Loftus and Murray 2004) and is more prevalent among whites than African-Americans (Brar et al. 2006), the gender and racial profile of the sample is consonant with that of the diagnosed population.

Interviews averaged 90 minutes, were recorded, and fully transcribed. Interviews focused on respondents' illness narratives, the stories patients tell about their illness, treatment, or illness management regimen (Frank 1995; Kleinman 1988). This chapter focuses on how participants managed the diet across diverse social settings, revealing the everyday advocacy and activism necessary for dietary adherence.

I analyzed the ethnographic data using an inductive approach (Glaser and Strauss 1967; Strauss and Corbin 1998), generating descriptive codes suggested by the content of the transcript or field notes (Esterberg 2002; Strauss and Corbin 1998). This permitted me to examine in detail the social experience of CD, GF eating, and everyday activism from the point of view of persons with CD. To ensure confidentiality, I assign pseudonyms to all respondents and mask organizations, restaurants, and other locations.

DETERMINANTS OF EVERYDAY ACTIVISM

The nature of symptoms and treatment make most persons with CD everyday activists, although some accept this role more eagerly than others. The social nature of eating and the ubiquity of gluten in the American diet make the personal act of eating politically charged. Avoiding adverse symptoms and long-term health consequences by remaining GF challenges mainstream foodways. The necessary and constant attention to minute details of all stages of food preparation transforms the mundane act of eating into a form of everyday health activism. Persons with CD attempting to follow a GF diet must advocate for themselves in social situations involving food, including dining in restaurants and others' homes. The embodied nature of the disease means persons with CD cannot dine out without considering the health implications. If one knowingly or accidentally consumes gluten, bodily changes, some active and immediate, others invisible within the intestine, will ensue. Thus, for those with CD, dining out is a high-risk activity and most proceed cautiously.

Despite some overlap, respondents generally fell into one of three categories, depending on their level of everyday activism. *Non-activists* do not advocate for GF options and include the noncompliant, who avoid disrupting established foodways, and the ultra-compliant, who err on the side of caution and restrict their food consumption unnecessarily. *Reluctant activists* hesitate to advocate for GF options due to social embarrassment, etiquette, lack of trust, and a belief that effective education is impossible within a brief conversation. Finally, *eager activists* enthusiastically advocate for GF options by putting their private illness into full public view. Eager activists are lay experts who have been living with CD longer. They are more likely than others to equate gluten with poison, and construe GF food as a medicine and right.

These categories comprise a continuum, with non-activists and eager activists occupying the two extremes (see Figure 41.1). Length of diagnosis, knowledge acquisition, and the significance of a CD

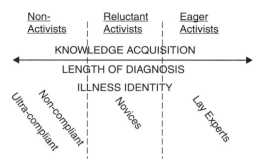

Figure 41.1 Continuum of CD Activism.

illness identity are related to activism. Generally, those diagnosed for longer periods, with greater knowledge of CD and the GF diet, and those for whom a celiac illness identity was especially salient were more likely to be eager activists.

NON-ACTIVISTS

Non-activists are fatalists who feel helpless in particular situations, especially dining out. The non-compliant non-activists do not adhere to the GF diet. They regularly and willingly consume glutenous foods, make few attempts to implement dietary changes, and feel powerless to alter established foodways. Ben, who does not belong to a support group, regularly "cheats" on the diet and manages symptoms by taking enzyme pills purporting to facilitate gluten digestion. His son was visiting the day we spoke and they planned to order pizza for dinner "to make it easy." He noted, "But, you know, I'm not supposed to eat it." When I asked what he would eat, he responded that he would eat the pizza and "take the pills." Such pills are widely criticized within the medical community as ineffective in halting the auto-immune reaction in CD. Nevertheless, Ben takes them regularly, prior to eating anything with known or suspected gluten. When dining out, he relies on the pills instead of instructing staff on ingredients and cross-contamination: "I have a bottle of these in each of our cars, so anytime we're out I have them with me because you don't know if they cross-contaminate ... It makes it a lot easier." Ease of dining was a key concern for Ben, a point he emphasized throughout our interview. Eating gluten was easier *for Ben* because he did not need to advocate for his dietary needs. Consuming gluten was easier for *his family*, who did not need to change their established foodways, and *for restaurant personnel*, who did not need to check ingredients or alter preparation methods. The enzyme pills worked well enough that Ben could withstand whatever GI discomfort consuming glutenous food might entail, despite the fact that intestinal damage was still occurring. The trade-off between avoiding GF advocacy and physical discomfort was one Ben was willing to accept if he did not need to disrupt established foodways. Despite having been diagnosed for two years, CD was not a large component of Ben's personal identity and whenever possible he minimized the extent to which CD and the GF diet impacted his social experience of food. Instead of putting his illness identity on public display by advocating for GF options, he downplays his illness identity by continuing to eat glutenous foods.

The *ultra-compliant* also do not advocate for GF options, but do so out of a strong commitment to remaining GF. Some have abundant knowledge about the GF-diet, understanding cross-contamination issues, hidden sources of gluten, and the different names under which gluten masquerades. They are unwilling to risk permitting anyone other than themselves to prepare their food, fearing it will be done incorrectly, and avoid social situations involving food as a result. Other ultra-compliant non-activists are uninformed about gluten sources, believing gluten resides in far more foods than is the case, and overly restrict their dining options as a precaution.

Confusion about safe and unsafe ingredients was a key rationale for why some respondents do not regularly or strongly advocate in social situations involving food. Knowledge of safe ingredients and cooking techniques is a necessary precursor to asking questions and offering instructions to ensure that food is uncontaminated. Lack of knowledge negatively impacts self-confidence, decreases everyday activism, and leads to unnecessary dietary limitations. Because of persistent misunderstandings about safe and unsafe ingredients that have only been partially resolved by FALCPA, some participants routinely avoided products and ingredients that are, in fact, GF. For example, Greg was not a support group member and was not highly informed about gluten sources. He previously enjoyed corn chips, but has given them up since going GF. When I mentioned that many conventional chips were GF, he was surprised, saying "I didn't know that," and immediately questioned companies' ability to keep chips free of cross-contamination. He concluded, "I just wouldn't chance it." Greg's ultra-compliance paired with his limited GF knowledge means that he may be unnecessarily restricting his diet and, consequently, his social and professional activities.

The only item Greg regularly consumes outside the home is black coffee. When travel prevents him from eating at home, he fasts, limiting excursions to a few days. Ultra-compliant fatalists like Greg feel powerless to change conventional foodways and do not advocate for GF options. Instead, they avidly avoid social situations involving food. Greg recalled missing several important family events, including weddings and graduations, because they necessitated longer trips. The last time Greg dined out was for an important business event six months prior. He took pains to emphasize his rationale for attending, noting the "very specific professional objective" of the dinner. For Greg, dining out is an event to be avoided, rather than a welcome social occasion. On the rare instance he does visit a restaurant Greg does not attempt to communicate his needs, maintaining, "My very specific dietary needs can't be satisfied. Avoiding food is pretty much what I need to do. It means no dining out." Plain meats, fish and chicken prepared in a clean pan, steamed vegetables or a baked potato are naturally GF items that most restaurants should be able to prepare on request. However, Greg was unaware of these options and never attempted to order them. In short, Greg's knowledge is so restricted that instead of reviewing menu options and ingredients with staff, he orders a menu item, pretends to eat, and makes excuses for not eating.

Jane was diagnosed less than two months when we spoke. She emphasized her difficulty maintaining an active social life post-diagnosis, recalling one occasion when she and a friend were planning a dinner out. After eliminating many of her favorite restaurants because she believed they could not accommodate her, Jane explained, "I finally said to her, 'The hell with it! Just come here, I'll fix something here.' And I cooked because it was less of a hassle than going out and trying to figure out what I could and couldn't have." Though Jane tried to locate a restaurant that could accommodate her, as a newcomer to the diet and her support group, she was unaware of local restaurants featuring GF options and felt more comfortable dining at home, where she could control the menu.

RELUCTANT ACTIVISTS

While reluctant activists advocate for GF options, they hesitate to do so. Like non-activists, many reluctant activists are novices lacking the knowledge to advocate effectively; but unlike non-activists, reluctant ones attempt it. Lorraine explained that being a novice prevented her from dining out more frequently: "We really stopped [dining out] for a while,

[but] now that I've learned what I can have we do go out a little bit more." Reluctant activists are hesitant to request changes in established foodways. They worry about inconveniencing others and dislike discussing ingredients and preparation methods with restaurant staff, friends and family, thus making a private issue public. Embarrassment, social etiquette, issues of trust, and beliefs about the ineffectiveness of GF education take center stage in their narratives. When advocacy fails or reluctant activists fail to advocate they may take chances by consuming suspect foods.

Embarrassment

Several respondents remarked that asking detailed questions of restaurant personnel was uncomfortable, even embarrassing. Melanie explained that she no longer enjoys dining out, which she called a "hassle" because of the need "to question and second guess everything." She assured me that she "ha[s] no problem conversing with the waiter," but noted that CD requires her "to be totally different now. You just hate to be different. You just want to get back with fitting in with the same old crowd and you can't. This is a disease you have to face head on . . . you always have to be aware and be your own advocate." Needing to always be aware of what she is eating and how it was prepared is a necessary chore that distinguishes Melanie's experiences from those of her friends.

Carrie repeatedly underscored how her shy demeanor and self-consciousness prevented her from being a more active advocate: "It's been three years, but I'm still not comfortable asking for the manager. People say it's good to educate people, but I never wanted to be a teacher. That's the hardest part." Questioning and instructing restaurant personnel made Carrie feel awkward in social situations: "A lot of people in [the support group] stress that you have to educate the wait staff, but I don't like being the center of attention. I've never been comfortable with that." Both Melanie and Carrie believe firmly that questioning restaurant staff is necessary to remain GF. However, they are reluctant to do so because questioning and instructing others makes them feel uncomfortable, partly because it calls attention to their illness and marks them as different, and partly because it violates entrenched rules of social decorum.

Social Etiquette

Many respondents expressed concern for matters of social etiquette. Leslie recalled an incident involving her well-intentioned relatives: "[My mother-in-law] was very proud that she purchased mustard she knew I could have, so I thanked her. And then my husband put out a squeeze container that I brought and explained that he was concerned about cross-contamination, but I whisked it away fearing she would be insulted." Leslie is careful to note that she thanked her mother-in-law for obtaining a safe brand of mustard, demonstrating an appropriate level of courtesy in response to the courtesy extended to her. She also acts quickly to minimize the insult her husband's continuing concern over cross-contamination might cause. Unfortunately, her father-in-law did cross-contaminate the fresh jar of mustard by "double dipping" his knife after using it on his hotdog bun. While Leslie's husband viewed the mustard incident "as an opportunity to educate his parents," she felt it was "not a good enough reason to insult them. It wasn't that important that I had mustard." Leslie's comments highlight the fine distinction many respondents make between educating and insulting others by pointing out or correcting their mistakes, and the tact required to skillfully maneuver such situations.

Melanie was similarly cautious when explaining her dietary restrictions to friends, as she felt they often "didn't want to hear it." She described how she handles dining at friends' homes to avoid socially uncomfortable situations: "I try to eat before I go, and then I just nibble on a salad and a lot of times they don't even have that, so then you make an excuse and just say that you're not hungry because they don't understand. You can explain it, but it's not what they want to hear . . . It's just from the way we grew up. You eat whatever's given to you and put on your plate." For Melanie, rules of social etiquette learned as a child demand that you "eat whatever's given to you." To do otherwise is to insult the host and exhibit bad manners. These etiquette rules (like her friends) are inflexible, even in situations of medical necessity. Instead of expecting her friends to accommodate her diet, Melanie accommodates her friends by eating in advance and not "making a fuss."

Later in our interview, Leslie described how she carefully introduces her dietary needs to restaurant staff:

> If they don't have a gluten-free menu I say, "I'm not giving you a hard time. I'm not a picky eater. I just need your help because I have a very bad food allergy." Normally when you open it that way it's not a problem. There's value in explaining that I'm not doing this to give you a hard time. I'm not asking you to leave the hamburger off the bun because I'm on Atkins.

Others made similar references to Atkins or vegetarian diets. Most were offended when people compared these to the GF diet and took pains to distinguish between them, stressing that Atkins and vegetarian diets are *voluntary*, whereas the GF diet is medically *necessary*. While vegetarians may be accused of being "picky" or giving wait staff "a hard time," people with CD cannot, as they have no choice. Leslie's careful approach to wait staff underscores respondents' sense that a fine line separates being picky and unjustly making work for restaurant personnel, and politely enlisting staff to create a safe meal because of medical necessity. Both how one approaches the situation and the rationale for making such requests differentiates them.

Respondents felt it was easier to make GF requests in restaurants than in friends' or family members' homes because norms of social etiquette were less flexible and the risk of insulting hosts was greater with friends and family. Recall that Leslie was more accommodating with her in-laws, and more assertive with restaurant personnel. Paying for a meal facilitates making special requests, while being a guest in another's home is a deterrent.

Issues of Trust

When available, most respondents preferred to dine in restaurants with GF menus, believing staff should have some knowledge of gluten and cross-contamination issues. Yet, as Carrie explained, "There are no guarantees," and persons with CD must trust that staff will prepare their meal correctly. Carrie continued: "I can't always trust even if they have a GF menu, so how can I trust places that don't? . . . All I have is their word that it's GF and they didn't pick off the croutons from the pre-made salad." Melanie agreed, saying:

> You have to put your trust in someone that they did the dish right so you don't get sick . . . You're always still thinking in the back of your mind, oh my god, do you think they prepared this correctly? Do you think they used the proper pans? . . . It's like you have to second guess everything now when you go out to eat.

Not trusting that restaurant staff will do what is required to prepare a GF meal is a key reason some respondents were reluctant to advocate in dining out situations. Some feared that if they were perceived as giving staff a "hard time," staff might sabotage their meal.

While dining at restaurants with GF menus increased respondents' confidence that the meal would be safe, ultimately reassurances rested on stereotypes. Respondents routinely disparaged teenage restaurant workers as uninformed safety risks. They viewed managers as more responsive than wait staff and "chefs" as more knowledgeable than "cooks." Thus, age and social status within the restaurant were determining factors in the level of trust respondents extended. Reputation and social standing of the restaurant also mattered, with higher class restaurants viewed as "safer bets" than middle-class or family style ones. Therefore, price affected trust in dining establishments both because higher priced restaurants were deemed safer, and because diners felt justified making special requests in higher priced environments.

Advocacy as Ineffective

Other reluctant activists believe strongly that educating food service personnel, friends, and family about the GF diet is impossible in the context of a brief conversation. Danielle explained that others often do not understand what gluten is: "You'll say, 'Does this have gluten in it?' and they'll say, 'No, it's sugar free.' You know, they think glucose." Karin recalled an incident at a well-known culinary school. Assuming the chef would have some knowledge of gluten because of his extensive culinary training, she asked her server to inquire if the main dish contained gluten. The server returned, claiming, "Oh no, Chef says only the finest semolina was used." Semolina is wheat and contains gluten.

Gabriella was diagnosed with CD as an infant and relied on her mother to advocate for her throughout primary and secondary school. As a college student, Gabriella learned to take responsibility for her diet, but her approach is decidedly reluctant. She complained, "I know you're supposed to say, 'I'm on this special diet.' Well at least that's what they say at these meetings that I go to . . . You're supposed to tell these people who don't understand this situation at all what's up, and something that's taken you years to understand yourself, you're supposed to explain to them in five minutes? Like that's possible?" Gabriella's point is well taken. Mastering the GF diet entails a steep learning curve, with most respondents admitting mistakes years after their diagnosis. It is therefore highly probable that a short conversation with someone unfamiliar with the diet will be insufficient to ensure a safe meal.

Although CD is an autoimmune disorder, in an earlier excerpt, Leslie recalled describing CD incorrectly as an "allergy" to restaurant staff. When I questioned her about the word "allergy," she explained that she deliberately used the inaccurate term:

> because people have a vision of having to call the ambulance because my throat has swollen shut. And that's ok for them to think that because if you explain that it's a dietary restriction, some people think that you can just have a little . . . You can have a little sugar if you have diabetes, you just take more insulin. Or you shouldn't have too much salt if you have high blood pressure. You should be reducing it, but people don't understand that it's all or nothing in this case.

According to many respondents, despite its inaccuracy, the term allergy carries more weight with restaurant personnel. Few people have heard of CD and even fewer understand what it means. Allergy, however, is a familiar term and conveys a powerful visual image. Moreover, it allows Leslie to avoid the dreaded descriptor of "dietary restriction," which many equate with moderation, rather than abstention.

Amy similarly bemoaned her friends' inability to comprehend the GF diet based on the term "diet," which implies weight loss:

> When you explain it you end up saying it's a gluten-free *diet* and that's the worst

because they immediately hear *diet* and think it's something that you're doing voluntarily, you know, for weight loss. So a lot of time I feel like the explanation was not even worth the time because people would just be like, "Well can't you quit your diet?"

In addition to the idea that diets are for weight loss, Gwen emphasized the related misconception that diets are temporary: "Friends have a hard time handling this diagnosis. They think it's like getting a cold. They keep saying 'Aren't you over that yet?' 'When will you not have to do that anymore?' They just can't believe that you're gonna have to do this for the rest of your life." Given the difficulty of overcoming these strong associations, many reluctant activists eventually stop trying.

Taking Chances

Despite sometimes advocating for GF options, reluctant activists may consume foods that are highly suspect out of convenience or to minimize making "extra work" for others. Gabriella spoke about "taking chances" with food, particularly when the possibility of cross-contamination is high. "I would just chance it, and then if I got sick I knew that I couldn't eat that again." Because she had been diagnosed as an infant, she rationalized taking chances by comparing the cumulative effect of her own gluten exposure to that of others diagnosed later in life. "I don't feel like it's that big of a deal for me because everyone else has been living with this for years and eating tons of [gluten], so it can't be doing that much damage to me. I mean, obviously it's doing damage, but the little bit that I chance is not even going to equal three months of just eating plain gluten." Gabriella emphasized that she does not intentionally eat obviously glutenous foods: "I don't go and eat Oreos, like I'm not stupid. It's pretty much like French fries, or if a hamburger's contaminated and I'm in a hurry, I'll take the bun off. You're not supposed to do that, but I absolutely hate sending it back. I feel like a huge jerk." To accommodate her busy schedule, minimize work for others, and avoid feeling "like a huge jerk," Gabriella takes chances in restaurants by eating foods she knows or suspects are contaminated, using her own embodied response to gauge whether or not she can safely do so again in the future.

Sheila explained her strategy for dealing with questionable food while attending a community event. She diligently avoided the pizza and crackers, which were obviously not GF, but took a chance on the cheese and vegetables (which could have been cross-contaminated on the buffet table) and the dip (which could have been made with glutenous ingredients). Given the uncomfortable and embarrassing GI symptoms contamination can cause, Sheila took a calculated risk: "I timed it so that if I do get symptoms, which usually start about an hour after I eat something, I should be home by then."

EAGER ACTIVISTS

Unlike non-activists and reluctant ones, eager activists advocate strongly for GF options in social situations involving food. These activists carefully explain the GF diet, including hidden gluten and cross-contamination, thus putting their illness in the public eye. Clive explained:

> I always carry a little card that says I've got celiac disease, that I require gluten-free food, and I always ask that they take that to the chef and ask that they recommend something or make something for me. Usually they come back and say, "Well, we can do you a salad with no croutons or we can do meat, plain meat with some vegetables." That's ok for me. And obviously if the server doesn't understand, I ask for the manager.

Asking for the manager when a server does not comprehend his dietary needs strikes Clive as "obvious," and he does this without hesitation whenever necessary.

Louise also offers detailed instructions and asks multiple questions to ensure her meal is GF. She recalled ordering a pork chop at a chain restaurant:

> The waiter came from the kitchen and said "The chef said he'll make that for you but not give you the pasta; he'll give you plain rice. And he won't give you the sauce," he said, "but otherwise the food will be gluten-free." So the meal came out and the meat looked like it had gravy on it and I thought oh no! So I called the waiter back and I said, "I can't eat this. It's got gravy on it. He probably made it with flour."

Louise eagerly advocates for GF options, asking questions before ordering and again after receiving what appeared to be suspect food. After consulting with the chef, the waiter reported that the gravy was a GF wine reduction, but Louise did not dare consume it without double checking first.

Eager activists regularly send incorrectly prepared dishes back, as when a salad is delivered with croutons or a steak is served on toast. Rhonda recalled an incident at an upscale restaurant when she ordered fish, one of the few menu items she could eat:

> I said, "No breadcrumbs because I'm allergic to gluten, so no wheat, rye or barley." And it came covered with crumbs so I said, "I said no breadcrumbs." And he responds, "Oh, they're not breadcrumbs, they're cracker crumbs." And I said, "Well I also said no gluten." And so he takes it back in and just scraped it off and brought it back, but I said, "You're going to have to fix a new piece of fish."

While they suffer some negative social consequences, such as eating after other dining companions when they send dishes back, or annoying some friends and family with their dietary needs, eager activists would rather suffer these relatively minor inconveniences than eat contaminated food and experience negative symptoms for days or weeks as a result.

Eager activists call ahead of special events to speak with caterers or restaurant personnel to request a GF meal and instruct them on how to prepare it. Stacey made extensive preparations prior to a wedding brunch, which involved speaking to the caterer, bringing some of her own food (something not all establishments will permit), and working closely with brunch staff: "I had my own thing. I took it in, handed it to the waitress and she plated it like everybody else's plate and when people went to the buffet, they came and brought it to me and nobody knew any different." Because staff plated her food for her, Stacey did not need to visit the buffet table where cross-contamination might be an issue. This also minimized differences between Stacey and other diners, allowing her to feel normal.

Eager activists also diverge from reluctant ones in how they frame eating, gluten, and GF food. Diagnosed six years prior to our interview, Geena is an eager activist for herself and her daughter, repeatedly referring to gluten as "poison" and GF foods as "medicine": "It's your prescription. Just because it isn't bottled in a pill or a drink doesn't mean you shouldn't take it as seriously as if it was in an IV or pill. It's your prescription to live longer and be free of symptoms, pain and other diseases." Likening GF food to medicine helped Rhonda justify its expense: "It's like medicine. We would figure out a way to get my medicine if I needed it and so that's what we did."

In contrast to reluctant activists, and in part because of their greater likelihood of framing gluten as poison and GF food as medicine, eager activists were less likely to feel guilty for challenging established

foodways and more likely to view GF food as a right rather than a favor. Geena argued forcefully, "A celiac person should not feel guilty because we're different. We have rights just like everybody else, but society makes us feel like we're sorry. I'm sorry I asked for that time to talk to the manager about my food. I'm sorry that you're busy and I'm asking you all the ingredients in your dish. It's terrible that we should feel that way, but we tend to." Geena believes strongly that she should not feel guilty about her dietary needs, even though she sometimes does. Viewing GF food as medicine and a right helps buffer feelings of guilt, but does not eliminate them.

Finally, eager activists believe that educating others and advocating for GF options benefits themselves and the wider celiac community. Rose explained, "I'm still explaining it after 30 years, but at this point I feel I'm educating people." Respondents who had been diagnosed for ten or more years acknowledged that GF eating is easier today compared to when they were first diagnosed, and credited the increased number of diagnosed persons and the everyday health activism of others for this positive change.

CONCLUSION

Most studies of compliance with medically mandated dietary modifications highlight the significant role of social support (Gallant 2003; Levy 1983; van Dama et al. 2005; Walker 2005). This study illuminates how persons with celiac disease obtain social support for a gluten-free diet via everyday activism. Whether or not GF foods are available in social settings, and the ability and willingness of others to follow preparation guidelines to avoid cross-contamination are forms of social support that significantly affect people's ability to follow a GF diet. Advocacy is important for expanding GF options and raising awareness. This research elucidates the key contributions of rank and file members (rather than CD and GF movement leaders), and highlights the important task individuals (rather than organizations) play in spreading the word about CD and the GF diet.

Dining out offers opportunities for educating others about CD and the GF diet, and promoting and expanding GF dining options. However, whereas Dauphinais et al. (1992) classify rank and file activism as involving "low risk" activities, for persons with celiac, dining out cannot be considered low risk. The risks of contamination and dangers to one's health are high whenever a person with CD dines outside the home, thereby necessitating advocacy to remain symptom-free. As a result, rank and file members constitute the greatest single source of advocacy within the CD movement and a large proportion of those with CD engage in everyday activism when dining out. Despite the importance of advocacy, persons with CD vary in their level of activism, with reluctant activists advocating for GF options only when convenient, non-activists avoiding advocacy at every turn, and eager activists advocating regularly and forcefully.

Reluctant activists were ambivalent about advocating for GF food, viewing it as a problem and favor that had to be carefully negotiated with others. Requesting GF options was embarrassing, as it implied special treatment, and required tact and respect for rules of social etiquette. Reluctant activists did not always trust others to prepare GF meals, and questioned the effectiveness of everyday advocacy. As a result, many reluctant activists took chances by consuming suspect food, skipped meals to avoid awkward social interactions, and felt guilty for asking others to alter established foodways. Reluctant activists were therefore hesitant to adopt a strong CD illness identity and were less likely than eager activists to put that identity on public display.

Non-activists were the least knowledgeable about GF options, and tended to overestimate the difficulty of obtaining GF meals or underestimate the importance of remaining GF. The non-compliant non-activists "cheated" on the diet regularly, minimizing the health effects, while the ultra-compliant took an extreme position by evading most social situations involving food. While ultra-compliant non-activists identify strongly with CD, their lack of knowledge prevents them from advocating effectively. Non-activists thereby avoid everyday advocacy and do not advance movement goals.

My study demonstrates the strong influence of social and cultural norms on both CD and GF advocacy and compliance with a GF diet. Cultural norms dictating that one should eat what they are served or completely clean their plate discourage GF advocacy. Questioning hosts about ingredients and cooking techniques seems rude within the context of these larger cultural norms, contributing to reluctant activism. The generalized social pattern of ordering off a pre-set menu in restaurants also discourages GF diners from making special requests to accommodate their dietary needs. In short, reluctant activists and non-activists demonstrate clearly that established foodways are a deterrent to advocacy. Because advocacy is necessary for dietary adherence when dining outside the home, established foodways are also a deterrent to compliance with the GF diet.

"Cheating" or "taking chances" by consuming known or suspected glutenous foods was often an attempt to hide one's illness identity. Avoiding social situations involving food was also a way to avert the potential social conflict and embarrassment frequently reported by reluctant activists. Both hiding and avoidance strategies are also reported by patients who lose the ability to eat and must obtain nourishment from feeding tubes (Walker 2005). This study therefore demonstrates that medical dietary modifications, in addition to the more extreme absence of eating, have significant social ramifications that are linked with social identity issues.

Eager activists in this study illuminate the personal beliefs and social constructs that can temper the power of established foodways, leading to higher levels of advocacy and dietary compliance. Eager activists were the most informed about the GF diet and had been diagnosed longer. Because they had lived with CD longer, they were more likely than both reluctant activists and non-activists to have incorporated CD as a central component of their personal identity and were less willing to compromise on the diet as a result. Instead of a problem, they viewed GF food as a medical solution and prescription for good health to which they had a right. Research on compliance with medically restrictive diets may therefore benefit from an examination of other studies that construe healthful food as a basic human right, while the CD and GF movement may find allies with other social movements employing a rights discourse (especially the anti-hunger or food security movement).

With ethnographic work such as this, it is difficult to generalize beyond the sample employed. Nevertheless, it is clear that for this sample, length of time diagnosed, the salience of a celiac illness identity, and knowledge acquisition were related to everyday activism. Additional research should test these relationships and identify other determinants of everyday activism.

NOTE

1. CD is distinct from wheat allergy and gluten intolerance. Wheat allergy involves a different autoimmune response (IgE antibodies) and produces an immediate reaction that may include inflammation, respiratory distress, and shock. Gluten intolerance involves difficulty digesting gluten that is resolved once gluten is removed from the diet. With wheat allergy or gluten intolerance, unpleasant symptoms

subside quickly and do not cause long-term damage (Green and Jones 2006).

WORKS CITED

Allsop, Judith, Kathryn Jones, and Rob Baggott. 2004. "Health Consumer Groups in the UK: A New Social Movement?" *Sociology of Health & Illness*, 26(6): 737–56.

Brar, Pardeep, Ann R. Lee, Suzanne K. Lewis, Govind Bhaget, and Peter Green. 2006. "Celiac Disease in African-Americans." *Digestive Diseases & Sciences*, 51: 1012–15.

Brown, Phil, Stephen Zavestoski, Sabrina McCormick, Brian Mayer, Rachel Morello-Frosch, and Rebecca Gasior Altman. 2004. "Embodied Health Movements: New Approaches to Social Movements in Health." *Sociology of Health & Illness*, 26(1): 50–80.

Buechler, Steven M. 1993. "Beyond Resource Mobilization? Emerging Trends in Social Movement Theory." *The Sociological Quarterly*, 34(2): 217–35.

Dauphinais, Pat Dewey, Steven Barkan, and Steven Cohn. 1992. "Predictors of Rank and File Feminist Activism: Evidence from the 1983 General Social Survey." *Social Problems*, 39(4): 332–44.

DeVault, Marjorie. 1991. *Feeding the Family: The Social Organization of Caring as Gendered Work*. Chicago: University of Chicago.

Esterberg, Kristin. 2002. *Qualitative Methods in Social Research*. NY: McGraw-Hill.

Food Allergen Labeling and Consumer Protection Act of 2004, Public Law 108–282, Title II (2004).

Frank, Arthur. 1995. *The Wounded Storyteller: Body, Illness and Ethics*. Chicago: University of Chicago Press.

Gallant, Mary. 2003. "The Influence of Social Support on Chronic Illness Self-management: A Review and Directions for Research." *Health Education & Behavior*, 3: 170–95.

Glaser, Barry and Anselm Strauss. 1967. *The Discovery of Grounded Theory*. Chicago: Aldine.

Green, Peter and Bana Jabri. 2006. "Celiac Disease." *Annual Review of Medicine* 57: 207–21.

Green, Peter and Rory Jones. 2006. *Celiac Disease: A Hidden Epidemic*. New York: HarperCollins.

Kleinman, Arthur. 1988. *The Illness Narratives: Suffering, Healing, and the Human Condition*. New York: Basic Books.

Levy, Rona L. 1983. "Social Support and Compliance: A Selective Review and Critique of Treatment Integrity and Outcome Measurement." *Social Science & Medicine*, 17(18): 1329–38.

Loftus, Conor G. and Joseph A. Murray. 2004. "Celiac Disease." Retrieved September 9, 2008. Available: http://acg.gi.org/patients/gihealth/pdf/celiac.pdf

Lupton, Deborah. 1996. *Food, the Body and the Self*. Thousand Oaks, CA: Sage.

Maurer, Donna. 2002. *Vegetarianism: Movement or Moment?* Philadelphia: Temple University Press.

Olsson, Cecilia, Phil Lyon, Agneta Hornell, Annelli Ivarsson, and Ylva Mattsson Sydner. 2009. "Food that Makes You Different: The Stigma Experienced by Adolescents with Celiac Disease." *Qualitative Health Research* 19(7): 976–984.

Strauss, Anselm and Juliet Corbin. 1998. *Basics of Qualitative Research, 2nd ed.* Thousand Oaks, CA: Sage.

Thompson, Tricia. 2008. *The Gluten Free Nutrition Guide*. New York: McGraw-Hill.

van Dama, Henk A., Frans G. van der Horsta, Lut Knoopsb, Richard M. Ryckmanc, Harry F.J.M. Creboldera, Bart H.W. van den Borneb. 2005. "Social Support in Diabetes: A Systematic Review of Controlled Intervention Studies." *Patient Education & Counseling*, 59: 1–12.

Walker, Ashby. 2005. "In the Absence of Food: A Case of Rhythmic Loss and Spoiled Identity for Patients with Percutaneous Endoscopic Gastrostomy Feeding Tubes." *Food, Culture & Society*, 8: 161–180.

Weinberg, Martin and Colin Williams. 2005. "Fecal Matters: Habitus, Embodiments, and Deviance." *Social Problems*, 52(3): 315–36.

42

The Year of Eating Politically[1]

Chad Lavin

Wendell Berry famously declared that "eating is an agricultural act," and recent trends in food activism have announced that eating is a political, economic, environmental, aesthetic, and ethical act as well.[2] High profile debates about free range eggs, grass fed beef, genetically modified corn, rising obesity rates, and the corporate control of seed technologies have captured the American imagination, producing not only a tremendous market for value added and responsible foods but also ubiquitous commentaries implicating the American food system in issues ranging from global warming and border security to intellectual property rights and national sovereignty. This politicization of the American diet often disrupts some of the more blindly fetishistic mechanisms of global capital by illuminating how a standard of living depends upon cheap, convenient calories often derived from the brutal exploitation of workers, animals, and land. Much more than parallel campaigns opposing sweatshop labor in the apparel industry, the focus on food immerses consumers in the contradictions of capital, emphasizing how diners literally incorporate these contradictions at every meal.

At the same time, current trends in food politics often correspond to a model of citizenship and responsibility that impoverishes traditional modes of political action and democratic control. Reducing politics to consumerism and political economy to ethics, current approaches to responsible foods tend to reflect the actual foreclosure of political opportunity. By locating political action to the actual and metaphorical space of the market, these trends reflect a reduction of political discourse to the terms of global capitalism to the extent that it is only in the rhetoric of free consumption that freedom can be imagined. These trends thus veer toward postpolitical fantasies that differ in content – but not in form – from the neoliberal promise of a harmonious society governed only by voluntary contracts and consumer sovereignty. Though food activism is typically couched in promises of democracy and equality, it often erects barriers to these ideals by charging the market with the responsibility for realizing them.

This trend is most evident in the recent shift from "organic" to "local" as the mark of responsible food. Despite their manifest overlap, these movements are rooted in distinct idioms that respond to very specific historical conditions; both are animated by anxieties about the health of individual bodies and bodies politic, but the turn to locals reflects a realization that this health is threatened less by industrial pollution and nuclear annihilation than by the erosion of national sovereignty and the exhaustion of the earth's oil supplies. But like its predecessor, the dominant articulation of the promise of local foods reflects more than anything else a deep suspicion of conventional politics and the wholesale colonization of the political imaginary by the logic of the market.

LOCAL IS THE NEW ORGANIC

Histories of organic foods in the U.S. invariably point to the 1960s, a periodization that owes to scientific, political, and ideological developments of the decade. Before the invention and rapid appropriation of chemical pesticides and fertilizers in the 1940s, all foods were what would today pass for "organic." And between Rachel Carson's Silent Spring (1962), which catalyzed concerns about chemical pesticides such as DDT, and Frances Moore Lappe's Diet for a Small Planet (1971), which tied global hunger to the industrialization of the American diet, Americans saw a rapid proliferation of books and organizations promoting a return to small-scale, organic agriculture and alternative diets (vegetarianism, macrobiotics) linking food choices not only to concerns about public health and global inequality, but also to individual authenticity, social solidarity, and the ethics of capitalist exchange. Symbolized by the Robin Hood Commission's 1969 christening of a vacant Berkeley lot "People's Park" in order to grow and distribute free meals, the organic foods movement has always been firmly rooted in and hardly distinguishable from the politics and ideals of the 1960s counterculture.

If rooting organic foods in this romanticized decade is both convenient and stereotypical, it is also illuminating for its demonstration of how even this most idealistic of countercultures remained enamored with a populist do-it-yourself ethos and belief in American entrepreneurialism that has always evoked a suspicion of institutional politics. This ethos would seem to be at odds with the culture's clear concerns about social justice, but a focus on food often opens into any number of conflicting issues and values. Attention to food reveals our bodies as complex assemblages inexorably implicated in other assemblages – not only the molecular assemblages that organize nutrition and ecology, but industrial assemblages of production and distribution, economic assemblages of labor and exchange, and cultural assemblages of cuisine and class.[3] As the artifact that most visibly demonstrates the unavoidability of these assemblages, food often contains our most distilled and intensified political commitments.

In the case of organics, these commitments have always been somewhat contradictory. Julie Guthman, in a comprehensive study of organic farming in California, identifies four broad concerns animating the organics movement: the alienating nature of industrial production, the health effects of processed foods, the social justice concerns endemic to the counterculture, and the environmental impact of industrial pollutants. But these concerns have rarely added up to a coherent political program, and so while the movement has always been organized around a broadly conceived back-to-the-land ethos that was a reaction to postwar suburbanization, the movement has typically found itself promoting rival (and often bluntly incompatible) value systems – one promoting social solidarity and civic engagement, and another promoting individual autonomy and "agrarian populism."[4]

Similarly, though Samuel Fromartz's summary claim that "organic food was supposed to be pure, wholesome, natural, and small-scale, a true alternative to conventional food" seems straightforward enough, it is curious that purity would be one of the organizing themes of the organics movement given that the foods the movement defines itself against – the processed foods and chain restaurants developed through the 1950s – were promoted primarily for their hygienic and sterilized packaging.[5] Organic food and fast food both capitalized on an American "obsession with food and filth;" just as restaurant franchises promised the same hygienic facilities at every location, organics allowed eaters to "purge oneself of the dirty things modern eating put in one's system" by eating "whole foods" uncontaminated by artificial sweeteners, preservatives, pesticides, and hormones, and by developing a food chain (and eventually a national economy) uncorrupted by fossil fuels and capitalist science.[6] So while organics promised a relationship with the land and one's food that was not mediated by industrial machinery, chemical toxins, or dubious profit maximizing enterprises, it also traded in an ideal of individual authenticity more typically associated with liberal politics.

Following Mary Douglas, we might see this midcentury obsession with dirt as indicative of broader concerns about political order. Just as Douglas illustrates how concerns about cleanliness typically reflect concerns about order more generally (the dietary prescriptions of Leviticus, for instance, have less to do with hygiene than with maintaining a covenant with God), it becomes clear that chain restaurants appeal because they offer not just protection against invasive bacteria, but predictability in an increasingly complex world.[7] Similarly, the appeal of organics lies beyond concerns about toxins in the industrial food supply, capturing instead much broader concerns about the corruption of the natural and political worlds. In his history of "the countercuisine," Warren Belasco explains how the movement saw the corrupted products of the industrial food supply as symbols of the corruption of American society:

> Wonder Bread ... aptly symbolized the white flight of the 1950s and 1960s. To make clean bread, ... bakers removed all colored ingredients (segregation), bleached the remaining flour (suburban school socialization), and then, to prevent discoloring decay, added strong preservatives and stabilizers.
>
> (law enforcement)[8]

It certainly did not hurt that the same corporations targeted for producing chemically laden food (e.g., Dow) were also implicated in manufacturing the napalm and Agent Orange that were being used in Vietnam.[9]

Just like the countercultural assemblage of which it was a part, the organics movement eventually found its way into a more conventional capitalist market. This actually happened quite rapidly in 1989, after 60 Minutes aired a report about Alar, a pesticide and probable human carcinogen then in wide use on apple crops. Within a year of this broadcast, the EPA banned Alar, Newsweek's cover declared "A Panic for Organic," and the US government passed the Organic Foods Production Act (OFPA) establishing the first formal regulations for the production, certification, and marketing of organic foods.[10] Within fifteen years, organics would metastasize into a $15 billion industry with firms like Heinz, General Mills, and ConAgra owning some of the most recognizable organic brands and with critics positioning "Big Organic" as an industry on the order of "Big Oil" and "Big Pharma."[11]

One could certainly predict conflict and growing pains in an organics movement linked into both the 1960s counterculture and Reagan-era concerns about individual health. And the assemblage of organic foods and the struggle of nonwhite peoples might contrast dramatically with the assemblage that links them to individual health and that sent throngs of shoppers to upscale grocers like Whole Foods in the 1990s. But it was surely only a matter of time before Big Food found a way to capitalize on the anxiety over industrial filth. As organics grew, it continued to thrive on a perceived deliverance from toxicity. In either case, it promised reconciliation with a purer, more natural order that was threatened or abandoned by industrial society and the new technologies symbolized by Twinkies, TV dinners, and white bread. So like the 1960s itself, the story of organics is by now a well-rehearsed narrative of dashed hopes, capitalist cooptation, and corporate corruption, such that, by 2006, retail leviathan Wal-Mart was selling organic produce and organic spinach had been tainted by E. coli 0157, a toxic bacteria that owes its very existence to the industrial farming practices that organics ostensibly opposed.

This disenchantment with organics has given rise to one of the more popular genres of food writing and narrative nonfiction in the last five years, something we might call "adventures in immediate food." In this genre, a mix of investigative journalism and public diary, writers investigate the operations of Big Food and attempt to develop a more immediate relationship with their own food. The genre's prototype is Michael Pollan's The Omnivore's Dilemma, in which the author investigates four distinct kinds of meals by systematically tracing the supply chains leading to each. Purchasing an "industrial meal" at McDonald's, Pollan follows the ingredients back to Iowa corn farms and Persian Gulf oil fields; procuring ingredients for a "Big Organic" meal from Whole Foods, he visits the corporate farms that the chain relies upon for vast quantities of organic foods; his "beyond organic" meal is made of ingredients garnered during his week living and working on a self-sustaining family farm in Virginia; and the book's final chapter chronicles the "Perfect Meal," comprising ingredients that Pollan has grown, foraged, or killed with his own two hands. This experiment in self-reliance proved a huge bestseller when it was released in the Spring of 2006, but it is anything but unique. In 2007 alone, the novelist Barbara Kingsolver, environmental writer Bill McKibben, and Canadian journalists Alisa Smith and JB MacKinnon each published their own books chronicling their yearlong adventures eating immediate foods, while The New Yorker ran a chronicle of Adam Gopnik's more audacious attempt to spend a week eating only food raised in the agricultural desert of New York City.[12] As a result of these and other books and some popular websites by journalists and food activists (100milediet.org, eatlocalchallenge.com, locavore.org) Time Magazine ran a cover proclaiming "Forget Organic. Eat Local" and Oxford University Press declared "locavore" to be the Word of the Year for 2007.[13]

Clearly, if there is a trend in responsible food, it is away from organics and toward locals.[14] And without overstating the distinction between local and organic foods movements, it does seem clear that if the villains in the organics movement were DDT and Alar, that role is played in the local foods narrative by "food miles" – the geographic distance food travels "from field to fork." One significance of this shift from the composition to the provenance of food is that the organic focus on chemicals draws attention to contamination and environmental runoff, whereas the locavore focus on distance draws attention to resources squandered in storing and transporting food. Put another way, organics is animated by concerns over purity, locals by efficiency. If organics exhibited anxieties about pollution, locals is quite specifically about peak oil.

I do not mean to overstate the distance between these two appeals for a revolution in our food supply; the issues and often the principals are the same in either case. Samuel Fromartz's Organic, Inc., for instance, treats locals as (literally) one chapter in a broader movement. But Bill McKibben offers a telling illustration of the distinction. In The End of Nature (1989), an early and still canonical warning about global warming, McKibben argued that scientific hubris had facilitated the wholesale colonization of "nature" such that there is (or soon will be) no undomesticated realm with which humans can commune. And in Enough (2003), he argued that the same hubris, now wielding nano- and bio-technologies, has destroyed humanity. In each case, the organizing logic was contamination, and the result was a story of (industrial or genetic) pollution. By 2007, however, if McKibben's tune was the same, his emphasis was not. In Deep Economy, the metaphorics of pollution has given way to that of spatiality; McKibben is now much less interested in purity than he is in locality; if the threat before was contamination, now it is distance. To be sure, the peril looming in Deep Economy is not contamination and the transgression of species boundaries, but environmental collapse due to the exhaustion of the world's oil supplies.

These arguments are not mutually exclusive, but their frames are quite distinct. The earlier books focus on the relations between species (we are species conquerors in The End of Nature; hybrids in Enough), whereas the latter one focuses on the relations between spaces; the earlier books speak to issues of species purity and individual integrity, the latter to issues of energy conservation and territoriality. Note this same shift in social theory more generally, with an earlier decade's fascination with cybernetics and hybridity (Haraway, et. al.) giving way to a focus on borders and sovereignty (Hardt and Negri, et. al.).[15] Following Douglas, we might see McKibben's earlier books as symptomatic of an anxiety about individual integrity in an age of media saturation and chemical living; his latest book to an anxiety about territorial borders in an age of globalization.

There is another significance of the shift from organics to locals. For locavores, the relevant currency for evaluating food systems is not price or environmental runoff, but rather calories. McKibben, for instance, notes how frozen peas burn an absurd number of "fossil fuel calories" in order to deliver hardly any "food calories," and Pollan notes a deplorable exchange rate for organic lettuce (57 fossil fuel calories burned for each for each food calorie delivered).[16] This attention to a caloric general equivalent opens into a strictly economic and properly thermodynamic understanding of food in which each object and link in the food chain is but a bearer of energy to be transferred to another through metabolism. This is quite explicit when McKibben and Pollan talk about our industrial food system as

essentially a machine for converting vast stores of petro-calories into digestible human food, just as a pastoral food system is a machine for converting solar calories and human labor power into digestible human food.[17] With calories as the general equivalent, locavores measure foods in terms of how much energy they deliver or squander, and they valuate national diets in the same way that economists calculate deficits and surpluses. Ultimately, locavores argue that the industrial food system, like the bloated US economy, operates at a loss, consuming many more calories than it delivers.[18] The locavore critique thus parallels concerns about the US national economy, and the debate over local food is inseparable from concerns about global geopolitics – especially the wars in the Middle East, the weakening US dollar, and the looming environmental crises of peak oil and climate change.

In this light, local is the new organic not because organics was co-opted by agribusiness, but because the organic ideal fails to speak to the defining crises of this new century – not only environmental and energy crises, but also the more immediately political crisis of sovereignty under the novel political formation of Empire. For if Cold War politics was organized around a grand opposition between East and West and US foreign policy was organized around a prophylactic pursuit of "containment," communications and financial technologies of recent decades have facilitated a compression of time-space, such that the dominant political anxieties so far this century – immigration, terrorism, global trade, and national sovereignty – have all surrounded the enduring viability of the territorial borders that underlie the institutions of governance. The renewed US commitment to "nation building" abroad, regional arrangements such as NAFTA and the EU that attempt to forge political alliances around populations sharing nothing but location, and crude efforts at border vigilantism – each of these trends endeavors to reassert traditional notions of space in response to the real political crisis defined by the challenge to state borders and what Michael Hardt calls a "decline of the distinction between inside and outside."[19]

In other words, local foods is but one symptom of a broader concern with political space, when traditional notions of space would seem to be collapsing. And to be sure, the significance of this collapse cannot be overstated: global politics since the 17th Century has been organized around the establishment and protection of clearly delineated spaces – with a clear distinction between public and private space, with the partition of common land into discrete estates, and with the relevant actors being states (not nations) confined by borders and occupying territories.[20] The ideal of political representation is anchored in the establishment of a fixed population bound to a particular territory over which the government has authority; the institutions charged with democratic governance are essentially tied to spaces. As Hardt and Negri have argued, what is at stake in 21st Century politics is not merely the current organization of governance and sovereignty, but the very notion of sovereignty itself. What is at stake in local foods is not only particular landscapes and communities, but the very idea of community itself.

TWO DISTINCT ALIENATIONS

Alongside the shift from chemicals to calories as the metric for responsible food, the locavore movement has also introduced as one of its primary virtues sociability. For if organics promises healthy land and pure bodies, locavores explicitly promise strong communities with immediate bonds between consumers and producers. Brian Halweil's esteemed Eat Here opens by noting how local food economies "build solidarity between farmers and their urban neighbors" and rests on the claim that the movement's appeal lies in its "preservation of the social value of good food in connecting people with each other, their communities, and their land."[21] With the standard refrain that farmers markets are more sociable spaces than supermarkets, facilitating more numerous and more meaningful conversations, this literature emphasizes that local foods build strong communities, implicitly assuming that weak communities are one of the primary concerns of political life today. McKibben, directly but hardly uniquely, argues that consumers are willing to pay a premium for local food precisely because conventional food offers a "surplus of individualism and a deficit of companionship."[22] Clearly, this literature appeals specifically to a loneliness that is presumed to be part of the urban experience.

Sociability was never a central claim of the organics movement, though that movement did respond directly to an alienation endemic to what Richard Bulliet calls "postdomestic" society in which very few Americans lived on or near farms.[23] Writing more narrowly about animals, Bulliet argues that because "people live far away, both physically and psychologically" from the origins of their food, they have come to experience "feelings of guilt, shame, and disgust" when they think about how their food is produced. That is, the mass migration from working farms through the 20th Century created an alienated and anxious population, eager to assuage their guilt and reestablish their connection to the land via an ethical commitment to things like organic foods and vegetarianism.

This postdomestic guilt resonates with Nietzschean ressentiment, and this is probably why Guthman finds an uneasy alliance between social and an individualistic values among both producers and consumers of organic foods. Promising an authentic relationship with nature, a relationship relinquished in the move to a suburban landscape and a relationship celebrated in a nostalgic model of American freedom, organics romantically conjures both a world of social and ecological reconciliation as well as one of strong, autonomous individuals. As such, it feeds on guilt about both the decadence of consumer society as well as the violence of capitalist markets. Michael Pollan's indictment of Whole Foods turns entirely on his claim that the chain capitalizes on this guilt with a marketing campaign that conjures a less mediate relationship with the land, even though the grocer relies on the same international commodity chains and regional distribution networks as other supermarkets.[24] While some tie Whole Foods' tremendous success in recent years to an environmental awakening or just another health-consciousness fad, the real lesson of this simulated pastoral's success might be that ressentiment is a growth industry.

But the rhetoric of community that pervades the locavore literature evokes a hopeful, rather than resentful, nostalgia. Emphasizing the provenance rather than the constitution of food, locavores promote a joy that is afforded by assemblages with peoples, cultures, and places. Though appeals to locals maintain the presuppositions of the organics movement regarding purity (the E. coli outbreaks of 2006 energized the locals more than the organics movement), locavores are clearly less concerned about biological purity than about alienation from a cultural and territorial history. It may be that the appeal to purity rings increasingly hollow to a population increasingly inured to chemical living such that a full 50% of Americans take at least one prescription medication every day.[25] But the point is that its model of authenticity is not biological, but rather cultural and geographical.

Localism, thus, appears as one more symptom of the political condition of postmodernity, of globalization, or of Empire. For just as Harvey argues that

19th Century social theory (Marx, Weber) was preoccupied with issues of temporality because the industrial revolution had fundamentally altered the rhythms of life and the experience of time, the contemporary preoccupation with locality arises from the disruption of space pursuant to recent developments in communication and financial technologies. The creation of non-localizable spaces on the internet; the blurring of public and private spaces by Total Information Awareness and the ubiquitous voyeurism of reality television and MySpace; the blurring of workplace and home by the some 25 million American who worked from home in 2006; and the concentration of political power in international finance organizations rather than territorially bound states – each of these trends upsets established ideas of what it means to occupy a space. And since established political institutions (national sovereignty, representative government, and private property) are all predicated on Enlightenment understandings of fixed borders and reliably discrete spaces, the stakes and disorientations of this disruption would be difficult to overstate. As Parkins and Craig put it, local foods insists on "the increased value of the specificity of place at a time when space seems less 'grounded' and more 'virtual'."[26]

One sees these same concerns animating familiar debates in social theory as well – not only those surrounding the democratic potential of online public spheres,[27] or the "quasi face-to-face" encounters facilitated by fair trade agreements,[28] but also attempts to update Foucault on the grounds that "discipline" is essentially rooted in a technique of spatial confinement that requires institutions (factories, prisons) that "everyone knows . . . are in more or less terminal decline."[29] The "generalization of discipline" that Hardt and Negri posit owes, in part, to recent developments in imaging technologies that not only allow the extension of surveillance networks throughout the increasingly smooth public space, but also allow for novel representations of that space in the interest of social control. These technologies have altered both the significance and possibility of public protest, but have also changed the spatial representation and control of criminals. Readily available and easily customizable online maps of sex offenders exemplify a new strategy of controlling populations not via confinement, but via perpetual visibility. Populations take solace from criminal threats today not by removing containing them at distant locales, but by monitoring their close proximity to the home.

Locavorism manifests an ambivalent relationship to this changing nature of space, simultaneously reclaiming and rejecting traditional public spaces. Alongside an unabashed celebration of open-air farmers markets, the literature on local foods also conveys a more or less explicit critique of urban space. That is, and as I'll discuss in the next section, local foods carries a notable bias against the topographies and the economies of cities, a bias that reflects a loss of faith in the conventional spaces of democratic politics and thus brings along a straightforward – if muted – retreat from democratic politics. The locavore literature trades in a utopian fantasy of postpolitical reconciliation with both neighbors and the land, a reconciliation that organics sacrificed when OFPA mandated that its ideal be mediated by the state and subject to legislative and regulatory struggle. And so, organics fails doubly: first, by failing to speak to the territorial anxieties of globalization, and, second, by offering an alternative to conventional food that was no less implicated in conventional politics. Today, localism speaks to the specific alienations and anxieties of globalization (from peak oil through national sovereignty) as well as to a population increasingly cynical about political struggle. Most crucially, it reflects a political condition in which it is only in their role as consumers that Americans can imagine political efficacy.

POSTPOLITICAL FANTASIES

Of course, local economies and even locavorism are nothing new. The locavore literature rarely strays too far from Jeffersonian ideals; when Kingsolver explains that her plan is "to eat deliberately" (23), the reference to Thoreau is unmistakable; and when Halweil, McKibben, and others promise that a local diet strengthens communities and increases social capital by promoting an ethics of neighborliness, it's clear that they've read Bowling Alone. The movement's promise of direct personal relations between producers and consumers (as well as subjects and objects), relations that were sacrificed first by industrialization and then by the inevitability of global supply chains, calls to mind nothing so much as the sovereign, responsible individuals that are the organizing conceit of American political lore.

But such localism often trades in a retreat from politics. Lizabeth Cohen notes how one version of localism – the mass migration to suburbs in the 1960s – was at least in part a retreat into racially and economically homogenous zones that could avoid many of the difficult political issues endemic to crowded and aging urban centers. These strategically segregated neighborhoods allowed citizens to erect barriers to entry and develop a narrow conception of "the public good" that included only the members of their specific community and was measured exclusively by the market value of their homes.[30] From the view of these constricted neighborhoods, Cohen continues, it was quite easy to justify the unequal funding of urban municipal services, especially schools, such that suburban localism was not necessarily a veil for racism, but it intensified racially-concentrated poverty just the same.

Today, Peter Singer opposes locavorism on precisely these grounds: it legitimates a specific interest over the general one, and justifies limiting economic support to an already privileged population that is unique only for its geographic proximity.[31] While Singer's concern is broadly cosmopolitan in its concern that local foods would shut down international grain markets that support third world farmers, Gopnik diagnoses a pro-rural, anti-urban bias in the local foods movement, a bias that is on clear display in Kingsolver's celebrations of country wisdom over urban naivete.[32] Kingsolver proactively denies that she is valorizing the country over the city, though this denial sits clumsily alongside her repeated mockery of people who cannot identify particular crops and her comparison of her family's leaving their home in Tucson to "rats leaping off the burning ship."[33] It is similarly difficult to read Smith and MacKinnon's locavore diary without noting their growing unease about life in a city, for even though they offer very few of the typical plaints of urban life (traffic, crime, noise), the book's central redemptive trope is a homestead 10 miles from the nearest highway, and Smith confesses more than once that the motivation for their project probably lies in her obsessive desire to own land.

This retreat from the city tends to carry with it a retreat from political life. Kingsolver, for instance, enjoying some local ice cream, declares that she "could hear the crash of corporate collapse with every bite. Tough work, but somebody's got to do it."[34] And while this is clearly a joke, the rest of her book bolsters the suggestion that the answer to the corporate control of food really does lie in an isolated realm divorced from political life. For not only does Kingsolver's yearlong experiment begin, literally, by leaving the city, the detailed calculations she provides at the close of her book are quintessentially bourgeois; though she estimates her year of homegrown food cost "well under 50¢ per meal," this calculation ignores the primary costs of the experiment: land (100 acres in Virginia) and lost income (two incomes, in her household).[35] More

than fuzzy math, this represents a characteristic effacement of such properly political issues as property rights and labor markets, an effacement that is only made more clear when Kingsolver visits Italy and introduces Slow Food as a movement founded by "chefs and consumers," even though it would be more accurate to say it was founded by farmers and communists.[36] Similarly, Halweil's landmark account of local foods explicitly derides "the initiative of well-meaning government officials," and dismisses the importance of conventional politics by identifying "more diffuse, but potentially more powerful, agent" that can fix our food system: "the food consumer."[37] Halweil proceeds then offers a list of subject positions capable of initiating real change: "farmer, restaurateur, politician, banker, entrepreneur, student looking for a career, or concerned parent."[38] The odd presence of "politician" and conspicuous absence of "citizen" from this list may reflect a real or perceived impotence, but it certainly exemplifies the trend for consumer activisms to ignore the broader political environment in which consumption happens.

Reading the literature on local foods, the flight from organics looks less like a concern about the cooptation of organics by agribusiness than a contamination of organics by conventional politics. Various commentators have pointed out that one of the themes of the organics movement has been trust – a trust embodied in an authentic and transparent relationship with the land and a trust threatened by a general cynicism in American politics and a specific lack of confidence in government.[39] But since 1990, "organic" has served less as a mark of an alternative to conventional food, a circumvention of the institutions of industrial production and processing, than as a legal category subject to frequent and contentious revision by the USDA. For not only is the fact that a food is labeled "organic" prima facie evidence that it is not part of an alternative food system (the label signifies, precisely, that it has been certified by the federal government), but the meaning of the term has been a constant source of conflict, with disagreement among producers, consumers, certifiers, legislators, and retailers over whether, for instance, crops fertilized with raw sewage or cows treated with antibiotics when sick can be called "organic."[40] Since OFPA, organic food has been implicated not only in global capitalism and industrial science, but also with all three branches of the federal government. The fact that the high cost of organic certification systematically excludes the smallest and often most "pure" producers from selling "organic" foods only exacerbates the movement's enduring skepticism toward the state.

As a result, the movement's pursuit of intimate relations with the land has veered toward classically liberal notions of individual autonomy and private property. Though it may be but a curious footnote that the primary retailer of these responsible foods, Whole Foods, remains steadfast in its opposition to the interference of both states and labor unions,[41] Guthman notes that organic farmers have always been "deeply suspicious of state intervention" and that consumers have "occasionally" responded to food contamination and safety scares (like Alar) with "demands for more state intervention (i.e., regulation); [but] more often, they began to buy so-called high-quality food."[42] So it is that Halweil explicitly dismisses the value of state regulation,[43] and the unmitigated and ubiquitous heroes of the locavore literature are rogue farmers who eschew institutional support or state assistance.[44]

This skepticism toward state intervention is not anomalous in a culture in which discourses of freedom are increasingly reliant on the rhetoric of the market, in which the rhetoric of citizenship has been largely abandoned for that of consumerism. Nor is there anything new in such a flight from politics; utopian movements on left and right have always promised of a world without conflict.

What is particularly interesting in this chapter of utopian literature is how it elevates the consumption (both the buying and the eating) of value added goods to the level of political action. Typically, this involves a celebration of backyard gardens, farmers markets, or, more ambitiously, Community Supported Agriculture (CSA) in which individuals buy subscriptions to particular farms. In each case, political action involves not mobilizing groups, organizing communities, running for office, or even voting, but rather making a series of ethically motivated consumer choices. As a result, the movement's skepticism toward the state informs a retreat from the one institution traditionally capable of (if only periodically interested in) resisting capital concentration: the state. Allowing the economic logic of liberalism to overshadow its political commitments to equality and freedom, the locavore movement participates in the conceptual apparatus that Wendy Brown calls neoliberalism.[45]

Of course, the locavore movement promises a food economy that could not be more different from the current concentration of agricultural resources under the likes of Monsanto and Archer Daniels Midland. The local ideal is of decentralized and autonomous family farms rather than the corporate "factory farms" that currently dominate the landscape. But the locavore literature is not only dismissive of state action, it is curiously silent on the issue of wage labor. When Smith and MacKinnon, for instance, speak about small farms as "the last redoubt of a gentler capitalism," what they mean is that market prices tend to be rounded down; they actually make no mention of labor in this gentle capitalism.[46] Even Michael Pollan, who seems most satisfied when he's visiting and working on farms, rarely mentions the existence of hired agricultural workers. Instead, Pollan casts farms as autonomous spaces where sovereign landholders mix their labor with the land to their mutual benefit; his accounts of individual farmers earning their title with their industry and rationality are straight out of American mythology and even evoke Locke.[47] Alongside his obvious concerns about the treatment of alienated fast food workers, this depiction of the and fulfilling labor of autonomous farmers exaggerates the contrast between city and country. With this aestheticization of labor, Pollan intimates that farms are innocent of the alienation and exploitation that drive urban economies.

The problem with this contrast is twofold. First, it is misleading. As Guthman points out, most labor even on the sorts of farms that locavores valorize is actually done by low-paid, itinerant, and abused immigrant labor, just as in conventional agriculture and industrial manufacture. In a systematic study of California's organic farms, Guthman turns up "no evidence to suggest that working conditions and remuneration on small 'family' farms are better than on large 'corporate' ones."[48] More than an unstated assumption that "small is beautiful," the locavore celebration of family farms represents a prototypically bourgeois effacement of wage labor. Pollan, again, barely mentions it, even in his excoriation of these same farms for their duplicitous marketing strategies and their abuses of both animals and the land.[49] More dishonestly, Fromartz profiles the benevolent labor practices at one unionized organic berry farm in California as evidence for the gentleness of this kind of capitalism, though he fails to mention that this is the only organized organic farm in the state.[50]

Second, and related, this effacement of wage labor by the productive power of consumption tends toward the fetishizing logic of capitalism, since it characterizes eating not only as a political act but also as a value creating activity. In one sense, this may be no different from Marx's argument that consumption is a form of production (since eating produces energy) and production a form of consumption (since farming burns fuel).[51] Like locavores, Marx offers a thermodynamic approach to food in which commodities are but bearers of a measurable quanta of energy; indeed, because the value of a commodity is precisely the amount of energy stored in it, Marx casts commerce – the production, distribution, exchange, and consumption of commodities – as transfers of energy from one form to another, both literally and metaphorically a "social metabolism."[52] Money is a convenient and nonperishable measure of value, but what is being bought and sold in commerce is another general equivalent – calories. (In fact, the nutritional literature at the opening of the 20th Century did refer to a food's caloric content as its "food value.") Marx thus offers a structural parallel between producing and consuming since both are metabolic transfers of energy, measured either in calories or in price.

But when locavores repeat this move – explaining how industrial agriculture metabolizes petrocalories into steak, and how buying local lettuce produces sustainable farms – their argument cannot be separated from a culture that systematically reduces the responsibilities of citizenship to the logic of consumerism. This same thermodynamic approach to food therefore has strikingly different effect in Marx and Pollan. In Marx, it illustrates how consumer goods embody exploited labor; in Pollan, it allows shopping as a proxy for labor. In the nineteenth century, it reflected the standardization of labor under industrial manufacture; today, it reflects the reduction of social and political life to market relations. To be sure: Pollan's assessment of food systems seems unimpeachable, his ethical call for a less mediate relationship with the energy sources that provide the conditions of our lives seems beyond reproach, and his resort to endorsing responsible shopping practices owes to the fact that large numbers of people simply cannot engage in raising their own food. (His vivid, first-person account of slaughtering chickens seems motivated, primarily, to demonstrate that something nonquantifiable – the experience not only of labor, but of death – is irretrievably lost in this transaction.)[53] Yet it inevitably participates in a political condition in which citizenship has been reduced to consumerism, and the very ability to conceptualize political action or individual freedom has been captured by the logic of the market. By establishing the market as the institution through which democratic citizenship can be effected, his argument participates in a neoliberal vogue for subordinating political struggle to market exchange. So while consuming local food does produce a market in sustainable agriculture, it also produces the market as the solution to political problems.[54]

Cohen points out that earlier versions of consumerist politics (such as the boycotts at the heart of the US Civil Rights movement) worked to reinforce social solidarity, whereas the consumer model of citizenship since the 1980s has worked to impoverish traditional models of political action. In particular, Cohen chronicles how niche marketing has fractured and segregated society into smaller and more homogenous consumer profiles with narrower and more personal interests, such that as market activity came to organize a greater segment of the public imagination it has become more difficult to envision an expansive collective identity or public good. For Cohen, the true irony is that while earlier instances of consumer activism promoted and fostered democratic participation, the success and popularity of consumer activism has corresponded with a steady decline in the most traditional and typical form of political action: voting.[55]

One interpretation of this correspondence is that consumerist politics is a ruse that distracts citizens from meaningful political engagement. But a slightly more sympathetic cast would say that the dominance of consumer politics owes to a real impotence of citizens in the traditional arenas of democratic politics. In other words, the point is not that locavores alibi capitalism, but that the locavore literature has wide appeal because it speaks to an actual lack of opportunities for political action. My argument here parallels recent analyses of other political trends, such as Jodi Dean's assessment of the democratic potential of the internet and Timothy Luke's study of the environmental movement's embrace of "green consumerism."[56] When Dean argues that blogs and chatrooms provide an illusion of meaningful participation in public discourse, and when Luke argues that that recycling does less to stall global warming than to give individual a sense that they are empowered to change the world, neither simply reduces these strategies to duplicitous redirections of publicly-minded energy toward "nonpolitical, nonsocial, noninstitutional solutions" to real problems.[57] Rather, both emphasize that these strategies appeal because they cover over "the real powerlessness" that individuals experience under globalization; they offer solace from a recognition that there are, in fact, very few opportunities for democratic action and that citizens are actually quite powerless to change the shape of their own lives.[58]

These narratives each offer a sense of empowerment in an age in which it has become all but unthinkable that agricultural policy, environmental regulation, or the global trade in information will be subject to democratic control. In each case, these agendas are animated by fantasies of political efficacy as well as postpolitical reconciliation, since they each posit a world in which global crises are forestalled not via representative politics and state regulation, but by smoothly functioning markets actually governed by individual ethics. The narratives of immediate food offer solace from the alienating logic of global capital and the exploitation of farmers by promising responsible consumption through the beneficent and mutually beneficial transactions of farmers markets and CSA. Finally, the bifurcated nostalgia for both Jeffersonian self-reliance and sixties solidarity that underlies popular approaches to food politics owes to a real loss of faith in the institutions traditionally charged with enacting political solutions.

SOME POLITICS IS LOCAL

Perhaps I've overstated the case. Though books like The Omnivore's Dilemma endeavor to reconcile agrarian populism with social conscience via responsible consumption, Pollan's more recent writings have recognized the inadequacy of consumerist politics. "Voting with our forks can advance reform only so far," he has since proclaimed; real change demands that people "wade into the muddy political waters of agricultural policy" and "vote with their votes as well."[59] Indeed, Pollan's activism surrounding the 2007 US Farm Bill inspired thousands of Americans to actually investigate this typically obscure and enduringly impenetrable piece of federal legislation, studying some very complex and decidedly unromantic dynamics guiding agricultural policy and budgetary process, all toward the end of a responsible assessment of the impossibility of redirecting international agricultural markets and trends without the active participation of states.

Similarly, Guthman identifies significant differences between various approaches to local foods. Most notably, she identifies two types of CSA: one in which eaters pay a nominal subscription fee in exchange for a share of the farm's yield, and another in which eaters invest in the equity of the farm and share its profits, its risks, and responsibilities. The former, which Guthman calls "more common and less radical," is a basic subscription arrangement in which consumers commit to a particular grower; they sacrifice some individual choice of goods, but do not significantly alter their role as consumer. But in the latter version, subscribers really are co-owners in the farm (albeit on a limited

basis), and Guthman makes a convincing case that it offers a significant decommodification of both food and land, especially as these farms rarely show a profit and typically depend upon grants for their viability.[60] The common version is benevolent consumerism, whereas the latter, while still organized around consumer activity, compels eaters to take on the responsibilities and risks required of community ownership. The common version strives for postpolitical assemblage, putting a class-biased air of harmonious exchange on the otherwise unchanged institution of the market; the radical version is self-consciously political, theorizing and enacting a form of collective action that transforms the nature of ownership, citizenship, and control.

Such social, political, and institutional projects are predicated on a belief in collective efficacy and the possibility of an alternative to the dominant trend toward neoliberalization. As such, their viability depends not merely on their offering creative and sustainable programs for a reworked food system, but also on an ability to imagine political agency and human freedom in terms that do not reduce to the logic of consumerism. They depend fundamentally on a belief in the practicality of collective action, and they depend on a belief in an alternative to the current market-based solutions to coordinating the production and distribution of essential resources like food and water. In this light, while the recent failure of the US Congress to significantly rework the terms of the Farm Bill certainly means several more years of unwise subsidies and corporate control of agriculture, the real significance could be more longstanding. Insofar as this failure is seen as yet more evidence that states are incapable or unwilling to address the environmental violations and human injustices endemic to the US food system, it offers yet another reason to doubt the possibility of institutional solutions to society's problems, and yet another reason to trade a politicization of consumption for a consumerist politics.

NOTES

1. Great thanks to Elizabeth Mazzolini for fostering my academic interest in food and for helpful feedback on an earlier draft of this essay, to Jodi Dean for encouraging this symposium, and to The Bill and Carol Fox Center for Humanistic Inquiry at Emory University for generously funding this research.

2. What Are People For? (San Francisco, CA: North Point Press, 1990), 145.

3. Elspeth Probyn, Carnal Appetites: FoodSexIdentities (NY: Routledge, 2000).

4. Julie Guthman, Agrarian Dreams: The Paradox of Organic Farming in California (Berkeley: University of California Press, 2004).

5. Samuel Fromartz, Organic, Inc.: Natural Foods and How They Grew (NY: Harcourt, 2006), ix; Harvey Levenstein The Paradox of Plenty: A Social History of Eating in America (Oxford University Press, 1993), ch15.

6. Levenstein, Paradox of Plenty, 183.

7. Mary Douglas, Purity and Danger (NY: Routledge, 1966). On the desire for predictable foods in a global economy, see Michael Pollan, The Botany of Desire: A Plant's-Eye View of the World (NY: Random House 2001), ch4. On the difficulties encountered and compromises required in marketing "ethnic" (i.e., Mexican, Italian, and Chinese) chain restaurants in the US, see Barry Glassner, The Gospel of Food: Everything You Think You Know About Food is Wrong (NY: Ecco, 2007), ch5.

8. Warren Belasco, Appetite for Change: How the Counterculture Took on the Food Industry (NY: Pantheon Books 1989), 49–50.

9. Nor is it entirely a coincidence that the man who won a 1920 Nobel Prize for developing synthetic fertilizer, Fritz Haber, also developed Zyklon B, the gas used in Hitler's concentration camps. See Michael Pollan, The Omnivore's Dilemma: A Natural History of Four Meals (NY: Penguin, 2006), 43.

10. Laura Shapiro, "Suddenly, It's a Panic for Organic," Newsweek (March 27, 1989).

11. For versions of this story, see Belasco, Appetite for Change; Levenstein, Paradox of Plenty; Fromartz, Organic, Inc.; Pollan, The Omnivore's Dilemma.

12. Bill McKibben, Deep Economy: The Wealth of Communities and the Durable Future (NY: Times Books, 2007); Barbara Kingsolver with Steven Hopp and Camille Kingsolver, Animal, Vegetable, Miracle: A Year of Food Life (NY: Harper Collins, 2007); Alisa Smith and JB MacKinnon, Plenty: One Man, One Woman, and a Raucous Year of Eating Locally (NY: Harmony Books, 2007); Adam Gopnik, "New York Local," The New Yorker (Sep 3 and 10, 2007).

13. See John Cloud, "Eating Better Than Organic," Time (Mar 2, 2007); Carlo Petrini, Slow Food Nation: Why Our Food Should Be Good, Clean, and Fair, trans. C. Furlan & J. Hunt (NY: Rizzoli Ex Libris, 2007); Daniel Imhoff, Food Fight: A Citizen's Guide to the Food and Farm Bill (Healdsburg, CA: Watershed Press, 2007).

14. I have not mentioned a competing trend, Slow Food, because the concern with slowness seems but one manifestation of a concern with locality. In their monograph on the Slow Food organization and philosophy, Wendy Parkins and Geoffrey Craig explicitly cast time and space as co-equal concerns, alongside pleasure (Slow Living [NY: Berg, 2006]). For more on concerns about speed owing to a postmodern collapse of space, see David Harvey, The Condition of Postmodernity (Oxford: Blackwell, 1990).

15. Frances Fukuyama has similarly traded his fear of the corrupting influence of genetic engineering (Our Posthuman Future [NY: Farrar, Strauss, and Giroux, 2002]) for a concern about American expansionism (America at the Crossroads [New Haven, CT: Yale University Press, 2006]).

16. McKibben, Deep Economy, 65; Pollan, Omnivore's Dilemma, 167.

17. Ibid. See also Richard Manning, "The Oil We Eat," Harper's (February 2004).

18. Nick Cullather shows how this thermodynamics thinking has directed US foreign policy since the early 20th Century, especially as it cast global hunger as a "caloric deficit," a measure that "can be tabulated as easily as currency or petroleum." Nick Cullather, "The Foreign Policy of the Calorie," American Historical Review 112.2 (April 2007), 339.

19. Michael Hardt, "Sovereignty," Theory & Event 5.4 (2002).

20. The list of relevant texts here could be very long. For a sampling of people making this argument, see Pierre Manent, A World Beyond Politics? (Princeton University Press, 2006); Henri Lefebvre, The Production of Space, trans. D. Nicholson-Smith (Oxford: Blackwell, 1991); Susan Bordo, The Flight to Objectivity (Albany: SUNY Press, 1987); and David Harvey, The Condition of Postmodernity.

21. Brian Halweil, Eat Here: Reclaiming Homegrown Pleasures in a Global Supermarket (NY: Norton, 2004), 10, 16.

22. Deep Economy, 109.

23. At the opening of the 20th Century, 40% of Americans lived on farms (meaning that most Americans at least visited a farm at some point). A century later, that number had declined to 2%. Richard Bulliet, Hunters, Herders, and

Hamburgers (NY: Columbia University Press, 2005), 3.

24. Omnivore's Dilemma, ch9. For Mackey's response and ensuing dialogue, see http://www2.wholefoodsmarket.com/blogs/jmackey/2006/05/26/an-open-letter-to-michael-pollan (accessed 27 May 2009).

25. Greg Critser, Generation Rx (NY: Houghton Mifflin, 2005); Ray Moynihan and Alan Cassels, Selling Sickness (NY: Nation Books, 2005).

26. Parkins and Craig, Slow Living, 62. For a parallel, see Fredric Jameson's argument that conspiracy theories, by explaining that the world is actually controlled by covert but unambiguous wielders of power, offer solace from a disorienting and increasingly anarchistic global market. "Cognitive Mapping" in Marxism and the Interpretation of Culture, ed. C. Nelson and L. Grossberg (Urbana: University of Illinois Press, 1988).

27. Jodi Dean, "Communicative Capitalism: Circulation and the Foreclosure of Politics," Cultural Politics 1.1 (March 2005).

28. J.K. Gibson-Graham, A Postcapitalist Politics (Minneapolis: University of Minnesota Press, 2007), ch4.

29. Gilles Deleuze, "Postscript on Societies of Control," in Negotiations 197201990, trans. M. Joughin. NY: Columbia University Press, 1997), 178. See also Michael Hardt and Antonio Negri, Empire (Cambridge: Harvard University Press, 2000), esp. 23–7.

30. Lizabeth Cohen, A Consumer's Republic: The Politics of Mass Consumption in Postwar America (NY: Vintage, 2004), 228.

31. Peter Singer and Jim Mason, The Way We Eat: Why Our Food Choices Matter (NY: Rodale, 2006).

32. Gopnik, "New York Local;" Kingsolver, Animal, Vegetable, Miracle, 7–8 and passim. For another critique of localist elitism, see Barry Glassner's "fast food populism" that celebrates the convenient and affordable foods that locavores malign but on which most city dwellers depend (Gospel of Food, ch6).

33. Kingsolver, Animal, Vegetable, Miracle, 2.

34. Ibid., 153.

35. Ibid., 307.

36. Ibid., 249. Other treatments of Slow Food are much more open about the links of the organization to radical, left-wing politics. See Petrini, Slow Food Nation; Parkins and Craig, Slow Living; and Corby Kummer, The Pleasures of Slow Food (San Francisco, CA: Chronicle Books, 2002).

37. Halweil, Eat Here, 157–8.

38. Ibid., 165.

39. Fromartz (Organic, Inc., ix) frames his book on organics as an issue of trust, and Levenstein (Paradox of Plenty, ch13) notes how the organics movement coincides with a proliferation of "alternative" medicines, signaling a similar lack of confidence in the American medical establishment.

40. Fromartz, Organic, Inc., ch6; Pollan, Omnivore's Dilemma, 155–6.

41. Whole Foods founder and CEO John Mackey is an avowed libertarian, and the chain is known for championing the benevolent labor practices designed to frustrate unions.

42. Guthman, Agrarian Dreams, 12, 24.

43. Halweil, Eat Here, ch9.

44. The most common personality here is Joel Salatin, owner/operator of Polyface Farms and self-described "Christian-conservative-libertarian-environmentalist-lunatic farmer" (Pollan, Omnivore's Dilemma, 125). A more striking character, however, is probably Arthur Harvey, an organic blueberry farmer who sued the USDA in 2002 and who (again evoking Thoreau) has refused to pay federal income taxes since 1959 due to his opposition to military spending (Fromartz, Organic, Inc., introduction). Such heroic individuals are a staple of the literature.

45. Wendy Brown, "Neo-liberalism and the End of Liberal Democracy," Theory & Event 7.1 (2003).

46. Plenty, 163.

47. Pollan celebrates Salatin for farming in a manner that his land "will be in no way diminished by the process—in fact, it will be the better for it, lusher, more fertile, even springier underfoot," casting the farmer as the quintessential Lockean subject, adding value to the land by cultivating it (Omnivore's Dilemma, 127).

48. Agrarian Dreams, 175.

49. Omnivore's Dilemma, ch9.

50. Organic, Inc., ch2. Thanks to Julie Guthman for confirming this.

51. Karl Marx, Grundrisse, trans. M. Nicolaus (NY: Penguin, 1973), 85–100.

52. Marx, Capital, Volume 1, trans. B. Fowkes (NY: Vintage, 1977), 198 and passim. On Marx's interest in thermodynamics, see Frederick Gregory, Scientific Materialism in the Nineteenth Century (Boston: D. Reidel Publishing Company, 1977); Anson Rabinbach, The Human Motor (NY: Basic Books, 1990); Amy Wendling, Alienation and Machine Production: Capitalist Embodiment in Marx. PhD Thesis (Penn State University, 2006).

53. Omnivore's Dilemma, 226–38.

54. Note how Carlo Petrini, the Italian founder of Slow Food, freely calls consumers "co-producers" in order to highlight the productive power of consumption, but finds himself openly disgusted by the "wealthy or very wealthy" patrons of a farmers market in San Francisco who seem to be buying self-righteousness as much as peppers (Slow Food Nation, 129–35). The lesson here seems that, with the current state of American

politics, Petrini's politicization of consumption freely translates into a consumerist politics. Similarly, while Evan Watkins uses the term "marketwork" to defetishize capitalism and explain how consumer activity amounts to "the process of constructing the market," the point here is that locavore marketwork does not merely construct a market for responsible agriculture, but constructs a particular understanding of political action. See Evan Watkins, Everyday Exchanges: Marketwork and Capitalist Common Sense (Stanford University Press, 1998).

55. Cohen, Consumer's Republic, 404–5.

56. Dean, "Communicative Capitalism;" Luke, Ecocritique: Contesting the Politics of Nature, Economy, and Culture (Minneapolis: University of Minnesota Press, 1997), ch 6.

57. Luke, Ecocritique, 119.

58. Ibid., Dean, "Communicative Capitalism," 61.

59. Pollan, "You Are What You Grow," in Manifestos on the Future of Food & Seed, ed. V. Shiva (South End Press, 2007); 139. See also Pollan, "Don't Call It the 'Farm Bill,' Call It the 'Food Bill,'" foreword to D. Imhoff, Food Fight.

60. Guthman, Agrarian Dreams, 184–5.

43

From Food Crisis to Food Sovereignty: The Challenge of Social Movements

Eric Holt-Giménez

The current global food crisis—decades in the making—is a crushing indictment against capitalist agriculture and the corporate monopolies that dominate the world's food systems. The role of the industrial agri-food complex in creating the crisis (through the monopolization of input industries, industrial farming, processing, and retailing) and the self-serving neoliberal solutions proposed by the world's multilateral institutions and leading industrial countries are being met with skepticism, disillusion, and indifference by a general public more concerned with the global economic downturn than with the food crisis. Neoliberal retrenchment has met growing resistance by those most affected by the crisis—the world's smallholder farmers.

Solutions to the food crisis advanced by the World Bank, the Food and Agriculture Organization (FAO), the Consultative Group for International Agricultural Research (CGIAR), and mega-philanthropy, propose accelerating the spread of biotechnology, reviving the Green Revolution, re-introducing the conditional lending of the World Bank and the International Monetary Fund, and re-centering the now fragmented power of the World Trade Organization (WTO) by concluding the Doha "Development Round" of trade negotiations. These institutions have a mandate from capital to mitigate hunger, diffuse social unrest, and reduce the overall numbers of peasant producers worldwide—without introducing any substantive changes to the structure of the world's food systems. Their neoliberal strategies are in stark contrast to the proposals for ecological approaches to agriculture (agroecology) and food sovereignty advanced by farmer federations and civil society organizations worldwide that instead seek to transform food systems. Clashes and declarations of protest at recent summits in Rome, Hokkaido, and Madrid, the growing public resistance to the industrial agrifood complex, and the rise, spread, and political convergence of movements for agroecology, land reform, food justice, and food sovereignty, all indicate that the food crisis has become the focal point in a class struggle over the future of our food systems.

THE FOOD CRISIS

Last year record numbers of the world's poor experienced hunger, this at a time of record harvests and record profits for the world's major agrifood corporations. The contradiction of increasing hunger in the midst of wealth and abundance sparked "food riots," not seen for many decades. Protests in Mexico, Morocco, Mauritania, Senegal, Indonesia, Burkina Faso, Cameroon, Yemen, Egypt, Haiti, and twenty other countries were sparked by skyrocketing food prices (see Walden Bello and Mara Baviera's article in this issue). In June 2008, the World Bank reported that global food prices had risen 83 percent over the last three years and the FAO cited a 45 percent increase in their world food price index in just nine months.[1] While commodity prices have since fallen due to the world economic downturn and speculators lessening their bets on commodities, food prices remain high and are not expected to return to pre-crisis levels.

The widespread food protests were not simply crazed "riots" by hungry masses. Rather, they were angry demonstrations against high food prices in countries that formerly had food surpluses, and where government and industry were unresponsive to people's plight. In some cases, starving people were just trying to access food from trucks or stores. Alarmed by the specter of growing social unrest, the World Bank announced that without massive, immediate injections of food aid, 100 million people in the South would join the swelling ranks of the word's hungry.[2] These shrill warnings immediately revived Malthusian mantras within the agrifood industry and unleashed a flurry of heroic industrial promises for new genetically engineered high-yielding, "climate-ready," and "bio-fortified" seeds. The World Bank called for a "New Deal" for Agriculture and trotted out a portfolio of $1.2 billion in emergency loans. The FAO appealed (unsuccessfully) to OECD governments to finance a $30 billion a year revival of developing country agriculture. Über-philanthropist Bill Gates invited multinational corporations to follow him into a new era of "creative capitalism," promising that his new Alliance for a Green Revolution in Africa (AGRA) would provide four million poor farmers with new seeds and fertilizers.

But with record grain harvests in 2007, according to the FAO, there was more than enough food in the world to feed everyone in 2008—at least 1.5 times current demand. In fact, over the last twenty years, food production has risen steadily at over 2.0 percent a year, while the rate of population growth has dropped to 1.14 percent a year. Globally, population is not outstripping food supply. Over 90 percent of the world's hungry are simply too poor to buy enough food. High food prices are a problem because nearly three billion people—half of the world's population—are poor and near-poor. Around half of the people in the developing world earn less than two dollars a day. Nearly 20 percent are "extremely poor" earning less than one dollar a day.[3] Many of those officially classified as poor are subsistence farmers who have limited access to land and water and cannot compete in global markets.[4] In addition, the diversion of large quantities of grains and oil crops for the growing industrial feedlots in the emerging economies, as well as the diversion of land and water for "green" agrofuels has put significant pressure on markets for many basic foods.

Unsurprisingly, the food crisis has provided the world's major agrifood monopolies with windfall profits. In the last quarter of 2007 as the world food crisis was breaking, Archer Daniels Midland's earnings jumped 42 percent, Monsanto's by 45 percent, and Cargill's by 86 percent. Cargill's subsidiary, Mosaic Fertilizer, saw profits rise by 1,200 percent.[5]

The steady concentration of profits and market power in the industrial North mirrors the loss of food producing capacity and the growth of hunger in the global South. Despite the oft-cited productivity gains of the Green Revolution, and despite decades of development campaigns—most recently, the elusive Millennium Development Goals—per capita hunger is rising and the number of desperately hungry people on the planet has grown steadily from 700 million in 1986 to 800 million in 1998.[6] Today, the number stands at over 1 billion. Fifty years ago, the developing countries had yearly agricultural trade surpluses of $1 billion. After decades of capitalist development and the global expansion of the industrial agrifood complex, the southern food *deficit* has ballooned to $11 billion a year.[7] The cereal import bill for low-income food-deficit countries is now over $38 billion and the FAO predicts it will grow to $50 billion by 2030.[8] This shift from food self-sufficiency to food dependency has been accomplished by colonizing national food systems and destroying peasant agriculture.

THE PERSISTENCE OF THE PEASANTRY

The last half-century of capitalist agricultural expansion has pummeled the world's peasantry, dispossessing them of land, water, and genetic resources through violent processes of enclosures, displacement, and outright piracy. The Green Revolution, the World Bank's structural adjustment programs, and global and regional trade agreements have driven differentiation and de-peasantization.[9] The same period has seen a fourfold increase in grain and oilseed production, with a steady decline in prices to farmers.[10] This has been accompanied by a relentless industrial trend of vertical and horizontal concentration within the world's food systems. Two companies, Archer Daniels Midland and Cargill, capture three-quarters of the world grain trade.[11] The top three seed companies Monsanto, Dupont, and Syngenta control 39 percent of the world's commercial seed market.[12]

However, high global rates of urbanization have not overcome the stubborn "persistence of the peasantry."[13] Whether this is due to the fact that historically new family-labor farms continually replace those lost through industrialization,[14] or because for much of the world's rural poor "there is hardly any alternative but farming," the fact is that despite massive out-migration and intense fractioning of peasant landholdings, the absolute numbers of peasant and smallholder farmers in the South have remained remarkably stable over the last forty years.[15] Smallholders continue to provide significant amounts of the food in the South, as high as 90 percent of all food production in African countries.[16]

This mix of de-peasantization and *re-peasantization* has led to shifts in crops, hybridized forms of production, and a heavy reliance on off-farm income and remittances. These processes are characterized by changes in the forms of production, livelihood strategies, and political demands. Reformulating the "peasant question," Araghi (see endnote 9) identifies not only historic demands for land, but also demands relating to the transnational and dispossessed character of today's smallholders, e.g., housing and homelessness, informal work, migration, identity, environment, and increasingly hunger.

The difficulty of confronting the extensive attacks on smallholders and politically mobilizing around the complexity of their livelihood demands has been a challenge for agrarian movements in the South. This has also been a problem for northern organizations seeking to protect family farms and counter the expansion of large-scale industrial agriculture with more sustainable forms of production. Only a decade ago, rural sociologists lamented the lack of an "underlying notion . . . to serve as a unifying force" for a sustainable agriculture movement, and pointed to the need for advocates to form coalitions to advance an agro-foods movement capable of contesting deregulation, globalization, and agro-ecosystem degradation.[17] With the current food crisis, the peasant-based call for *food sovereignty*—literally, people's self-government of the food system—can potentially fulfill this political function.

First defined in 1996 by the international peasant federation La Vía Campesina (The Peasant Way) as "people's right to healthy and culturally appropriate food produced through ecologically sound and sustainable methods, and their right to define their own food and agriculture systems," food sovereignty proposes that people, rather than corporate monopolies, make the decisions regarding our food. Food sovereignty is a much deeper concept than food security because it proposes not just guaranteed access to food, but democratic control over the food system—from production and processing, to distribution, marketing, and consumption. Whether applied to countries in the global South working to re-establish national food production, to farmers protecting their seed systems from GMOs, or to rural-urban communities setting up their own direct marketing systems, food sovereignty aims to democratize and transform our food systems.

For decades, family farmers, rural women, and communities around the world have resisted the destruction of their native seeds and worked hard to diversify their crops, protect their soil, conserve their water and forests, and establish local gardens, markets, businesses, and community-based food systems. There are many highly productive, equitable, and sustainable alternatives to the present industrial practices and corporate monopolies holding the world's food hostage, and literally millions of people working to advance these alternatives.[18] Contrary to conventional thinking, these practices are highly productive and could easily feed the projected mid-century global population of over nine billion people.[19]

Smallholders working with movements like Campesino a Campesino (Farmer to Farmer) of Latin America, and NGO networks for farmer-led sustainable agriculture like Participatory Land Use Management (PELUM) of Africa, and the Farmer Field Schools of Asia have restored exhausted soils, raised yields, and preserved the environment using highly effective agroecological management practices on hundreds of thousands of acres of land. These practices have given them important measures of autonomy in relation to the industrial agrifood system and have increased their environmental and economic resiliency, buffering them from climate-induced hazards and market volatility.

At the same time, peasant organizations struggling to advance agrarian reform have been busy confronting the neoliberal offensive.[20] Because the expansion of industrial agrifood both dispossesses smallholders and recruits them into a massive reserve army of labor, these peasant organizations have broadened their work across sectors and borders. The globalization of these movements—both in content and scale—responds in part to the intensification of capital's enclosures, and is pardy a strategic decision to engage in global advocacy. As a result, the new transnational agrarian movements regularly integrate social, environmental, economic, and cultural concerns with demands for land reform.

Two distinguishable currents can be identified from these trends. One is made up of peasant organizations and federations focusing primarily on new agrarian advocacy—like Vía Campesina. The other trend is made up of smallholders working with non-governmental organizations (NGOs) that focus primarily on developing sustainable agriculture—like Campesino a Campesino. The political and institutional origins of these currents are different, and this has at times led to contradictory, competitive and even adversarial relations, particularly between non-governmental organizations implementing programs in the interests of farmers, and farmer's organizations interested in implementing their own programs. Nonetheless, at both the farm and the international level, there is clear objective synergy between the agrarian demands of today's peasant organizations, and the needs of the growing base of smallholders practicing sustainable agriculture as a means of survival. The food crisis may be bringing these movements together.

ADVOCACY: WALKING ON THE PEASANT ROAD

In 1993 farm leaders from around the world gathered in Mons, Belgium for a conference on policy research put on by a Dutch NGO allied with the International Federation of Agricultural Producers (IFAP), an international farm federation dominated by large-scale, northern farmers. What emerged instead was an international peasant movement: La Vía Campesina. The emergence of an international *peasant-led* farmer federation signified both a break with conventional federations run by large producers and with the humanitarian NGOs typically concerned with peasant agricultural production. The Mons declaration asserted the right of small farmers to make a living in the countryside, the right of all people to healthy food, and the right of nations to define their own agricultural polices.[21]

Since its inception, Vía Campesina's main objective has been to halt neoliberalism and construct alternative food systems based on food sovereignty. It was formed with organizations mostly from the Americas and Europe, but has since expanded to include more than 150 rural social movements from over 79 countries, including 12 countries in Africa, and scores of organizations in South and East Asia. Unlike its large farmer counterpart IFAP, Vía Campesina is made up almost entirely of marginalized groups: landless workers, small farmers, sharecroppers, pastoralists, fisherfolk, and the peri-urban poor.

Vía Campesina has been remarkably successful in creating the political space in which to advance its platform of food sovereignty, getting the WTO out of agriculture, women's rights, sustainable agriculture, a ban on GMO's, and redistributive agrarian reform. The movement was instrumental in organizing protests at WTO ministerial meetings from Seattle to Hong Kong. Vía Campesina played the lead role in the FAO International Conference on Agrarian Reform and Rural Development in 2006, and mounted successful resistance campaigns to the World Bank's market-led land reform programs.

Vía Campesina has also been among the most vocal critics of institutional responses to the global food crisis. At the High Level Task force meeting on the food crisis in Madrid, Spain, Vía Campesina released a declaration demanding that solutions to the food crisis be completely independent of the institutions responsible for creating the crisis in the first place (i.e., the IMF, World Bank, WTO, and CGIAR). The declaration reaffirmed the call for food sovereignty, demanded an end to land grabs for industrial agrofuel and foreign food production, and called on the international community to reject the Green Revolution and instead support the findings of the UN's International Assessment of Agricultural Knowledge Science and Technology for Development (IAASTD). This seminal assessment, sponsored by five UN agencies and the World Bank, and authored by over four hundred scientists and development experts from more than eighty countries, concluded that there is an urgent need to increase and strengthen further research and adoption of locally appropriate and democratically controlled agroecological methods of production, relying on local expertise, local germplasm, and farmer-managed, local seed systems.

PRACTICE: AGROECOLOGICAL TRANSFORMATION—FARMER TO FARMER

> Farmers helping their brothers, so that they can help themselves ... to find solutions and not be dependent on a technician or on the bank: that is Campesino a Campesino.
> —Argelio González, Santa Lucía, Nicaragua, 1991

This is the farmer's definition of Latin America's thirty-year farmer-led movement for sustainable agriculture. El Movimiento Campesino a Campesino, the Farmer to Farmer Movement, is made up of hundreds of thousands of peasant-technicians farming and working in over a dozen countries.

Campesino a Campesino began with a series of rural projects among the indigenous smallholders of the ecologically fragile hillsides of the Guatemalan Highlands in the early 1970s. Sponsored by progressive NGOs, Mayan peasants developed a method for agricultural improvement using relatively simple methods of small-scale experimentation combined with farmer-led workshops to share their discoveries. Because they were producing at relatively low levels, they concentrated on overcoming the most commonly limiting factors of production in peasant agriculture, i.e., soil and water. By adding organic matter to soils, and by implementing soil and water conservation techniques, they frequently obtained yield increases of 100–400 percent. Rapid, recognizable results helped build enthusiasm among farmers and led to the realization that they could improve their own agriculture—without running the risks, causing the environmental damage, or developing the financial dependency associated with the Green Revolution. Initial methods of composting, soil and water conservation, and seed selection soon developed into a sophisticated "basket" of sustainable technologies and agroecological management approaches that included green manures, crop diversification, integrated pest management, biological weed control, reforestation, and agrobiodiversity management at farm and watershed scales.

The effective, low-cost methods for farmer-generated technologies and farmer-to-farmer knowledge transfer were quickly picked up by NGOs working in agricultural development. The failures of the Green Revolution to improve smallholder livelihoods in Central America, and the region's revolutionary uprisings and counterrevolutionary conflicts of the 1970s and '80s combined to create both the need and the means for the growth of what became the Campesino a Campesino movement.

As credit, seeds, extension services, and markets continually failed the peasantry, smallholders turned to NGOs rather than governments to meet their agricultural needs. The structural adjustment programs of the 1980s and '90s exacerbated the conditions of the peasantry. In response, the Campesino a Campesino movement grew, spreading through NGOs to hundreds of thousands of smallholders across the Americas.[22] Though the movement was routinely dismissed by the international agricultural research centers for "lacking science" and making unverified claims of sustainability, in Central America following Hurricane Mitch (1998), some 2,000 *promotores* from Campesino a Campesino carried out scientific research to prove that their farms were significantly more resilient and sustainable than those of their conventional neighbors.[23]

One of Campesino a Campesino most dramatic success stories has been in Cuba, where its farmer-driven agroecological practices helped the country transform much of its agriculture from high-external input, large-scale systems to smaller, low-input organic systems. This conversion was instrumental in helping Cuba overcome its food crisis during the Special Period following the collapse of the Soviet Union. The Cuban Campesino a Campesino Agroecology Movement (MACAC) was implemented through ANAP, the national association of small farmers. The MACAC grew in a structural environment in which Cuba's numerous agricultural research stations and agricultural universities worked to develop bio-fertilizers, integrated pest management, and other techniques for low external-input agriculture. Reforms were enacted to scale down collectives and cooperatives, placing greater control over farming and marketing directly into the hands of smallholders. Rural and urban farmers were provided easy access to land, credit, and markets.[24] In eight years, the Campesino a Campesino movement of Cuba grew to over 100,000 smallholders. It had taken the movement nearly twenty years in Mexico and Central America to grow to that size.[25]

The farmer-to-farmer approach has been fairly universalized among NGOs working in agroecological development, leading to highly successful farmer-generated agroecological practices worldwide (as well as a fair amount of methodological co-optation on the part of international agricultural research centers). The System of Rice Intensification (SRI) developed in Madagascar has raised yields to as high as eight metric tons per hectare and spread to a million farmers in over two dozen countries.[26] A survey of forty-five sustainable agriculture projects in seventeen African countries covering some 730,000 households revealed that agroecological approaches substantially improved food production and household food security. In 95 percent of these projects, cereal yields improved by 50–100 percent.[27] A study of organic agriculture on the continent showed that small-scale, modern, organic agriculture was widespread in sub-Saharan Africa, contributing significantly to improved yields, incomes, and environmental services.[28] Over 170 African organizations from nine countries in East and Southern Africa belong to the Participatory Land Use Management (PELUM) a network that has been sharing agroecological knowledge in East and South Africa for thirteen years. For twenty years, the Center for Low External Input Sustainable Agriculture (LEISA) has documented hundreds of agroecological alternatives that successfully overcome many of the limiting factors in African agriculture and elsewhere in the global South (http://www.leisa.info/).

THE DIVIDE BETWEEN PRACTITIONERS AND ADVOCATES

I think we should not fall in the trap of seeing the development of agroecology by just looking at the physical aspects of the farm or just at the economics. We as NGOs have a problem with our social position in which we are serving as a dike and often an obstacle to processes of agency within the people and greater local organization. . . . Agroecology is not just a collection of practices. Agroecology is a way of life. . . . We can't have an agroecological change without a campesino movement. We NGOs can accompany them, but we can't do it. We promote projects, and projects have a short life. They are unsustainable.
—Nelda Sánchez, Mesoamerican Information System for Sustainable Agriculture

Though the farmer-to-farmer-NGO partnership has been highly effective in supporting local projects and developing sustainable practices on the ground, unlike Vía Campesina, it has done little to address the need for an enabling policy context for sustainable agriculture. Given the unfavorable structural conditions, agroecological practices have not scaled up nationally to become the rule rather the exception.[29] Despite far-flung farmer-to-farmer networks linked by hundreds of NGOs, farmers in these movements have generally not lobbied, pressured, taken direct action, or otherwise organized in favor of sustainable agriculture in a significant way. The farmers of PELUM in West Africa excel in agroecological farming but until recently were largely uninvolved in policy work to halt the spread of the new internationally funded Green Revolution. The renowned Farmer Field Schools of Asia have revolutionized integrated pest management and pioneered participatory plant breeding, but have not been a political force in preserving agrobiodiversity or defending farmer's rights.

Ironically, the strength of these farmer-to-farmer networks—i.e., their capacity to generate farmer's agroecological knowledge in a horizontal, widespread, and decentralized fashion—is also a political weakness. On one hand, there are no coordinating bodies within these networks capable of mobilizing farmers for social pressure, advocacy, or political action. On the other, their effectiveness at developing sustainable agriculture at the local level has kept its promoters focused on improving agroecological practices rather than addressing the political and economic *conditions* for sustainable agriculture.

While the potential synergies between a global peasant federation advocating food sovereignty and far-flung smallholder movements practicing agroecology may seem obvious, efforts to bring agrarian advocacy to farmer-to-farmer networks have run up against the historical distrust between development NGOs implementing sustainable agriculture projects and the peasant organizations that make up the new agrarian movements. Aside from having assumed many of the tasks previously expected of the state, NGOs have become an institutional means to advance social and political agendas within the disputed political terrain of civil society. Within the institutional landscape of agricultural development some NGOs are enrolled either directly or indirectly in the neoliberal project. Others are simply doing what they do best and tend to look out for their own programs. But others are deeply concerned that advancing the practices of sustainable agriculture without addressing the conditions for sustainability will ultimately end in failure. These NGOs are potential links to vast informal networks of smallholders who are committed to transforming agriculture.

Over the last thirty years the farmers in these networks have demonstrated their capacity to share information and knowledge. Their commitment to agroecological practices has resulted in a body of agrarian demands specific to sustainable peasant agriculture. It is now common among these farmers to hear the term food sovereignty. However, because most of these farmers do not belong to the farmer organizations that make up Vía Campesina, there are few, if any,

avenues for them to exercise this commitment politically.

INTEGRATING ADVOCACY AND PRACTICE: BRAZIL'S LANDLESS WORKERS MOVEMENT

One example of the potential transformational power of integrating peasant advocacy with agroecological practice comes from a peasant movement that is actively integrating these two aspects into its own organization. Brazil's Landless Worker's Movement (MST), one of Vía Campesina's founding members, is the largest rural social movement in the Americas. The MST has had a significant influence within Vía Campesina and a profound effect on agrarian politics worldwide. The MST has settled more than a million landless peasants and forced the redistribution of thirty-five million acres of land (an area the size of Uruguay).

The MST has its roots in peasant land occupations dating back to the late 1970s. In December 1979 a group of landless rural workers set up a camp at a crossroads now known as Encruzihalda Natalino. Following a clause in the Brazilian constitution mandating that land serve a social function, the peasants demanded that the government redistribute idle land in the area. Three and a half years and many mass mobilizations later, the group was granted around 4,600 acres. Building on the success of Encruzihalda Natalino and several others like it, land occupations have been the primary tactic of the MST.[30]

Delegates from land occupations throughout Brazil met in 1984 in the state of Paraná and laid out four basic goals for the future of the movement: "a) to maintain a broadly inclusive movement of the rural poor in order; b) to achieve agrarian reform; c) to promote the principle that land belongs to the people who work on it and live from it; and d) make it possible to have a just, fraternal society and put an end to capitalism."[31] Since then the movement has established some 400 production associations, 1,800 elementary schools, adult literacy programs, credit co-ops, health clinics, and its own organic seed supplier for MST farmers.[32]

Though the MST initially promoted industrial agriculture among its members, this strategy proved unsustainable and economically disastrous on many of its settlements. In 1990 the movement reached out to other peasant movements practicing agroecology, and at its fourth national congress in 2000, the MST adopted agroecology as national policy to orient production on its settlements. Today, the seven organizations that participate in La Vía Campesina-Brasil have all adopted agroecology as an official policy, as have many organizations in Vía Campesina-International. The MST and La Vía Campesina-Brasil have established eleven secondary schools and introduced university courses in agroecology to train the movements' youth to provide technical assistance to campesino families in rural areas. The integration of agroecology into the new agrarian movements is a welcome development because it helps advance forms of production that are consistent with the political and social goals of food sovereignty, and the MST schools in and of themselves are a testament to the movements' capacity to advance agroeco-logical policies at state and federal levels.[33]

CULTIVATING CONVERGENCE

The global food crisis had reinforced neoliberal retrenchment in agricultural development and breathed new life into the sagging Green Revolution, now resurgent in Africa and parts of Asia. Like its predecessor, the new Green Revolution is essentially a *campaign* designed to mobilize resources for the expansion of capitalist agriculture. Similar to the role once played by the Ford and Rockefeller Foundations (albeit on a much smaller scale), the Bill and Melinda Gates Foundation is the new philanthropic flagship for the Green Revolution tasked with resurrecting the Consultative Group on International Agricultural Research and obtaining broad social and government agreement for the expansion of agro-industrial capital into peasant communities. The Alliance for a Green Revolution in Africa serves up shallow definitions of terms like agroecology, sustainability, and even food sovereignty in an effort to strip them of their deeper, agrarian content and enroll NGOs and their stakeholders into the Green Revolution.

The food crisis is bad, but another Green Revolution will make things much worse. The alternative, smallholder-driven agroecological agriculture, was recognized by the IAASTD as the best strategy for rebuilding agriculture, ending rural poverty and hunger, and establishing food security in the South. To be given a chance, however, this strategy requires a combination of strong political will *and* extensive on-the-ground agroecological practice to overcome opposition from the well-financed Green Revolution.

In the face of a renewed, neoliberal assault in the form of a Green Revolution, peasant movements and farmer-to-farmer networks do appear to be moving closer together. When PELUM brought over three hundred farmer leaders together in Johannesburg to speak on their own behalf at the World Summit on Sustainable Development, the Eastern and Southern Africa Farmers Forum was founded. African farm organizations and their allies have met in Mali, Bonn, and Senegal to advance African Agroecolgical Alternatives to the Green Revolution (2007, 2008). Following the Rome food crisis meeting, Vía Campesina met in Mozambique where they signed a declaration for a smallholder solution to the food crisis (2008). These developments and others suggest that the international call for food sovereignty is beginning to take root in specific smallholder initiatives to confront the food and farm crisis. New mixes of advocacy and practice across borders and sectors and between institutions are being forged on a daily basis.

These hopeful developments have the potential for bringing together the extensive local networks for agroecological practice with the transnational advocacy organizations. If the two currents merge into a broad-based movement capable of generating massive social pressure, they could tip the scales of political will in favor of food sovereignty.

Ultimately, to end world hunger, the monopolistic industrial agri-food complex will have to be replaced with agroecological and redistributive food systems. It is too early to tell whether or not the fledgling trend of convergence signals a new stage of integration between the main currents of peasant advocacy and smallholder agroecological practice. Nonetheless, the seeds of convergence have been sown. Successfully cultivating this trend may well determine the outcome of both the global food crisis and the international showdown over the world's food systems.

NOTES

1. S. Wiggins, and S. Levy, *Rising Food Prices: A Global Crisis* (London: Overseas Development Institute, 2008).
2. World Bank, "Rising Food Prices," http://siteresources.worldbank.org/NEWS/Resources/risingfoodprices_backgroundnote_apr08.pdf.
3. *Global Monitoring Report 2008* (World Bank, Washington, D.C., 2008).
4. E. Holt-Giménez, R. Patel, and A. Shattuck, *Food Rebellions* (Oakland: Food First/Fahamu, 2009).
5. G. Lean, "Rising Prices Threaten Millions with Starvation, Despite Bumper Crops," *The Independent* (2008).
6. F. M. Lappé, J. Collins, and P. Rosset, *World Hunger* (New York Food First, 1998).
7. FAO, "The State of Agricultural Commodity Markets 2004," ftp://ftp.fao.org/docrep/fao/007/y5419e/y5419e00.pdf.
8. O. De Schutter, "Promotion and protection of all human rights, civil, political, economic, social and cultural rights, including the right to development" (New York: Human Rights Council, United Nations, 2008).
9. F. Araghi, "The Great Global Enclosure of our Times," in Fred Magdoff, John Bellamy Foster, and Frederick H. Buttel, eds., *Hungry for Profit* (New York, Monthly Review Press, 2000), 145–60; D. F. Bryceson, C. Kay, and J. Mooij, eds., *Disappearing peosantries? Rural labor in Africa, Asia and Latin America* (London: Intermediate Technology Publications, 2000).
10. FAOSTAT, "ProdStat Crops" (2009), http://faostat.fao.org/site/567/default.aspx#ancor.
11. B. Vorley, "Food Inc.," (2003), http://www.ukfg.org.uk/docs/UKFG-Foodinc-Nov03.pdf.
12. ETC Group, "The World's Top 10 Seed Companies—2006," http://www.etcgroup.org/en/materials/publications.html?pub_id=656.
13. M. Edelman, "The Persistence of the Peasantry," *NACLA Report on the Americas* 33, no. 5 (2000).
14. A. V. Chayanov, *The Peasant Economy: Collected Works* (Moscow: Ekonomika, 1989).
15. J. D. van der Ploeg, *The New Peasantries* (London: Earthscan, 2008).
16. O. Nagayets, *Small Farms* (Washington, D.C.: IFPRI, 2005).
17. F. H. Buttel, "Some Observations on Agro-Food Change and the Future of Agricultural Sustainability Movements," in David Goodman and Michael J. Watts, eds., *Globalising Food* (New York Routledge, 1997) 344–65.
18. J. Pretty, *et al.*, "Resource-conserving agriculture increases yields in developing countries." *Environmental Science & Technology* 40, no. 4, (2006): 1114–19.
19. M. Jahi Chappell, "Shattering Myths," *Food First Backgrounder* 13, no. 3 (2008), http://www.foodfirst.org/files/pdf/backgrounders/bgr.100107final.pdf.
20. P. M. Rosset, R. Patel, and M. Courville, *Promised Land* (Oakland: Food First Books, 2006).
21. A. A. Desmarais, *Via Campesina* (Halifax: Fernwood Publishing 2006).
22. Brot fur die Welt, *Campesino a Campesino* (Stuttgart: Brot fur die Welt, 2006).
23. E. Holt-Giménez, "Measuring Farmers' Agroecological Resistance to Hurricane Mitch in Central America" (London: International Institute for Environment and Development, 2001).
24. S. Fernando Funes and Luis Garcia, *et al.*, eds., *Sustainable Agriculture and Resistance: Transforming Food Production in Cuba* (Oakland/Havana: Food First/ACTAF/CEAS, 2002).
25. E. Holt-Giménez, "The Campesino a Campesino Movement," Food *First Development Report* 10 (Oakland: Institute for Food and Development Policy/Food First, 1996).
26. N. Uphoff, "Agroecological Implications of the System of Rice Intensification (SRI) in Madagascar," *Environment, Development and Sustainability* 1, no. 3/4, (2000).
27. J. N. Pretty, J. I. L. Morison, and R. E. Hine, "Reducing Food Poverty by Increasing

Agricultural Sustainability in Developing Countries," *Agriculture, Ecosystems & Environment* 93 (2003): 87–105.

28. J. Pretty, Rachel Hine and Sofia Twarog, *Organic Agriculture and Food Security in Africa* (Geneva: United Nations Environment Program, 2008).

29. Holt-Giménez, "The Campesino a Campesino Movement."

30. A. Wright and W. Wolford, *To Inherit the Earth* (Oakland: Food First Books, 2003).

31. Wright and Wolford, *To Inherit the Earth*, 76.

32. J. P. Stedile, "MST Twenty Fifth Anniversary— 25 Years of Obstinacy" (2009), http://www. mstbrazil.org/?q=node/590.

33. J. M. Tardin and I. Kenfield in Holt-Giménez, *et al., Food Rebellions*.

Contributors

Abarca, Meredith E. (mabarca@utep.edu) Meredith E. Abarca holds a BA in English/ American Literature from the University of California at Santa Cruz and a Ph.D. in Comparative Literature from the University of California at Davis. She is the author of *Voices in the Kitchen: Views of Food and the World from Working-Class Mexican and Mexican American Women* (Texas A & M, 2006) and teaches courses in Chicana/o Literature, Mexican-American Folklore, 20th-Century US Literature and Women Philosophers in the Kitchen.

Allen, Patricia is Director of the Center of Agroecology and Sustainable Food Systems at the University of California, Santa Cruz. Her research focuses on the political economic structures that can constrain or enable social equity in sustainable food systems. Allen's recent work involves approaches to food-system localization; gender and labor inequities in the food system; and alternative agri-food institutions such as community supported agriculture, farm-to-school and farm-to-institution programs. She is author of numerous journal articles and book chapters and editor of *Food for the Future: Conditions and Contradictions of Sustainability* and of *Together at the Table: Sustainability* and of *Sustenance in the American Agrifood System*.

Boticello, Julie (ucsajbo@ucl.ac.uk) Julie Botticello is a post-doctoral research assistant on the *Waste of the World* program at University College London (UCL), a post-doctoral research Associate at the School of Oriental and African Studies (SOAS) in their Food Studies Centre, and an adjunct professor at Syracuse University in their London program. She gained her Ph.D. in Anthropology from University College London. Among others, her publications include "Fashioning Individuality and Social Connectivity among Yoruba Women in London" in D. Miller (ed.) *Anthropology and the Individual* (2009).

Buerkle, C. Wesley (Buerkle@mail.etsu. edu) C. Wesley Buerkle is Assistant Professor of Communication at East Tennessee State University. His research focuses on issues of masculinity in US culture, most often looking at issues of representing sexuality. Buerkle's essay, "Metrosexuality Can Stuff It," is dedicated to his late father who generously sent him shipments of frozen steaks throughout his graduate school career.

Caldwell, Alison (alisoncaldwell@mac. com) Alison Caldwell is a Southern California native who has lived in New York City for over 15 years. She has a background in television production and the arts, and is currently a Master of Arts candidate in the Food Studies program at New York University. Through new and traditional media, she develops content where food, culture, and politics overlap.

Copelton, Denise (dcopelto@brockport. edu) Denise Copelton is Assistant Professor of Sociology at The College at Brockport, State University of New York and co-editor for the book review section of *Gender & Society*. Her research centers on the social experience of illness, with a special focus on conditions requiring dietary modifications. Her publications have appeared in *Social Science & Medicine*, *Sociology of Health & Illness*, and *Deviant Behavior*. She is currently writing a book on the social experience of celiac disease and gluten-free eating.

Counihan, Carole (carole.counihan@ millersville.edu) Carole Counihan is Professor of Anthropology at Millersville University and editor-in-chief of *Food and Foodways* journal. She is author of *The Anthropology of Food and Body* (1999), *Around the Tuscan Table: Food, Family and Gender in Twentieth Century Florence* (2004), and *A Tortilla Is Like Life: Food and Culture in the San Luis Valley of Colorado* (2009). She is editor of *Food in the USA* (2002) and, with Penny Van Esterik, of *Food and Culture* (1997, 2008). She has been a visiting professor at Boston University, the University of Cagliari, the University of Gastronomic Sciences (Italy), and the University of Malta. Her new research focuses on food activism in Italy.

Deutsch, Jonathan (Jonathan.Deutsch@ kbcc.cuny.edu) Jonathan Deutsch, Ph.D. is a classically trained chef and Associate Professor of Culinary Arts at Kingsborough Community College, City University of New York and public health at the CUNY Graduate Center. He is the education editor of the journal *Food, Culture and Society* and author or editor of five books including (with Annie Hauck-Lawson) *Gastropolis: Food and New York City*, (with Sarah Billingsley) *Culinary Improvisation*, and (with Jeff Miller) *Food Studies: An Introduction to Research Methods* and numerous articles in scholarly journals.

Dollahite, Jamie S. (jsd13@cornell.edu) Jamie Dollahite is Associate Professor in Nutritional Sciences at Cornell University and Director of Cornell's Food and Nutrition Education in Communities Program, which includes large outreach programs targeted to low-income audiences. Her research focuses on effective, evidence-based practices, including community-based interventions that support healthy lifestyles and prevent obesity and chronic disease, best management practices that support successful program outcomes, assessing behavioral change among low-income program participants, and other factors that have an impact upon their access to the food supply and overall nutritional care.

Edwards, Ferne (ferne.edwards@rmit.edu. au) Ferne Edwards is a Ph.D. student at the Australian National University. She holds degrees in Anthropology, Spanish, and International Urban and Environmental Management from the University of Queensland, the University of Melbourne and RMIT University. Ferne's recent research includes climate change impacts on the food system for public health, the significance of non-monetarized foods in cities, and Venezuela's food sovereignty movement. Ferne has also coordinated many sustainability activities, including as initial moderator for Sustainable Melbourne.com and the Sustainable Cities Round Tables at the Victorian Eco-Innovation Lab, as a co-ordinator of the Sustainable Living Festival, and as a tour guide to Venezuela on the food sovereignty movement.

Ehrhardt, Julia C. (juliae@ou.edu) Julia Ehrhardt is Associate Professor of American and Women's and Gender Studies at the University of Oklahoma Honors College. The author of *Writers of Conviction: The Personal Politics of Zona Gale, Dorothy Canfield Fisher, Josephine Herbst, and Rose Wilder Lane* (2004), and several articles on American women writers, she is currently writing a literary history of fat and dieting in the United States.

Ferris, Marcie Cohen (ferrism@email.unc.edu) Marcie Cohen Ferris is Associate Professor and Director of Undergraduate Studies in the Department of American Studies at the University of North Carolina at Chapel Hill. Her research and teaching interests include the history of the Jewish South, women's history, and the foodways and material culture of the American South. Among her many publications is *Matzoh Ball Gumbo: Culinary Tales of the Jewish South* (2005), which was recognized by the International Association of Culinary Professionals for distinguished scholarship in research and presentation. Her current work, "The Edible South: Food and History in an American Region," is a social history of southern foodways.

Fitting, Elizabeth (Elizabeth.Fitting@Dal.Ca) Elizabeth Fitting is Associate Professor in the Department of Sociology and Social Anthropology at Dalhousie University in Nova Scotia, Canada. She is the author of *The Struggle for Maize: Campesinos, Workers, and Transgenic Corn in the Mexican Countryside* (2011). She has published articles in *Agriculture and Human Values*, *Focaal: the European Journal of Anthropology*, and has a chapter in *Food for the Few: Neoliberal Globalism and Agricultural Biotechnology in Latin America* (2008). Her work focuses on the relationship between transnational migration, rural livelihoods, and food sovereignty.

Garth, Hanna (hanna.garth@gmail.com) Hanna Garth is a Ph.D. Candidate in the Department of Anthropology at UCLA. Detailing the experiences of food rationing and scarcity, her research centers on household food acquisition and consumption in Santiago de Cuba. In addition to her work in Cuba she has conducted research in the Philippines, Chile, Peru, and the United States.

Gaytán, Marie Sarita (sarita.gaytan@nyu.edu) Marie Sarita Gaytán is a Faculty Fellow in Latino Studies at New York University. Her work has appeared in the *Journal of Contemporary Ethnography*, *Latino Studies*, and *Food, Culture, and Society*. She has taught at Lewis and Clark College and Bowdoin College. She is currently working on a book that examines the relationship between commodity culture and national identity.

Grieshop, J.I. (jigrieshop@ucdavis.edu) James Grieshop is Emeritus Specialist in Cooperative Extension in the Department of Human and Community Development at the University of California Davis. His research interests include community leadership, risk perception and health and safety, non-formal education, and communication and adoption of innovations. Among recent projects are studies and outreach education dealing with Hispanic leadership and risk perceptions and occupational safety among farmworkers. His work has appeared in several scholarly journals including *Human Organization*, *Agricultural and Human Values* and *Social Marketing Quarterly*.

Gross, Joan (jgross@oregonstate.edu) Joan Gross is Professor of Anthropology at Oregon State University. She is the author of *Speaking in Other Voices: An Ethnography of Walloon Puppet Theaters* (2001) and editor of *Teaching Oregon Native Languages* (2007). Her research focuses on linguistic anthropology and agrifood movements.

Guthman, Julie (jguthman@ucsc.edu) Julie Guthman is Associate Professor of Community Studies at the University of California at Santa Cruz. She is the author of *Agrarian Dreams: the Paradox of Organic Farming in California* (2004) and *Weighing In: Obesity, Food Justice, and the Limits of Capitalism* (forthcoming 2011). Her research on contemporary efforts to transform the way food is produced, distributed, and consumed has also been published in professional journals such as *Agriculture and Human Values*, *Antipode*, *Cultural Geographies*, *Environment and Planning A & D*, *Gastronomica*, and *Geoforum*, among many others.

Harper, A. Breeze (breezeharper@gmail.com) A. Breeze Harper is a Ph.D. Candidate at University of California-Davis focusing on Critical Food Geographies. She is the editor of *Sistah Vegan: Black Female Vegans Speak on Food, Identity, Health and Society* (2010). Her dissertation research focuses on applications of critical race and black feminist studies to vegan studies in the US.

Hassanein, Neva (Neva.Hassanein@mso.umt.edu) Neva Hassanein is Associate Professor of environmental studies at the University of Montana. An activist-scholar, Hassanein is the author of *Changing the Way America Farms: Knowledge and Community in the Sustainable Agriculture Movement* (1999), as well as academic articles, policy reports, and essays related to building sustainable, community-based, and democratic food systems. Hassanein has worked as an organizer and a volunteer in numerous non-profit organizations, and is now active in the Community Food and Agriculture Coalition, a food policy council in Missoula, Montana. She currently serves as the President of the Agriculture, Food, and Human Values Society.

Hayes-Conroy, Allison (anhc@temple.edu) and **Hayes-Conroy, Jessica** (hayes-conroy_jessica@wheatoncollege.edu) Allison and Jessica Hayes-Conroy locate much of their research at the intersection of feminist, political, and cultural geographies and agro-food studies. They have authored or co-authored papers in these areas for *Transactions of The Institute of British Geographers*, *Gender, Place and Culture*, *Geoforum*, *Environment and Planning A*, and *Geography Compass*. Allison has written two books on the culture of agriculture within suburban landscapes and

Jessica has authored chapters therein. They are both currently working on an edited volume on Critical Perspectives of Nutrition Intervention. Allison received her Ph.D. in Geography from Clark University, and her MA in Geography from the University of Hawai'i. Jessica received her Ph.D. in Geography and Women's Studies from Penn State University and her MA in Geography from the University of Vermont. Jessica is currently a visiting Post-Doctoral Mellon Fellow at Wheaton College and Allison is a visiting professor at Temple University.

Holt-Giménez, Eric (eholtgim@foodfirst.org) Eric Holt-Giménez is the Executive Director of Food First/Institute for Food and Development Policy, a people's think tank dedicated to ending the injustices that cause hunger. Eric has worked as an agroecologist and action-researcher for over thirty years in the US, Latin America, Africa and Asia. He holds a Masters in International Agricultural Development from UC Davis and a Ph.D. in Environmental Studies from UC Santa Cruz. He is the author of *Campesino a Campesino: Latin America's Farmer to Farmer Movement for Sustainable Agriculture* (2006) and *Food Rebellions: Crisis and the Hunger for Justice*, with Raj Patel and Annie Shattuck (2009).

Hoskins, Janet (jhoskins@usc.edu) Janet Hoskins is Professor of Anthropology at the University of Southern California, Los Angeles. She is the author of *The Play of Time: Kodi Perspectives on Calendars, History and Exchange* (1994, winner of the 1996 Benda Prize for Southeast Asian Studies), *Biographical Objects: How Things Tell the Story of People's Lives* (1998), and is the contributing editor of *Headhunting and the Social Imagination in Southeast Asia* (1996), *Anthropology as a Search for the Subject: The Space Between One Self and Another* (1999), and *Fragments from Forests and Libraries* (2000). She is now studying Caodaism and other indigenous Vietnamese religions from a transnational perspective.

Imbruce, Valerie (Vimbruce@bennington.edu) Valerie Imbruce is Director of Environmental Studies at Bennington College where she teaches courses on agrarianism, agroecology and environment and society. Her research and writing is focused on the globalization of agriculture and the influence of urban demands on regional agricultural systems. Her research has been supported by the National Science Foundation and she has held fellowships at the Center for Place, Culture, and Politics and the Center for Advanced Study in Education. Imbruce has also worked on urban sustainability with the United Nations Educational, Scientific, and Cultural Organization in New York City and agricultural development at Bioversity International in Rome, Italy and TechnoServe in Cajamarca, Peru.

Johnson, Adrienne Rose (adriennerose-johnson@gmail.com) Adrienne Johnson is a Ph.D. student at Stanford University in the Program in Modern Thought and Literature focusing on American Studies and Food Culture. She is interested in using popular culture to explore work-as-entertainment. Her previous research has included studies of gingerbread houses, factory tourism, virtual and miniature dollhouses, and dude ranching. She is the receipt of the 2009 Association for the Study of Food and Society Bill Whit Undergraduate Prize for "The American Grotesque: Competitive Eating and the Cultural Meaning of American Bodies."

Kirwan, James (jkirwan@glos.ac.uk) James Kirwan is a Senior Research Fellow at the Countryside and Community Research Institute, University of Gloucestershire. His principal research area is food supply chains and, in particular, their influence on the sustainability of rural areas. He has published on a range of issues in this area including, with Carol Morris, "Food

commodities, geographical knowledges and the reconnection of production and consumption: the case of naturally embedded food products" (*Geoforum*, 2010), with Bill Slee on "Exploring hybridity in food supply chains," in Canavari et al. *International Marketing and Trade of Quality Food Products* (2009) and "Alternative strategies in the UK agro-food system: interrogating the alterity of farmers' markets" (*Sociologia Ruralis*, 2004). His current research is focused on the place of meat within sustainable twenty-first century diets.

Kwate, Naa Oyo A. (kwate@aesop.rutgers.edu) Naa Oyo A. Kwate is Associate Professor in the Departments of Human Ecology Africana Studies at Rutgers University. Her research centers on determinants of African American health, with particular attention to individual experiences of identity and inequality, and the intersection of these variables with more structural factors. The recipient of a National Institute of Health Director's New Innovator Award (2009), and the Robert Wood Johnson Foundation's Investigator Award in Health Policy (2008), she has published in such journals as the *American Journal of Public Health*, *Preventive Medicine*, *Health & Place*, among many others.

Lance, G. Denise (dlance@ku.edu) G. Denise Lance is a Research Associate for the Kansas University Center on Developmental Disabilities at the University of Kansas. She holds a doctorate in special education and assistive technology from the University of Kansas. She has been an assistive technology consultant, web author, and freelance writer. She served as technical consultant for the Assistive Technology Educational Network (ATEN) of Florida for two years and has published several articles about assistive technology and her own experiences living with cerebral palsy. For ten years, she has been an online instructor for the University of San Diego, teaching a course on inclusion of students with disabilities.

Lang, Tim (t.lang@city.ac.uk) Tim Lang is Professor of Food Policy at City University and founder of the Centre for Food Policy. He was a hill farmer in Lancashire, NW England in the 1970s and for many years has been engaged in academic research and public debate about food policy. He has been advisor to four Parliamentary inquiries, a consultant to the World Health Organization, and served on multi-level government committees, commissions and working parties. He has authored/co-authored numerous articles, reports, chapters and books, most recently *Food Policy* (2009), *Atlas of Food* (2008), and *Food Wars* (Earthscan, 2004). In keeping with his research interests of defining sustainable living and food security he rides a bike to work.

Lavin, Chad (chadlavin@gmail.com) Chad Lavin is the author of *The Politics of Responsibility* (2008) and numerous essays in social and political theory. Currently Assistant Professor of Political Science and the Alliance for Social, Political, Ethical, and Cultural Thought (ASPECT) at Virginia Tech, he previously held a research fellowship at the Bill and Carol Fox Center for Humanistic Inquiry at Emory University, and teaching appointments at Penn State, Tulane University, and Hobart and William Smith Colleges. His current research focuses on digestive metaphors in political thought and food anxieties in contemporary politics.

Lawson, Laura (ljlawson@SEBS.Rutgers. edu) Laura Lawson is Professor and Chair of the Department of Landscape Architecture at the School of Environmental and Biological Sciences at Rutgers University. She is the recipient of numerous awards including the 2010 Great Places Book Award for *Greening*

Cities, Growing Communities: Lessons from Seattle's Urban Community Gardens (2009) co-authored with Jeff Hou and Julie Johnson and the inaugural Larine Y. Cowan "Make A Difference Award" in 2009 for her leadership on the East St. Louis Action Research Project, an interdisciplinary group of faculty, students, and staff interested in civic engagement and action research. She is the author of several publications including "Parks as Mirrors of Community Design Discourse and Community Hopes for Parks in East St. Louis" (2007).

Loh, Ji-Meng (jimengloh@gmail.com) Ji-Meng Loh works for ATT Labs and is a subject matter expert in spatial statistics.

Mannur, Anita (mannura@muohio.edu) Anita Mannur is Assistant Professor of English and Asian/Asian American Studies at Miami University, Ohio. She is the author of *Culinary Fictions: Food in South Asian Diasporic Culture* (Temple, 2010) and the co-editor (with Jana Evans Braziel) of Theorizing Diaspora (Blackwell 2003). She also edited a special issue on "Food Matters" for *The Massachusetts Review* and co-edited a special issue on Asian American Foodways (with Valerie Matsumoto) for *Amerasia Journal*.

Markowitz, Lisa (lisam@louisville.edu) Lisa Markowitz is Associate Professor and Chair of Anthropology at the University of Louisville. She has carried out long-term ethnographic fieldwork in the Andean highlands of Peru and worked in villages on the Bolivian *altiplano*. For the past decade, as an activist-researcher, she has been involved with alternative agrifood movements in Kentucky. Her most recent articles appear in *Research in Economic Anthropology* and in a special issue of *Food and Foodways* (which she edited with John Brett) on food policy and security. Her new project explores the construction of rural food supply chains in southern Peru.

Matejowsky, Ty (tmatejow@mail.ucf.edu) Ty Matejowsky is an Associate Professor with the Department of Anthropology at the University of Central Florida. He received his Ph.D. in anthropology from Texas A&M University in 2001. His ongoing research in the Philippines examines a number of issues related to globalization, including fast food, urban development, disaster responses, and international migration. Publications include "Like a 'Whopper Virgin': Anthropological Reflections on Burger King's Controversial Ad Campaign" (2010), "Fast Food and Nutritional Perceptions in the Age of 'Globesity': Perspectives from the Provincial Philippines" (2009), and "Jolly Dogs and McSpaghetti: Anthropological Reflections on Global/Local Fast Food Competition in the Philippines" (2008). He is currently working on a book about fast food globalization in the Philippines.

Maxey, Larch (larch.maxey@plymouth. ac.uk) Dr. Larch Maxey (LLB, MSc., Ph.D.) has written 40 publications, including a co-edited book on Low Impact Development. A Director of the Ecological Land Coop (ELC) and co-author of its ground-breaking report *Small is Successful: Creating Sustainable Livelihoods on 10 acres or less*. ELC establishes truly affordable eco-smallholdings, integrating Low Impact buildings with land-based, sustainable lifestyles.

Mercer, David (dave.mercer@rmit.edu. au) David Mercer is Associate Professor in the School of Global Studies, Social Science & Planning at RMIT University, Melbourne Australia. He is the Director of the postgraduate program in Environment & Planning and International Urban & Environmental Management. He has degrees in Geography from Cambridge University in the UK and Monash University in Australia. The author of over 140 publications in urban planning, social geography, environmental policy and international development, his most recent research has been on post-disaster recovery and reconstruction in Sri Lanka, Tamil Nadu, and Australia, as well as on food security in Australia.

Morris, Carol (Carol.Morris@nottingham. ac.uk) Carol Morris is Assistant Professor of Human Geography at the University of Nottingham, UK. Previously, she worked at the Countryside and Community Research Unit, University of Gloucestershire, and the Centre for Rural Research, at the University of Exeter where she contributed to numerous research projects concerned with the environmental governance of rural areas and food supply chains. She has a sustained publication record on these topics including, (with James Kirwan), "Food Commodities, Geographical Knowledges and the Reconnection of Production and Consumption: The Case of Naturally Embedded Food Products" (2010) and (with Henry Buller) "Growing Goods: The Market, The State and Sustainable Food Production" (2004). Her current research is focused on the scalar politics of meat production-consumption.

Nash, June (junenash27@gmail.com) June Nash is Distinguished Professor Emerita of Anthropology at the City University of New York. She has conducted extensive ethnographic research in Mexico and Bolivia, and authored numerous articles about gender and resistance among indigenous peoples as well as several books including *Mayan Visions: The Quest for Autonomy in an Age of Globalization*, *We Eat the Mines and the Mines Eat Us: Dependence and Exploitation in Bolivian Tin Mines*, *Practicing Ethnography in a Globalizing World: An Anthropological Odyssey*, and *In the Eyes of the Ancestors: Belief and Behavior in a Maya Community*.

Reichman, Daniel (daniel.reichman@ rochester.edu) Daniel Reichman is Assistant Professor of Anthropology at the University of Rochester. He is the author of *The Broken Village: Coffee,*

Migration, and Globalization in Honduras (2011). His current research focuses on the implementation of traceability standards for agricultural products.

Rouse, Carolyn (crouse@princeton.edu) Carolyn Rouse is a Professor in the Department of Anthropology and the Center for African American Studies at Princeton University. She is the author of *Engaged Surrender: African American Women and Islam* and *Uncertain Suffering: Racial Healthcare Disparities and Sickle Cell Disease*. She is finishing a co-written book entitled *Televised Redemption: The Media Production of Black Jews, Christians and Muslims*. Her current book project, *Development Hubris: Adventures Trying to Save the World*, examines discourses of charity and development and is tied to her own project building a high school in a fishing village in Ghana. In addition to being an anthropologist, Rouse is also a filmmaker whose documentaries include *Chicks in White Satin* (1994), and *Purification to Prozac: Treating Mental Illness in Bali* (1998).

Sachs, Carolyn is Professor of Rural Sociology and Head of the Women's Studies Department at Penn State University. Her research explores the new women agricultural entreperneurs and their opportunities and barriers to success. She is also engaged in a comparative international project on gender and climate change in India in collaboration with the Food and Agriculture Organization. Another project focuses on gender and the food system exploring gendered work in the food system from farm to table. Her extension and outreach interests include working with the Pennsylvania Women's Agriculture Network (PAWAgN) to provide hands-on agricultural, entrepreneurship, and leadership training. Dr. Sachs serves on an expert panel to the UN on Gender, Water, and Sanitation. She is author of numerous articles and the books *Invisible Farmers: Women in Agricultural Production* and *Gendered Fields: Rural Women, Agriculture, and Environment.*

Salazar, Melissa L. (melissa.salazar@gmail.com) Melissa Salazar works in the Española Valley of northern New Mexico on rural education, food and sustainability programs. She has a Ph.D. from University of California-Davis in Education and her research centers on health, food and identity. She has published several articles on children and school food and on how immigrants experience US food systems. She is currently working on a retail food cooperative in order to sustain traditional agricultural practices in the upper Rio Grande Valley, as well as continuing to visually document the food practices around her.

Schroeder, Kathleen (schroederk@appstate.edu) Kathleen Schroeder is Professor of Geography and Planning at Appalachian State University. She has authored numerous articles on global economic restructuring and issues of gender and development in Latin America and particularly in Bolivia where she has conducted research since 1992.

Sims, Rebecca (see Rebecca Whittle).

Sobal, Jeffery (js57@cornell.edu) Jeffery Sobal is Professor in the Division of Nutritional Sciences at Cornell University. He has co-edited three books with Donna Maurer: *Eating Agendas* (1995), *Weighty Issues* (1999), and *Intepreting Weight* (1999). His research uses a variety of social science theories and methods to analyze food, eating, and nutrition. His work focuses on the social causes and consequences of obesity, particularly marriage and body weight; food choice processes; commensality; family meals; and food systems.

Van Esterik, Penny (esterik@yorku.ca) Penny Van Esterik, Professor of Anthropology at York University, Toronto, has published widely on feminist approaches to food, culture, and breastfeeding primarily in Southeast Asia (Thailand and Lao PDR). She is the author of *Beyond the Breast-Bottle Controversy*, *Materializing Thailand*, *Taking Refuge: Lao Buddhists in North America*, and *Food Culture in Southeast Asia*. She is co-editor with Carole Counihan of *Food and Culture: A Reader* (1997, 2008).

Webber, Caroline B. (caroline.webber@ wmich.edu) Caroline Webber is Assistant Professor of Nutrition and Dietetics, Department of Family and Consumer Sciences, at Western Michigan University, and is a registered dietitian. Her research in sustainable food systems reflects broad, longstanding interests in public health and community nutrition. Her work focuses on the intersection of food security and food systems. The paper in this collection is based on her dissertation completed at Cornell University

Whittle, Rebecca (r.whittle@lancaster. ac.uk (formerly Rebecca Sims)) Rebecca Whittle is a senior research associate in the Lancaster Environment Centre at Lancaster University in the UK. Her research focuses on the sustainability of community-environment relations with a particular focus on concepts of resilience and equity in relation to social and environmental decision-making. She is author of "Putting place on the menu: the negotiation of locality in UK food tourism from production to consumption" (2010).

Williams, Donya (dwillia9@health.nyc. gov) Donya Williams is the Program Coordinator for the New York City Department of Health and Mental Hygiene's Healthy Bodegas.

Williams-Forson, Psyche (pwforson@umd. edu) Psyche Williams-Forson is Associate Professor of American Studies at the University of Maryland College Park and an affiliate faculty member of the Women's Studies and African American Studies departments and the Consortium on Race, Gender, and Ethnicity. She authored *Building Houses Out of Chicken Legs: Black Women, Food, and Power* (2006). Her new research explores the role of the value market as a immediate site of food acquisition and a project on class, consumption, and citizenship among African Americans by examining domestic interiors from the late nineteenth century to the early twentieth century.

Yau, Chun-Yip (cyyau@sta.cuhk.edu.hk) Chun-Yip Yau is Assistant Professor in the Department of Statistics at the Chinese University of Hong Kong. He received his Ph.D. in 2010 from Columbia University. His research interests include time series analysis, spatial statistics, and their environmental applications.

Credit Lines

Index